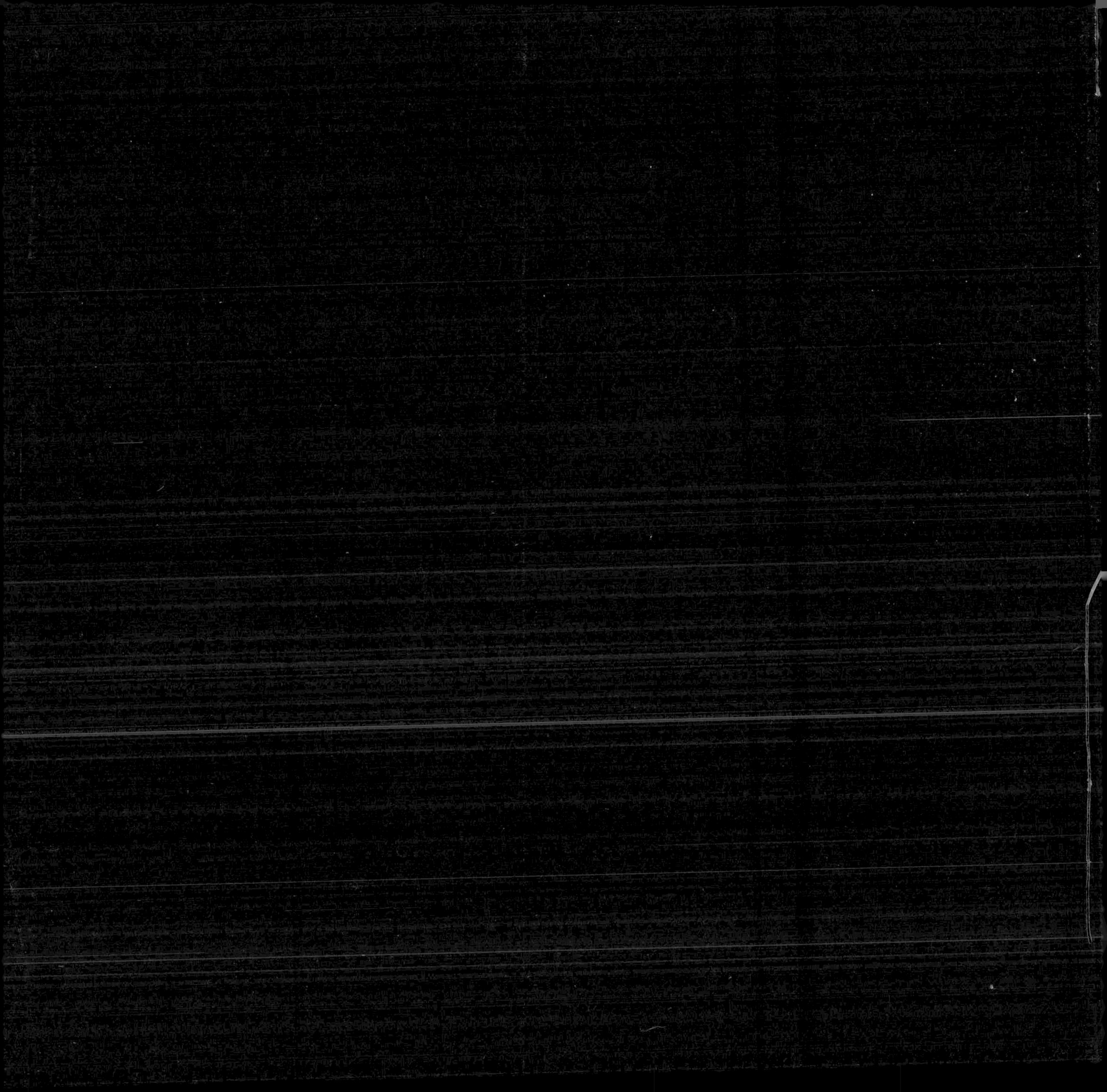

NEWCASTLE UNITED

The Ultimate Record 1881-2011

By Paul Joannou

with Alan Candlish & Bill Swann

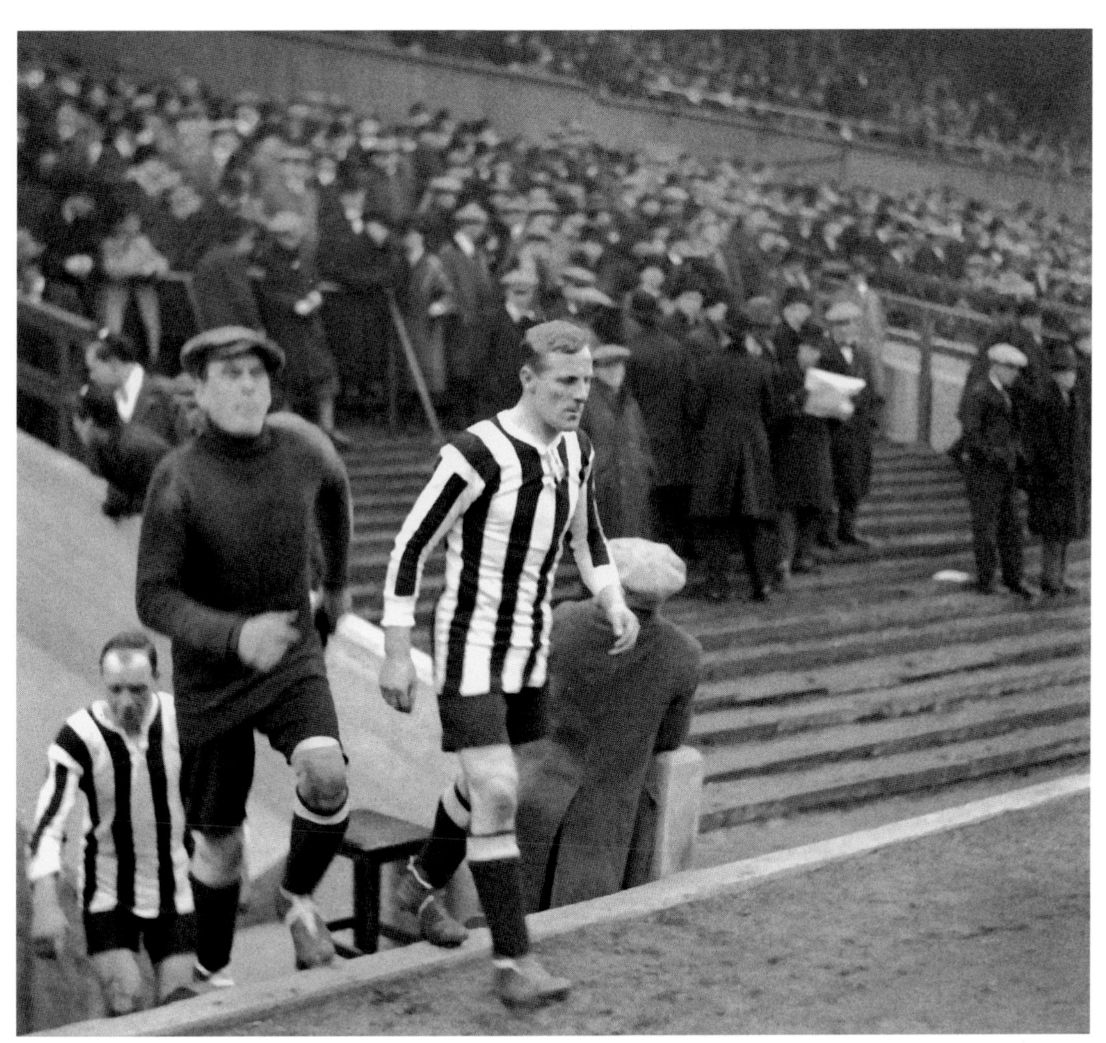

Frank Hudspeth followed by goalkeeper Willie Wilson and Wilf Low climbs the steps from the St James' Park dressing-room in 1925.

NEWCASTLE UNITED
AN OFFICIAL PUBLICATION

PUBLISHING

To the founders of Newcastle United Football Club; the men of Stanley FC in Byker and St Peter's who started it all 130 years ago.

First published November 2011 in Great Britain
by N Publishing, part of St James Ventures Ltd
Bolam White House, Belsay
Newcastle upon Tyne NE20 0HB
England

ISBN 978-0-9568156-0-6

Design & Layout: Paul Joannou and Dave Hewson & Simon Arbon, Team Digital.

Photographs & Illustrations are courtesy of:
Newcastle United FC Archive, Paul Joannou Archive, Ian Horrocks, Newcastle Chronicle & Journal, Dan Brannigan.

Printed and bound by CPI Group (UK) Ltd, CR0 4YY

JACKET ILLUSTRATIONS
Front cover: The original FA Cup winning shirt worn by centre-half Bob Stokoe in the 1955 final against Manchester City showing the famous black-and-white stripes and city crest.
Rear cover: Colours and designs of United's first choice kit over the years, from Stanley and East End to the present day Newcastle United.

Andy Aitken keeps fit c1905.

Worn with pride

1890s-1969

1969-1975

1976-1982

1983-1987

1988 to present

Over history Newcastle United have proudly displayed five different club badges on their shirts, although for well over 70 years, no crest was to be seen on the Magpies famous colours other than for special occasions, notably in FA Cup finals. Newcastle upon Tyne's coat-of-arms was generally used from Victorian times on most official club literature and when United were seen at special occasions in public; for those cup finals and at functions or on tour when club blazers displayed the City insignia.

That coat-of-arms is a historic motif, granted as far back as 1575. The central design of castles, not surprisingly goes back to earliest times as the town originally took the name from the 'New Castle' built by order of Robert Curthose, eldest son of William the Conqueror.
A castle was seen on the common seal in the 12th century while the three silver castles on the red shield, date from about 1400. A golden lion grasps a flag of St George, while two mythical seahorses on either side are a reminder of Newcastle's seaport heritage. The crest also carries a motto; Fortiter Defendit Triumphans – Triumphing by brave defence.

United experimented with their own badge for the first time during 1969 and 1970, a variant of the City's arms, a crest showing a black and white shield flanked by two magpies and a castle with a flag. But for the club's European success in Budapest during 1969, the City coat-of-arms was again emblazoned on the shirt. Newcastle then introduced a popular new circular crest in 1976, the club's first real trademark badge. This depicted the traditional themes of Newcastle United and of Tyneside; the magpie, the River Tyne and the city's castle. This badge was replaced in 1983 with a modern stream-lined design using the club's often used lettering of nufc and was worn on the club shirts for the next five years.

A brand new crest was introduced in 1988, one which is now very much a traditional part of Newcastle United Football Club and worn with pride by both players and supporters alike.

United's badge is modelled again on the long-established City Council coat-of-arms. The two sea-horses represent Tyneside's strong maritime connection, while the castle links with the city's Norman keep. The flag is similar to the council crest, a version of the cross of St George with the blue and red colours of East End while the shield signifies the club's black-and-white striped shirt.

Contents

A trio of United's centre-forward heroes; Alan Shearer, Jackie Milburn and Hughie Gallacher.

"Newcastle United's history is a quite remarkable one - they have a colourful past to say the least. Steeped in tradition, it is an institution in the North East, more than a mere football club"
SIR BOBBY ROBSON

Author's Introduction and Acknowledgements

NEWCASTLE UNITED
The Ultimate Record 1881-2011

When the first edition of Newcastle United's match by match history was published over 25 years ago in 1986 it was one of the earliest Complete Record books at a time when detailed historical works of that type on football clubs were in their infancy. Now almost every club in the country has such a volume. Since 1986 much new data has been researched on United's match record with even obscure and until recently, hidden friendly games now being discovered. This book takes the club's match record a stage further and brings everything up to date, a fitting way to mark 130 years of action since the founding of the club in the St Peter's district of Newcastle during November 1881.

Back then, Newcastle United were known as Stanley FC, soon to become Newcastle East End with a base at Chillingham Road in Heaton. Apart from the club's senior fixtures – Football League, Premier League, FA Cup, Football League Cup and European games – all other first-eleven matches are charted since Stanley FC first kicked a ball on the slopes of the Tyne valley amidst the industrial growth of Victorian Tyneside. Also added into this Ultimate Record are details of the club's reserve and junior sides for the very first time.

In addition, a complete player record is included giving appearances and goals for those players to have worn the famous Black'n'White shirt (and for an early period, the club's blue and then red shirts) in competitive action. Summaries of managers, trainers and coaches are incorporated, so too are United's Chairman, directors and officials. There is also a summary of Corporate Newcastle United over that century and more. A rundown of foremost matches and events at St James' Park is included as well, so too are the club's principal records.

The text contains a huge amount of collected data; facts and figures covering every United senior fixture and more besides. Accuracy has always been paramount and much care has been taken to resolve anomalies. It is inevitable though that a few errors will slip the net. Should you discover new information on United's match record, please forward details to the publisher or to myself at St James' Park.

Many hours of research has gone into investigating details of United's fixtures. This is especially to be noted for the first 20 years or so of United's history on Victorian Tyneside when both teams and scorers differed in the various local newspapers, and in the press elsewhere in the country. Where there were conflicts, such as historic information as to the identity of United's very first Football League goalscorers at Arsenal in 1893, the task was to gain a consensus by reviewing several reports, sometimes as many as six or seven versions. This gave the best possible judgement of the correct team or scorers for these early seasons to also compare with the official club ledgers as handwritten by United's Secretary. Over time, especially in early years, inconsistencies do occur. The club's highest ever scoreline is recorded as the 19-0 victory by East End over Point Pleasant back in 1888. This fixture infuriatingly notes star East Ender Alec White as scoring seven, eight or even nine goals. A consensus has been reached that the majority of reports note White hit the ball between the posts a mere seven times. Discrepancies also appear with attendances, certain team selections, own-goals and the like. More detailed notes on the data are included in the Introduction to the start of each section of the book.

Acknowledgements

My co-authors and knowledgeable United enthusiasts Alan Candlish and Bill Swann are thanked for all their work in preparing the statistical data. Alan has spent hour upon hour delving through newspapers to establish the most accurate match details, while Bill is largely responsible for charting the season by season electronic match summaries. This book could not have been produced in such a comprehensive manner without their invaluable input.

Several people have assisted in various ways and their help is appreciated: Richard Swann, John Edminson, Paul Tully, Jan Radwanski, John Allan, together with Peter Holme and Gordon Small at the National Football Museum. Mick Edmondson at The Back Page sporting bookshop in Newcastle, Paul Days, Malcolm Dix, Tony Fiddes, Jordon Tinniswood and Demandt Elf are also thanked while Steve Corke deserves acknowledgment for his work on the original Complete Record. In addition, fellow football historians around the country are acknowledged as are their individual club publications, all of which now produce a comprehensive library on the game with immense detail covering every senior club in this country.

Various archives have been reviewed and recognition of many organisations is due, including the National Football Museum, the British Library's newspaper collection in Colindale, the extensive Mitchell Library in Glasgow and the Scottish FA Collection housed at the National Library of Scotland in Edinburgh. The National Archive of Wales has also been visited.

Local newspaper collections have been invaluable in the North East, notably at North Tyneside, Gateshead, Darlington, Middlesbrough, Sunderland, Blyth Valley and especially at the Central Library Local Studies Department, Newcastle upon Tyne where the wide-ranging archive and knowledgeable staff have been of great assistance over many years of research. Tyne & Wear Archive Service at The Discovery Museum and the Woodhorn Northumberland Museum in Ashington have also been important points of reference.

Several municipal libraries out with the North East region have also been visited to research data, examples being those in Dundee, Inverness, Dumbarton, Bangor, Anglesey and even as far afield as Vancouver in Canada where details of United's North American tours of 1949 and 1970 were reviewed.

A special thanks to Ken Slater, Mike Bolam and Niall Mckenzie who have contributed a great deal to the production of this book. Dave Hewson and Simon Arbon at Team Digital have produced a first-class design and their involvement in pre-print artwork, and print management is appreciated. The long suffering wives and partners of myself, Bill and Alan are particularly thanked, for their tolerance and understanding over many months of research and preparation of The Ultimate Record.

Several individuals at Newcastle United FC are acknowledged; John Irving, Stuart Middlemiss, Simon Esland, Hazel Hebron, Dan Sheridan, John Hunter, Sharon Fletcher, Tony Toward and official photographer Ian Horrocks. Finally, Managing Director Derek Llambias and Peter Beardsley are thanked for their introductions to this 130th anniversary book.

PAUL JOANNOU
Club Historian
August 2011

Foreword

DEREK LLAMBIAS
Managing Director
Newcastle United Football Club

It's certainly no secret that I'm not from the North East, but as someone who has been a big football fan for many years, I have always been very aware of how passionate Newcastle United supporters are.

Now, having been involved with the Club over the past few years, that opinion has been confirmed time and time again, and it is clear to see what the team means to its legion of loyal fans.

Everywhere you go in the city, you are never far away from a black and white shirt, and there is a real connection between the Club and its followers that goes way beyond the norm.

The Club is the heartbeat of the city, and when St. James' Park is packed to the rafters and on song, there is not another football stadium like it anywhere in the UK.

We are lucky enough to have followers across the globe, and the old saying is very true - everywhere you go, you'll always meet a Geordie that holds the fortunes of Newcastle United close to their heart.

You only have to flick through the pages of this impressive book to appreciate the kind of history and tradition that goes hand-in-hand with this great footballing institution.

Make no mistake, this is a big club - a great club - and that sentiment is echoed throughout these pages through every game, every player and every trophy from the past 130 years.

Hopefully, the next few years will make a successful addition and a famous chapter to our long, proud history as we look to take the Club back to where it belongs.

The contents of this book and the twists and turns that the Club have taken since its inception demonstrates the size and the stature of Newcastle United and its imprint on English football over the decades.

I'm sure every Newcastle fan will enjoy this expertly written and comprehensive book - a fitting volume that tracks the history of this great football club every step of the way.

PETER BEARDSLEY, MBE
Reserve Team Manager
Newcastle United Football Club

As someone who was born and brought up in Longbenton, Newcastle United have always played a huge part in my life and having grown up on Tyneside, I've always had black and white blood running through my veins.

Even when I lived away from the North East and played my football elsewhere, I never lost that bond with the Club and I'm delighted to be part of things behind the scenes at St. James' Park today.

I was delighted to get the chance to come home back in 1983 after a spell in Canada with Vancouver Whitecaps. Pulling on a Newcastle shirt back then was the realisation of a childhood dream and remains one of the proudest moments of my career.

Having left the region for Liverpool in 1987, I was perhaps as surprised as anyone to be offered a second stint at St. James' six years later at the age of 32, but to be part of what was happening at the Club in the 1990s was a real honour and hugely exciting.

Now I am the Reserve Team Manager at the Club, and it gives me great pleasure to be able to play a part in bringing the next generation of talent through the ranks and into the first-team.

I am very lucky to have been able to entertain the Geordie public as a player and as a Tynesider, it filled me with immense pride to play in front of our magnificent fans during my two spells here.

The Club has a proud, esteemed history and the story of Newcastle United is nothing short of remarkable. From our romance with the FA Cup over the years to the more recent Champions League campaigns, it is a tale well worth documenting.

As someone that is keen on the history of the game - not to mention a bit of a stats buff - this book is a real Bible and one that every Newcastle supporter should not be without.

Our Club Historian Paul Joannou and his team have put together an impressive record to celebrate our 130th anniversary and I'm sure you'll enjoy it as much as I did.

United's FA Cup homecoming in 1952. The players show the trophy to the crowds at the top of Grey Street in a procession led by four police cars.

The good citizens of Tyneside and Newcastle upon Tyne in particular fly their black-and-white flag with pride. The famous colours of Newcastle United are the modern symbol of the community. Walk down the elegant Grainger Street or parade on the Quayside and someone will be wearing those black-and-white colours – whether on a warm summer's day or chilly winter evening. Newcastle United Football Club is at the very heart of the city. It is the life and soul of the Geordie region, an outpost in the north where football and Newcastle United are inbred into the population. Support of the Magpies is a way of life. Almost everyone takes an interest and becomes consumed with the colourful rollercoaster of the Black'n'Whites; day by day, year on year. It is a marvellous and remarkable soap-opera with over 130 years of action and much drama along the way.

Now one of the biggest clubs in Europe with sustainable support few can match, Newcastle United began life struggling to survive. The Magpies origins belong amidst the heavy engineering works, shipyards, pits and vast railway expansion of Victorian Tyneside. In this industrial growth the seeds were sown of the game of football. From the day the very first organised contest took place adhering to the rules of the association code on the 3rd March 1877 at the Elswick Rugby Club, Newcastle United were conceived.

The now mighty Magpies originated from a fledgling club at St Peter's alongside the Tyne in the east of the city, Stanley FC, formed in November 1881. Within a few months they changed their name and had become Newcastle East End FC with a base in Byker, then soon afterwards, at nearby Chillingham Road in Heaton. Their colours were originally dark blue – then Cambridge blue before wearing red. It was some time before the celebrated black-and-white stripes arrived.

Tyneside Football Development

March 1877	First game on Tyneside at the Elswick Rugby Club.
March 1877	First Tyneside club formed; Tyne Association FC.
Late 1878	Second club formed; Newcastle Rangers FC.
Jan 1880	Northumberland & Durham FA founded.
Oct 1880	Rangers play the first game at St James' Park.
Nov 1880	First competition; Northumberland & Durham Challenge Cup.
Nov 1881	Stanley FC (Newcastle United) formed in St Peter's, Byker.
Aug 1882	Newcastle West End founded.
Oct 1882	Stanley FC change their name to Newcastle East End.
May 1883	Northumberland FA formed.
April 1889	Northern League created.

East End and their great rivals to be across the city, Newcastle West End FC – based at St James' Park – started to develop slowly and attract growing support from their respective districts of the Geordie community. At first there was no league competition and matches were friendly contests or in local Football Association knockout competitions. While West End had the more favourable location and support at first, it was the East Enders who eventually became the stronger outfit. The region's first league competition was introduced in 1889 in the shape of the Northern League while the FA Cup too started to cause interest although it was a long time before the celebrated trophy was to cause a stir on Tyneside.

Both sides lured several big names to the area in an attempt to develop the game. At St James' Park Scottish internationals Bob Kelso and Ralph Aitken played for West End, while East End boasted the region's top locally developed talent in Alec White, one of the great pioneers of Newcastle United. Both sides were also served behind the scenes by Tom Watson who went onto guide Sunderland and Liverpool to a string of trophies.

Founding Fathers

The district of Byker is an important location in the history of Newcastle United; where the club originated and developed. They were formed from a local cricket team in St Peter's, alongside the River Tyne. Known as Stanley Cricket Club, their home field being located near Stanley Street on Walker Road. During November 1881, the annual meeting of the Stanley Cricket Club was held at the house of a Mr Allan in Shields Road, Byker. It was reported that the cricket club was in a very prosperous state while the meeting also saw the election of the principal officers for the following season: William Coulson (captain), James Bell (vice-captain), William Findlay (secretary) and Joseph Simpson (treasurer). All of these gentlemen were to play key roles in the foundation of the football club that was to be renamed in 12 years hence, Newcastle United. There was discussion on expanding the cricket club's sporting activities – and forming a football club. Soon the club's inaugural football match (against Elswick Leather Works 2nd XI) took place, on 26th November 1881 – two days after the meeting at Allan's house. The new club won 5-0 and Stanley FC's first line-up – and therefore Newcastle United's very first team – was: TS Phalp, J Hobson, J Gardner, A Marr, J Armstrong, JP Cook, R Findlay, WA Coulson, W Findlay, G McKenzie, J Dixon.

Most of the club's Founding Fathers lived and worked in the Byker or Heaton suburbs. William Armstrong Coulson, a teacher, was the side's first captain and recognised as the founder of the club, skipper of the cricket eleven too. The other prominent figure was William Findlay, secretary and soon to replace Coulson as the team's leader.

By the end of the 1890's decade East End were in a far stronger position. They played the better football and just about kept financially afloat. Support in those early days was poor and light years away from the 50,000 plus gates witnessed at St James' Park now. Consequently attempting to remain solvent was a constant struggle. It was clear that the city was not big enough for two senior teams. If football was to progress one club had to disappear.

During the 1891-92 season the battle for dominance came to its conclusion. West End were in a terrible state. Their form deteriorated and they were beaten heavily by East End. The East Enders by comparison also reached the First Round of the FA Cup and their progression as a football club was substantially ahead of the St James' Park organisation. The West Enders were also in a critical financial position. They had no money and by the end of the season called it a day.

The committee men of both clubs met with a view that the East Enders would take over the lease of St James' Park – a superior ground in terms of location and amenities, albeit at that stage still very primitive. East End decided to move from Chillingham Road and set-up base at the city-centre site. As part of the arrangement the remnants of the West End club would be passed to East End too – including a handful of directors and players! East End had won perhaps their greatest contest and became Tyneside's only professional side. They were determined to build a club which would be recognised as a big-time operator in football. First though they had to unite the community.

An element of East End's original support resented having to travel to West End's old home on the other side of the town, while West End's followers were bitter at the demise of their own club. In an attempt to heal the rift and attract more support it was decided to adopt a new name. At a meeting in the Bath Lane Hall close to St James' Park during December 1892, several names were proposed: Newcastle City, Newcastle United and Newcastle Rangers emerged as the favourites. The vote was almost unanimous for Newcastle United. The Football Association agreed to the change on 22nd December 1892, although the alteration in legal title from Newcastle East End was not completed until some time later, not until 1895.

The next step was to gain entry to the Promised Land of the recently introduced Football League. Tyneside's outfit had to start League competition in Division Two joining the Football League's second-tier along with Liverpool and Arsenal among others during the close-season of 1893. It was quite a momentous day in the history of the game as three of the country's leading clubs joined the ranks at the same time.

The Route to Newcastle United

Nov 1881	Stanley FC formed in St Peter's; playing at South Byker.
Aug 1882	Stanley affiliated with Northumberland & Durham FA.
Oct 1882	Stanley change their title to East End FC.
Late 1882	Rosewood FC merge with East End.
Aug 1883	Home ground now behind Byker Vicarage.
Aug 1884	East End move to Dalton Street, Byker.
Mar 1885	First senior trophy secured; Northumberland Challenge Cup.
Sept 1886	East End move to Chillingham Road in Heaton.
Sept 1887	Cheviot FC merge with East End.
Oct 1887	First FA Cup tie at South Bank.
Nov 1887	Union Harriers FC merge with East End.
Jan 1888	Record victory; 19-0 v Point Pleasant (Northumberland Cup).
June 1889	East End turn fully professional.
Sept 1890	Northern League commences, first game for East End.
Feb 1890	East End become a limited company & a share issue launched.
May 1892	Rivals Newcastle West End fold and are disbanded.
May 1892	East End take over the lease of St James' Park.
May 1892	East End fail in bid to join the Football League.
Sept 1892	East End's first home game at St James' Park; v Celtic.
Dec 1892	East End change their name to Newcastle United.
Dec 1892	First game as Newcastle United; v Middlesbrough.
May 1893	Newcastle United elected into the Football League (Division 2)
Sept 1893	First Football League fixture; v Woolwich Arsenal.

The new United were soon to ditch the red shirts of the past and switch to what were to become the famous black-and-white stripes – soon adopting the nickname of the Magpies.

United's first ever Football League match on 2nd September 1893 was against Arsenal – then known as Woolwich Arsenal. United travelled to the Londoner's new ground at Plumstead while the team's expenses had to be paid for by the directors, the club's cash box still being bare. United battled to gain a point in a 2-2 draw yet despite Football League action there was still public apathy and lack of support. What was to become a hotbed of football was only smouldering gently. The flames though were soon to be ignited.

Newcastle United finished that first season in a creditable fourth place and steady improvement followed during the following years although United did suffer record defeats in season 1894-95: 1-7 to Aston Villa in the FA Cup and 0-9 to Burton Wanderers in League action – still the club's heaviest reverse in both competitions. Despite a poor showing in that season, United's development on and off the field was heading at last in the right direction. Support was now steadily increasing to 10,000 and above with the East and West End baggage being buried with time. The financial position gradually improved. Newcastle United had turned the corner. They were now established and the hotbed was stoked.

With financial security United could now attempt to attract better quality footballers to Newcastle. A whole line of them started to flock to Tyneside, many from north of the border including Andy Aitken who became one of the club's stalwarts over the coming seasons. Apart from new players United also made an important signing off the field. In December 1895 Frank Watt was appointed Secretary. That was an important milestone as the Scot became a distinguished administrator. His aim was to turn Newcastle United into the top club in the country. Together with his directors he worked endlessly in making Newcastle United a first-class organisation. In days well before the advent of managers, the moustached Scotsman, filled the role magnificently and the Magpies went from strength to strength, rapidly so.

Heatonites to MAGPIES

During the pioneering years of the club's history the Tyneside media often gave Newcastle East End informal nicknames. The rallying call from the terraces back on Victorian Tyneside was Play Up East End and some newspaper reporters called the club The Reds or East Enders as well as the Heatonites. More traditionally, journalists from out of the area often referred to the club as The Novocastrians. It was not until East End became Newcastle United and black-and-white was adopted that the team were given the title of The Magpies. No precise date is certain but during the later years of the 1890s the tag became more frequent until it soon became commonplace throughout football.

United gained a place in football's elite at the end of the 1897-98 season although promotion in those days was not assured because a club had won the League, or finished as runners-up. The top two clubs from the Second Division, and the bottom two from Division One had to compete in a series of Test Matches to decide relegation and promotion issues. The top pairing of this Test Match mini-league would achieve success. So it was Burnley and Newcastle from the Second Division, against Stoke and Blackburn Rovers from the First. And in a manner to follow Newcastle United in the coming century and more, controversy was not far away.

In the decisive fixture only a draw was needed by Stoke and Burnley to send both clubs into the First Division. And they played out the game in such a fashion that a draw was the only outcome from the first kick of the ball to the last. An outcry followed on the so-called 'fixing' of the Stoke versus Burnley contest and on the general system of promotion and relegation. At the Football League's AGM the Test Match results were scrapped and the system abolished. The First Division was extended and both Blackburn Rovers and Newcastle United were elected into the higher sphere. Everyone was happy. Newcastle United were a First Division club.

BLACK'N'WHITE STRIPES ARRIVE

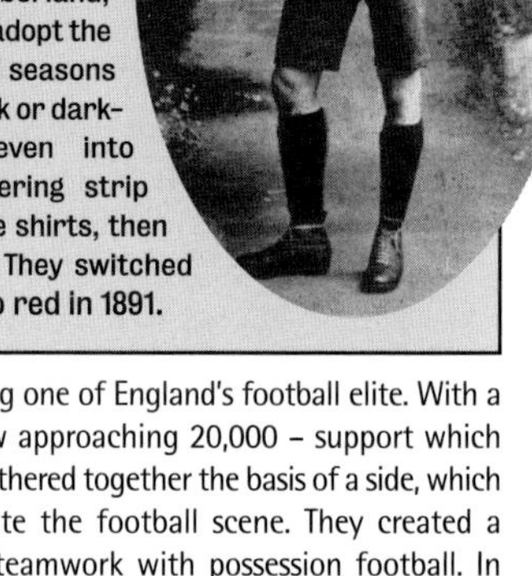

The famous black-and-white striped shirts of Newcastle United are now synonymous with the club and Tyneside in general. It wasn't until August 1894, almost 13 years after formation, that the club decided to change their colours from red shirts due to frequent colour clashes in Second Division action. United had already on a few occasions worn the county colours of Northumberland, black-and-white stripes, and decided to adopt the same kit. It should be noted for several seasons the club's attire was noted as having dark or dark-blue shorts rather than black, even into the 1920s decade. East End's pioneering strip consisted of white shorts and navy-blue shirts, then with the addition of an orange stripe. They switched to Cambridge blue in 1890, changing to red in 1891.

The Magpies were on their way to becoming one of England's football elite. With a loyal and almost guaranteed support, now approaching 20,000 – support which would soon hugely increase – United also gathered together the basis of a side, which during the Edwardian era would dominate the football scene. They created a celebrated eleven, one which combined teamwork with possession football. In Edwardian England, Newcastle United came of age and became the country's football masters. They lifted the League Championship on three occasions and reached five FA Cup finals.

Following the Black'n'Whites' promotion into the First Division, Newcastle's directors began to attract the players to form the nucleus of that great side. Figures like Colin Veitch, Jack Rutherford, Jimmy Lawrence, Alec Gardner, Bill McCracken and Peter McWilliam. All became household names throughout the country. Importantly they continued to add to their squad each year. Established internationals arrived on Tyneside in headline deals: Albert Shepherd, James Stewart and George Wilson to name a few of several big buys. United's side virtually became an all-international eleven, with even international reserves too.

Contests with neighbours Sunderland also started to mean something and there was an astonishing Good Friday encounter with their Wearside rivals that never was in 1901. Amazing scenes were witnessed on Tyneside which created news throughout the country. The attractive holiday fixture with Division One leaders Sunderland was fervently anticipated in the North East. Interest was huge and an estimated 70,000 fans converged on the St James' Park stadium, then with only a capacity of 30,000. Officials and police were swamped by supporters from both camps. Gates were broken down, barriers collapsed and thousands spilled onto the playing surface until the whole pitch was covered by a seething mass of people.

The referee and players attempted to start the game but they and the police were powerless to subdue and clear the crowd. Officials had no alternative but to announce that the match had been abandoned without a ball being kicked. And that led to uproar. A huge free-for-all followed between rival supporters. The Good Friday riot

BLACK'N'WHITE ORIGINS

There are various tales handed down from the past why, firstly Northumberland, then in 1894 Newcastle United chose the colours of black-and-white. The most popular surrounds a fervent supporter from the city's Blackfriars monastery, Father Dalmatius Houtmann. This Dutchman was often to be seen with United's players during the 1890s, the monastery being just a goal-kick away from St James' Park. He was dressed in a traditional black-and-white habit, and it has been suggested that the club decided to adopt his colours. Another legend is the story of a pair of magpies nesting in the old Victorian Stand. It was said that United's players of the time became so attached to the two birds that they picked their distinctive colours and named themselves the Magpies.

Another theory as the Northumberland side used the colours before United did, goes back deep into history. During the English Civil War the Royalist district force, known famously as the Newcastle Whitecoats went into battle wearing white shirts, dark pants, a flash of red, along with Cavalier hats, as well as black leather boots, belts and pouches. The largely black-and-white colours were distinctive and also to be seen on the crest of their commander the Duke of Newcastle. However, it is likely the origin comes from the traditional black-and-white colours of Northumberland's chequered tartan, worn by locals over the past and by the Duke of Northumberland's piper and now still widely seen in the region.

overshadowed everything during that year in the North East and prompted United's directors to plan a major transformation of the St James' Park arena in the coming years which made it one of the finest in the country.

Signs of United's celebrated eleven was clearly evident. In season 1901-02 Newcastle finished in third place while an important capture was the star of Scottish football, Bob McColl known as the Prince of Centre Forwards. That was a sensational deal, United's biggest transfer up to that point. McColl was recognised as one of the finest players in Britain, being an advocate of the possession game with the ball on the grass rather than in the air, and the Scot did much to develop Newcastle's masterful side in the next two years. He stamped his impression on the Magpies that was to last for a decade.

One player to become a huge personality for the Magpies first appeared for the club at that time too, winger Jackie Rutherford. He was a local Tyneside product and became a regular England forward and one of several Geordies to mix with United's big name buys. Along with the likes of full-back Jack Carr and Colin Veitch, Newcastle always made sure they had a local heart to their team.

More eminent players began to make an impression in the black-and-white shirt. Two were significant and both were Scots, Jimmy Howie and Peter McWilliam. And the pair were to develop into quality playmakers of the very best in the Football League.

United pictured before the 1905 FA Cup final.

The Masters at Work
1904-1915

The Magpies first lifted the Football League crown in season 1904-05. The Black'n'Whites were hailed as Champions with the most goals scored and the fewest conceded. They were worthy winners. The title race was settled on the last day of the season after United had dramatically faltered against Sunderland, falling 3-1 in their last home fixture. Despondency set-in amongst United's Edwardian Toon Army, but the Magpies showed character and in the last two games of the season – both away against Middlesbrough ad Sheffield Wednesday – recorded splendid victories to hold off the challenge of Everton and Manchester City. United did it in style too. They scored three goals in each match.

United almost completed what would have been a remarkable achievement of winning not only the League Championship but also the FA Cup. With little Cup pedigree up to then, at last the Magpies put together a sustained bid in the glamour competition and came close to the coveted double as they faced the side they were to replace as club of the era, Aston Villa.

At the Crystal Palace arena a vast crowd of 101,117 was attracted to the meeting of the country's two finest sides. Thousands of Geordies made the long trip to South London, the majority for the very first time visiting the capital. Newcastle United were favourites to lift the FA Cup but Villa showed only too well their proven qualities in the competition being past winners on three occasions. Those at the picturesque Sydenham enclosure saw a fine contest that was talked about for years. Yet Villa won 2-0 and few in Newcastle's camp complained about the result. It was the first of five appearances at the Crystal Palace national stadium in the coming years – each time though, United's form deserted them. They could never overcome what was to be called the Palace Hoodoo.

Edwardian Masters

Newcastle United's line-up from 1905 to the start of World War One in 1914 has been regarded as one of the finest English teams in all of football's history. The Edwardian Masters were a special group of players who took the Magpies to three Football League Championships and to five FA Cup finals, once as winners, all in the space of seven seasons. Each player was highly respected and was well known throughout football, talented performers, the majority being international players during the era. Three players took part in each of those campaigns and collected a full set of eight medals; goalkeeper Jimmy Lawrence, Colin Veitch and winger Jackie Rutherford.

After such a marvellous season United, not surprisingly, generated substantial profits. The cash they were to receive in the coming years made the Black'n'Whites the richest club in the country. Part of the money went on players, and part on an ambitious plan to convert their Gallowgate arena into what was to be among the best in the country. During 1905 St James' Park was ripped apart and converted into a stadium with a capacity noted as 60,000 – but which could hold well over that figure, and did. Vast terracing surrounded the playing surface and a new West Stand was constructed.

United continued where they had left off in the previous campaign. They were in the title race for most of the 1905-06 season but finished in fourth position, eight points behind Liverpool who lifted the trophy. Newcastle's top performance was a then record equalling 8-0 victory over Wolves during November, while in the FA Cup they matched their feat of the previous season by reaching the final for the second successive year.

Another FA Cup final in London, and another day which Newcastle's players and fans quickly tried to forget. The final was an enormous flop as the season's showpiece for the big crowd present at the Crystal Palace. United were again the bookies choice but played poorly. Everton were not much better but did have luck on their side and the one player in Jack Sharp on the wing who was at least playing to something like form. He made the only goal of the game for Sandy Young to fire past Lawrence. The Crystal Palace jinx had paralysed the Magpies again.

For the third year running Tyneside saw another bid for title silverware in season 1906-07. United were at the height of their mastery. If it wasn't the FA Cup that they focussed on, then it was the Football League Championship. United convincingly dominated matches from start to finish in a consistent fashion. Sheffield United, Everton and Bristol City were United's rivals for the title and the Black'n'Whites saw off all three challengers, lifting the trophy by three points. United's popularity and standing in the game was now immense. At St James' Park the club regularly had attendances of between 30,000 and 40,000.

However, even great teams are fallible and Newcastle United certainly caused a mighty sensation when the FA Cup arrived during January. The Geordies were paired with Crystal Palace of all clubs, then a non-league side, and near the bottom of the Southern League at that. It seemed a waste of time for the Londoners to travel north. It was a genuine battle of David and Goliath. No one gave Palace a chance. But with several exiled North Country men in their side, including ex-United players – and the advantage of the Palace Hoodoo – they not only put up a good show, but created one of the biggest FA Cup upsets ever as the Londoners sensationally won by a single goal – and with 10 men too! Newcastle's amazing FA Cup heritage was being created – both in terms of success and humiliation!

With that sensation rapidly forgotten, the 1907-08 campaign was boosted by the record purchase of Everton and Scotland winger George Wilson. The Magpies concluded their League season in fourth position and for the third time in four years reached the FA Cup final. Once more though the Crystal Palace jinx worked its fateful trick on United's players. In the run to the final Newcastle were ruthless, coasting to a meeting with Second Division Wolves.

So to the Crystal Palace again, this time as the hottest favourites up to then. Wolves were to be no competition for the magical Magpies everyone considered. But it all went wrong for the third time on a dismal wet day in London. Newcastle's flowing football was totally destroyed by the physical, fast tackling approach of Wolves who won 3-1.

After that disappointment the Magpies splashed out in the transfer market again and went for one of the best leaders in the country – Bolton Wanderer's England centre-forward Albert Shepherd. And what a buy he proved to be. Shepherd arrived at St James' Park at a time of unrest. Several of the club's stars were in dispute and out of favour. He had a good start in an unfamiliar line-up, netting in a convincing victory at Nottingham Forest. The stars were again ignored for the next match – an important local battle with Sunderland at St James' Park. What a home debut awaited Shepherd.

The date of 5th December 1908 will forever be etched on the minds of every Toon supporter. It was the day Sunderland of all clubs sensationally won 9-1 on Tyneside – still the biggest away victory in the top division. The Magpies new look side was at the time in second place in the table and a near record crowd of 56,000 packed into Gallowgate on a damp, dreary day. With a 1-1 half-time scoreline – Shepherd scoring on his first appearance on Tyneside with a penalty – there was little to indicate what was to follow. Yet United finished the game with only nine men, both Whitson and Duncan on the sidelines injured, and nine goals in their net!

Following this huge setback however, United's directors immediately brought back all their star names into the line-up. And they bounced back at once in the most convincing style. United only lost five games for the remainder of the season and walked away with the Football League Championship with a new record points haul of 53 – seven clear of nearest challengers Everton. It was a remarkable turn-a-round. After such a headlining defeat then to become title winners was astonishing. Never before – or since – has the League Championship trophy been won in such a fashion.

For season 1909-10 the pattern of previous years continued. United followed a Championship victory with a sustained bid to land the elusive FA Cup – and at last they did it, but again had to endure the Crystal Palace gremlin. With the Magpies still the attraction in the country, crowds flocked to watch the Novocastrians – including a reported new national League record of 70,000 at Stamford Bridge, Chelsea during December.

United met another Second Division side in Barnsley in the final. Just as when they faced Wolves in 1908 the Black'n'Whites were hot favourites. Yet that Crystal Palace jinx struck the Magpies not for the first time – and not for the last. Too many fouls and stoppages disrupted the first match at the Palace, Barnsley's spoiling tactics working a treat in a 1-1 draw. They halted Newcastle playing their flowing football and United left the equaliser to the dying moments. The trophy was in fact being decorated out of sight in Barnsley's red, when man-of-the-match Jackie Rutherford grabbed the equaliser.

Albert Shepherd fires home the first goal in the 1910 FA Cup final replay.

At Goodison Park the following Thursday, now away from the hypnotic Crystal Palace, United at last showed in a Cup final what a splendid side they were. The Tynesiders totally outplayed Barnsley and combined skill with brawn, countering the Yorkshire side's physical approach with a gritty, tough performance themselves. Centre-forward favourite Albert Shepherd was the hero of the day – he netted twice to take the FA Cup to Tyneside for the first time. And how Tyneside welcomed the trophy. The streets of the city were packed as the horse-drawn procession snaked its way through the elegant thoroughfares of Grainger and Dobson. The FA Cup at last made an appearance on Tyneside – and it was the last time the old version of the trophy was paraded. A brand new FA Cup was designed for the following year's competition. And Newcastle United were there again in the final.

The Crystal Palace arena is pictured at the bottom right of this panorama.

CRYSTAL PALACE HOODOO

Players, supporters and journalists all reckoned the past national arena of the Crystal Palace held a bizarre jinx over Newcastle United in the years up to World War One. The Magpies reached five FA Cup finals staged in Sydenham and lost them all. Situated in sprawling parkland amidst lakes and trees with the gigantic and inspiring Crystal Palace itself as a spectacular backdrop, United could never play to form there. Some said it the grass was too long for their short passing style of play others considered United's players couldn't cope with nerves or the razzamatazz of the Cup Final, even back then. In addition, as League Champions, United created a huge shock when the lost on home soil, to Crystal Palace of all clubs, in the FA Cup during 1907.

For the fifth occasion in only seven years the Magpies reached the FA Cup final in season 1910-11. Defending the trophy, Newcastle cruised into the final again. Bradford City, then a strong top division outfit, faced the Magpies. They were a good, all-round team with dour, defensive methods. A double blow struck United just before the final, setbacks to ultimately make the difference on the big day. Firstly, in a meaningless League contest at Blackburn, the man United relied on most, Albert Shepherd was carried off in a collision with the Rovers 'keeper. He injured a knee, a bad knock which kept him out of the showpiece and sadly wrecked the rest of his career. Then another mishap rocked United's camp. Peter McWilliam, one of the country's finest schemers, picked up a serious injury playing for Scotland against Wales. Not only was he to be missing from the final, but like Shepherd, it was an injury that was bad enough to force the talented Scot on to the sidelines for months, indeed, to stop him playing ever again.

Against City at the Crystal Palace a 0-0 draw was a big let down for the watching masses. The game was spoilt by a gusting wind and both defences were on top in a dull contest. Newcastle needed the thrust of Shepherd and play-making talent of McWilliam to unlock the door. In the replay at Old Trafford again a swirling wind hindered any chance of good football. Many thousands of fans were still trying to get into the stadium when the winning goal was scored. Bradford gained a somewhat lucky break after a collision in United's goalmouth. Jimmy Lawrence failed to collect the ball and in a melee it was a City boot, that of Jimmy Speirs which connected first. A scrappy goal, but one which sent the new FA Cup to Bradford – appropriately as fate had it, for the trophy was made in that Yorkshire town.

United's Twenties stars in 'gangster' pose. Hughie Gallacher is pictured in the centre.

had been restored they were older and many past their best. Several retired and sadly some did not return at all. Tommy Goodwill was the only senior United player to sacrifice his life while in action with the Northumberland Fusiliers. Young professionals, Tommy Cairns, Richard McGough, George Rivers, Tom Hughes and Dan Dunglinson also fell in action – the latter shoulder to shoulder with Goodwill at the Somme.

Football returned to Gallowgate in the shape of the Newcastle District United League in 1917, but this was some way from First Division action and matches against the likes of Aston Villa, Chelsea and Everton. Now a scratch Magpie eleven faced Aviation Athletic, Brighton West End and Pandon Temperance. Football was not up to a high standard as could be expected but in January 1919 the Northern Victory League was created to celebrate the Armistice. All senior clubs in the North East took part, including South Shields and Durham City, soon to field Football League teams along with Ashington. Middlesbrough lifted the title with United concluding the mini-season in fifth position. Football was on its way back.

With substantial revenue as a result of their year after year success, United continued to invest in top players. Scotland skipper Jimmy Hay arrived at Gallowgate while United paid a record fee for Bury's Billy Hibbert, an England striker who could also play at inside-forward. With this new blood in the side United turned their attention back to the Championship trophy for season 1911-12.

The Magpies almost lifted their fourth title in eight years, being well positioned during April, in second place only three points behind Blackburn Rovers. But in the final games of the programme, a defeat by Aston Villa and draws with Manchester United and Bradford City dashed United's hopes. They finished in third spot and were frustrated at letting points slip during April.

The years leading to the outbreak of World War One in 1914 saw United's celebrated side break-up. The names that had served the Magpies so well in the previous decade were now older, slower and most retired or moved on. The conclusion of the 1912-13 season marked the end of Newcastle's Edwardian heyday. United's performances in that era demand the highest praise. Champions on three occasions, and nearly more. They were only out of the top four placings on one occasion. FA Cup finalists on five occasions, winning the trophy once, and also getting to another semi-final. Peter McWilliam made the comment after he had retired: "The Newcastle team of the 1900's would give any modern side a two goal start and beat them, and further more beat them at a trot." The legendary Billy Meredith wrote: "They had the greatest side that was ever, in my opinion, possessed by any club."

War rather than football was soon on people's minds as hostilities had been declared against the Kaiser during August 1914 and this overshadowed anything and everything. It had been stated by the government that it was in the best interests of the nation that football should carry on, giving an outlet to other worries, and it did to the very end of the 1914-15 season. Included in the crowds were many of Lord Kitchener's army but as the season progressed and war in Europe deteriorated and looked to be prolonged, it was clear that normal football was unable to carry on. Players agreed to take a cut in wages and to donate sums to the War Fund. They also commenced military training too. Instead of shooting with balls at the goal, they now lined up with rifles at ranges set up on the Gallowgate turf.

Many of United's home games were watched increasingly by the walking-wounded from the nearby Rutherford College, now converted to a hospital and during May 1915 first-class football was suspended. Many clubs around the country went effectively into mothballs. Unofficial regional competitions were set-up in certain areas, but at St James' Park football ceased in any senior form until 1919. By the time football was ready to return Newcastle United had to rebuild almost from scratch. This they did very effectively as they launched into another highly eventful period.

War and Between
1915-1945

The signing of the Armistice in November 1918 signalled that football could now seriously start to plan for a relaunch of the country's national game. Like most clubs, Newcastle United's finances and playing squad had been decimated by the outbreak of war in 1914. Players had joined the forces; some went into the vast munitions and engineering works on Tyneside, others headed down the coal-pits. By the time peace

Newcastle United had to put in place a complete rebuilding strategy, on and off the pitch. A new side was needed. A mix of pre-war veterans, local talent and eventually big-name captures was put together which saw the Black'n'Whites develop an enterprising eleven to taste all the trimmings of glory. And this was just the answer the club's Bank Manager wanted. Success led to money streaming into the Gallowgate coffers once again.

At the same time the game also changed as the offside law was altered – a move which brought a feast of goals as new tactics evolved. Newcastle United were very much at the forefront of those important changes during the immediate post-war years while the club also saw the important rule change give them a cutting edge few sides could match. And with a new national arena at Wembley, the Magpies found the surroundings of the Twin Towers very much to their liking – at least for the first 50 years of its romantic life. It was to be an exciting and thrilling Twenties decade.

WEMBLEY GLORY, WEMBLEY WOE

Wembley was unveiled in 1923 and it was soon became the focus of a pilgrimage for football supporters. Newcastle took part in the first all-ticket final the following year and at first enjoyed their trek south to play in FA Cup finals, climbing the famous 39 steps to the Royal box and claim the trophy. They won five out of five played beneath the legendary twin towers and enjoyed all the glory of Wembley. Yet in more recent times, the Magpies found the surroundings of the North London suburb to be anything but enjoyable. From 1974 to the stadium's closure and later demolition in 2003, the Black'n'Whites played six games there and lost all six contests. Newcastle have yet to visit New Wembley, opened after total reconstruction in 2007.

The pre-FA Cup final formalities in 1924 are in progress as Guest of Honour HRH Duke of York meets the Aston Villa and United players.

For the 1919-20 season United fielded many new faces. Most were home grown players, or men signed for modest fees – in a period of financial prudence until their bank balance improved. Priority for the Black'n'Whites was to find a centre-forward. And in time for the following season's kick-off they headed north of the border to capture the services of Partick Thistle's Neil Harris. Also to head to Tyneside from Scotland were two names to be prominent as the club lifted both the FA Cup and Football League title in the coming years: County Durham-born Stan Seymour and Highlander Tom McDonald.

United's rebuilding was on stream. They finished the 1920-21 season in fifth place while the side developed well over the next two seasons. In defence – in days of a two-man rearguard – McCracken and Hudspeth ruled supreme. The pair held an almost telepathic understanding as well as tactical nous. They created an offside plan which worked a treat, catching forwards in a famed trap almost at will.

Season 1923-24 began in an ordinary, unspectacular way until the FA Cup came along in January. Newcastle were due a Cup run. They had not lived up to their Edwardian pedigree in the years since World War One, but 1924 was about to change all that. And in the year football fans were just becoming accustomed to a new showpiece venue, called then, The Empire Stadium, Wembley. Newcastle United and their Geordie following made sure they were going to be there and taste what was to become a magical Wembley experience.

Included in an absorbing FA Cup run that season was a tie with Derby County, one of the finest teams in Division Two. It took the Tynesiders all of four exciting and absorbing games in which 20 goals were scored to get past that Second Round hurdle. Those four games with Derby forged United into a splendid FA Cup side. A never-say-die spirit developed. The Magpies were set for Wembley. They took care of Manchester City in the semi-final and met Aston Villa in the final.

The Empire Stadium with its white stone façade and imposing towers was a vast monument in North London and in 1924 its surrounding grounds also housed the Empire Exhibition – a sprawling mass of pavilions, tents and razzmatazz from around the world and the British Empire. Geordies flocked to Wembley by all means at their disposal – by train, bus and steamers down the North Sea. Some supporters even went by foot – all 560 miles there and back! They spent hours wandering around the exhibits before entering the new Mecca of football.

In the final against old foes Villa, stand-in goalkeeper Bill Bradley at first stood alone between Villa and another FA Cup triumph for the famous Midland club. But the Gateshead-born 'keeper made several important saves and as the game went on, United became stronger and started to impose their brand of football on Villa. The match though appeared to be heading for extra-time when the Magpies rocked the Claret-and-Blues with a double strike in the dying minutes. United scored twice and the FA Cup was destined for the hands of skipper Frank Hudspeth.

It took Newcastle United only a couple of years to fashion their Wembley victors into Football League Champions. Two events made sure United became a more powerful outfit – that change in the laws of the game, and the signing of one of football's greatest ever centre-forwards. Firstly, the offside law had come under close scrutiny, especially as many clubs had copied the effective offside-trap originally laid to perfection by United's McCracken and Hudspeth. The game suffered and in the close-season of 1925 an important change occurred. The rule was altered in favour of the forwards. Goals, goals and more goals were the order of the day.

As a way of countering the new rule, clubs introduced a third defensive player, a stopper centre-half. Until that time the centre-half was a midfielder, with defensive duties solely being down to the two full-backs. Now tactics saw a three man defence in front of the goalkeeper – and a 3-2-5 formation evolved. Newcastle pioneered this tactical change along with a handful of other clubs. Charlie Spencer became arguably the first defensive centre-half as he was converted from a midfield role to the heart of United's back trio.

Any club who could master this new way of playing was halfway to success. The other part of the equation was to possess a striker capable of grabbing goals and taking advantage of hesitant defenders coming to terms with the new style of football. Neil Harris had proved an effective centre-forward during his time at Gallowgate, but he was now over 30 years old and United's directors sanctioned a near British record fee of £6,500 to be paid to Airdrie to secure the services of Scotland's centre-forward Hughie Gallacher. Almost immediately Wee Hughie, as he was to be nationally known, became a massive hero – perhaps surpassed only by Milburn and Shearer in the club's history. And he turned United into a Championship winning side.

The effervescent Scot went on a goal rampage in a black-and-white shirt for the next five seasons. It was a goal frenzy to last until the end of the decade. Before the 1926-27 season began the club's directors made a surprise decision to appoint Gallacher as skipper in place of respected and long serving full-back Frank Hudspeth. The move raised more than a few eyebrows as the controversial young Scot was a touch fiery in temperament, and was in trouble on and off the field throughout his headlining career. Yet Gallacher answered his critics in the only way he could – with goals, lots and lots of them, and by leading United to the title in majestic fashion. He was Newcastle's talisman. Led by Hughie, the Black'n'Whites fielded a brilliant, but lightweight attack – all five forwards averaging barely 5'6" in height!

Newcastle's triumphant FA Cup party manoeuvres its way through the packed streets of Newcastle in 1932.

By December United were placed in a handy position, in the top five along with Burnley, Tottenham Hotspur and Sunderland, as well as team of the era, Huddersfield Town. Then they moved to leaders of the pack. From Christmas to the end of the season Newcastle remained on top of the division for most of the time, powering their way to the club's fourth title victory. A new record crowd of 67,211 saw local rivals, and second-placed Sunderland beaten 1-0 in a crucial fixture then in the final run-in over Easter, United faced Huddersfield Town – with Sunderland, by then United's main challenger. The Terriers arrived on Tyneside for what was almost the deciding battle that resulted in a torrid and frantic struggle between two fine sides. And it was that man Gallacher who clinched the valuable points with the only goal of the game, a header which just about brought silverware to Tyneside.

The Magpies faced Spurs and won 3-2 on Tyneside the following day, lost a return encounter with Huddersfield, but grabbed the point that made absolutely certain that the Championship trophy headed to Tyneside with a draw in London at West Ham United. While United's success was centred on Hughie Gallacher at centre-forward and his record 36 goals in the season (39 in only 41 matches including FA Cup ties), praise was reaped on his forward colleagues, Seymour and McDonald in particular.

Much was expected for the 1927-28 season and the newly crowned Champions started like Champions. Huddersfield Town were defeated 3-1 on the opening day of the season with Gallacher starting off where he had finished. The Scot, who now could do no wrong on Tyneside, thumped in another hat-trick. Manchester United fell too, by 7-1 and all went well until a remarkable loss of form hit the side. They looked more like relegation candidates than Championship holders.

Another somewhat disappointing year followed in season 1928-29 as United's Championship eleven started to break up. It was frustrating for the club's supporters that United could not build on such a well balanced side, in the way that Huddersfield Town had done, and Arsenal were to achieve in the Thirties, and for that matter in the way that Newcastle had developed during Edwardian Britain.

The squad underwent substantial surgery. Part of that change saw the arrival of 39-year-old Scottish maestro Andy Cunningham – brought to Gallowgate to be groomed as United's first ever manager. The arrival of the Rangers and Scotland legend was to cause quite a rumpus on Tyneside with United's star centre-forward Hughie Gallacher never quite seeing eye to eye with the new manager-elect.

Despite Gallacher's goals, United's directors and new player-boss, Cunningham – one of the first in the top division – could not stop the rot. United finished the 1929-30 season in their worst position, in 19th place and just missed relegation by a single point. That campaign also saw the last appearance in a black-and-white shirt of Toon hero Hughie Gallacher. Although the mesmerising Scot had scored another hatful of goals in the season – 34 – and totalled over 140 in his five years at Newcastle, as well as being rated the finest in the country alongside Dixie Dean, United's directors had decided to sell him to Chelsea for a huge £10,000 fee. It was a highly controversial decision as Gallacher had no wish to depart, and United's supporters had no wish to see him head south.

There was uproar on Tyneside. The real reason why United sold Wee Hughie was never disclosed. The player wasn't told, the club said nothing. Rumour had it that the club's boardroom was fed up with the Scot's volatile temperament, seemingly always getting into trouble on and off the field. Or was it that Newcastle needed cash? They had made a loss on transfers, while the economic recession of the time had an effect too. There was also an apparent problem between manager Cunningham and his fellow countryman. Maybe that was the real reason one of United's greatest ever players was allowed to join the Blues of Stamford Bridge.

Tyneside was not a stable football community during the summer months of 1930. A new decade had begun in completely the wrong way. Manager Andy Cunningham and his directors had to put the remnants of a rattled side together again. It didn't take long to do so and not before long echoes of The Blaydon Races rang around Wembley Stadium again.

At first the club had to overcome the Gallacher sale. His exit was a demoralising blow to Newcastle United supporters. Most found the transfer hard to understand. Gallacher remained an icon on Tyneside and had done nothing wrong in the eyes of United's faithful. Ironically the very first home fixture of the following 1930-31 season saw Chelsea – and Gallacher – visit St James' Park. Interest in that First Division contest was intense, unsurpassed in the club's history. Seemingly everyone wanted to see Wee Hughie again and voice their backing of the player and at the same time dissatisfaction at his sale. A vast crowd massed around the St James' Park arena for the Wednesday fixture. Reports indicated that maybe as many as 80,000 tried to get into the Gallowgate stadium – then with a capacity of around 65,000 and at a severe strain approaching 70,000.

No.9 HEROES

A golden thread runs through tales of United's past, that of the club's now legendary centre-forward tradition. Since Victorian and Edwardian years, the Magpies have often fielded a special goalgetter in the centre-forward shirt. A whole line of them have become supporter favourites. And when shirt numbers were actually introduced to football in 1939, the No.9 shirt took on legendary status. Before the two wars the likes of Jock Peddie and Bob McColl started the tale. Then Bill Appleyard, Albert Shepherd, Neil Harris, Jack Allen and Wee Hughie Gallacher scored plenty of goals. Albert Stubbins followed, as did Wor Jackie Milburn, Len White, Wyn Davies and Supermac, Malcolm Macdonald. Modern stars arrived such as Chris Waddle, Andy Cole, Les Ferdinand and perhaps the finest of them all, Alan Shearer. Then Andy Carroll claimed the shirt for a brief period and kept the folklore very much alive.

Left to right: Jackie Milburn Alan Shearer, Hughie Gallacher. Malcolm Macdonald.

Thousands clambered in, thousands were locked out. A new record attendance of 68,386 (although the reported figure varies) was inside St James' Park as Gallacher ran out from the tunnel and onto the field. Hughie received a hero's welcome. Cloth caps waved, cheers and roars of appreciation for the ex-United star were astounding.

The opening of the Thirties decade saw United fare little better than at the end of the previous ten years. It was an experimental season for manager Andy Cunningham as he remodelled the United squad. In the close-season of 1931 United splashed out a modest £3,500 fee to bring Jack Allen back to his native Tyneside in a bid to solve the centre-forward problem. And the experienced Sheffield Wednesday leader was an immediate success as he spearheaded the Black'n'Whites on a return visit to Wembley.

By the time the FA Cup was due to kick-off Cunningham had worked hard to build unity. At the turn of the year, and with young, emerging players in the side like Sammy Weaver, Harry McMenemy and Jimmy Richardson, the Magpies appeared to have turned the corner. Newcastle were on the FA Cup trail, on a run which eventually saw them meet Chelsea – and of course Hughie Gallacher – in the semi-final.

The pre-match talk all surrounded Gallacher in the build up to the clash at Leeds Road, Huddersfield. Apart from the immortal Hughie, Chelsea fielded a side full of international talent but Newcastle came out on top in a 2-1 victory and reached their seventh FA Cup final.

Everyone's thoughts were on Wembley and facing up to the might of Arsenal, during the Thirties at the height of their mastery. The Londoners were to lift five Championship crowns and reach three FA Cup finals in this period. The Magpies were underdogs, however on the big day raised their game to oust the Gunners.

A classic final was witnessed, one that went down in history as one of the most talked about of all time, and a tie which produced one of the most controversial goals in the FA Cup's annals. Arsenal looked the more refined side and they started well. In fact the Gunners took the lead through winger Bob John after McInroy and Nelson had misjudged a cross.

Showing plenty of spirit, United hit back and went close on several occasions in a bid to grab an equaliser. And seven minutes before half-time they did so, creating one of the biggest talking points for years. As Jimmy Richardson chased for a deep pass which looked to be heading over the touchline and out of play, he wrapped his boot round the ball and fired in a cross for Jack Allen to power a shot into the Arsenal net. But was the ball out of play before United's inside-forward hit the centre? The referee thought not, the linesman agreed. But after the game many judges, backed by viewing early film footage, reckoned the ball was clearly over the line and the goal should not have stood.

Newcastle though were back in the match. And from that moment they started to impose themselves on the Gunners. United dominated the second-half and 18 minutes from the end Allen scored the winner with a tremendous piece of centre-forward play. On a 30-yard run, he went past three Arsenal defenders before striking a low drive into the net to secure the trophy.

United's FA Cup triumph had bonded together a decent side and for the 1932-33 season the Magpies' improvement even saw them make a bid for the Championship. They were back among the country's leading attractions and commenced the season in fine goalscoring form with Allen and Richardson, who played for England, proving a dangerous combination.

Andy Cunningham appeared to have put together a capable squad. Respected international players were at the heart of his side however in season 1933-34 the whole pack fell apart as Newcastle went through their worst season since entering the Football League over 40 years before. Although United gave their concerned fans a festive tonic by demolishing both Everton (7-3) and Liverpool (9-2) in quick succession, Newcastle slumped and failed to reproduce even a glimmer of that scintillating form. There were no more smiles. In the last 14 games of the programme United only won a single game and finished two points below Birmingham in a relegation position. The Magpies went down with Sheffield United. After 36 years in the top flight they were back in Division Two.

Newcastle United were now in a period of rapid decline. There was conflict in the boardroom in the wake of United's relegation, infighting at the top which lasted throughout the Thirties decade. United did not relish their first taste of demotion at all. In fact the club suffered a rude awakening. Revenue fell substantially after years of a good income stream, while the high prestige the Magpies held fast disappeared. And on the football field they found the more rough and tumble of Second Division football not to their liking. With Cunningham shown the door, the Black'n'Whites turned to Stoke City boss Tom Mather. He had earned a good reputation having fashioned Stoke into a useful First Division outfit after winning promotion in 1933. It was hoped he would do the very same for Newcastle United.

The Magpies second bite of Second Division football proved little better however. They ended two places lower with finances in free-fall. Gates were significantly down and the country's worsening economy had a major effect on the club, as with all other sides around the country.

Mather started a rapid rebuilding process but his new look United eleven with the enterprising Jack Smith at centre-forward fared little better. Although tipped for a serious promotion bid in 1937-38, as it turned out they certainly were involved in a sustained fight, but at the wrong end of the table! Indeed, the Magpies went through what would be recorded as their worst ever League campaign in almost 110 seasons and only missed the drop into Division Three North by a whisker.

Newcastle were trapped in a relegation dogfight with Barnsley, Nottingham Forest and Stockport County and the intense scrap became a nervous and desperate one. Placings at the bottom became extremely tight and as the finale to the season unravelled it was touch and go whether Newcastle would scrape clear or go tumbling out of the second tier of English football for the first time. In the end they were saved by the narrowest of margins - by one-tenth of a goal, finishing fourth from bottom of the table on the same points as Barnsley who went down.

After such a catastrophic season boardroom conflict and bickering resulted in decisive action. United's directorate made a monumental decision by inviting former star player Stan Seymour onto the top table. It was a shock move as Seymour had previously left the club in bitter dispute over payments and had since been a stinging critic at the fall from grace of the club he served so well for nine years. To the Board's credit, they knew that Seymour had the football know-how, respect and determination to turn the club's fortunes around. Seymour became a rarity in football then, a former player in the boardroom. And he was an inspiration, in time taking substantial control and completely revitalising the Magpies.

As the clouds of war started to hang over Europe again, season 1938-39 began in sombre mood. Nevertheless Seymour's influence on team matters made sure the Magpies did not repeat the previous campaign's pitiful failure. Newcastle's directors released almost £40,000 to buy new players and Seymour was at the heart of the talent search - almost becoming a second manager and the real power at St James' Park. Young players made their mark too, including inside-forward Albert Stubbins.

FOOTBALL HOTBED

Since the beginning of the 20th century, Newcastle United have always enjoyed a huge and wonderful support, the envy of most clubs around the country. Gates of 50,000 and over were often to be seen during pre-war years however the post-war boom saw attendances soar around the country - and nowhere more so than at St James' Park. In season 1947-48 the majestic Toon support created a new record average at any ground of over 56,000 at each home fixture. In modern day football only Manchester United and latterly Arsenal have bettered the Magpies' gates for Premier League fixtures. Since the club's stadium enlargement in 2001, Newcastle's average for Premier League action is an impressive 50,000-plus, just about fully 96% of capacity. Considering the lack of modern success witnessed on Tyneside, the region certainly deserves its 'Hotbed of Football' tag.

He was to develop into one of United's greatest goalscorers during wartime football. It was just the start of Seymour's flair of bringing talented players to St James' Park. His football knowledge and down-to-earth, yet sweet-talking charm, was to serve United with great results over the next 38 years.

Most supporters and critics were well satisfied with the Magpie revival. The club's books though showed a thumping loss in the year, but it was money worth losing if the investment meant that United were on their way back to becoming one of the top sides in the country. However that revival was to be interrupted for six long years as Hitler and his henchmen put an abrupt end to senior football.

Long before the 1939-40 programme began there had been an air of despondency about the mounting crisis on the Continent. And with only three matches recorded football was put on hold as Prime Minister Chamberlain declared war on Germany. A world-wide conflict was to erupt as never before. Wartime soccer replaced senior action and with football severely disrupted a lower grade of competition inevitably materialised. Newcastle possessed a potent striker in Albert Stubbins who took full advantage with goals by the hatful, while clubs could also field guest players who were stationed in the area, or on home leave, as a new registration system was introduced. Several noted names pulled on the black-and-white shirt during the war years including Tom Finney, Bill Nicholson and Stanley Mortensen.

Newcastle United spent the period of World War Two as something of an opportune break from their Thirties struggle. During the seven wartime seasons, supremo Stan Seymour searched the region for new young talent and groomed an eager squad of players in readiness for peacetime football.

As Seymour took control of team affairs he fielded a mix of local lads and guests. The tall, leggy frame of Stubbins developed into the country's most feared striker. No one could stop him. Albert netted the amazing total of over 230 goals in 187 wartime matches, including 29 hat-tricks. By the time season 1945-46 kicked-off football was fast returning to normal. And several of Seymour's youthful juniors showed their promise. Jackie Milburn, Bobby Cowell, Bobby Corbett, Ernie Taylor and Charlie Crowe all rubbed shoulders with pre-war professionals like Tommy Pearson and Jimmy Gordon. Those youngsters - and a few astute signings were very soon to create quite an impact on the football world. Newcastle United's decline was well and truly over.

Left:* *(top) Len Shackleton scores one of his six goals in the 13-0 record victory over Newport in 1946. (bottom) Jackie Milburn hits the net during the FA Cup-tie with Portsmouth in 1952.

Skipper Joe Harvey holds the FA Cup at Wembley in 1951. Left to right: Corbett, Crowe, Walker (behind), Taylor, Milburn, Harvey, Brennan, Cowell, Mitchell.

Wembley Kings
1945-1961

Newcastle United spent those war years extremely wisely. With Stan Seymour at the forefront of affairs – manager in all but name – he guided the club to a new period of prosperity as football returned to normal. The Magpies were rebuilt almost from scratch with a determination to get back to the top. As they had done after World War One, Newcastle created a side that went onto triumph and in an attacking, flamboyant way. Players emerged who became household names, a mix of home-grown talent and shrewd – yet sometimes expensive – buys in the transfer market. Newcastle United were a big spender and soon few clubs could match their purchasing power in the immediate post-war years.

Seymour's keen and sharp football mind harnessed together a side that entertained and which developed into the King's of Wembley during the Fifties. And the Twin Towers became very special to the Magpies and their supporters. United visited Wembley three times in the space of only five years and on each occasion lifted the FA Cup aloft in front of those white stone domes. Wembley was Newcastle's second home as a marvellous period in the history of the club unfolded.

With the trials of war over apart from the bickering, people wanted to relax and be entertained. Football was the working man's outlet and a boom was to hit the national game throughout the country – and nowhere more so than at St James' Park. Crowds flocked back to watch football and at Gallowgate youngsters like Jackie Milburn, Ernie Taylor, Bobby Cowell and Charlie Wayman were on show alongside notable signings such as Joe Harvey from Bradford City and centre-half Frank Brennan by way of Airdrie.

For the 1946-47 season as football returned in full swing, attendances rose everywhere. United's average gate went up to over 49,000. They were the best supported club in the country and within 12 months it had risen to more than 56,000, a national record until Manchester United only narrowly bettered it 20 years later in 1968. It was a remarkable achievement as the Magpies were still then a Second Division club.

United's eleven was full of exciting talent. For that 1946-47 campaign more new faces arrived and United fielded a side of exceptional quality. Newcastle broke the bank to attract Len Shackleton to St James' Park, a highly skilled inside-forward from Bradford Park Avenue. Shack of course was to become one of the game's most exhilarating players, a complete showman on the field. And what a debut awaited the Yorkshireman.

At Gallowgate against Newport County, the Magpies were irresistible. United equalled the Football League's highest ever score, smashed the First and Second Division record and Shackleton netted no fewer than six goals on his debut – and within 90 seconds United had missed a penalty! The scoreline ended 13-0, United's highest ever first-class victory. Everything the magical feet of Shackleton did on that afternoon came off. It was quite a show.

The Geordies main target was promotion to the First Division that season, but the FA Cup distracted the side as they reached the semi-final. And against Charlton Athletic at Elland Road in that semi-final, a club with a respected Division One pedigree at the time, the Magpies flopped controversially, losing 4-0. They were swept aside in a more than convincing manner and few at the time could understand why a free-flowing United eleven had played so dismally. But there had been trouble in the camp. Prior to the match top scorer Charlie Wayman – who ended the season as the division's most deadly striker with 30 goals – was sensationally dropped following a dispute with trainer Norman Smith. That rocked an already uneasy boat as other squabbles had been simmering in the background between officials and players. The team was unsettled and the Londoners took full advantage.

The fall-out from the semi-final defeat was quick. Wayman departed south while Len Shackleton was soon to move on too – joining rivals Sunderland in a record transfer. At the end of the season the directors, recognising that their footballers were in need of more direct management, rather than boardroom dictate, appointed George Martin as boss, although Stan Seymour remained with a huge influence. The ex-Luton Town manager turned out to be a wise appointment.

Within 12 months of Martin's arrival United were back with the elite of football, in the First Division. Season 1947-48 saw the Black'n'Whites promoted after a seven season absence and Martin took much of the credit, overcoming the discontentment of the previous campaign, then developing a resolute side with attacking flair. United's eleven possessed formidable spirit and teamwork, led on the field by an inspiring skipper in Joe Harvey, and backed by a huge, vociferous crowd which famously just about gave them a goal start in each home fixture.

The decisive promotion contest was against rivals Sheffield Wednesday at Gallowgate, a game that proved to be a battle royal. After an enthralling end to end tussle United finished winners by 4-2 and all but promoted. It was a good season all round for the Magpies in 1947-48. The club's reserve side lifted the Central League Championship too.

No impetus was lost after promotion as United took the First Division by storm and almost achieved a dramatic League Championship victory. Boosted by quality purchases of Bobby Mitchell and Chilean George Robledo, the energy and moral fibre showed in the previous campaign was again evident as the Toon challenged strongly for the title. Crucially though in the final run-in Newcastle met their main challengers Portsmouth in front of a 60,000 gate at St James' Park. The big crowd were stunned as Portsmouth comprehensively showed who was going to lift the trophy by winning 5-0!

The following season was much the same story; a programme that promised much but which in the end saw United frustrate supporters. Yet glory was soon to follow. As the Fifties decade opened Newcastle United were back as one of the country's finest teams. And for the next five years the Magpies were the club everyone was talking about. It was black-and-white scarves and black-and-white rattles kids asked for. It was autographs of Milburn, Mitchell and Robledo they wanted. The FA Cup and Wembley Stadium catapulted United into the limelight like never before.

MILESTONES • 1950-51 Two goals from Jackie Milburn at Wembley secures the FA Cup against Blackpool

The 1950-51 season saw the Geordies hit top spot in the First Division during September but it was in the FA Cup that United glittered most. And this despite losing manager George Martin, who took a lucrative offer with Aston Villa. Stan Seymour moved back into the spotlight, managing playing affairs, and the United director was instrumental in guiding the Tynesiders to a treble of FA Cup victories.

Newcastle reached the first of three finals in only a five year period and at the same time made a bid to challenge Spurs for the title. But Wembley and the glory of the FA Cup preyed on their mind and the Londoners raced away with League silverware. United met Blackpool at Wembley and the capacity crowd that witnessed the showpiece final was not disappointed in the way the FA Cup was won. With names such as Stanley Matthews and Tynesider Stan Mortensen, Blackpool were no pushovers. But Newcastle had the Wembley match-winner in Jackie Milburn who struck twice with breathtaking goals to secure a Tyneside victory. And those goals were two of the best ever scored at the famous stadium – the first a breakaway run half the length of the field, the second, a stunning long-range effort that flew into the top corner of the net.

With Newcastle still glowing with confidence they got off to a spectacular start to the 1951-52 season, thrashing Stoke City 6-0. Milburn fired the ball into the net three times and fellow striker George Robledo was also on the scoresheet. The partnership of Milburn and Robledo hit their peak that season. They were a deadly duo. The Chilean scored 39 goals, equalling Hughie Gallacher's record in a single season for United, while Milburn clocked up 28 goals.

Newcastle were in exhilarating form as 1952 opened and as their FA Cup defence began. United achieved a rare feat in English football by winning the FA Cup in successive years – the first time by any club since 1891. And after United's 1952 victory only three clubs have repeated that remarkable effort. The final with Arsenal was a match of no greatness with both United and the Londoners finding it difficult to find any sort of form. And the Gunners lost full-back Wally Barnes for most of the game after the Welsh defender twisted a knee attempting to stop a run of Milburn.

Newcastle's winner came in the closing moments. Appropriately Bobby Mitchell – the one man playing to ability, and who had been so important to United in the run to the final – created the opening with a characteristic wing sortie. He dribbled up the flank and sent over a deep, looping cross to the far post. George Robledo jumped to the ball and his well placed header went into the net, off the post. The FA Cup was in the hands of Joe Harvey again to equal Blackburn Rovers' Victorian achievement.

Before the club's next triumph, Newcastle spent heavily to bring Portsmouth and Scotland wing-half Jimmy Scoular to Tyneside as a replacement for Joe Harvey who had moved onto the coaching staff.
Indeed, by the time the 1954-55 season opened Newcastle United's side had gone through quite a change. Only Milburn, Cowell and Mitchell remained from the Magpies earlier FA Cup double and that trio were to be instrumental as the Black'n'Whites embarked on another Wembley trail.

Cup Treble

United's immediate post-war line-up developed into a prized combination. In 1951, 1952 and 1955 the Magpies reached the FA Cup final after thrill-a-minute Cup runs and lifted the trophy on each occasion. They first defeated Blackpool, then Arsenal and finally Manchester City. Newcastle were well-liked and respected throughout football. Three players took part in all 25 ties; full-back Bobby Cowell and star forwards Bobby Mitchell and Jack Milburn. Director Stan Seymour was in all but name, manager of the side. He had lifted the trophy as a player back in 1924. In 1955-56 United nearly reached another final, losing in the quarter-final to neighbours Sunderland.

Jack Milburn's dramatic opening goal inside the first minute of the 1955 FA Cup final.

United were an inconsistent eleven and during the opening months of the season frustrated many. The club's Board decided it was about time to appoint another manager and in came Duggie Livingstone who had a reputation of being a modern boss having impressed on the Continent. Manchester City had won through to meet United at Wembley – toppling Sunderland in the other semi-final at Villa Park and ending the region's dream of a Tyne versus Wear final.

By the time the Wembley showdown arrived United's camp had gone through a controversial episode which resulted in boss Duggie Livingstone's days at St James' Park become severely numbered. The manager's chosen FA Cup final eleven had not included Jackie Milburn and when his teamsheet was shown to Stan Seymour for approval with the rest of the Board, United's senior figure was not amused to say the least. Seymour was fuming. Diplomatically he organised a Board vote on United's Cup final line-up and made sure Milburn was in the side. Livingstone was told in no uncertain terms which team would face Manchester City. The manager was not to stay long on Tyneside thereafter.

The 1955 FA Cup final started sensationally. And of course it had to be Milburn who created the headlines. After only 45 seconds Wor Jackie rose to head in a White corner, powering the ball into the top corner of the net as if to prove a point. Milburn was a Wembley hero again. From that early moment United were the masters of City, although the Maine Road club did equalise before half-time only for United to take control, especially after Jimmy Meadows was forced to leave the field due to a ligament injury trying to stop the twisting turns of Bobby Mitchell.

Ten-man City were no match for United with Scoular controlling midfield and Mitchell reaping havoc on the flank. United's Scottish wing wizard netted a second, following a mazy run and acute angled shot which deceived City's German-born goalkeeper Bert Trautmann into expecting a cross. The game was wrapped up with a lovely goal by George Hannah, who crowned a fine individual display by finishing off a Scoular and Mitchell combination to score from 12 yards. It was United's FA Cup again. No one needed to tell the players how to climb those Wembley steps.

Those five years of glory were followed by five years of decay and eventual collapse. The Magpies though retained star quality in their side and still showed plenty of fighting spirit as they remained focussed at even more FA Cup success. United also continued to be an unpredictable team for the rest of the Fifties decade, able to play brilliant football at times, but also to look like woeful amateurs.

In season 1955-56 United defended the FA Cup with determination and took part in a wonderful tie against Fulham at Craven Cottage; a 5-4 victory after being 3-0 ahead, and 4-3 down! That season also recorded a memorable double victory over local rivals Sunderland at Christmas. On Boxing Day the Black'n'Whites almost matched that infamous and everlasting 9-1 humiliation of 1908. At Roker Park the Magpies stormed to a 4-0 first-half lead and then added two more goals after the interval. With a little better finishing United could have easily have reached the magic figure of nine. But six was enough and how the Toon supporters enjoyed their celebration that evening.

A day later United fans were hardly able to get the roars of Roker Park out of their ears before it all started again. This time United won 3-1 after being a goal down at half-time. But it was Sunderland who stopped the Magpies going all the way to Wembley yet again and in the process regained some pride. After that pulsating tie with Fulham, the Tyne-Wear rivals met in a quarter-final tie. The red-and-whites triumphed against all the odds by beating the Magpies at St James' Park.

Another remarkable FA Cup encounter took place the following campaign, in 1956-57. Few could believe that a match good enough to equal the thrilling end-to-end action of Craven Cottage could take place so quickly. But it did, in the Third Round against Manchester City. At Maine Road, City roared into attack from the kick-off and scored three quick goals to rock United. Yet United battled back to equalise at 3-3 then City were back in front at 4-3. United had it all to do again, and they amazingly did it, winning in extra-time by 5-4!

With that season ending in another year of mediocrity a new manager was appointed as the club decided to bring themselves into a football world which was starting to substantially alter. Although the Magpies had employed managers in the past, Newcastle United had always resisted their introduction – having been hesitant to lose control from the boardroom. But the game was changing and in stepped a bright and breezy moderniser in the shape of ex-Manchester United winger, Charlie Mitten for the start of the 1958-59 season.

The club certainly needed a new outlook. The days of director control and pre-war ideals were rapidly disappearing. Mitten immediately began to build a new squad and signed several players. His most important capture was the Golden Boy of Welsh football, Ivor Allchurch. Mitten's mini-revolution over the next three seasons saw the advent of many fresh ideas – including a stream-lined Continental style kit, United now ditching the baggy shirts and baggy shorts for good. Despite all the good intentions, Mitten though, never put together a side that could even begin to emulate the old-style Magpies. The team remained as erratic as ever. They thrilled many with some exciting performances as long serving Len White and emerging youngster George Eastham combined with Allchurch at the forefront of several memorable attacking displays which brought plenty of goals.

In season 1960-61 Mitten's Marvels as they were dubbed, flopped alarmingly. They continued to hit the net time and time again with White the spearhead, but in defence they were desperate. United conceded an incredible 109 goals, and as a result the Magpies tumbled to the bottom reaches of the First Division – and ultimately into Division Two.

Confidence was not helped either when lowly Colchester United knocked the Tynesiders out of the new Football League Cup tournament, an embarrassing 4-1 defeat at Layer Road. Additionally inside-forward George Eastham ran into a headlining dispute with the club over a transfer request, one which ended up in the High Court as the player took on, not only the Magpies, but football's archaic rules. Eastham was a loss. The Magpies ended up going down with Preston North End. Newcastle United were back where they started in 1946 and had to take stock and instigate a rebuilding process once more.

Harvey's Heroes
1961-1975

Newcastle United's fabulous Fifties era had come to a disappointing end. The glories of Wembley were now a distant memory. Charlie Mitten's attempt to take the Magpies into a rapidly changing football world had floundered and United found themselves in Division Two. Shocked and stunned, a past giant faced a period of uncertainty.

Newcastle United needed to continue to move with the times. On and off the field the Tynesiders needed a fresh outlook. Soon obsolete rules would be swept away; players would have unheard of freedom to select who they appeared for and unheard of wealth. The Sixties brought massive change in both football and society in general.

To guide United through this period the club turned to an old war-horse, former skipper of two FA Cup victories, Joe Harvey. While Harvey could never be said to be a great moderniser, he was black-and-white through and through and gained support of the fans for much of his 13 year period in charge at Gallowgate. He also was a players' manager – earning respect, if not for his tactical qualities, for his inspiration and enthusiasm, and for the many star players he brought to Tyneside. Joe steadily rebuilt the Magpies, initially based on solidity then with flair. United slowly dusted off the cobwebs of the old way and entered a new progressive football world – one that brought European glory, more Wembley drama and a host of Harvey's Heroes.

Manager Joe Harvey (left) and skipper Stan Anderson (right) hold the Second Division trophy in 1965 watched by Chairman Lord Westwood (behind).

Bob Moncur greets the Setubal captain at a snow-swept St James' Park in 1969.

Europeans

Newcastle United lead the way when it comes to flying the flag of the North East in Europe having played 120 competitive matches since their debut season of 1968-69. They won the Inter Cities Fairs Cup in that year and since have twice taken part in the prestigious Champions League, reaching Stage 2 in season 2002-03. Newcastle are one of only 10 English clubs to qualify in UEFA's premier competition and one of 16 in the European Cup since the tournament began. Apart from serious competitive football on the Continent, the Magpies have made regular visits to Europe since earliest times, in pre-war years to play exhibition games when British clubs educated the world in the sport. Newcastle's first game abroad was in 1904 when United travelled to Denmark to face a Copenhagen XI. Excluding the Home nations and the Republic of Ireland, Newcastle have faced clubs from 42 different countries.

Joe wheeled and dealed in the transfer market and fashioned almost a whole new side. He also targeted several of a batch of promising juniors for a future role. The Geordie kids had lifted the FA Youth Cup in 1962 for the first time and several of that side developed into star players, prominently Bob Moncur, Alan Suddick and David Craig.

Before Harvey's new team gained promotion though supporters had to endure some frustration and disappointment including one terrible lapse in the FA Cup.

Southern League Bedford Town had drawn the glamour tie in the 1964 tournament, a trip to FA Cup giants Newcastle United in the Third Round. And the blue-and-white shirts of the minnows were to be long remembered on Tyneside as they sensationally caused the shock of the season by winning 2-1, a notable upset in FA Cup history. After being tournament giants for so long, United found themselves in an extended run of Cup obscurity – both in the FA Cup and emerging Football League Cup. It was a dismal period to last for several years to come.

United's manager soon introduced some of the club's promising youngsters into action. Alan Suddick had already made his mark reaching the England Under-23 line-up, while full-backs Frank Clark and David Craig grabbed a place in defence, and both men stayed there for the next decade and more. Bobby Moncur and Bryan Robson were to be blooded too.

The Black'n'Whites made a determined bid the get back into the First Division in season 1964-65. All the manager's new faces had by then settled and Harvey put together a steadfast, hardworking eleven which ended up the best in the division as Second Division Champions. At the heart of the Magpies was a half-back line of quality: Stan Anderson, John McGrath and Jim Iley. A crowd of almost 60,000 knew that a Good Friday victory against Bolton Wanderers at Gallowgate would secure First Division football again for the Geordies and in a terrific atmosphere United ended up with the two vital points with a solid and professional 2-0 victory.

With football continuing to change, now seeing the advent of new formations such as 4-4-2 and 4-3-3 – gone were half-backs and inside-forwards, now midfielders and strikers reigned supreme – Newcastle found life difficult back in Division One. United's scouting network worked overtime to target new talent, especially up front. They needed a top centre-forward and Harvey plunged for Bolton's Wyn Davies in 1966 at a new club record fee of £80,000.

Davies took time to settle, but his arrival saw United steadily improve and steer clear of the relegation trap-door. By the time the 1967-68 programme began the Tynesiders had consolidated and were looking upwards. And being doomed before they had almost started by many critics, United surprised everyone during that campaign. Indeed, only a bad away record stopped the Magpies making a bid for a top three place, so good was their home form and the general revival.

MILESTONES • 1964-65 Following relegation, Newcastle are Second Division Champions and return to the top-tier

United finished the season well and because of one-club-per-city rules at the time, the Magpies actually qualified for European football for the very first occasion, in the Inter Cities Fairs Cup – the forerunner to the UEFA Cup and Europa League tournament. Jetting the highways of the Continent was something completely new for the whole North East region. And how the thousands upon thousands of supporters were to enjoy the club's opening three years of rousing European action which followed.

Season 1968-69 was to be United's most eventful for over a decade. The club's first ever European tie against seasoned campaigners Feyenoord during September 1968 saw many doubters. Few gave the Toon a hope, especially against a side of the Dutch team's standing. Yet Newcastle showed everyone they were not in the competition just to make up the numbers. In fact they were to show they could match the best on the Continent and lift the trophy at the very first attempt!

They destroyed Feyenoord 4-0 on Tyneside with a brilliant display and then took care of Lisbon's Sporting Clube and Real Zaragoza, two more experienced European sides. Another victory over Vitoria Setubal and the Tynesiders had confounded everyone by reaching the semi-finals. Harvey had now bonded a determined and gritty eleven expertly marshalled by skipper, and soon to be Scotland international, Bob Moncur. And up front the Davies and Robson partnership was a handful.

Bob Moncur and Willie McFaul hold the Fairs Cup to the St James' Park crowd.

The last four of the competition saw United in the draw along with Hungarians Ujpesti Dozsa, Goztepe of Turkey, and Scottish giants Glasgow Rangers. Newcastle were paired with Rangers, to give the country a fascinating Battle of Britain tie. A record Fairs Cup crowd of 75,580 packed into Ibrox for the first-leg encounter and the Black'n'Whites performed heroics in a resolute defensive display against the Glaswegians. Goalkeeper Willie McFaul took all the headlines by saving a vital Andy Penman spot-kick, diving the right way and pushing the ball around the post.

The events that occurred in the return leg, witnessed by nearly 60,000 were certainly worth waiting for – although probably not for the football played! The drama, tension and incident that unfolded completely overshadowed United's fine 2-0 victory in a very tough and physical match. It was more like Bannockburn or Culloden than an important European semi-final as the Scottish fans tried to call a halt to the game by invading the pitch and confronting police. Nevertheless the Geordies reached their first European final despite all the odds and they were handed much deserved praise, even from southern doubters.

Ujpesti Dozsa faced United in a two-legged final, a crack Hungarian side which at the time were recognised as one of the best combinations on the Continent. They included world stars Ferenc Bene and Janos Gorocs. All 60,000 tickets were sold for the first-leg at Gallowgate and Newcastle were in the right frame of mind. Newcastle wanted goals to take to Budapest and goals they got, although they were a long time in coming. It was skipper Bob Moncur who set the Magpies on course with an opening strike just after the hour in the 3-0 victory. He had never before scored a first-class goal, but the Scot amazingly went onto grab a hat-trick over the two legs.

On a hot and sticky evening alongside the Danube, United perhaps had wished they had stayed on Tyneside. The Magyars tore into the Magpies from the kick-off and by half-time were 2-0 ahead. But the interval perhaps saved the Geordies. They re-grouped, and with a short but famous dressing-room pep talk by Joe Harvey, turned the tables on the Hungarians after the break. Newcastle scored three times and astonishingly United lifted the Inter Cities Fairs Cup, 3-2 on the night and convincingly 6-2 on aggregate. It was a remarkable achievement.

The following two seasons saw United figure in more European deeds, with domestic football taking something of a back seat. They took part in noted ties with Belgian aristocrats Anderlecht and the might of Internazionale. The Milanese club was overflowing with star names – many from the World Cup in Mexico during the past summer of 1970, notably Facchetti, Burgnich, Mazzola and Bonninsegna. Yet the Magpies toppled them following a pulsating second-leg on Tyneside that even saw police on the pitch assisting the referee restore order.

At the end of the 1970-71 programme boss Joe Harvey decided on a major tactical change. He concluded that United's game-plan of the long ball to Wyn Davies had seen its day. Harvey splashed out a club record fee of £180,000 for the Second Division goalscoring sensation, Malcolm Macdonald. Self-confident and brash, Macdonald arrived on Tyneside in a Rolls Royce. A new era was born and a new batch of Harvey's Heroes came into action.

Joe Harvey always recognised United's centre-forward role meant something special to Geordie fans. He had lived through the days of Jackie Milburn and witnessed how Wyn Davies was elevated to hero status by the Tyneside faithful. Harvey saw that Malcolm Macdonald had all the qualities to become another huge icon. He was exciting and thrilling to watch on the field, and loved the razzmatazz off it. Macdonald developed into one of the biggest No. 9 heroes of all time.

The young Londoner began with headlines as he struck three goals to remember on his home senior debut against Liverpool, all in the style that was to make him the First Division's most deadly centre-forward. Supermac was born. The Magpies had found a new figure to worship. With other signings, the bargain capture of midfielder Terry Hibbitt from Leeds United for a modest fee and the much more expensive yet exciting talent of Tony Green in a black-and-white shirt, there was much expectation.

But Harvey's side was an inconsistent eleven, and managed to cause an almighty sensation in the Third Round of the FA Cup during 1972. One of the non-league's toughest competitors and feared giant-killers, Hereford United arrived on Tyneside

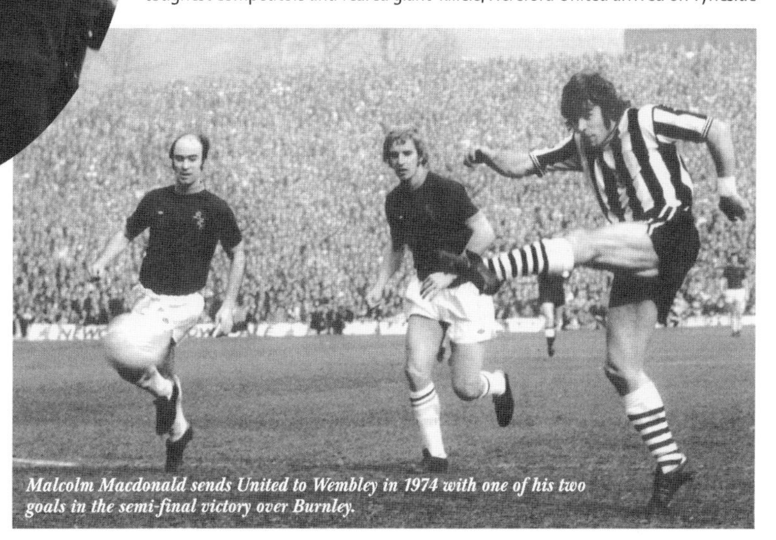

Malcolm Macdonald sends United to Wembley in 1974 with one of his two goals in the semi-final victory over Burnley.

for what was to become a calamitous tie for United – a moment in FA Cup history to be recalled time and time again to the grimace of every Toon supporter.

In a replay at Edgar Street the BBC cameras were in attendance. They were waiting for a shock and they certainly got one, although during the first period United should have comfortably wrapped the tie up after going a goal in front. Hereford battled for everything as Newcastle sat back on their lead. Then fate descended on Edgar Street. Hereford hit two goals and United had been felled once more by the Cup minnow.

That season was perhaps typical of United's exasperating line-up at that time. They could be brilliant on occasion, yet let everyone down with an unexplainable lack of consistency. The remaining years of Joe Harvey's reign in charge followed the same path and season 1973-74 gave Toon supporters a decent FA Cup run for more than a decade – and one that ended back at Wembley Stadium for the first time since 1955, a sentimental return for boss Joe Harvey.

With Macdonald at his peak spearheading the attack, after taking care of Nottingham Forest in a highly controversial quarter-final tie that went to three matches, talk was of Wembley. In the Hillsborough semi-final against Burnley two moments of Supermac magic took United into the final. United's rampaging centre-forward netted two marvellous breakaway goals and United were through to a record breaking eleventh FA Cup final.

Newcastle United however were to have no easy ride at Wembley, facing Liverpool, at the time the most feared side in the country. On their day United could beat anyone though, but which United would turn up beneath the Twin Towers – the dazzling, or the dreadful? Disappointingly it was the latter. Liverpool were commanding in every respect and the Magpies fell 3-0.

Harvey's days in charge were almost over. The Black'n'Whites needed to look forward. They had to find a manager with a different approach and add consistency to their game. They did that, but in the process created plenty of controversy.

Alan Gowling converts a Macdonald cross in the 1976 Football League Cup final.

Carousel of Change
1975-1991

Newcastle United selected a new manager to hold the reins at St James' Park who was largely unknown. Gordon Lee had proved to be a good boss at a lower level without the glitzy trimmings. He arrived at St James' Park in June 1975 as the new hope, a bright manager with fresh ideals. However it was soon to materialise that his philosophy of football clashed with his predecessor. Lee wanted hard graft, team-work and quick, neat football. And there was nothing wrong with that. But he did not favour superstars and their egos which big clubs like Newcastle United need. In the end Lee turned out to be a villain as the club went through a period of continual change for over a decade – a carousel for managers.

At first though, the injection of a new regime brought results and improvement in United's fortunes. From being a maddening, unpredictable eleven the new manager brought more consistency. With United in good shape they also at last made an impact on the Football League Cup tournament, for the first time in 15 years since the competition started. There was a real chance that United could reach another Wembley showpiece. In the semi-final they had to overcome Tottenham Hotspur, a high profile encounter with Spurs over two legs. And following a tough contest, United reached the final after a convincing 3-1 second-leg triumph.

Regular opponents in knock-out competition Manchester City faced the Tynesiders in United's first Football League Cup final. And the Maine Road club was in luck – they faced a United eleven which had been ravaged by both injury and illness in the week leading up to the Wembley day. An influenza bug hit the Toon camp and only a handful of players were not affected. Despite being under strength and only part fit, United still played their part in a fast-flowing match. But an amazing overhead bicycle-kick by Dennis Tueart – ironically born and bred in Newcastle – won the trophy for City. United were runners-up, but had gained much of the pride they had lost after a disappointing Wembley display two years earlier in 1974.

Gordon Lee's first season had been a success. Most were pleased; one figure who wasn't though was Malcolm Macdonald. Although Supermac had again shown he was perhaps the best striker in the country, he had several run-ins with his new boss. And in the summer Lee rocked Tyneside by selling Macdonald to Arsenal. Yet his decision appeared to be vindicated when United went onto have their best season in League action for over 25 years. Newcastle's boss then caused another mighty sensation by selling himself to Everton.

So United had to find a manager again, and that caused even bigger controversy. The fans undoubtedly wanted the big name they didn't get when Lee was appointed. The Newcastle Board looked for another young and aspiring manager, while the players wanted coach and ex-Lee aide, Richard Dinnis, an almost unknown figure in football. The outcome in an unsavoury well-publicised drama was that Dinnis was reluctantly put in charge but not until a mass transfer walk-out and players' strike had been threatened. The whole notorious affair eventually sent the Magpies back into the Second Division. Yet, at first Dinnis continued the good work of his previous boss, by guiding United into fifth place in the First Division and to UEFA Cup qualification. That good progress was to rapidly evaporate.

Following a close-season of more internal strife the 1977-78 season started in catastrophic fashion – and Newcastle never recovered. The Black'n'Whites quickly fell to bottom spot in the table, losing ten games in a row! The Magpies disintegrated from a title challenging outfit to a shambles within five months.

Dinnis went and Newcastle needed a steady head as their next new manager, and an experienced disciplinarian. They found one in the shape of ex-England player and former Wolves boss Bill McGarry. And McGarry was a hard-liner. He sorted the players out but McGarry couldn't keep the Magpies in Division One as they tumbled out of the top flight at the end of the 1977-78 season. And the former England wing-half couldn't make much of an impression in the second-tier. McGarry's days as boss of Newcastle United were soon numbered and United's directors were again thumbing over managerial CV's for yet another time. Chesterfield manager Arthur Cox landed the job in September 1980, another unsung name from the lower divisions.

There was no immediate impact and no instant success from the new boss. Cox's determined work and dedication took time, while he also had the substantial help of an inspirational signing which saw the Magpies take-off. Big-names were to soon return to the St James' Park dressing-room over the coming years – in the shape of four world-rated superstars: Keegan, Waddle, Beardsley and Gascoigne. The player who turned Cox's team of hopefuls into a side to make the whole country take notice was England skipper Kevin Keegan who joined the Magpies in a sensational deal during August 1982.

The former Liverpool legend moved to the North East in a blaze of publicity – Keegan returning to his roots, his father and grandfather being from County Durham. Keegan immediately put the football community of Tyneside back in the limelight. St James' Park was buzzing again. Keegan at 31 years old inspired the Black'n'Whites – both in terms of playing colleagues and supporters – like no other could. His charisma and talent on the field made a vast impact. And his mere presence saw other top international players join the Magpie bandwagon like Terry McDermott and David McCreery.

United stuttered after all the Keegan headlines as several players found it something of a culture shock fitting in with the glitz which now surrounded the club. After a season in which they missed out on promotion, for the start of the 1983-84 campaign Cox pulled off another master signing. Tynesider Peter Beardsley arrived back to his native North East from a stint in North America with Vancouver Whitecaps. Beardsley possessed skill galore and showed he had the potential to become an extra-special player. A superstar in the making had arrived. From the moment the little Geordie pulled on the black-and-white shirt alongside Keegan and the rapidly emerging Chris Waddle, Newcastle's destiny of promotion was assured.

Newcastle started the new season well and as the programme unfolded, United's exciting front trio showed a match-winning understanding that was dazzling and spectacular. United arrived at the final run-in of the programme in confident mood. The chasing four – big names all – Manchester City, Chelsea, Sheffield Wednesday and

A goal in the 1983-84 promotion campaign; Keegan celebrates with Waddle.

Paul Gascoigne, one of three highly talented Geordie footballers to head south during the 1980s.

United were the teams to beat. Promotion was all but confirmed against relegation threatened Derby County following one of several fabulous attacking performances, Newcastle winning 4-0. United were promoted and the front trio had netted 66 goals between them.

All that was left were the celebrations. And what celebrations. Not only to mark promotion, but also the departure of Kevin Keegan who had announced his retirement. Special K though would return, to be hailed The Messiah – and make an even bigger impact in time of dire need. First though, the Magpies found they couldn't build on all the hard work of promotion and lost all of their superstars – Waddle, Beardsley and a new megastar in the making, Paul Gascoigne (left), Gazza to all. And along the way the carousel continued to spin, indeed almost out of control.

The departure of Kevin Keegan left a chasm at St James' Park. United in fact could have done with his vast experience and magnetism as they started life back in the top division. And even more so when manager Arthur Cox sensationally resigned only days after securing promotion. A dispute between Newcastle's boss and Chairman Stan Seymour (Jnr) over finances and contract negotiations led to Cox remarkably dropping two divisions and being installed as manager of Derby County.

Newcastle supporters were stunned. From being in a position of building on the success Keegan had generated they not only had they lost their best player, but now had to find a new manager too. And as so often in the Magpies' recent past, the Black'n'Whites failed to consolidate effectively on a period of success. To begin with though, in came Jack Charlton to the manager's office, a Geordie idol. Everyone was happy.

Charlton had a tough task. Without Keegan, the Magpies were tipped to go straight back into the Second Division as the 1984-85 campaign got underway. Yet Big Jack was a manager who had proved at Middlesbrough and Sheffield Wednesday he could get the best out of players with limited ability and cope with capped resources. Without ever splashing out in the transfer market, the Ashington-born World Cup winner succeeded in keeping United in the First Division. Indeed Charlton did more than that to start with, leading the Magpies to the top-of-the-table in a dramatic opening to the season.

With Chris Waddle and Peter Beardsley rising to the challenge to step into Keegan's boots, Newcastle more than held their own. However, after the Geordies bright opening United gradually slid down the table eventually to end up in a disappointing, but secure, mid-table place. The summer of 1985 saw United's fans wait eagerly for a new batch of top names to arrive in a customary close-season spending spree. All they saw was Waddle move to White Hart Lane in a big deal and no-one land at St James' Park. Disgruntled supporters turned on Charlton in a pre-season friendly. He was given a rough ride and forthright as ever, quickly walked out of the Gallowgate entrance not to return. Long serving coach and ex-goalkeeper Willie McFaul stepped into the breach, the club's sixth manager in only 10 years.

Popular with players and supporters, McFaul replaced Waddle with another local product, a self-assured teenager from Dunston called Paul Gascoigne who was given an extended opportunity. Peter Beardsley flourished in the 1985-86 season and like Waddle before him, the Geordie was tipped for international honours, eventually capped by England alongside his former colleague.

However, Beardsley was soon to move to better things, to Liverpool for a national record transfer of £1.9m. After Waddle's exit, it was a major set-back to the club. McFaul made an effort to halt the mounting criticism of mediocrity and selling their best assets by completing an eye-catching deal. In August 1987 he splashed out on Brazilian international centre-forward Mirandinha, the first from the sun and sand of the Copa Cabaña to play in England. It was not enough and the season ended in dismay for McFaul – and for United's fans. Paul Gascoigne, 21 years old and now tipped to go to the very top, decided he had little choice but to venture south as well to further his career. Gazza joined Chris Waddle at Tottenham in a £2.6m deal.

With Gascoigne's departure coming quickly on the heels of the loss of United's other two big-names – Waddle and Beardsley – many of the Toon's faithful became increasingly frustrated. Political in-fighting started behind the scenes with dissatisfied shareholders and supporters beginning a determined campaign for massive change at St James' Park. It was revolution on Tyne. A full-scale hostile takeover mounted by the Magpie Group, led by powerful Tyneside entrepreneur John Hall, was to soon rock the club. Between 1988 and 1992 matters away from the action on the pitch took centre-stage as huge sums of money changed hands as a share-war for control of Newcastle United raged.

With the corporate brawling in the background, boss McFaul was sacked in October 1988 and remarkably United's beleaguered directorate – on and off the field – had a major problem finding a replacement, although with rebellion in full swing perhaps that was no surprise. Almost two months passed before QPR's Jim Smith filled the hot seat – and hot it was. He inherited a side destined for relegation.

Smith made multiple changes to his playing staff in an attempt to get back into the First Division quickly. He just missed promotion in 1990 as United competed in the Football League's recent innovation of a Play-Off contest for a final promotion spot – something of a blast from the past when United last competed in such a challenge way back in 1898. United faced a two-legged local derby with Sunderland of all clubs – with a prize of a one-off final at Wembley for a place in Division One. It was the biggest Tyne versus Wear confrontation for many a year and it resulted in a victory for the red-and-white section of the North East. United had been leap-frogged by a team six points worse off and who finished three places below the Magpies in the final analysis.

Manager Jim Smith found the mounting pressure too much. The Bald Eagle departed soon after that disappointment in March 1991. Newcastle's directors now turned to a big name, the former Argentinean World Cup winner and Spurs favourite, Ossie Ardiles who had impressed many during his managerial debut in charge of Swindon Town. Ardiles was a popular choice, but the little South American had little experience in the manager's chair and soon found it hard to come to terms with rebuilding an ailing club.

During the opening weeks of season 1991-92 Newcastle slumped to bottom of the Second Division table for only the fourth time in their history. The Magpies were in an almighty mess. Developments off the football field were creating headlines with John Hall's Magpie Group making a final bid to control the club as the Geordies slid into a financial crisis. United's worsening position required drastic action, and very quickly. Newcastle needed Hall's financial muscle and business acumen to transform United into the one of football's super-clubs with his enterprise and drive. In the coming months the Cameron-Hall empire would take full control and rapidly overhaul the club from top to bottom. Newcastle United never looked back.

Ardiles was sacked in February 1992 and immediately replaced by a certain Kevin Keegan – out of football since leaving the Magpies back in 1984. Newcastle's leadership was convinced that only one man could lead Newcastle out of the relegation mire. Keegan had the Midas touch, he was an inspiration and considered almost super-human to the legions of United supporters who longed for someone to lead and motivate them.

When Kevin Keegan took over at St James' Park it was a sensational appointment which captured the game's imagination. He had one job to start with – to save the club from relegation. Failure would almost certainly result in the club going bankrupt. That was unthinkable, but a real possibility. Keegan used all his motivating skills to gee up his team for the final weeks of the 1991-92 season. Before the concluding fixture against promotion chasing Leicester City at Filbert Street he noted: "We need a result, but we'll get it, survive and take-off." And Newcastle did exactly what the manager predicted. The Magpies recorded a deserved 2-1 victory; three points which guaranteed Second Division football and with it, the Magpies' future. United's triumph in adversity was the turning point in Newcastle's fortunes.

Struggle in 1992. Champions in 1993. Brian Kilcline holds the title trophy.

Premiership Extravaganza
1992-2000

Newcastle United's rescue from the brink of Third Division football and probable insolvency was in itself a remarkable achievement. It was though nothing compared to what was to follow. The way the club was transformed from a struggling giant into one of the country's super-clubs was sensational. Events at St James' Park have rarely been dull, and during the years leading towards the new century the football hotbed of Tyneside perhaps reached melting point. Led by John Hall – who was soon to be knighted – Newcastle United Football Club was turned upside down – and a modern, professional and determined organisation was put together – both on the St James' Park pitch and in the corridors of power behind the scenes.

At the start of the Nineties decade United were great under-achievers, they were modest in size possessing a turnover of a mere £4m and financially in turmoil. By the end of the decade the Magpies had grown into a major force in the glitter of the Premier League. Turnover surged upwards towards £100m while on the field of play they possessed a star-studded eleven able to challenge for the Premiership title – a dazzling super-league crown introduced in 1992 which transformed football. Yet in true Newcastle United fashion, having done all the hard work of reaching that status, they threw it all away. It was a must watch soap-opera that ran and ran.

Sparkling football and scintillating footballers were the order of the day. Peter Beardsley and David Ginola celebrate yet another Toon goal.

Following United's astonishing escape from oblivion, Kevin Keegan took a full-time appointment as boss during the summer of 1992. With gusto the new duo of Hall and Keegan swung into action. The Chairman began planning a vast transformation of St James' Park and overhaul of the club's finances. Keegan started to build for the coming 1992-93 season. Cash was released, despite the growing debts – now effectively underwritten by the Cameron-Hall empire. Together they proved a dynamic pairing and were utterly determined in making the Magpies fulfil their undoubted potential of becoming one of the most powerful clubs in Britain.

First though, Keegan had to get the Black'n'Whites out of the Second Division – now renamed Division One following the introduction of the Premier League. Keegan – a pied-piper who everyone cheerily followed – did it in spectacular fashion. They roared to a victorious start and simply could not stop winning! United registered ten wins out of ten games played, a maximum of 30 points, and galloped clear of the First Division field. They made it 11 from 11 with another victory, this time over Sunderland. The country took notice as the Tynesiders began to make headlines of a giant being reborn. Displaying a brand of football full of attacking ideas Newcastle were crowned Football League Champions with all the pomp and celebration of a club which had yearned for success for so long.

United made sure they were ready on and off the field for their first taste of the FA Carling Premiership. Major ground redevelopment was well underway that was to transform St James' Park and manager Keegan had money to spend to bolster his initial rebuilding when the likes of Rob Lee and John Beresford arrived on Tyneside. A new young centre-forward Andy Cole had also arrived and he teamed up with Peter Beardsley who returned to Tyneside from Everton. Beardsley was to be the side's most influential player in a United eleven that took the Premiership by storm.

United displayed a brand of football that gave Keegan's men the tag of The Entertainers. An emphatic 3-0 success over Liverpool was the benchmark in United's progress. For long the men from Liverpool had dominated in Tyne-Mersey clashes. Now it was Newcastle's turn. With record signing Cole breaking the 40-goal barrier for the club, Newcastle finished in a creditable third place behind Champions Manchester United in season 1993-94. They ended the programme as the Premiership's record goalscorers with 82 goals and with it entry into European action. Newcastle United were back in the big-time.

New faces flocked to Tyneside as Keegan continued his policy of being a buying manager while back in Europe United thrashed Royal Antwerp 10-2 on aggregate and made their mark within the corridors of UEFA. Newcastle registered a club record of nine wins in a row and not surprisingly were top of the Premiership. But that promising start was not sustained and the somewhat disappointing season also saw Keegan stun the football world by selling the new King of Tyneside, Andy Cole to rivals Manchester United for a record £7m – then an unheard of sum in England. United's manager was intent on a change in strategy and could rely on extra funds from his Board, the Magpies' ownership backing Keegan to the limit. The club's tremendous economic recovery continued unabated. They were now second only to Manchester United in financial standing.

United's boss was determined to make sure he had a squad to sustain a long Premiership season and make a serious bid for silverware. In the close-season of 1995 millions of pounds exchanged hands for top players from home and abroad, and Newcastle United led the way creating football fever on Tyneside. Keegan landed his replacement for Andy Cole, paying £6m for England leader Les Ferdinand from QPR. Soon after he brought the talented France and Paris St-Germain forward David Ginola to England, a signing that captivated the Toon Army. With other quality arrivals Keegan assembled a formidable squad, and more big names were to follow. It was one that was to take Manchester United all the way in the title race.

For much of the 1995-96 season Newcastle United did everything absolutely right. They roared to the top-of-the-table and had a comfortable points advantage over their rivals from Old Trafford. Their football was scintillating at times. United led the pack for most of the programme but agonisingly let the trophy slip in the closing weeks to a chasing Manchester United. Newcastle had only themselves to blame. United could have – and should have claimed the top prize.

The conclusion of that title race was disheartening and was to affect United in the following season, although to start with Keegan was doubly determined to win that elusive but most important trophy in the country. The football world was amazed as Newcastle United paid a world record fee of £15m plus add-ons to bring the country's top striker, Alan Shearer back to his native Tyneside from Blackburn Rovers during the summer. It was a deal which showed that the club was indeed a big mover – and intent in claiming success on the field.

Shearer's purchase was a coup. Hailed the best centre-forward in Europe at the time, his Geordie background gave him massive fan support and the pairing of Ferdinand and Shearer up front was to prove a devastating combination. Newcastle though, started 1996-97 with something of a hangover from the previous season's title race but soon the team clicked and goals flowed, culminating in a wonderful 5-0 revenge victory over Manchester United at St James' Park. Newcastle were back on top of the Premier League again and favourites to lift the Championship.

The Entertainers on Stage

During the club's resurgence at the start of the 1990s decade, The Black'n'Whites displayed a brand of attacking football only matched on a handful of occasions in the club's history. As United secured the First Division trophy in 1992-93 then entered the new world of the Premier League and a world-wide television audience, Newcastle were labelled The Entertainers due to their glitzy and delightful football. They displayed a quick and incisive style, with accurate passing, penetrating movement and plenty of goals. And with stars galore United's attacking vision was second to none. All that was missing was the prize of a trophy, The Entertainers just losing out on the Premiership crown in season 1995-96.

But fate was not on Newcastle's side. Injury disrupted plans with crucially both Shearer and Ferdinand out for spells. United slipped from top spot. Behind the scenes the club was going through a major corporate floatation to transform the club into a public limited company – a move that was to raise massive funds, but also rock the very foundations as Kevin Keegan became a high profile casualty during January 1997.

After Keegan's headlining and shock exit Newcastle's directors did not take long to appoint a new manager. Within days Kenny Dalglish was installed at St James' Park – one of the few men with a pedigree and standing in football who could step into Keegan's shoes. With a track record as a player and manager second to none, he appeared the ideal choice. But there was to be a stark contrast between the two as Dalglish soon began to dismantle Keegan's bright, entertaining line-up, full of goals and big names and develop his own less glamorous outfit which found goals hard to come by. The eventual result was the entertainment value dropped alarmingly and so did the Magpies new found status in football.

However, to start with most United supporters were content with the appointment. Many judges considered all the new manager had to do was to add two or three players to Keegan's squad and at first Dalglish guided United on the right tracks for

MILESTONES • 1995-96 United end as runners-up in the Premiership • **1996-97** With £15m Alan Shearer in the side, United end in second spot again

Tino Asprilla climbs to find the net in the very first Champions League clash at Gallowgate against Barcelona in 1997.

a European place again. Without hitting the headlines, the Magpies even found themselves with an outside chance of the title as the last month of the season unfolded. They clinched runners-up spot again and with that came a place in the new and highly lucrative Champions League. Dalglish – admittedly largely with Keegan's line-up – had made a successful beginning.

Season 1997-98 was to be another campaign of highs and lows. Dalglish began wheeling and dealing in the transfer market as Keegan's squad was dismantled. United's supporters were rocked when they sold Les Ferdinand then immediately lost Alan Shearer with a fractured fibula in pre-season action. As a result the Black'n'Whites entered the Champions League with a changed and patched up line-up. Qualifying following a dramatic two-legged victory against Croatia Zagreb, Newcastle were drawn in the group stage along with Dynamo Kyiv, PSV Eindhoven and the mighty Barcelona. It was a quite a test. But Newcastle did have one player in Tino Asprilla, one of Keegan's expensive imports, who kept his best football for European occasions. The temperamental and inconsistent Colombian had not been a great success in Premiership action, but did continually find the net when in Continental mode.

United opened their Champions League campaign with an epic against Barcelona at Gallowgate. It was a fixture beamed around the globe and Newcastle showed impressive style as they stormed into a 3-0 lead with a brilliant Asprilla hat-trick. Although the Spanish giants pulled two goals back late into the game, Newcastle's performance was hailed as one of their best ever. For an hour they outclassed Barcelona. After that opening though Newcastle struggled in Europe and also in League action. But in the FA Cup, United went all the way to Wembley with the influential return of Alan Shearer from injury giving the side a major boost.

Newcastle toppled Sheffield United in the semi-final at Old Trafford with a single close-in strike from Shearer yet United had never been too convincing. Many feared for the outcome in the meeting with eventual double winners Arsenal in front of the Twin Towers of Wembley. And on the day the Gunners were far too clever for a subdued and negative United side. The display was as disappointing as the Championship race in 1996, and Kenny Dalglish quickly lost many of his recently found Geordie allies on that afternoon.

During the summer of 1998 United's boss went on a spending spree, bringing in more players from around the world in a bid to revitalise his side, but few were of the standard United's fans or officials were used to. As a result not for the first time – or the last – Newcastle United hit the headlines just as the season began. Kenny Dalglish controversially departed with only two games of the 1998-99 programme completed and another high profile manager took control, this time former Chelsea boss and one of the world's finest players of recent times, Dutch ace Ruud Gullit. The appointment was heralded with much elation and as a new starting point in regaining the club's position as the country's most favourite side, gained with Kevin Keegan's Entertainers, but lost under the guidance of Dalglish.

Ruud Gullit was quick to point out that he would need time and money to rebuild the St James' Park staff. The new boss needed to make changes and not surprisingly as the remodelling took place, United's season was an inconsistent one. Gullit though guided the Magpies on another FA Cup run and provided Newcastle's fervent Toon Army with something to shout about. And just like the previous season the Black'n'Whites dished up a rousing run to Wembley – again though without being totally convincing on the field.

The Wembley occasion in 1999 had a déjà vu feeling about it. Against Manchester United this time, Newcastle were clearly second best, and although defeated by the eventual treble winners, the Magpies did perform better. For Newcastle United supporters though, runners-up positions in four successive seasons – two in the Premier League and two in the FA Cup – was hard to take.

Like Dalglish before him, Gullit's plans fell apart. The manager's relationship with his senior players as the new season's kick-off drew near – with the likes of Gary Speed, Rob Lee and big signing Duncan Ferguson, as well as Tyneside icon Alan Shearer – was not good and deteriorated further. Trouble was in the air.

Events on a wet, wild evening at St James' Park against Sunderland sealed Ruud Gullit's fate. The Dutch boss astonishingly left both Shearer and Ferguson on the bench – almost £24m of striking talent – and Rob Lee in the stand. Sunderland stole a victory in the torrential rain and the aftermath rapidly unfolded. Gullit resigned and United's hierarchy had no hesitation in choosing the man they wanted to reverse the Magpies' fortunes – former England and Barcelona coach, Bobby Robson.

Offered the job before when Keegan had departed, 66-year-old Robson eventually walked through the St James' Park doors as manager in September 1999. It was a sentimental return home to the club the experienced boss had supported as a kid. His arrival was unanimously hailed from all quarters. Newcastle had at last found the right man to replace Kevin Keegan albeit two-and-a-half years too late.

Bobby Robson's immediate challenge as he took control was to halt Newcastle United's League slide and to keep the Geordies in the Premier League as the Millennium arrived. That was essential. The vastly experienced County Durham-born manager was left with plenty of wounds to heal and a Magpie outfit which had suffered from enormous change during two management regimes that had ripped apart the earlier good work of Keegan. He had no easy task, but Robson knuckled down and completed the first stage of the job in a marvellous and much acclaimed way, then began the second stage of his task – rebuilding the Magpies to challenge with the best.

Not surprisingly Shearer and Ferguson were immediately recalled to the team as was the influential Rob Lee. In Robson's first fixture in front of the St James' Park crowd, against fellow strugglers Sheffield Wednesday, the Magpies ran riot winning 8-0. It was an astonishing homecoming for the new manager. Alan Shearer in particular enjoyed the management change, claiming the headlines alongside Wor Bobby by striking five goals.

Newcastle gradually regained confidence and collected points, slowly climbing up the table to safety. Robson had made an immediate impact and the buzz around Gallowgate, so evident when Keegan was in control, gathered momentum again.

As Bobby Robson's recovery plan was underway, they also found form in European football, and continued to shine in the FA Cup. Eventually knocked out by AS Roma in the UEFA Cup, for the third year running United ended up at Wembley stadium, and again there was plenty drama on the way. Newcastle's mixed Premiership form was in contrast to the spirit and potent attack shown in FA Cup action which ended with a semi-final clash staged at Wembley with one of the Premiership's best sides Chelsea.

Sir Bobby Robson takes in the special atmosphere of United's UEFA Cup semi-final in Marseille during 2004.

In the distant past Newcastle had enjoyed the surroundings of the national stadium – now on the road to demolition – but in modern times United had never won at the celebrated arena in their last eight matches. For two seasons running the Black'n'Whites had performed below standard in the Wembley bowl, had lost convincingly and emerged with little credit. Robson's side was to change that to a point. Against Chelsea they again were defeated, by 2-1, but they gave a performance packed with determination and style. They were the better side in the sunshine of Wembley. What they didn't have on the day was luck.

With Robson's rescue act successfully completed, the manager now began his make-over of the Black'n'Whites. He did have several quality players to build a team around. Apart from Shearer, Lee and Speed, Kieron Dyer had showed he was a midfielder with unlimited stamina and searing pace who could cause all sorts of problems for the opposition. Peruvian Nobby Solano emerged; he could also win matches on his own, while Shay Given had developed into both a spectacular and steady 'keeper, a regular for the Republic of Ireland.

As the new Millennium season of 2000-01 opened, a massive St James' Park enlargement programme was completed with capacity of almost 52,200. United's average attendance dramatically increased, back to the heady days of the immediate post-war years of over 50,000. Only Manchester United at the time (then, later Arsenal) could attract more through the turnstile. Robson – soon to be Sir Bobby as the popular boss was knighted – rapidly continued with his Magpie rebuilding. He guided United back into contention for the Premiership title with match-winners Laurent Robert and Craig Bellamy added to the squad for sizable fees.

The resultant Shearer and Bellamy partnership in attack was formidable in 2001-02 when they fired home 42 goals during the campaign. United started to look like title challengers displaying a popular attacking style again and by Christmas had become leaders of the pack. Many tipped United to take a trophy, but at a crucial stage in the season United lost both Bellamy and Dyer, two of the teams most important assets, players who gave the side a cutting edge with their devastating pace moving forward. Newcastle lost momentum going out of both the FA Cup and League Cup at the quarter-final stage and dropped to a final fourth position in the League race. However the Black'n'Whites did claim a consolation prize of Champions League qualification.

Robson continued wheeling and dealing in the transfer market. And there was an emphasis on youth as the manager looked to build a formidable squad that would serve the Magpies for the next few seasons. Included was highly rated midfielder Jermaine Jenas, but importantly the team was bonded together by the invaluable experience of three of the game's model professionals, Shearer, Speed and Given.

Having successfully qualified for the Champions League, Newcastle supporters looked forward to an exciting 2002-03 season. They had been drawn in the group stages of UEFA's five-star competition alongside Feyenoord, Dynamo Kyiv and Juventus, all seasoned European campaigners. And the travelling Toon Army were in for a fabulous adventure around the Continent as Newcastle showed they were fast becoming a European giant.

With the Shearer and Bellamy partnership one of the best around, United opened their Champions League campaign in the far edge of Europe, in Ukraine, but started miserably. Newcastle were beaten on the long trip to Kiev, then faced Feyenoord at Gallowgate, an encounter the Magpies needed to win to get their European season underway. The Dutch made Newcastle pay for a single defensive lapse and stole the points.

United then headed for Turin and few gave them any chance of breaking their duck against Italian champions, the might of Juventus in the Stadio Delle Alpi. They fell again and losing their first three games was a disaster. No-one gave the Magpies a hope – not even the most ardent member of the Toon Army. Yet amazingly Bobby Robson's men confounded everyone and won their next three matches, not only to create a Champion's League record, but also to qualify for the next stage and all in dramatic circumstances.

The Magpies' astonishing comeback began during October when Juventus arrived on Tyneside for a return clash. A single goal victory was the outcome and the comeback was underway. Dynamo Kyiv followed the Italians into the cauldron of St James' Park and suffered the same fate. United now had a chance of qualification to the next stage and all hinged on the final match with Feyenoord. In the De Kuip arena in Rotterdam one of the greatest nights in United's history unfolded as the Geordies took the game to Feyenoord and led 2-0, only for the Dutch to storm back into the match and level matters at 2-2. Then Craig Bellamy grabbed a truly dramatic winner in injury time to send United through into the next money-spinning phase of the competition.

Newcastle's Stage 2 opponents included Internazionale and Barcelona, as well as last season's finalist Bayer Leverkusen. The Black'n'Whites started as they did back in September, with a defeat. Worse was to follow. Just as in Stage 1, United began in disastrous fashion, losing their first two fixtures. A trip to Barcelona followed without their ace strikers both suspended. That was a blow and another defeat was recorded. Newcastle though had blended together into a resilient line-up.

United's form at the fortress of St James' Park was exceptional. Newcastle needed another dramatic comeback to stand any chance of reaching the quarter-finals. Following two convincing victories over Bayer that was amazingly on the cards again. United needed to win in the awesome San Siro against one of the favourites for the Champion's League trophy as well as Serie A title – Internazionale – and they almost did.

With Shearer and Bellamy back in tandem, over 10,000 of United's Toon Army travelled to Milan for a game probably not matched in the club's history for prestige. United's loyal and vociferous following played their part in the near 54,000 crowd as United outplayed the ill-tempered Italians for long periods of the game. Hitting the woodwork early on spurred the Black'n'Whites to attack Inter and they deservedly went in front when Shearer converted Bellamy's run and cross. Vieri equalised, but Shearer was on the spot again to fire home after Robert's fierce cross ball caused problems. A Cordoba goal settled the contest at 2-2 but few disagreed that the Magpies deserved to win. They had showed that on the big stage they could mix it with the best. Newcastle were at the peak of their modern history.

Robson continued to spend big before the season's end on yet another young international star in the making, bringing Leeds United's Jonathan Woodgate to St James' Park. For over a decade a succession of Newcastle managers had searched for a commanding central defender to marshal the back-line with authority. Most judges considered 23-year-old Woodgate was the answer; alas he was all too often injured. With the England defender in the line-up, Newcastle focussed on the League campaign as Easter approached, in touch with Arsenal and Manchester United at the top of the division. United were an outside bet for the title but United's Championship challenge disappointingly fizzled out as they finished in third place.

Trouble in Toon
2003-2011

By the end of season 2002-03 Sir Bobby Robson had completed the task of building an impressive squad and getting Newcastle United back into the top echelon of the Premier League alongside Arsenal, Manchester United, Liverpool and Chelsea. The Black'n'Whites achieved that on merit and continuing to display a brand of entertaining football.

But having spent around £190m on players and another £100m on facilities in the last decade they were to throw all that good work away to the anguish of their fanatical supporters. At first though Robson's hard work saw the Magpies continue to impress. In season 2003-04 they reached the semi-final of the UEFA Cup after the devastating blow of losing out on penalties in a Champions League qualifying tie with FK Partizan. They also challenged once more at the top of the Premier League. But for injuries at

Club Honours
First-team competitions; 1881-date

League Record

Northern League	1890-91 to 1892-93	4 seasons
Football League Division 2 (Tier 2)	1893-94 to 1897-98	5 seasons
Football League Division 1 (Tier 1)	1898-99 to 1933-34	32 seasons
Football League Division 2 (Tier 2)	1934-35 to 1947-48	7 seasons
Football League Division 1 (Tier 1)	1948-49 to 1960-61	13 seasons
Football League Division 2 (Tier 2)	1961-62 to 1964-65	4 seasons
Football League Division 1 (Tier 1)	1965-66 to 1977-78	13 seasons
Football League Division 2 (Tier 2)	1978-79 to 1983-84	6 seasons
Football League Division 1 (Tier 1)	1984-85 to 1988-89	5 seasons
Football League Division 2 (Tier 2)	1989-90 to 1992-93	4 seasons
FA Premier League (Tier 1)	1993-94 to 2008-09	16 seasons
Football League Championship (Tier 2)	2009-10	1 season
FA Premier League (Tier 1)	2010-11 to date	1 season

- Newcastle United are one of only eight clubs never to have played senior football other than in the top two divisions of the English game.

Senior Competitions

Football League/Premier League Champions: 1904-05, 1906-07, 1908-09, 1926-27
Football League/Premier League runners-up: 1995-6, 1996-97
Football League Div 2/1/Champ (Tier 2) Champions: 1964-65, 1992-93, 2009-10
Football League Div 2/1/Champ (Tier 2) Promotion: 1897-98, 1947-48, 1983-84
FA Cup Winners: 1910, 1924, 1932, 1951, 1952, 1955
FA Cup runners-up: 1905, 1906, 1908, 1911, 1974, 1998, 1999
Football League Cup runners-up: 1976
Inter Cities Fairs Cup Winners: 1969

Other Competitions

FA Charity Shield Winners: 1908-09
FA Charity/Community Shield runners-up: 1932-33, 1951-52, 1952-53, 1955-56, 1996-97
Sheriff of London Charity Shield Winners: 1906-07
Texaco Cup Winners: 1974, 1975
Anglo-Italian Cup Winners: 1973
Japan Cup Winners: 1983
Tyne-Tees-Wear Cup Winners: 1944
Cumberland Cup Winners: 1947, 1951
Shields Ingham Cup Winners: 1923
Norfolk & Norwich Charity Cup Winners: 1911
Northampton Hospital Charity Shield Winners: 1912
Newcastle & Sunderland Hospitals Cup Winners: 1912
Northumberland FA Challenge Cup (Senior Cup) Winners: 1885, 1889
Northumberland FA Tyne Charity Shield Winners: 1884-85, 1885-86, 1888-89, 1889-90
Northumberland FA Challenge Bowl Winners: 1884-85, 1885-86, 1888-89, 1889-90
Northumberland v Durham Inter-County Challenge Winners: 1888-89
Northern League runners-up: 1892-93

European Competitions entry

UEFA Champions League: 1997-98, 2002-03, 2003-04 (Qual)
Inter Cities/European Fairs Cup/UEFA Cup: 1968-69, 1969-70, 1970-71, 1977-78, 1994-95, 1996-97, 1999-00, 2003-04, 2004-05, 2006-07
UEFA Cup Winners Cup: 1998-99
Intertoto Cup: 2001-02, 2005-06, 2006-07
Anglo-Italian Cup: 1972-73, 1992-93

the crucial stage of the season in April, Robson may well have guided his side to silverware. But with the likes of Dyer, Jenas and Bellamy all sidelined, they fell to Olympique Marseille – and Didier Drogba in particular – in Europe. Then they lost Woodgate and saw Arsenal race away with the title as United finished in fifth spot.

Football life is rarely tedious at St James' Park and as the following season began a series of questionable and ruinous decisions took place, all of which sent United tumbling from their lofty status. Then ranked among the newly established Rich List of European football, they slid alarmingly, almost back to where they had started as the 1990s began. The entertaining roller-coaster turned into an embarrassing soap-opera at St James' Park.

Within the opening weeks of the new 2004-05 season Sir Bobby Robson was controversially sacked and in came Graeme Souness as boss. It was not a populist move. Although Newcastle reached the quarter-final of the UEFA Cup and FA Cup semi-final under the former Liverpool and Scotland star – pitifully losing 4-1 to Manchester United at Cardiff's Millennium Stadium – it was the start of a downward spiral.

With talisman Alan Shearer nearing the end of his fabulous career, United's hierarchy made another headlining and expensive trophy signing with the arrival of Shearer's former England colleague Michael Owen from Real Madrid for a record £16m fee. It was perhaps one big-deal too far. Could United really afford him? They could if Owen was a success and made sure the Black'n'Whites gained regular European action, notably in the money-spinning Champions League. Yet Owen was, but for a brief period alongside Shearer, not a success and all too often injured. Also to arrive on Tyneside was Deportivo's Albert Luque at more than £11m. He too was to be a very expensive flop.

Souness did not stay long as United languished in the Premier League. Former skipper Glenn Roeder moved from the Academy to take charge, steer the club clear of relegation, but afterwards was also replaced. Highly rated Sam Allardyce became Newcastle's sixth manager in only 10 years as the Bolton boss took control for season 2007-08. However, just as that deal had been completed and in a football world where rich billionaires from far and wide eyed Premier League clubs, the summer of 2007 saw huge upheaval in the corridors of St James' Park. The Hall family sold their controlling interest in Newcastle United to London-based entrepreneur Mike Ashley. He soon completed a total buy-out at a reported price of £134.4m and ousted Chairman Freddy Shepherd.

Allardyce's brand of football was not popular as Newcastle continued to hover in the lower half of the table. He departed after only eight months. Newcastle United's new ownership and structure included a Continental style approach with former England midfielder Dennis Wise as Director of Football. That appointment was not to be well-liked either. But the third coming of Kevin Keegan who was appointed manager in January 2008 was well received as Keegan-mania once more engulfed Tyneside.

Slowly but surely Keegan made a difference and Newcastle appeared to be on the right course. Then conflict between the manager and Dennis Wise as well as the club's ownership set the Newcastle ship on a calamitous bearing. Keegan resigned – and later forced a successful arbitration – Joe Kinnear filled the hot seat until illness forced him out of the picture, then modern icon Alan Shearer came out of retirement as boss in a last gasp bid to halt a dramatic slide. But it was too late. Instability on and off the pitch resulted in relegation after 16 years in the Premier League. That was a devastating bombshell and coincided with a world-wide economic recession. It was a double-blow.

Newcastle turned to experienced coach Chris Hughton to rebuild a broken super-club on the field. There was a huge gulf in both status and football between the Premier League and a second-tier of English football that was now branded The Championship. Several high wage-earners departed, but United had enough quality to make an impression. Hughton's side dominated the League programme from start to finish and lifted the title trophy with games to spare. United returned to the top-tier at the first attempt and the Premier League welcomed back the Magpies.

It was though to be a different Newcastle United which returned. The same massive support was evident with only Manchester United and Arsenal commanding bigger gates in England. But no longer were Newcastle United one of the game's big spenders in a football world that had undergone a severe financial reality check. No more world record transfers and super-stars. And no more high wage bills. Mike Ashley's Newcastle United was more thrifty and frugal in the use of its resources and determined to make more of its youth and Academy system. After such a woeful and ruinous five years, the club needed calm and stability – and patience from the fans whose relationship with the new owner was an uneasy one. Yet they still turned up in huge numbers and to Ashley's credit he steadied the finances and avoided meltdown.

With Alan Pardew appointed as manager (left) in December 2010 to lead the club into a new era, United finished season 2010-11 in a creditable mid-table position as they consolidated their regained Premier League place. As is Newcastle United's unique way, there were plenty of headlines during that first season back at the top level, none more so than the dramatic £35m sale to Liverpool of the club's new No. 9, Andy Carroll. Having reached the England line-up after a only a season-and-a-half of regular first-team action, the Gateshead-born striker was destined to follow in Alan Shearer's path. But Newcastle decided to cash-in and accept what was a new British record transfer fee.

With funds to spend Pardew was to be busy in the close-season of 2011 as he refashioned the Newcastle squad. Established players went and new blood arrived, including several from the Continent, adding to the club's cosmopolitan flavour. By the start of the 2011-12 programme a new look United was in place.

As Newcastle United headed towards their 130th Anniversary in November 2011, the Magpies continue to be one of the game's most captivating of football clubs. With a substantial, loyal and vocal support, a first-class stadium and training facility, the Black'n'Whites are one of England's biggest and best. They have a proud and colourful history, a never-ending rollercoaster of drama and incident.

Cheik Tiote races away in celebration after his equalising goal against Arsenal in 2011, United coming back from a 4-0 deficit.

- The Pioneering Era; Stanley & East End, FA Cup fixtures 1881-82 to 1888-89.
- East End & Newcastle United; Northern League, Football League, Premier League fixtures 1889-90 to 2010-11, including Test Matches & Play-Offs.
- East End & Newcastle United; FA Cup (including Qualifying matches), Football League Cup & European fixtures 1889-90 to 2010-11.
- Newcastle United; Anglo-Italian Cup, Texaco Cup, Anglo-Scottish Cup, FA Charity/Community Shield, Sheriff of London Charity Shield, Full Members Cup including later sponsored tournaments and the Mercantile Credit Centenary Trophy.

Notes on the statistics

Every senior fixture played by Newcastle United since formation in November 1881 to the end of the 2010-11 season, including games under previous titles of Newcastle East End FC and Stanley FC, are included in Sections 1 and 2 of this *Ultimate Record* of the club; season by season, game by game incorporating dates, results, scorers, teams and attendances.

Newcastle United's match data shown on the statistical spreadsheets is the culmination of many years of research by several enthusiastic United supporters. The data has been collected from a range of different sources; official Newcastle United ledgers, newspaper match reports, programmes, yearbooks as well as the National Football Museum archive incorporating the official Football League records.

Over the years a number of errors have occurred and been handed down, inaccuracies which have now been resolved. Anomalies exist in the early days of the game, generally up to the turn of the century in 1900. Differing match reports for many of these fixtures are in conflict with one another. As an example, in some cases over six different sources have been used to verify match details and there are still discrepancies.

Identification of players in the early years of the game must have been particularly difficult at times. With no numbers on the shirts, poor vantage points and no television recording, it is not surprising that such irregularities exist. Often the press reporter or club official could not decide who scored a particular goal, and the sometimes reported "scrimmage" was all that described the goal. And before football's authorities took a firm grip on proceedings, there were often disputes over the actual result, occasionally scorelines changed days later or even matches annulled and replayed.

Solutions to such problems are inevitably ones of compromise, a judgement taken from information gathered and due to this comprehensive review, differences in appearances and goals will occur to previous publications, although such cases are restricted to a handful of senior games in over 6,000 first-eleven matches and approaching 12,000 goals scored.

Fixtures

The season by season spreadsheets comprise full match details of all Newcastle United's first-class fixtures as scheduled above. Abandoned fixtures are included on the season breakdown but results, player appearances and goals are not included in the season totals. United's abandoned derby clash with Sunderland on Good Friday 1901 when according to some reports an estimated crowd approaching 70,000 tried to gain access to St James' Park, then with a capacity of only 30,000, is incorporated. Although the officials and players did make an attempt to start the action, this fixture was abandoned without a ball being kicked. Generally though, scheduled games which have been postponed before kick-off, usually due to weather or sometimes illness, or other unusual circumstances are not identified. One such unusual case surrounds a wartime Football League (North) game with Bradford Park Avenue in December 1945 which was postponed after the train United were travelling in broke down and the team could not get to the stadium.

Void Northern League games in season 1890-91 cancelled due to the state of the pitch are shown in a similar format to abandoned fixtures. The annulled FA Cup tie against Nottingham Forest in 1974 is likewise included in the match analysis but not in the totals, while the written off games before World War Two in season 1939-40 are classified as 'wartime' fixtures and included elsewhere. Where matches are played at a neutral stadium these venues are notated while if away fixtures have been switched to another ground these are also shown with a footnote.

Skipper Bob Moncur hoists the Inter Cities Fairs Cup, the forerunner of the present-day Europa League competition, as United's party returns from Budapest in 1969.

Club Titles

The titles for opposing clubs are those used at the point in time, eg Birmingham City will be noted as that title from 1945 to date, and as Small Heath from 1888, and Birmingham from 1905 to 1945. The former Football League club of Loughborough is also commonly referred to as *Loughborough Town*, but their official title was Loughborough Athletic & Football Club and is notated as Loughborough. The one exception is Sheffield Wednesday. Their title for many years was *The Wednesday*, but common practice throughout football was to call them Sheffield Wednesday.

European clubs are generally noted in the manner applied in their own country, and not as the Anglo version, eg Inter Milan is noted as *Internazionale* while Sporting Lisbon is referred to as *Sporting Clube de Portugal*. The same applies to Continental stadium names.

League Positions

The League position logged on the match records is generally United's placing in the table after the fixture in question and has been taken from the media or club publications. Some discrepancies will occur, especially so in modern football when matches are spread over the whole weekend and into Monday evening with changing League tables.

Attendances

Facts and figures relating to match attendances are something of a historian's nightmare. In the years up to 1925, no official attendances had to be recorded with football's authorities for League fixtures while afterwards, although a system existed for logging every match with the Football League – and later the Premier League – inconsistencies exist over the seasons. FA Cup and other knock-out competitions were more fully recorded, especially so in the game's early years.

For much of the first 30-odd years of football's League structure match gates were estimates, either given by club officials or gauged by the media present. Normally clubs kept accurate figures to themselves, Newcastle United being no different. In charting the Magpies' attendances up to 1925, varying figures have been collected from the newspaper reports and a consensus taken as to the gate present at the match. Sometimes up to six or seven differing attendances were recorded. Information is especially sketchy in the Victorian era.

From season 1925-26 all clubs had to record accurate figures of supporters passing through the turnstiles, and the Football League archive, now housed at the National Football Museum, holds the original record books for all League games. Yet, despite having a specific figure for every match a quandary still exists, as these ledgers also record a figure for what was called "members" present at each fixture. It is not conclusively known if such members were included in the gate figure, or in addition, although the convention appears is that they are included in the attendance. Also, these 'official' figures sometimes are in conflict with what appears to be accurate figures given by each club to the media, although this may be explained by a later adjustment exercise being carried out on the gate a few days after each game and before a figure is lodged with football's authorities. This early period also sometimes noted an accurate turnstile figure, being the number of supporters who paid through the gate. However such attendances require to be supplemented by the addition of 'member' and 'season-ticket' holders.

Typical of the problem faced is the attendance for United's record gate fixture with Chelsea in September 1930. The local press have recorded several figures for this match; 68,686, 68,586 and 68,386, the generally accepted gate confirmed some days after the game in the local press, and thereafter noted on club programmes. The official Football League papers log the figure of 68,089 with also a 'members' figure of 233 noted.

Within the season summary, average home attendances for the season are shown and these figures are for senior League (including Play-Offs & Test Matches) and Cup (including FA Cup, League Cup & European) fixtures only. They do not include secondary tournaments such as the Anglo-Italian Cup and Texaco Cup or abandoned and void games.

It should be remembered that over the years tactics and style of football have changed. A centre-half who played in the 1900s had a different role to that of say a centre-half of the Premier League years, while inside-forwards of the past are now known as midfielders, or second strikers. Football can be divided into largely three eras. Prior to 1925 the field of play was split into a 2-3-5 formation; two full-backs acting solely as defenders and rarely crossing the half-way line; three half-backs working both as creators and spoilers; and five forwards consisting of two wingers who usually stuck hard to their touchline, one centre-forward with two inside men alongside.

An important change in the offside law in 1925 led to the role of the centre-half being altered and, to a lesser extent, that of the inside-forwards. The two full-backs were now supported by a centre-back, the previous midfield role of the centre-half becoming a defensive one. The inside-forwards now often dropped into midfield to assist the under strength wing-half backs and the line-up became now 3-2-5.

Continental football's growing impact and England's World Cup victory in 1966 saw changes made with wingers becoming midfielders and full-backs starting to overlap down the flank. Tactical systems of 4-4-2, 4-3-3 and 4-2-4 were deployed which, as the decades evolved to the modern era, became at times more intricate with further variations.

Player Numbering & Team Notation

The traditional method of identifying players and positions of 1 to11 has been used throughout the charts. Player numbering on shirts was not introduced on a regular basis for Football League games until season 1939-40, while the introduction of squad numbering for the start of the Premier League in 1992-93 poses difficulties for all football statisticians.

However pre-1939 team line-ups in a 1 to11 formation was the norm although until a formal player numbering system was introduced, conflicts do exist in match reports as to the actual position of some players. In these instances, especially so in the earlier years, there is no definitive conclusion if a certain player figures in the number 4 role (right-half) or number 8 (inside-right) role.

Some conflicts have been decided by reference to the club's own team ledgers which give 1 to 11 positions.

Where squad numbers apply, the player's squad number is also identified. It should be noted that in recent seasons a handful of players had different squad numbers for European matches. In these instances the domestic squad number is used. Also, on a few occasions two different players were allocated the same squad number within a season, before and after transfers. Importantly, from Newcastle United's outlook, since the squad system was introduced, the club's iconic No. 9 shirt has been reserved exclusively for the Magpies' centre-forward, thus maintaining its historic status.

Player Appearances

A summary for appearances (including substitute appearances) in each season is shown and includes; Northern League, Football League & Premier League, including Test Matches & Play-Offs. FA Cup, including Qualifying matches, & Football League Cup. European competitions; UEFA Champions League, Inter Cities Fairs Cup, UEFA Cup, UEFA Cup Winners Cup & Intertoto Cup. Sheriff of London Charity Shield, FA Charity Shield, Wartime League & Cup, Texaco Cup, Anglo-Italian Cup, Anglo-Scottish Cup, Full Members Cup (and later sponsored variations) and Mercantile Credit Centenary Trophy.

Appearances in all other matches, including abandoned and void games, are not included. Each season summary includes a brief biography on a prominent player; games and goals statistics noted are for all senior competitive matches as above. A comprehensive player A-Z career register for all players is included in Section 3 of the book.

Goalscorers

There are instances of disputed goals in the early years of United's history, as noted previously, the varying information has been carefully scrutinised and a judgement made as to the probable scorer. After the end of the 19th century, disagreements were largely eliminated when it was up to the club to determine who scored goals and reported in returns to the governing bodies.

In modern football the Premier League's so-called 'Dubious Goals Committee' was introduced to adjudicate any instance where the identity of the scorer of a goal is disputed. A handful of United's Premier League goals have been referred to this committee, the likes of Alan Shearer's strike against Manchester United in 2001 attributed to Wes Brown as an own-goal. A few goals still cause debate, including Charles N'Zogbia's effort against Coventry is noted by UEFA as an own-goal by 'keeper Buffon, although to almost all at the game it was Andy's goal. Footnotes have been added as clarification.

Own-goals are included throughout including the identity of the opposition scorer. As these have been reviewed discrepancies have materialised such as goals scored direct from a corner and credited to a United player before 1924-25. In these instances the rules did not permit goals to be scored in this way. These have been changed to an own-goal by the goalkeeper in question.

Penalties are shown, and again a review of these spot-kicks has thrown up certain differences. As an example Bill Imrie has previously been credited with a penalty against Swansea Town in 1937, although the actual spot-kick was saved and then netted by Imrie in the follow up. In addition, the use of the terminology of 'penalty' in reports during the early years of football has led to some confusion. Some reporters described an incident as a 'penalty' when, in fact, the decision was a free-kick. This led, if a player scored from the free-kick, for the goal to be termed a 'penalty'! Alec Gardner's goal against Sunderland in April 1900 is one such instance. Only with very careful reading of several reports can this be ascertained.

As for player appearances, a summary of goalscorers for each season is shown while career totals are included within the player register in Section 3.

Substitutes

Although the occasional substitute was recorded in early friendly matches, senior League and Cup action only allowed the use of substitutes from season 1965-66 and initially only when a player had been injured. The rules for the use of substitutes were soon eased and greatly expanded during the 1990s and after, to such an extent that now in the Premier League three players can be used from a bench of a selected seven. Substitute records from recent seasons do contain inconsistencies especially when double or even triple changes have been made at the same time and where the identity of who replaced who is open to debate.

Dismissals

Included for the first time is a record of all United's players sent-off in senior fixtures. Prior to 1980 there were very few dismissals in a near century of football. The introduction of rigid rules and the yellow-red card system saw many more players ordered off the field. Each player sent-off is indicated in the team charts with a suffix, eg *8d*. On occasions dismissals were decided, or revoked, after the game. These are clarified as a footnote. The players sent-off in any one season are also indicated on the season summary page.

Season Summary

Each season includes a comprehensive summary page. Identified are individuals who have held various posts during the season, from Chairman to manager and coach including the side's regular captain. Also charted are the team's primary colours and change strip over the years, as well as in the modern era, the club's kit supplier and principal sponsor. Sections highlight major signings to take place as well as those players to have made their senior debut from the club's junior set-up and go onto to make an impact.

Player Transfers

Throughout the book player transfer fees are noted as either official club fees or those amounts generally reported in the media. Throughout the last century and more, and especially so in modern football where transfers have become more and more complicated, clubs, including Newcastle United, have at times been reluctant to divulge exact transfer figures. When United secured Hughie Gallacher in 1925 it was initially reported as being a new national record fee of £10,000, then reduced to quoted amounts of both £7,000 and £6,500.

Fees noted do not generally include add-on amounts such as the League levy, agent's fees if any and certain taxes (which can be later reclaimed). Due to these factors, discrepancies do occur in the transfer amounts. In 1969 the purchase of Jimmy Smith was generally reported as being £100,000, the club's first six-figure transfer. Yet it appears the fee was more like £80,000 topped up with add-ons to a figure approaching £100,000. Alan Shearer's world record transfer purchase is circulated as a £15m fee, however the amount the deal cost United is more, at around £15.75m. Michael Owen's overall fee is around £16.8m rather than the publicised £16m.

General Abbreviations

Abbreviations used throughout the data can be found at the end of the book on page 344. Specific abbreviations for fixture competitions are included before each section.

SEASONS
1887-88
1888-89

East End begin the FA Cup tradition

As Newcastle East End slowly but steadily developed in the Byker and Heaton area of Newcastle during the mid-years of the 1880s, football elsewhere was making giant strides forward. While national league competition in the shape of the Football League was not to arrive until 1888, the Football Association much earlier introduced what was to become the flagship trophy in football, the FA Cup. First competed for in 1877, East End took to the field some 10 years later in their first FA Cup match, a qualifying tie on Teesside with South Bank. On a miserable wet day and on a treacherous pitch, South Bank went ahead before the break before East End equalised with a goal from William Muir. The match went into extra-time, and Muir scored again before the Teesside club eventually won 3-2.

The following season of 1888-89 saw the East Enders progress further and take part in their first ever competitive meeting with their great rivals to be, Sunderland. Although, at that time, the East End versus West End clash was very much the local clash, a match with the Wearsiders was eagerly awaited and 5,000 at Sunderland's old ground on Newcastle Road saw the contest. East End were not disgraced against the home club – then well on their way to becoming the best in the country. Second-half goals from Davison and Jobling gave Sunderland victory.

Newcastle had started what was to become a fêted association in the illustrious competition. They were also to soon join the emerging network of league football around the country, locally in the form of the Northern League. Top level Football League action was just around the corner.

Pictured above: Jock Smith who had two spells with the club as a talented forward.

IN CHARGE

President: JT Oliver
Manager: Club Committee
Captain: Alec White/
Tom Hoban/Jock Smith
Trainer/Coach: Tom Dodds

MAJOR SIGNINGS

Joe McKane (Clydebank)
Robert Creilly (Dunmore)

SEASON REVIEW

1887-88

Appearances (1m): Blackett W 1, Chard W 1, Coldwell W 1, Hiscock E 1, Hoban T 1, Marshall T 1, Muir A 1, Muir W 1, Scott M 1, Stones S 1, White AH 1.

Goals (2g): Muir W 2.

Dismissals: 0 players.

1888-89

Appearances (3m): Coldwell W 3, Collins J 3, Creilly R 3, Henderson D 3, Hoban T 3, Miller Jas 3, Muir A 3, Raylstone J 3, Smith J 3, Young W 3, White AH 2, Mulvey M 1.

Goals (5g): Hoban T 1, Muir A 1, Raylstone J 1, White AH 1, unknown 1.

Dismissals: 0 players.

TEAM COLOURS Navy-blue shirts with orange stripe, white shorts.

PLAYER FOCUS Alec White

Born Glamis. Centre-half, 5'10"
1884 to 1892: 11 app 4 goals.

The most prominent figure in the early pioneering years of Newcastle United was Scot Alexander Henry White. A schoolteacher from the historic village of Glamis, White settled in the Heaton area of Tyneside. He started playing the fledgling game of football with the Rangers club which soon became the strongest on Tyneside, twice winning the Northumberland & Durham Challenge Cup. When they folded in 1884 Alec, by then a Northumberland county player, joined East End and was to become their leading figure. Tough and clever in midfield from the old-style centre-half position, he was soon appointed captain and reached national recognition by taking part in the 1886 North versus South match, an unofficial international trial contest, while he also appeared for the celebrated Corinthians eleven. Always able to score goals – once striking seven against Point Pleasant – White did much to develop the East Enders into Newcastle's foremost club and by the time they had switched to St James' Park White had guided them to two Northumberland Challenge Cup victories and seen off rivals West End. Alec retired firstly in 1889, but then returned to the field, to bow out once more in February 1892 shortly before East End were to change their name to Newcastle United. He was afterwards often to be seen at St James' Park over the following decades and was associated with the Northumberland FA as an administrator for over 50 years. He was also awarded the FA's Long Service Medal. White was one of the original shareholders in the East End – and Newcastle United – company when equity was launched in 1890. He was also elected as one of the club's first directors.

SEASON 1887-88 & 1888-89

FA Cup

Round	Date	Venue	Opponent	Res	F	A	HT	Att	Scorers	Chard	Stones	Coldwell	Marshall	White	Blackett W	Scott	Muir A	Muir W	Hoban	Hiscock E	Round
1Q	15 Oct	A	South Bank	Le	2	3	(0 1)		Muir W 2	1	2	3	4	5	6	7	8	9	10	11	1Q

Le Lost after extra time

FA Cup

Round	Date	Venue	Opponent	Res	F	A	HT	Att	Scorers	Coldwell	White	Muir A	Hoban	Henderson	Creilly	Miller Jas	Young W	Raylstone	Collins	Smith	Mulvey	Round
1Q	06 Oct	H	**Port Clarence**	W	3	1	(2 0)		Raylstone, Muir A, White	6	9	11	10	1	2	3	4	5	7	8		1Q
2Q	27 Oct	H	**Stockton**	W	2	1	(1 0)		Hoban, unknown	6	9	10	11	1	2	3	4	5	7	8		2Q
3Q	17 Nov	A	Sunderland	L	0	2	(0 0)	5,000		6		11	10	1	2	3	4	5	7	8	9	3Q

League action makes a start

The introduction of the Northern League competition was an important milestone in the development of the game in the North East. Sunderland apart, who were to soon join the Football League, in 1890, all local clubs up to then only tasted competitive action in regional cup tournaments and the odd brief sortie into the FA Cup. Regular league action was different. Newcastle East End took part in one of the opening three Northern League fixtures during September 1889 facing Darlington at Chillingham Road. A crowd approaching 3,000 turned up and saw the East Enders victorious by 2-1 with two of the three East End Millers scoring the club's first League goals.

The side started well, then found a mid-table place in that inaugural season finishing fourth behind winners St Augustine's from Darlington. East End's great rivals did better though, West End were runners-up and did win the first League clash. They won an early season confrontation at St James' Park, a rough match which saw two players sent-off – East End's James Miller becoming the first Newcastle United man ordered off in competitive action. East End won the return derby at Chillingham Road and such was the importance of the contest that the players received a sovereign each as a bonus. St Augustine's knocked East End out of the FA Cup in the qualifying stage, 2-1 in Darlington.

During the season a major corporate decision was taken when East End became a limited company with the issue of 2,000 shares at a price of 10 shillings (50p) each. The majority of the initial shareholding hailed from the Heaton and Byker areas of Tyneside, and included several players. The company's first Board of Directors was announced too, their occupations varied from clerk to pattern-maker and iron founder.

Pictured above: James Miller, a noted pioneer of the club in both Northern League and Football League action.

The colours are black-and-white stripes, but the team is Northumberland not East End, pictured at St James' Park and containing United pioneers. Unfortunately the players are not identified.

SEASON REVIEW

Northern League: P18 W9 D3 L6 F32 A28 Pts 21.
Position: 4th (Champions; Darlington St Augustine's).
FA Cup: Q2 (Winners; Blackburn Rovers).

Appearances (20m): Collins J 19, Creilly R 19, McCurdie A 18, Mulvey M 18, Miller Jas 15, Scott M 13, Gibbon P 10, Miller Jn1 10, Watson R 10, Calder H 9, Sawyers A 9, McInnes T 7, McKane J 7, McLaughlin H 7, Coupe J 6, Henderson D 6, Miller Jn2 6, Broughton JR 5, Thompson WK 5, White AH 5, Tinn 2, Blackett F 1, Blackett W 1, Coldwell W 1, Hoban T 1, Wood L 1, Unknown 9.

Goals (37g): Gibbon P 5, McInnes T 5, Miller Jn2 5, McLaughlin H 4, Mulvey M 4, Miller Jn1 3, White AH 3, Collins J 2, Creilly R 1, McCurdie A 1, Thompson WK 1, unknown 3.

Dismissals: 1 player; Miller Jas.

MAJOR SIGNINGS

Tom McInnes (Cowlairs)
Willie Thompson
(Shankhouse Black Watch)

FROM THE RANKS

None

Memorabilia CORNER

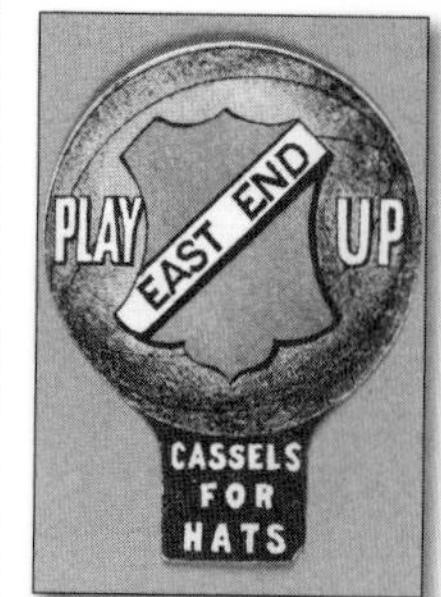

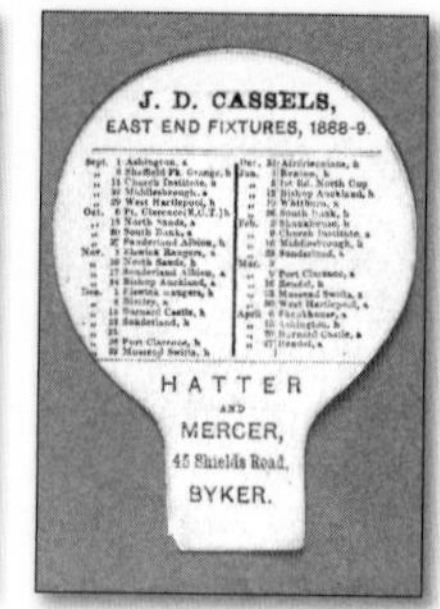

J. D. CASSELS,
EAST END FIXTURES, 1888-9

HATTER
AND
MERCER,
45 Shields Road,
BYKER.

Popular collector cards featured East End in the Victorian era, this one issued by a Byker clothier.

IN CHARGE

Chairman: Adam Gilchrist
Manager: Club Committee
Captain: James Miller
Trainer/Coach: Tom Dodds

CHILLINGHAM RD

Average Attendance
Lg 2,500 Lg & Cup 2,600

PLAYER FOCUS Bobby Creilly

Born Scotland. Half-back, 5'10"
1889 to 1895: 123 app 6 goals.

Half-back Bobby Creilly became a dependable player during the pioneering years of Newcastle United. Arriving from the Dunmore club in Scotland, like many in that era, he was tough and uncompromising as well as a touch fiery and temperamental. Creilly was a battler and looked the part too with short cropped hair. A noted footballer with East End's side, he appeared in the club's inaugural Northern League fixture against Darlington, first FA Cup proper match with Nottingham Forest and went onto appear in the opening match they played on moving to St James' Park when Celtic were the visitors. Often at odds with others, Bobby was once suspended for using bad language on the pitch at officials while he also on one occasion stormed off the field due to his colleagues' lack of effort. Creilly later appeared for Newcastle United in Second Division action, on over 50 occasions, he was also on the field for United's first ever Football League encounter with Arsenal. The Scot appeared for the Northumberland County XI and was a well known figure in the region. Following good service to the club, Bobby served Hebburn Argyle with credit in local football and during the Edwardian era fell on hard times, described as being in "destitute circumstances". He later was "removed to Coxlodge Hospital" then a sanatorium in Newcastle.

*East End's heartland.
Location plan of East End's grounds:
(1) Stanley Street (2) Byker Vicarage
(3) Dalton Street (on the edge of the plan)
(4) Chillingham Road.*

TEAM COLOURS Navy-blue shirts with orange stripe, white shorts.

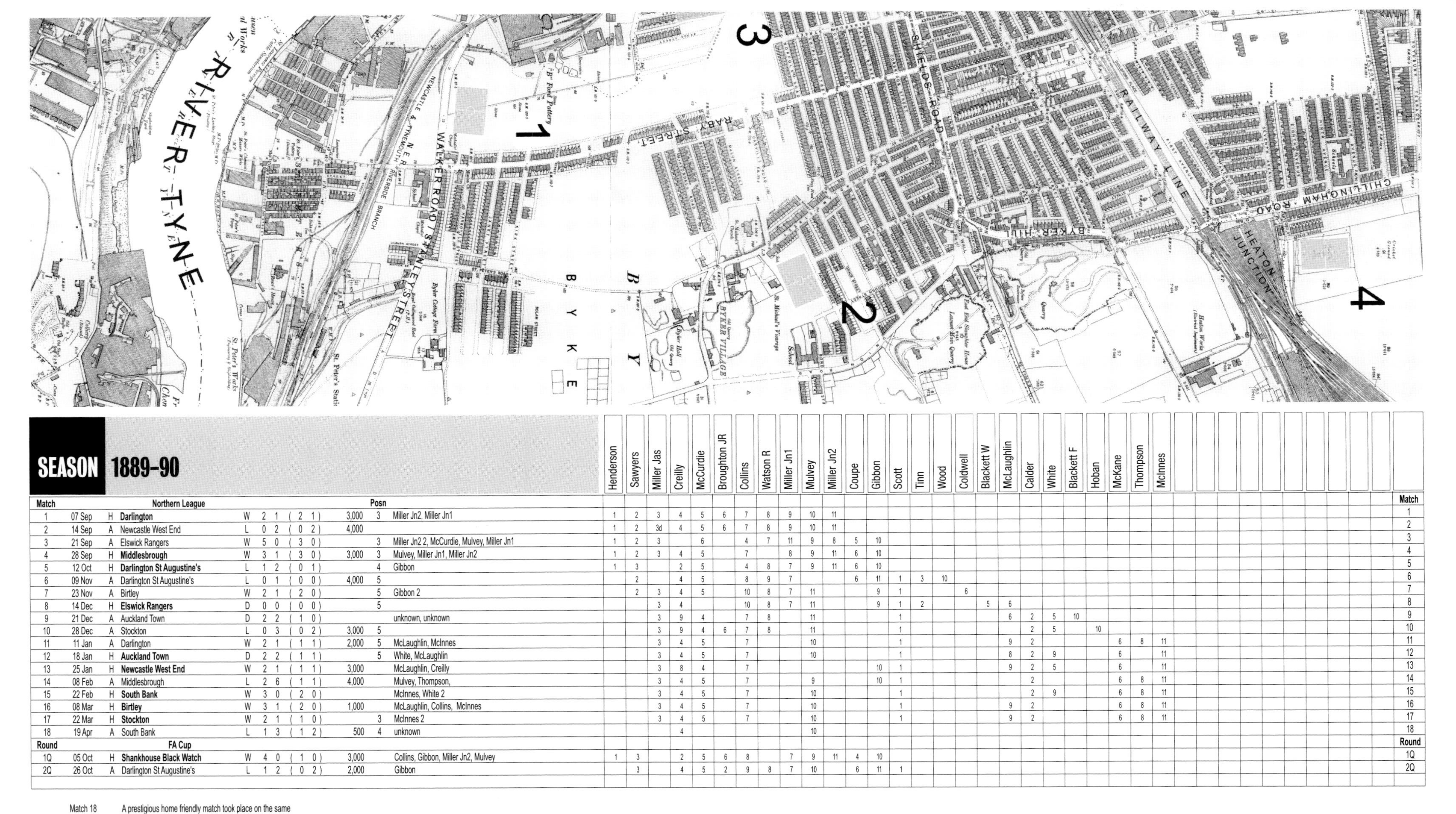

SEASON 1889-90

Match	Date		Northern League	Result		HT	Att	Posn	Scorers
1	07 Sep	H	**Darlington**	W	2 1	(2 1)	3,000	3	Miller Jn2, Miller Jn1
2	14 Sep	A	Newcastle West End	L	0 2	(0 2)	4,000		
3	21 Sep	A	Elswick Rangers	W	5 0	(3 0)		3	Miller Jn2 2, McCurdie, Mulvey, Miller Jn1
4	28 Sep	H	**Middlesbrough**	W	3 1	(3 0)	3,000	3	Mulvey, Miller Jn1, Miller Jn2
5	12 Oct	H	**Darlington St Augustine's**	L	1 2	(0 1)		4	Gibbon
6	09 Nov	A	Darlington St Augustine's	L	0 1	(0 0)	4,000	5	
7	23 Nov	A	Birtley	W	2 1	(2 0)		5	Gibbon 2
8	14 Dec	H	**Elswick Rangers**	D	0 0	(0 0)		5	
9	21 Dec	A	Auckland Town	D	2 2	(1 0)			unknown, unknown
10	28 Dec	A	Stockton	L	0 3	(0 2)	3,000	5	
11	11 Jan	A	Darlington	W	2 1	(1 1)	2,000	5	McLaughlin, McInnes
12	18 Jan	H	**Auckland Town**	D	2 2	(1 1)		5	White, McLaughlin
13	25 Jan	H	**Newcastle West End**	W	2 1	(1 1)	3,000		McLaughlin, Creilly
14	08 Feb	A	Middlesbrough	L	2 6	(1 1)	4,000		Mulvey, Thompson,
15	22 Feb	H	**South Bank**	W	3 0	(2 0)			McInnes, White 2
16	08 Mar	H	**Birtley**	W	3 1	(2 0)	1,000		McLaughlin, Collins, McInnes
17	22 Mar	H	**Stockton**	W	2 1	(1 0)		3	McInnes 2
18	19 Apr	A	South Bank	L	1 3	(1 2)	500	4	unknown
Round			**FA Cup**						
1Q	05 Oct	H	**Shankhouse Black Watch**	W	4 0	(1 0)	3,000		Collins, Gibbon, Miller Jn2, Mulvey
2Q	26 Oct	A	Darlington St Augustine's	L	1 2	(0 2)	2,000		Gibbon

Match	Henderson	Sawyers	Miller Jas	Creilly	McCurdie	Broughton JR	Collins	Watson R	Miller Jn1	Mulvey	Miller Jn2	Coupe	Gibbon	Scott	Tinn	Wood	Coldwell	Blackett W	McLaughlin	Calder	White	Blackett F	Hoban	McKane	Thompson	McInnes	Match
1	1	2	3	4	5	6	7	8	9	10	11																1
2	1	2	3d	4	5	6	7	8	9	10	11																2
3	1	2	3		6		4	7	11	9	8	5	10														3
4	1	2	3	4	5		7		8	9	11	6	10														4
5	1	3		2	5		4	8	7	9	11	6	10														5
6		2		4	5		8	9	7			6	11	1	3	10											6
7		2	3	4	5		10	8	7	11			9	1			6										7
8			3	4			10	8	7	11			9	1	2			5	6								8
9			3	9	4		7	8		11				1					6	2	5	10					9
10			3	9	4	6	7	8		11				1						2	5		10				10
11			3	4	5		7			10				1					9	2				6	8	11	11
12			3	4	5		7			10				1					8	2	9			6		11	12
13			3	8	4		7						10	1					9	2	5			6		11	13
14			3	4	5		7			9			10	1						2				6	8	11	14
15			3	4	5		7			10				1						2	9			6	8	11	15
16			3	4	5		7			10				1					9	2				6	8	11	16
17			3	4	5		7			10				1					9	2				6	8	11	17
18				4						10																	18
Round																											**Round**
1Q	1	3		2	5	6	8		7	9	11	4	10														1Q
2Q		3		4	5	2	9	8	7	10		6	11	1													2Q

Match 18 — A prestigious home friendly match took place on the same day as the South Bank fixture and a predominately reserve side was sent to Teesside. Full details of that team have not been recorded. As a consequence total appearances remain incomplete.

DateLine ... 7 Sept: First league contest, a 2-1 victory in the Northern League against Darlington. **14 Sept:** East End and West End contest a fiery Northern League derby with two players sent-off. **8 Feb:** For the fixture against Boro, East End start with 10 men, then field 12 players, before getting to the regulation 11.

SEASON
1890-91
NORTHERN LEAGUE

Painful local defeats

While the Northern League brought more competitive football to the region, it had to overcome hurdles to be a success. Like anything new there were growing pains, with clubs incurring more costs as a result of increased travelling. After an encouraging start with a 6-0 victory over Darlington, East End endured a disappointing season, being in the bottom reaches of the table for the campaign. They were demolished by eventual champions Ironopolis – indeed, winners for three of those years – by all of eight goals. Teesside neighbours Middlesbrough also inflicted a painful defeat (6-0) as did Wearside club Sunderland Albion (7-0). Yet East End sent West End packing 7-1 in League action, and 5-0 in the traditional Christmas contest while they also recorded another 4-0 win. The East Enders at least were top-dog on Tyneside.

The FA Cup qualifying competition brought Sunderland Albion to Chillingham Road just before that painful seven-goal defeat occurred at Christmas. Albion had been formed in 1888, a breakaway club to Sunderland, by then on their way to becoming a force in football. A close battle took place in front of 5,000 crowd, the match swinging from end-to-end with both clubs taking the lead. The contest went into extra-time but was abandoned at 2-2 due to darkness descending on the Heaton pitch. The replay again at Chillingham Road saw another thrilling game, Albion winning 2-0 with a double strike in the closing stages.

Although East End had a poor season, there was a rapidly developing gap between the club and other local sides, including West End. In 1890-91 East End remained unbeaten against their rivals in six meetings in which they scored 24 goals to only four against, while they also defeated Elswick Rangers 9-1 and 10-2, as well as Rendel 6-1. Football was changing quickly on Tyneside.

Scot Tom McInnes had a fine season after arriving from Cowlairs in Glasgow, then a ranked club north of the border. He was a noted Scottish international and went onto have a fine spell with Nottingham Forest at the top level.

Pictured above: Tom McInnes, one of the first big names to join East End, capped by Scotland.

Another vintage group photograph featuring certain East End footballers in Northumberland's line-up. Again though the players are not identified.

SEASON REVIEW

Northern League: P14 W5 D2 L7 F25 A39 Pts 12.
Position: 6th (Champions; Middlesbrough Ironopolis).
FA Cup: Q4 (Winners; Blackburn Rovers).

Appearances (17m): Collins J 17, McInnes T 17, McKane J 17, Scott M 17, Wilson WA1 17, McCurdie A 16, Miller Jas 16, Mulvey M 16, Creilly R 13, Thompson WK 13, McLaughlin H 7, Sorley J 5, Wallace J 5, Watson P 3, White AH 3, Carr R, 1, Gardner C 1, Tinlin C 1, Young P 1, Young W 1.

Goals (32g): McInnes T 11, Collins J 5, Thompson WK 5, Creilly R 2, Mulvey M 2, Sorley J 2, Wallace J 2, Young W 1, own goal 1, unknown 1.

Dismissals: 0 players.

MAJOR SIGNINGS

Peter Watson (Newmilns)
Joe Wallace (Newmilns)
Jock Sorley (Newmilns)

FROM THE RANKS

None

Memorabilia CORNER

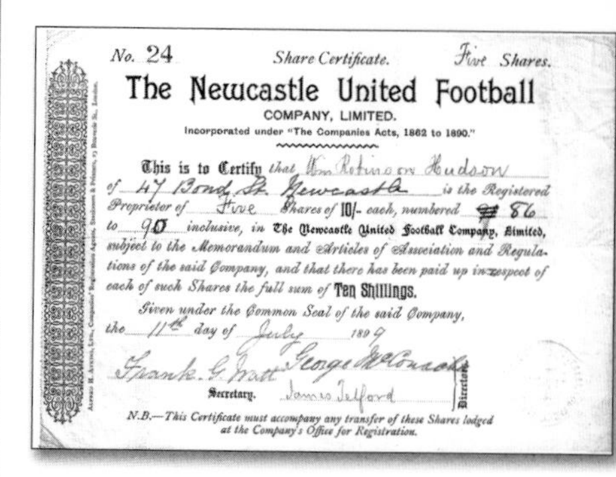

No. 24 Share Certificate. Five Shares.
The Newcastle United Football
COMPANY, LIMITED.
Incorporated under "The Companies Acts, 1862 to 1890."

This is to Certify that Wm Robinson Hudson of 47 Bond St. Newcastle is the Registered Proprietor of Five Shares of 10/- each, numbered 86 to 90 inclusive, in The Newcastle United Football Company, Limited, subject to the Memorandum and Articles of Association and Regulations of the said Company, and that there has been paid up in respect of each of such Shares the full sum of Ten Shillings.

Given under the Common Seal of the said Company, the 11th day of July 189

Frank G. Watt, Secretary.
George McConachie, James Telford, Directors.

N.B.—This Certificate must accompany any transfer of these Shares lodged at the Company's Office for Registration.

East End became a Limited Company in 1890, shares were sold at 10 shillings (50p) each.

IN CHARGE

Chairman: Adam Gilchrist
Manager: Director Committee
Captain: H McLaughlin
Trainer/Coach: Tom Dodds/William Bayles

CHILLINGHAM RD

Average Attendance
Lg 2,629 Lg & Cup 2,622

PLAYER FOCUS Joe McKane

Born Scotland. Left-half, 5'10"
1889 to 1895: 96 app 0 goals.

A Scot from the Glasgow area, Joe McKane served the club with distinction and a fair bit of controversy during the pioneer days of East End and the club's earliest season as Newcastle United. A bit fiery on the pitch, he was a tough competitor who never shirked from the tackle. Joe took part in several of the club's landmark fixtures like his fellow midfielder from over the Cheviots, Bobby Creilly. McKane was on the field for the club's first FA Cup proper match with Nottingham Forest as well as the inaugural Football League contest with Arsenal. Indeed, McKane was an influential figure in the Tynesiders team during that initial season of 1893-94 with senior company. Joe was an ever-present in the midfield battleground. Having arrived from the Clydebank club in January 1889, the Scot stayed with Newcastle for six years before heading to non-league football with Blyth in 1895. He once missed a fixture at Middlesbrough and forced United to play with ten men having failed to catch a train from Newcastle. He was fined for that mishap while he also was once docked two weeks wages for using what was described as "most insulting language" towards the players of Notts County.

TEAM COLOURS Cambridge-blue shirts, white shorts.

Location plan of Chillingham Road showing the ground at the end of Hartford Street. The complex of railway lines and junctions adjoins.

SEASON 1890–91

Match	Date		Northern League				Att	Posn	Scorers	Scott	Wilson	Miller Jas	McCurdie	McLaughlin	McKane	Creilly	Collins	Thompson	Mulvey	McInnes	Carr	White	Tinlin	Watson P	Sorley	Wallace	Young P	Gardner	Young W	Match
1	13 Sep	H	**Darlington**	W	6 0	(4 0)	1,200	2	Collins, unknown, McInnes 2, Mulvey, Thompson	1	2	3	4	5	6	7	8	9	10	11										1
2	20 Sep	A	Middlesbrough Ironopolis	L	0 8	(0 1)	3,500	4		1	2	3	4	5	6		8	9	10	11	7									2
3	27 Sep	H	**Newcastle West End**	W	7 1	(2 1)	5,000	3	Creilly, McInnes 3, Collins 2, Mulvey	1	2	3	4		6	7	8	9	10	11		5								3
4	01 Nov	H	**Stockton**	L	0 1	(0 0)	3,000	7		1	2	3	4	5	6	7	8	9	10	11										4
5	22 Nov	H	**Middlesbrough**	W	4 1	(1 0)	2,000	5	Collins, McInnes, Thompson 2	1	2		4	3	6	7	8	9	10	11		5								5
6	26 Dec	A	Sunderland Albion	L	0 7	(0 2)	5,000			1	2	3	4		6	7	8	9	10	11		5								6
7	27 Dec	A	Middlesbrough	L	0 6	(0 4)	4,000	7		1	2	3	4		6	7	8	9	10	11			5							7
	10 Jan	A	Newcastle West End	W*	4 1	(2 1)	4,000		*McInnes, White, Thompson, Creilly*	1	5	3	4		6	7		8		11		9		2		10				
	17 Jan	H	**Darlington St Augustine's**	W*	6 1	(5 0)			*Collins 2, Creilly, Wallace, Thompson, McInnes*	1	5	3	4		6	8	10	9		11				2		7				
8	24 Jan	A	Stockton	L	0 5	(0 1)	3,000	7		1	5	3	4		6	7	8	9	10	11				2						8
9	31 Jan	H	**Middlesbrough Ironopolis**	L	0 2	(0 1)	2,000	7		1	2	3	4		6	5	8	9		7					10	11				9
	14 Mar	A	Newcastle West End	W*	2 0	(0 0)			*Sorley, Mulvey*	1	5	3	4		6		8	7	10					2	9	11				
10	21 Mar	H	**Darlington St Augustine's**	W	2 0	(2 0)	1,200	6	Wallace, Sorley	1	4	3			6		5	7	8	11					9	10	2			10
11	04 Apr	A	Darlington	L	1 4	(0 2)	1,200	6	og (Theakston)	1	2	3	4		6	5	8		10	11					9			7		11
12	18 Apr	H	**Sunderland Albion**	W	1 0	(1 0)	4,000	6	Wallace	1	5	3	4		6		8		10	11				2	9	7				12
13	25 Apr	A	Darlington St Augustine's	D	2 2	(2 2)	1,000	6	Sorley, Collins	1	2	3	4		6	5	7		10	11					9	8				13
14	29 Apr	A	Newcastle West End	D	2 2	(2 0)	2,000	6	McInnes, Creilly	1	5	3	4		6	9	7		10	11				2		8				14
Round			FA Cup																											Round
2Q	25 Oct	A	Bishop Auckland Town	W	2 1	(1 1)	1,000		Young W, McInnes	1	2	3	4	5	6		8	9	10	11									7	2Q
3Q	15 Nov	H	**Shankhouse Black Watch**	W	5 0	(3 0)	1,200		Thompson 2, McInnes 3	1	2	3	4	5	6	7	8	9	10	11										3Q
4Q	06 Dec	H	**Sunderland Albion**	Ab	2 2	(1 1)	5,000		*Collins, Mulvey*	1	2	3	4		6	7	8	9	10	11		5								4Q
4Q	20 Dec	H	**Sunderland Albion**	L	0 2	(0 0)	4,000			1	2	3	4	5	6	7	8	9	10	11										4Q

Ab Abandoned during extra time due to bad light

W* Match declared void due to state of pitch and later replayed

DateLine ... 20 Sept: East End lose by 8-0 on Teesside against Ironopolis. **27 Sept:** Local rivals West End are given a 7-1 hiding by East End at Chillingham Road. **6 Dec:** The FA Cup Qualifying tie with Sunderland Albion is abandoned in extra-time due to bad light when all level at 2-2. **26 Dec:** Sunderland Albion score seven goals in a Boxing Day clash against East End.

SEASON
1891-92
NORTHERN LEAGUE

Tyne supremacy for East End

With Sunderland very much a respected member of the elite Football League camp – winning the title – and Ironopolis having a grip on the Northern League, the best East End could do was at least make sure they were again local kings on Tyneside. And this they did with ease. They surged ahead of West End again, for a second season running. The campaign saw East End dominate local matters and crush their rivals West End on no fewer than five occasions scoring 19 goals in the process, including a 7-1 romp in the Northern League. With a 4-1 victory over Champions Ironopolis at Chillingham Road, they finished a creditable fourth in the League table. That victory was a noted scalp. Ironopolis – the professional breakaway outfit from Middlesbrough – were a formidable side, winning the fledgling Northern League title in three of the opening four years. A crowd of 6,000 turned up and after an opening 1-1 stalemate, East End ran away with the match by scoring three more goals. It was the first defeat inflicted on the Teessiders in League action all season.

In the FA Cup, East End reached the First Round proper for the first time after qualifying wins over Tow Law, West End – with 8,000 in attendance – Shankhouse Black Watch and Bishop Auckland Town. They met Nottingham Forest, the Champions of the Football Alliance competition, a rival to the Football League.

East End sported a new red strip that season but due to a colour clash with Forest, East End borrowed the shirts of the Northumberland County side, black-and-white stripes. Alongside the River Trent, East End showed up well, although they lost 2-1. Yet against a Forest side including plenty of notable names in their line-up, defeat was no disgrace. Sorley and Thompson were a handful up front for East End, and they scored 30 goals between them in competitive action.

Pictured above: One of several pioneering Scots to serve United, Tom Crate was an effective striker.

Memorabilia CORNER

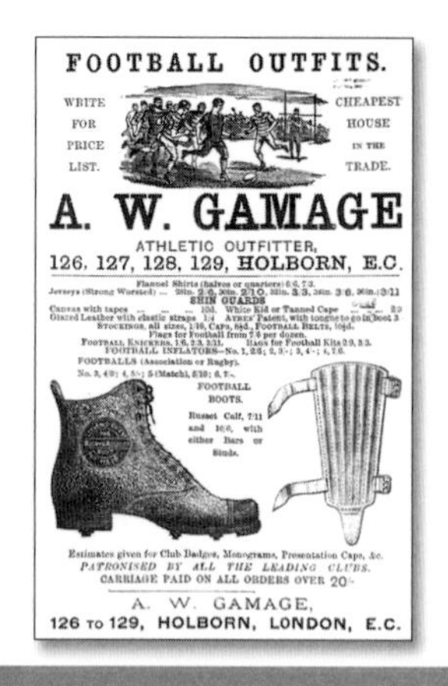

Football was all a bit different over a century ago, outfitters Gamages display their goods.

IN CHARGE

Chairman: Alex Turnbull
Manager: Director Committee
Captain: William Wilson/Jock Sorley
Trainer/Coach: William Bayles

CHILLINGHAM RD

Average Attendance
Lg 3,375 Lg & Cup 3,100

East End pictured at Chillingham Road. Back row, left to right: Forster (committee), Cameron (committee), Jeffrey (behind with cap), Creilly, Hardisty (referee), Watson, Scott, Golding (secretary), Wilson, Miller, McKane, Bell (committee), Turnbull (committee). Front: unknown, Barker, Crate, Thompson, Sorley, Wallace, Bayles (trainer), Peel (committee).

PLAYER FOCUS Willie Thompson

Born North Seaton. Centre-forward, 5'7"
1889 to 1897: 135 app 65 goals.

A locally born product of the pioneering era, Willie Thompson can be said to be the first in a long line of centre-forward heroes to lead United's attack. He began with Bedlington Burradon, then made a name for himself with one of the strongest clubs in the region, neighbours Shankhouse Black Watch, and often showed up well when facing Newcastle East End. He joined the club in December 1889 not long after facing Aston Villa in a high profile FA Cup-tie and taking part in Northumberland Challenge Cup finals for Shankhouse. Sporting a magnificent moustache in the style of the Victorians, Willie was an extremely popular character for Shankhouse and became equally so when wearing the colours of East End and ultimately Newcastle United. One of the best strikers around the North East at the time, he was a Northumberland County player and showed he could more than hold his own when Thompson appeared in the Football League on Newcastle's admittance in 1893. He scored a hat-trick – the first for the club at that level – against Arsenal in the opening month and went onto score 10 goals in that first League season. Not big, but quick and with the eye for the goal, he proved a deadly marksman netting over 60 for the club, a goal every second match. Suffering from a knee injury later in his career, he was replaced in the leader's role by Richard Smellie in 1896-97. Willie left St James' Park in 1897 to join Jarrow and afterwards also appeared for Ashington.

SEASON REVIEW

Northern League: P16 W9 D2 L5 F37 A20 Pts 20.
Position: 4th (Champions; Middlesbrough Ironopolis).
FA Cup: R1 (Winners; West Bromwich Albion).

Appearances (21m): McKane J 21, Scott M 21, Creilly R 20, Reay H 20, Sorley J 20, Crate T 19, Wallace J 19, Thompson WK 18, Wilson WA1 18, Miller Jas 17, Spence J 17, Watson P 12, Barker J 5, Gardner C 2, Blackett F 1, Connolly J1 1.

Goals (56g): Sorley J 17, Thompson WK 13, Reay H 9, Wallace J 4, Crate T 3, Spence J 3, Barker J 2, Creilly R 1, own goals 2, unknown 2.

Dismissals: 1 player; Connolly.

MAJOR SIGNINGS

Harry Reay (Shankhouse Black Watch)
Tom Crate (New Cumnock)
John Barker (Newcastle West End)

FROM THE RANKS

None

TEAM COLOURS Red shirts, white shorts (Change; black & white striped shirts, dark shorts)

SEASON 1891-92

Match	Date	Venue	Northern League	Res	F	A	HT	Att	Posn	Scorers	Scott	Watson P	Wilson	McKane	Creilly	Crate	Reay	Thompson	Connolly	Sorley	Wallace	Spence	Miller Jas	Blackett F	Gardner	Barker	Match
1	19 Sep	A	Darlington	D	1	1	(1 1)	1,500	7	Wallace	1	2	3	4	5	6	7	8	9d	10	11						1
2	10 Oct	A	Newcastle West End	W	2	0	(1 0)	5,000	5	Wallace, Thompson	1	2	3	6	4	8	7	9		10	11	5					2
3	17 Oct	A	Stockton	W	3	1	(3 0)	5,000	3	Reay 2, Thompson	1	2	3	6	4	8	7	9		10	11	5					3
4	31 Oct	A	South Bank	D	3	3	(2 2)	1,200	4	Thompson 2, Sorley	1	2	4	6	11	8	7	9		10		5	3				4
5	07 Nov	H	**Darlington**	W	4	0	(3 0)	2,000	3	Sorley 3, Crate	1		2	6	4	8	7	9		10		5	3	11			5
6	21 Nov	A	Middlesbrough	L	1	2	(1 0)	5,000	4	Sorley	1		2	6	4	8	7	9		10	11	5	3				6
7	19 Dec	H	**South Bank**	W	4	0	(1 0)	2,000	4	Thompson 3, Spence	1	2		6	4	10	7	9			11	5	3		8		7
8	26 Dec	H	**Sheffield United**	L	1	2	(0 1)	4,000	4	Crate	1		2	6	4	8	7	9		10	11	5	3				8
9	06 Feb	H	**Newcastle West End**	W	7	1	(5 1)	3,000	4	Sorley 2, unknown, Barker 2, Reay, Wallace	1		2	6	4		7			9	11	5	3		8	10	9
10	27 Feb	H	**Stockton**	W	3	2	(2 1)	3,000	4	Sorley 2, Reay	1	2	4	6	5	8	7			9	10		3			11	10
11	05 Mar	A	Sunderland Albion	W	3	0	(2 0)	3,000	3	Spence, Creilly, Sorley	1		2	6	4	9	8			10	11	5	3			7	11
12	02 Apr	H	**Sunderland Albion**	W	1	0	(0 0)	4,000	2	Sorley	1	2	4	6		8	7	9		10	11	5	3				12
13	13 Apr	A	Middlesbrough Ironopolis	L	0	3	(0 0)	4,000	4		1	2	3	6	4	8	7	9		10	11	5					13
14	16 Apr	A	Sheffield United	L	0	3	(0 0)	3,000	4		1		2	6	4		7	9		10	11	5	3			8	14
15	19 Apr	H	**Middlesbrough Ironopolis**	W	4	1	(2 1)	6,000	4	Reay, Sorley, Thompson, og (Langley)	1	2	5	6	4	8	7	9		10	11		3				15
16	30 Apr	H	**Middlesbrough**	L	0	1	(0 1)	3,000	4		1	2	5	6	4	8		9		10	11		3			7	16
Round			**FA Cup**																								**Round**
1Q	03 Oct	A	Tow Law Town	W	5	1	(4 0)	1,000		Reay 3, Thompson, Sorley	1		2	6	4	8	7	9		10	11	5	3				1Q
2Q	24 Oct	A	Newcastle West End	W	3	0	(1 0)	8,000		Sorley 2, Spence	1		2	6	4	8	7	9		10	11	5	3				2Q
3Q	14 Nov	H	**Shankhouse Black Watch**	W	3	2	(0 2)	3,000		Wallace, Thompson, Reay	1	2		6	4	8	7	9		10	11	5	3				3Q
4Q	05 Dec	H	**Bishop Auckland Town**	W	7	0	(1 0)	1,000		Sorley 2, Thompson 3, Crate, unknown	1	2		6	4	8	7	9		10	11	5	3				4Q
1	16 Jan	A	Nottingham Forest	L	1	2	(0 1)	7,000		og (Brown)	1		2	6	4	8	7	9		10	11	5	3				1

DateLine ... 19 Sept: Goalkeeper Matt Scott faces a penalty kick for the first time and sees the ball fly over the bar. **24 Oct:** East End win a big FA Cup clash with West End at St James' Park in front of an 8,000 crowd. **16 Jan:** First FA Cup Proper match, a 2-1 reverse to Nottingham Forest. **6 Feb:** West End thrashed once more by East End in a Northern League derby, by 7-1. **19 April:** Champions Ironopolis are beaten 4-1 in Heaton.

SEASON 1892-93

NORTHERN LEAGUE

A move west and United arrive

Season 1892-93 was to be a landmark year in the history of the club. Towards the end of the previous season it became clear that one half of the city's ranked clubs were in dire trouble. West End were in financial mess and folded during the summer of 1892. The remnants' of the West End club, including officials and players, as well as the lease of their ground at St James' Park, were offered to East End. Following a historic meeting in Heaton during May 1892, the East Enders decided to move across the city to Barrack Road and takeover the much more prestigious site of St James' Park. Several directors and a few players of the West End club went with them.

Before the start of the new season, East End's officials attempted to gain entry to the Football League. They were admitted to the newly formed Second Division, but the club rejected that proposal due to the lack of drawing-power opponents would have as compared to the First Division. So another season in the Northern League followed. After an exhibition opening match at St James' Park in front of around 6,000 against Glasgow Celtic, they fell to Sheffield United in Northern League action then defeated Middlesbrough. Mid-way through the season and in a bid to foster better support, East End decided to change their name, selecting Newcastle United at a public meeting on Friday 9th December 1892. The first game under that title was a friendly contest against Middlesbrough at St James' Park on Christmas Eve, a 2-1 victory in front of a gate of around 1,500.

The new United could have lifted the Northern League Championship that year but were beaten by Ironopolis. They faltered in the last two games and ended as runners-up to the Teessiders.

In spite of the change in venue and being now the sole major club on Tyneside, success in financial terms was not immediate. A big financial loss was recorded. Newcastle United needed the full backing of the community. That was slow to develop, but when it did, United rapidly surged ahead.

Pictured above: Harry Jeffrey was a big personality on Tyneside, strong tackling and often controversial.

Season 1892-93 was to be the first season at St James' Park. East End are pictured in red shirts before a fixture.

SEASON REVIEW

Northern League: P10 W5 D1 L4 F30 A19 Pts 11.
Position: 2nd (Champions; Middlesbrough Ironopolis).
FA Cup: R1 (Winners; Wolverhampton Wanderers).

Appearances (11m): Collins J 11, Graham W 11, Miller Jas 11, Whitton D 11, Creilly R 10, Reay H 10, Crate T 9, McKane J 9, Sorley J 9, Thompson WK 9, Wallace J 9, Jeffrey H 8, Watson P 3, Barker J 1.

Goals (32g): Sorley J 7, Thompson WK 7, Wallace J 6, Reay H 5, Crate T 2, Graham W 2, Collins J 1, Creilly R 1, own goal 1.

Dismissals: 0 players.

MAJOR SIGNINGS

Willie Graham (New Cumnock)
Harry Jeffrey (Newcastle West End)
James Collins (Newcastle West End)

FROM THE RANKS

None

Memorabilia CORNER

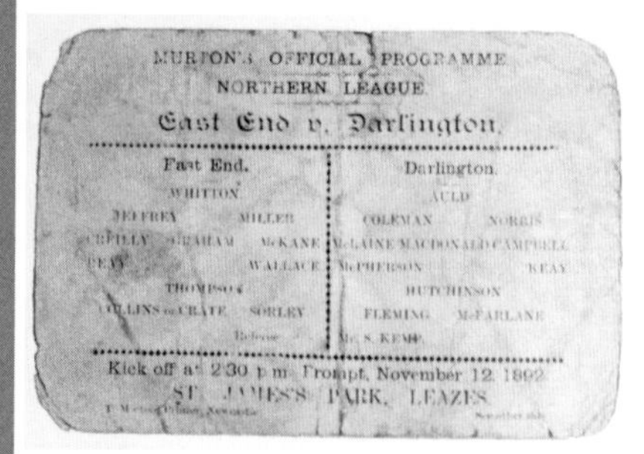

MURTON'S OFFICIAL PROGRAMME
NORTHERN LEAGUE
East End v. Darlington.

East End.	Darlington.
WHITTON	AULD
JEFFREY MILLER	COLEMAN NORRIS
CREILLY GRAHAM McKANE	McLAINE MACDONALD CAMPBELL
REAY WALLACE	McPHERSON KEAY
THOMPSON	HUTCHINSON
COLLINS or CRATE SORLEY	FLEMING McFARLANE
Referee	Mr. S. KEMP.

Kick off at 2.30 p.m. Prompt, November 12, 1892
ST. JAMES'S PARK, LEAZES.

The earliest known programme – or match card – from a fixture with Darlington in 1892.

IN CHARGE

Chairman: Alex Turnbull
Manager: Director Committee
Captain: Jock Sorley/Willie Graham
Trainer/Coach: William Bayles

ST JAMES' PARK

Average Attendance
Lg 2,800 Lg & Cup 3,000

PLAYER FOCUS Jock Sorley

Born Muirkirk. Inside-left/Centre-forward, 5'10"
1891 to 1893: 35 app 27 goals.

Signed from Newmilns in Ayrshire during January 1891, Jock Sorley was eventually to become captain of East End and Newcastle United. He was one of several popular Scots to land on Tyneside and serve United well in the club's earliest years. When on form, few defenders could cope with his darting runs and eye for goal and he once scored five goals in a friendly over Scottish club Annbank. Jock appeared in the club's Northern League campaigns of 1890-91, 1891-92 and 1892-93 often a scorer in those early years of competitive action in the North East. After taking part in Newcastle's bow in the Football League against Arsenal and scoring one of the historic opening goals, the equaliser in a 2-2 draw, Sorley only left the club at a time of financial struggle after being told – along with everyone else – he needed to take a reduction in wages. Sorley refused, but was awarded a valuable gold medal when he left Gallowgate as a mark of his popularity. Jock then assisted Middlesbrough, Blackburn Rovers and Burton Swifts after his stint on Tyneside before he returned to the region in 1896 to play with distinction in non-league circles with Hebburn Argyle winning the Northern Alliance title. At Ewood Park, he reached the FA Cup semi-final with Rovers in 1894 when they missed reaching the final after a defeat by Notts County. His family variously used the surname of McSorland, McSorley and Sorley, while his actual birth certificate notes the latter. After leaving football Jock worked as a miner and railway worker.

TEAM COLOURS Red shirts, white shorts (Change; black & white striped shirts, dark shorts)

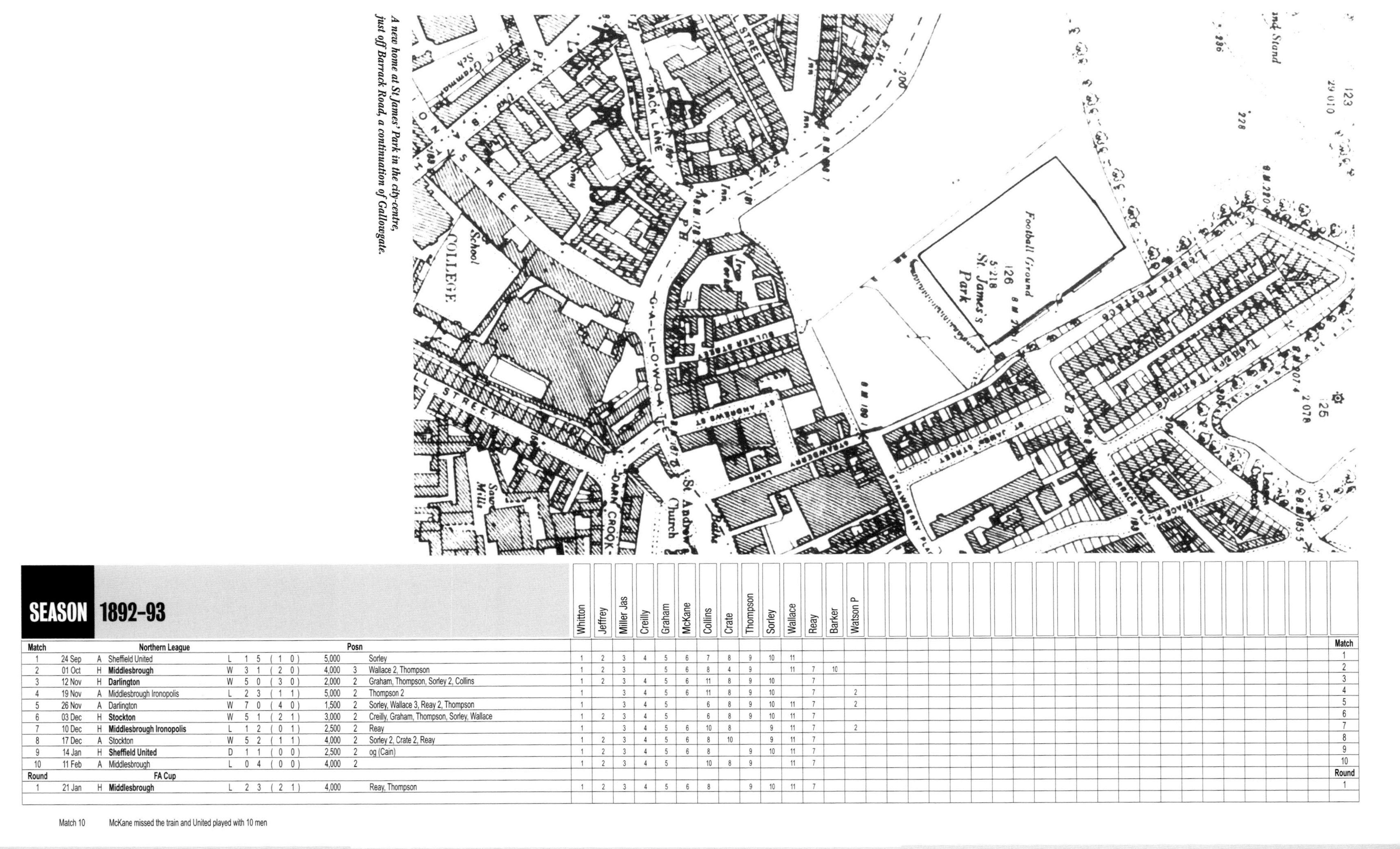

A new home at St James' Park in the city-centre, just off Barrack Road, a continuation of Gallowgate.

SEASON 1892-93

Match	Date		Northern League					Att	Posn	Scorers	Whitton	Jeffrey	Miller Jas	Creilly	Graham	McKane	Collins	Crate	Thompson	Sorley	Wallace	Reay	Barker	Watson P	Match
1	24 Sep	A	Sheffield United	L	1	5	(1 0)	5,000		Sorley	1	2	3	4	5	6	7	8	9	10	11				1
2	01 Oct	H	**Middlesbrough**	W	3	1	(2 0)	4,000	3	Wallace 2, Thompson	1	2	3		5	6	8	4	9		11	7	10		2
3	12 Nov	H	**Darlington**	W	5	0	(3 0)	2,000	2	Graham, Thompson, Sorley 2, Collins	1	2	3	4	5	6	11	8	9	10		7			3
4	19 Nov	A	Middlesbrough Ironopolis	L	2	3	(1 1)	5,000	2	Thompson 2	1		3	4	5	6	11	8	9	10		7		2	4
5	26 Nov	A	Darlington	W	7	0	(4 0)	1,500	2	Sorley, Wallace 3, Reay 2, Thompson	1		3	4	5		6	8	9	10	11	7		2	5
6	03 Dec	H	**Stockton**	W	5	1	(2 1)	3,000	2	Creilly, Graham, Thompson, Sorley, Wallace	1	2	3	4	5		6	8	9	10	11	7			6
7	10 Dec	H	**Middlesbrough Ironopolis**	L	1	2	(0 1)	2,500	2	Reay	1		3	4	5	6	10	8		9	11	7		2	7
8	17 Dec	A	Stockton	W	5	2	(1 1)	4,000	2	Sorley 2, Crate 2, Reay	1	2	3	4	5	6	8	10		9	11	7			8
9	14 Jan	H	**Sheffield United**	D	1	1	(0 0)	2,500	2	og (Cain)	1	2	3	4	5	6	8		9	10	11	7			9
10	11 Feb	A	Middlesbrough	L	0	4	(0 0)	4,000	2		1	2	3	4	5		10	8	9		11	7			10
Round			FA Cup																						Round
1	21 Jan	H	**Middlesbrough**	L	2	3	(2 1)	4,000		Reay, Thompson	1	2	3	4	5	6	8		9	10	11	7			1

Match 10 McKane missed the train and United played with 10 men

DateLine ... 3 Sept: First fixture at the new home of St James' Park, a 1-0 defeat to Glasgow Celtic in a friendly. **26 Nov:** East End hit seven goals past Darlington in a Northern League fixture. **24 Dec:** First game under the new title of Newcastle United, a 2-1 friendly success over Middlesbrough. **1 Jan:** United defeat the celebrated Corinthians by 8-1 in the New Year's Day holiday attraction.

SEASON
1893-94
DIVISION 2

Into Football League action

The club's hierarchy were convinced that the only way for the Tynesiders to develop further and flourish was to enter the Football League battleground. Sunderland had showed the way, swiftly becoming one of the country's finest teams. Costs and expenses would increase, resulting in financial struggle to start with, but if they could emulate their Wearside rivals and reach the First Division, as well as foster the town's support, a sustainable football club could be established.

Before the season's start United were again admitted to the Second Division of the Football League, and this time the Geordies accepted the invite, along with other noted clubs as Liverpool and Arsenal. Their debut was against the Londoners, a draw at the Manor Ground in Plumstead. The Newcastle party travelled through the night by train to get to London and the fare had to be paid by the team's directors, so short of cash was the club. They arrived early morning, hardly the best preparation. On a fine day, Arsenal held a 1-0 half-time advantage and increased their lead soon after the break. But the Tynesiders battled to level matters at 2-2. Scots Tom Crate and Jock Sorley are credited with scoring the club's first ever League goals. Newspaper reports though also note that yet another Scot, Willie Graham, may have grabbed Newcastle's first ever strike, not Crate.

They had a winning start on home soil, a 6-0 victory in the return contest with Arsenal. Once they found their feet, Newcastle almost sneaked into a Test Match place – being the promotion system then – but in the end they finished six points away in fourth place. They also did relatively well in the FA Cup, defeating First Division Sheffield United in front of 7,000, the club's first big victory in the competition. United then met another top side, Bolton Wanderers. A huge crowd turned up on Tyneside – real evidence that support was there to be tapped. Over 10,000 saw United knocked out by 2-1. The club needed that regular support desperately. They were in fact on the brink of collapse. At one stage the FA even suspended Newcastle for a non-payment of just over £26 to Derby County. But fund raising as well as loans from directors and shareholders kept the club afloat.

Pictured above: Tom Rodger, a Scot who impressed quickly at left-back in a United shirt.

Memorabilia CORNER

How one cartoonist captured the very first Football League contest for both Arsenal and United.

IN CHARGE

Chairman: Alex Turnbull/David McPherson
Manager: Director Committee
Captain: Willie Graham
Trainer/Coach: William Bayles/ D Veitch/John Pears

ST JAMES' PARK

Average Attendance
Lg 3,093 Lg & Cup 3,769

The first group labelled 'Newcastle United' for season 1893-94, the club's debut season in the Football League. Note the white shorts. As the club did not change to black-and-white striped shirts until late in 1894, their colours were still red.

PLAYER FOCUS Joe Wallace

Born Ayrshire. Forward, 5'4"
1891 to 1895: 77 app 33 goals.

Arriving on Tyneside at the same time as Jock Sorley from the Newmilns club, near Kilmarnock, Joe Wallace proved a worthwhile acquisition from Ayrshire. He quickly became a firm favourite of the crowd and could operate in any forward position. At only 5'4" tall, Wallace was a handful in attack despite his size during the clubs early years of competitive football. Joe initially became one of the mainstays of the club's Northern League side, then in Newcastle's first Football League season. He was top scorer with 15 goals during that historic opening campaign in Division Two, indeed he started on fire, netting six times in the first six fixtures. Joe was a regular during the club's initial two seasons in the Football League. He scored a hat-trick in the Magpies first home victory in League competition against Arsenal. The diminutive Wallace also scored the two goals which defeated Sheffield United during January 1893, Newcastle's first FA Cup victory in the senior stage of the tournament. Wallace started his career with the marvellously named Glenbuck Cherrypickers, a club which also much later developed the noted Shankley brothers. After helping Newcastle to make an impact on football's senior League competition, Joe joined local Tyneside club Rendel and he remained in the area for much of his life after hanging up his boots.

SEASON REVIEW

Football League Div 2: P28 W15 D6 L7 F66 A39 Pts 36.
Position: 4th (Champions; Liverpool).
FA Cup: R2 (Winners; Notts County).

Appearances (30m): Crate T 30, Creilly R 30, Graham W 30, McKane J 30, Lowery W 28, Thompson WK 28, Jeffrey H 27, Wallace J 27, Quinn C 25, Rodger T 18, Willis R 16, Law JH 10, Miller Jas 9, Gillespy T 4, Bartlett T 3, Inglis J 3, Laverick J 3, Barr JW 1, Bowman J 1, Keir M 1, Patten JT 1, Ramsey A 1, Ryder I 1, Ryder J 1, Simm W 1, Sorley J 1.

Goals (69g): Wallace J 17, Crate T 13, Thompson WK 10, Graham W 5, Quinn C 5, Willis R 5, Bartlett T 3, Jeffrey H 3, Law JH 2, Creilly R 1, Sorley J 1, own goals 2, unknown 2.

Dismissals: 0 players.

MAJOR SIGNINGS

John Law (Everton)
Bobby Willis (Shankhouse Black Watch)
Tom Rodger (St Johnstone)

FROM THE RANKS

Toby Gillespy (Arthur's Hill)
W Lowery (Blyth)

TEAM COLOURS Red shirts, white shorts (Change; black & white striped shirts, dark shorts)

SEASON 1893-94

Match			FL Division 2				Posn	
1	02 Sep	A	Woolwich Arsenal	D	2 2	(0 1)	6,000		Sorley, Crate
2	23 Sep	A	Burton Swifts	L	1 3	(0 2)		14	unknown
3	30 Sep	H	**Woolwich Arsenal**	W	6 0	(2 0)	2,000	10	Wallace 3, Thompson 3
4	07 Oct	A	Lincoln City	L	1 2	(1 1)	1,000	12	Wallace
5	14 Oct	A	Notts County	L	1 3	(1 2)	5,000	12	Wallace
6	21 Oct	A	Ardwick	W	3 2	(0 2)	3,000	9	Wallace, Crate, og
7	28 Oct	H	**Small Heath**	L	0 2	(0 0)	3,000	10	
8	04 Nov	A	Liverpool	L	1 5	(1 3)	8,000	11	Thompson
9	18 Nov	A	Northwich Victoria	L	3 5	(1 0)	400	12	Crate, Thompson, og (Scanlan)
10	25 Nov	H	**Liverpool**	D	0 0	(0 0)	2,000	12	
11	09 Dec	H	**Notts County**	W	3 0	(1 0)	3,500	11	Wallace 2, Thompson
12	16 Dec	A	Small Heath	W	4 1	(1 0)	2,500	8	Crate, Wallace, Willis, Graham
13	25 Dec	A	Middlesbrough Ironopolis	D	1 1	(1 1)	2,000	9	Crate
14	26 Dec	A	Walsall Town Swifts	W	2 1	(2 1)	5,000	8	Wallace 2
15	27 Dec	A	Crewe Alexandra	D	1 1	(1 1)	2,000	8	Graham
16	30 Dec	H	**Burslem Port Vale**	W	2 1	(1 1)	3,000	7	Crate, Creilly
17	01 Jan	H	**Lincoln City**	W	5 1	(0 1)	4,000	6	Bartlett 3, Thompson, Quinn
18	02 Jan	H	**Middlesbrough Ironopolis**	W	7 2	(4 1)	3,000	5	Law, Thompson, Willis 2, Quinn 2, Graham
19	06 Jan	H	**Ardwick**	W	2 1	(1 1)	1,200	5	Thompson, Graham
20	13 Jan	H	**Northwich Victoria**	W	3 0	(0 0)	2,000	5	Crate 3
21	20 Jan	A	Rotherham Town	L	1 2	(1 0)	1,000	5	Wallace
22	03 Feb	A	Burslem Port Vale	D	1 1	(1 0)	2,000	5	Wallace
23	17 Feb	H	**Rotherham Town**	W	4 0	(2 0)	600	4	Wallace, Crate, Quinn, Graham
24	24 Feb	H	**Grimsby Town**	W	4 1	(0 1)	4,000	4	Crate, Thompson, Quinn, Jeffrey
25	10 Mar	H	**Walsall Town Swifts**	W	2 0	(1 0)	2,000	4	Crate, Jeffrey (pen)
26	23 Mar	H	**Crewe Alexandra**	W	2 1	(0 1)	10,000	4	Jeffrey, unknown
27	24 Mar	H	**Burton Swifts**	W	4 1	(2 1)	3,000	4	Law, Wallace, Willis 2
28	14 Apr	A	Grimsby Town	D	0 0	(0 0)	2,000	4	
Round			**FA Cup**						
1	27 Jan	H	**Sheffield United**	W	2 0	(2 0)	7,000		Wallace 2
2	10 Feb	H	**Bolton Wanderers**	L	1 2	(0 2)	10,000		Crate

Match	Ramsay	Jeffrey	Miller	Creilly	Graham	McKane	Bowman	Crate	Thompson	Sorley	Wallace	Ryder J	Barr	Quinn	Lowery	Ryder I	Gillespy	Keir	Inglis	Patten	Simm	Rodger	Bartlett	Willis	Law	Laverick
1	1	2	3	4	5	6	7	8	9	10	11															
2		2	3	7	5	6		8	9		11	1	4	10												
3		2	3	4	5	6		7	9		11			8	1	10										
4		2	3	4	5	6		8	9		11			7	1		10									
5		2	3	4	5	6		8	9		10				1			7	11							
6		2	3	4	5	6		8	9		10				1				11	7						
7		2	3	4	5	6		8	9		11				1				7		10					
8		2	3	4	5	6		8	9		11			7	1		10									
9		2	3	4	5	6		10	9		7			11	1		8									
10		2		4	5	6		8	9		11			7	1		10					3				
11		2		4	5	6		8	9		11			7	1							3	10			
12		2		4	5	6		10	9		11			7	1							3		8		
13		2		4	5	6		10	9		11			7	1							3		8		
14		2		4	5	6		8	9		10			7	1							3			11	
15		2		4	5	6		10	9		11			7	1							3		8		
16		2		4	5	6		10	9					7	1							3		8	11	
17				2	5	6		4	9					7	1							3	10	8	11	
18				2	5	6		4	9					7	1							3	10	8	11	
19				2	5	6		4	9		11			7	1							3		8	10	
20		2		4	5	6		10	9		11			7	1									8		3
21		2		4	5	6		10	9		11			7	1									8		3
22		2		4	5	6		8			10			7	1							3		9	11	
23		2		4	5	6		8			10			7	1							3		9	11	
24		2		4	5	6		10	9		11			7	1							3		8		
25		2		4	5	6		9	11		10			7	1							3		8		
26		2		4	5	6		10	9		11			7	1							3		8		
27		2		4	5	6		7	9		10				1							3		8	11	
28		2		4	5	6		11	9		10			7	1									8		3
Round																										
1		2		4	5	6		8	9		11			7	1							3			10	
2		2		4	5	6		8	9		11			7	1							3			10	

Match 12 Various reports note different scorers
Match 24 Jeffrey's goal was possibly an og by Lundie
Match 28 Rodger may have played instead of Laverick

DateLine ... 2 Sept: First Football League contest, a 2-2 draw in London against Woolwich Arsenal. **30 Sept:** First Football League victory, 6-0 against Woolwich Arsenal at St James' Park. **27 Jan:** First FA Cup Proper victory, 2-0 against Sheffield United. **10 March:** United's first penalty-kick in Football League action, v Walsall Town Swifts.

SEASON 1894-95

DIVISION 2

Longstanding record defeats

Newcastle United's heaviest defeats in both League action and the FA Cup have stood for over 115 years. They were both recorded in a disastrous 1894-95 campaign. The club's second taste of senior football was not good enough, finishing in 10th place. In Victorian England the Midland town of Burton alongside the River Trent boasted two clubs; the Swifts and the Wanderers, both in Division Two with United. It was on a last day of the season in April at the Wanderers' Derby Turn ground that the Magpies registered their worst ever League defeat by all of nine goals. Brothers Art and Andrew Capes destroyed United, hitting seven of their tally of nine strikes.

Aston Villa faced the Tynesiders in the FA Cup during February at Villa Park. The country's top side – rivalled only by Sunderland – fired seven goals past 'keeper Ward, who was also to face the wrath of Burton. It could have been much worse too, Villa being five ahead at the interval.

Despite that double blow, United did consolidate in 1894-95 and the setbacks they received forced the club's directorate to have an in-depth review of how the Newcastle were structured and managed.

Up to the start of that season, United on occasion found their red shirts clashed with opponents, so on 2nd August 1894 they decided to ditch East End's colours and adopt shirts of black-and-white stripes with dark shorts, usually blue, not black, for many years to come. The first game after the change was the season's opener against Darwen at the old Barley Bank ground. United lost 0-5, then quickly lost again, 0-3 to Grimsby. New talent had arrived that season, but few really impressed during the miserable campaign which saw 92 goals conceded. Forward arrivals Dickson and Smith did impress at times though, grabbing 21 goals between them.

Pictured above: John McNee at only 5'4" tall was a noted player in Scotland before heading to Tyneside.

Memorabilia CORNER

By now East End were Newcastle United, but the cry from the terraces was still "Play Up"!

IN CHARGE

Chairman: David McPherson/John Cameron
Manager: Director Committee
Captain: Willie Graham
Trainer/Coach: William Bayles/John Pears/Harry Kirk

ST JAMES' PARK

Average Attendance
Lg 4,433 Lg & Cup 4,656

Newcastle pictured at St James' Park. Prominent supporters and directors John Graham (left) and John Black (right) are featured in the rear of the group, right, in bowler hats.

PLAYER FOCUS Willie Graham

Born Ayr. Centre-half, 5'10"
1892 to 1899: 109 app 13 goals.

Willie Graham, formerly of Preston North End and New Cumnock, was a player who stamped his authority in Newcastle's team after settling on Tyneside in the summer of 1892, just as East End moved to St James' Park. A tireless worker in the middle of the pitch and an inspiration on the field, Graham totalled over 100 games for the Geordies as the club focussed on joining the Football League and becoming recognised as a major club. Appointed captain for United's debut in the Football League, he more than anyone else organised United's team tactics during a period well before managers and coaches arrived on the scene. He was the leader in the dressing-room. Willie hailed from a footballing family, his more famous brother, John, also appearing for Preston and for Scotland too – the pair turning out together in Preston's historic first Football League title victory in the competitions inaugural year of 1888-89. Indeed Willie played in the very first Football League game against Burnley, a 5-2 victory. After more than six years service with United, he returned north to Scotland following a dispute with club officials and without permission to do so. As a result, United held his registration making sure he could not play senior football south of the border again.

SEASON REVIEW

Football League Div 2: P30 W12 D3 L15 F72 A84 Pts 27.
Position: 10th (Champions; Bury).
FA Cup: R2 (Winners; Aston Villa).

Appearances (32m): Graham W 30, Thompson WK 30, Creilly R 28, Smith Jn 27, Rendell T 25, McNee J 23, Dickson C 22, McDermid R 22, Jeffrey H 20, Ward WA 20, Willis R 20, Wallace J 17, McKane J 13, O'Brien PG 12, Crate T 11, Hynd J 9, Rodger T 6, Milne WJ 5, Hedley R 3, Cambell T 2, Donaldson 2, Lowery W 2, Haynes 1, Laverick J 1, Ryder J 1.

Goals (75g): Thompson WK 19, Willis R 13, Dickson C 11, Smith Jn 10, McNee J 4, Wallace J 4, Graham W 3, Crate T 2, O'Brien PG 2, Rendell T 2, Hedley R 1, McDermid R 1, Milne WJ 1, own goals 2.

Dismissals: 0 players.

MAJOR SIGNINGS

John McNee (Bolton Wand)
Jock Smith (Sheffield Wed)
Charles Dickson (Preston NE)
Bob McDermid (Dundee Wand)
Pat O'Brien (Sheffield Utd)
W Ward (Loughborough)

FROM THE RANKS

William Milne (Rutherford College)

TEAM COLOURS Black & white striped shirts, dark shorts (Change; red shirts, white shorts)

SEASON 1894-95

Match	Date		FL Division 2					Posn		Lowery	Jeffrey	Rendell	Creilly	Graham	McKane	Cambell	Willis	Thompson	Crate	Smith	Ryder	Wallace	Ward	Rodger	Laverick	Hedley	McNee	Dickson	McDermid	Hynd	O'Brien	Milne	Haynes	Donaldson	Match
1	01 Sep	A	Darwen	L	0 5	(0 1)	5,000			1	2	3	4	5	6	7	8	9	10	11															1
2	08 Sep	H	**Burton Swifts**	W	6 3	(2 0)	6,000	9	Wallace 2, Smith 2 (1 pen), Willis 2		2	3	4	5	6	7	8	9		10	1	11													2
3	15 Sep	H	**Grimsby Town**	L	0 3	(0 1)	5,000	12			2		4	5	6		8	7	10	9		11	1	3											3
4	22 Sep	H	**Notts County**	D	2 2	(1 1)	3,000	11	Thompson, Willis			4		5	6		8	11	10	9			1	3	2	7									4
5	29 Sep	H	**Leicester Fosse**	W	2 0	(1 0)	5,000	9	Thompson 2			2	4	5	6		8	11	7	9		10	1	3											5
6	06 Oct	A	Burslem Port Vale	D	4 4	(1 3)	2,000	10	Dickson, McNee, Thompson, Willis		2		4	5	6		8	9		7			1	3			10	11							6
7	13 Oct	H	**Darwen**	W	3 2	(1 0)	6,000	7	Dickson 2, McNee		2		4	5	6		8	9		7			1	3			10	11							7
8	20 Oct	A	Leicester Fosse	D	4 4	(4 2)	8,000	9	Dickson, Thompson, Willis, Smith (pen)		2		4	5	6		8	9		7			1	3			10	11							8
9	27 Oct	H	**Manchester City**	W	5 4	(2 2)	3,000	6	Dickson, Thompson 3, Graham	1	2	3	4	5	6		7	9				8					10	11							9
10	03 Nov	A	Bury	L	1 4	(1 3)	4,000	8	Thompson		2	3	4	5	6			11		8		7	1				9	10							10
11	10 Nov	H	**Burton Wanderers**	W	3 1	(2 1)	6,000	6	Thompson, Smith, McDermid		2	4		5	6			9		8		7	1				10	11	3						11
12	17 Nov	A	Lincoln City	L	1 3	(1 2)	2,000	7	Wallace		2	6	4	5				9		8		7	1				10	11	3						12
13	24 Nov	H	**Woolwich Arsenal**	L	2 4	(1 2)	3,000	8	Dickson 2		2		4	5	6			9		8		7	1				10	11	3						13
14	01 Dec	A	Grimsby Town	L	1 4	(1 2)	1,500	8	Thompson		2	6	4	5				9	8	7							10	11	3	1					14
15	15 Dec	H	**Rotherham Town**	W	5 2	(3 0)	4,000	8	Dickson 2, Willis 2, Graham		2		4	5	6		7	11	9	8								10	3	1					15
16	22 Dec	H	**Walsall Town Swifts**	W	7 2	(5 0)	1,500	5	Crate 2, Smith 3, Willis, og (Holmes)		2	6	4	5			7		9	8		11							3	1	10				16
17	25 Dec	H	**Crewe Alexandra**	W	6 0	(3 0)	7,000	5	Wallace, O'Brien, Willis, Smith 3		2	6	4	5			8		9	7		11							3	1	10				17
18	26 Dec	A	Rotherham Town	L	0 1	(0 1)	4,000	5			2	6	4	5			8	10	9	7		11							3	1					18
19	29 Dec	A	Walsall Town Swifts	W*	3 2	(3 0)	2,000	5	Willis 3		2	6	4	5			8	9		7							10		3	1		11			19
20	01 Jan	H	**Lincoln City**	W	4 2	(1 1)	4,000	4	Dickson, Willis, Thompson 2		2	6		5			8	7	4								10	11	3	1	9				20
21	05 Jan	A	Burton Swifts	L	3 5	(1 1)	3,000	5	og (Lawrence), O'Brien, Graham		2	6		5			8	7	4								9	11	3	1	10				21
22	12 Jan	A	Woolwich Arsenal	L	2 3	(0 1)	5,000	5	Thompson 2		2	6	4	5			8	7				11					9		3	1	10				22
23	09 Feb	A	Manchester City	L	0 4	(0 2)	3,500	7				6	4	5			8	9		7			1				10	11	3		2				23
24	09 Mar	A	Crewe Alexandra	L	1 2	(1 1)	7,000	10	Hedley				4	5				9		11		7	1			10	8	6	2				3		24
25	16 Mar	H	**Bury**	W	1 0	(1 0)	6,000	9	Thompson			6	2	5				9		4		7	1				10	11	3			8			25
26	23 Mar	A	Notts County	L	1 2	(1 1)	5,000	10	Thompson			6	4	5				9		8		7	1				10	11	3		2				26
27	06 Apr	A	Newton Heath	L	1 5	(1 1)	6,000	10	Dickson			6	4	5				9				8	1				10	11	3		2	7			27
28	12 Apr	H	**Burslem Port Vale**	L	1 2	(0 0)	3,000	10	McNee			6	2	5				9		4		10	1				8	11	3			7			28
29	13 Apr	H	**Newton Heath**	W	3 0	(3 0)	4,000	10	McNee, Thompson, Milne			6	5					9		4			1				10	11	3		2	7		8	29
30	15 Apr	A	Burton Wanderers	L	0 9	(0 4)	3,000	10				6	5					9		4			1			7	10	11	3		2			8	30
Round			**FA Cup**																																**Round**
1	02 Feb	H	**Burnley**	W	2 1	(1 1)	8,000		Rendell 2			6	4	5			8	9		7			1				10	11	3		2				1
2	16 Feb	A	Aston Villa	L	1 7	(1 6)	10,000		Thompson			6	4	5			8	9		7			1				10	11	3		2				2

W* Match abandoned after 80 mins due to a storm, but the result stood

Match 7 Some reports note Dickson 1 and McNee 2 goals
Match 9 The 5th goal given here to Thompson is also credited by some sources to Dickson
Match 16 One of Smith's goals is also attributed by some sources to Creilly
Match 24 Some reports note Hynd played instead of Haynes
02 Feb Some reports credit one of Rendell's goals to Willis

DateLine ... 1 Sept: United's worst start to a season, a 0-5 defeat at Darwen, a match in which United fielded a forward-line with an average height of 5'6". **29 Dec:** United win 3-2 at Walsall, but the fixture is left unfinished after 80m as their players walk off the pitch. **16 Feb:** Newcastle fall 1-7 to Aston Villa in the FA Cup, the club's worst defeat in the competition. **15 April:** United record their heaviest defeat in League football, 0-9 to Burton Wanderers.

SEASON
1895-96
DIVISION 2

Recovery and progress

Officials were shocked at the awful season last time round and were determined to change direction and set in place a recovery. New faces arrived in the dressing-room and importantly off the field too. And all hailed from north of the Cheviots. Tough half-back Jimmy Stott and Scottish international full-back Bob Foyers joined the ranks. So did forwards Willie Wardrope, Malcolm Lennox and James Logan – scorer of a FA Cup final hat-trick for Notts County. Another player forced a place in young Andy Aitken, who alongside Wardrope and Lennox headed the goals charts. All were a success. Also to settle on Tyneside was an imposing Scot, Frank Watt who took over the important Secretary's role in December 1895. That was to be a significant appointment.

Newcastle finished their third campaign in senior company in a much improved fifth place and instead of conceding goals they were free scoring themselves. Newcastle hit seven past Darwen, scored six against Crewe and Rotherham. They also recorded an 8-0 whitewash of West Hartlepool in the FA Cup. And they gained revenge over Burton Wanderers; defeating them home and away comfortably by scoring seven goals. Gates increased too. A reported 10,500 saw the game against Manchester City and a record 16,328 watched the FA Cup contest with Bury. That was the best by some way at St James' Park up to then. Newcastle led through a Willie Thompson strike at the turnaround, but Bury hit back after the interval. With a noted line-up then and in the top division – soon to lift the FA Cup twice – the Lancashire club went onto win 3-1. Despite that Cup reverse, with crowds improving and an average of just over 7,000 on Tyneside, but with the ability to attract over twice that number, Newcastle United were on the road to success.

Pictured above: Bob Foyers became a prominent defender and skipper of United for a period.

Memorabilia CORNER

Pitch markings before the turn of the century were unlike the present layout.

IN CHARGE

Chairman: William Nesham
Manager: Director Committee
Captain: Bob Foyers
Trainer/Coach: John Pears

ST JAMES' PARK

Average Attendance
Lg 7,300 Lg & Cup 7,041

The Magpies during 1895. Back row, left to right (players only): McKay, Henderson, Stott. Middle: Collins, McDermid, Foyer, Miller, Graham, Wardrope. On ground, centre: Thompson, Aitken.

PLAYER FOCUS Jimmy Stott

Born Middlesbrough. Left-half, 5'10"
1895 to 1899: 131 app 11 goals.

An important arrival from Grimsby Town's Second Division line-up for United, Jimmy Stott was to become part of a steadfast half-back line for the Tynesiders as they moved into their next level of development. Born on Teesside and starting his career with South Bank and Middlesbrough, he combined with Ghee and Ostler in the Magpies' midfield to great purpose after joining the club in June 1895 for a £15 fee. By then Stott was an experienced player at the peak of performance. Broad shouldered and powerful, he was soon appointed skipper and was a commanding figure on the field in midfield. Clever and swift, Jimmy was afraid of no man in the tackle – indeed, being censored by the club in 1896 for "continual fouling of his opponents"! His gritty determination aside, Jimmy displayed a grand all-round talent on the pitch. With Liverpool also, he was part of the Merseysider's first promotion team in 1894 as they became Second Division Champions and won the deciding Test Match against Newton Heath (Manchester United). He was top scorer with 14 goals in only 16 outings at Anfield. Stott went onto guide United to promotion for the first time in 1897-98. Moving back to Middlesbrough the following year, Jimmy afterwards resided on Tyneside. Often a hearty character, he became a popular publican in the city, often parading in snappy attire of the day with at times a top-hat and tailored suit.

SEASON REVIEW

Football League Div 2: P30 W16 D2 L12 F73 A50 Pts 34.
Position: 5th (Champions; Liverpool).
FA Cup: R2 (Winners; Sheffield Wednesday).

Appearances (36m): Graham W 36, McDermid R 36, Stott J 36, Wardrope W 36, Henderson Jn 35, Aitken A 32, Miller W 31, Collins J 30, Foyers R 30, Lennox M 26, Thompson WK 23, McKay W 21, Logan J 9, McDonald J1 6, Warburton J 3, Reid O 2, Adams G 1, Carr JR 1, Quinn C 1, Ward WA 1.

Goals (99g): Wardrope W 22, Lennox M 13, Aitken A 12, Collins J 9, Thompson WK 9, Logan J 8, McKay W 7, Stott J 6, Graham W 3, McDonald J1 2, McDermid R 1, Miller W 1, own goals 5, unknown 1.

Dismissals: 0 players.

MAJOR SIGNINGS

James Logan (Dundee)
Andy Aitken (Ayr Parkhouse)
Willie Wardrope (Linthouse)
Jimmy Stott (Grimsby Town)
Bob Foyers (St Bernards) £100
John Henderson (Clyde)
Malcolm Lennox (Glasgow Perthshire)
William Miller (Kilmarnock)
Willie McKay (Rangers)
John McDonald (Glasgow Ashfield)

FROM THE RANKS

Jack Carr (Science & Art)

TEAM COLOURS Black & white striped shirts, dark shorts (Change; red shirts, white shorts)

SEASON 1895-96

Match	Date		FL Division 2				HT	Att	Posn	Scorers	Henderson	McDermid	Foyers	Miller	Graham	Stott	Thompson	McKay	Logan	Aitken	Wardrope	Quinn	Collins	Lennox	Carr	Warburton	McDonald	Reid	Adams	Ward	Match
1	07 Sep	H	**Loughborough**	W	3	0	(2 0)	7,000	2	Wardrope, Aitken, Logan	1	2	3	4	5	6	7	8	9	10	11										1
2	14 Sep	A	Liverpool	L	1	5	(0 4)	10,000	8	Logan	1	2	3	4	5	6		8	9	10	11	7									2
3	21 Sep	H	**Notts County**	W	5	1	(3 0)	7,000	7	Aitken 3, Logan, McKay	1	2	3	4	5	6	7	8	9	10	11										3
4	28 Sep	A	Rotherham Town	D	1	1	(0 0)	2,000	7	Logan	1	2	3	4	5	6	7	8	9	10	11										4
5	05 Oct	H	**Liverpool**	W	1	0	(1 0)	10,000	7	Wardrope	1	2	3	4	5	6	9	8		10	11		7								5
6	19 Oct	A	Newton Heath	L	1	2	(0 0)	8,000	8	Logan	1	2	3	4	5	6	7	8	9	10	11										6
7	26 Oct	H	**Newton Heath**	W	2	1	(1 0)	7,000	6	Wardrope, og (Perrins)	1	2	3	4	5	6	7	8	9	10	11										7
8	09 Nov	A	Darwen	D	4	4	(0 3)	2,000	6	Wardrope, Aitken, Thompson, Collins	1	2	3	4	5	6	9			10	11		8	7							8
9	16 Nov	H	**Darwen**	W	7	2	(5 0)	6,000	6	Wardrope 3, Aitken, Collins, Lennox, McDermid	1	2	3	4	5	6	9			10	11		8	7							9
10	07 Dec	A	Burton Swifts	L	1	3	(0 3)	2,000	8	Wardrope	1	2		5	3	6	9	4		10	11		8	7							10
11	21 Dec	H	**Rotherham Town**	W	6	1	(1 0)	5,000	8	Wardrope 2, McKay, Lennox 2, Stott	1	2	3	4	5	6		9		10	11		8	7							11
12	25 Dec	H	**Crewe Alexandra**	W	6	0	(5 0)	8,000	6	Wardrope, Aitken, McKay 2, Collins, Lennox	1	2	3		5	6		9		10	11		8	7	4						12
13	26 Dec	A	Grimsby Town	L	1	2	(1 2)	4,000	8	Collins	1	2	3	4	5	6		9		10	11		8	7							13
14	28 Dec	A	Lincoln City	L	0	4	(0 3)	1,500	8		1	2	3	4	5	6		9		10	11		8	7							14
15	01 Jan	H	**Leicester Fosse**	W	1	0	(1 0)	5,000	7	Aitken	1	2			5	6		9		10	11		4	7		3	8				15
16	02 Jan	H	**Lincoln City**	W	5	0	(2 0)	5,000	5	Aitken, Lennox 2, Stott, Wardrope	1	2			5	6		9		10	11		4	7		3	8				16
17	04 Jan	A	Manchester City	L	2	5	(2 3)	10,000	7	McKay, Lennox	1	2			5	6		9		10	11		8	7		3		4			17
18	11 Jan	H	**Grimsby Town**	L	1	5	(1 3)	7,000	7	Collins	1	2			3	6		5	9	10	11		8	7				4			18
19	18 Jan	H	**Woolwich Arsenal**	W	3	1	(2 0)	8,000	6	McKay, Stott, Miller	1	2	3	4	5	6		9		10	11		8	7							19
20	25 Jan	A	Crewe Alexandra	L	0	3	(0 2)	8,000	6		1	2	3	4	5	6		9		10	11		8	7							20
21	08 Feb	H	**Burton Wanderers**	W	4	0	(1 0)	7,000	6	Lennox 2, Graham 2	1	2	3	4	5	6				10	11		8	7			9				21
22	22 Feb	A	Burton Wanderers	W	3	0	(2 0)	3,000	4	Thompson, Lennox 2	1	2	3	4	5	6	9			10	11		8	7							22
23	07 Mar	A	Loughborough	L	0	1	(0 0)	2,000	6		1	2	3	4	5	11				9	10		8	7					6		23
24	14 Mar	A	Notts County	W	1	0	(1 0)	5,000	5	Wardrope	1	2	3	4	5	6	9			11	10		8	7							24
25	21 Mar	H	**Manchester City**	W	4	1	(3 0)	10,500	5	Wardrope, Thompson, Collins, Lennox	1	2	3	4	5	6	9			10	11		8	7							25
26	03 Apr	H	**Burslem Port Vale**	W	4	2	(2 2)	10,000	5	McDonald 2, Collins, og (Morse)	1	2	3	4	5	6	9				11		8	7			10				26
27	04 Apr	H	**Burton Swifts**	W	5	0	(2 0)	7,000	5	Wardrope 2, Thompson 2, Stott	1	2	3	4	5	6	9				11		8	7			10				27
28	06 Apr	A	Woolwich Arsenal	L	1	2	(0 1)	16,000	5	og (Powell)	1	2	3	4	5	6	9				11		8	7			10				28
29	07 Apr	A	Leicester Fosse	L	0	2	(0 0)	5,000	5		1	2	3	4	5	6	9			10	11		8	7							29
30	20 Apr	A	Burslem Port Vale	L	0	2	(0 0)	2,000	5		1	2	3	4	5	6	9			10	11		8	7							30
Round			**FA Cup**																												**Round**
QP	05 Oct	A	Leadgate Exiles	WO																											QP
Q1	12 Oct	H*	**West Hartlepool NER**	W	8	0	(4 0)	3,000		Logan 2, Thompson, Collins 2, Stott, Graham, og (Baxter)		2	3	4	5	6	7	8	9		11		10							1	Q1
Q2	02 Nov	H	**Middlesbrough**	W	4	1	(2 1)	6,000		Wardrope 2 (1 pen), McKay, unknown	1	2	3	4	5	6	9	8		10	11		7								Q2
Q3	23 Nov	H	**Rendel**	W	5	0	(4 0)	3,000		Wardrope, Aitken 2 (1 pen), Logan, Thompson	1	2	3	4	5	6	7		9	10	11		8								Q3
Q4	14 Dec	H	**Tow Law Town**	W	4	0	(1 0)	3,000		Wardrope, og (Temperley), Lennox, Stott	1	2		4	3	6	9	5		10	11		8	7							Q4
1	01 Feb	A	Chesterfield	W	4	0	(3 0)	5,000		Wardrope 2, Aitken, Thompson	1	2	3	4	5	6	9			10	11		8	7							1
2	15 Feb	H	**Bury**	L	1	3	(1 0)	16,328		Thompson	1	2	3	4	5	6	9			10	11		8	7							2

WO Newcastle awarded a walkover when Leadgate scratched

H* Scheduled for Hartlepool, but played at Newcastle by agreement

Match 24 Aitken is also noted as the scorer, but the majority of reports give the goal to Wardrope

12 Oct Some reports note Henderson appeared in goal, not Ward

02 Nov Some reports credit McKay's goal to Collins

DateLine ... 5 Oct: The gates are locked for the first time at St James' Park for a League match as 10,000 see the visit of Liverpool. **25 Dec:** Against Crewe, Willie Wardrope strikes his 13th goal in nine successive League & Cup games, a record. **8 Feb:** United start the game against Burton Wanderers with only eight players. **15 Feb:** A new record crowd at St James' Park established of 16,328 against Bury in the FA Cup.

SEASON
1896-97
DIVISION 2

Promotion bid ends short

With a decent squad of players, including a new 'keeper in Charlie Watts and centre-forward in Richard Smellie, United's advancement continued as they looked upwards. For much of the season they were in promotion contention. With an average attendance of now 8,500 and big gates at St James' Park of 17,000 against Notts County and over 16,000 for the New Year's Day clash with Newton Heath, the financial crisis was well behind the club. A 2-0 victory over the future Manchester United club with goals from Willie Wardrope and Andy Aitken secured the points in a 2-0 triumph. That win started a good run in January. United went onto win four of the next five games in League fare. They defeated Lincoln City, Blackpool, Arsenal and Manchester City. Newcastle challenged at the top with Notts County and Newton Heath. But defeats in March to Gainsborough and Blackpool left United with too much to do in the promotion race.

There were plenty of unusual names in Second Division opposition over a century ago. Apart from Newton Heath, the Magpies faced Small Heath (later Birmingham City), Darwen, Loughborough and Gainsborough Trinity as well as Burton Wanderers and their neighbours Burton Swifts.

Although able to compete strongly in the Second Division there was still a marked gap to the top level. United faced Aston Villa in the FA Cup once more. And just like two years earlier in 1895, Villa ravaged the Magpies again, winning 5-0 in the Midlands at their old Perry Barr ground. They went onto lift the League and Cup double.

During the season goals were largely shared between Smellie, Aitken and Wardrope. Andy Aitken confirmed his development and was soon to become noted as one of the brightest stars in the country.

Pictured above: Charlie Watts filled a problem goalkeeping position for the club for two seasons.

Memorabilia CORNER

Newcastle United Official Card.
BURNLEY v. NEWCASTLE UNITED FIRST TEAM.
St. James's Park, Saturday, October 31st, 1896.
KICK-OFF AT THREE P.M.
NEWCASTLE UNITED FIRST TEAM.
E. SIMPSON, WINE & SPIRIT MERCHANT, NELSON STREET. QUALITY ONLY.
VISITORS to the FOOTBALL MATCH should call at Smiths' Cocoa Palace, 72, GALLOWGATE,
POSITIONS.
NEWCASTLE UNITED.
BURNLEY.
SHANKS, GROCER, Royal Court Buildings, BIGG MARKET.
SHANKS' Wholesale Cash Supply Stores, Royal Court Buildings, BIGG MARKET.
R. E. RUDDOCK, PHOTOGRAPHER, Grand Studio, Top of Pilgrim Street, NEWCASTLE.
Footballers and Football Groups a Speciality. Terms on Application at Studio.

United's 'official card' for a game with Burnley at the end of October.

IN CHARGE

Chairman: William Nesham
Manager: Director Committee
Captain: Jimmy Stott
Trainer/Coach: William Leach

ST JAMES' PARK

Average Attendance
Lg 8,532 Lg & Cup 8,532

Newcastle's squad in 1896-97. Back row, left to right: Watt (secretary), Foyer, Graham, White, Smellie, Watts, Leach (trainer). Sitting: McDermid, Thompson, Miller, Collins, Adam. On ground: Lennox, Aitken, Wardrope.

PLAYER FOCUS Willie Wardrope

Born Wishaw. Outside-left, 5'6"
1895 to 1900: 145 app 55 goals.

Small and delightful to watch, Willie Wardrope was a dangerous and versatile forward, able to play across the line but usually at outside-left. The Scot impressed many in his native land with Linthouse in Glasgow then made the move to Tyneside in May 1895 for a small fee. For the next five seasons Wardrope was an automatic choice, being a very effective forward, both at making goals and scoring them. In his first season he netted 13 goals in a nine-game sequence, a club record. Small and well built, the Scot scored 22 goals in that opening year and Willie helped enormously to develop United from a novice League club into one to be reckoned with. A key player in the Magpies promotion to the top flight during 1897-98 – scoring 13 goals – the Scot possessed a terrific shot and just missed getting into the full Scotland side, being a trialist at international level in 1898-99. Later Wardrope also won promotion with Middlesbrough while at Third Lanark he lifted the Scottish title in 1903-04 being an influential forward in the Third's victory. Willie moved to the capital following that success to join Fulham where he helped to secure the Southern League Championship at Craven Cottage. Wardrope then headed for Swindon and back north to his native Scotland. Afterwards he spent a period in North America coaching before the Great War. His younger brother Alex also played football for a number of clubs.

SEASON REVIEW

Football League Div 2: P30 W17 D1 L12 F56 A52 Pts 35.
Position: 5th (Champions; Notts County).
FA Cup: R1 (Winners; Aston Villa).

Appearances (31m): Aitken A 31, Watts C 31, Stott J 30, Wardrope W 30, White J 29, Smellie RD 27, Connell J 25, Lennox M 19, Stewart T 18, Miller W 17, Ostler J 16, Auld JR 15, Adams G 12, Collins J 11, Foyers R 9, Thompson WK 9, McDermid R 6, Graham W 2, Kinsella J 2, Blyth TH 1, Carr JR 1.

Goals (56g): Smellie RD 15, Aitken A 11, Wardrope W 11, Lennox M 4, Auld JR 3, Connell J 3, Stott J 3, Adams G 1, Blyth TH 1, Collins J 1, Miller W 1, Ostler J 1, Thompson WK 1.

Dismissals: 0 players.

MAJOR SIGNINGS

Charlie Watts (Burton Wand)
James Auld (Sunderland)
Tom Stewart & Jack Ostler (Motherwell) £200 joint fee
Richard Smellie (Nottingham Forest)
John White (Clyde)

FROM THE RANKS

Tom Blyth (Durham Univ)

TEAM COLOURS Black & white striped shirts, dark shorts (Change; Light blue shirts)

SEASON 1896-97

Match	Date	Venue	FL Division 2	Res	F	A	HT	Att	Posn	Goalscorers	Watts	White	Foyers	Miller	Graham	Stott	Thompson	Lennox	Smellie	Aitken	Wardrope	Carr	McDermid	Adams	Auld	Connell	Collins	Stewart	Ostler	Kinsella	Blyth	Match
1	05 Sep	A	Small Heath	L	1	3	(0 3)	4,000		Thompson	1	2	3	4	5	6	7	8	9	10	11											1
2	12 Sep	H	**Small Heath**	W	4	3	(3 2)	10,853	12	Smellie 3, Lennox	1	2	3	4	5	6	7	8	9	10	11											2
3	19 Sep	A	Notts County	L	1	3	(1 2)	5,000	12	Stott	1	2	3	4		5	7	8	9	10	11	6										3
4	26 Sep	A	Newton Heath	L	0	4	(0 1)	7,000	13		1	2		4		5	10	7	9	8	11		3	6								4
5	03 Oct	H	**Darwen**	W	5	1	(1 1)	8,000	11	Wardrope, Smellie 4	1	2		4		5	7	8	9	10	11		3	6								5
6	10 Oct	H	**Grimsby Town**	W	3	0	(1 0)	5,000	9	Aitken 2 (1 pen), Stott	1	2		4		5	8	7	9	10	11		3	6								6
7	17 Oct	A	Manchester City	W	2	1	(0 0)	7,000	7	Smellie, Auld	1	2		4		6		7	9	10	11		3		5	8						7
8	24 Oct	A	Lincoln City	W	2	1	(1 0)	2,000	6	Wardrope, Connell	1	2		4		6	9	7		10	11		3		5	8						8
9	07 Nov	A	Darwen	L	1	2	(0 2)		7	Miller	1	2		4		6		7	9	10	11		3		5	8						9
10	14 Nov	H	**Leicester Fosse**	W	3	1	(2 0)	7,000	5	Wardrope 2, Smellie	1	2	3	4		6			9	10	11				5	8	7					10
11	28 Nov	H	**Loughborough**	W	4	1	(2 0)	7,000	5	Wardrope, Aitken, Connell, Lennox	1	2	3	4		6		7	9	10	11				5	8						11
12	05 Dec	A	Burton Wanderers	W	1	0	(0 0)		4	Aitken	1	2	3	4		6			9	10	11				5	8	7					12
13	12 Dec	H	**Notts County**	D	2	2	(1 0)	17,000	4	Wardrope, Aitken	1	2	3	4		6			9	10	11				5	8	7					13
14	26 Dec	A	Grimsby Town	L	2	3	(1 2)	10,000	5	Wardrope, Stott	1	3		4		6		7	9	10	11					8		2	5			14
15	28 Dec	A	Gainsborough Trinity	L	0	2	(0 1)	2,000	5		1	3		4		6		7	9	10	11					8		2	5			15
16	01 Jan	H	**Newton Heath**	W	2	0	(1 0)	16,125	4	Wardrope, Aitken	1	3				6	9			10	11			4		8	7	2	5			16
17	02 Jan	H	**Lincoln City**	W	2	1	(2 0)	10,000	4	Aitken, Smellie	1	3		4					9	10	11			6	5	8	7	2				17
18	09 Jan	A	Leicester Fosse	L	0	5	(0 2)	3,000	5		1	3				6	7		9	10					5	8	11	2	4			18
19	16 Jan	H	**Blackpool**	W	4	1	(1 0)	9,000	3	Wardrope, Smellie, Collins, Auld	1	3				6			9	10	11				5	8	7	2	4			19
20	23 Jan	H	**Woolwich Arsenal**	W	2	0	(2 0)	6,000	3	Aitken, Auld	1	3				6			9	10	11				5	8	7	2	4			20
21	06 Feb	H	**Manchester City**	W	3	0	(1 0)	9,000	3	Wardrope 2, Aitken	1		3			6			9	10	11			4		8	7	2	5			21
22	20 Feb	A	Loughborough	L	0	3	(0 2)	2,000	4		1	3				6			9	10	11			4		8	7	2	5			22
23	06 Mar	H	**Walsall**	W	2	0	(0 0)	6,000	3	Connell, Ostler (pen)	1		3			6		7		9	11				4	8		2	5	10		23
24	13 Mar	A	Blackpool	L	1	4	(1 3)	3,000	4	Smellie	1	3				6			9	7	11				4	8		2	5	10		24
25	20 Mar	H	**Gainsborough Trinity**	L	1	2	(1 1)	6,000	4	Lennox	1	3		4		6		7	9	10	11				5	8		2				25
26	27 Mar	H	**Burton Swifts**	W	2	1	(1 1)	4,000	4	Blyth, Lennox	1	3				6		7		10	11			4		8		2	5		9	26
27	03 Apr	A	Walsall	W	2	0	(1 0)	4,000	4	Aitken (pen), Smellie	1	3				6		7	9	10	11			4		8		2	5			27
28	10 Apr	H	**Burton Wanderers**	W	3	0	(3 0)	7,000	4	Aitken, Smellie 2	1	3				6		7	9	10	11			4		8		2	5			28
29	12 Apr	A	Burton Swifts	L	0	3	(0 2)	2,000	4		1	3				6		7	9	10	11			4		8		2	5			29
30	16 Apr	A	Woolwich Arsenal	L	1	5	(0 3)	7,000	5	Adams	1	3				6		7	9	10	11			4		8		2	5			30
Round			**FA Cup**																													**Round**
1	30 Jan	A	Aston Villa	L	0	5	(0 4)	7,000			1	3				6			9	10	11				5	8	7	2	4			1

Match 11 Some reports credit Connell's goal to Smellie

Match 13 Goalscorers vary in reports with Smellie also noted as a scorer

DateLine ... 12 Dec: A reported crowd of 17,000 watch the visit of Notts County on Tyneside. **30 Jan:** Another heavy defeat to Aston Villa recorded, this time by five goals in FA Cup action. **16 April:** The referee was not pleased with his own officials in the match with Arsenal and sends off a linesman for being unsatisfactory.

NEWCASTLE UNITED

SEASON
1897-98
DIVISION 2

Test Match controversy

Season 1897-98 was an eventful season, United for the first time being promoted to the top level of English football. And for the first time also, gates averaged over 10,000.

Financially the club had turned the corner. New signings Jock Peddie at centre-forward and right-half Tommy Ghee were influential additions before the season began. Also to arrive from neighbours Sunderland – and their Team of all the Talent were the experienced pair of John Harvey and Johnny Campbell. All four were Scots, and they made a difference.

United were soon in contention at the top of the division along with Burnley and the Christmas clash between the two rivals attracted a record crowd approaching 30,000 to Gallowgate, which at the time was a crush. Burnley secured both points with a single goal, yet that defeat apart, United's home form was outstanding. Newcastle won 14 of their 15 games on home soil. In the second half of the season a run during February and March made sure the black-and-whites would be in with a chance of securing First Division football. Six victories in a row saw the Tynesiders net 21 goals to only four conceded. Five of the matches were at Gallowgate with Lincoln, Manchester City, Luton, Gainsborough and Grimsby all soundly beaten. Newcastle also travelled to Lancashire to claim full points at Darwen. Centre-forward Jock Peddie grabbed nine goals in that spree. They ended the scheduled programme just behind Burnley by three points.

Promotion was not achieved though just because a club finished as Champions or as runner-up. Back then a Test Match mini-league of games took place between the top placed clubs in the Second Division and the bottom clubs of the First Division to see who would end up in the top-tier. At the conclusion to the extra round of fixtures United were left in third spot, out of the promotion places, but only because Stoke and Burnley – who faced each other in the last round of matches – all but contrived the 0-0 result to ensure their own success. United were not happy, neither was the Football League. At the League's AGM the Test Match results and whole system were ditched. As a way out of the problem, the First Division was extended and the Tynesiders found themselves in the top division after all.

Pictured above: John Campbell was a noted acquisition, a veteran from Sunderland's Team of all the Talent.

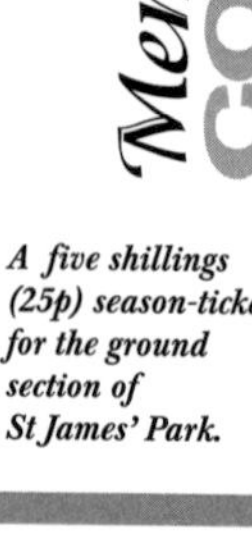

1898-9.
NEWCASTLE UNITED
Football Club.
SEASON TICKET.
BOYS' TICKET.
GROUND ONLY.
Not Transferable.

A five shillings (25p) season-ticket for the ground section of St James' Park.

IN CHARGE

Chairman: William Nesham
Manager: Director Committee
Captain: Jimmy Stott
Trainer/Coach: Tom Dodds

ST JAMES' PARK

Average Attendance
Lg 12,471 Lg & Cup 12,111

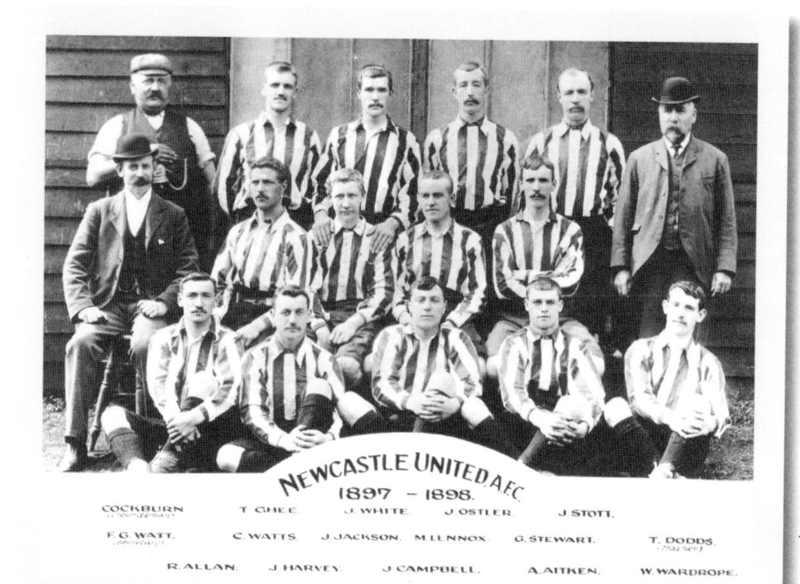

The squad which took United to promotion and into the top level of football at the end of the 1897-98 season.

PLAYER FOCUS Tommy Ghee

Born Kilmarnock. Right-half, 5'11"
1897 to 1902: 144 app 5 goals.

Probably the outstanding player of United's promotion campaign in 1898, Tommy Ghee was a dogged performer. Sturdy and vigorous on the field, he was a hearty competitor and did much to ensure the Magpies reached the top-tier of English football. Joining United from Kilmarnock in May 1897 after having served St Mirren and Darwen as well, Ghee was close to full international recognition, appearing in Scotland trial fixtures just before the close of the century. After becoming a corner-stone to promotion, Tommy was influential in United's initial season in the top division and as they consolidated with football's best. An automatic choice at right-half over four seasons, he played in the inaugural Division One contest with Wolves and in the club's first victory in the top flight against Liverpool. His rugged style linked perfectly with half-back colleagues Ostler and Stott in midfield. Jimmy was a good all-round sportsman; he excelled at aquatic events being an excellent swimmer as well as water-polo player, a popular pastime then. When reaching the veteran stage of his career, Tommy badly injured his leg and was forced to retire from playing in 1902 being replaced by fellow Scots Alex Caie and then the emerging Alec Gardner. He was then attached to United's training staff until 1920, a popular and respected aide at St James' Park alongside senior trainer James McPherson. He also looked after the Gallowgate billiards room, then an important meeting point for United's stars.

SEASON REVIEW

Football League Div 2: P30 W21 D3 L6 F64 A32 Pts 45.
Position: 2nd (Champions; Burnley).
FA Cup: R2 (Winners; Nottingham Forest).

Appearances (39m): Watts C 39, Ghee T 37, Jackson J 36, Stott J 35, Wardrope W 35, Ostler J 34, Harvey Jn 32, Aitken A 31, Allan R 29, Campbell JM 27, Peddie JH 24, White J 24, Smith W 14, Stewart T 12, Lindsay WA 9, Lennox M 4, Carr JR 2, Lockey J 2, Allen J 1, Milne WJ 1, Niblo TB 1.

Goals (87g): Peddie JH 19, Wardrope W 15, Campbell JM 12, Aitken A 9, Harvey Jn 9, Smith W 6, Allan R 4, Jackson J 3, Ghee T 2, Stott J 2, Ostler J 1, White J 1, own goals 4.

Dismissals: 0 players.

MAJOR SIGNINGS

John Harvey & John Campbell (Sunderland)
Jock Peddie (Third Lanark) £135
Tommy Ghee (Kilmarnock)
James Jackson (Rangers)
Billy Lindsay (Grimsby Town)
Tom Niblo (Linthouse) £90
William Smith (Hibs)

FROM THE RANKS

James Lockey (Willington Ath)

TEAM COLOURS Black & white striped shirts, dark shorts (Change; untraced)

SEASON 1897–98

Match	Date		FL Division 2				HT	Att	Posn	Scorers
1	04 Sep	H	**Woolwich Arsenal**	W	4	1	(3 0)	10,000		Wardrope 3, Campbell
2	11 Sep	A	Walsall	W	3	2	(2 1)	4,000	4	Wardrope, og 2 (Peers, Aston)
3	18 Sep	H	**Burton Swifts**	W	3	1	(2 0)	9,000	4	Wardrope, Allan, Stott
4	25 Sep	A	Lincoln City	W	3	2	(1 1)	4,000	4	Wardrope 2, Campbell
5	02 Oct	A	Burnley	L	0	3	(0 3)	8,000	5	
6	09 Oct	H	**Newton Heath**	W	2	0	(2 0)	14,000	4	Aitken, Harvey
7	16 Oct	A	Woolwich Arsenal	D	0	0	(0 0)	12,000	3	
8	23 Oct	H	**Blackpool**	W	2	0	(1 0)	10,000	3	Aitken, Campbell
9	06 Nov	A	Grimsby Town	L	0	2	(0 2)	5,000	4	
10	13 Nov	A	Newton Heath	W	1	0	(0 0)	6,000	3	Wardrope
11	27 Nov	H	**Small Heath**	W	4	0	(4 0)	12,000	3	Wardrope, Peddie, Campbell 2
12	04 Dec	A	Gainsborough Trinity	W	3	1	(2 0)	700	2	Campbell, Harvey, Peddie
13	18 Dec	A	Burton Swifts	L	1	3	(0 2)	4,000	3	White
14	25 Dec	A	Blackpool	W	3	2	(3 1)	4,000	3	Wardrope, Campbell, Stott
15	27 Dec	H	**Burnley**	L	0	1	(0 0)	30,000	3	
16	01 Jan	H	**Walsall**	W	2	1	(1 0)	16,000	3	Peddie, Allan
17	03 Jan	H	**Loughborough**	W	3	1	(2 1)	4,000	3	Peddie, Ostler (pen), og (Bailey)
18	08 Jan	A	Manchester City	D	1	1	(1 1)	20,000	3	Allan
19	15 Jan	H	**Darwen**	W	1	0	(1 0)	10,000	3	og (Leach)
20	22 Jan	H	**Leicester Fosse**	W	4	2	(3 0)	10,000	2	Aitken, Peddie 3
21	19 Feb	A	Luton Town	L	1	3	(0 2)	3,500	3	Allan
22	26 Feb	H	**Lincoln City**	W	3	0	(2 0)	10,000	2	Wardrope 2, Smith
23	05 Mar	A	Darwen	W	3	1	(1 1)	2,000	2	Peddie 3
24	12 Mar	H	**Luton Town**	W	4	1	(3 1)	15,000	2	Wardrope, Harvey 3
25	16 Mar	H	**Manchester City**	W	2	0	(1 0)	17,000	2	Peddie, Aitken
26	26 Mar	H	**Grimsby Town**	W	4	0	(3 0)	4,000	2	Campbell, Smith, Peddie 2
27	02 Apr	H	**Gainsborough Trinity**	W	5	2	(4 0)	12,000	2	Smith 2, Peddie 3
28	09 Apr	A	Leicester Fosse	D	1	1	(1 0)	6,000	2	Peddie
29	11 Apr	A	Loughborough	W	1	0	(1 0)	2,000	2	Campbell
30	12 Apr	A	Small Heath	L	0	1	(0 1)	5,000	2	
			Test Matches							
31	20 Apr	H	**Stoke**	W	2	1	(1 0)	13,000	2	Smith, Harvey
32	23 Apr	A	Stoke	L	0	1	(0 0)	14,000	2	
33	28 Apr	A	Blackburn Rovers	L	3	4	(1 3)	3,000	3	Wardrope, Smith, Aitken
34	30 Apr	H	**Blackburn Rovers**	W	4	0	(1 0)	16,000	3	Campbell, Harvey, Ghee, Jackson
Round			**FA Cup**							
Q3	30 Oct	H	**Willington Athletic**	W	6	0	(2 0)	6,000		Aitken 4, Campbell, Jackson
Q4	20 Nov	A	Stockton	W	4	1	(2 0)	8,000		Campbell, Harvey, Ghee, Jackson
Q5	11 Dec	A	Middlesbrough	W	2	0	(0 0)	6,000		Wardrope, Harvey
1	29 Jan	A	Preston North End	W	2	1	(1 1)	4,042		Peddie 2
2	12 Feb	A	Southampton	L	0	1	(0 0)	14,000		

Match	Watts	Stewart	Jackson	Ghee	Ostler	Stott	Lennox	Harvey	Campbell	Aitken	Wardrope	White	Allan	Milne	Peddie	Allen	Smith	Lindsay	Carr	Niblo	Lockey
1	1	2	3	4	5	6	7	8	9	10	11										
2	1	2	6	4	5		8	9		10	11	3	7								
3	1	2		4	5	6		8	9	10	11	3	7								
4	1	2		4	5	6			9	10	11	3	7	8							
5	1		3	4	5	6		8	9	10	11	2	7								
6	1		3	4	5	6		8	9	10	11	2	7								
7	1	2	5	4		6	7	8	9	10	11	3									
8	1	2	3	4	5	6	8		9	10	11		7								
9	1	2	3	4	5	6		8	9	10	11		7								
10	1		3	4	5	6		8		10	11	2	7		9						
11	1	2	4	5		6			8	10	11	3	7		9						
12	1		3	4	5	6		8	10		11	2	7		9						
13	1		3	4	5	6		8	10		11	2	7		9						
14	1		3	4	5	6			8	10	11	2	7		9						
15	1		3	4	5	6			8	10	11	2	7		9						
16	1		3		5	6		8	10	4	11	2	7		9						
17	1		3		5	6		8	10	4	11	2	7		9						
18	1		3	4	5	6		8		10	11	2	7		9						
19	1	2	6	5				8		4	11	3	7		10	9					
20	1	2		4	5	6		8		10	11	3	7		9						
21	1		3	4	5	6		8	11			2	7		9		10				
22	1		3	4	5				8		11		7		9		10	2	6		
23	1		3	4	5	6		8			11		7		9		10	2			
24	1		3	4	5	6		7		8	11				9		10	2			
25	1		3	4	5	6		7		8	11				9		10	2			
26	1		3	4	5	6		7	11	8					9		10	2			
27	1		3	4	5	6		8	11				7		9		10	2			
28	1		3	4	5	6				8	11		7		9		10	2			
29	1		3	4	5			8	9			2	7				10		6	11	
30	1		3	5		6		7	8	4	11	2			9		10				
TM																					
31	1		3	4	5	6		7		8	11				9		10	2			
32	1		3	4	5	6		7	10	8	11						9				2
33	1		3	4	5	6		7	9	8	11						10				2
34	1		3	4	5	6		7	9	8	11						10	2			
Round																					
Q3	1	2	3	4	5	6		8	9	10	11		7								
Q4	1	2	4	5		6		8	9	10	11	3	7								
Q5	1		3	4	5	6		8	10		11	2	7		9						
1	1		3	4	5	6		8		10	11	2	7		9						
2	1		3	4	5	6		8		10	11	2	7		9						

Match 3 Some reports credit Stott's goal to Aitken
Match 12 One source attributes Ostler with Peddie's goal
Match 13 Differences exist as to the identity of the scorer
Match 33 Some reports credit Smith's goal to Stott or Aitken

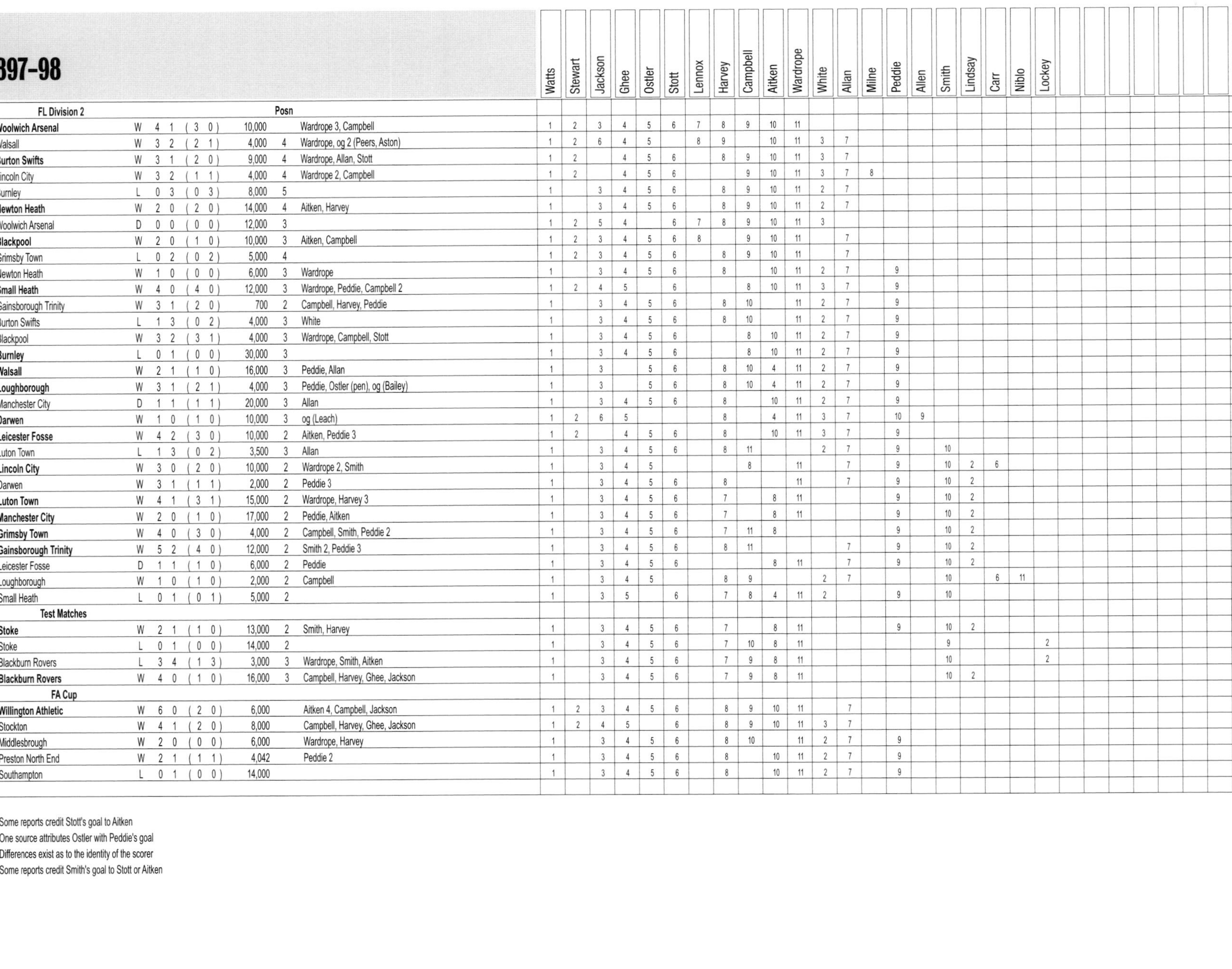

DateLine ... 2 Oct: Against Burnley, goalkeeper Charlie Watts saves a penalty three times. **27 Dec:** A record gate of 30,000 watches the top of the table clash with Burnley. **20 April:** United kick-off the Football League Test Matches for a place in the First Division with a clash against Stoke.

SEASON
1898-99
DIVISION 1

Survival in the top-tier

The higher standard of football in the top division was noticeable and United did not find it easy to start with. However, after this inaugural campaign in the top-tier United found their feet and the Magpies rapidly developed into one of England's elite clubs. Newcastle's squad was improved with the addition of experienced players Sandy MacFarlane, Willie Higgins, James Stevenson and Joe Rogers. With the St James' Park arena also improved for their top level debut, United opened their First Division record with a home fixture against Wolves. A crowd of 20,000 turned up and saw a fine game, although the Black'n'Whites lost 4-2. United were 3-0 down by the interval yet perked up following the break. Jock Peddie claimed Newcastle's first goals in Division One as the Scot struck twice.

Newcastle found it tough to begin with, losing their first three matches and not recording a victory until the 11th attempt, a 3-0 win over Liverpool. At St James' Park during November, Peddie was again a handful as he fired the ball past Liverpool 'keeper Storer while Sandy MacFarlane was also on the scoresheet as the Magpies got their winning record started. Newcastle though slipped to the bottom of the table. But with Jock Peddie continuing to be a force in attack – scoring 19 goals all told – United climbed to safety helped by four successive victories on Tyneside in the spring. Last season's Test match rivals Burnley and Stoke were toppled, as were Bury and Preston.

League derby encounters with Sunderland began too that season. In the very first meeting Newcastle travelled to Wearside and won a thrilling 90 minutes of football on Christmas Eve. United ended victors by 3-2 while on the last day of the season Sunderland took the points on Tyneside with a 1-0 win.

Pictured above: Jimmy Stevenson was on the fringe of a Scotland cap and possessed plenty of craft.

Memorabilia CORNER

WHITFIELD & CARR.
You may as well have it Nicely Made while you are at it.
THEREFORE CALL AT . . .
WHITFIELD & CARR'S
. . . For 50/- Suits to Order.
89, NORTHUMBERLAND STREET.

No. 5.
NEWCASTLE UNITED
OFFICIAL CARD
Containing Names and Positions of Teams.
Newcastle United v. Notts County.
SATURDAY, September 17th, 1898.
St. James' Park, Gallowgate. Kick-off at 3-30 p.m.

FIRST TEAM. "A" TEAM.

For well over a decade United's 'official card' comprised a single sheet of two pages.

IN CHARGE

Chairman: William Nesham
Manager: Director Committee
Captain: Jack Ostler
Trainer/Coach: Tom Dodds

ST JAMES' PARK

Average Attendance
Lg 16,882 Lg & Cup 16,882

United's first taste of football's elite in Division One. Back row, left to right: Cockburn (groundsman), Lindsay (W), Watts, W Nesham (director), Kingsley, Jackson, Campbell, Dodds (trainer). Sitting: Watt (secretary), Ghee, Ostler, Higgins, Aitken, Stott. On ground: Rogers, Harvey, Peddie, Smith, Niblo.

PLAYER FOCUS Jock Peddie

Born Glasgow. Centre-forward, 5'11"
1897 to 1902: 136 app 76 goals.

A ram-raiding Scot who became a hugely popular figure in United's centre-forward shirt, Jock Peddie headed to Tyneside from Third Lanark for a £135 fee in September 1897, initially on trial after impressing in a friendly against the Magpies. Peddie was an instant hit. He was a powerful striker and had a stinging shot, indeed, reckoned to be the hardest seen at St James' Park at the time. His prowess in attack was crucial as Newcastle gained promotion in 1898 when he netted 17 goals. The Scot scored the Black'n'Whites first goal in top level football, a brace against Wolves, while he also grabbed a couple in the earliest League derby with Sunderland, a 3-2 victory on Wearside. In First Division action, a record of almost 60 goals in four seasons is evidence enough of his danger man reputation. Peddie though was a touch temperamental and moody, sometimes running into trouble with authority. He refused to play on one occasion, more than once missed training and was suspended by the club. Yet along the way, he always scored goals, the fans on the terraces making him probably United's first hero-figure. Yet Newcastle sold their star asset in the summer of 1902, to Manchester United where he continued to score goals – another 58 for the Reds. Newcastle missed his free-scoring talent for two seasons. Jock was unlucky not to win a Scotland cap, being a trialist for his country. Also assisting Plymouth and Hearts, he later emigrated to North America where he continued to play and coach football.

SEASON REVIEW

Football League Div 1: P34 W11 D8 L15 F49 A48 Pts 30.
Position: 13th (Champions; Aston Villa).
FA Cup: R2 (Winners; Sheffield United).

Appearances (36m): Kingsley M 36, Ghee T 34, Jackson J 32, Peddie JH 31, Lindsay WA 30, Stott J 30, Rogers JJ 29, Aitken A 28, Ostler J 27, Stevenson J 26, Wardrope W 26, MacFarlane A 21, Higgins W 19, Niblo TB 10, Smith W 5, Reid W 4, Harvey Jn 3, Campbell JM 2, Birnie EL 1, Lockey J 1, Mowatt A 1.

Goals (51g): Peddie JH 19, Rogers JJ 8, Stevenson J 7, MacFarlane A 5, Higgins W 3, Aitken A 2, Wardrope W 2, Harvey Jn 1, Lindsay WA 1, Reid W 1, own goals 2.

Dismissals: 0 players.

MAJOR SIGNINGS

Alex MacFarlane (Airdrie) £30
Matt Kingsley (Darwen)
William Higgins (Bristol City)
Joe Rogers (Grimsby Town)
James Stevenson (Derby Co) £225

FROM THE RANKS

Ted Birnie (Sunderland Seaburn)

TEAM COLOURS Black & white striped shirts, dark shorts (Change; untraced)

SEASON 1898-99

Match	Date		FL Division 1				Att	Posn	Scorers	Kingsley	Lindsay	Higgins	Ghee	Ostler	Aitken	Harvey	Campbell	Peddie	Smith	Wardrope	Jackson	Stott	Niblo	Lockey	Birnie	Rogers	MacFarlane	Stevenson	Mowatt	Reid	Match
1	03 Sep	H	**Wolverhampton Wanderers**	L	2 4	(0 3)	20,000	15	Peddie 2	1	2	3	4	5	6	7	8	9	10	11											1
2	10 Sep	A	Everton	L	0 3	(0 2)	16,000	18		1	2	5	4		8		9	7	10		3	6	11								2
3	17 Sep	H	**Notts County**	L	1 2	(1 2)	18,000	18	Aitken	1			4	5	8			7	10	11	3	6		2	9						3
4	24 Sep	A	Stoke	D	0 0	(0 0)	12,000	18		1	2	9	4	5	8			11	10		3	6				7					4
5	26 Sep	A	Sheffield United	D	2 2	(2 2)	4,000	17	og (Bradshaw), Higgins	1	2	9	4	5	8			11			3	6	10			7					5
6	01 Oct	H	**Aston Villa**	D	1 1	(1 0)	25,000	18	Rogers	1	2	9	4	5	8			11			3	6	10			7					6
7	08 Oct	A	Burnley	L	1 2	(0 1)	6,000	18	Rogers	1	2	9	4	5	8			11	10		3	6				7					7
8	15 Oct	H	**Sheffield United**	L	1 2	(1 0)	7,000	18	Harvey	1	2		4	5	9	8		11		10	3	6				7					8
9	22 Oct	A	Bury	D	1 1	(1 0)	1,032	18	Rogers	1	2		4	5	10	8		9		11	3	6				7					9
10	29 Oct	A	Preston North End	L	0 1	(0 1)	4,000	18		1	2		4	5	10			8		11	3	6				7	9				10
11	05 Nov	H	**Liverpool**	W	3 0	(0 0)	20,000	18	Peddie 2, MacFarlane	1	2		4	5				11		10	3	6				7	9	8			11
12	12 Nov	A	Nottingham Forest	L	0 2	(0 1)	8,000	18		1			4	5	2			11		10	3	6				7	9	8			12
13	19 Nov	H	**Bolton Wanderers**	W	4 1	(1 1)	18,000	18	Peddie 2, MacFarlane, Rogers	1	2		4	5				11		10	3	6				7	9	8			13
14	26 Nov	A	Derby County	L	1 3	(0 2)	7,000	18	Wardrope	1	2		4	5				11		10	3	6				7	9	8			14
15	03 Dec	H	**West Bromwich Albion**	W	3 0	(2 0)	16,000	17	Aitken, Peddie, Rogers	1	2		4	5	10			9		11	3	6				7		8			15
16	10 Dec	A	Blackburn Rovers	L	2 4	(0 3)	7,000	17	Stevenson 2	1	2		4	5				11		10	3	6				7	9	8			16
17	17 Dec	H	**Sheffield Wednesday**	D	2 2	(1 2)	15,000	17	Peddie, MacFarlane	1	2		4		5			11		10	3	6					9	8	7		17
18	24 Dec	A	Sunderland	W	3 2	(2 1)	30,000	17	Wardrope, Peddie 2	1	2		4	5	10			9		11	3	6				7		8			18
19	26 Dec	A	Aston Villa	L	0 1	(0 1)	30,000	17		1	2		4	5	10			9		11	3	6				7		8			19
20	31 Dec	A	Wolverhampton Wanderers	D	0 0	(0 0)	6,000	16		1	2		4	6	10					11	3	5				7	9	8			20
21	07 Jan	H	**Everton**	D	2 2	(0 2)	15,000	17	og (Balmer), Stevenson	1	2		4	5	10					11	3	6				7	9	8			21
22	14 Jan	A	Notts County	L	1 3	(0 1)	12,000	17	Peddie	1		2		5	4			9		11	3	6				7	10	8			22
23	21 Jan	H	**Stoke**	W	3 0	(1 0)	12,000	17	Peddie 2 (1 pen), Rogers	1		2	4	5				9		11	3	6				7	10	8			23
24	04 Feb	H	**Burnley**	W	4 1	(2 1)	20,000	17	Peddie, Rogers 2, Lindsay	1	2	3	4	5	10			9		11		6				7		8			24
25	18 Feb	H	**Bury**	W	2 0	(0 0)	16,000	16	Peddie 2	1	2		4	5				9		11	3	6				7	10	8			25
26	25 Feb	H	**Preston North End**	W	2 1	(1 0)	15,000	13	MacFarlane, Peddie (pen)	1	2	3	4	5				9		11		6				7	10	8			26
27	11 Mar	H	**Nottingham Forest**	L	0 1	(0 1)	20,000	14		1	2		4	5				9		11	3	6				7	10	8			27
28	18 Mar	A	Bolton Wanderers	D	0 0	(0 0)	5,000	15		1	2	5	4		6			10			3		11			7	9	8			28
29	25 Mar	H	**Derby County**	W	2 0	(1 0)	16,000	15	Stevenson, Reid	1	2	5			4			9			3	6	11				7	8		10	29
30	01 Apr	A	West Bromwich Albion	L	0 2	(0 1)	2,304	14		1	2	5	4		6			9			3		11				7	8		10	30
31	03 Apr	A	Liverpool	L	2 3	(1 2)	15,000	14	Stevenson (pen), Higgins	1	2	5	4		6					7	3		11				9	8		10	31
32	08 Apr	H	**Blackburn Rovers**	W	1 0	(0 0)	12,000	15	MacFarlane	1		5	4		2						3	6	11			7	9	8		10	32
33	15 Apr	A	Sheffield Wednesday	W	3 1	(1 1)	4,000	13	Higgins, Stevenson 2	1	2	5	4		6					11	3		10			7	9	8			33
34	22 Apr	H	**Sunderland**	L	0 1	(0 0)	22,000	13		1	2	5	4		6			9			3		11			7	10	8			34
Round			FA Cup																												Round
1	28 Jan	A	Glossop North End	W	1 0	(1 0)	7,000		Peddie	1		2	4	5	10			9		11	3	6				7		8			1
2	11 Feb	A	Liverpool	L	1 3	(0 1)	7,000		Peddie	1	3	2	4	5	10			9		11		6				7		8			2

Match 33 Some reports credit one of Stevenson's goals to Higgins or Aitken

DateLine ... 3 Sept: United's first top-level fixture, against Wolves, a 4-2 defeat. **5 Nov:** The Magpies record their first victory in the top-tier, 3-0 against Liverpool. **24 Dec:** The first League derby meeting with Sunderland, United win 3-2 on Wearside.

SEASON
1899-1900
DIVISION 1

Competing with the best

At the turn of the century, Aston Villa and North East rivals Sunderland were the country's best. Newcastle though could now compete against this quality of opposition, defeating both sides in the season. United also recorded a 6-0 thrashing of Notts County. That win during October over the black-and-whites of the Trent equalled the club's best ever victory in senior company – in Football League or FA Cup matches proper. A crowd of 20,000 saw United completely swamp their rivals. All six goals were scored by Scots – Fraser (2), MacFarlane, Peddie, Stevenson and Wardrope – illustrating the importance footballers from north of the border had at Newcastle United, a trend to continue for over 50 years.

The Magpies consolidated their First Division status as the new century opened. By January 1900 they were in a mid-table position and gradually the Black'n'Whites were improving and developing, step by step. They defeated Aston Villa 3-2 in March, a notable result against the League Champions to be. Peddie netted twice with Alec Gardner also claiming a goal. That was the first victory recorded over Villa in six meetings in League or Cup. Newcastle had claimed only a single draw and suffered two heavy FA Cup defeats. It was a most satisfying triumph. United finished in a merited fifth place and Peddie was top scorer for the third season in a row. He had become the supporters' favourite.

The club though could still make little inroads into the FA Cup. They were knocked out in the Second Round to Southampton, the eventual finalists, this after defeating Reading in the opening stage of the competition.

The club's hierarchy led by Chairman William Nesham and Secretary Frank Watt steadily built an infrastructure platform to build upon, both in terms of facilities and the playing squad. St James' Park was given an overhaul for the season, now with a capacity of 30,000 – or at a squeeze a bit more – with a full-house watching the draw with Sheffield United during October.

Pictured above: Sandy MacFarlane was an influential forward over three seasons for the Magpies.

Memorabilia CORNER

STREET, Up-to-Date HATTERS.
THE SECRET OF HEALTH: ANDREWS' LIVER SALT.
THE FREE FOOTBALL PROGRAMME
NEWCASTLE UNITED
OFFICIAL CARD.
NEWCASTLE UNITED v. READING, E.C.T.
Smoke M[...]at's Royal Standard Cigars.
CIGAR, AND CIGARETTE MANUFACTURERS

Noted as a "Free Football Programme", this edition was for the "English Cup-tie" against Reading.

IN CHARGE

Chairman: William Nesham
Manager: Director Committee
Captain: Andy Aitken
Trainer/Coach: Tom Dodds

ST JAMES' PARK

Average Attendance
Lg 16,624 Lg & Cup 16,326

Newcastle as the century turned. Back row, left to right: Cockburn (groundsman), Jackson, Ghee, Stewart, Ostler, Lennox, Watt (secretary). Sitting: Allen, Harvey, Aitken, Smith, Stott, Watts, White, Wardrope – and Frank Watts's dog.

SEASON REVIEW

Football League Div 1: P34 W13 D10 L11 F53 A43 Pts 36.
Position: 5th (Champions; Aston Villa).
FA Cup: R2 (Winners; Bury).

Appearances (36m): Aitken A 36, Gardner DR 35, Kingsley M 35, Fraser J 32, MacFarlane A 32, Ghee T 31, Peddie JH 29, Rogers JJ 25, Carr J 23, Lindsay WA 23, Gardner Alec 21, Higgins W 20, Wardrope W 18, Niblo TB 11, Stevenson J 11, Birnie EL 8, Lindsay J 2, Mole G 1, Ostler J 1, Veitch CCM 1, Watts C 1.

Goals (56g): Peddie JH 16, Fraser J 8, Gardner Alec 6, MacFarlane A 6, Stevenson J 6, Wardrope W 5, Rogers JJ 3, Carr J 1, Gardner DR 1, Ghee T 1, Mole G 1, Niblo TB 1, own goal 1.

Dismissals: 0 players.

MAJOR SIGNINGS

Alec Gardner (Leith Ath)
Dave Gardner (Third Lanark)
John Fraser (Notts Co)

FROM THE RANKS

Jack Carr (Seaton Burn)
Colin Veitch (Rutherford College)
James Lindsay (Jarrow)

PLAYER FOCUS Jack Carr

Born Seaton Burn. Left-back, 5'10"
1897 to 1912: 278 app 5 goals.

Jack Carr was one of a select group of local footballers at the heart of United's great Edwardian side. Along with the likes of Colin Veitch and Jackie Rutherford, the Seaton Burn-born full-back became a key and reliable defender for the club in a 13 season period wearing the black-and-white stripes. Joining the club's staff in November 1897 from local football, he first operated at left-half but switched to defence in season 1904-05. That change to the heart of United's rearguard as the club developed as an eminent Division One side, earned Carr the right to wear the Three Lions badge of England in the same season, the first of two caps for the Geordie. Physical and rugged in the last line for the Magpies, Jack went onto take part in a treble of Football League title wins with Newcastle while he also played in three FA Cup finals, his last when in his thirties as victor in 1910 when he was a replacement for the injured Tony Whitson. A fine servant to the region, Carr was also a noted cricketer before World War One, appearing for Northumberland during the summer months. He spent the whole of his playing career at Gallowgate and when he retired in 1912 Jack moved onto the coaching staff. Carr tasted management with Blackburn Rovers, becoming the very first boss at Ewood Park in 1922. He found the position something of a struggle reviving Rovers' past glory and following a period as Secretary later returned to Tyneside and became a licensee in Newcastle's city-centre.

TEAM COLOURS Black & white striped shirts, dark shorts (Change; white shirts, dark shorts)

SEASON 1899-1900

Match	Date		FL Division 1				Att	Posn	Scorers	Kingsley	Lindsay WA	Gardner DR	Ghee	Higgins	Aitken	Rogers	Stevenson	Peddie	MacFarlane	Wardrope	Niblo	Fraser	Veitch	Ostler	Birnie	Gardner Alec	Carr	Mole	Lindsay J	Watts	Match
1	02 Sep	A	West Bromwich Albion	D	1 1	(0 0)	6,135	9	Peddie (pen)	1	2	3	4	5	6	7	8	9	10	11											1
2	09 Sep	H	**Everton**	W	2 0	(2 0)	25,000	3	Peddie, Niblo	1	2	3	4	5	6			9	10	7	8	11									2
3	16 Sep	A	Blackburn Rovers	W	3 2	(1 1)	8,000	4	Fraser, Peddie, Wardrope	1	2	3	4	5	6			9	10	7	8	11									3
4	23 Sep	H	**Derby County**	W	2 0	(2 0)	19,000	3	Peddie, Wardrope	1	2	3	4	5	6			9	10	7	8	11									4
5	30 Sep	A	Bury	L	1 2	(0 2)	3,568	6	Wardrope	1	2	3	4	5	6			9	10	7	8	11									5
6	07 Oct	H	**Notts County**	W	6 0	(3 0)	20,000	4	Fraser 2, MacFarlane, Peddie, Stevenson, Wardrope	1	2	3	4	5	6		8	9	10	7		11									6
7	14 Oct	A	Manchester City	L	0 1	(0 0)	25,000	4		1	2	3	4	5	6			9	10	7	8	11									7
8	21 Oct	H	**Sheffield United**	D	0 0	(0 0)	30,000	5		1	2	3	4	5	6	7		9	10	8		11									8
9	28 Oct	H	**Wolverhampton Wanderers**	L	0 1	(0 1)	20,000	5		1	2	3			6			9	10	7	8	11	4	5							9
10	04 Nov	A	Aston Villa	L	1 2	(0 2)	18,000	7	Ghee	1	2	3	4	5	6	7			10	8	9	11									10
11	11 Nov	H	**Liverpool**	D	1 1	(1 1)	12,000	9	MacFarlane	1	2	3	4	5	6	7			10	8	9	11									11
12	18 Nov	A	Burnley	W	3 1	(1 0)	5,000	5	Fraser, Wardrope, Rogers	1		3	4	5	6	7			10	8	9	11			2						12
13	25 Nov	H	**Preston North End**	D	0 0	(0 0)	17,000	5		1		3	4	5	6				10	8	9	11			2	7					13
14	02 Dec	A	Nottingham Forest	L	0 1	(0 0)	9,000	8		1		3		5	4		8	9	10			11			2	7	6				14
15	16 Dec	A	Stoke	D	2 2	(0 1)	3,000	9	Gardner A, MacFarlane	1		3		5	4	7	8		10			11			2	9	6				15
16	23 Dec	H	**Sunderland**	L	2 4	(2 1)	21,000	10	MacFarlane, Gardner A	1	2	3		5	4	7	8		10			11				9	6				16
17	30 Dec	H	**West Bromwich Albion**	W	4 2	(3 1)	10,887	9	Fraser, Peddie, Stevenson 2	1		3	4		5	7	8	9	10			11			2		6				17
	01 Jan	H	**Glossop North End**	Ab1	2 3	(1 3)	15,000		*MacFarlane, Peddie*	*1*		*3*	*4*		*5*	*7*	*8*	*9*	*10*			*11*			*2*		*6*				
18	06 Jan	A	Everton	L	2 3	(2 3)	5,000	11	Fraser (pen), Peddie	1		3	4		5	7		9	10			11			2	8	6				18
19	13 Jan	H	**Blackburn Rovers**	W	4 1	(2 1)	15,000	10	MacFarlane, Peddie 2, Carr	1		3	4	5	2	7	8	9	10			11					6				19
20	20 Jan	A	Derby County	L	1 2	(1 1)	10,000	11	Stevenson	1		3	4	5	2	7	8	9	10			11					6				20
21	03 Feb	H	**Bury**	W	2 1	(2 1)	10,000	10	Stevenson, og (Darroch)	1		3	4	5	2	7	8			10		11				9	6				21
22	03 Mar	A	Wolverhampton Wanderers	D	1 1	(0 1)	8,000	10	Peddie	1	2	3	4		5	7		9	10			11				8	6				22
23	10 Mar	H	**Aston Villa**	W	3 2	(2 1)	21,500	9	Peddie 2, Gardner A	1	2	3	4		5	7		9	10	11						8	6				23
24	14 Mar	H	**Glossop North End**	W	1 0	(0 0)	7,000	7	Peddie	1	3	2	4		5	7		9	10	11						8	6				24
25	17 Mar	A	Liverpool	L	0 2	(0 0)	18,000	7		1	2	3	4		5	7		9		11	10					8	6				25
26	24 Mar	H	**Burnley**	W	2 0	(2 0)	12,000	6	Fraser, Rogers	1	2	3	4		5	7		9	10			11				8	6				26
27	26 Mar	A	Sheffield United	L	1 3	(0 2)	3,000	6	Gardner A	1	2	3	4		5	7		9	10			11				8	6				27
28	31 Mar	A	Preston North End	L	1 4	(0 1)	4,000	6	Mole	1	2	3	4		5	7		10				11				8	6	9			28
29	07 Apr	H	**Nottingham Forest**	W	3 1	(2 0)	14,224	8	MacFarlane, Peddie, Gardner D (pen)	1	2	3	4		5			9	10	8		11				7	6				29
30	13 Apr	H	**Manchester City**	D	0 0	(0 0)	16,000	7		1	2	3	4		5	7		9	10			11				8	6				30
31	14 Apr	A	Glossop North End	D	0 0	(0 0)	2,000	6		1		3	4		5	7		9	10			11				8	6		2		31
32	16 Apr	A	Notts County	D	0 0	(0 0)	10,000	6		1	2	3	4		5	7		9	10			11				8	6				32
33	21 Apr	H	**Stoke**	D	2 2	(0 1)	12,000	6	Peddie, Gardner A	1		3			6	7		9	10			11			5	8	4		2		33
34	28 Apr	A	Sunderland	W	2 1	(2 1)	22,000	5	Fraser, Gardner A	1	2	3	4		5	7		9	10			11				8	6				34
Round			**FA Cup**																												**Round**
1	27 Jan	H	**Reading**	W	2 1	(1 0)	11,259		Stevenson, Rogers			3	4	5	2	7	8	10				11				9	6			1	1
2	10 Feb	A	Southampton	Ab2	0 0	(0 0)	10,000			*1*		*3*	*4*	*5*	*2*		*8*	*9*	*10*			*11*				*7*	*6*				2
2	17 Feb	A	Southampton	L	1 4	(1 2)	8,000		Peddie	1			4	5	2		8	9	10			11			3	7	6				2

Ab1 Abandoned after 72 mins due to fog
Ab2 Abandoned after 50 mins due to snow

Match 5 Initially some reports credited Niblo with the goal, but this was later adjusted to Wardrope
Match 10 One report gives the goal to Niblo

DateLine ... 5 Sept: United's first game against foreign opponents, a 6-3 victory over South African tourists, the Kaffirs. **21 Oct:** Another 30,000 gate at St James' Park is recorded for the visit of Sheffield United. **28 Oct:** Local product Colin Veitch makes his debut against Wolves at St James' Park.

SEASON 1900-01

DIVISION 1

United start to impress

The Tynesiders were now beginning to get noticed in football around the country. After last season's good show, United again did well, finishing this time in sixth position. A 3-1 success over Wolves on Tyneside in November had seen United lose only a single game – narrowly to Bolton – since the start of the season. They won seven games and were looking good.

In fact, the Magpies held second spot for a part of the campaign during December and maintained their challenge over Christmas and New Year. However, a poor run of form as the year developed had its effect. In March, Newcastle lost three games in succession, including an action packed 5-3 defeat to Preston at St James' Park. United then lost by three goals to the eventual Champions Liverpool. It resulted in a slide down the table. The season was dominated by a local meeting with Sunderland on Good Friday 1901 – a notorious match that never was. Sunderland were leaders of the table with United not far behind in seventh place. There was enormous interest in the confrontation between Tyne and Wear in the region with a crowd reported of between 45,000 to 50,000, even as high as 70,000 according to some reports, converging on United's stadium – then with a capacity less than half that number. The gates were forced open, walls scaled and the playing surface was covered with a mass of fans. It was impossible for a game of football to be played and the match was abandoned without a ball being kicked. And that made matters even worse as a full scale riot developed. A human disaster was averted only by good fortune and the incident was the talking point for weeks. As a result, plans were soon being considered to totally transform the Gallowgate arena into a stadium that could never repeat such a fiasco.

Several footballers started to pull on the black-and-white stripes to become household names in the near future, to turn the club into Edwardian England's footballing Masters; Alec Gardner, Jack Carr and Colin Veitch all entered the fray.

Pictured above: Tom Niblo had two periods with the club, a well-built Scot capped by his country.

Memorabilia CORNER

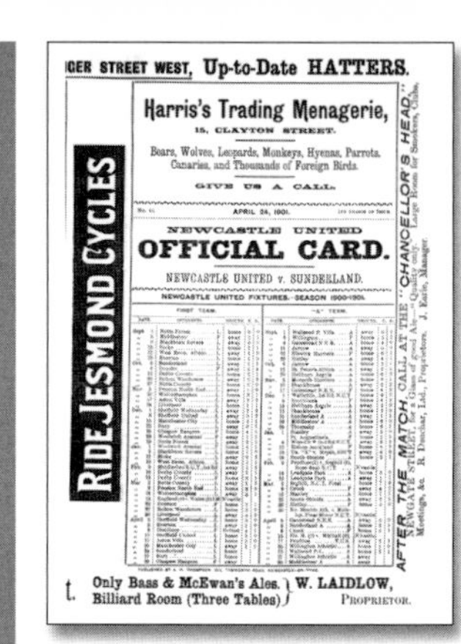

IGER STREET WEST, Up-to-Date HATTERS.

RIDE JESMOND CYCLES

Harris's Trading Menagerie,
15, CLAYTON STREET.
Bears, Wolves, Leopards, Monkeys, Hyenas, Parrots, Canaries, and Thousands of Foreign Birds.
GIVE US A CALL.

APRIL 24, 1901.

NEWCASTLE UNITED
OFFICIAL CARD.
NEWCASTLE UNITED v. SUNDERLAND.
NEWCASTLE UNITED FIXTURES.–SEASON 1900-1901.
FIRST TEAM. "A" TEAM.

AFTER THE MATCH, CALL AT THE "CHANCELLOR'S HEAD," NEWGATE STREET

Only Bass & McEwan's Ales. Billiard Room (Three Tables) W. LAIDLOW, PROPRIETOR.

Programmes at the turn of the century were filled with adverts, including "Harris's Trading Menagerie"!

IN CHARGE

Chairman: William Nesham/James Telford
Manager: Director Committee
Captain: Andy Aitken
Trainer/Coach: Tom Dodds

ST JAMES' PARK

Average Attendance
Lg 15,394 Lg & Cup 15,394

As a new century begins the Magpies pose for the camera at St James' Park.

SEASON REVIEW

Football League Div 1: P34 W14 D10 L10 F42 A37 Pts 38.
Position: 6th (Champions; Liverpool).
FA Cup: R1 (Winners; Tottenham Hotspur).

Appearances (35m): Carr J 35, Gardner Alec 35, Peddie JH 34, Aitken A 33, Ghee T 33, Kingsley M 33, Burgess C 31, MacFarlane A 31, Gardner DR 30, Niblo TB 26, Fraser J 20, Heywood F 13, Laidlaw JA 11, Scott MM 5, Allen E 4, Rogers JJ 3, Innerd W 2, Littlefair J 2, Watts C 2, Birnie EL 1, Veitch CCM 1.

Goals (43g): Peddie JH 14, Gardner Alec 6, MacFarlane A 6, Heywood F 3, Laidlaw JA 3, Aitken A 2, Ghee T 2, Niblo TB 2, Carr J 1, Fraser J 1, Gardner DR 1, own goals 2.

Dismissals: 0 players.

MAJOR SIGNINGS

Charles Burgess (Millwall Ath)
Matt Scott (Airdrie)

FROM THE RANKS

Wilf Innerd (Wallsend Park Villa)
James Littlefair (Burradon)

PLAYER FOCUS Matt Kingsley

Born Turton. Goalkeeper, 5'11"
1898 to 1904: 189 app 0 goals.

Joining United from Darwen in April 1898 to solve a problem goalkeeping position for United's bow in Division One, Kingsley was such a success in United's colours – 'keepers wearing the black-and-white striped jersey then along with the outfield players – he quickly became the club's very first player to be capped at full international level when on the St James' Park staff. A rival to Derby's Jack Robinson and Villa's Billy George, Matt appeared for England against Wales in season 1900-01 on his home ground, an easy 6-0 romp as it turned out. He was also to be selected for the Football League XI and was rated as one of the top custodians of the day. Matt was a regular for the club over six seasons before Jimmy Lawrence arrived on the scene in 1904. Efficient between the posts and noted for strong fisted clearances in the style of the day, Kingsley had a well built frame at over 14 stones and possessed the habit of continually swinging his arms to and fro as he waited for action. He actually once netted two goals for the Magpies when playing as a goalkeeper – in friendly contests against Brampton and Coventry. After leaving Tyneside at the end of season 1903-04, Kingsley served West Ham United and Queens Park Rangers in London – both then in the Southern League – as well as Rochdale and Barrow. He left the Hammers following an on the field fracas and suspension. Matt later resided in his native Lancashire.

TEAM COLOURS Black & white striped shirts, dark shorts (Change; white shirts, dark shorts)

SEASON 1900-01

Match	Date		FL Division 1	Result				Attendance	Posn	Scorers	Kingsley	Burgess	Gardner DR	Ghee	Aitken	Carr	Rogers	Gardner Alec	Peddie	MacFarlane	Fraser	Allen	Niblo	Laidlaw	Watts	Scott	Veitch	Heywood	Birnie	Innerd	Littlefair	Match
1	01 Sep	H	**Nottingham Forest**	D	0	0	(0 0)	20,000			1	2	3	4	5	6	7	8	9	10	11											1
2	08 Sep	A	Blackburn Rovers	D	0	0	(0 0)	10,000	10		1	2	3	4	5	6	7	8	9	10	11											2
3	15 Sep	H	**Stoke**	W	2	1	(1 1)	18,000	6	MacFarlane, Peddie	1	2		4	5	6		8	9	10		3	7	11								3
4	22 Sep	A	West Bromwich Albion	W	1	0	(0 0)	11,859	5	Peddie	1	2	3	4	5	6		8	9	10			7	11								4
5	29 Sep	H	**Everton**	W	1	0	(1 0)	22,500	2	Gardner D (pen)	1	2	3	4	5	6	7	8	9	10			11									5
6	06 Oct	A	Sunderland	D	1	1	(1 0)	28,688	4	og (McCombie)	1	2	3	4	5	6		8	9	10	11		7									6
7	13 Oct	H	**Derby County**	W	2	1	(2 0)	18,000	4	Fraser, Peddie	1	2	3	4	5	6		8	9	10	11		7									7
8	20 Oct	A	Bolton Wanderers	L	2	3	(1 1)	18,000	6	Peddie, Ghee	1	2	3	4	5	6		8	9	10	11		7									8
9	27 Oct	H	**Notts County**	W	2	0	(0 0)	12,000	3	MacFarlane, Gardner A	1	2	3	4	5	6		8	9	10	11		7									9
10	03 Nov	A	Preston North End	W	1	0	(0 0)	7,000	2	Laidlaw	1	2	3	4	5	6		8	9		11		7	10								10
11	10 Nov	H	**Wolverhampton Wanderers**	W	3	1	(1 1)	16,000	2	MacFarlane, Peddie, Niblo		2	3	4	5	6		8	9	10			7	11	1							11
12	17 Nov	A	Aston Villa	D	2	2	(1 2)	20,000	2	og (Evans), Gardner A	1	2	3	4	5	6		8	9	10			7	11								12
13	24 Nov	H	**Liverpool**	D	1	1	(1 1)	19,000	2	Laidlaw	1		3	4	5	6		8	9	10		2	7	11								13
14	01 Dec	A	Sheffield Wednesday	D	2	2	(1 1)	12,000	2	Peddie, Niblo	1	2	3	4	5	6		8	9	10			7	11								14
15	08 Dec	A	Sheffield United	L	0	2	(0 0)	15,594	2		1	2		4	5	6		8	9	10	11		7			3						15
16	15 Dec	H	**Manchester City**	W	2	1	(1 0)	14,500	2	Laidlaw, Peddie	1	2		4	5	6		8	9		11		7	10		3						16
17	22 Dec	A	Bury	L	0	1	(0 0)	4,631	2		1	2		4	5	6		8	9		11		7	10		3						17
18	29 Dec	A	Nottingham Forest	W	2	1	(1 1)	10,000	3	Peddie 2	1	2		4	5	6		8	9	10	7	3	11									18
19	05 Jan	H	**Blackburn Rovers**	W	1	0	(0 0)	10,000	3	Peddie	1	2	3	4	5	6		8	9	10	7		11									19
20	12 Jan	A	Stoke	L	0	2	(0 1)	6,000	4		1	2	3		5	6		8	9	10	7		11				4					20
21	19 Jan	H	**West Bromwich Albion**	D	1	1	(1 0)	10,500	4	Peddie	1	2	3	4	5	6		8	9	7	11			10								21
22	16 Feb	A	Derby County	D	1	1	(1 1)	7,000	5	Peddie	1	2	3	4	5	6		8	9	7			11					10				22
23	02 Mar	A	Notts County	L	1	3	(0 3)	4,000	6	Gardner A	1		2	4	5	6		8		7	11		9			3		10				23
24	09 Mar	H	**Preston North End**	L	3	5	(1 4)	17,000	8	Heywood, Peddie, Aitken	1	2	3		4	6		8	9	7			11					10	5			24
25	16 Mar	A	Wolverhampton Wanderers	L	0	1	(0 1)	5,000	8			2	3	4	5	6		8	7	10	11				1			9				25
26	27 Mar	H	**Bolton Wanderers**	W	3	0	(1 0)	16,000	7	Heywood, MacFarlane, Gardner A	1	2	3	4	5	6		7	9	8	11							10				26
27	30 Mar	A	Liverpool	L	0	3	(0 1)	10,000	7		1	2	3	4		6		7	9	8	11							10		5		27
	05 Apr	H	**Sunderland**	Ab	0	0		45,000			1	2	3	4	5	6		7	9	8			11					10				
28	06 Apr	H	**Sheffield Wednesday**	D	0	0	(0 0)	13,000	7		1	2	3	4	5	6		7	9	8								10			11	28
29	08 Apr	A	Everton	W	1	0	(1 0)	20,000	7	Gardner A	1	2	3	4	5	6		7	9	8			11					10				29
30	13 Apr	H	**Sheffield United**	W	3	0	(0 0)	16,000	7	MacFarlane, Carr, Ghee	1		2	4	5	6		7	9	8			11			3		10				30
31	17 Apr	H	**Aston Villa**	W	3	0	(1 0)	12,000	6	Heywood, MacFarlane, Gardner A	1	2	3	4	5	6		7	9	8			11					10				31
32	20 Apr	A	Manchester City	L	1	2	(1 1)	18,000	6	Peddie	1	2	3	4	5	6		7	9	8			11					10				32
33	24 Apr	H	**Sunderland**	L	0	2	(0 1)	18,694	7		1	2	3	4	5	6		7	9		11		8					10				33
34	27 Apr	H	**Bury**	D	0	0	(0 0)	8,500	6		1		2	4		6		7	9	8		3						10		5	11	34
Round			**FA Cup**																													**Round**
1	09 Feb	A	Middlesbrough	L	1	3	(0 1)	16,000		Aitken	1	2	3	4	5	6		8	9	7	11			10								1

Ab Abandoned before kick off due to riot

Match 8 Some reports note that Peddie scored both goals

Match 12 Some reports attribute the og to Carr, while others note Peddie or MacFarlane as the scorer

DateLine ... 18 March: St James' Park hosts its first international fixture as England defeat Wales 6-0. **18 March:** Matt Kingsley becomes United's first international player appearing for England against the Welsh. **5 April:** The derby match with Sunderland at Gallowgate is abandoned without a ball being kicked due to a riot with an estimated 45,000 in the ground and thousands outside.

SEASON
1901-02
DIVISION 1

A taste of what was to follow

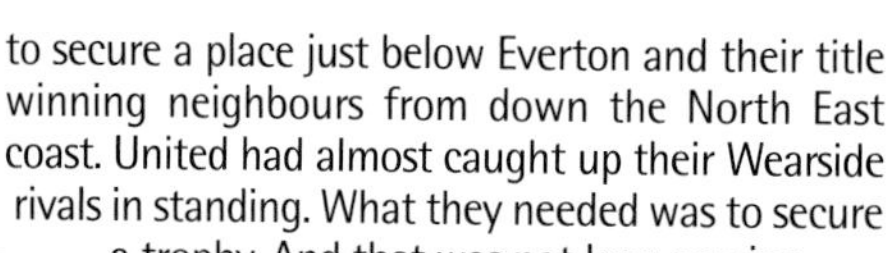

As the Victorian era closed and the country entered the Edwardian age there was a sense of expectancy, if not in the pubs of Tyneside, within the closed doors of St James' Park. Newcastle's directors and officials were confident they were on the right tracks and the building of the club into an organisation that could match the very best was taking shape. Season 1901-02 was evidence of that progress. United concluded their programme in third place, seven points behind Champions Sunderland. The Magpies put down a marker when they demolished Notts County 8-0 in October. That rout of Notts County registered a new goals record for United in senior football, bettering the previous best margin of six goals. Newcastle were 5-0 ahead at half-time. New arrival Ronald Orr hit four of the goals with Jock Peddie claiming a hat-trick.

United then won three games in a row to challenge near the top of the table. Although slipping over Christmas, Newcastle recovered during the spring to secure a place just below Everton and their title winning neighbours from down the North East coast. United had almost caught up their Wearside rivals in standing. What they needed was to secure a trophy. And that was not long coming.

At last Newcastle progressed a little further in the FA Cup, this time to the old Second Round stage when a North Eastern glamour tie was dished up; an epic tie with title foes Sunderland. The Red'n'Whites were favourites, but the Magpies shocked the bookies by winning 1-0. Ronald Orr, to make quite an impact in the season, netted in the dying minutes to take United into the quarter-final. Eventual winners Sheffield United though knocked United out at Bramall Lane.

Apart from Orr, two other significant players were additions on the team-sheet. One of the biggest names north of the border, centre-forward Bob McColl arrived on Tyneside while young teenager Jack Rutherford burst onto the scene. Both players had much influence – one short-term, one long-term – on the Magpies immediate success.

Pictured above: Richard Roberts was fast and direct down the left flank and became a terrace favourite.

Memorabilia CORNER

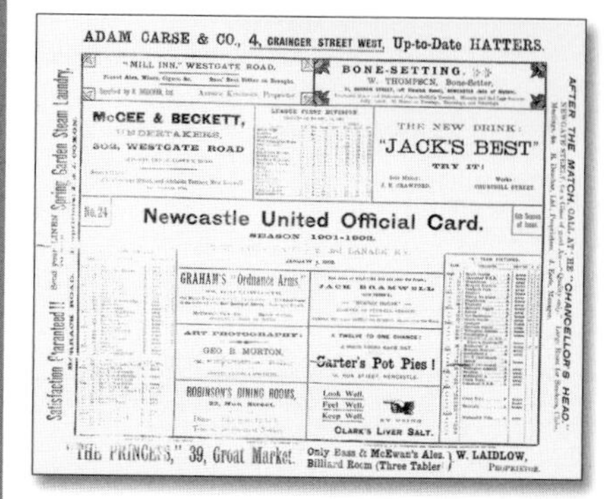

ADAM CARSE & CO., 4, GRAINGER STREET WEST, Up-to-Date HATTERS.

"MILL INN," WESTGATE ROAD.

BONE-SETTING. W. THOMPSON, Bone-Setter,

McGEE & BECKETT, UNDERTAKERS, 302, WESTGATE ROAD

THE NEW DRINK: "JACK'S BEST" TRY IT!

No. 24 Newcastle United Official Card. SEASON 1901-1902.

GRAHAM'S "Ordnance Arms"

JACK BRAMWELL

ART PHOTOGRAPHY: GEO. B. MORTON,

Carter's Pot Pies!

ROBINSON'S DINING ROOMS,

Look Well. Feel Well. Keep Well. CLARK'S LIVER SALT.

Satisfaction Guaranteed!! Send your LINEN Spring Garden Steam Laundry.

AFTER THE MATCH, CALL AT THE "CHANCELLOR'S HEAD,"

"THE PRINCESS," 39, Groat Market. Only Bass & McEwan's Ales. Billiard Room (Three Tables) W. LAIDLOW, PROPRIETOR.

United's large size two-sided 'official card' for the friendly with Scottish visitors, the "3rd Lanark RV".

IN CHARGE

Chairman: William Nesham/James Telford
Manager: Director Committee
Captain: Andy Aitken
Trainer/Coach: Tom Dodds

ST JAMES' PARK

Average Attendance
Lg 14,235 Lg & Cup 14,848

United's first team squad ready for action in season 1901-02.

PLAYER FOCUS Andy Aitken

Born Ayr. Half-back, 5'8"
1895 to 1906: 349 app 39 goals.

One of many celebrated Scots to wear United's colours in both the formative years, and the period up to World War One, Andy Aitken moved south from Ayr Parkhouse as a teenager in the summer of 1895. He quickly became a pivotal member of the Magpie side at half-back and ultimately the foundation stone to United's early trophy success. At first he was a blossoming midfielder as the black-and-whites won promotion in 1898 while in the opening years of the new century, Andy matured into a player of international quality. He was first capped by Scotland during 1900-01 against England, being a regular contender for the handful of international fixtures every season up to 1911. He skippered his country and was also appointed Newcastle captain for a period. Nicknamed Daddler, he led the Tynesiders almost to the prized Football League and FA Cup double in 1905, only to lose by a single goal in the FA Cup to Aston Villa. Versatile to several roles, Andy possessed terrier-like drive and stamina while he always looked to get in to attacking positions. Recognised as one of football's elite, when he approached his thirties younger stars took his place in United's ranks. Aitken moved down the North East coast and joined Middlesbrough as player-boss. At Ayresome Park he continued to impress before moving into a similar management role with Leicester Fosse. Aitken returned as a veteran player north of the border at Dundee and Kilmarnock before settling on Tyneside where he was Gateshead Town boss. He was related by marriage to teammate Alec Gardner, the pair marrying sisters.

SEASON REVIEW

Football League Div 1: P34 W14 D9 L11 F48 A34 Pts 37.
Position: 3rd (Champions; Sunderland).
FA Cup: QF (Winners; Sheffield United).

Appearances (38m): Kingsley M 37, Orr R 36, Aitken A 34, Carr J 33, Roberts RJ 32, Bennie RB 31, Davidson T 30, Gardner Alec 30, Stewart WG 29, Caie AS 25, Peddie JH 18, Gardner DR 13, McColl RS 12, Niblo TB 12, Veitch CCM 12, Rutherford J 11, Ghee T 9, Graham JR 6, Bamlett T 2, Birnie EL 2, MacFarlane A 2, Pattinson D 1, Watts C 1.

Goals (53g): Roberts RJ 12, Orr R 10, Peddie JH 8, Rutherford J 5, McColl RS 4, Veitch CCM 4, Gardner Alec 3, Stewart WG 3, Aitken A 1, Carr J 1, Niblo TB 1, Pattinson D 1.

Dismissals: 0 players.

MAJOR SIGNINGS

Bob McColl (Queen's Park)
Ronald Orr (St Mirren)
Bob Bennie (St Mirren)
Alex Caie (Millwall Ath)
Tom Davidson (Millwall Ath)
Richard Roberts (West Brom Albion)
Willie Stewart (Queen's Park)

FROM THE RANKS

Jack Rutherford (Willington Ath)
Tom Bamlett (Kibblesworth)
John Graham (Workington Diamonds)
Fred Heywood (Turton)

TEAM COLOURS Black & white striped shirts, dark shorts (Change; white shirts, dark shorts)

SEASON 1901-02

Match	Date		FL Division 1				Posn		Kingsley	Gardner DR	Bennie	Ghee	Aitken	Carr	Gardner Alec	MacFarlane	Peddie	Orr	Roberts	Stewart	Niblo	Davidson	Bamlett	Caie	Birnie	McColl	Veitch	Graham	Rutherford	Watts	Pattinson	Match
1	07 Sep	A	Blackburn Rovers	D 0 0	(0 0)	7,000			1	2	3	4	5	6	7	8	9	10	11													1
2	14 Sep	H	**Stoke**	W 5 1	(3 0)	20,000	6	Roberts 2, Orr 2, Niblo	1	2	3	4	5	6	8			10	11	7	9											2
3	21 Sep	A	Everton	D 0 0	(0 0)	20,000	6		1	2	3	4	5	6	8			10	11	7	9											3
4	28 Sep	H	**Sunderland**	L 0 1	(0 1)	25,000	13		1	2		4	5	6	7	8		10	11		9	3										4
5	03 Oct	A	Notts County	W 2 0	(0 0)	10,000	4	Peddie, Gardner A	1				5	6	7		9	10	11		8	3	2	4								5
6	05 Oct	A	Small Heath	L 1 3	(0 1)	12,000	7	Roberts	1				5	6	7		9	10	11		8	3	2	4								6
7	12 Oct	H	**Derby County**	L 0 1	(0 0)	15,000	12		1	2			5	6	7		9	10	11		8	3		4								7
8	19 Oct	A	Sheffield Wednesday	D 0 0	(0 0)	15,000	10		1	2		4	5	6	7			8	11			3		10	9							8
9	26 Oct	H	**Notts County**	W 8 0	(5 0)	12,000	7	Roberts, Peddie 3, Orr 4	1		2	4	5	6	7		9	8	11		10	3										9
10	02 Nov	A	Bolton Wanderers	L 1 3	(0 2)	11,951	11	Gardner A	1		2	4	5		7		9	8	11		10	3		6								10
11	09 Nov	H	**Manchester City**	W 3 0	(1 0)	8,000	9	Roberts, McColl (pen), Orr	1		2		5	6			9	8	11	7		3		4		10						11
12	23 Nov	H	**Liverpool**	W 1 0	(0 0)	20,000	8	McColl	1		2		5	6			9	8	11	7		3		4		10						12
13	30 Nov	H	**Grimsby Town**	W 5 1	(2 0)	15,000	5	Roberts, Peddie 3, Orr	1		2		5	6			9	8	11	7		3		4		10						13
14	07 Dec	A	Aston Villa	D 0 0	(0 0)	20,000	4		1		2		5	6			9	8	11	7	10	3		4								14
15	14 Dec	H	**Sheffield United**	D 1 1	(0 0)	18,000	5	Peddie (pen)	1		2		5	6			9	8	11	7	10	3		4								15
16	26 Dec	A	Derby County	L 0 1	(0 1)	20,000	11		1		2		5	6			9	8	11	7	10	3		4								16
17	28 Dec	H	**Bury**	D 1 1	(0 0)	7,000	10	Roberts	1		2		5	6				8	7		9	3		4			10	11				17
18	04 Jan	H	**Blackburn Rovers**	L 0 3	(0 2)	12,000	11		1		2	4		6			9	8	11	7		3		5			10					18
19	11 Jan	A	Stoke	D 0 0	(0 0)	5,000	12		1	2			5	6	7			9		8		3		4			10	11				19
20	18 Jan	H	**Everton**	D 1 1	(0 0)	17,000	12	Roberts	1	2				6	9			8	11	7		3		4	5		10					20
21	01 Feb	H	**Small Heath**	W 2 0	(0 0)	13,000	9	Veitch, Carr	1	3	2		5	6	9			8		7				4			10	11				21
22	15 Feb	H	**Sheffield Wednesday**	W 2 1	(2 0)	15,000	8	Roberts, Veitch	1		2	5		6	9		10		11	7		3		4			8					22
23	01 Mar	H	**Bolton Wanderers**	W 4 1	(1 0)	12,000	7	Roberts 2, Rutherford, McColl	1		2		5		8				11	7		3		4		9	6		10			23
24	08 Mar	A	Manchester City	L 0 2	(0 2)	20,000	9				2		5		10		9	8	11	7		3		4			6			1		24
25	10 Mar	A	Wolverhampton Wanderers	L 0 3	(0 2)	2,000	9		1		2		5		4		9	8	11	7		3		6					10			25
26	15 Mar	H	**Wolverhampton Wanderers**	W 3 1	(1 0)	7,000	7	Veitch, Rutherford 2	1	3	2		5	6	4			8		7							10	11	9			26
27	19 Mar	A	Nottingham Forest	W 2 0	(0 0)	20,000	3	Pattinson, Aitken	1	3	2		5	6	4			8		7								11	9		10	27
28	22 Mar	A	Liverpool	W 1 0	(1 0)	15,000	3	Orr	1	3	2		5	6	4			8		7							10	11	9			28
29	28 Mar	A	Grimsby Town	L 0 3	(0 1)	8,000	3		1	3	2		5	6	4			8	11	7						9			10			29
30	31 Mar	A	Sunderland	D 0 0	(0 0)	34,819	3		1		2		5	6	4			8	11	7		3				9			10			30
31	05 Apr	H	**Aston Villa**	W 2 1	(1 1)	14,000	3	Stewart 2	1		2			6	5			8	11	7		3		4		9			10			31
32	12 Apr	A	Sheffield United	L 0 1	(0 1)	7,837	3		1		2		5	6	4			8	11	7		3				10			9			32
33	19 Apr	H	**Nottingham Forest**	W 3 0	(1 0)	12,000	3	Roberts, Rutherford 2	1		2		5	6	4			8	11	7		3				10			9			33
34	26 Apr	A	Bury	L 0 4	(0 3)	2,325	3		1		2		5	6	4			8	11	7		3				10			9			34
Round			**FA Cup**																													**Round**
1	25 Jan	A	Woolwich Arsenal	W 2 0	(0 0)	15,000		Veitch, Gardner A	1		2		5	6	9		11	8		7		3		4			10					1
2	12 Feb	H	**Sunderland**	W 1 0	(0 0)	19,700		Orr	1		2		5	6	9		10	8	11	7		3		4								2
3	22 Feb	H	**Sheffield United**	D 1 1	(0 1)	20,418		Stewart	1		2		5	6	9			8	11	7		3		4		10						3
3r	27 Feb	A	Sheffield United	L 1 2	(1 1)	25,100		McColl	1		2		5		10			8	11	7		3		4		9	6					3r

DateLine ... 26 Oct: United register an 8-0 victory over Notts County, a record win at the time. **1 March:** Jack Rutherford comes through the ranks and makes his debut against Bolton as a 17-year-old, and finds the net. **29 April:** United play the first of three fixtures in aid of the Ibrox Disaster Fund, a 5-0 win over Glasgow Rangers.

SEASON 1902-03

DIVISION 1

Trouble in the Boardroom

Although United had showed they now had the know-how and ability on the field to mix-it with the best, behind the scenes all was not a happy camp. A Boardroom power struggle began to rock the club as influential director James Telford was to be challenged by the Bell family. And this off the field rumpus seemed to affect the side following three seasons of excellent progress. After starting well, being leaders of the pack in September they slid down the table due to what was recorded as perplexing team selections. West Bromwich Albion hit six against United, Aston Villa recorded seven goals. Fortunately though, it was only to be a one season blip.

The fall-out from what was to become a Boardroom coup was that several players were far from happy at the way Telford had been treated, notably Bob McColl. He headed north at the end of the following season. Despite the unrest in the Boardroom, at least the power at the club, still Telford at the time, had the foresight to invite their senior players, notably Veitch, Aitken and Carr to rectify matters on the field. This they did bringing in young Scottish playmaker Peter McWilliam into the line-up. As a result Newcastle United recovered to end in 14th position. And for the next nine years the side only finished out of the top four places on a single occasion.

On the last day of the programme the Black'n'Whites defeated Sunderland at Gallowgate for the first time – and in the process deprived the Wearsiders of the Championship. The title race went to the wire. And Sunderland's visit to Gallowgate on the 25th April proved crucial. Bob McColl popped up and grabbed the only goal of the game to make sure the title trophy went to Sheffield Wednesday by a single point.

Another Scot, established international Bobby Templeton pulled on United's shirt that season. He was a headline signing and a hugely gifted player. Another international, England's Arthur Turner arrived too. Big names were starting to land at St James' Park.

Pictured above: Bobby Templeton was one of the personality players of the era, a celebrated outside-left.

Memorabilia CORNER

United's popular mascot of Edwardian times, Rex, a black-and-white Great Dane.

IN CHARGE

Chairman: James Telford
Manager: Director Committee
Captain: Andy Aitken
Trainer/Coach: Tom Dodds

ST JAMES' PARK

Average Attendance
Lg 18,042 Lg & Cup 18,082

Newcastle United in 1902. Back row, left to right: Ghee (trainer), Davidson, Watts, Caie, Kingsley, Carr, Agnew, Bennie, Cockburn (groundsman). Middle: Watt (secretary), Stewart, Rutherford, Orr, unknown, Roberts, Dodds (trainer). Front: Gardner (Alec), Aitken, McColl, Turner, Graham, McWilliam.

PLAYER FOCUS Bob McColl

Born Glasgow. Centre-forward, 5'9"
1901 to 1904: 67 app 20 goals.

The signing of Scottish international centre-forward Bob McColl during November 1901 was a milestone in United's development. The transfer from Queen's Park of one of Scotland's biggest stars, nicknamed The Prince of Centre-forwards, showed that the club had become a power in the land. An amateur north of the border, McColl was acclaimed as Scotland's finest player having just scored a celebrated hat-trick against England. A slightly-built striker, he showed lightning quick acceleration and preferred to be at the hub of scientific movements with finesse on the ball – the beautiful way of playing the game. Many of United's players hailed McColl as the man who created the Magpies philosophy of a neat passing style of football, which became legendary in the decade before the First World War. But Bob was not at Gallowgate to see his plan bear fruits as he became disillusioned with the power struggle behind the scenes at St James' Park which led to his close ally James Telford being ousted from the Board. McColl moved back to Scotland where he continued to be an influence with Rangers and Queen's Park. His brother also had a short period in United's reserves, while on Bob's retirement from football in 1910; McColl entered the confectionary and retail trade, building up a large family business which stretched the width and breadth of the country. Nicknamed Toffee Bob, his RS McColl newsagency chain is still evident in certain locations a century later.

SEASON REVIEW

Football League Div 1: P34 W14 D4 L16 F41 A51 Pts 32.
Position: 14th (Champions; Sheffield Wednesday).
FA Cup: R1 (Winners; Bury).

Appearances (35m): Agnew WB 35, Aitken A 33, Carr J 32, Kingsley M 32, McColl RS 30, Gardner Alec 27, Orr R 24, Roberts RJ 22, Rutherford J 22, Veitch CCM 18, Davidson T 13, Stewart WG 12, Turner AD 12, Caie AS 10, Gardner And 10, Templeton RB 10, McWilliam P 7, Birnie EL 6, Stenhouse H 6, Bennie RB 5, Wilson W2 4, McIntyre EP 3, Watson J 3, Watts C 3, Appleyard W 2, Graham S 2, Benson RW 1, Richardson O 1.

Goals (42g): McColl RS 10, Rutherford J 6, Gardner Alec 5, Orr R 5, Roberts RJ 5, Gardner And 3, Carr J 2, Stewart WG 2, Caie AS 1, McIntyre EP 1, Templeton RB 1, Turner AD 1.

Dismissals: 0 players.

MAJOR SIGNINGS

Bobby Templeton (Aston Villa) £400 club record fee
Arthur Turner (Derby County)
Bill Appleyard (Grimsby Town) £350
John Watson (Clyde) £200

FROM THE RANKS

Peter McWilliam (Inverness Thistle)
Bob Benson (Swalwell)
Sam Graham (Galston)
Ted McIntyre (Allendale Park)
Ord Richardson (Wallsend Park Villa)
Harry Stenhouse (Blyth Spartans)
Billy Wilson (South Shields Ath)

TEAM COLOURS Black & white striped shirts, dark shorts (Change; white shirts, dark shorts)

SEASON 1902-03

Match	Date		FL Division 1					Posn	Scorers	Kingsley	Bennie	Agnew	Gardner Alec	Aitken	Carr	Stewart	Orr	McColl	Rutherford	Roberts	Davidson	McWilliam	Caie	Graham	Richardson	Veitch	Gardner And	Watson	Birnie	Stenhouse	Wilson	Watts	Turner	Benson	Templeton	McIntyre	Appleyard	Match
1	06 Sep	H	**Stoke**	W	5 0	(1 0)	17,000		Rutherford, McColl 2, Orr 2	1	2	3	4	5	6	7	8	9	10	11																		1
2	13 Sep	A	Everton	W	1 0	(1 0)	20,000	3	Stewart	1	2	3	4	5	6	7	8	9	10	11																		2
3	20 Sep	H	**Sheffield Wednesday**	W	3 0	(1 0)	25,000	1	Roberts 2, Rutherford	1		2	4	5	6	7	8	9	10	11	3																	3
4	27 Sep	A	West Bromwich Albion	L	1 6	(1 3)	22,160	5	Rutherford	1		2	4	5	6	7	8	9	10	11	3																	4
5	04 Oct	H	**Notts County**	W	6 1	(5 0)	17,000	4	Rutherford 2, McColl, Orr, Stewart, Carr	1		2	4	5	6	7	8	9	10	11	3																	5
6	11 Oct	A	Bolton Wanderers	W	2 0	(2 0)	10,000	1	Orr, Carr	1	2	3	4	5	6	7	8	9	10	11																		6
7	18 Oct	H	**Middlesbrough**	L	0 1	(0 1)	26,000	6		1	2	3		5	6	7	8	9	10	11		4																7
8	25 Oct	A	Derby County	D	0 0	(0 0)	12,000	4		1		3		5	6	7	8	9	10	11	2		4															8
9	01 Nov	A	Wolverhampton Wanderers	L	0 3	(0 1)	8,000	6		1		3		5	6			9	10	11	2		4	7	8													9
10	08 Nov	H	**Liverpool**	L	1 2	(1 1)	8,000	9	Roberts	1		3		5	6			9	10	7	2		4			8	11											10
11	15 Nov	A	Sheffield United	L	1 2	(0 0)	14,040	10	Roberts	1		3		5				9	10	7			4	8			11	2	6									11
12	22 Nov	H	**Grimsby Town**	W	1 0	(1 0)	11,000	8	Rutherford	1		3		5	6	7		9	10	11			4			8		2										12
13	29 Nov	A	Aston Villa	L	0 7	(0 4)	10,000	11		1		3		5	6	7	8		10	11			4					2		9								13
14	06 Dec	H	**Nottingham Forest**	L	0 2	(0 1)	12,000	13		1	2	3	4	5		7	8	10	9	11			6															14
15	13 Dec	A	Bury	L	0 1	(0 1)	4,749	13		1		3	4	5	6		8	10		11									9	7	2							15
16	20 Dec	H	**Blackburn Rovers**	W	1 0	(1 0)	12,000	13	Caie	1		3		5	6			10	8	11			9			4				7	2							16
17	27 Dec	A	Sunderland	D	0 0	(0 0)	28,000	14		1		3	9	5	6				10				4			8			11	7	2							17
18	03 Jan	A	Stoke	L	0 5	(0 2)	6,000	14		1		3	9	5	6				10				4			8			11	7	2							18
19	17 Jan	A	Sheffield Wednesday	L	0 3	(0 1)	12,000	16				3	4	5	6		8	9	10		2								11	7		1						19
20	24 Jan	H	**West Bromwich Albion**	W	1 0	(1 0)	20,156	15	Gardner And	1		3	4	5	6		8	9	7		2					10	11											20
21	31 Jan	A	Notts County	D	2 2	(2 1)	11,000	14	Gardner And, Orr	1		2	4	5	6		8	9	10		3						11						7					21
22	14 Feb	A	Middlesbrough	L	0 1	(0 1)	20,000	15		1		3	4		6		8	9			2					10	11		5				7					22
23	28 Feb	H	**Wolverhampton Wanderers**	L	2 4	(1 2)	16,000	15	Gardner And, Gardner Alex	1		3	4	5	6		8	10	9		2						11						7					23
24	07 Mar	A	Liverpool	L	0 3	(0 3)	15,000	15		1		3	4	5	6			9		8							10						7	2	11			24
25	14 Mar	H	**Sheffield United**	D	0 0	(0 0)	20,000	15				3	4	2	6				9	8						5	10					1	7		11			25
26	21 Mar	A	Grimsby Town	L	0 1	(0 1)	4,000	17		1		3	4	2	6		9			8						5	10						7		11			26
27	28 Mar	H	**Aston Villa**	W	2 0	(0 0)	20,000	15	McColl 2	1		3	9	2	6		8	10				4				5							7		11			27
28	01 Apr	H	**Everton**	W	3 0	(2 0)	18,000	15	Gardner Alex 2, McIntyre (pen)	1		3	10	2			8	9				4				5							7		11	6		28
29	04 Apr	A	Nottingham Forest	L	2 3	(2 3)	4,000	15	Gardner Alex 2	1		3	10		6		8	9		11	2	4				5							7					29
30	10 Apr	H	**Derby County**	W	2 1	(1 0)	25,000	15	Templeton, Roberts	1		3	8	2	6		10	9		7		4				5									11			30
31	11 Apr	H	**Bury**	W	1 0	(1 0)	18,000	15	Turner	1		3	8	2	6		10	9				4				5							7		11			31
32	13 Apr	H	**Bolton Wanderers**	W	2 0	(0 0)	15,000	15	McColl 2	1		3	8	2	6	7	10	9								5									11	4		32
33	18 Apr	A	Blackburn Rovers	L	1 3	(0 2)	8,000	15	McColl	1		3	8	2	6			9								5							7		11	4	10	33
34	25 Apr	H	**Sunderland**	W	1 0	(0 0)	26,562	14	McColl			3	8	2	6			9				4				5						1	7		11		10	34
Round			FA Cup																																			Round
1	07 Feb	A	Grimsby Town	L	1 2	(0 2)	6,000		McColl	1		3	4	5	6		8	9		7	2					10	11											1

DateLine ... 20 Sept: United reach the top of the table for the first time after a victory over Sheffield Wednesday. **4 Oct:** Notts County are swamped once more by United, this time 6-1. **18 Oct:** Peter McWilliam makes his debut against Middlesbrough. **18 April:** Sunderland beat Middlesbrough 2-1 at St James' Park due to closure of Roker Park. **25 April:** A 1-0 victory over Sunderland deprives the Wearsiders of the League title.

SEASON
1903-04
DIVISION 1

Title challenge by the Magpies

In spite of the Boardroom unrest which continued into the 1903-04 season, Newcastle United made a concerted bid to lift the Football League Championship as their team building neared completion – possessing now a professional staff of some 44 players. And United's approach was to assemble a mix of home grown players and expensive buys, now that they could afford to compete with anyone in the transfer market with solid support of gates approaching 20,000 and often close to the capacity 30,000. Even the reserve eleven could attract a crowd of 9,000 for the derby with the Sunderland 'A' line-up. For this season Bill Appleyard started his first full campaign and was one of those pricey arrivals, but his purchase was surpassed by the record – both a club and national fee of £700 – for Sunderland's Scottish international full-back Andy McCombie.

Newcastle continued their steady climb up the table, finishing in fourth position, not far away – five points – from Champions Sheffield Wednesday. They did have an outside chance of the title in a late rally – winning five of their last seven games, including a 4-0 romp over the eventual Champions.

The FA Cup though continued to be a competition the Magpies could not come to terms with. They fell in the opening round, to holders Bury. However, that lack of progress would very soon change.

For much of the season, the Black'n'Whites began to display slick football, a brand of short passing in a possession style to become United's hallmark in the next decade. They were making their mark with four of the side appearing in the prestigious England versus Scotland contest, the biggest game of the season next to the FA Cup final. Newcastle also started to fly the flag on the Continent. At the end of the season the Magpies travelled by a Neilson & Anderson steamer for a series of games in Denmark's capital Copenhagen.

Pictured above: Joining United for a record fee, Andy McCombie remained with United for over 46 years.

Memorabilia CORNER

ART PHOTOGRAPHY!!
GEO. R. MORTON,
140, Northumberland Street.
Athletic Groups a Speciality.

THOMAS LEE,
CYCLE BUILDER & REPAIRER
362½, WESTGATE ROAD, NEWCASTLE.
BEST REPAIRS ONLY ARE CHEAP.

Hedley's Cafe,
Corner of Blackett Street and Clayton Street.
DINNERS DAILY FROM 11 TO 3.
TEAS ON THE SHORTEST NOTICE.

PHOTOGRAPHIC GROUPS (Copyright)
Newcastle United Football 1st Team
NOW READY.
AND MAY BE HAD FROM
J. H. THOMPSON, 255, Tamworth Rd.

LEAGUE FIRST DIVISION.

EXCEPTIONAL VALUE AT
GEO. KAY SMITH'S ESTABLISHMENTS
4 and 6, Scotswood Road, South Benwell, and 119, Stanhope Street, Newcastle.
See the New American Shirts & Pants, Fleecy Inside, 1s. 11½d.
FOOTBALL KNICKERS, SHIRTS, &c., ALWAYS IN STOCK.

OFFICIAL PROGRAMME OF NEWCASTLE UNITED A.F.C.

SEASON 1903-1904.
NEWCASTLE UNITED v. MIDDLESBRO'.
No. 12. NOVEMBER 14, 1903.

FIRST TEAM FIXTURES

"THE LAUNDRY." "PAR EXCELLENCE."
Spring Garden Laundry, Barrack Road.
Proprietors: J. & J. COXON.
Orders promptly attended to and executed with dispatch, combined with Moderate Charges.

Warren & Co.,
Ladies' and Gentlemen's Tailors,
2a & 4, Grainger Street,
Newcastle-on-Tyne.

"A" TEAM FIXTURES

By 1903 an 'official programme' had arrived, but still a two-sided sheet.

IN CHARGE

Chairman: James Telford
Manager: Director Committee
Captain: Andy Aitken
Trainer/Coach: James McPherson

ST JAMES' PARK

Average Attendance
Lg 18,500 Lg & Cup 18,500

United about to launch a Championship bid. Note the lighter shorts, dark-blue not black at the time.

PLAYER FOCUS Jack Rutherford

Born Percy Main. Outside-right, 5'9"
1902 to 1913: 336 app 94 goals.

Along with Colin Veitch and Jimmy Lawrence, Tynesider Jack Rutherford played in all eight of United's Championship and FA Cup finals sides during the Edwardian era; three titles and five finals. Dubbed The Newcastle Flier, he was one of the most dangerous and respected forwards in the country during those years. A teenage debutant at 17 years old, one of United's youngest ever – and the youngest to score for the club in senior action – Jack also became one of most youthful to play for England, at 19 years of age when he pulled on the white shirt of his country during 1903-04. Swift of foot on the right touchline, Rutherford was a dangerman throughout the years before the Great War. He could create openings and was also able to find the net, scoring almost a century of goals for the Magpies, while the Geordie had a long career in top football. Following 13 seasons as a regular with the Magpies, and when almost 30 years old, he moved to Arsenal in 1913 where he proceeded to total another 323 games and not retire until he was over 42. A brief spell in charge of Stoke followed before Jack wound down his career with Clapton Orient and settled in the Neasden area of London. From a footballing family, one of his seven brothers, Sep was a FA Cup finalist with Portsmouth while his son John James turned also out for Arsenal, in the same season Jack was on the books. Another two brothers, Andrew and George were on Newcastle's staff for short spells while also related to the family was Laybourne McDougall who appeared notably for Gateshead during their League years.

SEASON REVIEW

Football League Div 1: P34 W18 D6 L10 F58 A45 Pts 42.
Position: 4th (Champions; Sheffield Wednesday).
FA Cup: R1 (Winners; Manchester City).

Appearances (35m): Gardner Alec 35, Rutherford J 34, Veitch CCM 34, Aitken A 33, Appleyard W 32, Templeton RB 32, Howie J 30, McColl RS 25, Carr J 21, Watts C 19, Tildesley J 17, Wills T 17, Kingsley M 16, Orr R 13, Agnew WB 9, McCombie A 6, McWilliam P 5, Birnie EL 2, Bennie RB 1, McIntyre EP 1, Roberts RJ 1, Thompson GA 1, Turner AD 1.

Goals (59g): Appleyard W 16, Howie J 14, Orr R 11, Rutherford J 7, McColl RS 6, Templeton RB 4, Veitch CCM 1.

Dismissals: 0 players.

MAJOR SIGNINGS

Andy McCombie (Sunderland) £700 club & national record fee
James Howie (Bristol Rovers) £300
Tom Wills (Ayr)

FROM THE RANKS

James Tildesley (Halesowen St John)
George Thompson (Halesowen St John)

TEAM COLOURS Black & white striped shirts, dark shorts (Change; white shirts, dark shorts)

SEASON 1903-04

Match	Date		FL Division 1					Att	Posn	Scorers	Kingsley	Aitken	Carr	Gardner	Veitch	McWilliam	Rutherford	Howie	Appleyard	McColl	Templeton	Agnew	Watts	Orr	Tildesley	Roberts	McIntyre	Wills	Turner	McCombie	Birnie	Bennie	Thompson	Match
1	02 Sep	H	**Aston Villa**	D	1	1	(0 0)	8,000		Templeton	1	2	3	4	5	6	7	8	9	10	11													1
2	05 Sep	A	West Bromwich Albion	W	2	1	(2 1)	10,352	5	Appleyard, Rutherford	1	2	6	4	5		7	8	9	10	11	3												2
3	12 Sep	H	**Small Heath**	W	3	1	(1 0)	17,000	3	McColl, Appleyard, Howie	1	2	6	4	5		7	8	9	10	11	3												3
4	19 Sep	A	Everton	L	1	4	(0 1)	20,000	6	Howie	1	2	6	4	5		7	8	9	10	11	3												4
5	26 Sep	H	**Stoke**	W	1	0	(0 0)	16,000	5	Rutherford		2	6	4	5		7	8	9	10	11	3	1											5
6	03 Oct	A	Derby County	W	3	1	(1 1)	10,000	4	McColl, Howie, Rutherford	1	2	6	4	5		7	8	9	10	11	3												6
7	10 Oct	H	**Manchester City**	W	1	0	(0 0)	19,730	2	Appleyard	1	2	6	4		5	7	8	9	10	11	3												7
8	17 Oct	A	Notts County	L	2	3	(1 2)	9,000	4	Templeton, Howie	1	2	6	4	5		7	8	9	10	11	3												8
9	24 Oct	H	**Sheffield United**	L	0	1	(0 1)	29,000	4		1	2	6	4	5		7	8	9		11	3		10										9
10	31 Oct	H	**Wolverhampton Wanderers**	W	3	0	(3 0)	18,000	4	Orr, Appleyard, Howie	1	3	6	4	5		7	8	9		11			10	2									10
11	07 Nov	A	Aston Villa	L	1	3	(0 3)	20,000	7	Templeton		3	6	4	8	5	10		9		11		1		2	7								11
12	14 Nov	H	**Middlesbrough**	W	2	1	(1 1)	28,000	6	Rutherford 2	1	3	6	4	5		7	8	9	10	11				2									12
13	21 Nov	A	Liverpool	L	0	1	(0 0)	9,000	6		1	3	6	4	5		7	8		10	11				2		9							13
14	28 Nov	H	**Bury**	W	3	2	(1 1)	8,000	6	Appleyard, Howie 2	1	6		4	5		7	8	9	10	11				2			3						14
15	05 Dec	A	Blackburn Rovers	L	0	4	(0 2)	8,000	7		1	6		4	5		7	8	9	10	11				2			3						15
16	12 Dec	H	**Nottingham Forest**	W	3	1	(2 1)	15,000	6	McColl, Appleyard, Howie	1	6		4	5		7	8	9	10	11				2			3						16
17	19 Dec	A	Sheffield Wednesday	D	1	1	(1 0)	10,000	6	McColl		6		4	5		7	8	9	10	11		1		2			3						17
18	25 Dec	A	Sheffield United	D	2	2	(0 1)	20,237	5	Appleyard, Howie	1	6		4	5		7	8	9	10	11				2			3						18
19	26 Dec	H	**Sunderland**	L	1	3	(0 2)	28,397	7	Rutherford	1	6		4	5		8		9	10	11				2			3	7					19
20	01 Jan	A	Sunderland	D	1	1	(0 0)	37,000	7	Orr		5		4	6		7		9	10	11		1	8	2			3						20
21	02 Jan	H	**West Bromwich Albion**	W	1	0	(0 0)	13,376	5	Orr		5		4	6		7		9	10	11		1	8	2			3						21
22	09 Jan	A	Small Heath	L	0	3	(0 2)	8,000	7			5		4	6		7		9	10	11		1	8	2			3						22
23	16 Jan	H	**Everton**	W	1	0	(0 0)	16,000	5	Appleyard		5		4	6		7	8	9	10	11		1		2			3						23
24	23 Jan	A	Stoke	W	3	2	(2 0)	8,000	5	McColl, Appleyard 2		5		4	6		7	8	9	10	11		1		2			3						24
25	30 Jan	H	**Derby County**	D	0	0	(0 0)	16,000	6					4	6	5	7	8	9	10	11		1		2			3						25
26	13 Feb	H	**Notts County**	W	4	1	(1 0)	16,000	5	Orr 2, Appleyard, Howie		5		4	6		7	8	9		11		1	10				3		2				26
27	27 Feb	A	Wolverhampton Wanderers	L	2	3	(0 1)	5,000	6	McColl, Howie		5	6	4	9		7	8		10	11	3	1							2				27
28	12 Mar	A	Middlesbrough	W	3	1	(3 1)	15,000	5	Appleyard, Howie, Rutherford		5	2	4	6		7	8	9		11		1	10				3						28
29	19 Mar	H	**Liverpool**	D	1	1	(1 1)	20,000	4	Howie		5	3	4	6		7	8		9	11		1	10						2				29
30	26 Mar	A	Bury	W	3	0	(1 0)	2,570	4	Orr 2, Appleyard		5	3	4	6		7	8	9		11		1	10						2				30
31	01 Apr	A	Manchester City	W	3	1	(1 1)	25,000	2	Orr, Appleyard, Howie		5	3	4	6		7	8	9				1	10						2	11			31
32	02 Apr	H	**Blackburn Rovers**	W	2	1	(1 0)	20,000	2	Orr, Veitch		5	2	4	6		7	8	9				1	10				3			11			32
33	09 Apr	A	Nottingham Forest	L	0	1	(0 0)	10,000	2				6	4	10	5		8	9	11			1					3				2	7	33
34	16 Apr	H	**Sheffield Wednesday**	W	4	0	(3 0)	26,000	4	Orr 2, Appleyard 2		5	3	4	6		7	8	9		11		1	10						2				34
Round			**FA Cup**																																**Round**
1	06 Feb	A	Bury	L	1	2	(1 1)	12,635		Templeton		5		4	6		7	8	9		11		1	10	2			3						1

DateLine ... 10 Oct: A 1-0 victory over Manchester City takes United into second place in Division One. **26 March:** A 3-0 victory at Gigg Lane against Bury sets up United's late Championship bid. **9 April:** A defeat against Nottingham Forest halts the Magpies title charge. **7 May:** United's first fixture on foreign soil; a 6-1 exhibition game against a Copenhagen XI in Denmark.

SEASON
1904-05
DIVISION 1

Champions and almost the double

After only six years since joining England's top-tier, Newcastle were now ready to claim the top prize. Indeed the Black'n'Whites failed by a whisker to claim the coveted double of Championship and FA Cup. United were now recognised as a new force to be reckoned with. They reached the top of the table as winter approached following a run of 10 victories out of 11 fixtures played including a record seven wins in a row. Newcastle joined a race for the title trophy with Everton and Manchester City. With Everton and City meeting each other – City winning – a two-horse race was left on the season's climax at the end of April. The title was settled on the last day of the season, this after United had been felled by arch rivals Sunderland at St James' Park. But the Geordies bounced back in their final two away games. Winning first at Sheffield Wednesday, they needed another success in the Tyne-Tees derby at Ayresome Park to have a chance of the Championship crown for the first time. With closest rivals Manchester City losing at Villa, United cruised home with a convincing 3-0 victory. Ronald Orr netted the opener then Jack Rutherford hit a beauty before Bill Appleyard wrapped up the title with a third goal. Newcastle claimed a well earned triumph and lifted the Championship by a single point.

Newcastle reached the FA Cup final after two difficult ties of five games with Plymouth then Tottenham. With a semi-final victory over Sheffield Wednesday, the Black'n'Whites faced Aston Villa at the national stadium in London, The Crystal Palace – an arena which was to prove something of a jinx ground for the Geordies. The biggest crowd ever to watch the Magpies congregated at the Palace – over 101,000 – and witnessed a fine tussle. But it was Villa who had the edge, claiming the trophy by a single goal from centre-forward Harry Hampton.

Pictured above: Bert Gosnell appeared for England and was one of the unsung heroes of United's success.

JOHN PIGGOTT.
117, CHEAPSIDE, AND MILK STREET, E.C.
NOTHING BETTER THAN
John Piggott's Cup Tie Football 9/8
HIT OF THE SEASON.
John Piggott's Surrey Driver Bat 15/9

SCOTCH WHISKY,
"BERTRAM BLEND."
EIGHT YEARS OLD.

MANFIELD'S
BOOTS.
WHITE CRICKET BOOTS
THE "M" CYCLING SHOES

WELCOME ALWAYS,
KEEP IT HANDY,
GRANT'S MORELLA
CHERRY BRANDY.
The best Tonic for Football Players

OFFICIAL PROGRAMME.
Great Association Football Match
FINAL TIE
ASTON VILLA
NEWCASTLE UNITED
At the CRYSTAL PALACE,
ON SATURDAY APRIL 15.

POSITIONS IN THE FIELD
ASTON VILLA
George
Spencer Miles
Pearson Leake Windmill or (Wilkes)
Brown Garraty Hampton Bache Hall
Gosnell Veitch Appleyard Howie Rutherford
McWilliam Aitken Gardner
Carr McCombie
Lawrence
NEWCASTLE UNITED

ELLIMAN'S FOR BRUISES
ACHES AND PAINS.
1d. ARE YOU A FOOTBALLER? 1d.
SPORTS
IS THE PAPER YOU WANT.

CARTERS GRASS SEEDS
HIGH HOLBORN, LONDON.

The FA Cup final programme from the tie with Aston Villa, United first showpiece final.

IN CHARGE

Chairman: John Cameron
Manager: Director Committee
Captain: Andy Aitken
Trainer/Coach: James McPherson

ST JAMES' PARK

Average Attendance
Lg 21,950 Lg & Cup 22,541

Newcastle's FA Cup final line-up. Left to right: McPherson (trainer), McWilliam, Rutherford, Howie, Gardner, Aitken, Veitch (with ball), Lawrence, Appleyard, McCombie, Carr, Gosnell, Watt (secretary). Note 'keeper Jimmy Lawrence wore a striped shirt.

SEASON REVIEW

Football League Div 1: P34 W23 D2 L9 F72 A33 Pts 48.
Position: 1st, Champions.
FA Cup: Finalist (Winners; Aston Villa).

Appearances (42m): Gardner Alec 40, Howie J 39, McCombie A 39, Lawrence J 37, Aitken A 36, Rutherford J 36, Carr J 35, McWilliam P 34, Appleyard W 33, Gosnell AA 33, Veitch CCM 28, Orr R 26, McCracken WR 13, Templeton RB 10, McClarence JP 8, Graham S 4, Watts C 4, McIntyre EP 2, Wills T 2, Crumley RJ 1, Innerd W 1, Thompson GA 1.

Goals (84g): Howie J 17, Appleyard W 15, Orr R 14, Rutherford J 10, Veitch CCM 10, Gosnell AA 6, McClarence JP 4, McWilliam P 4, Aitken A 2, Gardner Alec 1, own goal 1.

Dismissals: 0 players.

MAJOR SIGNINGS

Bill McCracken (Distillery) £50
Bert Gosnell (Chatham)
Jimmy Lawrence (Glasgow Perthshire)

FROM THE RANKS

Joe McClarence (Wallsend Park Villa)
Bob Crumley (Lochee Utd)

PLAYER FOCUS Jimmy Howie

Born Galston. Inside-right, 5'10"
1903 to 1910: 237 app 82 goals.

Every great side needs playmakers, the men to create everything going forward. Newcastle United had two of the finest during the years before World War One; Peter McWilliam and Jimmy Howie. Both hailed from north of the border and Ayrshire-born Howie arrived at St James' Park by way of Bristol Rovers for a £300 fee in May 1903. Having started his career with Kilmarnock where he won the Scottish Division Two crown, Howie was tempted to move into Southern League football where he impressed Newcastle's scouts. Known as Gentleman Jim during the period, Howie oozed class, had poise on the ball with the flair go past opponents and craft a chance. Possessing a somewhat distinctive and unique hopping-running action, Jimmy soon became an influential player in England's top level and was capped by his country on three occasions. Always able to score himself, he formed a match-winning partnership with Rutherford on the right of United's team formation and was a member of three title winning sides for the Black'n'Whites while Jimmy also played in four FA Cup finals, a victor in 1910. He was top scorer with 17 goals as the Magpies went close to the double in 1905 and scored Newcastle's first ever goal in a FA Cup final, against Wolves, in 1908. The Scot later pulled on the shirt of Huddersfield Town before moving into management as boss of Queens Park Rangers and Middlesbrough during the Twenties. A younger relation, David, was on United's books just before World War One and turned out in senior action for Bradford Park Avenue.

TEAM COLOURS Black & white striped shirts, dark shorts (Change; white shirts, dark shorts)

SEASON 1904-05

Match	Date		FL Division 1					Posn		Watts	McCracken	McCombie	Gardner	Aitken	Carr	Rutherford	Howie	Appleyard	Orr	Templeton	Veitch	McWilliam	Lawrence	Gosnell	Graham	McClarence	Wills	Innerd	McIntyre	Crumley	Thompson	Match
1	03 Sep	H	**Woolwich Arsenal**	W	3 0	(1 0)	21,897		Orr 2, Rutherford	1	2	3	4	5	6	7	8	9	10	11												1
2	10 Sep	A	Derby County	D	1 1	(1 0)	12,000	6	Appleyard	1	2	3	4	5	6	7	8	9	10	11												2
3	17 Sep	H	**Everton**	W	3 2	(2 1)	21,000	6	Veitch 2, Rutherford	1	2	3	4	5	6	7	8			11	9	10										3
4	24 Sep	A	Small Heath	L	1 2	(1 2)	15,000	7	Veitch	1	2	3	4	5	6	7	8	9		11	10											4
5	01 Oct	H	**Manchester City**	W	2 0	(2 0)	20,971	4	Veitch, Appleyard		3	2	4	5		7	8	9		11	10	6	1									5
6	08 Oct	A	Notts County	W	3 0	(1 0)	10,000	3	Howie, Rutherford 2		2	3	4	5		7	8	9		11	10	6	1									6
7	15 Oct	H	**Sheffield United**	D	1 1	(1 0)	23,263	3	Howie		2	3	4	5		7	8	9		11	10	6	1									7
8	22 Oct	A	Stoke	L	0 1	(0 1)	10,000	5			2	3	4	5		7	8	9	10	11	6		1									8
9	29 Oct	A	Preston North End	L	0 1	(0 0)	13,000	7			2	3	4	5	6	7	8		10	11	9		1									9
10	05 Nov	H	**Middlesbrough**	W	3 0	(1 0)	23,262	7	Orr, Howie, Rutherford			2	4	5	3	7	8		10		9	6	1	11								10
11	12 Nov	A	Wolverhampton Wanderers	W	3 1	(0 0)	6,000	5	Howie 2, Orr			2	4	5	3	7	8	9	10			6	1	11								11
12	19 Nov	H	**Bury**	W	3 1	(1 0)	18,262	3	Gosnell, Appleyard, Veitch			2	4	5	3	7		9	10		8	6	1	11								12
13	26 Nov	A	Aston Villa	W	1 0	(1 0)	13,000	3	Appleyard			2	4	5	3			9	10	7	8	6	1	11								13
14	03 Dec	H	**Blackburn Rovers**	W	1 0	(1 0)	20,000	1	McClarence			2	4		3		8	9			5	6	1	11	7	10						14
15	10 Dec	A	Nottingham Forest	W	3 1	(2 1)	10,000	1	Gosnell, Appleyard, Veitch			2	4		3	7	8	9	10		5	6	1	11								15
16	17 Dec	H	**Sheffield Wednesday**	W	6 2	(2 0)	18,000	1	Orr, Appleyard, Howie, Rutherford 2, McWilliam			2	4		3	7	8	9	10		5	6	1	11								16
17	24 Dec	A	Sunderland	L	1 3	(1 2)	29,500	1	McWilliam			2	4		3	7	8	9	10		5	6	1	11								17
18	31 Dec	A	Woolwich Arsenal	W	2 0	(0 0)	30,000	3	Rutherford, Veitch			2	4		3	7	8	9	10		5	6	1	11								18
19	02 Jan	H	**Notts County**	W	1 0	(0 0)	18,000	1	Orr		3	2	4	5		7	8	9	10			6	1	11								19
20	07 Jan	H	**Derby County**	W	2 0	(2 0)	20,000	1	Veitch, Gardner			2	4	5	3	7	8	9			10	6	1	11								20
21	14 Jan	A	Everton	L	1 2	(1 0)	27,000	1	Howie			2	4	5	3	7	8	9				6	1	11	10							21
22	21 Jan	H	**Small Heath**	L	0 1	(0 1)	24,000	1				2	4	5	3	7	8	9	10			6	1	11								22
23	28 Jan	A	Manchester City	L	2 3	(2 2)	35,000	4	Howie 2			2	4	5	3	7	8	9	10			6	1	11								23
24	11 Feb	A	Sheffield United	W	3 1	(0 0)	15,000	3	Gosnell, McClarence, og (Groves)			2	4	5	3		8		10		7	6	1	11		9						24
25	25 Feb	H	**Preston North End**	W	1 0	(1 0)	20,000	2	Appleyard			2	4	5		7	8	9	10			6	1	11			3					25
26	11 Mar	H	**Wolverhampton Wanderers**	W	3 0	(1 0)	20,000	3	Appleyard, Rutherford, McWilliam			2	4	5	3	7	8	9				6	1	11		10						26
27	18 Mar	A	Bury	W	4 2	(2 1)	14,216	2	Appleyard 3, Aitken			2	4	5	3	7	8	9			10	6	1	11								27
28	01 Apr	A	Blackburn Rovers	L	0 2	(0 1)	6,000	3			2		5		3	7		9					1	11	8	10		4	6			28
29	05 Apr	H	**Aston Villa**	W	2 0	(1 0)	25,000	2	Veitch, Appleyard			2	4	5	3	7	8	9			10	6	1	11								29
30	08 Apr	H	**Nottingham Forest**	W	5 1	(2 0)	22,000	2	Gosnell, McClarence, Howie 2, Aitken			2	4	5	3	7	8				10	6	1	11		9						30
31	21 Apr	H	**Stoke**	W	4 1	(4 0)	25,000	2	Orr 2, McClarence, Howie		2		4	5	3	7	8		10		6		1	11		9						31
32	22 Apr	H	**Sunderland**	L	1 3	(1 2)	32,493	3	Veitch			2	4	5	3	7	8	9			10	6	1	11								32
33	26 Apr	A	Sheffield Wednesday	W	3 1	(0 1)	12,000	2	Orr (pen), Howie, McWilliam			2		5		7	8	9	10		6	4		11			3			1		33
34	29 Apr	A	Middlesbrough	W	3 0	(1 0)	12,000	1	Orr, Appleyard, Rutherford		2			5	3	7	8	9	10		6		1	11					4			34
Round			**FA Cup**																													**Round**
1	04 Feb	H	**Plymouth Argyle**	D	1 1	(1 1)	28,385		Gosnell			2	4	5	3		8	9	10			6	1	11	7							1
1r	08 Feb	A	Plymouth Argyle	De	1 1	(1 1)	17,641		Gosnell			2	4	5	3		8		10			6	1	11		9					7	1r
1rr	13 Feb	N1	Plymouth Argyle	W	2 0	(1 0)	11,570		Orr 2 (1 pen)			2	4	5	3		8		10		7	6	1	11		9						1rr
2	18 Feb	A	Tottenham Hotspur	D	1 1	(1 0)	19,013		Howie			2	4	5	3	7	8		10		9	6	1	11								2
2r	22 Feb	H	**Tottenham Hotspur**	W	4 0	(2 0)	26,755		Orr 2, Appleyard, Howie			2	4	5	3	7	8	9	10			6	1	11								2r
3	04 Mar	A	Bolton Wanderers	W	2 0	(1 0)	35,574		Appleyard, Howie			2	4	5	3	7	8	9	10			6	1	11								3
SF	25 Mar	N2	Sheffield Wednesday	W	1 0	(1 0)	40,000		Howie			2	4	5	3	7	8	9			10	6	1	11								SF
F	15 Apr	N3	Aston Villa	L	0 2	(0 1)	101,117					2	4	5	3	7	8	9			10	6	1	11								F

N1 Played at Manor Ground, Plumstead, London
N2 Played at Hyde Road, Manchester
N3 Played at Crystal Palace, London

De Drawn after extra time

DateLine ... 3 Sept: Bill McCracken pulls on United's senior shirt for the first time against Arsenal. **1 Oct:** Jimmy Lawrence makes his debut against Manchester City, the first of a record 496 appearances. **15 April:** A crowd of 101,117 watches Newcastle's first FA Cup final at the Crystal Palace, the largest to see United. **22 April:** A record crowd on Tyneside of 32,493 watch the derby with Sunderland at St James' Park. **29 April:** United clinch the title with a 3-0 victory at Middlesbrough.

SEASON
1905-06
DIVISION 1

The Palace jinx takes hold

The Magpies were rapidly developing into the team of the era with what would be recognised as a celebrated line-up in football's history – and one which displayed an attractive style of football. Yet, they did have an Achilles heel, that of The Crystal Palace in South London. Set in vast parkland with boating lakes and an imposing backdrop of the famous glass palace itself, United never liked playing at the picturesque Sydenham arena. In the 1905 FA Cup final they failed, a year later in 1906 the Black'n'Whites returned and failed again, this time to Everton. And they were to find the surroundings of the Palace cast its spell on United in the future too. Newcastle started the Cup run with an emphatic 6-0 triumph over Grimsby while they also hammered Blackpool 5-0 before taking care of Arsenal in the semi-final. United were hot favourites to claim the FA Cup in 1906. Against their Merseyside rivals from Goodison Park – formidable opponents to the Magpies in this era – much was expected in the showpiece final. But the game was a total let down and far from the hoped season's showpiece. Everton triumphed by a single goal from Sandy Young in a drab contest.

United again challenged for the Football League title that season. They were on the fringe of the race for most of the campaign but fell short of Liverpool by some way as the FA Cup took over their focus. During a hot-spot of form in which six victories in a row were recorded, United did hammer Wolves 8-0 during November to equal the club's record scoreline.

During the season a substantially remodelled St James' Park was opened in September against Manchester City, now with a far bigger capacity of over 60,000. And with gates now approaching that level for big matches, that made United an affluent and extremely prosperous club, one of the richest in the country.

Pictured above: Sandy Higgins hailed from a footballing family. He was a versatile forward capped by the Scots.

Memorabilia CORNER

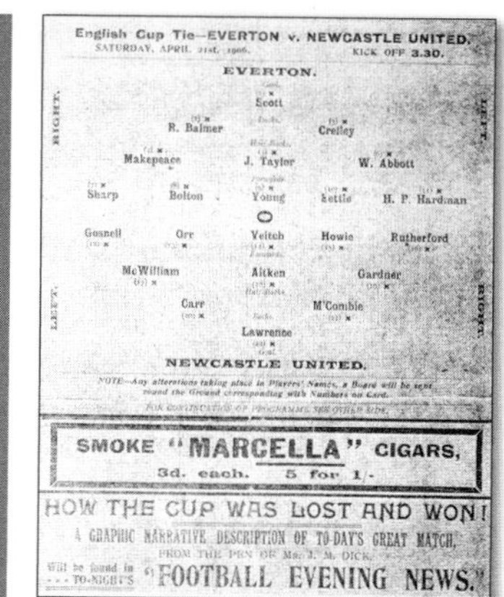
English Cup Tie—EVERTON v. NEWCASTLE UNITED.
SATURDAY, APRIL 21st, 1906. KICK OFF 3.30.

EVERTON.

Scott

R. Balmer, Crelley

Makepeace, J. Taylor, W. Abbott

Sharp, Bolton, Young, Settle, H. P. Hardman

Gosnell, Orr, Veitch, Howie, Rutherford

McWilliam, Aitken, Gardner

Carr, M'Combie

Lawrence

NEWCASTLE UNITED.

SMOKE "MARCELLA" CIGARS, 3d. each. 5 for 1/-

HOW THE CUP WAS LOST AND WON!
A GRAPHIC NARRATIVE DESCRIPTION OF TO-DAY'S GREAT MATCH,
FROM THE PEN OF Mr. J. M. DICK,
Will be found in TO-NIGHT'S "FOOTBALL EVENING NEWS."

FA Cup final programme from The Crystal Palace.

IN CHARGE

Chairman: John Cameron
Manager: Director Committee
Captain: Alec Gardner
Trainer/Coach: James McPherson

ST JAMES' PARK

Average Attendance
Lg 23,557 Lg & Cup 24,912

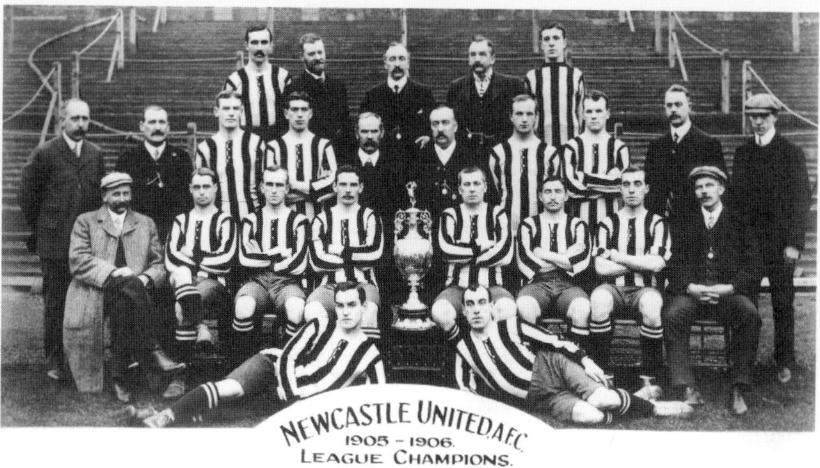

United proudly show off the Football League Championship trophy at the start of the 1905-06 season.

PLAYER FOCUS Ronald Orr

Born Bartonholm. Inside-forward, 5'5"
1901 to 1908: 180 app 70 goals.

Very much one of United's unsung heroes of the Edwardian era, Ronald Orr appeared for the Magpies over six seasons at inside-right or inside-left. Another to hail from the Ayrshire football hotbed, Orr was small and stocky; he was very effective despite never becoming one of the crowd favourites. Having made a name with St Mirren in the Scottish League, Newcastle brought him to Tyneside in a joint deal with full-back Bob Bennie during May 1901. Orr could pack a stinging drive and reached Scotland recognition during seasons 1901-02 and 1903-04. Described as clever and constructive with an unselfish approach, he once netted four goals for the Magpies against Notts County, won two Football League Championship medals and pulled on the Toon's shirt in the 1906 FA Cup final. Ronald fed off the bustling approach of Bill Appleyard well and despite his size, was good in the air too. However, for a time at Gallowgate he was somewhat unfairly singled out by the boo-boys when performances dipped and he left Tyneside after a period of barracking. Orr moved to Liverpool in April 1908 where he quickly made the Magpies suffer by striking four goals against his former club. He enhanced his reputation in over 100 games for the Reds, being a runner-up in the title race in 1909-10. Ronald ended his career with Raith Rovers then back on Tyneside with South Shields before World War One.

SEASON REVIEW

Football League Div 1: P38 W18 D7 L13 F74 A48 Pts 43.
Position: 4th (Champions; Liverpool).
FA Cup: Finalist (Winners; Everton).

Appearances (46m): Gosnell AA 43, Orr R 42, Rutherford J 42, Lawrence J 41, McWilliam P 38, Howie J 37, McCombie A 37, Gardner Alec 36, Veitch CCM 36, Carr J 31, Appleyard W 26, McCracken WR 20, Aitken A 19, McClarence JP 13, Hardinge HTW 9, Kirkaldy JW 8, Tildesley J 5, Raine JE 4, Crumley RJ 3, Higgins A 3, Donnachie J 2, Findlay J 2, Liddell R 2, Blake S 1, Bolton H 1, Dodds JT 1, Rowlandson TS 1, Rutherford RE 1, Watts C 1, Whitson TT 1.

Goals (94g): Orr R 21, Appleyard W 17, Howie J 14, Rutherford J 11, Veitch CCM 10, Gosnell AA 9, McClarence JP 5, McWilliam P 2, Gardner Alec 1, Hardinge HTW 1, Higgins A 1, Raine JE 1, own goal 1.

Dismissals: 0 players.

MAJOR SIGNINGS

Sandy Higgins (Kilmarnock) £250
Joe Donnachie (Morton)

FROM THE RANKS

'Tony' Whitson (Walker Parish)
Harry Hardinge (Maidstone Utd)
John Findlay (Knibshill Utd)
John Dodds (Hexham Star)
Sid Blake (Whitley Ath)
James Kirkcaldy (Northern Temperance)
Bob Liddell (Westwood)
James Raine (Scotswood/Univ football)

TEAM COLOURS Black & white striped shirts, dark shorts (Change; white shirts, dark shorts)

SEASON 1905-06

Match	Date		FL Division 1	Res	F	A	HT	Att	Posn	Scorers
1	02 Sep	A	Sunderland	L	2	3	(1 1)	30,000		Orr, Howie,
2	06 Sep	H	**Manchester City**	D	2	2	(1 1)	20,000	12	Gosnell, Orr
3	09 Sep	H	**Birmingham**	D	2	2	(1 0)	23,912	13	Orr, Howie
4	13 Sep	H	**Sheffield Wednesday**	L	0	3	(0 1)	20,000	14	
5	16 Sep	A	Everton	W	2	1	(1 1)	16,000	10	Orr, Howie
6	23 Sep	H	**Derby County**	L	0	1	(0 0)	31,600	11	
7	30 Sep	A	Sheffield Wednesday	D	1	1	(1 0)	16,000	15	McClarence
8	07 Oct	H	**Nottingham Forest**	W	3	2	(2 1)	15,000	12	Orr, McClarence, Howie
9	21 Oct	H	**Bury**	W	3	1	(2 0)	20,000	11	Orr, Appleyard, Veitch
10	28 Oct	H	**Middlesbrough**	W	4	1	(2 0)	35,000	7	Appleyard 3, McWilliam
11	04 Nov	H	**Preston North End**	W	1	0	(1 0)	28,000	6	Howie
12	11 Nov	H	**Wolverhampton Wanderers**	W	8	0	(5 0)	15,000	4	Orr 2, Appleyard 3, Howie 2, Veitch (pen),
13	18 Nov	A	Aston Villa	W	3	0	(2 0)	30,000	3	Orr 2, Veitch
14	25 Nov	H	**Liverpool**	L	2	3	(1 1)	32,000	5	Orr, McWilliam
15	02 Dec	A	Sheffield United	L	0	2	(0 1)	13,980	6	
16	09 Dec	H	**Notts County**	W	3	1	(1 0)	17,073	5	Appleyard, Rutherford J, Veitch
17	16 Dec	A	Stoke	L	0	1	(0 1)	8,000	8	
18	23 Dec	H	**Bolton Wanderers**	W	2	1	(2 0)	20,000	6	Orr, McClarence
19	25 Dec	A	Woolwich Arsenal	L	3	4	(3 4)	20,000	8	Howie 2, Rutherford J
20	26 Dec	A	Manchester City	W	4	1	(3 1)	35,000	5	Gosnell, McClarence, Rutherford J, Veitch (pen)
21	30 Dec	H	**Sunderland**	D	1	1	(1 1)	56,000	5	Orr
22	01 Jan	A	Blackburn Rovers	L	0	1	(0 0)	30,000	8	
23	06 Jan	A	Birmingham	W	1	0	(0 0)	8,000	6	Gosnell
24	20 Jan	H	**Everton**	W	4	2	(2 0)	22,000	5	Orr, Appleyard, Howie, Rutherford J
25	27 Jan	A	Derby County	L	1	2	(1 1)	7,000	5	McClarence
26	10 Feb	A	Nottingham Forest	L	1	2	(1 1)	7,000	7	Gosnell
27	03 Mar	A	Middlesbrough	L	0	1	(0 0)	20,000	11	
28	17 Mar	A	Wolverhampton Wanderers	W	2	0	(0 0)	9,000	9	Gosnell, Rutherford J
29	24 Mar	H	**Aston Villa**	W	3	1	(3 0)	16,000	8	Gosnell, Orr, Rutherford J
30	04 Apr	H	**Sheffield United**	W	2	1	(2 1)	20,000	10	Appleyard, Hardinge
31	09 Apr	A	Liverpool	L	0	3	(0 0)	18,000	11	
32	13 Apr	A	Bury	W	4	1	(1 1)	19,354	6	Gosnell, Veitch (pen), Howie, Rutherford J
33	14 Apr	A	Notts County	L	0	1	(0 0)	18,000	9	
34	16 Apr	H	**Woolwich Arsenal**	D	1	1	(1 1)	20,000	9	Orr
35	24 Apr	H	**Stoke**	W	5	0	(1 0)	12,000	7	Orr, Howie, Rutherford J 2, Veitch
36	26 Apr	A	Preston North End	D	0	0	(0 0)	5,000	5	
37	28 Apr	A	Bolton Wanderers	D	1	1	(1 1)	12,000	5	Appleyard
38	30 Apr	H	**Blackburn Rovers**	W	3	0	(3 0)	24,000	4	Gosnell, Higgins, Raine
Round			**FA Cup**							
1	13 Jan	H*	**Grimsby Town**	W	6	0	(2 0)	23,672		Gosnell, Orr 2, Appleyard 2, Rutherford J
2	03 Feb	A	Derby County	D	0	0	(0 0)	18,000		
2r	07 Feb	H	**Derby County**	W	2	1	(2 0)	28,257		Appleyard, Rutherford J
3	24 Feb	H	**Blackpool**	W	5	0	(2 0)	34,405		Orr 2, Appleyard, Gardner, og (Crewdson)
4	10 Mar	A	Birmingham	D	2	2	(0 2)	25,000		Veitch 2 (1 pen)
4r	14 Mar	H	**Birmingham**	We	3	0	(0 0)	39,059		Appleyard 2, Howie
SF	31 Mar	N1	Woolwich Arsenal	W	2	0	(1 0)	19,964		Veitch, Howie
F	21 Apr	N2	Everton	L	0	1	(0 0)	75,609		

Match	Lawrence	McCombie	Carr	Gardner	Aitken	Veitch	Rutherford J	Howie	Hardinge	Orr	Gosnell	Appleyard	McWilliam	Donnachie	McCracken	Crumley	McClarence	Rowlandson	Bolton	Tildesley	Findlay	Raine	Liddell	Kirkaldy	Higgins	Rutherford RE	Watts	Whitson	Blake	Dodds
1	1	2	3	4	5	6	7	8	9	10	11																			
2	1	2	3	4	5	6	7	8		10	11	9																		
3	1	2	3	4	5		7	8		10		9	6	11																
4	1		3	4	5		7	8		10		9	6	11	2															
5	1	3		4		5	7	8	9	10	11		6		2															
6		3		4		5	7	8	9	10	11		6		2	1														
7		3		4		5	7	8		10	11		6		2	1	9													
8		3		4		5	7	8		10	11		6		2	1	9													
9		3		4		5	7	8		10	11	9	6		2			1												
10	1	3		4		5	7	8		10	11	9	6		2															
11	1	3	6	4		5	7	8		10	11	9			2															
12	1	3		4		5	7	8		10	11	9	6		2															
13	1	3		4		5	7	8		10	11	9	6		2															
14	1	3		4		5	7			10	11	9	6		2		8													
15	1	3		4		5	7			10	11	9	6		2				8											
16	1		3	4		5	7	8		10	11	9	6							2										
17	1	3		4		5	7	8		10	11		6				9			2										
18	1	3				5	7	8		10	11		6				9			2	4									
19	1	3		4		5	7	8		10	11		6				9			2										
20	1	2	3	4		5	7	8		10	11		6				9													
21	1	2	3	8	4	5	7			10	11		6				9													
22	1	2	3	4		5	7		8	10	11		6				9													
23	1	2	3	4		5	7	8		10	11		6				9													
24	1	2	3		4	5	7	8		10	11	9	6																	
25	1		3	4	5		7	8		10	11		6				9			2										
26	1	2	3		4	5	7	8		10	11		6				9													
27	1	2	3	4		5		8		10	11	9	6									7								
28	1		3		5		7	8	9		11		6		2		10						4							
29	1	2		4	5		7			10	11	9			3									6	8					
30	1		3	5			7		8	10	11	9			2						4			6						
31	1		3	4			10		8		11	9			2							7		6		5				
32	1	2	3	4	5	9	7	8		10	11		6																	
33					5			8	7	10		9	4		2									6			1	3	11	
34	1	2	3		5				9	10	11		6		4							7								8
35	1	2	3			5	7	8		10	11	9	4											6						
36	1	2	3		4	5	7	8		10	11	9												6						
37	1		3		5		7	8			11	9	4		2									6	10					
38	1		3			5				10	11	9			2							7	4	6	8					
Round																														
1	1	2	3	4		5	7	8		10	11	9	6																	
2	1	2	3	4		5	7	8		10	11	9	6																	
2r	1	2	3	4		5	7	8		10	11	9	6																	
3	1	2	3	4		5	7	8		10	11	9	6																	
4	1	2	3	4	5	9	7	8		10	11		6																	
4r	1	2	3	4	5	10	7	8			11	9	6																	
SF	1	2	3	4	5	9	7	8		10	11		6																	
F	1	2	3	4	5	9	7	8		10	11		6																	

H* Scheduled for Grimsby, but played at Newcastle by agreement

N1 Played at Victoria Ground, Stoke

N2 Played at Crystal Palace, London

We Won after extra time

DateLine ... 6 Sept: A remodelled and enlarged St James' Park is formally opened against Manchester City. **11 Nov:** The Magpies equal their record victory with eight goals against Wolves. **30 Dec:** A new home record attendance established of 56,000 against Sunderland. **21 April:** United lose their second FA Cup final at The Crystal Palace, 1-0 to Everton.

NEWCASTLE UNITED

SEASON
1906-07
DIVISION 1

Masters make their mark

A pattern developed in the Edwardian era; a season with sights on the FA Cup followed by a determined bid to land the Championship trophy. It was as if United's Cup final disappointments spurred on the players to secure title silverware. In season 1906-07 it was the turn of the League trophy and United started with a bang, a 4-2 derby victory over Sunderland at Gallowgate – all in sweltering heat recorded at over 90 degrees Fahrenheit. A new record crowd at St James' Park was established at that match. A gate of 56,875 watched the sun-drenched derby. The Geordies were dominant throughout the programme, consistent and classy. They took the top position following a 5-0 triumph over Manchester United and stayed leading the following pack of Sheffield United, Bristol City and Everton. It was City who posed the biggest threat, yet United won 3-0 in an important clash at the end of March. Two goals from often match-winner Jack Rutherford guided United to a convincing victory.

Newcastle won every home League game – bar one – the last fixture at St James' Park of the campaign against Sheffield United. By then the Magpies were just about home and dry and the point secured silverware. The title victory reinforced the club's growing stature. They were now recognised as the finest side in the country.

United's FA Cup year was not without its headlines. Newcastle were paired with Crystal Palace of all clubs, then in the Southern League, a team bristling with North East connections. At St James' Park the non-leaguers fought like the proverbial minnows and sensationally won 1-0 – United's only defeat on Tyneside all season. Few Champions-elect in the whole of history have been dumped out of the Cup in such circumstances. It just added to the curious influence the Crystal Palace had over Newcastle United.

Pictured above: To appear in seven different roles for United, Finlay Speedie was highly respected.

Memorabilia CORNER

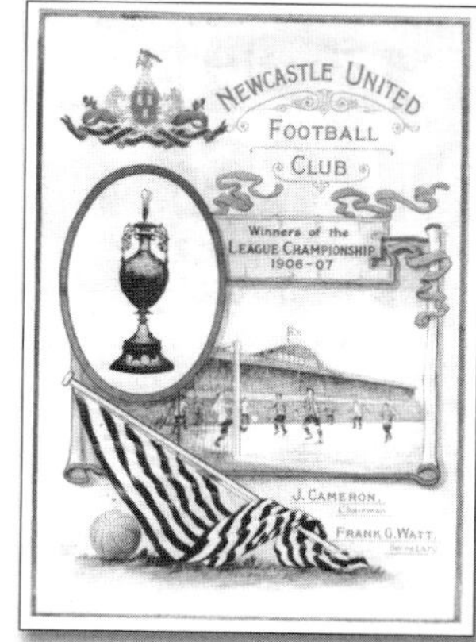

United's 1907 title winning party celebrated with a grand dinner on Tyneside, this menu-card survives.

IN CHARGE

Chairman: John Cameron
Manager: Director Committee
Captain: Alec Gardner
Trainer/Coach: James McPherson

ST JAMES' PARK

Average Attendance
Lg 33,625 Lg & Cup 33,344

The Black'n'Whites are pictured with the Sheriff of London Charity Shield. Back row, left to right: McCombie, McWilliam (behind), McCracken, McPherson (trainer), Watt (secretary), Carr, Veitch (behind), Speedie. Sitting: Rutherford, Howie, Appleyard, Lawrence (on ground), Gardner (on ground), Orr, Brown, Gosnell.

PLAYER FOCUS Alec Gardner

Born Leith. Right-half, 5'8"
1899 to 1910: 314 app 26 goals.

The club's finest uncapped player of the period, and perhaps of all time, Alec Gardner deserved to play at international level. In midfield he commanded respect and in many games controlled the play, being the focal point, continually feeding United's playmakers. Although not one to have the touch of brilliance, he was though a model of consistency and Gardner made United tick. Impressing many scouts when with Leith Athletic, Newcastle's officials were quick to spot his talent and just before the new century in November 1899 had to endure the wrath of his club when they went on a raiding party to Scotland's capital. Despite being literally "chased" out of Leith, they had Gardner's agreement to join the Magpies. A fixture in the Magpies' eleven for almost a decade, a period in which he won three titles and played in three FA Cup finals, Alec was consistently good in midfield having the knack of keeping moves flowing and specialising in an accurate low direct pass. Although he was selected for Scotland trial matches, he was overlooked at international level. Handed the soubriquet of Punky, Gardner was captain of the Magpies. 'Alick' – as he signed his name – would have totalled many more games for the Magpies had it not been for a broken leg in 1909 sustained in an FA Cup-tie against Blackpool. Although he had a short spell with Blyth Spartans, that bad injury finished his career, afterwards becoming a well-known publican in the heart of Newcastle.

SEASON REVIEW

Football League Div 1: P38 W22 D7 L9 F74 A46 Pts 51.
Position: 1st, Champions.
FA Cup: R1 (Winners; Sheffield Wednesday).

Appearances (40m): Rutherford J 36, Gardner Alec 35, Lawrence J 35, McWilliam P 34, Howie J 33, Veitch CCM 30, Speedie FB 29, Gosnell AA 28, Carr J 27, McCombie A 27, Appleyard W 24, McCracken WR 24, Brown H 23, Orr R 20, Duffy CF 7, McClarence JP 5, Dodds JT 4, Aitken A 3, Blackburn R 3, Kirkaldy JW 3, Sinclair TS 3, Kelsey WJ 2, Higgins A 1, Jobey G 1, Liddell R 1, Nicholson B 1, Soye J 1.

Goals (79g): Appleyard W 18, Rutherford J 11, Brown H 10, Speedie FB 10, Howie J 7, Veitch CCM 7, Orr R 4, Gosnell AA 3, McClarence JP 2, McWilliam P 2, Duffy CF 1, Gardner Alec 1, Kirkaldy JW 1, McCracken WR 1, own goal 1.

Dismissals: 0 players.

MAJOR SIGNINGS

Finlay Speedie (Rangers) £600
Dick Pudan (Bristol Rovers) £150
Tom Sinclair (Rangers) £375
James Soye (Southampton)

FROM THE RANKS

George Jobey (Morpeth Harriers)
Ben Nicholson (Morpeth Harriers)
William Kelsey (Boldon Star)

TEAM COLOURS Black & white striped shirts, dark shorts (Change; white shirts, dark shorts)

SEASON 1906-07

Match			FL Division 1						Posn		Lawrence	McCombie	Carr	Aitken	Veitch	McWilliam	Rutherford	Howie	Appleyard	Orr	Gosnell	McCracken	Gardner	Kirkaldy	Blackburn	Higgins	Brown	Soye	Speedie	Dodds	McClarence	Duffy	Nicholson	Kelsey	Sinclair	Liddell	Jobey	Match
1	01 Sep	H	**Sunderland**	W	4	2	(1 0)	56,875		Appleyard, Howie, Rutherford 2	1	2	3	4	5	6	7	8	9	10	11																	1
2	03 Sep	A	Sheffield Wednesday	D	2	2	(2 1)	8,000	4	Appleyard 2	1		3		5				9	10	11	2	4	6	7	8												2
3	08 Sep	A	Birmingham	W	4	2	(3 2)	17,000	2	Brown 3, Veitch (pen)	1	2	3		5		7	8	9		11		4	6			10											3
4	15 Sep	H	**Everton**	W	1	0	(0 0)	38,000	3	McWilliam	1	2	3		5	6	7	8			11		4				10	9										4
5	22 Sep	A	Woolwich Arsenal	L	0	2	(0 1)	30,000	5		1		3		5	6	7	8	9	10	11	2	4															5
6	29 Sep	H	**Sheffield Wednesday**	W	5	1	(1 0)	40,000	3	Appleyard, Gosnell, Kirkaldy, Speedie 2	1		3			5	7		9		11	2	4	6			10		8									6
7	06 Oct	A	Bury	L	2	3	(1 1)	10,221	6	Appleyard, Veitch (pen)	1		3		6	5	7		9		11	2	4				10		8									7
8	13 Oct	H	**Manchester City**	W	2	0	(0 0)	20,000	6	Appleyard 2	1	3		5		6	7	8	9	10	11	2	4															8
9	20 Oct	A	Middlesbrough	W	3	0	(1 0)	17,000	4	Appleyard 3	1	2	3	4	5	6	7	8	9		11								10									9
10	27 Oct	H	**Preston North End**	W	2	1	(2 0)	30,000	2	Brown, Howie	1	2	3		5	6	7	8	9		11		4				10											10
11	03 Nov	A	Derby County	D	0	0	(0 0)	9,000	2		1	2			5	6	7	8	9			3	4				10			11								11
12	10 Nov	A	Aston Villa	D	0	0	(0 0)	30,000	2		1	2	3		5	6	7	8			11		4				10				9							12
13	17 Nov	H	**Liverpool**	W	2	0	(0 0)	36,000	2	Gardner, Speedie	1	2	3		5	6	7	8			11		4				9		10									13
14	24 Nov	A	Bristol City	L	1	2	(1 1)	25,000	4	Brown	1	2	3		5	6	7	8			11		4				9		10									14
15	01 Dec	H	**Notts County**	W	4	3	(3 1)	20,000	3	Appleyard 2, Speedie, Veitch	1		3		5	6	7		9	10	11	2	4						8									15
16	08 Dec	A	Sheffield United	D	0	0	(0 0)	16,000	3		1	2			5	6	7			10		3	4				9		8			11						16
17	15 Dec	H	**Bolton Wanderers**	W	4	0	(3 0)	22,000	2	McClarence, Orr, Speedie 2	1	2			5	6	7			10		3	4						8		9	11						17
18	22 Dec	A	Manchester United	W	3	1	(0 1)	18,000	2	Speedie, McClarence, Veitch (pen)	1	2			5	6	7	8			11	3	4						10		9							18
19	25 Dec	A	Blackburn Rovers	L	0	4	(0 3)	35,000	2		1	2	3		5	6	7	8			11		4						10		9							19
20	26 Dec	A	Stoke	W	2	1	(1 1)	10,000	2	Howie, Speedie	1	2	6		5	4	7	8		10	11	3							9									20
21	01 Jan	H	**Derby County**	W	2	0	(0 0)	30,000	2	Orr, Speedie	1		3		5	6	7	8		10	11	2	4						9									21
22	05 Jan	H	**Birmingham**	W	2	0	(1 0)	26,000	2	Rutherford 2	1	2			5	6	7	8		10		3	4				11		9									22
23	19 Jan	A	Everton	L	0	3	(0 1)	45,000	2		1		3		5	6	7			10		2	4				9		8			11						23
24	26 Jan	H	**Woolwich Arsenal**	W	1	0	(1 0)	35,000	2	Howie	1		3			6	7	8	9	10		2	4				11		5									24
25	02 Feb	H	**Manchester United**	W	5	0	(3 0)	35,000	1	Gosnell, Orr, Rutherford, Veitch 2	1		3		6		7	8	9	10	11	2	4						5									25
26	09 Feb	H	**Bury**	W	3	2	(0 1)	25,000	1	Brown, Howie, Rutherford	1	2			6		7	8	9		11	3	4				10		5									26
27	16 Feb	A	Manchester City	D	1	1	(0 0)	35,000	1	Brown	1	2				6		8					4		7		10		5	11	9		3					27
28	23 Feb	H	**Middlesbrough**	W	4	0	(2 0)	47,000	1	Appleyard 2, McWilliam, McCracken (pen)	1		3			6	7	8	9			2	4				10		5	11								28
29	02 Mar	A	Preston North End	D	2	2	(2 2)	12,000	1	Gosnell, Howie	1	2	3			6	7	8	9		11		4				10		5									29
30	16 Mar	H	**Aston Villa**	W	3	2	(3 1)	48,000	1	Appleyard 2, Rutherford	1		3		5	6	7	8	9		11	2	4				10											30
31	20 Mar	A	Sunderland	L	0	2	(0 0)	32,000	1			3				6	7	8	9		11	2	4				10		5					1				31
32	23 Mar	A	Liverpool	L	1	4	(0 4)	20,000	1	Brown		2			5	6	7	8		10	11		4				9		3					1				32
33	29 Mar	H	**Stoke**	W	1	0	(0 0)	30,000	1	Rutherford		3			6	5	7	8	9		11	2	4				10								1			33
34	30 Mar	H	**Bristol City**	W	3	0	(1 0)	40,000	1	Howie, Rutherford 2			3			6	7	8	9	10		2	4						5			11			1			34
35	01 Apr	H	**Blackburn Rovers**	W	3	1	(2 0)	30,000	1	Duffy, Appleyard, Speedie (pen)		2			5	6	7	8	9	10			4						3			11			1			35
36	06 Apr	A	Notts County	L	0	1	(0 0)	12,000	1		1	2	3					8	9	10			4		7				5			11				6		36
37	13 Apr	H	**Sheffield United**	D	0	0	(0 0)	30,000	1		1	2	3		4	6	7	8		10							9		5			11						37
38	20 Apr	A	Bolton Wanderers	L	2	4	(2 2)	5,000	1	Orr, Veitch	1	2	3		4			8	9	10	11								5	7							6	38
Round			FA Cup																																			Round
1	12 Jan	H	**Crystal Palace**	L	0	1	(0 1)	28,000			1	2			5	6	7	8		10	11	3	4						9									1
			Sheriff of London Charity Shield																																			CS
	09 Mar	N	Corinthians	W	5	2	(1 1)	30,000		Rutherford, Appleyard, Brown 2, og (Norris)	1		3			6	7	8	9		11	2	4				10		5									

N Played at Craven Cottage, Fulham

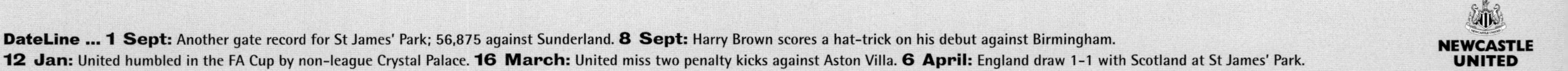

DateLine ... 1 Sept: Another gate record for St James' Park; 56,875 against Sunderland. **8 Sept:** Harry Brown scores a hat-trick on his debut against Birmingham. **12 Jan:** United humbled in the FA Cup by non-league Crystal Palace. **16 March:** United miss two penalty kicks against Aston Villa. **6 April:** England draw 1-1 with Scotland at St James' Park.

NEWCASTLE UNITED

SEASON
1907-08
DIVISION 1

Cup shock for the Black'n'Whites

Over the decades few clubs have been such hot-favourites to land the FA Cup as Newcastle United in 1908. At the peak of their ascendancy, they again reached the final in dominant form with four convincing home victories and 12 goals scored. Then in the semi-final they rocked Fulham by winning 6-0, still a record victory in that stage of the competition. United faced Division Two outfit Wolves, a side that finished in mid-table in football's second-tier. All judges considered the Magpies would lift the trophy. Yet remarkably they didn't. Wolves hustled and harried United and convincingly won 3-1. The defeat was a huge shock in football. Newcastle had performed way below their high standard and had lost their third final in only four years.

United again concluded the League programme in fourth spot, and at one stage were in second place challenging strongly with Manchester United, who earlier in the campaign during October had stunned Tyneside by defeating an off-colour Magpies 6-1 at Gallowgate. It was shock home reverse, but one to be sensationally exceeded during the following season. The Black'n'Whites did equal their best scoreline by walloping Birmingham the following month by 8-0, and they did take care of both Liverpool and Sunderland by scoring another nine goals soon after. In the final analysis though, United drew too many games – 12 – and at times looked weary when distracted by the FA Cup between late-January and the end of the season, winning only three of the 14 League fixtures. The season ended on a low. Apart from losing the Cup final, the concluding League fixtures also ended in defeat – to both Sunderland and Middlesbrough.

Newcastle spent heavily in the transfer market, notably unveiling a national record buy in Scottish winger George Wilson who arrived from Everton for a £1,600 fee.

Pictured above: Londoner Dick Pudan found a place at left-back, featured on this Sinclair cigarette-card.

Memorabilia CORNER

Football Association
Final Tie
.. Smoke ..
Lambert & Butler's
Waverley Cigarettes
3d. Per Packet of 10

It was back to the Crystal Palace in 1908, on this occasion yet another FA Cup final defeat.

IN CHARGE

Chairman: John Cameron
Manager: Director Committee
Captain: Alec Gardner
Trainer/Coach: James McPherson

ST JAMES' PARK

Average Attendance
Lg 28,895 Lg & Cup 31,682

A marvellously arranged staff group pictured in front of the West Stand. The six trophies are, left to right; Northumberland Senior Cup, Football League Championship, Sheriff of London Charity Shield, RVI Cup (foreground), Tynemouth Infirmary Cup, NE League Championship.

PLAYER FOCUS Bill Appleyard

Born Caistor. Centre-forward, 5'10"
1903 to 1908: 146 app 88 goals.

Big Bill Appleyard was a terror to goalkeepers in every sense of the word. A former North Sea fisherman from a family of 13 children, at over 14-stone he joined United in April 1903 from Grimsby Town for a near record fee that was said to be £700, but which was probably some way below that, noted by The Mariners at £350. He was a physical, full-bodied centre-forward who contrasted wonderfully well to the more skilful and elegant playmakers in the side. During the early part of Newcastle's Edwardian heyday, Appleyard was a highly effective striker. He was feared by 'keepers not only for his goal prowess, but also in an era when they were then largely unprotected by referees, for Bill's sometimes brute approach. Appleyard had little hesitation in banging into the goalie time and time again with his sizeable frame. A reserve for England, he had a potent shot, especially on his right. Nicknamed Cockles, Bill registered the club's first senior FA Cup hat-trick and helped win two League Championships for the Magpies, in 1905 and 1907. Appleyard also took part in two FA Cup finals in 1905 and 1908. Averaging more than a goal every second game, he was extremely popular with the Geordie fans, one of the heartiest in a long line of centre-forward heroes. When almost 30 years old, he left United in 1908 to join Oldham Athletic then moved back to Grimsby Town for second spell. Later Bill settled in Newcastle working and living in the city's West End.

SEASON REVIEW

Football League Div 1: P38 W15 D12 L11 F65 A54 Pts 42.
Position: 4th (Champions; Manchester United).
FA Cup: Finalist (Winners; Wolverhampton Wanderers).

Appearances (44m): Lawrence J 44, Gardner Alec 41, McWilliam P 36, Speedie FB 31, Appleyard W 29, Howie J 29, Veitch CCM 29, McCracken WR 27, Pudan AE 27, Rutherford J 25, Willis DL 23, Orr R 19, McCombie A 18, Wilson GW 18, Carr J 13, Higgins A 12, Duffy CF 9, Gosnell AA 8, Ridley J 7, Hall AN 6, McClarence JP 6, Soye J 6, Duncan ASM 4, Jobey G 4, Blackburn R 2, Brown H 2, McCormack JA 2, Whitson TT 2, Brown N 1, Hedley G 1, Hughes WJ 1, Liddell R 1, McCulloch A 1.

Goals(84g): Appleyard W 22, Rutherford J 15, Howie J 13, Wilson GW 6, Orr R 5, Speedie FB 4, Gardner Alec 3, Veitch CCM 3, Hall AN 2, Higgins A 2, McClarence JP 2, Soye J 2, Jobey G 1, McCormack JA 1, McWilliam P 1, Willis DL 1, own goal 1.

Dismissals: 0 players.

MAJOR SIGNINGS

George Wilson (Everton) £1,600 club & national record fee
Scott Duncan (Dumbarton) £150
Alex Hall (St Bernards) £200
Alex McCulloch (Middlesbrough) £200

FROM THE RANKS

James Ridley (Willington Ath)
William Hughes (Rhyl Ath)

TEAM COLOURS Black & white striped shirts, dark shorts (Change; white shirts, dark shorts)

SEASON 1907-08

Match	Date		FL Division 1					Posn		Lawrence	McCracken	Carr	Gardner	Veitch	McWilliam	Rutherford	Howie	Appleyard	Orr	Gosnell	Speedie	Hall	McCombie	Brown H	Duffy	Willis	Hedley	McClarence	Pudan	Soye	Ridley	Higgins	Wilson	McCormack	Whitson	Blackburn	McCulloch	Jobey	Liddell	Hughes	Duncan	Brown N	Match
1	04 Sep	H	**Notts County**	D	1 1	(0 1)	25,000		Rutherford	1	2	3	4	5	6	7	8	9	10	11																							1
2	07 Sep	A	Sheffield Wednesday	L	1 3	(0 1)	20,000	14	Orr (pen)	1	2	3	4		6	7	8		10	11	5	9																					2
3	14 Sep	H	**Chelsea**	W	1 0	(0 0)	35,000	12	Orr	1	2		4	7	6		8	9	10	11	5		3																				3
4	21 Sep	A	Bristol City	D	1 1	(1 1)	18,000	14	Orr	1	2		4		6	7			8		5	9	3	10	11																		4
5	23 Sep	A	Chelsea	L	0 2	(0 0)	25,000	15		1	2	3	4		6	7			8		5	9		10	11																		5
6	28 Sep	H	**Nottingham Forest**	W	3 0	(2 0)	25,000	8	Gardner, Hall, Speedie	1		3	7	5	6				10	11	8	9	2			4																	6
7	05 Oct	A	Notts County	W	1 0	(0 0)	20,000	7	Hall	1		3	7	5	6		8		10	11		9	2			4																	7
8	12 Oct	H	**Manchester United**	L	1 6	(0 3)	30,000	11	McWilliam	1		3	7	5	6				10		8	9	2			4	11																8
9	19 Oct	A	Manchester City	L	0 1	(0 0)	25,000	14		1	2		7	6	4		8		10		5		3		11			9															9
10	26 Oct	H	**Blackburn Rovers**	W	3 0	(0 0)	28,000	9	Howie, McClarence, Rutherford	1			4		6	7	8		10	11	5		2					9	3														10
11	02 Nov	A	Preston North End	L	0 2	(0 1)	12,000	13		1			4	5	6	7	8		10				2		11			9	3														11
12	09 Nov	H	**Bolton Wanderers**	W	3 0	(1 0)	28,000	8	Appleyard, Orr, Rutherford	1	2			5	6	7	8	9	10		4				11				3														12
13	16 Nov	A	Bury	W	2 1	(1 1)	18,000	8	Appleyard, Rutherford	1			4	5	6	7	8	9					2		11				3	10													13
14	23 Nov	H	**Birmingham**	W	8 0	(2 0)	16,000	4	Appleyard, Howie 2, Rutherford 3, Veitch 2	1			4	5	6	7	8	9	10				2		11				3														14
15	30 Nov	A	Aston Villa	D	3 3	(2 1)	25,000	3	Appleyard, Howie, Orr	1			4	5	6	7	8	9	10				2		11				3														15
16	07 Dec	H	**Everton**	W	2 1	(0 0)	30,000	3	Appleyard (pen), Rutherford	1			4	5	6	7	8	9	10				2						3		11												16
17	14 Dec	A	Liverpool	W	5 1	(3 0)	20,000	3	Appleyard, Rutherford 2, Wilson 2	1	2		4	5	6	7		9			10								3			8	11										17
18	21 Dec	A	Sunderland	W	4 2	(3 2)	30,000	3	Rutherford, Veitch, Wilson 2	1	2		4	5	6	7		9			10								3			8	11										18
19	25 Dec	A	Woolwich Arsenal	D	2 2	(2 1)	30,000	2	Appleyard, Higgins	1	2		4	5	6	7		9			10								3			8	11										19
20	26 Dec	H	**Sheffield United**	L	2 3	(1 1)	35,000	2	Appleyard, Howie	1	2		4		6	7	8	9	10						11				3					5									20
21	28 Dec	H	**Middlesbrough**	D	1 1	(0 1)	38,000	2	McCormack	1		3	7		6		8	9			2					4				10		11		5									21
22	01 Jan	A	Sheffield United	D	1 1	(1 0)	21,591	3	Appleyard	1		3	7		6			9			5					4					11	8	10		2								22
23	04 Jan	H	**Sheffield Wednesday**	W	2 1	(0 1)	30,000	2	Appleyard 2	1	2		7		6			9	10		5					4						8	11		3								23
24	18 Jan	H	**Bristol City**	W	2 0	(1 0)	30,000	2	McClarence, Soye	1	2		4		6	7	8									5		9	3	10			11										24
25	25 Jan	A	Nottingham Forest	D	0 0	(0 0)	12,000	2		1	2		4		6						10					5		9	3		11	8				7							25
26	08 Feb	A	Manchester United	D	1 1	(0 1)	50,000	2	Howie	1	2		4		6	7	8	9			10					5			3		11												26
27	15 Feb	H	**Manchester City**	D	1 1	(0 1)	27,000	2	Willis	1				5	6		8	9	10				2			4			3		11					7							27
28	11 Mar	H	**Preston North End**	D	0 0	(0 0)	17,000	2		1	2			5	6	7			10				3			4						8	11				9						28
29	14 Mar	H	**Bury**	W	3 0	(2 0)	25,000	2	Appleyard 2, Howie	1	2		7	5	6		8	9			10		3			4							11										29
30	21 Mar	A	Birmingham	D	1 1	(1 1)	20,000	2	Howie	1	2		4	5		7	8	9			10					6			3				11										30
31	23 Mar	A	Blackburn Rovers	D	1 1	(0 1)	15,000	2	Appleyard	1		3	7	5			8	9					2			6		10			11							4					31
32	01 Apr	A	Bolton Wanderers	L	0 4	(0 2)	15,000	2		1		3	7					9					2			5				10		8	11					6	4				32
33	04 Apr	A	Everton	L	0 2	(0 0)	10,000	2		1		3	5					9			10					6			2	11		8								4	7		33
34	08 Apr	H	**Aston Villa**	L	2 5	(1 2)	15,000	2	Wilson, Soye	1	2		4	5			8				10					6			3	9			11									7	34
35	11 Apr	H	**Liverpool**	W	3 1	(2 0)	30,000	2	Howie, Jobey, Wilson	1	2		4	5			8				10					6			3				11					9			7		35
36	17 Apr	H	**Woolwich Arsenal**	W	2 1	(1 1)	35,000	2	Speedie 2	1	2		4	5	6		8			11	10								3									9			7		36
37	18 Apr	H	**Sunderland**	L	1 3	(0 1)	50,000	2	Howie	1		3	4	5			8	9		11	10		2			6															7		37
38	20 Apr	A	Middlesbrough	L	1 2	(1 0)	20,000	4	Higgins	1		2	7	5	6			9			10					4			3		11	8											38
Round			FA Cup																																								Round
1	11 Jan	H	**Nottingham Forest**	W	2 0	(0 0)	41,637		Appleyard, Rutherford	1	2		4		5	7		9			10					6			3			8	11										1
2	01 Feb	H	**West Ham United**	W	2 0	(0 0)	47,285		Appleyard 2	1	2		4		5	7	8	9			10					6			3				11										2
3	22 Feb	H	**Liverpool**	W	3 1	(0 1)	45,987		Speedie, Appleyard, Rutherford	1	2		4	5	6	7	8	9			10								3				11										3
4	07 Mar	H	**Grimsby Town**	W	5 1	(3 0)	44,788		Appleyard 3, Gardner, og (Vincett)	1	2		4	5	6	7	8	9			10								3				11										4
SF	28 Mar	N1	Fulham	W	6 0	(2 0)	45,571		Appleyard, Gardner, Howie 2, Rutherford 2	1	2		4	5		7	8	9			10					6			3				11										SF
F	25 Apr	N2	Wolverhampton Wanderers	L	1 3	(0 2)	74,967		Howie	1	2		4	5	6	7	8	9			10								3				11										F

N1 Played at Anfield, Liverpool
N2 Played at Crystal Palace, London

DateLine ... 12 Oct: Manchester United win by a big margin, 6-1 at Gallowgate. **23 Nov:** The 8-0 triumph over Birmingham equals the club's best League scoreline.
5 Feb: United score 14 goals in a friendly against non-leaguers Beaumaris, Appleyard claiming nine. **28 March:** United thump Fulham 6-0 in the FA Cup semi-final, the biggest win in any semi-final.
25 April: United lose again in the FA Cup final, this time 3-1 to Wolves.

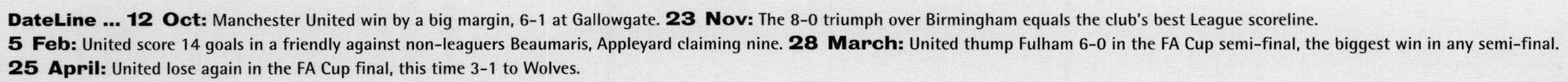

NEWCASTLE UNITED

SEASON
1908-09
DIVISION 1

Champions by a record margin

United's inadequate and somewhat humiliating performance in the 1908 FA Cup final provoked the players to a new level of high-performance. They started with a flourish by winning the first five games of the new season. Indeed by the end of the campaign they created a new record margin by lifting the League title by seven points. However, that was not achieved until a quite remarkable internal quarrel and on-field sensation was played out during November and December. Several top names had run into dispute with club officials and were temporarily ostracised just as new star centre-forward, Albert Shepherd, had arrived on Tyneside in a big deal.

An unfamiliar line-up took to the field for a local derby with Sunderland at Gallowgate – the upshot being a truly sensational 9-1 defeat with no fewer than eight second-half goals being fired into United's net, although it has to be noted that the Magpies were down to nine men due to injury for part of the time. As could be expected there was a huge outcry. The big names were swiftly reinstated and equally as remarkable was the reaction from the Magpies. They proceeded to win 14 of the next 18 games – seven victories in a row included – and lifted the title trophy with a record 53 points. Newcastle's nearest challengers, Everton, were crushed 3-0, a telling victory over the Merseyside club at Easter. A penalty for Bill McCracken and two goals for James Stewart saw the Magpies get the better of their rivals.

Newcastle went close to another FA Cup final too. They met their Wearside rivals again, United dishing out some kind of retribution by winning 3-0 in a quarter-final replay. United were drawn with Manchester United in the semi-final at Bramall Lane, but lost to a single goal from Harry Halse.

Pictured above: Andrew Anderson played the team game and fitted into United's possession style perfectly.

The FA Cup semi-final programme from the contest with Manchester United at Bramall Lane, Sheffield.

Memorabilia CORNER

IN CHARGE

Chairman: Joseph Bell
Manager: Director Committee
Captain: Colin Veitch
Trainer/Coach: James McPherson

ST JAMES' PARK

Average Attendance
Lg 31,526 Lg & Cup 32,378

For many years United arranged their annual photo-call on the steps and amidst the shrubbery of the Gallowgate End access. Local photographers such as John Taylor, Gladstone Adams and Arthur Hackett produced skilfully and orderly photographs, as is the case with this 1908 group.

PLAYER FOCUS Peter McWilliam

Born: Inverness. Left-half, 5'9"
1902 to 1911: 242 app 12 goals.

From the Highlands of Scotland, as soon as the elegant skills of Peter McWilliam were added to United's line-up on a regular basis in midfield for season 1904-05, Newcastle's team really started to blend together. Arriving as something of a raw youngster from Inverness Thistle in August 1902, he was left out by United's selection committee to begin with, however the club's Directors were persuaded to include the young Scot by his senior teammates, such was the impact he made on his colleagues. And the Magpies never looked back, winning the title in his first full season. Forming a highly respected midfield with Gardner, Veitch and Howie, Peter often was the player to make the difference. He appeared on eight occasions for his country, being skipper of the side, but was unluckily injured appearing for Scotland against Wales, knee ligament damage putting him out of the 1911 FA Cup final and thereafter forcing his retirement. Known everywhere in football as Peter the Great, he played a key part in three title sides and appeared in all four of the club's previous FA Cup finals. McWilliam later became a noted manager, being in charge of Tottenham for almost 18 years in two spells, and winning the FA Cup in 1921 – one of a handful of men to have played in, then managed a winning side. Also boss of Middlesbrough where he developed another good line-up, Peter was awarded the Football League's Long Service medal in 1939.

SEASON REVIEW

Football League Div 1: P38 W24 D5 L9 F65 A41 Pts 53.
Position: 1st, Champions.
FA Cup: SF (Winners; Manchester United).

Appearances (46m): Lawrence J 46, Veitch CCM 42, Whitson TT 38, McCracken WR 37, Wilson GW 36, McWilliam P 35, Howie J 33, Higgins A 31, Rutherford J 30, Stewart J 27, Anderson AL 25, Willis DL 22, Shepherd A 21, Duncan ASM 16, Gardner Alec 14, Carr J 11, Allan SJE 10, Jobey G 10, Gosnell AA 5, Liddell R 5, Ridley J 5, Pudan AE 3, McCombie A 2, Blanthorne R 1, Randall CE 1.

Goals (81g): Shepherd A 15, Wilson GW 10, Veitch CCM 9, Rutherford J 8, Stewart J 8, Howie J 7, Allan SJE 6, Anderson AL 5, Higgins A 5, Duncan ASM 2, Jobey G 1, Liddell R 1, McCracken WR 1, Ridley J 1, Willis DL 1, own goal 1.

Dismissals: 0 players.

MAJOR SIGNINGS

Albert Shepherd (Bolton Wand) £850
James Stewart (Sheffield Wed) £1,000
Bob Blanthorne (Grimsby Town) £350

FROM THE RANKS

Charles Randall (Hobson Wand)

TEAM COLOURS Black & white striped shirts, dark shorts (Change; white shirts, dark shorts)

SEASON 1908-09

Match	Date		FL Division 1	Result	HT	Att	Posn	Scorers	Lawrence	McCracken	Carr	Gardner	Veitch	McWilliam	Rutherford	Howie	Blanthorne	Stewart	Wilson	Whitson	Allan	Anderson	Liddell	Willis	Higgins	Duncan	Jobey	Ridley	Pudan	Shepherd	Gosnell	McCombie	Randall	Match
1	02 Sep	H	**Bradford City**	W 1 0	(0 0)	26,000		Veitch	1	2	3	4	5	6	7	8	9	10	11															1
2	05 Sep	H	**Leicester Fosse**	W 2 0	(0 0)	32,000	1	Howie, Veitch	1	2		4	5	6	7	8		10	11	3	9													2
3	09 Sep	H	**Bristol City**	W 2 1	(0 1)	22,000	1	Howie 2	1	2		4	5	6	7	8		10	11	3	9													3
4	12 Sep	A	Woolwich Arsenal	W 2 1	(1 0)	20,000	1	Rutherford, Stewart	1	2		4	5	6	7	8		9	10	3		11												4
5	19 Sep	H	**Notts County**	W 1 0	(1 0)	31,000	1	Wilson	1	2		4	5	6	7	8		9	10	3		11												5
6	26 Sep	A	Sheffield Wednesday	L 0 2	(0 0)	20,000	2		1	2		4	5		7	8		9	10	3		11	6											6
7	03 Oct	A	Bristol City	D 3 3	(0 1)	18,000	2	Higgins, Veitch 2 (1pen)	1	2		4	5		7	8		10	11	3				6	9									7
8	10 Oct	H	**Preston North End**	W 2 0	(1 0)	26,000	2	Higgins, Stewart	1	2			5	6		8		10	11	3				4	9	7								8
9	17 Oct	A	Middlesbrough	D 0 0	(0 0)	20,000	2		1	2			5	6	7	8		10	11	3				4	9									9
10	24 Oct	H	**Manchester City**	W 2 0	(0 0)	33,000	2	Howie 2	1	2			5	6	7	8		10	11	3					9		4							10
11	31 Oct	A	Liverpool	L 1 2	(0 1)	28,000	2	Wilson	1	2			5	6	7	8		10	11	3					9		4							11
12	07 Nov	H	**Bury**	W 3 1	(3 0)	30,000	2	Ridley, Rutherford, Veitch	1		2		5	6	7	8			10	3					9		4	11						12
13	14 Nov	A	Sheffield United	D 1 1	(1 1)	18,000	2	Veitch (pen)	1	2			5	6	7	8		10		3					9		4	11						13
14	21 Nov	H	**Aston Villa**	L 0 2	(0 1)	35,000	3		1	2			5	6	7	8		10	11	3					9		4							14
15	28 Nov	A	Nottingham Forest	W 4 0	(3 0)	8,000	2	Wilson, Shepherd, Higgins, Liddell	1				5						10	2			4	6	8	7			3	9	11			15
16	05 Dec	H	**Sunderland**	L 1 9	(1 1)	56,000	2	Shepherd (pen)	1				5						10	2			4	6	8	7			3	9	11			16
17	12 Dec	A	Chelsea	W 2 1	(0 1)	30,000	2	Allan, Veitch (pen)	1	2	3		5					10			9			6	8	7	4				11			17
18	19 Dec	H	**Blackburn Rovers**	W 2 0	(2 0)	22,000	2	Anderson, Duncan	1	2			5	6					10	3		11		4	8	7				9				18
19	25 Dec	H	**Manchester United**	W 2 1	(1 1)	40,000	2	Shepherd, Wilson	1	2			5	6					10	3		11		4	8	7				9				19
20	26 Dec	A	Manchester United	L 0 1	(0 1)	45,000	2		1	2			5	6					10	3		11		4	8	7				9				20
21	01 Jan	A	Everton	W 1 0	(1 0)	40,000	2	Howie	1			4	5	6	7	8			10	3		11								9		2		21
22	02 Jan	A	Leicester Fosse	W 4 0	(3 0)	15,000	2	Higgins 2, Shepherd, Stewart	1			4	2	6				10		3		11		5	8	7				9				22
23	09 Jan	H	**Woolwich Arsenal**	W 3 1	(0 1)	30,000	2	Anderson, Shepherd, Veitch (pen)	1	2		4	5	6	7	8				3		11			10					9				23
24	23 Jan	A	Notts County	W 4 0	(0 0)	20,000	1	Shepherd 4	1		2	4	5	6	7				10	3		11			8					9				24
25	30 Jan	H	**Sheffield Wednesday**	W 1 0	(0 0)	33,000	1	Veitch	1	2		4	5	6	7			10		3		11			8					9				25
26	13 Feb	A	Preston North End	W 1 0	(0 0)	10,000	1	Anderson	1	2				6	7	5			10	3		11		4	8					9				26
27	27 Feb	A	Manchester City	W 2 0	(0 0)	25,000	1	Jobey, Stewart	1	2	3		5			8		10				11		4	9	7	6							27
28	13 Mar	A	Bury	D 1 1	(0 1)	17,311	1	og (Parkin)	1	2						5		10		3				4	8	7	6			9	11			28
29	20 Mar	H	**Sheffield United**	W 4 0	(3 0)	31,000	1	Duncan, Shepherd, Stewart, Willis	1	2	3		5	6				8	10					4		7		11		9				29
30	23 Mar	A	Bradford City	W 2 1	(1 1)	15,000	1	Allan, Stewart	1		2		5		7			8		3	9			4			6	11					10	30
31	31 Mar	H	**Middlesbrough**	W 1 0	(0 0)	45,000	1	Allan	1	2			5			4			10		9			6	8	7		11	3					31
32	03 Apr	H	**Nottingham Forest**	D 1 1	(0 1)	22,000	1	Allan	1	2	3		5			4		10			9	11		6	8	7								32
33	10 Apr	A	Sunderland	L 1 3	(1 0)	27,493	1	Shepherd	1	2			5	6	7	4		8	10	3		11								9				33
34	12 Apr	H	**Everton**	W 3 0	(1 0)	30,000	1	Stewart 2, McCracken (pen)	1	2	3		5	6	7	4		8	10			11			9									34
35	17 Apr	H	**Chelsea**	L 1 3	(0 1)	25,000	1	Wilson	1	2			5	6	7	4		8	10	3		11			9									35
36	24 Apr	A	Blackburn Rovers	W 4 2	(2 1)	7,000	1	Allan, Rutherford 3	1	2	3		5	6	7	8		10			9	11		4										36
37	26 Apr	A	Aston Villa	L 0 3	(0 1)	8,000	1		1	2									10	3	9		5	4	8	7	6				11			37
38	30 Apr	H	**Liverpool**	L 0 1	(0 0)	30,000	1		1		2			6	7	8			10	3	9	11	5	4										38
Round			**FA Cup**																															**Round**
1	16 Jan	H	**Clapton Orient**	W 5 0	(2 0)	23,670		Anderson, Shepherd, Wilson 3	1			4	5	6	7	8			10	3		11								9		2		1
2	06 Feb	H	**Blackpool**	W 2 1	(1 1)	32,137		Howie, Rutherford	1	2		4	5	6	7	8			10	3		11								9				2
3	20 Feb	A	West Ham United	D 0 0	(0 0)	17,000			1	2			5	6	7				10	3		11		4	8					9				3
3r	24 Feb	H	**West Ham United**	W 2 1	(0 0)	36,526		Anderson, Shepherd (pen)	1	2			5	6	7	4			10	3		11			8					9				3r
4	06 Mar	H	**Sunderland**	D 2 2	(2 2)	53,353		Rutherford, Wilson	1	2			5	6	7	4			10	3		11			8					9				4
4r	10 Mar	A	Sunderland	W 3 0	(1 0)	27,512		Shepherd 2, Wilson	1	2			5	6		4		10	11	3					8	7				9				4r
SF	27 Mar	N1	Manchester United	L 0 1	(0 0)	40,118			1	2			5	6		4		10	11	3					8	7				9				SF
			FA Charity Shield																															CS
	28 Apr	N2	Northampton Town	W 2 0	(1 0)	7,000		Allan, Rutherford	1	2			5	6	7	8			10	3	9	11		4										

N1 Played at Bramall Lane, Sheffield

N2 Played at Stamford Bridge, London

DateLine ... 2 Sept: Bob Blanthorne breaks his leg on his debut against Bradford City. **5 Dec:** Sunderland register a 9-1 victory at St James' Park, the best in the top division. **23 Jan:** Albert Shepherd scores all four goals in a victory over Notts County, and then leaves early! **12 April:** United take care of Everton 3-0 in a near Championship decider. **28 April:** The Magpies lift the FA Charity Shield after a 2-0 success over Northampton.

NEWCASTLE UNITED

SEASON
1909-10
DIVISION 1

At last, United win the FA Cup

The 1909-10 campaign was to be the season United lifted the FA Cup for the very first time...at the fifth attempt, and even then, they still could not win at the dreaded Crystal Palace. The Black'n'Whites remained a huge attraction and that was evident when a reported crowd of 70,000 turned up to see the Geordies at Chelsea just before the FA Cup got underway. Comfortable in League action – finishing in fourth spot again – they cruised through to another Cup final, although had to resolve a series of controversial moments before their trip to London. They were carpeted for fielding weak sides and embroiled in a headlining bribery scandal surrounding crowd favourite Albert Shepherd.

United faced a rugged and tough opponent in Barnsley, then in football's second-tier but the game at the Crystal Palace was to be a drab showpiece and there was to be no after-match celebrations. Yet United received a slice of fortune they had up to then never seen at the Palace. A goal down with only seven minutes left, and as the wife of the Barnsley manager was tying red ribbons to the trophy, Rutherford ran clear and headed a dramatic equaliser from close in. All ended at 1-1 and everyone now turned their attention to a replay in Liverpool the following Thursday.

At a wet Goodison Park the Tynesiders at last found their form, although United's delicate short passing game was mixed with long balls, swift exchanges and some gutsy and rugged play. Newcastle dominated the replay and only miracles prevented United from scoring in the opening half. After the break it was much the same story. But Albert Shepherd ended the hero of the day, scoring the two goals which brought the trophy to Tyneside, including the first penalty in a FA Cup final. The trophy was presented to Colin Veitch by the Earl of Derby and United's triumphant party was welcomed on Tyneside by vast crowds as the Cup was paraded through the streets.

Pictured above: Although born in South Africa, Tony Whitson was raised a Geordie and a regular at left-back.

Memorabilia CORNER

At last victory in the FA Cup final – the official programme from Goodison Park, home of Everton.

IN CHARGE

Chairman: James Lunn
Manager: Director Committee
Captain: Colin Veitch
Trainer/Coach: James McPherson

ST JAMES' PARK

Average Attendance
Lg 25,895 Lg & Cup 28,248

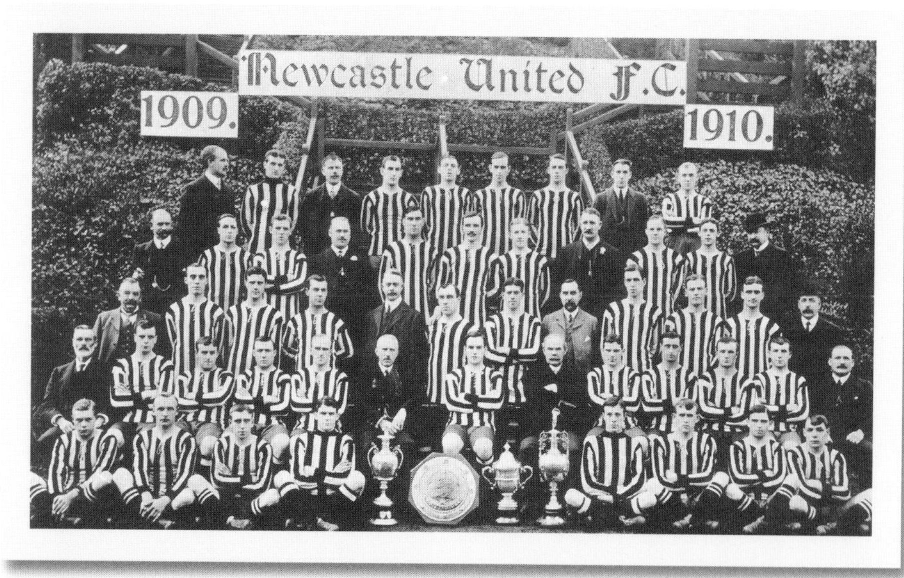

Trophies were again on display at the start of the 1909-10 season. Left to right: Northumberland Senior Cup, FA Charity Shield, NE League Championship, Football League Championship. And the FA Cup was to arrive at St James' Park for the first time at the end of the campaign.

PLAYER FOCUS Albert Shepherd

Born Great Lever. Centre-forward, 5'8"
1908 to 1914: 123 app 92 goals.

Replacing the robust play of Bill Appleyard at centre-forward was a difficult task, but United did it supremely well with the purchase of England leader Albert Shepherd. A big fee of £850 was paid to Bolton Wanderers in November 1908 for a player who had proved he could score goals on a regular basis at the top level, 90 in 123 games – and with panache to go with it. Shepherd was an instant hit. He became the first United player to claim 30 goals in a season and was a devastating centre-forward who thrilled the crowds with characteristic dashes through the middle when he made use of his lightning speed off the mark. A personality on and off the field as well, Albert was hugely popular. Especially strong running through the channels, he often netted with fabulous goals and on five occasions rattled four goals in a single game for the Magpies. Caught up in a headlining bribery allegation prior to the 1910 FA Cup final, Albert answered his critics by striking the goals to bring the trophy back to Tyneside for the first time. Also winning the Championship in 1909, he averaged 26 goals a season for United until a knee ligament injury just before the following year's final placed him on the sidelines for many months. Shepherd was never the same dynamic striker again and moved on to conclude his career with Bradford City. He afterwards was a publican in Bolton. His home debut for the Black'n'Whites coincided with Sunderland's remarkable 9-1 victory.

SEASON REVIEW

Football League Div 1: P38 W19 D7 L12 F70 A56 Pts 45.
Position: 4th (Champions; Aston Villa).
FA Cup: Winners.

Appearances (46m): Lawrence J 42, Wilson GW 37, McCracken WR 36, Shepherd A 36, Howie J 33, Whitson TT 33, Veitch CCM 32, Low WL 31, McWilliam P 31, Rutherford J 31, Higgins A 24, Stewart J 20, Anderson AL 19, Duncan ASM 14, Willis DL 14, Finlay J 11, Jobey G 11, Carr J 10, Gosnell AA 8, Waugh R 8, Liddell R 5, Allan SJE 4, Metcalf A 4, Blake S 3, McCombie A 2, Randall CE 2, Ridley J 2, Thompson H 2, Sinclair TS 1.

Goals (88g): Shepherd A 31, Rutherford J 12, Howie J 10, Higgins A 9, Stewart J 9, Wilson GW 5, Duncan ASM 2, McWilliam P 2, Anderson AL 1, Finlay J 1, Liddell R 1, McCracken WR 1, Randall CE 1, Veitch CCM 1, Waugh R 1, own goal 1.

Dismissals: 1 player; Shepherd.

MAJOR SIGNINGS

Wilf Low (Aberdeen) £800
John Finlay (Airdrie) £775

FROM THE RANKS

Arthur Metcalf (North Shields Ath)
Henry Thompson (North Shields Ath)
Bob Waugh (Newcastle Bentonians)

TEAM COLOURS Black & white striped shirts, dark shorts (Change; white shirts, dark shorts)

SEASON 1909-10

Match	Date	Venue	Opponent	Res	Score	HT	Att	Posn	Scorers	Blake	McCracken	Whitson	Jobey	Low	McWilliam	Rutherford	Howie	Shepherd	Wilson	Anderson	Lawrence	Veitch	Finlay	Stewart	Gosnell	Higgins	Willis	Carr	Liddell	Duncan	Allan	Waugh	Ridley	Thompson	Metcalf	Sinclair	McCombie	Randall
FL Division 1																																						
1	01 Sep	H	**Bolton Wanderers**	W	1 0	(0 0)	25,000		Rutherford	1	2	3	4	5	6	7	8	9	10	11																		
2	04 Sep	A	Blackburn Rovers	L	0 2	(0 1)	16,000	10			2	3	4			7	8	9	11		1	5	6	10														
3	06 Sep	A	Everton	W	4 1	(2 1)	30,000	5	Wilson, Stewart, Howie, Rutherford		2	3	4	6		7	8		10		1	5		9	11													
4	07 Sep	A	Bolton Wanderers	W	4 0	(3 0)	18,000	2	Shepherd 3, Rutherford		2	3	4	6		7	8	9	10		1	5			11													
5	11 Sep	H	**Nottingham Forest**	L	1 2	(1 0)	25,000	4	Shepherd		2	3	4	6		7	8	9	10		1	5			11													
6	18 Sep	A	Sunderland	W	2 0	(1 0)	40,000	1	Shepherd, Stewart		2	3	4	6		7		9	10		1	5		8	11													
7	25 Sep	H	**Everton**	L	1 2	(1 2)	35,000	2	Shepherd		2	3	4	6		7		9	10		1	5		8	11													
8	02 Oct	A	Manchester United	D	1 1	(0 1)	40,000	3	Rutherford		2	3			6	7	4	9	10		1	5		8	11													
9	09 Oct	H	**Bradford City**	W	1 0	(1 0)	25,000	2	Wilson		2	3			6	7	4	9	10	11	1	5				8												
10	16 Oct	A	Sheffield Wednesday	L	1 3	(0 2)	15,000	4	Shepherd (pen)		2	3			6	7		9	10	11	1	5		8			4											
11	23 Oct	H	**Bristol City**	W	3 1	(1 1)	10,000	4	Anderson, Shepherd 2		2		4		6	7		9	10	11	1			8				3	5									
12	30 Oct	A	Bury	W	2 1	(1 1)	15,204	3	Shepherd 2		2	3	4		6			9	10	11	1	5		8						7								
13	06 Nov	H	**Tottenham Hotspur**	W	1 0	(1 0)	26,000	2	Duncan		2	3	4		6			9	10	11	1	5		8						7								
14	13 Nov	A	Preston North End	L	0 4	(0 1)	16,000	5			2	3			5			9	10	11	1		6	8			4			7								
15	20 Nov	H	**Notts County**	L	1 3	(1 0)	18,000	8	Rutherford		2	3			6	7		9		11	1	5	4			10					8							
16	27 Nov	H	**Middlesbrough**	W	2 0	(1 0)	28,000	6	Shepherd, Howie		2	3		5	6	7	8	9	11		1	4				10												
17	04 Dec	A	Liverpool	L	5 6	(5 2)	20,000	7	Shepherd 4, Howie		2	3		5	6	7	8	9	11		1	4				10												
18	11 Dec	H	**Aston Villa**	W	1 0	(0 0)	19,000	6	Higgins			3		5	6	7	4	9	10		1					8						2	11					
19	18 Dec	A	Sheffield United	L	0 4	(0 1)	15,500	8				3	4	5	6	7	8	9			1					10		2					11					
20	25 Dec	A	Woolwich Arsenal	W	3 0	(3 0)	25,000	7	Shepherd 2, Rutherford		2	3		5		7	4	9		11	1	6		10		8												
21	27 Dec	A	Chelsea	L	1 2	(1 1)	70,000	7	Veitch		2	3		5				9	10	11	1	4	6	8		7												
22	01 Jan	H	**Chelsea**	W	1 0	(0 0)	30,000	8	Shepherd		2	3		5	6	7	8	9	10	11	1	4																
23	03 Jan	H	**Preston North End**	W	5 2	(2 0)	26,000	7	Shepherd 4, og (Winchester)		2			5	6	7	8	9	10	11	1	4												3				
24	08 Jan	H	**Blackburn Rovers**	W	4 1	(4 0)	35,000	6	Higgins, Shepherd 2, Howie		2			5	6		8	9		11	1					10	4			7				3				
25	22 Jan	A	Nottingham Forest	W	1 0	(1 0)	8,000	3	McWilliam		2			5	6	7	8		11		1					10	4	3			9							
26	12 Feb	H	**Manchester United**	L	3 4	(3 0)	30,000	5	Wilson, Higgins 2		2	3		5	6	7	8		10		1				11	9	4											
27	26 Feb	H	**Sheffield Wednesday**	W	3 1	(1 1)	8,000	5	Shepherd, Howie, McWilliam			3		5	6		8	9	11		1	4				10				7		2						
28	09 Mar	A	Bradford City	D	3 3	(2 3)	10,000	5	Stewart 2, Shepherd									9		11	1	5	6	10			4	3		7		2			8			
29	12 Mar	H	**Bury**	D	2 2	(1 2)	20,000	3	Wilson, Waugh (pen)			3		5	6		8	9	11		1	4		10						7		2						
30	19 Mar	A	Tottenham Hotspur	W	4 0	(3 0)	30,000	3	Stewart 2, Howie, Rutherford		2	3		5	6	7	8		10	11	1	4		9														
31	25 Mar	H	**Woolwich Arsenal**	D	1 1	(0 1)	30,000	2	Finlay									9d		11			6				4	3	5	7	10	2			8	1		
32	02 Apr	A	Notts County	D	2 2	(0 1)	8,000	6	Shepherd, Liddell		2	3					8	9		11	1	4	6	10					5	7								
33	09 Apr	A	Middlesbrough	D	1 1	(0 0)	10,000	5	Duncan					5	6		8	9	11		1	4				10				7		2					3	
34	13 Apr	H	**Sunderland**	W	1 0	(0 0)	40,000	3	Higgins		2			5			8	9	11		1	4	6			10		3		7								
35	16 Apr	H	**Liverpool**	L	1 3	(0 3)	22,000	4	Rutherford		2	3		5	6	7	8	9	11		1	4				10												
36	25 Apr	A	Bristol City	W	3 0	(1 0)	4,000	4	Randall, Stewart 2	1										11			6	9			4	3	5	7		2			8			10
37	27 Apr	A	Aston Villa	L	0 4	(0 2)	25,000	4		1										11			6				4		5	7	9	2			8		3	10
38	30 Apr	H	**Sheffield United**	D	0 0	(0 0)	40,000	4			2					7	8	9	11		1	4	6			10	5	3										
Round	**FA Cup**																																					
1	15 Jan	A	Stoke	D	1 1	(1 1)	18,080		Howie		2	3		5	6	7	8		11		1			9		10	4											
1r	19 Jan	H	**Stoke**	W	2 1	(1 0)	14,545		Higgins, Howie		2	3		5	6	7	8		11		1			9		10	4											
2	05 Feb	H	**Fulham**	W	4 0	(1 0)	35,846		Higgins 2, Rutherford, McCracken (pen)		2			5	6	7	8		10		1				11	9	4	3										
3	19 Feb	H	**Blackburn Rovers**	W	3 1	(2 1)	54,772		Higgins, Howie, Rutherford		2	3		5	6	7	8	9	11		1	4				10												
4	05 Mar	H	**Leicester Fosse**	W	3 0	(1 0)	52,544		Wilson, Shepherd, Howie			3		5	6		8	9	11		1	2				10	4			7								
SF	26 Mar	N1	Swindon Town	W	2 0	(0 0)	33,000		Stewart, Rutherford		2	3		5	6	7	8		11		1	4		9		10												
F	23 Apr	N2	Barnsley	D	1 1	(0 1)	76,980		Rutherford		2	3		5	6	7	8	9	11		1	4				10												
Fr	28 Apr	N3	Barnsley	W	2 0	(0 0)	69,364		Shepherd 2 (1 pen)		2			5	6	7	8	9	11		1	4				10		3										

N1 Played at White Hart Lane, London
N2 Played at Crystal Palace, London
N3 Played at Goodison Park, Liverpool

Match 31 Shepherd not actually sent off but left the field without the referee's permission and not allowed to return

DateLine ... 7 Sept: Albert Shepherd strikes a hat-trick against his former club in a 4-0 win over Bolton. **4 Dec:** United lose 6-5 at Liverpool after being 5-2 ahead at half-time. **27 Dec:** A reported 70,000 watch United's League contest at Chelsea. **25 April:** Newcastle field a reserve side against Bristol City and still win 3-0. **28 April:** Albert Shepherd scores the first penalty in a FA Cup final as United win 2-0 and becomes the first to hit 30 goals in a season.

SEASON 1910-11
DIVISION 1

Another final, another defeat

In League football, United looked jaded during season 1910-11 and slipped down the table to finish in eighth position, their lowest placing for eight years.

By Newcastle's high standards that was disappointing. On occasion they performed to their scintillating best; hitting six goals past both Liverpool and Bradford City with Albert Shepherd scoring seemingly at will. He claimed 33 goals for the season, including two four-goal strikes. The Magpies should have been placed higher in Division One but too many games they usually won, were either draws or defeats.

United did do well again in the FA Cup when the First Round began in January. There was a newly commissioned trophy for the 1910-11 season – the current famous silver pot all in football is familiar with – and Newcastle reached the season's showpiece once more, their fifth final in only seven seasons. As Cup holders they defended their crown with purpose en-route to the final. They were convincing in the opening tie, winning 6-1 against Bury, and after close and typical Cup battles over Northampton and Hull City, were comprehensive victors in the latter stages against Derby County and Chelsea. The tie with the Rams saw a new record crowd of 59,717 established at St James' Park.

Injury to key players – and that dreaded Crystal Palace curse – was to be the Tynesiders downfall though. Pivotal internationals Albert Shepherd and Peter McWilliam were both crocked in the run-up to the final. And that made a colossal difference. Against Bradford City – who finished above United in the First Division table but who had been beaten 6-1 by the Magpies in League action – Newcastle failed in London once more as a dour 0-0 draw was played out, then lost by a scrappy early goal in the replayed final at Old Trafford.

Pictured above: George Jobey came through the ranks to claim a place up front in the FA Cup final.

Memorabilia CORNER

Match programme at Old Trafford for the FA Cup final with Bradford City.

IN CHARGE

Chairman: James Lunn
Manager: Director Committee
Captain: Colin Veitch
Trainer/Coach: James McPherson

ST JAMES' PARK

Average Attendance
Lg 25,706 Lg & Cup 29,080

United's senior players pose with the 'English Cup' at the start of the 1910-11 season. Standing, left to right: McCracken, Low, Shepherd, McWilliam, Carr. Sitting: Rutherford, Howie, Veitch, Higgins, Wilson, Whitson. On ground: Watt (secretary), Lawrence, McPherson (trainer).

PLAYER FOCUS Colin Veitch

Born Newcastle upon Tyne. Half-back, 5'6"
1899 to 1915: 322 app 49 goals.

One of the most eminent names in Newcastle United's history, Colin Veitch was a versatile player, able to operate in any outfield role for both club and country. Joining United as a kid in January 1899 from local football, he took part in 16 seasons of action, winning three title medals and taking part in five FA Cup finals with the club, skipper when the Magpies lifted the trophy for the first time in 1910. Although not tall and commanding in physique, Veitch was a master on the field, the Tynesider always used the ball to good purpose while he could also score goals and combined effectively with both his attack and defence. Honoured by England, he would have won more than his six caps had it not been for his adaptability, being proficient in various roles which meant he stood as reserve on several occasions. Identified as the leading spirit behind the Magpies' Edwardian glory, he was also a celebrated individual off the field – an educated man of many talents not least being a leading activist in the Player's Union and heavily involved in the region's People's Theatre and Operatic Society. Retiring in 1915, Veitch later organised Newcastle's first junior set-up – the Newcastle Swifts – and sampled management with Bradford City in a short spell between 1926 and 1928. He afterwards became a distinguished journalist for the Newcastle Chronicle until his early death of pneumonia.

SEASON REVIEW

Football League Div 1: P38 W15 D10 L13 F61 A43 Pts 40.
Position: 8th (Champions; Manchester United).
FA Cup: Finalist (Winners; Bradford City).

Appearances (46m): Lawrence J 44, Low WL 39, McCracken WR 38, Shepherd A 38, Stewart J 37, Higgins A 34, Veitch CCM 34, Whitson TT 34, Wilson GW 27, Duncan ASM 26, McWilliam P 22, Rutherford J 20, Anderson AL 19, Finlay J 18, Randall CE 16, Willis DL 14, Hudspeth FC 12, Jobey G 9, Carr J 6, Metcalf A 4, Howie J 3, Ridley J 3, Allan SJE 2, Hewison R 2, Sinclair TS 2, Waugh R 2, Scott JG 1.

Goals (79g): Shepherd A 33, Stewart J 13, Higgins A 9, Duncan ASM 6, Randall CE 5, Metcalf A 2, Rutherford J 2, Willis DL 2, Wilson GW 2, Low WL 1, McCracken WR 1, McWilliam P 1, Ridley J 1, Veitch CCM 1.

Dismissals: 0 players.

MAJOR SIGNINGS

None

FROM THE RANKS

Bob Hewison (Whitley Ath)
Frank Hudspeth (North Shields Ath)
John Scott (Wallsend Slipway)

TEAM COLOURS Black & white striped shirts, dark shorts (Change; white shirts, dark shorts)

SEASON 1910-11

Match	Date		FL Division 1	Result	HT	Att	Posn	Scorers	Lawrence	McCracken	Whitson	Veitch	Low	McWilliam	Rutherford	Stewart	Shepherd	Higgins	Wilson	Carr	Finlay	Duncan	Randall	Ridley	Waugh	Hewison	Anderson	Sinclair	Howie	Jobey	Hudspeth	Willis	Allan	Metcalf	Scott	Match
1	01 Sep	A	Sunderland	L 1 2	(0 1)	30,000		Shepherd (pen)	1	2	3	4	5	6	7	8	9	10	11																	1
2	03 Sep	H	**Bristol City**	L 0 1	(0 0)	26,000	19		1	2			5	6		8	9	10	11	3	4	7														2
3	10 Sep	A	Oldham Athletic	W 2 0	(1 0)	34,000	10	Shepherd 2	1	2	3	4	5	6		8	9					7	10	11												3
4	17 Sep	A	Tottenham Hotspur	W 2 1	(1 0)	35,000	8	Ridley, Rutherford	1	2	3	4	5	6	7	8	9						10	11												4
5	24 Sep	H	**Middlesbrough**	D 0 0	(0 0)	40,000	8		1	2	3	4	5			8	9		11		6	7	10													5
6	01 Oct	A	Preston North End	L 1 2	(0 1)	18,000	10	Higgins	1		3	4	5			8	9	10	11		6	7			2											6
7	08 Oct	H	**Notts County**	W 2 0	(0 0)	30,000	9	Shepherd, Higgins	1	2	3		5		7		9	8	10		6					4	11									7
8	15 Oct	A	Manchester United	L 0 2	(0 1)	50,000	12		1	2	3	4	5	6	7		9	8	10								11									8
9	22 Oct	H	**Liverpool**	W 6 1	(3 0)	23,000	8	Stewart, Shepherd 4, Higgins	1	2	3	4	5	6	7	10	9	8									11									9
10	29 Oct	A	Bury	D 1 1	(0 1)	14,986	8	Shepherd	1	2	3	4	5	6		10	9	8				7					11									10
11	05 Nov	H	**Sheffield United**	D 1 1	(0 0)	20,000	9	Duncan		2	3	4	5	6		10	9	8	11			7						1								11
12	12 Nov	A	Aston Villa	L 2 3	(2 3)	40,000	9	Stewart 2	1	2	3	4	5			10	9				6	7					11		8							12
13	19 Nov	H	**Sunderland**	D 1 1	(1 1)	57,416	9	Shepherd	1	2	3	4	5	6	7	10	9										11		8							13
14	26 Nov	A	Woolwich Arsenal	W 2 1	(2 0)	13,000	9	Shepherd, Duncan	1	2	3		5	6			9	10				7					11		8	4						14
15	03 Dec	H	**Bradford City**	W 6 1	(2 0)	18,000	8	Stewart, Shepherd 3, Higgins 2 (1 pen)	1	2			5	6		10	9	8				7					11			4	3					15
16	10 Dec	A	Blackburn Rovers	L 1 3	(0 0)	12,000	9	Duncan	1		3		5			10	9	8			6	7			2		11			4						16
17	17 Dec	H	**Nottingham Forest**	W 4 1	(0 1)	15,000	7	Shepherd 4	1				5			10	9	8		3	6	7					11			4	2					17
18	24 Dec	A	Manchester City	L 0 2	(0 0)	15,000	8		1	2			5			10	9	8			6	7					11			4	3					18
19	26 Dec	H	**Everton**	W 1 0	(1 0)	40,000	7	Shepherd	1	2		4	5				9	8	10		6	7					11				3					19
20	27 Dec	A	Sheffield Wednesday	W 2 0	(1 0)	20,000	7	Shepherd 2	1	2		4	5			10	9	8	11		6	7									3					20
21	31 Dec	A	Bristol City	L 0 1	(0 1)	14,000	8		1	2		4	5	6		10	9	8	11			7									3					21
22	02 Jan	A	Everton	W 5 1	(0 1)	40,000	7	Randall, Shepherd 2, Stewart, Duncan	1			4				8	9	5	11	3	6	7	10								2					22
23	03 Jan	H	**Preston North End**	D 1 1	(1 1)	30,000	6	Wilson	1	2		5		6			9	8	11		4	7	10								3					23
24	07 Jan	H	**Oldham Athletic**	W 3 0	(0 0)	20,000	5	Shepherd, Stewart, Duncan	1	2		5		6		8	9		11			7	10			4					3					24
25	21 Jan	H	**Tottenham Hotspur**	D 1 1	(0 1)	22,000	4	Low	1		3		5	6		8	9	10				7		11							2	4				25
26	28 Jan	A	Middlesbrough	W 2 0	(1 0)	20,000	4	Randall, Stewart	1	2	3	4	5	6		8		9				7	10				11									26
27	11 Feb	A	Notts County	D 2 2	(1 1)	10,000	5	Randall, Stewart	1		2	4			7	8				3	6		10				11					5	9			27
28	18 Feb	H	**Manchester United**	L 0 1	(0 0)	45,000	5		1	2	3	4	5	6	7	8	9		11				10													28
29	27 Feb	A	Liverpool	L 0 3	(0 1)	8,000	5		1				5	6	7		9	8	11	3			10								2	4				29
30	04 Mar	H	**Bury**	W 5 1	(2 0)	12,000	5	Randall 2, Stewart, Metcalf, Higgins	1	2	3				7	9		4			6		10				11					5		8		30
31	18 Mar	H	**Aston Villa**	W 1 0	(0 0)	15,000	5	Shepherd	1	2	3	4	5		7	8	9		11				10									6				31
32	01 Apr	H	**Woolwich Arsenal**	L 0 1	(0 0)	15,000	6			2	3	4			7		9				5		10					1				6		8	11	32
33	03 Apr	A	Sheffield United	D 0 0	(0 0)	5,500	5		1	2		4	5			8	9					7	10				11				3	6				33
34	05 Apr	A	Nottingham Forest	W 1 0	(0 0)	2,500	5	Higgins	1	2	3	4			7			9			6		10				11					5		8		34
35	08 Apr	A	Bradford City	L 0 1	(0 1)	30,000	5		1		3		5			8	9	10		2	4	7					11					6				35
36	14 Apr	H	**Sheffield Wednesday**	L 0 2	(0 0)	30,000	6		1	2	3	4	5		7	8	9	10	11											6						36
37	15 Apr	H	**Blackburn Rovers**	D 2 2	(1 1)	25,000	6	Higgins, Stewart	1	2	3		5		7	8	9	10	11		6									4						37
38	29 Apr	H	**Manchester City**	D 3 3	(1 2)	5,000	8	Metcalf, Willis, McCracken (pen)	1	2	3	4	5			10			11			7										6	9	8		38
Round			**FA Cup**																																	**Round**
1	14 Jan	H	**Bury**	W 6 1	(3 1)	33,044		Shepherd 3, Stewart, Duncan, McWilliam	1	2	3	4	5	6		8	9	10	11			7														1
2	04 Feb	H	**Northampton Town**	D 1 1	(1 1)	42,023		Higgins	1	2	3	4	5	6		8		9	10			7					11									2
2r	08 Feb	H*	**Northampton Town**	W 1 0	(1 0)	28,200		Shepherd (pen)	1	2	3	4	5	6		8	9	10	11			7														2r
3	25 Feb	H	**Hull City**	W 3 2	(3 1)	46,531		Shepherd 2, Veitch	1	2	3	4	5	6	7		9	8	11				10													3
4	11 Mar	H	**Derby County**	W 4 0	(2 0)	59,717		Shepherd, Stewart, Rutherford, Willis	1	2	3	4	5		7	8	9	10	11													6				4
SF	25 Mar	N1	Chelsea	W 3 0	(2 0)	40,000		Wilson, Shepherd, Stewart	1	2	3	4	5		7	8	9	10	11													6				SF
F	22 Apr	N2	Bradford City	D 0 0	(0 0)	69,800			1	2	3	4	5		7	8		10	11											9		6				F
Fr	26 Apr	N3	Bradford City	L 0 1	(0 1)	66,646			1	2	3	4	5		7	8		10	11											9		6				Fr

H* Scheduled for Northampton, but played at Newcastle by agreement

N1 Played at St Andrew's, Birmingham
N2 Played at Crystal Palace, London
N3 Played at Old Trafford, Manchester

DateLine ... 3 Dec: Frank Hudspeth makes his debut in the match with Bradford City, the first of 482 games. **2 Jan:** United score five second-half goals to defeat Everton 5-1. **11 March:** A record gate of 59,717 creates record receipts of £2,128 for the FA Cup tie with Derby. **25 March:** Shepherd hits his 33rd goal of the season against Chelsea. **26 April:** In the FA Cup final replay, United fall 1-0 to Bradford City.

Title race with Rovers

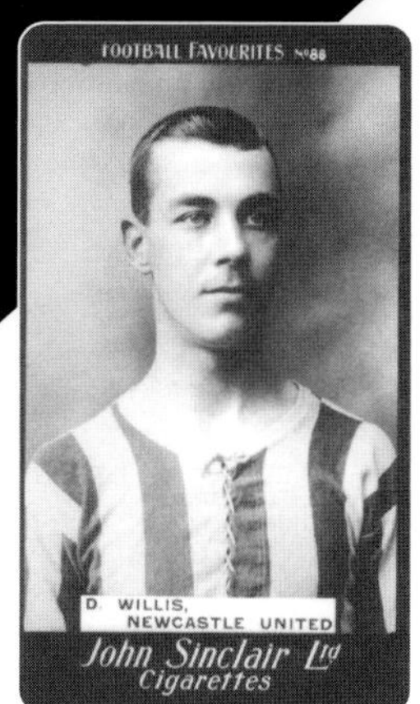

After FA Cup disappointment, it was all eyes on Championship silverware for season 1911-12 as United's own particular pattern continued. With the loss of two highly influential players in Shepherd and McWilliam, Newcastle's cheque book came out in a big way. They signed one of Scotland's best to replace McWilliam, Celtic midfielder James Hay, and also England striker Billy Hibbert from then top division outfit Bury. The Magpies' remodelled line-up challenged at the top of the table for honours with North East rivals Sunderland and Middlesbrough, then Everton and Blackburn Rovers. An early exit in the FA Cup to Derby County saw United concentrate on League action. Following a draw with Boro in November, the Teessiders led the table followed by United and Sunderland in third spot. Newcastle proceeded to lead the way mid-season with big wins over Aston Villa, Oldham and Bolton in which United netted 15 goals. The Magpies had the look of Champions once more.

As the New Year arrived though results were not as good with the Geordies going through a rough patch, losing six fixtures. They did get back to winning ways with a 4-1 success over Notts County and by April they held second spot, on the heels of Blackburn Rovers. But draws against Oldham, Bradford City and Liverpool and a crucial 2-0 defeat to Aston Villa, when they needed full points gave the momentum to Rovers. By the time United travelled to Lancashire for the last fixture of the season, the race was over. The title trophy was already destined for Ewood Park, Blackburn winning the Championship by five points.

An extraordinary contest took place during January against Manchester City. At their old Hyde Road ground, the home side missed all of three spot-kicks as the game ended 1-1. Stand-in goalkeeper Sid Blake ended the hero.

Pictured above: Half-back Dave Willis hailed from Byker and appeared for both Sunderland and United.

Memorabilia CORNER

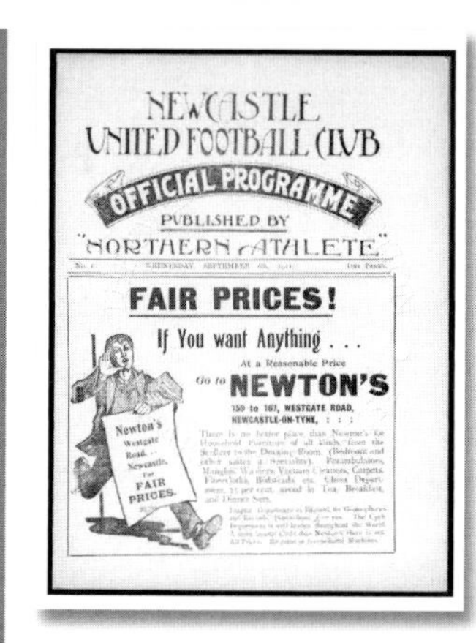

Match programme from 1912-13, by this time a substantial issue published by Northern Athlete.

IN CHARGE

Chairman: George Milne
Manager: Director Committee
Captain: Bill McCracken
Trainer/Coach: James McPherson

ST JAMES' PARK

Average Attendance
Lg 25,211 Lg & Cup 25,211

The Magpies were reaching the end of their Edwardian Mastery, but still showed off silverware. Left to right: Norfolk & Norwich Hospitals Charity Cup, NE League Championship, RVI Cup, Northumberland Senior Cup.

SEASON REVIEW

Football League Div 1: P38 W18 D8 L12 F64 A50 Pts 44.
Position: 3rd (Champions; Blackburn Rovers).
FA Cup: R1 (Winners; Barnsley).

Appearances (39m): Hay J 36, Low WL 36, McCracken WR 35, Stewart J 34, Willis DL 33, Wilson GW 33, Hibbert W 28, Lawrence J 27, Rutherford J 24, Whitson TT 20, Hudspeth FC 18, Higgins A 15, Lowes T 13, Duncan ASM 12, Blake S 10, Finlay J 8, Peart JG 8, Kelly WB 6, Scott JG 6, Veitch CCM 6, Anderson AL 5, Metcalf A 4, Jobey G 3, Gibson RJ 2, Sinclair TS 2, Carr J 1, Hewison R 1, McTavish JK 1, Thomas JW 1, Waugh R 1.

Goals (64g): Hibbert W 14, Stewart J 14, Hay J 7, Higgins A 4, Rutherford J 4, Finlay J 3, Low WL 3, Lowes T 3, McCracken WR 3, Peart JG 3, Wilson GW 2, Anderson AL 1, Duncan ASM 1, Scott JG 1, Veitch CCM 1.

Dismissals: 0 players.

MAJOR SIGNINGS

James Hay (Celtic) £1,250
Jack Peart (Stoke) £600
Billy Hibbert (Bury) £1,950 club & national record fee
Bill Kelly (Watford) £200
John McTavish (Tottenham Hot) £650

FROM THE RANKS

Tommy Lowes (Wallsend Park Villa)

PLAYER FOCUS George Wilson

Born Lochgelly. Outside-left, 5'6"
1907 to 1919: 218 app 33 goals.

United spent a national record fee of £1,600 in November 1907 when they secured the services of tricky winger George Wilson from Everton. The Scot had fallen out with the club's management after a series of disagreements which led to him being omitted from the FA Cup final eleven. One of the top players in the country at the time, although diminutive at only 5'6" tall, he was a match-winner on the left touchline, just as Rutherford in a different style was on the right flank. Appearing for his country and a Scottish Cup winner with Hearts – scoring the winning goal in the 1906 final – during the early part of his career, Wilson had built up a first-class reputation at Goodison Park and proceeded to continue that standing on Tyneside. Scoring twice on his debut against Liverpool, although small, George was stocky, able to ride tackles and create openings in the opponent's box. He was a cunning forward, an important player for United for eight seasons, winning the Division One Championship with the Magpies in 1909 and reaching three FA Cup finals, including the Black'n'Whites triumph in 1910. The First World War effectively ended his senior career, the Scot afterwards moving back to Scotland where he concluded his football career with East Fife, Albion Rovers and with Raith Rovers as boss. Known as Wee Geordie on Tyneside, he later emigrated to Vancouver in Canada. His brother David also appeared for Hearts and Everton.

TEAM COLOURS Black & white striped shirts, dark shorts (Change; white shirts, dark shorts)

SEASON 1911-12

Match	Date		FL Division 1					Posn		Lawrence	McCracken	Whitson	Willis	Low	Hay	Duncan	Kelly	Stewart	Higgins	Wilson	Waugh	Jobey	Anderson	Finlay	Scott	Metcalf	Sinclair	Gibson	Rutherford	Hibbert	Lowes	Blake	Hudspeth	Veitch	Carr	Hewison	Thomas	Peart	McTavish	Match
1	02 Sep	A	Bolton Wanderers	W	2 0	(1 0)	30,000		Stewart 2	1	2	3	4	5	6	7	8	9	10	11																				1
2	06 Sep	H	**Everton**	W	2 0	(2 0)	20,000	1	Low, Stewart	1		3	4	5	6	7	8	9	10	11	2																			2
3	09 Sep	H	**Bradford City**	L	0 2	(0 0)	40,000	5		1	2	3	4	5	6	7	8	9	10	11																				3
4	16 Sep	A	Woolwich Arsenal	L	0 2	(0 1)	20,000	8		1	2	3		5	6	7		8	9	10		4	11																	4
5	23 Sep	H	**Manchester City**	W	1 0	(0 0)	11,000	5	Stewart	1	2		4	5	3	7	9	8		10				6	11															5
6	30 Sep	A	Everton	L	0 2	(0 1)	15,000	9		1	2	3	4	5	6	7	9	10		11						8														6
7	07 Oct	H	**West Bromwich Albion**	D	0 0	(0 0)	22,000	8			2	3	4	5	6		9	8		10					11		1	7												7
8	14 Oct	A	Sunderland	W	2 1	(1 0)	30,000	8	Scott, McCracken (pen)	1	2	3	4	5	6	7		8	9	10					11															8
9	21 Oct	H	**Blackburn Rovers**	W	4 2	(3 1)	30,000	4	Hay, Stewart 2, Wilson	1	2	3	4	5	6			8	10	11									7	9										9
10	28 Oct	A	Sheffield Wednesday	W	2 1	(1 0)	18,000	2	Hibbert, Higgins	1	2	3	4	5	6			8	10	11									7	9										10
11	04 Nov	H	**Bury**	W	3 2	(0 0)	18,000	1	Hibbert, Higgins 2	1	2	3	4	5	6			8	10	11									7	9										11
12	11 Nov	A	Middlesbrough	D	1 1	(0 0)	32,986	2	Stewart	1	2	3	4	5	6	7		8	10	11										9										12
13	18 Nov	H	**Notts County**	W	3 2	(1 0)	18,000	1	Low, Rutherford 2	1	2	3	4	5	6			8	10	11									7	9										13
14	25 Nov	A	Tottenham Hotspur	W	2 1	(2 1)	37,541	1	Hay, Hibbert	1	2	3	4	5	6			8	10	11									7	9										14
15	02 Dec	H	**Manchester United**	L	2 3	(1 1)	25,000	1	Stewart, McCracken (pen)	1	2	3	4	5	6			8	10	11									7	9										15
16	09 Dec	A	Liverpool	W	1 0	(0 0)	15,000	1	Stewart	1	2	3	4	5	6			8	10						11				7	9										16
17	16 Dec	H	**Aston Villa**	W	6 2	(3 2)	30,000	1	Higgins, Hibbert, Stewart, Rutherford, Hay, McCracken (pen)	1	2	3	4	5	6			8	10	11									7	9										17
18	23 Dec	A	Preston North End	L	1 2	(1 1)	12,000	1	Hibbert	1	2	3	4	5	6			8					11						7	9	10									18
19	25 Dec	A	Oldham Athletic	W	4 2	(0 0)	25,000	1	Hay, Hibbert 2, Low	1	2	3	4	5	6			8		11									7	9	10									19
20	26 Dec	H	**Sheffield United**	D	2 2	(1 1)	40,000	1	Hibbert, Rutherford	1	2	3	4	5	6			8		11									7	9	10									20
21	30 Dec	H	**Bolton Wanderers**	W	5 2	(2 0)	28,000	1	Hay, Hibbert 3, Veitch		2		4	5	6										11				7	9	10	1	3	8						21
22	01 Jan	A	Sheffield United	L	1 2	(0 2)	38,825	1	Stewart				4		3			9		11		5		6					7		10	1	2	8						22
	06 Jan	A	Bradford City	Ab	0 0	(0 0)	8,000						4	5				8		11	2			6					7	9	10	1	3							
23	20 Jan	H	**Woolwich Arsenal**	L	1 2	(1 2)	10,000	3	Stewart					5	6			8		11						10	1		7	9			2		3	4				23
24	27 Jan	A	Manchester City	D	1 1	(1 0)	28,000	3	Lowes					5	3			9		11		6							7		10	1	2	4			8			24
25	10 Feb	A	West Bromwich Albion	L	1 3	(0 1)	30,252	3	Lowes		2	3	4	5	6			8		11									7	9	10	1								25
26	17 Feb	H	**Sunderland**	W	3 1	(1 0)	45,000	2	Anderson, Lowes, Stewart		2		4	5	6			9		10			11						7		8	1	3							26
27	24 Feb	H	**Preston North End**	W	1 0	(1 0)	25,000	2	Hay		2		4	5	6			9		11									7	10	8	1	3							27
28	02 Mar	H	**Sheffield Wednesday**	L	0 2	(0 1)	22,000	2		1	2		4	5						10				6	11				7	9	8		3							28
29	09 Mar	A	Bury	L	1 2	(0 0)	8,512	3	Stewart	1	2		4	5	6			10					11						7	9	8		3							29
30	16 Mar	H	**Middlesbrough**	L	0 1	(0 0)	35,000	3		1	2		4		6			8		11									7	10			3	5				9		30
31	23 Mar	A	Notts County	W	4 1	(1 1)	6,000	3	Finlay 2, Peart, Wilson		2		4	5						11				6		8		7		10		1	3					9		31
32	30 Mar	H	**Tottenham Hotspur**	W	2 0	(1 0)	15,000	2	Hibbert, Peart		2			5	4	7				11				6		8				10		1	3					9		32
33	05 Apr	H	**Oldham Athletic**	D	1 1	(1 0)	30,000	4	Hay		2			5	4	7		8		11				6						10		1	3					9		33
34	06 Apr	A	Manchester United	W	2 0	(1 0)	15,000	2	Duncan, Finlay	1	2		4			7		8		11				6						10			3	5				9		34
35	09 Apr	A	Bradford City	D	1 1	(1 0)	18,000	2	Hibbert	1	2		4	5	6			8		11									7	10			3					9		35
36	13 Apr	H	**Liverpool**	D	1 1	(0 1)	15,000	2	Hibbert	1	2		4	5	6			9					11						7	10	8		3							36
37	20 Apr	A	Aston Villa	L	0 2	(0 0)	20,000	2		1	2		4	5	6	7				11										10	8		3					9		37
38	27 Apr	A	Blackburn Rovers	D	1 1	(1 0)	10,000	3	Peart	1	2		4	5	6			8	11											10			3					9	7	38
Round			FA Cup																																					Round
1	13 Jan	A	Derby County	L	0 3	(0 1)	21,500				2			5	6			8		11				4					7	9		1	3	10						1

Ab Abandoned after 51 mins due to snow and fading light

DateLine ...11 Nov: A draw with Middlesbrough sees Boro head the table with United second and Sunderland third. **16 Dec:** United score six goals against Aston Villa and record six different goalscorers. **25 Dec:** Newcastle retain top spot in the table with a Christmas Day victory over Oldham. **27 Jan:** Manchester City miss three penalties in a 1-1 draw.

Epic rivalry with Sunderland

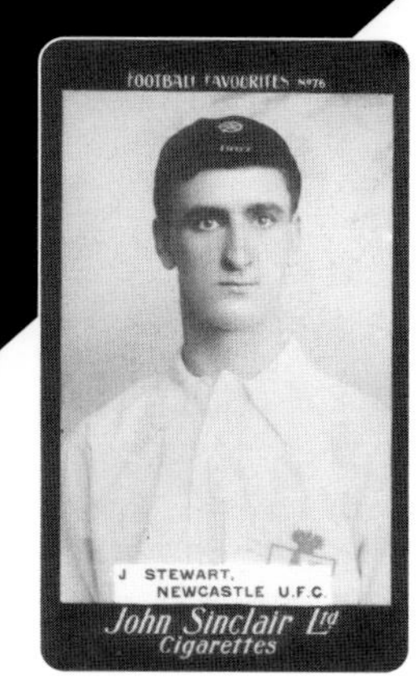

North East football was in a healthy state as the Edwardian era came to a close. Not only had Newcastle United reached their goal of becoming the country's finest side, not far behind were rivals Sunderland – of course, a club that held that prestigious label as the century turned. Few clubs in the country could match the North Eastern giants; they stood alongside Aston Villa as the nation's elite. In season 1912-13 Tyne and Wear clashed as never before in the quarter-final of the FA Cup. A heavyweight confrontation was played out over three hotly contested games; firstly a 0-0 draw at Roker Park, then an epic 2-2 free-flowing match with extra-time watched by nearly 57,000 at Gallowgate. Newcastle won ground advantage for the third clash but Sunderland had the edge. They won comfortably by 3-0 on a snow covered surface at St James' Park.

United's Wearside rivals were also the team to beat in the League programme, Sunderland eventually claiming the title trophy. Although the Magpies started well, romping home 6-0 against Everton, from November onwards United were no-where close to the red-and-whites. Season 1912-13 was a big let-down in League action, at one stage losing five in a row in December. The Black'n'Whites concluded the programme way off the pace in 14th spot, their worst placing since 1902. They even flirted with relegation worries for a period in April.

One of the principal reasons for their slump was that Newcastle struggled to replace Albert Shepherd in attack. Although he was on his way back from injury, the striker was never quite the same again. His flair and ruthless streak in front of goal was a huge loss. No-one reached double figures in the scoring chart with England international James Stewart the highest goal-getter with only nine strikes.

Pictured above: Nicknamed Tadger, James Stewart was an elegant footballer selected for England.

The characters of 'Magpie' and 'Geordie' as featured in the local press in 1912 became hugely popular.

Memorabilia CORNER

IN CHARGE

Chairman: George Milne
Manager: Director Committee
Captain: Bill McCracken
Trainer/Coach: James McPherson

ST JAMES' PARK

Average Attendance
Lg 25,642 Lg & Cup 28,220

Just in view on this 1912-13 group of players and officials is the club's mascot, Rex (bottom left). The Great Dane was extremely popular and often tied to the railings during fixtures at St James' Park.

SEASON REVIEW

Football League Div 1: P38 W13 D8 L17 F47 A47 Pts 34.
Position: 14th (Champions; Sunderland).
FA Cup: QF (Winners; Aston Villa).

Appearances (46m): Lawrence J 42, Hay J 39, Low WL 39, McTavish JK 38, Hudspeth FC 35, McCracken WR 35, Wilson GW 31, Hibbert W 29, Rutherford J 25, McDonald J2 24, Hewison R 22, Higgins A 20, Stewart J 20, Finlay J 17, Jobey G 15, Veitch CCM 12, Whitson TT 12, Cooper E 9, Duncan ASM 9, Peart JG 9, Shepherd A 8, Fleming JBM 4, Hughes T 2, Little R 2, Willis DL 2, Wilson JH 2, Alderson JT 1, Blake S 1, Lowes T 1, Scott JG 1.

Goals (55g): Stewart J 9, Higgins A 8, McTavish JK 7, Hudspeth FC 6, Hibbert W 4, Wilson GW 4, Peart JG 3, Rutherford J 3, Shepherd A 3, Low WL 2, McDonald J2 2, Veitch CCM 2, Cooper E 1, Hay J 1.

Dismissals: 0 players.

MAJOR SIGNINGS

John McDonald (Liverpool) £650
Edward Cooper (Glossop) £1,300
James Fleming (St Bernards) £250

FROM THE RANKS

Tom Hughes (Wallsend Park Villa)
John Alderson (Shildon Ath)
Dick Little (Jarrow Croft)
James Wilson (Newcastle Bentonians)

PLAYER FOCUS James Hay

Born Beith. Left-half, 5'8"
1911 to 1919: 149 app 8 goals.

To replace the talent of the injured Peter McWilliam, United looked to one of the best half-backs in Britain. Club directors headed north in July 1911 and paid a big fee of £1,250 for Celtic and Scotland captain Jimmy Hay. An experienced campaigner of six titles, five Scottish Cup finals and 255 games with the Hoops, there were few more experienced in midfield. Earning the nickname of The General and from Ayrshire, 30-year-old Hay slotted into United's midfield with ease as the Magpies started to rebuild their Edwardian Masters eleven. Cool and poised with the ball, Jimmy was a gifted player, but also possessed a vigorous edge to his game. He was a sturdy character, only 5'8" tall, but with broad shoulders. Jimmy was dubbed The Man with the Iron Chest by the press, although always known best by his Scots nickname of Dun Hay. A fixture in Newcastle's line-up for four seasons, his career at the top was halted by World War One. On returning to Scotland after the hostilities, he appeared for Ayr United where after a spell with Clydebank as boss, he returned as manager. Jimmy was embroiled in controversy at Ayr during the Twenties and was rather unjustifiably suspended sine-die from the game for a time following a bribery scandal in which he accused officials, referees and directors of illegal dealings. Hay was later a Newcastle scout for a period.

TEAM COLOURS Black & white striped shirts, dark shorts (Change; white shirts, dark shorts)

SEASON 1912-13

Match	Date		FL Division 1	Res			HT	Att	Posn	Scorers	Lawrence	McCracken	Hudspeth	Veitch	Low	Hay	Rutherford	McTavish	Shepherd	Hibbert	McDonald	Higgins	Wilson GW	Whitson	Jobey	Finlay	Peart	Stewart	Willis	Hewison	Fleming	Duncan	Little	Wilson JH	Alderson	Hughes	Cooper	Lowes	Scott	Blake	Match
1	02 Sep	A	Bolton Wanderers	W	2	1	(1 1)	30,000		McDonald, Rutherford	1	2	3	4	5	6	7	8	9	10	11																				1
2	07 Sep	H	**Sunderland**	D	1	1	(1 0)	54,200	6	Shepherd	1	2	3	4	5	6	7	8	9	10	11																				2
3	11 Sep	H	**Bolton Wanderers**	W	2	1	(0 1)	12,000	3	Wilson G, McTavish	1	2	3	4	5	6	7	8		9		10	11																		3
4	14 Sep	A	Oldham Athletic	L	0	1	(0 1)	30,000	5		1	2	3	4	5	6	7	8		9		10	11																		4
5	21 Sep	H	**Chelsea**	W	3	2	(1 2)	38,000	6	Stewart 2, Peart	1	2			5		7	8					11	3	4	6	9	10													5
6	28 Sep	A	Woolwich Arsenal	D	1	1	(1 0)	16,000	5	Stewart	1	2			5			8			7		11	3	4	6	9	10													6
7	05 Oct	H	**Bradford City**	D	1	1	(0 0)	35,000	5	Hudspeth (pen)	1	2	3		5		7					8	11		4	6	9	10													7
8	12 Oct	A	Manchester City	W	1	0	(1 0)	35,000	4	Stewart	1	2	3		5	4	7	8		9			11			6		10													8
9	19 Oct	H	**West Bromwich Albion**	D	1	1	(0 1)	30,000	4	McTavish	1	2	3		5	4	7	8		9			11			6		10													9
10	26 Oct	A	Everton	W	6	0	(2 0)	10,000	2	Stewart 2, McTavish 2, Low 2	1	2	3		5	4	7	8				10	11			6		9													10
11	02 Nov	H	**Sheffield Wednesday**	W	1	0	(0 0)	25,000	2	Higgins	1	2	3		5	4	7	8				10	11			6		9													11
12	09 Nov	A	Blackburn Rovers	L	0	2	(0 2)	32,485	3		1	2	3		5	4	7	8				10	11			6		9													12
13	16 Nov	H	**Derby County**	L	2	4	(2 3)	25,000	6	Hibbert, McTavish	1	2	3		5	4	7	8		9	11							10	6												13
14	23 Nov	A	Tottenham Hotspur	L	0	1	(0 0)	25,000	7		1	2	3		5	6	7	8		10			11							4	9										14
15	30 Nov	H	**Middlesbrough**	W	3	1	(3 1)	25,000	7	Wilson G, Peart, Hay	1	2	3		5	6	7	8			11		10				9			4											15
16	07 Dec	A	Notts County	W	1	0	(1 0)	10,000	5	Peart	1	2	3		5	6	7	8			11		10				9			4											16
17	14 Dec	H	**Manchester United**	L	1	3	(0 3)	20,000	8	Rutherford	1	2	3		5	6	7	8			11		10				9			4											17
18	21 Dec	A	Aston Villa	L	1	3	(1 2)	30,000	10	Hudspeth (pen)	1	2	3		5	6		8		10	11						9			4		7									18
19	25 Dec	H	**Sheffield United**	L	1	2	(0 1)	18,000	11	Higgins	1	2			5	6		8		11		10		3			9			4		7									19
20	26 Dec	A	Liverpool	L	1	2	(0 2)	35,000	11	Wilson G	1								9	11			10	3	5	6		8		4		7	2								20
21	28 Dec	A	Sunderland	L	0	2	(0 1)	35,000	12		1	2			5	6		8		11		9	10							4		7	3								21
22	30 Dec	A	Sheffield United	D	1	1	(0 0)	22,000	12	McTavish	1	2				3		7		11		9	10		5	6		8		4											22
23	01 Jan	H	**Liverpool**	D	0	0	(0 0)	30,000	11			2				3		8		11		9	10		5	6				4		7		1							23
24	04 Jan	H	**Oldham Athletic**	W	4	1	(2 0)	25,000	11	McDonald, Stewart, Higgins 2			2		5	3		8			11	9			6			10		4		7		1							24
25	18 Jan	A	Chelsea	L	0	1	(0 0)	45,000	12		1	2	3		5			8		10	11					6	9			4		7									25
26	25 Jan	H	**Woolwich Arsenal**	W	3	1	(2 0)	20,000	11	Stewart, Higgins, Hudspeth (pen)			2		5	3	7			8	11	9			6			10		4					1						26
27	08 Feb	A	Bradford City	L	0	2	(0 1)	20,000	13		1		2			6	7	8		9	11			3	5					4						10					27
28	15 Feb	H	**Manchester City**	L	0	1	(0 1)	35,000	13		1	2	3		5	4	7	8	9				11			6		10													28
29	01 Mar	H	**Everton**	W	2	0	(2 0)	25,000	12	Shepherd, Stewart	1		2	5		3		7	9		11		10		6			8		4											29
30	15 Mar	H	**Blackburn Rovers**	L	0	1	(0 0)	18,000	13		1							8						3	5	6			4	2	9						7	10	11		30
31	22 Mar	A	Derby County	L	1	2	(1 1)	9,000	13	Hudspeth (pen)	1		2		5	6		8		11		10		3						4	9						7				31
32	29 Mar	H	**Tottenham Hotspur**	W	3	0	(1 0)	20,000	14	Higgins 2, Hibbert	1		2		5	6		8		9		10	11	3						4							7				32
33	05 Apr	A	Middlesbrough	D	0	0	(0 0)	10,370	15		1		2		5						11	8	10	3		6		9		4							7				33
34	09 Apr	A	West Bromwich Albion	L	0	1	(0 0)	8,277	15		1		2		5	3		8			11					6				4	9					10	7				34
35	12 Apr	H	**Notts County**	D	0	0	(0 0)	12,000	15		1	2		4	5	6	9			8	11		10	3													7				35
36	14 Apr	A	Sheffield Wednesday	W	2	1	(2 0)	14,000	13	Hibbert, Cooper	1	2		4	5	6		8		9	11	10		3													7				36
37	19 Apr	A	Manchester United	L	0	3	(0 1)	17,000	13		1			5		2		8		9	11	10		3		6				4							7				37
38	26 Apr	H	**Aston Villa**	L	2	3	(0 3)	20,000	14	Higgins, Veitch		2	3	4	5	6		8		9	11	10															7			1	38
Round			FA Cup																																						Round
1	11 Jan	H	**Bradford City**	Ab	1	0	(1 0)	15,928		*Wilson G*	1	2	3		5	4		8				9	11		6			10				7									1
1	16 Jan	H	**Bradford City**	W	1	0	(1 0)	11,953		Wilson G	1	2	3		5	4		8				9	11		6			10				7									1
2	01 Feb	A	Hull City	D	0	0	(0 0)	18,250			1	2	3		5	4	7	8				9	11		6			10													2
2r	05 Feb	H	**Hull City**	W	3	0	(2 0)	32,278		Hibbert, Rutherford, Hudspeth (pen)	1	2	3		5	4	7	8		9	11		10		6																2r
3	22 Feb	A	Liverpool	D	1	1	(0 1)	37,093		Shepherd	1	2	3		5	4	7		9	8	11		10		6																3
3r	26 Feb	H	**Liverpool**	W	1	0	(1 0)	39,769		Hudspeth (pen)	1	2	3		5	6	7		9	8	11		10							4											3r
4	08 Mar	A	Sunderland	D	0	0	(0 0)	29,111			1	2	3	4	5	6	7			9	11		10					8													4
4r	12 Mar	H	**Sunderland**	De	2	2	(1 1)	56,717		McTavish, Veitch	1	2	3	4	5	6		7	9	8	11		10																		4r
4rr	17 Mar	H	**Sunderland**	L	0	3	(0 2)	49,354			1	2	3	4	5	6		8		9			11					10				7									4rr

Ab Abandoned after 45 mins due to snow and fading light

De Drawn after extra time

DateLine ... 26 Oct: United win 6-0 at Everton, United's best on their travels at the time. **16 Jan:** Only 11,953 watch the FA Cup-tie with Bradford City, the lowest FA Cup crowd since the start of the 1900s. **17 March:** An epic FA Cup quarter-final treble with Sunderland decided with a 3-0 Reds win. **26 April:** United fall three goals behind against Aston Villa after only 18 minutes and lose 3-2.

SEASON
1913-14
DIVISION 1

War looms as the Masters fade

All great sides come to pass in football. Although United's directors had continually refreshed their squad by adding more international quality to the ranks, United's Edwardian Masters had their finale as discord in Europe was smouldering towards a horrendous conflict. While Newcastle improved their League placing – in the end to a comfortable mid-table 11th – the Masters era was well and truly over.

Although Shepherd returned to full action, he was pale shadow of the vibrant centre-forward once ranked with the best in the country. Albert did get goals as he returned in earnest during January and February. He grabbed 10 in 16 games. They were important ones too, strikes which lifted the Magpies away from the lower reaches of the table. Injury also hit the side, but that gave opportunities to younger reserves. Local lad Tommy Goodwill was one who seized his chance, until he was sidelined too. Highlight of the League programme was a double victory over Sunderland, the reigning Champions. United won 2-1 at Roker Park, the Magpies spoiling the red-and-whites title party at the first home game of the season. Newcastle later recorded the same scoreline on Tyneside over Christmas.

There was a big FA Cup shock for the Black'n'Whites too. Sheffield United arrived at Gallowgate in the First Round and raced to a 3-0 lead in the opening minutes. The Blades eventually won 5-0 with Newcastle down to eight fit men at one stage, and no recognised goalkeeper. By the end of the season the clouds of war began to affect day to day activities at St James' Park. Training methods changed, to now include military exercises controlled by the Company Sergeant Major from the local garrison on Barrack Road.

Pictured above: Striker Tom Hall made the move from Wear to Tyne and had an immediate impact.

Memorabilia CORNER

The Gamage's yearbook for 1913-14.

IN CHARGE

Chairman: George Archibald
Manager: Director Committee
Captain: Bill McCracken
Trainer/Coach: James McPherson

ST JAMES' PARK

Average Attendance
Lg 26,958 Lg & Cup 27,019

United's playing staff and director photographs usually had a hierarchy. Young professionals were at the back, while seniors held a prominent seated position to the right and left of the club Chairman, Vice-Chairman and captain. Bill McCracken holds the central spot flanked by George Archibald and John Graham.

PLAYER FOCUS Billy Hibbert

Born Golborne. Inside-forward, 5'8"
1911 to 1920: 159 app 50 goals.

United were always in the hunt for highly rated players during the era and were never shy to spend big. Then in the top-tier of football, Bury's Billy Hibbert had showed he could mix it with the best, scoring 105 goals and capped by England in 1909-10. A Lancashire product, United spent a British record fee of £1,950 during October 1911 for his goal talent in the aftermath of Shepherd's failure to recapture his best form following injury. Billy operated at mainly inside-forward for United, although he was always reported as being better suited in the leader's role. Agile, slim and fast in attack, he scored 50 goals for United, being an effective goal-poacher in the seasons up to World War One, the club's top scorer in 1911-12 and 1914-15. Wearing his country's shirt, Hibbert once netted a remarkable 34 goals for the unofficial England line-up on tour in South Africa during 1910. Returning to action at Gallowgate after war, Billy was now a veteran at 35 years old but still managed to make headlines, netting hat-tricks against Liverpool and Bradford Park Avenue. He left United in May 1920 and subsequently continued to bag goals for Bradford City and Oldham Athletic before heading to North America to coach the game. Something of an errant traveller, Hibbert was also with Valencia in Spain and after a spell back in England with Wigan Borough, he also coached in Hungary before retirement.

SEASON REVIEW

Football League Div 1: P38 W13 D11 L14 F39 A48 Pts 37.
Position: 11th (Champions; Blackburn Rovers).
FA Cup: R1 (Winners; Burnley).

Appearances (39m): Hudspeth FC 37, Hibbert W 36, Low WL 35, Hay J 34, Wilson GW 28, Douglas A 23, Finlay J 21, Lawrence J 21, McCracken WR 21, Hall T 20, Hewison R 20, Shepherd A 20, Goodwill T 19, Mellor WG 16, King J 15, Cooper E 14, McDonald J2 12, Hampson W 10, Veitch CCM 6, Whitson TT 6, Spink J 5, Hardy S 3, Lowes T 2, Wilson JH 2, Dixon ES 1, Grey TJ 1, Higgins A 1.

Goals (39m): Shepherd A 10, Hall T 6, Hibbert W 6, Hudspeth FC 4, Wilson GW 4, Goodwill T 2, Low WL 2, McDonald J2 2, Douglas A 1, Hardy S 1, King J 1.

Dismissals: 0 players

MAJOR SIGNINGS

Billy Hampson (Norwich City) £1,250
Bill Bradley (Portsmouth) £300
Angus Douglas (Chelsea) £1,100
Tom Hall (Sunderland) £425
John King (Partick Thistle) £600
Bill Mellor (Norwich City) £765

FROM THE RANKS

Stan Dixon (Barrington Albion)
Jimmy Spink (Craghead Utd)
Tommy Goodwill (Seaton Delaval)
Tom Grey (Bedlington Utd)
Stan Hardy (Rutherford College)

TEAM COLOURS Black & white striped shirts, dark shorts (Change; white shirts, dark shorts)

SEASON 1913-14

Match	Date		FL Division 1				Att	Posn	Scorers	Lawrence	McCracken	Hudspeth	Hay	Low	Finlay	Cooper	King	Shepherd	Higgins	Wilson GW	Hall	Hibbert	McDonald	Goodwill	Lowes	Whitson	Hewison	Douglas	Hardy	Veitch	Wilson JH	Spink	Mellor	Hampson	Dixon	Grey	Match
1	01 Sep	A	Blackburn Rovers	L	0 3	(0 1)	20,000			1	2	3	4	5	6	7	8	9	10	11																	1
2	06 Sep	A	Sunderland	W	2 1	(1 1)	40,000	11	Hall, King	1	2	3	4	5	6	7	8				9	10	11														2
3	13 Sep	H	**Everton**	L	0 1	(0 1)	30,000	16		1	2	3	4	5	6		8			10	9	7		11													3
4	20 Sep	A	West Bromwich Albion	D	1 1	(0 1)	29,147	15	Hudspeth (pen)	1	2	3	4	5	6	7	8			11	9	10															4
5	27 Sep	H	**Sheffield Wednesday**	W	3 1	(1 0)	30,000	11	Hall, Hibbert, Low	1	2	3	4	5	6	7	8			11	9	10															5
6	04 Oct	A	Bolton Wanderers	L	1 3	(1 0)	32,000	14	Hall	1	2	3	4	5	6	7	8				9	10	11														6
7	11 Oct	H	**Chelsea**	W	1 0	(0 0)	22,000	13	McDonald	1	2	3	4	5	6	7					9	10	11		8												7
8	18 Oct	A	Oldham Athletic	L	0 3	(0 1)	20,000	14		1		2	4	5	6	7					9	10	11		8	3											8
9	25 Oct	H	**Manchester United**	L	0 1	(0 1)	35,000	15		1	2	3	4	5	6			9			8	10	11				7										9
10	01 Nov	A	Burnley	L	0 1	(0 1)	25,000	17		1	2	3	4	5	6			9		11	8	10						7									10
11	08 Nov	H	**Preston North End**	W	2 0	(1 0)	12,000	16	Hall, Wilson G	1		2	6	5			8			11	9	10				3	4	7									11
12	15 Nov	H	**Tottenham Hotspur**	W	2 0	(1 0)	25,000	13	Hall 2	1		2	6	5			8			11	9	10				3	4	7									12
13	22 Nov	A	Liverpool	D	0 0	(0 0)	30,000	12		1		2	6	5			8			11	9	10				3	4	7									13
14	29 Nov	H	**Aston Villa**	D	2 2	(1 2)	34,000	14	Low, Hudspeth (pen)	1		2	6	5			8			11	9	10				3	4	7									14
15	06 Dec	A	Middlesbrough	L	0 3	(0 1)	15,300	15		1	2	3	6	5			8				9	10		11			4	7									15
16	13 Dec	H	**Sheffield United**	W	2 1	(0 0)	25,000	12	Hibbert, Hudspeth (pen)	1		2	3	5	6						9	8		11			4	7	10								16
17	20 Dec	A	Derby County	L	0 2	(0 2)	15,000	16		1		2	3	5	6						9	8		11			4	7	10								17
18	25 Dec	H	**Bradford City**	D	0 0	(0 0)	25,000	17		1	2	3	4	5	6					10		9		11			8	7									18
19	26 Dec	A	Bradford City	L	0 2	(0 2)	18,000	18		1	2	3	4		6	7	8	9		10				11						5							19
20	27 Dec	H	**Sunderland**	W	2 1	(0 0)	50,000	17	Goodwill, Hibbert	1	2	3	6	5						10	9	8		11			4	7									20
21	01 Jan	H	**Manchester City**	L	0 1	(0 1)	20,000	17		1	2	3	6	5						10	9	8		11			4	7									21
22	03 Jan	A	Everton	L	0 2	(0 1)	25,000	19			2	3	4	5	6		8			10		9		11				7			1						22
23	17 Jan	H	**West Bromwich Albion**	D	3 3	(3 1)	18,200	19	Hardy, McDonald, Shepherd			2	6	5				9				8	11			3		7	10			4	1				23
24	24 Jan	A	Sheffield Wednesday	D	0 0	(0 0)	30,000	19					3	5	6			9		10		8	11					7				4	1	2			24
25	07 Feb	H	**Bolton Wanderers**	W	4 3	(3 1)	35,000	17	Wilson G 2, Shepherd 2 (1 pen)				3	5	6	7		9		10		8	11				4						1	2			25
26	14 Feb	A	Chelsea	W	1 0	(0 0)	35,000	15	Shepherd			3	6	5		7		9		10		8	11				4						1	2			26
27	21 Feb	H	**Oldham Athletic**	D	0 0	(0 0)	30,000	13				3	6	5		7	8	9				10	11				4						1	2			27
28	28 Feb	A	Manchester United	D	2 2	(2 2)	25,000	13	Hibbert, Shepherd			3	6	5		7		9		10		8	11				4						1	2			28
29	14 Mar	A	Preston North End	L	1 4	(0 2)	18,000	15	Shepherd			3		5	6	7		9		10		8	11				4						1	2			29
30	18 Mar	H	**Burnley**	W	3 1	(1 0)	15,000	12	Douglas, Goodwill, Hibbert			3	6					9		10		8		11			5	7				4	1	2			30
31	21 Mar	A	Tottenham Hotspur	D	0 0	(0 0)	20,000	13				3	6					9			10	8		11			5	7				4	1	2			31
32	01 Apr	H	**Liverpool**	L	1 2	(0 0)	20,000	15	Hudspeth (pen)			3		5		7		9		10				11			6					4	1	2	8		32
33	04 Apr	A	Aston Villa	W	3 1	(1 0)	20,000	12	Shepherd 2, Wilson G		2	3			6			9		10		8		11				7		4			1			5	33
34	10 Apr	H	**Blackburn Rovers**	D	0 0	(0 0)	40,000	15			2	3	6	5				9		10		8		11				7		4			1				34
35	11 Apr	H	**Middlesbrough**	W	1 0	(1 0)	30,000	13	Shepherd		2	3	6	5				9		10		8		11				7		4			1				35
36	13 Apr	A	Manchester City	W	1 0	(0 0)	30,000	10	Shepherd		2	3		5	6			9		10		8		11				7		4			1				36
37	18 Apr	A	Sheffield United	L	0 2	(0 0)	17,000	11				3	6	5				9		10		8		11			4	7					1	2			37
38	25 Apr	H	**Derby County**	D	1 1	(1 1)	16,000	11	Hibbert		2	3		5			4	9		10		8		11				7		6			1				38
Round			**FA Cup**																																		**Round**
1	10 Jan	H	**Sheffield United**	L	0 5	(0 1)	28,185				2	3	4	5	6					10	9	8		11				7			1						1

DateLine ... 6 Sept: Tom Hall nets on his debut against his former club Sunderland. **10 Jan:** A 5-0 FA Cup shock at the hands of Sheffield United on Tyneside, a record home defeat in the competition. **10 Jan:** United are reduced for a period to eight men in the whitewash by Sheffield United.

NEWCASTLE UNITED

SEASON
1914-15
DIVISION 1

Football continues as war rages

War was declared before the 1914-15 season kicked off, a conflict that was to develop into a horrifying and dreadful confrontation on the Continent and elsewhere. Football, however, continued largely unaffected through the first months of fighting and as the giant armies gathered in France and Belgium in particular. Indeed, the season was completed although as the battles developed and intensified as well as worsened, it was clear the sport could not keep going as normal. To start with fixtures at St James' Park saw many fans dressed in forces uniform as the call to arms gathered pace. Gradually, injured soldiers were to be seen in the crowd too. Then players began joining local regiments, and firing practice was carried out by United's footballers on the Gallowgate pitch – with rifles rather than footballs.

Newcastle again only returned an average mark in Division One, finishing out of trouble but too close to the relegation mire for comfort. They even once had to play without a recognised goalkeeper when Bill Mellor was injured in the pre-match warm-up against Spurs. Forward Jock King deputised and kept a clean sheet. A terrific festive double with Sunderland was served up for local supporters. On Tyneside the red-and-whites won 5-2 on Christmas Day but Newcastle gained revenge on Boxing Day at Roker Park, winning 4-2.

Newcastle did head on a mini-FA Cup run after an opening round victory over Southern League West Ham United. They met Chelsea in the quarter-final but after doing all the hard work in London at Stamford Bridge, securing a 1-1 draw; the Pensioners won the replay on Tyneside by a single goal.

On the seasons conclusion football was suspended and player's contracts cancelled. For the first time the game entered a period of severe disruption – and for some, total closure. Newcastle United were one of the clubs to bring down the shutters, the Magpies all but closing down during July 1915.

Pictured above: Jock Finlay joined United as a teenager and gave the club grand service for 14 seasons.

Memorabilia CORNER

BRITONS "WANTS" YOU JOIN YOUR COUNTRY'S ARMY! GOD SAVE THE KING

Several United players joined the forces, answering Kitchener's call-to-arms.

IN CHARGE

Chairman: George Archibald
Manager: Director Committee
Captain: Jimmy Hay
Trainer/Coach: James McPherson

ST JAMES' PARK

Average Attendance
Lg 15,289 Lg & Cup 18,112

Newcastle in their change kit during 1914-15. Back row, left to right: J Cameron (director), Hay, Watt (secretary), McCracken, Low, McPherson (trainer), Lawrence, Finlay, Hudspeth, JP Oliver (director). Front: Cooper, King, Hall, Hibbert, Wilson.

SEASON REVIEW

Football League Div 1: P38 W11 D10 L17 F46 A48 Pts 32.
Position: 15th (Champions; Everton).
FA Cup: QF (Winners; Sheffield United).

Appearances (45m): Hudspeth FC 42, Low WL 42, Goodwill T 41, Hay J 40, Hibbert W 36, Lawrence J 36, McCracken WR 36, Douglas A 33, King J 25, Hall T 24, Hewison R 22, Booth CT 19, Spink J 19, Pailor R 16, Cooper E 12, Finlay J 12, Higgins A 9, Hampson W 8, Mellor WG 8, Wilson GW 8, McGough R 2, Cairns T 1, Dixon ES 1, Little R 1, Soulsby JN 1, Veitch CCM 1.

Goals (57g): Hibbert W 16, Hall T 8, King J 7, Pailor R 5, Goodwill T 4, Hudspeth FC 4, Higgins A 3, Booth CT 2, Finlay J 2, Cooper E 1, Douglas A 1, McCracken WR 1, own goals 3.

Dismissals: 0 players

MAJOR SIGNINGS

Bob Pailor (West Brom Albion) £1,550

FROM THE RANKS

Curtis Booth (Wallsend Elm Villa)

PLAYER FOCUS Tommy Goodwill

Born Bates Cottages. Outside-left, 5'7"
1913 to 1916: 60 app 6 goals.

Born and bred in the Northumberland coalfield village of Bates Cottages near Cramlington, Tommy Goodwill began with local side Seaton Delaval. He joined the Gallowgate staff in May 1913 for £100 and soon graduated from United's ranks making an impression at outside-left. He claimed a position in the Magpies' team at the expense of the experienced Scottish international George Wilson for season 1913-14 and became the latest in an impressive line of home-grown stars at the time. Much liked by the fans on the terraces, Tommy was quick and direct on the ball with the urge to move into the box. Importantly, he was able to send over a telling cross into the box. As war broke out on the Continent, Tommy impressed even more in a black-and-white shirt as football continued for the 1914-15 programme. But his footballing career was to soon come to a close. One of the first to sign up on the call to arms by Lord Kitchener, Goodwill joined the Northumberland Fusiliers with other local United footballers at the end of the season. Sadly, he became the only regular United first-teamer to be killed in action, on the first day of the Battle of the Somme, on 1st July 1916, alongside his United reserve colleague Dan Dunglinson. He was only 21 years old and his name is included along with that of his teammate at the huge and poignant Thiepval Memorial in France.

TEAM COLOURS Black & white striped shirts, dark shorts (Change; white shirts with a broad diamond stripe, dark shorts)

SEASON 1914-15

Match	Date		FL Division 1					Posn		Lawrence	McCracken	Hudspeth	Hewison	Low	Hay	Douglas	Hibbert	Pailor	Wilson	Goodwill	Veitch	King	Hall	Booth	Hampson	Finlay	Mellor	Higgins	Spink	Cooper	Little	McGough	Soulsby	Dixon	Cairns	Match
1	02 Sep	H	**West Bromwich Albion**	L	1 2	(1 1)	15,000		Hibbert	1	2	3	4	5	6	7	8	9	10	11																1
2	05 Sep	H	**Everton**	L	0 1	(0 0)	12,000	19		1	2	3		5	6	7	8	9	10	11	4															2
3	09 Sep	H	**Sheffield Wednesday**	D	0 0	(0 0)	8,000	17		1	2	3		5	6	7	8			11		4	9	10												3
4	12 Sep	A	Chelsea	W	3 0	(2 0)	20,000	11	Hall 2, Hibbert	1	2	3	4	5	6	7	8			11			9	10												4
5	19 Sep	H	**Bradford City**	W	1 0	(1 0)	15,000	6	Douglas	1	2	3	4	5	6	7	8			11			9	10												5
6	26 Sep	A	Burnley	L	0 2	(0 1)	15,000	10		1	2		4	5	6	7	8			11			9	10	3											6
7	03 Oct	H	**Tottenham Hotspur**	W	4 0	(2 0)	22,000	6	Booth, Hall 2, Hibbert	1	2		4	5	6	7	8			11			9	10	3											7
8	10 Oct	A	Manchester City	D	1 1	(0 1)	25,000	6	Pailor	1	2	3	4	5		7		9		11			8	10		6										8
9	17 Oct	A	Middlesbrough	D	1 1	(0 0)	18,000	7	Hall	1	2	3	4	5	6	7	8			11			9	10												9
10	24 Oct	H	**Sheffield United**	W	4 3	(1 1)	27,500	6	Booth, Hall 2, Hudspeth (pen)	1	2	3	4	5	6	7	8			11			9	10												10
11	31 Oct	A	Aston Villa	L	1 2	(0 0)	15,000	10	Hibbert	1	2	3	4	5	6	7	8			11			9	10												11
12	07 Nov	H	**Liverpool**	D	0 0	(0 0)	24,000	9		1	2	3	4	5	6	7	8			11			9	10												12
13	14 Nov	A	Bradford Park Avenue	L	0 1	(0 1)	10,000	11		1	2	3	4	5	6	7		9		11			8	10												13
14	21 Nov	H	**Oldham Athletic**	L	1 2	(1 0)	12,000	11	Hudspeth (pen)	1	2	3	4	5	6	7	10	9		11			8													14
15	28 Nov	A	Manchester United	L	0 1	(0 1)	5,000	13		1		3	4	5	6	7	10	9	11				8		2											15
16	05 Dec	H	**Bolton Wanderers**	L	1 2	(1 1)	15,000	15	Hibbert	1	2	3	4	5	6	7	8			11			9	10												16
17	12 Dec	A	Blackburn Rovers	W	3 2	(0 2)	5,000	14	King 2, Hudspeth (pen)	1	2	3	4	5	6	7	9			11		8	10													17
18	19 Dec	H	**Notts County**	D	1 1	(1 0)	15,000	14	Hibbert	1	2	3	4	5	6	7	9			11		8	10													18
19	25 Dec	H	**Sunderland**	L	2 5	(0 3)	40,000	14	og 2 (Scott, Ness)	1	2	3	4	5	6	7	9			11		8	10													19
20	26 Dec	A	Sunderland	W	4 2	(2 2)	20,000	13	Higgins, Hibbert 2, Hudspeth		2	3	4	5	6	7	8	9	11								1	10								20
21	01 Jan	A	Sheffield Wednesday	L	1 2	(1 0)	11,000	14	King			3	4	5	6	7	8	9	11			10			2		1									21
22	02 Jan	A	Everton	L	0 3	(0 1)	20,000	15				3	4	5	6	7	8		11			10	9		2		1									22
23	23 Jan	A	Bradford City	D	1 1	(1 0)	12,000	15	Pailor		2	3		5	4	7	8	9		11		10				6	1									23
24	13 Feb	H	**Manchester City**	W	2 1	(1 1)	18,000	15	King, Hibbert	1	2	3		5	6	7	8	9		11		10							4							24
25	27 Feb	A	Sheffield United	L	0 1	(0 1)	17,500	16		1	2	3		5	6					11		10	9					8	4	7						25
26	10 Mar	H	**Middlesbrough**	L	1 2	(0 2)	10,000	18	Goodwill	1		3			6	7				11			8					10	4		2	5	9			26
27	17 Mar	H	**Chelsea**	W	2 0	(1 0)	5,000	17	Finlay 2	1	2	3		5			8	9		11						6		10	4	7						27
28	20 Mar	H	**Bradford Park Avenue**	D	1 1	(0 1)	10,000	16	Higgins	1	2	3		5						11			9			6		10	4	7				8		28
29	27 Mar	A	Oldham Athletic	L	0 1	(0 0)	7,836	17			2	3		5						11		8		10		6	1	9	4	7						29
30	29 Mar	A	Liverpool	D	2 2	(0 0)	3,000	15	Hall, King		2	3			5					11		8	9	10		6	1		4	7						30
31	02 Apr	A	Tottenham Hotspur	D	0 0	(0 0)	18,000	16			2	3		5	6		9			11		1		10		8			4	7						31
32	03 Apr	H	**Manchester United**	W	2 0	(1 0)	12,000	15	Hibbert 2	1	2	3		5	6		9			11		8		10					4	7						32
33	05 Apr	A	West Bromwich Albion	L	0 2	(0 1)	11,858	15		1	2	3								11			9	10		6		8	4	7		5				33
34	10 Apr	A	Bolton Wanderers	D	0 0	(0 0)	15,000	15		1		3		5	6	7	9			11		8		10	2				4							34
35	14 Apr	H	**Burnley**	L	1 2	(1 2)	6,000	16	Hibbert	1		3		5	6	7	9			11		8		10	2				4							35
36	17 Apr	H	**Blackburn Rovers**	W	2 1	(1 1)	14,000	15	Higgins, Hibbert	1		2		5	3		9			11		8				6		10	4	7						36
37	24 Apr	A	Notts County	L	0 1	(0 0)	10,000	15		1		2		5	3		9			11		8				6		10	4	7						37
38	28 Apr	H	**Aston Villa**	W	3 0	(0 0)	10,000	15	Goodwill, Hibbert, Cooper	1		2		5	3		9			11		8				6			4	7					10	38
Round			**FA Cup**																																	**Round**
1	09 Jan	A	West Ham United	D	2 2	(2 0)	15,000		Goodwill, og (Hughes)		2	3	4	5	6	7	9			11		8	10				1									1
1r	**16 Jan**	H	**West Ham United**	W	3 2	(2 1)	28,130		Pailor 2, Hibbert		2	3	4	5	6	7	8	9		11		10					1									1r
2	**30 Jan**	H	**Swansea Town**	De	1 1	(0 0)	30,005		McCracken (pen)	1	2			5	4	7	8	9		11		10			3	6										2
2r	06 Feb	A	Swansea Town	W	2 0	(1 0)	15,000		King, Pailor	1	2	3		5	6	7	8	9		11		10							4							2r
3	20 Feb	A	Sheffield Wednesday	W	2 1	(1 0)	25,971		King, Hibbert	1	2	3		5	6		8	9		11		10							4	7						3
4	06 Mar	A	Chelsea	De	1 1	(0 1)	58,760		Goodwill	1	2	3		5	6	7	9		10	11		8							4							4
4r	**13 Mar**	H	**Chelsea**	Le	0 1	(0 0)	49,827			1	2	3		5	6	7		9	10	11		8							4							4r

De Drawn after extra time
Le Lost after extra time

DateLine ... 25 Dec: Sunderland win 5-2 and score all seven goals including two own-goals. **2 April:** Goalkeeper Mellor is injured in the warm-up, forward John King steps in between the posts and keeps a clean sheet. **28 April:** The last fixture before World War One halts football; Tommy Goodwill scores but does not return, killed in action.

Rebuilding at Gallowgate

Football returned to full-swing after the Great War for the 1919-20 season. Much had changed since 1915 including an enlargement of the division to 22 clubs and very soon a widening of the Football League structure. At each club in the country there was a colossal overhaul needed in order that the football industry recovered. Club finances had been decimated everywhere, including at St James' Park. As a result there were few big transfer deals with cash needed to revamp a deteriorating and neglected Gallowgate. Although the stadium had not been bomb damaged, it had been taken over by the forces for much of the period of war and was in dire need of refurbishment. With many old faces retiring, the Magpies concentrated on rebuilding their squad by blending local, young talent with a few faces from pre-war years such as Bill McCracken, Wilf Low and the ever-green Jimmy Lawrence. Eager lads like Andy Smailes, Tom Curry, Bill Bradley, Stan Dixon and Tom Phillipson were introduced.

The new era opened in the capital with a fixture against Arsenal. Newcastle won 1-0, the first top flight match to be played at Highbury. The Magpies began the new age well. A run of six consecutive victories established the Black'n'Whites as leaders of the table by the time the derby double with Sunderland arrived at the end of November. The red-and-whites though won both games and knocked United off top place. A new record gate of 61,761 was set at St James' Park when Sunderland recorded a 3-2 victory.

By the turn of the year Newcastle were still doing well, challenging at the head of the table, youthful in attack and experienced at the back where a defensive pairing of two from Frank Hudspeth, Billy Hampson and Bill McCracken proved a formidable combination. But they were not to get back into the leaders spot. A bad run in January – losing four games in a row – saw United slip and continue in an inconsistent manner to end in eighth place.

Pictured above: Inside-forward Andy Smailes was one of several local products given a chance after war.

Memorabilia CORNER

Bill McCracken featured on a collector card of the time.

IN CHARGE

Chairman: John Oliver
Manager: Director Committee
Captain: Bill McCracken
Trainer/Coach: James McPherson

ST JAMES' PARK

Average Attendance
Lg 38,036 Lg & Cup 37,401

The Great War is over and football gets back to normal. United's playing staff, directors and officials are ready for the new era.

PLAYER FOCUS Wilf Low

Born Aberdeen. Centre-half, 5'11"
1909 to 1924: 378 app 9 goals.

When purchased from Aberdeen in a £800 fee plus player deal during May 1909, Wilf Low was already a noted footballer north of the border appearing on 119 occasions for the Dons and the club never once regretted his acquisition. His determined and sometimes hard-hitting style as a centre-half – in days before the defensive role – in the middle of the park became a feature of United's play. Low was the Magpies' enforcer on the field and few opponents relished a confrontation with the tenacious Scot. He was an important player to United as the Magpies reached the FA Cup final in 1910 and 1911, earning a winners' medal against Barnsley in the first of those replayed ties. Somewhat paradoxically nicknamed The Laughing Cavalier, Wilf pulled on his country's blue shirt on five occasions before and after the Great War. Skipper of the club during the early Twenties, Wilf retired in the summer of 1924 and like several of United's long-serving stars of the time, joined the coaching team. He was later groundsman at St James' Park and remained associated with the Magpies until his untimely death in a road accident in the city in 1933. Wilf's brother Harry Low also started with Aberdeen, the pair making the trip south to the North East, Harry earning fame with Sunderland, part of their Championship winning side in 1913, while his son, Norman, turned out for Newport County – in their line-up demolished 13-0 by United in 1946. A cousin, William Low, also played for Aberdeen and for Barnsley.

SEASON REVIEW

Football League Div 1: P42 W17 D9 L16 F44 A39 Pts 43.
Position: 8th (Champions; West Bromwich Albion).
FA Cup: R2 (Winners; Aston Villa).

Appearances (44m): Hudspeth FC 41, Low WL 40, Curry T 39, Finlay J 37, McCracken WR 35, Ramsay AP 34, Robinson RW 29, Hibbert W 26, Dixon ES 23, Smailes A 23, Bradley W 22, Lawrence J 21, Booth CT 15, Hall T 14, Hampson W 12, Cooper E 11, Phillipson TW 10, King J 9, Mooney E 9, Wilson JT 7, Henderson Jas 6, Bertram W 3, Hagan A 3, Hewison R 3, Pyke GW 3, Swan CS 3, Best J 2, Wake HW 2, Mellor WG 1, Rainnie A 1.

Goals (46g): Smailes A 10, Hibbert W 9, Dixon ES 6, Booth CT 4, Robinson RW 4, Phillipson TW 3, Hall T 2, Ramsay AP 2, Wilson JT 2, Hagan A 1, Henderson Jas 1, Hudspeth FC 1, own goal 1.

Dismissals: 0 players

MAJOR SIGNINGS

Ray Robinson (Grimsby Town) £400

FROM THE RANKS

Tom Phillipson (Scotswood, Es)
Andy Smailes (Blyth Spartans)
Chris Swan (Tyneside sch, Es)
Harry Wake (Birtley, Es)
Jack Wilson (Leadgate Utd)
Alex Rainnie (South Shields)
Willie Bertram (Durham City)
Jerry Best (Mickley CW)
Ed Mooney (Walker Celtic)
George Pyke (Rutherford College)

TEAM COLOURS Black & white striped shirts, dark shorts (Change; white shirts with broad black diamond stripe, dark shorts)

SEASON 1919-20

Match	Date		FL Division 1					Posn		Lawrence	McCracken	Hudspeth	Curry	Low	Finlay	Robinson	Henderson	Wilson	Hall	Hibbert	Dixon	Cooper	Booth	Pyke	Ramsay	Hampson	Bradley	Mellor	Smailes	Hagan	Rainnie	Phillipson	Mooney	Hewison	King	Best	Swan	Wake	Bertram	Match
1	30 Aug	A	Arsenal	W	1 0	(1 0)	55,000		Henderson	1	2	3	4	5	6	7	8	9	10	11																				1
2	03 Sep	H	**West Bromwich Albion**	L	0 2	(0 2)	50,000	16		1	2	3	4	5	6	7	8	9	10	11																				2
3	06 Sep	H	**Arsenal**	W	3 1	(2 0)	45,000	10	Wilson 2, Hudspeth (pen)	1	2	3	4	5	6	7	8	9		11	10																			3
4	08 Sep	A	West Bromwich Albion	L	0 3	(0 1)	20,082	15		1	2	3	4	5	6	7	8	9		11	10																			4
5	13 Sep	A	Chelsea	D	0 0	(0 0)	60,000	14		1	2	3		5	6	7	8		10	9	4	11																		5
6	20 Sep	H	**Chelsea**	W	3 0	(2 0)	40,000	10	Dixon 3	1	2	3	4	5	6				7	9	8	11	10																	6
7	24 Sep	H	**Derby County**	D	0 0	(0 0)	25,000	7		1	2	3	4	5	6				7		8	11	10	9																7
8	27 Sep	A	Liverpool	D	1 1	(0 1)	30,000	9	Booth	1	2	3	4	5	6	7			11		8		10	9																8
9	04 Oct	H	**Liverpool**	W	3 0	(1 0)	45,000	4	Hibbert 3	1	2	3	4	5	6	7				9	8		10		11															9
10	11 Oct	A	Bradford Park Avenue	W	1 0	(1 0)	12,000	2	Dixon	1	2	3	4	5	6	7				9	8		10		11															10
11	18 Oct	H	**Bradford Park Avenue**	W	4 0	(1 0)	44,000	2	Dixon, Hibbert 3	1	2		4	5	6	7				9	8		10		11	3														11
12	25 Oct	A	Preston North End	W	3 2	(2 0)	18,000	2	Hibbert, Ramsay 2	1		3	4	5	6	7				9	8		10		11	2														12
13	01 Nov	H	**Preston North End**	W	1 0	(0 0)	48,000	1	Robinson		2	3	4	5	6	7				9	8		10		11		1													13
14	08 Nov	A	Middlesbrough	W	1 0	(1 0)	30,000	1	Booth		2	3	4	5	6	7				9	8		10		11		1													14
15	22 Nov	A	Sunderland	L	0 2	(0 1)	47,148	1			2	3	4	5	6	7				9	8		10		11		1													15
16	29 Nov	H	**Sunderland**	L	2 3	(2 0)	61,761	3	Hibbert, Robinson		2	3	4	5	6	7			10	9	8				11		1													16
17	03 Dec	H	**Middlesbrough**	D	0 0	(0 0)	40,000	3			2	3	4	5	6	7			10	9	8				11		1													17
18	06 Dec	A	Sheffield United	L	1 2	(1 2)	17,500	4	Hall		2		4	5	6	7			10		8				11	3		1	9											18
19	13 Dec	H	**Sheffield United**	W	2 1	(1 1)	30,000	4	Robinson, Smailes			3	4	5	6	7			10		8				11	2	1		9											19
20	20 Dec	A	Manchester United	L	1 2	(1 2)	20,000	4	Hagan		2	3	4	5	6	7					8				11		1		9	10										20
21	26 Dec	H	**Burnley**	D	0 0	(0 0)	45,000	4			2	3	4	5	6	7					8				11		1		9	10										21
22	27 Dec	H	**Manchester United**	W	2 1	(1 0)	35,000	3	Hibbert, Smailes		2	3	4	5	6	7				10	8				11		1		9											22
23	01 Jan	H	**Aston Villa**	W	2 0	(1 0)	40,000	3	Smailes 2		2	3	4	5	6	7				10	8				11		1		9											23
24	03 Jan	H	**Oldham Athletic**	L	0 1	(0 0)	35,000	3			2	3	4	5	6	7	8						10	9	11		1													24
25	17 Jan	A	Oldham Athletic	L	0 1	(0 1)	20,460	5			2	3	4	5	6				7	10					11		1		9	8										25
26	24 Jan	A	Everton	L	0 4	(0 2)	20,000	6			2	3	4	5					7	10					11		1		9		6	8								26
27	07 Feb	A	Bradford City	L	0 1	(0 1)	25,000	8			2		4	5		7		9							11	3	1		10			8	6							27
28	11 Feb	H	**Everton**	W	3 0	(3 0)	20,000	5	Robinson, Smailes 2			3		5		7		9							11	2	1		10				6	4	8					28
29	14 Feb	H	**Bradford City**	L	0 1	(0 0)	45,000	7				3		5		7		9							11	2	1		10				6	4	8					29
30	21 Feb	A	Bolton Wanderers	W	3 0	(2 0)	25,000	5	Booth 2, Smailes			3	4		6	7							10		11	2	1		9				5		8					30
31	28 Feb	H	**Bolton Wanderers**	L	0 1	(0 0)	40,000	7				3			6	7							10		11	2	1		9				5	4	8					31
32	06 Mar	H	**Blackburn Rovers**	D	0 0	(0 0)	35,000	6		1	2	3	4	5	6							7							10			9			8	11				32
33	13 Mar	A	Blackburn Rovers	L	0 2	(0 0)	25,000	8		1	2	3	4		6							7							10			9	5		8	11				33
34	20 Mar	H	**Notts County**	W	2 1	(0 0)	30,000	7	Smailes 2	1	2	3	4	5	6							7			11				10			9			8					34
35	22 Mar	A	Sheffield Wednesday	W	1 0	(0 0)	15,000	6	Smailes	1	2	3	4	5	6							7	10		11				8			9								35
36	27 Mar	A	Notts County	D	0 0	(0 0)	15,000	6			2	3	4	5	6					8		7	10		11		1		9											36
37	02 Apr	A	Burnley	L	0 1	(0 0)	30,000	7		1	2	3	4	5	6					8		7			11				9								10			37
38	03 Apr	H	**Sheffield Wednesday**	D	1 1	(0 1)	20,000	6	Phillipson			3	4	5						10		7			11	2	1					9	6				8			38
39	05 Apr	A	Aston Villa	L	0 4	(0 2)	50,000	7				3	4		6					10		7			11	2	1		9				5				8			39
40	17 Apr	H	**Manchester City**	W	3 0	(0 0)	25,000	7	Phillipson 2, og (Tyler)	1	2	3		5	6										11				9			7			8			4	10	40
41	24 Apr	A	Manchester City	D	0 0	(0 0)	25,000	7		1	2	3	4	5	6					8					11				9			7							10	41
42	01 May	A	Derby County	L	0 1	(0 0)	21,366	8		1		3	4	5											11	2			9			7			8			6	10	42
Round			FA Cup																																					Round
1	10 Jan	H	**Crystal Palace**	W	2 0	(2 0)	15,000		Dixon, Hall		2	3	4	5	6	7			9	10	8				11		1													1
2	31 Jan	H	**Huddersfield Town**	L	0 1	(0 1)	46,462			1	2	3	4	5		7			9	10	8				11								6							2

DateLine ... 30 Aug: The Black'n'Whites open a new era with a fine 1-0 victory at Arsenal. **29 Nov:** A gate of 61,761 watches the Tyne-Wear battle with Sunderland, a new home record. **10 Jan:** Newcastle take care of the Crystal Palace gremlin this time with a 2-0 victory in the FA Cup.

NEWCASTLE UNITED

SEASON 1920-21
DIVISION 1

Back challenging at the top

Newcastle's post-war revamp was a success, and without much of an outflow of cash in the transfer market. That would soon change as the club again shortly became big spenders.

A financial outlay did begin to increase in season 1920-21, United splashing out a combined £10,300 to bring four players from Scotland; centre-forward Neil Harris, as well as Billy Aitken and Tom McDonald while County Durham winger Stan Seymour returned to his native North East via Greenock and a successful spell with Morton. They were a huge success and in attack Harris and Seymour scored 29 goals. United contested the top places and stood nestled in second or third place for most of the programme. An October double over Sunderland – including a 6-1 win at St James' Park – gained revenge for last season's reverse. Seymour and Harris in particular rocked Newcastle's Wearside neighbours, netting five of the eight goals scored.

At that time Newcastle won 11 out of 14 games played. Newcastle sustained their bid at the top into April, chasing Burnley. But, Newcastle again faltered; only winning one in eight matches which effectively ended their title chase. Picking up only two points from four fixtures, and matches against chasing rivals Bolton and Manchester City did not go well, saw United fall out of the race. They dropped to a final fifth position as a result.

A high-profile FA Cup encounter took place with Liverpool at the end of January, between clubs second and third in the First Division. A new record crowd of 62,073 turned up at Gallowgate to witness the feast of football, an enthralling tie won by a Neil Harris strike. Liverpool's neighbours across Stanley Park, Everton, knocked United out in the next round in another big Cup-tie. They won comfortably 3-0 on Merseyside.

Pictured above: Billy Aitken arrived from Scotland to delight the fans with his runs on the right wing.

The Magpies' senior playing staff comprised 34 footballers when this group was taken at the start of the 1920-21 season.

Memorabilia CORNER

Programmes throughout the 1920s had a simila format, featuring a prominent advert on the cover.

IN CHARGE

Chairman: John Oliver
Manager: Director Committee
Captain: Wilf Low
Trainer/Coach: James McPherson

ST JAMES' PARK

Average Attendance
Lg 41,243 Lg & Cup 41,921

PLAYER FOCUS Jimmy Lawrence

Born Glasgow. Goalkeeper, 5'10"
1904 to 1922: 507 app 0 goals.

United's first choice goalkeeper for all of 14 seasons, Jimmy Lawrence was at the heart of United's great team spirit during the club's heyday. A jovial character, full of wit and jokes in the dressing-room, Jimmy arrived at Gallowgate in July 1904 from his local Glasgow Perthshire club. The Scot proceeded to stay between the posts for all of Newcastle's title and FA Cup sides of the era before World War One, rewarded also by a cap for his country in 1910-11 against England. Consistent and always at the forefront of team affairs, Jimmy was something of an intellectual in the club's inner-sanctum while he was rarely shy of a witty remark, often raising team morale. Returning to St James' Park following the worldwide conflict, Lawrence played on until he was over 37 years old, his final game for the club during 1921-22 being nearly 18 years after his debut. Jimmy became boss of South Shields in May 1922 and was also in charge of Preston before heading to Germany as a coach. On returning to Britain, Jimmy was associated with Stranraer as a director to his death. The club's record appearance holder with 496 League and Cup matches – 507 senior outings all told – no-one bar modern goalkeeper Shay Given, has come close to his overall total of matches for the Magpies in a century. He was also an early Player's Union activist and did much to lay the foundations of the modern PFA.

SEASON REVIEW

Football League Div 1: P42 W20 D10 L12 F66 A45 Pts 50.
Position: 5th (Champions; Burnley).
FA Cup: R3 (Winners; Tottenham Hotspur).

Appearances (46m): Lawrence J 46, Aitken WJ 38, Low WL 38, Smailes A 38, Harris NL 37, McCracken WR 34, McIntosh RA 33, Seymour GS 33, Hudspeth FC 32, Finlay J 29, Hampson W 25, Ward E 25, Curry T 24, Mooney E 14, McDonald TH 13, Dixon ES 12, King J 12, Pyke GW 7, Phillipson TW 5, Hagan A 3, Ramsay AP 3, Gray AD 2, Mitchell TM 1, Roxburgh R 1, Russell SR 1.

Goals (70g): Harris NL 19, Smailes A 18, Seymour GS 10, Ward E 5, Aitken WJ 3, Pyke GW 3, Hagan A 2, King J 2, McDonald TH 2, Curry T 1, Dixon ES 1, Finlay J 1, Hudspeth FC 1, Phillipson TW 1, own goal 1.

Dismissals: 0 players.

MAJOR SIGNINGS

Stan Seymour (Morton) £2,500
Billy Aitken (Rangers) £2,500
Tom McDonald (Rangers) £2,000
Robert McIntosh (Dundee) £1,250
Neil Harris (Partick Thistle) £3,300 club record fee

FROM THE RANKS

Tom Mitchell (Spennymoor Utd)
Robert Roxburgh (Morpeth Comrades)
Sam Russell (Old Park Corinthians)
Ted Ward (Blyth Spartans)
Andrew Gray (Jesmond Villa)

TEAM COLOURS Black & white striped shirts, dark shorts (Change; white shirts with broad black diamond stripe, dark shorts)

SEASON 1920-21

Match	Date		FL Division 1					Att	Posn	Scorers	Lawrence	McCracken	Hudspeth	Curry	Low	Finlay	Aitken	Ward	Harris	Smailes	Seymour	McIntosh	King	Hagan	Hampson	Mooney	Pyke	Dixon	Gray	Phillipson	Mitchell	Ramsay	McDonald	Roxburgh	Russell	Match
1	28 Aug	H	**West Bromwich Albion**	D	1	1	(1 1)	61,080		Seymour	1	2	3	4	5	6	7	8	9	10	11															1
2	01 Sep	A	Everton	L	1	3	(0 1)	45,000	16	Harris	1	2	3	4	5	6	7	8	9	10	11															2
3	04 Sep	A	West Bromwich Albion	D	0	0	(0 0)	29,202	17		1	2	3		5	6	7	8	9	10	11	4														3
4	08 Sep	H	**Everton**	W	2	0	(1 0)	35,000	9	Smailes, Finlay	1	2	3		5	6	7		9	10	11	4	8													4
5	11 Sep	H	**Preston North End**	W	4	2	(3 2)	48,000	7	Hagan 2, Harris, og (Doolan)	1	2	3		5	6	7		9		11	4	8	10												5
6	18 Sep	A	Preston North End	L	2	3	(2 1)	20,000	8	King, Harris	1	2	3		5	6	7	8	9		11	4	10													6
7	25 Sep	H	**Sheffield United**	W	3	0	(2 0)	40,000	8	Seymour 2, Harris	1	2			5	6	7	8	9		11	4	10		3											7
8	02 Oct	A	Sheffield United	W	3	0	(1 0)	28,000	7	Pyke 2, Ward	1	2				6	7	8		10	11	4			3	5	9									8
9	09 Oct	H	**Sunderland**	W	6	1	(2 0)	58,016	3	Seymour, Smailes 2, Harris 2, Ward	1	2			5	6	7	8	9	10	11	4			3											9
10	16 Oct	A	Sunderland	W	2	0	(0 0)	40,000	3	Seymour, Harris	1	2			5	6	7	8	9	10	11	4			3											10
11	23 Oct	H	**Bradford Park Avenue**	W	2	1	(2 0)	48,000	2	Harris, Ward	1	2			5	6	7	8	9	10	11	4			3											11
12	30 Oct	A	Bradford Park Avenue	W	2	0	(0 0)	15,000	1	Harris, Aitken	1	2	6		5		7	8	9		11	4			3			10								12
13	06 Nov	H	**Burnley**	L	1	2	(0 2)	50,000	2	Harris	1	2			5	6	7	8	9		11	4			3			10								13
14	13 Nov	A	Burnley	L	1	3	(1 2)	38,860	4	Dixon	1	2	3		5	6	7		9	10	11	4						8								14
15	20 Nov	H	**Liverpool**	W	2	0	(1 0)	50,000	3	Seymour, Ward	1	2	3		5		7	8	9	10	11	4				6										15
16	27 Nov	A	Liverpool	W	1	0	(1 0)	25,000	2	Smailes	1		3		5		7	8	9	10	11	4			2	6										16
17	04 Dec	H	**Aston Villa**	W	2	1	(1 1)	25,000	2	Seymour, Smailes	1		3		5	6			9	10	11	4			2		8		7							17
18	11 Dec	A	Aston Villa	D	0	0	(0 0)	35,000	2		1	2			5	6	7		9	10	11	4	8		3											18
19	18 Dec	A	Manchester United	L	0	2	(0 1)	30,000	2		1	2	3		5	6	7		9	10	11	4	8													19
20	25 Dec	H	**Tottenham Hotspur**	D	1	1	(1 1)	45,000	2	Harris	1	2	3		5		7		9	10	11	4	8			6										20
21	27 Dec	A	Tottenham Hotspur	L	0	2	(0 0)	54,500	4		1		3		5				9	10	11	4	8		2	6			7							21
22	01 Jan	H	**Manchester United**	W	6	3	(2 2)	40,000	4	Seymour 2, Smailes, Harris 2, Phillipson	1	2	3		5	6		8	9	10	11					4				7						22
23	15 Jan	H	**Bradford City**	W	4	0	(3 0)	40,000	2	Smailes 2, Harris, Aitken	1	2	3	4	5	6	7	8	9	10	11															23
24	22 Jan	A	Bradford City	D	1	1	(1 1)	19,000	2	Ward	1	2	3	4	5	6	7	8	9	10	11															24
25	05 Feb	A	Chelsea	L	0	2	(0 2)	50,000	4		1	2	3	4	5	6	7		9	10								8			11					25
26	09 Feb	H	**Chelsea**	W	1	0	(0 0)	40,000	2	Smailes	1		3	4			7	8	9	10	11	5			2	6										26
27	12 Feb	H	**Huddersfield Town**	W	1	0	(0 0)	45,000	2	Smailes	1		3	4		6	11	8	9	10		5			2					7						27
28	23 Feb	A	Huddersfield Town	W	3	1	(3 0)	10,000	2	Smailes 2, Harris	1		3	4			7		9	10		5			2	6		8				11				28
29	26 Feb	H	**Middlesbrough**	W	2	0	(0 0)	40,000	2	Smailes, Aitken	1		3	6	5		7	8	9	10		4			2							11				29
30	05 Mar	A	Middlesbrough	D	0	0	(0 0)	38,000	2		1		3	6	5		7			10		4			2		9	8					11			30
31	12 Mar	H	**Blackburn Rovers**	L	1	2	(0 2)	44,000	3	Hudspeth (pen)	1		3		5	6	7		9	10		4			2			8					11			31
32	19 Mar	A	Blackburn Rovers	D	3	3	(1 3)	25,000	3	McDonald, Smailes, Harris	1		3	6	5		7		9	10		4			2			8					11			32
33	25 Mar	H	**Oldham Athletic**	L	1	2	(0 1)	32,000	3	Curry	1	2		6	5		7		9	10		4			3			8					11			33
34	26 Mar	A	Derby County	W	1	0	(0 0)	18,000	3	Smailes	1	2		4	5	6		8	7	9					3			10					11			34
35	28 Mar	A	Oldham Athletic	D	0	0	(0 0)	16,801	3		1	2		4	5	6	7					8			3		9	10					11			35
36	02 Apr	H	**Derby County**	L	0	1	(0 0)	35,000	3		1	2	3	4	5	6		8					10				9			7			11			36
37	09 Apr	A	Bolton Wanderers	L	1	3	(0 2)	25,000	4	McDonald	1	2	3	4			7					5	10			6	9	8					11			37
38	16 Apr	H	**Bolton Wanderers**	W	1	0	(0 0)	15,000	4	Smailes	1	2	3	4			7			9	11	5	8			6							10			38
39	23 Apr	A	Arsenal	D	1	1	(0 0)	30,000	5	King	1	2		6	5		7			9	11	4	8		3								10			39
40	30 Apr	H	**Arsenal**	W	1	0	(0 0)	40,000	4	Smailes	1			6			7			9	11	4		8	3	5							10	2		40
41	02 May	A	Manchester City	L	1	3	(0 1)	25,000	5	Smailes	1			4	5					9	11			8	2	6				7			10		3	41
42	07 May	H	**Manchester City**	D	1	1	(1 0)	35,000	5	Pyke	1	2		6					9	8	11	4			3	5	7						10			42
Round			FA Cup																																	Round
1	08 Jan	H*	**Nottingham Forest**	D	1	1	(0 1)	47,652		Harris	1	2	3		5	6		8	9	10	11					4				7						1
1r	12 Jan	H	**Nottingham Forest**	W	2	0	(2 0)	30,278		Seymour, Harris	1	2	3	4	5	6	7	8	9	10	11															1r
2	29 Jan	H	**Liverpool**	W	1	0	(0 0)	62,073		Harris	1	2	3	4	5	6	7	8	9	10	11															2
3	19 Feb	A	Everton	L	0	3	(0 1)	54,205			1	2	3	4	5	6	7	8	9	10												11				3

H* Scheduled for Nottingham but played at Newcastle by agreement

DateLine ... 9 Oct: United win 6-1 against Sunderland, the biggest triumph over their local rivals. **1 Jan:** United record a 6-3 victory on New Year's Day against Manchester United. **29 Jan:** The FA Cup fixture with Liverpool attracts a record crowd of 62,073 to Gallowgate. **17 May:** Barcelona defeat United 3-2 on tour, the first reverse in 17 years on the Continent.

NEWCASTLE UNITED

SEASON
1921-22
DIVISION 1

Mid-table consolidation

Newcastle flattered to deceive for much of the 1921-22 season, but it could be said that another season of consolidation took place following war. Funds were now replenished and United's bank balance again looked healthy, yet after last year's fine performance, it was a disappointing show throughout the programme, even though in the end they still finished in seventh place. But for much of the campaign United languished in mid-table and falling early in the FA Cup to Preston, gave United's support little to shout about.

Newcastle though had started the campaign well, with opening victories over Huddersfield Town and Everton. That fine form continued until November when the side failed to pick up full points for nine fixtures. A New Year contest with Champions-elect Liverpool ended in a 1-1 draw and a double over Manchester United showed Newcastle had regained form. A resounding 6-0 FA Cup success against lowly Newport County followed but then United fell in the competition to Preston. Newcastle had a dismal spring after that knock-out, unable to collect a win for five games. However they ended the season with a flourish. Four victories in a row saw the Geordies climb from mid-table, and a 5-1 stroll over Manchester City was the ideal way to end the home programme. Tom McDonald scored a hat-trick on that day and had proved a valuable find. Neil Harris was a success at centre-forward again, with 23 goals – now 42 strikes in two seasons.

The season also marked the final curtain for long serving goalkeeper Jimmy Lawrence who ended his 15-season career with United. His position between the posts in the coming years was shared by Bill Bradley and another veteran of the game, Huddersfield Town's experienced Sandy Mutch. He stayed with United for 36 years!

Pictured above: Jimmy Low was one of many Scots to appear between the wars, a cunning outside-right.

Memorabilia CORNER

Local sports outfitter Murtons were often linked with the Magpies, here on the front of the programme.

IN CHARGE

Chairman: John Oliver
Manager: Director Committee
Captain: Wilf Low
Trainer/Coach: James McPherson

ST JAMES' PARK

Average Attendance
Lg 35,238 Lg & Cup 34,935

United pictured on tour before a game with Barcelona. Back row, left to right: Low, Wilson, Curry, McCracken, Lawrence, Hampson, Hudspeth, Aitken. Front: McPherson (trainer), Pyke, McDonald, Seymour.

PLAYER FOCUS Stan Seymour

Born Kelloe. Outside-left, 5'7"
1920 to 1929: 266 app 84 goals.

A native of County Durham, Stan Seymour was later to be known in football circles in his long career on and off the field simply as Mr Newcastle. Joining the Magpies in a £2,500 deal during May 1920 as a potent outside-left by way of Bradford City and Greenock Morton, Seymour was a first-class player for eight seasons always able to net from the flank. He won both the FA Cup and Championship trophies with United in the Twenties. Stan was an influential figure, on the fringe of a full cap for his country – appearing for England in unofficial internationals during 1925. But when he retired and left Gallowgate in the close-season of 1929 it was with bitterness over benefit payments. Always likely to be a touch controversial, he then became a critic of the club as Newcastle declined during the Thirties. Surprisingly to many, Stan returned to the fold as a director in June 1938 and from that moment the forthright yet shrewd Seymour dedicated his life to United's cause. Quickly he became a powerful Board member, manager of the club in all but name, indeed appointed to the title of Honorary Manager for two spells. Later Chairman too, he guided the club to promotion and to a treble of FA Cup victories. His son, Stan Junior, was also Chairman, while another son, Colin, appeared for the Black'n'Whites during wartime soccer. Seymour spent almost 50 years with the Geordies and remained associated with the club as Vice-President to his death in Newcastle during 1978.

SEASON REVIEW

Football League Div 1: P42 W18 D10 L14 F59 A45 Pts 46.
Position: 7th (Champions; Liverpool).
FA Cup: R2 (Winners; Huddersfield Town).

Appearances (44m): Hudspeth FC 42, McDonald TH 41, Curry T 37, Harris NL 36, Low WL 31, Mooney E 30, McCracken WR 28, Bradley W 27, Low J 26, McIntosh RA 24, Mitchell TM 22, Seymour GS 20, Aitken WJ 16, Lawrence J 16, Paton HD 13, Dixon ES 12, Smailes A 11, Hagan A 9, Roxburgh R 9, Woods H 8, Russell SR 7, Finlay J 5, Spencer CW 5, Pyke GW 3, Hampson W 2, Archibald J 1, Swan CS 1, Thain JW 1, Wake HW 1.

Goals (66g): Harris NL 23, McDonald TH 18, Curry T 3, Dixon ES 3, Mooney E 3, Hagan A 2, Low J 2, Paton HD 2, Seymour GS 2, Smailes A 2, Finlay J 1, Hudspeth FC 1, Low WL 1, McIntosh RA 1, Mitchell TM 1, Woods H 1.

Dismissals: 0 players.

MAJOR SIGNINGS

Jimmy Low (Rangers) £1,300
Harry Paton (Clydebank) £410
Harry Woods (South Shields) £2,600

FROM THE RANKS

Charlie Spencer (Washington Chemicals)
John Thain (Pelaw Jnrs)

TEAM COLOURS Black & white striped shirts, dark shorts (Change; white shirts with broad black diamond stripe, dark shorts)

SEASON 1921-22

Match	Date	Venue	FL Division 1	Res	F	A	HT	Att	Posn	Scorers
1	27 Aug	A	Huddersfield Town	W	2	1	(1 0)	25,000		McDonald 2
2	31 Aug	H	**Everton**	W	3	0	(1 0)	40,000	1	Harris, Paton 2
3	03 Sep	H	**Huddersfield Town**	L	1	2	(0 2)	50,000	5	McDonald
4	07 Sep	A	Everton	W	3	2	(3 1)	30,000	3	Harris, McDonald 2
5	10 Sep	A	Burnley	L	0	2	(0 1)	28,016	7	
6	17 Sep	H	**Burnley**	W	2	1	(0 0)	48,000	4	Harris 2
7	24 Sep	A	Sheffield United	D	1	1	(0 1)	25,000	4	Harris
8	01 Oct	H	**Sheffield United**	W	2	1	(1 1)	40,000	3	Mooney, Smailes
9	08 Oct	A	Chelsea	D	1	1	(1 1)	35,000	4	Harris
10	15 Oct	H	**Chelsea**	W	1	0	(1 0)	40,000	3	Harris
11	22 Oct	A	Preston North End	L	0	2	(0 1)	12,680	5	
12	29 Oct	H	**Preston North End**	W	3	1	(2 1)	40,000	4	Curry, McDonald 2
13	05 Nov	A	Tottenham Hotspur	L	0	4	(0 2)	34,448	7	
14	12 Nov	H	**Tottenham Hotspur**	L	0	2	(0 0)	30,000	9	
15	19 Nov	H	**Sunderland**	D	2	2	(2 0)	49,000	9	McDonald, McIntosh
16	26 Nov	A	Sunderland	D	0	0	(0 0)	49,483	9	
17	03 Dec	H	**Middlesbrough**	D	0	0	(0 0)	50,000	10	
18	10 Dec	A	Middlesbrough	D	1	1	(1 1)	36,000	9	Harris
19	17 Dec	H	**Aston Villa**	L	1	2	(1 1)	30,000	10	Mooney
20	24 Dec	A	Aston Villa	L	0	1	(0 0)	32,000	11	
21	26 Dec	A	Liverpool	L	0	1	(0 0)	45,000	12	
22	31 Dec	H	**Manchester United**	W	3	0	(1 0)	30,000	12	Harris 2, McDonald
23	02 Jan	H	**Liverpool**	D	1	1	(0 1)	43,000	12	Harris
24	14 Jan	A	Manchester United	W	1	0	(1 0)	20,000	11	McDonald
25	21 Jan	A	Birmingham	W	4	0	(2 0)	20,000	10	Dixon, Finlay, Low W, Hudspeth (pen)
26	04 Feb	A	Arsenal	L	1	2	(0 1)	30,000	10	McDonald
27	08 Feb	H	**Birmingham**	L	0	1	(0 0)	25,000	10	
28	11 Feb	H	**Arsenal**	W	3	1	(2 0)	30,000	9	Harris 2, McDonald
29	25 Feb	H	**Blackburn Rovers**	W	2	0	(0 0)	25,000	9	Low J, Woods
30	04 Mar	A	Bolton Wanderers	L	2	3	(2 3)	22,000	9	Harris, McDonald
31	06 Mar	A	Blackburn Rovers	W	2	0	(1 0)	20,000	9	Harris, Seymour
32	11 Mar	H	**Bolton Wanderers**	W	2	1	(2 0)	30,000	8	Curry, Harris
33	18 Mar	H	**Oldham Athletic**	D	1	1	(0 1)	30,000	8	Harris
34	25 Mar	A	Oldham Athletic	D	0	0	(0 0)	15,600	7	
35	01 Apr	H	**Cardiff City**	D	0	0	(0 0)	28,000	7	
36	08 Apr	A	Cardiff City	L	0	1	(0 1)	25,000	9	
37	14 Apr	H	**Bradford City**	L	1	2	(1 1)	20,000	11	Harris
38	15 Apr	H	**West Bromwich Albion**	W	3	0	(2 0)	28,000	10	Harris 2, Mitchell
39	17 Apr	A	Bradford City	W	3	2	(0 0)	25,000	8	Harris, Low J, Smailes
40	22 Apr	A	West Bromwich Albion	W	2	1	(0 1)	32,063	7	Curry, Harris
41	29 Apr	H	**Manchester City**	W	5	1	(3 0)	34,000	5	Hagan 2, McDonald 3
42	06 May	A	Manchester City	L	0	1	(0 0)	15,000	7	
Round			FA Cup							
1	07 Jan	H	**Newport County**	W	6	0	(1 0)	28,567		McDonald 2, Harris, Dixon 2, Mooney
2	28 Jan	A	Preston North End	L	1	3	(1 1)	28,416		Seymour

Match	Lawrence	McCracken	Hudspeth	McIntosh	Low WL	Curry	Aitken	Paton	Smailes	McDonald	Seymour	Mooney	Harris	Finlay	Mitchell	Swan	Bradley	Hagan	Russell	Pyke	Roxburgh	Dixon	Low J	Thain	Hampson	Woods	Spencer	Wake	Archibald	Match
1	1	2	3	4	5	6	7	8	9	10	11																			1
2	1	2	3	4		6	7	8		10	11	5	9																	2
3	1	2	3	4		6	7	8		10	11	5	9																	3
4	1	2	3	4		6	7	8		10	11	5	9																	4
5	1	2	3	4		6	7	8		10	11	5	9																	5
6	1	2	3	4		6	7	8		10	11	5	9																	6
7	1	2	3	4			7		8	10		5	9	6	11															7
8	1	2	3	4	6				8	10		5	9		11	7														8
9		2	3	4	5		7		8	10			9	6	11		1													9
10		2	3	4	5	6	7		8				9		11		1	10												10
11			3	4	5	6	7		8				9		11		1	10	2											11
12		2	3		5	4	7	8		10		6			11		1			9										12
13	1	2	3		5	4	7	8		10		6			11					9										13
14	1		3	4	5	6	7	8		10					11					9	2									14
15	1		3	4	5	6	7			10					11			8			2	9								15
16			3	4	5	6	7			10			9		11		1	8			2									16
17			3	4	5					10		6	9		11		1	8			2		7							17
18			3		5	6				10		4	9		11		1				2	8	7							18
19			3	4	5	6				10		11	9				1	8			2			7						19
20		2	3	4	5	6		8		10			9		11		1						7							20
21		2	3	4	5	6		8		10			9		11		1						7							21
22		2	3		5	6		10		11		4	9				1					8	7							22
23		2	3		5	6				10	11	4	9				1					8	7							23
24		2	3		5	6		8		10		4			11		1					9	7							24
25		2	3		5					10	11	4	9	6			1					8	7							25
26		2			5	6				10	11	4					1					9	7		3	8				26
27		2	3		5					10	11	4	9	6			1						7			8				27
28		2	3	4	5					10	11	6	9				1						7			8				28
29		2	3	4	5	6				10	11		9				1						7			8				29
30			3	4	5	6				10			9		11		1				2		7			8				30
31	1		3	5		4				10	11		9	6							2		7			8				31
32	1		3	4		6				10	11		9								2		7			8	5			32
33		2	3	4		6				10	11	5	9				1						7			8				33
34	1	2	3		5	4				10	11	6	9									8	7							34
35			3		5	4				10	11	6	9				1		2			8	7							35
36	1	2	3		5	4	7		8	10		6	9		11															36
37	1	2	3		5	4				10		6	9		11							8	7							37
38			3			4			8	10		6	9		11		1		2				7				5			38
39			3			6			8	10			9		11		1		2				7				5	4		39
40			3			4			8		11	6	9				1	10	2				7				5			40
41			3		5	4				10		6	9		11			8	2				7						1	41
42			3			4			9	10		6			11		1	8	2				7				5			42
Round																														Round
1		2	3		5	6				10	11	4	9				1					8	7							1
2		2			5	6				10	11	4	9				1					8	7		3					2

DateLine ... 7 Jan: United's first meeting with Newport ends in a 6-0 victory. **4 Feb:** HRH Duke of York watches United in the League fixture at Highbury against Arsenal. **14 April:** Jimmy Lawrence appears in his last game for United against Bradford City.

SEASON
1922-23
DIVISION 1

Close, but not close enough

For the fourth season in a row since World War One, United once more finished the season below the chasing pack in the Championship race after being tipped for silverware in some quarters. Completing the programme in fourth position this time, the closest yet, had United's late season push been evident earlier, they could have gone very close to lifting title silverware again. With Huddersfield Town and Sunderland, they chased leaders Liverpool, and made a strong bid during March after three consecutive victories on Tyneside when they defeated West Bromwich Albion, Cardiff and Blackburn, scoring 10 goals in the process. But United then faced no fewer than five away fixtures. It was a tough ask although any potential Champion would have raised their game and produced results. Newcastle didn't win a game and fell behind in the title chase. Newcastle ended a long way behind the Anfield club, with a 12 point gap between top and fourth place.

United's veteran defensive full-back pair of Billy Hampson and Bill McCracken hit a milestone at Ninian Park during February. In a game that finished in a heavy defeat, Hampson was over 38 years of age, while McCracken was 40 years old. Sandy Mutch behind them in United's goal, was over 38 as well. The Welsh club gave the elder statesmen of football a run-a-round on that afternoon, netting five goals.

The FA Cup had a new home that season, at the brand new national arena in the North London suburb of Wembley. United were not to get anywhere near the first final, losing after a reply at The Dell in the opening round to Southampton, who were something of a bogey side to the Magpies then. However, it did not take long for the Magpies to find themselves in front of the white stone domes of The Empire Stadium, Wembley.

Pictured above: Billy Hampson served the club in defence and became United's oldest ever player.

Memorabilia CORNER

By now Newcastle's municipal coat-of-arms was featured on all club publications.

IN CHARGE

Chairman: John Oliver
Manager: Director Committee
Captain: Wilf Low
Trainer/Coach: James McPherson

ST JAMES' PARK

Average Attendance
Lg 26,690 Lg & Cup 26,763

By 1922 Newcastle United were building a fine squad, skipper Wilf Low sits at the centre of the pre-season photo-call.

PLAYER FOCUS Tom McDonald

Born Inverness. Inside-left, 5'8"
1921 to 1931: 367 app 113 goals.

Highlander Tom McDonald was one of United's key players during the FA Cup and League Championship victories in 1924 and 1927. An unsung hero of those glory days, he was an effective inside-forward following a £2,000 move from Rangers in March 1921, able to strike plenty of goals – over a century for the Magpies. An unselfish team-man on the field, at 5'8" tall he was as professional as they come and worked hard in midfield too. Blessed with craft and guile, he had a sure touch on the ball and often a deadly finish. McDonald forged a great partnership with colleagues Seymour and Gallacher in United's attack, the primary factor to the black-and-whites success in that era. Appearing for the Scotland B and trial line-ups during the mid-Twenties, he was unlucky to be overlooked at full international level, yet his worth to United was never in doubt; Tom figuring in both the club's top appearance and top goals chart. He was a regular support striker for the Magpies over seven campaigns, averaging 15 goals a season and claiming 23 goals as the Tynesiders won the title trophy. On leaving St James' Park in May 1931, he finished his career with York City, soon becoming their trainer. He later returned to Tyneside, for many years McDonald was a club steward at Gallowgate looking after the lofty bird's-eye press-box high up on the old West Stand. He lived the rest of his life in Newcastle's western suburbs.

SEASON REVIEW

Football League Div 1: P42 W18 D12 L12 F45 A37 Pts 48.
Position: 4th (Champions; Liverpool).
FA Cup: R1 (Winners; Bolton Wanderers).

Appearances (44m): Harris NL 39, Low J 39, Curry T 38, McDonald TH 38, Hampson W 31, Bradley W 29, Hudspeth FC 29, McIntosh RA 29, Seymour GS 29, Aitken WJ 26, Low WL 26, Mooney E 22, Spencer CW 18, McCracken WR 15, Mutch A 15, Roxburgh R 11, Mitchell TM 10, Woods H 8, Hagan A 6, Clark JnR 5, Smailes A 5, Dixon ES 4, Clark JasR 3, Scott WH 3, Keen JF 2, Richardson EG 2, MacKenzie RR 1, Russell SR 1.

Goals (46g): McDonald TH 15, Harris NL 14, Aitken WJ 4, Seymour GS 4, Low J 2, Clark JasR 1, Clark JnR 1, Hudspeth FC 1, McIntosh RA 1, Mitchell TM 1, Spencer CW 1, Woods H 1.

Dismissals: 1 player; McCracken.

MAJOR SIGNINGS

Sandy Mutch (Huddersfield Town) £850
William Scott (Airdrie) £800

FROM THE RANKS

Bob Clark (Prudhoe Castle)
Roddie MacKenzie (Inverness Clackn)
James Clark (Jarrow)

TEAM COLOURS Black & white striped shirts, dark shorts (Change; white shirts with broad black diamond stripe, dark shorts)

SEASON 1922-23

Match	Date	Venue	FL Division 1	Result	HT	Att	Posn	Scorers	Mutch	McCracken	Hudspeth	McIntosh	Low WL	Curry	Low J	Smailes	Harris	McDonald	Seymour	Hampson	Russell	Mitchell	Keen	Spencer	Hagan	Bradley	Richardson	Roxburgh	Mooney	Dixon	Aitken	Woods	Clark JasR	Scott	MacKenzie	Clark JnR	Match
1	26 Aug	H	**Everton**	W 2 0	(1 0)	50,000		McDonald 2	1	2	3	4	5	6	7	8	9	10	11																		1
2	28 Aug	A	Birmingham	W 2 0	(0 0)	35,000	1	Harris 2	1	2	3	4	5	6	7	8	9	10	11																		2
3	02 Sep	A	Everton	L 2 3	(1 3)	35,000	2	Harris, McDonald	1			4	5	6	7	8	9	10		2	3	11															3
4	06 Sep	H	**Birmingham**	D 0 0	(0 0)	20,000	4		1	2		4	5	6	7	8	9	10		3			11														4
5	09 Sep	H	**Sheffield United**	W 3 0	(0 0)	35,000	2	McDonald, Harris, Hudspeth (pen)	1	2	3	4		6	7		9	10				11		5	8												5
6	16 Sep	A	Sheffield United	L 0 2	(0 1)	20,000	6		1	2d	3	4		6	7	10	9	11						5	8												6
7	23 Sep	H	**Preston North End**	W 3 1	(2 1)	35,000	3	Harris 2, McDonald		2	3	4		6	7		9	10						5	8	1	11										7
8	30 Sep	A	Preston North End	L 0 1	(0 0)	17,695	4				3	4		6	7		9	10						5	8	1	11	2									8
9	07 Oct	H	**Burnley**	L 0 2	(0 1)	38,000	9				3	4	5		7		9	10		2		11			8	1			6								9
10	14 Oct	A	Burnley	D 0 0	(0 0)	25,000	10				3	4	5		7		9	10		2		11				1			6	8							10
11	21 Oct	H	**Arsenal**	D 1 1	(1 0)	30,000	10	Low J			3	4	5	6	7		9	10	11	2						1				8							11
12	28 Oct	A	Arsenal	W 2 1	(0 0)	30,000	8	Aitken, Low J			3		5	4	7		9	10	11	2						1			6		8						12
13	04 Nov	H	**Sunderland**	W 2 1	(1 0)	60,000	5	Aitken, McDonald			3		5	4	7		9	10	11	2						1			6		8						13
14	11 Nov	A	Sunderland	L 0 2	(0 0)	47,000	9				3		5	4	7		9	10	11	2						1			6		8						14
15	18 Nov	A	Tottenham Hotspur	W 1 0	(1 0)	30,300	6	McDonald			3	4	5	6	7		9	10	11	2						1					8						15
16	25 Nov	H	**Tottenham Hotspur**	D 1 1	(0 0)	25,000	6	McDonald			3	4	5	6	7		9	10	11	2						1					8						16
17	02 Dec	A	Liverpool	W 2 0	(1 0)	35,000	5	Harris, McIntosh			3	4	5	6	7		9	10	11	2						1					8						17
18	09 Dec	H	**Liverpool**	L 0 1	(0 0)	30,000	7				3	4	5	6	7		9	10	11	2						1					8						18
19	16 Dec	A	Aston Villa	D 1 1	(1 1)	16,000	6	Harris		2		4	5	6	7		9		11	3					10	1					8						19
20	23 Dec	H	**Aston Villa**	D 0 0	(0 0)	20,000	8			2		4	5	6	7		9	10	11	3						1					8						20
21	25 Dec	H	**Middlesbrough**	D 1 1	(1 0)	30,000	7	Aitken		2		4	5	6	7		9	10	11	3						1					8						21
22	26 Dec	A	Middlesbrough	D 1 1	(1 1)	40,000	8	Woods		2		4	5	6	7		9		11	3						1					8	10					22
23	30 Dec	A	Nottingham Forest	W 1 0	(0 0)	12,000	7	Mitchell				4	5					10		3		11				1		2	6	9	8	7					23
24	01 Jan	H	**Oldham Athletic**	W 1 0	(0 0)	30,000	5	McDonald (pen)					5	4	7			10	11	3						1		2	6	9	8						24
25	06 Jan	H	**Nottingham Forest**	W 1 0	(1 0)	20,000	4	McDonald				4	5		7			10		3		11				1		2	6		8	9					25
26	20 Jan	A	Chelsea	L 0 3	(0 0)	30,000	4			2			5	4	7		9		11	3						1			6		8	10					26
27	27 Jan	H	**Chelsea**	D 0 0	(0 0)	15,000	4		1	2			5	4	7		9			3		11							6			8	10				27
28	10 Feb	A	Cardiff City	L 0 5	(0 1)	18,000	6		1	2		4	5	6	7		9		11	3									8				10				28
29	14 Feb	H	**West Bromwich Albion**	W 2 0	(1 0)	10,000	4	Seymour, Clark JasR						4	7		9		11	3				5		1		2	6		8		10				29
30	28 Feb	H	**Cardiff City**	W 3 1	(1 1)	11,000	3	Harris, McDonald, Seymour			3			4	7		9	10	11	2				5		1			6		8						30
31	03 Mar	H	**Blackburn Rovers**	W 5 1	(2 1)	30,000	3	Harris 3, Seymour 2			3			4	7		9	10	11	2				5		1			6		8						31
32	10 Mar	A	Blackburn Rovers	D 1 1	(0 1)	15,000	3	McDonald			3	4		2	7		9	10	11					5		1			6		8						32
33	14 Mar	A	West Bromwich Albion	L 1 2	(0 0)	5,520	3	Harris			3	4		6	7		8	10	11					5		1		2						9			33
34	17 Mar	A	Bolton Wanderers	L 0 1	(0 1)	25,000	3				3	4		6	7		9	10	11					5		1		2			8						34
35	30 Mar	A	Oldham Athletic	D 0 0	(0 0)	19,149	5		1		3	4		6	7		9	10	11	2				5							8						35
36	31 Mar	A	Huddersfield Town	L 0 2	(0 0)	16,500	6		1		3	4		6	7			10	11	2				5							8	9					36
37	07 Apr	H	**Huddersfield Town**	W 1 0	(1 0)	22,500	6	Clark JnR	1		3			6	7		9	10	11	2				5											4	8	37
38	14 Apr	A	Stoke	L 0 1	(0 0)	20,000	8		1		3			4			9	10		2		11		5					6		7					8	38
39	16 Apr	H	**Bolton Wanderers**	W 1 0	(0 0)	22,000	6	McDonald	1					4			9	10		3		11	7	5				2	6							8	39
40	21 Apr	H	**Stoke**	W 1 0	(1 0)	15,000	4	Spencer	1					4			7	10	11	3				5				2	6					9		8	40
41	28 Apr	A	Manchester City	D 0 0	(0 0)	25,000	4		1		3			4			9	10	11					5				2	6		7					8	41
42	05 May	H	**Manchester City**	W 3 1	(1 1)	12,000	4	Aitken, McDonald 2			3			4	7			10				11		5		1		2	6		8			9			42
Round			FA Cup																																		Round
1	13 Jan	H	**Southampton**	D 0 0	(0 0)	28,287				2	3	4	5		7		9	11								1			6		8	10					1
1r	17 Jan	A	Southampton	L 1 3	(1 2)	20,060		Harris		2	3	4	5		7		9	10	11							1			6			8					1r

DateLine ... 26 Aug: Goalkeeper Sandy Mutch is almost 38 years old when he makes his debut against Everton. **17 Jan:** Southampton are a thorn to United once more in the FA Cup as they win 3-1 at The Dell. **10 Feb:** At Cardiff, United's full-backs of McCracken (40 years old) and Hampson (38) with 'keeper Mutch (38) form United's oldest defensive formation.

NEWCASTLE UNITED

The Toon savours Wembley

Since before the First World War football's authorities had set in place plans for a new national stadium. In fact during the transition period between the Crystal Palace and Wembley, United's St James' Park was even considered to host FA Cup finals. That never transpired and in 1923 a new venue in North London was unveiled, The Empire Stadium, Wembley, to rapidly become an inspiration to all in football. Newcastle were soon to experience its wonderful atmosphere as they took part in only the second final to be staged beneath its huge Twin Towers. By the time Newcastle ran out for the First Round in January, the Magpies had rarely caught the eye. Having started the season well, then sliding to just above mid-table, the cut and thrust of Cup football forged United into a potent unit. The new Wembley was soon in their sights.

Pictured above: Bill Bradley stepped into the FA Cup final eleven at the last moment and was inspired.

A four-match Second Round classic with Derby County did much to bond the Geordies together. All of 420 minutes of football and 20 goals saw United win in the end by 5-3 – only just – in a terrific third replay at Gallowgate. United then took care of Watford and Liverpool in the quarter-final, then Manchester City were beaten 2-0 in the semi-final and United faced Aston Villa at Wembley in what was the first all-ticket final.

Before the trip to London, United placed their players in cotton-wool, all that is except 'keeper Sandy Mutch who appeared in a Wembley rehearsal with Villa in Division One action. In a 6-1 hammering, ironically it was the unlucky goalkeeper who was injured, missing the Wembley big-day. In stepped reserve custodian Bill Bradley who went on to perform brilliantly at Wembley, one of the star performers as United lifted silverware with a 2-0 victory. Other top displays came from centre-forward Neil Harris and winger Stan Seymour, both to score on the Wembley turf in a late rally by the Magpies.

Memorabilia CORNER

The FA Cup had a new home, The Empire Stadium, Wembley. United's first visit there was a triumphant one.

IN CHARGE

Chairman: John Oliver
Manager: Director Committee
Captain: Frank Hudspeth
Trainer/Coach: James McPherson

ST JAMES' PARK

Average Attendance
Lg 25,952 Lg & Cup 28,520

United's FA Cup squad which took the club to Wembley. Back row, left to right: McPherson (trainer), Mooney, Harris, Hudspeth, Clark (Robert), Spencer, McCombie (trainer), Watt (secretary). Sitting: Low (J), Curry, Hampson, Bradley, Russell, McDonald, Cowan. On ground: Gibson, Seymour. Inset: Mutch.

PLAYER FOCUS Neil Harris

Born Glasgow. Centre-forward, 5'7"
1920 to 1925: 194 app 101 goals.

A dashing centre-forward, Neil Harris had an eye for goal and possessed a stinging shot. At just over 5'7" tall he wasn't a big leader, but was fast and joined a handful of strikers to score over 100 goals for the Magpies. Having created a reputation with Partick Thistle of being a deadly marksman before, during and after the First World War in Scottish football, he was often linked with a move south when peace was restored. Having won the wartime Victory Cup with Fulham as a guest player, Harris signed for the Black'n'Whites in May 1920 for a then hefty fee of £3,300. It took Neil a while to gain the favour of the Geordie crowd and was at one point transfer-listed before finding a rich seam of form as United headed for FA Cup victory in 1924. Then he rapidly became the hero. With an aggressive style he netted seven goals in an exciting run to the Wembley final before claiming one of the two goals that lifted the trophy for the Magpies. Harris was capped by Scotland that year too. Following another good season in 1924-25, Neil moved to Notts County in November 1925 while the Glaswegian also turned out for Oldham Athletic and Third Lanark before entering senior management with Swansea and Swindon. From a well-known family, his brother Joshua did well in the game as well, while his two sons Neil (Jnr) and John also saw first-class action, the latter becoming manager of Sheffield United for a period too.

SEASON REVIEW

Football League Div 1: P42 W17 D10 L15 F60 A54 Pts 44.
Position: 9th (Champions; Huddersfield Town).
FA Cup: Winners.

Appearances (51m): McDonald TH 44, Harris NL 42, Seymour GS 42, Hudspeth FC 37, Hampson W 36, Curry T 35, Mooney E 33, Aitken WJ 30, Cowan WD 30, Low J 29, Gibson WM 28, Mutch A 26, Bradley W 25, Spencer CW 25, McIntosh RA 17, Russell SR 16, Clark JnR 11, Low WL 10, Mitchell TM 9, Clark JasR 8, Hunter JA 8, Keating AE 7, MacKenzie RR 4, Finlay J 3, Roxburgh R 3, Thompson F 2, Scott WH 1.

Goals (81g): Harris NL 23, Seymour GS 21, McDonald TH 12, Cowan WD 8, Aitken WJ 3, Hudspeth FC 3, Gibson WM 2, Low J 2, Mitchell TM 2, Clark JasR 1, Clark JnR 1, Hampson W 1, Keating AE 1, Thompson F 1.

Dismissals: 1 player; Hudspeth.

MAJOR SIGNINGS

Willie Cowan (Dundee) £2,250
Willie Gibson (Ayr Utd) £2,500
James Hunter (Falkirk) £3,500

FROM THE RANKS

Bert Keating (Prudhoe Castle)
Frank Thompson (St Peter's Albion)

TEAM COLOURS Black & white striped shirts, black shorts (Change; white shirts with broad black diamond stripe, black shorts)

SEASON 1923-24

Match	Date		FL Division 1					Posn		Bradley	Hampson	Hudspeth	McIntosh	Spencer	Curry	Low J	Aitken	Harris	McDonald	Seymour	Clark JnR	Cowan	Roxburgh	Mooney	Scott	Clark JasR	Russell	Low WL	Finlay	Mitchell	Gibson	Mutch	Hunter	Keating	MacKenzie	Thompson	Match
1	25 Aug	A	Arsenal	W	4 1	(1 1)	45,000		Seymour, McDonald, Harris 2	1	2	3	4	5	6	7	8	9	10	11																	1
2	29 Aug	H	**Blackburn Rovers**	W	2 1	(1 0)	11,000	2	Seymour, Harris	1	2	3	4	5	6	7	8	9	10	11																	2
3	01 Sep	H	**Arsenal**	W	1 0	(1 0)	40,000	1	Aitken	1	2	3	4	5	6		7	9	10	11	8																3
4	08 Sep	H	**Sheffield United**	D	2 2	(2 1)	40,000	3	Harris, Hudspeth (pen)	1	2	3	4	5	6		7	9	10	11		8															4
5	12 Sep	H	**Bolton Wanderers**	W	1 0	(0 0)	25,000	1	Seymour	1	2	3	4	5	6		7	9	10	11		8															5
6	15 Sep	A	Sheffield United	L	1 2	(1 1)	25,000	3	Hudspeth (pen)	1	2	3	4	5	6	7		9	10	11		8															6
7	17 Sep	A	Blackburn Rovers	L	1 2	(0 0)	26,000	3	Seymour	1	2	3d	4	5	6	7		9	10	11		8															7
8	22 Sep	H	**Cardiff City**	D	1 1	(1 0)	40,000	4	McDonald	1		3	4	5		7	8		10	11			2	6	9												8
9	29 Sep	A	Cardiff City	L	0 1	(0 1)	45,000	7		1	2	3	4		6	7	8		9	11				5		10											9
10	06 Oct	A	West Ham United	L	0 1	(0 0)	30,000	9		1	3		4	5	6	7	8	9	10	11			2														10
11	13 Oct	H	**West Ham United**	D	0 0	(0 0)	21,000	9		1	3		4	5	6	7	8		10	11			2			9											11
12	20 Oct	A	Middlesbrough	L	0 1	(0 0)	25,000	13		1	2		4				7	9	10	11		8					3	5	6								12
13	27 Oct	H	**Middlesbrough**	W	3 2	(2 1)	30,000	12	Seymour 2, Hampson (pen)	1	2		4				7	9		11		8				10	3	5	6								13
14	03 Nov	A	Manchester City	D	1 1	(1 1)	27,652	13	Mitchell	1	2	3			4		7	9	10			8		6				5		11							14
15	10 Nov	H	**Manchester City**	W	4 1	(3 0)	28,000	10	Harris 2, Cowan, Aitken	1	2	3			4		7	9	10	11		8		6				5									15
16	17 Nov	A	Preston North End	W	2 1	(2 1)	12,500	8	Harris 2	1	2	3			4		7	9	10	11		8		5							6						16
17	24 Nov	H	**Preston North End**	W	3 1	(1 1)	25,000	5	Seymour, Cowan 2	1		3			4		7	9	10	11		8		5			2				6						17
18	01 Dec	A	Burnley	L	2 3	(1 3)	8,000	8	Seymour, Harris	1	2	3			4		7	9	10	11		8		5							6						18
19	08 Dec	H	**Burnley**	W	2 0	(1 0)	25,000	7	Seymour, McDonald	1	2	3			4		7	9	10	11		8		5							6						19
20	15 Dec	A	Sunderland	L	2 3	(2 3)	45,000	8	Seymour, Harris	1	2	3			4		7	9	10	11		8		5							6						20
21	22 Dec	H	**Sunderland**	L	0 2	(0 1)	50,000	9			2	3			4		7	9	10	11	8							5			6	1					21
22	25 Dec	A	Liverpool	W	1 0	(0 0)	25,000	9	Clark JnR		2		4				7	9	10	11	8			5			3				6	1					22
23	26 Dec	H	**Liverpool**	W	2 1	(1 0)	23,000	6	McDonald 2		2				4	7		9	10	11	8			5			3				6	1					23
24	29 Dec	A	Nottingham Forest	D	0 0	(0 0)	12,000	7			2				4	7		9	10		8			5		11	3				6	1					24
25	01 Jan	H	**Aston Villa**	W	4 1	(2 1)	30,000	6	Seymour 2, McDonald, Harris	1		3			4	7		9	10	11	8			5			2				6						25
26	05 Jan	H	**Nottingham Forest**	W	4 0	(2 0)	28,000	5	Harris 2, Cowan 2	1		3			4	7		9	10	11		8		5			2				6						26
27	19 Jan	A	Tottenham Hotspur	L	0 2	(0 1)	25,649	5				3	4					9	10	11		8		5			2			7	6	1					27
28	26 Jan	H	**Tottenham Hotspur**	D	2 2	(2 1)	34,000	6	Seymour, McDonald	1		2	4			7		9	10	11		8		5							6		3				28
29	09 Feb	H	**Huddersfield Town**	L	0 1	(0 0)	25,000	8				3	4	5			7		10		8						2			11	6	1		9			29
30	16 Feb	A	Notts County	L	0 1	(0 0)	10,000	9				3		5			7				8			6		10	2			11		1		9	4		30
31	27 Feb	A	Huddersfield Town	D	1 1	(1 1)	6,000	9	Seymour		2			5		7		9	10	11		8		6								1	3		4		31
32	01 Mar	A	Everton	D	2 2	(2 0)	30,000	9	McDonald, Cowan		2			5	4	7		9	10			8		6						11		1	3				32
33	15 Mar	H	**West Bromwich Albion**	D	1 1	(1 0)	20,000	9	Harris		2	3		5	4	7	8	9		11				6								1		10			33
34	19 Mar	H	**Notts County**	L	1 2	(1 1)	10,000	10	McDonald		2			5	4		7	9	10	11											6	1	3	8			34
35	22 Mar	A	West Bromwich Albion	D	0 0	(0 0)	16,053	10			2	3		5		7		9	10			8		4						11	6	1					35
36	02 Apr	H	**Everton**	W	3 1	(2 1)	12,000	9	Seymour, Harris, Gibson			3		5			7	9	10	11		8		4			2				6	1					36
37	05 Apr	A	Birmingham	L	1 4	(1 2)	20,000	9	Aitken		2				4		7		10		8							5		11	6	1	3			9	37
38	09 Apr	H	**Birmingham**	W	2 1	(1 1)	8,000	9	Mitchell, Thompson		2	3					7							6		10		5		11		1		8	4	9	38
39	12 Apr	H	**Chelsea**	W	2 1	(1 0)	20,000	9	Seymour, Keating			3			4	7				11	8			6		10	2	5				1		9			39
40	18 Apr	A	Bolton Wanderers	W	1 0	(1 0)	20,000	8	Low J		2	3			6	7		9	10	11		8		4				5				1					40
41	19 Apr	A	Chelsea	L	0 1	(0 1)	30,000	9				3		5	4	7		9	10	11		8						2			6	1					41
42	21 Apr	A	Aston Villa	L	1 6	(1 1)	40,000	9	Clark JasR						2		7				8					10			5	11	6	1	3	9	4		42
Round			FA Cup																																		Round
1	12 Jan	A	Portsmouth	W	4 2	(0 2)	26,422		Seymour, Harris, Low J, Gibson	1		3			4	7		9	10	11		8		5			2				6						1
2	02 Feb	A	Derby County	D	2 2	(1 0)	27,873		McDonald 2						4	7		9	10	11		8		5			2				6	1	3				2
2r	06 Feb	H	**Derby County**	De	2 2	(2 0)	50,393		Harris, Cowan						4	7		9	10	11		8		5			2				6	1	3				2r
2rr	11 Feb	N1	Derby County	De	2 2	(1 1)	17,300		Seymour, Hudspeth (pen)		2	3		5	4	7	8	9		11		10									6	1					2rr
2rrr	13 Feb	H	**Derby County**	W	5 3	(3 2)	32,496		Seymour, Harris 3, Cowan		2	3		5		7		9	10	11		8		4							6	1					2rrr
3	23 Feb	A	Watford	W	1 0	(1 0)	23,444		Seymour		2	3		5		7		9	10	11		8		4							6	1					3
4	08 Mar	H	**Liverpool**	W	1 0	(1 0)	56,594		McDonald		2	3		5	4	7	8	9	10	11				6								1					4
SF	29 Mar	N2	Manchester City	W	2 0	(1 0)	50,039		Harris 2		2	3		5		7		9	10	11		8		4							6	1					SF
F	26 Apr	N3	Aston Villa	W	2 0	(0 0)	91,695		Seymour, Harris	1	2	3		5		7		9	10	11		8		4							6						F

N1 Played at Burnden Park, Bolton
N2 Played at St Andrew's, Birmingham
N3 Played at Wembley Stadium, London

De Drawn after extra time

DateLine ... 13 Feb: A four game FA Cup epic with Derby results in triumph by 5-3, the longest tie for another 65 years. **21 April:** The Magpies field almost a reserve side against Villa and lose 6-1. Goalkeeper Mutch did play, was injured and missed the FA Cup final. **26 April:** The first all-ticket FA Cup final, United defeat Aston Villa 2-0.

SEASON 1924-25
DIVISION 1

Offside, offside! was the call

For years tactics of football had developed in such a manner that thoughtful defenders of the day – then the two full-backs – could catch forwards in a well-drilled offside trap. Season by season United's prominent backs of Hampson, Hudspeth and McCracken devised the plan to almost perfection. They were the best in the business. Many clubs tried to emulate the tactic to such a telling effect that football as a spectacle suffered. By the end of season 1924-25 the game's rulers decided on a change. It was to be the last season of such defensive football.

United conceded only 42 goals as their back-line stood firm again, and that gave the Black'n'Whites a good footing to improve their League standing. They still ended the programme well behind team of the era Huddersfield Town – winners of the title for three seasons in a row – but could have, and should have been much closer than their sixth place. With three convincing wins in the space of 14 days during March they went top of the table with only five games left. Preston, Burnley and Leeds were defeated, however, two crucial home set-backs by West Bromwich Albion and Bolton – both in the title race too – and an away reverse to Tottenham was not good enough. The Terriers took control and lifted the title ahead of Albion with Newcastle claiming only three points from a possible 12 in the final run-in.

The FA Cup holders went out of the tournament early, in Round Two, this after a local derby with a difference – a rare contest with Hartlepools United. The Tynesiders won 4-1 at Gallowgate but then faltered badly against Second Division Leicester City, losing in a replay when a record crowd turned up at Filbert Street.

Pictured above: Willie Cowan was one of several Scottish playmakers and hugely effective during the Twenties.

Memorabilia CORNER

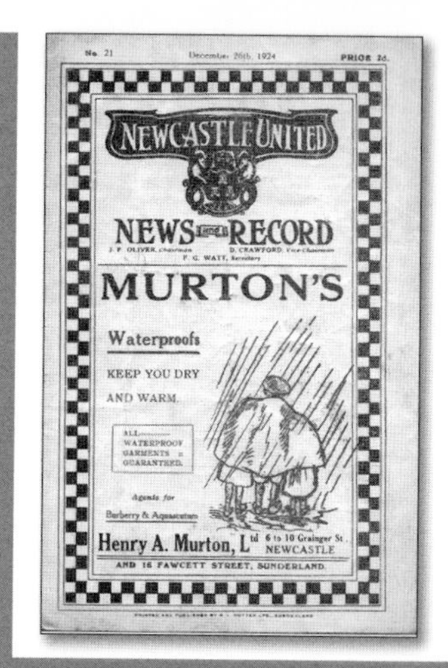

Match programme from the Boxing Day fixture with Everton in 1924.

IN CHARGE

Chairman: John Oliver
Manager: Director Committee
Captain: Frank Hudspeth
Trainer/Coach: James McPherson

ST JAMES' PARK

Average Attendance
Lg 26,019 Lg & Cup 27,902

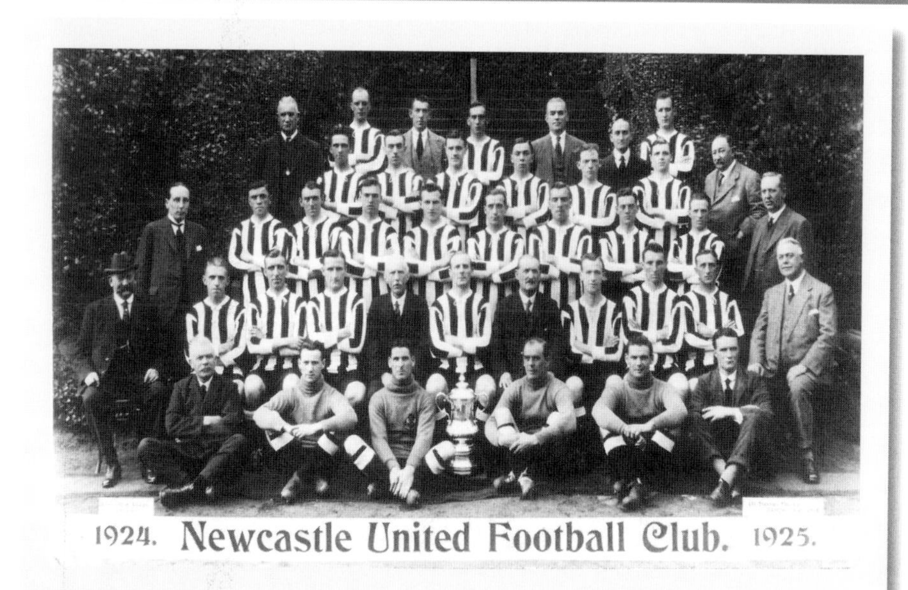

Skipper Frank Hudspeth has the FA Cup trophy at his feet as Newcastle players and officials pose for the camera at the beginning of the 1924-25 season.

SEASON REVIEW

Football League Div 1: P42 W16 D16 L10 F61 A42 Pts 48.
Position: 6th (Champions; Huddersfield Town).
FA Cup: R2 (Winners; Sheffield United).

Appearances (45m): Bradley W 39, Cowan WD 38, Seymour GS 38, Spencer CW 38, Gibson WM 37, Hudspeth FC 37, Harris NL 36, McDonald TH 36, Hampson W 32, Urwin T 32, MacKenzie RR 26, Clark JnR 18, Curry T 18, Low J 17, Mooney E 16, Maitland AE 11, Russell SR 6, Keating AE 5, Hunter JA 4, Mitchell TM 4, Tate IH 4, Mutch A 2, Loughlin J 1.

Goals (67g): Harris NL 20, McDonald TH 13, Cowan WD 12, Seymour GS 7, Clark JnR 4, Urwin T 4, Keating AE 2, Low J 2, Hudspeth FC 1, MacKenzie RR 1, Mooney E 1.

Dismissals: 1 player; Urwin.

MAJOR SIGNINGS

Tommy Urwin (Middlesbrough) £3,200
Alf Maitland (Middlesbrough) £1,000

FROM THE RANKS

James Loughlin (Darlington Railway Ath)
Isaac Tate (Marley Hill)

PLAYER FOCUS Bill McCracken

Born Belfast. Right-back, 5'11"
1904 to 1923: 444 app 8 goals.

One of the most celebrated footballers of his time, Irishman Bill McCracken spent almost 19 years on United's playing staff after signing from the Lisburn Distillery club in May 1904 for £50. During that long period Bill became an idol to the Geordie crowd as he won three titles and played in three FA Cup finals, yet he was very much a villain on the field elsewhere. A tactical genius on the pitch, his defensive acumen at mainly right-back was renowned, and when his partnership at various times with either Frank Hudspeth and Billy Hampson developed an offside-trap to almost perfection, football's rules were changed in 1925 largely as a result. McCracken was a colourful and controversial character, often at odds with referees and officials, yet he was a terrific footballer, a regular for the Irish (until he fell-out with his country's hierarchy over payments). Captain of club and country, on concluding his lengthy playing career during the 1922-23 season when aged over 40 years old, he started a period as manager of a number of lower division and somewhat struggling clubs. In February 1923 he began with Hull City, then was in charge of Gateshead, Millwall and Aldershot. Bill did taste a degree of success, taking the Tigers close to a Wembley FA Cup final appearance, only losing in the semi-final replay by a single goal. McCracken afterwards became well-known as a scout for United and Watford, remarkably active until into his nineties. He deservedly was awarded the FA's Long Service Medal. His cousin Robert McCracken also played for Northern Ireland, in the same line-up as Bill.

TEAM COLOURS Black & white striped shirts, black shorts (Change; white shirts with broad black diamond stripe, black shorts)

SEASON 1924-25

Match			FL Division 1				Posn	
1	30 Aug	H	**Huddersfield Town**	L 1 3	(1 1)	47,000		Cowan
2	01 Sep	A	Blackburn Rovers	D 1 1	(0 1)	30,000	16	Seymour
3	06 Sep	A	Aston Villa	D 0 0	(0 0)	40,000	15	
4	08 Sep	A	West Ham United	D 0 0	(0 0)	23,000	16	
5	10 Sep	H	**Blackburn Rovers**	W 4 0	(2 0)	30,000	6	Harris 3, Hudspeth (pen)
6	13 Sep	H	**Arsenal**	D 2 2	(1 1)	22,000	4	McDonald, Mooney
7	17 Sep	H	**West Ham United**	W 4 1	(3 1)	30,000	2	Harris 3, McDonald
8	20 Sep	A	Manchester City	L 1 3	(1 2)	35,000	4	McDonald
9	27 Sep	H	**Bury**	D 2 2	(1 0)	35,000	8	Seymour, Urwin
10	04 Oct	A	Nottingham Forest	D 1 1	(1 1)	15,000	8	Seymour
11	11 Oct	H	**Liverpool**	D 0 0	(0 0)	25,000	7	
12	18 Oct	A	Sunderland	D 1 1	(1 1)	55,642	8	Clark
13	25 Oct	H	**Cardiff City**	L 1 2	(1 2)	22,000	13	Cowan
14	01 Nov	A	Preston North End	W 1 0	(1 0)	12,347	9	Harris
15	08 Nov	H	**Burnley**	W 3 0	(0 0)	20,000	6	Clark 2, Cowan
16	15 Nov	A	Leeds United	D 1 1	(0 1)	35,000	6	Seymour
17	22 Nov	H	**Birmingham**	W 4 0	(1 0)	18,000	4	Cowan, Harris 3
18	29 Nov	A	West Bromwich Albion	L 0 2	(0 2)	13,141	8	
19	06 Dec	H	**Tottenham Hotspur**	D 1 1	(0 1)	28,000	7	Seymour
20	13 Dec	A	Bolton Wanderers	L 2 3	(1 3)	15,000	10	Keating, Low
21	20 Dec	H	**Notts County**	W 1 0	(1 0)	25,000	8	McDonald
22	25 Dec	A	Everton	W 1 0	(0 0)	30,000	6	Keating
23	26 Dec	H	**Everton**	D 1 1	(0 1)	25,000	6	Seymour
24	27 Dec	A	Huddersfield Town	D 0 0	(0 0)	15,000	5	
25	01 Jan	H	**Sheffield United**	D 0 0	(0 0)	20,000	6	
26	03 Jan	H	**Aston Villa**	W 4 1	(3 0)	28,000	5	Cowan 3, McDonald
27	17 Jan	A	Arsenal	W 2 0	(1 0)	30,000	3	Harris, Seymour
28	24 Jan	H	**Manchester City**	W 2 0	(2 0)	26,000	3	Cowan, Urwin
29	07 Feb	H	**Nottingham Forest**	W 4 1	(3 1)	21,000	5	Harris 2, McDonald, Urwin
30	11 Feb	A	Bury	D 0 0	(0 0)	5,066	3	
31	14 Feb	A	Liverpool	D 1 1	(0 1)	35,000	3	Clark
32	21 Feb	H	**Sunderland**	W 2 0	(2 0)	52,000	3	Cowan, Urwin
33	28 Feb	A	Cardiff City	L 0 3	(0 0)	25,000	4	
34	07 Mar	H	**Preston North End**	W 3 1	(1 0)	20,000	3	Cowan, Harris, Low
35	14 Mar	A	Burnley	W 3 1	(1 0)	12,000	3	Harris 2, McDonald
36	21 Mar	H	**Leeds United**	W 4 1	(2 1)	19,000	2	Harris 2, McDonald 2
37	28 Mar	A	Birmingham	D 1 1	(0 0)	36,000	1	Harris
38	04 Apr	H	**West Bromwich Albion**	L 0 1	(0 0)	25,400	3	
39	11 Apr	A	Tottenham Hotspur	L 0 3	(0 1)	23,144	4	
40	13 Apr	A	Sheffield United	W 2 1	(1 1)	20,000	4	McDonald 2
41	18 Apr	H	**Bolton Wanderers**	L 0 1	(0 0)	8,000	5	
42	25 Apr	A	Notts County	L 0 2	(0 1)	8,000	6	
Round			**FA Cup**					
1	10 Jan	H	**Hartlepools United**	W 4 1	(1 0)	36,632		Cowan, Harris, McDonald, MacKenzie
2	31 Jan	H	**Leicester City**	D 2 2	(0 1)	58,713		McDonald (pen), Cowan
2r	05 Feb	A	Leicester City	L 0 1	(0 1)	40,350		

Match	Mutch	Hampson	Hudspeth	Mooney	Spencer	Gibson	Low	Cowan	Harris	McDonald	Seymour	Bradley	Hunter	Keating	Urwin	Clark JnR	Tate	Curry	Russell	Mitchell	MacKenzie	Maitland	Loughlin
1	1	2	3	4	5	6	7	8	9	10	11												
2	1	2	3	4	5	6	7	8	9	10	11												
3		2	3	4	5	6	7	8	9	10	11	1											
4		2		4	5	6	7	8		10	11	1	3	9									
5		2	3	4	5	6			9	10	11	1			7	8							
6		2	3	4	5	6			9	10	11	1			7	8							
7		2	3	4	5	6	7		9	10	11					8	1						
8		2	3	4	5	6	7	8	9	10	11						1						
9		2	3		5	6		8	9	10	11				7		1	4					
10			3		5	6		8	9		11	1			7			4	2	10			
11			3		5	6		8	9	10	11	1			7			4	2				
12			3	4	5	6			9	10	11	1			7	8			2				
13			3		5	6		8		10	11	1			7	9		4	2				
14			3	5		6		8	9	10	11	1			7			4	2				
15		2	3	4	5	6		10	9		11	1			7	8							
16		2	3	4	5	6		10	9		11	1			7	8							
17		2		4	5	6		10	9		11	1	3		7	8							
18		2			5	6		10	9		11	1			7	8		4	3				
19		2		4	5	6		10	9		11	1	3		7	8							
20		2		6	5		7	10	9		11	1	3	8							4		
21		2	3	6	5		7			10	11	1		9		8					4		
22		2			5			8		10	11	1		9	7			6			4	3	
23		2			5			8		10	11	1		9	7			6			4	3	
24			2		5			8		10	11	1			7			6			4	3	9
25		2	3		5			9		10	11	1			7	8		6			4		
26		2	3		5			9		10	11	1			7	8		6			4		
27		2	3		5	6		8	9	10	11	1			7						4		
28		2	3		5	6		8	9	10	11	1			7						4		
29			2		5	6			9	10	11	1			7	8					4	3	
30			2		5	6		10	9		11	1			7	8					4	3	
31			2		5		7	10	9			1			11d	8		6			4	3	
32		2	3		5	6		8	9	10	11	1			7						4		
33		2				6		8	9	10	11				7		1	5			4	3	
34		2	3		5	6	7	8	9	10	11	1									4		
35		2	3		5	6	7	8	9	10		1								11	4		
36		2	3		5	6	7	8	9	10	11	1									4		
37		2	3		5	6	7	8	9	10	11	1									4		
38		2	3			6	7	8	9	10		1						5		11	4		
39			2			6		8	9	10		1			7			5		11	4	3	
40			2			6	7		9	10		1			11	8		5			4	3	
41			2			6	7	8	9	10		1			11			5			4	3	
42			2			6	7	9		10		1			11	8		5			4	3	
Round																							
1		2	3		5	6		8	9	10	11	1			7						4		
2		2	3		5	6		8	9	10	11	1			7						4		
2r		2	3		5	6		8	9	10	11	1			7						4		

DateLine ... 10 Sept: A hat-trick for Neil Harris against Blackburn Rovers gets United's season on winning track. **10 Jan:** The first senior local derby with Hartlepools United, a 4-1 victory in the FA Cup. **14 Feb:** Three players are sent-off in the Liverpool clash, one for United and two for the Reds. **21 March:** United's third victory in a row sees the Magpies in with a shot at the title.

SEASON 1925-26
DIVISION 1

Record signing dazzles and sparkles

With the new offside rule introduced for the start of the season, clubs had to quickly come to terms with a different style of football. A new formation evolved with the previous midfield role of the centre-half now turned into a defensive pivot to counter freedom in attack. The Magpies were at the forefront of this change, with arguably Charlie Spencer becoming one of the first players to successfully make the switch. In the bedding-in period goals flowed. United thrashed Arsenal 7-0 in October, yet before United themselves fully came to terms with the change, they fell 7-1 to Blackburn Rovers.

Any team with a noted scorer reaped the benefit and United's directors were determined to land one of the best strikers in the business to replace the aging Neil Harris. In December of that season they smashed the club record transfer fee to bring 22-year-old Scot Hughie Gallacher to Tyneside for £6,500. It proved to be a landmark deal. Gallacher immediately made his mark and the new approach to defending had no answer to his trickery. He scored 15 goals in his first nine games as United jumped between brilliant and awful in an inconsistent season – a year though that saw the black-and-whites net 90 goals.

United couldn't maintain winning form on a steady basis in League competition and also went out of the FA Cup to lowly placed Second Division club Clapton Orient in Round Five. They finished in mid-table, yet they would make amends in the following campaign. The man who would lead them to Championship silver, Hughie Gallacher, finished the season as he started his time on Tyneside with goals. Against relegation threatened Manchester City he scored a hat-trick to seal their fate, his 25th for United in just 22 matches and his 42nd strike in the season as a whole.

Pictured above: Originally a midfielder, Charlie Spencer became one of the first defensive centre-backs.

Memorabilia CORNER

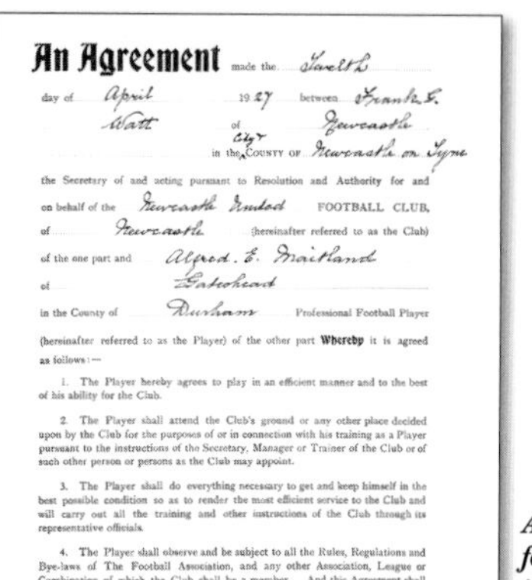

An Agreement made the Twelfth day of April 1927 between Frank G. Watt of Newcastle in the City County of Newcastle on Tyne the Secretary of and acting pursuant to Resolution and Authority for and on behalf of the Newcastle United FOOTBALL CLUB, of Newcastle (hereinafter referred to as the Club) of the one part and Alfred. E. Maitland of Gateshead in the County of Durham Professional Football Player (hereinafter referred to as the Player) of the other part **Whereby** it is agreed as follows:—

1. The Player hereby agrees to play in an efficient manner and to the best of his ability for the Club.

2. The Player shall attend the Club's ground or any other place decided upon by the Club for the purposes of or in connection with his training as a Player pursuant to the instructions of the Secretary, Manager or Trainer of the Club or of such other person or persons as the Club may appoint.

3. The Player shall do everything necessary to get and keep himself in the best possible condition so as to render the most efficient service to the Club and will carry out all the training and other instructions of the Club through its representative officials.

4. The Player shall observe and be subject to all the Rules, Regulations and Bye-laws of The Football Association, and any other Association, League or Combination of which the Club shall be a member. And this Agreement shall be subject to any action which shall be taken by The Football Association under their Rules for the suspension or termination of the Football Season and if any such suspension or termination shall be decided upon the payment of wages shall likewise be suspended or terminated as the case may be.

5. The Player shall not engage in any business or live in any place which the Directors (or Committee) of the Club may deem unsuitable.

All professional footballers were issued with a standard contra[ct] this one signed [by] Alf Maitland.

IN CHARGE

Chairman: John Oliver
Manager: Director Committee
Captain: Frank Hudspeth
Trainer/Coach: James McPherson

ST JAMES' PARK

Average Attendance
Lg 29,862 Lg & Cup 30,252

The time-honoured new season group for 1925-26, later supplemented by a record signing as an inset, Hughie Gallacher (centre top). He was to turn United into title contenders.

PLAYER FOCUS Frank Hudspeth

Born Percy Main. Left-back, 5'9"
1910 to 1929: 482 app 38 goals.

Tyneside born and bred, Frank Hudspeth was a grand servant to the Magpies in his near 19 year career at St James' Park – equal record service for United for many years while no other outfield player has appeared more for the club. At left-back, Frank was dependable and consistent as well as having a tactical mind, forming the notorious Magpie offside-trap with Bill McCracken. Joining United in March 1910 as a youngster from North Shields Athletic, he gained a regular place just as United's Edwardian era was coming to a close in season 1912-13. After the war, Frank was one of the club's mainstays, Hudspeth skippering the side to their next triumph, to FA Cup glory in 1924. The older and wiser he became, he seemingly became a better player, indeed gaining his only full England cap against Ireland at Windsor Park when almost 36 years of age in 1925-26. A year on, he was an ever-present as the Magpies lifted the title trophy with his experience and cool head being an important factor in the success. Something of a penalty expert, he netted more than 30 goals from the spot, including eight in season 1925-26. Frank headed south from Gallowgate in January 1929 and served Stockport County before moving into a coaching career with Rochdale and Burnley during the 1930s. He afterwards lived in Lancashire. Frank once led out an England XI in a Victory International during season 1919-20.

SEASON REVIEW

Football League Div 1: P42 W16 D10 L16 F84 A75 Pts 42.
Position: 10th (Champions; Huddersfield Town).
FA Cup: R5 (Winners; Bolton Wanderers).

Appearances (45m): Urwin T 44, McDonald TH 43, Wilson W1 43, Hudspeth FC 35, Cowan WD 33, Chandler A 32, Spencer CW 28, Seymour GS 26, Gibson WM 25, MacKenzie RR 25, Curry T 24, Gallacher HK 22, Clark JnR 21, Harris J 19, Hampson W 16, Mitchell TM 15, Mooney E 8, Loughlin J 7, Maitland AE 5, Mordue T 5, Harris NL 4, Low J 4, Park O 4, Dowsey JR 3, Crown L 2, Bradley W 1, Taylor A 1.

Goals (90g): Gallacher HK 25, McDonald TH 11, Hudspeth FC 8, Seymour GS 8, Urwin T 8, Cowan WD 7 Clark JnR 6, Loughlin J 5, Gibson WM 2, Harris NL 2, Mordue T 2, Curry T 1, Mitchell TM 1, own goals 4.

Dismissals: 0 players.

MAJOR SIGNINGS

Hughie Gallacher (Airdrie) £6,500 club record fee
Bert Chandler (Derby County) £3,250
Jimmy Boyd (St Bernards) £600
Joe Harris (Middlesbrough) £750
Willie Wilson (Peebles Rvs) £600

FROM THE RANKS

Ossie Park (Darlington Railway Ath)
John Dowsey (Hunswick Villa)
Tom Mordue (Horden Ath)
Allan Taylor (North Shields)

TEAM COLOURS Black & white striped shirts, black shorts (Change; white shirts with broad black diamond stripe, black shorts)

SEASON 1925-26

Match	Date	Venue	FL Division 1	Res	F	A	HT F	HT A	Att	Posn	Scorers
1	29 Aug	A	Bolton Wanderers	D	2	2	2	1	30,998		Cowan, og (Pym)
2	05 Sep	H	**Notts County**	W	6	3	3	1	33,264	7	Mitchell, McDonald, Harris N, Cowan 2, og (Dinsdale)
3	09 Sep	H	**Blackburn Rovers**	L	1	7	0	3	21,582	14	McDonald
4	12 Sep	A	Aston Villa	D	2	2	0	1	38,819	14	Hudspeth (pen), og (Spiers)
5	16 Sep	A	Leeds United	L	0	2	0	1	21,291	15	
6	19 Sep	H	**Leicester City**	W	3	2	2	0	29,925	12	Loughlin 3
7	26 Sep	A	West Ham United	L	0	1	0	1	24,722	17	
8	03 Oct	H	**Arsenal**	W	7	0	6	0	40,683	12	Clark 3, Loughlin, Seymour 2, Urwin
9	10 Oct	A	Manchester United	L	1	2	0	1	39,651	16	Seymour
10	12 Oct	A	Blackburn Rovers	W	2	1	2	0	12,094	11	Harris N, McDonald
11	17 Oct	H	**Sunderland**	D	0	0	0	0	51,604	11	
12	24 Oct	A	Huddersfield Town	W	1	0	1	0	18,285	8	McDonald
13	31 Oct	H	**Birmingham**	L	1	3	0	1	26,475	12	Hudspeth (pen)
14	07 Nov	A	Bury	D	1	1	1	1	7,582	13	Cowan
15	14 Nov	H	**Tottenham Hotspur**	W	3	1	3	1	23,391	10	Gibson, Seymour, og (Clay)
16	21 Nov	A	Cardiff City	D	0	0	0	0	25,539	9	
17	05 Dec	A	West Bromwich Albion	L	0	4	0	2	15,633	12	
18	09 Dec	H	**Sheffield United**	W	3	1	2	0	12,996	10	Mordue, Cowan, Hudspeth (pen)
19	12 Dec	H	**Everton**	D	3	3	1	1	36,274	10	Gallacher 2, Seymour
20	19 Dec	A	Manchester City	D	2	2	1	0	28,616	11	McDonald (pen), Gallacher
21	25 Dec	A	Liverpool	L	3	6	1	2	31,409	12	Gallacher 3
22	26 Dec	H	**Liverpool**	W	3	0	3	0	48,809	11	Clark, Gallacher, Urwin
23	01 Jan	H	**Burnley**	L	1	3	0	1	34,903	13	Urwin
24	02 Jan	H	**Bolton Wanderers**	W	5	1	3	0	34,136	11	Gallacher 4, Urwin
25	16 Jan	A	Notts County	W	3	1	2	1	10,700	9	Gallacher 2, McDonald
26	23 Jan	H	**Aston Villa**	D	2	2	1	0	39,305	9	McDonald, Hudspeth (pen)
27	06 Feb	H	**West Ham United**	W	4	1	1	0	27,034	6	Cowan, Gallacher 2, Seymour
28	13 Feb	A	Arsenal	L	0	3	0	2	48,346	8	
29	22 Feb	A	Leicester City	L	2	3	1	2	16,700	10	Gallacher 2
30	27 Feb	A	Sunderland	D	2	2	1	1	34,902	10	Mordue, Urwin
31	06 Mar	H	**Huddersfield Town**	L	0	2	0	2	54,496	12	
32	13 Mar	A	Birmingham	D	1	1	0	0	24,333	11	Urwin
33	20 Mar	H	**Bury**	W	4	0	3	0	26,170	9	Clark, Gallacher 2, McDonald
34	25 Mar	A	Tottenham Hotspur	L	0	1	0	1	11,774	9	
35	02 Apr	A	Burnley	L	0	1	0	1	27,674	13	
36	03 Apr	H	**Cardiff City**	L	0	1	0	0	26,205	16	
37	05 Apr	H	**Leeds United**	W	3	0	1	0	16,666	12	Curry, Gallacher, McDonald
38	10 Apr	A	Sheffield United	L	3	4	1	2	18,920	15	McDonald, Hudspeth 2 (2 pens)
39	14 Apr	H	**Manchester United**	W	4	1	3	1	9,829	11	McDonald, Clark, Urwin, Hudspeth (pen)
40	17 Apr	H	**West Bromwich Albion**	W	3	0	2	0	13,084	9	Loughlin, Urwin, Hudspeth (pen)
41	24 Apr	A	Everton	L	0	3	0	3	20,517	10	
42	01 May	H	**Manchester City**	W	3	2	1	1	20,262	10	Gallacher 3
Round			**FA Cup**								
3	09 Jan	H	**Aberdare Athletic**	W	4	1	1	0	38,452		Cowan, Gallacher 2, Gibson
4	30 Jan	A	Cardiff City	W	2	0	1	0	38,270		Seymour 2
5	20 Feb	A	Clapton Orient	L	0	2	0	2	31,400		

Match	Bradley	Chandler	Hudspeth	MacKenzie	Park	Curry	Urwin	Clark JnR	Cowan	McDonald	Mitchell	Taylor	Spencer	Harris NL	Wilson	Low	Maitland	Loughlin	Gibson	Mooney	Seymour	Hampson	Dowsey	Mordue	Gallacher	Harris J	Crown
1	1	2	3	4	5	6	7	8	9	10	11																
2		2	3	4		6	7		8	10	11	1	5	9													
3		2	3	4		6	7		8	10	11		5	9	1												
4		2	3	4		6	7	8	9	10	11		5		1												
5		2	3	4		6	7		8	10	11		5		1	9											
6			2	4		6	7		8	10	11		5		1		3	9									
7			2			4	7	8		10	11		5		1		3	9	6								
8		2	3	4			7	8		10			5		1			9		6	11						
9		2	3	4			7	8		10			5		1			9		6	11						
10		2	3	4		6	7		8	10			5	9	1						11						
11		2	3	4			7		8	10			5	9	1					6	11						
12		2		4			7		8	10			5		1			9		6	11	3					
13			3			4	7		8	10			5		1			9		6	11	2					
14		2		4			7	8	9	10			5		1				6		11	3					
15		2					7		9	10			5		1				6	4	11	3	8				
16		2					7		9	10			5		1				6	4	11	3	8				
17		2					7		9	10			5		1				6	4	11	3	8				
18		2	3	4			7		8	10			5		1				6		11			9			
19			3	4			7		8	10			5		1				6		11	2			9		
20		2		4			7		8	10	11		5		1		3		6						9		
21		2							8	10	11		5		1	7			6			3			9	4	
22		2	3			6	7	8	10	5	11				1										9	4	
23		2	3			6	7	8	10	5	11				1										9	4	
24		2	3			5	7	8		10	11				1				6						9	4	
25		2	3			5	11		8	10					1	7			6						9	4	
26		2	3	4			7		8	10			5		1						11				9	6	
27		2	3			5	7		8	10					1				6		11				9	4	
28		2	3	6		5	7		8	10					1						11			9		4	
29		2	3	6			7	8		10			5		1						11				9	4	
30		2	3	4	5		7	8	10		11				1				6					9			
31				4		5	7	8		10	11				1							2			9	6	3
32				4		5	7	8		10					1				6		11	2			9		3
33			3	4	5		7	8	10	11					1				6			2			9		
34			3	4	5		7	8	10	11					1				6			2			9		
35		2		4		5	7		8	10					1		3		6		11				9		
36			3	4		5	11		8	10					1	7			6			2		9			
37			3			6	7	8		10			5		1						11	2			9	4	
38			3			6	7	8		10			5		1						11	2			9	4	
39			3				7	8		10			5		1				6		11	2		9		4	
40		2	3				7	8	10				5		1			9	6		11					4	
41		2	3				7	8		10			5		1				6		11				9	4	
42			2			5	7	8		10					1		3		6		11				9	4	
Round																											
3		2	3			5	7		8	10	11				1				6						9	4	
4		2	3			5	7		8	10					1				6		11				9	4	
5		2	3				7		8	10			5		1				6		11				9	4	

DateLine ... 31 Aug: The Magpies defeat Real Madrid 6-1 in a friendly at Gallowgate. **9 Sept:** Blackburn win 7-1 on Tyneside with Ted Harper netting five goals. **3 Oct:** United defeat Arsenal 7-0 as the offside change proves a test for some. **12 Dec:** Hughie Gallacher scores twice on his debut against Everton after a record move. **1 May:** Manchester City miss a penalty and lose 3-2 when a draw would have saved them from relegation.

SEASON
1926-27
DIVISION 1

Goal-power takes United to the title

With Hughie Gallacher a threat up front no club could tame, Newcastle were tipped for honours at the very start of the season. United started on fire with the Scot scoring all four goals in a home victory over Aston Villa. Local foes Sunderland were rivals for the Championship that year, but it was Huddersfield Town – title winners for the last three years – who ran neck and neck with the Magpies for much of the campaign. The Black'n'Whites took over at the top after New Year with a run of six victories in a row, but then almost created a huge FA Cup shock. After Newcastle demolished Notts County 8-1 in the opening FA Cup sortie, they played out an intriguing tie against famous amateurs The Corinthians – and returned to their old bogey ground of The Crystal Palace. The Sydenham enclosure almost proved a jinx once more, the amateurs taking a shock lead before United levelled and netted two late goals. Surprisingly Newcastle fell to Southampton in Round Five and now had only the League title to focus on.

With all three clubs in the race consistently picking up points, the contests with both Sunderland and Huddersfield were decisive as the race reached fever pitch. Firstly, United's great rivals from Wearside were toppled 1-0, when a new Gallowgate crowd record was established of 67,067, then Huddersfield suffered the same fate. United had their noses in front.

Gallacher was the big difference, netting a record 39 goals in the season. Although United's line-up and diminutive forward five in particular included several other players at the top of their game – men like Tom McDonald, Stan Seymour and Tommy Urwin in particular – it was the Scottish leader who more than any won the title for the Black'n'Whites. A 3-2 victory over Spurs at Gallowgate was crucial, then a draw in East London at West Ham secured the point which earned the Magpies' first Championship victory for 18 years.

Pictured above: Bob McKay made headlines on his debut, striking a hat-trick against West Bromwich Albion.

Memorabilia CORNER

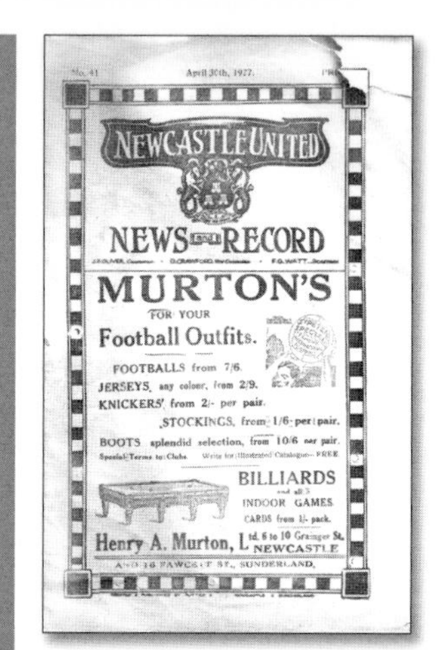

Now called the 'News & Record', this issue from United's last home game of the title winning season.

IN CHARGE

Chairman: John Oliver
Manager: Director Committee
Captain: Hughie Gallacher
Trainer/Coach: James McPherson

ST JAMES' PARK

Average Attendance
Lg 36,513 Lg & Cup 36,333

Hughie Gallacher was appointed captain for the 1926-27 season, pictured with the ball. The Scot led United to the Championship trophy.

SEASON REVIEW

Football League Div 1: P42 W25 D6 L11 F96 A58 Pts 56.
Position: 1st, Champions.
FA Cup: R5 (Winners; Cardiff City).

Appearances (45m): Hudspeth FC 45, Seymour GS 45, Wilson W1 45, McDonald TH 44, Urwin T 42, Gallacher HK 41, MacKenzie RR 41, Maitland AE 39, Spencer CW 37, Gibson WM 35, McKay R 28, Clark JnR 17, Harris J 9, Curry T 5, Park O 5, Chandler A 4, Loughlin J 4, Mooney E 3, Boyd JM 2, Hampson W 2, Low J 2.

Goals (108g): Gallacher HK 39, McDonald TH 23, Seymour GS 19, McKay R 11, Urwin T 5, Clark JnR 4, Hudspeth FC 3, MacKenzie RR 2, Low J 1, own goal 1.

Dismissals: 0 players.

MAJOR SIGNINGS

Bob McKay (Rangers) £2,750

FROM THE RANKS

None

PLAYER FOCUS Hughie Gallacher

Born Bellshill. Centre-forward, 5'5"
1925 to 1930: 174 app 143 goals.

Considered by judges to be one of the very best centre-forwards of all time, even though Hughie Gallacher was only 5'5" tall, the Scot was a handful for any defence. He possessed a powerful, accurate shot with both feet, expert dribbling ability, and the knack of scoring with his head despite his size. He was also an intimidating opponent, frequently losing his cool with, not only defenders, but also referees. In a long career Hughie totalled 463 goals in 624 matches, formidable statistics which prove his undoubted quality. On his arrival to Tyneside in December 1925 from Airdrie in a near British record transfer of £6,500, he was quickly elevated to cult status. Gallacher captained United's side to the Championship trophy in 1927 and with 39 goals in that season, held the club's scoring record for decades to come. A personality player, he was also outstanding for the Scottish international side, a Wembley Wizard in 1928. In the summer of 1930 and following over 140 goals for the Magpies, Hughie was controversially sold to Chelsea for a near record £10,000 fee against his wishes and amidst uproar on Tyneside. And on his first game back to Gallowgate with Chelsea, a record breaking St James' Park crowd of over 68,000 was present to see him. A player who created headlines throughout his career, Gallacher also had both productive and problematic stays at Derby County, Grimsby Town, Notts County and Gateshead. He remained on Tyneside for the rest of his life until his tragic suicidal death beneath an express train on Tyneside in 1957.

TEAM COLOURS Black & white striped shirts, black shorts (Change; white shirts with broad black diamond stripe, black shorts)

SEASON 1926-27

Match	Date		FL Division 1						Posn		Wilson	Chandler	Hudspeth	MacKenzie	Mooney	Gibson	Urwin	Clark	Gallacher	McDonald	Seymour	Curry	Loughlin	Maitland	Spencer	Boyd	Park	Harris	McKay	Low	Hampson	Match
1	28 Aug	H	**Aston Villa**	W	4	0	(1 0)	36,057		Gallacher 4	1	2	3	4	5	6	7	8	9	10	11											1
2	01 Sep	H	**Burnley**	L	1	5	(1 2)	33,069	10	Hudspeth (pen)	1	2	3	4	5	6	7	8	9	10	11											2
3	04 Sep	A	Bolton Wanderers	L	1	2	(0 1)	25,049	15	Seymour	1	2	3	4	5		7	8		10	11	6	9									3
4	06 Sep	A	Burnley	D	3	3	(2 0)	25,374	14	Gallacher, McDonald, Seymour	1		2	4		6	7	8	9	10	11			3	5							4
5	11 Sep	H	**Manchester United**	W	4	2	(1 1)	28,050	11	Gallacher, McDonald 2, Seymour	1		2	4		6	7	8	9	10	11			3	5							5
6	18 Sep	A	Derby County	D	1	1	(1 0)	26,306	12	og (Crilly)	1	2	3	4		6	7	8	9	10	11				5							6
7	20 Sep	A	Cardiff City	D	1	1	(0 0)	14,048	13	Urwin	1		3	4		6	8		9	10	11			2	5	7						7
8	25 Sep	H	**Sheffield United**	W	2	0	(1 0)	27,611	10	Gallacher 2	1		3	4		6	7		9	10	11		8	2	5							8
9	02 Oct	A	Arsenal	D	2	2	(2 0)	38,842	10	Clark, Seymour	1		3	4		6	7	8	9	10	11			2	5							9
10	09 Oct	H	**Liverpool**	W	1	0	(1 0)	21,575	9	Gallacher	1		3	4			7	8	9	10	11			2			5	6				10
11	16 Oct	A	Everton	W	3	1	(1 0)	41,746	6	Clark, Gallacher, McDonald	1		3	4			7	8	9	10	11			2	5			6				11
12	23 Oct	H	**Blackburn Rovers**	W	6	1	(4 0)	27,145	6	Clark, McDonald, MacKenzie, Seymour 3	1		3	4		6	7	8	9	10	11			2	5							12
13	30 Oct	A	Sunderland	L	0	2	(0 1)	31,152	8		1		3	4		6	7	8		10	11		9	2	5							13
14	06 Nov	H	**West Bromwich Albion**	W	5	2	(3 1)	28,864	7	Gallacher 2, McKay 3	1		3	4		6	7		9	10	11			2	5				8			14
15	13 Nov	A	Bury	L	2	3	(1 2)	19,973	10	Gallacher, Hudspeth (pen)	1		3	4		6	7		9	10	11			2	5				8			15
16	20 Nov	H	**Birmingham**	W	5	1	(2 0)	30,056	6	Gallacher, Hudspeth, McDonald, McKay, Seymour	1		3	4		6	7		9	10	11			2	5				8			16
17	27 Nov	A	Tottenham Hotspur	W	3	1	(2 0)	33,325	5	Gallacher 3	1		3			6	7		9	10	11			2	5			4	8			17
18	04 Dec	H	**West Ham United**	W	2	0	(1 0)	35,079	5	Gallacher, Seymour	1		3			6	7		9	10	11			2	5			4	8			18
19	11 Dec	A	Sheffield Wednesday	L	2	3	(1 1)	38,422	5	McDonald, McKay	1		3			6	7		9	10	11			2	5			4	8			19
20	18 Dec	H	**Leicester City**	D	1	1	(1 1)	35,702	5	Seymour	1		3	4		6			9	10	11			2	5	7			8			20
21	25 Dec	H	**Cardiff City**	W	5	0	(3 0)	36,250	3	Gallacher 2, McDonald 3	1		3	4		6	7		9	10	11			2	5				8			21
22	27 Dec	A	Leeds United	W	2	1	(1 1)	48,590	3	Seymour, Urwin	1		3			6	7		9	10	11			2			5	4	8			22
23	01 Jan	H	**Leeds United**	W	1	0	(0 0)	51,343	2	Gallacher	1		3	4			7		9	10	11	6		2			5		8			23
24	15 Jan	A	Aston Villa	W	2	1	(1 1)	46,723	1	Gallacher, McDonald	1		3	4		6	7		9	10	11			2	5				8			24
25	22 Jan	H	**Bolton Wanderers**	W	1	0	(1 0)	57,431	1	McKay	1		3	4		6	7		9	10	11			2	5				8			25
26	05 Feb	H	**Derby County**	W	3	0	(1 0)	30,849	1	Gallacher, McDonald (pen), Urwin	1		3	4		6	7		9	10	11			2	5				8			26
27	09 Feb	A	Manchester United	L	1	3	(1 1)	25,402	1	McDonald	1		3	4		6	7		9	10	11			2	5				8			27
28	12 Feb	A	Sheffield United	L	1	2	(1 1)	31,633	2	Seymour	1		3	4		6	7		9		11		10	2	5				8			28
29	26 Feb	A	Liverpool	W	2	1	(1 1)	34,493	2	Seymour 2	1		3	4		6	7	9		10	11			2	5				8			29
30	05 Mar	H	**Everton**	W	7	3	(2 1)	40,202	1	Gallacher 3, McDonald (pen), McKay, MacKenzie, Seymour	1		3	4		6	7		9	10	11			2	5				8			30
31	12 Mar	A	Blackburn Rovers	W	2	1	(1 0)	35,334	1	Gallacher 2	1		3	4		6	7		9	10	11			2	5				8			31
32	19 Mar	H	**Sunderland**	W	1	0	(1 0)	67,067	1	Gallacher	1		3	4		6			9	10	11			2	5				8	7		32
33	26 Mar	A	West Bromwich Albion	L	2	4	(2 2)	21,046	2	Gallacher, McDonald	1		3	4		6	7		9	10	11			2			5		8			33
34	02 Apr	H	**Bury**	W	3	1	(2 0)	26,059	2	Clark, McDonald (pen), McKay	1		3	4		6	7	9		10	11			2	5				8			34
35	06 Apr	H	**Arsenal**	W	6	1	(2 1)	33,635	1	Gallacher 3, McDonald, McKay 2	1		3	4		6	7		9	10	11				5				8		2	35
36	09 Apr	A	Birmingham	L	0	2	(0 0)	27,918	1		1		3	4			7		9	10	11	6			5				8		2	36
37	15 Apr	H	**Huddersfield Town**	W	1	0	(0 0)	60,149	1	Gallacher	1		3	4		6	7		9	10	11			2	5				8			37
38	16 Apr	H	**Tottenham Hotspur**	W	3	2	(2 2)	32,151	1	Seymour 2, Urwin	1		3	4			7	8	9	10	11			2	5			6				38
39	19 Apr	A	Huddersfield Town	L	0	1	(0 0)	44,636	1		1		3	4			7	8	9	10	11			2	5			6				39
40	23 Apr	A	West Ham United	D	1	1	(1 1)	29,722	1	Seymour	1		3	4			7	8	9	10	11			2	5			6				40
41	30 Apr	H	**Sheffield Wednesday**	W	2	1	(1 1)	28,421	1	Gallacher 2	1		3	4			7	8	9	10	11	6		2	5							41
42	07 May	A	Leicester City	L	1	2	(1 1)	26,621	1	Low	1		3	4					9	10	11	6		2			5		8	7		42
Round			FA Cup																													Round
3	08 Jan	H	**Notts County**	W	8	1	(6 0)	32,564		Gallacher 3, McDonald 3 (1 pen), Seymour, Urwin	1		3	4		6	7		9	10	11			2	5				8			3
4	29 Jan	A	Corinthians	W	3	1	(0 1)	56,338		McDonald 2, McKay	1		3	4		6	7		9	10	11			2	5				8			4
5	19 Feb	A	Southampton	L	1	2	(0 0)	21,408		McDonald (pen)	1		3	4		6	7		9	10	11			2	5				8			5

DateLine ... 28 Aug: A great opening day for United and for Hughie Gallacher who nets all four goals in a win over Aston Villa. **6 Nov:** Bob McKay scores a hat-trick on his debut against West Bromwich Albion. **8 Jan:** United rack up eight goals in a FA Cup victory over Notts County and are six up at half-time. **19 March:** A new record home gate established of 67,067 for the match against Sunderland. **9 April:** Billy Hampson becomes United's oldest player against Birmingham City at almost 42 years and 8 months old. **23 April:** Newcastle pick up the point needed to lift the title with a 1-1 draw with West Ham Utd. **30 April:** Gallacher nets a then record 39th goal of the season against Sheffield Wednesday.

SEASON
1927-28
DIVISION 1

Title hangover at Gallowgate

The Football League Champions swaggered into the new season as the action started at St James' Park. Hughie Gallacher, now a massive name in the football world, started where he had left off, striking a hat-trick on the opening day against their closest rivals at that time Huddersfield Town. But perhaps United were over confident as soon the Magpies looked anything but Champions. For an unexplainable reason that happens in football so often, Newcastle suffered a hangover after their title victory. Gallacher continued to grab plenty of goals – 21 in United's total of 80 – but as a team, they were not up to scratch for much of the programme.

The Magpies did begin well with victories such as a 7-1 defeat of Manchester United and a 3-1 triumph over Sunderland putting United among the top placings, but as winter approached they alarmingly slid down the division not winning a game for 12 matches – with their star centre-forward a lengthy absentee, suspended for a headlining two months due to a much publicised fracas with officials following something of a grudge match with Huddersfield on New Year's Eve. The Geordies were down to a mid-table place at one point yet as ever, football was often entertaining.

A remarkable clash with Aston Villa took place on Tyneside during March. In weather that at times deteriorated into a snowstorm, Villa were 4-0 down, and by the 77th minute United had registered goal number seven and were comfortably 7-2 in front. Then the visitors hit three quick goals before the whistle halted the amazing game at 7-5. Supporters left the ground shaking their heads, baffled at what they had just witnessed. Going out of the FA Cup early – to eventual winners Blackburn Rovers – United fans were mystified as why the League Champions had deteriorated so rapidly.

Pictured above: At right-back, Scot Alf Maitland was a solid and at times dashing defender.

Memorabilia CORNER

NEWCASTLE UNITED

News and Record.

MURTON'S
FOR YOUR
Football Outfits

FOOTBALLS from 7/6
JERSEYS any colour from 2/9.
KNICKERS from 2/- per pair.
STOCKINGS from 1/6 per pair.
BOOTS splendid selection from 10/6 per pair.

Billiards
Indoor Games

HENRY A. MURTON LTD
6 to 10 GRAINGER STREET, NEWCASTLE.
AND 18 FAWCETT STREET, SUNDERLAND

The cover advert noted that footballs could be purchased for 7s 6d (38p) and boots from 10s 6d (53p).

IN CHARGE

Chairman: John Oliver
Manager: Director Committee
Captain: Hughie Gallacher
Trainer/Coach:
James McPherson/Andy McCombie

ST JAMES' PARK

Average Attendance
Lg 30,195 Lg & Cup 30,195

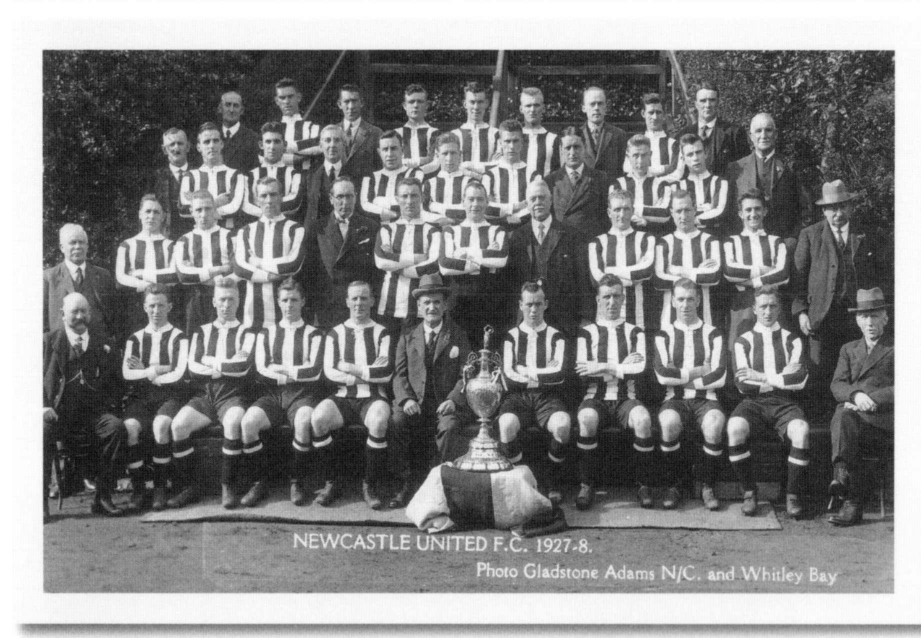

Chairman John Oliver and skipper Hughie Gallacher sit proudly next to the coveted League Championship prize.

SEASON REVIEW

Football League Div 1: P42 W15 D13 L14 F79 A81 Pts 43.
Position: 9th (Champions; Everton).
FA Cup: R3 (Winners; Blackburn Rovers).

Appearances (43m): Harris J 42, McDonald TH 41, Maitland AE 39, Urwin T 39, Gallacher HK 33, McKay R 33, Wilson W1 33, Seymour GS 30, Hudspeth FC 24, Spencer CW 24, Park O 20, Wilkinson JM 16, Curry T 14, Evans TJ 12, Gibson WM 11, Boyd JM 10, Burns MT 10, MacKenzie RR 10, Gillespie WF 7, Clark JnR 5, McCurley J 5, Low J 4, Carlton W 3, Little J 3, Barber S 1, Bradley R 1, Chalmers W 1, Halliday W 1, Lang T 1

Goals (80g): Gallacher HK 21, McDonald TH 13, Seymour GS 13, McKay R 11, Wilkinson JM 9, Boyd JM 3, McCurley J 3, Chalmers W 1, Evans TJ 1, Harris J 1, Hudspeth FC 1, Urwin T 1, own goals 2.

Dismissals: 1 player; Gallacher.

MAJOR SIGNINGS

Tom Evans (Clapton Orient) £3,650
Willie Chalmers (Rangers) £2,500
John McCurley (Third Lanark) £2,500

FROM THE RANKS

Micky Burns (Chilton CW)
Tommy Lang (Larkhall Thistle)
Jonathan Wilkinson (Crook Town)
John Little (Crook Town)
Stan Barber (Wallsend)

PLAYER FOCUS Tommy Urwin

Born Haswell. Outside-right, 5'6"
1924 to 1930: 200 app 23 goals.

Tommy Urwin was one of only a handful of players to have appeared with distinction for the North East's big-three clubs. A former England schools international, Tommy first made a name for himself with Middlesbrough as a diminutive outside-right who was full of craft and cunning. Joining the Ayresome Park set up as a teenager from Shildon just before the Great War, Tom had to wait until 1919 before he could show he was a prized find. A regular in those post-war seasons and totalling 200 games for Boro, Urwin was first capped by England against Sweden in 1923 before joining the Black'n'Whites, claiming four games for his country all told. Following a row over payments and a near switch to Manchester United, the County Durham product moved from Tees to Tyne in August 1924 for a £3,200 fee and proceeded to be part of a celebrated forward-line to lift the Football League title in 1927. Part of United's team plan for six seasons, his last port of call was Roker Park, completing the North East set when he joined Sunderland in February 1930 when 34 years old. Urwin retired at the end of the 1933-34 season when almost 40 years old with 455 senior appearances and 44 goals to his name for the North East clubs. Urwin then became Sunderland's assistant-trainer for several years afterwards. Tom once missed an England call-up when a telegram notifying him of arrangements for the international never arrived, while at the end of his fine career he appeared on 12 occasions for the FA XI on tour to Canada in 1931.

TEAM COLOURS Black & white striped shirts, black shorts (Change; white shirts with broad black diamond stripe, black shorts)

SEASON 1927-28

Match	Date		FL Division 1				Attendance	Posn	Scorers
1	27 Aug	A	Huddersfield Town	W	3 1	(1 0)	24,465		Gallacher 3
2	03 Sep	H	**Tottenham Hotspur**	W	4 1	(3 0)	41,038	3	Seymour 2, McDonald (pen), Gallacher
3	05 Sep	A	Derby County	D	1 1	(0 0)	20,829	3	Seymour
4	10 Sep	A	Manchester United	W	7 1	(2 0)	50,217	2	Seymour 2, McDonald, Gallacher, og (Moore), Urwin, Harris
5	14 Sep	H	**Derby County**	W	4 3	(1 1)	36,965	1	Gallacher, McKay 3
6	17 Sep	H	**Everton**	D	2 2	(1 1)	50,359	1	McDonald, McKay
7	24 Sep	A	Cardiff City	L	1 3	(1 3)	30,590	1	Gallacher
8	01 Oct	H	**Blackburn Rovers**	L	0 1	(0 1)	30,869	4	
9	08 Oct	A	Bolton Wanderers	W	2 1	(2 1)	30,676	2	Gallacher, McKay
10	15 Oct	H	**Sheffield Wednesday**	W	4 3	(2 3)	29,886	1	McDonald 2 (1 pen), Gallacher 2
11	22 Oct	H	**Sheffield United**	W	1 0	(0 0)	12,376	1	Gallacher
12	29 Oct	A	Aston Villa	L	0 3	(0 2)	50,797	2	
13	05 Nov	H	**Sunderland**	W	3 1	(1 1)	44,780	2	McDonald, McKay, Seymour
14	12 Nov	A	Bury	W	4 1	(3 0)	20,844	2	Seymour, McDonald (pen), Gallacher, McKay
15	19 Nov	H	**Burnley**	D	1 1	(1 1)	26,991	2	Gallacher
16	26 Nov	A	Leicester City	L	0 3	(0 1)	33,375	2	
17	03 Dec	H	**Liverpool**	D	1 1	(0 1)	26,534	2	McKay
18	10 Dec	A	Arsenal	L	1 4	(1 2)	42,630	3	Seymour
19	17 Dec	H	**Portsmouth**	L	1 3	(1 2)	19,584	4	McDonald
20	24 Dec	A	West Ham United	L	2 5	(1 3)	19,296	6	Boyd, Evans
21	26 Dec	A	Middlesbrough	D	1 1	(1 0)	37,478	5	Gallacher
22	27 Dec	H	**Middlesbrough**	D	3 3	(1 1)	40,208	6	Boyd, Gallacher, McDonald
23	31 Dec	H	**Huddersfield Town**	L	2 3	(1 1)	33,640	7	Gallacher 2
24	02 Jan	H	**Birmingham**	D	1 1	(1 1)	34,434	6	Gallacher
25	07 Jan	A	Tottenham Hotspur	L	2 5	(0 3)	34,731	8	McKay, Hudspeth (pen)
26	21 Jan	H	**Manchester United**	W	4 1	(4 1)	25,912	5	McKay, Seymour, Wilkinson 2
27	04 Feb	H	**Cardiff City**	W	2 0	(2 0)	26,439	4	McKay, Wilkinson
28	11 Feb	A	Blackburn Rovers	L	0 1	(0 0)	12,504	7	
29	18 Feb	H	**Bolton Wanderers**	D	2 2	(1 1)	28,932	6	McCurley, og (Finney)
30	25 Feb	A	Sheffield Wednesday	D	0 0	(0 0)	25,462	7	
31	10 Mar	H	**Aston Villa**	W	7 5	(4 2)	23,053	7	McCurley 2, McDonald, Seymour, Wilkinson 3
32	17 Mar	A	Sunderland	D	1 1	(1 1)	40,071	7	McDonald
33	24 Mar	H	**Bury**	L	2 3	(2 0)	28,871	7	Gallacher, McDonald
34	31 Mar	A	Burnley	L	1 5	(1 4)	12,454	12	Wilkinson
35	07 Apr	H	**Leicester City**	L	1 5	(1 3)	32,492	18	Chalmers
36	10 Apr	A	Birmingham	W	2 0	(2 0)	23,436	11	Wilkinson 2
37	14 Apr	A	Liverpool	D	0 0	(0 0)	28,669	13	
38	18 Apr	A	Everton	L	0 3	(0 1)	28,266	14	
39	21 Apr	H	**Arsenal**	D	1 1	(1 1)	22,819	12	Seymour
40	23 Apr	A	Sheffield United	D	1 1	(0 0)	16,895	10	Gallacher
41	28 Apr	A	Portsmouth	W	1 0	(0 0)	28,364	9	Seymour
42	05 May	H	**West Ham United**	W	3 1	(0 1)	17,909	9	McDonald (pen), Gallacher, Boyd
Round			**FA Cup**						
3	14 Jan	A	Blackburn Rovers	L	1 4	(0 1)	27,652		Seymour

Match	Wilson	Maitland	Hudspeth	MacKenzie	Spencer	Harris	Urwin	McKay	Gallacher	McDonald	Seymour	Little	Lang	Burns	Curry	Low	Park	Clark	Wilkinson	Boyd	Halliday	Carlton	Evans	Gibson	Gillespie	McCurley	Barber	Bradley	Chalmers
1	1	2	3	4	5	6	7	8	9	10	11																		
2	1	2	3	4	5	6	7	8	9	10	11																		
3	1	2	3	4	5	6	7	8	9	10	11																		
4	1	2	3	4	5	6	7	8	9	10	11																		
5	1	2	3	4	5	6	7	8	9	10	11																		
6	1	2	3	4	5	6	7	8	9	10	11																		
7	1		3	4	5	6	7	8	9	10		2	11																
8			3	4	5	6	7	8	9	10	11	2		1															
9	1	2	3		5	6	11	8	9	10					4	7													
10	1	2	3		5	6	11	8	9	10					4	7													
11	1	2	3	4		6	11	8	9	10						7	5												
12	1	2	3		5	6	11			10						7	4	8	9										
13	1	2	3		5	6	7	8	9	10	11				4														
14	1	2	3		5	6	7	8	9	10	11				4														
15	1	2	3		5	6		8	9	10	11				4					7									
16	1	2	3		5	6	7	8	9		11				4						10								
17	1	2	3		5	6	7	8	9	10	11											4							
18	1	2		4	5	6	7	8	9	10	11												3						
19	1	2			5	6		8	9	10	11									7		4	3						
20	1	2			5	6	11	8		10					4				9	7			3						
21	1	2	3		5	4	11	10	9	6								8		7									
22	1	2	3		5	4	11	10	9	6								8		7									
23	1	2	3		5	4	11	10	9d	6								8		7									
24	1		3			4	11	10	9	6							5	8		7			2						
25	1		3		5	4	11	8	9	10										7			2	6					
26	1	2				4	7	8		10	11						5		9					6	3				
27	1	2				4		8		10	11						5		9	7				6	3				
28	1	2				4	7	8		10	11						5		9				3	6					
29	1	2	3			4	7			10	11						5		9					6		8			
30	1	2					7			10	11						5		9			4	3	6		8			
31	1	2				4	7			10	11						5		9				3	6		8			
32	1	2				4	7	8		10	11						5		9				3	6					
33		2				4	7	8	9	10				1			5						3	6		11			
34	1	2				4	7	8		10	11	3					5		9								6		
35		3				4	7	8	9	10				1			5							6				2	11
36		2				4	7		8	10	11			1	6		5		9				3						
37		2				4	7		8	10	11			1	6		5		9				3						
38		2				4	7		8	10	11			1	6		5		9						3				
39		2				4	7		8	10	11			1	6		5		9						3				
40		2				4	7		8	10	11			1	6		5		9						3				
41		2				4	7		8	10	11			1	6		5		9						3				
42		2				4		8	9	10	11			1	6		5			7					3				
Round																													
3	1	2	3		5	4	7	8	9		11													6		10			

Match 23 Gallacher not sent off, but was involved in an altercation with the referee as they left the field. He was reported and received double the usual suspension for a dismissal

DateLine ... 10 Sept: The Champions win 7-1 at Old Trafford against Manchester United. **31 Dec:** Hughie Gallacher embroiled in a fracas with referee Bert Fogg after the match with Huddersfield which results in a lengthy suspension. **10 March:** A remarkable contest with Aston Villa ends 7-5 to the Magpies at St James' Park.

SEASON
1928-29
DIVISION 1

Championship side breaks up

There was much disappointment around Tyneside in both official circles and in supporter ranks that United's title winning line-up of 1927 did not develop into a more lasting success, building on the dexterity of Hughie Gallacher who remained the country's top goal-getter alongside Everton's Dixie Dean. Instead, the victory was a one-off with the title side breaking up. Season 1928-29 was another frustrating one and there were several changes in personnel. England centre-half Jack Hill arrived as a new skipper and defensive king-pin; while veteran Scottish international schemer Andy Cunningham landed on Tyneside as well, to be primed as the club's first ever boss.

Newcastle went through another mediocre season, with friction in the dressing-room. In Division One they finished in mid-table and recorded some perplexing results, none more so than the early season 7-2 defeat by Burnley on Tyneside. The visitors were sensationally 6-1 ahead at the interval and without doubt tension was evident in the ranks. Newcastle were in relegation trouble by the start of November, thankfully however, the players sorted themselves out, won five games in a row to climb the table as Christmas approached.

The Magpies were humbled in the FA Cup by Third Division Swindon Town who won 2-0 at the County Ground while in an inconsistent second half of the season, United took part in an eye-catching derby with Sunderland, won 4-3 at St James' Park in front of nearly 66,000. Gallacher crowned a fabulous match with a headed 87th minute winner for the Magpies. As an added irritant to United's hierarchy, United toured the Continent during the close-season and arrived back to British soil amidst much controversy following a less than hospitable few weeks in Central Europe. There was discord in the camp which needed a quick cure. The new manager-elect was to have plenty to consider with his Chairman and directors when he took charge during the following season.

Pictured above: England stopper Jack Hill was a record purchase, and new skipper of the Magpies.

Memorabilia CORNER

In Loving Memory of
NEWCASTLE UNITED
Who fell fighting for the Cup
At the County Ground, Swindon,
On Saturday, January 12th, 1929
IN THE 3rd ROUND.

They came, but for the briefest stay
To meet the "Robins" gay;
They tasted the 3rd League's fare, and fell
Upon this fatal day.

Funeral cards were commonly issued when clubs were knocked out of the FA Cup, on this occasion when United fell to Swindon.

IN CHARGE

Chairman: John Oliver/David Crawford
Manager: Director Committee
Captain: Joe Harris/Jack Hill
Trainer/Coach: Andy McCombie

ST JAMES' PARK

Average Attendance
Lg 31,667 Lg & Cup 31,667

Throughout the Twenties, United sported the much later termed 'granddad' shirt, immensely popular to Newcastle supporters when rebranded in the mid-1990s. Note also goalkeepers Wilson and Burns are wearing outfield shirts.

SEASON REVIEW

Football League Div 1: P42 W19 D6 L17 F70 A72 Pts 44.
Position: 10th (Champions; Sheffield Wednesday).
FA Cup: R3 (Winners; Bolton Wanderers).

Appearances (43m): Maitland AE 41, Harris J 40, Lang T 39, Gallacher HK 34, Burns MT 30, McDonald TH 30, Thomson RW 30, Boyd JM 28, Hill JH 26, McCurley J 26, MacKenzie RR 24, Urwin T 23, Chalmers W 19, Wilson W1 13, Park O 12, Wilkinson JM 11, Cunningham AN 10, Gibson WM 6, Hudspeth FC 6, McKay R 5, Wood EE 5, Carlton W 3, Flannigan D 3, Seymour GS 3, Gillespie WF 2, Curry T 1, Evans TJ 1, Fairhurst DL 1, Mathison G 1.

Goals (70g): Gallacher HK 24, Lang T 10, Chalmers W 8, Boyd JM 7, McCurley J 4, Hudspeth FC 3, Urwin T 3, Cunningham AN 2, MacKenzie RR 2, Wilkinson JM 2, Carlton W 1, Harris J 1, McDonald TH 1, own goals 2.

Dismissals: 0 players.

MAJOR SIGNINGS

Jack Hill (Burnley) £8,100 club record fee
Andy Cunningham (Rangers) £2,300
Dave Fairhurst (Walsall) £1,750
Dave Flannigan (Third Lanark) £2,500
Bob Thomson (Sunderland) exchange
Ed Wood (Rhyl Ath) £750

FROM THE RANKS

George Mathison (Walker Celtic, Es)

PLAYER FOCUS Tommy Lang

Born Larkhall. Outside-left, 5'7"
1926 to 1934: 230 app 58 goals.

A characteristic winger once described by United's programme editor in the enduring words of Kipling: "He's little but he's wise, he's a terror for his size." Lang cost United a mere £110 when he moved from his local side Larkhall Thistle as a 20-year-old in October 1926. The Lanarkshire youngster proved to be a good prospect, taking over from Stan Seymour on the left touchline in United's line-up and becoming a regular for the Magpies during seven seasons. Gallant and trusted, Lang was one of several celebrated 'wee uns' to wear the black-and-white shirt in pre-war years. He was steady and possessed deft footwork on the wing. Lang always wanted to cut in from the flank and have a go at goal himself, pitching in with several important goals. The Scot was especially compelling during the Black'n'Whites run to Wembley in the FA Cup during 1932. He was an ever-present and in the semi-final Tom created one goal, and scored the other, in Newcastle's 2-1 victory over Chelsea. Lang moved to Leeds Road, Huddersfield in an exchange deal during December 1934, but headed for Old Trafford when he joined Manchester United a year later. Tommy ran down his playing days with Swansea Town and Queen of the South before the Second World War, and Ipswich Town afterwards. He played on very much as an old hand and retired in 1947 when over 40. Lang then became trainer at Portman Road for a period.

TEAM COLOURS Black & white striped shirts, black shorts (Change; white shirts with broad black diamond stripe, black shorts)

SEASON 1928-29

Match	Date	Venue	FL Division 1	Result	HT	Att	Posn	Scorers	Wilson	Maitland	Gillespie	MacKenzie	Park	Harris	Urwin	McKay	Gallacher	McDonald	Seymour	Wood	Boyd	Chalmers	Evans	Hudspeth	Lang	Flannigan	Curry	Thomson	McCurley	Hill	Wilkinson	Burns	Gibson	Carlton	Mathison	Cunningham	Fairhurst	Match
1	25 Aug	H	**Cardiff City**	D 1 1	(1 0)	36,964		Gallacher	1	2	3	4	5	6	7	8	9	10	11																			1
2	29 Aug	H	**Burnley**	L 2 7	(1 6)	19,648	15	Chalmers 2	1	2	3	4		6			9	10	11	5	7	8																2
3	01 Sep	A	Sheffield United	L 1 3	(0 0)	23,094	20	Chalmers	1	2		4	5	6	11	8		10			7	9	3															3
4	08 Sep	H	**Bury**	W 2 1	(0 1)	25,994	19	Gallacher 2	1	2		4	5	6	7		9	10				8		3	11													4
5	10 Sep	A	Burnley	L 3 4	(0 0)	19,976	19	Lang, Hudspeth 2 (2 pens)	1	2		4	5	6	7		9	10				8		3	11													5
6	15 Sep	A	Aston Villa	D 1 1	(1 1)	33,811	19	Chalmers	1	2			5	4			9	10			7	8		3	11	6												6
7	22 Sep	H	**Leicester City**	W 1 0	(0 0)	30,816	17	Hudspeth	1	2			5	4		8	9	10			7			3	11	6												7
8	24 Sep	A	Blackburn Rovers	L 0 2	(0 1)	14,750	17		1	2			5	4		8	9	10			7			3	11	6												8
9	29 Sep	A	Manchester United	L 0 5	(0 3)	25,243	20		1	2			5	4		8	9	10			7			3	11		6											9
10	06 Oct	H	**Leeds United**	W 3 2	(1 2)	39,166	17	Boyd, Lang, McDonald	1	2				4			9	6		5	7	8			11			3	10									10
11	13 Oct	A	Liverpool	L 1 2	(1 0)	32,845	18	Boyd	1	2				4			9	6		5	7	8			11			3	10									11
12	20 Oct	H	**Arsenal**	L 0 3	(0 1)	30,121	21		1	2		4	5	6			9	10	11		7	8						3										12
13	27 Oct	A	Sunderland	L 2 5	(1 3)	50,519	21	Boyd, MacKenzie	1	2		4						6			7	8			11			3	10	5	9							13
14	03 Nov	H	**Huddersfield Town**	W 4 1	(2 0)	38,620	21	Boyd, Gallacher 2, Lang		2		4					9	6			7				11			3	10	5	8	1						14
15	10 Nov	A	Manchester City	W 4 2	(3 1)	19,987	18	Lang, Gallacher 3		2		4					9	6			7				11			3	10	5	8	1						15
16	17 Nov	H	**Birmingham**	W 1 0	(0 0)	29,566	14	Wilkinson		2		4		6			9				7				11			3	10	5	8	1						16
17	24 Nov	A	Portsmouth	W 1 0	(0 0)	19,227	13	Harris		2		4		6			9				7				11			3	10	5	8	1						17
18	01 Dec	H	**Bolton Wanderers**	W 4 1	(3 0)	31,420	12	Boyd, McCurley, MacKenzie, Wilkinson		2		4		3			9				7				11				10	5	8	1	6					18
19	08 Dec	A	Sheffield Wednesday	L 1 3	(0 1)	25,835	13	Gallacher (pen)		2		4		3			9				7				11				10	5	8	1	6					19
20	15 Dec	H	**Derby County**	W 4 1	(1 1)	27,549	10	Boyd, Chalmers, Gallacher, McCurley				4		2			9				7	8			11			3	10	5		1	6					20
21	22 Dec	A	Everton	L 2 5	(1 2)	23,295	11	Chalmers, Lang				4		2			9				7	8			11			3	10	5		1	6					21
22	25 Dec	A	West Ham United	L 0 1	(0 1)	23,794	14			2		4		3			9				7				11				10	5	8	1	6					22
23	26 Dec	H	**West Ham United**	W 1 0	(1 0)	43,237	13	McCurley		2		4	5	6			9				7	8			11			3	10			1						23
24	29 Dec	A	Cardiff City	L 0 2	(0 0)	12,254	14			2		4		6			9				7	8			11			3	10	5		1						24
25	01 Jan	H	**Blackburn Rovers**	L 0 2	(0 0)	36,964	14			2				6	7		9					8			11			3	10	5		1		4				25
26	05 Jan	H	**Sheffield United**	W 4 2	(3 2)	17,587	13	Boyd, Carlton, McCurley, og (Webster)		2				6	7		9				8				11			3	10	5		1		4				26
27	19 Jan	A	Bury	L 0 2	(0 1)	13,536	14			2				6	7		8			5					11			3	10		9	1			4			27
28	02 Feb	A	Leicester City	D 1 1	(1 1)	20,796	14	Gallacher		2		4		6	7		9	10							11			3		5		1				8		28
29	09 Feb	H	**Manchester United**	W 5 0	(3 0)	34,134	14	Lang, Gallacher 3 (1 pen), Urwin		2		4		6	7		9	10							11			3		5		1				8		29
30	16 Feb	A	Leeds United	D 0 0	(0 0)	16,036	10			2		4		6	7		9	10							11			3		5		1				8		30
31	23 Feb	H	**Liverpool**	D 2 2	(2 1)	27,376	12	Lang 2		2		4	5	6	7			10							11			3			9	1				8		31
32	09 Mar	H	**Sunderland**	W 4 3	(2 2)	65,838	10	Gallacher 2 (1 pen), Urwin, og (Allan)		2		4		6	7		9	10							11			3		5		1				8		32
33	13 Mar	H	**Aston Villa**	W 2 1	(1 1)	30,168	8	Gallacher 2		2				4	7		9	10							11			3		5		1	6			8		33
34	16 Mar	A	Huddersfield Town	L 1 2	(1 1)	16,411	10	Cunningham (pen)		2				4	7			10							11			3	6	5	9	1				8		34
35	23 Mar	H	**Manchester City**	W 4 0	(1 0)	27,613	10	Lang, Gallacher 2 (2 pens), Urwin		2				4	7		9	10							11			3	6	5		1				8		35
36	30 Mar	A	Birmingham	D 0 0	(0 0)	21,052	9			2		4		6	7			10			9				11			3		5		1				8		36
37	02 Apr	A	Arsenal	W 2 1	(1 0)	21,699	9	Cunningham, Lang		2				4	7			10			9				11			3	6	5		1				8		37
38	06 Apr	H	**Portsmouth**	L 0 1	(0 0)	26,092	12			2				4	7			10			9	8			11			3	6	5		1						38
39	13 Apr	A	Bolton Wanderers	L 0 1	(0 1)	10,463	12			2				4	9			10			7	8			11			3	6	5		1						39
40	20 Apr	H	**Sheffield Wednesday**	W 2 1	(2 0)	26,401	10	Gallacher 2 (1 pen)		2				4	7		9	10		5		8			11			3	6			1						40
41	27 Apr	A	Derby County	W 2 1	(1 0)	13,228	10	Chalmers 2		2				4	7			10			9	8			11				6	5		1					3	41
42	04 May	H	**Everton**	W 2 0	(0 0)	19,743	10	Gallacher 2		2				4	7		9	10				8			11			3	6	5		1						42
Round			**FA Cup**																																			**Round**
3	12 Jan	A	Swindon Town	L 0 2	(0 1)	17,689				2			5	6	7		9				8				11			3	10			1		4				3

DateLine ... 29 Aug: United find themselves 6-1 down at half-time against Burnley at Gallowgate. **6 Oct:** United field a side of 10 Scots and one Englishman in the match against Leeds United. **2 Feb:** Andy Cunningham becomes United's oldest debutant against Leicester at 39 years 2 days old. **9 March:** A crowd of 65,838 witness an end-to-end clash with Sunderland result in a 4-3 victory.

SEASON
1929-30
DIVISION 1

United's first boss takes the hot-seat

During the inter-war years several clubs started to create a post of team manager, moving away from director rule in the dressing-room, albeit it would be many decades before the suits of the boardroom relinquished full control. There were some notable managers around, notably Herbert Chapman of Huddersfield and Arsenal. Newcastle decided to join the trend by handing Andy Cunningham the hot-seat. United needed someone to have a more direct relationship with the playing squad with team spirit at a low-point, while there was a simmering row between Gallacher and United's Board. Finishing the last two seasons in ninth and 10th positions was unacceptable, and 1929-30 was to be no better. Indeed, United struggled to stay in the top division. They slid to 22nd place during February while as often occurs in a poor League campaign, they did progress in the FA Cup, to the quarter-final before being beaten by Bill McCracken's Hull City. Over 63,000 saw a 1-1 draw with the Tigers before United's ex-star full-back guided Hull to a famous 1-0 victory on Humberside.

With League points needed, Cunningham was appointed player-manager formally in January 1930. The tall Scot rarely saw eye-to-eye with Hughie Gallacher, but United's goal-getter-in-chief was the main reason the Black'n'Whites kept hold of their First Division status that year. The relegation scrap went to the end and Gallacher's 29 League goals were vital. United needed to pick up two points on the last day of the season in May against Burnley at St James' Park. A 40,000 crowd saw Joe Devine net a dramatic 63rd minute goal with a strike to save United's hide.

Newcastle had survived, but the close-season brought a bombshell – the sale of star centre-forward Hughie Gallacher against his wishes...and for that matter the will of United's support too.

Pictured above: Joe Harris was an experienced midfielder in Scotland before switching to Tyneside.

Memorabilia CORNER

For the first time, a touch of colour was included on the front cover in an enlarged programme.

IN CHARGE

Chairman: James Lunn
Manager: Director Committee/Andy Cunningham
Captain: Jack Hill
Trainer/Coach: Andy McCombie

ST JAMES' PARK

Average Attendance
Lg 32,463 Lg & Cup 35,540

Jack Hill is now the club captain in prime central position, seated. He is flanked by previous skippers Gallacher (left) and Harris (right).

PLAYER FOCUS Roddie MacKenzie

Born Inverness. Right-half, 5'7"
1922 to 1935: 256 app 7 goals.

On the St James' Park staff for almost 13 years, at right-half Roddie MacKenzie found a regular place in United's midfield for season 1924-25. Landing on Tyneside during September 1922 having played for the local Inverness clubs, Clacknacuddin and Thistle, he impressed in a trial and proceeded to become a resolute character in a black-and-white shirt. Roddie was to be a fixture in the Magpie line-up for the next ten campaigns – and all at a transfer fee of £100. MacKenzie was tenacious and big-hearted, the engine-room to Newcastle's midfield and often an inspiration to his colleagues on the field – especially when against the odds. He relished a contest against the big-names of football, occasions when he held little respect for reputations. In an era of very few dismissals, Roddie was sent-off against Manchester City, then in the same 1930-31 season was handed a further month's suspension after striking an Arsenal player. He was a regular as the Magpies lifted the title trophy in 1927 and also experienced a Wembley triumph in the 1932 FA Cup final, an ever-present in the nine matches to glory. Alas, the Scot also featured as United were relegated at the end of season 1933-34. Aged 34, the following summer of 1935 saw his career with the Magpies came to a close. Roddie remained on Tyneside joining Gateshead, appearing over two seasons for the Redheugh Park side when they were members of the Football League.

SEASON REVIEW

Football League Div 1: P42 W15 D7 L20 F71 A92 Pts 37.
Position: 19th (Champions; Sheffield Wednesday).
FA Cup: QF (Winners; Arsenal).

Appearances (48m): Gallacher HK 44, Harris J 41, Hill JH 37, McInroy A 36, McDonald TH 34, Lang T 32, Thomson RW 29, Maitland AE 28, Weaver S 21, Urwin T 20, Hutchison D 18, MacKenzie RR 18, Boyd JM 17, Fairhurst DL 17, Chalmers W 16, Devine JC 16, Richardson J 16, McCurley J 14, Mathison G 13, Richardson JR 11, Cape JP 10, Scott G 10, Burns MT 7, Nevin GW 6, Cunningham AN 5, Fidler A 5, Wood EE 4, Davidson DL 2, Wilson JW 1.

Goals (81g): Gallacher HK 34, Devine JC 8, Hutchison D 6, Lang T 5, McDonald TH 5, Weaver S 5, Chalmers W 4, Richardson JR 4, Hill JH 2, Scott G 2, Urwin T 2, Boyd JM 1, Cape JP 1, McCurley J 1, own goal 1.

Dismissals: 0 players.

MAJOR SIGNINGS

Duncan Hutchison (Dundee Utd) £4,050
Sam Weaver (Hull City) £2,500
Albert McInroy (Sunderland) £2,750
Dave Davidson (Liverpool) £4,000
Joe Devine (Burnley) £5,575
Jackie Cape (Carlisle Utd) £1,750
George Scott (South Shields) £1,250

FROM THE RANKS

Jimmy Richardson (Blyth Spartans, Es)
Joe Richardson (Blyth Spartans)
Albert Fidler (Gosforth British Legion)
George Nevin (Dipton Utd)
Joe Wilson (Stanley Utd)

TEAM COLOURS Black & white striped shirts, black shorts (Change; white shirts with broad black diamond stripe, black shorts)

SEASON 1929-30

Match	Date	H/A	Opponent	Res	F	A	HT	Att	Posn	Scorers	Burns	Maitland	Thomson	MacKenzie	Hill	Harris	Urwin	Gallacher	Hutchison	McDonald	Lang	Richardson JR	Fidler	Nevin	McCurley	Mathison	Boyd	Wood	Chalmers	McInroy	Weaver	Wilson	Scott	Fairhurst	Cunningham	Cape	Davidson	Devine	Richardson J
			FL Division 1																																				
1	31 Aug	H	**Manchester United**	W	4	1	(1 0)	43,489		Gallacher 3, McDonald	1	2	3	4	5	6	7	8	9	10	11																		
2	04 Sep	H	**Blackburn Rovers**	W	5	1	(2 1)	36,263	2	Gallacher, Lang, McDonald, Richardson JR, Urwin	1	2	3	4	5	6	7	9		10	11	8																	
3	07 Sep	A	Grimsby Town	L	0	4	(0 2)	22,390	9		1	2	3	4	5	6	7	9		10	11	8																	
4	09 Sep	A	West Ham United	L	1	5	(1 2)	15,536	10	Gallacher		2		4	5	6	7	9		10	11		1	3	8														
5	14 Sep	H	**Leicester City**	W	2	1	(0 1)	29,791	7	Gallacher 2 (1 pen)		2		4		5	7	9		10	11	8	1	3	6														
6	16 Sep	A	Blackburn Rovers	L	2	4	(1 3)	19,163	9	Gallacher, og (O'Dowd)		2				5		9		10	11	8	1	3	6	4	7												
7	21 Sep	A	Birmingham	L	1	5	(1 2)	25,707	13	Lang		2			5	4	7	9		10	11		1	3	6		8												
8	28 Sep	H	**Huddersfield Town**	W	5	2	(2 0)	29,629	12	Chalmers, Gallacher 2, McCurley, Urwin		2	3			6	7	9			11		1		10	4		5	8										
9	05 Oct	A	Sheffield United	L	0	1	(0 1)	21,150	15			2	3			6	7	9		10	11					4		5	8	1									
10	12 Oct	H	**Burnley**	W	2	1	(0 1)	33,306	14	Chalmers, Gallacher		2	3		5	6	7	9		10	11					4			8	1									
11	19 Oct	A	Sunderland	L	0	1	(0 1)	58,519	18			2	3	4	5	6	7	9			11				10				8	1									
12	26 Oct	H	**Bolton Wanderers**	L	2	3	(1 0)	28,636	19	McDonald 2		2	3		5	4	11		9	10					6		7		8	1									
13	02 Nov	A	Everton	L	2	5	(1 2)	31,543	19	Gallacher 2		2	3		5	6	7	9	8	10	11					4				1									
14	09 Nov	H	**Sheffield Wednesday**	L	1	3	(0 2)	27,505	20	McDonald		2	3		5	4	7	9	8	10	11				6					1									
15	16 Nov	A	Manchester City	L	0	3	(0 1)	34,500	21			2	3		4	6	11	9	8								7	5	10	1									
16	23 Nov	H	**Portsmouth**	W	4	1	(1 0)	17,895	20	Gallacher 4		2	3		5	6	11	9				8				4	7		10	1									
17	30 Nov	A	Arsenal	W	1	0	(0 0)	40,365	19	Weaver		2	3		5	4	11	9							10		7		8	1	6								
18	07 Dec	H	**Aston Villa**	D	2	2	(1 0)	30,758	19	Gallacher (pen), Weaver		2	3			4	11	9							10		7		8	1	6	5							
19	14 Dec	A	Leeds United	L	2	5	(1 3)	21,097	20	Gallacher 2		2	3		5	4	11	9							10		7		8	1	6								
20	21 Dec	H	**Derby County**	L	2	3	(0 0)	16,974	20	Chalmers, Hill	1	2	3		5	4		9			11	8					7		10		6								
21	25 Dec	H	**Middlesbrough**	W	3	2	(2 1)	38,922	20	Chalmers, Gallacher, Weaver	1	2	3		5	4		9	7	10									8		6		11						
22	26 Dec	A	Middlesbrough	D	2	2	(0 1)	40,538	19	Scott, Hutchison	1	2			5	6	7		9	10				3		4			8				11						
23	28 Dec	A	Manchester United	L	0	5	(0 5)	14,862	20		1				5	4		9	7	10				3					8		6		11	2					
24	04 Jan	H	**Grimsby Town**	W	3	1	(0 0)	31,803	20	Gallacher, Hutchison, Scott		2	3		5	4		9	7						10					1	6		11		8				
25	18 Jan	A	Leicester City	L	1	6	(0 3)	20,941	21	Hutchison			3	4	5			9	8	10										1	6		11	2		7			
26	01 Feb	A	Huddersfield Town	L	0	2	(0 0)	14,661	22			2	3	4		6		9	7			8								1			11				5	10	
27	08 Feb	H	**Sheffield United**	L	3	5	(2 2)	36,960	22	Devine, Gallacher, Hutchison		2	3	4				9	7		11									1	6				8		5	10	
28	22 Feb	H	**Sunderland**	W	3	0	(1 0)	49,304	21	Boyd, Hutchison, Lang			3			5			9	10	11					4	7			1	6							8	2
29	08 Mar	H	**Everton**	W	1	0	(1 0)	43,278	22	Gallacher		3				5		9		10						4	7			1	6		11					8	2
30	11 Mar	A	Burnley	W	3	0	(2 1)	12,487	21	Cape, Devine, Lang					5	4		9		10	11									1	6			3		7		8	2
31	15 Mar	A	Sheffield Wednesday	L	2	4	(0 3)	9,350	21	Devine, Weaver					5	4		9		10	11									1	6			3		7		8	2
32	22 Mar	H	**Manchester City**	D	2	2	(1 2)	29,586	20	Devine, Gallacher			3		5	4		9		10	11									1	6			2		7		8	
33	29 Mar	A	Portsmouth	L	0	2	(0 1)	21,208	20						5	6		9		10	11					4				1				3		7		8	2
34	02 Apr	H	**Birmingham**	D	1	1	(0 0)	18,113	20	Devine					5						11					4	9	6	10	1				3		7		8	2
35	05 Apr	H	**Arsenal**	D	1	1	(0 1)	36,309	20	Devine				4	5	6		9		10	11									1				3		7		8	2
36	09 Apr	A	Bolton Wanderers	D	1	1	(0 0)	6,990	20	Gallacher				4	5	6		9		10	11	8					7			1				3					2
37	12 Apr	A	Aston Villa	L	0	2	(0 0)	25,801	20					4	5	6		9			11	8					7			1				3				10	2
38	18 Apr	H	**Liverpool**	W	3	1	(2 1)	40,757	20	Gallacher, Hill, Weaver				4	5			9		10	11									1	6			3		7		8	2
39	19 Apr	H	**Leeds United**	W	2	1	(1 0)	23,066	19	Gallacher 2				4	5	6		9		10	11									1				3		7		8	2
40	21 Apr	A	Liverpool	D	0	0	(0 0)	26,793	18						5	4		9		6	11				10					1				3		7		8	2
41	26 Apr	A	Derby County	L	1	3	(1 1)	9,975	19	Devine					5	4		9		6	11				10		7			1				3				8	2
42	03 May	H	**West Ham United**	W	1	0	(0 0)	39,389	19	Devine				4	5	6		9	7	10	11									1				3				8	2
Round			**FA Cup**																																				
3	11 Jan	H	**York City**	D	1	1	(1 0)	38,674		Gallacher			3		5	4	7	9		10										1	6		11	2	8				
3r	15 Jan	A	York City	W	2	1	(1 1)	12,583		Gallacher, Hutchison			3	4	5			9	7										10	1	6		11	2	8				
4	25 Jan	H	**Clapton Orient**	W	3	1	(1 1)	48,141		Richardson JR 3		2	3	4	5			9	7	10		8								1	6		11						
5	15 Feb	H	**Brighton & Hove Albion**	W	3	0	(2 0)	56,469		Gallacher 3			3			5		9		10	11					4	7			1	6				8				2
6	01 Mar	H	**Hull City**	D	1	1	(1 0)	63,486		Lang			3			5		8	9	10	11					4	7			1	6								2
6r	05 Mar	A	Hull City	L	0	1	(0 0)	32,930				2	3	4	5			9	7	10	11	8								1	6								

DateLine ... 23 Nov: Hughie Gallacher scores all four goals in a 4-1 win over Portsmouth. **11 Jan:** Andy Cunningham's first game as boss against York City in the FA Cup, a 1-1 draw. **1 March:** Over 63,000 watch Bill McCracken's Hull City in a FA Cup clash. **19 April:** Gallacher scores his 34th goal of the season against Leeds United. **3 May:** A single goal victory over West Ham United saves United from the drop.

Record return for Wee Hughie

The new season began without the goals of Hughie Gallacher in a black-and-white shirt, sold to Chelsea in a near British record fee of £10,000. United's directors, and boss Cunningham, had decided to offload a player who had become something of a regular trouble-maker on and off the field, although at the same time sacrifice his flow of goals. Uproar followed as United's fans adored the Scot, while Hughie had no wish to end up in London. Yet the deal went through nevertheless. Remarkably, Newcastle's first home game of the season saw Chelsea and Gallacher on Tyneside. A huge crowd turned up to see the little Scot again, with the gates locked and some 10,000 to 20,000 estimated congregating outside the stadium, a reported 68,386 (a ground record) were inside St James' Park. United won 1-0 and went onto have another indifferent season, losing by five goals to both Middlesbrough (on Tyneside) and Sunderland which did not go down well. There were two bizarre games; both featuring 11 goals in each match. United won 7-4 at Old Trafford against Manchester United, then lost by the same scoreline to Portsmouth at St James' Park.

Cunningham shuffled his pack with a notable arrival being experienced Scottish international full-back Jimmy Nelson, one of the Wembley Wizards like Gallacher. Youthful vigour – and plenty of ability – was given its chance in the shape of Jimmy Richardson, Harry McMenemy and Sam Weaver. All made an impact. Newcastle though struggled to replace Gallacher, trying a number of players in the striker's role without success. One of them, Scottish newcomer Duncan Hutchison, hit a hat-trick in a 4-0 FA Cup victory over Nottingham Forest. He scored again in the Fourth Round defeat to Leeds, but never capitalised on his opportunity. The manager's team building was to take shape in time, and eventually he found a replacement for Wee Hughie with the return home of a noted Geordie-born centre-forward.

Pictured above: One of several centre-forwards who tried to fill Gallacher's shirt, Dundee United's Duncan Hutchison.

Memorabilia CORNER

United's programme in 1930-31 had a full colour cover displaying an advert for the local Evening Chronicle

IN CHARGE

Chairman: James Lunn
Manager: Andy Cunningham
Captain: Jack Hill
Trainer/Coach: James McPherson (Jnr)

ST JAMES' PARK

Average Attendance
Lg 27,118 Lg & Cup 27,440

The club's first manager, Andy Cunningham is featured on United's staff group at the start of the 1930-31 season (far right) seated in a suit.

SEASON REVIEW

Football League Div 1: P42 W15 D6 L21 F78 A87 Pts 36
Position: 17th (Champions; Arsenal).
FA Cup: R4 (Winners; West Bromwich Albion).

Appearances (44m): Starling RW 38, Weaver S 36, Fairhurst DL 34, Wilkinson J 32, McInroy A 29, Hutchison D 27, Davidson DL 26, Bedford H 25, Boyd JM 25, Nelson J 25, Naylor J 24, Lindsay DM 19, MacKenzie RR 19, Thomson RW 16, Burns MT 15, Cape JP 15, Hill JH 15, Lang T 12, Richardson J 12, Richardson JR 12, Chalmers W 6, Devine JC 6, Harris J 6, McDonald TH 3, Mathison G 2, Park O 2, Betton A 1, Keen ERL 1, Robinson JW 1.

Goals (83g): Hutchison D 14, Bedford H 13, Lindsay DM 12, Boyd JM 9, Cape JP 7, Wilkinson J 7, Starling RW 6, Lang T 4, Richardson JR 4, Devine JC 3, MacKenzie RR 1, Weaver S 1, own goals 2.

Dismissals: 2 players; MacKenzie (2)

MAJOR SIGNINGS

Jimmy Nelson (Cardiff City) £7,000
Jack Wilkinson (Sheffield Wed) £3,000
Harry Bedford (Derby County) £4,000
Jimmy Naylor (Huddersfield Town) £4,000
Duncan Lindsay (Cowdenbeath) £2,700
Ron Starling (Hull City) £3,750

FROM THE RANKS

'Ike' Keen (Nuns Moor)

PLAYER FOCUS Jimmy Boyd

**Born Glasgow. Outside-right, 5'10"
1925 to 1935: 215 app 64 goals.**

Another of the many Scots on the club's books during the inter-war years, Jimmy Boyd developed initially with Edinburgh St Bernards and as a teenager settled on Tyneside in May 1925 for a £600 fee. He was a versatile forward, filling the inside-right and outside-right berths on United's forward line. Although he made two appearances in the title winning campaign of 1926-27 as an able deputy, Jimmy didn't become a regular choice until 1928-29. By season 1931-32 Jimmy was on top form as United headed for Wembley, grabbing 23 goals during the programme from largely the wide position and forming a highly dangerous front line along side Jack Allen. Never flamboyant or one with a bag of tricks, Boyd nevertheless was a very effective forward supplying plenty of decisive crosses into the danger area. And he could find the net as well, having a first-class goals-to-games ratio. Boyd was always immaculately turned out, on and off the field, as smart as they come, while he was also a bit of a dressing-room joker. Leaving United following a decade of fine service in May 1935, Boyd served both Derby County and Bury as well as Dundee and Grimsby Town before hanging up his boots shortly after World War Two. Afterwards he coached in Sweden and was on United's scouting roster for a period. Capped by Scotland in season 1933-34, against Ireland at Parkhead, in later years he took up indoor-bowls and represented England.

TEAM COLOURS Black & white striped shirts, black shorts (Change; white shirts, black shorts)

SEASON 1930-31

Match	Date	Venue	FL Division 1	Res	Score	HT	Att	Posn	Scorers	McInroy	Nelson	Fairhurst	Naylor	Hill	Weaver	Cape	Starling	Lindsay	Chalmers	Wilkinson	Mathison	McDonald	Richardson J	Burns	Thomson	Harris	Richardson JR	Park	MacKenzie	Hutchison	Devine	Keen	Lang	Boyd	Davidson	Bedford	Robinson	Betton	Match
1	30 Aug	A	Sheffield Wednesday	L	1 2	(1 0)	23,673		Cape	1	2	3	4	5	6	7	8	9	10	11																			1
2	03 Sep	H	**Chelsea**	W	1 0	(0 0)	68,386	8	Cape	1	2	3	6	5		7	8	9		11	4	10																	2
3	06 Sep	H	**Grimsby Town**	L	1 2	(1 2)	27,155	17	Lindsay	1		3	6	5		7	8	9		11	4	10	2																3
4	10 Sep	A	Birmingham	D	1 1	(0 0)	13,893	14	Lindsay					5	6	7	10	9		11			2	1	3	4	8												4
5	13 Sep	A	Manchester United	W	7 4	(3 2)	10,907	9	Starling 2, Lindsay, Richardson JR, Cape 3			3		5	6	7	10	9		11			2	1		4	8												5
6	17 Sep	H	**Birmingham**	D	2 2	(0 1)	19,902	10	Lindsay, Richardson JR	1		3			6	7	10	9		11			2			4	8	5											6
7	20 Sep	H	**West Ham United**	W	4 2	(2 2)	18,971	6	Cape, Starling, Wilkinson, og (Cox)	1		3	4	5	6	7	10	9		11			2				8												7
8	27 Sep	A	Bolton Wanderers	W	3 0	(2 0)	17,988	6	Lindsay 2, Richardson JR	1		3	4	5		7	10	9		11			2			6	8												8
9	04 Oct	H	**Liverpool**	L	0 4	(0 2)	52,887	7		1		3	4	5		7	10	9		11			2			6	8												9
10	11 Oct	A	Middlesbrough	L	1 3	(1 2)	24,827	10	Cape	1		3	6			7				11			2				8	5	4	9	10								10
11	18 Oct	H	**Derby County**	L	2 5	(1 3)	26,028	14	Lang 2 (1 pen)	1				5		7	8						2		3	4				9	10	6	11						11
12	25 Oct	A	Sheffield United	L	1 3	(0 1)	22,149	14	Richardson JR	1		2	4	5	6	7	10			11					3		8			9									12
13	01 Nov	H	**Leeds United**	W	4 1	(2 1)	13,534	14	Devine 2, Lindsay 2	1		2	4	5	6			9							3		8			7	10		11						13
14	08 Nov	A	Blackpool	D	0 0	(0 0)	14,516	12		1		2	4	5	6			9							3		8			7	10		11						14
15	15 Nov	H	**Portsmouth**	L	4 7	(2 4)	20,604	14	Devine, Lindsay 2, Wilkinson	1			4	5	6			9		11			2		3		8			7	10								15
16	22 Nov	A	Sunderland	L	0 5	(0 2)	24,120	17		1		3	4	5	6			9	8	11			2							7	10								16
17	29 Nov	H	**Blackburn Rovers**	L	2 3	(1 1)	20,271	18	Boyd, Lindsay	1	2	3		5	6		10	9	8	11									4					7					17
18	06 Dec	A	Manchester City	L	0 2	(0 1)	21,076	18		1	2				6		10	9	8	11					3				4d					7	5				18
19	13 Dec	H	**Leicester City**	W	5 2	(3 1)	21,916	18	Bedford, Boyd, Hutchison 2, og (Black)	1	2				6		10			11					3				4	9				7	5	8			19
20	20 Dec	A	Arsenal	W	2 1	(1 0)	32,212	17	Bedford, Hutchison	1	2				6		10			11					3				4	9				7	5	8			20
21	26 Dec	A	Huddersfield Town	W	3 0	(3 0)	15,956	15	Boyd 2, Starling	1	2				6		10		9	11					3				4					7	5	8			21
22	27 Dec	H	**Sheffield Wednesday**	L	1 2	(1 1)	37,194	16	Bedford	1	2				6		10		9	11					3				4					7	5	8			22
23	01 Jan	H	**Aston Villa**	W	2 0	(0 0)	45,045	15	Starling, Wilkinson	1	2	3	4		6		10			11										9				7	5	8			23
24	03 Jan	A	Grimsby Town	D	2 2	(1 0)	10,565	15	Boyd, Hutchison	1	2	3	4		6		8			11		10								9				7	5				24
25	17 Jan	H	**Manchester United**	W	4 3	(3 1)	24,835	15	Bedford 2, Boyd, Hutchison	1		3	4		6		10			11			2							9				7		8	5		25
26	26 Jan	A	West Ham United	L	2 3	(1 1)	9,090	15	Bedford, Weaver	1	2		4		6		10			11										9				7	5	8		3	26
27	31 Jan	H	**Bolton Wanderers**	W	4 0	(3 0)	9,159	13	Starling, Hutchison, Boyd 2	1	2	3	6				10			11									4	9				7	5	8			27
28	07 Feb	A	Liverpool	L	2 4	(1 2)	28,268	15	Hutchison, Wilkinson	1	2	3	6				10			11									4	9				7	5	8			28
29	14 Feb	H	**Middlesbrough**	L	0 5	(0 2)	31,945	16		1	2	3	4		6		10			11										9				7	5	8			29
30	21 Feb	A	Derby County	W	5 1	(3 0)	17,547	15	Bedford, Hutchison, Wilkinson 3		2	3			6		10			11				1					4	9				7	5	8			30
31	28 Feb	H	**Sheffield United**	W	1 0	(1 0)	22,810	13	Hutchison		2	3			6		10			11				1					4	9				7	5	8			31
32	07 Mar	A	Leeds United	L	0 1	(0 1)	6,845	13				2			6		10			11				1	3				4	9				7	5	8			32
33	14 Mar	H	**Blackpool**	L	0 2	(0 1)	13,303	14				2			6					11				1	3		10		4	9				7	5	8			33
34	21 Mar	A	Portsmouth	W	2 1	(2 0)	14,733	11	Bedford, Lang		2	3	4		6	7	10	9						1									11		5	8			34
35	28 Mar	H	**Sunderland**	W	2 0	(0 0)	33,419	11	Bedford 2		2	3	4		6	7	10	9						1									11		5	8			35
36	03 Apr	H	**Huddersfield Town**	D	1 1	(0 0)	24,262	11	Lindsay		2	3	4		6	7	10	9						1									11		5	8			36
37	04 Apr	A	Blackburn Rovers	L	0 1	(0 0)	12,381	12				2			6		10	9						1	3				4				11	7	5	8			37
38	07 Apr	A	Aston Villa	L	3 4	(3 2)	29,975	13	Hutchison, Bedford (pen), Boyd		2	3			6		10							1					4	9			11	7	5	8			38
39	11 Apr	H	**Manchester City**	L	0 1	(0 1)	16,097	16			2				6		10							1	3				4	9			11	7	5	8			39
40	18 Apr	A	Leicester City	L	1 3	(0 3)	12,148	17	Bedford		2	3			6		10							1					4	9			11	7	5	8			40
41	25 Apr	H	**Arsenal**	L	1 3	(1 1)	21,747	18	Lang		2	3			6		10							1					4d	9			11	7	5	8			41
42	02 May	A	Chelsea	D	1 1	(0 1)	22,860	17	MacKenzie			2			6		10							1	3				4	9			11	7	5	8			42
Round			**FA Cup**																																				**Round**
3	10 Jan	H	**Nottingham Forest**	W	4 0	(2 0)	34,219		Bedford, Hutchison 3	1	2	3	4		6		10			11										9				7	5	8			3
4	24 Jan	A	Leeds United	L	1 4	(0 2)	40,261		Hutchison (pen)	1	2	3	4		6		10			11										9				7	5	8			4

Match 2 — The Chelsea fixture is the record attendance at St James' Park. Several conflicting crowd figures have been published. 68,386 is considered the record gate

Match 41 — MacKenzie not sent off during the game, but afterwards received a month's ban for striking an opponent

DateLine ... 3 Sept: A record crowd established of 68,386 for Hughie Gallacher's return with Chelsea. **13 Sept:** United score seven goals at Old Trafford and win 7-4 against Manchester United. **15 Nov:** Portsmouth win by 7-4 in a remarkable match at St James' Park. **14 Feb:** A local Tyne-Tees derby ends in a shock 5-0 win for Boro on Tyneside.

SEASON 1931-32

DIVISION 1

Another victory at Wembley

Manager Andy Cunningham's plans came to fruition in season 1931-32. He fashioned a new Black'n'White combination with experienced centre-forward Jack Allen an important addition, in the short term adequately replacing Gallacher up front. Although performances were much improved, Newcastle's early season form was nothing too spectacular, but during the winter months the Magpies knitted together, recording good League results – a 4-1 win on Wearside included – to even challenge in the chasing pack at the top of the table. However they were inconsistent, having conceded eight goals to Everton on one decidedly off-day at the end of October. Like so often in football that unpredictability saw the club have a fêted run to Wembley in the FA Cup. They were perhaps the typical Cup side, able to raise their form for a one-off big match and perfectly suited to knock-out football.

United were handed favourable draws in the opening rounds, facing Blackpool then Southport. Neither game proved easy though, the Magpies needing replays – indeed a third match against the Haig Avenue outfit. At a neutral Hillsborough the Tynesiders went nap, running up a 9-0 scoreline, a record FA Cup victory for the club. Fate continued to favour Newcastle, coming out of the hat with relegation threatened Leicester. Then Third Division Watford were their next victim. So to the semi-final...and a much tougher test in Chelsea. It was also a reunion with Hughie Gallacher. Although their former star found the net, United rallied to win 2-1 and faced the might of Arsenal, to be Thirties footballs' finest. Being the underdogs suited Newcastle, and on the Wembley stage they defied the odds to lift the trophy thanks to a brace of goals from Geordie hero-to-be Jack Allen, one of which has gone down in history as an infamous equalising strike, the ball being rifled into the Gunner's net after the ball had arguably crossed the goal line and gone out of play. It mattered little to United fans. The FA Cup returned to Tyneside.

Pictured above: Aberdonian Dave Davidson quickly established himself in the defensive pivot's role.

Memorabilia CORNER

Wembley's match programme for the 1932 FA Cup final with the Gunners.

IN CHARGE

Chairman: James Lunn
Manager: Andy Cunningham
Captain: Jimmy Nelson
Trainer/Coach: James McPherson (Jnr)

ST JAMES' PARK

Average Attendance
Lg 30,367 Lg & Cup 33,408

Newcastle's FA Cup winning squad. Back row, left to right: Cape, Thomson, Weaver, Davidson, Naylor, Starling. Middle: Cunningham (manager), Allen, Nelson, McInroy, Fairhurst, MacKenzie, McPherson Jnr (trainer). On ground: Boyd, Richardson, McMenemy, Lang.

PLAYER FOCUS Jack Allen

Born Newcastle upon Tyne. Centre-forward, 5'10"
1931 to 1934: 91 app 41 goals.

By the time Tynesider Jack Allen pulled on the black-and-white stripes of the team he supported as a lad, he was an adept striker of the finest order. Appearing for Leeds United and Brentford before settling at Hillsborough in 1927, Jack made a name for himself in a first-rate Sheffield Wednesday side that lifted the title in successive years of 1929 and 1930. Allen was at the forefront of both triumphs, netting 85 goals in only 114 games. When he moved to St James' Park in June 1931 for a £3,500 fee, the aggressive leader was a long overdue replacement for Hughie Gallacher. Although Jack took time to settle, he found the same eye-catching form as the Magpies set their sights on Wembley in 1932. Jack became the Toon's danger man on the way to FA Cup victory – scoring five times and then twice in the final against Arsenal with a man-of-the-match performance. Included was the infamous Over The Line strike. Allen was a robust centre-forward and didn't mind mixing it with the opposition, while his eye for goal made sure he was the player opponents feared most. Leaving Gallowgate in November 1934 when over 31 years old, the striker concluded playing with Bristol Rovers, Gateshead and Ashington. After his career Jack settled back in his native North East, becoming a well known publican to his death. His brother Ralph turned out for both Charlton and Brentford.

SEASON REVIEW

Football League Div 1: P42 W18 D6 L18 F80 A87 Pts 42.
Position: 11th (Champions; Everton).
FA Cup: Winners.

Appearances (51m): Lang T 51, Davidson DL 50, Nelson J 49, Weaver S 49, Fairhurst DL 48, McInroy A 47, Boyd JM 46, Richardson JR 45, MacKenzie RR 39, McMenemy H 38, Allen JWA 37, Starling RW 15, Cape JP 9, Naylor J 8, Bedford H 7, Burns MT 4, Feeney WT 4, Bell D 3, Mathison G 3, Thomson RW 3, Richardson J 2, Betton A 1, Ford JC 1, Hutchison D 1, McBain T 1.

Goals (105g): Boyd JM 23, Allen JWA 19, Lang T 15, Richardson JR 14, Weaver S 8, Cape JP 7, McMenemy H 7, Bedford H 5, Starling RW 2, Feeney WT 1, Hutchison D 1, MacKenzie RR 1, own goals 2.

Dismissals: 0 players.

MAJOR SIGNINGS

Jack Allen (Sheffield Wed) £3,500

FROM THE RANKS

Harry McMenemy (Strathclyde Jnrs)
Joe Ford (Rosewell Rosedale)
'Daniel' Bell (Wallyford Bluebell)
Wilf Feeney (Whitby Utd)

TEAM COLOURS Black & white striped shirts, black shorts (Change; white shirts, black shorts)

SEASON 1931-32

Match	Date		FL Division 1					Posn		Burns	Nelson	Fairhurst	MacKenzie	Davidson	Weaver	Boyd	Bedford	Allen	Starling	Lang	McIlroy	Naylor	Bell	Richardson JR	McMenemy	Mathison	Cape	Hutchison	Ford	Thomson	Feeney	Richardson J	Betton	McBain	Match
1	29 Aug	H	**Liverpool**	L	0 1	(0 0)	30,298			1	2	3	4	5	6	7	8	9	10	11															1
2	02 Sep	A	Birmingham	L	1 4	(0 3)	12,313	22	Boyd		2	3		5	6	7	8	9	10	11	1	4													2
3	05 Sep	A	Grimsby Town	W	2 1	(0 1)	12,248	18	Boyd, Richardson JR		2	3		5	6	7		9		11	1		4	8	10										3
4	12 Sep	H	**Chelsea**	W	4 1	(1 0)	28,562	16	Boyd, Lang, Richardson JR 2		2	3		5	6	7		9		11	1		4	8	10										4
5	19 Sep	A	West Ham United	L	1 2	(0 2)	21,558	20	Allen		2	3		5	6	7		9		11	1		4	8	10										5
6	26 Sep	H	**Sheffield Wednesday**	W	4 1	(1 1)	31,892	16	Bedford (pen), Allen, Boyd 2		2	3		5	6	7	10	9		11	1			8		4									6
7	03 Oct	A	Bolton Wanderers	L	1 2	(1 1)	13,833	17	Richardson JR		2	3		5	6	7	10	9		11	1			8		4									7
8	10 Oct	H	**Middlesbrough**	W	3 1	(1 0)	41,569	15	Boyd 2, Lang		2	3	4	5	6	7		9		11	1			8	10										8
9	17 Oct	A	Blackburn Rovers	W	3 0	(2 0)	11,947	13	Allen, Boyd, Lang		2	3	4	5	6	7		9		11	1			8	10										9
10	24 Oct	H	**Manchester City**	W	2 1	(0 0)	21,772	11	Lang, McMenemy		2	3	4	5	6	7		9		11	1			8	10										10
11	31 Oct	A	Everton	L	1 8	(0 6)	30,765	13	Richardson JR		2	3	4	5	6	7		9		11	1			8	10										11
12	07 Nov	H	**Arsenal**	W	3 2	(3 0)	28,949	12	Allen, Boyd, McMenemy		2	3	4	5	6	7		9		11	1			8	10										12
13	14 Nov	A	Derby County	D	1 1	(1 1)	12,661	12	Boyd		2	3	4	5	6	7		9		11	1			8	10										13
14	21 Nov	H	**West Bromwich Albion**	W	5 1	(3 0)	35,871	10	Allen, Boyd, Richardson JR 2, Weaver		2	3	4	5	6	7		9		11	1			8	10										14
15	28 Nov	A	Sunderland	W	4 1	(3 0)	34,195	9	Boyd, Lang, McMenemy, Richardson JR		2	3	4	5	6	7		9		11	1			8	10										15
16	05 Dec	H	**Portsmouth**	D	0 0	(0 0)	27,901	9			2	3	4	5	6	7		9		11	1			8	10										16
17	12 Dec	A	Blackpool	L	1 3	(1 1)	13,410	9	Lang		2	3	4	5	6	7		9		11	1			8	10										17
18	19 Dec	H	**Sheffield United**	W	5 3	(3 2)	25,740	8	Bedford 3, Boyd, Lang		2	3		5	6	7	9			11	1	4		8	10										18
19	25 Dec	H	**Huddersfield Town**	W	2 1	(2 0)	43,493	7	Bedford, McMenemy		2	3	4	5	6	7	9			11	1			8	10										19
20	26 Dec	A	Huddersfield Town	W	2 1	(2 0)	25,424	5	Allen, og (Young)		2	3	4	5	6	7	8	9	10	11	1														20
21	28 Dec	A	Aston Villa	L	0 3	(0 1)	42,441	6			2	3		5	6	7		9		11	1			8	10	4									21
22	01 Jan	H	**Aston Villa**	W	3 1	(1 1)	43,391	3	Lang, Richardson JR, Cape		2	3	4	5	6			9		11	1			8	10		7								22
23	02 Jan	A	Liverpool	L	2 4	(1 2)	22,717	5	Cape, Hutchison		2	3	4	5	6					11	1			8	10		7	9							23
24	16 Jan	H	**Grimsby Town**	W	2 0	(0 0)	27,837	5	Cape 2		2	3		5	6					11	1	4		8	10		7		9						24
25	30 Jan	H	**West Ham United**	D	2 2	(1 0)	31,942	4	Weaver 2		2			5	6	7			8	11	1	4		9						3	10				25
26	06 Feb	A	Sheffield Wednesday	L	0 2	(0 1)	16,290	7				3	4	5	6	7				11	1			8			9				10	2			26
27	17 Feb	H	**Bolton Wanderers**	W	3 1	(3 0)	22,618	6	Cape, Lang, Weaver		2	3	4	5	6				9	11	1			8	10		7								27
28	20 Feb	A	Middlesbrough	L	1 2	(0 1)	18,694	7	Feeney		2	3	4	5	6			9	8	11	1						7				10				28
29	02 Mar	H	**Blackburn Rovers**	W	5 3	(3 1)	16,760	6	Allen 2, Boyd, Lang, Richardson JR		2	3	4	5	6	7		9		11	1			8	10										29
30	05 Mar	A	Manchester City	L	1 5	(0 2)	28,322	7	Allen			3		5	6	7		9		11	1	4		8							10	2			30
31	19 Mar	A	Arsenal	L	0 1	(0 1)	57,516	9			2	3	4	5	6	7		9		11	1			8	10										31
32	25 Mar	H	**Leicester City**	W	3 2	(0 0)	34,697	7	Starling, Allen, Boyd		2	3	4	5	6	7		9	10	11	1			8											32
33	26 Mar	H	**Derby County**	D	3 3	(0 0)	27,805	8	Boyd, Starling, Weaver		2		4	5	6	7		9	10	11	1			8						3					33
34	29 Mar	A	Leicester City	L	2 4	(2 0)	20,578	8	Allen, Weaver (pen)		2	3	4	5	6	7		9	10	11	1			8											34
35	02 Apr	A	West Bromwich Albion	L	1 2	(0 2)	18,547	9	Allen		2	3	4	5	6	7		9	10	11	1			8											35
36	09 Apr	H	**Sunderland**	L	1 2	(0 1)	43,599	10	Lang		2	3	4	5		7		9		11	1	6		8	10										36
37	14 Apr	A	Chelsea	L	1 4	(1 4)	12,605	10	MacKenzie		2	3	4	5		7			9	11	1	6		8	10										37
38	16 Apr	A	Portsmouth	L	0 6	(0 3)	14,959	13			2	3			6	7			8	11	1	4			10								5	9	38
39	27 Apr	H	**Blackpool**	D	2 2	(0 2)	31,348	11	Boyd, McMenemy		2	3	4	5	6	7				11	1			8	10		9								39
40	30 Apr	A	Sheffield United	W	3 0	(1 0)	15,377	11	Boyd, McMenemy, og (Gibson)	1	2		4	5	6	7			8	11				9	10					3					40
41	04 May	H	**Everton**	D	0 0	(0 0)	30,898	11		1	2	3	4	5	6	7			8	11				9	10										41
42	07 May	H	**Birmingham**	L	0 3	(0 1)	10,757	11		1	2	3	4	5	6	9			8	11					10		7								42
Round			**FA Cup**																																**Round**
3	09 Jan	A	Blackpool	D	1 1	(0 0)	14,000		Lang		2	3	4	5	6	7		9		11	1			8	10										3
3r	13 Jan	H	**Blackpool**	W	1 0	(0 0)	46,104		Boyd		2	3	4	5	6	7		9		11	1			8	10										3r
4	23 Jan	H	**Southport**	D	1 1	(1 1)	50,155		Boyd		2	3	4	5	6	7		9		11	1			8	10										4
4r	26 Jan	A	Southport	De	1 1	(1 1)	20,010		Boyd		2	3	4	5	6	7		9		11	1			8	10										4r
4rr	01 Feb	N1	Southport	W	9 0	(4 0)	19,181		Lang, McMenemy, Cape 2, Weaver, Boyd, Richardson JR 3		2	3	4	5	6	7				11	1			8	10		9								4rr
5	13 Feb	H	**Leicester City**	W	3 1	(2 1)	43,354		Allen, Lang, Weaver		2	3	4	5	6	7		9		11	1			8	10										5
6	27 Feb	H	**Watford**	W	5 0	(3 0)	57,879		Allen 3, Boyd, Richardson JR		2	3	4	5	6	7		9		11	1			8	10										6
SF	12 Mar	N2	Chelsea	W	2 1	(2 1)	36,709		Allen, Lang		2	3	4	5	6	7		9		11	1			8	10										SF
F	23 Apr	N3	Arsenal	W	2 1	(1 1)	92,298		Allen 2		2	3	4	5	6	7		9		11	1			8	10										F

N1 Played at Hillsborough, Sheffield
N2 Played at Leeds Road, Huddersfield
N3 Played at Wembley Stadium, London

De Drawn after extra time

DateLine ... 31 Oct: Everton score eight times to collect the points at Goodison Park. **16 Jan:** Joe Ford suffers a double fracture of his leg on his debut against Grimsby Town. **1 Feb:** Newcastle record their highest victory in League (up to then) and FA Cup football, a 9-0 win over Southport. **23 April:** Newcastle lift the FA Cup with a 2-1 triumph over Arsenal, the *Over The Line* final. **27 April:** HRH Prince of Wales, later King Edward VIII watches the Blackpool fixture at St James' Park.

SEASON 1932-33

DIVISION 1

The Cup holders eye the title

As FA Cup winners Newcastle United were back at the forefront of the game. They looked the part for much of the programme, chasing the League title alongside Aston Villa, Arsenal and Sheffield Wednesday. Andy Cunningham's side impressed many judges with the effervescence of McMenemy, Richardson and Weaver pulling the strings. Five victories in succession at the height of winter when they climbed to fourth place proved the point. It was United's best ever festive haul. Christmas Eve and Boxing Day wins over Blackpool and Birmingham brought much cheer. Newcastle then did the double over the Brummies before picking up full points against Bolton, and in the New Year meeting with Middlesbrough.

However, after that they did not quite have what it needed to take the League prize. Influential half-back Sam Weaver was injured and a late season dip in form saw the Black'n'Whites drop out of the race after a woeful April. They lost to Sunderland (0-1), Leeds United (1-6) and Aston Villa (0-3). The derby defeat to the mid-table Wearsiders at St James' Park was a blow and United never recovered. Leeds United were a thorn to United in that season. Apart from that six-goal thrashing, the Tykes knocked the Magpies out of the FA Cup. On that afternoon, Newcastle were affected by a flu-bug and were well below their best losing 3-0 on Tyneside – all three goals coming from centre-forward Arthur Hydes.

As FA Cup holders Newcastle took part in the FA Charity Shield challenge match staged at St James' Park for the one and only time. Against Everton a fabulous contest was played out, won 5-3 by the League Champions with Dixie Dean putting on an exhibition show by scoring four goals. There was also an unofficial English versus Scottish Cup winners' challenge. United met Rangers twice during September and won 5-0 at Gallowgate, but lost 4-1 at Ibrox.

Pictured above: England international Albert McInroy moved from Roker Park to become United's 'keeper.

Memorabilia CORNER

United's 'News & Programme' promoted Gosforth Stadium's greyhound meetings.

IN CHARGE

Chairman: James Lunn
Manager: Andy Cunningham
Captain: Jimmy Nelson
Trainer/Coach: James McPherson (Jnr)

ST JAMES' PARK

Average Attendance
Lg 25,992 Lg & Cup 26,972

The FA Cup is back at St James' Park, the centre-piece to United's photo-shot at the start of the 1932-33 season.

SEASON REVIEW

Football League Div 1: P42 W22 D5 L15 F71 A63 Pts 49.
Position: 5th (Champions; Arsenal).
FA Cup: R3 (Winners; Everton).

Appearances (44m): Fairhurst DL 44, Nelson J 42, McMenemy H 41, Boyd JM 39, Lang T 39, Allen JWA 38, Richardson JR 36, Betton A 35, MacKenzie RR 33, Murray JJ 27, McInroy A 25, Weaver S 20, Burns MT 19, Davidson DL 11, Cape JP 10, Bell D 6, Dryden JR 5, Heward HA 5, Mathison G 3, Dennison RS 2, Richardson J 2, Gallantree WL 1, Leighton WA 1.

Goals (74g): Allen JWA 19, Boyd JM 14, McMenemy H 11, Richardson JR 10, Lang T 9, Cape JP 3, Weaver S 3, Bell D 1, Betton A 1, Dryden JR 1, Murray JJ 1, own goal 1.

Dismissals: 0 players.

MAJOR SIGNINGS

John Murray (Rangers) £2,500

FROM THE RANKS

Billy Leighton (Walker Park)
Billy Gallantree (Harton CW)
Bob Dennison (Radcliffe CW)
John Dryden (Ashington)
Harry Heward (Herrington Swifts)

PLAYER FOCUS Sam Weaver

Born Pilsley. Left-half, 5'9"
1929 to 1936: 230 app 43 goals.

One of the biggest names in football during the Thirties decade, Sammy Weaver was a sturdy and power-packed midfielder who was developed at Hull City after moving to Humberside from his native Derbyshire as a teenager. Under the guidance of former United star Bill McCracken at Hull, Sam quickly had many scouts watching him at Anlaby Road. Remembered in the game as the man who perfected the long-throw tactic, Weaver was also a terrific player in the middle of the park. Joining United as a 20-year-old in November 1929 for £2,500, he scored on his debut and possessed stamina, grit as well as determination and a compelling urge to go forward. Appearing for England on three occasions, Weaver could also score goals and he became an influential player in United's line-up as they lifted the FA Cup in 1932. Captain of the side on many occasions, it was only Newcastle's relegation which saw him move on, joining Chelsea for £4,166 in August 1936, but not until he had tried to haul the Magpies back to the top stage for two seasons. Weaver was a success at Stamford Bridge as well, also skippering his team before war halted his career. A guest player for several teams in the wartime leagues, afterwards Sammy remained in the game for the rest of his life, connected prominently with Mansfield Town for over 25 years as coach, manager and scout. He also was a first-class cricketer, appearing for Somerset and Derbyshire where he became masseur for a lengthy period.

TEAM COLOURS Black & white striped shirts, black shorts (Change; white shirts, black shorts)

SEASON 1932-33

Match	Date	Venue	FL Division 1	Res	F	A	HT	Att	Posn	Scorers	McInroy	Nelson	Fairhurst	MacKenzie	Davidson	Weaver	Boyd	Richardson JR	Allen	McMenemy	Lang	Murray	Betton	Mathison	Burns	Bell	Cape	Richardson J	Gallantree	Dryden	Leighton	Heward	Dennison	Match
1	27 Aug	A	Bolton Wanderers	D	2	2	(2 0)	16,245		Allen, Richardson JR	1	2	3	4	5	6	7	8	9	10	11													1
2	31 Aug	H	**Middlesbrough**	W	5	1	(1 0)	35,109	5	Lang, McMenemy 2, Allen, Weaver (pen)	1	2	3	4	5	6	7		9	10	11	8												2
3	03 Sep	H	**Liverpool**	W	4	3	(3 0)	28,261	5	Allen, Lang, McMenemy, og (Steele)	1	2	3	4	5	6	7		9	10	11	8												3
4	10 Sep	A	Leicester City	W	3	0	(1 0)	22,103	4	Boyd 2, Lang	1	2	3	4	5	6	7	8	9	10	11													4
5	17 Sep	H	**Portsmouth**	D	1	1	(1 1)	39,567	5	Allen	1	2	3	4	5	6	7		9	10	11	8												5
6	24 Sep	A	Chelsea	W	1	0	(1 0)	51,857	3	Boyd	1	2	3	4		6	7		9	10	11	8	5											6
7	01 Oct	H	**Huddersfield Town**	L	0	4	(0 1)	24,766	5		1	2	3	4	5		7		9	10	11	8		6										7
8	08 Oct	A	Sheffield United	L	1	3	(0 2)	11,472	7	Allen		2	3	4	5	6	7	8	9	10	11				1									8
9	15 Oct	H	**Wolverhampton Wanderers**	W	3	2	(2 2)	23,453	6	Boyd 2, McMenemy		2	3			6	7	8		10	11		5		1	4	9							9
10	22 Oct	H	**West Bromwich Albion**	W	3	0	(1 0)	26,026	4	Cape, McMenemy, Richardson JR		2	3			6	7	8		10	11	4	5		1		9							10
11	29 Oct	A	Sheffield Wednesday	L	0	2	(0 1)	9,496	9			2	3			6	7	8		10	11	4	5		1		9							11
12	05 Nov	H	**Everton**	L	1	2	(1 0)	30,877	9	Richardson JR		2	3				7	8	9	10	11	4	5	6	1									12
13	12 Nov	A	Arsenal	L	0	1	(0 1)	56,498	10			2	3	4			7	8	9	10	11	6	5		1									13
14	19 Nov	H	**Manchester City**	W	2	0	(1 0)	20,551	10	Cape 2			3	4				8	9	10	11	6	5		1		7	2						14
15	26 Nov	A	Sunderland	W	2	0	(1 0)	38,401	7	Allen, Lang		2	3	4				8	9	10	11	6	5		1		7							15
16	03 Dec	H	**Leeds United**	W	3	1	(0 0)	20,965	7	Allen 2, Lang		2	3	4		6		8	9	10	11		5		1		7							16
17	10 Dec	A	Blackburn Rovers	L	1	2	(1 0)	10,028	7	Lang		2	3	4		6		8	9	10	11		5		1		7							17
18	17 Dec	H	**Derby County**	D	0	0	(0 0)	22,138	6			2	3	4			7	8	9	10	11	6	5		1									18
19	24 Dec	A	Blackpool	W	4	0	(3 0)	14,053	6	Allen 2, Boyd, Lang		2	3	4			7	8	9	10	11	6	5		1									19
20	26 Dec	H	**Birmingham**	W	2	1	(1 1)	41,748	6	Boyd, Richardson JR		2	3	4		6	7	8	9	10	11		5		1									20
21	27 Dec	A	Birmingham	W	2	1	(0 1)	29,371	5	Lang, Murray			3	4			7	8	9	10	11	6	5		1			2						21
22	31 Dec	H	**Bolton Wanderers**	W	3	1	(1 1)	18,101	4	Allen, Boyd 2		2	3	4		10	7	8	9		11	6	5		1									22
23	02 Jan	A	Middlesbrough	W	3	2	(0 1)	20,218	4	Allen, Boyd, McMenemy		2	3	4			7	8	9	10	11	6	5		1									23
24	07 Jan	A	Liverpool	L	0	3	(0 1)	21,417	4			2	3				8			10	11		5	6	1	4	9		7					24
25	21 Jan	H	**Leicester City**	W	2	1	(1 0)	12,659	4	Boyd, Richardson JR	1	2	3		4		7	8	9	10		6	5							11				25
26	28 Jan	A	Portsmouth	L	0	2	(0 0)	12,465	4		1	2	3		4		7	8	9	10		6	5							11				26
27	04 Feb	H	**Chelsea**	W	2	0	(1 0)	29,460	4	Lang (pen), Allen	1	2	3	4			7		9	10	11	6	5								8			27
28	11 Feb	A	Huddersfield Town	L	0	4	(0 2)	10,837	4		1	2	3	4			7	8	9	10	11		5									6		28
29	18 Feb	H	**Sheffield United**	W	2	0	(1 0)	7,620	4	Betton, Richardson JR	1	2	3	4			7	8	9		11		5									6	10	29
30	04 Mar	A	West Bromwich Albion	L	2	3	(0 0)	21,847	4	Bell, Boyd	1	2	3				7	8	9	10	11	6	5			4								30
31	06 Mar	A	Wolverhampton Wanderers	D	1	1	(0 0)	16,314	4	McMenemy	1	2	3				7	8	9	10	11	6	5			4								31
32	11 Mar	H	**Sheffield Wednesday**	W	3	1	(0 0)	32,351	4	Allen 2, McMenemy	1	2	3	4		6	7	8	9	10	11		5											32
33	25 Mar	H	**Arsenal**	W	2	1	(2 0)	51,215	4	Boyd, Weaver (pen)	1	2	3	4		6	7	8	9	10	11		5											33
34	01 Apr	A	Manchester City	W	2	1	(0 1)	34,686	3	Allen, Richardson JR	1	2	3	4			7	8	9	10	11	6	5											34
35	05 Apr	A	Everton	D	0	0	(0 0)	14,455	3		1	2	3	4			7	8	9	10	11	6	5											35
36	08 Apr	H	**Sunderland**	L	0	1	(0 1)	35,618	3		1	2	3	4			7	8	9	10	11	6	5											36
37	15 Apr	A	Leeds United	L	1	6	(1 3)	14,967	4	Allen	1	2	3	4		6	7	8	9	10	11		5											37
38	17 Apr	H	**Aston Villa**	W	3	1	(1 1)	21,649	4	Richardson JR 2, Weaver (pen)	1	2	3	4		6	7	9		10	11	8	5											38
39	18 Apr	A	Aston Villa	L	0	3	(0 1)	23,700	4		1	2	3	4	5	6		9		10	11	8					7							39
40	22 Apr	H	**Blackburn Rovers**	W	2	1	(1 1)	12,247	4	Allen, Dryden	1	2	3	4			7	8	9	10			5							11		6		40
41	29 Apr	A	Derby County	L	2	3	(0 2)	6,465	5	Allen, Richardson JR	1	2	3	4			7	8	9				5							11		6	10	41
42	06 May	H	**Blackpool**	L	1	2	(1 0)	11,443	5	McMenemy	1	2	3	4			7	8	9	10	11		5									6		42
Round			FA Cup																															Round
3	14 Jan	H	**Leeds United**	L	0	3	(0 2)	47,554				2	3				8		9	10		6	5		1	4	7			11				3
			FA Charity Shield																															
	12 Oct	H	**Everton**	L	3	5	(1 3)	15,000		Boyd, McMenemy 2		2	3		5	6	7	8	9	10	11				1	4								CS

DateLine ... 21 Sept: United defeat Glasgow Rangers 5-0 in an English Cup v Scottish Cup winners contest. **12 Oct:** Everton claim the Charity Shield, defeating United 5-3 with Dixie Dean netting four goals. **8 April:** United are knocked out of the title race after a 1-0 defeat by Sunderland.

SEASON
1933-34
DIVISION 1

A first taste of relegation

A stark contrast was in store for United's fans as the 1933-34 season got underway. The Magpies went from FA Cup winners and title challengers to relegation certs in a disastrous campaign. No-one could quite understand why. Newcastle's squad looked good on paper. It included nine full internationals with two more on the way, as well as the unlucky Harry McMenemy who would have been capped but for injury. On the field though, just about nothing went right, especially in a ruinous second half of the programme.

That injury to play-maker McMenemy was crucial. He was one of the division's top schemers, a rising star, but during September against Blackburn Rovers he damaged a knee and was in and out of the side for almost six months as he recovered. He was solely missed. Up to New Year, after recovering from an unsteady start, United never looked in real trouble. They defeated Sunderland in the big local derby, by 2-1 at St James' Park then recorded a remarkable festive double against Merseyside clubs. They first won 7-3 at Goodison Park against Everton and on New Year's Day thumped Liverpool 9-2 at Gallowgate. In that encounter with Liverpool the half-time whistle was blown with the contest even at 2-2. Then United crushed their visitors with a seven goal assault. Jimmy Richardson and Sam Weaver completed hat-tricks in that eventful 45 minutes of football.

Newcastle were in 13th place which was comfortable enough. But then they dramatically collapsed. In the last 14 fixtures of the season from February onwards, United won just once, a late season 5-1 victory over Wolves. In a tight relegation scrap, at a crucial time United lost several players including the influential Weaver – a reported nine being in the treatment room. Newcastle had to win at Stoke on the last day, but lost 2-1, while rivals Birmingham won emphatically. The Magpies went down for the first time and after 36 distinguished years at the top level.

Pictured above: Harry McMenemy broke through and impressed many in the schemer's role.

Memorabilia CORNER

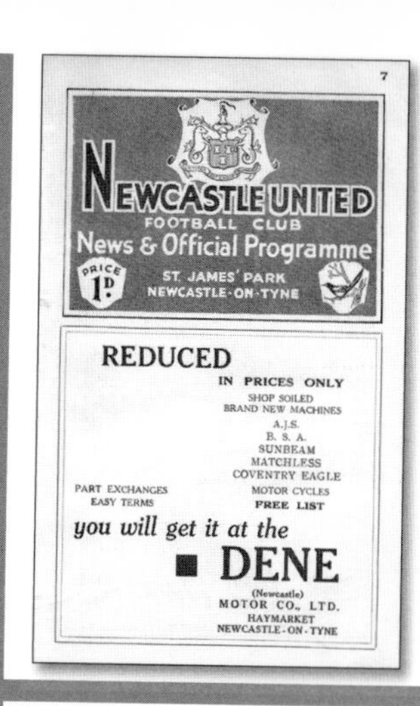

By 1930 United's programmes contained a few illustrations, rarely though any match action.

IN CHARGE

Chairman: James Lunn
Manager: Andy Cunningham
Captain: Jimmy Nelson
Trainer/Coach: James McPherson (Jnr)

ST JAMES' PARK

Average Attendance
Lg 24,142 Lg & Cup 24,142

Newcastle's squad included many seasoned campaigners, captain Jimmy Nelson is at the centre of the club's playing staff. Yet they couldn't stop United's relegation.

SEASON REVIEW

Football League Div 1: P42 W10 D14 L18 F68 A77 Pts 34.
Position: 21st, Relegated (Champions; Arsenal).
FA Cup: R3 (Winners; Manchester City).

Appearances (43m): Fairhurst DL 41, Nelson J 41, Lang T 39, Richardson JR 37, Boyd JM 34, Weaver S 33, Betton A 26, Murray JJ 25, Williams R 25, McInroy A 23, Davidson DL 17, McMenemy H 17, MacKenzie RR 16, Allen JWA 15, Bell D 15, McPhillips WP 14, Imrie WN 10, Cape JP 9, Dennison RS 9, Burns MT 6, Hughes Jn 5, Leighton WA 5, Pearson TU 4, Kelly J 2, Richardson J 2, Thomson RW 2, Dryden JR 1.

Goals (68g): Weaver S 14, Williams R 13, Richardson JR 12, Lang T 9, Imrie WN 4, Allen JWA 3, McMenemy H 3, Boyd JM 2, Cape JP 2, Dennison RS 2, Murray JJ 2, Leighton WA 1, Pearson TU 1.

Dismissals: 0 players.

MAJOR SIGNINGS

Bill Imrie (Blackburn Rvs) £6,500
Ronnie Williams (Swansea Town) £1,500

FROM THE RANKS

Bill McPhillips (Musselburgh Bruntonians)
Ernie Hall (West Wylam)
John Hughes (Tanfield Lea Inst)
Tommy Pearson (Murrayfield Amat)

PLAYER FOCUS Jimmy Nelson

Born Greenock. Right-back, 5'8"
1930 to 1935: 160 app 0 goals.

During the years between the two wars, Jimmy Nelson was a venerable defender. A Scot from the banks of the Clyde estuary, he actually started his career as a forward in Belfast with Crusaders when an apprentice boiler-maker before heading for Wales and joining Cardiff City in 1921. Part of a fine Bluebirds side in the top level – Cardiff's finest ever line-up – Jimmy just missed winning a Championship medal in 1923-24, losing the title by goal average. But Nelson twice reached the FA Cup final with the Welsh club, becoming one of the heroes of City as they lifted the trophy in 1927. Jimmy totalled 270 games for Cardiff and headed for St James' Park joining the Tynesiders in July 1930 for a sizable £7,000 fee. Nelson made the right-back berth his own for the next four seasons. As skipper, he led United back to Wembley and to another FA Cup triumph in 1932. Jimmy read the game well from the back and marshalled Newcastle's defence with an ice-cool temperament. In June 1935 he headed south to join Southend United in the lower divisions when reaching the veteran stage of his playing days. Afterwards the Scot served Newcastle again, a scout for a period after World War Two. Nelson was also a solid full-back at international level for Scotland, one of the famous Wembley Wizards in 1928, winning four caps for his country. His son Tony also appeared in the Football League while his son-in-law, Stan Montgomery, did likewise.

TEAM COLOURS Black & white striped shirts, black shorts (Change; white shirts, black shorts)

SEASON 1933-34

Match	Date		FL Division 1				HT	Att	Posn	Scorers	McInroy	Nelson	Fairhurst	MacKenzie	Betton	Weaver	Boyd	Richardson JR	Allen	McMenemy	Lang	Kelly	Dennison	Cape	Davidson	Murray	Bell	Pearson	Williams	McPhillips	Hughes	Thomson	Richardson J	Imrie	Burns	Leighton	Dryden	Match
1	26 Aug	H	**Portsmouth**	D	2	2	(0 2)	26,891		Allen, Lang	1	2	3	4	5	6	7	8	9	10	11																	1
2	02 Sep	A	Leeds United	L	0	3	(0 1)	17,721	21		1	2	3	4	5	6	7	8	9	10	11																	2
3	06 Sep	H	**Blackburn Rovers**	W	3	1	(3 1)	17,506	15	Lang 2, McMenemy	1	2	3	4	5	6	7	8	9	10	11																	3
4	09 Sep	H	**Derby County**	D	1	1	(1 1)	23,948	16	Richardson JR	1	2	3	4	5	6	7	8			11	9	10															4
5	16 Sep	A	West Bromwich Albion	D	1	1	(0 1)	24,386	16	Weaver (pen)	1	2	3	4	5	6		8	9		11		10	7														5
6	18 Sep	A	Blackburn Rovers	L	2	3	(1 2)	14,066	16	Cape, Richardson JR	1	2	3	4	5	6		8	9		11		10	7														6
7	23 Sep	H	**Birmingham**	D	0	0	(0 0)	21,667	18		1	2	3	4	5	6		8			11	9	10	7														7
8	30 Sep	A	Sheffield Wednesday	L	1	3	(0 1)	14,278	19	Lang	1	2	3	4		6	7	8	9		11				5	10												8
9	07 Oct	H	**Manchester City**	D	2	2	(1 0)	19,044	19	Cape, Weaver	1	2	3			6		8	9		11			7	5	10	4											9
10	14 Oct	A	Arsenal	L	0	3	(0 1)	32,821	20		1	2	3		5		7	8	9	10						6	4	11										10
11	21 Oct	H	**Sunderland**	W	2	1	(1 0)	43,439	20	Weaver 2	1	2	3		5	6	7	8	9		11					10	4											11
12	28 Oct	A	Chelsea	L	1	2	(0 0)	26,657	20	Murray	1	2	3		5	6	7	8	9		11					10	4											12
13	04 Nov	H	**Sheffield United**	W	3	1	(2 1)	15,107	19	Allen, Dennison, Lang	1	2	3		5	6		8	9		11		10	7		4												13
14	11 Nov	A	Tottenham Hotspur	L	0	4	(0 1)	41,379	20		1	2	3	4	5	6	7		9	10	11					8												14
15	18 Nov	H	**Leicester City**	D	1	1	(0 1)	8,098	17	McMenemy	1	2	3	4	5	6		9		10	11			7		8												15
16	25 Nov	A	Aston Villa	W	3	2	(1 1)	25,009	17	Lang, Williams, Weaver	1	2	3	4		6		8		10	11			7	5				9									16
17	02 Dec	H	**Huddersfield Town**	D	3	3	(2 1)	24,946	18	Lang, Williams 2	1	2	3	4		6		8		10	11			7	5				9									17
18	09 Dec	A	Wolverhampton Wanderers	L	1	2	(1 2)	17,569	18	Richardson JR	1	2	3	4		6		8		10	11			7	5				9									18
19	16 Dec	H	**Stoke City**	D	2	2	(0 0)	18,633	18	Richardson JR, Weaver (pen)	1	2	3	4	5	6	7	8		10	11								9									19
20	23 Dec	A	Liverpool	W	2	1	(1 1)	22,037	16	Richardson JR, Williams	1	2	3	4	5	10	7	8			11					6			9									20
21	25 Dec	H	**Everton**	L	1	2	(1 1)	34,211	17	Williams	1	2	3	4	5	10	7	8			11					6			9									21
22	26 Dec	A	Everton	W	7	3	(4 1)	39,109	15	Lang, Weaver (pen), Williams 3, Richardson JR, Boyd	1	2	3		5	10	7	8			11					6	4		9									22
23	30 Dec	A	Portsmouth	L	0	2	(0 1)	16,883	17		1	2	3		5	10	7	8			11					6	4		9									23
24	01 Jan	H	**Liverpool**	W	9	2	(2 2)	17,242	13	Boyd, Lang, Richardson JR 3, Weaver 3, Williams		2	3		5	10	7	8			11					6	4		9	1								24
25	06 Jan	H	**Leeds United**	W	2	0	(0 0)	21,587	13	Weaver, Williams		2	3		5	10	7	8			11					6	4		9	1								25
26	20 Jan	A	Derby County	D	1	1	(0 1)	18,751	13	Richardson JR		2	3			10	7	8			11				5	6	4		9	1								26
27	27 Jan	H	**West Bromwich Albion**	L	1	2	(0 2)	21,148	13	Richardson JR		2	3			10	7	8			11				5		4		9	1	6							27
28	03 Feb	A	Birmingham	W	2	1	(1 0)	16,366	12	Weaver, Williams		2	3			10	7	8			11				5	6	4		9	1								28
29	10 Feb	H	**Sheffield Wednesday**	D	0	0	(0 0)	23,023	12			2	3				7	8			11		10		5	6	4		9	1								29
30	24 Feb	H	**Arsenal**	L	0	1	(0 0)	40,065	15			2				10	7	8			11				5	6	4		9	1		3						30
31	03 Mar	A	Sunderland	L	0	2	(0 1)	31,776	16			2				6	7	8			11		10		5		4		9	1		3						31
32	10 Mar	H	**Chelsea**	D	2	2	(1 1)	14,108	16	McMenemy, Weaver (pen)		2	3			6	7	8		10	11				5	4			9	1								32
33	17 Mar	A	Sheffield United	L	0	4	(0 2)	16,272	17				3			6	7		9	10	11				5				8	1			2	4				33
34	21 Mar	A	Manchester City	D	1	1	(1 0)	11,964	17	Leighton		2	3				7			10					5	6		11	9					4	1	8		34
35	24 Mar	H	**Tottenham Hotspur**	L	1	3	(1 2)	25,246	18	Imrie (pen)		2	3				7			10	11				5	6			9					4	1	8		35
36	30 Mar	H	**Middlesbrough**	D	1	1	(1 1)	35,142	16	Weaver		2	3		5	10	7	8			11					6			9					4	1			36
37	31 Mar	A	Leicester City	L	2	3	(0 1)	17,920	18	Allen, Pearson		2	3		5		7		9	10								11			6			4	1	8		37
38	02 Apr	A	Middlesbrough	L	0	1	(0 0)	17,535	18				3		5		7	9			10										6		2	4	1	8	11	38
39	07 Apr	H	**Aston Villa**	D	1	1	(1 0)	30,344	19	Dennison		2	3		5		7	8	9		11		10								6			4	1			39
40	14 Apr	A	Huddersfield Town	L	1	4	(0 1)	10,356	21	Williams		2	3		5		7						10					11	9	1	6			4		8		40
41	21 Apr	H	**Wolverhampton Wanderers**	W	5	1	(4 1)	25,587	20	Williams, Richardson JR, Imrie 3 (1 pen)		2	3				7	8		10	11				5	6			9	1				4				41
42	28 Apr	A	Stoke City	L	1	2	(1 1)	12,255	21	Murray		2	3				7	8		10	11				5	6			9	1				4				42
Round			FA Cup																																			Round
3	13 Jan	A	Wolverhampton Wanderers	L	0	1	(0 0)	33,850				2	3		5	10	7	8			11					6	4		9	1								3

DateLine ... 15 Nov: St James' Park hosts the England versus Wales clash, a 2-1 win for the Welsh. **26 Dec:** A thrilling clash with Everton finishes 7-3 in United's favour. **1 Jan:** Liverpool are trounced by 9-2 at St James' Park, United's highest tally in League action up to then. **28 April:** United lose at Stoke by 2-1 and are relegated for the first time.

NEWCASTLE UNITED

SEASON
1934-35
DIVISION 2

Gloom in the Second Division

In the aftermath of relegation there was much criticism of all at St James' Park from many quarters. The 1932 FA Cup side broke up as Cunningham and his directors refashioned the team built around an all-international half-back line of Weaver, Bill Imrie – who had arrived late in the relegation season – and England signing and newly appointed skipper Tom Leach. There was another new face up front, as United relied on a young striker from Huddersfield Town, Jack Smith to spearhead a quick promotion challenge. He was one of the bright spots in a dismal campaign. Smith grabbed 16 goals and was soon a budding talent.

Newcastle though were in for a shock. Instead of quickly asserting themselves in the promotion race, they slumped to the bottom of the second-tier. They did not like the flavour of relegation at all and took time to come to terms with the hustle and bustle of Second Division football. United lost their first four games of the programme, conceding 17 goals in the process and were soon in trouble at the foot of the division. They slowly came to terms with the new football environment and matches against the likes of Oldham, Port Vale and Plymouth. With four victories out of the next five games played they recovered in November and December to steadily climb the ladder into sixth spot, some 13 points from Champions Brentford.

An ill-tempered FA Cup meeting with Tottenham Hotspur was the highlight of the season. At White Hart Lane a crowd of over 61,000 saw United's captain and experienced campaigner Tom Leach sent-off as Spurs won 2-0. United ended with only eight men, two ending up in the dressing-room injured.

It was not a surprise when Andy Cunningham resigned at the end of the season. His departure was inevitable one way or another. Several candidates were interviewed for the post, Stoke City boss Tom Mather being appointed in the close-season.

Pictured above: Experienced Bill Imrie was brought to Tyneside to revitalise the Magpies.

Memorabilia CORNER

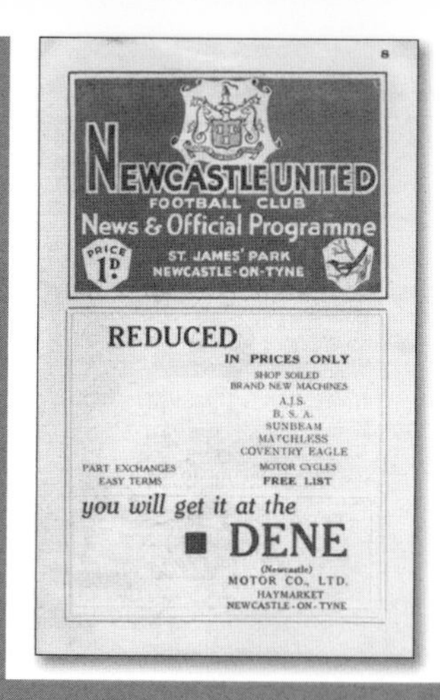

Programme adverts showed a changing lifestyle with adverts for BSA and Sunbeam motor cycles.

IN CHARGE

Chairman: James Lunn
Manager: Andy Cunningham
Captain: Jimmy Nelson/Tom Leach
Trainer/Coach: James McPherson (Jnr)

ST JAMES' PARK

Average Attendance
Lg 20,081 Lg & Cup 20,081

Boss Andy Cunningham was still in charge as Newcastle attempted to get out of the second-tier of football, pictured with his staff (far right, seated).

SEASON REVIEW

Football League Div 2: P42 W22 D4 L16 F89 A68 Pts 48.
Position: 6th (Champions; Brentford).
FA Cup: R4 (Winners; Sheffield Wednesday).

Appearances (44m): Richardson J 41, Leach TJ 38, Fairhurst DL 37, Murray JJ 36, Weaver S 35, Smith Jk 28, Pearson TU 27, Tapken NH 27, Imrie WN 24, McMenemy H 23, Bott WE 20, Lang T 17, Wilson JA 16, Leighton WA 15, Boyd JM 14, Burns MT 13, Cairns WH 12, Williams R 11, Gallantree WL 8, Richardson JR 8, Russell T 7, Davidson DL 6, Shankley R 6, Kelly J 3, Nelson J 3, Docking SH 2, Gordon J 2, McPhillips WP 2, Swinburne TA 2, Allen JWA 1.

Goals (94g): Smith Jk 16, Pearson TU 14, Bott WE 9, McMenemy H 7, Murray JJ 7, Lang T 6, Weaver S 6, Boyd JM 5, Cairns WH 4, Richardson JR 4, Wilson JA 4, Gallantree WL 2, Leach TJ 2, Imrie WN 1, Kelly J 1, Leighton WA 1, Richardson J 1, Williams R 1, own goals 3.

Dismissals: 2 players; Weaver, Leach.

MAJOR SIGNINGS

Jack Smith (Huddersfield Town) £2,500
Tom Leach (Sheffield Wed) £1,100
Wilf Bott (Huddersfield Town) £1,000+player
Archie Livingstone (Dundee)
Tom Russell (Rangers) £650

FROM THE RANKS

Jimmy Gordon (Wishaw Jnrs)
Billy Cairns (Stargate Rvs)
Tom Swinburne (Herrington CW)
Norman Tapken (Wallsend Thermal Welfare)
Joe Wilson (Tanfield Lea Inst)
Stan Docking (Birtley, Es)
Bob Shankley (Rutherglen Glencairn)

PLAYER FOCUS Jimmy Richardson

Born Ashington. Inside-right, 5'7"
1928 to 1938: 164 app 51 goals.

Locally born and bred in Ashington and a prized international schoolboy footballer, Jimmy Richardson rapidly developed through the ranks at Gallowgate after being secured from Blyth Spartans in April 1928. He became a fixture in United's side during 1931 having just turned 20 years of age and showed that he could be a big threat up front from the inside-forward positions. Jimmy grabbed 15 goals in the 1931-32 campaign and 22 over the following two seasons to become a noted support striker. Fast over 10 yards and with close control of the ball as well as the gifted eye for goal in surging runs forward at pace, Jimmy found the net on his debut and was soon rated highly. He grafted too and became one of the central figures in Newcastle's FA Cup run and triumph at Wembley in 1932. Richardson was soon in his country's side, twice capped the following season when he scored two goals wearing the Three Lions shirt. Jimmy was transferred to Huddersfield Town during October 1934 only to return to Gallowgate three years later for a second spell in a £4,500 deal. He was then 26 years old and never captured his previous sparkling form for the Magpies, although he was then in an inferior line-up. Millwall signed him in March 1938 for a £4,000 fee and after appearing in wartime football, Jimmy closed his playing career with Leyton Orient where he was appointed trainer. He also held a similar post with Millwall during the Fifties. His brother John appeared for Oldham Athletic.

TEAM COLOURS Black & white striped shirts, black shorts (Change; white shirts, black shorts)

SEASON 1934-35

Match			FL Division 2					Posn		Burns	Nelson	Fairhurst	Imrie	Leach	Weaver	Gallantree	Richardson JR	Williams	Shankley	Lang	Kelly	Pearson	McPhillips	Davidson	Richardson J	Allen	Murray	Swinburne	Boyd	Russell	Smith	McMenemy	Tapken	Leighton	Wilson	Bott	Cairns	Docking	Gordon	Match
1	25 Aug	A	Nottingham Forest	L	1 5	(0 1)	21,409		Lang	1	2	3	4	5	6	7	8	9	10	11																					1
2	27 Aug	A	Blackpool	L	1 4	(1 1)	25,303	18	Richardson JR	1	2	3	4	5	6	7	8		10		9	11																			2
3	01 Sep	H	**Brentford**	L	2 5	(1 1)	23,714	21	Gallantree, Kelly		2	3	4		6	7	8		10		9	11	1	5																3
4	08 Sep	A	Fulham	L	2 3	(0 2)	26,937	22	Richardson JR 2			3	4		10	7	8			11	9		1	5	2		6												4
5	12 Sep	H	**Blackpool**	W	4 1	(1 1)	23,404	19	Boyd, Lang, Richardson JR, Weaver			3	4		10		8	9		11				5	2		6	1	7											5
6	15 Sep	H	**Bradford Park Avenue**	L	0 1	(0 0)	26,504	21				3	4		10		8			11				5	2	9	6	1	7											6
7	22 Sep	A	Plymouth Argyle	W	3 1	(0 0)	13,404	20	Boyd, Leach, Smith	1			4	5	10		8			11						2		6		7	3	9								7
8	29 Sep	H	**Norwich City**	W	2 0	(0 0)	20,067	16	Lang, og (Ramsay)	1			4	5	10		8			11						2		6		7	3	9								8
9	06 Oct	A	Swansea Town	W	4 3	(2 2)	5,875	14	Boyd, McMenemy, Murray, Weaver	1			4	5	10					11						2		6		7	3	9	8							9
10	13 Oct	A	West Ham United	L	2 3	(1 0)	26,799	16	Lang, Weaver	1			4	5	10					11						2		6		7	3	9	8							10
11	20 Oct	H	**Manchester United**	L	0 1	(0 0)	24,782	16		1			4	5	10					11						2		6		7	3	9	8							11
12	27 Oct	A	Port Vale	W	3 1	(1 0)	11,036	15	Murray, Smith 2	1		3	4	5	6			10		11						2		8		7		9								12
13	03 Nov	H	**Barnsley**	W	4 1	(3 1)	7,959	12	Boyd, Murray, Smith 2	1		3	4	5	6			10		11						2		8		7		9								13
14	10 Nov	A	Sheffield United	L	1 5	(0 4)	18,362	17	Smith	1		3	4	5	6			10		11						2		8		7		9								14
15	17 Nov	H	**Bradford City**	W	4 2	(2 1)	13,727	12	Boyd, Leighton, Smith 2			3		5	6			10		11						2		4		7		9		1	8						15
16	24 Nov	A	Notts County	W	1 0	(0 0)	9,616	11	Smith					5	6			10		11						2		4		7	3	9		1	8						16
17	01 Dec	H	**Southampton**	W	1 0	(0 0)	16,144	10	Lang					5	6			7		11						2		4			3	9	10	1	8						17
18	08 Dec	A	Bolton Wanderers	L	0 1	(0 0)	22,170	11				3		5	6					11						2		4		7		9	10	1	8						18
19	15 Dec	H	**Oldham Athletic**	W	4 2	(1 0)	13,112	11	Lang, McMenemy, Smith 2			3		5	6d					11						2		4		7		9	10	1	8						19
20	22 Dec	A	Burnley	W	3 0	(1 0)	14,792	7	McMenemy, Pearson, Smith			3		5	6	7						11			2		4				9	10	1	8						20
21	25 Dec	H	**Hull City**	W	6 2	(2 0)	26,943	7	Gallantree, Pearson 2, Smith 2, Wilson			3		5	6	7						11			2		4				9	10	1		8					21
22	26 Dec	A	Hull City	D	1 1	(1 0)	21,788	7	Pearson			3		5	6	7						11			2		4				9	10	1		8					22
23	29 Dec	H	**Nottingham Forest**	W	2 0	(1 0)	23,029	7	Murray, Pearson			3		5	6	7						11			2		4				9	10	1		8					23
24	01 Jan	H	**Bury**	W	5 1	(2 1)	26,644	6	Bott 3, Pearson, Smith			3		5	6							11			2		4				9		1		8	7	10			24
25	05 Jan	A	Brentford	L	0 3	(0 1)	26,079	7				3		5	6							11			2		4				9	10	1		8	7				25
26	19 Jan	H	**Fulham**	D	1 1	(0 0)	24,542	7	og (Hindson)			3	4	5								11			2		6				9		1		8	7		10		26
27	30 Jan	A	Bradford Park Avenue	W	3 1	(1 1)	4,487	6	Bott, Williams, Wilson			3	4	5				10				11			2		6						1		8	7	9			27
28	02 Feb	H	**Plymouth Argyle**	W	3 0	(1 0)	23,317	5	McMenemy, Pearson, Smith			3	6	5								11			2						9	10	1	4	8	7				28
29	09 Feb	A	Norwich City	L	0 2	(0 0)	16,128	6				3	6	5								11			2						9	10	1	4	8	7				29
30	16 Feb	H	**Swansea Town**	W	5 1	(0 1)	9,203	6	Cairns 3, Imrie, Murray			3	6	5								11			2		4					10	1	8		7	9			30
31	23 Feb	H	**West Ham United**	W	3 0	(1 0)	27,439	4	Murray, Pearson 2			3	6									11		5	2		4				9		1	8		7	10			31
32	02 Mar	A	Manchester United	W	1 0	(1 0)	20,728	3	Pearson			3	6									11		5	2		4				9		1		8	7	10			32
33	09 Mar	H	**Port Vale**	L	1 2	(1 1)	23,934	5	Pearson			3	6	5								11			2		4				9		1		8	7	10			33
34	16 Mar	A	Barnsley	L	1 2	(0 1)	14,511	6	Wilson			3		5	6							11			2		4					10	1		8	7	9			34
35	23 Mar	H	**Sheffield United**	W	4 1	(1 0)	18,851	6	Weaver 2 (1 pen), McMenemy, Bott			3		5	10							11			2		6					8	1	4		7	9			35
36	30 Mar	A	Bradford City	D	3 3	(1 1)	8,323	6	McMenemy, Bott, Richardson J			3		5	10							11			2		6					8	1	4		7	9			36
37	06 Apr	H	**Notts County**	D	1 1	(1 0)	12,394	6	Pearson			3		5	10							11			2		6				9	8	1	4		7				37
38	13 Apr	A	Southampton	L	0 2	(0 1)	9,159	6				3		5				9	8			11			2		6					10	1	4		7				38
39	19 Apr	A	Bury	W	2 0	(2 0)	12,634	6	Bott, Murray			3		5	6							11			2		8					10	1	4		7		9		39
40	20 Apr	H	**Bolton Wanderers**	L	1 3	(1 1)	28,277	6	Leach			3	4	5	6			9	8			11			2							10	1			7				40
41	27 Apr	A	Oldham Athletic	L	2 3	(2 1)	3,851	7	Wilson, Weaver (pen)	1		3		5	6							11			2							10			8	7	9		4	41
42	04 May	H	**Burnley**	W	2 0	(2 0)	7,718	6	McMenemy, Pearson	1		3		5	6				7			11			2						9	10			8				4	42
Round			FA Cup																																					Round
3	12 Jan	A	Hull City	W	5 1	(2 0)	23,000		Bott 2, Cairns, Pearson, og (Quantick)	1		3	4	5	10							11			2		6								8	7	9			3
4	26 Jan	A	Tottenham Hotspur	L	0 2	(0 0)	61,195				3		5d	6							11			2		4				9		1		8	7	10			4

DateLine ... 25 Aug: Newcastle get underway in Division Two with a disastrous 5-1 defeat at Nottingham Forest. **1 Jan:** Wilf Bott registers a hat-trick on his debut against Bury. **5 Jan:** Brentford complete the double over the Magpies with a 3-0 victory. **26 Jan:** United fall by two goals to Spurs in the FA Cup and end with eight men, two injured and one sent-off.

NEWCASTLE UNITED

SEASON 1935-36

DIVISION 2

League mediocrity, epic Cup double

Under the stewardship of new chief Tom Mather, it was much the same story for Newcastle United – lots of changes, promotion also-rans and a big-match FA Cup exit. Newcastle did compete adequately in the first portion of the season, reaching a place just below the division's pace-setters, but a poor return in January and February when they couldn't register a win for eight games cost the Magpies dearly in pursuit of promotion back to the top level. United finished a full ten points off the pack.

Newcastle reached the FA Cup Fifth Round and met team of the era, Arsenal – at the height of their mastery – in an epic encounter. It was an absorbing tie to get their downhearted fans shouting again. A record FA Cup gate at the time of 65,484 crowded into the Barrack Road stadium, all to see the big names from the Gunners, James, Bastin and company. There was a reported 20,000 locked out around St James' Park and the lucky ones inside the ground witnessed a terrific match; Arsenal leading three times and United battling back to equalise on each occasion. Another 60,000-plus attendance was at Highbury for the replay against the reigning Champions but this time Newcastle could not match the best in the country. They lost 3-0; the Gunners going onto win the trophy. In that tie one player stood out, United's up and coming centre-forward Jack Smith. He netted twice and scored 26 goals in the season – becoming hot property and destined for a bigger stage than United could offer at the time.

While United could attract gates of that magnitude, apathy also set in among supporters. There was a stark contrast in support. A crowd of only 3,964 watched the Second Division match against Norwich City during February, the lowest at Gallowgate since 1900. As Newcastle's fortunes declined, even less would very soon turn up at St James' Park.

Pictured above: Capped by England at centre-half, Tom Leach attempted to steady the Newcastle camp.

Memorabilia CORNER

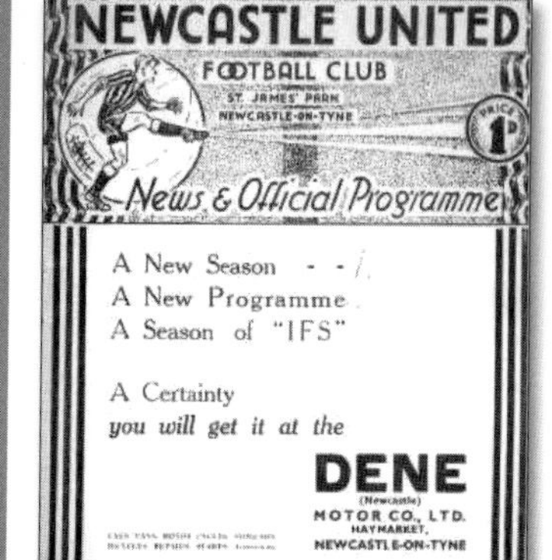

In 1935-36 United introduced a dashing caricatured footballer – to feature for several years.

IN CHARGE

Chairman: James Lunn
Manager: Tom Mather
Captain: Tom Leach
Trainer/Coach: James McPherson (Jnr)

ST JAMES' PARK

Average Attendance
Lg 19,483 Lg & Cup 21,839

A new manager in Tom Mather replaced Cunningham at Gallowgate. He is pictured (far right, seated) at the start of the 1935-36 season.

PLAYER FOCUS Dave Fairhurst

Born Blyth. Left-back, 5'8"
1929 to 1946: 285 app 2 goals.

A Blyth lad from a family of ten children, and with a characteristic Northumbrian pit background, Dave Fairhurst was another who made an impression with Blyth Spartans. Emerging as a tough and steadfast left-back as the Thirties decade opened, he had been through trial matches with United as a kid and arrived at Gallowgate for a second time in March 1929 after a spell in the lower divisions with Walsall. He learned the defender's trade in a two-year stay in the Midlands totalling 59 appearances and rapidly made the left-back position his own at St James' Park as he replaced Scottish international Bob Thomson. Fairhurst's progress in a black-and-white shirt was such that he was soon to be in contention for England recognition, eventually capped in 1933-34 against France, a 4-1 victory at White Hart Lane. Curley haired and rarely to be flustered on the field, he was of the steady and reliable type rather than the flamboyant and risky. Dave was a FA Cup winner with the Black'n'Whites in 1932, an ever-present in the run to face Arsenal. Following more than a decade in Newcastle's defence in which he rarely missed a fixture, Fairhurst called it a day on the resumption of normal football after the Second World War. In the Forties he was appointed as Birmingham City trainer. From footballing stock, his father played for Spartans too while three brothers also took up the game.

SEASON REVIEW

Football League Div 2: P42 W20 D6 L16 F88 A79 Pts 46.
Position: 8th (Champions; Manchester United).
FA Cup: R5 (Winners; Arsenal).

Appearances (47m): Pearson TU 45, Tapken NH 41, Richardson J 37, Ware H 37, Smith Jk 36, Weaver S 36, Gordon J 32, Fairhurst DL 28, Davidson DL 27, Imrie WN 25, Bott WE 24, Connelly EJ 22, Garnham A 21, McMenemy H 20, Leach TJ 15, Wilson JA 14, Harris A 12, Cairns WH 10, Murray JJ 8, Bulloch HC 5, Johnson H 5, Livingstone A 5, Burns MT 4, Hall E 2, Leighton WA 2, McPhillips WP 2, Forster WB 1, Smith D 1.

Goals (97g): Smith Jk 26, Pearson TU 14, Cairns WH 9, Connelly EJ 9, Ware H 9, Bott WE 6, Weaver S 6, Imrie WN 5, McMenemy H 5, Harris A 4, Fairhurst DL 2, Livingstone A 1, Wilson JA 1.

Dismissals: 0 players.

MAJOR SIGNINGS

Harry Ware (Stoke City) £2,400
Hugh Bulloch (Portadown) £1,325

FROM THE RANKS

Alf Garnham (Birtley)
Ed Connelly (Rosslyn Jnrs)
William Forster (Howdon British Legion)
Albert Harris (Blackhall CW)
Henry Johnson (Walker Park)
Dave Smith (Reyrolles)

TEAM COLOURS Black & white striped shirts, black shorts (Change; white shirts, black shorts)

SEASON 1935-36

Match	Date		FL Division 2					Posn		Tapken	Richardson	Fairhurst	Imrie	Leach	Murray	Bott	Leighton	Cairns	McMenemy	Pearson	Wilson	Burns	Weaver	Davidson	Harris	Ware	Smith J	Gordon	Livingstone	Bulloch	Garnham	Connelly	Forster	Smith D	McPhillips	Johnson	Hall	Match
1	31 Aug	H	**Bradford Park Avenue**	D	3 3	(0 0)	27,843		Cairns, McMenemy, Pearson	1	2	3	4	5	6	7	8	9	10	11																		1
2	04 Sep	H	**Barnsley**	W	3 0	(1 0)	21,150	5	Cairns 2, Pearson	1	2	3	4	5	6	7		9	10	11	8																	2
3	07 Sep	A	Tottenham Hotspur	W	2 1	(2 0)	47,442	1	Cairns 2		2	3	4	5	6	7		9	10	11	8	1																3
4	09 Sep	A	Barnsley	L	2 3	(1 2)	12,796	3	Cairns, McMenemy		2	3	4	5	6	7		9	10	11	8	1																4
5	14 Sep	H	**Manchester United**	L	0 2	(0 1)	28,520	10			2	3	4	5		7		9	10	11	8	1	6															5
6	21 Sep	A	Port Vale	L	0 3	(0 1)	9,356	18			2	3	4	5	8	7		9	10	11		1	6															6
7	28 Sep	H	**Fulham**	W	6 2	(3 1)	24,736	14	Cairns, Harris, Pearson 3, Ware	1	2	3	4					9	10	11			6	5	7	8												7
8	05 Oct	A	Burnley	W	2 1	(1 0)	10,765	9	Cairns, McMenemy	1	2	3	4	5				9	10	11			6		7	8												8
9	12 Oct	H	**Charlton Athletic**	L	1 2	(1 2)	26,797	14	Harris	1	2	3	4	5				9	10	11			6		7	8												9
10	19 Oct	H	**Leicester City**	W	3 1	(0 1)	14,017	11	Cairns, Harris, Ware	1	2	3	4					9	10	11			6	5	7	8												10
11	26 Oct	A	Swansea Town	W	2 1	(1 0)	12,776	9	McMenemy, Smith J	1	2	3	4			7			10	11			6	5		8	9											11
12	02 Nov	H	**West Ham United**	D	3 3	(0 1)	22,873	8	Bott, Smith J, Ware	1	2	3	4			7			10	11			6	5		8	9											12
13	09 Nov	A	Bury	W	4 3	(2 1)	12,098	7	Bott, Smith J 3	1	2	3	4			7			10	11			6	5		8	9											13
14	16 Nov	H	**Doncaster Rovers**	W	2 1	(2 0)	26,845	5	Pearson, Smith J	1	2	3				7			10	11			6	5		8	9	4										14
15	23 Nov	A	Sheffield United	L	1 5	(0 1)	14,789	7	Livingstone	1	2	3				7				11			6	5		8	9	4	10									15
16	30 Nov	H	**Nottingham Forest**	W	5 1	(2 1)	23,885	6	Fairhurst 2, Harris, Smith J 2	1	2	3							10	11			6		7	8	9	4		5								16
17	07 Dec	A	Norwich City	L	0 1	(0 0)	11,995	7		1	2								10	11			6	5	7	8	9	4			3							17
18	14 Dec	H	**Southampton**	W	4 1	(1 1)	18,498	6	Imrie, Pearson, Smith J 2	1	2		6						10	11				5	7	8	9	4			3							18
19	26 Dec	H	**Bradford City**	W	3 2	(1 0)	14,662	8	McMenemy, Smith J, Weaver	1	2		7	3					10	11			6	5		8	9	4										19
20	28 Dec	A	Bradford Park Avenue	L	2 3	(2 0)	12,609	11	Pearson 2	1	2				6				10	11				5	7	8	9	4			3							20
21	01 Jan	H	**Plymouth Argyle**	W	5 0	(3 0)	19,630	8	Weaver 2 (1 pen), Smith J 2, Ware	1	2				6	11							10			7	9	4	8	5	3							21
22	04 Jan	H	**Tottenham Hotspur**	L	1 4	(0 2)	35,389	9	Bott	1				2	6	11							10			7	9	4	8	5	3							22
23	18 Jan	A	Manchester United	L	1 3	(0 1)	22,968	11	Ware	1	2					7				11			6	5		8	9	4			3	10						23
24	01 Feb	A	Fulham	L	1 3	(0 3)	24,882	11	Ware	1		2								11			6	5	7	8	9	4			3	10						24
25	05 Feb	H	**Port Vale**	D	2 2	(1 1)	9,238	11	Smith J, Ware	1	2					7	4			11			6			8	9		10	5	3							25
26	08 Feb	H	**Burnley**	D	1 1	(0 1)	17,487	11	Imrie	1		3	6							11				5			9	4	8			10	2	7				26
	22 Feb	A	Leicester City	Ab	1 2	(0 1)	13,449		*Weaver (pen)*	1	2	3				7				11			6	5		8	9	4				10						
27	26 Feb	A	Charlton Athletic	L	2 4	(1 3)	13,544	12	Smith J, Imrie (pen)		2	3	6			7				11				5		8	9	4				10			1			27
28	29 Feb	H	**Norwich City**	D	1 1	(1 1)	3,964	12	Imrie		2		4			7				11	8		6	5			9				3	10			1			28
29	07 Mar	A	Doncaster Rovers	D	2 2	(1 1)	14,245	12	Pearson, Smith J	1	2		4	5						11	8		6				9	7			3	10						29
30	14 Mar	H	**Bury**	W	3 0	(1 0)	14,287	11	Connelly 2, Smith J	1	2			5						11	8		6		7		9	4			3	10						30
31	19 Mar	A	Leicester City	L	0 1	(0 0)	10,000	11		1	2			5		7				11			6			8	9	4			3	10						31
32	21 Mar	A	West Ham United	L	1 4	(1 1)	37,298	13	Wilson	1	2			5						11	7		6			8	9	4			3	10						32
33	28 Mar	H	**Sheffield United**	W	3 0	(2 0)	22,613	10	Connelly, Smith J, Weaver	1	2									11	7		6	5		8	9	4			3	10						33
34	01 Apr	A	Bradford City	L	2 3	(1 1)	3,916	10	Connelly 2	1	2	3								11	7		6	5		8	9	4				10						34
35	04 Apr	A	Nottingham Forest	W	2 1	(2 0)	6,107	9	Bott, Ware	1	2	3				7				11	8		6	5		9		4				10						35
36	10 Apr	H	**Hull City**	W	4 1	(3 1)	16,928	9	Pearson, Connelly 2, Weaver (pen)	1		2								11	7		6	5		8	9	4			3	10						36
37	11 Apr	H	**Swansea Town**	W	2 0	(0 0)	12,010	8	Connelly, Smith J	1		2	6							11	7			5		8	9	4			3	10						37
38	13 Apr	A	Hull City	W	3 2	(1 1)	5,638	8	Pearson, Smith J, Imrie (pen)	1		2	4							11			6	5		8	9	7				10				3		38
39	18 Apr	A	Southampton	W	3 1	(2 0)	8,547	7	Smith J 2, Ware	1		2	6							11	8					7	9	4		5		10				3		39
40	22 Apr	A	Blackpool	L	0 6	(0 3)	7,935	8		1		2	6	5					8	11			10			7	9	4								3		40
41	25 Apr	H	**Blackpool**	W	1 0	(0 0)	7,765	8	Weaver	1		2	6							11			10		7	8	9	4								3	5	41
42	02 May	A	Plymouth Argyle	L	0 1	(0 0)	12,933	8		1		2	6							11					7	8	9	4				10				3	5	42
Round			FA Cup													7																						Round
3	11 Jan	A	Walsall	W	2 0	(2 0)	19,882		Connelly, Smith J	1	2					7				11			6	5		8	9	4			3	10						3
4	27 Jan	A	Sheffield Wednesday	D	1 1	(1 1)	25,355		Pearson	1	2					7				11			6	5		8	9	4			3	10						4
4r	29 Jan	H	**Sheffield Wednesday**	W	3 1	(1 0)	27,680		Bott 2, Smith J	1	2					7				11			6	5		8	9	4			3	10						4r
5	15 Feb	H	**Arsenal**	D	3 3	(1 2)	65,484		Pearson, Smith J 2	1	2					7				11			6	5		8	9	4			3	10						5
5r	19 Feb	A	Arsenal	L	0 3	(0 1)	62,391			1	2									11			6	5		8	9	4			3	10						5r

Ab Abandoned after 80 mins due to waterlogged pitch

DateLine ... 31 Aug: New boss Tom Mather's first game in charge against Bradford Park Avenue, a 3-3 draw. **15 Feb:** An absorbing FA Cup tie with Arsenal ends 3-3 at St James' Park in front of 65,484. **29 Feb:** The 3,964 gate for the visit of Norwich is at the time the lowest home attendance since 1900.

SEASON
1936-37
DIVISION 2

Promotion push ends short

Tom Mather's influence was slowly making a difference, but to many inpatient United supporters, improvement was not quick enough. Indeed, due to the club's inability to get back into the First Division they lost England midfielder Sam Weaver to Chelsea, and were to soon see their new star asset, centre-forward Jack Smith move on as well after netting 66 goals in the last three seasons. Season 1936-37 ended again short of the mark, but only just, in fourth spot, six points away from a promotion place. The Black'n'Whites were strong contenders up to Easter, the usual make-or-break time in football.

There were several fine displays in the early months of the programme including a 7-0 pounding of Doncaster Rovers when Jack Smith netted four goals. Fulham were beaten 4-3 at Craven Cottage in a compelling spectacle while Swansea and Norwich both conceded five goals to the Magpies. The victory on the long trip to face the Canaries at the end of December put United in a decent position to make a concerted push towards the top of the table. However United's form after the festive period was a disappointment, points being thrown away which would have made the difference. They lost five games in a row and by March supporters had turned their back, even though a good recovery was being made which saw the Magpies win eight of the last ten fixtures. Only 3,867 arrived at St James' Park for the Division Two clash with Nottingham Forest, the lowest since the turn of the century.

Another attractive FA Cup match took place, United being tied with Preston North End who were to reach the final, only to be beaten by North East rivals Sunderland that year. But United had to travel to Deepdale and the First Division side took care of the Black'n'Whites, comfortably by 2-0.

Pictured above: Tom Mooney was quick and a danger when he cut in from the left flank.

Memorabilia CORNER

NEWCASTLE UNITED
FOOTBALL CLUB
ST. JAMES' PARK, NEWCASTLE-ON-TYNE
PRICE 1D
News & Official Programme

WHAT A DRAW!
YOU CANNOT AFFORD TO MAKE YOUR PURCHASE WITHOUT INSPECTING THE SHOWROOMS OF THE
DENE
(Newcastle)
MOTOR CO., LTD.
HAYMARKET,
NEWCASTLE-ON-TYNE
WE CAN SUPPLY ANY MAKE OF MACHINE

Match programme from the game with Doncaster Rovers, a 7-0 victory.

IN CHARGE

Chairman: James Lunn
Manager: Tom Mather
Captain: Harry McMenemy
Trainer/Coach: James McPherson (Jnr)

ST JAMES' PARK

Average Attendance
Lg 24,427 Lg & Cup 24,427

The Magpies before a Second Division fixture in 1936-37. Back row, left to right: Smith, Carver, Garnham, Tapken, Docking, Ancell, Imrie. Front: McPherson Jnr (trainer), Rogers, Gordon, Livingstone, Richardson (Joe), Pearson, Mather (manager).

SEASON REVIEW

Football League Div 2: P42 W22 D5 L15 F80 A56 Pts 49.
Position: 4th (Champions; Leicester City).
FA Cup: R3 (Winners; Sunderland).

Appearances (43m): Gordon J 41, Richardson J 41, Rogers E 39, Pearson TU 38, Carver J 37, Tapken NH 35, Imrie WN 31, Smith Jk 29, Ancell RFD 26, Mooney T 21, Cairns WH 19, Leighton WA 16, Garnham A 15, Livingstone A 15, Fairhurst DL 14, Ware H 12, McMenemy H 10, Park JB 9, McPhillips WP 8, Docking SH 7, Davidson DL 6, Forster WB 2, Connelly EJ 1, Grundy AJ 1.

Goals (80g): Smith Jk 24, Cairns WH 16, Rogers E 10, Pearson TU 7, Leighton WA 6, Imrie WN 5, McMenemy H 4, Docking SH 2, Mooney T 2, Park JB 2, Garnham A 1, Livingstone A 1.

Dismissals: 0 players.

MAJOR SIGNINGS

Jesse Carver (Blackburn Rvs) £2,000
Bobby Ancell (St Mirren) £2,750
Tom Mooney (Airdrie) £2,650
John Park (Hamilton) £1,800
'Tim' Rogers (Arsenal) £2,500

FROM THE RANKS

Arnold Grundy (Dunston CWS)

PLAYER FOCUS Jack Smith

Born Batley. Centre-forward, 5'11"
1934 to 1938: 112 app 73 goals.

With the club struggling to replace the goal-power of Hughie Gallacher, United turned to a young ex-England schoolboy star of Huddersfield Town in Jack Smith. Out of favour at Leeds Road, the 19-year-old Yorkshireman moved north to Tyneside in September 1934 for a modest £2,500 and immediately was a hit up front for the Magpies. He found the net on his debut against Plymouth Argyle and was hungry for action. Jack scored 14 in his next 20 matches for the Geordies showing an energetic style up front. A total of 16 goals in his first season was a terrific start, and then he claimed 26 and 24 in the next two campaigns. Scoring four goals in a contest with Doncaster, he could strike the ball true and hard with both feet while he was quick off the mark, acceleration and pace which worried defenders. With United unable to make a sustained bid to get out of the second-tier, it was no surprise when their star centre-forward moved to a club with better prospects of top level football, a transfer which did not please United's support. In February 1938 for a £6,500 fee he joined rivals Manchester United who went onto win promotion. Jack wasn't quite the same forceful striker at Old Trafford, only scoring 15 goals all told for the Reds. After the war he played for Blackburn Rovers and Port Vale until leaving the senior level in 1948.

TEAM COLOURS Black & white striped shirts, black shorts (Change; white shirts, black shorts)

SEASON 1936-37

Match	Date	H/A	FL Division 2	Res	Score	HT	Att	Posn	Scorers	Tapken	Richardson	Ancell	Gordon	Carver	Garnham	Rogers	Ware	Smith	McMenemy	Pearson	Imrie	Cairns	McPhillips	Park	Davidson	Livingstone	Mooney	Connelly	Fairhurst	Leighton	Docking	Forster	Grundy	Match
1	29 Aug	H	**Barnsley**	L	0 1	(0 1)	30,097			1	2	3	4	5	6	7	8	9	10	11														1
2	31 Aug	A	West Ham United	W	2 0	(1 0)	21,854	7	McMenemy, Pearson	1	2	3	4	5		7	8		10	11	6	9												2
3	05 Sep	A	Sheffield United	L	1 2	(0 2)	20,236	15	McMenemy	1	2	3	4	5		7	8		10	11	6	9												3
4	09 Sep	H	**West Ham United**	W	5 3	(3 1)	23,560	10	Cairns 4, McMenemy	1	2	3	4	5		7	8		10	11	6	9												4
5	12 Sep	H	**Tottenham Hotspur**	L	0 1	(0 0)	28,314	13			2	3	4	5		7	8		10	11	6	9	1											5
6	14 Sep	A	Bradford Park Avenue	W	3 0	(1 0)	7,921	6	Cairns 2, Imrie		2	3	4	5		11	8		10		6	9	1	7										6
7	19 Sep	A	Blackpool	L	0 3	(0 3)	26,962	15			2	3	4				8		10	11	6	9	1	7	5									7
8	26 Sep	H	**Blackburn Rovers**	W	2 0	(0 0)	21,866	10	Cairns 2	1	2	3	4			8				11	6	9		7	5	10								8
9	03 Oct	A	Bury	W	2 1	(2 1)	17,893	5	Cairns, Park	1	2	3	4			8				11	6	9		7	5	10								9
10	10 Oct	H	**Leicester City**	W	1 0	(0 0)	34,877	5	Cairns	1	2	3	4			8					6	9		7	5	10	11							10
11	17 Oct	H	**Chesterfield**	L	1 2	(1 0)	27,442	8	Cairns	1	2	3	4			8					6	9		7	5		11	10						11
12	24 Oct	A	Nottingham Forest	W	2 0	(1 0)	20,171	6	Cairns, Rogers	1	2	3	4			7	8			10	6	9			5		11							12
13	31 Oct	H	**Plymouth Argyle**	D	1 1	(1 0)	29,079	5	Smith	1	2		4	5		7		9		10	6						11		3	8				13
14	07 Nov	A	Coventry City	D	2 2	(1 1)	33,150	6	Mooney (pen), Smith	1	2	3	4	5	6	7		9		10							11			8				14
15	14 Nov	H	**Doncaster Rovers**	W	7 0	(4 0)	22,406	6	Leighton 2, Rogers, Smith 4	1	2	3	4	5	6	7		9		10							11			8				15
16	21 Nov	A	Fulham	W	4 3	(3 1)	23,633	5	Pearson, Rogers 2, Smith	1	2	3	4	5	6	7		9		10							11			8				16
17	28 Nov	H	**Burnley**	W	3 0	(1 0)	27,465	4	Garnham, Leighton, Smith	1	2	3	4	5	6	7		9		10							11			8				17
18	05 Dec	A	Southampton	L	0 2	(0 2)	16,038	5		1	2		4	5	6	7		9		10							11		3	8				18
19	12 Dec	H	**Swansea Town**	W	5 1	(3 0)	14,306	4	Pearson, Rogers 2, Smith 2	1	2		4	5	6	7		9		10							11		3	8				19
20	19 Dec	A	Bradford City	L	0 2	(0 1)	9,618	4		1	2		4	5	6	7		9		10							11		3	8				20
21	25 Dec	H	**Norwich City**	L	0 1	(0 0)	38,372	6		1	2	3	4	5		7		9		10	6						11			8				21
22	26 Dec	A	Barnsley	L	0 1	(0 0)	22,760	7		1	2		4	5		7				10	6	9					11		3	8				22
23	28 Dec	A	Norwich City	W	5 1	(1 0)	19,244	6	Pearson, Smith 3, Leighton	1	2		4	5		7		9		10	6						11		3	8				23
24	01 Jan	H	**Bradford Park Avenue**	D	1 1	(0 1)	29,327	6	Leighton	1	2		4	5		7		9		10	6						11		3	8				24
25	02 Jan	H	**Sheffield United**	W	4 0	(3 0)	33,408	5	Cairns, Mooney, Smith 2		2		4	5		7		8		10	6	9	1				11		3					25
26	09 Jan	A	Tottenham Hotspur	W	1 0	(1 0)	30,505	3	Rogers	1	2			5	6	7		8		10	4	9							3		11			26
27	23 Jan	H	**Blackpool**	L	1 2	(0 2)	34,122	4	Pearson		2	3	4	5	6			8	10	11		9	1	7										27
28	30 Jan	A	Blackburn Rovers	L	1 6	(0 4)	7,928	5	Park		2		4	5				9		10	6		1	7			11		3	8				28
29	06 Feb	H	**Bury**	L	1 3	(1 2)	22,160	7	Leighton	1	2			5	6		4	9		10				7			11		3	8				29
30	13 Feb	A	Leicester City	L	2 3	(2 1)	24,252	7	Cairns, Smith	1		3	4	5		7		8			6	9				10	11					2		30
31	20 Feb	A	Chesterfield	L	0 4	(0 2)	10,163	9		1		3	4	5		7		8			6	9				10	11					2		31
32	06 Mar	A	Plymouth Argyle	D	1 1	(0 1)	18,365	11	Imrie	1	2		4	5	3	7	8	9		11	6					10								32
33	13 Mar	H	**Coventry City**	W	4 2	(4 0)	12,924	10	Imrie, Pearson, Smith 2	1	2		4	5	3	7	8	9		11	6					10								33
34	17 Mar	H	**Nottingham Forest**	W	3 2	(2 2)	3,867	7	Smith, Rogers, Imrie (pen)	1	2		4	5	3	7	8	9		11	6					10								34
35	20 Mar	A	Doncaster Rovers	W	2 1	(1 0)	11,782	8	Imrie, McMenemy	1	2		4	5		7		9	10	11	6					8			3					35
36	26 Mar	H	**Aston Villa**	L	0 2	(0 1)	46,213	8		1	2		4	5		7		9	10	11	6					8			3					36
37	27 Mar	H	**Fulham**	D	1 1	(0 1)	10,160	7	Smith	1	2	3	4	5		7		9		11	6									8	10			37
38	30 Mar	A	Aston Villa	W	2 0	(1 0)	65,437	7	Smith 2	1	2	3	4	5		7		9		11	6					8					10			38
39	03 Apr	A	Burnley	W	3 0	(2 0)	10,574	6	Cairns, Docking 2		2	3	4	5	6	7				11		9	1			8					10			39
40	10 Apr	H	**Southampton**	W	3 0	(2 0)	12,399	5	Cairns, Livingstone, Pearson		2	3	4	5		7				11	6	9	1			8					10			40
41	17 Apr	A	Swansea Town	W	2 1	(1 0)	9,310	5	Rogers, Smith	1	2	3	4	5		7		9		11	6					8					10			41
42	24 Apr	H	**Bradford City**	W	2 0	(2 0)	10,608	4	Rogers, Smith	1	2	3	4	5		7		9		11						8					10		6	42
Round			FA Cup																															Round
3	16 Jan	A	Preston North End	L	0 2	(0 1)	25,387			1	2		4	5		7		9		10	6						11		3	8				3

DateLine ... 9 Sept: United defeat West Ham United 5-3 with Billy Cairns hitting four and West Ham's Tudor Martin a hat-trick on his debut.
14 Nov: Jack Smith scores four goals in a 7-0 demolition of Doncaster Rovers. **17 March:** Only 3,867 turn up for the home match against Nottingham Forest, the club's lowest at Gallowgate since 1900.

SEASON
1937-38
DIVISION 2

Survival by goal average

Newcastle's progress since they had changed manager had been steady. However, as had occurred just four years ago so soon after winning the FA Cup, events took a swift and dramatic turn for the worse – and without any real indication of the appalling turnaround. Instead of looking upwards towards the First Division, they faced the Third Division (North) trapdoor and only scraped clear by a whisker. Season 1937-38 was to be the worst campaign in the club's history – almost matched only by a similar near-disaster and last gasp escape in 1991-92.

Tom Mather's initial plans were hit by injury. Several regulars were soon on the sidelines and then new purchase, the highly talented ex-Arsenal and England star Ray Bowden was also to be found in the treatment room and out of action for a period, notably at the crucial end of season run-in. Then worse, top striker Jack Smith was lured to First Division-bound Manchester United.

As the season progressed United continued to hover in the relegation mire. A slight recovery took place in the spring, but then they slipped back into trouble in a table which had several clubs at the bottom separated by a handful of points. Six defeats in eight games sent the Magpies into a tense and anxious climax to the season. They defeated Chesterfield 3-1 in their last fixture on Tyneside, then faced three matches on the road. United lost in a re-arranged return match with Chesterfield then fell at Swansea and Luton. They stared Third Division football for the very first time full in the face – in the pre-war era, the lowest level of senior football. Newcastle needed other clubs to do them a favour – and Nottingham Forest's point in a 2-2 draw against Barnsley proved a lifeline. It sent the Tykes down and kept the Magpies up. But only just, on goal average, by one-tenth of a goal!

Pictured above: Geordie Billy Cairns became the first United centre-forward to actually wear the No. 9 shirt.

Memorabilia CORNER

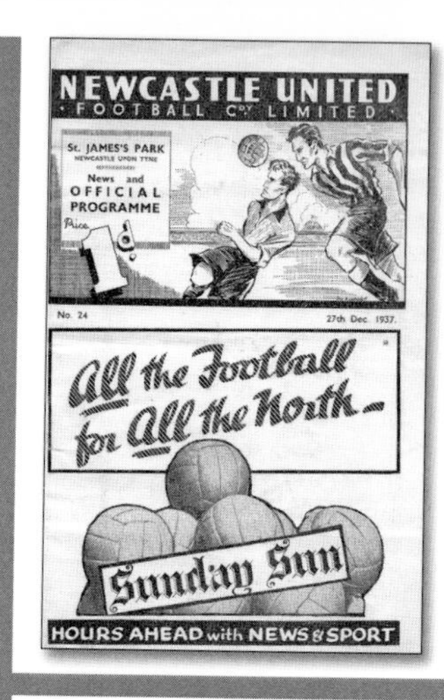

The local Sunday Sun was to feature on the cover of United's 1937-38 programme.

IN CHARGE

Chairman: James Lunn
Manager: Tom Mather
Captain: Jesse Carver
Trainer/Coach: Harry Bedford/Andy McCombie

ST JAMES' PARK

Average Attendance
Lg 21,276 Lg & Cup 21,276

Newcastle in change colours. Left to right: Imrie, Murray, Park, Gordon, McPhillips, McMenemy, Ware, Ancell, Richardson (Joe), Cairns, Pearson.

SEASON REVIEW

Football League Div 2: P42 W14 D8 L20 F51 A58 Pts 36.
Position: 19th (Champions; Aston Villa).
FA Cup: R3 (Winners; Preston North End).

Appearances (43m): Pearson TU 42, Gordon J 40, Imrie WN 38, Park JB 37, Richardson J 36, Ancell RFD 30, Carver J 28, Swinburne TA 25, Bowden ER 21, Smith Jk 19, Fairhurst DL 18, Denmark J 17, Mooney T 17, Cairns WH 16, Richardson JR 15, Rogers E 14, Livingstone A 13, Docking SH 12, Tapken NH 10, McPhillips WP 8, Connelly EJ 7, Garnham A 6, Grundy AJ 1, Leighton WA 1, Shiel J 1, Stubbins A 1.

Goals (51g): Imrie WN 9, Park JB 9, Smith Jk 7, Mooney T 5, Bowden ER 4, Cairns WH 4, Pearson TU 4, Livingstone A 3, Richardson JR 3, Docking SH 1, Gordon J 1, own goal 1.

Dismissals: 0 players.

MAJOR SIGNINGS

Ray Bowden (Arsenal) £5,000
Jimmy Richardson (Huddersfield Town) £4,500
Jimmy Denmark (Third Lanark) £2,550

FROM THE RANKS

Albert Stubbins (Whitley & Monkseaton Jnrs)
John Shiel (Seahouses)

PLAYER FOCUS Tommy Pearson

Born Edinburgh. Outside-left, 5'8"
1933 to 1948: 277 app 60 goals.

From a footballing family, his father appearing for Hearts and uncle for Arsenal, Tommy Pearson ran the left touchline for over 13 seasons at Newcastle and was a big favourite of the Gallowgate faithful. With finesse on the ball, he could deliver a constructive pass into the danger area on a regular basis and also find the net himself. Born in Scotland's capital, Edinburgh, Pearson was brought to Tyneside as a kid in March 1933. With immaculate ball control and the ability to go past defenders with bamboozling shuffles and body-swerves, he claimed a regular place during season 1934-35. Unorthodox and often to produce a brilliant touch which the crowd treasured, the Second World War probably stopped Tommy becoming a big international star for his country. Yet he did play for the Scots when nearly 34 years old in 1946-47 – ironically this after pulling on England's shirt in a wartime fixture at St James' Park at the beginning of the conflict. Appearing for several clubs in wartime football, after the hostilities Tommy again pulled on United's shirt with distinction, this time as a experienced campaigner, part of the club's promotion side in 1947-48. He then headed for Aberdeen before the end of that successful season where he played on for some time, totalling 115 games for the Dons before being appointed coach and ultimately manager in 1959. In the Sixties he was on Newcastle's scouting team.

TEAM COLOURS Black & white striped shirts, black shorts (Change; white shirts, black shorts)

SEASON 1937-38

Match	Date		FL Division 2						Posn		Tapken	Richardson J	Garnham	Gordon	Carver	Imrie	Rogers	Livingstone	Smith	Docking	Pearson	Leighton	Denmark	Park	Fairhurst	Shiel	Ancell	Connelly	Mooney	Swinburne	Richardson JR	Bowden	Cairns	McPhillips	Grundy	Stubbins	Match
1	28 Aug	A	Manchester United	L	0	3	(0 0)	29,446			1	2	3	4	5	6	7	8	9	10	11																1
2	01 Sep	H	**Barnsley**	L	0	1	(0 0)	19,065	20		1	2			3	6	7	8		10	11	4	5	9													2
3	04 Sep	H	**Sheffield United**	W	6	0	(2 0)	22,144	15	Pearson 2, Livingstone 2, Imrie (pen), Gordon	1	2		4		6		8	9	10	11		5	7	3												3
4	06 Sep	A	Barnsley	L	0	3	(0 2)	13,117	19		1	2		4	5	6		8		10	11			7	3	9											4
5	11 Sep	A	Tottenham Hotspur	D	2	2	(0 0)	25,577	18	Park, Imrie (pen)	1	2		4	5	6		8	9	10	11			7			3										5
6	15 Sep	H	**Luton Town**	L	1	3	(1 2)	17,622	20	Livingstone	1	2		4		6	7	8	9		11		5				3	10									6
7	18 Sep	H	**Burnley**	D	2	2	(0 2)	14,982	18	Smith, Imrie (pen)	1	2		4	5	6		8	9	10	11			7			3										7
8	25 Sep	A	Bury	D	1	1	(0 1)	10,315	17	Imrie	1	2		4	5	6		8	9	10	11			7			3										8
9	02 Oct	H	**Coventry City**	L	1	2	(0 0)	22,687	19	Smith	1	2		4	5	6			9		10			7			3	8	11								9
10	09 Oct	A	Nottingham Forest	D	0	0	(0 0)	20,266	18			2		4	5	6			9		10			7	3			8	11	1							10
11	16 Oct	A	Aston Villa	L	0	2	(0 0)	50,192	20			2		4	5	6			9		10			7	3			8	11	1							11
12	23 Oct	H	**Bradford Park Avenue**	W	3	0	(1 0)	21,280	18	Imrie, Mooney, Richardson JR		2	6		5	4	7		9		10				3				11	1	8						12
13	30 Oct	A	West Ham United	L	0	1	(0 0)	29,915	20			2	6		5	4	7		9		10				3				11	1	8						13
14	06 Nov	H	**Southampton**	W	3	0	(1 0)	29,656	19	Park, Richardson JR, Smith		2		4	5	6			9		11			7	3					1	8	10					14
15	13 Nov	A	Blackburn Rovers	L	1	2	(1 0)	17,468	19	Bowden		2		4	5	6			9		11			7	3					1	8	10					15
16	20 Nov	H	**Plymouth Argyle**	W	3	1	(2 1)	21,476	19	Mooney, Smith, Imrie (pen)		2		4	5	6			9		10			7			3		11	1		8					16
17	27 Nov	A	Fulham	W	2	1	(1 1)	12,369	18	Park, Smith		2		4	5	6			9		10			7			3		11	1		8					17
18	04 Dec	H	**Sheffield Wednesday**	W	1	0	(0 0)	9,502	17	Mooney		2		4	5	6			9		10			7			3		11	1		8					18
	11 Dec	A	Chesterfield	Ab1	0	1	(0 1)	10,219				2		4	5	6					10			7			3		11	1	8		9				
19	18 Dec	H	**Swansea Town**	W	1	0	(0 0)	16,322	14	Imrie		2		4	5	6					10			7			3		11	1	8		9				19
20	25 Dec	H	**Stockport County**	D	0	0	(0 0)	29,736	13					4	5	6					10			7	2		3		11	1	8		9				20
	27 Dec	A	Stockport County	Ab2	2	2	(2 0)	18,417		*Smith, Park*				4	5	6			9		10			7	2		3		11	1	8						
21	01 Jan	H	**Manchester United**	D	2	2	(0 2)	40,088	16	Smith 2				4	5	6			9					7	2		3		11	1	10	8					21
22	15 Jan	A	Sheffield United	L	0	4	(0 1)	14,912	17			2		4	5	6	7		9		11						3			1	10	8					22
23	29 Jan	A	Burnley	L	1	2	(0 1)	10,550	18	Park		2		4	5	6					11			7			3			1	8	10	9				23
24	02 Feb	H	**Tottenham Hotspur**	W	1	0	(0 0)	11,249	16	Cairns		2		4	5	6					11			7			3				8	10	9	1			24
25	05 Feb	H	**Bury**	W	1	0	(1 0)	20,109	14	Cairns (pen)		2		4	6						11		5	7	3					1	8	10	9				25
26	12 Feb	A	Coventry City	L	0	1	(0 1)	20,977	15			2		4		6					11		5	7			3			1	8	10	9				26
27	19 Feb	H	**Nottingham Forest**	W	3	1	(1 0)	17,550	13	Bowden, og (McCall), Imrie (pen)		2		4		6					11		5	7			3			1	8	10	9				27
28	26 Feb	H	**Aston Villa**	W	2	0	(2 0)	48,434	13	Cairns, Park		2		4		6					11		5	7			3	10		1		8	9				28
29	02 Mar	A	Stockport County	W	3	1	(2 1)	8,629	10	Bowden 2, Park		2		4		6					11		5	7			3	10		1		8	9				29
30	05 Mar	A	Bradford Park Avenue	L	0	2	(0 2)	12,187	11			2		4		6					11		5	7			3	10		1		8	9				30
31	12 Mar	H	**West Ham United**	D	2	2	(1 0)	22,361	11	Docking, Richardson JR		2		4		6				10	11		5	7			3			1	8		9				31
32	19 Mar	A	Southampton	L	0	1	(0 1)	20,204	12		1	2		4		6				10	11		5	7			3					8	9				32
33	26 Mar	H	**Blackburn Rovers**	W	2	0	(1 0)	14,422	11	Cairns, Park			6	4						10	11		5	7	2		3			1		8	9				33
34	02 Apr	A	Plymouth Argyle	L	1	2	(1 1)	22,810	12	Pearson			6	4							10		5	7	2		3		11	1		8	9				34
35	09 Apr	H	**Fulham**	L	1	2	(0 1)	12,426	13	Pearson		2	6	4							10		5	7			3		11	1		8	9				35
36	15 Apr	H	**Norwich City**	L	0	1	(0 0)	20,336	14			2		4		6	8	9		10	11		5	7			3							1			36
37	16 Apr	A	Sheffield Wednesday	L	0	3	(0 1)	30,137	15			2		4		6	8	10		9	11		5	7			3							1			37
38	18 Apr	A	Norwich City	D	1	1	(0 1)	22,576	16	Imrie (pen)				4	5	6	7	8			10			9	2		3		11					1			38
39	23 Apr	H	**Chesterfield**	W	3	1	(1 0)	15,345	14	Mooney 2, Park				4	5	6	7	8			10			9	2		3		11					1			39
40	25 Apr	A	Chesterfield	L	0	2	(0 0)	6,311	14					4	5	6	7	8			10			9	2		3		11					1			40
41	30 Apr	A	Swansea Town	L	0	2	(0 1)	11,428	17			2		4	5	6	8				10			7	3				11				9	1			41
42	07 May	A	Luton Town	L	1	4	(0 2)	15,344	19	Park		2		4			7				11		5	9	3							10		1	6	8	42
Round			**FA Cup**																																		**Round**
3	08 Jan	A	West Bromwich Albion	L	0	1	(0 0)	33,932				2		4	5	6	7		9		11						3			1	10	8					3

Ab1 Abandoned after 76 mins due to bad light
Ab2 Abandoned after 77 mins due to bad light

DateLine ... 15 Sept: The Magpies slip into 20th place with a home defeat to Luton Town. **16 April:** Newcastle's fourth defeat in a row to Sheffield Wednesday puts the Magpies in relegation trouble. **23 April:** The Black'n'Whites secure two points with a 3-1 victory over Chesterfield, a life-line in the drop-zone battle. **7 May:** A 2-2 draw between Nottingham Forest and Barnsley secures United's survival, and the Tyke's relegation.

NEWCASTLE UNITED

SEASON
1938-39
DIVISION 2

Seymour begins a makeover

After the previous season's struggle Newcastle United were at a low ebb – a dire situation only to be matched in the club's 130-year history by similar circumstances at the start of the 1990s. They had little money, dwindling crowds, a poor line-up, inadequate leadership – and not least, faced another world conflict on the horizon. Yet out of all of that doom and despondency came one shining light, the arrival of ex-player Stan Seymour into the Boardroom. It was a surprise move, but a welcome one with Seymour bringing football know-how and fresh ideas as well as dynamic leadership to St James' Park. From that point Newcastle United never looked back.

Despite finances being decimated, United invested on the playing squad and went into debt to bring Harry Clifton and Ralph Birkett to St James' Park, two players in the England reckoning. Joining Bowden, United's line-up had quality. Also to arrive was a new trainer, Norman Smith, to be Seymour's right-hand man for the next 25 years.

Season 1938-39 saw a vast change for the better. Confidence returned and United looked the part being up at the top during November with five wins in six games, including successive victories over Bradford Park Avenue, Sheffield Wednesday and Fulham. But as the season developed they never quite reached promotion contention, slipping up during March and April with only one victory in nine games. But they were on the right tracks, and crowds came through the turnstiles again – over 64,000 watching the Division Two clash with leaders Fulham during November when a 2-1 victory put United top of the table. All the good work was however to be suddenly halted by the outbreak of World War Two.

There was a headline FA Cup meeting. Reaching the Fifth Round, United met Preston once more and in front of over 62,000 lost by the odd goal in three at Gallowgate.

Pictured above: Tall and thoughtful, Duggie Wright's form in midfield earned a call-up for England.

Memorabilia CORNER

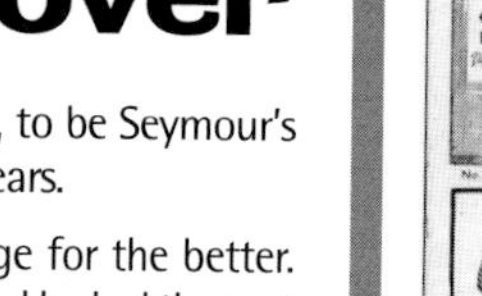

Note that United's programme during the 1930s used St James's Park, rather than St James' Park.

IN CHARGE

Chairman: James Lunn
Manager: Tom Mather
Captain: Jimmy Denmark
Trainer/Coach: Norman Smith

ST JAMES' PARK

Average Attendance
Lg 32,691 Lg & Cup 34,500

United just prior to World War Two. Back row, left to right: Smith (trainer), Richardson, Stubbins, Swinburne, Wright, Ancell, Mather (manager). Front: Birkett, Gordon, Park, Clifton, Mooney, Denmark.

PLAYER FOCUS Joe Richardson

Born Bedlington. Right-back, 5'8"
1929 to 1945: 337 app 1 goal.

A grand servant to Newcastle United for almost half-a-century of his life as a player, trainer, physio and then back-stage aide, Joe Richardson was black-and-white through and through. A solid and mean right-back, good enough to wear England's shirt against Scotland in a wartime international during season 1939-40, Richardson was a former blacksmith and as strong and as gritty as they come. Another to begin at the Blyth Spartans breeding ground, Joe became a one-club man in senior football with the Magpies. He rivalled Alf Maitland as a youngster for the defender's role then took over from Jimmy Nelson in Newcastle's line-up during 1934-35. Robust, but fair in the tackle, Joe featured through the lean years of the 1930s as the Magpies struggled to cope with relegation to the second tier. He then was a regular during the war seasons for United and skippered the side on occasion before retiring from action in 1945 when he joined the coaching staff. In later years at St James' Park, Richardson became a huge personality both loved and feared by young professionals as they climbed the Gallowgate ladder of fame. Usually wearing the traditional white trainers coat of the day, Joe was always on hand to give generous advice, or indeed, a short sharp bark in his rich Geordie vernacular. He holds record service of over 46 years on the playing and coaching staff. Along with Benny Craig, Alex Mutch and Joe Harvey, he was at the very heart and soul of the club following World War Two.

SEASON REVIEW

Football League Div 2: P42 W18 D10 L14 F61 A48 Pts 46.
Position: 9th (Champions; Blackburn Rovers).
FA Cup: R5 (Winners; Portsmouth).

Appearances (46m): Ancell RFD 46, Wright JD 46, Mooney T 42, Denmark J 34, Richardson J 34, Cairns WH 33, Clifton H 33, Bowden ER 31, Swinburne TA 31, Gordon J 28, Birkett RJE 26, Stubbins A 24, Park JB 15, Theaker CA 15, Carver J 11, Craig B 9, Scott W 9, Garnham A 8, Woodburn J 8, Pearson TU 6, Frost AD 5, Rogers E 5, Fairhurst DL 3, Pears W 2, Bradley GJ 1, Kelly D 1.

Goals (68g): Cairns WH 20, Clifton H 17, Mooney T 12, Stubbins A 4, Birkett RJE 3, Bowden ER 2, Gordon J 2, Pearson TU 2, Scott W 2, Ancell RFD 1, Frost AD 1, Park JB 1, Wright JD 1.

Dismissals: 0 players.

MAJOR SIGNINGS

Ralf Birkett (Middlesbrough) £5,900
Doug Wright (Southend Utd) £3,250
Benny Craig (Huddersfield Town) £4,000
Arthur Frost (New Brighton) £2,515
Clarence Theaker (Grimsby Town) £1,250
Willie Scott (Aberdeen) £3,750
Harry Clifton (Chesterfield)
£8,500 club record fee

FROM THE RANKS

Jimmy Woodburn (Coltness Utd)
William Pears (Crook Town, Es)

TEAM COLOURS Black & white striped shirts, black shorts (Change; white shirts, black shorts)

SEASON 1938-39

Match	Date		FL Division 2				Att	Posn	Scorers
1	27 Aug	H	**Plymouth Argyle**	W	2 1	(2 1)	38,300		Birkett, Clifton
2	31 Aug	A	Luton Town	L	1 2	(0 0)	17,689	14	Clifton
3	03 Sep	A	Sheffield United	D	0 0	(0 0)	17,648	14	
4	07 Sep	A	West Bromwich Albion	L	2 5	(2 3)	17,025	14	Mooney, Stubbins
5	10 Sep	H	**Burnley**	W	3 2	(3 1)	30,824	12	Bowden, Cairns, Stubbins
6	14 Sep	H	**West Bromwich Albion**	W	5 1	(1 0)	31,128	6	Cairns 4, Stubbins
7	17 Sep	A	Tottenham Hotspur	L	0 1	(0 1)	37,694	10	
8	24 Sep	H	**Southampton**	W	1 0	(1 0)	34,816	7	Cairns
9	01 Oct	A	Coventry City	L	0 1	(0 1)	18,774	9	
10	08 Oct	H	**Nottingham Forest**	W	4 0	(4 0)	31,154	6	Birkett, Cairns 3
11	15 Oct	H	**Tranmere Rovers**	W	5 1	(3 1)	34,955		Cairns 3, Mooney 2
12	22 Oct	A	West Ham United	D	1 1	(0 1)	26,721	3	Cairns
13	29 Oct	H	**Bradford Park Avenue**	W	1 0	(0 0)	40,758	2	Cairns
14	05 Nov	A	Sheffield Wednesday	W	2 0	(0 0)	25,373	2	Cairns 2
15	12 Nov	H	**Fulham**	W	2 1	(2 0)	64,166	1	Birkett, Bowden
16	19 Nov	A	Blackburn Rovers	L	0 3	(0 3)	20,876	2	
17	26 Nov	H	**Millwall**	D	2 2	(1 1)	38,166	4	Clifton, Mooney
18	03 Dec	A	Manchester City	L	1 4	(1 1)	43,114	5	Cairns
19	10 Dec	H	**Bury**	W	6 0	(3 0)	27,972	5	Mooney 3 (1 pen), Clifton 3
20	17 Dec	A	Swansea Town	W	1 0	(1 0)	11,151	4	Clifton
21	24 Dec	A	Plymouth Argyle	W	1 0	(1 0)	17,615		Mooney
22	27 Dec	H	**Norwich City**	W	4 0	(2 0)	26,156	2	Mooney 2 (2 pens), Clifton 2
23	31 Dec	H	**Sheffield United**	D	0 0	(0 0)	46,536		
24	02 Jan	H	**Chesterfield**	L	0 1	(0 0)	33,701	3	
25	14 Jan	A	Burnley	L	0 2	(0 1)	12,745		
26	28 Jan	A	Southampton	D	0 0	(0 0)	15,802	5	
27	04 Feb	H	**Coventry City**	L	0 4	(0 1)	43,443	7	
28	15 Feb	A	Nottingham Forest	L	0 2	(0 1)	7,365		
29	18 Feb	A	Tranmere Rovers	W	3 0	(3 0)	9,155	7	Clifton, Stubbins, Gordon
30	25 Feb	H	**West Ham United**	W	2 0	(1 0)	29,587	5	Pearson (pen), Cairns
31	01 Mar	H	**Tottenham Hotspur**	L	0 1	(0 1)	18,503		
32	04 Mar	A	Bradford Park Avenue	W	1 0	(0 0)	10,148	4	Wright
33	11 Mar	H	**Sheffield Wednesday**	W	2 1	(0 1)	29,578		Frost, Scott
34	16 Mar	A	Norwich City	D	1 1	(0 1)	7,764	2	Clifton
35	18 Mar	A	Fulham	D	1 1	(0 0)	20,182	2	Clifton
36	25 Mar	H	**Blackburn Rovers**	D	2 2	(2 2)	40,237	2	Scott, Clifton
37	01 Apr	A	Millwall	D	1 1	(0 1)	25,951		Cairns
38	07 Apr	A	Chesterfield	L	0 2	(0 2)	28,268		
39	08 Apr	H	**Manchester City**	L	0 2	(0 1)	24,487	9	
40	15 Apr	A	Bury	D	1 1	(0 1)	6,656		Ancell
41	22 Apr	H	**Swansea Town**	L	1 2	(0 0)	11,705		Clifton
42	29 Apr	H	**Luton Town**	W	2 0	(1 0)	10,341	9	Pearson (pen), Clifton
Round			**FA Cup**						
3	07 Jan	A	Brentford	W	2 0	(1 0)	27,551		Clifton, Mooney
4	21 Jan	A	Cardiff City	D	0 0	(0 0)	42,060		
4r	25 Jan	H	**Cardiff City**	W	4 1	(1 0)	44,649		Clifton, Gordon, Mooney, Park
5	11 Feb	H	**Preston North End**	L	1 2	(1 1)	62,327		Cairns

Match	Swinburne	Richardson	Ancell	Gordon	Denmark	Wright	Birkett	Bowden	Cairns	Clifton	Mooney	Park	Stubbins	Woodburn	Craig	Bradley	Garnham	Fairhurst	Rogers	Carver	Scott	Theaker	Kelly	Pearson	Frost	Pears
1	1	2	3	4	5	6	7	8	9	10	11															
2	1	2	3	4	5	6	7		8	10	11	9														
3	1	2	3	4	5	6	7			10	11	9	8													
4	1	2	3	4	5	6	7			10	11	9	8													
5	1	2	3	4	5	6	7	10	9		11		8													
6	1	2	3	4	5	6	7	10	9		11		8													
7	1	2	3	4	5	6	7	10	9		11		8													
8	1	2	3	4	5	6	7	10	9		11		8													
9	1	2	3		5	6	7	10	9		11		8	4												
10	1	2	3		5	6	7	10	9		11		8	4												
11	1	2	3		5	6	7	10	9		11		8	4												
12	1	2	3		5	6	7	10	9		11		8	4												
13	1	2	3		5	6	7	10	9		11		8	4												
14	1	2	3		5	6	7	10	9		11		8	4												
15	1	2	3		5	6	7	10	9		11		8	4												
16	1		3		5	6	7	10	9		11		8		2	4										
17	1		3		5	6	7	10	9	8	11				2		4									
18	1		3		5	6	7		9	10	11		8				4	2								
19	1	2	3		5	6	7	10	9	8	11						4									
20	1	2	3		5	6		10	9	8	11						4		7							
21	1	2	3		5	6		10	9	8	11						4		7							
22	1	2	3		5	6		10	9	8	11						4		7							
23	1	2	3		5	6		10	9	8	11						4		7							
24	1	2	3		5	6		10	9	8	11						4		7							
25	1		3	4		6	7	10		8	11							2		5	9					
26		2	3	4		6	7	10	9	8	11									5		1				
27			3	4		6		10		9	11	7	8					2				1	5			
28		2	3	4	5	6	7		9	10	11		8									1				
29		2	3	4	5	6			9	8		7	10									1		11		
30		2	3	4	5	6			9	8		7	10									1		11		
31		2	3	4	5	6			9	8		7	10									1		11		
32	1	2	3	4		10			9		11	7		6						5	8					
33	1	2	3	4		6				10	11	7								5	8				9	
34	1	2	3	4		6				10	11	7								5	8				9	
35	1	2	3	4		6		10	9	8	11	7								5						
36	1		3	4		6		10		8	11	7			2					5	9					
37			3	4	5	6		9	10	8	11	7			2							1				
38			3	4	5	6		9	10	8	11	7			2							1				
39			3	4	5	6		8	9	7	11		10		2							1				
40			3		5	6				8	11		10		2							1		7	9	4
41			3		5	6				10	11		8		2							1		7	9	4
42			3	4	5	6	7			10					2						8	1		11	9	
Round																										
3	1	2	3	4		6	7	10		8	11									5	9					
4		2	3	4		6	7	10		8	11									5	9	1				
4r		2	3	4		6		10		8	11	7								5	9	1				
5		2	3	4		6	7		9	10	11		8							5		1				

DateLine ... 20 Aug: The celebration Football League Jubilee fixture with Gateshead takes place, a 2-1 win. **9 Nov:** England face Norway at Gallowgate and secure a comfortable 4-0 victory. **21 Jan:** United have three goals disallowed in the FA Cup-tie with Cardiff City.

SEASON 1946-47
DIVISION 2

A goal-feast return to action

With everything back to routine, the 1946-47 season kicked off with the same Second Division fixture list before war called a halt seven years earlier. United's squad included a few of their pre-war stars – Benny Craig, Tommy Pearson and Duggie Wright to name three – now a bit older, but experienced heads to mix with an eager batch of youngsters and several big-money purchases. For the new era, Newcastle were skippered now by Joe Harvey, who was to lead the club by example.

Although United lost the scoring prowess of Stubbins who departed to the First Division in a record deal, the Black'n'Whites still had goal power. His replacement, Charlie Wayman went onto net 34 goals in the season as the wartime goal-feast continued. That was evident when Newport County arrived on Tyneside during October. With star signing Len Shackleton making his debut for United, the Magpies went goal-crazy, hitting the Welshmen by all of 13-0; a club record scoreline, and still the biggest victory in the English top two divisions.

Remarkably, Shackleton netted not only one hat-trick, but two – although his sixth goal these days would be registered as an own-goal by full-back Ken Wookey. Nevertheless the club and most reporters were content to let the rare six-goal debut haul stand in the record books. Newcastle also missed a penalty in the massacre of poor Newport – Wayman failing from the spot in the opening exchanges.

Newcastle challenged well for promotion, indeed, were leaders of the pack until the FA Cup became a full-size distraction. The Magpies reached the semi-final, beating First Division Sheffield United on the way, then self-destructed at Elland Road against Charlton Athletic. There was discord in the camp and a player-management fall-out led to a resounding four goal defeat to the Londoners. The consequence was a new manager entered the corridors at St James' Park as the season came to a close with United just out of the promotion race. Luton Town's George Martin landed the job, at a salary of £1,250 a year with a bonus payment of £250 if promotion was secured.

Pictured above: Len Shackleton developed into a complete showman, a huge personality in the game.

NEWCASTLE UNITED
ASSOCIATION FOOTBALL CLUB
ST. JAMES'S PARK, NEWCASTLE UPON TYNE
OFFICIAL PROGRAMME - 2d. No. 8.
You can obtain an Excellent Meal at a Moderate Price at any of Carricks Cafes
The Big Five – NEWCASTLE JOURNAL, EVENING CHRONICLE, SUNDAY SUN, WEEKLY CHRONICLE, SPORTING MAN
FOOTBALL LEAGUE FIXTURE
NEWCASTLE UNITED versus NEWPORT Co.
KICK-OFF 3-15 P.M.
SATURDAY, OCT. 5th, 1946.

The four-page match programme for the 13-0 rout against Newport County.

Memorabilia CORNER

IN CHARGE

Chairman: George Rutherford
Manager: Director Committee
Captain: Joe Harvey
Trainer/Coach: Norman Smith

ST JAMES' PARK

Average Attendance
Lg 49,384 Lg & Cup 49,434

United are ready for a new post-war era. Back row, left to right: Watt Jnr (secretary), Harvey, Craig, Garbutt, Corbett, Wright, Smith (trainer), GS Seymour (director). Front: Milburn, Woodburn, King (G), Wayman, Pearson, Brennan.

PLAYER FOCUS Charlie Wayman

Born Bishop Auckland. Centre-forward, 5'6"
1941 to 1947: 124 app 71 goals.

Small and explosive with the instinct of a natural striker, Charlie Wayman was a handful for defences throughout the immediate post-war years and bagged over 300 goals in a respected career. Alas, his contribution to United's cause was limited due to a dressing-room bust-up with trainer Norman Smith on the eve of the 1947 FA Cup semi-final. A wartime find at Spennymoor United, joining the Gallowgate set-up in September 1941, at the time of that Cup run he was then making a big name for himself as Newcastle's top scorer (eventually to hit 34 goals in the 1946-47 season), but found himself dropped for the semi-final (United losing 4-0) and on the way out of St James' Park. Charlie joined Southampton soon after in a £10,000 deal during October 1947 and became an extremely popular footballer on the south coast. In one contest with Leicester City he struck five goals into the net. Composed and skilful with a turn of pace that worried defenders, Wayman did well at all his clubs. Especially dangerous on his left, he netted plenty of goals at The Dell, as well as for Preston North End and later Middlesbrough and Darlington. Wayman reached the FA Cup final with Preston in 1954 when he netted in every round to Wembley while Charlie three times headed the Football League's divisional scoring list. Unlucky not to reach England recognition, Wayman retired due to a knee injury. His brother Frank appeared for Chester.

SEASON REVIEW

Football League Div 2: P42 W19 D10 L13 F95 A62 Pts 48.
Position: 5th (Champions; Manchester City).
FA Cup: SF (Winners; Charlton Athletic).

Appearances (48m): Wayman C 46, Pearson TU 44, Bentley RTF 42, Harvey Jos 38, Shackleton LF 38, Brennan F 36, Graham D 36, Wright JD 36, Milburn JET 27, Swinburne TA 26, Woodburn J 22, Stobbart GC 21, Garbutt EJE 20, Burke RJ 17, Cowell RG 17, Craig B 14, Corbett R 12, Walker TJ 9, Smith T 7, Crowe CA 4, Fraser R 3, Hair G 3, Stubbins A 3, King G 2, Sibley A 2, Anderson WR 1, Donaldson A 1, Theaker CA 1.

Goals (109g): Wayman C 34, Bentley RTF 22, Shackleton LF 22, Milburn JET 8, Stobbart GC 8, Pearson TU 6, Harvey Jos 3, Walker TJ 2, Woodburn J 2, Hair G 1, Stubbins A 1.

Dismissals: 0 players.

MAJOR SIGNINGS

Frank Brennan (Airdrie) £7,500
Albert Sibley (Southend Utd) £6,500+player
George Stobbart (Middlesbrough) £4,650
Roy Bentley (Bristol City) £8,500
Bob Fraser (Hibernian) £3,750
Len Shackleton (Bradford Park Avenue) £13,000 club record fee

FROM THE RANKS

George King (Northb sch, RAF)
Tommy Thompson (Lumley YMCA)

TEAM COLOURS Black & white striped shirts, black shorts (Change; white shirts, black shorts)

SEASON 1946-47

Match	Date		FL Division 2					Posn	Scorers
1	31 Aug	A	Millwall	W	4 1	(2 1)	39,187		Bentley 2, Milburn, Stubbins
2	05 Sep	A	Nottingham Forest	W	2 0	(1 0)	32,691		Bentley, Harvey
3	07 Sep	H	**Swansea Town**	D	1 1	(0 0)	54,966		Woodburn
4	11 Sep	H	**Coventry City**	W	3 1	(2 0)	55,313	1	Wayman, Stobbart 2 (1 pen)
5	14 Sep	A	Tottenham Hotspur	D	1 1	(0 1)	52,213	2	Harvey
6	16 Sep	A	Coventry City	D	1 1	(0 1)	26,024	2	Milburn
7	21 Sep	H	**Burnley**	L	1 2	(0 2)	61,255	3	Wayman
8	28 Sep	A	Barnsley	D	1 1	(0 1)	34,192	3	Stobbart
9	05 Oct	H	**Newport County**	W	13 0	(7 0)	52,137	2	Bentley, Milburn 2, Shackleton 6, Wayman 4
10	12 Oct	A	Southampton	D	1 1	(0 0)	25,746	2	Shackleton
11	19 Oct	A	Bradford Park Avenue	L	1 2	(1 2)	26,533	7	Pearson
12	26 Oct	H	**Manchester City**	W	3 2	(1 0)	65,798	5	Wayman 3
13	02 Nov	A	West Ham United	W	2 0	(1 0)	32,617	3	Bentley, Shackleton
14	09 Nov	H	**Sheffield Wednesday**	W	4 0	(1 0)	46,916	1	Wayman 4
15	16 Nov	A	Fulham	W	3 0	(0 0)	44,000	1	Bentley, Wayman 2
16	23 Nov	H	**Bury**	D	1 1	(0 1)	49,656	1	Bentley
17	30 Nov	A	Luton Town	L	3 4	(3 0)	25,410	1	Bentley, Shackleton, Wayman
18	07 Dec	H	**Plymouth Argyle**	W	3 2	(0 2)	47,661	1	Bentley 3
19	14 Dec	A	Leicester City	W	4 2	(0 1)	35,262	1	Bentley, Pearson, Shackleton, Wayman
20	21 Dec	H	**Chesterfield**	W	2 1	(2 0)	53,675	1	Wayman 2
21	25 Dec	H	**West Bromwich Albion**	L	2 4	(1 3)	44,722		Shackleton, Stobbart
22	26 Dec	A	West Bromwich Albion	L	2 3	(0 2)	31,794	4	Wayman 2
23	28 Dec	H	**Millwall**	L	0 2	(0 2)	53,305	4	
24	01 Jan	H	**Nottingham Forest**	W	3 0	(2 0)	56,827	4	Bentley, Wayman, Woodburn
25	04 Jan	A	Swansea Town	W	2 1	(1 0)	22,836	4	Shackleton, Wayman
26	18 Jan	H	**Tottenham Hotspur**	W	1 0	(0 0)	62,873	2	Shackleton
27	28 Jan	A	Burnley	L	0 3	(0 2)	25,309	3	
28	01 Feb	H	**Barnsley**	W	4 2	(4 0)	40,182	3	Bentley, Shackleton, Stobbart, Wayman
29	15 Feb	H	**Southampton**	L	1 3	(1 1)	50,516	4	Pearson
30	22 Mar	H	**Fulham**	L	1 3	(0 2)	43,647	5	Shackleton
31	04 Apr	H	**Birmingham City**	D	2 2	(1 1)	57,259	5	Bentley, Milburn
32	05 Apr	H	**Luton Town**	W	7 2	(5 1)	40,372	5	Wayman 2, Stobbart 2, Shackleton, Milburn, Harvey
33	07 Apr	A	Birmingham City	L	0 2	(0 1)	41,639	5	
34	12 Apr	A	Plymouth Argyle	W	1 0	(1 0)	32,460	5	Shackleton
35	19 Apr	H	**Leicester City**	D	1 1	(0 0)	36,739	5	Wayman
36	26 Apr	A	Chesterfield	L	0 1	(0 0)	14,672	5	
37	03 May	A	Manchester City	W	2 0	(0 0)	46,492	5	Walker, Wayman
38	10 May	H	**Bradford Park Avenue**	W	5 0	(2 0)	33,131	5	Bentley 3, Walker, Wayman
39	17 May	A	Bury	D	2 2	(1 2)	17,298	5	Bentley, Wayman
40	24 May	A	Sheffield Wednesday	D	1 1	(0 1)	28,405	5	Hair
41	26 May	H	**West Ham United**	L	2 3	(0 2)	30,112	5	Milburn, Shackleton
42	07 Jun	A	Newport County	L	2 4	(1 3)	8,798	5	Pearson, Shackleton
Round			**FA Cup**						
3	11 Jan	H	**Crystal Palace**	W	6 2	(4 0)	43,183		Bentley, Pearson, Shackleton 2, Stobbart, Wayman
4	25 Jan	H	**Southampton**	W	3 1	(0 1)	55,878		Wayman 3
5	08 Feb	H	**Leicester City**	D	1 1	(0 0)	50,301		Shackleton
5r	20 Feb	A	Leicester City	W	2 1	(2 1)	28,424		Bentley, Pearson
6	01 Mar	A	Sheffield United	W	2 0	(2 0)	46,911		Bentley (pen), Milburn
SF	29 Mar	N	Charlton Athletic	L	0 4	(0 3)	47,821		

Match	Garbutt	Craig	Graham	Harvey	Brennan	Wright	Milburn	Bentley	Stubbins	Wayman	Pearson	Swinburne	Woodburn	Theaker	Walker	Stobbart	King	Corbett	Cowell	Shackleton	Smith	Burke	Crowe	Fraser	Sibley	Anderson	Donaldson	Hair
1	1	2	3	4	5	6	7	8	9	10	11																	
2	1	2	3	4	5	6	7	8	9	10	11																	
3		2	3	4	5	6	7		9	10	11	1	8															
4		2	3	4	5	6	8			10	11			1	7	9												
5	1	2	3	4	5	6	8			10	11				7		9											
6	1	2		4	5	6	7			10	11		8				9	3										
7	1	2	3	4	5	6	7	8		10	11					9												
8	1	2	3	4	5	6	7	8		10	11					9												
9	1		3	4	5	6	7	8		9	11								2	10								
10	1		3	4	5	6	7	8		9	11								2	10								
11	1	2	3	4		6	7	8		9	11									10	5							
12	1	2	3	4	5	6	7	8		9	11									10								
13	1	2	3	4	5		7	8		9	11		6							10								
14			3	4	5		7	8		9	11	1	6						2	10								
15			3	4	5	6	7	8		9	11	1							2	10								
16			3	4	5	6	7	8		9	11	1							2	10								
17		2	3	4		6	7	8		9	11	1								10	5							
18			3	4		5		8		9	11	1				7				10		2	6					
19			3	4				8		9	11	1				7				10	5	2	6					
20			3	4				8		9	11	1				7				10	5	2	6					
21			3			6		8		9	11	1				7				10	5	2	4					
22			3			6	7	8		9	11	1	4							10	5	2						
23			3			6	7	8		9	11	1	4							10	5	2						
24	1		3			6		8		9	11		4			7				10		2		5				
25	1		3			6		8		9	11		4			7				10		2		5				
26				4	5	6		8		9	11	1				7		3		10		2						
27				4	5	6		8		9	11	1				7		3		10		2						
28					5	6		8		9	11	1	4			7		3	2	10								
29					5	6		8		9	11	1	4					3	2	10					7			
30	1			4	5		7	8		9	11		6					3		10		2						
31	1		3		5	6	7	8		10	11		4			9						2						
32	1		3	4	5	6	7			10	11					9				8		2						
33	1		3	4	5	6	7			10	11					9				8		2						
34	1		3	4	5	6		8		11					7	9				10		2						
35		2		4				8		10	11		6					3						5	7	1	9	
36	1		3	4	5	6		9		10	11				7				2	8								
37			3	4	5			9		10	11	1	6		7				2	8								
38			3	4	5			9		10	11	1	6		7				2	8								
39			3	4	5			9		10		1	6		7				2	8								11
40			3	4	5			8		9		1	6		7				2	10								11
41			3	4	5		7	8		9		1	6						2	10								11
42		2	3	4	5			8			11	1	6		7	9				10								
Round																												
3	1		3	4		6		8		9	11		5			7				10		2						
4				4	5	6		8		9	11	1				7		3		10		2						
5					5	6		8		9	11	1	4			7		3	2	10								
5r				4	5	6	7	8		9	11	1						3	2	10								
6					5	6	7	8		9	11	1	4					3	2	10								
SF				4	5	6	7	8			11	1				9		3	2	10								

N — Played at Elland Road, Leeds

Match 9 — Shackleton's 6th goal could also be given as an own goal by Wookey

DateLine ... 5 Oct: A record 13-0 scoreline racked up against Newport County; the best in the top two divisions. **5 Oct:** Len Shackleton scores an amazing six goals on his United debut against Newport. **6 Nov:** A then record friendly crowd of 46,124 watch the clash with Swedish champions Norrkoping. **29 March:** Charlton reach Wembley by comprehensively beating United 4-0 in the semi-final of the FA Cup. **17 May:** Charlie Wayman scores his 34th goal of the season against Bury. **26 May:** George Martin takes charge for the first time for the game with West Ham United, a 3-2 defeat.

SEASON
1947-48
DIVISION 2

Boom time and promotion

With Stan Seymour still very much influential, new manager George Martin had one priority, to get the Magpies back into the top flight. He first had to sort out dressing-room issues and a flurry of transfer activity followed, in and out of Gallowgate. Substantial sums were exchanged as United hit the headlines as one of the game's big buyers and sellers. Martin put together an altered line-up and were the favourites to claim one of the two promotion places – especially after an exiting the FA Cup. The race was between any two clubs of Birmingham City, Southampton, Sheffield Wednesday and United.

With a formidable home record – winning 18 of their 21 fixtures – Newcastle would have cruised into the First Division had their away record been better. But at Gallowgate, a vociferous Geordie support of almost 56,300 at every match – an English record for many years until 1968 – gave the Magpies the proverbial goal start. And at Easter when the crunch came, that support was crucial. Against Fulham they roared United to a single goal victory, then on Good Friday promotion rivals Sheffield Wednesday arrived on Tyneside. Over 66,000 saw United win 4-2 and just about seal promotion, a terrific contest that see-sawed from end-to-end and which saw the Owls in front at one stage. A point at Tottenham mathematically made sure.

United went up with Birmingham and were ready to become one of football's elite again. And at the same time, a few of the new Magpie players were to be elevated as huge stars; Frank Brennan, Joe Harvey and none more so than Jackie Milburn, who had taken over the No. 9 shirt and become the local hero. He was touted for a place in the England side and was quickly to make an impression wearing the white shirt of his country. Within a few months two more footballers arrived for big fees who were also to become household names; Bobby Mitchell and George Robledo.

Pictured above: Tall and composed, Norman Dodgin was born and bred in Sheriff Hill from a footballing family.

Memorabilia CORNER

Programme from the match against Chesterfield, note the advert for Newcastle's five local newspapers.

IN CHARGE

Chairman: George Rutherford
Manager: George Martin
Captain: Joe Harvey
Trainer/Coach: Norman Smith

ST JAMES' PARK

Average Attendance (Record)
Lg 56,298 Lg & Cup 56,298

The Black'n'Whites en-route to promotion. Back row, left to right: Smith (trainer), Brennan, Fraser, Garbutt, Craig, Houghton, Dodgin. Front: Sibley, Thompson, Harvey, Stobbart, Taylor, McCall.

PLAYER FOCUS Joe Harvey

Born Edlington. Right-half, 6'0"
1945 to 1954: 281 app 13 goals.

Joe Harvey served United as a player with distinction then returned to Gallowgate to guide the Magpies from the manager's office with equal merit. A rugged right-half and down-to-earth Yorkshireman, Joe cost the club £4,250 from Bradford City in October 1945 and led the Black'n'Whites as skipper, first to promotion in 1948 and then to a double FA Cup triumph in 1951 and 1952. Tall, commanding and with a growl from his days as a wartime sergeant-major, Harvey was an uncompromising figure in United's midfield, at his best when players needed to roll up their sleeves and graft. Retiring from action on the pitch as 1954 opened, he was on the coaching staff to another FA Cup victory in 1955 and then, after learning the ropes of management at Barrow and Workington, returned to St James' Park as boss in June 1962. Joe rebuilt the Geordies, winning the Second Division Championship in 1965 before leading the Magpies to a celebrated Inter Cities Fairs Cup triumph four years later. A manager of the old school, he wasn't a tactical boss but knew a good footballer and was an inspiration, while Joe held the respect of his players. He reached Wembley again in the FA Cup during 1974 and moved upstairs a year after that defeat becoming Chief Scout and both assistant and caretaker boss. Totally dedicated to the club, Joe remained associated with the Magpies to his death. Harvey had spent almost 37 years in the ranks of the Tynesiders, one of the club's finest servants.

SEASON REVIEW

Football League Div 2: P42 W24 D8 L10 F72 A41 Pts 56.
Position: 2nd, Promoted (Champions; Birmingham City).
FA Cup: R3 (Winners; Manchester United).

Appearances (43m): Brennan F 43, Milburn JET 40, Harvey Jos 38, Craig B 27, Dodgin N 27, Stobbart GC 27, Fairbrother J 26, Shackleton LF 26, Pearson TU 22, Fraser R 21, Cowell RG 19, Sibley A 19, Garbutt EJE 17, Woodburn J 17, Graham D 16, McCall W 15, Houghton FC 13, Bentley RTF 12, Taylor E 8, Walker TJ 8, Hair G 6, Wayman C 6, Donaldson A 5, Lowrie G 5, Corbett R 4, Thompson T 4, Crowe CA 2.

Goals (73g): Milburn JET 20, Stobbart GC 9, Shackleton LF 7, McCall W 4, Pearson TU 4, Sibley A 4, Bentley RTF 3, Harvey Jos 3, Walker TJ 3, Hair G 2, Houghton FC 2, Thompson T 2, Wayman C 2, Woodburn J 2, Dodgin N 1, Donaldson A 1, Lowrie G 1, own goals 3.

Dismissals: 0 players.

MAJOR SIGNINGS

Jack Fairbrother (Preston NE) £6,500
Willie McCall (Aberdeen) £8,400
George Lowrie (Coventry City) £18,500 club record fee

FROM THE RANKS

None

TEAM COLOURS Black & white striped shirts, black shorts (Change; white shirts, black shorts)

SEASON 1947-48

Match			FL Division 2					Posn		Fairbrother	Craig	Graham	Harvey	Brennan	Woodburn	Walker	Bentley	Wayman	Shackleton	Pearson	Milburn	Dodgin	Cowell	Corbett	Fraser	Stobbart	Taylor	Donaldson	Hair	Garbutt	Sibley	McCall	Houghton	Thompson	Lowrie	Crowe	Match
1	23 Aug	H	**Plymouth Argyle**	W	6 1	(1 0)	52,642		Bentley, Pearson, Shackleton 2, Walker, Wayman	1	2	3	4	5	6	7	8	9	10	11																	1
2	27 Aug	A	Chesterfield	W	1 0	(0 0)	20,159		Wayman	1	2	3	4	5	6		8	9	10	11	7																2
3	30 Aug	A	Luton Town	L	1 2	(1 2)	26,000	5	Bentley	1	2	3	4	5	6		8	9	10	11	7																3
4	03 Sep	H	**Chesterfield**	L	2 3	(2 1)	58,334	11	Bentley, Milburn	1	2	3		5	6		10	9	8	11	7	4															4
5	06 Sep	H	**Brentford**	W	1 0	(0 0)	56,622	9	Woodburn	1				5	6		8			11	7		2	3	4	9	10										5
6	10 Sep	A	Birmingham City	D	0 0	(0 0)	51,704			1		3	4	5	6	7	8						2				10	9	11								6
7	13 Sep	A	Leicester City	D	2 2	(2 2)	35,472	7	Donaldson, Shackleton	1		3	4	5	6	7	8		10				2					9	11								7
8	17 Sep	H	**Birmingham City**	W	1 0	(0 0)	51,704	4	Hair				4	5	6		8	9	10		7		2	3					11	1							8
9	20 Sep	H	**Leeds United**	W	4 2	(1 1)	57,275	3	Hair, Shackleton 2, Stobbart				4	5	6		8		10		7		2	3		9			11	1							9
10	27 Sep	A	Fulham	L	0 3	(0 2)	41,264	5					4	5	6		8		10		7		2	3		9			11	1							10
11	04 Oct	H	**Coventry City**	D	0 0	(0 0)	55,569	6				3	4	5			8	9	10		7	6			2				11	1							11
12	11 Oct	H	**West Ham United**	W	1 0	(1 0)	55,767	4	Milburn			3	4	5		7			10	11	8	6			2			9		1							12
13	18 Oct	A	Bury	W	5 3	(2 1)	23,827	4	Milburn 3, Shackleton, og (Bickerstaffe)	1		3	4	5		7			8	11	9	6			2	10											13
14	25 Oct	H	**Southampton**	W	5 0	(2 0)	57,184	3	Milburn, Pearson, Stobbart, Walker 2	1		3	4	5		7			8	11	9	6			2	10											14
15	01 Nov	A	Doncaster Rovers	W	3 0	(1 0)	28,340	2	Harvey, Milburn 2	1		3	4	5					8	11	9	6			2	10					7						15
16	08 Nov	H	**Nottingham Forest**	L	0 2	(0 2)	60,244	3		1		3	4	5			10		8	11	9	6			2	7											16
17	15 Nov	A	Bradford Park Avenue	W	3 0	(3 0)	24,654	3	Stobbart, Sibley, og (White)	1		3	4	5					8	11	9	6			2	10					7						17
18	22 Nov	H	**Cardiff City**	W	4 1	(2 1)	56,904	3	Milburn 2, Shackleton, Stobbart	1		3	4	5					8	11	9	6			2	10					7						18
19	29 Nov	A	Sheffield Wednesday	L	0 1	(0 0)	41,355	4		1		3	4	5					8	11	9	6			2	10					7						19
20	06 Dec	H	**Tottenham Hotspur**	W	1 0	(1 0)	57,950	3	Milburn	1		3	4	5					8	11	9	6			2	10					7						20
21	13 Dec	A*	Millwall	L	1 2	(1 1)	33,362	3	Pearson	1	3		4	5					8	11	9	6			2	10					7						21
22	20 Dec	A	Plymouth Argyle	L	0 3	(0 1)	27,069	3		1	3		4	5					8	11	9	6			2	10					7						22
23	26 Dec	A	West Bromwich Albion	W	1 0	(0 0)	48,322		og (Millard)	1	3		4	5					10	11	9	6			2	8					7						23
24	01 Jan	H	**West Bromwich Albion**	W	3 1	(0 0)	61,301	2	Dodgin, Milburn 2	1	3		4	5					10	11	9	6			2	8					7						24
25	03 Jan	H	**Luton Town**	W	4 1	(2 1)	64,931	2	Milburn 3, Stobbart	1	3		4	5					10	11	9	6			2	8					7						25
26	17 Jan	A	Brentford	L	0 1	(0 1)	29,684	2			3		4	5					10	11	9	6			2	8				1		7					26
27	24 Jan	A	Leeds United	L	1 3	(1 2)	30,367	2	Milburn		3		4	5					8	11	9	6			2	10				1		7					27
28	31 Jan	H	**Leicester City**	W	2 0	(2 0)	51,675	2	McCall, Sibley		3		8	5	6						10				2			9		1	7	11	4				28
29	21 Feb	A	Coventry City	D	1 1	(0 1)	22,047	3	McCall (pen)		3		4	5							9				2		10			1	7	11	6	8			29
30	28 Feb	A	West Ham United	W	2 0	(0 0)	30,000	3	Milburn, Thompson		3		4	5							9		2				10			1	7	11	6	8			30
31	06 Mar	H	**Bury**	W	1 0	(0 0)	56,444	3	Milburn		3		4	5							9		2				10			1	7	11	6	8			31
32	13 Mar	A	Southampton	L	2 4	(0 3)	26,780	3	Milburn, Sibley		3		4	5							8		2				10			1	7	11	6		9		32
33	20 Mar	H	**Doncaster Rovers**	W	2 0	(1 0)	48,724	3	Lowrie, Thompson		3		4	5							7		2				10			1		11	6	8	9		33
34	26 Mar	H	**Barnsley**	W	1 0	(1 0)	64,757	3	McCall		3		4	5							10		2			8				1	7	11	6		9		34
35	27 Mar	A	Nottingham Forest	D	0 0	(0 0)	28,856	3			3			5							7	4	2			8	10			1		11	6		9		35
36	29 Mar	A	Barnsley	D	1 1	(1 0)	30,247	2	McCall		3			5							8	4	2					9		1		11	7		10	6	36
37	03 Apr	H	**Bradford Park Avenue**	W	2 0	(2 0)	50,367	2	Stobbart, Woodburn		3			5	10						9	4	2			8				1		11	7			6	37
38	10 Apr	A	Cardiff City	D	1 1	(1 0)	49,209	2	Stobbart	1	3		4	5	10						9	6	2			8						11	7				38
39	14 Apr	H	**Fulham**	W	1 0	(0 0)	54,061	2	Stobbart (pen)	1	3		4	5	10						9	6	2			8						11	7				39
40	17 Apr	H	**Sheffield Wednesday**	W	4 2	(1 1)	66,483	2	Harvey, Houghton 2, Stobbart	1	3		4	5	10	11					9	6	2			8							7				40
41	24 Apr	A	Tottenham Hotspur	D	1 1	(0 1)	44,164	2	Sibley	1	3		4	5	10	11					9	6	2			8					7						41
42	01 May	H	**Millwall**	W	1 0	(1 0)	43,328	2	Harvey	1	3		4	5	10						9	6	2			8					7	11					42
Round			FA Cup																																		Round
3	10 Jan	A	Charlton Athletic	L	1 2	(1 1)	53,428		Pearson	1	3		4	5					10	11	9	6			2	8					7						3

A* Played at Selhurst Park, London

DateLine ... 22 Nov: Jack Milburn scores in around ten seconds of the game with Cardiff City, the quickest until 2003. **17 March:** A gate of 64,938 are at St James' Park for the 1-1 draw between the Football League and Scottish League. **17 April:** United clinch promotion with two late goals in a thrilling 4-2 win over Sheffield Wednesday. **1 May:** United's last home gate of the season creates a record average attendance of over 56,000.

SEASON 1948-49

DIVISION 1

United go close to Championship silver

Newcastle United were now on a roll. Momentum was kept going as United romped to the top placings in the First Division as crowds continued to pack St James' Park. A substantial sum of £55,000 was spent during the season on George Robledo (together with his brother Ted), Colin Gibson and Bobby Mitchell. Only a handful of clubs then had that purchasing power. Although Welsh international Gibson was dogged by injury, George Robledo and Mitchell proved to be exceptional buys – and probably turned a good side into a trophy winning one.

There was no time for steady consolidation; United challenged forcefully for the Football League Championship with six wins in a row during the autumn. They went to the top after a 1-0 victory over Everton just before Christmas and became a big attraction around the country. A gate of 70,787 saw the fixture with Manchester United played at Maine Road (due to war repairs to Old Trafford).

Surprisingly knocked out of the FA Cup by Second Division Bradford Park Avenue, the race for the title was between United and Portsmouth. During April a near decisive confrontation took place on Tyneside. Pompey arrived at St James' Park with the aim of heading south unbeaten. They did that all right, but also gave United a lesson, by netting five goals, all scored by wingers Froggatt and Harris. Over 60,000 at Gallowgate were stunned to silence. United's challenge faded and they slipped from second place – in the end disappointingly – to fourth position.

At the close of the season the club headed off on a milestone tour of North America, United's first voyage out of Europe. Their exhibition trek lasted some six weeks during which they both spread the game of football and the prestige of Newcastle United. They were back in time for another crack at Portsmouth – and the title trophy.

Pictured above: Ron Batty was a tough competitor, at St James' Park for almost 13 years.

Memorabilia CORNER

A restyling of United's programme with a rather accurate sketch of St James' Park at the time.

IN CHARGE

Chairman: George Rutherford
Manager: George Martin
Captain: Joe Harvey
Trainer/Coach: Norman Smith

ST JAMES' PARK

Average Attendance
Lg 54,011 Lg & Cup 53,701

A return to the top flight for the Magpies. Back row, left to right: Thompson, Harvey, Cowell, Fairbrother, Craig, Dodgin, Smith (trainer). Front: Gibson, Stobbart, Donaldson (A), Martin (manager), Milburn, Walker, Brennan.

SEASON REVIEW

Football League Div 1: P42 W20 D12 L10 F70 A56 Pts 52.
Position: 4th (Champions; Portsmouth).
FA Cup: R3 (Winners; Wolverhampton Wanderers).

Appearances (43m): Brennan F 42, Dodgin N 42, Fairbrother J 42, Cowell RG 39, Harvey Jos 39, Milburn JET 35, Batty RR 31, Taylor E 29, Gibson CH 24, Stobbart GC 24, Walker TJ 22, Hair G 15, Robledo GO 15, Donaldson A 13, Mitchell RC 13, Craig B 10, Thompson T 10, Sibley A 8, Houghton FC 6, Graham D 4, Lowrie G 4, Fraser R 3, Clark AH 1, Garbutt EJE 1, McCall W 1.

Goals (70g): Milburn JET 19, Robledo GO 6, Donaldson A 5, Gibson CH 5, Stobbart GC 5, Walker TJ 5, Hair G 4, Lowrie G 3, Mitchell RC 3, Taylor E 3, Harvey Jos 2, Sibley A 2, Houghton FC 1, Thompson T 1, own goals 6.

Dismissals: 0 players.

MAJOR SIGNINGS

Bobby Mitchell (Third Lanark) £17,000
Colin Gibson (Cardiff City) £15,000
George & Ted Robledo (Barnsley) £23,000 (joint fee)

FROM THE RANKS

Ron Batty (East Tanfield CW)
Albert Clark (North Shields)

PLAYER FOCUS Frank Brennan

Born Annathill. Centre-half, 6'3"
1946 to 1956: 349 app 3 goals.

When United purchased 6'3" tall Frank Brennan from Airdrie for a £7,500 fee during May 1946, the club needed a powerful central defender they could build a defence around. Brennan fitted the bill perfectly. Having recently impressed for the Scotland national side against England's Tommy Lawton, he showed he could handle the best strikers in the business. Brennan was a no-nonsense centre-half; he was tough, strong and cleared the ball positively and with distance either by head or his size 12 boots. At the core of United's great Fifties combination, along with Joe Harvey, Bobby Mitchell and Jack Milburn, Frank became something of a cult figure on Tyneside. The granite Scot helped United to promotion in 1948 and was an influence in both FA Cup victories of 1951 and 1952 when he commanded the defence with mean authority. Immensely popular with Newcastle's crowd, Brennan then ran into dispute with the club's hierarchy during 1955 and his career as a top defender was all but over. Many judges at the time considered he was treated badly by the club in days of a dictatorial master, but after Player's Union and even TUC involvement, Frank was forced out of Gallowgate in March 1956 when aged nearly 32 to the non-league scene with North Shields. He later returned to Wembley when the Scot guided Shields to FA Amateur Cup victory as manager in 1969. He also had a brief spell as Darlington boss and coached around the world as part of the British Council organisation.

TEAM COLOURS Black & white striped shirts, black shorts (Change; white shirts, black shorts)

Match	Date		FL Division 1		Score	HT	Att	Posn	Scorers	Fairbrother	Fraser	Craig	Harvey	Brennan	Dodgin	Gibson	Taylor	Milburn	Lowrie	Walker	Cowell	Sibley	Donaldson	Stobbart	McCall	Thompson	Batty	Hair	Garbutt	Clark	Houghton	Robledo GO	Mitchell	Graham	Match
1	21 Aug	A	Everton	D	3 3	(2 2)	57,279		Walker, Lowrie 2	1	2	3	4	5	6	7	8	9	10	11															1
2	25 Aug	H	**Chelsea**	D	2 2	(1 1)	59,020		Lowrie, Milburn	1	2	3	4	5	6	7	8	9	10	11															2
3	28 Aug	H	**Preston North End**	L	2 5	(1 3)	63,549	15	Donaldson, Stobbart	1	5	3	4		6	8					2	7	9	10	11										3
4	01 Sep	A	Chelsea	W	3 2	(1 0)	43,840		Gibson, Milburn, Thompson	1		3	4	5	6	7		10		11	2		9			8									4
5	04 Sep	A	Burnley	W	3 0	(2 0)	32,947	7	Donaldson 2, Milburn	1		3	4	5	6	7		10		11	2		9			8									5
6	08 Sep	H	**Aston Villa**	W	2 1	(1 1)	56,110	5	Gibson, Milburn	1		3	4	5	6	7		10		11	2		9			8									6
7	11 Sep	H	**Stoke City**	D	2 2	(0 1)	59,265	5	Walker, Donaldson (pen)	1		3	4	5	6	7		10		11	2		9			8									7
8	13 Sep	A	Aston Villa	W	4 2	(2 1)	35,824	5	Donaldson, Gibson, Milburn, Walker	1		3	4	5	6	7		10		11	2		9	8											8
9	18 Sep	A	Charlton Athletic	D	0 0	(0 0)	56,711	5		1		3	4	5	6	7		10		11	2		9	8											9
10	25 Sep	H	**Manchester City**	D	0 0	(0 0)	49,729	5		1		3	4	5	6	7				11	2		9	10		8									10
11	02 Oct	A	Portsmouth	L	0 1	(0 0)	45,827	6		1			4	5	6			10		11	2	7	9	8			3								11
12	09 Oct	A	Sunderland	D	1 1	(1 1)	51,399	8	Hair	1			4	5	6	8	10				2	7	9				3	11							12
13	16 Oct	H	**Wolverhampton Wanderers**	W	3 1	(1 1)	60,958	6	Milburn 2, og (McLean)	1			4	5	6	8	10	9			2	7					3	11							13
14	23 Oct	A	Bolton Wanderers	W	5 1	(2 0)	39,071	3	Gibson 2, Milburn, Sibley, Taylor	1			4	5	6	8	10	9			2	7					3	11							14
15	30 Oct	H	**Liverpool**	W	1 0	(1 0)	67,362	3	Milburn	1			4	5	6	8	10	9			2	7					3	11							15
16	06 Nov	A	Blackpool	W	3 1	(1 0)	30,676	3	Hair,Stobbart, og (Crosland)	1			4	5	6	8	10	9			2			7			3	11							16
17	13 Nov	H	**Derby County**	W	3 0	(0 0)	64,061	3	Hair, Milburn, Stobbart	1			4	5	6	8	10	9			2			7			3	11							17
18	20 Nov	A	Arsenal	W	1 0	(0 0)	62,000	2	og (Mercer)	1			4	5	6	8	10	9			2			7			3	11							18
19	27 Nov	H	**Huddersfield Town**	L	2 4	(2 4)	49,332	3	Hair, Milburn	1			4	5	6	8	10	9			2			7			3	11							19
20	04 Dec	A*	Manchester United	D	1 1	(1 0)	70,787	3	Stobbart	1			4	5	6	8	10				2		9	7			3	11							20
21	11 Dec	H	**Sheffield United**	W	3 2	(2 1)	42,862	2	Milburn, Stobbart, og (Cox)					5	6	8	10	9			2			7			3	11	1	4					21
22	18 Dec	H	**Everton**	W	1 0	(0 0)	43,515	1	Taylor	1			4	5	6	8	10	9			2			7			3	11							22
23	25 Dec	A	Birmingham City	L	0 2	(0 1)	42,000	2		1			4	5	6		10	8		7	2		9				3	11							23
24	27 Dec	H	**Birmingham City**	W	1 0	(0 0)	49,457	2	Milburn	1			4	5	6		10	9			2			7		8	3	11							24
25	01 Jan	A	Preston North End	L	1 2	(0 1)	39,428	2	Taylor	1			4	5	6		10	9			2			7		8	3	11							25
26	15 Jan	H	**Burnley**	D	1 1	(0 1)	33,439	2	Houghton	1			4	5	6	7		10		11	2		9				3				8				26
27	22 Jan	A	Stoke City	D	1 1	(1 0)	39,777	2	Milburn	1			4	5	6	7	10	11			2			9			3				8				27
28	05 Feb	H	**Charlton Athletic**	W	2 0	(1 0)	56,143	2	Walker 2	1			4	5	6		10	9		11	2			7			3					8			28
29	19 Feb	A	Manchester City	L	0 1	(0 0)	48,624	2		1			4	5	6		10	7		11	2			8			3					9			29
30	05 Mar	H	**Sunderland**	W	2 1	(0 1)	58,250	2	Milburn, Robledo	1			4	5	6			9	10	7	2						3					8	11		30
31	12 Mar	A	Wolverhampton Wanderers	L	0 3	(0 0)	41,152	2		1			4	5					10	7	2			9			3				6	8	11		31
32	19 Mar	H	**Arsenal**	W	3 2	(2 2)	55,248	2	Harvey, Mitchell, Robledo	1			4	5	6		10	9		7	2						3					8	11		32
33	26 Mar	A	Huddersfield Town	W	2 0	(2 0)	25,745	2	og 2 (Hepplewhite, Stewart)	1			4	5	6		10	9		7	2						3					8	11		33
34	02 Apr	H	**Blackpool**	W	3 1	(2 1)	62,672	2	Milburn 2, Robledo	1			4	5	6		10	9		7	2						3					8	11		34
35	06 Apr	H	**Portsmouth**	L	0 5	(0 3)	60,611	2		1			4	5	6		10			7	2			9			3					8	11		35
36	09 Apr	A	Derby County	W	4 2	(1 2)	24,076	2	Harvey, Robledo 2, Sibley	1			4	5	6		10				2	7		9			3					8	11		36
37	15 Apr	H	**Middlesbrough**	W	1 0	(0 0)	64,381	2	Milburn	1			4	5	6		10	9			2	7					3					8	11		37
38	16 Apr	H	**Bolton Wanderers**	D	1 1	(0 1)	39,999	2	Robledo	1			4	5	6		10	9			2			7			3					8	11		38
39	18 Apr	A	Middlesbrough	L	2 3	(2 1)	44,037	2	Milburn, Mitchell	1			4	5	6		10	9						7			3					8	11	2	39
40	23 Apr	A	Liverpool	D	1 1	(0 0)	43,488	2	Mitchell	1				5	6		10	9								7	3				4	8	11	2	40
41	30 Apr	H	**Manchester United**	L	0 1	(0 0)	38,266	4		1				5	6			9		7	2					10					4	8	11	3	41
42	07 May	A	Sheffield United	D	0 0	(0 0)	43,107	4		1				5	6					7	2			9		10					4	8	11	3	42
Round			FA Cup																																Round
3	08 Jan	H	**Bradford Park Avenue**	L	0 2	(0 1)	47,196			1			4	5	6	8	10	9			2			7			3	11							3

A* Played at Maine Road, Manchester

DateLine ... 4 Dec: A crowd of 70,787 at Maine Road watch the fixture with Manchester United. **6 April:** A crucial title chasing clash with Portsmouth ends in five headed goals and a 5-0 victory for Pompey. **1 June:** Newcastle defeat Alberta All Stars 16-2 on tour in North America.

NEWCASTLE UNITED

SEASON 1949-50
DIVISION 1

A late title bid, another close miss

As the 1940s came to a close and the game was to explode into the fabulous Fifties era, Champions Portsmouth possessed a terrific line-up, a team at its peak, and including gritty Scot Jimmy Scoular – to later join United – at its heart. They were again the line-up to beat in the Championship race during 1949-50, and once more United pressed the Fratton Park club hard in a tight table – three points eventually separating the top five clubs. Desperate to lift a trophy, the Magpies started badly though. They lost their opening three games, including a first day reverse at St James' Park to Pompey, and slipped to the wrong end of the division.

Results improved although inconsistency was a thorn, and a double festive defeat by Middlesbrough did not help confidence. A seven goal spree against Oldham in the FA Cup restored some faith but then they were knocked out convincingly by Chelsea in Round Four. Undoubtedly United took time to recover from the long tour of America.

But they started to click after their Cup exit with the strike pairing of Milburn and Robledo served to almost perfection by wingers Mitchell and Tommy Walker, as well as the slight frame of 5'4" Ernie Taylor in midfield. Newcastle raced up the table with a sequence of good results during April and May. The Geordies picked up full points in six of their eight matches played including a 5-1 victory over Liverpool and they had Portsmouth in their sights again. But the Magpies' surge was too late and they ran out of games, reaching fifth spot. Had that form been half as good in the opening months of the season that narrow three point difference could well have been made up. The title silverware headed back to Fratton Park and United had to wait for another season to land a trophy. But this time they were to bring silver back to Tyneside.

Pictured above: Jack Fairbrother held the 'keeper's jersey as United became a top side in the country.

Memorabilia CORNER

Match programme for the Tyne v Wear clash which attracted almost 58,000 to Gallowgate.

IN CHARGE

Chairman: George Rutherford/John Lee
Manager: George Martin
Captain: Joe Harvey
Trainer/Coach: Norman Smith

ST JAMES' PARK

Average Attendance
Lg 46,456 Lg & Cup 46,456

By 1949 the Magpies were fast becoming a top side. Back row, left to right: Cowell, Harvey, Fairbrother, McNeil, McMichael, Crowe. Front: Mitchell, Walker, Taylor, Milburn, Robledo (G).

SEASON REVIEW

Football League Div 1: P42 W19 D12 L11 F77 A55 Pts 50.
Position: 5th (Champions; Portsmouth).
FA Cup: R4 (Winners; Arsenal).

Appearances (44m): Brennan F 43, Mitchell RC 40, Walker TJ 40, Houghton FC 34, Milburn JET 32, Robledo GO 32, Crowe CA 28, Hannah GL 27, Fairbrother J 24, Harvey Jos 22, Taylor E 22, Batty RR 20, Cowell RG 20, Dodgin N 17, Graham D 17, Garbutt EJE 15, Corbett R 13, McMichael A 11, Craig B 7, Thompson T 6, Lowery J 5, Lowrie G 3, Sibley A 3, Graver AM 1, Robledo EO 1, Smith T 1.

Goals (84g): Milburn JET 21, Walker TJ 13, Robledo GO 11, Mitchell RC 9, Hannah GL 7, Houghton FC 7, Taylor E 7, Thompson T 3, Corbett R 1, Harvey Jos 1, Lowrie G 1, own goals 3.

Dismissals: 1 player; Lowrie.

MAJOR SIGNINGS

Matt McNeil (Hibernian) £6,400
Alf McMichael & George Hannah (Linfield) £23,000 (joint fee)

FROM THE RANKS

Andy Graver (Annfield Plain)
Jerry Lowery (CA Parsons Ath)

PLAYER FOCUS Tommy Walker

Born Cramlington. Outside-right, 5'10"
1941 to 1954: 235 app 39 goals.

A consistent performer at outside-right for the Magpies, Tommy Walker's more direct style was a significant contrast to the tricky Bobby Mitchell on the opposite flank in United's celebrated line-up of the time. Extremely quick – taking part in race meetings at the noted Powderhall event – and always able to strike the net, Walker landed at Gallowgate in October 1941 having been spotted appearing for the local Netherton junior side. Walker was one of an eager group of several forwards to challenge for places during the war years, making an impression on both flanks and at inside-forward to start with. After finding a slot in 1948-49 he became a regular in the number seven shirt over the next four seasons. He often picked up the ball in a deep position, then would storm forward down his flank using his sprinting ability to good effect. Tommy won two FA Cup winners' medals with the Geordies in 1951 and 1952 when his direct thrusts at the heart of opponent's back-lines caused bedlam and goal opportunities on many occasions. Included was one special moment when a characteristic penetrating run in the final against Blackpool led to a Milburn's spectacular strike which won the trophy. During February 1954, when over 30 years old, he was transferred to Oldham Athletic for a £2,500 fee. Walker also appeared in the lower divisions for Chesterfield before he retired. His grandson was in United's junior ranks during the late 1990s.

TEAM COLOURS Black & white striped shirts, black shorts (Change; white shirts, black shorts)

SEASON 1949-50

Match	Date	Venue	FL Division 1	Result	HT	Att	Posn	Goalscorers	Fairbrother	Craig	Batty	Houghton	Brennan	Dodgin	Walker	Robledo GO	Milburn	Lowrie	Mitchell	Taylor	Garbutt	Graham	McMichael	Harvey	Hannah	Cowell	Crowe	Thompson	Smith	Sibley	Robledo EO	Graver	Corbett	Lowery	Match
1	20 Aug	H	**Portsmouth**	L 1 3	(0 2)	54,258		Robledo G	1	2	3	4	5	6	7	8	9	10	11																1
2	24 Aug	A	Everton	L 1 2	(1 1)	49,504		Lowrie	1	2	3	4	5	6	7	8	9	10	11																2
3	27 Aug	A	Wolverhampton Wanderers	L 1 2	(1 0)	50,922	21	Milburn	1	2	3	4	5	6	7	8	9	10d	11																3
4	31 Aug	H	**Everton**	W 4 0	(2 0)	42,689	17	Milburn, Mitchell, Robledo G, Walker	1	2	3	4	5	6	7	8	9		11	10															4
5	03 Sep	H	**Aston Villa**	W 3 2	(2 1)	57,669	13	Milburn 3 (1pen)	1	2	3	4	5	6	7	8	9		11	10															5
6	05 Sep	A	Blackpool	D 0 0	(0 0)	27,182	12		1	2	3	4	5	6	7	8	9		11	10															6
7	10 Sep	A	Charlton Athletic	L 3 6	(0 3)	40,582	17	Milburn 2, Mitchell	1	2	3	4	5	6	7	8	9		11	10															7
8	17 Sep	H	**Manchester City**	W 4 2	(2 1)	58,141	15	Hannah, Milburn, Robledo G, Walker					5	6	7	8	9		11		1	2	3	4	10										8
9	24 Sep	A	Fulham	L 1 2	(1 0)	40,000	17	Milburn (pen)					5	6	7	8	9		11		1	2	3	4	10										9
10	01 Oct	H	**Stoke City**	W 4 1	(2 0)	49,903	13	Houghton 2, Milburn, Thompson			3	10	5		7		9		11		1			4		2	6	8							10
11	08 Oct	A	Burnley	W 2 1	(1 0)	37,319	9	Harvey, Walker				10	5		7		9		11		1		3	4		2	6	8							11
12	15 Oct	H	**Sunderland**	D 2 2	(2 1)	57,999	10	Robledo G, Walker				10	5		7	9			11		1		3	4		2	6	8							12
13	22 Oct	A	Liverpool	D 2 2	(2 1)	48,987	11	Mitchell, Thompson					5		7	9			11		1		3	4	10	2	6	8							13
14	29 Oct	H	**Arsenal**	L 0 3	(0 1)	54,670	14					10	5		7	9			11		1		3	4		2	6	8							14
15	05 Nov	A	Bolton Wanderers	D 2 2	(1 1)	31,728	12	Milburn, Taylor				4			11	9	7			8	1	2	3		10		6		5						15
16	12 Nov	H	**Birmingham City**	W 3 1	(2 1)	30,113	10	Robledo G 2, og (Harris)				4	5		11	10	9			8	1	2	3				6			7					16
	19 Nov	A	Derby County	Ab 0 1	(0 1)	29,973					3	8	5	4	7	9				10	1	2					6			11					
17	26 Nov	H	**West Bromwich Albion**	W 5 1	(4 1)	32,415	10	Houghton, Milburn 2, Robledo G, Walker			3	8	5	4	7	10	9		11		1	2					6								17
18	03 Dec	A	Manchester United	D 1 1	(1 1)	30,343	10	Walker			3	8	5	4	7	10	9		11		1	2					6								18
19	10 Dec	H	**Chelsea**	D 2 2	(0 1)	43,239	10	Milburn, Mitchell			3	8	5	4	7	10	9		11		1	2					6								19
20	17 Dec	A	Portsmouth	L 0 1	(0 1)	30,455	13				3	8	5	4	7	10	9		11		1	2					6								20
21	24 Dec	H	**Wolverhampton Wanderers**	W 2 0	(1 0)	56,048		Taylor, og (McLean)			3		5	4		9	7		11	8	1	2			10		6								21
22	26 Dec	H	**Middlesbrough**	L 0 1	(0 1)	61,184					3		5	4		9	7		11	8	1	2			10		6								22
23	27 Dec	A	Middlesbrough	L 0 1	(0 0)	53,802	15		1		3		5	4		9	7		11	8		2			10		6								23
24	31 Dec	A	Aston Villa	W 1 0	(1 0)	39,803	12	Hannah	1		3	4	5			8	9		11			2			10					7	6				24
25	14 Jan	H	**Charlton Athletic**	W 1 0	(0 0)	48,557		Robledo G	1		3	4	5		7	8	9		11			2			10		6								25
26	21 Jan	A	Manchester City	D 1 1	(0 0)	42,986	11	Hannah	1		3	4	5		7	8			11			2			10		6					9			26
27	04 Feb	H	**Fulham**	W 3 1	(0 1)	41,120		Hannah, Robledo G, Thompson	1				5	6	11	9	7					2	3	4	10			8							27
28	18 Feb	A	Stoke City	L 0 1	(0 0)	31,473	12		1				5		7	9			11	8				4	10	2	6						3		28
29	25 Feb	H	**Burnley**	D 0 0	(0 0)	30,032	12		1			9	5		7	8			11					4	10	2	6						3		29
30	04 Mar	A	Sunderland	D 2 2	(2 1)	68,004	11	Houghton, Taylor	1			9	5		7				11	8				4	10	2	6						3		30
31	11 Mar	H	**Derby County**	W 2 1	(2 0)	40,784	10	Mitchell, Corbett (pen)	1			9	5		7				11	8				4	10	2	6						3		31
32	18 Mar	A	West Bromwich Albion	D 1 1	(0 1)	33,469	10	Houghton	1			9	5		7				11	8				4	10	2	6						3		32
33	25 Mar	H	**Bolton Wanderers**	W 3 1	(1 1)	33,752	9	Houghton, Mitchell, Taylor	1			9	5		7				11	8				4	10	2	6						3		33
34	29 Mar	A	Derby County	D 1 1	(0 1)	16,029	9	Hannah	1			8	5		7		9		11					4	10	2	6						3		34
35	01 Apr	A	Birmingham City	W 2 0	(0 0)	37,249	8	Taylor, Walker	1				5		7		9		11	8				4	10	2	6						3		35
36	07 Apr	H	**Huddersfield Town**	D 0 0	(0 0)	46,886	8		1				5		7		9		11	8				4	10	2	6						3		36
37	08 Apr	H	**Liverpool**	W 5 1	(2 1)	48,639	7	Hannah, Mitchell 2, Taylor, Walker	1			6	5		7		9		11	8				4	10	2							3		37
38	11 Apr	A*	Huddersfield Town	W 2 1	(0 1)	37,700	7	Houghton, Robledo G				6	5		11	9				8				4	10	2				7			3	1	38
39	15 Apr	A	Arsenal	L 2 4	(2 2)	51,997	7	Hannah, Robledo G				6	5		7	9			11	8				4	10	2							3	1	39
40	22 Apr	H	**Manchester United**	W 2 1	(0 0)	52,203	7	Milburn, Walker				6	5		7		9		11	8				4	10	2							3	1	40
41	29 Apr	A	Chelsea	W 3 1	(2 0)	24,667	6	Milburn, Walker 2				4	5		7	10	9		11	8			3			2	6							1	41
42	06 May	H	**Blackpool**	W 3 0	(1 0)	35,274	5	Milburn 2, Taylor				6	5		7		9		11	8			3	4	10	2								1	42
Round			FA Cup																																Round
3	07 Jan	A	Oldham Athletic	W 7 2	(3 1)	41,706		Milburn 3, Mitchell, Walker 2, og (McCormack)	1		3	4	5		7	8	9		11			2			10		6								3
4	28 Jan	A	Chelsea	L 0 3	(0 2)	64,446			1		3	4	5		7	8	9		11			2			10		6								4

Ab Abandoned after 75mins due to fog

A* Played at Elland Road, Leeds

DateLine ...15 Oct: Jack Milburn grabs a hat-trick for England against Wales at Cardiff. **31 Dec:** Brothers George and Ted Robledo play in the same line-up for the first time against Aston Villa. **4 March:** The Newcastle and Sunderland clash is watched by 68,004 at Roker Park, the largest ever derby attendance.

NEWCASTLE UNITED

SEASON 1950-51
DIVISION 1

FA Cup magic at Wembley

Season 1950-51 was the year a trophy ended back in the St James' Park Boardroom, 19 years since United's victory in the 1932 FA Cup final. Many judges noted the Magpies should have in reality done better – and even lifted the double, so good was their side that season. Despite losing manager George Martin to Aston Villa, in League action the Tynesiders led the pack early on, then relinquished control to Arsenal and afterwards Tottenham. But the Black'n'Whites hung close to the London pair, although Spurs did give United a hiding at White Hart Lane, losing by seven goals during November. However by the time the FA Cup was in full swing, Newcastle's focus was elsewhere never really making a sustained push to close the gap. They finished in fourth place only picking up a single victory in a run of 11 fixtures.

With Stan Seymour back at the forefront of United's team plans, a pulsating run to Wembley began with an easy win against Bury followed by an awe-inspiring tie against Bolton Wanderers. United were 2-1 behind with time fast running out. A famous fight-back was launched and the Magpies won 3-2 with two late goals in front of a new record Gallowgate FA Cup crowd of 67,596. Stoke City and Bristol Rovers were then dispatched, although not until Rovers had battled with classic FA Cup spirit to hold United at St James' Park to a goalless draw.

Newcastle went onto meet Wolves in a tough semi-final before facing Blackpool in the final – a side to boast both Stanley Mathews and Geordie Stan Mortensen in their ranks. The final belonged to neither of Blackpool's stars though, rather to United's own hero Jackie Milburn. He scored two breathtaking goals within five minutes of the second half to give United a 2-0 victory. It was a deserved triumph and an estimated 200,000 welcomed United home with the trophy.

Pictured above: Bobby Corbett was one of several home-grown full-backs to wear United's colours with credit.

Memorabilia CORNER

FA Cup final match programme for the tie with Blackpool at Wembley.

IN CHARGE

Chairman: John Lee
Manager: George Martin/Stan Seymour/Director Committee
Captain: Joe Harvey
Trainer/Coach: Norman Smith

ST JAMES' PARK

Average Attendance
Lg 46,670 Lg & Cup 47,692

Tyneside's FA Cup heroes in 1951. Back row, left to right: Cowell, Milburn, Fairbrother, Robledo (G), Corbett, Crowe. Front: Walker, Taylor, GS Seymour (director), Harvey, Smith (trainer), Brennan, Mitchell.

PLAYER FOCUS Jackie Milburn

Born Ashington. Centre-forward, 5'11"
1943 to 1957: 494 app 239 goals.

The Geordies' folk-hero during the Fifties, Wor Jackie Milburn scored three goals in a trio of FA Cup triumphs at Wembley to be heralded like few before or since in the region. Included was a special double strike against Blackpool in the 1951 final while in 1955 Milburn headed, what was then, the quickest goal in a Wembley final – after only 45 seconds. From the illustrious Ashington Milburn and Charlton footballing clan, he impressed a drooling Stan Seymour in a public trial during August 1943 and was immediately blooded in the first eleven. A left winger at first, Milburn was a versatile forward and became something of a reluctant centre-forward when handed the shirt in 1948 as United won promotion. Yet he was a huge success in the role, possessing sprinter's pace – appropriately with the initials of JET – and a thundering drive. He could swivel and shoot in tight situations and possessed fantastic control of the ball when running at speed. Capped by England on 13 occasions, Jackie featured in United's team for 14 seasons until he moved to Linfield as player-boss in June 1957. After a short spell in charge at Ipswich Town, Milburn later returned to his native North East becoming a respected journalist. Earning the Freedom of the City, a statue of Jackie stands close to United's stadium, while at St James' Park the Milburn Stand is an everlasting memory of one of the club's greatest and much loved players. Only Alan Shearer has scored more than Jackie's 200 League and Cup goals for the Magpies, while no-one can better his overall total.

SEASON REVIEW

Football League Div 1: P42 W18 D13 L11 F62 A53 Pts 49.
Position: 4th (Champions; Tottenham Hotspur).
FA Cup: Winners.

Appearances (50m): Cowell RG 50, Fairbrother J 50, Walker TJ 50, Mitchell RC 48, Taylor E 48, Robledo GO 46, Harvey Jos 44, Crowe CA 43, Milburn JET 39, Brennan F 38, Corbett R 25, McMichael A 23, Hannah GL 13, McNeil MA 11, Stokoe R 9, Houghton FC 4, Robledo EO 4, Batty RR 3, Graham D 1, Paterson TA 1.

Goals (80g): Milburn JET 25, Robledo GO 17, Mitchell RC 10, Taylor E 10, Walker TJ 10, Hannah GL 2, Brennan F 1, Crowe CA 1, Harvey Jos 1, Stokoe R 1, own goals 2.

Dismissals: 0 players.

MAJOR SIGNINGS

Ronnie Simpson (Third Lanark) £8,750
Reg Davies (Southend Utd) £9,000
John Duncan (Ayr Utd) £8,250
Tom Paterson (Leicester City) £2,500

FROM THE RANKS

Bob Stokoe (Spen Jnrs)

TEAM COLOURS Black & white striped shirts, black shorts (Change; white shirts, black shorts)

SEASON 1950-51

Match	Date		FL Division 1					Att	Posn	Scorers	Fairbrother	Cowell	McMichael	Harvey	Brennan	Houghton	Walker	Taylor	Milburn	Hannah	Mitchell	Robledo GO	Crowe	Graham	Corbett	Batty	McNeil	Stokoe	Paterson	Robledo EO	Match
1	19 Aug	A	Stoke City	W	2	1	(1 0)	28,547		Milburn 2 (1 pen)	1	2	3	4	5	6	7	8	9	10	11										1
2	23 Aug	H	**West Bromwich Albion**	D	1	1	(0 1)	48,720		Brennan	1	2	3	4	5	6	7	8	9		11	10									2
3	26 Aug	H	**Everton**	D	1	1	(0 0)	49,096		Taylor	1	2	3	4	5	6	7	8	9		11	10									3
4	30 Aug	A	West Bromwich Albion	W	2	1	(1 1)	29,377	3	Milburn, Mitchell	1	2	3	4	5		7	8	9		11	10	6								4
5	02 Sep	A	Portsmouth	D	0	0	(0 0)	43,244	5		1	2	3	4	5		7	8	9		11	10	6								5
6	06 Sep	H	**Huddersfield Town**	W	6	0	(3 0)	34,031		Milburn 3, Mitchell, Robledo G, Taylor	1	2	3	4	5		7	8	9		11	10	6								6
7	09 Sep	H	**Chelsea**	W	3	1	(1 0)	56,903	1	Milburn, Walker 2	1	2	3	4	5		7	8	9		11	10	6								7
8	13 Sep	A	Huddersfield Town	D	0	0	(0 0)	30,323	1		1	2	3	4	5		7	8	9		11	10	6								8
9	16 Sep	A	Burnley	D	1	1	(0 1)	33,373	1	Milburn	1	2	3	4	5		7	8	9		11	10	6								9
10	23 Sep	H	**Arsenal**	W	2	1	(1 1)	66,926	1	Milburn, Taylor	1	2	3	4	5		7	8	9		11	10	6								10
11	30 Sep	A	Sheffield Wednesday	D	0	0	(0 0)	40,096	1		1	2	3	4	5		7	8	9		11	10	6								11
12	07 Oct	A	Aston Villa	L	0	3	(0 1)	44,240			1	2		4	5	9	7	8			11	10	6	3							12
13	14 Oct	H	**Derby County**	W	3	1	(2 0)	54,793	3	Milburn, Mitchell, Walker	1	2	3	4	5		7	8	9		11	10	6								13
14	21 Oct	A	Bolton Wanderers	W	2	0	(1 0)	49,213	2	Robledo G, Taylor	1	2	3	4	5		7	8	9		11	10	6								14
15	28 Oct	H	**Blackpool**	W	4	2	(2 1)	61,008	2	Milburn, Robledo G 3	1	2	3	4	5		7	8	9		11	10	6								15
16	04 Nov	A	Liverpool	W	4	2	(2 1)	48,810	2	Robledo G 3, Taylor	1	2	3	4	5		7	8	9		11	10	6								16
17	11 Nov	H	**Fulham**	L	1	2	(1 1)	54,234	2	og (Quested)	1	2	3	4	5		7	8	9		11	10	6								17
18	18 Nov	A	Tottenham Hotspur	L	0	7	(0 3)	70,026	4		1	2	3	4	5		7	8	9		11	10	6								18
19	25 Nov	H	**Charlton Athletic**	W	3	2	(0 1)	48,670	3	Milburn 2, Walker	1	2	3	4	5		7		8	10	11	9	6								19
20	02 Dec	A	Manchester United	W	2	1	(0 1)	40,000	3	Hannah, Walker	1	2	3	4	5		7	8		10		9	6		11						20
21	09 Dec	H	**Wolverhampton Wanderers**	D	1	1	(1 0)	48,492	3	Walker	1	2	3	4	5		7	8		10		9	6		11						21
22	16 Dec	H	**Stoke City**	W	3	1	(2 0)	29,505	3	Hannah, Mitchell, Robledo G	1	2		4	5		7	8		10	11	9	6			3					22
23	23 Dec	A	Everton	L	1	3	(1 3)	35,880		Taylor	1	2		4	5		7	8		10	11	9	6			3					23
24	25 Dec	A	Middlesbrough	L	1	2	(1 1)	41,318		Stokoe	1	2		4			7	8			11		6			3	5	9	10		24
25	13 Jan	A	Chelsea	L	1	3	(1 1)	43,840	5	Mitchell	1	2	3	4			7	8	9		11	10	6				5				25
26	20 Jan	H	**Burnley**	W	2	1	(2 0)	40,666	4	Milburn 2	1	2		4			7	8	9		11	10	6		3		5				26
27	03 Feb	A	Arsenal	D	0	0	(0 0)	55,073	4		1	2		4	5		7	8	9		11	10	6		3						27
28	17 Feb	H	**Sheffield Wednesday**	W	2	0	(1 0)	47,075	5	Robledo G, Taylor	1	2		4	5		7	8	9		11	10			3					6	28
29	03 Mar	A	Derby County	W	2	1	(0 0)	25,999	5	Robledo G, Walker	1	2		4			7	8	9		11	10	6		3			5			29
30	17 Mar	A	Blackpool	D	2	2	(1 2)	24,825	5	Milburn, Robledo G	1	2			5		7		9	8	11	10	6		3			4			30
31	23 Mar	H	**Sunderland**	D	2	2	(1 1)	62,173	5	Harvey, Milburn	1	2		4	5		7	8	9		11	10	6		3						31
32	24 Mar	H	**Liverpool**	D	1	1	(1 1)	45,535	5	Mitchell	1	2			5		7	8	9		11	10	6		3			4			32
33	26 Mar	A	Sunderland	L	1	2	(1 2)	55,150	6	Mitchell	1	2			5		7	8	9	10	11		6		3			4			33
34	31 Mar	A	Fulham	D	1	1	(1 1)	30,000	6	Walker	1	2		4			7	8			11	10	6		3		5	9			34
35	04 Apr	H	**Aston Villa**	L	0	1	(0 1)	38,543	6		1	2			5		7	8	9		11	10	6		3			4			35
36	07 Apr	H	**Tottenham Hotspur**	L	0	1	(0 1)	41,241	6		1	2					7	8	9		11	10	6		3		5	4			36
37	11 Apr	H	**Portsmouth**	D	0	0	(0 0)	32,222	6		1	2					7	8		10	11	9			3		5	4		6	37
38	14 Apr	A	Charlton Athletic	W	3	1	(1 1)	25,798	5	Robledo G, Taylor, og (Phipps)	1	2		4			7	8		10	11	9			3		5			6	38
39	18 Apr	H	**Bolton Wanderers**	L	0	1	(0 1)	39,099	5		1	2		4			7	8	9	10	11		6		3		5				39
40	21 Apr	H	**Manchester United**	L	0	2	(0 2)	45,209	5		1	2		4	5		7	8	9		11	10	6		3						40
41	02 May	A	Wolverhampton Wanderers	W	1	0	(0 0)	27,015	4	Robledo G	1	2		4	5		7	8		10	11	9	6		3						41
42	05 May	H	**Middlesbrough**	W	1	0	(0 0)	35,935	4	Walker	1	2	3	4			7	8		10	11	9	6				5				42
Round			**FA Cup**																												**Round**
3	06 Jan	H	**Bury**	W	4	1	(4 1)	33,944		Milburn, Robledo G, Taylor, Walker	1	2	3	4			7	8	9		11	10					5			6	3
4	27 Jan	H	**Bolton Wanderers**	W	3	2	(1 2)	67,596		Milburn 2, Mitchell	1	2		4			7	8	9		11	10	6		3		5				4
5	10 Feb	A	Stoke City	W	4	2	(2 0)	48,500		Milburn, Mitchell, Robledo G 2	1	2		4	5		7	8	9		11	10	6		3						5
6	24 Feb	H	**Bristol Rovers**	D	0	0	(0 0)	63,000			1	2		4	5		7	8	9		11	10	6		3						6
6r	28 Feb	A	Bristol Rovers	W	3	1	(3 1)	30,724		Crowe, Milburn, Taylor	1	2		4	5		7	8	9		11	10	6		3						6r
SF	10 Mar	N1	Wolverhampton Wanderers	D	0	0	(0 0)	62,191			1	2		4	5		7	8	9		11	10	6		3						SF
SFr	14 Mar	N2	Wolverhampton Wanderers	W	2	1	(2 1)	47,349		Milburn, Mitchell	1	2		4	5		7	8	9		11	10	6		3						SFr
F	28 Apr	N3	Blackpool	W	2	0	(0 0)	100,000		Milburn 2	1	2		4	5		7	8	9		11	10	6		3						F

N1 Played at Hillsborough, Sheffield
N2 Played at Leeds Road, Huddersfield
N3 Played at Wembley Stadium, London

DateLine ...18 Nov: Eventual Champions Spurs crush United 7-0 in front of 70,026 at White Hart Lane. **27 Jan:** A gate of 67,596 see the clash with Bolton, the highest for any FA Cup-tie at St James' Park. **24 Feb:** The first all-ticket match recorded on Tyneside and 63,000 see the FA Cup meeting with Bristol Rovers. **28 April:** United lift the FA Cup with a 2-0 glory day at Wembley against Blackpool.

More Cup glory at Wembley

Newcastle United ended the 1951-52 season having successfully defended their FA Cup title, the first club to do so since 1891, and having scored over a century of goals. They were recognised as England's most captivating side. The team glowed with confidence and zest after their Wembley victory against Blackpool and they defeated Stoke City 6-0 on the opening day of the new campaign. After that appetizer it just got better. United then scored seven goals against League Champions Tottenham, and another seven two weeks later when Burnley arrived on Tyneside.

United were again tipped for the title trophy and were in fourth place by the festive holiday, but once more the glitter of the FA Cup took over. The Magpies had a demanding Cup run back to Wembley, and in the end deserved their trophy victory for overcoming what was a daunting challenge. Aston Villa were seen off in the opening round, then United faced a trip to White Hart Lane to face another meeting with Tottenham. A brilliant display in the mud was the outcome, Newcastle winning 3-0, before defeating Swansea and moving to another testing game in the quarter-final, a tie against Portsmouth at Fratton Park. Again United's team rose to the occasion and recorded a 4-2 success after a wonderful contest, Jackie Milburn netting a superb hat-trick in the process. Blackburn Rovers had to be overcome in the semi-final – yet another difficult task – a tie which went to a replay and a last-ditch spot-kick winner from Bobby Mitchell.

Newcastle had to tackle Arsenal in the final, a club to finish third in the League table. In a tight match at Wembley, United at last had a bit of fortune, as the Londoners were forced to play with ten men for almost most of the game due to an early injury to Wally Barnes. The Magpies had the advantage and grabbed a late winner with a Robledo header in the 84th minute.

Pictured above: Inside-forward Billy Foulkes had a meteoric rise to fame, quickly winning both a Welsh cap and the FA Cup.

Memorabilia CORNER

United are back in front of the Twin Towers of Wembley, the FA Cup final programme with Arsenal.

IN CHARGE

Chairman: John Lee/Robert Rutherford
Manager: Stan Seymour/Director Committee
Captain: Joe Harvey
Trainer/Coach: Norman Smith

ST JAMES' PARK

Average Attendance
Lg 50,473 Lg & Cup 50,765

Newcastle's 1952 FA Cup winning eleven. Back row, left to right: Cowell, Harvey, Simpson, Brennan, McMichael, Robledo (E). Front: Walker, Foulkes, Milburn, Robledo (G), Mitchell.

SEASON REVIEW

Football League Div 1: P42 W18 D9 L15 F98 A73 Pts 45.
Position: 8th (Champions; Manchester United).
FA Cup: Winners.

Appearances (50m): Cowell RG 47, Robledo GO 47, Simpson RC 47, Brennan F 46, Harvey Jos 45, McMichael A 44, Walker TJ 42, Milburn JET 40, Robledo EO 40, Mitchell RC 38, Foulkes WI 31, Hannah GL 20, Crowe CA 10, Taylor E 9, Davies ER 8, Prior KG 6, Stokoe R 6, Duncan JG 5, Keeble VAW 5, Corbett R 4, Batty RR 2, Cameron HG 2, Fairbrother J 2, Lackenby G 2, Lowery J 1, Paterson TA 1.

Goals (114g): Robledo GO 39, Milburn JET 29, Mitchell RC 14, Foulkes WI 7, Davies ER 5, Hannah GL 5, Duncan JG 3, Keeble VAW 3, Prior KG 2, Walker TJ 2, Brennan F 1, Crowe CA 1, Harvey Jos 1, Taylor E 1, own goal 1.

Dismissals: 0 players.

MAJOR SIGNINGS

Billy Foulkes (Chester) £11,500
Vic Keeble (Colchester Utd) £15,000

FROM THE RANKS

George Lackenby (Newcastle sch)

PLAYER FOCUS George Robledo

Born Iquique. Inside-forward, 5'9"
1949 to 1953: 166 app 91 goals.

The first South American to make an impact at the very top of English football, George Robledo became an immense favourite at St James' Park after making a name for himself with Barnsley in the latter years of World War Two. With an English mother, George wasn't tall, but was stocky and powerful, the Chilean joined United in January 1949 for a substantial fee of £23,000, a package including his younger brother Ted, who also appeared for the club. Having become a noted goalscorer with the Tykes claiming 93 goals, Robledo teamed up with Jackie Milburn up front and the partnership became one of the most feared in the country for the next four years. He was a grafter in attack, lethal in front of goal and frequently picked up the pieces in and around the box to great effect often striking the ball true and hard. During season 1951-52 Robledo netted the winner at Wembley in United's FA Cup final triumph while he also equalled Hughie Gallacher's longstanding goals tally of 39 strikes in a single season. A regular for Chile, he appeared in the World Cup finals and was enticed by a hefty financial package to return to his native country during May 1953 where he remained involved in football for several years at both club and international level. Nicknamed Pancho by his colleagues, George scored seven goals for United in a friendly contest against Border Province on tour in South Africa during 1952.

TEAM COLOURS Black & white striped shirts, black shorts (Change; white shirts, black shorts)

SEASON 1951–52

Match	Date		FL Division 1	Res	F	A	HT F	HT A	Att	Posn	Scorers
1	18 Aug	H	**Stoke City**	W	6	0	3	0	47,047		Crowe, Milburn 3, Mitchell, Robledo G
2	22 Aug	A	Bolton Wanderers	D	0	0	0	0	49,587		
3	25 Aug	A	Manchester United	L	1	2	1	0	51,850	9	Robledo G
4	29 Aug	H	**Bolton Wanderers**	L	0	1	0	1	49,587	9	
5	01 Sep	H	**Tottenham Hotspur**	W	7	2	4	1	52,541	9	Mitchell 2, Robledo G 3, Taylor, Walker
6	05 Sep	A	West Bromwich Albion	D	3	3	3	2	29,311	10	Hannah, Robledo G 2
7	08 Sep	A	Preston North End	W	2	1	1	0	39,452	7	Robledo G 2
8	15 Sep	H	**Burnley**	W	7	1	4	1	51,278	7	Hannah 2, Mitchell, Robledo G 4
9	22 Sep	A	Charlton Athletic	L	0	3	0	1	52,168	10	
10	29 Sep	H	**Fulham**	L	0	1	0	0	55,531	12	
11	06 Oct	H	**Wolverhampton Wanderers**	W	3	1	2	1	57,558	10	Davies, Milburn 2
12	13 Oct	A	Huddersfield Town	W	4	2	2	1	32,945	10	Hannah, Milburn 2, Robledo G
13	20 Oct	H	**Chelsea**	W	3	1	2	0	52,168	7	Milburn 2 (1 pen), Robledo G
14	27 Oct	A	Portsmouth	L	1	3	0	0	39,944	8	Milburn
15	03 Nov	H	**Liverpool**	D	1	1	0	0	50,132	8	Foulkes
16	10 Nov	A	Blackpool	L	3	6	1	3	28,611	9	Milburn, Robledo G 2
17	17 Nov	H	**Arsenal**	W	2	0	2	0	61,192	8	Robledo G, og (Daniel)
18	24 Nov	A	Manchester City	W	3	2	0	0	39,358	8	Milburn, Mitchell, Robledo G
19	01 Dec	H	**Derby County**	W	2	1	2	1	49,880	8	Robledo G 2
20	08 Dec	A	Aston Villa	D	2	2	1	2	32,884	7	Duncan 2
21	15 Dec	A	Stoke City	W	5	4	2	2	30,000	5	Davies 2, Duncan, Robledo G 2
22	22 Dec	H	**Manchester United**	D	2	2	2	2	45,414	5	Foulkes, Milburn
23	25 Dec	A	Sunderland	W	4	1	2	0	52,274	5	Foulkes, Milburn, Robledo G 2
24	26 Dec	H	**Sunderland**	D	2	2	0	1	63,665	4	Milburn 2 (1 pen)
25	29 Dec	A	Tottenham Hotspur	L	1	2	0	1	55,219	5	Robledo G
26	05 Jan	H	**Preston North End**	W	3	0	2	0	42,410	4	Foulkes, Milburn, Robledo G
27	19 Jan	A	Burnley	L	1	2	0	1	33,719	5	Milburn
28	26 Jan	H	**Charlton Athletic**	W	6	0	3	0	45,905	4	Foulkes, Milburn 2, Robledo G 2, Walker
29	09 Feb	A	Fulham	D	1	1	0	0	46,000	4	Robledo G
30	16 Feb	A	Wolverhampton Wanderers	L	0	3	0	1	41,420	5	
31	01 Mar	H	**Huddersfield Town**	W	6	2	3	1	51,394	5	Mitchell 2, Robledo G, Milburn 3 (1 pen)
32	12 Mar	A	Chelsea	L	0	1	0	0	42,948	5	
33	15 Mar	H	**Portsmouth**	D	3	3	2	1	62,870	6	Milburn, Mitchell, Robledo G
34	22 Mar	A	Liverpool	L	0	3	0	1	48,996	6	
35	07 Apr	H	**Blackpool**	L	1	3	0	1	47,316	11	Foulkes
36	11 Apr	H	**Middlesbrough**	L	0	2	0	1	59,364	11	
37	12 Apr	H	**Manchester City**	W	1	0	1	0	46,645	11	Robledo G
38	14 Apr	A	Middlesbrough	L	1	2	1	0	36,448	11	Keeble
39	16 Apr	A	Arsenal	D	1	1	1	0	53,203	11	Keeble
40	19 Apr	A	Derby County	W	3	1	0	0	18,940	9	Harvey, Keeble, Prior
41	23 Apr	H	**West Bromwich Albion**	L	1	4	0	1	31,188	9	Prior
42	26 Apr	H	**Aston Villa**	W	6	1	4	0	36,852	8	Brennan, Davies 2, Hannah, Milburn, Mitchell
Round			**FA Cup**								
3	12 Jan	H	**Aston Villa**	W	4	2	1	2	56,897		Foulkes, Mitchell 2, Robledo G
4	02 Feb	A	Tottenham Hotspur	W	3	0	2	0	69,009		Mitchell, Robledo G 2
5	23 Feb	A	Swansea Town	W	1	0	1	0	27,801		Mitchell
6	08 Mar	A	Portsmouth	W	4	2	1	1	44,699		Milburn 3, Robledo G
SF	29 Mar	N1	Blackburn Rovers	D	0	0	0	0	65,000		
SFr	02 Apr	N2	Blackburn Rovers	W	2	1	0	0	53,920		Mitchell (pen), Robledo G
F	03 May	N3	Arsenal	W	1	0	0	0	100,000		Robledo G
			FA Charity Shield								
	24 Sep	A	Tottenham Hotspur	L	1	2	1	1	27,760		Milburn

Match	Lowery	Cowell	Corbett	Harvey	Brennan	Crowe	Walker	Taylor	Milburn	Robledo GO	Mitchell	Fairbrother	Hannah	Simpson	McMichael	Duncan	Robledo EO	Batty	Davies	Foulkes	Stokoe	Paterson	Cameron	Lackenby	Keeble	Prior	Match
1	1	2	3	4	5	6	7	8	9	10	11																1
2		2	3	4	5	6	7	8	9	10	11	1															2
3		2	3	4	5	6	7	8		9	11	1	10														3
4		2	3	4	5	6		8	7	9	11		10	1													4
5		2		4	5	6	7	8		9	11		10	1	3												5
6		2		4	5	6	7	8		9	11		10	1	3												6
7				4	5		7	8		9	11		10	1	3	2	6										7
8		2		4	5		7		9	8	11		10	1	3		6										8
9				4	5		7		9	8	11		10	1	3	2	6										9
10		2		4	5	6		8	9	7	11		10	1	3												10
11		2		4	5			8	9	10			11	1			6	3	7								11
12		2		4	5				9	10			11	1	3		6		8	7							12
13		2			5		7		9	8			10	1	3		6				4	11					13
14		2		4	5				9	8	11		10	1	3		6			7							14
15		2			5				9	8			10	1	3		6			7	4		11				15
16		2		4	5				9	10				1	3		6		8	7			11				16
17		2		4	5		7		9	10	11			1	3		6			8							17
18		2		4	5		7		9	10	11			1	3		6			8							18
19		2		4	5		7		9	10	11			1	3		6			8							19
20		2		4	5		7			10	11			1	3	9	6			8							20
21		2		4	5		7			10				1	3	9	6		11	8							21
22		2		4	5		7		9	10	11			1	3		6			8							22
23		2		4	5		7		9	10	11			1	3		6			8							23
24		2		4	5		7		9	10	11			1	3		6			8							24
25		2			5				9	10	11			1	3		6		8	7				4			25
26		2		4	5		7		9	10	11			1	3		6			8							26
27		2		4	5		7		9	10	11			1	3		6			8							27
28		2		4	5		7		9	10	11			1	3		6			8							28
29		2		4	5		7		9	10	11			1	3		6			8							29
30		2		4	5		7		9	10	11			1	3		6			8							30
31		2		4	5		7		9	10	11			1	3		6			8							31
32		2		4	5		7				11		10	1	3		6			8					9		32
33		2			5		7		9	10	11			1	3		6			8				4			33
34		2		4	5		7		9	10	11			1	3		6			8							34
35		2		4	5		7		9	10	11			1	3		6			8							35
36		2		4	5	6	7		9	8			10	1	3											11	36
37		2		4		6	7		9	8				1	3						5				10	11	37
38		2		4		6	7			8			10	1	3						5				9	11	38
39		2					7			4			10	1			6	3	8		5				9	11	39
40		2		4			7						10	1	3		6		8		5				9	11	40
41		2		4	5		7		9	10				1	3		6			8						11	41
42		2		4	5		7		9		11		10	1	3		6		8								42
Round																											Round
3		2		4	5		7		9	10	11			1	3		6			8							3
4		2		4	5		7		9	10	11			1	3		6			8							4
5		2		4	5		7		9	10	11			1	3		6			8							5
6		2		4	5		7		9	10	11			1	3		6			8							6
SF		2		4	5		7		9	10	11			1	3		6			8							SF
SFr		2		4	5		7		9	10	11			1	3		6			8							SFr
F		2		4	5		7		9	10	11			1	3		6			8							F
CS				4	5		7		9	8	11		10	1	3	2	6										CS

N1 Played at Hillsborough, Sheffield
N2 Played at Elland Road, Leeds
N3 Played at Wembley Stadium, London

DateLine ... 18 Aug: Stoke are flattened 6-0 on the opening day of the season; United's best start ever. **1 Sept:** United gain revenge against Tottenham with a 7-2 headline win over the reigning Champions. **12 Sept:** The Cup winners clash between United and Glasgow Celtic attracts 61,300 to Parkhead, the largest for any United friendly. **2 April:** A penalty in the dying minutes by Bobby Mitchell defeats Blackburn and sends United to the FA Cup final. **3 May:** Newcastle regain the FA Cup, defeating Arsenal 1-0 with George Robledo equalling Gallacher's 39 goal record for a season. **2 July:** Robledo fires home seven goals as United defeat Border Province 10-0 on tour in South Africa.

South African tour takes its toll

The FA Cup kings headed for South Africa in the close season of 1952, taking the famous trophy with them. They were given almost royal status on the exhibition tour in which United played all of 16 matches in 70 days. It was enjoyable, it was rewarding, but the expedition took its toll when the 1952-53 season began. Injury hit the squad, with Jack Milburn missing two chunks of the season with a cartilage problem while Joe Harvey had his foot in plaster for a long period. Several players were also jaded. As a consequence Newcastle never reached the heights of performance of the last few years and in Division One they slipped down the table during the winter not recording a victory for 11 games. They dropped to even become embedded in the relegation scrap. Four defeats in succession, to Portsmouth, Manchester United, Middlesbrough and Bolton during April left the Black'n'Whites needing other clubs to do them a favour. Rivals in the drop zone, Stoke City, lost at Derby and United were safe.

In the FA Cup there was to be no headlining treble victory. In the middle of that bad run, form deserted them, going out to Second Division Rotherham United at Gallowgate – a mighty Cup shock. The previous Third Round tie against Swansea Town caused news also when the scheduled match at St James' Park was abandoned after only eight minutes of play due to a descending thick fog – with over 63,000 in the ground. Newcastle won the replay and another 60,000 went through the turnstile.

Away from competitive action, Glasgow giants Celtic arrived at Barrack Road to mark the opening of the club's first floodlighting system during February. The game was billed as an England versus Scotland Cup winners challenge and a crowd of 41,888 saw the spectacle, a 2-0 victory. Newcastle also drew an absorbing return match at Parkhead, 3-3, in front of over 60,000.

Pictured above: A workhorse in midfield, Tommy Casey was tenacious and full of vigour.

Memorabilia CORNER

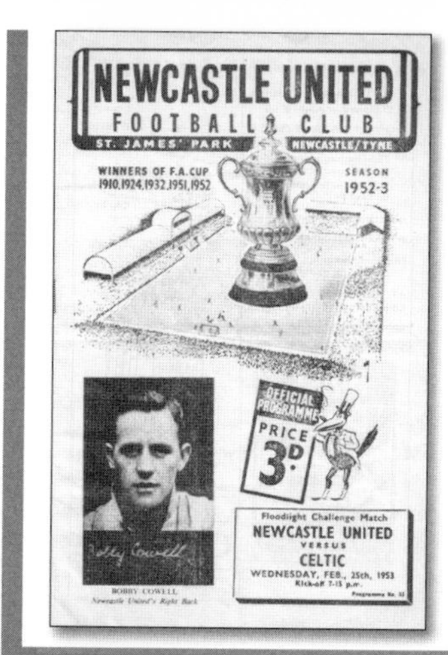

Programme for the first floodlit game on Tyneside, against Glasgow Celtic.

IN CHARGE

Chairman: Robert Rutherford
Manager: Stan Seymour/Director Committee
Captain: Joe Harvey
Trainer/Coach: Norman Smith

ST JAMES' PARK

Average Attendance
Lg 44,521 Lg & Cup 45,668

The FA Cup is on show again for the club's photo-call on the Gallowgate steps. Skipper Joe Harvey is flanked by Chairman Robert Rutherford (right) and director Stan Seymour (left).

SEASON REVIEW

Football League Div 1: P42 W14 D9 L19 F59 A70 Pts 37.
Position: 16th (Champions; Arsenal).
FA Cup: R4 (Winners; Blackpool).

Appearances (45m): Brennan F 40, Simpson RC 40, Cowell RG 39, Mitchell RC 38, Casey T 35, McMichael A 35, Walker TJ 30, Robledo GO 26, Hannah GL 24, Crowe CA 23, Davies ER 22, Harvey Jos 20, Keeble VAW 20, Stokoe R 19, Foulkes WI 18, Milburn JET 16, Mulgrew T 14, Batty RR 12, Brander GM 5, Robinson R 5, Cahill T 3, White LR 3, Prior KG 2, Robledo EO 2, Black N 1, Duncan JG 1, Keery S 1, Woollard AJ 1.

Goals (65g): Robledo GO 18, Mitchell RC 11, Keeble VAW 10, Davies ER 6, Milburn JET 5, Hannah GL 4, Brander GM 2, Foulkes WI 2, Walker TJ 2, Brennan F 1, Harvey Jos 1, Prior KG 1, own goals 2.

Dismissals: 0 players.

MAJOR SIGNINGS

Len White (Rotherham Utd) £12,500
Tommy Casey (Bournemouth) £7,000
Stan Keery (Shrewsbury Town) £8,250
Tommy Mulgrew (Northampton Town) £9,000
Arnold Woollard (Peterborough Utd) £5,000

FROM THE RANKS

None

PLAYER FOCUS Bobby Mitchell

Born Glasgow. Outside-left, 5'11"
1949 to 1961: 410 app 113 goals.

An influential and popular winger, Bobby Mitchell took part in all three Fifties FA Cup victories. He was a key player for Newcastle, a magician at outside-left who could step-up a gear and become a match-winner – which he did on numerous occasions, especially in those three FA Cup runs. His transfer from Third Lanark in February 1949 for a fee of £17,000 – a record for a winger – was money exceptionally well spent. Highly talented, tall and willowy, he was nicknamed Bobby Dazzler, and loved to take on defenders in a style that became famous – with close ball control and mazy dribbles. He was Gallowgate's exhibitionist, yet Mitchell could be direct too. He scored plenty of goals, over a century for the Magpies, many fiercely driven shots as the Glaswegian cut in from the left flank. He was rarely one to become heated, having a cool head once scoring a decisive spot-kick in the dying minutes of the 1952 FA Cup semi-final. Towards the end of his long career of 13 seasons with United, Mitchell moved into a midfield role. Capped by Scotland and scoring on his debut against Denmark, after leaving United when over 36 years old in June 1961 he assisted Berwick and became Gateshead player-boss for a period during the Sixties. Bobby later became a well-known publican in Newcastle. With Alan Shearer, Mitchell is one of only two players to have appeared over 400 times and scored more than 100 goals for the club in League and Cup football.

TEAM COLOURS Black & white striped shirts, black shorts (Change; white shirts, black shorts)

SEASON 1952-53

Match	Date		FL Division 1		Att	Posn	Goalscorers	Simpson	Cowell	McMichael	Stokoe	Brennan	Crowe	Foulkes	Hannah	Milburn	Robledo GO	Mitchell	Harvey	Robinson	Batty	Casey	Walker	Davies	Robledo EO	Prior	Duncan	Keeble	Brander	Mulgrew	Cahill	Keery	White	Woollard	Black	Match
1	23 Aug	A	Sheffield Wednesday	D 2 2 (2 0)	55,126		Hannah, Robledo G	1	2	3	4	5	6	7	8	9	10	11																		1
2	27 Aug	A	West Bromwich Albion	L 0 1 (0 1)	46,206			1	2	3		5	6	7	8	9	10	11	4																	2
3	30 Aug	H	**Tottenham Hotspur**	D 1 1 (0 1)	59,629	18	Robledo G	1	2	3		5	6	7	8	9	10	11	4																	3
4	06 Sep	A	Burnley	L 1 2 (1 1)	35,068	21	Robledo G			3		5	6	7	8	9	10	11		1	2	4														4
5	10 Sep	H	**Sunderland**	D 2 2 (0 1)	60,727	18	Davies, og (Stelling)			3		5	6			9	10	11		1	2	4	7	8												5
6	13 Sep	H	**Preston North End**	W 4 3 (1 2)	52,020	15	Davies 2, Robledo G 2	1		3		5			10		9	11			2	6	7	8	4											6
7	17 Sep	A	Sunderland	W 2 0 (1 0)	59,665	12	Mitchell, Robledo G	1	2	3		5	6		10		9	11				4	7	8												7
8	20 Sep	A	Stoke City	L 0 1 (0 0)	32,353	15		1	2	3		5	6		10		9	11				4	7	8												8
9	27 Sep	H	**Manchester City**	W 2 0 (1 0)	48,961	12	Hannah, Milburn (pen)	1	2	3		5	6		10	9		11				4	7	8												9
10	04 Oct	A	Liverpool	L 3 5 (1 2)	48,002	15	Prior, Robledo G 2 (1 pen)	1	2			5	6		10		9				3	4	7	8		11										10
11	11 Oct	A	Wolverhampton Wanderers	L 0 2 (0 2)	45,404	15			2			5	6		10		9			1	3	4	7	8		11										11
12	18 Oct	H	**Charlton Athletic**	W 3 2 (1 1)	41,532	13	Keeble 2, Robledo G			3	5		6		8		10	11		1		4	7				2	9								12
13	25 Oct	A	Arsenal	L 0 3 (0 1)	63,744	17			2	3		5					10	11	4	1		6	7	8				9								13
14	01 Nov	H	**Derby County**	W 1 0 (1 0)	44,571	17	Walker	1	2	3		5			10				4			6	7	8				9	11							14
15	08 Nov	A	Blackpool	W 2 0 (2 0)	33,712	12	Brander, Robledo G	1	2	3	4	5			10		9					6	7						11	8						15
16	15 Nov	H	**Chelsea**	W 2 1 (1 1)	37,178	10	Robledo G (pen), Brennan	1	2	3	4	5	10				9					6	7						11	8						16
17	22 Nov	A	Manchester United	D 2 2 (1 0)	33,528	10	Keeble, Robledo G	1	2	3	4	5					9	11				6	7					10		8						17
18	29 Nov	H	**Portsmouth**	W 1 0 (1 0)	46,721	8	Robledo G	1	2	3	4	5					9	11				6	7					10		8						18
19	06 Dec	A	Bolton Wanderers	L 2 4 (1 1)	41,420	8	Keeble, Walker	1	2	3	4	5					9	11				6	7					10		8						19
20	13 Dec	H	**Aston Villa**	W 2 1 (1 1)	38,046	8	Keeble, og (Parkes)	1	2	3	4	5					9	11				6	7					10		8						20
21	20 Dec	H	**Sheffield Wednesday**	L 1 5 (0 2)	37,927	9	Mitchell (pen)	1	2	3		5	6				9	11				4	7					10		8						21
22	25 Dec	H	**Cardiff City**	W 3 0 (1 0)	36,143	9	Mitchell (pen), Foulkes 2	1	2		4	5		9				11				6	7					10		8	3					22
23	27 Dec	A	Cardiff City	D 0 0 (0 0)	51,592	9		1	2		4	5		9				11				6	7	10						8	3					23
24	01 Jan	H	**West Bromwich Albion**	L 3 5 (2 2)	48,944	9	Davies, Milburn, Mitchell	1	2		4	5				9		11				6	7	10						8	3					24
25	03 Jan	A	Tottenham Hotspur	L 2 3 (2 2)	52,648	12	Davies, Milburn	1	2	3		5				9		11	4			6	7	8				10								25
26	17 Jan	H	**Burnley**	D 0 0 (0 0)	49,366	12		1	2	3	9	5							4			6	7	10					11	8						26
27	24 Jan	A	Preston North End	L 1 2 (0 1)	26,394	12	Brander	1		3	5				8				4		2	6	7					9	11			10				27
28	07 Feb	H	**Stoke City**	L 1 2 (1 1)	31,426	12	Robledo G	1	2	3	5		6			9	8	11	4			10	7													28
29	14 Feb	A	Manchester City	L 1 2 (0 1)	24,898	13	Milburn	1	2			5	6			8		11	4		3	10	7					9								29
30	21 Feb	H	**Liverpool**	L 1 2 (1 2)	40,345	16	Mitchell	1	2			5	6	8		9		11	4		3	10											7			30
31	28 Feb	H	**Wolverhampton Wanderers**	D 1 1 (1 1)	46,254	15	Robledo G	1	2		4	5		8		9	10	11			3	6											7			31
32	07 Mar	A	Charlton Athletic	D 0 0 (0 0)	33,222	15		1	2	3		5		8	10			11	4			6	7					9								32
33	14 Mar	H	**Arsenal**	D 2 2 (0 1)	51,618	15	Mitchell, Robledo G	1	2	3		5		7	10		9	11	4			6		8												33
34	21 Mar	A	Derby County	W 2 0 (0 0)	19,741	12	Robledo G 2	1	2	3		5		7	10		9	11	4			6		8												34
35	28 Mar	H	**Blackpool**	L 0 1 (0 1)	41,205	14		1	2	3		5		7	10		9	11	4			6		8												35
36	03 Apr	H	**Middlesbrough**	W 1 0 (1 0)	48,434	13	Hannah	1	2	3		5	6	7	10			11	4					8				9								36
37	04 Apr	A	Chelsea	W 2 1 (0 1)	40,218	13	Mitchell 2	1	2	3		5	6	7	10			11	4					8				9								37
38	06 Apr	A	Middlesbrough	L 1 2 (0 1)	37,926	13	Mitchell (pen)	1	2	3		5	6	7	10			11	4					8				9								38
39	11 Apr	H	**Manchester United**	L 1 2 (1 1)	39,078	15	Mitchell	1	2	3		5	6		10	9		11	4				7							8						39
40	18 Apr	A	Portsmouth	L 1 5 (1 1)	27,835	15	Keeble	1	2	3	4		6	8		9		11										10					7	5		40
41	25 Apr	H	**Bolton Wanderers**	L 2 3 (0 2)	34,824	15	Hannah, Harvey	1		3		5	6	7	10	9		11	4		2			8												41
42	01 May	A	Aston Villa	W 1 0 (1 0)	19,387	16	Milburn	1	2			5	6	7	10	9		11	4		3									8						42
Round			FA Cup																																	Round
3	10 Jan	H	**Swansea Town**	Ab 0 0	63,499			1	2	3	4	5				9						6	7	11				10		8						3
3	14 Jan	H	**Swansea Town**	W 3 0 (1 0)	61,064		Davies, Keeble, Mitchell	1	2	3	4	5						11				6	7	10				9		8						3
4	31 Jan	H	**Rotherham United**	L 1 3 (0 0)	54,356		Keeble	1	2	3	4	5					9	11				6	7	8				10								4
			FA Charity Shield																																	CS
	24 Sep	A	Manchester United	L 2 4 (1 0)	11,381		Keeble 2	1	2		5						8	11			3	6	7		4			9							10	

Ab Abandoned after 8 mins due to fog

DateLine ... 24 Sept: Manchester United secure the Charity Shield with a 4-2 victory at Old Trafford. **1 Jan:** United crash 5-3 at Gallowgate to West Bromwich Albion on New Year's Day. **10 Jan:** The FA Cup-tie at St James' Park with Swansea is abandoned after only eight minutes due to fog with a crowd of 63,499 inside the stadium. **14 Jan:** A victory over Swansea in the FA Cup sets a then national record of 16 Cup-ties unbeaten. **25 Feb:** The first floodlit match at St James' Park attracts 41,888 for the 2-0 win over Glasgow Celtic. **16 May:** United bow out of the Coronation Cup tournament in Glasgow after a 4-0 defeat to Hibs.

SEASON 1953-54

DIVISION 1

Another lacklustre season

Newcastle's line-up for the second year running looked weary with the squad which had developed so well from the immediate post-war years deteriorating fast. New blood was needed, notably to replace Joe Harvey, who had moved onto the training staff. United splashed out big-time, with the record purchase of Jimmy Scoular from Portsmouth. He was in the team for the season's start, a heated derby with Sunderland at Gallowgate which ended in a 2-1 triumph. Scoular though was sidelined with an injury and the Magpies found themselves again in the wrong half of the Division One table, as it transpired alongside North Eastern neighbours Sunderland and Middlesbrough. Up to the mid-point of the season United recorded only five victories.

Home form was well below standard. They lost ten games at Gallowgate, including nearly falling to non-league Wigan Athletic in the FA Cup during January. The future Premier League outfit, yet back then a football minnow, drew 2-2 on Tyneside after being in front 2-1, and earned a glamour replay at their old Springfield Park ground. United won 3-2, but the tie did little to improve confidence. Sliding to 18th spot in the League ranking at one stage, United needed points as the season came to its conclusion. They secured enough in the end with an end-of-season rally, notching up four wins in the last five matches. Newcastle had good wins over Manchester City, Sheffield Wednesday and Arsenal as well as against Chelsea, on the last day of the programme at Stamford Bridge.

But it had been a miserable programme. A vast improvement was needed, and the club's Board also considered what was to them, a thorny issue, that of employing a manager. Although most of the country's top clubs now had a full-time boss in charge of playing affairs, Newcastle were slow to accept the changing face of football and move with the times. But the side's poor showing pushed them into action again.

***Pictured above:** United spent heavily on the creative skills of Ivor Broadis who scored twice on his debut.*

Memorabilia CORNER

The Evening Chronicle 'Magpie' was by now prominent on United's programme cover.

IN CHARGE

Chairman: Robert Rutherford/Stan Seymour
Manager: Stan Seymour/Director Committee
Captain: Jimmy Scoular
Trainer/Coach: Norman Smith

ST JAMES' PARK

Average Attendance
Lg 45,392 Lg & Cup 45,814

United's playing squad numbered 36 by 1953 with four goalkeepers, front row, left to right: Robertson, Robinson, Simpson and Thompson.

PLAYER FOCUS Ronnie Simpson

Born Glasgow. Goalkeeper, 5'10"
1951 to 1960: 297 app 0 goals.

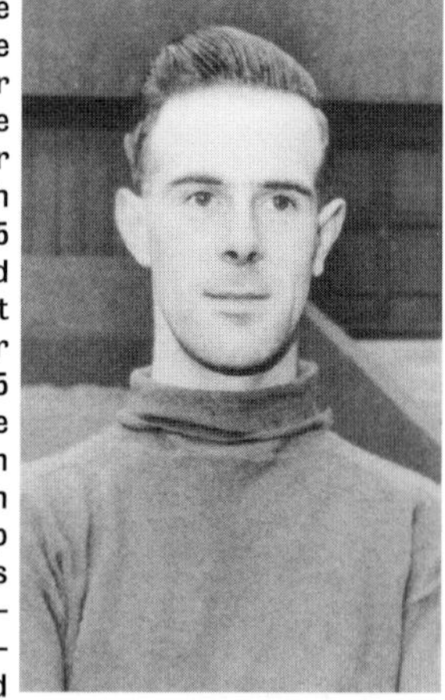

Goalkeeper Ronnie Simpson had a quite remarkable career in football. He made his first senior appearance with Queen's Park in 1945 as a 14-year-old and did not conclude his career until 1970, some 25 years later when he was almost 40! In between Simpson lifted two FA Cup winners medals with the Geordies – in 1952 and 1955 – then claimed everything there was to win in Scotland as one of Jock Stein's stars in a famous Celtic line-up, a member of the legendary Lisbon Lions European Cup winning eleven in 1967. And to crown an astonishing career Simpson was handed his international debut by Scotland when over 36 years of age. Taking over from Jack Fairbrother in Newcastle's ranks following a £8,750 transfer from Third Lanark during February 1951, Simpson was not big for a goalkeeper, but he possessed marvellous agility, often likened to the proverbial leaping cat. United's last line of defence for most of the Fifties decade, Ronnie returned to Scotland following a lengthy period on the sidelines due to injury in October 1960 when he joined Hibs. Simpson moved to Celtic in 1964 and proceeded to become a legend at Parkhead. He retired from playing in 1970 and then entered coaching, for a brief spell also managing Hamilton. Early into his career in 1948, Simpson represented the British Olympic side. Ronnie settled in Edinburgh, his father, Jimmy Simpson, appeared for Rangers and also played for Scotland.

SEASON REVIEW

Football League Div 1: P42 W14 D10 L18 F72 A77 Pts 38.
Position: 15th (Champions; Wolverhampton Wanderers).
FA Cup: R5 (Winners; West Bromwich Albion).

Appearances (47m): Simpson RC 47, Cowell RG 45, Brennan F 44, Milburn JET 44, Mitchell RC 40, McMichael A 33, Scoular J 32, Hannah GL 31, Stokoe R 29, Broadis IA 28, Davies ER 19, Foulkes WI 19, Crowe CA 17, Casey T 15, Monkhouse ATW 15, Batty RR 14, White LR 13, Keeble VAW 12, Keery S 6, Walker TJ 5, Greener R 3, Cooper J 2, Cahill T 1, Gaskell A 1, Mulgrew T 1, Punton WH 1.

Goals (81g): Milburn JET 18, Mitchell RC 16, Broadis IA 13, Monkhouse ATW 8, Hannah GL 7, Keeble VAW 7, Davies ER 6, White LR 3, Keery S 1, Mulgrew T 1, Scoular J 1.

Dismissals: 0 players.

MAJOR SIGNINGS

Ivor Broadis (Manchester City) £17,500
Alan Monkhouse (Millwall) £11,500
Bill Punton (Portadown) £6,000
Jimmy Scoular (Portsmouth) £22,250 club record fee

FROM THE RANKS

Joe Cooper (Winlaton Mill)
Ron Greener (Easington CW)
Ken Prior (Cambois Jnrs/Sunderland)

TEAM COLOURS Black & white striped shirts, black shorts (Change; white shirts, black shorts)

SEASON 1953-54

Match	Date		FL Division 1	Result	HT	Att	Posn	Scorers	Simpson	Cowell	Batty	Scoular	Brennan	Crowe	Milburn	Davies	Keeble	Hannah	Mitchell	Stokoe	Cooper	McMichael	Walker	Casey	White	Foulkes	Keery	Greener	Mulgrew	Broadis	Monkhouse	Gaskell	Cahill	Punton	Match
1	22 Aug	H	**Sunderland**	W 2 1	(1 1)	58,516		Mitchell (pen), Keeble	1	2	3	4	5	6	7	8	9	10	11																1
2	26 Aug	A	Liverpool	D 2 2	(1 1)	47,263		Davies, Hannah	1	2	3		5	6	7	8	9	10	11	4															2
3	29 Aug	A	Manchester United	D 1 1	(1 0)	27,837	10	Hannah	1	2	3		5	6	7	8	9	10	11	4															3
4	02 Sep	H	**Liverpool**	W 4 0	(2 0)	48,439	3	Keeble, Milburn, Mitchell 2	1	2	3		5	6	7	8	9	10	11	4															4
5	05 Sep	H	**Bolton Wanderers**	L 2 3	(1 2)	61,321	12	Hannah, Mitchell	1	2	3		5	6	7	8	9	10	11	4															5
6	09 Sep	A	West Bromwich Albion	D 2 2	(0 0)	40,220	10	Keeble, Mitchell	1	2	3		5	6	7	8	9	10	11	4															6
7	12 Sep	A	Preston North End	D 2 2	(0 1)	36,035	12	Keeble, Milburn	1	2	3		5	6	7	8	9	10	11		4														7
8	16 Sep	H	**West Bromwich Albion**	L 3 7	(0 3)	57,838	12	Keeble, Mitchell 2	1	2		4	5	6	7	8	9	10	11			3													8
9	19 Sep	H	**Tottenham Hotspur**	L 1 3	(0 1)	53,056	14	Milburn	1	2		4	5	6	7	8	9	10				3	11												9
10	23 Sep	A	Sheffield Wednesday	L 0 3	(0 3)	29,271	16		1	2	3	4	5		9	11								6	7	8	10								10
11	26 Sep	A	Burnley	W 2 1	(0 0)	33,738	13	Keery, Milburn	1	2	3	4	5		9	11								6	7	8	10								11
12	03 Oct	H	**Charlton Athletic**	L 0 2	(0 1)	47,516	14		1	2	3	4			9				11					6	7	8	10	5							12
13	10 Oct	H	**Wolverhampton Wanderers**	L 1 2	(1 0)	39,913	16	Mulgrew	1	2	3	4	5		7				11					6	9		10		8						13
14	17 Oct	A	Aston Villa	W 2 1	(0 1)	29,556	14	Davies, Milburn	1	2	3	4		6	9	8			11						7		10	5							14
15	24 Oct	H	**Huddersfield Town**	L 0 2	(0 1)	46,644	17		1			4	2		9	8			11			3		6		7	10	5							15
16	31 Oct	A	Sheffield United	L 1 3	(1 1)	30,412	17	Hannah	1	2		4	5	6	9			10	11			3				7				8					16
17	07 Nov	H	**Cardiff City**	W 4 0	(2 0)	42,355	15	Broadis 2, Hannah, Milburn	1	2		4	5	6	9			10				3				7				8	11				17
18	14 Nov	A	Manchester City	D 0 0	(0 0)	48,830	15		1	2		4	5	6	9	10						3				7				8	11				18
19	21 Nov	H	**Portsmouth**	D 1 1	(1 0)	48,853	15	Milburn	1	2		4	5	6	9			10				3	7							8	11				19
20	28 Nov	A	Arsenal	L 1 2	(1 0)	62,456	15	Milburn	1	2		4	5		9			10	11	6		3	7							8					20
21	05 Dec	H	**Chelsea**	D 1 1	(0 1)	41,728	15	Mitchell	1	2		4	5		9			10	11	6		3	7							8					21
22	12 Dec	A	Blackpool	W 3 1	(0 1)	19,896	15	Broadis, Hannah, Mitchell	1	2		4	5		7			10	11	6		3								8	9				22
23	19 Dec	A	Sunderland	D 1 1	(0 0)	49,923	17	Broadis	1	2		4	5		7			10	11	6		3								8	9				23
24	25 Dec	A	Middlesbrough	W 3 2	(2 1)	28,138		Mitchell, Monkhouse, Scoular	1	2		4	5		7			10	11	6		3								8	9				24
25	26 Dec	H	**Middlesbrough**	L 2 3	(0 0)	43,750	15	Broadis, Mitchell	1	2		4	5					10	11	6		3				7				8		9			25
26	01 Jan	H	**Blackpool**	W 2 1	(1 1)	44,343	12	Milburn 2	1	2		4	5		9			10	11	6		3				7				8					26
27	02 Jan	H	**Manchester United**	L 1 2	(0 2)	56,034	14	Broadis	1	2		4	5		9			10	11	6		3				7				8					27
28	16 Jan	A	Bolton Wanderers	D 2 2	(1 1)	29,476	13	Keeble, Broadis	1	2		4	5		10		9		11			3		6	7					8					28
29	23 Jan	H	**Preston North End**	L 0 4	(0 2)	40,340	15		1	2		4	5		10		9		11	6		3				7				8					29
30	06 Feb	A	Tottenham Hotspur	L 0 3	(0 0)	35,798	18		1	2		4	5					10	11	6					7					8	9		3		30
31	13 Feb	H	**Burnley**	W 3 1	(1 1)	29,114	14	Broadis 2, Milburn	1	2			5		9			10	11	4		3		6		7				8					31
32	25 Feb	A	Charlton Athletic	D 0 0	(0 0)	13,441			1	2		4	5		9			10	11	6		3				7				8					32
33	27 Feb	A	Wolverhampton Wanderers	L 2 3	(0 2)	38,592	16	Broadis, Milburn	1	2			5		9			10	11	4		3		6		7				8					33
34	06 Mar	H	**Aston Villa**	L 0 1	(0 0)	36,847	17		1	2			5		9			10	11	4		3		6		7				8					34
35	13 Mar	A	Huddersfield Town	L 2 3	(1 2)	25,710	17	Milburn, Monkhouse	1	2			5		10				11	4		3		6	7					8	9				35
36	20 Mar	H	**Sheffield United**	W 4 1	(1 1)	36,668	18	Milburn, Monkhouse 3	1	2		4	5		10				11			3		6	7					8	9				36
37	27 Mar	A	Cardiff City	L 1 2	(1 0)	26,242	17	Monkhouse	1	2		4	5		10				11			3		6	7					8	9				37
38	03 Apr	H	**Manchester City**	W 4 3	(2 1)	27,764	16	Milburn 2 (2 pens), Monkhouse, Davies	1	2	3				10	8				5	4			6		7					9			11	38
39	10 Apr	A	Portsmouth	L 0 2	(0 1)	26,604	17		1	2			5		7	10			11	4		3		6						8	9				39
40	16 Apr	H	**Sheffield Wednesday**	W 3 0	(1 0)	43,945	16	Mitchell 2, Monkhouse	1	2			5	6	7	8		10	11	4		3									9				40
41	17 Apr	H	**Arsenal**	W 5 2	(2 2)	48,243	16	Davies 3, Hannah, White	1	2			5	6	7	8		10	11	4		3			9										41
42	24 Apr	A	Chelsea	W 2 1	(0 0)	46,991	15	Mitchell, White	1	2			5	6		8		10	11	4		3			7						9				42
Round			FA Cup																																Round
3	09 Jan	H	**Wigan Athletic**	D 2 2	(1 0)	52,222		Broadis, Milburn	1		2	4	5		10				11	6		3	7							8	9				3
3r	13 Jan	A	Wigan Athletic	W 3 2	(2 1)	26,500		Broadis, Keeble, White	1	2		4	5		10		9		11			3		6	7					8					3r
4	30 Jan	A	Burnley	D 1 1	(0 1)	52,011		Broadis	1	2		4	5		9			10	11	6		3				7				8					4
4r	03 Feb	H	**Burnley**	W 1 0	(0 0)	48,284		Mitchell (pen)	1	2		4	5		9			10	11	6		3				7				8					4r
5	20 Feb	A	West Bromwich Albion	L 2 3	(0 2)	61,088		Milburn, Mitchell	1	2		4	5		9			10	11	6		3				7				8					5

DateLine ... 16 Sept: West Bromwich Albion inflict another home defeat on the Magpies, this time by 7-3. **9 Jan:** Non-league Wigan Athletic hold United at Gallowgate with a 2-2 draw. **19 April:** The FA Amateur Cup final replay between Bishop Auckland and Crook Town is watched by 56,008 at St James' Park.

SEASON 1954-55

DIVISION 1

A Wembley treble for the Magpies

A step up in performance was evident as the black-and-white shirts made an appearance in season 1954-55. That was much needed. Yet United were inconsistent with it, but finishing in the top half of the table and reaching their third FA Cup final in only five years was satisfying enough. Along the way the Magpies demonstrated highs of brilliance at times although they needed plenty of good fortune to get to another Wembley outing.

Following a bright opening to the programme, United slumped with a bad run in the autumn only to recover by New Year. As preparations were being made for the Third Round of the FA Cup, players were coming to terms with a new manager when Duggie Livingstone was appointed during the festive period. With a Continental approach, the former Everton player was to have a turbulent period in charge, being at odds for most of his brief stay with both his director masters and with many star players.

Livingstone guided United through the opening two rounds of the FA Cup before meeting Nottingham Forest in Round Five. An archetypal Cup battle of three matches saw United squeeze into the quarter-final to meet Huddersfield Town. Another testing confrontation was played out, this time over two riveting games and more hard work for United followed in the semi-final, a tie against giant-killers York City, from Division Three (North). The Magpies needed a replay at Roker Park to dispose of the minnows and reach Wembley to face Manchester City.

Livingstone's team selection for the big-day proved to be a controversial one, omitting Jack Milburn. Newcastle's Board though forced a change on the boss – the end of his time on Tyneside being cast – and of course it was Wor Jackie who hit the Wembley headlines again, opening the scoring with a flying header in a 3-1 victory after only 45 seconds – then the fastest ever goal at the famous stadium.

Pictured above: Slightly built, George Hannah often was the star of the show with his skill and craft.

Memorabilia CORNER

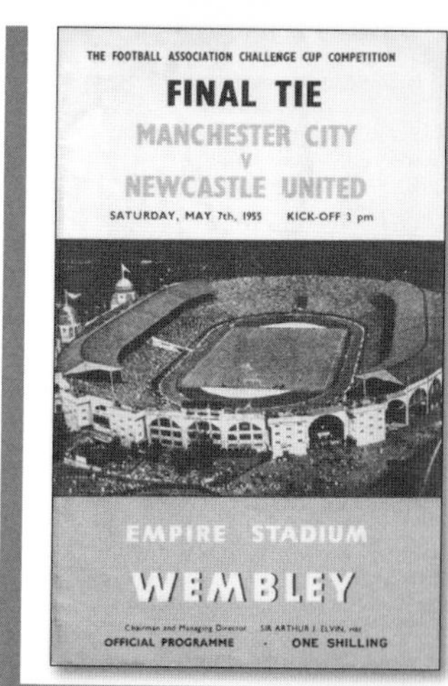

The largely uncovered Wembley Stadium was pictured on the cover of the 1955 FA Cup final programme.

IN CHARGE

Chairman: Stan Seymour
Manager: Director Committee/Duggie Livingstone
Captain: Jimmy Scoular
Trainer/Coach: Norman Smith

ST JAMES' PARK

Average Attendance
Lg 42,878 Lg & Cup 42,986

United are on their way to a third FA Cup victory in five years. Back row, left to right: Scoular, Woollard, Stokoe, Simpson, Batty, Crowe. Front: Milburn, Hannah, Keeble, Davies, Mitchell.

PLAYER FOCUS Bobby Cowell

Born Trimdon Grange. Right-back, 5'9"
1943 to 1956: 409 app 0 goals.

An important cog in United's treble of FA Cup victories at right-back in 1951, 1952 and 1955, indeed Bobby Cowell appeared in every one of the 25 games of those three Wembley runs. He was also part of Newcastle's 1947-48 promotion eleven. An ex-miner in County Durham and a product of United's wartime nursery, Bobby first appeared in United's line-up during 1943 and went onto make his Football League debut in an incredible game – United's 13-0 demolition of Newport County in 1946. From that point Cowell hardly missed a fixture in the number two shirt for the next decade as an honest and reliable professional. Only an injury picked up on a tour of Germany during 1955 halted his Toon career the following year when aged 33. Underrated by many, Cowell was fast and able to recover position quickly, as well as having a knack of making off-the-line clearances, once famously in the 1951 FA Cup final. He was on the fringe of an England call-up, noted by several judges as among the best uncapped defenders in the Fifties. But Bobby could never oust Alf Ramsay from the England shirt during those years. Although he pulled on United's jersey over 400 times, he never found the net. Like many of his era, Bobby started his career at his local pit welfare club, as a miner with a wage of £4 per week. On retirement in 1956, Cowell remained on Tyneside for the rest of his life.

SEASON REVIEW

Football League Div 1: P42 W17 D9 L16 F89 A77 Pts 43.
Position: 8th (Champions; Chelsea).
FA Cup: Winners.

Appearances (52m): Scoular J 52, Cowell RG 50, Mitchell RC 50, Milburn JET 48, Simpson RC 45, Stokoe R 42, White LR 37, Batty RR 35, Crowe CA 34, Hannah GL 31, Keeble VAW 28, Broadis IA 23, Davies ER 21, McMichael A 19, Casey T 15, Curry WM 11, Brennan F 6, Mitchell SA 4, Monkhouse ATW 4, Paterson WAK 4, Keery S 3, Thompson JH 3, Cooper J 2, Taylor JH 2, Woollard AJ 2, Tait A 1.

Goals (107g): Mitchell RC 23, Milburn JET 21, White LR 16, Keeble VAW 15, Hannah GL 13, Broadis IA 5, Curry WM 5, Davies ER 4, Monkhouse ATW 2, Crowe CA 1, McMichael A 1, Scoular J 1.

Dismissals: 0 players.

MAJOR SIGNINGS

Bill Paterson (Doncaster Rovers)
£22,250 equal club record fee

FROM THE RANKS

Bill Curry (Newcastle sch)
Stewart Mitchell (Benburb Jnrs)
Harry Taylor (Crawcrook Jnrs)
Alex Tait (Northb sch, Ey)
John Thompson (Newcastle sch)

TEAM COLOURS Black & white striped shirts, black shorts (Change; white shirts, black shorts)

SEASON 1954-55

Match			FL Division 1				Posn	
1	21 Aug	A	Arsenal	W	3 1	(2 1)	65,334		Davies, Mitchell R 2
2	25 Aug	H	**West Bromwich Albion**	W	3 0	(2 0)	58,548		Milburn, White 2
3	28 Aug	H	**Sheffield United**	L	1 2	(0 1)	52,341		Mitchell R
4	01 Sep	A	West Bromwich Albion	L	2 4	(1 4)	36,414	10	Hannah, Scoular
5	04 Sep	A	Preston North End	D	3 3	(0 1)	35,831	12	Hannah, Milburn, White
6	08 Sep	H	**Aston Villa**	W	5 3	(4 1)	39,960	9	Milburn, White 4
7	11 Sep	H	**Burnley**	W	2 1	(1 0)	47,346		Milburn, Mitchell R
8	13 Sep	A	Aston Villa	W	2 1	(1 0)	27,330	4	Milburn, Mitchell R
9	18 Sep	A	Leicester City	L	2 3	(2 0)	38,038	9	Mitchell R (pen), White
10	25 Sep	H	**Chelsea**	L	1 3	(0 3)	45,659	11	Milburn
11	02 Oct	A	Cardiff City	L	2 4	(0 2)	34,760		Milburn, White
12	09 Oct	A	Sunderland	L	2 4	(0 2)	66,654	15	Mitchell R (pen), Milburn
13	16 Oct	H	**Tottenham Hotspur**	D	4 4	(3 2)	45,306	14	Broadis 2, Crowe, White
14	23 Oct	A	Manchester United	D	2 2	(1 0)	37,247	13	Broadis, Mitchell R
15	30 Oct	H	**Wolverhampton Wanderers**	L	2 3	(1 2)	49,279	16	Milburn 2
16	06 Nov	A	Blackpool	L	0 2	(0 0)	20,701	16	
17	13 Nov	H	**Charlton Athletic**	W	3 1	(1 0)	35,988	15	Mitchell R (pen), Curry 2
18	20 Nov	A	Bolton Wanderers	L	1 2	(1 0)	25,936	15	Curry
19	27 Nov	H	**Huddersfield Town**	D	2 2	(1 2)	36,409	15	Curry, White
20	04 Dec	A	Sheffield Wednesday	W	3 0	(1 0)	20,221	15	Broadis, Mitchell R, White
21	11 Dec	H	**Portsmouth**	W	2 1	(0 1)	33,414	13	Keeble 2
22	18 Dec	H	**Arsenal**	W	5 1	(3 0)	35,122	12	Mitchell R 2 (1 pen), Keeble 2, Milburn
23	25 Dec	A	Manchester City	L	1 3	(1 1)	26,664	12	Keeble
24	27 Dec	H	**Manchester City**	W	2 0	(0 0)	52,874	12	Mitchell R 2 (1 pen)
25	01 Jan	A	Sheffield United	L	2 6	(2 5)	32,141	13	Keeble, Mitchell R
26	22 Jan	A	Burnley	W	1 0	(0 0)	23,460	12	Hannah
27	05 Feb	H	**Leicester City**	W	2 0	(1 0)	36,061	10	Hannah, Milburn
28	12 Feb	A	Chelsea	L	3 4	(0 1)	50,667	13	Keeble 2, Milburn
29	26 Feb	H	**Sunderland**	L	1 2	(0 1)	62,835	12	Milburn
30	05 Mar	A	Portsmouth	L	1 3	(0 2)	54,055	17	Keeble
31	19 Mar	A	Wolverhampton Wanderers	D	2 2	(0 1)	36,614		Milburn 2
32	02 Apr	A	Charlton Athletic	D	1 1	(1 1)	24,918	19	Hannah
33	08 Apr	A	Everton	W	2 1	(1 1)	60,080		Hannah, Keeble
34	09 Apr	H	**Sheffield Wednesday**	W	5 0	(2 0)	40,883		Davies 2, Hannah, Mitchell R, White
35	11 Apr	H	**Everton**	W	4 0	(1 0)	45,329	14	Mitchell R 2, Milburn 2
36	16 Apr	A	Huddersfield Town	L	0 2	(0 1)	29,913	11	
37	18 Apr	H	**Manchester United**	W	2 0	(0 0)	35,569	11	Hannah, White
38	20 Apr	H	**Preston North End**	D	3 3	(2 2)	38,681	11	Davies, Hannah, Milburn
39	23 Apr	H	**Bolton Wanderers**	D	0 0	(0 0)	48,194	11	
40	25 Apr	H	**Blackpool**	D	1 1	(0 1)	41,380		Broadis
41	27 Apr	H	**Cardiff City**	W	3 0	(3 0)	19,252	8	Hannah 2, McMichael
42	30 Apr	A	Tottenham Hotspur	L	1 2	(0 2)	37,262	8	Mitchell R
Round			**FA Cup**						
3	08 Jan	A	Plymouth Argyle	W	1 0	(1 0)	28,685		Keeble
4	29 Jan	H	**Brentford**	W	3 2	(0 0)	46,574		Curry, Hannah, Mitchell R
5	19 Feb	A	Nottingham Forest	D	1 1	(0 0)	25,252		Milburn
5r	28 Feb	H	**Nottingham Forest**	De	2 2	(2 0)	38,573		Keeble, Mitchell R
5rr	02 Mar	H	**Nottingham Forest**	W	2 1	(1 1)	36,631		Monkhouse 2
6	12 Mar	A	Huddersfield Town	D	1 1	(0 0)	54,960		White
6r	16 Mar	H	**Huddersfield Town**	We	2 0	(0 0)	52,449		Keeble, Mitchell R
SF	26 Mar	N1	York City	D	1 1	(1 1)	65,000		Keeble
SFr	30 Mar	N2	York City	W	2 0	(1 0)	59,239		Keeble, White
F	07 May	N3	Manchester City	W	3 1	(1 1)	100,000		Milburn, Mitchell R, Hannah

Match	Simpson	Cowell	McMichael	Scoular	Brennan	Crowe	Milburn	Davies	Monkhouse	Hannah	Mitchell RC	Stokoe	White	Broadis	Mitchell SA	Batty	Keeble	Keery	Paterson	Thompson	Curry	Casey	Cooper	Taylor	Woollard	Tait
1	1	2	3	4	5	6	7	8	9	10	11															
2	1	2	3	4		6	7	8		10	11	5	9													
3	1	2	3	4		6	7	8	9	10	11	5														
4	1	2	3	4		6	7			10	11	5	9	8												
5		2	3	4		6	7			10	11	5	9	8	1											
6	1	2	3	4		6	7			10	11	5	9	8												
7	1	2	3	4		6	7			10	11	5	9	8												
8	1	2	3	4	5	6	7	8		10	11		9													
9	1	2	3	4	5	6	7	8		10	11		9													
10	1	2	3	4	5	6	7	8			11		9	10												
11		2		4		6	7				11	5	8		1	3	9	10								
12		2	3	4		6	9			10	11	5	7	8	1											
13		2	3	4		6	7			10	11		9	8	1				5							
14		2	3	4		6	7				11		9	8					5	1	10					
15		2	3	4		6	7				11		9	8					5	1	10					
16		2		4		6	7			10	11		9	8		3			5	1						
17	1	2		4	5	6	9				11		7	8		3					10					
18	1	2		4		6	9				11	5	7	8		3					10					
19	1	2		4		6	9				11	5	7	8		3					10					
20	1	2		4		6	9				11	5	7	8		3	10									
21	1	2		4			8				11	5	7			3	9				10	6				
22	1	2		4			8				11	5	7			3	9				10	6				
23	1	2		4			8				11	5	7			3	9				10	6				
24	1	2		4			8				11	5	7			3	9				10		6			
25	1	2		4			8				11	5				3	9				10		6	7		
26	1	2		4			7			10	11	5		8		3	9					6				
27	1			4		6	7	8		10	11	5				3	9								2	
28	1			4		6	7	8		10	11	5				3	9								2	
29	1	2		4			7			10	11	5		8		3	9					6				
30	1	2		4	5		10				11			8		3	9					6		7		
31	1	2		4			8			10	11	5	7			3	9					6				
32	1	2	3	4		6	9	8		10	11	5	7													
33	1	2	3	4		6		8		10	11	5	7				9									
34	1	2	3	4		6		8		10	11	5	7				9									
35	1	2		4		6	9	8		10	11	5				3										7
36	1	2		4		6	9	8		10	11	5	7			3										
37	1	2		4		6		8		10	11	5	7			3	9									
38	1	2		4		6	7	8		10	11	5				3	9									
39	1	2		4		6	7	8		10	11	5				3	9									
40	1	2	11	4			9			10		5	7	8		3						6				
41	1	2	11	4					7	10		5		8		3		9				6				
42	1	2		4		6	7	8		10	11	5				3	9									
Round																										
3	1	2		4			10				11	5	7	8		3	9	6								
4	1	2		4			7			8	11	5				3	9				10	6				
5	1	2		4		6	7	8			11	5	9			3	10									
5r	1	2		4			7			10	11	5		8		3	9					6				
5rr	1	2		4		6	10	8	9		11	5	7			3										
6	1	2		4			10				11	5	7	8		3	9					6				
6r	1	2		4			10				11	5	7	8		3	9					6				
SF	1	2		4			10	8			11	5	7			3	9					6				
SFr	1	2		4		6	10	8			11	5	7			3	9									
F	1	2		4			8			10	11	5	7			3	9					6				

N1 Played at Hillsborough, Sheffield
N2 Played at Roker Park, Sunderland
N3 Played at Wembley Stadium, London

De Drawn after extra time
We Won after extra time

DateLine ... 8 Sept: Len White scores four goals against Aston Villa including three headers. **1 Jan:** United concede four goals in the first eight minutes at Bramall Lane against Sheffield United as new boss Duggie Livingstone watches. **30 March:** United take care of giant-killers York City in the replayed FA Cup semi-final at Roker Park. **7 May:** Newcastle lift the FA Cup for the third time in only five years by beating Manchester City 3-1.

SEASON **1955-56**

DIVISION 1

Revenge, after nearly 50 years

Newcastle soon reverted back to director control as Livingstone moved on half-way through the 1955-56 programme. In the comfort zone for most of the season, climbing to the dizzy height of third place in the table over Easter, the campaign was dominated by four matches with their nearest and dearest of rivals, Sunderland. In a festive double meeting with the red-and-whites, the Magpies at long last recorded some semblance of revenge for that long ago 1908 defeat. At Roker Park on Boxing Day they won by all of 6-1, and with more luck could have got close to that infamous tally of nine goals. The Black'n'Whites were 4-0 up at the interval with strikes from Milburn, Curry and a double hit from Vic Keeble. Then Jackie Milburn grabbed his second, as did Bill Curry to rack up six. After that United eased up, maybe with the knowledge they had a return match a day later. Sunderland avoided total humiliation, but had to face a rampant Magpie eleven on Tyneside in double-quick time. United gave their rivals another lesson 24-hours later by winning 3-1 at St James' Park.

United defended their title of FA Cup kings and looked to be even heading for another semi-final place with a real chance of getting to the Cup final again until neighbours Sunderland defied the odds and won the quarter-final tie at a packed St James' Park in March. Following victories over Sheffield Wednesday, Fulham – a truly remarkable tie which ended 5-4 at Craven Cottage after being 3-0 ahead and 4-3 behind – and then Stoke City, United entertained Sunderland in front of almost 62,000. United were firm favourites, but had a decidedly off-day and their Wear rivals took advantage by winning 2-0. That reverse was a blow, and United's good League form which had taken them to just behind leaders and eventual Champions Manchester United, waned as a result. The Black'n'Whites slipped into mid-table following a single win in a 10 game spell to the end of the season.

Pictured above: Welsh international Reg Davies could be a handful, being fast and robust up front.

Memorabilia CORNER

Programme from the derby with Sunderland. Over the festive period United hit nine goals over two days against the red-and-whites.

IN CHARGE

Chairman: Wilf Taylor
Manager: Duggie Livingstone/Director Committee
Captain: Jimmy Scoular
Trainer/Coach: Norman Smith

ST JAMES' PARK

Average Attendance
Lg 37,666 Lg & Cup 39,740

United pictured before a fixture against Atletico Madrid in Spain. Back row, left to right: Stokoe, Simpson, McMichael, Casey, Lackenby. Front: Scoular, White, Davies, Keeble, Curry, Mitchell.

PLAYER FOCUS Vic Keeble

Born Colchester. Centre-forward, 6'0"
1952 to 1957: 121 app 69 goals.

Spotted by United's celebrated veteran scout Bill McCracken during the early Fifties, Vic Keeble joined United for £15,000 as a promising goal-poacher in February 1952 from his home town club of Colchester United. Highly rated in Division Three at Layer Road, Keeble had been for a brief spell with Arsenal as a kid. On Tyneside it took him a while to claim a spot in the United line-up due to being away from Tyneside for periods on National Service as well as the form of Jackie Milburn in the leader's role. But he took over the No. 9 shirt when Milburn was switched to inside-forward and proved a very effective centre-forward. With little finesse, Keeble was a bustler up front and was noted for his aerial prowess. Vic was a handful for defenders and in season 1954-55 as United lifted the FA Cup he was a dangerous front man grabbing five goals in the run to Wembley. Then Keeble claimed 29 goals in 1955-56 when he combined with Milburn effectively in Newcastle's attack. Nicknamed Camel due to his stooped posture on the field, afterwards though Vic picked up a back injury and lost his place, eventually joining West Ham United for a £10,000 fee in October 1957. At Upton Park he scored 19 goals and was a key factor in the Hammers winning promotion during his first season. That back problem caused Keeble's retirement in 1960, afterwards being linked with Colchester and Chelmsford in administrative roles. His son Chris appeared for Ipswich Town and Colchester United in the 1990s.

SEASON REVIEW

Football League Div 1: P42 W17 D7 L18 F85 A70 Pts 41.
Position: 11th (Champions; Manchester United).
FA Cup: QF (Winners; Manchester City).

Appearances (47m): Milburn JET 43, Davies ER 41, Simpson RC 41, McMichael A 38, Keeble VAW 36, Mitchell RC 33, Scoular J 33, Stokoe R 31, Casey T 28, Batty RR 24, Curry WM 23, White LR 22, Paterson WAK 19, Crowe CA 18, Hannah GL 16, Lackenby G 16, Brennan F 11, Punton WH 8, Tait A 8, Waugh K 7, Woollard AJ 7, Thompson JH 6, Monkhouse ATW 4, Keery S 2, Ferguson RB 1, Taylor JH 1.

Goals (95g): Keeble VAW 29, Milburn JET 21, Curry WM 9, Davies ER 9, White LR 7, Mitchell RC 6, Hannah GL 3, Casey T 2, Crowe CA 2, Stokoe R 2, Monkhouse ATW 1, Paterson WAK 1, Scoular J 1, Tait A 1, own goal 1.

Dismissals: 0 players.

MAJOR SIGNINGS

None

FROM THE RANKS

Bobby Ferguson (Dudley Jnrs)
Ken Waugh (Film Renters)

TEAM COLOURS Black & white striped shirts, black shorts (Change; white shirts, black shorts)

SEASON 1955–56

Match	Date	Venue	Opponent	Result	Score	HT	Att	Posn	Scorers
			FL Division 1						
1	20 Aug	H	**Sheffield United**	W	4 2	(3 0)	42,559		Davies 2, Hannah, Keeble
2	24 Aug	H	**Birmingham City**	D	2 2	(1 2)	34,473	4	Davies, Keeble
3	27 Aug	A	Preston North End	L	3 4	(0 3)	39,583	8	Hannah, White 2
4	31 Aug	A	Birmingham City	L	1 3	(0 0)	38,690	8	White
5	03 Sep	H	**Burnley**	W	3 1	(3 0)	41,272	10	Davies, Mitchell, Scoular
6	07 Sep	A	West Bromwich Albion	D	1 1	(1 0)	20,555	10	Davies
7	10 Sep	A	Luton Town	L	2 4	(0 3)	25,719	14	Milburn 2
8	17 Sep	H	**Charlton Athletic**	W	4 1	(1 0)	39,040	12	Keeble, Milburn 3
9	24 Sep	A	Tottenham Hotspur	L	1 3	(0 3)	41,096	14	Milburn
10	01 Oct	H	**Everton**	L	1 2	(1 2)	40,493	15	Tait
11	08 Oct	H	**Portsmouth**	W	2 1	(1 0)	42,320	15	Mitchell 2
12	15 Oct	A	Arsenal	L	0 1	(0 1)	46,093	16	
13	22 Oct	H	**Wolverhampton Wanderers**	W	3 1	(0 0)	34,575	14	Davies, Keeble, Monkhouse
14	29 Oct	A	Aston Villa	L	0 3	(0 1)	26,851	16	
15	05 Nov	H	**Blackpool**	L	1 2	(0 0)	54,557	16	Milburn
16	12 Nov	A	Huddersfield Town	W	6 2	(2 0)	18,664	16	Crowe, Keeble 4, White
17	19 Nov	H	**Cardiff City**	W	4 0	(1 0)	35,603	16	Milburn 2 (1 pen), Keeble, Crowe
18	26 Nov	A	Manchester City	W	2 1	(2 1)	22,860	13	Hannah, Keeble
19	03 Dec	H	**Bolton Wanderers**	W	3 0	(1 0)	36,856	12	Davies, Keeble 2
20	10 Dec	A	Chelsea	L	1 2	(1 1)	37,327	13	Milburn (pen)
21	17 Dec	A	Sheffield United	L	1 2	(1 2)	17,961	15	Milburn
22	24 Dec	H	**Preston North End**	W	5 0	(2 0)	32,976		Mitchell (pen), Keeble 2, Milburn 2
23	26 Dec	A	Sunderland	W	6 1	(4 0)	55,723	6	Curry 2, Keeble 2, Milburn 2
24	27 Dec	H	**Sunderland**	W	3 1	(0 1)	61,058	6	Keeble, Milburn, White
25	31 Dec	A	Burnley	L	1 3	(1 2)	29,032	10	Keeble
26	02 Jan	H	**West Bromwich Albion**	L	0 3	(0 1)	50,768	13	
27	14 Jan	H	**Luton Town**	W	4 0	(1 0)	21,464	9	Curry, Davies, Keeble 2
28	21 Jan	A	Charlton Athletic	W	2 0	(0 0)	34,414	5	Casey, Mitchell
29	04 Feb	H	**Tottenham Hotspur**	L	1 2	(0 0)	29,597	8	Paterson
30	11 Feb	A	Everton	D	0 0	(0 0)	35,653	8	
31	22 Feb	A	Portsmouth	W	2 0	(1 0)	15,100		Curry, Keeble
32	25 Feb	H	**Arsenal**	W	2 0	(2 0)	50,822	3	Curry, Milburn
33	07 Mar	A	Cardiff City	D	1 1	(1 1)	31,265		Curry
34	10 Mar	H	**Aston Villa**	L	2 3	(1 2)	34,647	4	Curry, og (Dugdale)
35	17 Mar	A	Blackpool	L	1 5	(0 1)	23,740	5	Keeble
36	24 Mar	H	**Huddersfield Town**	D	1 1	(0 1)	20,008	4	Davies
37	30 Mar	A	Manchester United	L	2 5	(1 1)	58,748	4	Keeble, Stokoe
38	31 Mar	A	Wolverhampton Wanderers	L	1 2	(1 0)	31,940		Keeble
39	02 Apr	H	**Manchester United**	D	0 0	(0 0)	37,395	9	
40	07 Apr	H	**Manchester City**	W	3 1	(1 0)	26,181	8	Keeble, Milburn, White
41	14 Apr	A	Bolton Wanderers	L	2 3	(2 2)	17,173	10	Keeble, White
42	21 Apr	H	**Chelsea**	D	1 1	(0 1)	24,322	11	Milburn (pen)
Round			**FA Cup**						
3	07 Jan	A	Sheffield Wednesday	W	3 1	(0 0)	48,198		Curry, Keeble, Milburn
4	28 Jan	A	Fulham	W	5 4	(3 1)	39,200		Casey, Keeble 2, Milburn, Stokoe
5	18 Feb	H	**Stoke City**	W	2 1	(1 0)	61,550		Curry, Mitchell
6	03 Mar	H	**Sunderland**	L	0 2	(0 1)	61,474		
			FA Charity Shield						
	14 Sep	A	Chelsea	L	0 3	(0 0)	12,802		

Match	Simpson	Woollard	McMichael	Scoular	Stokoe	Crowe	Milburn	Davies	Keeble	Hannah	Mitchell	Brennan	Casey	White	Thompson	Lackenby	Punton	Tait	Batty	Monkhouse	Waugh	Keery	Curry	Paterson	Taylor	Ferguson
1	1	2	3	4	5	6	7	8	9	10	11															
2	1	2	3	4	5	6	7	8	9	10	11															
3	1		3	4	5		9	8		10	11	2	6	7												
4	1		3	4	5		7	8		10	11	2	6	9												
5			3	4			7	8		10	11	5	6	9	1	2										
6			3	4			7	8		10	11	5	6	9	1	2										
7			3	4			7	8		10		5	6	9	1	2	11									
8			3	4	5		9	8	10		11		6		1	2		7								
9			3	4	5		9	8	10		11		6		1	2		7								
10	1		3	4	5	6		8		10	11			9				7	2							
11	1			4	5	6	8		10		11	2						7	3	9						
12	1			5		6	9	8	10		11							7	3		2	4				
13	1			4		6		8	10			5					11	7	3	9	2					
14	1					6		8	10			5	4				11	7	3	9	2					
15	1			4	5	6	9	8	10			2					11	7	3							
16	1		3	4	5	6	11	8	9	10				7		2										
17	1		3	4	5	6	11	8	9	10				7		2										
18	1		3	4	5	6	11	8	9	10				7		2										
19	1		3	4	5	6	10	8	9					7		2							11			
20	1		3	4	5	6	10	8	9					7			11		2							
21	1		3	4			7	8	9	10							11		2			6		5		
22	1		3	4			7	8	9		11		6						2				10	5		
23	1		3	4			7	8	9		11		6						2				10	5		
24	1		3	4			7	8	9				6	11					2				10	5		
25	1		3			4	7	8	9				6	11					2				10	5		
26	1	2	3			4	7	8			11	5	6	9									10			
27	1	2	3		4		7	8	9		11		6										10	5		
28	1	2	3		4		7	8	9		11		6										10	5		
29	1		3		4		7	8			11		6						2	9			10	5		
30	1		3		4		7	8			11		6	9					2				10	5		
31	1		3		4		7	8	9		11		6						2				10	5		
32	1		3		4		7	8	9		11		6						2				10	5		
33	1			6	4		7	8	9		11								3		2		10	5		
34	1			6	4		7	8	9		11								3		2		10	5		
35	1		3	4	5		7		9		11		6	8							2		10			
36	1		3		4		7	8			11		6	9							2		10	5		
37	1		3		4		7	8	9	10	11		6			2								5		
38	1		3	4	5		8		9	10	11		6	7		2										
39	1			4	5	6	8		9	10	11					2			3						7	
40	1			4		6	8		9		11			7		5			2				10			3
41	1		3	4		6		8	9					7		5	11		2				10			
42	1		3	4			8		9		11		6	7		5			2				10			
Round																										
3	1	2	3		4		7	8	9		11		6										10	5		
4	1	2	3		4		7	8	9		11		6										10	5		
5	1		3		4		7	8	9		11		6						2				10	5		
6	1		3	6	4		7	8	9		11								2				10	5		
CS			3	4			9	8		10		5	6	7	1	2	11									

DateLine ... 26 Dec: United thrash Sunderland 6-1 at Roker Park, the first of a memorable derby Festive double. **28 Jan:** An epic FA Cup-tie with Fulham is played out at Craven Cottage, won 5-4 by United. **22 Feb:** United take part in the Football League's first floodlit match a 2-0 win at Portsmouth. **3 March:** Sunderland gain derby revenge by dumping United out of the FA Cup, winning a quarter-final tie by 2-0.

SEASON 1956-57

DIVISION 1

Managerless and rudderless

Newcastle decided not to appoint a manager after the departure of Duggie Livingstone, reverting back to the somewhat archaic director control. With unrest simmering in the Boardroom as well, on the pitch United were largely without guidance and inspiration; managerless and rudderless for most of the season. Rarely did the Magpies have a settled line-up and they slipped into the relegation zone and were in need of points. They went through a dismal autumn with a single victory in 13 games. Newcastle's Fifties heyday was now well and truly over. Alongside them in the basement scrap were Sunderland, and two victories in the season over their local rivals cheered-up all at St James' Park – including a six-goal spree at Christmas.

Stand-in centre-forward and part-timer Alex Tait grabbed a special hat-trick in that win against the Wearsiders at Gallowgate, watched by one of the smallest derby attendances in the era. Due to dense fog, only 29,727 turned up as many thought the game would be postponed. But it went ahead, even though visibility was difficult. In the next home match four days later when West Bromwich Albion faced United, another five goals hit the visitors net. United steadily moved clear of the drop following a good run in March, in the final analysis in 17th place with seven points to spare.

In the middle of League despair, the Black'n'Whites took part in a showpiece FA Cup-tie with 1955 finalists Manchester City – a classic encounter to match anything in both club's remarkable history. A rousing draw at Gallowgate took the contest to Maine Road and City had United reeling, ahead by three goals in the first half hour. But Newcastle's old FA Cup fighting spirit saw the Geordies level at 3-3 and earn extra-time. City went back in front at 4-3 and United had to do it all again. And they did it, equalising then remarkably claiming a winner with a Len White shot to make the score 5-4. After all that hard work though, the Magpies fell pitifully to Third Division Millwall in Round Four.

Pictured above: Bill Curry came through the junior ranks, United's first player capped by England at Under-23 level.

Memorabilia CORNER

FOOTBALL LEAGUE, DIVISION 1 • CENTRAL LEAGUE
NEWCASTLE UNITED FOOTBALL CLUB
ST. JAMES' PARK NEWCASTLE UPON TYNE
SEASON 1956-1957
OFFICIAL PROGRAMME PRICE 3d

Newcastle's programme throughout the 1950s had a striking design for the era.

IN CHARGE

Chairman: Wilf Taylor
Manager: Director Committee
Captain: Jimmy Scoular
Trainer/Coach: Norman Smith

ST JAMES' PARK

Average Attendance
Lg 35,202 Lg & Cup 36,235

The Black'n'Whites during 1956-57. Back row, left to right: Casey, Batty, Simpson, McMichael, Stokoe. Front: Davies, Milburn, Scoular, Keeble, Hannah, Prior.

PLAYER FOCUS Bob Stokoe

Born Mickley. Centre-half, 6'0"
1947 to 1961: 288 app 5 goals.

Although on United's staff since September 1947 it took Bob Stokoe a long time to claim a regular slot in the team. Joining the Magpies from local football with Spen Juniors as a half-back, he made his debut in the centre-forward role, scoring against Middlesbrough, and was destined to play a shadow part in the club's double Wembley victory in 1951 and 1952. Stokoe was tall, mobile and good in the air, but almost left the club on more than one occasion in search of first-team football. But he eventually claimed the centre-half position for his own on Frank Brennan's exit in season 1954-55. Bob appeared for United in the club's next FA Cup success in 1955 and he went onto skipper the Geordies in the years leading up to the Sixties decade, a dependable figure as United went through a mediocre period. Stokoe left Tyneside after loyal service during February 1961, joining Bury as a veteran. He soon was appointed player-manager, the start of a long career as a boss. Stokoe was also in charge of Charlton, Rochdale, Carlisle and Blackpool while he returned famously to Wembley with Sunderland in 1973, winning the trophy for a second time, on this occasion as a manager. After a brief spell on United's coaching team in 1989, Bob settled back in his native Tyne Valley, in Hexham on retirement. He was awarded the Football League's Long Service Medal in 1984.

SEASON REVIEW

Football League Div 1: P42 W14 D8 L20 F67 A87 Pts 36.
Position: 17th (Champions; Manchester United).
FA Cup: R4 (Winners; Aston Villa).

Appearances (45m): Stokoe R 41, Simpson RC 38, Keith RM 36, Scoular J 36, Milburn JET 33, White LR 33, Casey T 29, Davies ER 29, Batty RR 27, Mitchell RC 26, McMichael A 25, Curry WM 21, Eastham GE 18, Hannah GL 15, Keeble VAW 14, Tait A 13, Punton WH 12, Crowe CA 11, Keery S 8, Franks AJ 7, Mitchell SA 7, Taylor JH 4, Scott ME 3, Hughes G 2, Lackenby G 2, Prior KG 2, Cooper J 1, Paterson WAK 1, Redhead WS 1.

Goals (74g): Davies ER 13, White LR 13, Milburn JET 12, Casey T 7, Tait A 7, Curry WM 5, Keeble VAW 4, Scoular J 3, Eastham GE 2, Hannah GL 2, Mitchell RC 2, Crowe CA 1, Punton WH 1, Taylor JH 1, own goal 1.

Dismissals: 0 players.

MAJOR SIGNINGS

Dick Keith (Linfield) £9,000
George Eastham (Ards) £9,000

FROM THE RANKS

Albert Franks (Boldon CW/Sunderland)
Gordon Hughes (Tow Law Town)
Malcolm Scott (Cleadon Jnrs)
Bill Redhead (George Angus)

TEAM COLOURS Black & white striped shirts, black shorts (Change; white shirts, black shorts)

SEASON 1956-57

Match	Date		FL Division 1				HT	Att	Posn	Scorers	Simpson	Lackenby	McMichael	Scoular	Stokoe	Crowe	Taylor	Milburn	Keeble	Hannah	Mitchell RC	Davies	Batty	Prior	Casey	Keith	Keery	Hughes	Punton	White	Eastham	Paterson	Curry	Tait	Redhead	Scott	Cooper	Franks	Mitchell SA	Match
1	18 Aug	H	**Portsmouth**	W	2	1	(0 0)	30,191		Crowe, Taylor	1	2	3	4	5	6	7	8	9	10	11																			1
2	22 Aug	A	Cardiff City	L	2	5	(1 2)	35,833		Davies 2	1	2	3	4	5	6		7	9	10	11	8																		2
3	25 Aug	A	Sunderland	W	2	1	(1 0)	51,032	7	Davies, Milburn	1		3	4	5	6		8	9	10	11	7	2																	3
4	29 Aug	H	**Cardiff City**	W	1	0	(0 0)	34,859	7	Keeble	1		3	4	5	6		8	9	10	11	7	2																	4
5	01 Sep	A	Sheffield Wednesday	L	0	4	(0 3)	36,270	11		1		3	4	5	6		8	9	10	11	7	2																	5
6	05 Sep	A	Birmingham City	L	1	6	(0 3)	32,506	11	Keeble	1		3	4	5			8	9	10		7	2	11	6															6
7	08 Sep	H	**Manchester United**	D	1	1	(0 0)	50,133	13	Milburn	1				5	6		9		10		8	3	11		2	4	7												7
8	15 Sep	A	Arsenal	W	1	0	(0 0)	46,318	11	Hannah	1				5	6		7	9	10		8	3			2	4		11											8
9	22 Sep	H	**Burnley**	D	1	1	(1 1)	36,790	12	Keeble	1				5		7		9	10		8	3		6	2	4		11											9
10	29 Sep	A	Preston North End	L	0	1	(0 1)	29,189	13		1				5	6	7		9	10	11	8	3			2	4													10
11	06 Oct	H	**Luton Town**	D	2	2	(1 1)	36,941	12	Hannah, Milburn	1				5	6		9		10	11		3			2	4			7	8									11
12	13 Oct	A	Aston Villa	L	1	3	(1 3)	35,038	15	Eastham	1			4	5	6		9		10	11		3			2				7	8									12
13	20 Oct	H	**Manchester City**	L	0	3	(0 2)	34,802	16		1			4	5		7	9	10		11		3		6	2					8									13
14	27 Oct	A	Charlton Athletic	D	1	1	(1 1)	21,473	17	Curry	1		3								11	10			6	2	4			7	8	5	9							14
15	03 Nov	H	**Leeds United**	L	2	3	(1 1)	49,034	17	Davies, Keeble	1		3		5			7	9		11	10			6	2	4				8									15
16	10 Nov	A	Tottenham Hotspur	L	1	3	(1 1)	51,722	19	White	1		3	4	5			7	9			8	2		6					11			10							16
17	17 Nov	H	**Everton**	D	0	0	(0 0)	32,263	19		1			4	5			7	9				3		6	2	10			11	8									17
18	24 Nov	A	Blackpool	W	3	2	(2 2)	18,248	18	Casey, Milburn, White	1			4	5			8	9		11		3		6	2				7			10							18
19	01 Dec	H	**Wolverhampton Wanderers**	W	2	1	(1 0)	37,562	16	Curry, White	1			4	5			8					3		6	2		7		11	10		9							19
20	08 Dec	A	Bolton Wanderers	L	1	3	(1 2)	25,131	18	Davies	1			4	5			8			11	10	3		6	2				7			9							20
21	15 Dec	A	Portsmouth	D	2	2	(0 1)	18,453	18	Davies 2	1			4	5							8	3		6	2			11	7			10	9						21
22	22 Dec	H	**Sunderland**	W	6	2	(3 1)	29,727	18	Tait 3, Davies, White, Casey (pen)	1			4	5							8	3		6	2			11	7			10	9						22
23	25 Dec	A	West Bromwich Albion	L	0	1	(0 0)	13,730			1		3	4	5							8	2		6				11	7			10	9						23
24	26 Dec	H	**West Bromwich Albion**	W	5	2	(4 2)	20,319	12	Punton, Davies 2, Casey (pen), Scoular	1		3	4	5							8	2		6				11	7			10	9						24
25	29 Dec	H	**Sheffield Wednesday**	L	1	2	(0 1)	42,649	14	Curry	1			4	5								3			2			11	7	8		10	9	6					25
26	01 Jan	H	**Birmingham City**	W	3	2	(1 0)	29,383	12	Tait, Casey 2 (1 pen)	1			4	5			8					3		6	2			11	7			10	9						26
27	12 Jan	A	Manchester United	L	1	6	(0 3)	44,911	12	Milburn	1			4		6		8			11		3			2				7	10		9			5				27
28	19 Jan	H	**Arsenal**	W	3	1	(1 0)	46,815	14	Curry, White 2	1			4	5			7				8	3		6	2			11	9			10							28
29	02 Feb	A	Burnley	L	2	3	(1 0)	26,778	13	Milburn, Tait	1		3	4				10			11	8				2				7				9		5	6			29
30	09 Feb	H	**Preston North End**	L	1	2	(1 0)	43,086	14	Milburn	1		3	4	5			10				8			6	2			11	7				9						30
31	16 Feb	A	Luton Town	L	1	4	(0 2)	21,003	14	Milburn	1		3	4	5			7			11					2				8	10			9				6		31
32	23 Feb	H	**Charlton Athletic**	W	3	1	(3 1)	21,721	14	Casey, Eastham, Scoular			3	4	5						11				10	2				7	8			9				6	1	32
33	02 Mar	A	Manchester City	W	2	1	(1 0)	25,229	11	Mitchell R, White			3	4	5						11				10	2				7	8			9				6	1	33
34	09 Mar	H	**Bolton Wanderers**	W	4	0	(2 0)	34,073	11	Davies, Milburn, Scoular, White			3	4	5			7			11	8			6	2				9	10								1	34
35	16 Mar	A	Leeds United	D	0	0	(0 0)	32,541	11				3	4	5			7			11	8			6	2				9	10								1	35
36	23 Mar	H	**Tottenham Hotspur**	D	2	2	(2 2)	37,955	11	Davies, Milburn			3	4	5			7			11	8			6	2				9	10								1	36
37	30 Mar	A	Everton	L	1	2	(0 1)	29,775	11	og (Donovan)			3	4	5			7			11	8			6	2				9	10								1	37
38	06 Apr	H	**Blackpool**	W	2	1	(1 0)	31,777	10	Davies, Milburn			3	4	5			7				8			6	2				11	10		9						1	38
39	13 Apr	A	Wolverhampton Wanderers	L	0	2	(0 0)	22,335	12		1		3	4	5			7				8				2				11	10		9					6		39
40	19 Apr	H	**Chelsea**	L	1	2	(0 2)	30,708	12	White	1		3	4	5			7		8	11					2				9			10					6		40
41	20 Apr	H	**Aston Villa**	L	1	2	(1 0)	28,453	12	Mitchell R	1		3		5			8		10	11				6	2				7			9					4		41
42	22 Apr	A	Chelsea	L	2	6	(2 2)	20,795	17	Milburn, White	1		3		5			8		10	11				6	2				7			9					4		42
Round			**FA Cup**																																					**Round**
3	05 Jan	H	**Manchester City**	D	1	1	(0 0)	57,921		White	1			4	5			9				8	3		6	2			11	7			10							3
3r	09 Jan	A	Manchester City	We	5	4	(0 3)	46,990		Curry, Tait, White 2, Casey (pen)	1			4	5						11	8	3		6	2				7			10	9						3r
4	26 Jan	A	Millwall	L	1	2	(0 1)	45,646		Tait	1			4								8	3		6	2			11	7			10	9		5				4

We — Won after extra time

DateLine ... 22 Dec: The Black'n'Whites hit Sunderland for six again, this time 6-2 at St James' Park, Alex Tait striking a hat-trick. **9 Jan:** Another scintillating FA Cup thriller for the second year running, United winning 5-4 at Manchester City. **22 April:** Jackie Milburn scores his 200th and last senior goal for United against Chelsea, a club record until 2006.

NEWCASTLE UNITED

Magpies in need of direction

As the season began it was quickly apparent that Newcastle were going to have another season of toil and tears. They lacked almost everything, and were in dire need of direction. United were poor on Tyneside, winning only six games, yet more than good on their travels. With many new faces blooded, a mix of youngsters and fresh arrivals, yet few to impress, United again dropped into the lower reaches of the First Division. Once more they were alongside neighbours Sunderland. There was a real possibility that one – if not both – of the North East giants would drop into the second-tier. It was Sunderland who were relegated – for the first time – while United very nearly joined them, but scrambled to safety on goal-average. A 4-1 victory over Manchester City in April was crucial. Then two points were picked up with draws against Bolton and Manchester United before a nail-biting finale which saw worrying defeats on Tyneside to Leeds and Burnley.

There were more grumbles from the terraces and stands after another painful exit in the FA Cup, this time eventual Third Division (North) Champions Scunthorpe United arrived on Tyneside to inflict an embarrassing 3-1 defeat. Amidst all this doom, one player did blossom in the black-and-white stripes, Len White, who took over from Milburn as the fans' hero. At centre-forward he became a deadly striker.

With the club almost in free-fall, at last the Board decided to engage a manager once more, and come to terms with the times. They needed someone to take full control and thrust the club into a new rapidly changing world of football. There were several contenders for the post, and many who warned of an 'impossible job' on Tyneside. Ex-Manchester United star Charlie Mitten was the man to breeze into St James' Park as United's new boss. At 37 years of age, he was seen as the moderniser, to catapult United out of their old ways.

Pictured above: Albert Franks claimed a regular spot at half-back, a powerful player with a mighty throw-in.

Memorabilia CORNER

Programme from the FA Cup-tie with Scunthorpe United, a shock 3-1 defeat.

IN CHARGE

Chairman: Wilf Taylor/William McKeag
Manager: Director Committee
Captain: Bob Stokoe
Trainer/Coach: Norman Smith

ST JAMES' PARK

Average Attendance
Lg 36,246 Lg & Cup 36,382

The Magpies pictured at St James' Park during 1957-58. Back row, left to right: Scoular, Batty, Stokoe, Simpson, McMichael, Casey. Front: Hill, Davies, Curry, Eastham, Mitchell.

SEASON REVIEW

Football League Div 1: P42 W12 D8 L22 F73 A81 Pts 32.
Position: 19th (Champions; Wolverhampton Wanderers).
FA Cup: R4 (Winners; Bolton Wanderers).

Appearances (44m): Scoular J 43, Mitchell RC 38, McMichael A 37, Simpson RC 36, Stokoe R 36, Franks AJ 35, White LR 32, Eastham GE 31, Keith RM 27, Hughes G 26, Curry WM 23, Davies ER 22, Batty RR 14, Casey T 12, Hill JM 11, McKinney WE 10, Bottom AE 8, Tait A 8, Mitchell SA 7, Keeble VAW 6, Punton WH 5, Bell JR 4, Hale KO 3, Nesbitt J 3, Paterson WAK 3, Cooper J 1, Harker CJ 1, Scott ME 1, Whitehead R 1.

Goals (80g): White LR 25, Mitchell RC 13, Curry WM 11, Bottom AE 7, Davies ER 5, Eastham GE 5, Franks AJ 2, Hill JM 2, Hughes G 2, Batty RR 1, Bell JR 1, Casey T 1, Keeble VAW 1, Paterson WAK 1, Stokoe R 1, Tait A 1, own goal 1.

Dismissals: 0 players.

MAJOR SIGNINGS

Arthur Bottom (York City) £4,500
Jimmy Hill (Linfield) exchange

FROM THE RANKS

Jackie Bell (Evenwood Town)
Ken Hale (Newsham BC/Everton)
Bill McKinney (Wallsend St Lukes)
Bob Whitehead (Fatfield Jnrs)
Chris Harker (West Allotment)
John Nesbitt (South Shields)

PLAYER FOCUS Jimmy Scoular

Born Livingston. Right-half, 5'7"
1953 to 1961: 272 app 6 goals.

United's record signing from Portsmouth in June 1953 for a fee of £22,250, Jimmy Scoular was recognised as one of the game's best midfielders of the immediate post-war years. An experienced campaigner at the heart of Pompey's fine side which lifted two Football League titles in 1949 and 1950 – when United chased them hard – Jimmy was rugged, yet possessed skills on the ball and the ability to pin-point passes all over the field. Appearing for Portsmouth in over 280 matches and capped by Scotland on nine occasions, he replaced the leadership qualities of Joe Harvey in Newcastle's camp and guided the Black'n'Whites to FA Cup glory at Wembley in 1955. In that victory over Manchester City, Jimmy largely dominated the midfield and his sweeping cross-field passing was a feature of the final. He was at times controversial and a real competitor while he could fall out with individuals as he snarled at both colleagues and opponents on the pitch. With balding head and rolled-up sleeves, Scoular was one of the personality players of the 1940s and 1950s and served the Magpies with credit for seven full seasons. The Scot entered management with Bradford Park Avenue in January 1961, subsequently taking charge of Cardiff City and Newport County. At Ninian Park, he was boss for almost a decade and saw the Bluebirds feature on the European stage. His father Alec appeared for several Scottish clubs before the Second World War.

TEAM COLOURS Black & white striped shirts, black shorts (Change; white shirts, black shorts)

SEASON 1957–58

Match	Date		FL Division 1					Att	Posn	Scorers	Simpson	Keith	McMichael	Scoular	Stokoe	Casey	White	Davies	Keeble	Curry	Mitchell RC	Batty	Hill	Eastham	Mitchell SA	Nesbitt	Franks	Hughes	Whitehead	Punton	Scott	Tait	Bell	McKinney	Hale	Paterson	Cooper	Bottom	Harker	Match
1	24 Aug	A	West Bromwich Albion	L	1	2	(0 0)	31,410		White	1	2	3	4	5	6	7	8	9	10	11																			1
2	31 Aug	H	**Tottenham Hotspur**	W	3	1	(2 0)	37,742	12	Eastham, Keeble, Mitchell R	1		3	4	5	6		8	9		11	2	7	10																2
3	04 Sep	A	Sheffield Wednesday	L	0	1	(0 0)	23,060	16		1		3	4	5	6		8	9		11	2	7	10																3
4	07 Sep	A	Birmingham City	W	4	1	(0 0)	29,784	10	Mitchell R (pen), Curry 2, Hill	1		3	4	5	6		8		9	11	2	7	10																4
5	11 Sep	H	**Portsmouth**	W	2	0	(1 0)	39,027	8	Davies, Mitchell R	1		3	4	5	6		8		9	11	2	7	10																5
6	14 Sep	H	**Chelsea**	L	1	3	(1 1)	44,560	11	Mitchell R (pen)	1		3	4	5	6		8		9	11	2	7	10																6
7	18 Sep	A	Portsmouth	D	2	2	(1 2)	32,093	13	Curry, Hill		2	3	4	5	6		8	9	10	11		7		1															7
8	21 Sep	A	Sunderland	L	0	2	(0 1)	45,718	15			2	3	4	5	6		8	9	10	11		7		1															8
9	25 Sep	H	**Sheffield Wednesday**	D	0	0	(0 0)	27,651			1	2		4			9			10	11	3	8			5	6	7												9
10	28 Sep	A	Burnley	W	2	0	(1 0)	18,405	10	Curry 2	1			4	5		7			9	11	3	8	10			6		2											10
11	05 Oct	H	**Preston North End**	L	0	2	(0 1)	36,131	11		1	2		4	5		7			9	11	3	8	10			6													11
12	12 Oct	H	**Everton**	L	2	3	(1 1)	30,472	14	Curry, Davies	1	2		4	5		7	8	10	9		3					6			11										12
13	19 Oct	A	Aston Villa	L	3	4	(1 3)	27,660	16	Curry 2, Eastham	1	2		4			8			9		3		10			6			11	5	7								13
14	26 Oct	H	**Wolverhampton Wanderers**	D	1	1	(1 1)	44,361	18	Curry	1	2		4	5		8	10		9		3					6			11		7								14
15	02 Nov	A	Leicester City	L	1	2	(0 1)	31,884	18	Batty	1	2		4	5			8		9		3		10			6			11		7								15
16	09 Nov	H	**Blackpool**	L	1	2	(1 2)	36,410	18	og (Gratrix)	1	2	3	4	5		8			9				10			6			11		7								16
17	16 Nov	A	Luton Town	W	3	0	(3 0)	19,670	18	Bell, White 2	1	2	3	4	5		9				11			8			6	7					10							17
18	23 Nov	H	**Manchester United**	L	1	2	(1 0)	53,950	18	Mitchell R	1	2	3	4	5		9				11			8			6	7					10							18
19	30 Nov	A	Arsenal	W	3	2	(1 1)	41,649	17	Hughes, Mitchell R 2 (1 pen)	1	2	3	4			9			10	11			8		5	6	7												19
20	07 Dec	H	**Bolton Wanderers**	L	1	2	(0 2)	29,886	19	Eastham	1	2	3	4	5		9				11			8			6	7					10							20
21	14 Dec	A	Leeds United	L	0	3	(0 2)	23,363	20		1		3	4				10		9	11	2		8		5	6	7												21
22	21 Dec	H	**West Bromwich Albion**	W	3	0	(0 0)	31,699	18	Davies, White 2	1	2	3	4	5		9	8			11			10			6	7												22
23	25 Dec	H	**Nottingham Forest**	L	1	4	(1 1)	25,214	19	Hughes	1	2	3	4	5		9	8			11			10			6	7												23
24	26 Dec	A	Nottingham Forest	W	3	2	(3 1)	32,359		Casey, Mitchell R, White	1	2	3	4	5	10	9				11			8			6	7												24
25	28 Dec	A	Tottenham Hotspur	D	3	3	(1 1)	51,649	17	Mitchell R (pen), White 2	1		3	4	5	10	9				11						6	7						2	8					25
26	11 Jan	H	**Birmingham City**	L	1	2	(0 0)	34,825	17	White	1		3	4	5	10	9				11			8			6	7						2						26
27	18 Jan	A	Chelsea	L	1	2	(1 2)	37,327	18	White	1		3	4			9			10	11			8			6	7						2		5				27
28	01 Feb	H	**Sunderland**	D	2	2	(2 0)	47,739	19	Curry, Tait			3					10		9	11			8	1		6					7		2		5	4			28
29	22 Feb	A	Everton	W	2	1	(0 1)	22,448	19	Bottom 2			3	4	5					9	11			8	1		6					7		2				10		29
30	01 Mar	H	**Aston Villa**	L	2	4	(2 2)	40,135	19	Mitchell R (pen), Bottom			3	4	5					9	11			8	1		6					7		2				10		30
31	08 Mar	A	Wolverhampton Wanderers	L	1	3	(0 0)	34,058	20	White			3	4	5		9			10	11				1		6	7						2				8		31
32	15 Mar	H	**Leicester City**	W	5	3	(3 2)	33,840	18	Bottom 2, White 3			3	4	5		9				11			10	1		6	7						2				8		32
33	19 Mar	A	Preston North End	L	1	2	(1 2)	24,793		White	1	2	3	4	5		9				11		8	10			6	7												33
34	29 Mar	H	**Luton Town**	W	3	2	(2 1)	16,775	18	Bottom, Davies, White	1	2	3	4	5		9	10			11						6	7										8		34
35	05 Apr	A	Blackpool	L	2	3	(0 3)	18,719		Mitchell R (pen), Franks	1	2	3	4	5		9	10			11						6	7										8		35
36	07 Apr	A	Manchester City	L	1	2	(0 1)	36,995	21	White	1	2	3	4	5		9			10	11						6	7										8		36
37	12 Apr	H	**Arsenal**	D	3	3	(1 3)	43,221	20	Curry, White, Stokoe	1	2	3	4	5		9	8		10	11						6	7												37
38	14 Apr	H	**Manchester City**	W	4	1	(1 1)	53,326	20	Davies, Franks, White 2	1	2	3	4	5		9	8			11			10			6	7												38
39	19 Apr	A	Bolton Wanderers	D	1	1	(0 0)	19,284	19	White	1	2	3	4	5		9	8			11			10			6	7												39
40	23 Apr	A	Manchester United	D	1	1	(0 1)	28,393	18	White	1	2	3	4	5		9	8			11			10			6	7												40
41	26 Apr	H	**Leeds United**	L	1	2	(0 1)	32,594	18	Mitchell R	1	2	3	4	5		9	8			11			10			6	7												41
42	28 Apr	H	**Burnley**	L	1	3	(0 1)	21,610	19	Bottom		5	3	4			11											7				9	6	2	8			10	1	42
Round			**FA Cup**																																					**Round**
3	04 Jan	A	Plymouth Argyle	W	6	1	(2 0)	38,129		Eastham 2, Mitchell R, White 3	1		3	4	5	10	9				11	2		8			6	7												3
4	25 Jan	H	**Scunthorpe United**	L	1	3	(0 1)	39,234		Paterson	1		3	4			9				11			10			6	7						2	8	5				4

DateLine ... 25 Jan: FA Cup woe for United as they are eliminated by Third Division Scunthorpe United. **28 April:** Newcastle miss the drop by goal-average after a 3-1 defeat against Burnley. **28 April:** United's reverse to Burnley is the club's 11th home failure of the season, a record at the time.

NEWCASTLE UNITED

SEASON
1958-59
DIVISION 1

Mitten's modernisation plan

Charlie Mitten brought much needed inventive and novel ideas to St James' Park and had much to do in reshaping Newcastle United. He soon introduced modern techniques as well as a new stylish Continental style kit. And he brought in new faces, notably making the record purchase of Ivor Allchurch, a midfielder of real quality. Also to make an appearance was the bosses own son, teenager John Mitten.

Following an awful opening for the often controversial Mitten – a 5-1 home defeat to Blackburn Rovers – his overhauled line-up quickly knitted together and began to entertain. There were some terrific displays as his midfield and attack clicked, as the ball was played through a sparkling triangle of Allchurch, George Eastham – a highly rated starlet – and Len White.

United's up and down form was baffling though. Chelsea took part in an amazing League fixture with United during September, a football spectacular which had all of 11 goals and the outcome never guaranteed until the closing stages. At Stamford Bridge the Londoners were ahead 3-2 at half-time, then United went in front 4-3 and 5-3, only for Chelsea to strike three times in 16 minutes and incredibly win 6-5!

United claimed a 4-4 draw with Manchester United at Old Trafford after being 4-1 down at the interval. In the next match, the Magpies lost 4-3 to Wolves at St James' Park in another terrific encounter, while in March they defeated Portsmouth 5-1 then three days later lost by the same scoreline to Manchester City. United scored 81 goals in the season and conceded 84 – that added up to plenty goalmouth action.

Going out of the FA Cup early, to Chelsea, United had reached seventh position in the table, a huge improvement on the last two seasons of struggle. Although they slid to mid-table at the end of the season, it was still a satisfying turn-around.

Pictured above: George Eastham developed as a rising star, only to become embroiled in a headline dispute.

Memorabilia CORNER

Newcastle's programme underwent a revamp and noted that St James' Park's capacity was set at 70,000.

IN CHARGE

Chairman: William McKeag
Manager: Charlie Mitten
Captain: Bob Stokoe
Trainer/Coach: Norman Smith

ST JAMES' PARK

Average Attendance
Lg 39,482 Lg & Cup 40,280

Newcastle show off a modernised kit for 1958. Back row, left to right: Scoular, Nesbit, Stokoe, Simpson, Keith, McMichael, Franks. Front: Wright (Billy), Eastham, White, Hale, Mitchell.

PLAYER FOCUS Alf McMichael

Born Belfast. Left-back, 5'8
1949 to 1963: 433 app 1 goal.

Northern Ireland international Alf McMichael was a respected full-back during the Fifties. He had ability to raise his game against the top wingers while Alf was level-headed, polished and assured. He crossed the Irish Sea for Tyneside from Linfield during September 1949 as a 21-year-old in a £23,000 joint deal with another youngster, George Hannah. McMichael took over from Bobby Corbett as United's regular left-back and appeared in the 1952 FA Cup final. Alf though was unluckily injured for both the 1951 and 1955 victories and had to watch Newcastle's triumph from the sidelines on each occasion. With first-rate positional sense in defence, McMichael spent all of 14 seasons in Newcastle's line-up, while he played an important role in Northern Ireland's celebrated 1958 World Cup campaign in Sweden. The Irishman also skippered his country on many of his 40 appearances. He led out the Magpies as well during his lengthy service at St James' Park. One of a handful of United players to total over 400 games for the club, McMichael left the first-class scene in the summer of 1963 moving across the Tyne to become South Shields player-manager. He returned to his native Belfast in 1971 becoming boss of Bangor for a short period. For many years McMichael was the club's most capped player. He only netted one goal for the Magpies in over a decade wearing the black-and-white shirt, that against Cardiff City at the end of the 1954-55 season when he appeared as an emergency outside-left.

SEASON REVIEW

Football League Div 1: P42 W17 D7 L18 F80 A80 Pts 41.
Position: 11th (Champions; Wolverhampton Wanderers).
FA Cup: R3 (Winners; Nottingham Forest).

Appearances (43m): McMichael A 40, Eastham GE 36, Keith RM 33, Scoular J 33, Harvey BR 32, White LR 31, Franks AJ 30, Hughes G 29, Allchurch IJ 27, Bell JR 24, Stokoe R 23, McGuigan JJ 22, Taylor JH 17, Mitchell RC 16, Scott ME 16, Mitchell SA 11, Curry WM 10, Davies ER 9, Whitehead R 7, Hale KO 5, Wright WJ 5, Evans R 4, Bottom AE 3, McKinney WE 3, Marshall TWJ 2, Mitten JE 2, Ferguson RB 1, Gibson J 1, Wilson CA 1.

Goals (81g): White LR 25, Allchurch IJ 16, Curry WM 10, Eastham GE 7, McGuigan JJ 5, Taylor JH 4, Bottom AE 3, Wright WJ 3, Davies ER 2, Franks AJ 2, Bell JR 1, Hughes G 1, Keith RM 1, own goal 1.

Dismissals: 0 players.

MAJOR SIGNINGS

Ivor Allchurch (Swansea Town) £28,000 club record fee
Bryan Harvey (Wisbech Town) £3,000
Terry Marshall (Wisbech Town) £7,000
John McGuigan (Southend Utd) £2,250+player
Billy Wright (Leicester City) £7,500

FROM THE RANKS

Reg Evans (Durham sch)
Carl Wilson (Delves Lane Jnrs)

TEAM COLOURS Black & white striped shirts, black shorts (Change; white shirts, black shorts)

SEASON 1958-59

Match	Date		FL Division 1						Posn		Mitchell SA	Keith	McMichael	Scoular	Scott	Bell	Hughes	Eastham	Curry	Hale	Mitchell RC	Franks	Wilson	Wright	Davies	McGuigan	Stokoe	White	Harvey	Bottom	Evans	McKinney	Ferguson	Allchurch	Mitten	Whitehead	Taylor	Marshall	Gibson	Match
1	23 Aug	H	**Blackburn Rovers**	L	1	5	(0 2)	52,497		og (Whelan)	1	2	3	4	5	6	7	8	9	10	11																			1
2	25 Aug	A	Blackpool	L	0	3	(0 1)	25,531			1	2	3	4	5	6	7	10				8	9	11																2
3	30 Aug	A	Everton	W	2	0	(0 0)	36,602	17	McGuigan, Wright	1	2	3	4	5	6	7	10						9	8	11														3
4	03 Sep	H	**Blackpool**	W	1	0	(0 0)	44,979	12	White	1	2	3	4		6	7	10							8	11	5	9												4
5	06 Sep	A	Tottenham Hotspur	W	3	1	(0 1)	41,805	10	McGuigan, White 2	1	2	3	4		6	7	10							8	11	5	9												5
6	10 Sep	A	Chelsea	L	5	6	(2 2)	46,601		Wright 2, White, Davies, Franks	1	2	3			6	7					4		10	8	11	5	9												6
7	13 Sep	H	**Manchester United**	D	1	1	(1 1)	60,670	13	Davies	1	2	3	4		6	7				11			9	10		5	8												7
8	17 Sep	H	**Chelsea**	L	1	2	(1 1)	50,283	14	White	1	2	3	4		6	7					8		11	10		5	9												8
9	20 Sep	A	Wolverhampton Wanderers	W	3	1	(2 1)	39,130	12	Bottom, White 2		2	3			6	7					4			10		5	9	1	8	11									9
10	27 Sep	H	**Portsmouth**	W	2	0	(1 0)	42,302	10	Bottom 2 (1 pen)		2	3			6	7					4			10		5	9	1	8	11									10
11	04 Oct	A	Aston Villa	L	1	2	(0 1)	29,335		White				4		6	7				11				10		5	9	1	8		2	3							11
12	11 Oct	H	**Leicester City**	W	3	1	(1 1)	46,686	8	Allchurch 2, White		2	3	4		6	7	8								11	5	9	1					10						12
13	18 Oct	A	Preston North End	W	4	3	(2 0)	25,525	7	Franks, White 3		2	3			6	7	10		8		4				11	5	9	1											13
14	25 Oct	H	**Manchester City**	W	4	1	(2 0)	54,837	7	Eastham, McGuigan, White 2		2	3			6	7	8				4				11	5	9	1					10						14
15	01 Nov	A	Arsenal	L	2	3	(0 1)	62,801	7	McGuigan, Allchurch (pen)		2	3			6	7	8				4				11	5	9	1					10						15
16	08 Nov	H	**Luton Town**	W	1	0	(1 0)	53,488	7	White		2	3			6	7	8				4				11	5	9	1					10						16
17	15 Nov	A	Birmingham City	L	0	1	(0 0)	28,720	8			2	3			6	7	8				4				11	5	9	1					10						17
18	22 Nov	H	**West Bromwich Albion**	L	1	2	(1 2)	51,636	9	Allchurch		2	3			6	7	8				4					5	9	1					10	11					18
19	29 Nov	A	Leeds United	L	2	3	(1 0)	23,732	12	Allchurch 2		2	3	4	5	6	7	8										9	1					10	11					19
20	06 Dec	H	**Burnley**	W	5	2	(3 1)	42,561	10	Allchurch 2, White, Eastham, Bell (pen)	1		3	4		6	7	8			11						5	9				2		10						20
21	13 Dec	A	Bolton Wanderers	D	1	1	(1 0)	23,020	10	White	1		3	4		6	7	8			11						5	9						10		2				21
22	20 Dec	A	Blackburn Rovers	L	0	3	(0 2)	25,207	11		1		3	4		6	7	8			11						5	9						10		2				22
23	26 Dec	H	**Nottingham Forest**	L	1	3	(1 1)	49,447		Curry		2	3	4		6	7	8	10							11	5	9	1											23
24	27 Dec	A	Nottingham Forest	L	0	3	(0 2)	39,907	15			2	3	4		6	7	8								10	5	9	1		11									24
25	03 Jan	H	**Everton**	W	4	0	(3 0)	42,475	12	White 2, Allchurch 2		2	3	4			7	11				6				10	5	9	1					8						25
26	17 Jan	H	**Tottenham Hotspur**	L	1	2	(0 1)	32,503	12	White		2	3		6		7	11				4				10	5	9	1					8						26
27	31 Jan	A	Manchester United	D	4	4	(1 4)	48,777	13	Allchurch, McGuigan, White 2		2	3	4	5			10				6				11		9	1					8			7			27
28	07 Feb	H	**Wolverhampton Wanderers**	L	3	4	(2 1)	42,377		Eastham 2 (2 pens), White		2	3	4	5			10				6				11		9	1					8			7			28
29	21 Feb	H	**Aston Villa**	W	1	0	(0 0)	20,182	13	Taylor		2	3	4	5			10				6				11		9	1					8			7			29
30	28 Feb	A	Leicester City	W	1	0	(0 0)	24,362	12	Eastham			3	4	5			10				6						9	1		11	2		8			7			30
31	07 Mar	H	**Preston North End**	L	1	2	(0 1)	31,962	12	White			3	4	5			10			11	6						9	1					8		2	7			31
32	11 Mar	A	Portsmouth	W	5	1	(2 0)	19,404	12	Eastham (pen), Curry 3, Taylor			3	5				10	9		6	4						11	1					8		2	7			32
33	14 Mar	A	Manchester City	L	1	5	(1 2)	25,417	13	White			3	4	5			10	9			6						11	1					8		2	7			33
34	21 Mar	H	**Arsenal**	W	1	0	(1 0)	32,774	13	Curry		2	3	5	6		7	10	9			4							1					8			11			34
35	27 Mar	A	West Ham United	L	0	3	(0 2)	35,000				2	3	5			7	10			6	4							1					8			11	9		35
36	28 Mar	A	Luton Town	L	2	4	(1 2)	20,878		Allchurch, Hughes		2	3	5			7	10			6	4							1					8			11	9		36
37	30 Mar	H	**West Ham United**	W	3	1	(2 0)	20,911	14	Allchurch, Keith, Taylor		2	3	5				10			6	4				11			1					8			7		9	37
38	11 Apr	A	West Bromwich Albion	D	2	2	(2 1)	23,750		Curry 2		2	3	5	11			8	9	10	6	4							1								7			38
39	18 Apr	H	**Leeds United**	D	2	2	(0 1)	19,321	15	Allchurch, Curry		2	3	5	11				9	8	6	4							1					10			7			39
40	22 Apr	H	**Bolton Wanderers**	W	2	0	(2 0)	17,451		Curry, Taylor				5	3			10	9	8	6	4				11			1							2	7			40
41	25 Apr	A	Burnley	D	2	2	(1 1)	15,430	12	Curry, Allchurch				5	3			10	9		6	4				11			1					8		2	7			41
42	29 Apr	H	**Birmingham City**	D	1	1	(1 0)	19,776	11	Allchurch		2	3	5				10	9		6	4				11			1					8			7			42
Round			FA Cup																																					Round
3	19 Jan	H	**Chelsea**	L	1	4	(0 3)	57,038		Eastham		2	3	4				11				6				10	5	9	1					8			7			3

DateLine ... 23 Aug: A 5-1 home defeat marks Charlie Mitten's first game in charge against Blackburn Rovers. **10 Sept:** A remarkable end-to-end fixture at Stamford Bridge ends 6-5 to Chelsea. **1 Oct:** Newcastle entertain Brazilian club Bela Vista and rack up a 12-1 scoreline, White and Bottom netting five goals each. **11 Oct:** Ivor Allchurch scores twice on his debut against Leicester following a record move. **31 Jan:** Newcastle end all level at 4-4 with Manchester United after a thrilling contest at Old Trafford.

NEWCASTLE UNITED

SEASON 1959-60

DIVISION 1

Mitten's Marvels entertain all

With Boardroom feuding making headlines, manager Charlie Mitten was tempted to make tracks for Elland Road following an approach from Leeds, but a crisis was averted when the boss was persuaded to continue with his rebuilding plans. Remarkably for the second season in a row, United fell heavily on the opening day of the new campaign, this time Tottenham winning 5-1 at St James' Park. But that shock was not to deter the Magpies. Although always at risk in defence from conceding goals, Newcastle could frequently bang home plenty at the other end of the field. And that blend of the brilliant and the infuriating resulted in more entertaining football.

After a poor opening in which they dropped to the bottom places at one stage the Black'n'Whites recovered during November with a string of good results. They toppled Everton 8-2 and went onto win four matches in succession. United fired all of 15 goals into the opponents net as Blackburn, Manchester City, Arsenal and Luton were all blown away. The defeat of City saw another gripping contest take place at Maine Road, so soon after the blockbuster FA Cup-tie. Newcastle were 2-1 behind at half-time and turned the match round to win 4-3.

At New Year Manchester United were swamped by 7-3 in a terrific contest at Gallowgate. Dubbed by one media-hack, "Mitten's Marvels", they finished the season in eighth place, although could have ended higher had it not been for an end of term slump in which they claimed only a single win in seven outings.

A classic FA Cup challenge took place too, with one of the top sides of the era, reigning Champions Wolves. At Gallowgate a crowd of over 62,000 witnessed a dazzling encounter finish 2-2, then in the replay at Molineux another end-to-end match took place. Wolves though recorded a 4-2 victory and went all the way to secure the trophy.

Pictured above: Dick Keith proved to be a top-class full-back, and a regular for Northern Ireland.

Memorabilia CORNER

The club's new floodlighting system with four giant pylons was featured on the programme.

IN CHARGE

Chairman: William McKeag/Wallace Hurford
Manager: Charlie Mitten
Captain: Bob Stokoe
Trainer/Coach: Norman Smith

ST JAMES' PARK

Average Attendance
Lg 36,037 Lg & Cup 37,237

Manager Charlie Mitten (left) gives last minute instructions to United's side. Back row, left to right: Mitten (J), Scott, Whitehead, Eastham, McGuigan. Front: Mitchell, Scoular, Curry, Taylor, Allchurch, Harvey.

PLAYER FOCUS Ivor Allchurch

Born Swansea. Inside-forward, 5'10"
1958 to 1962: 154 app 51 goals.

One of the most prominent players in football during the Fifties era, Ivor Allchurch spent most of his career in his native South Wales, with lower division clubs, Swansea Town and Cardiff City. He was a regular for his country – capped 68 times – an exquisite inside-forward who commanded respect. Allchurch scored twice on his debut at Gallowgate against Leicester City and went onto dominate and control games from midfield, spraying passes around the field. When he added his exceptional talent in attack the Welshman could prove a match-winner. Allchurch made the move to the top level late in his career by joining the Magpies in October 1958 from Swansea. He was nearly 29 years old and cost United a club record fee of £28,000, the deal being a headline story. Despite his ability and although Ivor delighted the Geordie crowd time and time again with his link play and strong shooting, the Tynesiders eventually slid into Division Two in 1961. Captain of the Black'n'Whites for a period, Allchurch returned to Wales heading for Ninian Park in August 1962 to conclude his senior playing career as Newcastle rebuilt. Playing on in non-league football until he was 50 years of age, Ivor totalled over 700 first-class matches and netted more than 250 goals. He was awarded the MBE during 1966. His brother Len also had a distinguished career in football during the same era, appearing for Swansea and notably Sheffield United as well as alongside Ivor for Wales.

SEASON REVIEW

Football League Div 1: P42 W18 D8 L16 F82 A78 Pts 44.
Position: 8th (Champions; Burnley).
FA Cup: R3 (Winners; Wolverhampton Wanderers).

Appearances (44m): Eastham GE 44, Allchurch IJ 43, McMichael A 43, White LR 42, Bell JR 40, Scoular J 34, Hughes G 33, Stokoe R 33, Harvey BR 32, Luke GT 25, Keith RM 24, Mitchell RC 15, Whitehead R 12, Heslop GW 9, Mitchell SA 9, McKinney WE 8, Mitten JE 6, Gilfillan RI 5, Scott ME 5, Taylor JH 5, Tait A 4, Franks AJ 3, Simpson RC 3, Wright BG 2, Ferguson RB 1, Hale KO 1, Malcolm WGL 1, Marshall TWJ 1, McGuigan JJ 1.

Goals (86g): White LR 29, Eastham GE 20, Allchurch IJ 14, Bell JR 5, Hughes G 5, Mitten JE 3, Hale KO 2, Luke GT 2, Scott ME 2, Tait A 1, own goals 3.

Dismissals: 0 players.

MAJOR SIGNINGS

Bob Gilfillan (Cowdenbeath) £4,000

FROM THE RANKS

George Heslop (Dudley Jnrs)
George Luke (Newcastle sch, Es)
Brian Wright (Sunderland sch)

TEAM COLOURS Black & white striped shirts, black shorts (Change; white shirts, black shorts)

SEASON 1959-60

Match	Date		FL Division 1				HT	Att	Posn	Scorers	Simpson	Keith	McMichael	Franks	Scoular	Bell	Taylor	Eastham	White	Allchurch	McGuigan	Harvey	Scott	Stokoe	Mitchell RC	Tait	Whitehead	Hughes	Mitchell SA	Ferguson	Malcolm	Hale	Luke	Gilfillan	McKinney	Heslop	Mitten	Marshall	Wright	Match
1	22 Aug	H	**Tottenham Hotspur**	L	1	5	(0 1)	40,782		Eastham	1	2	3	4	5	6	7	8	9	10	11																			1
2	26 Aug	A	Birmingham City	L	3	4	(0 3)	26,981		White, Eastham 2 (2 pens)		2	3	4	5	6	7	8	9	10		1	11																	2
3	29 Aug	A	Manchester United	L	2	3	(1 3)	53,257	22	Allchurch, White		2	3		4	6	7	8	9	10		1	11	5																3
4	02 Sep	H	**Birmingham City**	W	1	0	(0 0)	35,395	21	White		2	3		4		7	8	11	10		1		5	6	9														4
5	05 Sep	H	**Preston North End**	L	1	2	(0 1)	37,683	21	Eastham		2	3		4		7	8	11	10		1		5	6	9														5
6	09 Sep	A	West Bromwich Albion	D	2	2	(1 2)	28,200	19	Eastham, White	1		3		4	6		10	9	8				5	11		2	7												6
7	12 Sep	A	Leicester City	W	2	0	(1 0)	24,318	20	Bell 2	1		3		4	6		10	9	8				5	11		2	7												7
8	16 Sep	H	**West Bromwich Albion**	D	0	0	(0 0)	39,266	20			2	3		4	6		10	9	8				5	11			7	1											8
9	19 Sep	H	**Burnley**	L	1	3	(1 1)	38,576	20	Tait		2	3		4	6		10		8				5	11	9		7	1											9
10	26 Sep	A	Leeds United	W	3	2	(1 2)	28,306	17	Allchurch, Scott 2			3		4	6		10	7	8			9	5	11		2		1											10
11	03 Oct	H	**West Ham United**	D	0	0	(0 0)	41,924	18						4	6		10	7	8			9	5	11		2		1	3										11
12	10 Oct	H	**Nottingham Forest**	W	2	1	(0 0)	33,764	14	White, og (Whare)			3		4	6		10	9	8				5	11		2		1		7									12
13	17 Oct	A	Fulham	L	3	4	(1 3)	37,200	17	Eastham, Hale 2			3		4	6		10	9					5		7	2		1			8	11							13
14	24 Oct	H	**Bolton Wanderers**	L	0	2	(0 1)	34,679	18				3		4	6		10	7	8				5	11		2		1					9						14
15	31 Oct	A	Wolverhampton Wanderers	L	0	2	(0 2)	33,999	18				3		4	6		8	9	10				5	11			7	1						2					15
16	07 Nov	H	**Everton**	W	8	2	(4 0)	23,727	18	Luke, Allchurch 2, White 3, Eastham (pen), Hughes			3		4	6		8	9	10							2	7	1				11			5				16
17	14 Nov	A	Blackpool	L	0	2	(0 1)	15,667	18				3		4	6		8	9	10		1					2	7					11			5				17
18	21 Nov	H	**Blackburn Rovers**	W	3	1	(2 0)	31,368	15	Eastham, White 2			3		4	6		8	9	10		1					2	7					11			5				18
19	28 Nov	A	Manchester City	W	4	3	(1 2)	29,416	16	Allchurch, Bell, White, og (McTavish)			3		4	6		8	9	10		1					2	7					11			5				19
20	05 Dec	H	**Arsenal**	W	4	1	(2 1)	40,031	12	Allchurch 2, White 2		2	3		4	6		8	9	10		1						7					11			5				20
21	12 Dec	A	Luton Town	W	4	3	(2 2)	14,524	11	Eastham 2, Hughes, Luke		2	3		4	6		8	9	10		1						7					11			5				21
22	19 Dec	A	Tottenham Hotspur	L	0	4	(0 1)	32,824	12			2	3		4	6		8	9	10		1		5				7					11							22
23	26 Dec	A	Chelsea	D	2	2	(0 2)	47,462	12	Allchurch, White			3		4	6		8	9	10		1		5			2	7					11							23
24	28 Dec	H	**Chelsea**	D	1	1	(1 0)	43,295	12	Eastham		2	3		4	6		8	9	10		1		5				7					11							24
25	02 Jan	H	**Manchester United**	W	7	3	(3 1)	57,200	12	Allchurch, White 3, Eastham (pen), Hughes, Bell		2	3		4	6		8	9	10		1		5				7					11							25
26	16 Jan	A	Preston North End	W	2	1	(0 0)	24,355	12	Eastham, og (Cunningham)		2	3		4	6		8	9	10		1						7					11			5				26
27	23 Jan	H	**Leicester City**	L	0	2	(0 1)	32,353	12			2	3	4		6		8	9	10		1						7					11			5				27
28	06 Feb	A	Burnley	L	1	2	(0 1)	26,998	12	Allchurch		2	3		4	6		8		10		1	9	5				7					11							28
29	13 Feb	H	**Leeds United**	W	2	1	(1 1)	16,148	12	Hughes, White		2	3		4	6		8	9	10		1		5				7					11							239
30	20 Feb	A	West Ham United	W	5	3	(3 2)	27,000	9	Allchurch, Eastham, Hughes, White 2		2	3		4	6		8	9	10		1		5				7					11							30
31	27 Feb	A	Arsenal	L	0	1	(0 0)	47,657	9			2	3			4		8	9	10		1		5	6			7					11							31
32	05 Mar	H	**Fulham**	W	3	1	(2 1)	33,993	9	Allchurch, Eastham, White		2	3			4		8	9	10		1		5	6			7									11			32
33	12 Mar	A	Bolton Wanderers	W	4	1	(3 1)	24,648	7	Eastham, Mitten 2, White		2	3			4		8	9	10		1		5	6			7									11			33
34	19 Mar	H	**Luton Town**	W	3	2	(2 1)	29,269	7	Eastham, White 2		2	3			4		8	9	10		1		5	6			7									11			34
35	25 Mar	A	Everton	W	2	1	(2 1)	54,868	5	Allchurch, White			3			4		8	9	10		1		5				7					6		2		11			35
36	02 Apr	H	**Blackpool**	D	1	1	(0 0)	32,152	6	Mitten			3			4		8	9	10		1		5				7					6		2		11			36
37	09 Apr	A	Blackburn Rovers	D	1	1	(0 0)	21,962	7	Eastham			3			4		8	9	10		1		5				7					6		2		11			37
38	15 Apr	H	**Sheffield Wednesday**	D	3	3	(2 2)	39,942	7	Bell, White 2		2	3		4	6		8	11	10		1		5										9				7		38
39	16 Apr	H	**Wolverhampton Wanderers**	W	1	0	(0 0)	47,409	7	White			3		4			8	11	10		1		5				7					6	9	2					39
40	18 Apr	A	Sheffield Wednesday	L	0	2	(0 1)	33,332	6				3		4			8	11	10		1		5				7					6	9	2					40
41	23 Apr	A	Nottingham Forest	L	0	3	(0 1)	28,066	7				3			6		8	9	10		1		5				7					11		2				4	41
42	30 Apr	H	**Manchester City**	L	0	1	(0 0)	27,812	8				3			6		8	11	10		1		5				7						9	2				4	42
Round			FA Cup																																					Round
3	09 Jan	H	**Wolverhampton Wanderers**	D	2	2	(1 2)	62,443		Allchurch, Eastham		2	3		4	6		8	9	10		1		5				7					11							3
3r	13 Jan	A	Wolverhampton Wanderers	L	2	4	(2 3)	39,082		Eastham, White		2	3		4	6		8	9	10		1						7					11			5				3r

DateLine ... 22 Aug: United crash 5-1 on Tyneside for the second year running as the season opens, this time to Tottenham. **7 Nov:** Newcastle strike eight goals to thrash Everton 8-2. **2 Jan:** The Magpies get the better of Manchester United after an enthralling 7-3 contest.

Glory days come to an end

Since gaining their place back in the top division Newcastle United had enjoyed 13 seasons of being one of the country's elite. Season 1960-61 was to see United's glory days come to an abrupt end. The Tynesiders made a good start, scoring 10 times in their opening two games, but after that a suspect defence was to be the side's downfall. Indeed, they went onto concede no fewer than 117 goals that year (109 in League matches) – the worst on record – and all this when an enterprising attack, led by White, scored plenty at the right end of the field, 100 (86 League), one of the best in the division.

It was end-to-end football all season with Newcastle locked in a relegation fight. At the vital stage of the dog-fight, United gave supporters hope with a terrific 2-1 victory at the home of eventual double winners, Tottenham Hotspur. But those two points were expensive, as they also lost Len White through injury and out of the final relegation scrap. United never recovered. They lost 6-1 to Chelsea at Gallowgate three days later and couldn't claim another victory for six games. Newcastle were relegated with Preston North End.

Perhaps the FA Cup was a factor in a poor second half of the season. Newcastle entered the chase for the trophy and reached the quarter-final. They had played well to see off Fulham and Stockport County convincingly, 5-0 and 4-0, then defeated Stoke City 3-1. United held home advantage on each occasion and received more fortune with another plum home draw in the Sixth Round. But their luck ran out as Sheffield United inflicted a 3-1 defeat in front of a near 55,000 crowd. The Magpies did have another tournament to compete in, but one which did not distract them long. The new Football League Cup began that season, and United – like several clubs – took little interest in the competition for many years. They were humbled 4-1 by little Colchester United, joint bottom of Division Three. Newcastle's decline was complete.

Pictured above: Graduating through the ranks, Bill McKinney was an able defender at right-back.

Memorabilia CORNER

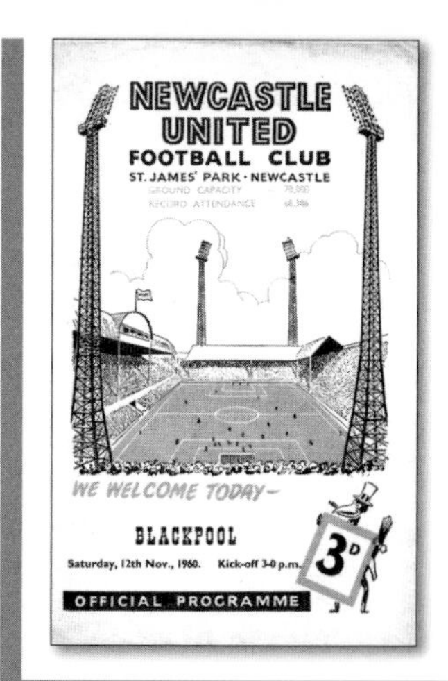

There were plenty of thrilling games in this era, the programme from the 4-3 contest with Blackpool.

IN CHARGE

Chairman: Wallace Hurford
Manager: Charlie Mitten
Captain: Bob Stokoe/Ivor Allchurch/Bill McKinney
Trainer/Coach: Norman Smith

ST JAMES' PARK

Average Attendance
Lg 26,500 Lg & Cup 29,694

Newcastle are on the decline, but still have five internationals in this group. Back row, left to right: Scoular, Keith, Harvey, Stokoe, McMichael, Bell. Front: Marshall, Allchurch, White, McGuigan, Tuohy.

PLAYER FOCUS Len White

Born Skellow. Centre-forward, 5'7"
1953 to 1962: 270 app 153 goals.

Originally an outside-right signed from Rotherham United in February 1953, for the opening four years of his Gallowgate career, Len White proved to be a sound and versatile forward, filling in across the front line without ever being guaranteed a regular place. But when both Jackie Milburn and Vic Keeble moved on, the stocky White was handed the No. 9 shirt and the Yorkshireman burst into goalscoring action and was full value for what turned out to be a bargain £12,500 transfer fee. From 1957 to 1961, White had few equals as a striker in England – although to the disappointment and anger of many, he never gained full international selection. He did get into the Football League line-up when he struck an eight-minute hat-trick. Hitting over a century of goals in those four seasons, Len developed into a huge crowd favourite at St James' Park. White's weaving runs and powerful shooting had United's fans roaring support. Len helped the Magpies to FA Cup glory in 1955, but an injury during United's relegation season of 1960-61 left him with a badly damaged ankle, a knock which saw the effervescent White struggle to reclaim his destructive ability in the box. He headed back to Yorkshire in February 1962 joining Huddersfield Town where he continued to play local football until past 50 years of age. White hailed from footballing pedigree, three brothers also appearing in Football League soccer.

SEASON REVIEW

Football League Div 1: P42 W11 D10 L21 F86 L109 Pts 32.
Position: 21st, Relegated (Champions; Tottenham Hotspur).
FA Cup: QF (Winners; Tottenham Hotspur).
FL Cup: R1 (Winners; Aston Villa).

Appearances (47m): Neale DF 43, Allchurch IJ 41, White LR 38, McMichael A 36, Hughes G 34, Keith RM 31, Bell JR 30, Harvey BR 27, Woods CMP 26, McKinney WE 25, Scanlon AJ 25, Stokoe R 19, McGuigan JJ 18, Mitchell RC 15, McGrath JT 13, Tuohy W 12, Hollins DM 9, Scoular J 9, Heslop GW 8, Mitchell SA 8, Thompson W 8, Wright BG 8, Hodgson K 7, Dalton G 5, Luke GT 4, Garrow HA 3, Harrower J 3, Wilson J 3, Gilfillan RI 2, Marshall TWJ 2, Mitten JE 2, Ferguson RB 1, Gibson J 1, Scott ME 1.

Goals (100g): White LR 29, Allchurch IJ 10, Neale DF 10, Woods CMP 9, Hughes G 8, McGuigan JJ 6, Mitchell RC 6, Scanlon AJ 6, Tuohy W 4, Gilfillan RI 2, Luke GT 2, McKinney WE 2, Bell JR 1, Gibson J 1, Keith RM 1, Marshall TWJ 1, Stokoe R 1, own goal 1.

Dismissals: 1 player; Thompson.

MAJOR SIGNINGS

John McGrath (Bury) £24,000+player
Albert Scanlon (Manchester Utd) £17,500
Dave Hollins (Brighton) £11,000
Liam Tuohy (Shamrock Rvs) £9,500
Jimmy Harrower (Liverpool) £15,000

FROM THE RANKS

George Dalton (Newcastle sch)
Duncan Neale (Ilford)
Charlie Woods (Cleator Moor Celtic)
Bill Thompson (Northb sch)
Ken Hodgson (Montague & N Fenham YC)
Jimmy Wilson (Shotts Bon Accord)
Bert Garrow (Fochabars)

TEAM COLOURS Black & white striped shirts, black shorts (Change; white shirts, black shorts)

SEASON 1960-61

Match	Date	Venue	Opponent	Result	Att	Posn	Scorers
			FL Division 1				
1	20 Aug	A	Preston North End	W 3 2 (1 1)	17,363		White 3
2	24 Aug	H	**Fulham**	W 7 2 (5 1)	23,498		Gilfillan 2, Neale 2, Tuohy 2, White
3	27 Aug	H	**Burnley**	L 0 1 (0 0)	35,485	5	
4	31 Aug	A	Fulham	L 3 4 (1 3)	21,361		Allchurch, Hughes, Woods
5	03 Sep	A	Nottingham Forest	W 2 0 (0 0)	23,806	8	Gibson, og (McDonald)
6	05 Sep	A	West Bromwich Albion	L 0 6 (0 3)	22,661	13	
7	10 Sep	H	**Manchester City**	L 1 3 (0 1)	25,904	13	Marshall
8	14 Sep	H	**West Bromwich Albion**	W 3 2 (1 2)	16,107	11	Hughes, Tuohy, White
9	17 Sep	A	Arsenal	L 0 5 (0 1)	34,885	12	
10	24 Sep	H	**Leicester City**	L 1 3 (0 1)	21,161	14	McGuigan
11	01 Oct	H	**Cardiff City**	W 5 0 (2 0)	17,627	14	Luke 2, Mitchell R, White 2
12	08 Oct	A	Aston Villa	L 0 2 (0 1)	25,336	15	
13	15 Oct	H	**Wolverhampton Wanderers**	D 4 4 (2 3)	23,401	15	Hughes, Mitchell R 2, White
14	22 Oct	A	Manchester United	L 2 3 (0 1)	37,516	16	Hughes, Stokoe (pen)
15	29 Oct	H	**Tottenham Hotspur**	L 3 4 (2 1)	51,369	17	Hughes, White 2
16	05 Nov	A	Chelsea	L 2 4 (1 2)	30,489	18	White 2
17	12 Nov	H	**Blackpool**	W 4 3 (0 1)	26,657	15	Neale 2, White 2
18	19 Nov	A	Everton	L 0 5 (0 1)	41,123	16	
19	26 Nov	H	**Blackburn Rovers**	W 3 1 (1 1)	22,623	14	Mitchell R, White 2
20	03 Dec	A	Bolton Wanderers	L 1 2 (1 1)	12,921	16	White
21	10 Dec	H	**West Ham United**	D 5 5 (1 2)	20,106	16	Bell, McGuigan, Mitchell R, White 2
22	17 Dec	H	**Preston North End**	D 0 0 (0 0)	21,514	16	
23	24 Dec	H	**Birmingham City**	D 2 2 (0 0)	20,354		Mitchell R, Scanlon
24	26 Dec	A	Birmingham City	L 1 2 (0 1)	29,435	18	Woods
25	31 Dec	A	Burnley	L 3 5 (2 2)	24,972	19	White, Hughes 2
26	14 Jan	H	**Nottingham Forest**	D 2 2 (2 0)	25,845	20	White, Woods
27	21 Jan	A	Manchester City	D 3 3 (1 0)	19,746	20	Allchurch, White, Woods
28	04 Feb	H	**Arsenal**	D 3 3 (2 2)	34,394	20	Hughes, Scanlon, White
29	11 Feb	A	Leicester City	L 3 5 (2 3)	26,449	20	Allchurch, White 2
30	22 Feb	A	Cardiff City	L 2 3 (0 2)	22,502	20	Allchurch, White
31	25 Feb	H	**Aston Villa**	W 2 1 (1 0)	21,275	20	White 2
32	08 Mar	A	Wolverhampton Wanderers	L 1 2 (1 0)	24,970	20	Allchurch
33	11 Mar	H	**Manchester United**	D 1 1 (1 1)	28,867	20	Scanlon
34	22 Mar	A	Tottenham Hotspur	W 2 1 (0 1)	46,470	19	Allchurch, Scanlon
35	25 Mar	H	**Chelsea**	L 1 6 (0 0)	28,975	20	Neale
36	31 Mar	H	**Sheffield Wednesday**	L 0 1 (0 0)	42,181	20	
37	01 Apr	A	West Ham United	D 1 1 (1 1)	17,103	20	Scanlon
38	03 Apr	A	Sheffield Wednesday	D 1 1 (1 1)	35,273	20	Woods
39	08 Apr	H	**Everton**	L 0 4 (0 2)	30,342	21	
40	15 Apr	A	Blackpool	L 1 2 (0 1)	19,381	21	Woods
41	22 Apr	H	**Bolton Wanderers**	W 4 1 (3 0)	18,820	21	Tuohy, McGuigan, Keith, McKinney (pen)
42	29 Apr	A	Blackburn Rovers	W 4 2 (2 2)	12,746	21	Allchurch, McGuigan 2, Neale
Round			**FA Cup**				
3	07 Jan	H	**Fulham**	W 5 0 (3 0)	36,037		Allchurch, Neale 3, Woods
4	01 Feb	H	**Stockport County**	W 4 0 (1 0)	48,715		Allchurch, White, Woods 2
5	18 Feb	H	**Stoke City**	W 3 1 (1 0)	46,253		Scanlon, Allchurch, McKinney (pen)
6	04 Mar	H	**Sheffield United**	L 1 3 (0 3)	54,829		McGuigan
Round			**FL Cup**				
1	10 Oct	A	Colchester United	L 1 4 (0 3)	9,130		Neale

Match	Harvey	Keith	McMichael	Wright	Stokoe	Bell	Marshall	Allchurch	White	McGuigan	Tuohy	Hughes	Neale	Gilfillan	Woods
1	1	2	3	4	5	6	7	8	9	10	11				
2	1	2	3	4	5	6			10		11	7	8	9	
3	1	2	3	4	5			6	10		11	7	8	9	
4	1	2	3	6	5			10	9		11	7	4		8
5	1	2	3	6	5			10			11	7	4		8
6	1	2	3	6	5			10	9		11	7	4		8
7	1	2	3	4			7	10	9		11		6		8
8	1	2	3		5			8	9	10	11	7	6		
9	1	2	3					8	9	10	11	7	6		
10	1	2			5			10	9	11		7	6		8
11	1	2	3					8	9	11			4		
12	1		3					8	9				4		
13	1	2	3		5			10	9			7	6		8
14	1	2	3		5			10	9			7	6		8
15	1	2	3		5	6		10	9			7			8
16	1	2	3			6		10	9			7			8
17	1		3		5	6		10	9			7	8		
18	1		3			6		10	9			7	8		
19			3		5	6		8	9			7	4		
20			3		5	6		8	9			7	4		
21			3		5	6			9	8		7	4		
22	1	2	3		5	6			9			7	4		8
23	1	2	3		5	6			9			7	4		8
24	1	2				6			9			7	4		8
25	1	2		4		6			9			7			8
26		2				6		10	9				4		8
27	1	2				6		10	9				4		8
28	1	2			5	6		10	9			7	4		8
29	1							10	9			7	4		8
30		2	3			6		8	9			7	4		
31			3			6		8	9	10			4		
32			3					8	9	10		7	4		
33			3			6		8	9	10		7	4		
34		2	3			6		8	9				4		
35		2	3			6		8		9			4		
36			3			6		10		9		7	4		
37			3			6		10		9		7	4		
38			3			6		10		9		7	4		8
39		2	3			6		10		9		7	4		8
40			3			6		10		9	11		4		8
41		7	3					10		9	11		4		8
42								10		9	11	7	4		8
Round															
3		2				6		10	9			7	4		8
4	1	2			5	6		10	9				4		8
5		2				6		10	9			7	4		8
6			3			6		8	9	10		7	4		
Round															
1	1	2	3					8	9				4		10

Match	Gibson	Heslop	Scoular	Scott	Mitchell RC	Wilson	Luke	McKinney	Mitten	Thompson	Garrow	Scanlon	Mitchell SA	Hodgson	McGrath	Dalton	Hollins	Harrower	Ferguson
1																			
2																			
3																			
4																			
5	9																		
6																			
7		5																	
8			4																
9		5	4																
10			4	3															
11		5			6	7	10												
12		5			6	7	10	2	11										
13			4		11														
14			4		11														
15			4		11														
16			4		11					5									
17			4		11			2											
18		5	4		11			2											
19					10			2			1	11							
20					10			2			1	11							
21					10			2			1	11							
22					10							11							
23					10							11							
24							10	3		5d		11							
25							10	3		5		11							
26								3		5		11	1	7					
27								3		5		11		7					
28								3				11							
29		2						3				11			5	6			
30					10							11	1		5				
31								2				11	1	7	5				
32								2				11	1		5	6			
33								2				11	1		5				
34												11		7	5		1	10	
35												11		7	5		1	10	
36					11			2				8			5		1		
37								2				11			5		1	8	
38								2				11			5		1		
39												11			5		1		
40								2						7	5		1		
41								2							5	6	1		
42		5						2								6	1		3
Round																			
3								3		5		11	1						
4								3				11		7					
5								3		5		11	1						
6								2		5		11	1						
Round																			
1		5				7			11							6			

DateLine ... 24 Aug: Newcastle's opening home game of the season sees Fulham hit for seven in a 7-2 triumph. **10 Oct:** United's first Football League Cup match ends in an embarrassing 4-1 defeat at Colchester. **10 Dec:** United draw 5-5 with West Ham after being three goals behind with 11 minutes to go. **22 March:** United defeat Spurs, the double winners elect, 2-1 at White Hart Lane, Dave Hollins saving a penalty on his debut. **25 March:** Chelsea win 6-1 at St James' Park with six second-half goals and almost seal United's relegation. **29 April:** United concede their 117th goal of the season against Blackburn, a club record.

SEASON
1961-62
DIVISION 2

A big shock to the system

It was a big surprise to most supporters and critics that Charlie Mitten was still in charge as the 1961-62 season began with United in the second-tier of English football. But the former Manchester United star's retention was to be brief. He was sacked in October as United grappled with the different style of football a division lower. It was a shock to the system for all connected with the club. Newcastle had no immediate plan for a successor and returned to Board control, before appointing long-serving trainer Norman Smith to the post, but only as a stop-gap.

As could be expected after relegation there were changes in personnel. United broke their transfer record by bringing Barrie Thomas to St James' Park for a £45,000 fee. He was something of a tearaway centre-forward and took the place of terrace hero Len White who never really recovered from that telling injury in 1960-61. A few eager youngsters from the club's junior set-up – they won the FA Youth Cup that season – were blooded in the first eleven, notably Alan Suddick. More big names of the future would soon also get their chance.

Newcastle were mediocre in League action. A dismal opening half of the season saw United slip to 18th place by January – a period only interrupted by a three game winning spurt during October in which they netted an impressive 16 goals. Afterwards victories over Leeds and Southampton signalled an upturn in form and further wins during March saw the Magpies finish in mid-table. They were knocked out of both cup tournaments early, another embarrassing exit included. In the FA Cup, Football League newcomers Peterborough United sneaked a single goal victory at Gallowgate. The Magpies were in a mess. They needed inspiration and plenty hard work to resurrect their fortunes.

Pictured above: Barrie Thomas became United's record buy and scored plenty of goals at centre-forward.

Manager Charlie Mitten is at the centre of his staff of 43 players as United begin life in the Second Division, pictured outside the recently constructed West Stand main entrance. His stay on Tyneside was not to last much longer.

Memorabilia CORNER

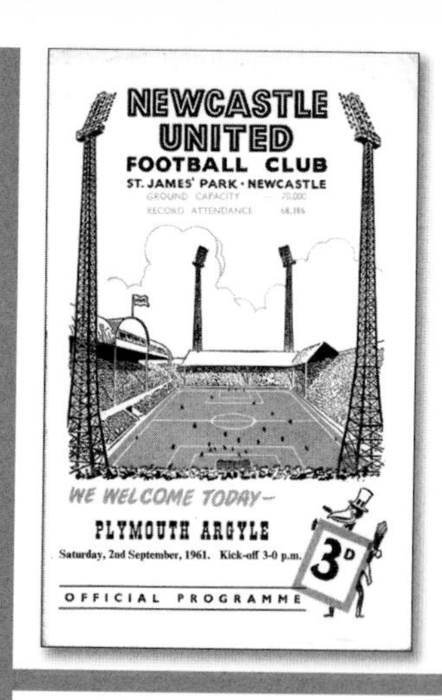

The programme remained the same...but the competition changed, now in Division Two.

IN CHARGE

Chairman: Wallace Hurford
Manager: Charlie Mitten/Norman Smith
Captain: Bill McKinney
Trainer/Coach: Norman Smith

ST JAMES' PARK

Average Attendance
Lg 27,946 Lg & Cup 27,359

PLAYER FOCUS Alan Suddick

Born Chester-le-Street. Forward, 5'11"
1961 to 1966: 152 app 43 goals.

When Alan Suddick burst onto the scene at a 17-year-old as the Sixties opened, the highly skilled forward was destined for the very top. Becoming an apprentice professional at St James' Park in October 1961 and winning the FA Youth Cup with United, he was soon elevated to the England Under-23 line-up showing ability to create and a potent shot to score goals. Able to operate in a wide position, or in midfield as well as an extra striker, Suddick often delighted United's fans and he soon became a valued asset. In season 1965-66 he was especially prominent, netting 15 goals including a double strike against Sunderland. With a touch of flair and showmanship, his career may have reached the very top had United's formation at the time been competing at the highest level, rather than initially fighting to get back into the First Division then surviving the drop. Like many players of his ilk, Alan was inconsistent. Newcastle though sacrificed his undoubted talent in a bid to raise funds to rebuild the side in December 1966. Moving to Blackpool for a record sale of £63,000, Suddick also became a highly popular player in the tangerine shirt and spent over a decade at Bloomfield Road totalling 348 games, again though in a team which largely struggled. Also to play for Stoke City, Bury and Southport as well as Barrow and Workington, he helped both United and Blackpool to promotion.

SEASON REVIEW

Football League Div 2: P42 W15 D9 L18 F64 A58 Pts 39.
Position: 11th (Champions; Liverpool).
FA Cup: R3 (Winners; Tottenham Hotspur).
FL Cup: R2 (Winners; Norwich City).

Appearances (46m): Hollins DM 46, Allchurch IJ 43, McMichael A 37, Keith RM 30, Wright BG 29, Dalton G 27, Tuohy W 27, Thompson W 21, Bell JR 19, White LR 19, Thomas EB 18, Neale DF 17, McKinney WE 16, Heslop GW 15, Kerray JR 15, Hale KO 14, Leek K 14, McGuigan JJ 14, Suddick A 14, Fell JI 11, Hughes G 11, McGrath JT 10, Wilson J 10, Day W 9, Ferguson RB 6, Woods CMP 4, Clish C 3, Harrower J 3, Scanlon AJ 2, Turner DJ 1, Wilson WS 1.

Goals (68g): Allchurch IJ 11, Thomas EB 10, Hale KO 8, Leek K 6, McGuigan JJ 6, White LR 6, Tuohy W 4, Suddick A 3, Kerray JR 2, Neale DF 2, Wilson J 2, Day W 1, Fell JI 1, Hughes G 1, McKinney WE 1, Woods CMP 1, Wright BG 1, own goals 2.

Dismissals: 0 players.

MAJOR SIGNINGS

Ken Leek (Leicester City) £25,000
Jimmy Fell (Everton) £3,000+player
Billy Day (Middlesbrough) £12,000
Jimmy Kerray (Huddersfield Town) £10,000
Barrie Thomas (Scunthorpe Utd) £45,000 club record fee

FROM THE RANKS

Alan Suddick (Chester Old Boys, Ey)
Colin Clish (Durham sch)
Dave Turner (sch)
Billy Wilson (Walkerburn Jnrs)

TEAM COLOURS Black & white striped shirts, black shorts (Change; white shirts, black shorts)

SEASON 1961-62

Match	Date		FL Division 2					Posn		Hollins	Keith	McMichael	Neale	McGrath	Bell	Hughes	Harrower	McGuigan	Allchurch	Tuohy	Dalton	White	Woods	Leek	Thompson	Wright	Scanlon	Heslop	Hale	McKinney	Suddick	Wilson J	Ferguson	Thomas	Kerray	Fell	Day	Clish	Turner	Wilson WS	Match
1	19 Aug	H	**Leyton Orient**	D	0 0	(0 0)	26,638			1	2	3	4	5	6	7	8	9	10	11																					1
2	23 Aug	H	**Walsall**	W	1 0	(1 0)	33,821		Tuohy	1	2	3	4	5					10	11	6	7	8	9																	2
3	26 Aug	A	Preston North End	W	1 0	(1 0)	14,122	3	Woods	1	2	3	4						10	11	6	7	8	9	5																3
4	29 Aug	A	Walsall	L	0 1	(0 1)	25,453	5		1	2	3	4						10		6	7		9	5	8	11														4
5	02 Sep	H	**Plymouth Argyle**	L	0 2	(0 2)	28,235	14		1	2	3	4			7			8	11	6	9		10				5													5
6	09 Sep	A	Huddersfield Town	L	1 2	(0 1)	18,087	17	White	1	2	3						9	8	11	6	7		10		4		5													6
7	16 Sep	H	**Swansea Town**	D	2 2	(2 1)	23,644	17	Leek, Allchurch	1	2	3							8	11	6	7		10		4		5	9												7
8	20 Sep	H	**Liverpool**	L	1 2	(0 2)	38,192	18	Hale	1	2	3			4				8	11	6	7		10				5	9												8
9	23 Sep	A	Southampton	L	0 1	(0 1)	20,064	19		1		3	4			7			10	11	6			8				5	9	2											9
10	30 Sep	H	**Luton Town**	W	4 1	(3 0)	22,452	18	Allchurch, White, Hale, Hughes	1		3	4			7			10	11	6	9						5	8	2											10
11	04 Oct	A	Liverpool	L	0 2	(0 1)	52,419	18		1		3	4			7		10	8	11	6	9						5		2											11
12	07 Oct	H	**Charlton Athletic**	W	4 1	(1 0)	22,957	17	McGuigan 2, Allchurch, og (Sewell)	1		3	4					10	8	11	6	9						5		2	7										12
13	14 Oct	A	Bury	W	7 2	(2 1)	13,809	14	McGuigan, Leek 2, Hale 2, Suddick, Neale	1	2	3	4					10		11	6			9				5	8		7										13
14	21 Oct	H	**Brighton & Hove Albion**	W	5 0	(2 0)	24,408	12	Tuohy, Leek 3, Hale	1	2	3	4						10	11	6			9				5	8		7										14
15	27 Oct	A	Scunthorpe United	L	2 3	(2 0)	13,987	14	Allchurch, Suddick	1	2	3	4						10	11	6			9				5	8		7										15
16	04 Nov	H	**Norwich City**	D	0 0	(0 0)	25,895	14		1	2	3	4		6			10	8	11				9				5			7										16
17	11 Nov	A	Rotherham United	D	0 0	(0 0)	11,427	14		1	2	3	8	5	6	7			10					9		4						11									17
18	18 Nov	H	**Bristol Rovers**	W	5 2	(3 1)	23,215	9	Wilson J, Allchurch, White 3	1	2	3		5	6	7			10			9				4			8			11									18
19	25 Nov	A	Stoke City	L	1 3	(0 0)	22,009	11	Hale (pen)	1	2	3		5	6				10			9				4			8		7	11									19
20	02 Dec	H	**Sunderland**	D	2 2	(1 0)	53,991	14	McGuigan, White	1	2	3		5	6	7		10	8			9				4						11									20
21	16 Dec	A	Leyton Orient	L	0 2	(0 1)	13,261	14		1		3		5	6	7		10	8			9				4				2		11									21
22	23 Dec	H	**Preston North End**	L	0 2	(0 0)	18,775	15		1		3		5	6			10	8			9				4				2	7	11									22
23	26 Dec	H	**Middlesbrough**	L	3 4	(1 2)	21,038	18	Tuohy, Allchurch, McGuigan	1				5		7	8	9	10	11	6					4				2			3								23
24	13 Jan	A	Plymouth Argyle	D	1 1	(0 1)	17,457	18	Allchurch	1								9	10	11	6		8		5	4				2		7	3								24
25	20 Jan	H	**Huddersfield Town**	D	1 1	(0 0)	31,950	18	Wilson J	1									10	11	6				5	4			8	2		7	3	9							25
26	27 Jan	A	Leeds United	W	1 0	(1 0)	17,209	18	Tuohy	1									8	11	6	10			5	4				2	7		3	9							26
27	02 Feb	A	Swansea Town	L	2 3	(1 1)	20,000	16	Thomas, Wright	1									10	11	6		8		5	4				2	7		3	9							27
28	10 Feb	H	**Southampton**	W	3 2	(3 2)	30,564	15	Thomas, Kerray, Neale	1		3	4	5	6				10	11										2	7			9	8						28
29	17 Feb	A	Luton Town	L	0 1	(0 0)	9,040	15		1		3	4		6				10	11					5					2	7			9	8						29
30	24 Feb	A	Charlton Athletic	D	1 1	(1 0)	16,935	15	Allchurch	1	2	3							10		6				5	4					7	11		9	8						30
31	03 Mar	H	**Bury**	L	1 2	(0 2)	25,853	16	Thomas	1	2	3							10	11	6				5	4						7		9	8						31
32	07 Mar	A	Middlesbrough	L	0 3	(0 2)	21,023	15		1	2	3			6				10						5	4					7			9	8	11					32
33	10 Mar	A	Brighton & Hove Albion	W	4 0	(2 0)	12,286	15	Allchurch, Thomas, Kerray, Suddick	1	2	3			6				10						5	4					7			9	8	11					33
34	17 Mar	H	**Scunthorpe United**	W	2 1	(2 0)	37,931	14	Thomas, Day	1	2	3			6				10						5	4								9	8	11	7				34
35	24 Mar	A	Norwich City	D	0 0	(0 0)	18,022	13		1	2	3			6				10						5	4								9	8	11	7				35
36	31 Mar	H	**Rotherham United**	W	1 0	(0 0)	21,865	13	Thomas	1	2	3			6				10						5	4								9	8	11	7				36
37	07 Apr	A	Bristol Rovers	L	1 2	(0 0)	10,770	14	Thomas	1	2	3			6				10						5	4								9	8	11	7				37
38	14 Apr	H	**Stoke City**	W	2 0	(0 0)	20,593	15	Thomas, og (Allen)	1	2	3			6				10						5	4								9	8	11	7				38
39	20 Apr	H	**Derby County**	W	3 0	(2 0)	33,138	15	Fell (pen), Hale, Thomas	1	2										6				5	4			10					9	8	11	7	3			39
40	21 Apr	A	Sunderland	L	0 3	(0 1)	57,666	15		1	2	3							10		6				5	4								9	8	11	7				40
41	23 Apr	A	Derby County	W	2 1	(1 1)	10,745	15	Allchurch, Thomas	1	2	3			6				10						5	4								9	8	11	7				41
42	28 Apr	H	**Leeds United**	L	0 3	(0 1)	21,708	11		1	2								10						5	4								9	8	11	7	3	6		42
Round			FA Cup																																						Round
3	06 Jan	H	**Peterborough United**	L	0 1	(0 0)	42,782			1							8	9	10	11	6	7			5	4				2			3								3
Round			FL Cup																																						Round
1	13 Sep	H	**Scunthorpe United**	W	2 0	(1 0)	14,372		Hale, Allchurch	1	2	3							8	11	6	7		10		4		5	9												1
2	02 Oct	A	Sheffield United	D	2 2	(0 1)	12,065		McGuigan, McKinney	1			4			7		9	10	11	6							5	8	2								3			2
2r	11 Oct	H	**Sheffield United**	L	0 2	(0 0)	12,595			1		3						10		11	6	9					7	5	8	2										4	2r

DateLine ...13 Sept: Newcastle's first League Cup triumph, a 2-0 win over Scunthorpe. **7 Oct:** Alan Suddick makes his debut against Charlton as a 17-year-old. **9 Oct:** A gate of 40,993 turns up for Bobby Mitchell's testimonial. **25 Nov:** Trainer Norman Smith steps up from caretaker to manager against Stoke, a 3-1 defeat. **2 May:** The Magpies lift the FA Youth Cup for the first time, defeating Wolves 2-1 on aggregate.

SEASON
1962-63
DIVISION 2

Warhorse Harvey takes control

For over eight years as skipper Joe Harvey roared and growled as he led from the front in a black-and-white shirt. In the summer of 1962 he returned as manager with the club in a desperate state. He had to restructure the club from the bottom upwards, and did a marvellous job in doing so. Within four seasons they regained their top flight status, then entered Europe, landed a trophy and returned to Wembley with a flamboyant line-up. It was the beginning of a 13 year period in charge. The Yorkshireman-cum-adopted Geordie totally remodelled the Magpie squad. He discarded old colleagues from the Fifties – White and Allchurch included – and brought to Tyneside several new names over the coming seasons. Importantly though he also developed from within, the Magpies having a good crop of youngsters from their youth system.

Not surprisingly with so much reconstruction under way at Gallowgate, the 1962-63 programme offered little but work in progress. The new season opened with a flurry of goals – no fewer than 23 being scored in the opening four games. United drew 4-4 with Cardiff at Ninian Park after being 3-1 up at the interval, and to follow in a double with Middlesbrough the Magpies lost 4-2 on Teesside and won 6-1 at Gallowgate.

There were plenty more goals to come as at times Newcastle looked the part. They won 6-0 at Walsall – equalling the club's best win on their travels – and hit another six against both Swansea and Bradford City. In the end they finished below the promotion pack and were knocked out of both cup tournaments convincingly; by Leyton Orient in the League Cup and Norwich City in the FA Cup – by five goals at Carrow Road. That Fourth Round tie in East Anglia was delayed several weeks due to a severe winter which saw little football played in January and February.

Pictured above: Ron McGarry, a sturdy and useful forward with an entertaining personality to go with it.

Memorabilia CORNER

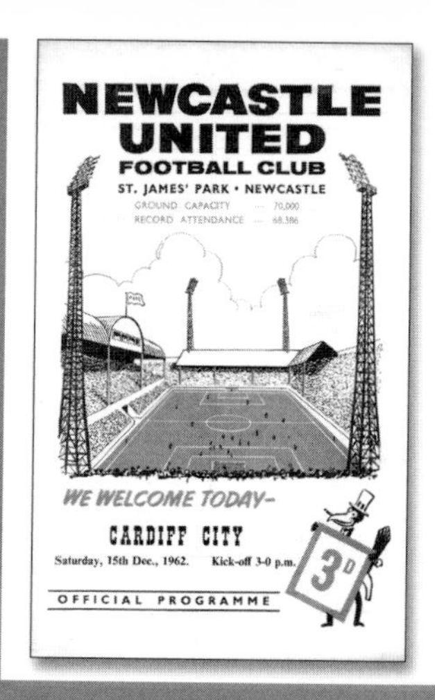

Programme issued for United's clash with Cardiff City, a 2-1 victory.

IN CHARGE

Chairman: Wallace Hurford
Manager: Joe Harvey
Captain: Dick Keith
Trainer/Coach: Norman Smith/Jimmy Greenhalgh

ST JAMES' PARK

Average Attendance
Lg 31,625 Lg & Cup 31,208

A new manager, a new start. Joe Harvey (front centre) is now in charge and a rebuilding process is underway.

SEASON REVIEW

Football League Div 2: P42 W18 D11 L13 F79 A59 Pts 47.
Position: 7th (Champions; Stoke City).
FA Cup: R4 (Winners; Manchester United).
FL Cup: R2 (Winners; Birmingham City).

Appearances (46m): Hilley D 46, Hollins DM 43, Fell JI 42, Iley J 38, Neale DF 38, Keith RM 34, Suddick A 32, Thompson W 30, Thomas EB 26, Kerray JR 25, Dalton G 21, McGarry RJ 20, Clish C 19, McGrath JT 16, Hale KO 12, McKinney WE 12, McMichael A 12, Hughes G 8, Wright BG 8, Penman WST 6, Day W 5, Moncur R 3, Tuohy W 3, Ferguson RB 2, Mitchell SA 2, Garrow HA 1, Turner DJ 1, Watkin G 1.

Goals (88g): Fell JI 16, Thomas EB 16, Suddick A 11, Kerray JR 8, McGarry RJ 8, Hilley D 7, Hale KO 6, McKinney WE 4, Hughes G 3, Penman WST 3, Dalton G 1, McGrath JT 1, Tuohy W 1, own goals 3.

Dismissals: 1 player; McGarry.

MAJOR SIGNINGS

Dave Hilley (Third Lanark) £40,000
Jim Iley (Nottingham Forest) £17,000
Ron McGarry (Bolton Wand) £17,500
Willie Penman (Rangers) £11,500

FROM THE RANKS

Bob Moncur (W Lothian sch, Ss)
George Watkin (Chopwell)

PLAYER FOCUS Dave Hilley

Born Glasgow. Inside-forward, 5'9"
1962 to 1967: 209 app 33 goals.

Costing Newcastle a near club record fee of £40,000 in August 1962 as a replacement for Ivor Allchurch in United's midfield, Dave Hilley was one of Joe Harvey's first signings as he rebuilt the Magpies following relegation. A Scottish playmaker from Third Lanark, Hilley was slightly built, with the ability to create openings and dance into the box into threatening positions. Scoring on his debut and always able to find the net, he became a fundamental part of United's side which lifted the old Second Division title in 1965 netting 12 goals in that trophy success. Dave was afterwards a prominent midfielder as Newcastle consolidated back in the top flight. An automatic choice in the black-and-white shirt for almost five seasons, Hilley moved to Nottingham Forest in December 1967 and afterwards the Scot had a spell in South Africa with the Highlands Park and Hellenic clubs. Hilley concluded his career in the non-leagues with Scarborough, South Shields and Bedlington Terriers, winning the FA Trophy at Wembley in 1976. Dave later settled back in Newcastle and was a correspondent covering North East football for the Sunday Post for many years. From a footballing family, his brother also appeared for Third Lanark and Hilley was unlucky not to reach the full Scotland side, appearing at Under-23 and Scottish League level and in other representative matches for his country just before heading for Tyneside.

TEAM COLOURS Black & white striped shirts, black shorts (Change; white shirts, black shorts)

SEASON 1962-63

Match	Date	V	FL Division 2	Res	F	A	HT	Att	Posn	Scorers	Hollins	Keith	McMichael	Wright	Thompson	Dalton	Suddick	Hilley	Thomas	Kerray	Fell	McKinney	Hale	Ferguson	Neale	Iley	McGrath	Clish	Day	Watkin	Tuohy	McGarry	Hughes	Moncur	Mitchell	Penman	Garrow	Turner	Match
1	18 Aug	A	Cardiff City	D	4	4	(3 1)	27,569		Fell (pen), Kerray, Hilley, og (Rankmore)	1	2	3	4	5	6	7	8	9	10	11																		1
2	22 Aug	A	Middlesbrough	L	2	4	(1 1)	30,611		Fell, Thomas	1	2	3	4	5	6	7	8	9	10	11																		2
3	25 Aug	H	**Portsmouth**	D	1	1	(0 1)	35,214	15	Thomas	1		3	4	5	6		8	9	10	11	2	7																3
4	29 Aug	H	**Middlesbrough**	W	6	1	(2 1)	41,550	15	Thomas 3, Hilley, Hale 2	1				5	6		8	9	10	11	2	7	3	4														4
5	01 Sep	A	Preston North End	L	1	2	(1 1)	13,884	12	Hale	1				5	6		7	9	10	11	2	8	3	4														5
6	04 Sep	A	Scunthorpe United	L	1	2	(0 0)	13,953	12	Kerray	1	2	3		5	6	8	7		9	11		10		4														6
7	08 Sep	H	**Plymouth Argyle**	W	3	1	(2 0)	34,375	13	Fell, Kerray 2	1	2	3		5			7	9	10	11		8		4	6													7
8	12 Sep	H	**Derby County**	D	0	0	(0 0)	34,465	13		1	2	3		5			7	9	10	11		8		4	6													8
9	15 Sep	A	Grimsby Town	W	1	0	(1 0)	12,318	13	Kerray	1	2	3		5			7	9	10	11		8		4	6													9
10	19 Sep	A	Derby County	W	1	0	(1 0)	14,901	10	Fell	1	2	3		5		8	7	9	10	11				4	6													10
11	22 Sep	H	**Norwich City**	W	2	1	(2 0)	36,345	10	Fell (pen), Thomas	1	2	3				8	7	9	10	11				4	6	5												11
12	29 Sep	A	Walsall	W	6	0	(3 0)	10,336	5	Fell, Kerray, Thomas 2, Suddick, Hilley	1	2	3		5		8	7	9	10	11				4	6													12
13	06 Oct	A	Stoke City	L	1	3	(0 3)	26,775	9	Thomas	1	2	3		5		8	7	9	10	11				4	6													13
14	13 Oct	H	**Sunderland**	D	1	1	(1 1)	62,262	9	Kerray	1	2		4	5		8	7	9	10	11					6		3											14
15	20 Oct	A	Leeds United	L	0	1	(0 1)	23,250	7		1	2		4	5		10	7	9	8	11					6		3											15
16	27 Oct	H	**Swansea Town**	W	6	0	(4 0)	24,005	7	Fell 2, Suddick 2, Thomas, og (Sanders)	1	2			5		10	8	9		11				4	6		3	7										16
17	03 Nov	A	Chelsea	L	2	4	(1 3)	34,428	7	Fell, Suddick	1	2					10	8	9		11				4	6	5	3	7										17
18	10 Nov	H	**Luton Town**	W	3	1	(1 0)	27,428	8	Fell, Thomas 2	1	2			5		10	8	9		11				4	6		3	7										18
19	17 Nov	A	Southampton	L	0	3	(0 1)	13,582	7		1	2			5		10	8		7	11		9		4	6		3											19
20	24 Nov	H	**Scunthorpe United**	D	1	1	(0 1)	25,864	7	Hale	1	2			5			8	9		11		10		4	6		3	7										20
21	01 Dec	A	Bury	D	0	0	(0 0)	12,633	8		1	2			5			7		10			8		4	6		3		9	11								21
22	08 Dec	H	**Rotherham United**	W	4	1	(1 0)	21,955	7	Tuohy, Kerray, Hale 2	1	2			5		8	7		10			9		4	6		3			11								22
23	15 Dec	H	**Cardiff City**	W	2	1	(0 1)	27,916	5	Fell 2	1	2			5		8	7		10	11				4	6		3				9							23
24	22 Dec	A	Portsmouth	L	1	3	(0 1)	18,373	5	McGarry	1	2			5		8	7		10	11				4	6		3				9							24
25	19 Jan	A	Plymouth Argyle	W	2	0	(1 0)	11,940	7	Thomas, McGarry	1	2			5			7	9	10	11				4	6		3				8							25
26	02 Mar	A	Sunderland	D	0	0	(0 0)	62,420	7		1	2			5		11	7	9	10					4	6		3				8							26
27	09 Mar	H	**Leeds United**	D	1	1	(0 1)	29,575	7	Hilley	1	2			5		10	8			11				4	6		3				9	7						27
28	16 Mar	A	Swansea Town	L	0	1	(0 0)	7,725	10		1	2				3		8		10	11				4	6	5					9d	7						28
29	23 Mar	H	**Chelsea**	W	2	0	(1 0)	39,418	9	Fell, Thomas	1	2				3		8	9		11				4	6	5					10	7						29
30	27 Mar	H	**Grimsby Town**	D	0	0	(0 0)	27,884	8		1	2				3	7	8	9		11				4	6	5					10							30
31	30 Mar	A	Luton Town	W	3	2	(1 0)	7,281	4	Fell, Thomas, Suddick	1					3	7	8	9		11	2			4	6						10		5					31
32	03 Apr	H	**Charlton Athletic**	W	3	2	(1 1)	30,360	4	Penman, Hilley, Suddick					5	3	7	8			11	2			4	6						9			1	10			32
33	06 Apr	H	**Southampton**	W	4	1	(2 0)	28,744	4	Fell, Penman, Suddick, Dalton	1				5	6	7	8			11	2			4			3				9				10			33
34	12 Apr	H	**Huddersfield Town**	D	1	1	(1 1)	49,672	5	McGarry	1	2					7	8			11				4	6	5	3				9				10			34
35	16 Apr	A	Huddersfield Town	L	1	2	(1 1)	22,022	4	Penman	1	2				6	7	8			11					4	5	3				9				10			35
36	20 Apr	H	**Bury**	L	1	3	(0 1)	25,017	8	McGarry		2				3	7	8							4	6	5				11	9			1	10			36
37	23 Apr	A	Charlton Athletic	W	2	1	(1 1)	12,341	7	Suddick, McKinney	1					3	8	10			11	2			4	6	9						7	5					37
38	27 Apr	A	Rotherham United	L	1	3	(1 1)	9,384	7	McGrath	1					3	8	10			11	2			4	6	9						7	5					38
39	01 May	H	**Stoke City**	W	5	2	(3 2)	26,781	6	Hilley, McGarry, Suddick, McKinney 2 (1 pen)	1			4		3	7	10			11	2			8	6	5					9							39
40	04 May	A	Norwich City	W	2	1	(1 0)	16,665	5	McGarry, McKinney				4		3	7	10			11	2			8	6	5					9					1		40
41	08 May	H	**Walsall**	L	0	2	(0 0)	21,797	5		1			4		3	7	8			11	2				6	5					9				10			41
42	11 May	H	**Preston North End**	D	2	2	(1 1)	13,502	7	Suddick, Hughes	1					3	10	8			11	2				6	5					9	7					4	42
Round			FA Cup																																				Round
3	07 Mar	A	Bradford City	W	6	1	(2 1)	13,605		McGarry 2, Thomas, Hilley, Hughes 2	1	2			5			8	9		11				4	6		3				10	7						3
4	13 Mar	A	Norwich City	L	0	5	(0 2)	34,770			1	2			5			8		10	11				4	6		3				9	7						4
Round			FL Cup																																				Round
2	26 Sep	H	**Leyton Orient**	D	1	1	(0 0)	22,452		Fell (pen)	1	2	3					8	9		11		10		4	6	5		7										2
2r	01 Oct	A	Leyton Orient	Le	2	4	(1 2)	8,037		Suddick, og (Lucas)	1	2			5	6	8	7	9	10	11				4		3												2r

Le Lost after extra time

DateLine ... 18 Aug: Joe Harvey's first game as United's manager ends in a 4-4 draw at Cardiff. **29 Aug:** Local rivals Middlesbrough are toppled 6-1 on Tyneside. **29 Sept:** United win 6-0 at Walsall and equal their biggest away victory. **7 March:** The Third Round FA Cup-tie with Bradford City is finally played, after 12 postponements due to weather. **30 March:** Bob Moncur pulls on the senior shirt for the first time at Kenilworth Road, Luton.

Humbled by Bedford in the Cup

The glamour of the FA Cup is such that every now and then, the proverbial David of the football world slays a Goliath. And that makes the competition such an attraction. The Tynesiders are one of those giants with a marvellous Cup history. Yet United have a track record of not only reaching plenty of finals, but also of being the victim of the Cup minnow. During the Sixties, so soon after their exploits and glory in the 1950s, one of those famous giant-killing feats occurred. Little Bedford Town of the Southern League arrived on Tyneside in January. The bold part-timers were as brilliant as United were bad and sensationally won 2-1 at St James' Park. And this was after another ignominious League Cup exit, this time to Bournemouth.

United's main focus though was on promotion and they fell short. Ten miles or so away, rivals Sunderland were a step ahead of the Magpies. Indeed, the Red'n'Whites pushed hard at the end of the season and finished in runners-up spot, and back in the top flight. United had kept just in touch of the chasing pack, but in the final tally were a long way short in eighth position. United started with a bang, winning four of the opening five matches then fell out of form alarmingly until a sparkling run of results over the winter saw a climb up the ladder. They secured full points in 10 of 13 fixtures played. By mid-March Newcastle were in a handy position to, if not claim top spot from Leeds United in the promotion race, have a real go at the second position with Sunderland. They defeated their Wear neighbours 1-0, but a late season run of five defeats – including twice at the hands of eventual Champions Leeds – halted any surge into a promotion place. Yet signs were evident – the Bedford embarrassment aside – that boss Joe Harvey had the making of team that could follow their Roker Park foes back to the top.

Pictured above: Gordon Marshall had a good record with Hearts before becoming United's No 1.

Memorabilia CORNER

A new programme design for season 1963-64, and a 1-0 victory over Sunderland.

IN CHARGE

Chairman: Wallace Hurford
Manager: Joe Harvey
Captain: Stan Anderson
Trainer/Coach: Jimmy Greenhalgh

ST JAMES' PARK

Average Attendance
Lg 29,435 Lg & Cup 29,028

Joe Harvey's overhaul starts to take shape, United's line-up in 1964. Back row, left to right: McGrath, Marshall, Clark, Burton, Craig, Iley. Front: Suddick, Hilley, Anderson, Thomas, Hockey.

PLAYER FOCUS Jim Iley

Born South Kirkby. Left-half, 5'11"
1962 to 1969: 249 app 16 goals.

Knowledgeable and seasoned, the balding head of Jim Iley became an influential figure on United's team during the Sixties. An experienced midfielder having served Sheffield United, Tottenham Hotspur and Nottingham Forest in over 260 games, Iley had the know-how to blend with a group of young, emerging players at Gallowgate. In midfield alongside another model professional in Stan Anderson, the pair guided United back into the First Division in 1965, Jim netting a 20-yard screamer to clinch promotion against Bolton Wanderers. Often captain of the Magpies before and after that Second Division Championship success, Iley cost £17,000 when he journeyed north from the City Ground during September 1962. Having appeared for the England Under-23 eleven and both the FA and Football League sides, the Yorkshireman was recognised as an able and respected footballer possessing composure with the ball at his feet and ability to drive forward. Before leaving St James' Park when nearly 34 years old, he briefly took part in United's first European venture, and triumphant Fairs Cup run in 1968-69. He later tried management on a budget with a string of clubs including Peterborough United, Bury – once knocking United out of the League Cup in 1980 – Barnsley, Blackburn Rovers and Exeter City. Iley made his Football League debut for the Blades as a 17-year-old while he is related by marriage to England winger Colin Grainger.

SEASON REVIEW

Football League Div 2: P42 W20 D5 L17 F74 A69 Pts 45.
Position: 8th (Champions; Leeds United).
FA Cup: R3 (Winners; West Ham United).
FL Cup: R3 (Leicester City).

Appearances (45m): Iley J 45, McGrath JT 41, Dalton G 40, Hilley D 40, Marshall G 35, Suddick A 34, McGarry RJ 33, Thomas EB 27, Taylor C 26, Anderson S 25, Penman WST 24, Burton AD 19, McKinney WE 18, Cummings RD 16, Craig DJ 14, Hockey T 13, Hollins DM 10, Keith RM 8, Kirkman AJ 5, Thompson W 5, Butler JW 4, Moncur R 3, Clark FA 2, Markie J 2, Walker L 2, Allen GB 1, Clish C 1, O'Neil LA 1, Turner DJ 1.

Goals (79g): Thomas EB 21, McGarry RJ 12, Penman WST 8, Suddick A 7, Hilley D 6, Anderson S 5, Cummings RD 5, Taylor C 5, Burton AD 3, Iley J 3, Dalton G 1, Kirkman AJ 1, McKinney WE 1, own goal 1.

Dismissals: 0 players.

MAJOR SIGNINGS

Stan Anderson (Sunderland) £19,000
Ollie Burton (Norwich City) £37,500
Gordon Marshall (Hearts) £18,500
Trevor Hockey (Notts Forest) £25,000
Colin Taylor (Walsall) £20,000
Bobby Cummings (Aberdeen) £5,000
Alan Kirkman (Rotherham Utd) £12,300

FROM THE RANKS

Frank Clark (Crook Town, Ey/Ea)
David Craig (N Ireland BB)
Len Walker (Spennymoor Utd)
Geoff Allen (Newcastle sch, Ey)
Joe Butler (Newcastle sch)
John Markie (Bathgate St Marys, Ss)
Les O'Neil (Blyth Spartans)

TEAM COLOURS Black & white striped shirts, black shorts (Change; white shirts, black shorts)

SEASON 1963-64

Match			FL Division 2					Posn		Marshall	McKinney	Dalton	Burton	Thompson	Iley	Suddick	Hilley	McGarry	Penman	Taylor	Keith	Thomas	McGrath	Kirkman	Hollins	Walker	Clish	Moncur	O'Neil	Markie	Cummings	Craig	Anderson	Hockey	Butler	Clark	Allen	Turner	Match
1	24 Aug	H	**Derby County**	W	3 1	(2 1)	35,269		Taylor, Penman, McGarry	1	2	3	4	5	6	7	8	9	10	11																			1
2	26 Aug	A	Middlesbrough	L	0 3	(0 3)	37,803			1	2	3	4	5	6	7	8	9	10	11																			2
3	31 Aug	A	Plymouth Argyle	W	4 3	(3 3)	13,960	12	Taylor, Thomas 3	1	5	3	4		6		7	8	10	11	2	9																	3
4	04 Sep	H	**Middlesbrough**	W	2 0	(0 0)	56,918	7	Penman, McGarry	1		3	4		6		7	8	10	11	2	9	5																4
5	07 Sep	H	**Charlton Athletic**	W	5 0	(3 0)	33,225	4	Penman 2, Thomas, Suddick 2	1		3	4		6	8	7		10	11	2	9	5																5
6	11 Sep	H	**Southampton**	D	2 2	(1 1)	42,879	4	Thomas, McGarry (pen)	1		3	4		6		7	8	10	11	2	9	5																6
7	14 Sep	A	Grimsby Town	L	1 2	(0 1)	9,828	5	McGarry (pen)	1		3	4		6	7	10	8		11	2	9	5																7
8	18 Sep	A	Southampton	L	0 2	(0 2)	18,540	9		1		3	4		6		7	8		11	2	9	5	10															8
9	21 Sep	H	**Preston North End**	L	2 4	(0 2)	29,710	11	Kirkman, Burton	1	2	3	4		6		7	8		11		9	5	10															9
10	28 Sep	A	Leyton Orient	L	0 1	(0 1)	12,989	13				3	8	5	6	7		9		11			2	10	1	4													10
11	02 Oct	H	**Portsmouth**	W	1 0	(0 0)	22,118	13	Dalton			6	4		10	8		9		11			2	7	1		3	5											11
12	05 Oct	H	**Swansea Town**	W	4 1	(1 0)	23,711	8	Taylor, Thomas, Hilley 2			3	4		6	8	7	10		11		9	2		1			5											12
13	09 Oct	A	Sunderland	L	1 2	(1 1)	56,980	9	Taylor			3	4		6	7	8	10		11	2	9	5		1														13
14	19 Oct	A	Portsmouth	L	2 5	(0 4)	14,996	10	McGarry, Hilley			3	4		6	7	8	9		11	2		5		1				10										14
15	26 Oct	H	**Northampton Town**	L	2 3	(1 1)	25,943	12	Taylor, Iley (pen)			3		5	6	7	8			11			2	10	1					4	9								15
16	02 Nov	A	Norwich City	L	1 3	(1 2)	17,660	16	McGarry		2	3			6	10	7	8		11					1			5		4	9								16
17	09 Nov	H	**Cardiff City**	L	0 4	(0 2)	38,495	18				3			6			8	10	11			5		1						9	2	4	7					17
18	16 Nov	A	Swindon Town	D	0 0	(0 0)	20,699	17		1	2	3			6	11	8		10			9	5										4	7					18
19	23 Nov	H	**Manchester City**	W	3 1	(1 0)	22,557	15	Penman, Thomas 2	1	2	3			6	11	8		10			9	5										4	7					19
20	30 Nov	A	Bury	W	2 1	(1 0)	9,848	13	Thomas, og (Bunner)	1	2	3			6	11	8		10			9	5										4	7					20
21	07 Dec	H	**Scunthorpe United**	W	3 1	(2 0)	24,988	10	Suddick, Penman, Thomas	1	2	3			6	11	8		10			9	5										4	7					21
22	14 Dec	A	Derby County	W	2 1	(1 0)	9,237	10	Thomas, Hilley	1	2	3			6	11	8		10			9	5										4	7					22
23	21 Dec	H	**Plymouth Argyle**	D	1 1	(0 1)	23,572	10	Thomas	1	2	3			6	11	8		10			9	5										4	7					23
24	26 Dec	H	**Huddersfield Town**	W	2 0	(1 0)	37,898	10	Thomas, Hilley	1	2	3			6	7	8		10	11		9	5										4						24
25	28 Dec	A	Huddersfield Town	L	0 3	(0 2)	12,832	10		1	2	3			6	7	8		10	11		9	5										4						25
26	11 Jan	A	Charlton Athletic	W	2 1	(2 0)	18,588	8	McGarry, Thomas	1	2	3			6	8	7	10		11		9	5										4						26
27	18 Jan	H	**Grimsby Town**	W	4 0	(3 0)	23,681	7	Thomas 2, Anderson 2	1	2	3			6	8	7	10		11		9	5										4						27
28	01 Feb	A	Preston North End	L	0 3	(0 2)	18,982	7		1	2	3	8		6	11		10				9	5										4	7					28
29	08 Feb	H	**Leyton Orient**	W	3 0	(1 0)	20,670	5	Penman, Cummings, McKinney	1	2	3	4		6	8	7		10	11			5								9								29
30	22 Feb	A	Rotherham United	W	3 2	(1 2)	9,727	6	Suddick 2, Penman	1		3	2		6	11	7	8	10				5								9		4						30
31	29 Feb	H	**Swindon Town**	W	4 1	(1 0)	23,565	6	Suddick, Cummings, Hilley, Burton	1		3	4		6	11	7	8	10				5								9	2							31
32	07 Mar	A	Northampton Town	D	2 2	(1 1)	11,440	6	Suddick, Cummings	1		3			6	11	7	8	10				5								9	2	4						32
33	14 Mar	H	**Sunderland**	W	1 0	(1 0)	27,341	5	McGarry (pen)	1		3			6	11	7	8	10				5								9	2	4						33
34	17 Mar	A	Swansea Town	W	1 0	(0 0)	9,000	5	Anderson	1		3			6	11	7	8	10				5								9	2	4						34
35	20 Mar	A	Cardiff City	D	2 2	(1 2)	9,096	5	Cummings, McGarry (pen)	1		3			6	11	7	8	10				5								9	2	4						35
36	27 Mar	H	**Leeds United**	L	0 1	(0 1)	55,039	5		1		3			6	11	7	8	10				5								9	2	4						36
37	30 Mar	A	Leeds United	L	1 2	(1 1)	40,105	5	Iley	1		3			6	11	7	10				9	5								8	2	4						37
38	04 Apr	A	Manchester City	L	1 3	(0 2)	15,450	6	Thomas	1					6		7	10		11		9	5								8	2	4		3				38
39	08 Apr	H	**Rotherham United**	W	5 2	(2 2)	18,308	5	McGarry, Thomas 3, Anderson	1					6		7	10				9	5								8	2	4	11	3				39
40	11 Apr	H	**Bury**	L	0 4	(0 1)	20,001	6		1					6		7	10				9	5								8	2	4	11	3				40
41	18 Apr	A	Scunthorpe United	L	0 2	(0 0)	6,433	7							6		8	10		11		9	5		1							2	4	7		3			41
42	25 Apr	H	**Norwich City**	W	2 0	(1 0)	12,256	8	Cummings, Iley	1					6		8	10					5								9	2	4	7		3	11		42
Round			FA Cup																																				Round
3	04 Jan	H	**Bedford Town**	L	1 2	(0 2)	34,585		Anderson	1	2	3			6	11	8		10			9	5										4	7					3
Round			FL Cup																																				Round
2	25 Sep	H	**Preston North End**	W	3 0	(1 0)	14,906		McGarry (pen), Thomas, Burton			3	8	5	6	7		10		11		9	2		1	4													2
3	06 Nov	A	Bournemouth & BA	L	1 2	(1 0)	11,735		McGarry (pen)	1		6			10	7	8	9		11			5									2			3			4	3

DateLine ... 6 Nov: David Craig's first game for the senior side in the League Cup match with Bournemouth. **4 Jan:** Non-league minnows Bedford Town create FA Cup headlines by winning 2-1 on Tyneside. **18 April:** Frank Clark makes his debut in the match at Scunthorpe.

NEWCASTLE UNITED

SEASON
1964-65
DIVISION 2

United return as Champions

With Wearside rivals Sunderland being promoted, the pressure was on the Magpies to do the same as 1964-65 commenced. And it was a former Roker Park favourite and Reds' skipper who did much to lead United to the Second Division crown. Ex-England player Stan Anderson had joined the Magpies in a controversial Wear to Tyne move in 1963, and the experienced right-half forged a dominant combination with Jim Iley and John McGrath at the heart of United's side which was pivotal to the club's success. The development of young full-backs Craig and Clark was crucial too, the Black'n'Whites having a solid back-line throughout the season, conceding only 45 goals.

Elimination by Blackpool and Swansea Town in knock-out football mattered little. The focus was on promotion and from the early weeks of the season United reached the top and became favourites for a return to Division One, chased by Bolton, Southampton, Norwich and surprise outfit Northampton Town. Supporters began to believe promotion could be a reality following a seven match winning spree from November to the beginning of January. The Cobblers were thrashed 5-0 and a rewarding Tyne-Tees derby double provided full points. There was a spirit in the side too. After that winning sequence, at Coventry, United found themselves 4-1 down at the break. They battled back and only narrowly lost by 5-4.

Easter was a crucial stage of the campaign as often is the case. Newcastle claimed the required points to secure promotion with four successive victories in the spring, with a deciding clash against Bolton Wanderers – a 2-0 triumph on Good Friday in front of 60,000 at St James' Park. After four years in charge Joe Harvey had achieved his first target. For good measure the Magpies went onto lift the Second Division trophy with a point against Manchester City. Now the boss turned his attention to his next objective – survival in the highest grade.

Pictured above: A star of Sunderland, Stan Anderson moved to Tyneside and guided United to promotion.

Memorabilia CORNER

United's programm now featured the city crest once mor The fixture with Bury was a controversial one.

IN CHARGE

Chairman: Wallace Hurford/Lord Westwood
Manager: Joe Harvey
Captain: Stan Anderson
Trainer/Coach: Jimmy Greenhalgh

ST JAMES' PARK

Average Attendance
Lg 35,197 Lg & Cup 35,197

United's Second Division winning players are featured in the front row of this pre-season group. Left to right: Hockey, Anderson, McGrath, Penman, Hilley, Thomas, Harvey (manager), Suddick, Thompson, Burton, Taylor, McGrath, Iley. Goalkeepers Hollins (left) and Marshall (right) are behind.

PLAYER FOCUS Frank Clark

Born Highfield. Left-back, 6'0"
1962 to 1975: 486 app 2 goals.

When ex-youth international Frank Clark left Newcastle United on a free transfer to Nottingham Forest after almost 13 years consistent service at the end of the 1974-75 season no-one could have imagined what glory was to follow for the County Durham defender. At 32 years of age, Clark found himself a part of an emerging Brian Clough revolution that went onto lift a string of trophies including the European Cup in 1979! It was an astonishing end to a fine career as one of the game's unsung heroes. Joining the Black'n'Whites' junior ranks from Crook Town in October 1962, Clark recovered from a broken leg and graduated to United's first eleven becoming a regular from season 1964-65 when he lifted a Second Division title medal. With a calm temperament Clark was a steady influence as the Magpies secured the Inter Cities Fairs Cup four years later and then reached the FA Cup final in 1974. Dependable at left-back rather than spectacular, Frank has appeared for United more than any other outfield player in post-war football. After retiring from playing in 1979 he entered coaching then became manager at Orient – where he was also Managing Director – as well as back at Nottingham Forest and at Manchester City. Afterwards Frank became part of the League Managers Association executive team. Before joining the Black'n'Whites, Clark lifted the FA Amateur Cup with Crook in 1961 and played for England at that level. He also turned out for the Football League XI in 1969-70.

SEASON REVIEW

Football League Div 2: P42 W24 D9 L9 F81 A45 Pts 57.
Position: 1st, Champions.
FA Cup: R3 (Winners; Liverpool).
FL Cup: R2 (Winners; Chelsea).

Appearances (44m): Clark FA 44, Marshall G 44, McGrath JT 44, Anderson S 42, Craig DJ 42, Iley J 40, Hilley D 36, McGarry RJ 33, Hockey T 26, Cummings RD 25, Penman WST 23, Suddick A 22, Robson BS 20, Moncur R 12, Taylor C 10, Knox T 9, Thomas EB 7, Burton AD 2, McKinney WE 2, Allen GB 1.

Goals (81g): McGarry RJ 16, Hilley D 12, Anderson S 8, Cummings RD 8, Penman WST 7, Robson BS 7, Suddick A 6, Iley J 5, Thomas EB 3, Hockey T 2, Taylor C 2, Burton AD 1, Knox T 1, own goals 3.

Dismissals: 1 player; McGarry.

MAJOR SIGNINGS

Tommy Knox (Chelsea) £10,000

FROM THE RANKS

Bryan Robson (Clara Vale Jnrs)

TEAM COLOURS Black & white striped shirts, black shorts (Change; white shirts, black shorts)

SEASON 1964-65

Match	Date		FL Division 2		Score	HT	Att	Posn	Scorers	Marshall	Craig	Clark	Anderson	McGrath	Iley	Hilley	McGarry	Thomas	Penman	Hockey	Robson	Moncur	Taylor	Cummings	McKinney	Burton	Suddick	Allen	Knox	Match
1	24 Aug	H	**Charlton Athletic**	D	1 1	(1 1)	32,805		Hilley	1	2	3	4	5	6	7	8	9	10	11										1
2	29 Aug	H	**Southampton**	W	2 1	(1 1)	24,531		Thomas, Hilley	1	2	3	4	5	6	7	8	9	10	11										2
3	01 Sep	A	Charlton Athletic	W	1 0	(0 0)	22,939	5	Robson	1	2	3	4	5	6	8	10	9		11	7									3
4	05 Sep	A	Huddersfield Town	W	1 0	(1 0)	8,770	4	McGarry	1	2	3	4	5	6	8	10	9		11	7									4
5	08 Sep	A	Northampton Town	L	0 1	(0 0)	15,365	6		1	2	3	4	5		8	10	9		11	7	6								5
6	12 Sep	H	**Coventry City**	W	2 0	(0 0)	37,481	5	Taylor, Thomas	1	2	3	4	5		8	10d	9		7		6	11							6
7	16 Sep	H	**Plymouth Argyle**	W	2 1	(0 0)	21,639	5	Taylor, Thomas	1	2	3	4	5		8	10	9		7		6	11							7
8	19 Sep	A	Cardiff City	D	1 1	(0 1)	12,016	1	Cummings	1	2	3	4	5		8	10			7		6	11	9						8
9	26 Sep	H	**Preston North End**	W	5 2	(2 2)	34,219	1	McGarry 2, Cummings, Hilley, og (Kendall)	1		3	4	5	6	8	10			7			11	9	2					9
10	30 Sep	A	Plymouth Argyle	L	1 2	(0 0)	21,639	1	McGarry	1	2	3	4	5	6	8	10			7			11	9						10
11	03 Oct	A	Ipswich Town	L	1 3	(0 3)	14,447	6	Burton	1		3	4	5	6	10				7			11	9	2	8				11
12	10 Oct	H	**Leyton Orient**	W	5 0	(3 0)	28,454	3	Iley, Robson 2, Anderson 2	1	2	3	4	5	10	8					7	6	11	9						12
13	14 Oct	A	Manchester City	L	0 3	(0 3)	10,215	3		1	2	3	4	5	10	8					7	6	11	9						13
14	17 Oct	A	Bury	W	2 1	(1 0)	8,950	3	Cummings, Robson	1	2	3	4	5	10	8					7	6	11	9						14
15	24 Oct	H	**Crystal Palace**	W	2 0	(0 0)	30,050	2	Suddick, McGarry	1	2	3	4	5	10		8				7	6		9			11			15
16	31 Oct	A	Norwich City	D	1 1	(1 0)	19,380	2	Robson	1	2	3	4	5	10		8				7	6		9			11			16
17	07 Nov	H	**Rotherham United**	W	3 1	(1 0)	32,870	2	Suddick, Iley, McGarry	1	2	3	4	5	10		8				7	6		9			11			17
18	14 Nov	A	Swansea Town	L	1 3	(0 2)	10,457	2	McGarry	1	2	3	4	5	10		8				7	6		9			11			18
19	21 Nov	H	**Derby County**	D	2 2	(1 0)	31,041	2	Cummings, McGarry	1	2	3	4	5	6	10	8				7			9			11			19
20	28 Nov	A	Swindon Town	W	6 1	(4 1)	15,866	2	Suddick, Penman 2, Hilley, Anderson 2	1	2	3	4	5	6	8	9		10	7							11			20
21	05 Dec	H	**Portsmouth**	W	3 0	(2 0)	29,135	2	Hockey, Iley, Anderson	1	2	3	4	5	6	8	9		10	7							11			21
22	12 Dec	H	**Northampton Town**	W	5 0	(4 0)	40,376	1	McGarry 3, Hockey, og (Everitt)	1	2	3	4	5	6	8	9		10	7							11			22
23	19 Dec	A	Southampton	W	1 0	(0 0)	22,365	1	Suddick	1	2	3	4	5	6	8	9		10	7							11			23
24	26 Dec	A	Middlesbrough	W	2 0	(2 0)	38,184	1	Hilley, og (Nurse)	1	2	3	4	5	6	8	9		10	7							11			24
25	28 Dec	H	**Middlesbrough**	W	2 1	(2 1)	54,750	1	Hilley 2	1	2	3	4	5	6	8	9		10	7							11			25
26	02 Jan	H	**Huddersfield Town**	W	2 1	(1 0)	45,315	1	McGarry 2	1	2	3	4	5	6	8	9		10	7							11			26
27	16 Jan	A	Coventry City	L	4 5	(1 4)	28,038	1	McGarry 2, Hilley 2	1	2	3	4	5	6	8	9			7				10			11			27
28	23 Jan	H	**Cardiff City**	W	2 0	(1 0)	37,291	1	Hilley, Anderson	1	2	3	4	5	6	8	9		10	7								11		28
29	06 Feb	A	Preston North End	L	0 2	(0 0)	18,961	1		1	2	3	4	5	6	8	9		10	7							11			29
30	13 Feb	H	**Ipswich Town**	D	2 2	(1 0)	29,459	1	Suddick, Anderson	1	2	3	4	5	6	8	9		10	7							11			30
31	20 Feb	A	Leyton Orient	L	1 2	(0 1)	8,319	1	McGarry (pen)	1	2	3	4	5	6	10	8				7			9					11	31
32	27 Feb	H	**Bury**	L	2 3	(0 2)	33,923	2	Suddick, Anderson	1	2	3	4	5	6	8	9			7							10		11	32
33	06 Mar	A	Portsmouth	W	2 1	(1 1)	19,399	2	Cummings, Robson	1	2	3	4	5	6				10		7			9			8		11	33
34	13 Mar	H	**Norwich City**	W	2 0	(2 0)	41,441	1	Cummings, Robson	1	2	3	4	5	6		8		10		7			9					11	34
35	20 Mar	A	Rotherham United	D	1 1	(1 0)	9,693	1	Penman	1	2	3	4	5	6		8		10		7			9					11	35
36	27 Mar	H	**Swansea Town**	W	3 1	(0 0)	28,634	1	Penman 3	1	2	3	4	5	6		8		10					9			7		11	36
37	03 Apr	A	Derby County	W	3 0	(0 0)	19,668	1	Knox, Hilley, Iley	1	2	3	4	5	6	8			10		7			9					11	37
38	10 Apr	H	**Swindon Town**	W	1 0	(1 0)	32,503	1	Hilley	1	2	3	4	5	6	8			10		7			9					11	38
39	16 Apr	H	**Bolton Wanderers**	W	2 0	(1 0)	59,960	1	Penman, Iley	1	2	3	4	5	6	8			10		7			9					11	39
40	17 Apr	A	Crystal Palace	D	1 1	(0 0)	21,756	1	Cummings	1	2	3		5	6	8			10	11				9		4	7			40
41	19 Apr	A	Bolton Wanderers	D	1 1	(0 1)	15,762	1	Cummings	1	2	3	4	5	6	8			10		7			9			11			41
42	24 Apr	H	**Manchester City**	D	0 0	(0 0)	33,259	1		1	2	3	4	5	6	8			10		7			9			11			42
Round			FA Cup																											Round
3	09 Jan	A	Swansea Town	L	0 1	(0 1)	18,951			1	2	3	4	5	6	8	9		10	7							11			3
Round			FL Cup																											Round
2	23 Sep	A	Blackpool	L	0 3	(0 1)	13,670			1	2	3		5	6	8	10			7		4	11	9						2

DateLine ...1 Sept: Bryan Robson finds a place in United's attack for the first time, scoring against Charlton. **16 Jan:** A fabulous contest at Coventry sees City win 5-4, with United 5-1 behind at one stage. **20 Feb:** United are featured on BBC's *Match of the Day* for the first time at Leyton Orient. **27 Feb:** All of 11 minutes are added by the referee and Bury score in injury time to win 3-2. **16 April:** United clinch promotion on Good Friday in front of almost 60,000 with a 2-0 victory over Bolton. **24 April:** A 0-0 draw with Manchester City gives United the point to secure the Second Division trophy.

SEASON 1965-66

DIVISION 1

Survival is the priority

By the start of the 1965-66 season football was developing rapidly. The coming World Cup in England was to see the game boom while tactics on the field, and corporate dealing in the Boardroom – as well as huge social changes in the country – were to sweep through the national sport. United were rarely at the forefront of all this change, and for several years lagged behind the mini-revolution. They were more focussed on making sure the club survived in Division One – that was a priority.

Newcastle supporters endured a couple of seasons of watching United in a relegation scrap – and suffered more cup tears, this time falling to Peterborough United again – before the corner turned for the better.

The Black'n'Whites struggled throughout the programme in their first year back at the top. Goalscoring was a major deficiency; Newcastle netted only 50 in League action and by the New Year meeting with Sunderland had slid to 19th place following a run of six games without a victory. And then the Wearsiders inflicted another painful reverse.

The signing of experienced midfielder Keith Kettleborough was a key point in the season during January. Although he only cost a modest £22,500 in an era which saw transfer fees escalate, he made a difference to United's midfield. In a tight League table, United collected points and climbed the table with a run of five wins in seven outings. West Ham were beaten 2-1 and three more victories over Nottingham Forest, Sheffield Wednesday and Stoke eased worries. Then, at the beginning of March, Sunderland were flattened 2-0 in the return derby at Gallowgate – a day when Alan Suddick netted two suburb goals. But United were then sucked back into the scrap at the bottom and went through a tense final period. Newcastle though finished with a flurry, recording a wonderful 2-0 victory over runners-up in the title race, Leeds United.

Pictured above: John McGrath mixed pure football with rugged endeavour at the heart of United's defence.

Memorabilia CORNER

A fine aerial picture of St James' Park was featured on the 1965-66 programme cover.

IN CHARGE

Chairman: Lord Westwood

Manager: Joe Harvey

Captain: Jim Iley

Trainer/Coach: Jimmy Greenhalgh

ST JAMES' PARK

Average Attendance

Lg 33,793 Lg & Cup 33,273

United returned to the top division with this squad. Back row, left to right: Iley, Burton, Craig, Anderson, Marshall, Clark, Cummings, Thompson, McGrath. Front: Hockey, Hilley, McGarry, Harvey (manager), Penman, Allen, Suddick.

PLAYER FOCUS David Craig

Born Comber. Right-back, 5'10"

1960 to 1978: 434 app 12 goals.

From the outskirts of Belfast, David Craig joined the club's junior squad as a raw teenager following a trial period at Scunthorpe and helped the Black'n'Whites lift the FA Youth Cup in 1962. Like teammate and fellow full-back Frank Clark, he was soon elevated to the senior eleven and by season 1964-65 became an automatic choice at right-back when he won the a Second Division title medal. For the next decade and more Craig gave United grand service as a cultured defender, solid in a contest and with the urge to go forward. Always reliable and professional in everything he did on and off the field, Craig was admired by colleagues and supporters. In regular contention for his country, winning 25 caps, David was regarded as one of the best defenders around during the Seventies being an intelligent player, constructive with the ball and seldom rash with a challenge. Craig was part of the Newcastle side to hold aloft the Inter Cities Fairs Cup in 1969, then was unluckily injured and missed both of the Magpies visits to Wembley for the 1974 FA Cup final and 1976 League Cup final after appearing in each run to the twin towers. Firstly the Irishman dislocated an elbow, then injured a knee – two cruel mishaps. A one-club servant at Gallowgate, David left the senior game in the summer of 1978 and after a brief period in non-league football with Blyth Spartans entered business on Tyneside.

SEASON REVIEW

Football League Div 1: P42 W14 D9 L19 F50 A63 Pts 37.
Position: 15th (Champions; Liverpool).
FA Cup: R4 (Winners; Everton).
FL Cup: R2 (Winners; West Bromwich Albion).

Appearances (45m): Hilley D 45, Iley J 42, Craig DJ 40, McGrath JT 39, Clark FA 38 (1), Marshall G 36, Suddick A 31, Bennett A 26, Robson BS 25, McGarry RJ 24 (2), Kettleborough KF 20, Moncur R 20 (3), Burton AD 18 (1), Anderson S 17, Hockey T 17, Penman WST 11 (1), Thompson W 11, Hollins DM 9, Knox T 9, Napier CRA 8, Noble P 6 (3), Cummings RD 3 (1).

Goals (57g): Suddick A 15, Bennett A 10, Robson BS 10, Hilley D 6, McGarry RJ 5, Iley J 4, Anderson S 1, Craig DJ 1, Cummings RD 1, Hockey T 1, McGrath JT 1, Thompson W 1, own goal 1.

Dismissals: 0 players.

MAJOR SIGNINGS

Albert Bennett (Rotherham Utd) £27,500

Keith Kettleborough (Sheffield Utd) £22,500

Kit Napier (Workington) £17,500

FROM THE RANKS

Peter Noble (Consett)

TEAM COLOURS Black & white striped shirts, black shorts (Change; white shirts, black shorts/all white shirts & shorts)

SEASON 1965-66

Match	Date		FL Division 1						Posn		Marshall	Craig	Clark	Anderson	McGrath	Iley	Hockey	Hilley	McGarry	Penman	Suddick	Bennett	Knox	Burton	Cummings	Moncur	Hollins	Noble	Thompson	Robson	Napier	Kettleborough	Craggs	Melling	Match
1	21 Aug	H	**Nottingham Forest**	D	2	2	(1 1)	37,230		Suddick, McGarry	1	2	3	4	5	6	7	8	9	10	11	u													1
2	25 Aug	H	**West Bromwich Albion**	L	0	1	(0 1)	43,901			1	2	3	4	5	6	7	8	9	10	11	u													2
3	28 Aug	A	Sheffield Wednesday	L	0	1	(0 1)	23,391	18		1	2	3	4	5	6	7	10	9			8	11	u											3
4	01 Sep	A	West Bromwich Albion	W	2	1	(1 0)	22,043	16	Hilley, McGarry	1	2	3	4	5	6	7	10	8		11			u	9										4
5	04 Sep	H	**Northampton Town**	W	2	0	(0 0)	28,051	10	Suddick, Cummings	1	2	3	4	5	6	7	10	8		11			s7	9										5
6	08 Sep	H	**Manchester United**	L	1	2	(0 1)	57,436	10	Hockey	1	2	3	4	5	6	7	10	8		11			u	9										6
7	11 Sep	A	Stoke City	L	0	4	(0 1)	25,702	17		1	2	3	4	5	6	7	10	9		11	8			s5										7
8	15 Sep	A	Manchester United	D	1	1	(1 0)	30,401	17	McGarry (pen)	1		3	4		6	7	10	9	u		8	11	2		5									8
9	18 Sep	H	**Burnley**	W	3	2	(1 1)	35,883	14	Hilley, Bennett, Anderson	1		3	4		6	7	10	9	s6		8	11	2		5									9
10	25 Sep	A	Chelsea	D	1	1	(1 1)	30,856	14	Bennett		2	u	4	5		7	10				9	11	3		6	1	8							10
11	02 Oct	H	**Arsenal**	L	0	1	(0 1)	42,841	15			2	s7	4	5		7	10			8	9	11	3		6	1								11
12	09 Oct	H	**Aston Villa**	W	1	0	(0 0)	31,382	14	McGarry		2		4	5	6		10	9		7	8	11	3		s8	1								12
13	16 Oct	A	Liverpool	L	0	2	(0 2)	47,948	14			2	3	4	5	10	7	8	9	u			11			6	1								13
14	23 Oct	H	**Tottenham Hotspur**	D	0	0	(0 0)	42,430	14			2	3	4	5	6	11	10	9		7	8				u	1								14
15	30 Oct	A	Fulham	L	0	2	(0 0)	19,226	15			2	3			6	11	10	8		7			4		u	1		5	9					15
16	06 Nov	H	**Blackpool**	W	2	0	(1 0)	33,853	15	Robson 2		2	3	4	5	6	11	10		u		8					1			7	9				16
17	13 Nov	A	Blackburn Rovers	L	2	4	(2 1)	12,293	15	Bennett, og (Harrison)		2	3	4	5	6	11	10			u	8					1			7	9				17
18	20 Nov	H	**Leicester City**	L	1	5	(1 2)	27,603	17	Robson		2	3		5	6		10	9		u	8				4	1			7	11				18
19	27 Nov	A	Sheffield United	L	2	3	(2 0)	13,880	19	Thompson, Iley	1	u	3		5	6		8	10	7				2		4			9		11				19
20	11 Dec	A	West Ham United	L	3	4	(0 3)	23,758	20	Robson, Bennett, Iley	1	2	3		5	6		10				8		u		4			9	11	7				20
21	18 Dec	H	**Liverpool**	D	0	0	(0 0)	34,153	19		1		3		5	6		10		u		8		2		4			9	11	7				21
22	01 Jan	A	Aston Villa	L	2	4	(1 2)	19,402	19	Bennett 2	1	2			5	6		10		u		8		3		4			9	11	7				22
23	03 Jan	A	Sunderland	L	0	2	(0 0)	54,668	19		1	2			5	6		10		u		8		3		4			9	11	7				23
24	08 Jan	H	**West Ham United**	W	2	1	(1 0)	31,754	18	Bennett, Suddick	1	2			5	6		7	u		8	9		3		4				11		10			24
25	15 Jan	A	Tottenham Hotspur	D	2	2	(1 2)	26,683	19	Bennett, Suddick	1	2			5	6		7	s9		8	9		3		4				11		10			25
26	29 Jan	A	Nottingham Forest	W	2	1	(1 1)	21,659	19	Suddick, Hilley	1	2	3		5	6		7	9		8			4						11		10	u		26
27	05 Feb	H	**Sheffield Wednesday**	W	2	0	(1 0)	31,207	18	Suddick 2	1	2	3		5	6		7	9		8			4				u		11		10			27
28	19 Feb	A	Northampton Town	L	1	3	(0 2)	14,541	18	Iley	1	2	3		5	6		7			8	9				4		s9		11		10			28
29	26 Feb	H	**Stoke City**	W	3	1	(2 0)	26,201	16	Suddick 2, Hilley	1	2	3		5	6		8	9		11					s9			4	7		10			29
30	05 Mar	H	**Sunderland**	W	2	0	(1 0)	52,051	15	Suddick 2	1	2	3		5	6		8			11	7		9				s9	4			10			30
31	12 Mar	A	Burnley	L	0	1	(0 0)	16,257	16		1	2	3		4			8		7	11	9				5		6				10	u		31
32	19 Mar	H	**Chelsea**	L	0	1	(0 0)	35,118	17		1	2	3			6		8	7	u	11	9				5		4				10			32
33	26 Mar	A	Arsenal	W	3	1	(2 0)	13,979	17	Suddick, Robson 2	1	2	3			6		8	9		11					5		4		7		10		u	33
34	08 Apr	H	**Everton**	D	0	0	(0 0)	30,731	18		1	2	3		4	6		8	9		11					5		u		7		10			34
35	09 Apr	H	**Blackburn Rovers**	W	2	1	(2 0)	21,607	19	Hilley, Robson	1	2	3		4	6		8		9	11					5		u		7		10			35
36	11 Apr	A	Everton	L	0	1	(0 0)	32,598	16		1	2	3		5	6		8		9	11							4		7		10		u	36
37	16 Apr	A	Leicester City	W	2	1	(0 1)	18,535	13	Bennett, Robson (pen)	1	2	3		5	6		10		9	11	8								7		4		u	37
38	20 Apr	A	Blackpool	D	1	1	(1 0)	12,446	14	Suddick	1	2	3		5	6		10	u	9	11	8								7		4			38
39	23 Apr	H	**Sheffield United**	L	0	2	(0 1)	25,733	14		1	2	3		5	6		8	s9	9	11	10								7		4			39
40	30 Apr	A	Leeds United	L	0	3	(0 1)	29,531	19		1	2	3		5	6		10			7		11			s8		9	4			8			40
41	07 May	H	**Fulham**	D	1	1	(1 1)	18,818	19	McGrath	1	2	3		4	6		10		9	11							s8	5	7		8			41
42	16 May	H	**Leeds United**	W	2	0	(1 0)	21,669	15	Suddick, Robson	1	2	3		4	6		8		10	11	9				u			5	7					42
Round			FA Cup																																Round
3	22 Jan	A	Chester	W	3	1	(1 1)	18,251		Robson, McGarry, Craig	1	2	3		5	6		7	9		8			4						11		10			3
4	12 Feb	H	**Sheffield Wednesday**	L	1	2	(1 2)	39,495		Suddick	1	2	3		5	6		7	9		8			4						11		10			4
Round			FL Cup																																Round
2	22 Sep	H	**Peterborough United**	L	3	4	(1 3)	16,132		Hilley, Bennett, Iley	1		3	4		6	7	10	9			8	11	2		5									2

DateLine ... 21 Aug: Albert Bennett becomes United's first named substitute for the opening match with Nottingham Forest. **4 Sept:** Ollie Burton appears from the bench for Trevor Hockey in the match with Northampton, United's first substitute to take the field. **20 Nov:** Leicester record a 5-1 triumph at Gallowgate. **16 May:** A final day 2-0 victory over Leeds ensures survival in the top flight.

SEASON 1966-67

DIVISION 1

Relegation battle won again

It was another campaign of toil for the Tynesiders as they battled for survival at the wrong end of the table. Yet amidst the struggle there was optimism for the future as players such as Bob Moncur and Bryan Robson emerged as men while record purchase, Welsh leader Wyn Davies showed he could become the focal point of the team.

Although Newcastle opened the campaign in steady fashion, with two victories and a draw in the first four games, from September through the winter the Magpies looked favourites for the drop. They played 24 games and won only three times, suffering at the hands of several clubs – including a six-goal hammering at Blackpool, who were eventually relegated. By Christmas United were toiling in 21st place, and Joe Harvey gambled. With limited cash resources he sold prized asset Alan Suddick to relegation rivals Blackpool and with the £60,000 proceeds brought in three players; rugged centre-back John McNamee, midfielder worker Dave Elliott and flying winger Tommy Robson.

The manager's wheeling and dealing worked... just. The Magpies continued to struggle recording some woeful results, including a 3-0 home set-back by Sunderland and heavy defeats at Leeds, Tottenham and Fulham all in quick succession. United secured the points they required in the last two home games of the season. Against West Ham United the Magpies needed the lifeline of a Jack Burkett own-goal which relieved much tension. Confidence returned and a 3-1 victory over Southampton brought delight and survival with the comfort of those four points. From then on Newcastle took giant leaps forward to become one of the division's stronger line-ups.

Once more there was little joy in cup action, although a compelling match was played out against Coventry City at Highfield Road in the FA Cup. United won 4-3 in the style of bygone Cup days. Wyn Davies netted his only hat-trick for the Magpies on that afternoon when he gave the City defence the run-a-round.

Pictured above: Becoming something of a cult-figure, John McNamee relished a contest with opposing forwards.

Memorabilia CORNER

Included in club programmes for 1966-67 was the free issue Football League Review.

IN CHARGE

Chairman: Lord Westwood
Manager: Joe Harvey
Captain: Jim Iley
Trainer/Coach: Ron Lewin

ST JAMES' PARK

Average Attendance
Lg 32,085 Lg & Cup 32,085

During this era, the customary location to take the club's photo-shoot was on the steps to the West Stand main entrance, as pictured in 1966. Soon the pitch at St James' Park would act as the studio setting.

PLAYER FOCUS Bryan Robson

Born Sunderland. Striker, 5'8"
1962 to 1971: 244 app 97 goals.

Recognised as one of the finest strikers of his generation not to be capped by his country, Bryan Robson's playing days lasted until he was over 40 years of age. Hitting the net over 300 times, his outstanding total included almost a century of goals for the Magpies during the early period of his career. Robson was born in Sunderland, was small, sturdy and nicknamed Pop at St James' Park. Signing forms for Newcastle in November 1962 as a 17-year-old from the local Clara Vale junior club, he took time to find a regular place in United's attack after developing through the junior ranks, but when he did Bryan was always capable of hitting spectacular efforts from the edge of the box. Plenty of those stinging shots were evident as Newcastle lifted the Inter Cities Fairs Cup in 1969 – Robson banging home six goals as the Magpies reached the concluded leg of the final in Budapest. He claimed 30 goals in total during that eventful season. Robson continued to claim goals, gaining England Under-23 and Football League recognition, until a bust-up with boss Joe Harvey led to his club record and controversial sale to West Ham United for £120,000 in February 1971. He then proceeded to serve several clubs with credit, Chelsea and his home town eleven, Sunderland, as well as most notably, the Hammers where he scored over 100 times. Robson brought an end to his playing days in 1987, afterwards coaching and scouting with a number of top clubs.

SEASON REVIEW

Football League Div 1: P42 W12 D9 L21 F39 A81 Pts 33.
Position: 20th (Champions; Manchester United).
FA Cup: R4 (Winners; Tottenham Hotspur).
FL Cup: R2 (Winners; Queens Park Rangers).

Appearances (45m): Clark FA 42, Robson BS 39, Iley J 37, Hilley D 33, Marshall G 33, Bennett A 32, Davies RW 30, Craig DJ 26, Moncur R 25, McNamee J 21, McGarry RJ 19 (1), Suddick A 19, Elliott D 18, Burton AD 17 (1), Noble P 15, Kettleborough KF 13, Thompson W 13 (1), Craggs JE 11 (2), Allen GB 10, McFaul WS 8, Knox T 7 (1), McGrath JT 7, Guthrie RG 5 (1), Robson TH 5, Alderson S 4, Hollins DM 4, Dalton G 1, Winstanley G 1 (1).

Goals (43g): Robson BS 11, Davies RW 9, Noble P 7, McGarry RJ 5, Bennett A 3, Hilley D 2, Craggs JE 1, Craig DJ 1, McNamee J 1, Suddick A 1, own goals 2.

Dismissals: 0 players.

MAJOR SIGNINGS

Willie McFaul (Linfield) £7,000
Dave Elliott (Sunderland) £10,000
John McNamee (Hibernian) £26,000
Tommy Robson (Chelsea) £13,000
Wyn Davies (Bolton Wand) £80,000 club record fee

FROM THE RANKS

John Craggs (Durham sch, Ey)
Ron Guthrie (Newcastle sch)
Stuart Alderson (Evenwood Town)
Graham Winstanley (Durham sch)

TEAM COLOURS Black & white striped shirts, black shorts (Change; white shirts, black shorts/all blue shirts & shorts)

SEASON 1966-67

Match			FL Division 1			Posn		Marshall	Craig	Guthrie	Burton	Thompson	Iley	Robson BS	Kettleborough	McGarry	Hilley	Suddick	Bennett	Dalton	Moncur	Clark	Knox	Alderson	Noble	Craggs	Hollins	Davies	Allen	McGrath	McFaul	Winstanley	Elliott	McNamee	Robson TH	Match
1	20 Aug	A	Aston Villa	D 1 1 (0 1)	17,673		McGarry	1	2	3	4	5	6	7	8	9	10	11	u																		1
2	23 Aug	A	Sheffield United	W 1 0 (0 0)	15,188		McGarry (pen)	1	2	3	4	5	6	7	8	9	10	11	u																		2
3	27 Aug	H	**Tottenham Hotspur**	L 0 2 (0 1)	35,780	13		1	2		4	5		7	8	9	10	11	u	3	6																3
4	31 Aug	H	**Sheffield United**	W 1 0 (1 0)	21,876	13	og (Wagstaffe)	1	2			5		u	4	9	10	7	8		6	3	11														4
5	03 Sep	A	Manchester United	L 2 3 (0 0)	44,448	13	Craig, McGarry	1	2		4	5	6		8	9	10	7			u	3	11														5
6	07 Sep	H	**West Bromwich Albion**	L 1 3 (1 2)	24,748	14	Robson B	1	2		4	5	6	11	8	9	10		7			3	s6														6
7	10 Sep	H	**Burnley**	D 1 1 (1 1)	25,485	15	McGarry	1	2		4	5			u	9	10	11	8		6	3		7													7
8	17 Sep	A	Nottingham Forest	L 0 3 (0 1)	21,732			1	2		s8	5			4	9	10	11	8		6	3		7													8
9	24 Sep	H	**Fulham**	D 1 1 (0 1)	20,427	16	Noble	1		3	4			7	6	9	10	11			5	2	u		8												9
10	01 Oct	A	Everton	D 1 1 (1 0)	38,364	15	Bennett	1					6	7	4	9	u	10	8		5	3	11			2										10
11	08 Oct	A	Arsenal	L 0 2 (0 2)	24,595			1	2			s1	6	7	4	9	11	10	8		5	3														11
12	15 Oct	H	**Manchester City**	W 2 0 (0 0)	16,523	16	McGarry, Suddick				u	5	6			9		10	8		4	3	11	7		2	1										12
13	22 Oct	A	Blackpool	L 0 6 (0 4)	21,202	17						5	6	7	u	9		10	8		4	3	11			2	1										13
14	29 Oct	H	**Sunderland**	L 0 3 (0 2)	57,643	20						5	6	7	u	8	10	11			4	3				2	1	9								14
15	05 Nov	A	Manchester City	D 1 1 (0 1)	26,137	20	Robson B (pen)			u			6	7	4			10	8			3				2	1	9	11	5						15
16	12 Nov	H	**Liverpool**	L 0 2 (0 1)	36,920	21				s5			6	7	4			10	8			3				2		9	11	5	1					16
17	19 Nov	A	West Ham United	L 0 3 (0 1)	31,285	21				3	4		6	7				10	8		5	2				s3		9	11		1					17
18	26 Nov	H	**Sheffield Wednesday**	W 3 1 (2 1)	26,873	21	Bennett, Davies, Robson B				4		6	10		u		7	8		5	3				2		9	11		1					18
19	03 Dec	A	Southampton	L 0 2 (0 0)	21,488	21					4		6	10		u	7		8		5	3				2		9	11		1					19
20	10 Dec	H	**Chelsea**	D 2 2 (1 1)	32,529	20	Davies, Robson B		2		4		6	10			u		8		5	3				7		9	11		1					20
21	17 Dec	H	**Aston Villa**	L 0 3 (0 1)	25,406	20			2		4		6	10				7	8		5	3				u		9	11		1					21
22	24 Dec	H	**Leeds United**	L 1 2 (1 1)	29,165	21	Craggs		2		4		6	8			10				5	3				7		9	11		1	s4				22
23	26 Dec	A	Leeds United	L 0 5 (0 2)	40,680	21			2				6	7		8	10				5	3	11		4			9			1	u				23
24	31 Dec	A	Tottenham Hotspur	L 0 4 (0 2)	27,948	22		1	2				10	7		u					6	3			8			9					4	5	11	24
25	14 Jan	A	Burnley	W 2 0 (1 0)	17,369	21	Bennett, Robson B	1			2		10	7					8		u	3						9		6			4	5	11	25
26	21 Jan	H	**Nottingham Forest**	D 0 0 (0 0)	37,079	21		1			2	u	10	7					8			3						9		6			4	5	11	26
27	04 Feb	A	Fulham	L 1 5 (0 2)	21,612	21	Robson B	1					10	7		s4	11		8			3				2		9		6			4	5		27
28	11 Feb	H	**Everton**	L 0 3 (0 3)	31,214	21		1		3		4	6	7			10		8			2	11					9		u				5		28
29	25 Feb	H	**Arsenal**	W 2 1 (2 0)	27,463	21	Davies, Hilley	1	2					7		8	10				4	3			u			9		6				5	11	29
30	04 Mar	A	Sunderland	L 0 3 (0 0)	50,442	21		1	2					7		8	10				6	3			u			9					4	5	11	30
31	11 Mar	H	**Manchester United**	D 0 0 (0 0)	38,203	21		1	2				6	11			10		7		u	3			8			9					4	5		31
32	18 Mar	H	**Blackpool**	W 2 1 (0 0)	30,568	20	Robson B 2	1	2				6	11			10		7		u	3			8			9					4	5		32
33	24 Mar	H	**Stoke City**	W 3 1 (1 0)	39,408	19	McNamee, Noble 2	1	2				6	11			10		7		u	3			8			9					4	5		33
34	25 Mar	A	Chelsea	L 1 2 (1 2)	26,388	20	Noble	1				u	6	11			10		7		2	3			8			9					4	5		34
35	27 Mar	A	Stoke City	W 1 0 (1 0)	17,802	20	Robson B	1					6	7			10				2	3			8	s8		9	11				4	5		35
36	01 Apr	H	**Leicester City**	W 1 0 (0 0)	35,183	19	Hilley	1					6	11			10		7		2	3			8			9		u			4	5		36
37	07 Apr	A	Liverpool	L 1 3 (0 0)	44,824	21	Davies	1	2				6	11			10		7		u	3			8			9					4	5		37
38	22 Apr	A	Sheffield Wednesday	D 0 0 (0 0)	25,007	21		1	2				6	11			10		7		u	3			8			9					4	5		38
39	26 Apr	H	**West Ham United**	W 1 0 (1 0)	38,863	19	og (Burkett)	1	2				6	11			10		7		u	3			8			9					4	5		39
40	29 Apr	H	**Southampton**	W 3 1 (1 0)	42,426	19	Davies, Noble, Robson B	1	2				6	11			10		7		u	3			8			9					4	5		40
41	06 May	A	Leicester City	L 2 4 (1 2)	13,951	19	Davies, Noble	1	2				6	11			10		7		u	3			8			9					4	5		41
42	13 May	A	West Bromwich Albion	L 1 6 (0 4)	19,928	20	Noble	1	2				6	11			10		7		u	3			8			9					4	5		42
Round			FA Cup																																Round
3	28 Jan	A	Coventry City	W 4 3 (3 2)	35,569		Davies 3, Robson B	1			2		10	7		u	11		8			3						9		6			4	5		3
4	18 Feb	A	Nottingham Forest	L 0 3 (0 1)	45,962			1	u		2		10	7		9	8				4	3							11			6		5		4
Round			FL Cup																																Round
2	13 Sep	A	Leeds United	L 0 1 (0 1)	18,131			1	2	u		5			4	9	10	11	8		6	3		7													2

DateLine ... 28 Jan: United win a thrilling FA Cup-tie at Coventry by 4-3 with a Wyn Davies hat-trick. **26 April:** Two points against West Ham United courtesy of an own-goal saves United's First Division status. **10 May:** A belated Jackie Milburn testimonial match attracts 45,404 to Gallowgate.

NEWCASTLE UNITED

SEASON 1967-68

DIVISION 1

The corner turned and an unlikely prize

An enormous improvement in fortunes for the Black'n'Whites took place in season 1967-68. There were no more relegation scraps, in contrast, United showed a pleasing transformation being solid at the back where Moncur marshalled a resolute defence, and now dangerous in attack where Davies was a threat alongside – at first Albert Bennett – then Pop Robson. An exceptional home record saw United blend together a decent side. Indeed, had their away results been somewhat better, a top-six place was a reality. They even got the better of local rivals Sunderland in a Festive double. United won 2-1 at Gallowgate then an outstanding 3-3 draw was witnessed on Wearside. In an action packed encounter at Roker Park, Ollie Burton banged home two penalty kicks and cult-figure, big John McNamee grabbed an 88th minute equaliser with a power header from a corner.

Yet the Magpies could make little headway in neither the League Cup – knocked out by lowly Lincoln City – nor the FA Cup where a derby with a difference took place when Carlisle United arrived at Gallowgate. The Cumbrians recorded a shock result, winning 1-0 in front of over 56,000.

Yet, those painful exits were soon put to one side, somewhat as being the norm for the Magpies now. United went onto cap a satisfying League campaign, qualifying for European football for the very first time, even by finishing as low as in 10th place. Back then, such were the rules that entry into the Inter Cities Fairs Cup – the forerunner of the UEFA Cup and Europa League – allowed only one team from a particular city. That gave Newcastle the opportunity and what drama was to follow. They even had a taster of the European format with a home and away double with European Cup holders Glasgow Celtic. Both matches were far from friendly encounters and United won both, 1-0 on Tyneside and 3-2 in Scotland.

Pictured above: Nicknamed Ankles, Albert Bennett did much to catapult United into European qualification.

Memorabilia CORNER

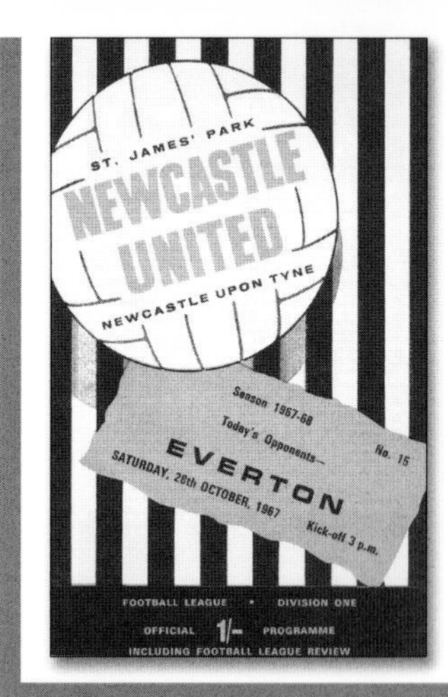

A striking programme design for what was a fiery clash with Everton on Tyneside.

IN CHARGE

Chairman: Lord Westwood
Manager: Joe Harvey
Captain: Bob Moncur
Trainer/Coach: Ron Lewin

ST JAMES' PARK

Average Attendance
Lg 37,239 Lg & Cup 38,117

Newcastle at the start of the 1967-68 season. The majority of senior players are in the middle and front rows. Middle, left to right: Mutch (physio), Duffy, Craggs, Craig (D), Elliott, Burton, Guthrie (R), McNamee, McGrath, Clark, Moncur, Iley, Richardson (physio). Sitting: Clapham, Allen, Hilley, Noble, Lewin (coach), Harvey (manager), Smith (coach), Craig (B) (coach), Robson (B), Robson (T), Bennett, Davies. Goalkeepers: McFaul, Clarke, Marshall, Woods, Crane.

PLAYER FOCUS Ollie Burton

Born Chepstow. Centre-half, 5'11"
1963 to 1973: 229 app 8 goals.

Although Ollie Burton played most of his football for United at centre-half, he began his career as a wing-half or full-back with Newport County. Norwich City signed the forceful Welsh schools and Under-23 international and in June 1963 Ollie headed to Tyneside in a £37,500 transfer. One of the clubs most expensive imports at the time, to start with at St James' Park, he operated at right-back and occasionally in the old wing-half role for United where he could be effective, especially around the box with his ferocious shooting. Then on the tactical introduction of the twin centre-back game following the 1966 World Cup, Burton moved into the heart of the defence and never looked back. He contested the second central defender's slot with Scot John McNamee to become first-choice partner to skipper Bobby Moncur as United lifted the Inter Cities Fairs Cup in 1969. Capped nine times for Wales, Ollie was a hard-hitting defender, but a player who always could play a bit too. He became the club's first ever substitute to enter the field in a senior match during September 1965, while he was also the first from the bench to score two years later. Burton was a winner in one of the earliest League Cup finals with Norwich in 1961-62 as the Canaries defeated Rochdale. A knee injury halted his career, being forced to retire in 1973; afterwards he resided in East Anglia.

SEASON REVIEW

Football League Div 1: P42 W13 D15 L14 F54 A67 Pts 41.
Position: 10th (Champions; Manchester City).
FA Cup: R3 (Winners; West Bromwich Albion).
FL Cup: R2 (Winners; Leeds United).

Appearances (44m): Davies RW 43, Elliott D 42, Robson TH 40 (1), Iley J 39 (1), Marshall G 39, Burton AD 37 (3), Clark FA 37, Scott J 37 (1), Moncur R 35, McNamee J 32, Bennett A 28, Sinclair JEW 17, Robson BS 12 (1), Craig DJ 11 (1), McGrath JT 10 (1), Hilley D 9, McFaul WS 5, Guthrie RG 4 (1), Winstanley G 3, Ross EW 2, Foggon A 1, Noble P 1.

Goals (55g): Davies RW 12, Robson TH 11, Bennett A 10, Iley J 4, Robson BS 4, Burton AD 3, Elliott D 3, Scott J 3, Sinclair JEW 3, McNamee J 2.

Dismissals: 1 player; Burton.

MAJOR SIGNINGS

Jim Scott (Hibernian) £35,000
Jackie Sinclair (Leicester City) £67,500

FROM THE RANKS

Alan Foggon (Durham sch)

TEAM COLOURS Black & white striped shirts, black shorts (Change; all blue shirts & shorts)

SEASON 1967-68

Match	Date		FL Division 1				Att	Posn	Goalscorers	Marshall	Burton	Clark	Elliott	McGrath	Iley	Scott	Bennett	Davies	Hilley	Robson TH	Robson BS	Moncur	Craig	McFaul	Guthrie	McNamee	Noble	Winstanley	Craggs	Sinclair	Foggon	Ross	Match
1	19 Aug	H	**Southampton**	W	3 0	(0 0)	33,709		Bennett, Robson T, Scott	1	2	3	4	5	6	7	8	9	10	11	s6												1
2	23 Aug	A	Chelsea	D	1 1	(1 1)	32,677		Bennett	1	2	3	4	5	6	7	8	9	10	11		u											2
3	26 Aug	A	Liverpool	L	0 6	(0 3)	51,829			1	2	3	4	5	6	7	8	9	10	11		u											3
4	30 Aug	H	**Chelsea**	W	5 1	(3 1)	34,809	6	Bennett, Davies 2, Elliott, Robson T	1	2	3	4	5	6	7	8	9	10	11			u										4
5	02 Sep	H	**Stoke City**	D	1 1	(1 1)	38,924	7	Davies	1	2	3	4	5	6	7	8	9	10	11			u										5
6	06 Sep	A	Manchester City	L	0 2	(0 1)	29,978	10		1	2	3	4	5	6	7	8	9	10	11			u										6
7	09 Sep	A	Nottingham Forest	L	0 4	(0 1)	30,155	13		1	2	3	4	5	6	7	8	9	10	11			u										7
8	16 Sep	H	**Coventry City**	W	3 2	(2 2)	28,892	13	Bennett, Davies, Iley		u		4	5	10	8	7	9		11		6	2	1	3								8
9	23 Sep	A	Sheffield United	L	1 2	(0 1)	16,387	13	Robson B (pen)	1	2		4	s8	6		8	9		11	7		3			5	10						9
10	30 Sep	H	**Arsenal**	W	2 1	(1 0)	33,377	13	Davies, Robson B (pen)	1	2		4		10		8	9	u	11	7	6	3			5							10
11	07 Oct	A	Wolverhampton Wanderers	D	2 2	(1 2)	32,386	13	Robson B, Robson T	1	2		4		10		8	9	u	11	7	6			3	5							11
12	14 Oct	H	**Fulham**	W	2 1	(0 1)	27,664	10	Bennett 2	1	2		4		10		8	9		11	7	6	3		s7	5							12
13	25 Oct	A	Leeds United	L	0 2	(0 1)	30,347	11		1	2		4		10	8	7	9		11		6			3	5		u					13
14	28 Oct	H	**Everton**	W	1 0	(0 0)	34,030	11	Iley (pen)	1	2d		4		10	7	8	9		11		6			3	5		u					14
15	04 Nov	A	Leicester City	D	2 2	(2 0)	18,001	11	Bennett, Robson T	1	2	3	4		10	7	8	9		11		6				5		u					15
16	11 Nov	H	**West Ham United**	W	1 0	(0 0)	32,869	9	Davies	1	2	3	4		10	7	8	9		11		6			u	5							16
17	18 Nov	A	Burnley	L	0 2	(0 0)	15,546	12		1	2	3	4			7	8	9	10	11		6				5			u				17
18	25 Nov	H	**Sheffield Wednesday**	W	4 0	(2 0)	28,101	9	Bennett 2, Davies, Elliott	1	2	3	4		10	7	8	9	u	11		6				5							18
19	02 Dec	A	Tottenham Hotspur	D	1 1	(1 1)	34,494	8	Davies	1	2	3	4		10	7	8	9		11		6				5		u					19
20	09 Dec	H	**Manchester United**	D	2 2	(0 0)	48,639	8	Iley, Robson T	1	2	3	4		10	7	8	9		11		6				5		u					20
21	16 Dec	A	Southampton	D	0 0	(0 0)	19,498	6		1	2	3	4		10	7	8	9		11		6				5		u					21
22	23 Dec	H	**Liverpool**	D	1 1	(1 1)	46,204	6	Scott	1	2	3	4		10	7	8	9		11		6				5		u					22
23	26 Dec	H	**Sunderland**	W	2 1	(1 1)	59,579	6	Bennett, Davies	1	2	3	4		10	7	8	9		11		6				5		u					23
24	30 Dec	A	Sunderland	D	3 3	(1 2)	46,030	6	McNamee, Burton 2 (2 pens)	1	2	3	4		10	7	8	9		11		6				5		u					24
25	06 Jan	A	Stoke City	L	1 2	(0 1)	17,623	7	Davies	1	2	3	4		10	7	8	9		11		6	u			5							25
26	13 Jan	H	**Nottingham Forest**	D	0 0	(0 0)	43,274	6		1	2	3	4		10	u	8	9		11		6				5				7			26
27	20 Jan	A	Coventry City	W	4 1	(1 1)	33,760	5	Davies, Robson T, Scott, Sinclair	1	2	3	4		10	s8	8	9		11		6				5				7			27
28	03 Feb	H	**Sheffield United**	W	1 0	(1 0)	32,191	5	Davies	1	2	3	4		10	7		9			8	6				5		u		11			28
29	10 Feb	A	Arsenal	D	0 0	(0 0)	36,996	5		1	2	3	10	5		7				s8	9	6						4		11	8		29
30	24 Feb	H	**Wolverhampton Wanderers**	W	2 0	(0 0)	35,431	5	Elliott, Robson T	1	2	3	4			8		9		11	10	6				5		u		7			30
31	02 Mar	A	Sheffield Wednesday	D	1 1	(0 0)	24,762	5	Robson T	1	2	3	4			8		9		11	10	6						5	u	7			31
32	16 Mar	H	**Leeds United**	D	1 1	(0 0)	46,075	5	Robson T	1	2	3	4		10	8		9		11	u	6				5				7			32
33	23 Mar	A	Everton	L	0 1	(0 0)	43,519	5		1	2	3	4		10	8		9		11	u	6				5				7			33
34	03 Apr	H	**Leicester City**	D	0 0	(0 0)	33,932	6		1	2	3	4		10	u		9		11	8	6				5				7			34
35	06 Apr	A	West Ham United	L	0 5	(0 1)	27,780	7		1	2	3			4	8		9		11	10	6	s7			5				7			35
36	12 Apr	H	**West Bromwich Albion**	D	2 2	(2 0)	40,308	7	Iley, Robson T	1	2	3	4		10	8		9		11	7	6				5				u			36
37	13 Apr	H	**Burnley**	W	1 0	(0 0)	27,229	7	Sinclair	1	u	3	4		10	8		9		11		6	2			5				7			37
38	15 Apr	A	West Bromwich Albion	L	0 2	(0 2)	22,367	8		1	s8	3	4		10	8		9		11		6	2			5				7			38
39	20 Apr	A	Fulham	L	0 2	(0 2)	21,612	9		1	s8	3	4		10	11		9				6	2			5				7		8	39
40	27 Apr	H	**Tottenham Hotspur**	L	1 3	(0 2)	30,281	10	Robson T	1	u	3	4		10	8		9		11		6	2			5				7			40
41	04 May	A	Manchester United	L	0 6	(0 3)	59,697	10			4	3	10		s5	8		9		11		6	2	1				5		7			41
42	11 May	H	**Manchester City**	L	3 4	(2 2)	46,492	10	McNamee, Robson B, Sinclair			3	u		6	8		9		11	10	4	2	1		5				7			42
Round			FA Cup																														Round
3	27 Jan	H	**Carlisle United**	L	0 1	(0 1)	56,569				2	3	4		10	8		9		11		6	u	1		5				7			3
Round			FL Cup																														Round
2	13 Sep	A	Lincoln City	L	1 2	(0 0)	15,454		Burton		s3	3	4	5	6	7	8	9	10				2	1								11	2

DateLine ... 30 Aug: United show they have turned the corner with a 5-1 victory over Chelsea. **13 Sept:** Ollie Burton becomes United's first substitute to score, against Lincoln City. **30 Dec:** A derby-day thriller at Roker Park ends 3-3 with Sunderland. **27 Jan:** The first senior meeting with Carlisle takes place, a shock 1-0 defeat in the FA Cup. **8 March:** United complete the double over European Cup holders Celtic with a 3-2 victory in Glasgow. **11 May:** Manchester City lift the Championship on the last day of the season after a 4-3 triumph at Gallowgate.

European run turns silver

United's most eventful season for over a decade started with much expectation. The whole campaign was dominated by Newcastle's first venture onto the European stage – during the Sixties just starting to have an impact on the domestic game. Although the Magpies had another decent season in League action – finishing mid-table once more – their Fairs Cup run overshadowed everything, even a mouth-watering FA Cup-tie with reigning Champions Manchester City which attracted gates of 60,000-plus to each match. United lost that clash narrowly, but by then the spotlight was on Europe.

Newcastle's first game in European action in September saw experienced campaigners Feyenoord take on the novices from Tyneside. No-one really gave United a chance. But with a Tyneside crowd energized by the new type of contest, the black-and-whites shocked everyone – even themselves – by going all the way to the final. Feyenoord were dispatched by an impressive scoreline of 4-0, a performance which could quite easily have ended up with six or seven goals in the Dutch net.

More of the Continent's elite suffered at the hands of the Magpie machine, Sporting Clube from Lisbon, Real Zaragoza, Glasgow Rangers – in a Battle of Britain clash – and then Hungarians Ujpesti Dozsa in the final, a club then rated as one of the very best in Europe.

Newcastle won the first leg by a convincing 3-0 margin and set-up what was going to be a difficult trip behind the Iron Curtain to Budapest. And tough it proved to be as the Magyars raced to a 2-0 advantage and reduced the deficit to a single goal. United were rocking, but were saved by the half-time whistle. The interval came just at the right time for the Magpies. They regrouped and came out a different side, scoring twice to stun the home crowd, then went onto grab a winner on the night and lift the trophy by a convincing 6-2 margin in the end.

Pictured above: Alan Foggon burst onto the scene as United entered Europe, he scored in the Fairs Cup final.

Memorabilia CORNER

Programme from the deciding leg of the Fairs Cup final in Budapest with Ujpesti Dozsa.

IN CHARGE

Chairman: Lord Westwood
Manager: Joe Harvey
Captain: Bob Moncur
Trainer/Coach: Dave Smith

ST JAMES' PARK

Average Attendance
Lg 33,714 Lg & Cup 39,296

United are heading for Europe. Back row, left to right: Burton, Clark, McNamee, Marshall, Craig, Moncur. Front: Elliott, Sinclair, Iley, Bennett, Robson (B), Robson (T).

SEASON REVIEW

Football League Div 1: P42 W15 D14 L13 F61 A55 Pts 44.
Position: 9th (Champions; Leeds United).
FA Cup: R4 (Winners; Manchester City).
FL Cup: R3 (Winners; Swindon Town).
Inter Cities Fairs Cup: Winners.

Appearances (59m): Robson BS 59, Gibb T 58, McFaul WS 58, Clark FA 54, Davies RW 52, Burton AD 49 (1), Moncur R 43, Scott J 40 (2), Craig DJ 38, Foggon A 27 (7), McNamee J 27 (2), Sinclair JEW 25 (4), Dyson K 21 (1), Craggs JE 20, Elliott D 19 (2), Allen GB 14, Arentoft P 14, Horsfield A 8 (2), Guthrie RG 6 (1), Bennett A 3 (1), Robson TH 3 (1), Winstanley G 3 (1), Hindson G 2, Iley J 2 (5), Ross EW 2, Duffy A 1, Hope JWM 1.

Goals (92g): Robson BS 30, Davies RW 15, Foggon A 7, Gibb T 7, Scott J 7, Dyson K 6, Sinclair JEW 5, Arentoft P 3, Horsfield A 3, McNamee J 3, Moncur R 3, Allen GB 1, Burton AD 1, Craig DJ 1.

Dismissals: 0 players.

MAJOR SIGNINGS

Tommy Gibb (Partick Thistle) £45,000
Ben Arentoft (Morton) £18,000

FROM THE RANKS

Keith Dyson (Durham sch, Es)
Alan Duffy (Durham sch, Ey)
Gordon Hindson (Durham sch)

PLAYER FOCUS Bobby Moncur

Born Perth. Centre-half, 5'10"
1960 to 1974: 360 app 9 goals.

Joining United as an apprentice professional during October 1960 from schools football in Scotland, Bob Moncur developed from a promising inside-forward – scoring the goal to win the FA Youth Cup in 1962 – to reserve centre-half, then international central defender; captain of both club and country. Moncur's playing career ran in parallel with Joe Harvey's management on Tyneside. He was appointed skipper in 1967-68 and marshalled the Magpies defence where the solidly built defender read the game well and made sure opponents knew he was around. A durable and rock-solid competitor, he was a driving leader on the pitch. The Scot steered United to European triumph in 1969 when Bob scored a remarkable hat-trick over the two legged final. Moncur went onto lead the Magpies out at Wembley in the 1974 FA Cup final then departed in the summer of that year and wound down his playing career with a brief stint at neighbours Sunderland, where he won promotion, and at Carlisle. Bob stepped up to management at Brunton Park during 1976-77, afterwards being in charge at Hearts and Plymouth Argyle. A good all-round sportsman, Moncur also excelled at golf, squash and especially sailing, a sport in which he took part in prestige international events. He left the game at the end of 1989 and settled on Tyneside becoming a hugely popular local radio commentator as well as St James' Park match-day host.

TEAM COLOURS Black & white striped shirts, black shorts (Change; all blue shirts & shorts/all white shirts & shorts)

SEASON 1968–69

Match	Date		FL Division 1						Posn	
1	10 Aug	H	**West Ham United**	D	1	1	(0 0)	37,307		Robson B
2	14 Aug	A	Sheffield Wednesday	D	1	1	(1 1)	27,258		Robson B
3	17 Aug	A	Burnley	L	0	1	(0 1)	13,579	18	
4	21 Aug	H	**Chelsea**	W	3	2	(0 2)	39,048		Gibb, Robson B 2
5	24 Aug	H	**Everton**	D	0	0	(0 0)	38,851	9	
6	28 Aug	H	**Nottingham Forest**	D	1	1	(1 0)	34,613		Robson B
7	31 Aug	A	Sunderland	D	1	1	(1 0)	49,807	9	Robson B
8	07 Sep	A	Coventry City	L	1	2	(1 1)	34,361		Sinclair
9	14 Sep	H	**West Bromwich Albion**	L	2	3	(1 2)	35,128		Davies, Robson B
10	21 Sep	A	Manchester United	L	1	3	(0 2)	47,262	20	Gibb
11	28 Sep	H	**Tottenham Hotspur**	D	2	2	(0 2)	30,469	17	Allen, McNamee
12	05 Oct	H	**Leeds United**	L	0	1	(0 1)	41,999	20	
13	08 Oct	A*	Nottingham Forest	W	4	2	(2 0)	17,651	16	Davies, Dyson, Foggon, Robson B
14	12 Oct	A	Ipswich Town	W	4	1	(0 1)	20,763	14	Foggon, Robson B 2 (1 pen), Dyson
15	19 Oct	H	**Queens Park Rangers**	W	3	2	(2 1)	35,503	12	Burton, Dyson, Gibb
16	26 Oct	A	Liverpool	L	1	2	(1 1)	45,323	13	Gibb
17	02 Nov	H	**Leicester City**	D	0	0	(0 0)	20,374	12	
18	09 Nov	A	Arsenal	D	0	0	(0 0)	34,168	12	
19	16 Nov	H	**Manchester City**	W	1	0	(0 0)	36,420	11	Davies
20	23 Nov	A	Wolverhampton Wanderers	L	0	5	(0 2)	25,425	14	
21	30 Nov	H	**Southampton**	W	4	1	(3 1)	29,515	11	Dyson, Foggon, Robson B 2
22	07 Dec	A	Stoke City	L	0	1	(0 0)	11,594	14	
23	14 Dec	H	**Ipswich Town**	W	2	1	(1 1)	26,454	12	Davies 2
24	21 Dec	A	Queens Park Rangers	D	1	1	(1 0)	16,444	12	Foggon
25	26 Dec	A	Leeds United	L	1	2	(0 2)	44,995	13	McNamee
26	11 Jan	A	Leicester City	L	1	2	(0 2)	21,673	15	Robson B
27	18 Jan	H	**Arsenal**	W	2	1	(0 0)	34,227	13	Davies, Robson B
	01 Feb	A	Manchester City	Ab	1	1		30,160		*Horsfield*
28	15 Feb	A	Southampton	D	0	0	(0 0)	22,213	13	
29	01 Mar	A	West Ham United	L	1	3	(0 2)	26,336	15	Davies
30	08 Mar	H	**Burnley**	W	1	0	(1 0)	32,460	16	Horsfield
31	22 Mar	H	**Sunderland**	D	1	1	(1 0)	48,588	16	Sinclair
32	29 Mar	H	**Coventry City**	W	2	0	(1 0)	26,750	14	Robson B (pen), McNamee
33	02 Apr	A	Tottenham Hotspur	W	1	0	(0 0)	22,528	11	Horsfield
34	04 Apr	A	Chelsea	D	1	1	(1 1)	42,078	11	Robson B (pen)
35	09 Apr	H	**Sheffield Wednesday**	W	3	2	(1 0)	25,973	11	Arentoft, Dyson, Horsfield
36	12 Apr	H	**Manchester United**	W	2	0	(1 0)	46,379	11	Foggon, Robson B (pen)
37	14 Apr	A	Everton	D	1	1	(1 0)	36,335	11	Davies
38	19 Apr	A	West Bromwich Albion	L	1	5	(1 2)	23,087	11	Robson B
39	21 Apr	H	**Wolverhampton Wanderers**	W	4	1	(1 0)	24,986	10	Davies, Robson B 2, Sinclair
40	30 Apr	H	**Stoke City**	W	5	0	(1 0)	28,015	9	Arentoft, Davies, Robson B, Scott 2
41	05 May	A	Manchester City	L	0	1	(0 0)	20,108	9	
42	17 May	H	**Liverpool**	D	1	1	(1 0)	34,927	9	Davies
Round			**FA Cup**							
3	04 Jan	H	**Reading**	W	4	0	(2 0)	41,255		Craig, Dyson, Robson B, Scott
4	25 Jan	H	**Manchester City**	D	0	0	(0 0)	57,994		
4r	29 Jan	A	Manchester City	L	0	2	(0 1)	60,844		
Round			**FL Cup**							
2	02 Sep	A	Southport	W	2	0	(1 0)	8,521		Robson B (pen), Sinclair
3	25 Sep	A	Southampton	L	1	4	(0 2)	13,840		Robson B
Round			**Inter Cities Fairs Cup**							
1(1)	11 Sep	H	**Feyenoord (N)**	W	4	0	(3 0)	46,348		Davies, Gibb, Robson B, Scott
1(2)	17 Sep	A	Feyenoord (N)	L	0	2	(0 1)	45,000		
2(1)	30 Oct	A	Sporting Clube de Portugal (P)	D	1	1	(1 0)	9,000		Scott
2(2)	20 Nov	H	**Sporting Clube de Portugal (P)**	W	1	0	(1 0)	53,747		Robson B
3(1)	01 Jan	A	Real Zaragoza (Sp)	L	2	3	(2 2)	22,000		Davies, Robson B
3(2)	15 Jan	H	**Real Zaragoza (Sp)**	Wa	2	1	(2 1)	56,055		Gibb, Robson B
4(1)	12 Mar	H	**Vitoria Setubal (P)**	W	5	1	(2 0)	57,662		Davies, Foggon, Gibb, Robson B 2
4(2)	26 Mar	A**	Vitoria Setubal (P)	L	1	3	(1 1)	34,000		Davies
SF(1)	14 May	A	Glasgow Rangers	D	0	0	(0 0)	75,580		
SF(2)	21 May	H	**Glasgow Rangers**	W	2	0	(0 0)	59,303		Scott, Sinclair
F(1)	29 May	H	**Ujpesti Dozsa (H)**	W	3	0	(0 0)	59,234		Moncur 2, Scott
F(2)	11 Jun	A	Ujpesti Dozsa (H)	W	3	2	(0 2)	34,000		Moncur, Arentoft, Foggon

Match	McFaul	Craig	Clark	Elliott	McNamee	Burton	Robson BS	Bennett	Davies	Ross	Sinclair	Robson TH	Gibb	Iley	Scott	Allen	Guthrie	Duffy	Dyson	Young	Moncur	Foggon	Winstanley	Johnson	Craggs	Horsfield	Hindson	Arentoft	Hope	Marshall	Clarke
1	1	2	3	4	5	6	7	8	9	10	11	s8																			
2	1	2	3		5	6	8		9		7	11	4	10	u															
3	1	2	3	10	5	6	8		9		7	11	4		s11															
4	1	2	3	10	5	6	8		9		7		4		u	11															
5	1	2	3	10	5	6	8		9		7		4		u	11															
6	1	2	3	10	5	6	8		9		7		4	u		11															
7	1	2	3	10	5	6	8		9				4	s11	7	11															
8	1	2	3	10	5	6	8		9		7		4	s2		11															
9	1	2	3	10	5	6	8		9				4	s10	7	11															
10	1	2		4		5	10				7		6	s7	9	11	3	8													
11	1	2		10	5	6	8						4		9	11	3		7	u											
12	1	2			5	6	8		9				4		10	11	3		7		u									
13	1	2			5	6	8		9				4			11	3		7		10	s11								
14	1	2	3	u	5	6	8		9				4						7		10	11								
15	1	2	3	u	5	6	8		9				4						7		10	11								
16	1	2	3	u		6	8		9				4						7		10	11	5							
17	1	2	3			6	8		9		11		4		7				u		10		5							
18	1	2	3	10		5	8		9		11		4		7				u		6									
19	1	2	3	10		5	8		9		11		4		7						6		s11							
20	1	2	3	10		5	8		9				4		7				11		6		u							
21	1	2	3	u		5	8		9				4		10				7		6	11								
22	1	2	3			5	8	7	9				4		10						6	11		u						
23	1	2	3			5	8	u	9				4		10				7		6	11								
24	1	2	3		u	5	8		9				4		10				7		6	11								
25	1	2	3		s7	5	8		9				4		10				7		6	11								
26	1	2	3		5		8	7	9		11		4		10						6	s11								
27	1		2	s3		5	8		9				4		10		3		7		6	11								
	1		3		5		10		9				4		7				u		6				2	8	11				
28	1		3		5		10		9				4		7						6	s7			2	8	11				
29	1		3			5	10		9				4		7						6	s11			2	8	11				
30	1		3		u	5	10		9				4		7						6	11			2	8					
31	1		3			5	8		9		7		4		10						6	11			2	s11					
32	1		3	10	5		8		9		7		4								6	11			2	u					
33	1		3	u	5		7						4						8		6	11			2	9		10		
34	1		3		5	u	7						4						8		6	11			2	9		10		
35	1		3		5		7		9				4			11			8		6				2	s11		10		
36	1		3		5		7		9		s8		4								6	11			2	8		10		
37	1		3		5	s5	8		9		7		4								6	11			2			10		
38	1		3			5	8		9		7		4		u						6	11			2			10		
39	1		3			5	8		9		7		4		s11						6	11			2			10		
40	1		3			5	8		9		11		4		7						6	u			2			10		
41			3		5		8				11		4		7						6	s11			2	9		10	1	
42	1	u	3			5	8		9		11		4		7						6				2			10		
Round																															
3	1	2	3			5	8		9		s11		4		10				7		6	11								
4	1		3	s7		5	8		9				4		10				7		6	11			2					
4r	1		3	u		5	8		9				4		10				7		6	11			2					
Round																															
2	1	2	3	10	5	6	8				7	11	4	u	9															
3	1	2		6		5	8			7			4	10	9	11	3					u								
Round																															
1(1)	1	2	3	10	5	6	8		9		u		4	u	7	11														u	
1(2)	1	2	3	10	5	6	8		9		u		4	s3	7	11														u	
2(1)	1	2	3	u		6	8		9				4		7				s11		10	11	5								u
2(2)	1	2	3	10		5	8	s11	9				4		7				11		6		u								u
3(1)	1	2	3		u	5	8		9		u		4		10				7		6	11										u
3(2)	1	2	3		u	5	8		9				4		10		s2		7		6	11										u
4(1)	1		3		u	5	7		9		s8		4		10						6	11			2	8					u
4(2)	1		3	u	s5	5	8		9		7		4		10						6	11			2				u		
SF(1)	1		3		5	u	8		9		s7		4		7						6	11			2			10	u		
SF(2)	1	2	3			5	8		9		11		4		7						6	u			u			10	u		
F(1)	1	2	3			5	8		9		11		4		7						6	s11			u			10	u		
F(2)	1	2	3		u	5	8		9		11		4		7						6	s7					10	u		

A* Played at Meadow Lane, Nottingham
A** Played at Estadio Jose Alvalade, Lisbon

Ab Abandoned after 41 mins due to rain
Wa Tie won on away goals

DateLine ... 11 Sept: United's first ever European fixture, a 4–0 victory over Feyenoord under the Gallowgate lights. **30 April:** For the first time in 17 years, a United striker claims 30 goals as *Pop* Robson scores against Stoke. **14 May:** A crowd of 75,580 watch the Fairs Cup semi-final with Glasgow Rangers at Ibrox. **11 June:** Newcastle claim the Fairs Cup with a terrific 3–2 triumph in Budapest against Ujpesti Dozsa. **11 June:** Newcastle record their 59th senior match of the season, the most in the club's history.

SEASON 1969-70
DIVISION 1

Cruel exit in trophy defence

Tyneside's public took to European football from the start. In the six home matches of the previous 1968-69 season an average of almost 55,400 watched the action. It was no different as the Magpies defended their crown with close to 60,000 watching the tie with Anderlecht. This time United held respect and were no longer dismissed before a ball was kicked.

Ties with Dundee United and Southampton were something of a disappointment in the draw, but then United faced Porto and Belgian aristocrats Anderlecht. The quarter-final meeting with an experienced Anderlecht eleven proved memorable. Having to claw back a two-goal deficit from their trip to Brussels, a charged crowd at Gallowgate roared United first to level the tie at 2-2, then into the lead at 3-2. Another semi-final beckoned for the Geordies, but in the dying minutes all of Tyneside was stunned to silence when Thomas Nordahl rifled home a crucial away goal which sent the Belgians through and United out.

In domestic football, again which largely took a back seat to the Euro feast, Newcastle finished the season in seventh place, their best placing for 19 years. With a mean defence which conceded just 35 goals, only Champions Everton had a better rearguard. Newcastle got the better of rivals Sunderland, winning soundly 3-0 on Tyneside and claiming a 1-1 draw at Roker Park. Two late victories at St James' Park as the season ended, a 5-1 success over Manchester United and a 4-0 whitewash of Coventry City, made sure they qualified for the now renamed European Fairs Cup, once more, as many noted, through the back-door and the controversial one-club-per-city rule. Although being knocked out at the first stage of both the League Cup and FA Cup, qualifying for another season of European football was satisfying enough.

Pictured above: One half of a talented pair of footballing brothers, Jim Scott had a dainty touch and scored vital goals.

Memorabilia CORNER

Artwork was still the norm for programme design in 1969. Print techniques would soon change.

IN CHARGE

Chairman: Lord Westwood
Manager: Joe Harvey
Captain: Bob Moncur
Trainer/Coach: Dave Smith

ST JAMES' PARK

Average Attendance
Lg 37,531 Lg & Cup 38,717

The Inter Cities Fairs Cup stands in front of the 1969-70 squad. Back row, left to right: Burton, Foggon, Smith (coach), Clark, Ross. Middle: McNamee, Craggs, Hope, McFaul, Gibb, Davies. Front: Scott, Sinclair, Moncur, Harvey (manager), Robson, Craig, Arentoft.

PLAYER FOCUS Tommy Gibb

Born Bathgate. Midfield, 5'10"
1968 to 1975: 269 app 19 goals.

Having made over 150 appearances for Partick Thistle, Tommy Gibb was something of a low-key signing for a modest £45,000 in August 1968. A lean Scot, Gibb was a player to be groomed for the future, a promising midfielder having just appeared for the Scotland Under-23 line-up. However, he wasn't to see much Central League action for the Magpies as Tom was soon given a chance in United's senior line-up. He made an immediate impact and became a permanent fixture in the side during 1968-69. Indeed, the slim midfielder went onto create a club record 171 consecutive appearances in first team action for the Magpies. With plenty of energy and the knack of making late runs into the penalty area, Gibb was perfectly suited to the new tactical form of the game, and midfield engine-room in particular. Born and raised in Central Scotland, the Scot was a prominent figure in United's European success during 1968-69 scoring in the Geordies debut match against Feyenoord then taking part in every contest en route to Budapest. Rarely to claim match headlines or receive plaudits, he was though highly valued by his boss and colleagues. Tommy also appeared in the 1974 FA Cup final for Newcastle while a year later Gibb made the short move to Sunderland, joining the Roker Park staff in the close-season of 1975. He then spent two seasons with Hartlepool, his last club before retirement. Afterwards Tommy returned north to his native West Lothian.

SEASON REVIEW

Football League Div 1: P42 W17 D13 L12 F57 A35 Pts 47.
Position: 7th (Champions; Everton).
FA Cup: R3 (Winners; Chelsea).
FL Cup: R2 (Winners; Manchester City).
European Fairs Cup: QF (Winners; Arsenal).

Appearances (52m): Gibb T 52, McFaul WS 52, Robson BS 52, Davies RW 50, Moncur R 50, Clark FA 40, Burton AD 35 (2), Craig DJ 33, Arentoft P 27 (5), Foggon A 27 (2), Dyson K 26 (1), Smith Jas 26 (1), Guthrie RG 17 (2), McNamee J 17 (1), Craggs JE 16, Scott J 15 (3), Ford D 13 (1), Elliott D 6 (2), Sinclair JEW 6, Thomson JA 4 (1), Cowan J 3 (1), Young D 3 (1), Duffy A 1 (2), Hindson G 1.

Goals (65g): Robson BS 25, Dyson K 12, Davies RW 11, Foggon A 5, Smith Jas 3, Scott J 2, Craig DJ 1, Elliott D 1, Ford D 1, Gibb T 1, Guthrie RG 1, McNamee J 1, own goal 1.

Dismissals: 0 players.

MAJOR SIGNINGS

David Ford (Sheffield Wed) exchange
Jimmy Smith (Aberdeen) £100,000 club record fee

FROM THE RANKS

David Young (Newcastle sch)
John Cowan (Crusaders)
Jimmy Thompson (Petershill Jnrs)

TEAM COLOURS Black & white striped shirts, black shorts (Change; all blue shirts & shorts/all red shirts & shorts)

SEASON 1969-70

Match	Date		FL Division 1				Att	Posn	Scorers	McFaul	Craig	Clark	Gibb	Burton	Moncur	Sinclair	Robson	Davies	Arentoft	Foggon	Duffy	Craggs	Scott	Smith	Dyson	Elliott	Guthrie	McNamee	Cowan	Thomson	Hindson	Ford	Young	Hope	Match
1	09 Aug	A	West Ham United	L	0 1	(0 0)	33,323			1	2	3	4	5	6	7	8	9	10	11	s2														1
2	13 Aug	H	**Sheffield Wednesday**	W	3 1	(2 0)	41,341		Foggon, Robson 2	1		3	4	5	6	u	8	9	10	11		2	7												2
3	16 Aug	H	**Manchester City**	W	1 0	(1 0)	46,860	7	Robson (pen)	1		3	4	5	6	u	8	9	10	11		2	7												3
4	20 Aug	A	Sheffield Wednesday	L	0 1	(0 1)	19,121	9		1		3	4	5	6		8	9	10	11		2	7	s10											4
5	23 Aug	A	Leeds United	D	1 1	(0 1)	40,403	9	Scott	1		3	4	5	6		8	9	10	11		2	7	u											5
6	27 Aug	A	Manchester United	D	0 0	(0 0)	53,267	10		1		3	4	5	6		8	9	10	11		2	7	u											6
7	30 Aug	H	**Arsenal**	W	3 1	(1 1)	47,208	8	Foggon, Davies, Robson	1		3	4	5	6		8	9	10	11		2	7	u											7
8	06 Sep	A	Ipswich Town	L	0 2	(0 2)	18,229	9		1		3	4	5	6		8		10	11		2	7		9	s11									8
9	13 Sep	H	**Derby County**	L	0 1	(0 0)	39,382	12		1		3	4	5	6		8	9	s7	11		2	7	10											9
10	17 Sep	H	**Everton**	L	1 2	(1 1)	37,094		Elliott	1			4	5	6	11	7	9	8		u	2				10	3								10
11	20 Sep	A	Southampton	D	1 1	(0 1)	19,130	14	Robson	1			4	5	6	11	7	9	8		s10	2				10	3								11
12	27 Sep	H	**Wolverhampton Wanderers**	D	1 1	(1 1)	38,072	14	Robson (pen)	1			4		6	11	7	9	10		8	2		u			3	5							12
13	04 Oct	A	Crystal Palace	W	3 0	(1 0)	28,407	12	Davies, Dyson, Robson	1	2	3	4	u	6		7	9	11					10	8			5							13
14	08 Oct	A	Manchester City	L	1 2	(0 1)	32,172	12	Robson	1	2	3	4	s8	6		7	9	11					10	8			5							14
15	11 Oct	H	**Liverpool**	W	1 0	(0 0)	44,576	11	Foggon	1	2	3	4	5	6		7	9	10	11				8					u						15
16	18 Oct	A	Tottenham Hotspur	L	1 2	(0 0)	33,286	12	Robson	1	2	3	4	5	6		7	9	10	11				8					u						16
17	25 Oct	H	**Chelsea**	L	0 1	(0 0)	40,088	15		1	2	3	4	5	6		8	9	u	11			7	10											17
18	01 Nov	A	Burnley	W	1 0	(0 0)	16,444	13	Davies	1	2	3	4	5	6		7	9	s10						8				10	11					18
19	08 Nov	H	**Sunderland**	W	3 0	(1 0)	56,317	13	Davies, Dyson 2	1	2	3	4	5	6	11	7	9	10				u		8										19
20	15 Nov	H	**Nottingham Forest**	W	3 1	(2 1)	24,307	13	Dyson, Craig, og (Hindley)	1	2	3	4	5	6	11	7	9	10				s9		8										20
21	22 Nov	A	Coventry City	L	0 1	(0 0)	31,825	13		1	2	3	4	5	6	u	7		10				9	8			11								21
22	06 Dec	A	Stoke City	W	1 0	(0 0)	17,767	13	Robson	1	2	3	4	5	6		8	9		11			7	10			s10								22
23	13 Dec	A	Derby County	L	0 2	(0 0)	30,057	14		1	2	3	4	5	6		8	9		10			7							u	11				23
24	20 Dec	H	**Ipswich Town**	W	4 0	(0 0)	19,411	13	Ford, Dyson, Robson 2	1	2	3	4	5	6		7	9	10				u		8							11			24
25	26 Dec	H	**Leeds United**	W	2 1	(2 0)	54,517	12	Davies, Robson	1	2	3	4	5	6		7	9	10						8			s5				11			25
26	27 Dec	A	Arsenal	D	0 0	(0 0)	39,646	12		1	2	3	4		6		7	9	10			u			8			5				11			26
27	17 Jan	A	Wolverhampton Wanderers	D	1 1	(1 1)	29,665	11	Guthrie	1	2	3	4		6		7	9	u					8			10	5				11			27
28	24 Jan	A	Everton	D	0 0	(0 0)	42,845	11		1	2	3	4		6		7	9	s10					8			10	5				11			28
29	31 Jan	H	**Crystal Palace**	D	0 0	(0 0)	36,008	11		1	2	3	4		6		7	9	10	s11				8				5				11			29
30	06 Feb	H	**West Bromwich Albion**	W	1 0	(1 0)	32,054	11	Dyson	1	2	3	4		6		7	9						8	11	10		5		s2					30
31	11 Feb	H	**Southampton**	W	2 1	(1 0)	30,738	9	Davies, Smith	1		3	2		6		7	9						8	11	4		5		10		s11			31
32	16 Feb	A	Liverpool	D	0 0	(0 0)	38,218	10		1		2	4		6		7	9						8		u	3	5		10		11			32
33	25 Feb	A	Chelsea	D	0 0	(0 0)	35,341	9		1	2	3	4		6		7	9						8	u		10	5				11			33
34	28 Feb	H	**Tottenham Hotspur**	L	1 2	(0 1)	34,827	9	McNamee	1	2	3	4		6		7	9						8	s10			5		10		11			34
35	02 Mar	H	**West Ham United**	W	4 1	(2 1)	27,726	6	Dyson, Foggon, Davies, Robson	1	2		4		6		7	9		10		3		8	11			5				u			35
36	14 Mar	A	West Bromwich Albion	D	2 2	(1 1)	19,641	6	Dyson, Robson	1			4	5			7	9		11					8	u	3		6			10	2		36
37	21 Mar	H	**Stoke City**	W	3 1	(1 0)	28,485	6	Davies, Robson 2 (1 pen)	1			2	5			7	9	u	10					8	4			6			11	3		37
38	27 Mar	A	Sunderland	D	1 1	(0 0)	51,950	6	Smith	1	2		4	5	6		7	9		11				10	8	u	3								38
39	28 Mar	A	Nottingham Forest	D	2 2	(2 2)	21,360	6	Dyson, Robson	1	2		4	5	6		7	9		11				10	8		3		u						39
40	30 Mar	H	**Burnley**	L	0 1	(0 1)	33,264	7		1	2		4	5	6		7	9		11					8	10	3		s10						40
41	04 Apr	H	**Manchester United**	W	5 1	(2 0)	43,024	7	Smith, Davies, Robson 3 (2 pens)	1			4	5	6		7	9	s1	11		2		10	8		3								41
42	14 Apr	H	**Coventry City**	W	4 0	(2 0)	32,858	7	Foggon, Dyson, Robson, Gibb	1	2		4	5	6		7	9		11		u		10	8		3								42
Round			**FA Cup**																																**Round**
3	03 Jan	A	Southampton	L	0 3	(0 1)	19,010			1	2	3	4		6		7	9	10				s8		8			5				11			3
Round			**FL Cup**																																**Round**
2	02 Sep	A	Sheffield United	L	0 2	(0 2)	22,101			1		3	4	5	6		8	9	u	11		2	7	10											2
Round			**Inter Cities Fairs Cup**																																**Round**
1(1)	15 Sep	A	Dundee United	W	2 1	(0 0)	15,500		Davies 2	1		3	4	5	6	u	7	9	10			2		11	8	u								u	1(1)
1(2)	01 Oct	H	**Dundee United**	W	1 0	(0 0)	37,470		Dyson	1	2	3	4	u	6		7	9	s11	11				10	8			5						u	1(2)
2(1)	18 Nov	A	FC Porto (P)	D	0 0	(0 0)	25,000			1	2	3	4	5	6		7	9	10			u	s11		8		11		u					u	2(1)
2(2)	26 Nov	H	**FC Porto (P)**	W	1 0	(1 0)	44,833		Scott	1	2	3	4	5	6	u	8	9	10	11			7	u			u							u	2(2)
3(1)	17 Dec	H	**Southampton**	D	0 0	(0 0)	38,163			1	2	3	4	5	6		7	9	10	s11		u	11		8									u	3(1)
3(2)	14 Jan	A	Southampton	Da	1 1	(0 1)	25,182		Robson	1	2	3	4		6		7	9						8	u		s10	5				11	10	u	3(2)
4(1)	11 Mar	A	RSC Anderlecht (Bel)	L	0 2	(0 1)	30,000			1			4	s5	6		7	9		11		2		10	8	s10	3	5				u	u	u	4(1)
4(2)	18 Mar	H	**RSC Anderlecht (Bel)**	Wa	3 1	(2 0)	59,309		Dyson, Robson 2	1	2	3	4	5	6		7	9		11					8	u	10		u			u	s3	u	4(2)

Da — Tie won on away goals
Wa — Tie lost on away goals

DateLine ... 18 March: Heartache for United as a late goal by Anderlecht knocks the club out of Europe. **27 March:** Newcastle and Sunderland share the points in front of almost 52,000, a 1-1 draw. **4 April:** Manchester United are demolished in a 5-1 show at St James' Park.

SEASON
1970-71
DIVISION 1

Inter no match for the Mighty Magpies

United's newly found status in Europe was further enhanced when the opening round of the Fairs Cup was drawn. United faced one of the game's heavyweights in Internazionale, past winners of the European Cup and full of stars of the summer's World Cup in Mexico. The Magpies not only matched their esteemed opponents, but convincingly defeated the Milan giants after an enthralling and notorious clash during September. Newcastle almost brought home a celebrated victory in the famous San Siro, Inter equalising in the final minutes, but a 1-1 scoreline was satisfying enough.

The return leg on Tyneside was to be 90 minutes of football to be talked about for years. United tore into their distinguished opponents and opened up a 2-0 advantage, only for the Italians to resort to a nasty and vicious side of the game. United's players were targeted and at times the fouls were violent. Indeed, at one stage police were on the field helping to restore order. And they were also needed when the referee was assaulted by goalkeeper Vieri. He was sent-off which just added to the mayhem. United held their cool and progressed into the next round where they faced another journey to the then communist world of Eastern Europe. Hungarians Pecsi Dozsa were an unknown quantity, yet after failing to claim enough goals in the first leg on Tyneside, Newcastle were eliminated after a 2-2 draw on aggregate and a penalty shoot-out.

On the domestic scene, it was much the same as the previous three campaigns; steady in League action, but a dismal showing in knock-out ties frustrating supporters who now longed for a FA Cup run to get excited about. Manager Joe Harvey decided on a Magpie makeover. Having lost star striker Bryan Robson to West Ham United for a big fee following a publicised bust-up, United's boss was to completely overhaul his side and also make a change in the tactical style of the black-and-whites.

Pictured above: A thoughtful striker, Keith Dyson often looked the part up front for United.

Memorabilia CORNER

Decimalisation arrives for 1970-71. United's programme now cost '5 new pence'.

IN CHARGE

Chairman: Lord Westwood
Manager: Joe Harvey
Captain: Bob Moncur
Trainer/Coach: Dave Smith

ST JAMES' PARK

Average Attendance
Lg 29,762 Lg & Cup 31,841

United's 1970-71 squad. Back row, left to right: Craig (David), Foggon, Craggs, Young, Kennedy (K), Ellison, Mather, Hindson, McGovern. Middle: Nattrass, Craig (Derek), Cowan, Johnson, Hope, McFaul, Burleigh, Dyson, Guthrie (R), Burton. Front: McNamee, Smith, Thomson, Elliott, Moncur, Arentoft, Robson, Ford, Clark, Gibb.

PLAYER FOCUS Wyn Davies

Born Caernarfon. Centre-forward, 6'1"
1966 to 1971: 216 app 53 goals.

Welsh international Wyn Davies may not have been the most deadly of strikers in the goal stakes for United, nor was he the most skilled of footballers, but his impact and contribution to United's cause was immense. After a long transfer chase, he cost the Magpies a club record fee of £80,000 in October 1966 from Bolton Wanderers where he had found the net on 74 occasions. Davies made his first appearance for the club in a derby contest with Sunderland and soon was to be hailed as one of the club's celebrated No. 9 heroes. Davies was a perfect target man up front and was quite brilliant in the air. He became the spearhead to lead the club to European trophy success in 1969 when Continental defenders could not handle his physical style at all. Nicknamed The Mighty Wyn, he proved difficult to harness and created plenty of chances for his co-strikers to capitalise on. Having a whole-hearted, brave and committed approach, United's supporters turned Davies into something of a cult figure for five seasons – and for many a year afterwards to anyone who saw him play. The arrival though of Malcolm Macdonald in 1971 saw a change of tactics and Davies moved on, appearing for both Manchester giants as well as Blackpool, Stockport County, Crystal Palace and Crewe Alexandra. Davies won 34 caps for his country and after leaving the game at the end of the 1970s, Wyn returned to Bolton where he settled.

SEASON REVIEW

Football League Div 1: P42 W14 D13 L15 F44 A46 Pts 41.
Position: 12th (Champions; Arsenal).
FA Cup: R3 (Winners; Arsenal).
FL Cup: R2 (Winners; Tottenham Hotspur).
European Fairs Cup: R2 (Winners; Leeds United).

Appearances (49m): Gibb T 49, McFaul WS 48, Moncur R 48, Davies RW 41, Dyson K 39 (1), Craig DJ 38, Clark FA 37, Robson BS 36, McNamee J 30, Smith Jas 28, Young D 28 (1), Arentoft P 18, Burton AD 17 (1), Tudor JA 16, Ford D 15 (2), Foggon A 14 (2), Guthrie RG 13 (1), Craggs JE 11, Cassidy T 3 (1), Mitchell I 3 (2), Barrowclough SJ 2 (1), Hindson G 2 (1), Burleigh MS 1, Elliott D 1, Nattrass I 1 (3).

Goals (52g): Robson BS 10, Dyson K 7, Davies RW 6, Tudor JA 5, Foggon A 4, Moncur R 3, Smith Jas 3, Ford D 2, Gibb T 2, Young D 2, Barrowclough SJ 1, Craig DJ 1, Hindson G 1, McNamee J 1, Mitchell I 1, own goals 3.

Dismissals: 0 players.

MAJOR SIGNINGS

John Tudor (Sheffield United) exchange
Stewart Barrowclough (Barnsley) £33,000
Ian Mitchell (Dundee Utd) £50,000
Tommy Cassidy (Glentoran) £25,000

FROM THE RANKS

Irving Nattrass (Durham sch)
Martin Burleigh (Willington)

TEAM COLOURS Black & white striped shirts, black shorts (Change; all blue shirts & shorts/all red shirts & shorts)

SEASON 1970–71

Match	Date	H/A	FL Division 1	Res	Score	HT	Att	Posn	Scorers	McFaul	Craig	Guthrie	Gibb	McNamee	Moncur	Dyson	Robson	Davies	Smith	Foggon	Arentoft	Young	Hindson	Barrowclough	Clark	Burton	Ford	Cassidy	Elliott	Mitchell	Burleigh	Tudor	Craggs	Hope	Nattrass	Match
1	15 Aug	H	**Wolverhampton Wanderers**	W	3 2	(1 0)	38,346		Foggon, Smith, Gibb	1	2	3	4	5	6	7	8	9	10	11	u															1
2	19 Aug	A	Stoke City	L	0 3	(0 2)	15,197			1	2	3	4	5	6	7	8	9	10	11	u															2
3	22 Aug	A	Crystal Palace	L	0 1	(0 1)	27,287	18		1	2	3	4	5	6	7	8	9		11	10	u														3
4	26 Aug	H	**Nottingham Forest**	D	1 1	(0 1)	35,132		McNamee	1	2	3	4	5	6	7	8	9	10				11	u												4
5	29 Aug	H	**Blackpool**	L	1 2	(1 1)	34,041	19	Hindson	1	2	3	4	5	6	7	8	9	10				11	s7												5
6	02 Sep	A	West Bromwich Albion	W	2 1	(1 1)	25,183		Dyson, og (Wilson)	1	2		4		6	8	7	9	10	u		11			3	5										6
7	05 Sep	A	Derby County	W	2 1	(2 1)	30,466	11	Young, Dyson	1	2		4		6	8	7	9	10	u		11			3	5										7
8	12 Sep	H	**Liverpool**	D	0 0	(0 0)	35,595	12		1	2		4		6	8	7	9		11	10	u			3	5										8
9	19 Sep	A	West Ham United	W	2 0	(1 0)	25,841	8	Robson 2	1	2		4		6	8	7	9			10	11	u		3	5										9
10	26 Sep	H	**Coventry City**	D	0 0	(0 0)	32,095	10		1	2		4		6	8	7	9			10	11			3	5	s8									10
11	03 Oct	A	Manchester City	D	1 1	(0 0)	31,159	8	Ford	1	2	u	4		6	8	7	9			10				3	5	11									11
12	10 Oct	H	**Arsenal**	D	1 1	(0 0)	38,024	10	Robson	1	2		4		6	8	7	9			10	u			3	5	11									12
13	17 Oct	A	Wolverhampton Wanderers	L	2 3	(1 0)	24,083	11	Davies, og (Holsgrove)	1	2		4		6	8	7	9			10	s5			3	5	11									13
14	24 Oct	A	Everton	L	1 3	(0 2)	43,135	13	og (Wright)	1	2		4		6	8	7	9	10		u	5			3		11									14
15	31 Oct	H	**Manchester United**	W	1 0	(0 0)	45,176	11	Davies	1	2		4	5	6	8	7	9				10			3		11	u								15
16	07 Nov	A	Southampton	L	0 2	(0 0)	19,250	13		1	2		4	5	6	s8	7	9			10				3		11	8								16
17	14 Nov	H	**Ipswich Town**	D	0 0	(0 0)	25,657	13		1	2		4	5	6		7	9		s8					3		11	8	10							17
18	21 Nov	A	Tottenham Hotspur	W	2 1	(1 0)	38,873	11	Gibb, Craig	1	2		4	5	6	8	7	9		u	10				3		11									18
19	28 Nov	H	**Burnley**	W	3 1	(1 1)	20,994	11	Ford, Robson, Moncur	1	2		4	5	6	8	7	9			10				3		11			s8						19
20	05 Dec	A	Chelsea	L	0 1	(0 1)	39,413	11		1	2		4	5	6	8	7	9			10			u	3		11									20
21	12 Dec	H	**Huddersfield Town**	W	2 0	(1 0)	21,254	10	Dyson, Robson	1	2		4	5	6	8	7	9			10				3	s7	11									21
22	19 Dec	H	**Crystal Palace**	W	2 0	(1 0)	21,779	10	Robson 2 (1 pen)	1		3	4	5	6	8	7	9			10			u	2		11									22
23	26 Dec	A	Leeds United	L	0 3	(0 1)	46,758	10			2		4	5	6	8	7	9			u	10			3		11				1					23
24	09 Jan	H	**Stoke City**	L	0 2	(0 1)	25,708	12		1	2		4	5	6	8	7	9				11			3		u			10						24
25	16 Jan	A	Nottingham Forest	L	1 2	(0 2)	21,978	13	Robson	1	2	u	4	5	6	7	8	9		11	10				3											25
26	30 Jan	A	Burnley	D	1 1	(0 1)	12,521	12	Barrowclough	1	2	3	4		6		7	8	10			u		11		5						9				26
27	06 Feb	H	**Chelsea**	L	0 1	(0 1)	34,336	14		1	2	3	4		6		7	8	10					11		5				u		9				27
28	13 Feb	A	Huddersfield Town	D	1 1	(1 0)	15,580	13	Smith	1	2	3	4		6		7	9	10			11				5				u		8				28
29	20 Feb	H	**Tottenham Hotspur**	W	1 0	(0 0)	31,718	12	Robson	1	2	3	4		6		7	9	10			11				5				u		8				29
30	27 Feb	A	Manchester United	L	0 1	(0 1)	41,902	14		1	2	3	4		6			9	10			11				5		u		7		8				30
31	13 Mar	A	Ipswich Town	L	0 1	(0 0)	17,060	13		1	2	3	4		6	u		9	10			11				5		7				8				31
32	17 Mar	H	**Everton**	W	2 1	(1 0)	22,874		Tudor, Moncur	1		3	4	5	6	7		9	10			11						s3				8	2			32
33	20 Mar	H	**Southampton**	D	2 2	(1 0)	15,683	14	Dyson 2	1			4	5	6	9			10	7		11			3							8	2		u	33
34	27 Mar	H	**Derby County**	W	3 1	(2 0)	26,502	13	Dyson, Foggon 2	1			4	5	6	9			10	7		11			3							8	2		s2	34
35	03 Apr	A	Blackpool	W	1 0	(0 0)	14,637	9	Foggon	1			4	5	6	9			10	7		11			3							8	2		s10	35
36	06 Apr	A	Liverpool	D	1 1	(1 1)	44,289	9	Tudor	1			4	5	6	9			10	7		11			3							8	2		u	36
37	10 Apr	H	**Leeds United**	D	1 1	(0 0)	49,699		Tudor	1			4	5	6	9			10	7		11			3							8	2		u	37
38	12 Apr	H	**Manchester City**	D	0 0	(0 0)	29,148	9		1			4	5	6	9			10	7		11			3							8	2		s11	38
39	17 Apr	A	Arsenal	L	0 1	(0 0)	48,106	11		1			4	5	6	9			10	7		11			3							8	2		u	39
40	24 Apr	H	**West Ham United**	D	1 1	(1 1)	22,790	12	Tudor	1	u		4	5	6	9			10	7		11			3							8	2			40
41	28 Apr	H	**West Bromwich Albion**	W	3 0	(0 0)	18,444	11	Young, Smith, Tudor	1	u		4	5	6	9		7	10			11			3							8	2			41
42	01 May	A	Coventry City	L	0 2	(0 1)	20,596	12		1	2		7	5		9		8	10			11			3			u					4		6	42
Round			FA Cup																																	Round
3	11 Jan	H	**Ipswich Town**	D	1 1	(1 0)	32,150		Mitchell	1	2		4	5	6		8	9	7		10				3		s11			11						3
3r	13 Jan	A	Ipswich Town	L	1 2	(1 0)	21,449		Robson	1	2	s7	4	5	6		8	9	7	11	10				3											3r
Round			FL Cup																																	Round
2	08 Sep	A	Bristol Rovers	L	1 2	(0 1)	16,824		Dyson	1	2		4		6	8	7	9	10	s10		11			3	5										2
Round			Inter Cities Fairs Cup																																	Round
1(1)	23 Sep	A	Internazionale Milano (I)	D	1 1	(1 0)	14,460		Davies	1	2	u	4		6	8	7	9			10	11	u		3	5	u		u					u		1(1)
1(2)	30 Sep	H	**Internazionale Milano (I)**	W	2 0	(1 0)	56,495		Davies, Moncur	1	2	u	4		6	8	7	9	u		10	11	u		3	5	u							u		1(2)
2(1)	21 Oct	H	**Pecsi Dozsa (H)**	W	2 0	(1 0)	50,550		Davies 2	1	2		4	u	6	8	7	9	10		u	5	u		3		11				u		u			2(1)
2(2)	04 Nov	A	Pecsi Dozsa (H)	Lep	0 2	(0 1)	25,000			1	2		4	5	6	8	7	9			u	10	s8		3		11			s11			u	u		2(2)

Lep Lost after extra time, tie lost on penalties (2-5)

DateLine ... 30 Sept: United entertain and beat Internazionale in a fiery contest in which 'keeper Vieri is sent-off for punching the referee. **4 Nov:** United are eliminated from Europe after a penalty shoot-out to unknowns Pecsi Dozsa. **17 March:** Newcastle defeat Champions Everton by 2-1 at St James' Park.

NEWCASTLE UNITED

SEASON 1971-72

DIVISION 1

All change, Supermac unveiled

While United's tactical plan during the last few seasons based on a solid rearguard and long-ball game to Wyn Davies was highly effective, especially so in European football, during the summer of 1971 manager Joe Harvey decided on a change in direction. United's boss was to discard the popular Davies and embark on a more flamboyant and entertaining style of football. The nucleus of his strategy was the arrival of Malcolm Macdonald to take over the No. 9 shirt.

The new-look Magpies needed time to blend and were an infuriatingly inconsistent eleven. They caused an almighty sensation when the FA Cup reached the Third Round stage in January. Drawn against non-league Hereford United – a noted giantkiller in the competition – Newcastle placed themselves in a tricky position after an archetypal Cup-tie full of fervour at St James' Park. With Hereford taking the lead, the match ended all level at 2-2 and United faced an awkward and challenging replay at Edgar Street. In a much disrupted tie due to snow and rain, the Magpies went a goal up and should have put Hereford to the sword in the opening 45 minutes. But they didn't, and paid for it. Hereford famously scored in the closing minutes to first equalise, then grab an extra-time winner and United were humbled from the competition.

By the time of that ignominy, the Magpies had recovered from a meagre haul of points in Division One, being bottom of the table by the end of October. Slowly the team knitted together and Macdonald made a difference, expertly served by the bargain capture of Terry Hibbitt from Leeds as well as Tony Green who arrived for another huge fee. They started to look good, and in a pleasing style – with panache and flair – even winning at Old Trafford against Manchester United following the Hereford debacle. United climbed the table and finished in 11th spot. With Macdonald a huge success and into the England reckoning after he grabbed 30 goals in all games, much was expected of Harvey's refreshed line-up in the future.

Pictured above: Solid at the back, Pat Howard became immensely popular with United's crowd.

Memorabilia CORNER

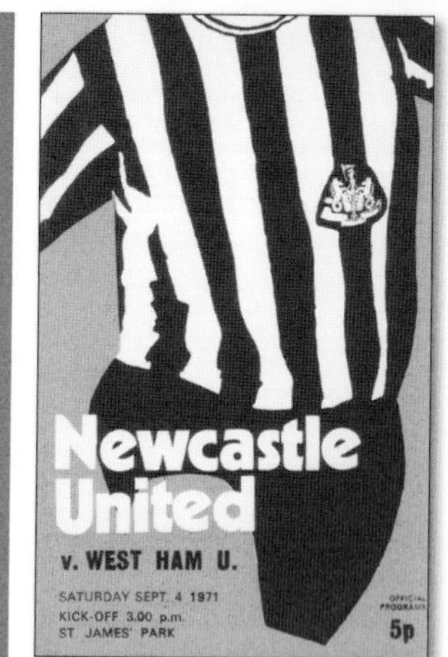

Another eye-catching programme design for 1971-72, albeit simple and uncomplicated.

IN CHARGE

Chairman: Lord Westwood
Manager: Joe Harvey
Captain: Bob Moncur
Trainer/Coach: Keith Burkinshaw

ST JAMES' PARK

Average Attendance
Lg 32,659 Lg & Cup 32,397

Two No. 9 heroes are featured on this group, but they never played together. Back row, left to right: Craig (David), Mitchell, Barrowclough, Burkinshaw (coach), Burleigh, Cassidy, Nattrass, Gibb. Middle: Davies, Dyson, McNamee, Macdonald, Tudor, Clark, Smith, Burton. Front: Young, Craggs, Moncur, Harvey (manager), Foggon, Arentoft, Guthrie (R).

PLAYER FOCUS Malcolm Macdonald

Born London. Centre-forward, 5'11"
1971 to 1976: 257 app 138 goals.

United splashed out what was a huge sum of £180,000 in May 1971 for Luton Town's prolific goal-getter Malcolm Macdonald, a player who had never appeared in the top flight. Yet manager Joe Harvey saw something special in Macdonald; he saw pace to scare defenders, dynamic shooting and also the built-in showbiz image which the Geordie fans would take too big-style. And how spot-on was his judgement. Macdonald burst onto the First Division scene in sensational fashion, netting a fabulous hat-trick on his senior Gallowgate debut against Liverpool. Supermac was born. Raised in Fulham, he was brash and powerfully built being especially strong with his favoured left boot. Malcolm was under-rated on his right too and deceivingly good in the air. Goals flowed in a black-and-white shirt, including many spectacular efforts and in the process Supermac became one of the club's biggest No. 9 legends. He could do little wrong on Tyneside. Malcolm reached Wembley with United in the 1974 FA Cup – spectacularly scoring twice in the semi-final against Burnley – and again in the 1976 League Cup. He became Newcastle's first England player for a generation but the appointment of Gordon Lee as boss eventually led to Macdonald's departure to Arsenal for a near record £333,333 fee in August 1976, a deal which caused uproar. More goals followed at Highbury until a knee injury halted his career in 1979 when only 29 years old. He later became manager at Fulham and Huddersfield Town, afterwards settling in the North East as a football columnist and local radio broadcaster. He once famously netted five goals for England against Cyprus at Wembley in 1975 to equal an international scoring record.

SEASON REVIEW

Football League Div 1: P42 W15 D11 L16 F49 A52 Pts 41.
Position: 11th (Champions; Derby County).
FA Cup: R3 (Winners; Leeds United).
FL Cup: R3 (Winners; Stoke City).

Appearances (52m): Macdonald MI 52, McFaul WS 51, Clark FA 50, Tudor JA 46 (1), Craig DJ 45, Hibbitt TA 45, Howard P 41, Barrowclough SJ 32 (2), Green A 32, Gibb T 30 (5), Nattrass I 30 (4), Burton AD 26, Moncur R 22, Reid AD 12 (7), Guthrie RG 11, Young D 8 (1), Ellison R 7, Cassidy T 6 (4), Dyson K 6 (3), Busby VD 5, Guthrie CW 4, Hindson G 2, McNamee J 2, Smith Jas 2 (2), Burleigh MS 1, Coulson WJ 1, Craig DM 1, Hodgson GH 1, Kennedy KV 1.

Goals (64g): Macdonald MI 30, Tudor JA 11, Barrowclough SJ 3, Cassidy T 3, Hibbitt TA 3, Busby VD 2, Green A 2, Nattrass I 2, Craig DJ 1, Dyson K 1, Gibb T 1, Howard P 1, Smith Jas 1, own goals 3.

Dismissals: 0 players.

MAJOR SIGNINGS

Tony Green (Blackpool) £150,000
Terry Hibbitt (Leeds Utd) £30,000
Pat Howard (Barnsley) £23,000
Alex Reid (Dundee Utd) exchange
Malcolm Macdonald (Luton Town) £180,000 club record fee

FROM THE RANKS

Derek Craig (Gateshead sch)
Ray Ellison (Newcastle sch)
Chris Guthrie (Northb sch, Es/Ey)
Gordon Hodgson (Newcastle sch, Es/Ey)
Keith Kennedy (Sunderland sch)

TEAM COLOURS Black & white striped shirts, black shorts (Change; all blue shirts & shorts/all red shirts & shorts)

SEASON 1971-72

Match	Date	Venue	Opponent	Result	Score	HT	Attendance	Posn	Goalscorers
			FL Division 1						
1	14 Aug	A	Crystal Palace	L	0 2	(0 1)	25,281		
2	18 Aug	A	Tottenham Hotspur	D	0 0	(0 0)	42,715		
3	21 Aug	H	Liverpool	W	3 2	(2 1)	39,736		Macdonald 3 (1 pen)
4	25 Aug	H	Huddersfield Town	D	0 0	(0 0)	40,989	13	
5	28 Aug	A	Coventry City	L	0 1	(0 0)	22,638	15	
6	01 Sep	A*	Leeds United	L	1 5	(0 2)	18,623	18	og (Hunter)
7	04 Sep	H	West Ham United	D	2 2	(1 2)	31,972	18	Tudor, Cassidy
8	11 Sep	A	Manchester City	L	1 2	(1 1)	32,710	21	Macdonald
9	18 Sep	H	Wolverhampton Wanderers	W	2 0	(2 0)	29,347	16	Hibbitt, Tudor
10	25 Sep	A	Ipswich Town	D	0 0	(0 0)	18,724	17	
11	02 Oct	H	Derby County	L	0 1	(0 0)	31,972	19	
12	09 Oct	A	Arsenal	L	2 4	(0 2)	40,509	19	Macdonald 2
13	16 Oct	H	Crystal Palace	L	1 2	(0 1)	20,711	20	Dyson
14	23 Oct	H	Manchester United	L	0 1	(0 0)	55,603	21	
15	30 Oct	A	Everton	L	0 1	(0 0)	38,811	22	
16	06 Nov	H	Southampton	W	3 1	(0 0)	32,677	21	Macdonald 2, Green
17	13 Nov	A	Leicester City	L	0 3	(0 2)	28,792	21	
18	20 Nov	H	Nottingham Forest	W	2 1	(1 0)	24,583	19	Macdonald 2
19	27 Nov	A	Stoke City	D	3 3	(1 1)	16,855	19	Macdonald 2, Craig DJ
20	04 Dec	H	Chelsea	D	0 0	(0 0)	37,586	19	
21	11 Dec	A	West Bromwich Albion	W	3 0	(0 0)	18,036	17	Busby, Macdonald 2
22	18 Dec	A	West Ham United	W	1 0	(1 0)	21,991	16	Busby
23	27 Dec	H	Sheffield United	L	1 2	(0 1)	53,079	16	Hibbitt
24	01 Jan	A	Wolverhampton Wanderers	L	0 2	(0 1)	26,571	18	
25	08 Jan	H	Coventry City	W	4 2	(2 1)	25,875	17	Hibbitt, Tudor 2, Macdonald (pen)
26	22 Jan	H	Tottenham Hotspur	W	3 1	(1 0)	30,113	17	Tudor, Macdonald, Nattrass
27	29 Jan	A	Huddersfield Town	D	0 0	(0 0)	12,829	16	
28	12 Feb	A	Manchester United	W	2 0	(1 0)	44,983	12	Tudor, Barrowclough
29	19 Feb	H	Everton	D	0 0	(0 0)	29,584	12	
30	26 Feb	A	Southampton	W	2 1	(0 0)	18,884	11	Macdonald (pen), Barrowclough
31	04 Mar	H	Leicester City	W	2 0	(2 0)	25,256	11	Macdonald, Gibb
32	11 Mar	H	Arsenal	W	2 0	(0 0)	33,907	11	Macdonald, Smith
33	18 Mar	A	Liverpool	L	0 5	(0 3)	43,899	11	
34	25 Mar	H	Manchester City	D	0 0	(0 0)	37,506	11	
35	01 Apr	A	Sheffield United	L	0 1	(0 0)	28,103	12	
36	03 Apr	A	Derby County	W	1 0	(0 0)	38,119	11	Cassidy
37	05 Apr	H	Ipswich Town	L	0 1	(0 0)	22,979	11	
38	08 Apr	A	Nottingham Forest	L	0 1	(0 0)	12,470	13	
39	19 Apr	H	Leeds United	W	1 0	(0 0)	42,164	13	Macdonald
40	22 Apr	A	Chelsea	D	3 3	(2 2)	33,000	12	Tudor 2, Macdonald
41	03 May	H	West Bromwich Albion	W	4 2	(2 0)	18,927	11	Macdonald 2 (1 pen), Green, og (Wile)
42	08 May	H	Stoke City	D	0 0	(0 0)	21,264	11	
Round			**FA Cup**						
3	24 Jan	H	Hereford United	D	2 2	(2 2)	39,381		Tudor, Macdonald (pen)
3r	05 Feb	A	Hereford United	Le	1 2	(0 0)	14,313		Macdonald
Round			**FL Cup**						
2	08 Sep	H	Halifax Town	W	2 1	(2 0)	19,930		Macdonald, Cassidy
3	06 Oct	A	Arsenal	L	0 4	(0 0)	34,071		
Round			**Texaco Cup**						
1(1)	15 Sep	A	Heart of Midlothian	L	0 1	(0 0)	18,000		
1(2)	28 Sep	H	Heart of Midlothian	Wep	2 1	(0 0)	24,380		Macdonald 2
2(1)	19 Oct	A	Coventry City	D	1 1	(0 0)	12,311		Howard
2(2)	03 Nov	H	Coventry City	W	5 1	(2 1)	25,230		Macdonald, Tudor 2, Nattrass, og (Blockley)
SF(1)	24 Nov	A	Derby County	L	0 1	(0 1)	20,201		
SF(2)	08 Dec	H	Derby County	Le	2 3	(1 0)	37,151		Macdonald, Barrowclough

Match	McFaul	Craig DJ	Clark	Gibb	McNamee	Nattrass	Dyson	Tudor	Macdonald	Young	Hibbitt	Cassidy	Burton	Moncur	Guthrie RG	Hindson	Howard	Barrowclough	Ellison	Guthrie CW	Green	Reid	Coulson	Busby	Burleigh	Smith	Kennedy	Hodgson	Craig DM
1	1	2	3	4	5	6	7	8	9	10	11	s7																	
2	1	2	3	4			7	8	9	10	11		5	6	u														
3	1	2	3	4			7	8	9	10	11	s9	5	6															
4	1	2	3	4			7	8	9	10	11	u	5	6															
5	1	2	3	4				8	9	10	11	7	5	6		u													
6	1	2	3	4	5			8	9		11	7		6	10	u													
7	1	2	3	4				8	9		11	s6	5	6	10	7													
8	1	2	6	4		10		8	9	s11	11	7	5		3														
9	1	2	6	4		10		8	9	u	11				3		5	7											
10	1	2	6	4		10	u	8	9		11				3		5	7											
11	1	2	6	4		10	u	8	9		11						5	7	3										
12	1		6	u		2	8	4	9	10	11					7	5		3										
13	1		3	4		u	8	10	9	6	11	7					5		2										
14	1		3	7		10		8	9		11		5				6	s8	2	4									
15	1		3			s2		10	9		11		5				6	7	2	4	8								
16	1	2	3	s11		4		10	9		11		5				6	7			8								
17	1	2	3	s4		4		10	9		11		5				6	7			8								
18	1	2	3	u		6		10	9		11						5	7			8	4							
19	1	2	3			4		10	9		11		5				6	7			8	s7							
20	1	2	3			4		10	9				5				6	11			8	7	u						
21	1	2	3			4			9		11		5				6	s8			8	7		10					
22	1		2	s7		4			9		11		5		3		6	7				10		8					
23	1		2			4			9		11		5		3		6	u			8	7		10					
24	1	2	3			4		10	9	u	11		5				6				8	7							
25		2	3			4		10	9		11		5				6	7			8	s4			1				
26	1	2	3			4		10	9		11		5				6	7			8	s8							
27	1	2	3			4		10	9		11		5				6				8	s5		7					
28	1	2	3	4		s7		10	9		11			6			5	7			8								
29	1	2		4		s11		10	9		11			6	3		5	7			8								
30	1	2	3	4				10	9		11			6	u		5	7			8								
31	1	2	3	4				10	9		11			6			5	7			8					s11			
32	1	2	3	4				10	9		11			6			5	7			8					s10			
33	1	2	3	4				s10	9		11			6			5	7			8					10			
34	1	2	3	4				10	9		11			6			5	7			8	s6							
35	1	2	3	4				10	9			u		6			5	7			8	11							
36	1	2	3	4				10	9			s4		6			5	7			8	11							
37	1	2	3			u		10	9			11		6			5	7			8	4							
38	1	2				4			9					6			5	7		10	8	u					3	11	
39	1	2	3	4		u		10	9					6			5	7			8	11							
40	1	2	3	4		u		10	9					6			5	7			8	11							
41	1	2	3	4				10	9		11			6			5	7			8	s7							
42	1	2	3	4		s7		10	9		11			6			5				8	7							
Round																													
3	1	2	3			4		10	9		11		5				6	7			8	s7							
3r	1	2	3			4		10	9	u	11			6			5				8			7					
Round																													
2	1	2	6	4		10		8	9		11	7	5		3					u									
3	1	2	6			4	s7	8	9	10	11								3							7			5
Round																													
1(1)	1	2	6	4		10	s5	8	9		11		5		3			7							u				
1(2)	1	2	6	4		10	s3	8	9		11				3		5	7							u				
2(1)	1		3	7		10		8	9		11		5				6	u	2	4					u				
2(2)	1	2	3	u		4		10	9		11		5				6	7			8				u				
SF(1)	1	2	3	s8		6		10	9		11		5				4	7			8				u				
SF(2)	1	2	3	s11		4			9		10		5				6	7			8		11		u				

A* Played at Hillsborough, Sheffield

Wep Won after extra time, tie won on penalties (4-3)
Le Lost after extra time

DateLine ... 21 Aug: Record signing Malcolm Macdonald nets a hat-trick on his home League debut against Liverpool. **6 Nov:** United's recovery starts as new signing Tony Green inspires a 3-1 victory over Southampton. **5 Feb:** A huge FA Cup shock as non-league Hereford United dismiss First Division United in the Third Round replay. **12 Feb:** The Magpies bounce back after Cup humiliation with a 2-0 win at Old Trafford, the club's only victory there in over 40 years.

SEASON
1972-73
DIVISION 1

The Seventies Entertainers

Football in the 1970s decade saw a multitude of colourful and electrifying footballers on view at the top level of Division One. There were plenty of entertaining stars at St James' Park as Harvey gathered an impressive squad. Apart from Supermac up front, midfield boasted the enterprising trio of Smith, Green and Hibbitt, but the side was rocked by an injury to the magical talent of Tony Green during an early season match with Crystal Palace. And Joe Harvey had to plan without key players Macdonald and Moncur for periods too. Yet, Newcastle's squad was good enough to still maintain their mid-to-upper position in Division One. For a period they held fifth spot during March and could have climbed even higher had the Magpies managed to convert a few of the eight draws into victories in the second half of the season. But without a win for six matches, Newcastle slipped to a final ninth place.

Little impact was made in either the League Cup or FA Cup to more supporter exasperation. The Black'n'Whites did get past the opening rounds in both competitions this time, defeating Port Vale and Bournemouth from the lower divisions, but then they failed on home soil at the next hurdle. Firstly, Blackpool won 3-0 in the League Cup, then Luton Town claimed United's scalp in the FA Cup. Both results were shocks, against so-called inferior opponents.

Newcastle did win another tournament – the Anglo-Italian Cup. In a series of fiery games against Roma, Bologna, Como and Torino, Newcastle reached the final and faced Fiorentina in their home city of Florence at the end of the season. Without ace striker Malcolm Macdonald – on England duty – the Black'n'Whites returned to Tyneside with the trophy. While it was a distinctly second-rate competition and everyone knew it, the victory was a foundation for the side to launch a serious bid at long last on the FA Cup in the following season.

Pictured above: Stewart Barrowclough, fast and energetic down the right wing, often provided a telling cross.

Memorabilia CORNER

United's new East Stand was featured on the programme cover throughout 1972-73.

IN CHARGE

Chairman: Lord Westwood
Manager: Joe Harvey
Captain: Bob Moncur
Trainer/Coach: Keith Burkinshaw

ST JAMES' PARK

Average Attendance
Lg 27,779 Lg & Cup 28,308

Joe Harvey (far right, back row) had fashioned a new squad. Back row, left to right: Burkinshaw (coach), Gibb, Young, Reid, Howard, Nattrass, Smith. Middle: Craig (David), Cowan, Hodgson, McFaul, Burleigh, Ellison, Guthrie (R), Burton. Front: Tudor, Green, Hibbitt, Moncur, Barrowclough, Clark, Macdonald.

PLAYER FOCUS Tony Green

Born Glasgow. Midfield, 5'7"
1971 to 1973: 39 app 3 goals.

Becoming a Magpie icon after less than 40 games for the Black'n'Whites is testament to the impact the little Glaswegian Tony Green had on everyone who watched him. When a heavy tackle by a Crystal Palace defender wrecked the effervescent Scot's career at Selhurst Park in September 1972 Newcastle lost one of their most gifted talents of post-war years. Green was at the peak of his career but a knee injury kept him on the sidelines for months and eventually forced him out of the game and into teaching during December 1973 when only 27 years old. Small and slight, but never to baulk from a challenge, Green made a name for himself with Blackpool under the guidance of Geordie managers Stan Mortensen and Bob Stokoe as a buzzing midfielder who had skill, pace and a thundering shot. He gave defenders nightmares, having the match-winning ability to tip-toe at pace with the ball at his feet in and around the penalty area. He joined United in October 1971 for a £150,000 fee, the biggest ever paid at the time for a Scotsman. Tony made an immediate influence on United's fortunes, instrumental as the Magpies climbed away from relegation trouble then developed into something of a flamboyant eleven. Starting his senior career with Albion Rovers, he won six caps for Scotland and was destined to be a regular in the blue shirt of his country before injury struck. After football, Green settled near to Blackpool and for many years was a member of the Pools Panel.

SEASON REVIEW

Football League Div 1: P42 W16 D13 L13 F60 A51 Pts 45.
Position: 9th (Champions; Liverpool).
FA Cup: R4 (Winners; Sunderland).
FL Cup: R3 (Winners; Tottenham Hotspur).

Appearances (59m): Tudor JA 59, Clark FA 58, Craig DJ 57, Hibbitt TA 57, Howard P 57, Barrowclough SJ 55, McFaul WS 48, Macdonald MI 47, Moncur R 46, Smith Jas 46, Nattrass I 28 (4), Gibb T 21 (2), McDermott T 13 (1), Young D 13 (1), Burleigh MS 11, Hodgson GH 7 (2), Green A 6 (1), Guthrie RG 4, Kennedy AP 4, Reid AD 4 (3), Cowan J 3 (3), Cassidy T 2 (3), Robson K 2, Cannell PA 1.

Goals (89g): Macdonald MI 24, Tudor JA 24, Barrowclough SJ 8, Smith Jas 7, Hibbitt TA 6, Craig DJ 5, Gibb T 4, Nattrass I 3, Green A 1, Guthrie RG 1, Howard P 1, McDermott T 1, Moncur R 1, own goals 3.

Dismissals: 3 players; Macdonald, Smith, Craig.

MAJOR SIGNINGS

Terry McDermott (Bury) £25,000

FROM THE RANKS

Alan Kennedy (Sunderland sch)
Keith Robson (Durham sch)

TEAM COLOURS Black & white striped shirts, black shorts (Change; all blue shirts & shorts)

SEASON 1972–73

Match	Date	H/A	Opponent	Result	Att	Posn	Scorers
			FL Division 1				
1	12 Aug	H	**Wolverhampton Wanderers**	W 2 1 (2 1)	33,790		Tudor, Green
2	15 Aug	A	Birmingham City	L 2 3 (2 2)	35,831	9	Macdonald, Barrowclough
3	19 Aug	A	Sheffield United	W 2 1 (0 0)	23,078	9	Tudor, Macdonald
4	23 Aug	H	**West Bromwich Albion**	D 1 1 (1 1)	29,695	9	Macdonald
5	26 Aug	H	**Ipswich Town**	L 1 2 (0 2)	24,601	10	Macdonald
6	30 Aug	H	**Tottenham Hotspur**	L 0 1 (0 0)	27,912	13	
7	02 Sep	A	Crystal Palace	L 1 2 (1 1)	21,749	15	Tudor
8	09 Sep	H	**Arsenal**	W 2 1 (1 0)	23,878	13	Macdonald, Craig
9	16 Sep	A	Coventry City	W 3 0 (2 0)	17,592	11	Macdonald 3
10	23 Sep	H	**Leeds United**	W 3 2 (2 2)	38,964	9	Tudor, Macdonald, Smith
11	30 Sep	A	Everton	L 1 3 (1 1)	33,028	12	Barrowclough
12	07 Oct	H	**Norwich City**	W 3 1 (1 1)	18,103	11	Tudor 2, Guthrie
13	14 Oct	A	Stoke City	L 0 2 (0 0)	16,609	12	
14	21 Oct	H	**Manchester United**	W 2 1 (0 0)	38,214	11	Hibbitt, Tudor
15	28 Oct	A	Chelsea	D 1 1 (0 0)	35,273	10	Smith
16	04 Nov	A	West Bromwich Albion	W 3 2 (1 1)	14,379	9	Tudor 2, Smith
17	11 Nov	H	**Birmingham City**	W 3 0 (2 0)	26,042	6	Macdonald, Howard, Gibb
18	18 Nov	A	Liverpool	L 2 3 (1 2)	46,153	8	Tudor, Macdonald
19	02 Dec	A	West Ham United	D 1 1 (0 0)	23,785	8	Craig
20	09 Dec	H	**Southampton**	D 0 0 (0 0)	20,436	8	
21	16 Dec	A	Derby County	D 1 1 (1 0)	28,826	8	Tudor
22	23 Dec	H	**Manchester City**	W 2 1 (1 1)	28,274	6	Macdonald (pen), Barrowclough
23	26 Dec	A	Leeds United	L 0 1 (0 0)	45,486	9	
24	30 Dec	H	**Sheffield United**	W 4 1 (2 1)	28,620	5	Macdonald, Tudor, Nattrass, Craig
25	01 Jan	H	**Leicester City**	D 2 2 (1 0)	30,868	5	Tudor, Smith
26	06 Jan	A	Ipswich Town	L 0 1 (0 1)	19,609	6	
27	20 Jan	H	**Crystal Palace**	W 2 0 (1 0)	24,676	5	Hibbitt, Nattrass
28	27 Jan	A	Arsenal	D 2 2 (1 0)	37,906	6	Macdonald, Smith
29	10 Feb	H	**Coventry City**	D 1 1 (1 1)	23,051	5	Barrowclough
30	17 Feb	A	Wolverhampton Wanderers	D 1 1 (0 1)	22,147	6	Hibbitt
31	24 Feb	A	Norwich City	W 1 0 (1 0)	26,411	5	Macdonald
32	28 Feb	H	**Derby County**	W 2 0 (0 0)	34,286	5	Tudor, Macdonald
33	10 Mar	H	**Stoke City**	W 1 0 (0 0)	24,020	5	Macdonald
34	17 Mar	A	Manchester United	L 1 2 (0 1)	48,426	5	Nattrass
35	24 Mar	H	**Chelsea**	D 1 1 (1 0)	24,663	5	Barrowclough (pen)
36	31 Mar	A	Leicester City	D 0 0 (0 0)	18,712	5	
37	07 Apr	H	**West Ham United**	L 1 2 (1 1)	24,075	6	Tudor
38	14 Apr	A	Southampton	D 1 1 (0 0)	14,785	7	Barrowclough
39	18 Apr	A	Manchester City	L 0 2 (0 1)	25,156	7	
40	21 Apr	H	**Liverpool**	W 2 1 (1 1)	36,810	6	Tudor 2
41	25 Apr	H	**Everton**	D 0 0 (0 0)	22,390	6	
42	28 Apr	A	Tottenham Hotspur	L 2 3 (2 0)	21,721	9	Tudor, McDermott
Round			**FA Cup**				
3	13 Jan	H	**AFC Bournemouth**	W 2 0 (2 0)	33,930		Macdonald, og (Cave)
4	03 Feb	H	**Luton Town**	L 0 2 (0 2)	42,276		
Round			**FL Cup**				
2	05 Sep	A	Port Vale	W 3 1 (2 1)	10,370		Macdonald, Barrowclough, Craig
3	04 Oct	H	**Blackpool**	L 0 3 (0 1)	19,810		
Round			**Texaco Cup**				
1(1)	13 Sep	A	Ayr United	D 0 0 (0 0)	8,500		
1(2)	27 Sep	H	**Ayr United**	W 2 0 (1 0)	14,550		Smith, Tudor
2(1)	25 Oct	A	West Bromwich Albion	L 1 2 (0 2)	7,927		Hibbitt
2(2)	08 Nov	H	**West Bromwich Albion**	W 3 1 (1 1)	20,420		Tudor, Gibb, Hibbitt
SF(1)	14 Mar	H	**Ipswich Town**	D 1 1 (0 1)	22,531		Macdonald
SF(2)	10 Apr	A	Ipswich Town	Le 0 1 (0 0)	18,627		
Round			**Anglo-Italian Cup**				
Gp	21 Feb	A	AS Roma	W 2 0 (1 0)	18,919		Tudor 2
Gp	21 Mar	H	**Bologna**	W 1 0 (1 0)	15,220		Gibb
Gp	04 Apr	A	Como	W 2 0 (0 0)	3,000		Moncur, Tudor
Gp	02 May	H	**Torino**	W 5 1 (1 0)	9,580		Tudor, Macdonald, Smith, Hibbitt, og (Masiello)
SF(1)	11 May	A	Crystal Palace	D 0 0 (0 0)	12,001		
SF(2)	21 May	H	**Crystal Palace**	W 5 1 (2 0)	12,510		Macdonald 3, Barrowclough, Gibb
F	03 Jun	A	ACF Fiorentina	W 2 1 (1 0)	45,000		Craig, og (Superchi)

Match	McFaul	Craig	Clark	Gibb	Howard	Moncur	Barrowclough	Green	Macdonald	Tudor	Hibbitt	Smith	Young	Cowan	Reid	Cassidy	Nattrass	Robson	Hodgson	Guthrie	Ellison	McDermott	Burleigh	Kennedy	Cannell	Steele
1	1	2	3	4	5	6	7	8	9	10	11	u														
2	1	2	3	4	5	6	7	8	9	10	11		u													
3	1	2	3	4	5		7	8	9	10	11		6	s7												
4	1	2	3		5			8	9	10	11	7	6	4	u											
5	1	2	3		5				9	10	11	7	6	4	8	s8										
6	1	2	3		5		7	8	9	10	11		6	4			s4									
7	1	2	3		5		7	8	9	10	11		6	s4			4									
8	1	2	3		5	6	7		9	10	11	8	4		u											
9	1	2	3		5	6	7		9	10	11	8	4					u								
10	1	2	3	4	5		7		9	10	11	8	6						s9							
11	1	2	3	4	5		7			9	11	8	6		s11				10							
12	1	2		4	5	6	7			9	11	8	u						10	3						
13	1	2	6	4	5		7			9	11	8	u						10	3						
14	1	2	3	4	5	6	7			9	11	8							10	u						
15	1	2	3	4	5	6	7			9	11	8				s10			10							
16	1	2	5	4		6	7		9	10	11	8							u	3						
17	1	2	3	4	5	6	7		9	10	11	8					s4									
18	1	2	3		5	6	7		9	10	11	8					4		u							
19	1	2	3		5	6	7		9	10	11	8					4		u							
20	1	2	3		5	6	7		9	10	11	8					4		u							
21	1	2	3		5	6	7		9	10	11	8					4			u						
22	1	2	3		5	6	7		9	10	11	8					4		u							
23	1	2	3		5	6	7		9	10	11	8					4		u							
24	1	2	3		5	6	7		9	10	11	8					4		u							
25	1	2	3		5	6	7		9	10	11	8					4		u							
26	1	2	3		5	6	7		9	10	11	8					4		u							
27	1	2	3		5	6			9	10	11	8				7	4		u							
28	1	2	3		5	6	7		9	10	11	8					4				u					
29	1	2	3		5	6	7		9	10		8			11		4				u					
30	1	2	3		5	6	7		9	10	11	8			s8		4									
31	1	2	3		5	6	7		9	10	11				8		4					u				
32		2	3		5	6	7		9	10	11	8					4					u	1			
33		2	6		5		7		9	10	11	8					4					u	1	3		
34		2	6		5		7		9	10	11	8					4					s8	1	3		
35		2	3		5	6	7			9	11						4	10				8	1	u		
36		2	3	u	5	6	7			9	11						4	10				8	1			
37		2	3		5	6	7		9	10	11	8					4					u	1			
38		2	3	4	5	6	7		9	10	11						s8					8	1			
39	1	2	3	4	5	6	7		9	10	11						s4					8				
40	1	2	3		5	6	7		9	10	11	8					u					4				
41	1	2	3		5	6	7		9	10	11	8					u					4				
42	1	2	3		5	6	7		9	10	11	8					u					4				
FA Cup Round																										
3	1	2	3		5	6	7		9	10	11	8					4		u							
4	1	2	3		5	6	7		9	10		8			s11		4		11							
FL Cup Round																										
2	1	2	3		5	6	7		9	10	11	8	4	s10												
3	1	2	3	10	5	6	7			9	11	8	4						u							
Texaco Cup Round																										
1(1)	1	2	3		5	6	7		9	10	11	8	4		u								u			
1(2)	1	2	3	4	5		7			10	11	8	6						s9				u		9	
2(1)	1	2	3	4	5	6	7			9	11	8	s7						10				u			
2(2)	1	2	5	4		6	7		9	10	11	8					u			3			u			
SF(1)		2	6		5		7		9	10	11	8					4					u	1	3		u
SF(2)	u	2	3	4	5	6	7		9	10	11	u										8	1			
Anglo-Italian Cup Round																										
Gp	1	2	3		5	6	7		9	10	11				8		4	u				u	u			
Gp	u		6	4	5		7		9d	10	11	8					2	u				u	1	3		
Gp	u	2	3	s10	5	6	7	s8		9	11	10					4	u				8	1			
Gp	1	2d	3	u	5	6	7		9	10	11	8d					u					4				u
SF(1)	1		3	8	5	6	7		9	10	11					u	2	u				4				u
SF(2)	1	2	3	s8	5	6	7		9	10	11	8				s7	u					4				u
F	1	2	3	10	5	6				9	11	8				7	u	u				4				u

Le Lost after extra time

DateLine ... 29 July: *Supermac* scores one of the quickest goals of all time against St Johnstone, after only four seconds. **23 Sept:** A marvellous encounter with Leeds is 2-2 after eight minutes and ends in a 3-2 victory for the Magpies. **2 May:** Four players are sent-off in a fiery match against Torino; Smith and Craig for United. **3 June:** The Black'n'Whites lift the Anglo-Italian Cup in Florence with a 2-1 success over Fiorentina.

SEASON 1973-74

DIVISION 1

Howay the Lads to Wembley

It had been almost a generation since the Magpies had reached the final of the FA Cup. Newcastle's reputation as a giant in the famous competition was at the time waning fast and younger supporters were becoming tired of old-timer stories of the Fifties glory days. Steeped in those magical triumphs was manager Joe Harvey. More than anyone else he wanted another Cup run and in season 1973-74 he guided United through a campaign as good as any of the past – all that is until the big day at Wembley Stadium.

Before the Cup started in January, United began the season well, even in reach of top spot during November while they also enjoyed a mini-run in the League Cup too. United could be brilliant on occasions, however often pitiful and depressingly bad. Yet that lack of consistency threw up absorbing contests when the FA Cup began as the year turned. There were visions of another Hereford catastrophe when United could only draw with non-leaguers Hendon on Tyneside, but this time the Geordies made no mistake in the replay, winning 4-0. It was the same story against Scunthorpe – stalemate on Tyneside and a convincing victory at the second attempt. Then a terrific display was put together to demolish West Bromwich Albion by 3-0 at The Hawthorns.

The quarter-final meeting with Nottingham Forest proved a gripping contest. At St James' Park United stormed back from a 3-1 deficit to win 4-3 with 10 men only for the authorities to nullify the result due to a pitch invasion. Two highly charged replays followed at a neutral Goodison Park with a single Supermac strike taking United into the semi-final for the second time. Against Burnley, Malcolm Macdonald had his finest hour, propelling the Tynesiders to Wembley with two breathtaking breakaway goals. And so to Liverpool in the final. There was to be no sparkling United on show, instead the dire and dreadful side of the black-and-whites turned up. Liverpool – and notably Kevin Keegan – swept United aside with a 3-0 victory.

John Tudor forged a telling partnership with Supermac in attack.

Memorabilia CORNER

The Magpies face all-conquering Liverpool in the FA Cup final at Wembley.

IN CHARGE

Chairman: Lord Westwood
Manager: Joe Harvey
Captain: Bob Moncur
Trainer/Coach: Keith Burkinshaw

ST JAMES' PARK

Average Attendance
Lg 32,861 Lg & Cup 31,923

The Black'n'Whites first-team squad which took the club to Wembley in 1974. Back row, left to right: Burleigh, Barrowclough, Gibb, Nattrass, McFaul. Middle: Harvey (manager), Craig (David), Hodgson, Cassidy, Howard, Smith, McDermott, Burkinshaw (coach). Front: Macdonald, Moncur, Clark, Tudor, Green, Hibbitt.

SEASON REVIEW

Football League Div 1: P42 W13 D12 L17 F49 A48 Pts 38.
Position: 15th (Champions; Leeds United).
FA Cup: Finalist (Winners; Liverpool).
FL Cup: R3 (Winners; Wolverhampton Wanderers).

Appearances (61m): McFaul WS 59, Howard P 55, Clark FA 54, McDermott T 53, Moncur R 50, Hibbitt TA 48, Cassidy T 46 (1), Tudor JA 44, Macdonald MI 43 (1), Smith Jas 42 (1), Craig DJ 36 (1), Barrowclough SJ 26 (7), Gibb T 24 (8), Kennedy AP 23 (4), Nattrass I 18 (1), Robson K 16, Crosson D 8 (1), Bruce AR 7 (1), Hope G1 6, Laughton D 6, Burleigh MS 2, Cannell PA 2, Hodgson GH 2 (1), Craig DM 1, Hudson RW 0 (1).

Goals (85g): Macdonald MI 28, Tudor JA 12, McDermott T 7, Cassidy T 6, Robson K 6, Barrowclough SJ 4, Gibb T 4, Clark FA 2, Hibbitt TA 2, Howard P 2, Moncur R 2, Nattrass I 2, Smith Jas 2, Bruce AR 1, Hope G1 1, own goals 4.
(Appearances & goals exclude the annulled FA Cup fixture with Nottingham Forest.)

Dismissals: 3 players; Smith, Cassidy, Howard.

MAJOR SIGNINGS

Alex Bruce (Preston NE) £150,000

FROM THE RANKS

Paul Cannell (Newcastle sch)
Ray Hudson (Gateshead sch)
David Crosson (Durham sch)
George Hope (Northb sch)

PLAYER FOCUS Jimmy Smith

Born Glasgow. Midfield, 5'11"
1969 to 1976: 178 app 16 goals.

Joe Harvey added a touch of finesse and panache to his side when he purchased Aberdeen's 22-year-old international midfielder Jimmy Smith in July 1969. A talented ball-player from Glasgow, Smith cost United a much publicised new club record fee and when all the add-ons were included, first £100,000 signing. Smith became an instant favourite with the crowd, able to lay on chances with exquisite passes while he always attempted to play to the audience. And with the female section of United's support, Smith was also a huge hit – being the proverbial tall, dark and handsome Scotsman and stylish with it. Yet Jinky, as he was known, was also a frustrating enigma to many. Having a languid manner, for six seasons he was in and out of the side, could win a game with one brilliant pass then look totally disinterested for the rest of the contest. After appearing in the 1974 FA Cup final, the arrival of Gordon Lee as boss marked the end of Smith's Gallowgate career, coincidently with an unlucky injury which wrecked his footballing days. Jimmy was forced to retire in July 1976 due to knee problems following a brief loan spell with Celtic. Smith appeared on four occasions for his country, while in 1973 he was sent-off within the first minute of a Texaco Cup contest against Birmingham City, one of the fastest dismissals on record. His brother also appeared in Scottish football.

TEAM COLOURS Black & white striped shirts, black shorts (Change; all blue shirts & shorts/yellow shirts with green trim & sky-blue shor

SEASON 1973–74

Match	Date	Venue	Opponent	Res	F	A	HT	Att	Posn	Scorers	McFaul	Craig DJ	Clark	Gibb	Nattrass	Moncur	Barrowclough	Smith	Macdonald	Tudor	Hibbitt	Cassidy	Hodgson	Kennedy	McDermott	Howard	Robson	Crosson	Hudson	Hope	Laughton	Bruce	Burleigh	Cannell	Craig DM	Steele	Match
			FL Division 1																																		
1	25 Aug	A	West Ham United	W	2	1	(0 1)	28,169		Macdonald 2	1	2	3	4	5	6	7	8	9	10	11	u															1
2	29 Aug	H	**Southampton**	L	0	1	(0 1)	25,531			1	2	3	4	5	6	7	8			11	9	10	s2													2
3	01 Sep	H	**Arsenal**	D	1	1	(1 1)	30,665		McDermott	1		3		2	6	7	8			11	9		u	4	5	10										3
4	04 Sep	A	Ipswich Town	W	3	1	(2 1)	21,696	6	Robson, Cassidy, Smith	1		3		2	6	7	8			11	9		u	4	5	10										4
5	08 Sep	A	Sheffield United	D	1	1	(0 1)	26,897	8	Robson	1		3		2	6	s8	8	9		11	7			4	5	10										5
6	12 Sep	H	**Ipswich Town**	W	3	1	(2 0)	30,604	6	Macdonald 2, og (Johnson)	1		3		2	6		8	9	u	11	7			4	5	10										6
7	15 Sep	H	**Wolverhampton Wanderers**	W	2	0	(0 0)	36,412	3	Howard, Nattrass	1		3		2	6	u	8	9	10	11	7			4	5											7
8	22 Sep	A	Coventry City	D	2	2	(1 2)	24,085	4	Tudor, Macdonald	1		3	u	2	6		8	9	10	11	7			4	5											8
9	29 Sep	H	**Queens Park Rangers**	L	2	3	(0 2)	31,402	5	Tudor 2	1		3	u	2	6		8	9	10	11	7			4	5											9
10	06 Oct	A	Liverpool	L	1	2	(0 1)	45,612	8	Nattrass	1	s10	3		2	6		8	9	10	11	7			4	5											10
11	13 Oct	H	**Manchester City**	W	1	0	(1 0)	35,346	7	Macdonald	1	2	3		10	6	s10	8	9		11	7			4	5											11
12	20 Oct	H	**Chelsea**	W	2	0	(0 0)	32,106	5	Macdonald 2 (1 pen)	1	2	3	s10		6		8	9		11	7			4	5	10										12
13	27 Oct	A	Tottenham Hotspur	W	2	0	(0 0)	31,259	5	Barrowclough, Gibb	1	2	3	7		6	11	8	9		10				4	5		u									13
14	03 Nov	H	**Stoke City**	W	2	1	(1 0)	28,135	2	Gibb, McDermott	1	2	3	7		6	10	8			11	9			4	5			s4								14
15	10 Nov	A	Leicester City	L	0	1	(0 1)	20,726	3		1	2	3	7	u	6		8			11	10			4	5				9							15
16	17 Nov	H	**Manchester United**	W	3	2	(1 2)	42,474	2	Cassidy 2, Hope	1	3		7	2	6	u	8			11	10			4	5				9							16
17	24 Nov	A	Everton	D	1	1	(1 1)	34,376	2	Gibb	1		3	7	2	6		8		10	11				4	5		u		9							17
18	08 Dec	A	Birmingham City	L	0	1	(0 1)	25,428	4		1		3	s2	2		7	8		9	11				4	5	10				6						18
19	15 Dec	H	**Derby County**	L	0	2	(0 1)	19,470	6		1		6	2			7			9	11	8	u	3	4	5	10										19
20	22 Dec	A	Queens Park Rangers	L	2	3	(0 2)	15,757	6	Moncur, McDermott	1	2	3	8		6	u			9	11	7			4	5	10										20
21	26 Dec	H	**Leeds United**	L	0	1	(0 1)	55,638	11		1	2	3	7		6		8	9	10	11	s8			4	5											21
22	29 Dec	H	**Sheffield United**	W	1	0	(0 0)	27,943	9	Tudor	1	2	3	7		6		8	9	10	11			u	4	5											22
23	01 Jan	A	Arsenal	W	1	0	(1 0)	29,258	7	Hibbitt	1	2	6	7				8	9	10	11			3	4	5	u										23
24	12 Jan	A	Wolverhampton Wanderers	L	0	1	(0 1)	22,235	9		1	2	6	7			s7		9	10	11	8		3	4	5											24
25	19 Jan	H	**West Ham United**	D	1	1	(1 0)	27,217	9	Macdonald	1	2	6	u			7	8	9	10		11		3	4	5											25
26	02 Feb	A	Derby County	L	0	1	(0 1)	24,992	9		1	2	3	s10		6	7	8	9		10	11			4	5											26
27	05 Feb	A	Southampton	L	1	3	(1 1)	16,497	11	Macdonald	1	2	3	4		6	u		9	10	11	8d				5						7					27
28	09 Feb	H	**Coventry City**	W	5	1	(1 0)	27,371	9	Tudor, Macdonald, Bruce, og 2 (Craven, Dugdale)	1	2	3	4		6	s7		9	10	11	8				5						7					28
29	23 Feb	H	**Liverpool**	D	0	0	(0 0)	45,192	9		1	2	3			6	7	11	9	10		8		s7	4	5											29
30	02 Mar	A	Leeds United	D	1	1	(0 0)	46,611	9	Barrowclough	1	2	5	u		6	7	11	9	10		8		3	4												30
31	16 Mar	A	Chelsea	L	0	1	(0 1)	24,207	14		1		2			6	7	8	9	10	11		u	3	4	5											31
32	23 Mar	H	**Leicester City**	D	1	1	(0 0)	32,116	13	McDermott (pen)	1	2	5			6	7		9		11	8		3	4		10					u					32
33	27 Mar	A	Manchester City	L	1	2	(0 2)	21,590	15	Cassidy		2	5			6				9		8	11	3	4							7	1	10	u		33
34	03 Apr	A	Stoke City	L	1	2	(1 1)	16,437	15	Tudor	1	2	3			6				9		8		11	4	5		u		10		7					34
35	06 Apr	H	**Everton**	W	2	1	(0 0)	45,497	13	Macdonald 2 (1 pen)	1	2	3			6			9	10	11	8		u		5				7		4					35
36	10 Apr	H	**Burnley**	L	1	2	(1 2)	30,168	15	Macdonald	1	2	3			6			9	10	11	8		s2		5				7		4					36
37	13 Apr	A	Manchester United	L	0	1	(0 1)	44,751	15		1					6	7		9			8		3	4	5	10	2			11	u					37
38	15 Apr	H	**Norwich City**	D	0	0	(0 0)	31,132	18		1					6	7		9	10	11	8		3	4	5		2				s7					38
39	17 Apr	A	Norwich City	D	1	1	(0 0)	18,408	14	Cassidy	1					6			9	10		8		3	4	5	7	2			11	u					39
40	20 Apr	H	**Birmingham City**	D	1	1	(1 1)	34,066	14	Robson	1					6			9	10		8		3	4	5	7	2			11	u					40
41	27 Apr	A	Burnley	D	1	1	(1 1)	21,340	15	Macdonald	1		2			6		7	9	10		8		3	4	5	u				11						41
42	11 May	H	**Tottenham Hotspur**	L	0	2	(0 0)	21,601	15					s7			7			9	11			3	4	5		2			6	10	1	8			42
Round			**FA Cup**																																		Round
3	05 Jan	H	**Hendon**	D	1	1	(1 0)	33,840		Howard	1	2	6	7			s7	8	9	10	11			3	4	5											3
3r	09 Jan	A*	Hendon	W	4	0	(1 0)	15,385		Hibbitt, Tudor, Macdonald, McDermott (pen)	1	2	6	7			s11		9	10	11	8		3	4	5											3r
4	26 Jan	H	**Scunthorpe United**	D	1	1	(0 1)	38,913		McDermott	1	2	6	u			7	8	9	10		11		3	4	5											4
4r	30 Jan	A	Scunthorpe United	W	3	0	(1 0)	19,028		Macdonald 2, Barrowclough	1	2	3	s8		6	7	8	9	10		11			4	5											4r
5	16 Feb	A	West Bromwich Albion	W	3	0	(1 0)	42,699		Tudor, Macdonald, Barrowclough	1	2	3			6	7	s11	9	10	11	8			4	5											5
6	09 Mar	H	**Nottingham Forest**	W*	4	3	(1 2)	52,551		*Tudor, Moncur, McDermott (pen), Craig DJ*	1	2	3			6	7	8	9	10	11			s2	4	5d											6
6	18 Mar	N1	Nottingham Forest	De	0	0	(0 0)	40,685			1		2			6	7	8	9	10	11			3	4	5	u										6
6r	21 Mar	N1	Nottingham Forest	W	1	0	(1 0)	31,373		Macdonald	1	2	5			6	u	8	9	10	11	7		3	4												6r
SF	30 Mar	N2	Burnley	W	2	0	(0 0)	55,000		Macdonald 2	1	2	3			6		8	9	10	11	7		s11	4	5											SF
F	04 May	N3	Liverpool	L	0	3	(0 0)	100,000			1		2	s7		6		7	9	10	11	8		3	4	5											F
Round			**FL Cup**																																		Round
2	08 Oct	H	**Doncaster Rovers**	W	6	0	(2 0)	15,948		Robson 2, Macdonald 3, Clark	1	u	3		2	6		8	9		11	7			4	5	10										2
3	30 Oct	A	Birmingham City	D	2	2	(1 1)	13,025		Gibb, McDermott	1	2	3	7		6		8	9		11	10			4	5		s8									3
3r	07 Nov	H	**Birmingham City**	Le	0	1	(0 0)	19,276			1	2	3	7	4	6	s10	8		10	11	9				5											3r
Round			**Texaco Cup**																																		Round
1(1)	19 Sep	A	Morton	W	2	1	(1 1)	4,326		Tudor, Smith	1		3	4	2	6	7	8		9		10			11	5		u								u	1(1)
1(2)	01 Oct	H	**Morton**	D	1	1	(0 0)	12,158		og (Laughton)	1	2	3	4	s8	6	7	8	9	10	11					5										u	1(2)
2(1)	22 Oct	A	Birmingham City	D	1	1	(0 1)	12,429		Macdonald (pen)	1	2	3	7		6	11	8	9					u	4	5		10								u	2(1)
2(2)	28 Nov	H	**Birmingham City**	Ab	1	1	(1 0)	5,529		*Tudor*	1		3		2	6	7	8		10	11				4	5		s8						9		u	2(2)
2(2)	05 Dec	H	**Birmingham City**	W	3	1	(3 0)	9,762		Tudor 2, Clark	1		3	s4	2		7	8d		9	11				4	5	10	6								u	2(2)
SF(1)	12 Dec	A	Dundee United	L	0	2	(0 2)	8,500			1			8			7			9	11		s9	3	4	6	10	2							5	u	SF(1)
SF(2)	19 Dec	H	**Dundee United**	We	4	1	(1 1)	5,009		Robson, Tudor, Macdonald, Cassidy	1	2	3	7		6			s10	9	11	8			4	5	10						u				SF(2)
F	24 Apr	H	**Burnley**	We	2	1	(0 1)	36,076		Macdonald, Moncur	1		2	s8		6		8	9	10	11	7		3	4	5							u				F

W* Match annulled by FA following crowd interruption

A* Played at Vicarage Road, Watford
N1 Played at Goodison Park,Liverpool
N2 Played at Hillsborough, Sheffield
N3 Played at Wembley Stadium, London

Le Lost after extra time
We Won after extra time
De Drawn after extra time
Ab Abandoned after 100 mins due to bad light

DateLine ... 8 Oct: Frank Clark scores his first senior goal in the 6-0 demolition of Doncaster in the League Cup. **16 Feb:** United seriously eye the FA Cup after a brilliant 3-0 display against West Bromwich Albion. **9 March:** United's 4-3 FA Cup thriller with Nottingham Forest is controversially annulled by the FA. **30 March:** *Supermac* hits the headlines with two goals in the FA Cup semi-final victory over Burnley. **20 April:** United face Birmingham for the seventh time in the season, the most fixtures against any club. **4 May:** Newcastle slump in the FA Cup final and are comprehensively beaten 3-0 by Liverpool.

SEASON 1974-75
DIVISION 1

Joe Harvey's last stand

Following the Geordies run to the FA Cup final – despite the convincing defeat by Liverpool – there was belief that United could take the next step, to eliminate that unpredictability tag and become, if not title challengers, at least seriously head for a place in the UEFA Cup. With arguably the country's best goalscorer leading the attack in Malcolm Macdonald, United should have done so. There was plenty of exciting football in the 1974-75 season, but with Bob Moncur allowed to depart, Newcastle's defence was not as strong as before and too many goals were conceded which meant United slipped to 15th place in the final analysis.

Youngsters emerged, Irving Nattrass and Alan Kennedy being highly rated and tipped for international honours, while a close to record fee was paid to Blackpool for the tricky skills of Micky Burns. An exit in the League Cup to lowly Chester when the latter stages of the competition were within United's reach was disappointing. In the FA Cup another disaster followed. Following a marvellous victory at Maine Road over Manchester City which saw a change in home venue on order of the Football Association as punishment for last season's quarter-final rumpus, United came a cropper, this time at the hands of lowly Walsall at a packed Fellows Park. Newcastle's inability to develop to a next level was exasperating.

The Cup shock in the Midlands saw initially United bounce back with some impressive First Division results, including a 4-1 victory against Liverpool on Tyneside. However, as March began a slump in League results followed – without a win in nine games – and that in many supporters' minds was the end of the road for Joe Harvey. On too many occasions United had fallen to an inferior club. The time was ready for change. Harvey was moved 'upstairs' in the summer and invitations went out to new candidates to take the club forward.

Pictured above: Tommy Cassidy arrived on Tyneside as a raw Irish lad and developed into a noted link man.

Memorabilia CORNER

Newcastle's 1974-75 programme was titled 'The Black'n'White' and had risen to 10p

IN CHARGE

Chairman: Lord Westwood
Manager: Joe Harvey
Captain: Frank Clark
Trainer/Coach: Keith Burkinshaw

ST JAMES' PARK

Average Attendance
Lg 34,614 Lg & Cup 33,690

Frank Clark had replaced Bob Moncur as skipper for season 1974-75. Back row, left to right: Robson (K), Laughton, Bruce, McFaul, Smith, Gibb. Middle: Howard, McDermott, Keeley, Crosson, Kennedy (A), Cassidy, Craig (David). Front: Burns, Barrowclough, Hibbitt, Clark, Tudor, Nattrass, Macdonald.

PLAYER FOCUS Willie McFaul

Born Coleraine. Goalkeeper, 5'10"
1966 to 1975: 386 app 0 goals.

For almost 22 years Ulsterman Willie McFaul was associated with the Magpies as player, coach and manager. Having impressed watching officials in a friendly against United – even although conceding seven goals at St James' Park – he joined the club in November 1966 for a modest £7,000 as a young goalkeeper from Linfield. The likable Irishman was stand-in to Gordon Marshall then became first choice custodian in 1968-69 and was a brilliant last line of defence as the black-and-whites lifted European silver at the end of that campaign. Although not tall for a 'keeper, McFaul was alert and able to spring to make an eye-catching save. Winning six caps for his country being reserve to Pat Jennings for a long period at international level, Willie was also in superb form as the club headed for Wembley in 1974 producing a series of match-winning stops in the FA Cup run. On retirement in 1975 McFaul was appointed to the coaching staff and became boss in September 1985 when Jack Charlton departed. In charge, he did well in the top flight for a couple of seasons but a crucial spending-spree during the close-season of 1988 did not produce the desired result and he was dismissed in October. Afterwards Willie continued coaching, for a period in charge of Coleraine and the Guam national team, while he also scouted and assisted the Northern Ireland FA and international side. McFaul is related to Barry, Allan and Vic Hunter, all to serve Northern Ireland as well.

SEASON REVIEW

Football League Div 1: P42 W15 D9 L18 F59 A72 Pts 39.
Position: 15th (Champions; Derby County).
FA Cup: R4 (Winners; West Ham United).
FL Cup: R5 (Winners; Aston Villa).

Appearances (59m): Macdonald MI 58, Keeley GM 55, McFaul WS 55, Howard P 53 (1), Nattrass I 47, Kennedy AP 42, Tudor JA 42 (2), Hibbitt TA 35, Burns ME 33 (1), Barrowclough SJ 28 (3), Clark FA 28 (1), Smith Jas 25 (5), Nulty GO 22, Craig TB 21 (1), McDermott T 20, Gibb T 17 (3), Cassidy T 16 (2), Craig DJ 16 (2), Cannell PA 14, Bruce AR 6 (3), Barker MA 2, Bell AW 2, Hudson RW 2, Kelly PA 2, Laughton D 2 (2), Mahoney MJ 2, McCaffery A 2 (1), Blackhall R 1, Crosson D 1.

Goals (91g): Macdonald MI 32, Tudor JA 18, Burns ME 10, Barrowclough SJ 5, Cannell PA 4, Howard P 4, Kennedy AP 4, Keeley GM 3, Bruce AR 2, Cassidy T 2, Craig TB 2, Nulty GO 2, Hibbitt TA 1, McDermott T 1, Nattrass I 1.

Dismissals: 0 players.

MAJOR SIGNINGS

Micky Burns (Blackpool) £170,000
Tommy Craig (Sheffield Wed) £110,000
Geoff Nulty (Burnley) £120,000
Glenn Keeley (Ipswich Town) £70,000
Mick Mahoney (Torquay Utd) £25,000

FROM THE RANKS

Peter Kelly (Scotland sch)
Aidan McCaffery (Tyneside sch, Ey)
Micky Barker (Durham sch)
Tony Bell (Tyneside sch)
Ray Blackhall (Northb sch)

TEAM COLOURS Black & white striped shirts, black shorts (Change; yellow shirts with green trim, sky-blue shorts)

SEASON 1974-75

Match	Date		Opponent				HT	Att	Posn	Scorers	McFaul	Nattrass	Kennedy	Smith	Keeley	Howard	Burns	Cassidy	Macdonald	Tudor	Hibbitt	Craig DJ	McDermott	Laughton	Clark	Gibb	Barrowclough	Cannell	Bruce	Bell	Nulty	Craig TB	Barker	McCaffery	Crosson	Blackhall	Kelly	Hudson	Mahoney	Tunks	Edgar	Match
			FL Division 1																																							
1	17-Aug	H	**Coventry City**	W	3	2	(1 0)	35,950		Macdonald, Howard, Kennedy	1	2	3	4	5	6	7	8	9	10	11	s3																				1
2	21-Aug	H	**Sheffield United**	D	2	2	(0 1)	34,283		Macdonald, Burns	1	2	3	8	5	6	7		9	10	11	u	4																			2
3	24-Aug	A	Wolverhampton Wanderers	L	2	4	(1 2)	23,526	13	Tudor 2	1	2	3	8	5	6	7		9	10	11	s2	4																			3
4	27-Aug	A	Sheffield United	L	1	2	(1 2)	17,650	14	Keeley	1	8	3		5	6	7		9	10	11	2	4	u																		4
5	31-Aug	H	**West Ham United**	W	2	0	(2 0)	30,782	11	Tudor, Macdonald	1	8		u	5	6	7		9	10	11	2	4		3																	5
6	7-Sep	A	Derby County	D	2	2	(1 1)	21,197	11	Macdonald, Burns	1	2		u	5	6	7	8	9	10	11				3	4																6
7	14-Sep	H	**Carlisle United**	W	1	0	(0 0)	40,568	8	Tudor	1	2		s4	5	6	7	8	9	10	11		4		3																	7
8	21-Sep	A	Queens Park Rangers	W	2	1	(0 0)	18,594	6	Tudor, Burns	1	2	u		5	6	7		9	10	11		4		3	8																8
9	28-Sep	H	**Ipswich Town**	W	1	0	(0 0)	43,526	6	Howard	1	2			5	6	7		9	10	11		4		3	8	u															9
10	5-Oct	A	Everton	D	1	1	(1 0)	40,000	7	McDermott	1	2	3		5	6	7		9	10	11		4	u		8																10
11	12-Oct	H	**Stoke City**	D	2	2	(2 1)	39,658	7	Tudor, Keeley	1	2	3		5	6	7		9	10	11		4			8	s7															11
12	16-Oct	H	**Wolverhampton Wanderers**	D	0	0	(0 0)	30,825			1	2	3		5	6	7	u	9	10	11		4			8																12
13	19-Oct	A	Birmingham City	L	0	3	(0 2)	33,339	9		1	2	3		5	6	7		9	10	11		4		u	8																13
14	26-Oct	H	**Leicester City**	L	0	1	(0 0)	34,988	10		1		3		5	6	7	s4	9	10	11		4		2	8																14
15	2-Nov	H	**Luton Town**	W	1	0	(0 0)	30,141	9	Tudor	1	2	8		5	6		4	9	10	11		u		3		7															15
16	9-Nov	A	Middlesbrough	D	0	0	(0 0)	38,380	10		1	2	8		5	6		4	9	10	11				3		7	u														16
17	16-Nov	H	**Chelsea**	W	5	0	(0 0)	35,236	8	Cannell, Macdonald 2, Kennedy, Barrowclough	1	2	8	s11	5	6		4	9		11				3		7	10														17
18	23-Nov	A	Burnley	L	1	4	(0 1)	19,523	10	Barrowclough	1	2	8	11	5	6		4	9	s9					3		7	10														18
19	30-Nov	H	**Manchester City**	W	2	1	(1 1)	37,684	8	Macdonald, Howard	1		8	11	5	6		4	9			2			3		7	10	s11													19
20	7-Dec	A	Tottenham Hotspur	L	0	3	(0 3)	23,422	10			2	8			6	7		9	u				5	3	4		10	11	1												20
21	14-Dec	A	Coventry City	L	0	2	(0 2)	15,562	12		1	2	8		5	6	7		9	10					3		s11	4	11													21
22	21-Dec	H	**Leeds United**	W	3	0	(0 0)	34,054	9	Tudor, Kennedy, Howard	1	2	8	11	5	6	u		9	10					3	4	7															22
23	26-Dec	A	Carlisle United	W	2	1	(1 0)	20,605	9	Tudor, Macdonald	1	2	3	4	5	6	u		9	10							7				8	11										23
24	11-Jan	H	**Tottenham Hotspur**	L	2	5	(0 4)	39,679	11	Craig T, Burns	1	2	3	4	5	6	7		9	10						u					8	11										24
25	18-Jan	A	Manchester City	L	1	5	(1 2)	32,021	10	Macdonald	1	2	3	4	5	6	7		9	10							s10				8	11										25
26	1-Feb	H	**Middlesbrough**	W	2	1	(0 1)	42,514	13	Macdonald, Burns	1	2	3	4	5	6	10		9								7		u		8	11										26
27	8-Feb	A	Luton Town	L	0	1	(0 0)	18,019	13		1		3	4	5		10		9			2			6	u	7				8	11										27
28	12-Feb	H	**Liverpool**	W	4	1	(3 0)	38,115	11	Tudor, Macdonald 2, Barrowclough	1	2	3	4	5	6	u		9	10							7				8	11										28
29	15-Feb	H	**Burnley**	W	3	0	(2 0)	40,602	10	Macdonald 2, Barrowclough	1	2	3	4	5	6	u		9	10							7				8	11										29
30	22-Feb	A	Chelsea	L	2	3	(0 2)	26,770	12	Tudor, Macdonald	1	2	3	4	5	6	s3		9	10							7				8	11										30
31	28-Feb	A	West Ham United	W	1	0	(1 0)	33,150	12	Macdonald	1	6		4	5		u		9	10		2					7				8	11	3									31
32	15-Mar	A	Ipswich Town	L	4	5	(3 2)	23,450	12	Tudor 2, Macdonald 2	1	6		4					9	10		2				s6	7				8	11	3	5								32
33	18-Mar	A	Arsenal	L	0	3	(0 3)	16,540	13		1			4					9	10		3					7		u		8	11		5	2	6						33
34	22-Mar	H	**Derby County**	L	0	2	(0 1)	32,201	13		1			4	5	6			9	10	3						7		u		8	11					2					34
35	25-Mar	A	Liverpool	L	0	4	(0 2)	41,147	13		1			4	5	6			9	10	3	2					7		s4		8	11										35
36	29-Mar	A	Leeds United	D	1	1	(1 0)	41,225		Nulty	1	2			5	6			9	10	4	3					7		u		8	11										36
37	31-Mar	H	**Queens Park Rangers**	D	2	2	(0 1)	29,819	14	Tudor, Macdonald	1	2			5	6			9	10	4	3					7		s10		8	11										37
38	5-Apr	A	Leicester City	L	0	4	(0 2)	23,132	14		1	2			5	6			9			3					7	10			8	11		s10				4				38
39	12-Apr	H	**Everton**	L	0	1	(0 0)	29,585	15			2			5				9		11	3			6	4	7	10			8	s7							1			39
40	19-Apr	A	Stoke City	D	0	0	(0 0)	32,302	15				3		5	s2			9		11	2			6		7		10		8	4							1			40
41	23-Apr	H	**Arsenal**	W	3	1	(1 1)	21,895	13	Bruce, Macdonald, Craig T	1		3		5	6	7		9		11				2	s7			10		8	4										41
42	26-Apr	H	**Birmingham City**	L	1	2	(1 2)	24,787	15	Macdonald	1		3		5	6			9		11				2	u	7		10		8	4										42
Round			FA Cup																																							Round
3	4-Jan	A*	Manchester City	W	2	0	(0 0)	37,625		Nulty, Burns	1	2	3	4	5	6	7		9	10					u						8	11										3
4	25-Jan	A	Walsall	L	0	1	(0 1)	19,998			1	2	3	4	5	6	7		9							s4		10			8	11										4
Round			FL Cup																																							Round
2	10-Sep	A	Nottingham Forest	D	1	1	(0 1)	14,183		Macdonald	1	2		s8	5	6	7	8	9	10	11				3	4																2
2r	25-Sep	H	**Nottingham Forest**	W	3	0	(2 0)	26,228		Macdonald, Burns, Keeley	1	2	u		5	6	7		9	10	11		4		3	8																2r
3	8-Oct	A	Queens Park Rangers	W	4	0	(3 0)	15,815		Tudor, Macdonald 3	1	2	3		5	6	7	s11	9	10	11		4			8																3
4	13-Nov	H	**Fulham**	W	3	0	(0 0)	23,774		Cannell, Macdonald, Cassidy	1	2	8	u	5	6		4	9		11				3		7	10														4
5	4-Dec	H	**Chester**	D	0	0	(0 0)	31,656			1	11	8		5	6		4	9					s4	3		7	10									2					5
5r	18-Dec	A	Chester	L	0	1	(0 0)	19,000			1	2	8	11	5	6	u		9						3	4	7	10														5r
Round			Texaco Cup																																							Round
Gp	3-Aug	A	Sunderland	L	1	2	(0 0)	28,738		Tudor	1		3	s9	6	5	7	8	9	10	11	2	4							u												Gp
Gp	6-Aug	A	Carlisle United	D	2	2	(1 0)	13,560		Burns 2	1		3	s8	5	6	7	8	9	10	11	2	4							u												Gp
Gp	10-Aug	H	**Middlesbrough**	W	4	0	(2 0)	11,571		Macdonald, Cassidy, Tudor, Burns	1	2	3	u	6	5	7	8	9	10	11		4																	u		Gp
2(1)	18-Sep	A	Aberdeen	D	1	1	(1 1)	13,500		Macdonald	1	2		8	5	6	7		9	10	11		4		3	u				u												2(1)
2(2)	2-Oct	H	**Aberdeen**	W	3	2	(1 1)	18,838		Macdonald 2, Hibbitt	1	2	3		5	6	7		9	10	11		4			8	u			u												2(2)
SF(1)	23-Oct	H	**Birmingham City**	D	1	1	(0 1)	20,559		Macdonald	1	2	3		5	6	7		9	10	11		4		s2	8				u												SF(1)
SF(2)	6-Nov	A	Birmingham City	W	4	1	(2 0)	17,754		Kennedy, Nattrass, Cannell, Barrowclough	1	2	8	11	5	6		4		10				s2	3		7	9		u												SF(2)
F(1)	27-Nov	A	Southampton	L	0	1	(0 0)	17,100					8	11	5	6	u	4	9			2			3		7	10		1											u	F(1)
F(2)	11-Dec	H	**Southampton**	We	3	0	(0 0)	20,615		Tudor, Bruce, Cannell	1	2	8			6	7		9	s4				5	3			10	11	u								4				F(2)

A* Match scheduled for Newcastle, but played at Maine Road by order of the FA

We Won after extra time

DateLine ... 4 Jan: United face Manchester City at Maine Road in a 'home' FA Cup fixture, switched by order of the FA. **11 Jan:** United lose 5-2 at St James' Park after being four goals down at half-time to Tottenham. **25 Jan:** A single goal FA Cup defeat to lowly Walsall marks the beginning of the end for Joe Harvey. **15 March:** The Magpies fall 5-4 at Ipswich in a match they led 3-2 at the interval. **16 April:** Malcolm Macdonald scores five goals at Wembley for England against Cyprus.

Gordon who? Lee surprises all

In a football world where the media started to gain significant importance, there were plenty of headlines as Newcastle pondered their choice of manager. Big-names were linked with the St James' Park post; however, it was a virtual unknown, Gordon Lee, who breezed into Gallowgate during June as new boss. Gordon who? Everyone asked, even United's players. The former Aston Villa player and latterly Blackburn manager was of the new track-suit breed of boss. He liked hard work and commitment, disliked egos and half-hearted effort. The glory or bust style of football was dumped and a more sedate, possession approach was unveiled. Some didn't like the change while United still had the power of Supermac up front – for now. He teamed up with a new strike partner in Alan Gowling.

Lee's new principles guided Newcastle to relative success, a run in the Football League Cup, for so long a limp competition for the Magpies. Never had they done well in the tournament which now had a Wembley climax and European prize. With the front two of Macdonald and Gowling a major threat, United reached the semi-final and faced Tottenham Hotspur in a two-legged contest. The Geordies won 3-1 at St James' Park to book their very first League Cup final place. Lady Luck though was not to be on United's side in the final against Manchester City during February. Lee's squad was laid low with influenza in the week before the final – even threatening the showpiece itself. United's side was clearly affected, but took part in a decent final, losing 2-1 to City, their winner being scored ironically by Newcastle-born Dennis Tueart with a sensational bicycle-kick.

There was also a FA Cup run to the quarter-final, and had it not been for that flu-bug, maybe even further. After a terrific three-game tie with Bolton Wanderers, United had to field a patched up line-up just after the League Cup final and fell to Derby County at the Baseball Ground. It had been a more than satisfactory start for new boss Gordon Lee. Yet, long before the season's end, fans were waiting for what was the inevitable bombshell. Centre-forward Malcolm Macdonald endured a strained relationship with his manager, and he joined Arsenal in a big move south.

Pictured above: Once a Busby Babe, Alan Gowling resurrected his career in black-and-white stripes.

Memorabilia CORNER

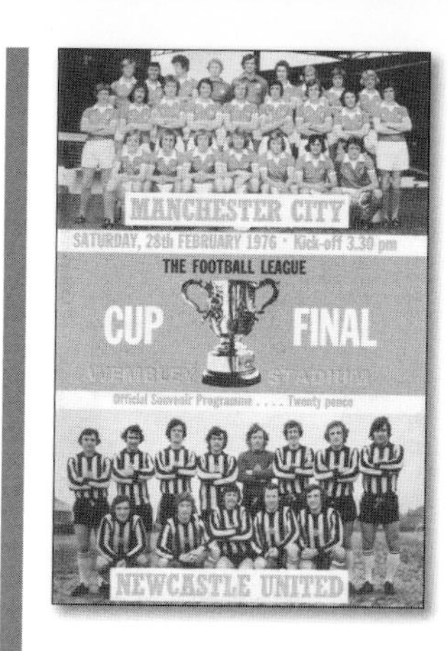

United returned to Wembley in 1976, match programme for the League Cup final with Manchester City.

IN CHARGE

Chairman: Lord Westwood
Manager: Gordon Lee
Captain: Geoff Nulty
Trainer/Coach: Richard Dinnis

ST JAMES' PARK

Average Attendance
Lg 33,057 Lg & Cup 34,269

Gordon Lee's first squad pictured at the start of the 1975-76 season. Back row, left to right: Mahoney, Craig (David), Smith, Nattrass, Kennedy (A), Cannell, Barrowclough, Macdonald, Craig (T), Tudor, McFaul. Front: Burns, Nulty, Bruce, Hibbitt, Lee (manager), Cassidy, Howard, Keeley.

PLAYER FOCUS Tommy Craig

Born Glasgow. Midfield, 5'7"
1974 to 1978: 157 app 29 goals.

Once the most expensive teenager in British football when he moved from Aberdeen to Sheffield Wednesday in 1969 for a £100,000 fee, Tommy Craig possessed an educated left-foot and could control the middle of the park with astute vision. Small, solidly built and with a powerful drive, he spent a long time at Hillsborough in a side on a downward spiral before Joe Harvey brought him back to top-level football in a £110,000 deal during December 1974. Replacing the injured Terry Hibbitt, he slipped into the midfield role perfectly in a Toon shirt and under Gordon Lee's guidance was influential as Newcastle took part in the 1976 Football League Cup final – leading the Magpies out at Wembley as skipper – and thereafter qualified for Europe. Tommy also captained his country at youth, Under-21 and Under-23 levels while he won a senior cap in 1975-76 when at the peak of form. But Lee's departure and United's rapid nose-dive saw Craig move on to join Aston Villa in January 1978 for a hefty £270,000. Craig never settled at Villa Park and concluded his playing days with Swansea and Carlisle before beginning a long period in coaching at Brunton Park. Tommy returned to Tyneside and was for over eight years on United's backroom staff as well as having spells at Hibernian, Celtic, Aberdeen, as well as on the Continent with Sporting Charleroi. Highly respected, he was also for a time on the Scottish FA coaching team. His brother John was also with Aberdeen.

SEASON REVIEW

Football League Div 1: P42 W15 D9 L18 F71 A62 Pts 39.
Position: 15th (Champions; Liverpool).
FA Cup: QF (Winners; Southampton).
FL Cup: Finalist (Winners; Manchester City).

Appearances (61m): Kennedy AP 60, Gowling AE 59, Burns ME 58 (1), Nattrass I 57, Craig TB 56 (1), Macdonald MI 56, Mahoney MJ 54, Howard P 53, Nulty GO 42, Cassidy T 34 (1), Barrowclough SJ 30 (10), Bird JC 20 (1), Craig DJ 20, Keeley GM 16 (1), Oates G 9 (1), Hudson RW 8 (2), Bruce AR 7, Hibbitt TA 7, Tudor JA 6 (1), Jones R 5, Blackhall R 4 (1), Cannell PA 4 (1), McCaffery A 3 (1), Edgar E 1, McFaul WS 1, McLean DJ 1 (1).

Goals (105g): Gowling AE 31, Macdonald MI 24, Craig TB 11, Nulty GO 9, Burns ME 8, Nattrass I 4, Cassidy T 3, Cannell PA 2, Tudor JA 2, Barrowclough SJ 1, Bird JC 1, Bruce AR 1, Craig DJ 1, Hibbitt TA 1, Howard P 1, Keeley GM 1, Kennedy AP 1, own goals 3.

Dismissals: 1 player; Burns.

MAJOR SIGNINGS

Alan Gowling (Huddersfield Town) £70,000
John Bird (Preston NE) exchange
Graham Oates & Roger Jones (Blackburn Rvs) joint £100,000

FROM THE RANKS

David McLean (Northb sch, Ey)
Eddie Edgar (Tyneside sch)

TEAM COLOURS Black & white striped shirts, black shorts (Change; yellow shirts with green trim, sky-blue shorts)

SEASON 1975–76

Match	Date	Venue	Opponent	Res	F	A	HT	Att	Posn	Scorers	Mahoney	Nattrass	Kennedy	Nulty	Howard	Hibbitt	Burns	Bruce	Macdonald	Gowling	Craig TB	Barrowclough	Bird	Blackhall	Cassidy	Tudor	Keeley	Craig DJ	McCaffery	Hudson	Cannell	Jones	Oates	McLean	Edgar	McFaul	Match
			FL Division 1						Posn																												
1	16-Aug	A	Ipswich Town	W	3	0	(2 0)	27,680		Craig T (pen), Macdonald 2	1	2	3	4	5	6	7	8	9	10	11	u															1
2	20-Aug	H	**Middlesbrough**	D	1	1	(0 1)	41,417		Macdonald	1	2	3	4	5	6	7	8	9	10	11	s8															2
3	23-Aug	H	**Leicester City**	W	3	0	(2 0)	36,084	2	Macdonald 2, Burns	1	2	3	4	5	6	7	8	9	10	11	u															3
4	27-Aug	A	Derby County	L	2	3	(1 0)	27,585		Macdonald, Bruce	1	2	3	4	5	6	7d	8	9	10	11	s8															4
5	30-Aug	A	Manchester City	L	0	4	(0 1)	31,875	11		1	2	3	4	6		8		9	10	11	7	5	u													5
6	6-Sep	H	**Aston Villa**	W	3	0	(2 0)	35,604	8	Craig T, Macdonald 2	1	2	3	4	6		7		9	10	11	u	5		8												6
7	13-Sep	A	Everton	L	0	3	(0 2)	28,938	10		1	2	3	4	6		7			10	11	s9	5		8	9											7
8	20-Sep	H	**Wolverhampton Wanderers**	W	5	1	(1 1)	30,876	10	Gowling 3, Tudor, Cassidy	1	2	3	4	6		7			10	11	u	5		8	9											8
9	23-Sep	A	Birmingham City	L	2	3	(1 3)	31,166	14	Craig T, Nulty	1	2	3	4	6		7			10	11		5		8	9	u										9
10	27-Sep	A	Queens Park Rangers	L	0	1	(0 1)	22,981	14		1	2	3	11	6		7		9	10	u		5			8	4										10
11	4-Oct	H	**Tottenham Hotspur**	D	2	2	(1 0)	33,284	14	Tudor, Barrowclough	1	2	3	4	6		7		9	10	11	s8	5			8											11
12	11-Oct	A	West Ham United	L	1	2	(0 1)	30,400	16	Howard	1	2	3	4	6		7		9	10	11	8	5		u												12
13	18-Oct	H	**Norwich City**	W	5	2	(1 1)	32,799	15	Gowling 2, Macdonald 2, og (Jones)	1	2	3	4	6		7		9	10	11	8	u					5									13
14	25-Oct	A	Stoke City	D	1	1	(0 0)	24,057	12	Gowling	1	2	3	4	6		7		9	10	11	8	s7					5									14
15	1-Nov	H	**Arsenal**	W	2	0	(1 0)	34,968	11	Gowling, Nattrass	1	2	3	4	6		7		9	10	11	8	u					5									15
16	8-Nov	A	Leeds United	L	0	3	(0 2)	39,304	11		1	2	3	4	6		7		9	10	11	8						5	u								16
17	15-Nov	H	**Liverpool**	L	1	2	(1 1)	41,145	13	Nulty	1	2	3	4	6		7		9	10	11	8			u			5									17
18	22-Nov	A	Norwich City	W	2	1	(0 1)	19,036	11	Nulty 2	1	2	3	4	6		7		9	10	11	8	u					5									18
19	29-Nov	A	Manchester United	L	0	1	(0 0)	52,264	15		1	2	3	4	6		7		9	10	11	8				s7		5									19
20	6-Dec	H	**Coventry City**	W	4	0	(2 0)	27,172	11	Craig T 2 (1 pen), Burns, Craig DJ	1	2	3	4	6		7		9	10	11	8			u			5									20
21	13-Dec	A	Leicester City	L	0	1	(0 0)	18,130	15		1	2	3	4	6		7		9	10	11	8						5		u							21
22	20-Dec	H	**Ipswich Town**	D	1	1	(0 1)	26,152	13	Nulty	1	2	3	4	6		7		9	10	11	8			u			5									22
23	26-Dec	A	Burnley	W	1	0	(0 0)	22,458		Craig T (pen)	1	2	3	4	6		s8		9	10	11				7	8		5									23
24	27-Dec	H	**Sheffield United**	D	1	1	(0 0)	31,762	12	Macdonald	1	2	3	4	6				9	10	11	8	u		7			5									24
25	10-Jan	H	**Everton**	W	5	0	(2 0)	31,726	12	Gowling 3, Nulty, Nattrass	1	2	3	4	6		8		9	10	11	u	5		7												25
26	17-Jan	A	Aston Villa	D	1	1	(1 1)	36,389	12	Gowling	1	2	3	4	6		7		9	10	11	s10	5		8												26
27	31-Jan	A	Middlesbrough	D	3	3	(0 1)	30,365	12	Gowling, Kennedy, Nattrass	1	2	3	4	6		7		9	10	11	u			8		5										27
28	7-Feb	H	**Derby County**	W	4	3	(0 0)	45,770	10	Craig T (pen), Macdonald, Nulty, og (Todd)	1	2	3	4	6		7		9	10	11	u					5	8									28
29	21-Feb	A	Liverpool	L	0	2	(0 1)	43,304			1	2	3		6		7		9	10	11	4			8		s5	5									29
30	3-Mar	H	**Stoke City**	L	0	1	(0 1)	38,822	17		1		3		6		7		9		11	4		2	8		5			s9	10						30
31	13-Mar	H	**West Ham United**	W	2	1	(0 1)	33,866		Craig T (pen), Macdonald			3		6		7		9	10	11	4	5	2	8							1	u				31
32	16-Mar	A	Arsenal	D	0	0	(0 0)	18,424	14				3		6		7		9	10	11	4	5	2	8							1	u				32
33	20-Mar	H	**Manchester United**	L	3	4	(0 2)	45,043	15	Gowling, Macdonald, Burns		2	3		6		7		9	10	11	4	5		8							1	s8				33
34	27-Mar	A	Coventry City	D	1	1	(0 1)	14,144	13	Bird	1	2	3		6		7		9	10	11	4	5							s6			8				34
35	31-Mar	H	**Leeds United**	L	2	3	(0 2)	32,685	14	Craig T (pen), Gowling	1	2	3				7		9	10	11	4	5		u					8			6				35
36	3-Apr	H	**Queens Park Rangers**	L	1	2	(0 1)	30,145	14	Gowling	1	2	3				7		9	10	11	4	5						u	8			6				36
37	7-Apr	H	**Birmingham City**	W	4	0	(0 0)	18,893	14	Gowling, Macdonald 2, Burns	1	2	3				7		9	10		4	5	u	11					8			6				37
38	10-Apr	A	Wolverhampton Wanderers	L	0	5	(0 0)	20,083	14		1	2	3				7		9	10	s4	4	5		11					8			6				38
39	14-Apr	H	**Manchester City**	W	2	1	(0 1)	21,095	14	Macdonald, Cassidy	1	2	3				7		9	10	11		5		4				s5	8			6				39
40	17-Apr	H	**Burnley**	L	0	1	(0 1)	24,897	14		1	2	3				7		9	10	11			u	4				5	8			6				40
41	19-Apr	A	Sheffield United	L	0	1	(0 1)	18,906	15			2	3				7		9	10	11				4				5	8		1	6	s6			41
42	24-Apr	A	Tottenham Hotspur	W	3	0	(0 0)	29,649	15	Macdonald 2, Burns		2	3				7		9	10	11				4				5	u		1	6	8			42
Round			**FA Cup**																																		**Round**
3	3-Jan	A	Queens Park Rangers	D	0	0	(0 0)	20,102			1	2	3	4	6		7		9	10	11	s5			8			5									3
3r	7-Jan	H	**Queens Park Rangers**	W	2	1	(1 0)	37,225		Craig T (pen), Gowling	1	2	3	4	6		7		9	10	11	u	5		8												3r
4	24-Jan	A	Coventry City	D	1	1	(1 0)	32,004		Gowling	1	2	3	4	6		7		9	10	11	u			8		5										4
4r	28-Jan	H	**Coventry City**	W	5	0	(2 0)	44,676		Gowling, Macdonald 2, Cassidy, Burns	1	2	3	4	6		7		9	10	11	u			8		5										4r
5	14-Feb	A	Bolton Wanderers	D	3	3	(2 1)	46,880		Gowling, Macdonald 2	1	2	3	4	6		7		9	10	11	s4			8		5										5
5r	18-Feb	H	**Bolton Wanderers**	De	0	0	(0 0)	52,760			1	2	3		6		7		9	10	11	s4			8		5	4									5r
5rr	23-Feb	N1	Bolton Wanderers	W	2	1	(1 0)	43,448		Gowling, Burns	1	2	3		6		7			10	11	4		s2	8		5				9						5rr
6	6-Mar	A	Derby County	L	2	4	(1 2)	38,362		Gowling 2			3		6		7		9	10		4		2	8		5			11	u				1		6
Round			**FL Cup**																																		**Round**
2	10-Sep	H*	**Southport**	W	6	0	(2 0)	23,352		Gowling 4, Cannell 2	1	2	3	4	6		7			10	11	s4			8		5				9						2
3	7-Oct	A	Bristol Rovers	D	1	1	(0 1)	17,141		Gowling	1	2	3	4	6		7		9	10	11	8			s5			5									3
3r	15-Oct	H	**Bristol Rovers**	W	2	0	(0 0)	26,294		Craig T (pen), Nattrass	1	2	3	4	6		7		9	10	11	8			u			5									3r
4	11-Nov	A	Queens Park Rangers	W	3	1	(2 1)	21,162		Macdonald, Burns, Nulty	1	2	3	4	6		7		9	10	11	8			u			5									4
5	3-Dec	H	**Notts County**	W	1	0	(1 0)	31,114		og (McManus)	1	2	3	4	6		7		9	10	11	8						5			u						5
SF(1)	14-Jan	A	Tottenham Hotspur	L	0	1	(0 1)	40,215			1	2	3	4	6		7		9	10	11	u			8		5										SF(1)
SF(2)	21-Jan	H	**Tottenham Hotspur**	W	3	1	(1 0)	49,902		Gowling, Keeley, Nulty	1	2	3	4	6		7		9	10	11	s2			8		5										SF(2)
F	28-Feb	N2	Manchester City	L	1	2	(1 1)	100,000		Gowling	1	2	3		6		7		9	10	11	4			8		5				u						F
Round			**Anglo-Scottish Cup**																																		**Round**
Gp	2-Aug	A	Carlisle United	L	0	2	(0 1)	9,209			1	2	3		4	6	10	8	9		11				7		5				s3					u	Gp
Gp	6-Aug	H	**Sunderland**	L	0	2	(0 2)	20,088			u	2		3	4	6	u	11	9	10					8		5				7					1	Gp
Gp	9-Aug	H	**Middlesbrough**	D	2	2	(0 1)	11,624		Hibbitt, Gowling	1	2	3	4	5	6	7	8	9	10	11				u										u		Gp

H* Match scheduled for Southport but played at Newcastle by agreement

N1 Played at Elland Road, Leeds

N2 Played at Wembley Stadium, London

De Drawn after extra time

DateLine ... 16 Aug: New manager Gordon Lee guides United to a 3-0 success at Ipswich in his first match. **10 Sept:** Newcastle equal their best League Cup victory with a 6-0 win over Southport. **21 Jan:** The Black'n'Whites see off Spurs in the League Cup semi-final deciding leg, 3-1 on the night. **14 Feb:** A scintillating end-to-end FA Cup tussle at Bolton ends all square at 3-3. **28 Feb:** United's first League Cup final ends in a close 2-1 defeat to Manchester City. **7 April:** Alan Gowling strikes his 30th goal of the season against Birmingham City.

SEASON
1976-77
DIVISION 1

Toon turmoil, yet Euro qualification

Manager Gordon Lee overcame the somewhat initial negative reaction and won over the fans. His kind of football management was getting results. United were more consistent, were team focussed and had just reached a Wembley final. Nevertheless the star system and the sale of Macdonald caused uproar in the ranks. The manager had to begin once more to prove his way was the right way.

All looked good for the first half of the season. Newcastle – without Supermac – and with the tricky Micky Burns now leading the line in a very different tactical forward plan, moved into the top three by December with Liverpool and Bobby Robson's Ipswich Town. There was even talk of a serious bid for the Championship title – not won by United since 1927. But then the boss created furore, selling himself to Everton in a shock departure during January. And what turmoil that caused. Just before a high profile FA Cup meeting with Manchester City at Gallowgate, news broke that Lee was defecting to Merseyside. The players were stunned, fans outraged. United tumbled out of the Cup and Lee became public-enemy number one.

Coach Richard Dinnis took control while the club's Board considered their options. His relationship with the players was first-class and he was championed for the job, although with little football pedigree. The Boardroom wanted a new face, the players wanted Dinnis. The result was turmoil, almost mutiny. Amidst all the bickering though United finished the season in their highest placing since 1951 in fifth spot and qualified for the UEFA Cup. Along the way they went on a record equalling unbeaten run at Gallowgate of 19 games. Reluctantly United appointed Dinnis as manager on a two year contract. The club's directors had many doubts but yielded to player-power. There was much unease in the Boardroom. Those misgivings were to unfold as the new season began.

Pictured above: Geoff Nulty skippered Newcastle, had terrific work-rate and was invaluable on the field.

Memorabilia CORNER

A full colour programme had largely arrived by 1976, as had the term 'match magazine'.

IN CHARGE

Chairman: Lord Westwood
Manager: Gordon Lee/Richard Dinnis
Captain: Geoff Nulty
Trainer/Coach: Richard Dinnis/Willie McFaul

ST JAMES' PARK

Average Attendance
Lg 33,529 Lg & Cup 33,872

A streamlined black-and-white strip for the 1976-77 season. Back row, left to right: Bird, Keeley, Gowling, Jones, Mahoney, Oates, Nattrass, Cassidy. Front: Burns, Craig (T), Howard, Craig (David), Nulty, Barrowclough, Kennedy (A), Tudor.

PLAYER FOCUS Alan Kennedy

Born Sunderland. Left-back, 5'10"
1971 to 1978: 215 app 10 goals.

One of two locally born Kennedy brothers to appear for United in the same era, Alan was the youngest of the pair and his career went to the very top; twice hitting the net to win the European Cup for Liverpool in 1981 and 1984. A teenage sensation at left-back with Newcastle, he was chosen for United's 1974 FA Cup final side when only 19 years old on an injury to David Craig. Kennedy's determined and surging runs from the back were a feature of United's play and soon he replaced Frank Clark and was noted as a future star. It was little of a surprise, when after internal turmoil at Gallowgate throughout 1977 and the club's subsequent relegation, he headed for Anfield in a sizeable £330,000 deal during August 1978. Also gaining a boxful of Championship and FA Cup winners' medals with Liverpool as well as taking part in a third European Cup final, Kennedy appeared for a string of clubs at the end of his fine career; Sunderland and Hartlepool United included while he also had a spell on the Continent. Brave and committed with a natural impulse to go forward, Kennedy was selected for his country at Under-23 and B level with the Magpies and reached the full England side in 1983-84. His older brother Keith was later a noted full-back for Bury. A popular character on Merseyside, Alan settled in Lancashire becoming a local radio commentator.

SEASON REVIEW

Football League Div 1: P42 W18 D13 L11 F64 A49 Pts 49.
Position: 5th (Champions; Liverpool).
FA Cup: R4 (Winners; Manchester United).
FL Cup: R4 (Winners; Aston Villa).

Appearances (52m): Barrowclough SJ 50, Kennedy AP 50 (1), Nulty GO 50, Mahoney MJ 49, Nattrass I 49, Burns ME 48, Craig TB 47, Cassidy T 43, McCaffery A 43 (1), Gowling AE 42, Cannell PA 35 (1), Oates G 19 (3), Blackhall R 8 (12), Hudson RW 8, Bird JC 7 (1), Craig DJ 4 (2), Guy A 4, Mitchell K 4, Jones R 2, Tudor JA 2, Barker MA 1, Chambers C 1, Howard P 1 (1), Keeley GM 1, Kelly PA 1, McFaul WS 1, Owens M 1, Smith Ant 1.

Goals (79g): Burns ME 17, Gowling AE 15, Cannell PA 13, Craig TB 10, Barrowclough SJ 5, McCaffery A 4, Nattrass I 4, Nulty GO 3, Oates G 3, Cassidy T 2, Kennedy AP 2, Hudson RW 1.

Dismissals: 0 players.

MAJOR SIGNINGS

Ralph Callachan (Hearts) £100,000
Steve Hardwick (Chesterfield) £80,000

FROM THE RANKS

Kenny Mitchell (Sunderland sch)
Alan Guy (Tyneside sch)

TEAM COLOURS Black & white striped shirts, black shorts (Change; yellow shirts with green trim, green shorts/blue shirts with white trim, white shorts

SEASON 1976-77

Match	Date		FL Division 1						Att	Posn	Scorers	Mahoney	Nattrass	Kennedy	Hudson	Bird	Nulty	Barrowclough	Oates	Burns	Gowling	Craig TB	McCaffery	Blackhall	Cannell	Tudor	Howard	Cassidy	Craig DJ	Guy	Mitchell	McLean	Jones	Keeley	McFaul	Kelly	Owens	Smith	Barker	Chambers	Match
1	21 Aug	H	**Derby County**	D	2	2	(1	1)	35,927		Craig T (pen), Hudson	1	2	3	4	5	6	7	8	9	10	11	u																		1
2	25 Aug	A	Tottenham Hotspur	W	2	0	(0	0)	24,022	6	Burns, Barrowclough	1	2	3	4	5	6	7	8	9	10	11		s9																	2
3	28 Aug	H	**Bristol City**	D	0	0	(0	0)	31,775	3		1	2	3	4	5	6	7	8			11			9	10	s11														3
4	04 Sep	A	Middlesbrough	L	0	1	(0	0)	26,014	10		1	2	3	4		6	7		9	10	11	5		s11			8													4
5	11 Sep	H	**Manchester United**	D	2	2	(1	2)	39,037	9	Burns, Cannell	1	2	3	u		6	7		9	10	11	5		8			4													5
6	18 Sep	A	Leeds United	D	2	2	(0	0)	35,098	10	Cannell, Cassidy	1	2	3			6	7	10	9		11	5		8			4	u												6
7	25 Sep	H	**Liverpool**	W	1	0	(1	0)	34,813	8	Cannell	1	2	3			6	7	10	9		11	5	s4	8				4												7
8	02 Oct	A	Norwich City	L	2	3	(0	3)	21,417	13	Craig T (pen), Gowling	1	2	3			6	7	u	9	10	11	5		8			4													8
9	06 Oct	H	**West Bromwich Albion**	W	2	0	(1	0)	28,746	7	Gowling, Cannell	1	2	3			6	7	s2	9	10	11	5		8			4													9
10	16 Oct	A	Coventry City	D	1	1	(0	0)	18,083	9	Gowling	1	2	3		u	6	7		9	10	11	5		8			4													10
11	23 Oct	H	**Birmingham City**	W	3	2	(1	1)	31,711	5	Craig T, Burns 2	1	2	3			6	7		9	10	11	5	s3	8			4													11
12	30 Oct	H	**Stoke City**	W	1	0	(0	0)	32,339	3	Cannell	1	2	3			6	7		9		11	5	u	8			4		10											12
13	06 Nov	A	Manchester City	D	0	0	(0	0)	40,049	5		1	2	3			6	7		9	10	11	5	u	8			4													13
14	20 Nov	A	West Ham United	W	2	1	(1	1)	21,324	5	Burns, Nulty	1	2	3			6	7		9	10	11	5		8			4			u										14
15	24 Nov	H	**Everton**	W	4	1	(1	0)	31,203	3	Craig T, Gowling 2, Cannell	1	2	3			6	7		9	10	11	5		8			4	s3												15
16	27 Nov	H	**Queens Park Rangers**	W	2	0	(2	0)	39,045	3	Burns, Cannell	1	2	3			6	7		9	10	11	5	u	8			4													16
17	04 Dec	A	Arsenal	L	3	5	(1	3)	34,054	3	Gowling, Burns 2	1	2	3	u		6	7		9	10	11	5		8			4													17
	11 Dec	H	**Ipswich Town**	Ab	1	0	(1	0)	39,257		*Barrowclough*	1	2	3	u		6	7		9	10	11	5		8				4												
18	18 Dec	A	Aston Villa	L	1	2	(1	1)	33,982	4	Gowling	1	2	3			6	7		9	10	11	5		8			4	u												18
19	27 Dec	H	**Sunderland**	W	2	0	(1	0)	50,048	5	Cannell, Kennedy	1	2	3			6	7		9	10	11	5		8			4	u												19
20	22 Jan	A	Derby County	L	2	4	(1	2)	23,036	7	Craig T (pen), Gowling	1	2	3			6	7		9	10	11	5		8			4	u												20
21	05 Feb	A	Bristol City	D	1	1	(0	0)	23,698	8	Burns	1	2	3			6	7	s8	9	10		5	11	8			4													21
22	16 Feb	H	**Manchester City**	D	2	2	(0	2)	28,954	9	Burns 2	1	2	3	u		6	7		9	10		5	11				4			8										22
23	19 Feb	A	Manchester United	L	1	3	(1	2)	51,828	10	Nulty	1	2	3			6	7		9	10	11	5	u				4			8										23
24	26 Feb	H	**Tottenham Hotspur**	W	2	0	(2	0)	30,230	8	Gowling, Burns	1	2	3			6	7	s7	9	10	11	5					4			8										24
25	02 Mar	H	**Leeds United**	W	3	0	(0	0)	33,714	7	Burns, Oates, McCaffery	1	2	3			6	7	8	9	10	11	5					4			u										25
26	05 Mar	A	Liverpool	L	0	1	(0	1)	45,553	7		1	2	3			6	7	8	9	10	11	5	s4				4													26
27	09 Mar	H	**Ipswich Town**	D	1	1	(1	0)	33,820	6	Nattrass	1	2	3			6	7	8	9	10	11	5	4								u									27
28	12 Mar	H	**Norwich City**	W	5	1	(2	1)	27,808	5	Craig T, Gowling, Oates, McCaffery 2	1	2	3			6	7	8	9	10	11	5	4								u									28
29	15 Mar	A	Stoke City	D	0	0	(0	0)	12,708	5		1	2	3			6	7	8	9	10	11	5	u				4													29
30	19 Mar	A	West Bromwich Albion	D	1	1	(0	0)	23,780	5	Barrowclough	1	2	3			6	7		9	10	11	5	s10				4		8											30
31	23 Mar	H	**Coventry City**	W	1	0	(1	0)	25,332	4	Burns	1	2	3			6	7		9	10	11	5	s10	8			4													31
32	26 Mar	H	**Middlesbrough**	W	1	0	(1	0)	33,643	4	Kennedy	1	2	3			6	7		9	10	11	5	u	8			4													32
33	02 Apr	A	Birmingham City	W	2	1	(1	0)	20,283	4	Craig T (pen), Barrowclough	1	2	3			6	7		9	10	11	5	u	8			4													33
34	08 Apr	A	Sunderland	D	2	2	(0	1)	46,056	4	Craig T, Cannell	1	2	3			6	7		9	10	11	5	u	8			4													34
35	09 Apr	H	**Leicester City**	D	0	0	(0	0)	30,443	4		1	2	3			6	7		9	10	11	5	8				4			u										35
36	16 Apr	H	**West Ham United**	W	3	0	(1	0)	30,967	4	Gowling, Cannell, Nulty	1	2	3			6	7		9	10	11	5	s4	8			4													36
37	23 Apr	A	Queens Park Rangers	W	2	1	(0	1)	20,544	4	Barrowclough, Nattrass	1	2	3			6	7		9	10	11	5	s10	8			4													37
38	30 Apr	H	**Arsenal**	L	0	2	(0	1)	44,677	4		1	2	3			6	7		9	10	11	5	s4	8			4													38
39	03 May	A	Leicester City	L	0	1	(0	0)	14,289	4		1	2	3		s2	6	7		9		11	5	10	8			4													39
40	07 May	A	Ipswich Town	L	0	2	(0	0)	24,760	4		1		3		u	6	7	10	9		11	5	2	8			4													40
41	14 May	H	**Aston Villa**	W	3	2	(3	1)	29,873	4	Cannell 2, Oates	1	2	3			6		7	9	10	11	5	s2	8			4													41
42	24 May	A	Everton	L	0	2	(0	2)	25,208	5		1		3		5	6	4	7	9	10	11		u	8				2												42
Round			FA Cup																																						Round
3	08 Jan	A	Sheffield United	D	0	0	(0	0)	30,513			1	2	3			6	7		9	10	11	5		8			4	u												3
3r	24 Jan	H	**Sheffield United**	W	3	1	(2	1)	36,375		Craig T, Burns, McCaffery	1	2	3			6	7		9	10	11	5		8			4	u												3r
4	29 Jan	H	**Manchester City**	L	1	3	(1	2)	45,300		Gowling	1	2	3	u		6	7		9	10		5		8			4	11												4
Round			FL Cup																																						Round
2	01 Sep	A	Gillingham	W	2	1	(1	0)	11,203		Cassidy, Cannell	1	2	3	4	5	6	7	8				s4		9			11		10											2
3	22 Sep	H	**Stoke City**	W	3	0	(2	0)	27,143		Craig T (pen), Burns, Nattrass	1	2	3			6	7	10	9		11	5		8			4	s4												3
4	27 Oct	A	Manchester United	L	2	7	(1	3)	52,002		Burns, Nattrass	1	2	3			6	7		9	10	11	5	s10	8			4													4
Round			Anglo-Scottish Cup																																						Round
Gp	07 Aug	A	Sheffield United	W	1	0	(1	0)	7,933		Gowling	1	2	3		5	6	7	8	9	10	11					u	4					u								Gp
Gp	10 Aug	A	Hull City	D	0	0	(0	0)	4,715			u	2	s2	10			7	8			11		3		9	6	4					1	5							Gp
Gp	14 Aug	H	**Middlesbrough**	W	3	0	(3	0)	15,703		Gowling 2, Barrowclough	u	2	3	4	5	6	7	8	9	10	11	u										1								Gp
2(1)	15 Sep	A	Ayr United	Ld	0	3	(0	1)	3,600			u			10				8					s11					4	9	7				1	2	3	5	6	11	2(1)

Ab Abandoned after 45 mins due to ice

Ld Disqualified from competition for fielding weakened side

DateLine ... 27 Oct: The Magpies lose 7-2 to Manchester United in the League Cup, their heaviest defeat. **4 Dec:** United fall 5-3 to Arsenal in London with Malcolm Macdonald doing the damage at Highbury. **29 Jan:** Gordon Lee departs following the FA Cup defeat to Manchester City on Tyneside. **5 Feb:** Richard Dinnis handed the manager's role for the game with Bristol City, a 1-1 draw. **9 March:** Floodlights fail against Ipswich at Gallowgate, but the match is completed in dim light. **14 May:** United qualify for the UEFA Cup with a 3-2 success over Aston Villa.

SEASON 1977-78

DIVISION 1

United in crisis

There was unease during the summer months at Gallowgate between directors, manager and players. Preparation for the new 1977-78 season was not ideal and by the time United kicked a ball in anger feuding was still taking place in the corridors of St James' Park. Following a decent opening victory over Leeds, the Magpies lost their next 10 League fixtures and were firmly embedded at the foot of the table. In addition they tumbled out of the League Cup to Millwall and then in the UEFA Cup, outclassed by eventual finalists, Bastia at Gallowgate. Dinnis was dismissed and in came ex-Wolves boss Bill McGarry, one of the old-school and with a reputation as a hardliner. He had a difficult task, not only keeping United in the top flight but also sorting out a mutinous and unhappy dressing-room.

Players came and went, but results only marginally improved. McGarry did deflect League worries for a brief period as Peterborough United were beaten in a FA Cup replay at St James' Park. But another inglorious FA Cup exit was recorded, beaten by Wrexham at the Racecourse Ground when a mouth-watering tie in the Fifth Round with giant-killers Blyth Spartans was on the cards. The local non-leaguers did eventually play at St James' Park, but not against the Magpies, their tie with Wrexham being switched to Gallowgate.

With the Black'n'Whites firmly in the relegation scrap and struggling to steer clear of the drop zone, few supporters had faith in a late recovery. United finished the season almost as badly as they had started it. They didn't win a League contest at all from January 3rd onwards, and picked up a mere three points from a possible 18 in the final crucial month of the season. It was of no surprise when they were relegated after a defeat by Aston Villa. Supporters gave their verdict on the sorry season. Less than 8,000 turned up for the last home fixture against Norwich – at the time the lowest attendance for a senior fixture at St James' Park since World War Two.

Pictured above: From the junior ranks, Paul Cannell challenged for a place in United's attack for three seasons.

Memorabilia CORNER

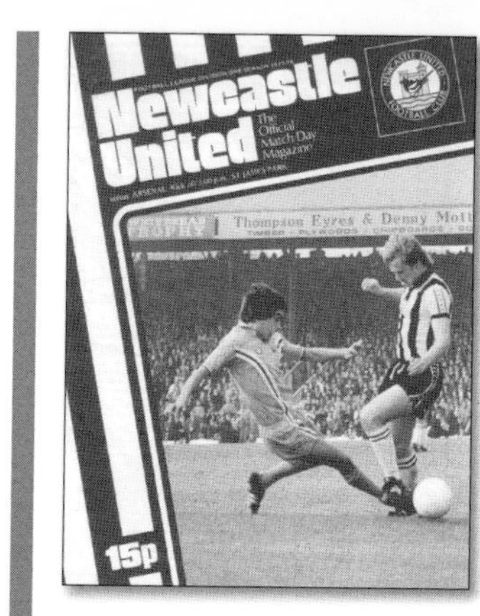

United's programme now highlighted a new club crest featuring the castle and magpie.

IN CHARGE

Chairman: Lord Westwood/Robert Rutherford
Manager: Richard Dinnis/Bill McGarry
Captain: Geoff Nulty
Trainer/Coach: Willie McFaul/Peter Morris

ST JAMES' PARK

Average Attendance
Lg 24,719 Lg & Cup 25,029

United's squad of 32 players for the start of the 1977-78 season. Manager Richard Dinnis had high hopes for the campaign.

PLAYER FOCUS Micky Burns

Born Preston. Striker, 5'7"
1974 to 1978: 191 app 51 goals.

When United purchased Micky Burns from Blackpool in June 1974 for a £170,000 fee, he was at the time United's biggest purchase next to Malcolm Macdonald. Having scored 62 goals in 203 matches for the Bloomfield Road club, Burns was highly rated. A pocket-sized, crafty forward, Micky could play wide, in a midfield role or alongside the main striker. Deft and thoughtful on the ball, Burns did not hit it off with his first boss, Joe Harvey, but with Gordon Lee in control, he flourished. Micky could weave in between defenders and always was a threat in and around the penalty area. When Supermac moved south, Burns took over the No. 9 shirt and proceeded to be a big success in a very different style, striking 17 goals during season 1976-77 as the Geordies qualified for Europe. A League Cup finalist with United in 1976, during the aftermath of player-director friction as well as relegation at St James' Park, he moved to Wales in August 1978 with Cardiff City when 31 years of age. However, Micky quickly returned to the North East joining Middlesbrough a month later. On retiring in 1981 he started coaching at Ayresome Park and afterwards he was for long associated with the PFA in Manchester. Burns earned a degree in economics when an amateur with Skelmersdale United while he won an England cap at that level and reached the FA Amateur Cup final in 1967.

SEASON REVIEW

Football League Div 1: P42 W6 D10 L26 F42 A78 Pts 22.
Position: 21st, Relegated (Champions; Nottingham Forest).
FA Cup: R4 (Winners; Ipswich Town).
FL Cup: R2 (Winners; Nottingham Forest).
UEFA Cup: R2 (Winners; PSV Eindhoven).

Appearances (51m): Burns ME 50, Nattrass I 46 (1), Barrowclough SJ 37 (5), Craig TB 31, Kennedy AP 31, Bird JC 29 (2), Mahoney MJ 29, Cassidy T 23 (1), Gowling AE 21 (1), Blackhall R 20 (1), Blackley JH 20, McCaffery A 20, McGhee ME 19 (1), Barker MA 18 (1), Barton D 14, Walker NS 14, Nulty GO 13, Larnach M 12 (2), Callachan R 11, Cannell PA 11 (1), Carr K 11, Hardwick S 11, Mitchell K 10, Martin DW 9 (2), Craig DJ 8, Kelly PA 8 (2), McLean DJ 8 (1), Robinson SA 7 (1), Scott JA 7 (1), Hudson RW 6 (2), Oates G 5 (6), Guy A 1, Smith Ant 1 (1), Gorry MC 0 (1), Parkinson AJ 0 (2).

Goals (54g): Burns ME 16, Craig TB 6, Gowling AE 6, Cassidy T 5, Kennedy AP 3, McGhee ME 3, Nattrass I 3, Bird JC 2, Blackhall R 2, Martin DW 2, Barrowclough SJ 1, Cannell PA 1, Hudson RW 1, McCaffery A 1, Mitchell K 1, Robinson SA 1.

Dismissals: 1 player; Mitchell.

MAJOR SIGNINGS

John Blackley (Hibernian) £100,000
Mark McGhee (Morton) £150,000
Mike Larnach (Clydebank) £100,000
Dennis Martin (Carlisle Utd) £40,000

FROM THE RANKS

Kevin Carr (Northb sch)
Nigel Walker (Whickham Jnrs)
David Barton (Durham sch)
Stuart Robinson (Murton CW)
Jamie Scott (Newcastle sch)
Tony Smith (Sunderland sch, Ey)

TEAM COLOURS Black & white striped shirts, black shorts (Change; yellow shirts with green trim, green shorts/blue shirts with white trim, white shorts)

SEASON 1977-78

Match	Date		Opponent		Score	HT	Att	Posn	Scorers
			FL Division 1						
1	20 Aug	H	**Leeds United**	W	3 2	(2 1)	36,491		Burns 2, Kennedy
2	23 Aug	A	Liverpool	L	0 2	(0 0)	48,267	11	
3	27 Aug	A	Middlesbrough	L	0 2	(0 1)	26,712	17	
4	03 Sep	H	**West Ham United**	L	2 3	(2 1)	26,942	20	Burns, Cassidy
5	10 Sep	H	**West Bromwich Albion**	L	0 3	(0 2)	22,705	22	
6	17 Sep	A	Birmingham City	L	0 3	(0 0)	18,953	22	
7	24 Sep	H	**Coventry City**	L	1 2	(1 1)	22,484	22	Gowling
8	01 Oct	A	Ipswich Town	L	1 2	(1 1)	21,797	22	McCaffery
9	05 Oct	A	Norwich City	L	1 2	(1 1)	16,630	22	Craig T
10	08 Oct	H	**Derby County**	L	1 2	(0 0)	26,578	22	Burns
11	15 Oct	A	Manchester United	L	2 3	(0 2)	55,056	22	Martin, Burns
12	22 Oct	H	**Chelsea**	W	1 0	(1 0)	23,683	22	Burns
13	29 Oct	A	Everton	D	4 4	(2 1)	37,574	22	Craig T, Gowling 2, Cassidy
14	05 Nov	H	**Bristol City**	D	1 1	(0 0)	23,321	21	Martin
15	12 Nov	A	Wolverhampton Wanderers	L	0 1	(0 1)	16,964	22	
16	19 Nov	H	**Arsenal**	L	1 2	(0 0)	23,679	22	Cassidy
17	03 Dec	H	**Leicester City**	W	2 0	(0 0)	20,112	22	Burns, Nattrass
18	10 Dec	A	Queens Park Rangers	W	1 0	(0 0)	15,251	21	Robinson
19	17 Dec	H	**Wolverhampton Wanderers**	W	4 0	(2 0)	22,982	20	Craig T, Mitchell, Cassidy, Nattrass
20	26 Dec	A	Manchester City	L	0 4	(0 0)	45,811	21	
21	28 Dec	H	**Nottingham Forest**	L	0 2	(0 1)	41,612	21	
22	31 Dec	H	**Liverpool**	L	0 2	(0 0)	36,499	21	
23	02 Jan	A	Leeds United	W	2 0	(1 0)	36,643	21	Burns 2
24	14 Jan	H	**Middlesbrough**	L	2 4	(1 1)	34,460	21	McGhee, Cassidy
25	21 Jan	A	West Ham United	L	0 1	(0 1)	25,461	21	
26	25 Feb	H	**Ipswich Town**	L	0 1	(0 0)	22,264	22	
27	04 Mar	A	Derby County	D	1 1	(1 1)	19,708	22	Burns
28	11 Mar	H	**Manchester United**	D	2 2	(1 2)	25,825	22	McGhee, Burns (pen)
29	15 Mar	H	**Birmingham City**	D	1 1	(0 1)	19,493	21	Nattrass
30	18 Mar	A	Chelsea	D	2 2	(1 0)	22,777	21	McGhee, Burns (pen)
31	24 Mar	H	**Everton**	L	0 2	(0 1)	28,933	21	
32	25 Mar	A	Nottingham Forest	L	0 2	(0 1)	35,552	21	
33	29 Mar	H	**Manchester City**	D	2 2	(0 1)	20,256	21	Bird, Kennedy
34	01 Apr	A	Bristol City	L	1 3	(0 1)	17,344	22	Barrowclough
35	04 Apr	A	Coventry City	D	0 0	(0 0)	22,135	21	
36	08 Apr	H	**Aston Villa**	D	1 1	(0 0)	19,330	21	Burns (pen)
37	12 Apr	A	West Bromwich Albion	L	0 2	(0 0)	17,053	21	
38	15 Apr	A	Arsenal	L	1 2	(0 0)	33,353	21	Burns
39	17 Apr	A	Aston Villa	L	0 2	(0 1)	25,495	21	
40	22 Apr	H	**Queens Park Rangers**	L	0 3	(0 2)	13,463	21	
41	26 Apr	H	**Norwich City**	D	2 2	(1 0)	7,986	21	Burns, Kennedy
42	29 Apr	A	Leicester City	L	0 3	(0 1)	11,530	21	
Round			**FA Cup**						
3	07 Jan	A	Peterborough United	D	1 1	(1 1)	17,621		Hudson
3r	11 Jan	H	**Peterborough United**	W	2 0	(0 0)	26,837		Craig T (pen), Blackhall
4	28 Jan	H	**Wrexham**	D	2 2	(0 0)	29,344		Bird, Blackhall
4r	06 Feb	A	Wrexham	L	1 4	(1 2)	18,676		Burns
Round			**FL Cup**						
2	31 Aug	H	**Millwall**	L	0 2	(0 1)	21,861		
Round			**UEFA Cup**						
1(1)	14 Sep	A	Bohemians (Ei)	D	0 0	(0 0)	25,000		
1(2)	28 Sep	H	**Bohemians (Ei)**	W	4 0	(1 0)	19,046		Craig T 2, Gowling 2
2(1)	19 Oct	A	SEC Bastia (F)	L	1 2	(1 0)	8,500		Cannell
2(2)	02 Nov	H	**SEC Bastia (F)**	L	1 3	(1 2)	34,560		Gowling

Match	Mahoney	Nattrass	Kennedy	Cassidy	McCaffery	Bird	Barrowclough	Cannell	Burns	Gowling	Craig TB	Blackhall	Hardwick	Oates	McLean	Mitchell	Craig DJ	Callachan	Blackley	Kelly	Martin	Nulty	Barker	Walker	Smith	Robinson	Carr	Hudson	Gorry	Larnach	Barton	McGhee	Parkinson	Scott	Guy
1	1	2	3	4	5	6	7	8	9	10	11	u																							
2		2	3	4	5	6	7		9	10	11	8	1	s8																					
3		2	3	4	5	6	7		9	10	11	s2	1	8																					
4	1	s8	3	4	5	6			9		11	2		10	7	8																			
5	1	6	3			5	7	8	9	10	11	4		s10			2																		
6	1	6	3			5	7	8	9		11			s4	4		2	10																	
7	1	6	3		5		7		9	10	11			s4	4		2	8																	
8	1	6	3		5		7		9	10	11			s2	8		2	4																	
9	1	6	3		5		7		9	10	11	2		s8	4			8																	
10	1	2			5		7		9	10	11	3		8	4				6	s10															
11					5	4	7	8	9		11	3	1		s4				6	2	10														
12		3		4	5		7	8	9	10	11		1						u	2		6													
13		2		4	5		7		9	10	11	u	1						3		8	6													
14		2				5	7		9	10	11		1						6		8		3	4	u										
15		6		4		5	7		9		11		1				2				8		3	10	s10										
16		6		4		5	7		9	10	11		1				2				s10		3		8										
17		2		4		5	u		8		10		1	9					6		7		3			11									
18		2		4		5		9	8		10								6		7		3			11	1	s8							
19		2		4		5	u		8		10					9			6		7		3			11	1								
20		2		4		5		9	8		10								6		7		3			11	1		s6						
21		2		4		5	s9	9	8		10	6									7		3			11	1								
22		2			5		7		8		10	6									s7		3			11	1	4		9					
23				4	5		s6		8		11	2											3				1	7		9	6	10			
24		6		4	5				8	10	11	2											3				1	7		s3		9			
25	1	2	6	4		5	11		7	s4													3					8		10		9			
26	1	2	10	4		5	7		8	11		u							6				3							9					
27	1	4	3			5	7		8										6	2			s10	11						9		10			
28	1	4	3			5	7		8										6	2				11						9		10	s7		
29	1	4	3			5			8										6	2				11		7				9		10	s11		
30	1	2	3			5			8										6	s6				11						9	4	10		7	
31	1	2	3			5	s8		8													6		11						9	4	10		7	
32	1	2	3			5	7		u							9			6			8		11							4	10			
33	1	2	3			5	7		8							9				u		6		11							4	10			
34	1	2	3			5	7		8			6										9		11							4	10		s5	
35	1	5	3				7		8			2						10				6								u	4	9		11	
36	1	5	3				7		8			2						10				6								s10	4	9		11	
37	1	5	3			s11	7		8			2				6d		10													4	9		11	
38	1	5	3			u	7		8										2			6		10							4	9		11	
39	1	5	3				7		8							9		u	2			6		10							4			11	
40	1	2	3				7		8							9			5				6	11						10	4	s11			
41			3				7		8							u		6	5	2				11			1			10	4	9			
42									8			3				6		11		2		5				s9	1			10	4	9			7
Round																																			
3		6		4	5		s9		8	10	11	2				9							3				1	7							
3r		2		4	5		s7		8	10	11	6				9							3				1	7							
4	1	4	10			5	7		8	11		2							6				3							u		9			
4r	1	4	11	s6		5	7		8	10		2							6				3									9			
Round																																			
2	1	2	3	4	5	6	7	s7	9		11			10	8																				
Round																																			
1(1)	1	6	3	4	u	5	7	8	9		11	u	u	u	u		2	10																	
1(2)	1	6	3		5		7	u	9	10	11		u	u	4	u	2	8											u						
2(1)		3		4	5	u	7	8	9	10	11	u	1		u					2		6			u		u								
2(2)		3		4	5	s6	7	8	9	10	11	2	1									6		u	u		u	s8							

DateLine ... 22 Oct: A 1-0 victory over Chelsea ends a run of 10 successive League defeats, a club record. **2 Nov:** United crash out of the UEFA Cup after a display of quality from French side Bastia. **19 Nov:** Bill McGarry's first game as boss ends in defeat, 2-1 to Arsenal. **27 Feb:** St James' Park hosts the Blyth v Wrexham FA Cup clash with 42,157 watching, the biggest crowd of the season. **26 April:** Only 7,986 turn up to see Norwich at St James' Park, the lowest gate for over 40 years. **29 April:** United's defeat against Leicester City marks the 26th reverse of the season, a club record.

SEASON 1978-79

DIVISION 2

McGarry cracks the whip

Newcastle United's rapid slide from the top, from fourth spot in Division One, a Wembley final and UEFA Cup football, was as eye-catching as it was catastrophic. Bill McGarry had a big task to put the shattered parts of the club back together. He continued to sort out the dressing-room and clear the bad feeling of the last 12 months. The downside was that players of real quality found new homes, the likes of Burns, Craig and Kennedy following Macdonald out of Gallowgate. A complete new squad had to be assembled, a mix of seasoned pros arrived – Mick Martin and record purchase Peter Withe included – local youngsters such as talented midfielder Nigel Walker, as well as a find from the non-leagues in Blyth's Alan Shoulder.

Newcastle's re-fashioned line-up was in a chasing promotion group at the top until a dreadful winter disrupted their plans, as did injury. Although Watford and Wolves saw United out of the knock-out cups, by the time 1979 opened their was real hope of a quick return into Division One. They were in ninth place, but five successive defeats signalled a slide. A wretched 4-1 home reverse by Sunderland was agony for United supporters. It marked the end of the season as far as promotion was concerned, United finishing in a disappointing eighth position after being down to 16th place in March when West Ham inflicted a heavy 5-0 defeat at the Boleyn Ground.

Those loyal fans had seen enough. Increasing disillusionment set-in and only 7,134 saw the final contest of the season against Wrexham at Gallowgate, a post-war low. With discontent came organised revolt. Pressure mounted on a beleaguered Boardroom, not only for instant change on the field, but also in the long-term management and ownership of the whole club. Seeds of revolution to last a decade were sprouting fast.

Pictured above: Alan Shoulder exchanged the pit-head for St James' Park and proved to be a popular striker.

Memorabilia CORNER

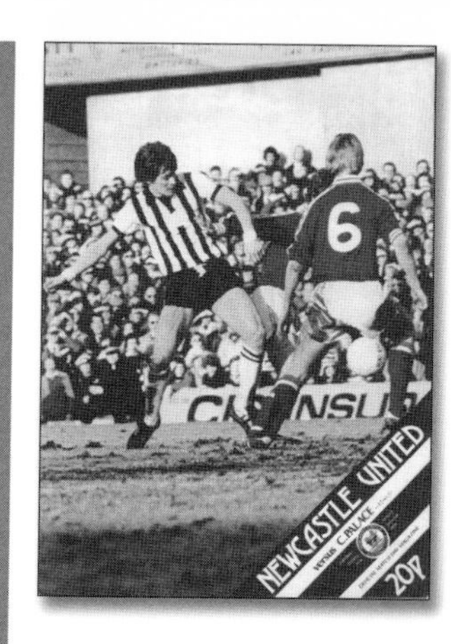

Newcastle's magazine for the game with Crystal Palace, a 1-0 victory.

IN CHARGE

Chairman: Robert Rutherford
Manager: Bill McGarry
Captain: Terry Hibbitt
Trainer/Coach: Peter Morris

ST JAMES' PARK

Average Attendance
Lg 20,494 Lg & Cup 20,926

A return to Division Two for United. Back row, left to right: Callachan, Barker, Parkinson, Mahoney, Bird, Carr, Barton, Blackley, Connolly. Sitting: Kennedy (A), Mitchell, McGhee, Cassidy, McGarry (manager), Larnach, Nattrass, Kelly, Hibbitt, Morris (asst manager). On ground: Guy (A), Walker, Scott, Blackhall.

PLAYER FOCUS Irving Nattrass

Born Fishburn. Right-back, 5'10"
1970 to 1979: 313 app 22 goals.

Newcastle United nurtured two exceptional full-backs in the Seventies era. Alan Kennedy was one; the other at right-back was Irving Nattrass. Another local product from County Durham, Nattrass first appeared for the Magpies in season 1970-71 as an 18-year-old and became a stylish defender able to operate also at centre-back or in midfield. An England Under-23 international, he was much tipped for a full call-up but the chaos in the Gallowgate camp towards the end of the that decade and his ultimate move to Middlesbrough for a big £375,000 fee, saw that dream fall by the wayside. Before that though, Nattrass showed a coolness and refinement just like his predecessor David Craig in defence. He oozed class and confidence, and was due to embark on England's tour of South America in 1977 – and win his first cap – but injury prevented his appearance. Irving pulled on the No. 2 shirt in the Magpies' 1976 League Cup final and later skippered the Black'n'Whites. On relegation, it was clear he was too good for Second Division football and he moved back to the top-tier by joining Boro in July 1979 opting to stay in the North East rather than join Spurs or Manchester City who both also wanted his signature. Dogged by mishaps during his career, after good service at Ayresome Park over seven seasons and 221 appearances he retired due to injury in June 1986.

SEASON REVIEW

Football League Div 2: P42 W17 D8 L17 F51 A55 Pts 42.
Position: 8th (Champions; Crystal Palace).
FA Cup: R4 (Winners; Arsenal).
FL Cup: R2 (Winners; Nottingham Forest).

Appearances (46m): Hibbitt TA 44, Withe P 43, Brownlie JJ 37, Connolly J 35, Hardwick S 34, Blackley JH 32, Bird JC 29, Mitchell K 29 (5), Martin MP 26, Nattrass I 24, Shoulder A 24, Barton D 22 (2), Cassidy T 21, Suggett C 21 (3), Walker NS 19 (2), Kelly PA 16, Pearson JF 10 (1), Carr K 8, Barker MA 6 (1), Nicholson GA 6(3), Robinson SA 6, Mahoney MJ 4, McGhee ME 4 (8), Guy A 2 (1), Manners PJ 2, Scott JA 2, Mulgrove KA 0 (1), Parkinson AJ 0 (1), Wharton K 0 (2).

Goals (56g): Withe P 16, Shoulder A 11, Connolly J 8, Pearson JF 4, Bird JC 3, Nattrass I 3, Barton D 2, McGhee ME 2, Robinson SA 2, Walker NS 2, Cassidy T 1, Martin MP 1, Mitchell K 1.

Dismissals: 0 players.

MAJOR SIGNINGS

Mick Martin (West Brom Albion) £100,000
Terry Hibbitt (Birmingham City) exchange
Colin Suggett (Norwich City) £60,000
John Brownlie (Hibernian) exchange
John Connolly (Birmingham City) exchange
Jim Pearson (Everton) £75,000
Alan Shoulder (Blyth Spartans) £20,000
Peter Withe (Nottingham Forest) £200,000 club record fee

FROM THE RANKS

Gary Nicholson (Newcastle sch)
Kenny Wharton (Grainger Park BC)
Peter Manners (sch)

TEAM COLOURS Black & white striped shirts, black shorts (Change; yellow shirts with green trim, green shorts/blue shirts with white trim, white shorts)

SEASON 1978-79

Match	Date		FL Division 2		Score (HT)	Att	Posn	Scorers	Mahoney	Kelly	Barker	Cassidy	Bird	Barton	Walker	Pearson	Mitchell	Hibbitt	Connolly	Guy	Blackley	Suggett	Withe	Hardwick	Brownlie	McGhee	Nattrass	Scott	Robinson	Nicholson	Martin	Shoulder	Mulgrove	Parkinson	Wharton	Carr	Manners	Match
1	19 Aug	A	Millwall	L	1 2 (1 0)	12,105		Barton	1	2	3	4	5	6	7	8	9	10	11	u																	1
2	23 Aug	H	**West Ham United**	L	0 3 (0 1)	27,167			1	2	3	4	5		7	9	u	10	11		6	8															2
3	26 Aug	H	**Luton Town**	W	1 0 (1 0)	24,112		Pearson	1	2	3	4	5		u	8		10	11		6	7	9														3
4	02 Sep	A	Cambridge United	D	0 0 (0 0)	8,174	20			2		4	5	6		8	u	10	11			7	9	1	3												4
5	09 Sep	H	**Blackburn Rovers**	W	3 1 (0 1)	23,751	10	Withe 2, McGhee		2		4		5		8		10	11		6	7	9	1	3	s4											5
6	16 Sep	A	Wrexham	D	0 0 (0 0)	14,091	12			2		4		5			s8	10	11		6	7	9	1	3	8											6
7	23 Sep	H	**Orient**	D	0 0 (0 0)	26,361	11			2		4					s6	10	11		6	7	9	1	3	8	5										7
8	30 Sep	A	Notts County	W	2 1 (1 0)	11,362	8	Connolly, Bird		2			5				s8	10	11		6	7	9	1	3	8		4									8
9	07 Oct	H	**Leicester City**	W	1 0 (0 0)	25,731	6	Walker		2			5		8		4	10	11		6	7	9	1	3	s2											9
10	14 Oct	A	Sunderland	D	1 1 (1 0)	35,405	6	Withe		2			5	6	8		4	10	11			7	9	1	3	u											10
11	21 Oct	A	Charlton Athletic	L	1 4 (1 1)	11,616	11	Walker		2			5	6	8	7	4	10				s7	9	1	3				11								11
12	28 Oct	H	**Cardiff City**	W	3 0 (1 0)	23,477	8	Connolly, Withe, Robinson		2			5		8			10	11		6	7	9	1	3	s4			4								12
13	04 Nov	A	Bristol Rovers	L	0 2 (0 1)	10,582	11			2			5		8	4	u	10	11		6	7	9	1	3												13
14	11 Nov	H	**Millwall**	W	1 0 (0 0)	23,087	10	Pearson		2			5		8	4		10	11		6	7	9	1	3	s4											14
15	18 Nov	A	Luton Town	L	0 2 (0 1)	10,434				2				5	8		4	10	11		6	7	9	1	3	s2											15
16	22 Nov	H	**Cambridge United**	W	1 0 (1 0)	20,004	7	Bird			3		5		8			10			6	7	9	1	2	s7	4			11							16
17	25 Nov	H	**Oldham Athletic**	D	1 1 (0 0)	20,563	10	McGhee			3		5		8		s4	10			6		9	1	2	7	4			11							17
18	02 Dec	A	Crystal Palace	L	0 1 (0 1)	19,761	11						5		8		3	10	11		6	7	9	1	2					s8	4						18
19	09 Dec	H	**Stoke City**	W	2 0 (0 0)	23,459	9	Connolly, Withe				7	5				3	10	11		6		9	1	2				u		4	8					19
20	16 Dec	A	Fulham	W	3 1 (2 1)	8,575	6	Connolly, Withe, Shoulder				8	5	s6			3	10	11		6		9	1	2						4	7					20
21	23 Dec	H	**Burnley**	W	3 1 (2 0)	23,639	6	Withe, Shoulder, Cassidy			s5	8	5				3	10	11		6		9	1	2						4	7					21
22	26 Dec	A	Sheffield United	L	0 1 (0 0)	23,118	6				u	8		5			3	10	11		6		9	1	2						4	7					22
23	30 Dec	A	Brighton & Hove Albion	L	0 2 (0 1)	25,812	9					8		5			3	10	11			6	9	1	2						4	7	s6				23
24	03 Feb	A	Orient	L	0 2 (0 0)	7,251	11							5			3	10		s11	6		9	1	2		8		11		4	7					24
25	17 Feb	A	Leicester City	L	1 2 (0 2)	15,106	12	Nattrass					5		s11		3				6		9	1	2		8	10	11		4	7					25
26	24 Feb	H	**Sunderland**	L	1 4 (0 2)	34,733	15	Connolly					5		8		s6	10	11		6		9	1	2		3				4	7					26
27	03 Mar	H	**Charlton Athletic**	W	5 3 (3 2)	14,998	11	Connolly, Shoulder 2 (1 pen), Martin, Mitchell						5	8		3	10	11				9	1	2		6				4	7		s4			27
28	10 Mar	A	Cardiff City	L	1 2 (0 1)	11,368	15	Connolly						5	8		3	10	11			s8	9	1	2		6				4	7					28
29	24 Mar	A	West Ham United	L	0 5 (0 4)	24,651	16						5		8		3	10	11				9	1	2		6				4	7			s8			29
	28 Mar	H	**Wrexham**	Ab	1 1 (1 1)	7,152		Cassidy				8	5				u	10	11		3		9	1	2		6				4	7			u			
30	31 Mar	A	Oldham Athletic	W	3 1 (1 1)	6,329	14	Withe, Shoulder (pen), Nattrass				8	5				u	10	11		3		9	1	2		6				4	7					30
31	04 Apr	H	**Preston North End**	W	4 3 (2 2)	12,167	13	Connolly, Withe, Shoulder, Barton				8		5			6	10	11		3		9	1	2						4	7			u			31
32	07 Apr	H	**Crystal Palace**	W	1 0 (0 0)	18,862		Shoulder				8		5			u	10	11		3		9	1	2		6				4	7					32
33	10 Apr	A	Burnley	L	0 1 (0 1)	7,851						8		5			u	10	11		3		9	1	2		6				4	7					33
34	14 Apr	H	**Sheffield United**	L	1 3 (0 2)	19,126	11	Shoulder				8					5	10	11		3	u	9	1	2		6				4	7					34
35	16 Apr	A	Preston North End	D	0 0 (0 0)	12,960						8			s4		5	10	11		3		9		2		6				4	7				1		35
36	18 Apr	H	**Notts County**	L	1 2 (0 1)	12,017		Withe				8			4		5	10	11		3	s11	9		2		6					7				1		36
37	21 Apr	H	**Fulham**	D	0 0 (0 0)	11,924	12						3	5	10		9					8			2		6			11	4	7			s2	1		37
38	25 Apr	A	Blackburn Rovers	W	3 1 (1 1)	4,902		Withe 3					6	5			3	10				8	9				2			11	4	7			u	1		38
39	28 Apr	A	Stoke City	D	0 0 (0 0)	23,217	11						6	5			3	10				8	9				2			11	4	7				1	u	39
40	02 May	H	**Bristol Rovers**	W	3 0 (2 0)	9,627	9	Withe, Shoulder, Bird					6	5			3	10	11			8	9				2			s3		7				1	4	40
41	05 May	H	**Brighton & Hove Albion**	L	1 3 (0 3)	28,434		Shoulder					6	5			3	10	11				9				2			s3	8	7				1	4	41
42	08 May	H	**Wrexham**	W	2 0 (1 0)	7,134	8	Pearson, Shoulder					6	5		8	3	10	11				9				2				4	7				1		42
Round			FA Cup																																			Round
3	16 Jan	H	**Torquay United**	W	3 1 (1 1)	21,366		Robinson, Withe, Nattrass (pen)				8		s7			3	10			6		9	1	2		5		11	7	4						3
4	27 Jan	H	**Wolverhampton Wanderers**	D	1 1 (0 0)	29,561		Withe						5			3	10		7	6		9	1	2	s11	8		11		4						4
4r	22 Feb	A	Wolverhampton Wanderers	L	0 1 (0 1)	19,588							5		11	s3	3	10		7	6		9	1	2		8				4						4r
Round			FL Cup																																			Round
2	29 Aug	A	Watford	L	1 2 (1 0)	15,346		Pearson	1	2	3	4	5			8		10	11		6	7	9			s8											2

Ab Abandoned after 45 mins due to rain

DateLine ... 26 Aug: A victory against Luton ends a club record run of 21 League games without a win. **24 Feb:** Sunderland win 4-1 on Tyneside with Gary Rowell netting a hat-trick. **8 May:** A gate of only 7,134 watch the last fixture of the season with Wrexham, the lowest post-war attendance at Gallowgate.

SEASON 1979-80
DIVISION 2

Promotion challenge falls flat

To keep hold of their star asset, centre-forward Peter Withe, United had to get back into the top level of football. If they didn't, without doubt Withe would move on, being already eyed by First Division suitors. Following an early League Cup derby with Sunderland ended in a penalty shoot-out defeat with all of 14 spot-kicks, Newcastle put together a string of good results. They scored four goals at Brisbane Road against Orient then defeated Leicester City 3-2 and Wrexham by a single goal to go out in front in the Second Division table. Up to the Christmas half-way mark of the campaign, the Black'n'Whites were on course for promotion. The Magpies then gained some revenge over their Wearside rivals by crushing the red-and-whites 3-1 on New Year's Day. They were top of the table and looking good.

However, a long term knock to midfield anchor-man Mick Martin following an injury against Luton Town proved a blow. It was a turning point as McGarry failed to find a replacement. Although results continued to be maintained at first, after that inspiring New Year victory over Sunderland, the Geordies slumped. The chance of promotion gradually slipped away, vanishing completely following a single goal defeat at Roker Park against Sunderland during April. The second-half of the season was a disaster. Newcastle only won twice after the New Year holiday – relegation, rather than promotion form. Yet remarkably they still finished in ninth place, which was an indication of the mediocre standard of competition that season. Promotion had been for the taking.

There was another knock-out blow in the FA Cup for United's long suffering fans to cope with. Chester – for the second time in five years – left United reeling with a young Ian Rush scoring as they won on Tyneside. Boss Bill McGarry was more and more under pressure. His tenure was not to last much longer as the embattled club Board soon made another change.

Pictured above: Peter Withe, tall and forceful, a class apart at centre-forward in the second-tier.

Memorabilia CORNER

United's magazine included an innovative 'scratch off' prize draw in season 1979-80.

IN CHARGE

Chairman: Robert Rutherford
Manager: Bill McGarry
Captain: Mick Martin
Trainer/Coach: Willie McFaul

ST JAMES' PARK

Average Attendance
Lg 23,345 Lg & Cup 23,710

A much changed United squad was on show for 1979-80. Back row, left to right: Connolly, Hardwick, Carr, Manners, Barton. Middle: Brownlie, Nicholson, Cassidy, Suggett, Scott, Mitchell, Pearson, Mulgrove, Robinson, Davies, Shoulder, Bird. Front: Cartwright, Martin, Withe, Walker, McGarry (manager), Hibbitt, Nattrass, Wharton.

PLAYER FOCUS Terry Hibbitt

Born Bradford. Midfield, 5'7"
1971 to 1981: 291 app 18 goals.

For the modest sum of £30,000, United secured the services of midfielder Terry Hibbitt in August 1971. It was perhaps the bargain of the Seventies decade. On the periphery of the great Leeds side of the period, Hibbitt possessed a quality left-foot and was too good for the Elland Road bench. He quickly showed he could hold his own in the First Division and immediately formed a partnership with another new Gallowgate arrival – Malcolm Macdonald. With Hibbitt's pin-point through balls the Magpies found they had a lethal combination that few opposition defences could handle. A touch fiery on the field, Terry played a major role as Newcastle reached Wembley in the 1974 FA Cup final. Extremely popular with the crowd, he was also tipped for full England recognition, but was one of the unlucky fringe players. An injury forced him out of the side in 1975 and by the time he was fit again Terry not only had a rival for the left-sided midfield spot in Tommy Craig, but also a new boss, Gordon Lee. And like Macdonald, Terry was never a Lee favourite. He was sent packing to St Andrews joining Birmingham City in September 1975 only to return to Gallowgate at the end of his footballing days for a second stint in April 1978. Injury halted his senior career in June 1981, Hibbitt concluding his playing days across the Tyne with Gateshead, where he eventually gained an England call-up at non-league level. Residing on Tyneside, he died when only 47 years old in 1994. His brother Kenny appeared over 500 times for Wolves during the same era.

SEASON REVIEW

Football League Div 2: P42 W15 D14 L13 F53 A49 Pts 44.
Position: 9th (Champions; Leicester City).
FA Cup: R3 (Winners; West Ham United).
FL Cup: R2 (Winners; Wolverhampton Wanderers).

Appearances (45m): Hardwick S 44, Shoulder A 43 (1), Brownlie JJ 41, Boam SW 40, Withe P 40, Davies IC 39 (1), Hibbitt TA 37, Barton D 35, Cartwright P 34 (5), Cassidy T 31 (1), Martin MP 21, Rafferty WH 20 (5), Walker NS 11 (2), Bird JC 10, Carney S 10 (1), Shinton RT 10, Connolly J 8 (8), Mitchell K 6, Ferguson BJ 4 (1), Cropley AJ 3, Nicholson GA 3 (1), Pearson JF 3, Carr K 1, Wharton K 1.

Goals (57g): Shoulder A 21, Withe P 11, Cassidy T 6, Cartwright P 4, Rafferty WH 4, Barton D 2, Connolly J 2, Davies IC 2, Hibbitt TA 2, Boam SW 1, Ferguson BJ 1, Shinton RT 1.

Dismissals: 0 players.

MAJOR SIGNINGS

Stuart Boam (Middlesbrough) £140,000
Bobby Shinton (Manchester City) £175,000
Billy Rafferty (Wolves) £175,000
Ian Davies (Norwich City) £175,000

FROM THE RANKS

Brian Ferguson (Mansfield Town)

TEAM COLOURS Black & white striped shirts, black shorts (Change; yellow shirts with green trim, green shorts/blue shirts with white trim, white shorts)

SEASON 1979–80

Match	Date		FL Division 2	Res	F	A	HT	Att	Posn	Scorers	Hardwick	Brownlie	Davies	Martin	Barton	Bird	Shoulder	Cassidy	Withe	Hibbitt	Pearson	Mitchell	Cartwright	Nicholson	Boam	Walker	Connolly	Rafferty	Carney	Cropley	Shinton	Ferguson	Wharton	Carr	Match
1	18 Aug	H	**Oldham Athletic**	W	3	2	(2 2)	19,099		Withe, Shoulder 2 (2 pens)	1	2	3	4	5	6	7	8	9	10	11	u													1
2	21 Aug	A	Preston North End	L	0	1	(0 0)	12,707			1	2	3	4	5	6	7	8	9	10	11		u												2
3	25 Aug	A	Charlton Athletic	D	1	1	(1 0)	6,849	12	Cassidy	1	2	3	4	5	6	7	8	9	10			s11	11											3
4	01 Sep	H	**Chelsea**	W	2	1	(0 1)	25,047	9	Withe 2	1	2	3	4	5		7	8	9	10			11	s8	6										4
5	08 Sep	A	Orient	W	4	1	(3 0)	5,700	2	Cartwright, Hibbitt, Withe, Shoulder (pen)	1	2	3	4	5		7	8	9	10			11		6	s8									5
6	15 Sep	H	**Leicester City**	W	3	2	(1 1)	26,443	1	Cartwright, Shoulder 2 (2 pens)	1	2	3	4	5		7	8	9	10			11		6	u									6
7	22 Sep	H	**Wrexham**	W	1	0	(0 0)	27,904	1	Shoulder (pen)	1	2	3	4	5		7	8	9	10			11		6	u									7
8	29 Sep	A	Birmingham City	D	0	0	(0 0)	19,967	1		1	2	3	4	5		7	8	9	10			11		6	u									8
9	06 Oct	A	West Ham United	D	1	1	(1 1)	23,206	1	Withe	1	2	3	4	5		7		9	10			11	u	6	8									9
10	10 Oct	H	**Preston North End**	D	0	0	(0 0)	25,154	1		1	2	3	4	5		7		9	10		u	11		6	8									10
11	13 Oct	H	**Shrewsbury Town**	W	1	0	(1 0)	21,603	1	Shoulder	1	2		4	5		7	8	9	10		3	u		6	11									11
12	20 Oct	A	Watford	L	0	2	(0 0)	17,715	3		1	2	3	4	5		7	8	9	10			s8		6		11								12
13	27 Oct	H	**Cambridge United**	W	2	0	(2 0)	24,104	2	Withe, Shoulder	1	2	3	4	5		7	s9	9				11		6	8		10							13
14	03 Nov	A	Oldham Athletic	L	0	1	(0 1)	11,486	4		1	2	s8	4	5		7		9			3	11		6	8		10							14
15	10 Nov	H	**Cardiff City**	W	1	0	(1 0)	22,867	2	Shoulder	1	2	3	4	5		7		9	11			u		6	8		10							15
16	17 Nov	A	Bristol Rovers	D	1	1	(0 0)	7,626	4	Shoulder	1	2	3	4	5		7		9	11			8		6		s11	10							16
17	24 Nov	A	Swansea City	W	3	2	(2 0)	15,442	3	Hibbitt, Rafferty, Shoulder	1	2	3	4	5		7		9	11			8		6		s8	10							17
18	01 Dec	H	**Fulham**	W	2	0	(1 0)	23,485	2	Rafferty, Withe	1			4	5		7		9	11		3	8		6		u	10	2						18
19	08 Dec	A	Luton Town	D	1	1	(0 1)	14,845	1	Rafferty	1	2		4	5		7		9	11			8		6		s4	10	3						19
20	15 Dec	H	**Queens Park Rangers**	W	4	2	(1 2)	25,027	1	Withe 2, Shoulder, Cassidy	1	2	3		5		7	4	9	11			8		6		s8	10							20
21	22 Dec	A	Notts County	D	2	2	(2 2)	11,224	1	Shoulder, Connolly	1	2	3		5		7	4	9	11			8		6		s9	10							21
22	26 Dec	A	Burnley	L	2	3	(1 1)	16,433	3	Shoulder, Barton	1	2	3		5		7	4		11			8		6		9	10	s4						22
23	29 Dec	H	**Charlton Athletic**	W	2	0	(0 0)	26,225	1	Shoulder, Cassidy	1	2	3		5		7	4		11			8		6		9	10	u						23
24	01 Jan	H	**Sunderland**	W	3	1	(1 1)	38,784	1	Cartwright, Shoulder (pen), Cassidy	1	2	3		5		7	4	9	11			8		6		u	10							24
25	12 Jan	A	Chelsea	L	0	4	(0 1)	32,281	2		1	2	3		5		7	4	9	11			8		6		s10	10							25
26	19 Jan	H	**Orient**	W	2	0	(0 0)	20,954	1	Connolly, Barton	1	2	3		5		7	4	9				8		6		11	u	10						26
27	02 Feb	A	Leicester City	L	0	1	(0 1)	24,549	2		1	2	3		5		7	4	9				8		6		11	s3	10						27
28	09 Feb	A	Wrexham	L	0	1	(0 0)	13,299	3		1	2	3				7	4	9				8		6		11	s7	5	10					28
29	20 Feb	H	**Birmingham City**	D	0	0	(0 0)	27,069	3		1		3				7	4	9			6	8		5		11	s10	2	10					29
30	23 Feb	A	Shrewsbury Town	L	1	3	(0 2)	10,833	5	Shoulder (pen)	1	2					7		9	11		6	8		5		s4	10	3	4					30
31	01 Mar	H	**Watford**	L	0	2	(0 1)	23,091	6		1	2	3		5		7	4	9	11			8		6		10	s3							31
32	08 Mar	A	Cambridge United	D	0	0	(0 0)	6,908	6		1	2	3			6	u	4	9	10			8		5	7					11				32
33	15 Mar	H	**West Ham United**	D	0	0	(0 0)	25,474	7		1	2	3			6	4			10			8	u	5	7		9			11				33
34	22 Mar	A	Cardiff City	D	1	1	(1 1)	9,304	7	Shinton	1	2	3			6	4	u	9	10			8		5	7					11				34
35	29 Mar	H	**Bristol Rovers**	W	3	1	(0 1)	18,975	5	Withe 2, Cassidy	1	2	3			6	s7	4	9	10			8		5	7					11				35
36	02 Apr	H	**Notts County**	D	2	2	(2 1)	22,005	4	Shoulder, Cassidy	1	2	3			6	7	4	9	10			8		5	u					11				36
37	05 Apr	A	Sunderland	L	0	1	(0 0)	41,752	7		1		3		6		7	4	9	10			8		5	s8			2		11				37
38	07 Apr	H	**Burnley**	D	1	1	(1 0)	18,863	7	Davies	1		3		6		7	4	9						5	8		10	2		11	s9			38
39	12 Apr	A	Fulham	L	0	1	(0 0)	7,152	7		1	2	3			6	11	4		10			u		5			9			7	8			39
40	19 Apr	H	**Swansea City**	L	1	3	(1 1)	14,314	7	Shoulder (pen)	1	2			5		11	4		10			s4					9	6		7	8	3		40
41	26 Apr	A	Queens Park Rangers	L	1	2	(1 0)	11,245	8	Ferguson	1	2	3				11	4	9			6	8		5			s11			7	10			41
42	03 May	H	**Luton Town**	D	2	2	(1 2)	13,765	9	Shoulder, Rafferty		2	3		6		11		9	10			4		5			7			u	8		1	42
Round			FA Cup																																Round
3	05 Jan	H	**Chester**	L	0	2	(0 1)	24,548			1	2	3		5		7	4	9	11			8		6		s11	10							3
Round			FL Cup																																Round
2(1)	29 Aug	A	Sunderland	D	2	2	(0 1)	27,746		Davies, Cartwright	1	2	3	4	5	6	7	8	9	10			s11	11											2(1)
2(2)	05 Sep	H	**Sunderland**	Dep	2	2	(0 0)	30,533		Shoulder, Boam	1	2	3	4	5		7		9	10	8		s11	11	6										2(2)

Dep — Drawn after extra time, tie lost on penalties (6-7)

DateLine ... 5 Sept: Newcastle exit the League Cup after a penalty shoot-out with Sunderland. **1 Jan:** A New Year's Day victory over Sunderland by 3-1 creates record receipts of £47,974. **15 March:** A petrol bomb is hurled at West Ham supporters in the fixture at St James' Park. **19 April:** Alan Shoulder scores his ninth penalty of the season against Swansea, a club record.

SEASON
1980-81
DIVISION 2

Arthur Cox's Black'n'White Army

Few connected with Newcastle United considered that Bill McGarry's position at St James' Park would last. The loss of popular centre-forward Peter Withe to Aston Villa was expected, but still a big blow despite the sizable £500,000 fee received. Following a less than satisfactory start in League action and an ignominious exit in the Football League Cup to Bury – managed by ex-skipper Jim Iley – the axe fell on McGarry. The once proud Magpies were in a mess, a position they would find themselves too often in the coming decades. It took the club's Board several weeks to find a replacement boss after many calls for high-profile names to be given the job. It was Chesterfield manager Arthur Cox who landed the vacancy, like Gordon Lee before him, an honest, hard-working young boss with potential, but one with little pedigree.

There was to be no overnight miracle at Gallowgate. Cox struggled to put together a side to make an impact and the Magpies stagnated in mid-table. Without the threat of Withe up front goals were in short supply, Bobby Shinton top scoring with a meagre seven in all competitions. There were few bright spots in a dismal season, but the arrival of Tow Law Town youngster Chris Waddle was a bonus. The raw winger burst onto the scene and shined in a FA Cup victory over Sheffield Wednesday. Yet Waddle could do little to stop yet more Cup woe. Against lowly Exeter City the Magpies fell by four goals at the other St James' Park some 370 miles south of the Tyne.

With club finances severely strained, season 1980-81 saw the first club sponsorship deal concluded, with Newcastle Breweries being allied to their neighbour across Barrack Road. The famous symbol of the Blue Star was now emblazoned on the equally celebrated black-and-white stripes. United needed the funds desperately as revenue was falling quickly with the average gate down to less than 18,000.

Pictured above: Locally born, John Trewick returned home in a record deal and assisted in the promotion push.

Memorabilia CORNER

Striker Billy Rafferty is featured on the cover of this programme against Swansea City.

IN CHARGE

Chairman: Robert Rutherford/Stan Seymour (Jnr)
Manager: Bill McGarry/Arthur Cox
Captain: Mick Martin
Trainer/Coach: Willie McFaul
Club Sponsor: Newcastle Breweries
Kit Supplier: Umbro

ST JAMES' PARK

Average Attendance
Lg 16,001 Lg & Cup 17,350

United's squad for 1980-81. Back row, left to right: Carney, Connolly, Shinton, Boam, Rafferty, Mitchell, Barton. Middle: Hibbitt, Suggett, Kelly, Carr, Hardwick, Walker, Nicholson, Clarke. Front: Davies, Leaver, Wharton, McGarry (manager), Martin, Cartwright, Shoulder, Montgomerie.

PLAYER FOCUS Mick Martin

Born Dublin. Midfield, 6'0"
1978 to 1983: 163 app 6 goals.

From a footballing family, the son of noted Aston Villa international Con Martin, the Dubliner made an early impression with Manchester United before joining West Bromwich Albion in 1975. At the Hawthorns, Mick established himself as a first-rate midfield player helping the Baggies to promotion as well as the FA Cup semi-final and it cost United £100,000 to bring him to Tyneside during November 1978. In a mediocre Newcastle team to start with, it took the Irishman a while to win over the fans, but he prospered in seasons 1981-82 and 1982-83. At that time Mick was nicknamed Zico by the St James' Park faithful after his dynamic displays in a Magpie shirt. An upright player, tall and polished, Martin rarely hit a pass astray. However he was discarded by United's boss Arthur Cox just as the Magpies were to embark on a successful promotion campaign. Wolves signed Mick in September 1983 but he moved on again soon afterwards appearing for a number of clubs in short spells before returning to Tyneside. During 1987 he joined United's back-room team and was part of the coaching staff up to 1990 for a period. Also with Celtic as a coach, Mick settled in Newcastle often linked to the media in the North East and in Ireland. A regular for the Republic of Ireland, winning 52 caps, he captained both club and country and later became a scout. His father unusually operated as both a goalkeeper and centre-half.

SEASON REVIEW

Football League Div 2: P42 W14 D14 L14 F30 A45 Pts 42.
Position: 11th (Champions; West Ham United).
FA Cup: R5 (Winners; Tottenham Hotspur).
FL Cup: R2 (Winners; Liverpool).

Appearances (48m): Carr K 43, Wharton K 40 (1), Boam SW 37, Shoulder A 35 (1), Martin MP 33, Carney S 28 (4), Davies IC 27, Shinton RT 27, Trewick J 25, Halliday B 23, Johnson PE 20, Walker NS 20 (1), Clarke RC 18, Harford MG 18 (1), Mitchell K 18 (1), Hibbitt TA 17 (1), Rafferty WH 17, Waddle CR 17, Barton D 15, Brownlie JJ 14 (1), Koenen FLA 13 (1), Kelly PA 9, Hardwick S 5, Cartwright P 4 (5), Nicholson GA 2 (1), Withe C 2, Leaver PH 1.

Goals (38g): Shinton RT 7, Shoulder A 6, Harford MG 4, Rafferty WH 4, Clarke RC 3, Hibbitt TA 3, Waddle CR 3, Martin MP 2, Boam SW 1, Halliday B 1, Koenen FLA 1, Trewick J 1, Walker NS 1, own goal 1.

Dismissals: 1 player; Carney.

MAJOR SIGNINGS

Mick Harford (Lincoln City) £216,000
Ray Clarke (Brighton) £180,000
Peter Johnson (Middlesbrough) £60,000
Frans Koenen (NEC) £80,000
John Trewick (West Brom Albion) £250,000 club record fee

FROM THE RANKS

Bruce Halliday (Sunderland sch)
Chris Waddle (Tow Law Town)
Phil Leaver (Tyneside sch)
Chris Withe (Liverpool sch)

TEAM COLOURS Black & white striped shirts, black shorts (Change; all yellow shirts & shorts with green trim)

SEASON 1980-81

Match	Date	Venue	Opponents	Result		HT	Att	Posn	Goalscorers
			FL Division 2						
1	16 Aug	A	Sheffield Wednesday	L	0 2	(0 0)	26,164		
2	20 Aug	H	**Notts County**	D	1 1	(0 0)	17,272		Shoulder
3	23 Aug	A	Bolton Wanderers	L	0 4	(0 2)	11,835	22	
4	30 Aug	H	**Luton Town**	W	2 1	(0 1)	13,175	21	Koenen, Hibbitt
5	06 Sep	H	**Cardiff City**	W	2 1	(2 0)	15,787	14	Clarke, Shoulder (pen)
6	13 Sep	A	Queens Park Rangers	W	2 1	(1 0)	10,865	8	Hibbitt, Boam
7	20 Sep	H	**Oldham Athletic**	D	0 0	(0 0)	19,786	9	
8	27 Sep	A	Bristol Rovers	D	0 0	(0 0)	5,171	8	
9	04 Oct	H	**West Ham United**	D	0 0	(0 0)	24,866	10	
10	07 Oct	A	Preston North End	W	3 2	(2 0)	5,301	7	Rafferty, Shinton 2
11	11 Oct	A	Bristol City	L	0 2	(0 0)	10,539	9	
12	18 Oct	H	**Swansea City**	L	1 2	(0 1)	16,278	10	Rafferty
13	22 Oct	H	**Shrewsbury Town**	W	1 0	(0 0)	11,985	7	Shinton
14	25 Oct	A	Chelsea	L	0 6	(0 3)	22,916	9	
15	01 Nov	H	**Watford**	W	2 1	(2 1)	14,590	8	Hibbitt, Shinton
16	08 Nov	A	Cambridge United	L	1 2	(0 1)	5,684	9	Shinton
17	11 Nov	A	Notts County	D	0 0	(0 0)	8,093	9	
18	15 Nov	H	**Sheffield Wednesday**	W	1 0	(1 0)	19,145	9	Shinton
19	22 Nov	H	**Wrexham**	L	0 1	(0 1)	15,941	10	
20	29 Nov	A	Orient	D	1 1	(0 0)	5,800	10	Shinton
21	13 Dec	A	Swansea City	L	0 4	(0 3)	11,672	14	
22	20 Dec	H	**Bristol City**	D	0 0	(0 0)	14,131	13	
23	26 Dec	A	Grimsby Town	D	0 0	(0 0)	17,623	14	
24	27 Dec	H	**Derby County**	L	0 2	(0 2)	20,886	16	
25	10 Jan	A	Wrexham	D	0 0	(0 0)	6,437	15	
26	17 Jan	A	Luton Town	W	1 0	(1 0)	10,774	13	Harford
27	31 Jan	H	**Bolton Wanderers**	W	2 1	(1 0)	19,143	13	Clarke, Martin
28	07 Feb	H	**Queens Park Rangers**	W	1 0	(0 0)	20,404	13	Waddle
29	21 Feb	H	**Bristol Rovers**	D	0 0	(0 0)	14,364	13	
30	25 Feb	A	Cardiff City	L	0 1	(0 1)	4,235	13	
31	28 Feb	A	Oldham Athletic	D	0 0	(0 0)	5,887	13	
32	07 Mar	A	West Ham United	L	0 1	(0 1)	26,274	14	
33	14 Mar	H	**Preston North End**	W	2 0	(1 0)	12,015	12	Harford 2
34	21 Mar	A	Shrewsbury Town	L	0 1	(0 0)	4,975	13	
35	28 Mar	H	**Chelsea**	W	1 0	(1 0)	17,297	12	Halliday
36	04 Apr	A	Watford	D	0 0	(0 0)	10,986	13	
37	11 Apr	H	**Cambridge United**	W	2 1	(1 1)	11,013	12	Shoulder, og (Turner)
38	15 Apr	H	**Blackburn Rovers**	D	0 0	(0 0)	13,128	11	
39	18 Apr	A	Derby County	L	0 2	(0 1)	14,139	11	
40	20 Apr	H	**Grimsby Town**	D	1 1	(0 1)	13,170	11	Shoulder
41	25 Apr	A	Blackburn Rovers	L	0 3	(0 2)	10,609	11	
42	02 May	H	**Orient**	W	3 1	(1 0)	11,639	11	Walker, Harford, Trewick
Round			**FA Cup**						
3	03 Jan	H	**Sheffield Wednesday**	W	2 1	(1 1)	22,458		Waddle 2
4	24 Jan	H	**Luton Town**	W	2 1	(1 0)	29,211		Clarke, Martin
5	14 Feb	H	**Exeter City**	D	1 1	(0 0)	36,984		Shoulder
5r	18 Feb	A	Exeter City	L	0 4	(0 3)	17,668		
Round			**FL Cup**						
2(1)	27 Aug	H	**Bury**	W	3 2	(1 1)	9,073		Rafferty 2, Shoulder (pen)
2(2)	02 Sep	A	Bury	La	0 1	(0 1)	4,348		

Match	Carr	Kelly	Davies	Cartwright	Boam	Carney	Rafferty	Shinton	Clarke	Wharton	Koenen	Hibbitt	Shoulder	Barton	Hardwick	Walker	Nicholson	Mitchell	Martin	Withe	Waddle	Halliday	Johnson	Trewick	Harford	Brownlie	Leaver
1	1	2	3	4	5	6d	7	8	9	10	11	u															
2	1	2	3	s8	5		7	8	9	10	11		4	6													
3	1	2	3	s11	5		7	8	9	10	11		4	6													
4			3		5	2	9			s6	11	10	7	6	1	4	8										
5			3		5	2	8		9	u	11	10	7		1	4		6									
6			3	s10	5	2	8		9		11	10	7		1	4		6									
7			3		5	2	8		9	u	11	10	7		1	4		6									
8	1	2	3	u	5	6	8		9		11	10	7			4											
9	1	2	3		5		10	9			11	8	7			4		6	u								
10	1	2	3		5		10	9			u	11	7			4		6	8								
11	1	2	3	s7	5		10	9		8		11	7					6	4								
12	1	2	3		5	u	10	9		8		11	7					6	4								
13	1				5	2	10	7		8		11				u		6	4	3	9						
14	1			8	5	2	10	7		11	s9								4	3	9	6					
15	1				5	2		7	9	8	u	11	10					6	4				3				
16	1				5	2		7	9	8	u	11	10					6	4				3				
17	1				5	2		7	9	8	u	11	10					6	4				3				
18	1				5	2		7	9	8	u	11	10					6	4				3				
19	1				5	2		7	9	8	u	11	10					6	4				3				
20	1			u	5	2	9	7		8	11		10					6	4				3				
21	1			9	5	2		7		8	11		10				s11	6	4				3				
22	1				5	2		7		11		u	10					6	4		9		3	8			
23	1				5	2		7		10		u						6	4		11		3	8	9		
24	1				5	2		7		10		s6						6	4		11		3	8	9		
25	1			u	5	2		7		10									4		11	6	3	8	9		
26	1				5	2		7		10						u			4		11	6	3	8	9		
27	1				5	2		7	9	10									4		11	6	3	8	u		
28	1				5	2		7	9	10									4		11	6	3	8	s4		
29	1				5	4				10			7			u					11	6	3	8	9	2	
30	1		7	4	5					10						s10					11	6	3	8	9	2	
31	1		3		5	s11				10			7						4		11	6		8	9	2	
32	1		3			s11				10			7	5					4		11	6		8	9	2	
33	1		3			u				10			7	5		11			4			6		8	9	2	
34	1		3			s5				10			7	5		11			4			6		8	9	2	
35	1		3			s4				10			7	5		11			4			6		8	9	2	
36	1		3			u				10			7	5		11			4			6		8	9	2	
37	1		3			u				10			7	5		11			4			6		8	9	2	
38	1		3			u				10			7	5		11			4			6		8	9	2	
39	1		3			u				10			7	5		11			4			6		8	9	2	
40	1		3			u				10			7	5		11			4			6		8	9	2	
41	1		3			u				10			7	5		11			4			6		8	9	2	
42	1		3							10			7	5		11	u		4			6		8	9	2	
Round																											
3	1				5	2		7	9	10						u			4		11	6	3	8			
4	1				5	2		7	9	10			u						4		11	6	3	8			
5	1				5	2		7	9	10			s7			4					11	6	3	8			
5r	1				5	2			9	10			7			4					11	6	3	8		s10	
Round																											
2(1)	1	2	3	s6	5		10				7	8	9	4			11										6
2(2)			3		5	2	9	8		6	11	10	7		1	4		s6									

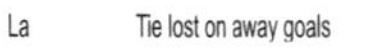

La Tie lost on away goals

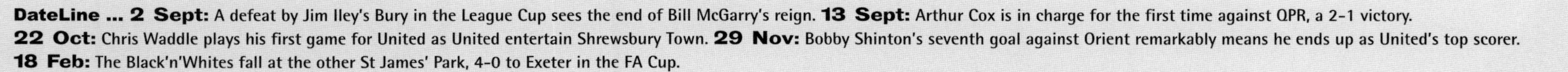

DateLine ... 2 Sept: A defeat by Jim Iley's Bury in the League Cup sees the end of Bill McGarry's reign. **13 Sept:** Arthur Cox is in charge for the first time against QPR, a 2-1 victory. **22 Oct:** Chris Waddle plays his first game for United as United entertain Shrewsbury Town. **29 Nov:** Bobby Shinton's seventh goal against Orient remarkably means he ends up as United's top scorer. **18 Feb:** The Black'n'Whites fall at the other St James' Park, 4-0 to Exeter in the FA Cup.

NEWCASTLE UNITED

SEASON 1981-82

DIVISION 2

In dire need 100 years on

In their centenary season – although it was not marked, never mind celebrated – Newcastle United's fortunes were at low ebb, the lowest since those months of despair in the Second Division just before World War Two. Arthur Cox failed to make an immediate impression on the Magpies. With a new three-points system introduced for season 1981-82, his side again never looked like entering the promotion race, stuck in the lower half of the table as the season unfolded. A new striker was introduced to replace the manager's expensive but ineffective purchase of Mick Harford. Livewire centre-forward Imre Varadi arrived and made a difference claiming 20 goals. He began a revival by claiming a hat-trick in a 4-0 victory at Cardiff at the beginning of October, but his effort still wasn't enough to push United into serious promotion contention.

Cox also turned to youth, fielding the club's youngest ever side at the time against Queens Park Rangers. Newcastle did improve. Being inconsistent, they leaped up the table, even to the lofty position of fourth at one point in April following a run of six games without defeat. But they ended some way off the top places in ninth spot.

More Cup anguish was heaped on the Geordie faithful as Malcolm Macdonald's Fulham dumped United out of the League Cup and managerless relegation candidates Grimsby Town did likewise in the FA Cup – this after a dramatic tie with Colchester United ended in a 4-3 victory at Layer Road. Gates dwindled further and with it finances fell too. By the end of the season the club was in need of inspiration. Within the corridors of power Chairman Stan Seymour – the son of Mr Newcastle himself – had a brainwave. And backed by local sponsors Newcastle Breweries a close-season move unfolded which was to shock the football world and set Tyneside alight.

Pictured above: Imre Varadi was a live-wire No. 9, highly praised by Newcastle's Black-and-White Army.

Memorabilia CORNER

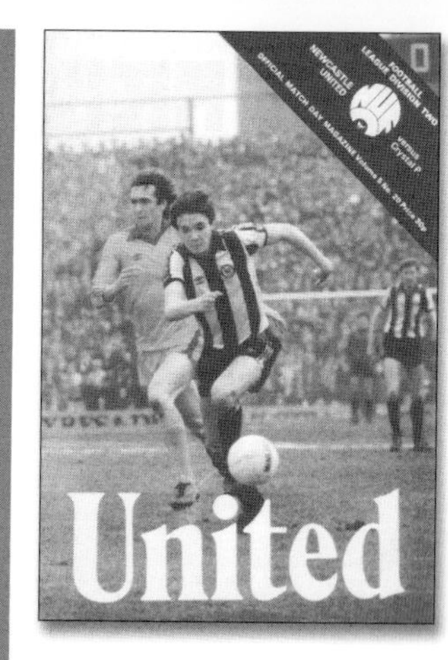

A new modern style club badge was in place by the time United faced Crystal Palace.

IN CHARGE

Chairman: Stan Seymour (Jnr)
Manager: Arthur Cox
Captain: Mick Martin
Trainer/Coach: Tommy Cavanagh
Club Sponsor: Newcastle Breweries
Kit Supplier: Umbro

ST JAMES' PARK

Average Attendance
Lg 17,276 Lg & Cup 17,736

Arthur Cox and his first United squad. Back row, left to right: Cavanagh (asst manager), Carney, Halliday, Waddle, Hardwick, Harford, Carr, Barton, Haddock, Shinton, McFaul (coach). Sitting: Wharton, Trewick, Walker, Martin, Cox (manager), Brownlie, Shoulder, Johnson, Davies.

PLAYER FOCUS Kenny Wharton

Born Newcastle upon Tyne. Midfield, 5'8"
1978 to 1989: 333 app 27 goals.

Born in Newcastle, for just about all of his playing and coaching career Kenny Wharton served Newcastle United with the sort of dedication expected from a lad raised in the city. Small and slender, but possessing a tenacious edge to his game, Kenny was given the nickname of Bones in the St James' Park dressing-room. He filled either a full-back or midfield role for the Magpies over 11 seasons and was a part of the club's celebrated promotion winning side in 1984. Having joined the Black'n'Whites as an apprentice in January 1978, Wharton became a first-team regular in 1980-81 and was at times a furious competitor while also could often get forward and support United's attack. Famously, Kenny once capped a period of showboating by a confident Magpie team against Luton during April 1988 by nonchalantly sitting on the ball, all to tease the opponents and rally the crowd. The incident is now captured on YouTube. He survived no less than six changes in management at Gallowgate before being forced to quit playing due to a cartilage injury in May 1989. Kenny tried to resurrect his senior career with several clubs, including Middlesbrough and Carlisle United, before switching to a lower grade of football. He then started on a coaching trade in Canada and at St Johnstone in 1992. Wharton joined the Newcastle coaching staff in 1999 and remained with the club for over a decade. For a spell his son Paul was also on the club's books, while he is also related by marriage to Victorian half-back Tommy Ghee.

SEASON REVIEW

Football League Div 2: P42 W18 D8 L16 F52 A50 Pts 62.
Position: 9th (Champions; Luton Town).
FA Cup: R4 (Winners; Tottenham Hotspur).
FL Milk Cup: R2 (Winners; Liverpool).

Appearances (47m): Carr K 47, Varadi I 47, Waddle CR 47, Trewick J 45, Brownlie JJ 43, Martin MP 42 (2), Wharton K 33 (5), Saunders W 32, Haddock PM 31 (2), Carney S 30 (1), Mills DJ 23, Barton D 22, Cartwright P 16 (1), Davies IC 15, Halliday B 15, Shinton RT 10 (2), Brown A 5, Walker NS 5, Shoulder A 4 (9), Todd K 3 (2), Bell DS 2, Ferris PJ 0 (2), Pugh KJ 0 (1).

Goals (59g): Varadi I 20, Waddle CR 8, Trewick J 6, Wharton K 5, Mills DJ 4, Brown A 3, Brownlie JJ 3, Barton D 2, Davies IC 2, Shinton RT 2, Todd K 2, Saunders W 1, own goal 1.

Dismissals: 1 player; Brownlie.

MAJOR SIGNINGS

Imre Varadi (Everton) £125,000

FROM THE RANKS

Peter Haddock (Cramlington Jnrs)
Wes Saunders (Durham sch, Ey)
Derek Bell (Newcastle sch)
Paul Ferris (Lisburn Jnrs, NIy)
Kevin Pugh (Northb sch)
Kevin Todd (Ryhope)

TEAM COLOURS Black & white striped shirts, black shorts (Change; all yellow shirts & shorts with green trim)

SEASON 1981-82

Match	Date		FL Division 2						Posn		Carr	Brownlie	Davies	Trewick	Barton	Halliday	Walker	Shoulder	Varadi	Wharton	Waddle	Martin	Haddock	Shinton	Carney	Todd	Saunders	Brown	Pugh	Mills	Cartwright	Bell	Ferris	Match
1	29 Aug	H	**Watford**	L	0	1	(0 1)	19,244			1	2	3	4	5	6	7	8	9	10	11	s6												1
2	05 Sep	A	Queens Park Rangers	L	0	3	(0 1)	14,176	22		1		3	4	5	6	7	8	9	10	11	s10	2											2
3	12 Sep	H	**Cambridge United**	W	1	0	(0 0)	14,666	19	Trewick	1	2	3	4	5	6	7		9	10	11	8		u										3
4	19 Sep	A	Norwich City	L	1	2	(1 1)	14,384	19	Waddle	1	2	3	4	5	6	7		9	10	11	8			s5									4
5	23 Sep	H	**Shrewsbury Town**	W	2	0	(1 0)	13,783	18	Wharton, Shinton	1	2	3	4	5	6		s9	9	10	11	8		7										5
6	26 Sep	H	**Orient**	W	1	0	(0 0)	13,737	16	Trewick	1	2	3	4	5	6		u	9	10	11	8		7										6
7	29 Sep	A	Bolton Wanderers	L	0	1	(0 1)	6,429	16		1	2	3	4	5	6			9	10	11	8		7	u									7
8	03 Oct	A	Cardiff City	W	4	0	(2 0)	5,764	10	Varadi 3, Davies (pen)	1	2	3	4	5	6			9	10	11	8	s10	7										8
9	10 Oct	H	**Derby County**	W	3	0	(2 0)	17,224	6	Wharton, Varadi 2	1	2	3	4	5	6			9	10	11	8		7		s11								9
10	17 Oct	A	Barnsley	L	0	1	(0 1)	18,477	11		1	2	3	4	5	6			9	10	11	8	u	7										10
11	24 Oct	H	**Rotherham United**	D	1	1	(0 0)	19,052	10	Shinton	1	2	3	4	5	6		s10	9	10	11	8		7										11
12	31 Oct	A	Oldham Athletic	L	1	3	(1 3)	9,010	13	Davies	1	2	3	4	5				9	10	11	8	s3	7	6									12
13	07 Nov	A	Chelsea	L	1	2	(0 2)	16,509	14	Waddle	1	2					4		9	10	11	8	6		5		3	7	s9					13
14	14 Nov	H	**Charlton Athletic**	W	4	1	(1 1)	15,254	12	Wharton, Varadi 2, Brown	1	2		4				u	9	10	11	8	6		5		3	7						14
15	21 Nov	H	**Luton Town**	W	3	2	(2 0)	21,084	8	Varadi, Brown 2	1	2		4				s7	9	10	11	8	6		5		3	7						15
16	24 Nov	A	Orient	L	0	1	(0 0)	4,026	8		1	2		4		u		7	9	10	11	8	6		5		3							16
17	28 Nov	A	Grimsby Town	D	1	1	(1 1)	9,256	10	Wharton	1	2		4				u	9	10	11	8	6		5		3	7						17
18	05 Dec	H	**Blackburn Rovers**	D	0	0	(0 0)	18,775	10		1	2		4				s7	9	10	11	8	6		5		3	7						18
19	16 Jan	A	Watford	W	3	2	(1 0)	12,333	11	Varadi, Todd 2	1	2		4					9	10	11	8	6	u	5	7	3							19
20	30 Jan	H	**Norwich City**	W	2	1	(0 0)	14,492	10	Varadi, Mills	1	2		4				u	9	10	11	8	6		5		3			7				20
21	03 Feb	H	**Bolton Wanderers**	W	2	0	(1 0)	14,714	10	Wharton, Trewick (pen)	1			4	5				9	10	11	8	6	u	2		3			7				21
22	06 Feb	A	Cambridge United	L	0	1	(0 1)	5,092	10		1			4	5				9	10	11	8	6	s4	2		3			7				22
23	13 Feb	H	**Cardiff City**	W	2	1	(2 0)	15,129	10	Varadi, Trewick	1	2		4	5			u	9	10	11	8	6				3			7				23
24	20 Feb	A	Shrewsbury Town	D	0	0	(0 0)	4,636	11		1	2		4					9	10	11	8	6		5		3			7	s8			24
25	24 Feb	H	**Sheffield Wednesday**	W	1	0	(1 0)	19,174	8	Varadi	1	2		4				u	9	10	11		6		5		3			7	8			25
26	27 Feb	A	Derby County	D	2	2	(0 1)	12,257	9	Waddle, Varadi	1	2		4				u	9	10	11		6		5		3			7	8			26
27	03 Mar	A	Leicester City	L	0	3	(0 2)	12,497	9		1	2	u	4					9	10	11		6		5		3			7	8			27
28	06 Mar	H	**Barnsley**	W	1	0	(1 0)	18,784	8	Varadi	1	2		4				s7	9		11	8	6		5		3			7	10			28
29	13 Mar	A	Rotherham United	D	0	0	(0 0)	16,905	8		1	2		4					9	u	11	8	6		5		3			7	10			29
30	20 Mar	H	**Oldham Athletic**	W	2	0	(2 0)	18,531	6	Mills, Brownlie	1	2		4				s6	9		11	8	6		5		3			7	10			30
31	27 Mar	H	**Chelsea**	W	1	0	(1 0)	26,994	6	Waddle	1	2		4				u	9		11	8	6		5		3			7	10			31
32	31 Mar	H	**Crystal Palace**	D	0	0	(0 0)	22,151	6		1	2		4				u	9		11	8	6		5		3			7	10			32
33	03 Apr	A	Charlton Athletic	W	1	0	(1 0)	6,357	4	Waddle	1	2		4					9	u	11	8	6		5		3			7	10			33
34	06 Apr	A	Wrexham	L	2	4	(1 1)	4,517	5	Varadi 2	1	2		4					9	s4	11	8	6		5		3			7	10			34
35	10 Apr	H	**Leicester City**	D	0	0	(0 0)	25,777	5		1	2		4	5			s8	9		11	8			6		3			7	10			35
36	12 Apr	A	Sheffield Wednesday	L	1	2	(1 2)	29,917	5	Barton	1	2		4	5				9	u	11	8			6		3			7	10			36
37	17 Apr	A	Luton Town	L	2	3	(1 0)	13,041	7	Mills, Trewick (pen)	1	2		4	5				9	s5	11	8	6				3			7	10			37
38	24 Apr	H	**Grimsby Town**	L	0	1	(0 0)	14,065	9		1	2		4					9	s3	11	8	6		5		3			7	10			38
39	01 May	A	Blackburn Rovers	L	1	4	(0 2)	5,207	10	Varadi	1	2d	3						9	10	11	8	6		5					7		4	s11	39
40	05 May	H	**Queens Park Rangers**	L	0	4	(0 3)	10,748	11		1	2		4					9		11	8	6		5		3			7		10	s4	40
41	08 May	H	**Wrexham**	W	4	2	(2 0)	9,419	9	Waddle, Varadi, Trewick (pen), Brownlie	1	2		4	5	6			9	s3	11	8					3			7	10			41
42	15 May	A	Crystal Palace	W	2	1	(0 0)	8,453	9	Waddle, Mills (pen)	1			4	5	6			9	s4	11	8	2				3			7	10			42
Round			FA Cup																															Round
3	04 Jan	H	**Colchester United**	D	1	1	(1 0)	16,977		Varadi	1	2		4				7	9	10	11	8	6		5	s4	3							3
3r	18 Jan	A	Colchester United	We	4	3	(2 1)	7,505		Waddle, Varadi, Saunders, Brownlie	1	2		4					9	10	11	8	6	u	5	7	3							3r
4	23 Jan	H	**Grimsby Town**	L	1	2	(0 0)	25,632		og (Crosby)	1	2		4					9	10	11	8	6	s4	5	7	3							4
Round			FL Cup																															Round
2(1)	07 Oct	H	**Fulham**	L	1	2	(0 0)	20,247		Barton	1	2	3	4	5	6		s10	9	10	11	8		7										2(1)
2(2)	28 Oct	A	Fulham	L	0	2	(0 1)	7,210			1	2	3	4	5	6		s6	9	10	11	8		7										2(2)

We Won after extra time

DateLine ... 3 Oct: Imre Varadi makes his mark with a hat-trick in a 4-0 victory at Cardiff. **24 Nov:** The 4,026 attendance at Orient is the lowest post-war gate to watch a United League match. **27 March:** Chris Waddle shines and grabs the winner in a clash with Chelsea on Tyneside. **1 May:** Paul Ferris becomes the club's youngest debutant aged 16 years 9 months and 21 days old against Blackburn.

SEASON 1982-83

DIVISION 2

On the Keegan bandwagon

The biggest name in English football over the past decade had been Kevin Keegan; twice European Footballer of the Year and recent skipper of the England side. When the news broke that Keegan was to sensationally join Newcastle United few could believe it. He wanted the challenge to guide United back to the top before hanging up his boots. Arthur Cox now had a personality to build a team around – and furthermore had a gem of a footballer even at 31 years old. And his presence at Gallowgate attracted other valued players to Tyneside, including England colleague Terry McDermott who had left Tyneside for fame and medals with Liverpool back in 1974, as well as experienced Northern Ireland regular David McCreery.

As a result crowds swarmed into St James' Park again, then with a much reduced capacity due to safety restrictions. There was a buzz of anticipation and excitement was at fever pitch. Keegan had a spectacular start, scoring the winner on the first day of the season against QPR, then in a dazzling display at Rotherham when he netted four goals in a 5-1 victory – both in front of the television cameras. United were back in the limelight and loving it, although during the first half of the season results were not as good as the hype.

But there was a vast improvement compared to before and a final surge in the last quarter of the season saw a Keegan-inspired Magpies improve, yet still finish short of promotion, in fifth place, three points from success. They could have sneaked into the last promotion frame but dropping points to little Cambridge United left too much to do and Leicester City pipped the Black'n'Whites for the third promotion slot. Hope remained though as Keegan announced he would give it another go. The club had a one season window to capitalise on the Keegan factor.

Pictured above: Experienced at the top level, David McCreery's non-stop attitude was important in midfield.

Memorabilia CORNER

Kevin Keegan pictured on the cover of the programme, now with the addition of sponsors Newcastle Breweries and the Blue Star.

IN CHARGE

Chairman: Stan Seymour (Jnr)
Manager: Arthur Cox
Captain: Kevin Keegan
Trainer/Coach: Tommy Cavanagh
Club Sponsor: Newcastle Breweries
Kit Supplier: Umbro

ST JAMES' PARK

Average Attendance
Lg 24,166 Lg & Cup 24,572

The old Gallowgate terrace is in the background to this group. Back row, left to right: McFaul (coach), Trewick, Halliday, Haddock, Hardwick, Hedworth, Clarke, Carr, Saunders, Waddle, Martin, Liversedge (physio). Sitting: Cartwright, Anderson, Varadi, Todd, McDermott, Cox (manager), Keegan, Craggs, Carney, McCreery, Wharton.

PLAYER FOCUS Kevin Keegan

Born Armthorpe. Striker, 5'8"
1982 to 1984: 85 app 49 goals.

The day Kevin Keegan arrived on Tyneside in August 1982 for a cut-price £100,000 fee was one of the most important in the history of the club. The catalyst to re-ignite the traditional football hotbed, his charisma rejuvenated Newcastle as he skippered United back to the First Division. Although born in Yorkshire, Keegan hailed from Durham stock and created a unique bond between player and supporter. His skills on the field saw United transformed into an attack minded outfit which displayed sweet football the envy of many. Starting his career with Scunthorpe, Kevin made himself into a mega-star. A hard-working bundle of energy up front, his career took off when he moved to Liverpool in 1971, going on to win every major honour and soon he was England's most influential player as well, appointed captain of his country. After a spell in Germany with Hamburg, twice becoming European Footballer of the Year he returned to England in 1980 with Southampton. Awarded the OBE for his services to the game in the same year he joined the Magpies, Keegan ended his playing career in a spectacular fan-fare at St James' Park at the end of the successful 1983-84 promotion season. Yet fate ensured he returned to Tyneside in February 1992 and Keegan was to make an even greater impact as manager. Creating The Entertainers and almost lifting the Premier League title, he departed in 1997 following five years of magical football which had placed United very firmly among the top sides in Europe. Going on to be in charge of Fulham, Manchester City and England, he was to re-appear for a third spell, again as boss, albeit briefly during 2008.

SEASON REVIEW

Football League Div 2: P42 W18 D13 L11 F75 A53 Pts 67.
Position: 5th (Champions; Queens Park Rangers).
FA Cup: R3 (Winners; Manchester United).
FL Milk Cup: R2 (Winners; Liverpool).

Appearances (46m): Clarke JD 43, Varadi I 43, Keegan JK 41, Wharton K 41 (4), Waddle CR 40, Carr K 36, Anderson JCP 35 (2), McDermott T 35, Martin MP 33 (6), Carney S 30 (2), McCreery D 25 (3), McDonald NR 24 (2), Haddock PM 18, Saunders W 15, Craggs JE 10 (3), Gayle HA 8, Hardwick S 7, Todd K 5 (1), Cartwright P 4, Channon MR 4, Hedworth C 3 (1), Thomas MR 3, Bell DS 1 (1), Ferris PJ 1 (4), Trewick J 1.

Goals (78g): Varadi I 22, Keegan JK 21, McDermott T 7, Waddle CR 7, Wharton K 5, McDonald NR 4, Martin MP 3, Clarke JD 2, Gayle HA 2, Anderson JCP 1, Channon MR 1, Todd K 1, own goals 2.

Dismissals: 3 players; Carney, McDermott (2).

MAJOR SIGNINGS

Kevin Keegan (Southampton) £100,000
Terry McDermott (Liverpool) £100,000
David McCreery (Tulsa Roughnecks) £75,000
John Anderson (Preston NE) free
Jeff Clarke (Sunderland) free
Martin Thomas (Bristol Rovers) £50,000

FROM THE RANKS

Neil McDonald (Carlisle Utd, Es)
Chris Hedworth (Tyneside sch)

TEAM COLOURS Black & white striped shirts, black shorts (Change; all yellow shirts & shorts with blue trim)

SEASON 1982-83

Match	Date	H/A	FL Division 2	Res	F	A	HT	Att	Posn	Scorers	Hardwick	Craggs	Saunders	Trewick	Clarke	Haddock	Keegan	Martin	Varadi	Cartwright	Waddle	Wharton	Anderson	Channon	Bell	McDonald	Todd	Carr	Carney	McDermott	McCreery	Hedworth	Gayle	Ferris	Thomas	Match
1	28 Aug	H	**Queens Park Rangers**	W	1	0	(0 0)	35,718		Keegan	1	2	3	4	5	6	7	8	9	10	11	s4														1
2	01 Sep	A	Blackburn Rovers	W	2	1	(2 0)	14,421	1	Keegan, Martin	1	2	3		5	6	7	4	9	8	11	10	s11													2
3	04 Sep	A	Bolton Wanderers	L	1	3	(0 3)	17,707	3	Keegan (pen)	1	2	3		5	6	7	4	9	8	11	10	u													3
4	08 Sep	H	**Middlesbrough**	D	1	1	(0 0)	27,984	6	Channon	1	2	3		5	6	7	4	9	10	11	u		8												4
5	11 Sep	H	**Chelsea**	D	1	1	(0 1)	29,136	8	Clarke	1	2	3		5	6	7	4	9		11	10		8	s11											5
6	18 Sep	A	Shrewsbury Town	L	1	2	(1 1)	7,907	9	Varadi	1	2	3		5	6	7	4	9			10	s11	8	11											6
7	25 Sep	H	**Barnsley**	L	1	2	(1 2)	24,522	12	Varadi	1	2	3		5	6	7	4	9			10		8		11	s4									7
8	02 Oct	A	Rotherham United	W	5	1	(2 0)	12,436	10	Keegan 4 (1 pen), Todd			3		5		7	4	9			11	2			u	8	1	6	10						8
9	09 Oct	A	Oldham Athletic	D	2	2	(2 2)	11,491	10	Varadi 2			3		5		7	4	9			s8	2				8	1	6d	10d	11					9
10	16 Oct	H	**Fulham**	L	1	4	(0 3)	29,647	13	Keegan (pen)			3		5		7	4	9			s8	2				8	1	6	10	11					10
11	23 Oct	H	**Crystal Palace**	W	1	0	(1 0)	22,616	11	Waddle			3		5	6	7	4	9		11	10	2			u		1			8					11
12	30 Oct	A	Leeds United	L	1	3	(1 1)	26,570	13	Anderson						6	7	4	9		11	3	2					1	5	10	8	s9				12
13	06 Nov	H	**Burnley**	W	3	0	(1 0)	20,961	9	Waddle, Varadi, Keegan						6	7	4	9		11	3	2			s4		1	5	10	8					13
14	13 Nov	A	Leicester City	D	2	2	(1 1)	15,044	10	Keegan 2		u				6	7	4	9		11	3	2					1	5	10	8					14
15	20 Nov	A	Carlisle United	L	0	2	(0 1)	16,276	13			s7			5	4			9		11	3	2				7	1	6	10	8					15
16	27 Nov	H	**Cambridge United**	W	2	0	(2 0)	20,385	10	McDermott, Martin		s9			5			4	9		11	3	2					1		10	8	6	7			16
17	04 Dec	A	Charlton Athletic	L	0	2	(0 1)	10,381	11						5			4			11	3	2					1	s7	10	8	6	9	7		17
18	11 Dec	H	**Wolverhampton Wanderers**	D	1	1	(1 1)	19,595	12	Wharton					5	u		4			9	3	2			11		1		10	8	6	7			18
19	18 Dec	A	Sheffield Wednesday	D	1	1	(1 0)	16,310	15	Varadi					5	6			9		11	3	2			4		1	s2	10	8		7			19
20	27 Dec	H	**Derby County**	W	1	0	(0 0)	30,558	13	Gayle		2			5	6	7	u	9		11	3						1		10	4		8			20
21	28 Dec	A	Grimsby Town	D	2	2	(0 1)	14,983	12	Varadi, Gayle					5	6	7	s4	9		11	3						1	2	10	4		8			21
22	01 Jan	H	**Carlisle United**	D	2	2	(1 1)	28,578	13	Keegan 2		2			5	6	7	s4	9		11	3						1		10	4		8			22
23	03 Jan	H	**Bolton Wanderers**	D	2	2	(0 1)	23,533	12	Waddle, Martin					5	6	7	4			9	3	2			s11		1		10d	11		8			23
24	15 Jan	A	Queens Park Rangers	L	0	2	(0 0)	13,972	14						5		7	4	9		11	3	2			8		1	6	10				s9		24
25	22 Jan	H	**Shrewsbury Town**	W	4	0	(1 0)	19,333	12	Wharton 2, Varadi, Keegan (pen)			3		5		7	4	9		11	10	2			8		1	6					s7		25
26	05 Feb	A	Middlesbrough	D	1	1	(1 1)	25,184	12	Keegan			3		5		7	4	9		11	10	2			8		1	6					u		26
27	19 Feb	H	**Oldham Athletic**	W	1	0	(1 0)	20,689	10	McDermott					5		7	4	9		11	3	2			8		1	6	10				s11		27
28	26 Feb	A	Fulham	D	2	2	(2 1)	14,277	11	McDermott, Varadi		u			5		7	4	9		11	3	2			8		1	6	10						28
29	05 Mar	A	Crystal Palace	W	2	0	(0 0)	10,239	10	Waddle, Varadi					5		7	4	9		11	3	2			8		1	6	10				u		29
30	12 Mar	H	**Leeds United**	W	2	1	(1 0)	24,543	6	Waddle, Keegan (pen)					5		7	4	9		11	3	2			8		1	6	10				u		30
31	19 Mar	A	Burnley	L	0	1	(0 0)	14,069	9						5		7	4	9		11	3	2			8		1	6	10	u					31
32	26 Mar	H	**Leicester City**	D	2	2	(0 1)	22,692	10	McDermott, Keegan					5		7	4	9		11	3	2			8		1	6	10	s8					32
33	02 Apr	H	**Grimsby Town**	W	4	0	(2 0)	20,202	10	Varadi 2, McDonald, Keegan					5		7	4	9		11	3	2			8		1	6	10	s10					33
34	04 Apr	A	Derby County	L	1	2	(0 2)	19,779	10	Waddle					5		7	4	9		11	3	2			8		1	6	10	s4					34
35	09 Apr	H	**Blackburn Rovers**	W	3	2	(2 0)	17,839	10	Waddle, Varadi, og (Metcalf)					5		7		9		11	3	2			8		1	6	10	4			s9		35
36	16 Apr	A	Chelsea	W	2	0	(1 0)	13,446	7	Varadi, Keegan (pen)					5		7	u	9		11	3	2			8		1	6	10	4					36
37	20 Apr	H	**Rotherham United**	W	4	0	(2 0)	18,523	5	McDermott, Varadi, Keegan, Wharton					5		7	s11	9		11	3	2			8		1	6	10	4					37
38	23 Apr	H	**Charlton Athletic**	W	4	2	(1 0)	20,567	5	McDermott, Varadi 2, Wharton					5		7	s2	9		11	3	2			8		1	6	10	4					38
39	30 Apr	A	Cambridge United	L	0	1	(0 1)	7,591	5			2			5		7	s8	9		11	3				8		1	6	10	4					39
40	04 May	A	Barnsley	W	5	0	(1 0)	10,958	5	Varadi 2, McDonald 2, Keegan					5		7	u	9		11	3	2			8			6	10	4				1	40
41	07 May	H	**Sheffield Wednesday**	W	2	1	(0 0)	29,874	5	Varadi, og (Sterland)					5		7	u	9		11	3	2			8			6	10	4				1	41
42	14 May	A	Wolverhampton Wanderers	D	2	2	(2 2)	22,446	5	Varadi, McDonald					5		7	s8	9		11	3	2			8			6	10	4				1	42
Round			FA Cup																																	Round
3	08 Jan	A	Brighton & Hove Albion	D	1	1	(0 0)	17,711		McDermott					5		7	4	9		11	3	2			8		1	6	10			u			3
3r	12 Jan	H	**Brighton & Hove Albion**	L	0	1	(0 0)	32,687							5		7	4	9		11	3	2			8		1	6	10				u		3r
Round			FL Cup (Milk Cup)																																	Round
2(1)	06 Oct	A	Leeds United	W	1	0	(1 0)	24,012		Varadi			3		5		7	4	9			s11	2				8	1	6	10	11					2(1)
2(2)	27 Oct	H	**Leeds United**	Le	1	4	(1 1)	24,984		Clarke		s5	3		5	6	7	4	9		11	10	2					1			8					2(2)

Le Lost after extra time

DateLine ... 28 Aug: Kevin Keegan marks his sensational arrival at St James' Park with the winner against QPR. **2 Oct:** United are on the right tracks under the glare of the BBC as they win 5-1 at Rotherham. **9 Oct:** McDermott and Carney ordered off against Oldham Athletic. **7 June:** United lift the Japan Cup in Tokyo after a 0-0 draw with Brazilian club Botafogo.

SEASON 1983-84

DIVISION 2

The Pied Piper signs off for now

With Kevin Keegan signing up for another season, labelled his last as a player, United had one opportunity to capitalise on his undoubted ability and aura. Two factors made sure the Magpies did so. One of the side effects of the Keegan-show was the development of local lad Chris Waddle from a raw Northern League winger into a real top-class find in the making. He was to flourish in season 1983-84 alongside his tutor, while the return of Newcastle-born Peter Beardsley to Tyneside, gave United an attack few defences could cope with.

The bookies not surprisingly made the Magpies favourites. By the time the new front trio settled, Newcastle began to turn on the style – the past and future England players scoring 66 goals in the process. Many of the displays were exhibition displays, notably a 5-0 demolition of Manchester City in October. It wasn't all plain sailing, but cultured defender Glenn Roeder steadied the defence and when the crunch of the season arrived during April, United were in a perfect spot, in third place. Earlier victories over Portsmouth and at Maine Road in another great show against Manchester City set Newcastle up nicely. Three successive wins over Leeds and Swansea on Tyneside, and at The Valley against Charlton, gave the Magpies the promotion impetus. On Easter Monday, United trounced Carlisle 5-1 at St James' Park and signalled a promotion charge. Despite dropping points at Cambridge, Newcastle bounced back to hit Derby County by four goals and picked up the required point at Huddersfield before the promotion party started against Brighton on Tyneside.

Keegan signed off in that match with style, and after a high-profile farewell against Liverpool. He was whisked out of Gallowgate in a helicopter and was gone as suddenly as he arrived. The Pied Piper of Tyneside was to return though when the club was again in need of inspiration.

Pictured above: Between the posts, Kevin Carr became United's regular 'keeper over five seasons.

Memorabilia CORNER

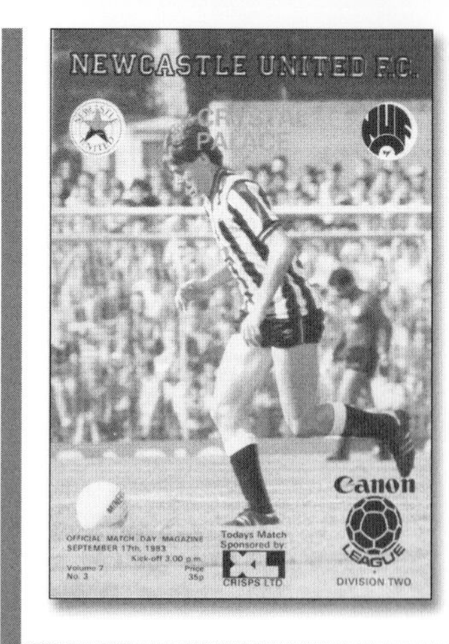

One player to flourish in 1983-84 was Chris Waddle, featured on the programme cover shot.

IN CHARGE

Chairman: Stan Seymour (Jnr)
Manager: Arthur Cox
Captain: Kevin Keegan
Trainer/Coach: Willie McFaul
Club Sponsor: Newcastle Breweries
Kit Supplier: Umbro

ST JAMES' PARK

Average Attendance
Lg 29,811 Lg & Cup 29,418

United's promotion squad before the start of the season. Back row, left to right: McFaul (coach), Carney, McDonald, Saunders, Thomas, Clarke, Carr, Waddle, Hedworth, Haddock, Liversedge (physio). Sitting: Anderson, Varadi, Ryan, Keegan, Cox (manager), McDermott, McCreery, Trewick, Wharton.

PLAYER FOCUS Terry McDermott

Born Kirkby. Midfield, 5'9"
1973 to 1984: 167 app 23 goals.

Signing for United initially as a virtual unknown link-man from lower division Bury in January 1973 for a bargain £25,000 fee, Terry McDermott rapidly developed into one of the leading midfielders not only in England, but in the whole of Europe. With a great engine, Terry quickly impressed all on Tyneside and after outstanding displays as United reached the FA Cup final in 1974, moved back to his native Merseyside when he joined Liverpool for £170,000 in November 1974. At Anfield Terry won the lot; not least three European Cups, four titles and 25 caps for England. With the ability to time late runs into the box, McDermott was frequently on the scoresheet, netting many stunning goals. Full of running and possessing vision and know-how to create an opening or get into a scoring position himself, McDermott was voted both Footballer of the Year and Player of the Year. He returned to Gallowgate as a 30-year-old in September 1982 to link up with Kevin Keegan and helped secure promotion in 1984 before departing again following a contract dispute. Settling on Tyneside, he was then assistant to no fewer than five different United managers during the period from 1992 to 2008. Hugely popular on both Merseyside and Tyneside, he later became Lee Clark's experienced assistant in the managerial team at Huddersfield Town. His sons Neale and Greg both began a career in the game with the Magpies while Terry also won trophies at the end of his playing career with Apoel in Cyprus.

SEASON REVIEW

Football League Div 2: P42 W24 D8 L10 F85 A53 Pts 80.
Position: 3rd, Promoted (Champions; Chelsea).
FA Cup: R3 (Winners; Everton).
FL Milk Cup: R2 (Winners; Liverpool).

Appearances (45m): McDermott T 45, Waddle CR 45, Anderson JCP 44, Keegan JK 44, McCreery D 43, Wharton K 41 (3), Beardsley PA 37 (1), Carney S 34 (1), Thomas MR 26, Ryan JB 25, Roeder GV 24, Carr K 19, Saunders W 19, Clarke JD 14, Trewick J 14 (2), McDonald NR 10 (3), Mills DJ 10 (8), Haddock PM 1 (2).

Goals (87g): Keegan JK 28, Beardsley PA 20, Waddle CR 18, McDermott T 7, Mills DJ 5, Wharton K 4, Anderson JCP 1, Ryan JB 1, Trewick J 1, own goals 2.

Dismissals: 0 players.

MAJOR SIGNINGS

Peter Beardsley (Vancouver Whitecaps) £120,000
Glenn Roeder (QPR) £120,000
John Ryan (Oldham Ath) £225,000
Malcolm Brown (Huddersfield Town) £100,000
David Mills (Sheffield Wed) exchange

FROM THE RANKS

None

TEAM COLOURS Black & white striped shirts, black shorts (Change; silver-grey shirts with a black pin-stripe, silver-grey shorts)

SEASON 1983-84

Match	Date		FL Division 2 (Canon)				HT	Att	Posn	Scorers	Carr	Anderson	Ryan	McCreery	Clarke	Carney	Keegan	McDonald	Mills	McDermott	Waddle	Wharton	Thomas	Trewick	Beardsley	Saunders	Haddock	Roeder	Match
1	27 Aug	A	Leeds United	W	1	0	(1 0)	30,806		Anderson	1	2	3	4	5	6	7	8	9	10	11	s1							1
2	29 Aug	H	**Shrewsbury Town**	L	0	1	(0 1)	29,140				2	3	4	5	6	7	8	9	10	11	s8	1						2
3	03 Sep	H	**Oldham Athletic**	W	3	0	(1 0)	22,573	3	Waddle, McDermott, Mills		2	3	4	5	6	7	8	9	10	11	u	1						3
4	06 Sep	A	Middlesbrough	L	2	3	(0 1)	19,648	7	Mills, Keegan		2	3	4	5	6	7	8	9	10	11	s8	1						4
5	10 Sep	A	Grimsby Town	D	1	1	(0 1)	9,000	9	Keegan		2	3	4	5	6	7		9	10	11	8	1	u					5
6	17 Sep	H	**Crystal Palace**	W	3	1	(1 0)	22,869	7	Waddle, Keegan, Ryan		2	3	4	5	6	7		9	10	11	8	1	s8					6
7	24 Sep	A	Barnsley	D	1	1	(0 0)	14,085	7	Waddle		2	3	4	5	6	7		9	10	11	8	1		s5				7
8	01 Oct	H	**Portsmouth**	W	4	2	(3 0)	25,488	4	Wharton, Waddle 2, Keegan (pen)		2	3	4		6	7		s9	10	9	11	1		8	5			8
9	08 Oct	H	**Charlton Athletic**	W	2	1	(0 1)	23,329	4	Keegan 2		2	3	4		6	7		s11	10	9	11	1		8	5			9
10	16 Oct	A	Swansea City	W	2	1	(1 0)	9,807	3	Wharton, Mills		2	3	4		6	7		s9	10	9	11	1		8	5			10
11	19 Oct	A	Cardiff City	W	2	0	(1 0)	9,926	2	Beardsley, Keegan		2	3	4		6	7		u	10	9	11	1		8	5			11
12	29 Oct	H	**Manchester City**	W	5	0	(2 0)	33,675	2	Waddle, Beardsley 3, Keegan		2	3	4		6	7		u	10	9	11	1		8	5			12
13	05 Nov	H	**Fulham**	W	3	2	(1 1)	31,660	2	Wharton, Keegan, Mills		2	3	4		6	7		s5	10	9	11	1		8	5			13
14	12 Nov	A	Chelsea	L	0	4	(0 2)	30,638	3			2	3	4		6	7		s4	10	9	11	1		8	5			14
15	19 Nov	A	Sheffield Wednesday	L	2	4	(1 1)	41,134	4	McDermott, Keegan (pen)		2	3			6	7	4	u	10	9	11	1		8	5			15
16	26 Nov	H	**Cambridge United**	W	2	1	(1 0)	25,065	3	Beardsley, Keegan (pen)		2	3			6	7	4	u	10	9	11	1		8	5			16
17	03 Dec	A	Derby County	L	2	3	(2 0)	18,691	4	Waddle, Keegan			3	4		6	7	s4		10	9	11	1		8	5	2		17
18	10 Dec	H	**Huddersfield Town**	W	5	2	(2 2)	25,747	3	McDermott, Waddle 2, Beardsley, Keegan		2	3	4		6	7		s3	10	9	11	1		8	5			18
19	17 Dec	A	Brighton & Hove Albion	W	1	0	(0 0)	13,896	3	Waddle		2		4		6	7	u	11	10	9	3	1		8	5			19
20	26 Dec	H	**Blackburn Rovers**	D	1	1	(0 1)	33,622	3	Waddle		2		4			7	s11	11	10	9	3	1		8	5		6	20
21	27 Dec	A	Carlisle United	L	1	3	(1 1)	14,756	4	Waddle		2		4		11	7			10	9	3	1	u	8	5		6	21
22	31 Dec	A	Oldham Athletic	W	2	1	(1 0)	8,518	4	Keegan 2		2	3	4			7	8		10	9	11	1	s9		5		6	22
23	02 Jan	H	**Barnsley**	W	1	0	(1 0)	29,842	3	Waddle		2	3	4			7	u		10	9	11	1		8	5		6	23
24	21 Jan	A	Crystal Palace	L	1	3	(0 3)	9,464	4	Beardsley	1	2	3	4	5		7	u		10	9	11			8			6	24
25	04 Feb	A	Portsmouth	W	4	1	(2 0)	18,686	4	Beardsley 2, Keegan 2	1	2	11	4	5	s11	7			10	9	3			8			6	25
26	11 Feb	H	**Grimsby Town**	L	0	1	(0 1)	28,633	5		1	2		4	5	u	7	11		10	9	3			8			6	26
27	18 Feb	A	Manchester City	W	2	1	(2 0)	41,767	4	Beardsley, Keegan	1	2		4	5	u	7			10	9	3		11	8			6	27
28	25 Feb	H	**Cardiff City**	W	3	1	(2 0)	27,964	4	Waddle, Keegan 2 (1 pen)	1	2		4	5		7		u	10	9	3		11	8			6	28
29	03 Mar	A	Fulham	D	2	2	(1 2)	12,290	3	Beardsley, Keegan		2		4	5	u	7			10	9	3	1	11	8			6	29
30	10 Mar	H	**Chelsea**	D	1	1	(0 0)	35,544	3	McDermott	1	2		4	5		7		u	10	9	3		11	8			6	30
31	17 Mar	H	**Middlesbrough**	W	3	1	(1 1)	30,421	4	McDermott, Beardsley, Keegan	1	2		4		5	7		u	10	9	3		11	8			6	31
32	24 Mar	A	Shrewsbury Town	D	2	2	(0 0)	8,313	3	Keegan, og (Johnson)	1	2		4		5	7		u	10	9	3		11	8			6	32
33	28 Mar	H	**Leeds United**	W	1	0	(1 0)	31,222	3	og (Irwin)	1	2		4		5	7			10	9	3		11	8		u	6	33
34	31 Mar	H	**Swansea City**	W	2	0	(0 0)	27,329	3	Beardsley, Wharton	1	2		4		5	7			10	9	3		11	8		u	6	34
35	07 Apr	A	Charlton Athletic	W	3	1	(1 1)	15,289	3	McDermott, Waddle, Beardsley	1	2		4		5	7			10	9	3		11	8		u	6	35
36	14 Apr	H	**Sheffield Wednesday**	L	0	1	(0 0)	36,288	3		1	2		4		5	7			10	9	3		11	8		u	6	36
37	20 Apr	A	Blackburn Rovers	D	1	1	(0 0)	19,196	3	Trewick	1	2		4		5	7			10	9	3		11	8		s11	6	37
38	23 Apr	H	**Carlisle United**	W	5	1	(2 0)	33,458	3	Waddle, Beardsley 2, Keegan 2	1	2		4		5	7	11	u	10	9	3			8			6	38
39	28 Apr	A	Cambridge United	L	0	1	(0 1)	7,720	3		1	2		4		5	7	11		10	9	3			8		s11	6	39
40	05 May	H	**Derby County**	W	4	0	(2 0)	35,866	3	Waddle, Beardsley 2, Keegan	1	2		4		5	7		u	10	9	3		11	8			6	40
41	07 May	A	Huddersfield Town	D	2	2	(2 2)	25,101	3	Mills, Beardsley	1	2		4		5			8	10	9	3		11	7		u	6	41
42	12 May	H	**Brighton & Hove Albion**	W	3	1	(1 1)	36,286	3	Keegan, Waddle, Beardsley	1	2		4		5	7		u	10	9	3		11	8			6	42
Round			FA Cup																										Round
3	06 Jan	A	Liverpool	L	0	4	(0 2)	33,566				2	3	4			7	s11		10	9	11	1		8	5		6	3
Round			FL Cup (Milk Cup)																										Round
2(1)	05 Oct	H	**Oxford United**	D	1	1	(0 1)	21,184		McDermott		2	3	4		6	7		s11	10	9	11	1		8	5			2(1)
2(2)	26 Oct	A	Oxford United	L	1	2	(0 2)	13,040		Keegan		2	3	4		6	7		s11	10	9	11	1		8	5			2(2)

DateLine ... 16 Oct: United face Swansea on a Sunday, the club's first fixture on the Sabbath, a 2-1 victory. **29 Oct:** A landmark 5-0 win over Manchester City shows United are determined to gain promotion. **5 May:** A 4-0 triumph in the sun over Derby County at St James' Park all but secures promotion. **7 May:** Newcastle gain a point in a 2-2 draw at Huddersfield and return to the top flight. **12 May:** The promotion party continues as Brighton are beaten 3-1 in Keegan's last senior game. **17 May:** A capacity crowd gives Keegan a send-off in a Farewell match against Liverpool.

Big Jack fills the breach

With the Black'n'Whites proudly back in the First Division, United should have been looking forward positively to a new era. Yet not long after the celebrations had died down manager Arthur Cox ran into a contract dispute with Chairman Stan Seymour. Astonishingly, differences could not be resolved and Cox headed south to take charge of Derby County. Several times in the past Newcastle's fans and the local media shouted loud and hard for a big-name manager to take the helm at St James' Park. The sudden departure of Cox on the eve of the new season pushed United's directorate to appoint someone all were familiar with, and a local hero at that, Jack Charlton, recently boss of Sheffield Wednesday.

The England World Cup winner filled the breach and knuckled down to make sure United stayed in the First Division. Without the flair and razzmatazz of Keegan, Charlton relied on the further development of Beardsley and especially of Waddle who rapidly rose to England recognition. United's boss also brought in lanky strikers in George Reilly and Tony Cunningham and this made sure the ball was more often in the air, tactics which did not go down too well. Yet Charlton achieved his objective with comfort, United finishing 14th in the table. In the process he also guided United to a rip-roaring New Year's Day derby success over Sunderland at Gallowgate. Peter Beardsley – not far behind Waddle in international recognition – grabbed a hat-trick in a match which saw six booked and two Wearsiders sent-off. There was also the assurance of more talent being developed as United's kids lifted the FA Youth Cup – with a very special teenager making the headlines, Paul Gascoigne. But the summer brought despair; Chris Waddle decided he needed to move to further his career, joining Tottenham in a big deal – the first of three Geordie superstars to head south in quick succession.

Pictured above: Malcolm Brown arrived with a first-class reputation at full-back, but was sidelined by injury.

Memorabilia CORNER

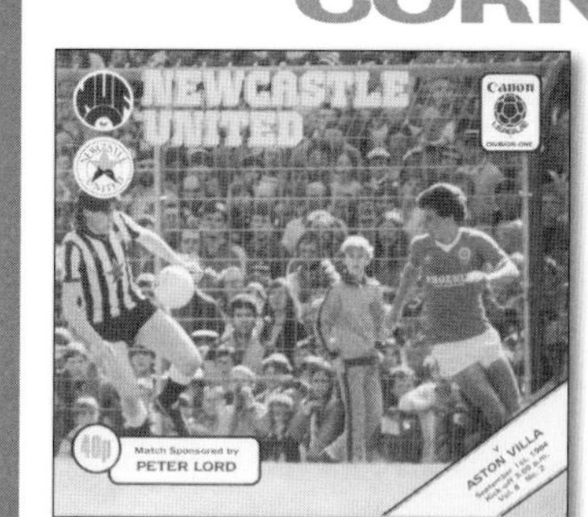

Programme from an early home fixture of the 1984-85 season, a 3-0 victory gave United top spot.

IN CHARGE

Chairman: Stan Seymour (Jnr)
Manager: Jack Charlton
Captain: Glenn Roeder
Trainer/Coach: Willie McFaul
Club Sponsor: Newcastle Breweries
Kit Supplier: Umbro

ST JAMES' PARK

Average Attendance
Lg 26,228 Lg & Cup 25,810

Back in the top flight. Back row, left to right: Hedworth, Carr, Saunders, Thomas, Brown. Middle: McFaul (coach), Melville, Wharton, McCreery, Ryan, McDonald, Anderson, Dawes, Charlton (manager). Sitting: Carver, Ferris, Beardsley, Roeder, Carney, Waddle, Haddock.

PLAYER FOCUS Chris Waddle

Born Gateshead. Forward, 6'0"
1980 to 1985: 191 app 52 goals.

At his peak, Chris Waddle would command the fourth highest transfer fee ever paid at the time when he joined Olympique Marseille from Tottenham for £4.25m in 1989. Winning 62 caps for England, he was something of a late developer in the pro-game and when with Tow Law Town, Chris was given a chance by United during July 1980 as a then gangly, raw winger costing the club a mere £1,000. He soon prospered having an eye for goal and expert ability to whip in a vicious cross. Waddler, as he was to be known, flourished as Newcastle won promotion in 1984 and he took United's famous centre-forward shirt operating as a roving leader across the front line. Deceivingly fast, he twisted and swerved, loved to run at defences and go past the opposition. Reaching England reckoning when at Gallowgate, the Tynesider moved to White Hart Lane during July 1985 for a £590,000 fee and his loss was a huge blow to United. After that Waddle just got better and better, turning into a top international player. He became a massive favourite on the Mediterranean coast, reaching the European Cup final with Marseille in 1991. Chris returned to England with Sheffield Wednesday during 1992. Playing in two Wembley finals and winning the Footballer of the Year award, the Geordie ended his career with a number of clubs when into his thirties. Retiring from first-class football in 1998 he afterwards became a columnist and radio broadcaster for BBC 5 Live. His cousin Alan Waddle appeared for Liverpool and Swansea.

SEASON REVIEW

Football League Div 1: P42 W13 D13 L16 F55 A70 Pts 52.
Position: 14th (Champions; Everton).
FA Cup: R3 (Winners; Manchester United).
FL Milk Cup: R3 (Winners; Norwich City).

Appearances (48m): Brown M 45, Beardsley PA 44, Waddle CR 41 (1), Wharton K 41, Roeder GV 39, McCreery D 38 (2), Anderson JCP 37 (4), Heard TP 36, McDonald NR 35 (7), Carr K 30, Saunders W 27, Clarke JD 25, Megson GJ 21 (1), Thomas MR 18, Reilly GG 14, Cunningham AE 13, Carney S 8, Ryan JB 6, Baird IJ 4 (1), Haddock PM 3, Hedworth C 2, Allon JB 1, Ferris PJ 0 (6), Gascoigne PJ 0 (2).

Goals (63g): Beardsley PA 17, Waddle CR 16, McDonald NR 8, Wharton K 7, Reilly GG 3, Heard TP 2, Megson GJ 2, Anderson JCP 1, Baird IJ 1, Carney S 1, Cunningham AE 1, Ferris PJ 1, McCreery D 1, own goals 2.

Dismissals: 0 players.

MAJOR SIGNINGS

Gary Megson (Nottingham Forest) £110,000
George Reilly (Watford) £200,000
Tony Cunningham (Manchester City) £75,000
Tim Heard (Sheffield Wed) exchange

FROM THE RANKS

Paul Gascoigne (Dunston Jnrs)
Joe Allon (Tyneside sch, Ey)

TEAM COLOURS Black & white striped shirts, black shorts (Change; silver-grey shirts with a black pin-stripe, silver-grey shorts)

SEASON 1984-85

Match	Date		FL Division 1 (Canon)		Score	HT	Att	Posn	Scorers	Carr	Brown	Ryan	Carney	Roeder	Saunders	McDonald	Wharton	Waddle	Beardsley	McCreery	Allon	Anderson	Ferris	Haddock	Heard	Hedworth	Clarke	Megson	Baird	Thomas	Cunningham	Reilly	Gascoigne	Match
1	25 Aug	A	Leicester City	W	3 2	(1 1)	18,636		McCreery, Waddle, Carney	1	2	3	4	5	6	7	8	9	10	11		u												1
2	27 Aug	H	**Sheffield Wednesday**	W	2 1	(1 1)	29,673		Beardsley (pen), Wharton	1	2	3	4	5	6	7	8	9	10	11		s11												2
3	01 Sep	H	**Aston Villa**	W	3 0	(0 0)	31,591	1	Beardsley, Waddle 2	1	2	3	4	5	6	7	8	9	10	11		u												3
4	04 Sep	A	Arsenal	L	0 2	(0 1)	37,078	1		1	2	3	4	5	6	7	8	9	10	11		u												4
5	08 Sep	A	Manchester United	L	0 5	(0 1)	54,915	5		1	2	3	4	5	6	7	8	9	10	11		s3												5
6	15 Sep	H	**Everton**	L	2 3	(1 1)	29,452	10	Beardsley (pen), Wharton	1	2	3	4	5	6	7	8	9	10	11			s4											6
7	22 Sep	A	Queens Park Rangers	D	5 5	(4 0)	14,144	9	Waddle 3, Wharton, McDonald	1	2			6	3	7	8	9	10	11		5	u	4										7
8	29 Sep	H	**West Ham United**	D	1 1	(1 0)	29,966	10	Beardsley	1	2			6	3	7	8	9	10	11		5	u		4									8
9	06 Oct	H	**Ipswich Town**	W	3 0	(2 0)	25,677	7	Waddle, Heard, og (Burley)	1	2			6	3	7	8	9	10	11		5	u		4									9
10	13 Oct	A	Coventry City	D	1 1	(0 0)	14,091	7	Beardsley (pen)	1	2			6	3	7	8	9	10	11		5	u		4									10
11	20 Oct	H	**Nottingham Forest**	D	1 1	(0 1)	28,328	9	Wharton	1	2				3	7	8	9	10	11		5	s6		4	6								11
12	27 Oct	A	Watford	D	3 3	(1 0)	18,753	10	Beardsley, Wharton, McDonald	1	2				3	7	8	9	10	11		5	u		4		6							12
13	03 Nov	A	Luton Town	D	2 2	(1 1)	10,009	11	Beardsley, Heard	1	2				3	7	8	9	10	11		5	u		4		6							13
14	10 Nov	H	**Chelsea**	W	2 1	(2 0)	24,542	8	Waddle, McDonald	1	2				3	7	8	9	10	11		5	s9		4		6							14
15	18 Nov	H	**Liverpool**	L	0 2	(0 1)	27,015	11		1	2			6	3	7	8	9	10	11		5	s7		4									15
16	24 Nov	A	Southampton	L	0 1	(0 0)	18,895	14		1	2			6	3	7	8	9	10	11		5			4			s10						16
17	01 Dec	H	**Stoke City**	W	2 1	(1 0)	21,564	12	Waddle, Anderson (pen)	1	2			6	3	s10	8	9		11	10	5			4			7						17
18	08 Dec	A	Tottenham Hotspur	L	1 3	(0 0)	29,695	13	Waddle	1	2			6	3	s4	8	9	10	11		5			4			7						18
19	15 Dec	H	**Norwich City**	D	1 1	(0 1)	20,423	14	Waddle	1	2			6	3		8	9	10	11		5	u		4			7						19
20	22 Dec	A	Aston Villa	L	0 4	(0 2)	14,491	14		1	2					8	11	9	u	4		5			3		6	7	10					20
21	26 Dec	A	West Bromwich Albion	L	1 2	(0 1)	20,248	16	Baird	1	2		u	4		11	8	9				5			3		6	7	10					21
22	29 Dec	H	**Arsenal**	L	1 3	(0 1)	27,828	18	Beardsley (pen)	1	2			4			8	9	10	11		5			3		6	7	s11					22
23	01 Jan	H	**Sunderland**	W	3 1	(1 0)	36,529	17	Beardsley 3 (1 pen)	1	2		u		3	11	8		10			5			4		6	7	9					23
24	12 Jan	A	Everton	L	0 4	(0 2)	32,156	17		1	2			4	3	s5	8	9		11		5					6	7	10					24
25	02 Feb	A	West Ham United	D	1 1	(0 1)	17,723	18	Waddle		2		u	6		7	3	9	10	11					4		5	8		1				25
26	09 Feb	H	**Manchester United**	D	1 1	(0 1)	32,555	16	Beardsley		2			6		4	3	9	10			u			11		5	7		1	8			26
27	16 Feb	A	Chelsea	L	0 1	(0 1)	21,806	16			2			6		7	3		10	4		s4			11		5	8		1	9			27
28	23 Feb	H	**Luton Town**	W	1 0	(0 0)	24,515	14	Wharton		2			6		u	3	9	10						11		5	4		1	8	7		28
29	02 Mar	H	**Watford**	W	3 1	(1 0)	24,875	12	Cunningham, Reilly, Megson		2			6				9	10	u		3			11		5	4		1	8	7		29
30	09 Mar	A	Nottingham Forest	D	0 0	(0 0)	17,425	12			2			6				9	10	u		3			11		5	4		1	8	7		30
31	20 Mar	H	**Leicester City**	L	1 4	(0 1)	21,764	13	Beardsley		2			6				9	10	s4		3			11		5	4		1	8	7		31
32	23 Mar	A	Ipswich Town	D	1 1	(0 0)	14,366	14	McDonald		2			6		7		s9	10	4		3			11		5			1	8	9		32
33	30 Mar	A	Sheffield Wednesday	L	2 4	(1 2)	26,525	15	Beardsley (pen), Waddle		2			6		s9		9	10	4		3			11		5			1	8	7		33
34	06 Apr	H	**West Bromwich Albion**	W	1 0	(0 0)	22,694	15	Beardsley		2			6		s7			10	4		3			11		5	7		1	8	9		34
35	08 Apr	A	Sunderland	D	0 0	(0 0)	28,246	15			2			6		7			10	4		3			11		5			1	8	9	u	35
36	13 Apr	H	**Queens Park Rangers**	W	1 0	(0 0)	21,733	12	Reilly		2			6		7	3		10			5			11			4		1	8	9	s9	36
37	17 Apr	H	**Coventry City**	L	0 1	(0 1)	19,577	12			2			6		s8	3		10	4		5			11			7		1	8	9		37
38	20 Apr	A	Liverpool	L	1 3	(0 0)	34,733	14	McDonald		2			6		s7	3	9	10	4		5			11			7		1		8		38
39	27 Apr	H	**Southampton**	W	2 1	(0 1)	20,845	14	Reilly, McDonald		2			6		7	3	9	10	4		s2			11		5			1		8		39
40	04 May	A	Stoke City	W	1 0	(1 0)	7,088	12	og (Dyson)					6		7	3	9	10	4		2			11		5			1		8	u	40
41	06 May	H	**Tottenham Hotspur**	L	2 3	(1 1)	29,652	13	Beardsley 2 (2 pens)					6		7	3	9	10	4		2			11		5			1		8	s4	41
42	11 May	A	Norwich City	D	0 0	(0 0)	18,399	14			u			6		7	3	9	10	4		2			11		5			1	8			42
Round			**FA Cup**																															**Round**
3	06 Jan	A	Nottingham Forest	D	1 1	(1 0)	23,582		Megson	1	2				3	11	8	9	10	u		5			4		6	7						3
3r	09 Jan	H	**Nottingham Forest**	Le	1 3	(1 1)	26,383		Waddle	1	2				3	11	8	9	10	s4		5			4		6	7						3r
Round			**FL Cup (Milk Cup)**																															**Round**
2(1)	26 Sep	H	**Bradford City**	W	3 1	(1 0)	18,884		Wharton, McDonald, Ferris	1	2			6	3	7	8	9	10	11		5	s4	4										2(1)
2(2)	10 Oct	A	Bradford City	W	1 0	(0 0)	10,210		Waddle	1	2			6	3	7	8	9	10	11		5	u	4										2(2)
3	30 Oct	A	Ipswich Town	D	1 1	(1 0)	15,084		McDonald	1	2		4	6	3	7	8	9	10	11		5	u											3
3r	07 Nov	H	**Ipswich Town**	L	1 2	(1 1)	23,372		Waddle	1	2		4		3	7	8	9	10	11		5	s4			6								3r

Le — Lost after extra time

DateLine ... 25 Aug: Jack Charlton takes charge for the first time and sees United win 3-2 at Leicester. **1 Sept:** A 3-0 win over Aston Villa takes United to top spot in the table for the first time since 1950.
22 Sept: On QPR's *Astroturf* pitch an amazing 5-5 draw with the Londoners is played out. **6 Oct:** George Burley scores a 20 second own-goal for United against Ipswich.
1 Jan: Sunderland are crushed 3-1 on Tyneside and Peter Beardsley strikes a hat-trick while the Red'n'Whites have two men sent-off. **13 April:** Paul Gascoigne appears in United's senior shirt for the first time against QPR.
10 May: The Geordies lift the FA Youth Cup against Watford, 4-1 on aggregate.

SEASON 1985-86

DIVISION 1

All change again in the hot-seat

Jack Charlton commanded much respect in the game, both for his football know-how and also his forthright manner. He was up-front and open with his views. A Newcastle United supporter as a lad in Ashington, he had the club at heart, but he would manage the Magpies his way or not at all. After losing the star quality of Chris Waddle to Spurs, and then being criticised for not bringing first-rate acquisitions to the squad in the close-season, a barrage of disapproval rained down from the terraces and stands towards the manager during a pre-season friendly with Sheffield United. That was enough for Big Jack. He walked out and could not be persuaded to stay. Newcastle had to find another manager.

Long-serving ex-goalkeeper and now coach Willie McFaul took control and he soon reverted back to a more fluent and precise style of football. Beardsley followed Waddle into the England team while Paul Gascoigne made a big impact in his first full season in senior action. United's line-up also had a distinct local flavour to it. Apart from Beardsley and Gascoigne, the likes of Wharton, McDonald, Haddock, Stephenson and Joe Allon all featured. McFaul guided the Magpies to a safe mid-table placing, recording along the way a run of five League victories on the bounce during February and March.

However, little progress was made in the League Cup or FA Cup, falling to Oxford United and Brighton. Both clubs were to shock Tyneside for a second time in recent seasons. As the programme came to its close, a wacky contest took place at Upton Park with West Ham United. The Black'n'Whites fielded three goalkeepers – Martin Thomas who was injured, then stand-ins Chris Hedworth and Peter Beardsley – as the Hammers scored eight goals. Cup elimination and that extraordinary defeat apart, it had been a campaign of consolidation. The big test was to take the next step forward.

Pictured above: Neil McDonald was another Tyneside raised player to impress and then move on.

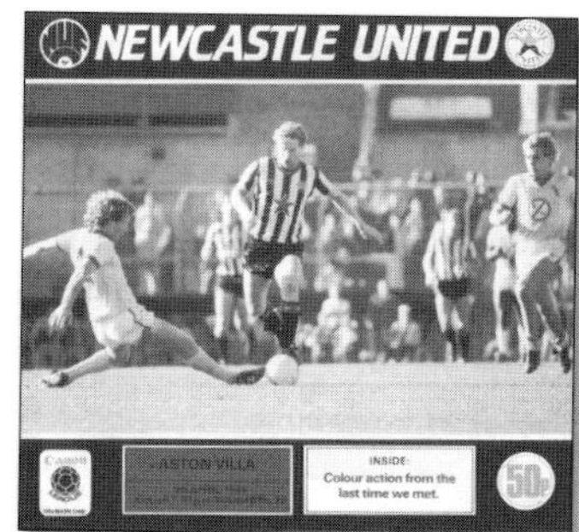

United's programme had now reached 50p, and top level action was in the Canon League.

IN CHARGE

Chairman: Stan Seymour (Jnr)
Manager: Willie McFaul
Captain: Glenn Roeder
Trainer/Coach: Colin Suggett
Club Sponsor: Newcastle Breweries
Kit Supplier: Umbro

ST JAMES' PARK

Average Attendance
Lg 23,434 Lg & Cup 23,306

Willie McFaul was now boss. Back row, left to right: McCreery, Davies, Haddock, Saunders, Gascoigne, McKinnon, Anderson. Middle: Clarke, Scott, McDonald, Thomas, Kelly, Reilly, Cunningham, Hedworth. Sitting: Wright (physio), Wharton, Ferris, Heard, Roeder, Beardsley, Allon, Megson, McFaul (manager).

SEASON REVIEW

Football League Div 1: P42 W17 D12 L13 F67 A72 Pts 63.
Position: 11th (Champions; Liverpool).
FA Cup: R3 (Winners; Liverpool).
FL Milk Cup: R3 (Winners; Oxford United).

Appearances (46m): Roeder GV 46, Beardsley PA 45, Clarke JD 45, McCreery D 42 (2), Anderson JCP 41, Thomas MR 36, Gascoigne PJ 32 (3), Bailey JA 29, Stewart IE 29 (3), McDonald NR 26 (5), Stephenson P 23, Whitehurst W 21, Reilly GG 19, Davies A 16 (1), Wharton K 15, Cunningham AE 12 (7), McKellar DN 10, Haddock PM 8, Hedworth C 4, Allon JB 3, Megson GJ 3 (3), McKinnon R 1.

Goals (69g): Beardsley PA 19, Gascoigne PJ 9, Reilly GG 7, Whitehurst W 7, Roeder GV 6, McDonald NR 4, Anderson JCP 3, Clarke JD 3, Cunningham AE 3, Stewart IE 2, Wharton K 2, Allon JB 1, Davies A 1, Stephenson P 1, own goal 1.

Dismissals: 1 player; Gascoigne.

MAJOR SIGNINGS

Ian Stewart (QPR) £150,000
Billy Whitehurst (Hull City) £232,500
Alan Davies (Manchester Utd) £50,000
John Bailey (Everton) £80,000

FROM THE RANKS

Paul Stephenson (St Mary's BC, Ey)
Rob McKinnon (Rutherglen Glencairn)

PLAYER FOCUS Peter Beardsley

Born Newcastle upon Tyne. Forward, 5'8"
1983 to 1997: 326 app 119 goals.

Peter Beardsley was three times at St James' Park as a player, first as a youngster on trial. Born and bred in the city, Peter though made a name for himself with Carlisle United, under Bob Moncur's guidance. He showed then he had mesmerising skills on the ball and was the type of player fans gladly paid to watch. Rejected by Manchester United when starring for Vancouver Whitecaps, he landed on Tyneside to team up with Keegan during September 1983 for £120,000. Beardsley's talent in attack, as well as his tremendous work-rate and enthusiasm, did much to secure promotion in 1984 and then consolidate United back in Division One. Peter reached the England side with the Magpies before switching to Liverpool in a national £1.9m record deal during July 1987. At Anfield he won the title and FA Cup before moving the short distance to Everton. Keegan always admired Peter's brilliance and he rejoined the Magpies in July 1993 for a £1.5m fee and proceeded to become an influential figure as the Black'n'Whites developed into a Premiership force. Beardsley perhaps displayed his best football during that resurgence in both midfield and attack. Scoring over a century of goals for the Magpies, the majority in dazzling fashion with stunning drives, delightful runs and strikes of pure genius, Peter played on until he was over 36 years old in Toon colours. Leaving Gallowgate during August 1997 he played out his career with Bolton, Manchester City, Fulham and Hartlepool. Peter eventually returned to Gallowgate for a fourth time as part of United's junior development staff, becoming reserve team coach in 2010. Nicknamed Pedro and winning 59 caps for England, Beardsley was awarded the MBE in 1995.

TEAM COLOURS Black & white striped shirts, black shorts (Change; silver-grey with a black-white band shirts, silver-grey shorts)

SEASON 1985-86

Match	Date		FL Division 1 (Canon)					Posn		Thomas	Anderson	Wharton	Davies	Clarke	Roeder	McDonald	Megson	Reilly	Beardsley	Gascoigne	McCreery	Stewart	McKinnon	Hedworth	Haddock	Cunningham	Bailey	Allon	Whitehurst	Stephenson	McKellar
1	17 Aug	A	Southampton	D	1 1	(0 1)	16,401		Beardsley (pen)	1	2	3	4	5	6	7	8	9	10	11	s11										
2	21 Aug	H	**Luton Town**	D	2 2	(0 1)	21,933		Roeder, Beardsley	1	2	3		5	6	7	8	9	10	4	s8	11									
3	24 Aug	H	**Liverpool**	W	1 0	(0 0)	29,941	8	Reilly	1	2	3		5	6	7	u	9	10	4	8	11									
4	26 Aug	A	Coventry City	W	2 1	(0 0)	12,097	3	Stewart, Reilly	1	2	3		5	6	7	u	9	10	4	8	11									
5	31 Aug	H	**Queens Park Rangers**	W	3 1	(1 0)	25,219	4	Beardsley, Reilly, McDonald	1	2	3		5	6	7	s11	9	10	4	8	11									
6	04 Sep	A	Manchester United	L	0 3	(0 2)	51,102	6		1	2	3		5	6	7	u	9	10	4	8	11									
7	07 Sep	A	Tottenham Hotspur	L	1 5	(1 2)	23,883	8	Davies	1	2		4	5	6	7		9	10	s3	8	11	3								
8	14 Sep	H	**West Bromwich Albion**	W	4 1	(2 0)	21,902	6	Reilly 2, McDonald, Clarke	1	3		4	5	6	7		9	10	s8	8	11		2							
9	21 Sep	H	**Oxford United**	W	3 0	(0 0)	23,642	4	Gascoigne, Beardsley, McDonald	1	3		4	5	6	7		9	10	s2	8	11		2							
10	28 Sep	A	Arsenal	D	0 0	(0 0)	24,104	4		1	3		4	5	6	7	u		10		8	11			2	9					
11	05 Oct	H	**West Ham United**	L	1 2	(0 2)	26,957	7	Reilly	1	3		4	5	6	7		9	10		8	11			2	u					
12	12 Oct	A	Ipswich Town	D	2 2	(1 2)	12,536	8	Beardsley, McDonald	1	3		4	5	6	7		9	10		8	11			2	u					
13	19 Oct	H	**Nottingham Forest**	L	0 3	(0 1)	23,304	10		1	3		4	5	6	7		9	10		8	11			2	s2					
14	26 Oct	A	Aston Villa	W	2 1	(1 1)	12,633	9	Beardsley, Gascoigne	1	2			5	6	7	s9	9	10	8	4	11					3				
15	02 Nov	H	**Watford**	D	1 1	(0 1)	20,640	8	Gascoigne	1	2			5	6	7		9	10	11	4	s7				8	3				
16	09 Nov	A	Birmingham City	W	1 0	(1 0)	8,162	8	Reilly	1	3		2	5	6	s11		9	10	7	4	11						8			
17	16 Nov	H	**Chelsea**	L	1 3	(1 1)	22,394	8	Roeder	1	2		11	5	6			9	10	7	4	s4					3	8			
18	23 Nov	A	Manchester City	L	0 1	(0 1)	25,179	11		1	2	11	7	5	6	s8		9	10	8	4						3				
19	30 Nov	H	**Leicester City**	W	2 1	(2 0)	17,311	9	Clarke, Beardsley	1	4	8	2	5	6	7			10			11				9	3	u			
20	07 Dec	A	Luton Town	L	0 2	(0 1)	10,319	9		1	7	8	2	5	6				10		4	11				u	3		9		
21	14 Dec	H	**Southampton**	W	2 1	(1 0)	19,340	9	Beardsley, Roeder	1	2	11	8	5	6				10		4	u					3		9	7	
22	21 Dec	A	Liverpool	D	1 1	(1 1)	30,746	9	Beardsley	1	2			5	6	u			10	8	4	11					3		9	7	
23	26 Dec	A	Sheffield Wednesday	D	2 2	(0 1)	30,269	10	Beardsley, Roeder	1	2			5	6	u			10	8	4	11					3		9	7	
24	01 Jan	H	**Everton**	D	2 2	(0 1)	28,031	11	Beardsley, Gascoigne	1	2			5	6	u			10	8	4	11					3		9	7	
25	11 Jan	A	West Bromwich Albion	D	1 1	(1 0)	9,106	10	Wharton	1	2	11		5	6	u			10	8	4						3		9	7	
26	18 Jan	A	Queens Park Rangers	L	1 3	(0 2)	13,159	11	Gascoigne	1	2	11		5	6	s7			10	8	4						3		9	7	
27	01 Feb	H	**Coventry City**	W	3 2	(2 1)	16,785	11	Wharton, Beardsley, Allon	1	2	11		5	6	s8			10	8	4						3	9		7	
28	08 Feb	A	Nottingham Forest	W	2 1	(0 0)	15,388	10	Beardsley 2	1	2	11		5	6	s2			10	8	4					9	3			7	
29	01 Mar	H	**Arsenal**	W	1 0	(0 0)	22,085	10	Roeder	1	2	11		5	6				10	8	4					s10	3		9	7	
30	15 Mar	H	**Ipswich Town**	W	3 1	(0 1)	19,451	9	Beardsley, Whitehurst, Gascoigne		2			5	6	11			10	8	4					s11	3		9	7	1
31	19 Mar	A	Oxford United	W	2 1	(1 0)	10,052	9	Gascoigne, Beardsley		2			5	6	u			10	8	4					11	3		9	7	1
32	22 Mar	H	**Tottenham Hotspur**	D	2 2	(1 1)	31,028	9	Whitehurst, Anderson		2			5	6	u			10	8	4					11	3		9	7	1
33	29 Mar	A	Everton	L	0 1	(0 1)	41,116	9			2			5	6				10	8	4	11				u	3		9	7	1
34	31 Mar	H	**Sheffield Wednesday**	W	4 1	(3 0)	25,714	9	Stephenson, Gascoigne, Beardsley, Whitehurst		2			5	6				10	8	4	11				s11	3		9	7	1
35	05 Apr	A	Watford	L	1 4	(0 2)	14,706	10	og (McClelland)		2			5	6				10	8	4	11				s11	3		9	7	1
36	09 Apr	H	**Aston Villa**	D	2 2	(1 1)	20,435	10	Whitehurst, Gascoigne					5	6				10	8	4	11		2		s11	3		9	7	1
37	12 Apr	H	**Birmingham City**	W	4 1	(1 0)	20,334	9	Beardsley 2, Anderson, Whitehurst	1	2			5	6	11			10	8d	4					u	3		9	7	
38	16 Apr	H	**Manchester United**	L	2 4	(1 3)	32,183	10	Stewart, Cunningham	1				5	6	2			10	8	4	11				s8	3		9	7	
39	19 Apr	A	Chelsea	D	1 1	(1 1)	18,970	10	Anderson		8			5	6	2			10		4	u				11	3		9	7	1
40	21 Apr	A	West Ham United	L	1 8	(0 4)	24,735	10	Whitehurst	1	5				6	2			10		4	s1		8		11	3		9	7	
41	26 Apr	H	**Manchester City**	W	3 1	(0 1)	23,479	10	Clarke, Roeder, Whitehurst					5	6	2			10		4	u			8	11	3		9	7	1
42	03 May	A	Leicester City	L	0 2	(0 1)	13,171	11					u	5	6	2			10		4	11			8	9	3			7	1
Round			FA Cup																												
3	04 Jan	H	**Brighton & Hove Albion**	L	0 2	(0 1)	25,112			1	2			5	6	u			10	8	4	11					3		9	7	
Round			FL Cup (Milk Cup)																												
2(1)	25 Sep	H	**Barnsley**	D	0 0	(0 0)	18,827			1			4	5	6	7	s9	9	10	8	3	11			2						
2(2)	08 Oct	A	Barnsley	Dea	1 1	(1 0)	10,084		Cunningham	1	3		4	5	6	7	u	9		8		11			2	10					
3	30 Oct	A	Oxford United	L	1 3	(1 1)	8,096		Cunningham	1	3		s4	5	6	2	7		10	4	8	11				9					

Dea — Drawn after extra time, tie won on away goals

DateLine ... 17 Aug: Coach Willie McFaul steps up to become boss and takes control against Southampton. **4 Jan:** Brighton knock the Magpies from the FA Cup following controversial refereeing decisions at St James' Park. **21 April:** United concede eight goals at West Ham with three different goalkeepers.

SEASON 1986-87

DIVISION 1

Seeds of revolution in Toon

Newcastle United's ambition – or the lack of it – was a hot topic on Tyneside during the mid-Eighties. The club was heavily criticised for not being able to find a formula both on the field and in the Boardroom that showed they had the drive and purpose to get the club amongst the best in the country. They could develop players, yet had lost first Waddle, and soon Peter Beardsley was to move on, to Liverpool in a record deal. Worse was to follow when new star in the making, Paul Gascoigne, did likewise. All decided to make their way to clubs that could fulfil their personal dream. Grumbles of discontent began to swiftly escalate....and trigger a revolution on Tyneside.

Willie McFaul's second season in charge started in dreadful fashion. They received a lesson by Champions Liverpool on the opening day and went six games without registering a victory, collecting only two points out of 18. They were lodged at the bottom of the table. At the end of November the Tynesiders did show signs that Newcastle could produce the goods, beating Chelsea and West Ham United. The Magpies were perhaps in a false position. What they needed was an influx of experience and new blood. That was provided by the addition of Paul Goddard, an intelligent striker who made the forward line tick.

Newcastle recovered and Goddard's goals – in each of seven successive games, and eight in nine played – as the Magpies rallied, kept United in Division One. With spring approaching they climbed away from the danger zone following an undefeated run of nine games, which included victories over Arsenal and Manchester United. Another success over Chelsea picked up the points that secured their top status.

Newcastle reached Round Five of the FA Cup that year, their first decent run for several seasons. They faced Tottenham – and Chris Waddle – but fell to a single and dubious penalty at White Hart Lane.

Pictured above: Paul Goddard led the line with intelligent play and frequently grabbed important goals.

Memorabilia CORNER

Paul Gascoigne took the eye in 1986-87, United's programme now featured Greenalls Beers.

IN CHARGE

Chairman: Stan Seymour (Jnr)
Manager: Willie McFaul
Captain: Glenn Roeder
Trainer/Coach: Colin Suggett
Club Sponsor: Greenalls Breweries
Kit Supplier: Umbro

ST JAMES' PARK

Average Attendance
Lg 24,750 Lg & Cup 24,554

A new sponsor for United in Greenalls. Back row, left to right: Wharton, Gascoigne, Tinnion, Stephenson, Davies, Anderson. Middle: Suggett (coach), Thomas, McDonald, Whitehurst, Cunningham, Clarke, Allon, Kelly, Wright (physio). Sitting: Bailey, Ferris, Beardsley, McFaul (manager), Roeder, McCreery, Stewart.

PLAYER FOCUS Glenn Roeder

Born Woodford. Centre-half, 6'1"
1983 to 1989: 217 app 10 goals.

A confident and stylish centre-half rated highly by many, Glenn Roeder had led his QPR team out as skipper in a Wembley FA Cup final and appeared for the England B side by the time he headed north for Tyneside from London. A £120,000 purchase in December 1983, he was an influential acquisition as Arthur Cox assembled his 1984 promotion winning line-up. Roeder always wanted to be constructive from the back-line and roused the crowd when he surged forward often displaying a characteristic double-shuffle in his stride when on the ball. Tall and slender, he was a class act as a player and skippered the Black'n'Whites over four seasons. Roeder headed south to join Watford in July 1989 when 33 years old soon joining Leyton Orient. From Essex, he moved into coaching at Brisbane Road and was later to be appointed manager at Gillingham and back at Watford as well as in the Premier League with West Ham United. Roeder returned to Gallowgate as Academy boss during 2005 and later took control of the first-team in February 2006 at the time of crisis. Steering United clear of relegation in season 2005-06, Glenn was in charge for 15 months before being dismissed in May 2007. Roeder was also part of the England coaching staff during 1997 and 1998. During his period in charge at Upton Park, Glenn was rushed to hospital after a game with Middlesbrough suffering from a brain tumour which required major surgery.

SEASON REVIEW

Football League Div 1: P42 W12 D11 L19 F47 A65 Pts 47.
Position: 17th (Champions; Everton).
FA Cup: R5 (Winners; Coventry City).
FL Littlewoods Cup: R2 (Winners; Arsenal).

Appearances (48m): McDonald NR 45 (1), Thomas MR 44, Roeder GV 43, Wharton K 41 (1), Beardsley PA 37, Anderson JCP 36, McCreery D 36, Jackson PA 34, Goddard P 29, Thomas AM 28 (4), Stephenson P 27, Gascoigne PJ 23 (4), Jackson D 19 (7), Cunningham AE 15 (4), Stewart IE 11 (7), Bailey JA 9, Whitehurst W 9 (1), Clarke JD 7, Allon JB 6, Craig AH 6 (1), Davies A 6 (1), Scott KW 5, Kelly GA 4, Tinnion B 3, Wrightson JG 3 (1), Bogie I 1, Nesbit A 1 (3).

Goals (54g): Goddard P 13, Thomas AM 9, McDonald NR 7, Beardsley PA 5, Gascoigne PJ 5, Jackson D 3, Roeder GV 3, Cunningham AE 2, Wharton K 2, Allon JB 1, Anderson JCP 1, Jackson PA 1, Scott KW 1, Stewart IE 1.

Dismissals: 2 players; Anderson, McDonald.

MAJOR SIGNINGS

Peter Jackson (Bradford City) £250,000
Albert Craig (Hamilton) £100,000
Darren Jackson (Meadowbank Thistle) £240,000
Andy Thomas (Oxford Utd) £100,000
Paul Goddard (West Ham Utd) £415,000 club record fee

FROM THE RANKS

Gary Kelly (Lancashire sch)
Kevin Scott (Eppleton CW)
Brian Tinnion (Durham sch)
Ian Bogie (Wallsend BC, Es)
Jeff Wrightson (Wallsend BC)
Tony Nesbit (Sunderland sch)

TEAM COLOURS Black & white striped shirts, black shorts (Change; silver-grey shirts with a black-white band, silver-grey shorts)

SEASON 1986–87

Match	Date	Venue	FL Division 1 (Today League)	Res	Score	HT	Att	Posn	Scorers
1	23 Aug	H	**Liverpool**	L	0 2	(0 1)	33,306		
2	25 Aug	A	Tottenham Hotspur	D	1 1	(0 1)	25,381		Beardsley
3	30 Aug	A	Luton Town	D	0 0	(0 0)	9,254	18	
4	03 Sep	H	**Queens Park Rangers**	L	0 2	(0 0)	23,080	18	
5	06 Sep	H	**Sheffield Wednesday**	L	2 3	(0 2)	22,010	21	Allon, Scott
6	13 Sep	A	Coventry City	L	0 3	(0 1)	11,370	22	
7	20 Sep	H	**Wimbledon**	W	1 0	(0 0)	21,545	20	Gascoigne
8	27 Sep	A	Norwich City	L	0 2	(0 1)	15,735	20	
9	04 Oct	A	Southampton	L	1 4	(1 1)	14,622	22	Thomas A
10	11 Oct	H	**Manchester City**	W	3 1	(1 1)	21,780	21	McDonald (pen), Gascoigne, Cunningham
11	18 Oct	H	**Arsenal**	L	1 2	(0 0)	22,368	21	Stewart
12	25 Oct	A	Aston Villa	L	0 2	(0 2)	14,614	21	
13	01 Nov	H	**Oxford United**	D	0 0	(0 0)	19,622	22	
14	08 Nov	A	Leicester City	D	1 1	(1 0)	9,836	22	McDonald (pen)
15	15 Nov	H	**Watford**	D	2 2	(0 0)	23,645	22	McDonald (pen), Anderson
16	22 Nov	A	Chelsea	W	3 1	(1 1)	14,544	22	Thomas A 2, Beardsley
17	30 Nov	H	**West Ham United**	W	4 0	(2 0)	22,077	18	Thomas A 2, McDonald, Jackson D
18	06 Dec	A	Charlton Athletic	D	1 1	(0 1)	7,333	16	Goddard
19	13 Dec	H	**Nottingham Forest**	W	3 2	(1 1)	26,191	15	Wharton, Thomas A, Beardsley
20	21 Dec	A	Sheffield Wednesday	L	0 2	(0 2)	28,897	17	
21	26 Dec	H	**Everton**	L	0 4	(0 1)	35,079	20	
22	27 Dec	A	Watford	L	0 1	(0 1)	18,011	21	
23	01 Jan	A	Manchester United	L	1 4	(1 2)	43,334	21	Jackson D
24	03 Jan	H	**Coventry City**	L	1 2	(0 1)	22,366	22	McDonald
25	24 Jan	A	Liverpool	L	0 2	(0 0)	38,054	22	
26	07 Feb	H	**Luton Town**	D	2 2	(2 1)	22,437	22	Jackson P, Goddard
27	14 Feb	A	Queens Park Rangers	L	1 2	(0 0)	10,731	22	Goddard
28	28 Feb	A	Wimbledon	L	1 3	(0 1)	6,779	22	Beardsley
29	07 Mar	H	**Aston Villa**	W	2 1	(1 1)	21,224	22	Cunningham, Beardsley
30	21 Mar	A	Manchester City	D	0 0	(0 0)	23,060	22	
31	25 Mar	H	**Tottenham Hotspur**	D	1 1	(0 1)	30,782	22	Goddard
32	28 Mar	H	**Southampton**	W	2 0	(1 0)	22,717	21	Goddard, Gascoigne
33	04 Apr	H	**Leicester City**	W	2 0	(2 0)	23,360	20	Goddard, Wharton
34	08 Apr	H	**Norwich City**	W	4 1	(1 1)	24,534	18	Goddard, Gascoigne, McDonald (pen), Jackson D
35	11 Apr	A	Oxford United	D	1 1	(1 0)	10,526	18	Goddard
36	14 Apr	A	Arsenal	W	1 0	(1 0)	17,353	17	Goddard
37	18 Apr	H	**Manchester United**	W	2 1	(1 1)	32,706	16	Goddard, Roeder
38	20 Apr	A	Everton	L	0 3	(0 0)	43,576	17	
39	25 Apr	H	**Chelsea**	W	1 0	(0 0)	21,962	17	Goddard
40	02 May	A	West Ham United	D	1 1	(1 0)	17,844	17	McDonald (pen)
41	04 May	H	**Charlton Athletic**	L	0 3	(0 2)	26,950	17	
42	09 May	A	Nottingham Forest	L	1 2	(0 2)	17,788	17	Gascoigne
Round			FA Cup						
3	21 Jan	H	**Northampton Town**	W	2 1	(1 0)	23,177		Thomas A, Goddard
4	31 Jan	H	**Preston North End**	W	2 0	(0 0)	30,495		Roeder, Goddard
5	21 Feb	A	Tottenham Hotspur	L	0 1	(0 1)	38,033		
Round			FL Cup (Littlewoods Cup)						
2(1)	23 Sep	A	Bradford City	L	0 2	(0 0)	6,384		
2(2)	08 Oct	H	**Bradford City**	W	1 0	(0 0)	15,893		Roeder
Round			Full Members Cup						
3	03 Dec	A	Everton	L	2 5	(0 4)	7,530		Thomas A 2

Match	Thomas MR	Anderson	Bailey	McCreery	Clarke	Roeder	Davies	Gascoigne	Whitehurst	Beardsley	Wharton	McDonald	Allon	Stewart	Bogie	Scott	Cunningham	Kelly	Thomas AM	Stephenson	Jackson D	Jackson PA	Goddard	Nesbit	Wrightson	Craig	Tinnion
1	1	2	3	4	5	6	7	8	9	10	11	s8															
2	1	2	3	4	5	6	7		9	10	11	8		u													
3	1	2	3	4		6		8	9	10	11	5		u	7												
4	1	2	3	4		6	7	8	9		11	5	10	s11													
5	1	2	3	4			7	8	9			5	10	11	u	6											
6	1	6	3	4	5		7	8	9			2	u	11			10										
7		2	3	4	5	6		8	9			7	u	11				1	10								
8	1	2	3	4	5	6		s2		10		11	9						8	7							
9	1	6		4	5			s4	11	10	3	2	9						8	7							
10		6		4		5		8		10	3	2	u	11			9	1		7							
11		6				5		8		10	3	2		11			9	1	4	7	s11						
12	1	3		4		6		s7		10		2		11			9		8	7		5					
13	1	3		4		6		7		10	s7	2		11			9		8			5					
14	1	2		4		6				10	3	7		11			s11		8			5	9				
15	1	2		4		6				10	3	7					s8		8	11		5	9				
16	1	2		4		6				10	3	7							8	11	s2	5	9				
17	1	2		4		6				10	3	7							8	11	s9	5	9				
18	1	2		4		6				10	3	7							8		11	5	9	s2			
19	1			4		6				10	3	2							8	7	11	5	9	s11			
20	1					6				10	3	2		u					8	7	11	5	9	4			
21	1					6				10	3	2		s7					8	7	11	5	9		4		
22	1					6				10	3	2		u					8	7	11	5	9		4		
23	1			4		6				10	3	2		s7					8	7	11	5	9				
24	1			4		6	2				3	7		s2					8		10	5	9		11		
25	1	4				6				10	3	2		11					8		7	5	9	u			
26	1			4		6				10	3	2					8		7		s4	5	9			11	
27	1					6				10	3	2				4	8		7		u	5	9			11	
28	1				6					10	3	2				4	8		7			5	9		s7	11	
29	1	6		4						10	3	2	8				9			7	s8	5				11	
30	1	11		4		6				10	3	2					9			7	s8	5	8				
31	1	11		4		6		8		10	3	2					s9			7		5	9				
32	1	11		4		6		8		10	3	2					u			7		5	9				
33	1	11		4		6		8		10	3	2								7	u	5	9				
34	1	11		4		6		8		10	3	2								7	s4	5	9				
35	1	11				6		8		10	3	2							s7	7	4	5	9				
36	1	11				6		8		10	3	2							s9	7	4	5	9				
37	1	11				6		8		10	3	2							s10	7	4	5	9				
38	1					6		8			3	2d		s7					10	7	4	5	9				11
39	1	11		4		6		8			3	2					10			u	7	5	9				
40	1	11d		4		6		8			3	2					10				7	5	9			s7	
41	1	2				6		8			3						10		s4	7	9	5				4	11
42	1	2		4		6	s7	8			3						9		10		7	5					11
Round																											
3	1			4		6				10	3	2		s9					8	7	11	5	9	u			
4	1	8		4		6					3	2		11			10		7	u	u	5	9				
5	1			4		6				10	3	2				u	s8		8		7	5	9			11	
Round																											
2(1)	1	2	3	4		6		8	s11	10		7	u	11		5			9								
2(2)		6		4	u	5		8	11	10	3	2	9	s11				1		7							
Round																											
3	1	2		4		6		s11		10	3	7				5			8	11	9			s4			

DateLine ... 20 Sept: At the seventh attempt United record their first win of the season against Wimbledon. **18 April:** Paul Goddard strikes his seventh goal in consecutive matches against Manchester United. **25 April:** Demolition of the Edwardian West Stand at St James' Park begins after the fixture with Chelsea. **25 April:** A 1-0 success over Chelsea makes sure United are safe in a relegation scrap.

SEASON
1987-88
DIVISION 1

Stars continue to head south

Manager Willie McFaul was conscious of the growing flak pointed towards the club. The departure of Peter Beardsley in the close-season for a new British record fee of almost £2m made sure the club had to appease supporters in some degree. McFaul was given funds, albeit not the level of cash received for Beardsley, and pulled off an eye-catching deal by bringing the very first Brazilian to top level football in England. Centre-forward Mirandinha arrived on Tyneside to a fanfare of waving Brazilian flags and yellow shirts. He certainly made an initial impact, but as the months unfolded it was clear he alone was not going to make a difference to United's fortunes. And more bad news was on the way for Toon followers. They were to lose another star to a so-called more proactive club.

To start with though Mirandinha teamed up with the blossoming Geordie talent of Paul Gascoigne and following another tutorial on the game from Liverpool and League Cup defeat to Wimbledon, the pair helped United recover from a poor start. Mira looked good at times, and scored in four games on the trot as United climbed to mid-table as winter approached. And they defeated Crystal Palace and Swindon Town in the FA Cup, all with Gazza standing out as a huge talent and fast becoming hot property. United then fell in Round Five to the gremlin that was Wimbledon again, but continued in good League form, moving into eighth spot by the end of the programme. Apart from Gazza, young Irishman Michael O'Neill prospered too – striking eight goals in only five games.

At the end of the season though there was another kick in the teeth for United's loyal fans. Gascoigne headed to the capital to join Chris Waddle at Spurs. Those grumbles became ever more vocal.

Pictured above: Michael O'Neill quickly made an impact up front following a move from Ulster.

Memorabilia CORNER

United's programme shows Mirandinha in full flow with the open Gallowgate End in the background.

IN CHARGE

Chairman: Stan Seymour (Jnr)/Gordon McKeag
Manager: Willie McFaul
Captain: Glenn Roeder
Trainer/Coach: John Pickering
Club Sponsor: Greenalls Breweries
Kit Supplier: Umbro

ST JAMES' PARK

Average Attendance
Lg 21,030 Lg & Cup 21,656

Pictured at United's training ground. Back row, left to right: Thomas (M), Bogie, Wharton, Thomas (A), Tinnion, Stephenson, Kelly. Middle: Gascoigne, McDonald, Cornwall, Scott, Jackson (P), Anderson. Sitting: Jackson (D), Goddard, Roeder, Mirandinha, McCreery.

SEASON REVIEW

Football League Div 1: P40 W14 D14 L12 F55 A53 Pts 56.
Position: 8th (Champions; Liverpool).
FA Cup: R5 (Winners; Wimbledon).
FL Littlewoods Cup: R3 (Winners; Luton Town).

Appearances (48m): McDonald NR 48, Kelly GA 44, Roeder GV 43, Gascoigne PJ 42 (1), Goddard P 41, McCreery D 39, Anderson JCP 38 (2), Jackson PA 36, Wharton K 33 (4), Mirandinha 31 (1), Jackson D 30 (7), Cornwell JA 25 (4), O'Neill MAM 22 (4), Tinnion B 18 (1), Hodges GP 7, Scott KW 6, Stephenson P 6 (3), Bogie I 5 (4), Thomas MR 4, Bailey JA 3 (1), Craig AH 3 (3), Lormor A 3 (2), Thomas AM 1 (3).

Goals (70g): Mirandinha 13, O'Neill MAM 13, Gascoigne PJ 11, Goddard P 10, McDonald NR 5, Jackson D 4, Jackson PA 2, Lormor A 2, Scott KW 2, Wharton K 2, Anderson JCP 1, Bogie I 1, Cornwell JA1, McCreery D 1, Roeder GV 1, Tinnion B 1.

Dismissals: 5 players; Gascoigne (2), Wharton (2), Jackson PA.

MAJOR SIGNINGS

Glyn Hodges (Wimbledon) £300,000
Michael O'Neill (Coleraine) £100,000
Tommy Wright (Linfield) £30,000
Mirandinha (SE Palmeiras) £575,000 club record fee
John Robertson (Hearts) £750,000 club record fee

FROM THE RANKS

Tony Lormor (Wallsend BC)

PLAYER FOCUS Paul Gascoigne

Born Gateshead. Midfield, 5'10"
1980 to 1988: 107 app 25 goals.

Joining the club as a schoolboy in 1980, Paul Gascoigne was the youngest of a trio of exceptional locally born players to appear for United with swagger and style and yet all were to move onto a bigger stage. Gazza, the extrovert of the three, rapidly advanced through the Magpies ranks, the star of the FA Youth Cup victory in 1985. He entered regular first-team action as a teenager during season 1985-86 and was at once under the spotlight as a precocious talent destined for the top. Well-built, strong and forceful, he mixed his power-play with amazing ball skills in midfield, always able to create or score goals. He also liked a laugh – in typical Geordie fashion and was something of a joker on and off the field. Controversial, at times calamitous, and always humorous, barely into his twenties Gazza was soon a show-biz star and his headline record £2.6m move as to Spurs in July 1988 took him to the capital and onto another level. His country called, so did the World Cup and Paul was the focus of attention as England almost reached the final under Bobby Robson in 1990. A money-spinning transfer to Italy's Serie A and Lazio followed, by then one of the world's top names. Often dogged by injury, he returned to Britain in 1995 appearing with distinction for Rangers as they won everything in Scotland, while he ended his senior career in the shirt of Everton, Middlesbrough and Burnley. Earning 57 caps for his country, Gascoigne went onto have a sometimes troubled life as he attempted to find a vocation on the fringe of the game. Paul won the prestigious BBC Sports Personality of the Year award in 1990.

TEAM COLOURS Black & white striped shirts, black shorts (Change; silver-grey shirts with a black-white band, silver-grey shorts/all blue shirts & shorts)

SEASON 1987-88

Match	Date		FL Division 1 (Barclays)	Result	Att	Posn	Scorers	Kelly	McDonald	Bailey	McCreery	Jackson PA	Roeder	Jackson D	Gascoigne	Goddard	Wharton	Hodges	Thomas AM	Tinnion	Scott	Thomas MR	Anderson	Mirandinha	Stephenson	Cornwell	Bogie	O'Neill	Craig	Lormor	Hallam	Match
1	19 Aug	A	Tottenham Hotspur	L 1 3 (0 3)	26,261		McCreery	1	2	3	4	5	6	7	8	9	10	11	s7	u												1
2	22 Aug	A	Sheffield Wednesday	W 1 0 (1 0)	22,031	13	Jackson D	1	2	3	4	5		7	8	9	10	11	u	u	6											2
3	29 Aug	H	**Nottingham Forest**	L 0 1 (0 1)	20,111	17			2	3	4	5	6	7	8	9	10	11	s10			1	s9									3
4	01 Sep	A	Norwich City	D 1 1 (0 0)	16,636	16	Jackson P		2		4	5	6	7	8		3	11	u	u		1	10	9								4
5	05 Sep	H	**Wimbledon**	L 1 2 (0 2)	22,734	18	McDonald (pen)		2		4	5	6	u	8	9	3	11	u			1	7	10								5
6	12 Sep	A	Manchester United	D 2 2 (2 2)	45,137	18	Mirandinha 2	1	2		4	5	6	s4		9	8	11		s11			3	10	7							6
7	20 Sep	H	**Liverpool**	L 1 4 (0 2)	24,141	19	McDonald (pen)	1	2		4	5	6	s11		9	8	11	u				3	10	7							7
8	26 Sep	H	**Southampton**	W 2 1 (0 0)	18,093	15	Goddard, Mirandinha	1	7		4	5	6	s2	8	9	u			3			2	10		11						8
9	03 Oct	A	Chelsea	D 2 2 (1 2)	22,071	15	Goddard, Wharton	1	7		4	5	6	s11	8	9	s7			3			2	10		11						9
10	17 Oct	H	**Everton**	D 1 1 (1 1)	20,266	16	Mirandinha	1	2		4	5	6	7	8	9	s4			3			u	10		11						10
11	24 Oct	A	Coventry City	W 3 1 (2 1)	18,585	12	Jackson D, Goddard, Gascoigne	1	2		4	5	6	7	8	9	s10			3			s11	10		11						11
12	31 Oct	H	**Arsenal**	L 0 1 (0 0)	23,662	15		1	7		4	5	6	10	8	9	u			3			2			11	u					12
13	07 Nov	A	Luton Town	L 0 4 (0 1)	7,638	18		1	7			5	6	11	8	9	4			3			2	10		u		s3				13
14	14 Nov	H	**Derby County**	D 0 0 (0 0)	21,698	17		1	7			5	6	10	8	9	4			3			2			11	u	s7				14
15	21 Nov	A	Queens Park Rangers	D 1 1 (0 1)	11,794	16	Jackson P	1	7		4	5	6		8d		3						2	9		u	10	u	11			15
16	28 Nov	H	**Charlton Athletic**	W 2 1 (1 1)	19,453	16	Mirandinha, Cornwell	1	7		4	5	6		8		3			u			2	10		11	u	9				16
17	05 Dec	A	Oxford United	W 3 1 (1 0)	8,190	15	McDonald (pen), O'Neill, Mirandinha	1	7		4	5	6				3			u			2	10		11	8	9	u			17
18	12 Dec	H	**Portsmouth**	D 1 1 (0 1)	20,255	13	Mirandinha	1	7		4	5d	6			9	3						2	10		11	8	u	u			18
19	19 Dec	A	West Ham United	L 1 2 (0 0)	18,679	15	Mirandinha	1	7		4	5	6	s3	8	9				3			2	10		11	u					19
20	26 Dec	H	**Manchester United**	W 1 0 (1 0)	26,461	12	Roeder	1	2		4		6	7	8	9	3						5	10		11	s3		s7			20
21	28 Dec	A	Liverpool	L 0 4 (0 1)	44,637	14		1	2		4		6	7	8	9	3						5	10		11	s7		u			21
22	01 Jan	A	Nottingham Forest	W 2 0 (1 0)	28,583	13	Gascoigne, Mirandinha	1	7		4	5	6	u	8	9	3						2	10		11			u			22
23	02 Jan	H	**Sheffield Wednesday**	D 2 2 (0 0)	25,503	12	Goddard 2	1	7		4	5	6	11	8	9	3						2	10		s2			s10			23
24	23 Jan	H	**Tottenham Hotspur**	W 2 0 (1 0)	24,616	12	Gascoigne 2	1	7			5	6	4	8	9	3						2	10		u		11		s10		24
25	06 Feb	A	Wimbledon	D 0 0 (0 0)	10,505	10		1	7			5	6	4	8	9	3						2	10		u		11		u		25
26	13 Feb	H	**Norwich City**	L 1 3 (1 1)	21,068	12	Gascoigne	1	7			5	6	4	8	9	3			u			2	10		s4		11				26
27	27 Feb	H	**Chelsea**	W 3 1 (2 0)	17,858	11	Mirandinha 2, Gascoigne	1	2		4	5	6	s10	8	9	3d							10		7		11	u			27
28	01 Mar	A	Southampton	D 1 1 (0 0)	13,380	10	O'Neill	1	2		4	5	6	u	8	9	3							10		7		11	u			28
29	05 Mar	A	Everton	L 0 1 (0 1)	25,674	11		1	7		4	5	6	s4	8	9				3			2	10		u		11				29
30	19 Mar	A	Arsenal	D 1 1 (0 1)	25,889	13	Goddard	1	2		4		6	10	8	9				3			5		s7	7	u	11				30
31	26 Mar	H	**Coventry City**	D 2 2 (0 0)	19,050	12	O'Neill 2	1	2		4		6	10	8	9				3			5		7	u	s7	11				31
32	02 Apr	H	**Luton Town**	W 4 0 (2 0)	20,565	11	O'Neill 3, Goddard	1	2		4	u	6		8	9	11			3			5		7	u		10				32
33	04 Apr	A	Derby County	L 1 2 (1 0)	18,591	11	O'Neill	1	2		4		6		8d	9	11			3			5	s7	7	s11		10				33
34	09 Apr	H	**Queens Park Rangers**	D 1 1 (1 1)	18,403	11	O'Neill	1	7		4	5	6	11	8	9	3			u			2				u	10				34
35	12 Apr	H	**Watford**	W 3 0 (1 0)	16,318	10	O'Neill, Wharton, Tinnion	1	2		4		6	7	8	9	11			3			5		s7	u		10				35
36	19 Apr	A	Watford	D 1 1 (0 1)	12,075	9	Anderson	1	2		4		6	8		9	3				7		5	10		s7		11		s10		36
37	23 Apr	A	Charlton Athletic	L 0 2 (0 2)	7,482	10		1	2		4		6	8	s3	9	11			3	u		5			7		10				37
38	30 Apr	H	**Oxford United**	W 3 1 (1 0)	16,617	10	Lormor, O'Neill, Goddard	1	2		4		6	7	8	9			s7		u		5			3		10		11		38
39	02 May	A	Portsmouth	W 2 1 (1 0)	12,468	8	Lormor, Scott	1	2	s10	4			7	8				9		6		5			3		10		11	u	39
40	07 May	H	**West Ham United**	W 2 1 (0 1)	23,731	8	O'Neill, Gascoigne	1	2		4			7	8	10			u		5		3			6	s10	11		9		40
Round			FA Cup																													Round
3	09 Jan	H	**Crystal Palace**	W 1 0 (1 0)	20,415		Gascoigne	1	7			5	6	11	8	9	3						2			4	u	10	s10			3
4	30 Jan	H	**Swindon Town**	W 5 0 (2 0)	28,699		Jackson D, Goddard, Gascoigne 2 (1 pen), O'Neill	1	7			5	6	4	8	9	3						2	10	u	u		11				4
5	20 Feb	H	**Wimbledon**	L 1 3 (0 1)	28,796		McDonald	1	7		4	5	6	11	8	9	3						2	10		u		s11				5
Round			FL Cup (Littlewoods Cup)																													Round
2(1)	23 Sep	A	Blackpool	L 0 1 (0 1)	7,959			1	2		4	5	6	11	8	9		u		3			u	10	7							2(1)
2(2)	07 Oct	H	**Blackpool**	W 4 1 (2 1)	21,228		Jackson D, Gascoigne, Goddard, Mirandinha		2		4	5	6	7	8	9	s8			3		1		10	s1	11						2(2)
3	28 Oct	A	Wimbledon	L 1 2 (1 1)	6,443		McDonald (pen)	1	7		4	5	6	10	8	9				3			2			11	u	u				3
Round			Full Members Cup (Simod Cup)																													Round
1	25 Nov	H	**Shrewsbury Town**	W 2 1 (1 0)	7,787		Mirandinha, Bogie	1	7			5			8		3			u	6		2	9		4	10	s11	11			1
2	02 Dec	A	Bradford City	L 1 2 (0 0)	8,866		Scott	1	2			5			8		3d			u	6			10		11	7	9	4	u		2

DateLine ... 12 Sept: Mirandinha gets onto the scoresheet for the first time in a 2-2 draw with Manchester United. **23 Jan:** United's new Milburn Stand opened before the fixture with Tottenham and Paul Gascoigne makes an impression by scoring both goals in a 2-0 win. **12 April:** Michael O'Neill nets his eighth goal in only five games against Watford.

SEASON
1988-89
DIVISION 1

Tumbling into turmoil

With a background of shareholder infighting, Newcastle used the Gascoigne transfer monies and more in a spending spree before the new 1988-89 programme got underway. McFaul had already splashed out to secure the service of Scottish striker John Robertson, then added Wimbledon duo Dave Beasant and Andy Thorn, both for club record fees. In addition John Hendrie arrived at Gallowgate for another substantial outlay. McFaul spent over £3m and his new look team made their debut at Goodison Park but did not gel at all, Everton winning 4-0. It took the Magpies six games to record a victory, that a wonderful 2-1 success at Anfield against Liverpool.

United were in the bottom places and were eliminated in the League Cup by Third Division Sheffield United. The pressure was on United's former goalkeeper and it was no surprise when McFaul was axed during October and in landed the Bald Eagle, QPR boss Jim Smith, with the uphill task of keeping United in the First Division.

He immediately started wheeling and dealing in the transfer market, the club going through an extraordinary level of activity in and out of Gallowgate. But Smith couldn't stop the rot, and found the corporate scrap behind the scenes difficult to cope with. That certainly affected United's performances on the field and after a brief window of hope during March when Mirandinha hit a patch of form, scoring in successive 2-0 victories over Everton and Norwich, Newcastle slumped. Having fallen in a marathon FA Cup meeting with Watford – of four games – they lost seven of the last nine fixtures and were relegated, rock bottom of the table with only 31 points. They recorded only three victories at Gallowgate all season, the club's worst ever on home soil. The Toon had gone down without a fight.

Pictured above: A record buy saw goalkeeper and FA Cup winning skipper Dave Beasant arrive on Tyneside.

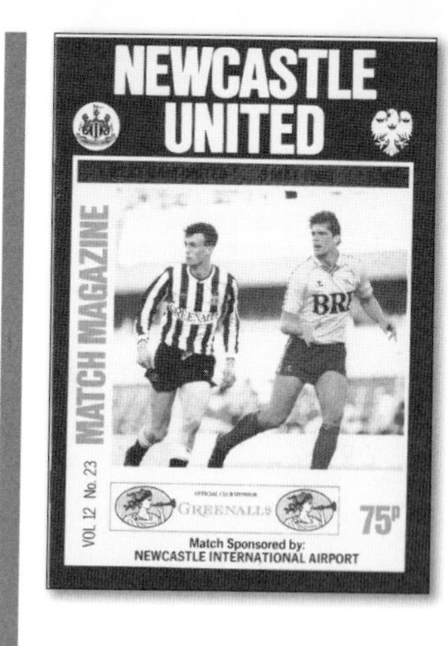

Michael O'Neill is pictured on United's magazine cover, along with a new club crest.

Memorabilia CORNER

IN CHARGE

Chairman: Gordon McKeag
Manager: Willie McFaul/Jim Smith
Captain: Andy Thorn
Trainer/Coach: John Pickering/Bobby Saxton
Club Sponsor: Greenalls Breweries
Kit Supplier: Umbro

ST JAMES' PARK

Average Attendance
Lg 22,907 Lg & Cup 22,861

Newcastle's senior players are in the middle and front rows. Middle, left to right: Wright (D)(physio), Stephenson, Wright (T), Beasant, Scott, Cornwall, Jackson (P), Tinnion, Thorn, Thomas (M), Kelly, Anderson, Pickering (coach). Front: Suggett (coach), Jackson (D), O'Neill, Robertson, Wharton, Roeder, McFaul (manager), Mirandinha, McCreery, Hendrie, Bogie, Craig.

PLAYER FOCUS Mirandinha

Born Fortaleza. Centre-forward, 5'8"
1987 to 1990: 67 app 24 goals.

With a formidable goals record in his native Brazil, Francisco Ernandi Lima da Silva – Mirandinha – to all, was an eye-catching signing, the first from that country to appear in England's top level. Having recently found the net wearing the famous yellow national shirt against England at Wembley, Newcastle paid a club record £575,000 to Palmeiras in August 1987 to bring the small and dusky South American to St James' Park. A striker who could delight and infuriate in equal measure, Mira did show flashes of genius but also a selfish and moody side to his game which did not fit to United's team plan, especially when in a relegation dog-fight. Packing a powerful shot and able to sprint clear of defenders, manager Willie McFaul's hope was that Mirandinha would deflect the growing supporter anger of star departures and form the nucleus of a stabilised Magpie eleven. That did happen for a short period in 1987-88 but as United's form waned; the Brazilian proved a luxury no-one wanted. The arrival of Jim Smith as boss saw something of a running battle between player and manager and it was of little surprise when the Brazilian headed back to South America after the Magpies' relegation during July 1989. He played on with a string of clubs in Japan, Portugal and Brazil. Mira began coaching too in Saudi Arabia and Malaysia. Two sons also played football, the eldest in the Dutch leagues for a period.

SEASON REVIEW

Football League Div 1: P38 W7 D10 L21 F32 A63 Pts 31.
Position: 20th, Relegated (Champions; Arsenal).
FA Cup: R3 (Winners; Liverpool).
FL Littlewoods Cup: R2 (Winners; Nottingham Forest).

Appearances (47m): Hendrie JG 43, McCreery D 42, Scott KW 36 (2), Thorn AC 31, Beasant DJ 27, Mirandinha 27 (8), Brock KS 26, Anderson JCP 24, Sansom KG 24, Wharton K 23 (4), O'Brien WF 22 (3), Roeder GV 22, O'Neill MAM 21 (11), Jackson D 18 (2), Ranson R 17 (1), Tinnion B 15 (2), Pingel FM 13 (1), Cornwell JA 11 (2), Wright TJ 11, Kelly GA 9, Robertson JG 9 (7), Stephenson P 9 (1), McDonald RR 8 (7), Payne LJ 6 (1), Sweeney PM 6 (2), Bogie I 5 (7), Kristensen B 4 (1), Brazil GN 3 (4), Lormor A 3, Jackson PA 2, Roche D 0 (2), Craig AH 0 (1), Gourlay AM 0 (1), Howey SN 0 (1), Robinson DJ 0 (1).

Goals (38g): Mirandinha 11, Hendrie JG 5, O'Brien WF 4, O'Neill MAM 4, Brock KS 3, Jackson D 2, McDonald RR 2, Anderson JCP 1, Lormor A 1, Pingel FM 1, Ranson R 1, Thorn AC 1, Tinnion B 1, own goal 1.

Dismissals: 0 players.

MAJOR SIGNINGS

John Hendrie (Bradford City) £500,000
Liam O'Brien (Manchester Utd) £300,000
Kenny Sansom (Arsenal) £300,000
Kevin Brock (QPR) £300,000
Bjorn Kristensen (Aarhus GF) £260,000
Frank Pingel (Aarhus GF) £260,000
Rob McDonald (PSV Eindhoven) £150,000
Lee Payne (Barnet) £25,000
Ray Ranson (Birmingham City) £175,000
Paul Sweeney (Raith Rvs) £100,000
Dave Beasant (Wimbledon) £850,000
club record fee
Andy Thorn (Wimbledon) £850,000
club record fee

FROM THE RANKS

Steve Howey (Sunderland sch)
David Roche (Wallsend BC)
David Robinson (Wallsend BC)

TEAM COLOURS Black & white striped shirts, black shorts (Change; yellow & green striped shirts, green shorts)

SEASON 1988-89

Match	Date		Opponent	Res	F	A	HT	Att	Posn	Goalscorers	Beasant	Anderson	Tinnion	McCreery	Jackson PA	Thorn	Hendrie	Robertson	Mirandinha	Wharton	O'Neill	Jackson D	Scott	Bogie	Craig	Cornwell	Gourlay	Stephenson	Payne	Robinson	O'Brien	McDonald	Roeder	Brock	Ranson	Sansom	Wright	Pingel	Brazil	Kelly	Sweeney	Kristensen	Roche	Lormor	Howey	Match
			FL Division 1 (Barclays)						Posn																																					Match
1	27 Aug	A	Everton	L	0	4	(0 2)	41,560			1	2	3	4	5	6	7	8	9	10	11	s9	u																							1
2	03 Sep	H	**Tottenham Hotspur**	D	2	2	(2 0)	33,508	17	Thorn, Jackson D	1	2	u	4		6	7	11		3	9	10	5	8	s2																					2
3	10 Sep	A	Derby County	L	0	2	(0 0)	16,014	19		1	2		4		6	7	11		3	9	10	5	8		u	u																			3
4	17 Sep	H	**Norwich City**	L	0	2	(0 1)	22,809	20		1	2	3	4		6	7	11			9	10	5	8			u	s9																		4
5	24 Sep	A	Charlton Athletic	D	2	2	(0 1)	6,088	19	Jackson D, Tinnion	1		s11	4		6	7	11	9	3		10	5	s2		2		8																		5
6	01 Oct	A	Liverpool	W	2	1	(1 1)	39,139	18	Hendrie, Mirandinha (pen)	1	2		4		6	7	s10	9	3	10	8	5			u		11																		6
7	08 Oct	H	**Coventry City**	L	0	3	(0 3)	22,890	19		1	2		4		6	7	s6	9	3	10	8	5			s10		11																		7
8	22 Oct	A	West Ham United	L	0	2	(0 0)	17,765	20		1	2	3	4		6	8	s4	9		11	10	5	s6				7																		8
9	26 Oct	H	**Middlesbrough**	W	3	0	(1 0)	23,845	18	Mirandinha 2, og (Pallister)	1	2	3				8	s11	9		10	4	5		u	6		7	11																	9
10	29 Oct	H	**Nottingham Forest**	L	0	1	(0 0)	24,642	18		1	2	3				8	s11	9		10	4	5		u	6		7	11																	10
11	05 Nov	A	Queens Park Rangers	L	0	3	(0 2)	11,013	19		1	2	3	4		6	8	9			11	10	5			u		7	s3																	11
12	12 Nov	H	**Arsenal**	L	0	1	(0 0)	23,807	20		1	2	3	4		6	8	7	9			10	u			5			11	s7																12
13	19 Nov	A	Millwall	L	0	4	(0 2)	15,767	20		1	2	3	4		6	8		s5	11		s11				5					7	9	10													13
14	27 Nov	H	**Manchester United**	D	0	0	(0 0)	20,234	20		1	2	3	4		6	7	u	10	s11						5			11		8	9														14
15	03 Dec	A	Luton Town	D	0	0	(0 0)	8,338	20		1	2	3	4		6	7		10			9	u			5	s10		11		8															15
16	10 Dec	H	**Wimbledon**	W	2	1	(1 0)	20,292	20	Hendrie 2	1	2	3	4		6	7		10	s10		9				5					8	s9		11												16
17	17 Dec	H	**Southampton**	D	3	3	(1 2)	20,103	19	Brock, O'Neill 2	1		3	4		5	7		9	10	s3			s9							2	8	6	11												17
18	26 Dec	A	Sheffield Wednesday	W	2	1	(2 1)	25,573	18	McDonald, O'Neill	1			4		5	7		s4	10	8										s8	9	6	11	2	3										18
19	31 Dec	A	Tottenham Hotspur	L	0	2	(0 2)	27,739	19		1			4			7		s4	10	8		5								s8	9	6	11	2	3										19
20	02 Jan	H	**Derby County**	L	0	1	(0 0)	31,079	19		1			4			7		9	10	s9		5								s10	8	6	11	2	3										20
21	14 Jan	A	Aston Villa	L	1	3	(1 1)	21,010	20	Mirandinha (pen)				4			7		9	10			5						8		6	u		11	2	3	1	s8								21
22	21 Jan	H	**Charlton Athletic**	L	0	2	(0 1)	19,076	20			5		4			7		s4	10	s10										9		6	11	2	3	1	8								22
23	04 Feb	H	**Liverpool**	D	2	2	(1 1)	30,983	19	Mirandinha, Pingel		5		4			7		9		u		2								10	u	6	11		3	1	8								23
24	11 Feb	A	Coventry City	W	2	1	(0 0)	16,577	19	Hendrie, Mirandinha (pen)		5		4			7		9		s9		2								10	u	6			3	1	8	11							24
25	26 Feb	A	Middlesbrough	D	1	1	(1 0)	24,385	19	O'Brien		u		4			7		9				5								10		6	11	2	3	1	8	s9							25
26	11 Mar	H	**Queens Park Rangers**	L	1	2	(0 0)	21,665	19	Ranson				4			7		s7		s10		5								10		6	11	2	3	1	8	9							26
27	15 Mar	A	Nottingham Forest	D	1	1	(0 1)	20,800	19	Brock				4		6	7			s9	s8		5								10			11	2	3		8	9	1						27
28	22 Mar	H	**Everton**	W	2	0	(1 0)	21,012	19	Mirandinha, O'Brien				4		6	7		9		s9		5								10			11	2	3		8	s8	1						28
29	25 Mar	A	Norwich City	W	2	0	(1 0)	22,440	19	Mirandinha, O'Brien				4		6	7		9		s9		5								10			11	2	3		8	s8	1						29
30	27 Mar	H	**Sheffield Wednesday**	L	1	3	(0 2)	31,010	19	Mirandinha (pen)				4		6	7		9		s8		5								10			11	2	3		8	s2	1						30
31	01 Apr	A	Southampton	L	0	1	(0 0)	16,175	19					4			7		9		s8		5								10		6	11	2	3		8		1	s9					31
32	08 Apr	H	**Aston Villa**	L	1	2	(0 1)	20,464	19	O'Brien				4			7		9		u		5								10		6	11	2	3				1	s9	8				32
33	15 Apr	A	Arsenal	L	0	1	(0 0)	38,023	19					4		9	7				10		5									s8	6			3		8		1	11	2	s11			33
34	22 Apr	H	**Luton Town**	D	0	0	(0 0)	18,636	19					4		9	7		s2	s10	10		5										6	11		3				1	8	2				34
35	29 Apr	A	Wimbledon	L	0	4	(0 1)	5,206	19					4		9					10		5									s2	6	11	s7	3		7		1	8	2				35
36	03 May	H	**West Ham United**	L	1	2	(1 1)	14,445	20	Lormor		2		4		9							5									s2	6	11		3	1	10			8	s10		7		36
37	06 May	H	**Millwall**	D	1	1	(0 1)	14,731	20	Anderson		2		4		9				8	10		5										6	11			1	u			3	u		7		37
38	13 May	A	Manchester United	L	0	2	(0 0)	30,379	20			2		4		6					10		5										9	11		3	1				8		s10	7	s7	38
Round			**FA Cup**																																											Round
3	07 Jan	H	**Watford**	D	0	0	(0 0)	24,217			1			4			7		s7	10	9		5	s9							6	8		11	2	3										3
3r	10 Jan	A	Watford	De	2	2	(1 1)	16,431		Brock, Mirandinha (pen)	1			4			7		9	10	u		5								8	s9	6	11	2	3										3r
3rr	16 Jan	H	**Watford**	De	0	0	(0 0)	28,498						4			7			10	s10		5	9							8	s9	6	11	2	3	1									3rr
3rrr	18 Jan	A	Watford	Le	0	1	(0 0)	24,065						4			7		9	10			5	s11							8	s9	6	11	2	3	1									3rrr
Round			**FL Cup (Littlewoods Cup)**																																											Round
2(1)	27 Sep	A	Sheffield United	L	0	3	(0 2)	17,900			1	2	11			6	7	s9	10	3	9	4	5	u		8																				2(1)
2(2)	12 Oct	H	**Sheffield United**	W	2	0	(1 0)	14,991		Hendrie, Mirandinha	1	2	3			6	8	s7	9	10	11	4	5	s4				7																		2(2)
Round			**Full Members Cup (Simod Cup)**																																											Round
3	13 Dec	A	Watford	L	1	2	(0 0)	6,186		McDonald	1	2				6	7		9	3		10	s7			s2					4	8	5	11												3
Round			**Mercantile Credit Centenary Trophy**																																											Round
1	29 Aug	H	**Wimbledon**	We	1	0	(0 0)	17,904		O'Neill	1		3	4	5	6	7	8		10	9	2	s4	s3		11																				1
SF	21 Sep	A	Manchester United	Le	0	2	(0 0)	14,968			1		s9	4		6	7	11	s4	3		10	5	8		2		9																		SF

Le Lost after extra time
De Drawn after extra time
We Won after extra time

DateLine ... 19 Nov: A 4-0 defeat at Millwall confirms United are in a relegation battle. **10 Dec:** Jim Smith arrives as manager and watches United win 2-1 against Wimbledon. **18 Jan:** Watford squeeze through in the FA Cup following a four-game battle, the longest on record. **29 April:** Wimbledon fire four goals past Gary Kelly as Newcastle slide towards the Second Division.

SEASON 1989-90

DIVISION 2

Play-off exit to Sunderland

United faced another period in the second-tier and with a new manager who had still work to do in rebuilding a squad. Jim Smith continued to move players in and out of St James' Park, bringing in a new centre-forward in Mick Quinn to replace the discarded Mira, while half-way through the season he captured the skipper of Scotland, Roy Aitken from Celtic. Hugely experienced and Smith's leader on the field, the Scot made a difference. United looked to be heading straight back into the top division as Quinn, along with partner up front Mark McGhee, rattled in the goals. The pairing claimed 61 in the season.

The Black'n'Whites were well placed as Christmas approached but then slipped up disastrously, dropping to seventh soon after a 4-1 reverse to Wolves at St James' Park. But Aitken steadied the ship, inspiring the Magpies on his debut to a dramatic late 5-4 victory over Leicester after being 4-2 behind. There was a brief diversion from their promotion target when Manchester United faced the Geordies in the Fifth Round of the FA Cup. The Reds won a thrilling game of five goals, and several contentious refereeing decisions.

Newcastle finished just short of an automatic promotion place in third position, critically drawing all of 14 games, and found themselves in for a taste of the Football League's blast from the Victorian past and the Test Matches – a Play-Off for promotion in a Wembley finale. And would you believe it, United faced Sunderland of all clubs who had finished some three places below the Magpies and six points worse off. In an ill-tempered double meeting and a stalemate at Roker Park, the Wearsiders won through to Wembley in a deciding contest at Gallowgate. The season ended on a real low.

Pictured above: Captain of Scotland, Roy Aitken added drive and know-how to United's midfield.

Memorabilia CORNER

An unusual cover design, featuring Mark McGhee as United magazine hits the £1 mark.

IN CHARGE

Chairman: Gordon McKeag
Manager: Jim Smith
Captain: Roy Aitken
Trainer/Coach: Bobby Saxton
Club Sponsor: Greenalls Breweries
Kit Supplier: Umbro

ST JAMES' PARK

Average Attendance
Lg 22,033 Lg & Cup 22,325

Jim Smith's squad in 1989-90. Back row, left to right: Saxton (asst manager), Fereday, Wright (T), Anderson, O'Brien, Thorn, McDonald (R), Scott, Kristensen, Quinn, Kelly, O'Neill, Wright (D)(physio). Sitting: Brazil, Gallacher, Sweeney, McGhee, Smith (manager), Dillon, Brock, Ranson, Stimson.

SEASON REVIEW

Football League Div 2: P46 W22 D14 L10 F80 A55 Pts 80.
Position: 3rd, Play-off (Champions; Leeds United).
FA Cup: R5 (Winners; Manchester United).
FL Littlewoods Cup: R3 (Winners; Nottingham Forest).

Appearances (58m): McGhee ME 58, Quinn M 55, Scott KW 53, Brock KS 52 (1), Dillon KP 52 (2), Stimson MN 45 (2), Ranson R 42, Burridge J 39, Kristensen B 35 (8), Anderson JCP 33 (9), Gallacher JA 29 (7), Aitken RS 28, Fereday W 24 (7), O'Brien WF 20 (7), Sweeney PM 19 (6), Wright TJ 14, Bradshaw DS 12 (4), Thorn AC 12, Askew W 6, Brazil GN 5 (15), Kelly GA 5, Robinson DJ 0 (2).

Goals (100g): Quinn M 36, McGhee ME 25, Gallacher JA 8, Anderson JCP 4, O'Brien WF 4, Scott KW 4, Brazil GN 3, Brock KS 3, Kristensen B 3, Thorn AC 2, Aitken RS 1, Robinson DJ 1, Stimson MN 1, own goals 5.

Dismissals: 0 players.

MAJOR SIGNINGS

Roy Aitken (Celtic) £500,000
Mark McGhee (Celtic) £200,000
Mick Quinn (Portsmouth) £680,000
Billy Askew (Hull City) £150,000
Kevin Dillon (Portsmouth) free
Wayne Fereday (QPR) £400,000
John Gallacher (Falkirk) £100,000
Mark Stimson (Tottenham Hotspur) £150,000

FROM THE RANKS

None

PLAYER FOCUS Mick Quinn

Born Liverpool. Centre-forward, 5'10"
1989 to 1992: 140 app 71 goals.

Few players in United's history have made such an impact on their debut in a black-and-white shirt. Mick Quinn netted four goals against Leeds United on the opening day of the 1989-90 season following a sizable £680,000 move north from Portsmouth during June. Having learned the striker's trade in the lower divisions with Wigan, Stockport and Oldham, Quinn showed he could score goals at the top level with Pompey. Despite being at times in the headlines for the wrong reasons, Mick was a key figure as the Fratton Park club were promoted to the top flight. Netting 34 goals in his first season with the Magpies – the League's top goalscorer – Mick nearly spearheaded Newcastle to promotion as well, United failing in the Play-Offs. A poacher supreme in the box, Quinn could turn and shoot in tight situations, ability which made up for an apparent languid style and lack of athleticism. A knee injury put him on the sidelines for a long period and when fit, he was discarded as Kevin Keegan took control, although he did play in five matches of the 1993 Championship winning season. Mick was transferred to Coventry City in November 1992, while the chirpy Merseysider also appeared for Watford and Plymouth before moving abroad for brief spells in Hong Kong and Greece. At the end of his career Quinn had netted almost 300 senior goals. After his playing days were concluded Mick trained race-horses and entered the media becoming a popular radio commentator notably for TalkSport.

TEAM COLOURS Black & white striped shirts, black shorts (Change; yellow & green striped shirts, green shorts)

SEASON 1989–90

Match	Date		FL Division 2 (Barclays)				HT	Att	Posn	Scorers	Wright	Ranson	Sweeney	Dillon	Scott	Thorn	Gallacher	Brock	Quinn	McGhee	Fereday	Brazil	Kristensen	Stimson	Anderson	Kelly	Burridge	O'Brien	Bradshaw	Aitken	Roche	Robinson	Askew	Lormor	Match
1	19 Aug	H	**Leeds United**	W	5	2	(1 2)	24,396		Quinn 4 (1 pen), Gallacher	1	2	3	4	5	6	7	8	9	10	11	s3	u												1
2	26 Aug	A	Leicester City	D	2	2	(1 1)	13,384	7	Quinn, Gallacher	1	2		4	5	6	7	8	9	10	11	u	s8	3											2
3	02 Sep	H	**Oldham Athletic**	W	2	1	(1 0)	21,092	5	Quinn 2 (1 pen)	1	2		4	5	6	7	8	9	10	11	s2	s7	3											3
4	09 Sep	A	AFC Bournemouth	L	1	2	(1 1)	9,982	8	Quinn	1	2	8	4	5	6	7		9	10	11		s7	3	s8										4
5	13 Sep	A	Oxford United	L	1	2	(1 1)	7,313	8	Quinn	1	2		4	5	6		8	9	10	11	7	s4	3	u										5
6	16 Sep	H	**Portsmouth**	W	1	0	(0 0)	19,766	6	Thorn		2			5	6	7	8	9	10	11	u	4	3	s4	1									6
7	24 Sep	A	Sunderland	D	0	0	(0 0)	29,499	7			u		4	5	6	7	8	9	10		s7	11	3	2	1									7
8	27 Sep	H	**Watford**	W	2	1	(2 1)	17,008	6	Quinn, Gallacher				4	5	6	7	8	9	10	11	u	u	3	2	1									8
9	30 Sep	A	Hull City	W	3	1	(1 1)	9,629	3	McGhee, Anderson, Brazil				4	5	6	7	8	9	10	11	s7	s9	3	2	1									9
10	07 Oct	A	Ipswich Town	L	1	2	(0 2)	15,220	5	McGhee				4	5	6	7	8	9	10	11	s6	s7	3	2		1								10
11	14 Oct	H	**Bradford City**	W	1	0	(0 0)	19,879	3	McGhee				4	5		7	8	9	10	u	u	6	3	2		1	11							11
12	18 Oct	H	**Blackburn Rovers**	W	2	1	(1 0)	20,702	2	Quinn, McGhee				4	5		7	8	9	10	s7	s8	6	3	2		1	11							12
13	21 Oct	A	Brighton & Hove Albion	W	3	0	(1 0)	10,756	2	Quinn 3				4	5		7	8	9	10	s2	s7	6	3	2		1	11							13
14	28 Oct	H	**Port Vale**	D	2	2	(1 0)	17,824	3	McGhee, Quinn		2		4	5	u		8	9	10	7	u	6	3			1	11							14
15	01 Nov	A	West Bromwich Albion	W	5	1	(2 1)	12,339	3	og (Robson), Brazil, Brock, McGhee, O'Brien		2	s11	4	5			8	9	10	7	11	6	3			1	s4							15
16	04 Nov	H	**Middlesbrough**	D	2	2	(1 1)	23,382	3	McGhee, O'Brien		2		4	5		s11	8	9	10	7	11	6	3			1	s2							16
17	11 Nov	A	West Ham United	D	0	0	(0 0)	25,892	3			2		4	5		s7	8	9	10		7	6	3	s8		1	11							17
18	18 Nov	A	Barnsley	D	1	1	(0 0)	10,475	3	Quinn		2		4	5			8	9	10	7	s2	6	3	s7		1	11							18
19	25 Nov	H	**Sheffield United**	W	2	0	(2 0)	27,170	3	Gallacher, Quinn		2		4	5		7	8	9	10	s7	u	6	3			1	11							19
20	02 Dec	A	Leeds United	L	0	1	(0 0)	31,715	3			2		4	5		7	8	9	10	s3		6	3	s7		1	11							20
21	09 Dec	H	**Oxford United**	L	2	3	(1 1)	16,645	4	Stimson, Quinn (pen)		2	s4	4	5			8	9	10	7		6	3	s10		1	11							21
22	26 Dec	A	Stoke City	L	1	2	(1 0)	14,878	6	Scott		2	3	4	5		7	8	9	10		s7	6	ss7			1	11							22
23	30 Dec	A	Swindon Town	D	1	1	(1 0)	11,657	6	Quinn			s7		5		u	8	9	10	7		6	3	2		1	11	4						23
24	01 Jan	H	**Wolverhampton Wanderers**	L	1	4	(0 0)	21,937	7	Brock			u		5		s4	8	9	10	7		6	3	2		1	11	4						24
25	13 Jan	H	**Leicester City**	W	5	4	(2 2)	20,785	7	McGhee 2, Quinn 2, Gallacher			s7	6	5		s6	8	9	10	7			3	2		1	11		4					25
26	20 Jan	A	Oldham Athletic	D	1	1	(0 0)	11,190	6	McGhee		7	3	6	5		9			10			8		2		1	11	u	4	u				26
27	04 Feb	H	**Sunderland**	D	1	1	(0 0)	31,665	6	McGhee			11	8	5		7	s11	9	10			6	3	s6		1		2	4					27
28	10 Feb	A	Portsmouth	D	1	1	(1 0)	14,204	7	Quinn	1		11	8	5			7	9	10		u	6	3	s6				2	4					28
29	24 Feb	A	Sheffield United	D	1	1	(1 0)	21,035	8	og (Morris)	1	6	u	8				7	9	10	11		u	3	5				2	4					29
30	28 Feb	H	**AFC Bournemouth**	W	3	0	(0 0)	15,163	6	Anderson, Quinn 2	1	6	u	8			u	7	9	10	11			3	5				2	4					30
31	03 Mar	H	**Barnsley**	W	4	1	(3 1)	18,999	5	Anderson, Scott, Aitken, McGhee (pen)	1	6	u	8	2		s11	7	9	10	11			3	5					4					31
32	07 Mar	H	**Hull City**	W	2	0	(1 0)	20,684	4	McGhee 2 (1 pen)	1	6	s3	8	2		11	7	9	10		u		3	5					4					32
33	10 Mar	A	Watford	D	0	0	(0 0)	12,069	4		1	6	3	8	2		11	7	9	10	u		u		5					4					33
34	17 Mar	H	**Ipswich Town**	W	2	1	(0 1)	20,554	4	Quinn 2	1	6	3	8			11	7	9	10		s8			5				2	4		s11			34
35	21 Mar	A	Bradford City	L	2	3	(1 1)	10,364	4	McGhee (pen), og (Aizlewood)	1	6	3	8			11	7	9	10		s11	s8		5				2	4					35
36	24 Mar	A	Blackburn Rovers	L	0	2	(0 0)	13,285	5		1	6	3	8	2			7	9	10		ss3			5				s3	4			11		36
37	31 Mar	H	**Brighton & Hove Albion**	W	2	0	(0 0)	18,742	4	Quinn, Gallacher		6	3	8	2		s7	7	9	10			u		5		1			4			11		37
38	03 Apr	H	**Plymouth Argyle**	W	3	1	(1 1)	16,528	3	Quinn, McGhee 2 (1 pen)		6	3	8	2		s7	7	9	10			s5		5		1			4			11		38
39	07 Apr	A	Port Vale	W	2	1	(2 0)	10,290	3	Quinn, McGhee		6	3	8	2		u	7	9	10			u		5		1			4			11		39
40	11 Apr	H	**West Bromwich Albion**	W	2	1	(1 0)	19,471	3	Quinn, Anderson		6	3	8	2			7	9	10	11		u	s11	5		1			4					40
41	14 Apr	A	Wolverhampton Wanderers	W	1	0	(1 0)	19,507	3	Scott		6		8	2			7	9	10			11	3	5		1	u		4	u				41
42	16 Apr	H	**Stoke City**	W	3	0	(2 0)	26,179	2	Kristensen 2, Quinn		6		8	2			7	9	10			11	3	5		1	s8	s6	4					42
43	21 Apr	A	Plymouth Argyle	D	1	1	(1 1)	11,702	3	McGhee				8	2			7	9	10			11	3	5		1	u	6	4		u			43
44	25 Apr	H	**Swindon Town**	D	0	0	(0 0)	26,548	3			6		8	2			7	9	10			11	3	5		1	u	u	4					44
45	28 Apr	H	**West Ham United**	W	2	1	(0 1)	31,461	3	Kristensen, Quinn		6		8	2			7	9	10			11	3	5		1	s8	u	4					45
46	05 May	A	Middlesbrough	L	1	4	(0 0)	18,484	3	og (McGee)		6		8	2			7	9	10			11	3	5		1	s2	s9	4					46
Round			**Play-Offs**																																**Round**
SF(1)	13 May	A	Sunderland	D	0	0	(0 0)	26,641				6		u	2			7	9	10			11	3	5		1	s6		4			8		SF(1)
SF(2)	16 May	H	**Sunderland**	L	0	2	(0 1)	32,216						s6	2			7	9	10			11	3	5		1	s8	6	4			8		SF(2)
Round			**FA Cup**																																**Round**
3	06 Jan	A	Hull City	W	1	0	(0 0)	10,743		O'Brien			u	4	5			8	9	10	7		6	3	2		1	11	u						3
4	27 Jan	A	Reading	D	3	3	(2 2)	11,989		McGhee 2, Quinn		3	8	s11	5		7		9	10	u		6	2			1	11		4					4
4r	31 Jan	H	**Reading**	W	4	1	(2 0)	26,658		McGhee 2, Quinn, Robinson		2	11	8	5		7		9	10			6	3			1		s4	4		s2			4r
5	18 Feb	H	**Manchester United**	L	2	3	(0 1)	31,805		McGhee (pen), Scott		2	11	8	5			7	9	10		s11		3	u		1		6	4					5
Round			**FL Cup (Littlewoods Cup)**																																**Round**
2(1)	19 Sep	A	Reading	L	1	3	(0 1)	7,960		Gallacher		2		4	5	6	7	8	9	10	11	u		3	u	1									2(1)
2(2)	04 Oct	H	**Reading**	W	4	0	(1 0)	15,211		Brazil (pen), Brock, Thorn, McGhee			s2	4	5	6	7	8		10		9	11	3	2		1							u	2(2)
3	25 Oct	H	**West Bromwich Albion**	L	0	1	(0 1)	22,619				2		4	5		7	8	9	10	s7	s8	6	3			1	11							3
Round			**Full Members Cup (Zenith Data Systems Cup)**																																**Round**
2	28 Nov	H	**Oldham Athletic**	W	2	0	(1 0)	6,167		Quinn 2		2		4			7	8	9	10	s3	s10	6	3			1	11	5						2
3	20 Dec	H	**Derby County**	We	3	2	(1 1)	6,704		O'Brien, Gallacher, og (Cross)		2	3	4	5		7	8	9	10	s8		6		s3		1	11							3
SF	23 Jan	A	Middlesbrough	L	0	1	(0 0)	16,948				6	3	7	5		9			10	2		8				1	11	u	4		u			SF

We   Won after extra time

DateLine ... 19 Aug: Mick Quinn nets four goals on his debut against Leeds in a 5–2 victory. **13 Jan:** The Magpies win a remarkable game with Leicester by 5–4 after being 4–2 behind. **28 April:** Mick Quinn scores his 36th goal of the season against West Ham United. **16 May:** Sunderland win the promotion Play-Off with a 2–0 triumph at Gallowgate.

Power struggle takes its toll

By the start of the Nineties discontent among supporters reached fury. Relegation and a Play-Off defeat to arch rivals Sunderland gave impetus to a bid for change at St James' Park. The Magpie Group had been formed in 1988 led by local tycoon John Hall with a plan to force ownership change at Newcastle United, and eventually revolutionise the club. They received huge backing from the mass of United's following. Without doubt this intensification impacted both on the manager and the players, and ultimately results on the pitch. It was impossible not to be affected by what became a high-profile takeover played out in the media every day.

Jim Smith had to try and close-off the power struggle behind the scenes from the dressing-room and pick his players up following the previous season's frustration. It was soon clear he was powerless to change the Black'n'Whites fortune.

Although Mick Quinn continued to score goals, United failed to make an impression on the promotion race with a growing injury list disrupting the manager's plans. By November the Tynesiders had dropped to as low as 19th in the table and had been dumped from the League Cup by neighbours Middlesbrough. Cash was found, although the club was in dire need of funds, and the signing of Gavin Peacock saw a revival. Yet by the spring there was little hope of getting into the race for the First Division and a change was made.

Smith departed at the end of March and the beleaguered Board turned to former World Cup winner in Ossie Ardiles, then a fledgling manager at Swindon Town. Quickly he discarded the old heads and gave youth its chance, selecting the club's youngest ever side at the time. Fans gave their judgement. The club's average gate plummeted to just over 17,000. Something had to change – and it certainly did.

Pictured above: Kevin Scott came through the junior ranks and was a resolute stopper at centre-back.

Memorabilia CORNER

By 1990 programmes were now full colour magazines. Scott Sloan is pictured on this edition.

IN CHARGE

Chairman: Gordon McKeag/George Forbes
Manager: Jim Smith/Ossie Ardiles
Captain: Roy Aitken
Trainer/Coach: Bobby Saxton/Tony Galvin
Club Sponsor: Greenalls Breweries/ Newcastle Breweries
Kit Supplier: Umbro

ST JAMES' PARK

Average Attendance
Lg 16,879 Lg & Cup 17,307

In 1990 an unusual redesigned shirt was on show. Back row, left to right: Dillon, Quinn, Simpson, Howey, Bradshaw, Anderson. Middle: Wright (D)(physio), Clark, Stimson, Kristensen, Wright (T), Burridge, Scott, O'Brien, McGhee, Saxton (asst manager). Sitting: Brazil, Brock, Sweeney, Askew, Smith (manager), Aitken, Gallacher, Ranson, Sloan.

PLAYER FOCUS John Anderson

Born Dublin. Right-back, 5'11"
1982 to 1992: 337 app 15 goals.

Newcastle United received sterling service from John Anderson following his arrival on a free transfer during the summer of 1982. Released by Gordon Lee at Preston after starting his senior career at The Hawthorns with West Bromwich Albion, the Dubliner proved United's ex-boss wrong as he became a terrace favourite at Gallowgate with his gutsy, never-say-die attitude on the pitch. Versatile at full-back, central defence or in the midfield anchor role, John had little of the finer skills on the ball, but was a workmanlike and honest professional respected by his team-mates. Consistent and reliable, he missed only one game during the Magpies promotion campaign of 1983-84 when he mixed his fearless and at times hard-hitting football with the Geordies playmakers. Winning 16 caps for the Republic of Ireland, an ankle injury then troubled him for almost four years and eventually forced him to quit first-class football in January 1992 after a decade at St James' Park. John later remained in the North East, for a time in charge of Berwick Rangers as well as playing non-league football. He had a short period on Newcastle's coaching staff in 1992 before covering the Magpies for local BBC radio where he became a well-liked broadcaster. For a time John assisted the Newcastle Kestrels' women's football club while Anderson played Gaelic football as a teenager and was also at Manchester United for trials.

SEASON REVIEW

Football League Div 2: P46 W14 D17 L15 F49 A56 Pts 59.
Position: 11th (Champions; Oldham Athletic).
FA Cup: R4 (Winners; Tottenham Hotspur).
FL Rumbelows Cup: R2 (Winners; Sheffield Wednesday).

Appearances (52m): Quinn M 49, Burridge J 45, Scott KW 45 (1), Kristensen B 43 (1), Brock KS 42 (2), Aitken RS 37, Anderson JCP 32, Ranson R 28 (3), Peacock GK 27, Stimson MN 27, O'Brien WF 26 (12), Watson SC 26 (2), Dillon KP 22, McGhee ME 21 (4), Clark LR 13 (6), Hunt A 13 (3), Sloan SM 13 (5), Sweeney PM 10 (1), Fereday W 8 (2), Bradshaw DS 7 (1), Srnicek P 7, Roche D 6 (3), Elliott RJ 5 (1), Gaynor T 4, Howey SN 4 (8), Gourlay AM 2 (1), Mitchell DS 2, Neilson AB 2 (1), Appleby MW 1 (1), Askew W 1 (1), Gallacher JA 1, Makel LR 1 (3), Moran P 1, Simpson N 1 (4), Robinson DJ 0 (4), Watson JI 0 (1).

Goals (55g): Quinn M 20, Peacock GK 7, McGhee ME 6, Brock KS 5, O'Brien WF 3, Anderson JCP 2, Clark LR 2, Hunt A 2, Stimson MN 2, Gaynor T 1, Kristensen B 1, Mitchell DS 1, Scott KW 1, Sloan SM 1, own goal 1.

Dismissals: 5 players; Quinn, Kristensen, Scott, Stimson, Howey.

MAJOR SIGNINGS

Gavin Peacock (Bournemouth) £450,000
Andy Hunt (Kettering Town) £210,000
Neil Simpson (Aberdeen) £100,000
Scott Sloan (Berwick Rangers) £65,000
Pavel Srnicek (FC Banik Ostrava) £350,000

FROM THE RANKS

Lee Clark (Wallsend sch, Es/Ey)
Robbie Elliott (Wallsend BC, Ey)
Alan Neilson (Cyprus sch)
Steve Watson (Wallsend BC, Ey)
John Watson (Wallsend BC)
Matty Appleby (Nunthorpe)
Lee Makel (Hilda Park Jnrs)

TEAM COLOURS Black & white striped shirts, black shorts (Change; canary yellow shirts with green trim, green shorts)

SEASON 1990-91

Match	Date	Venue	Opponent	Res	Score	HT	Att	Posn	Scorers
			FL Division 2 (Barclays)						
1	25 Aug	H	**Plymouth Argyle**	W	2 0	(1 0)	23,984	5	Kristensen, Quinn
2	01 Sep	A	Blackburn Rovers	W	1 0	(0 0)	11,329	5	O'Brien
3	08 Sep	H	**Millwall**	L	1 2	(0 1)	23,922	8	Quinn
4	15 Sep	A	Port Vale	W	1 0	(0 0)	10,025	5	Quinn
5	18 Sep	A	Sheffield Wednesday	D	2 2	(1 1)	30,628	4	McGhee 2
6	22 Sep	H	**West Ham United**	D	1 1	(1 1)	25,462	7	McGhee
7	29 Sep	A	Bristol City	L	0 1	(0 1)	15,858	10	
8	03 Oct	H	**Middlesbrough**	D	0 0	(0 0)	17,023	12	
9	06 Oct	H	**Portsmouth**	W	2 1	(1 0)	17,682	9	Quinn 2
10	13 Oct	A	Oxford United	D	0 0	(0 0)	6,820	9	
11	20 Oct	A	Ipswich Town	L	1 2	(0 2)	15,567	10	Quinn (pen)
12	24 Oct	H	**Charlton Athletic**	L	1 3	(0 2)	14,016	12	Brock
13	27 Oct	H	**West Bromwich Albion**	D	1 1	(0 1)	14,774	12	O'Brien
14	03 Nov	A	Hull City	L	1 2	(0 1)	8,375	16	McGhee
15	10 Nov	A	Wolverhampton Wanderers	L	1 2	(1 1)	18,721	19	Clark
16	17 Nov	H	**Barnsley**	D	0 0	(0 0)	15,548	19	
17	24 Nov	H	**Watford**	W	1 0	(0 0)	13,774	16	Quinn (pen)
18	01 Dec	A	Leicester City	L	4 5	(1 2)	11,045	16	Quinn 3, O'Brien
19	16 Dec	A	Plymouth Argyle	W	1 0	(0 0)	7,845	15	Peacock
20	22 Dec	A	Bristol Rovers	D	1 1	(0 0)	6,643	15	Gaynor
21	26 Dec	H	**Swindon Town**	D	1 1	(1 1)	17,003	15	Quinn
22	29 Dec	H	**Notts County**	L	0 2	(0 0)	17,557	16	
23	01 Jan	A	Oldham Athletic	D	1 1	(0 0)	14,550	15	Quinn
24	12 Jan	H	**Blackburn Rovers**	W	1 0	(0 0)	16,382	14	Mitchell
25	16 Jan	A	Brighton & Hove Albion	L	2 4	(0 1)	7,684	15	Quinn, Brock
26	19 Jan	A	Millwall	W	1 0	(1 0)	11,478	15	Peacock
27	02 Feb	H	**Port Vale**	W	2 0	(1 0)	14,602	12	Peacock, Quinn
28	23 Feb	H	**Wolverhampton Wanderers**	D	0 0	(0 0)	18,612	13	
29	27 Feb	H	**Brighton & Hove Albion**	D	0 0	(0 0)	12,692	13	
30	02 Mar	H	**Leicester City**	W	2 1	(2 0)	13,575	12	McGhee, Sloan
31	09 Mar	A	Watford	W	2 1	(1 0)	10,018	11	Anderson, Quinn
32	12 Mar	A	Middlesbrough	L	0 3	(0 2)	18,250	11	
33	16 Mar	H	**Bristol City**	D	0 0	(0 0)	13,578	11	
	20 Mar	H	**Oxford United**	Ab	1 0	(0 0)	9,658	11	*Quinn*
34	23 Mar	A	Portsmouth	W	1 0	(1 0)	9,607	11	Brock
35	30 Mar	A	Swindon Town	L	2 3	(1 1)	9,309	13	Peacock, Quinn
36	01 Apr	H	**Bristol Rovers**	L	0 2	(0 0)	17,509	14	
37	06 Apr	A	Notts County	L	0 3	(0 0)	7,806	16	
38	10 Apr	H	**Oxford United**	D	2 2	(1 1)	10,004	16	Hunt, og (Melville)
39	13 Apr	H	**Oldham Athletic**	W	3 2	(2 0)	16,615	13	Peacock, Hunt, Brock
40	17 Apr	H	**Sheffield Wednesday**	W	1 0	(1 0)	18,330	11	Brock
41	20 Apr	H	**Ipswich Town**	D	2 2	(1 2)	17,638	12	Stimson, Quinn
42	24 Apr	A	West Ham United	D	1 1	(1 0)	24,195	12	Peacock
43	27 Apr	A	Charlton Athletic	L	0 1	(0 0)	7,234	12	
44	04 May	A	West Bromwich Albion	D	1 1	(0 1)	16,706	11	Quinn
45	07 May	A	Barnsley	D	1 1	(1 0)	9,534	11	Peacock
46	11 May	H	**Hull City**	L	1 2	(0 1)	17,940	11	Clark
Round			**FA Cup**						
3	05 Jan	H	**Derby County**	W	2 0	(0 0)	19,748		Quinn, Stimson
4	13 Feb	H	**Nottingham Forest**	D	2 2	(2 0)	29,231		Quinn, McGhee
4r	18 Feb	A	Nottingham Forest	L	0 3	(0 1)	28,962		
Round			**FL Cup (Rumbelows Cup)**						
2(1)	25 Sep	A	Middlesbrough	L	0 2	(0 1)	15,042		
2(2)	10 Oct	H	**Middlesbrough**	W	1 0	(1 0)	12,778		Anderson
Round			**Full Members Cup (Zenith Data Systems Cup)**						
2	21 Nov	A	Nottingham Forest	L	1 2	(1 0)	9,567		Scott

Match	Burridge	Scott	Sweeney	Aitken	Kristensen	Ranson	Dillon	Anderson	Quinn	Howey	O'Brien	Brazil	Sloan	McGhee	Bradshaw	Brock	Fereday	Simpson	Gourlay	Gallacher
1	1	2	3	4	5	6	7	8	9	10	11	u	u							
2	1	2	3	4	5	6	7	8	9	s10	11			10	u					
3	1	2	3	4	5	6	7	8	9	s7	11			10		s11				
4	1	2		4	5	6	7	3	9		11			10		8	s7	s8		
5	1	2	u		5	6	7	3	9					10	4	8	11	s4		
6	1	2		4	5	6	7	3	9		s8			10		8	11	s3		
7	1	2		4	5	6			9					10	3			8	7	11
8	1	2	3	4	5	6	7		9		11			10		8				
9	1	2	3	4		6	7	5	9		11			10		8	u			
10	1	2		4		6		5	9		11		s7	10	3	8	7			
11	1	2	3	4	10d	s6		5	9		11		s11		6	8	7			
12	1	2	s3	4	5	6		3		9	11		7	10		8				
13	1	2	3		5	6				s7	11		7	10			9			
14	1	2	3			6		5			11		8	10					9	
15	1	2				6		5	9		11		8	10	4		3			
16	1	2				6		3	9		11		10		4	8	s4			
17	1	2		4	5			6	9		11		10			8				
18	1	2		4	5				9		11		10			8				
19	1	5		4	6	s6		2	9		s7		7			11				
20	1	5d		4	6	s11		2	9		7		u			11				
21	1	5		4	6	8	11	2	9		s10		10			7				
22	1	5		4	6	10	11	2	9		s4		s7			7				
23	1	5		4	6	2			9		s11		10			7				
24	1			4	6	2	7	5	9				u			s8				
25	1			4	6	2	10	5	9				s8			7				
26	1			4	6	2	7	5	9	u					s7	11				
27	1			4	6	2	7	5	9		u			u		11				
28	1	5		4	6	2	7		9					s10		11				
29	1	5		4	6	2	7		9		u			s8		11				
30	1	5		4	6			2	9	u	s7		7	10		11				
31	1	5		4	6			2	9		7			10		11				
32	1	5		4	6				9		7		s8			11				
33	1	5		4	6				9	10	s8			s10		11				
	1	*5*		*4*	*6*		*7*		*9*		*u*			*10*		*11*				
34	1	5		4	6		7		9		s11			10		11				
35	1	5		4			7	6	9					u	u	11				
36	1	5		4	s7		7	6	9					s10		11				
37	1	5		4	6			7	9					10		11				
38	1	5			6				9						u	11				
39	1	5			6				9							11				
40		5			6				9	s10	s7					11				
41		5			6				9	s10	s4					11				
42		5			6				9		4				u	11				
43		5			6				9	s10d	4					11				
44		5			6				9	s10	4									
45		5			6				9	s10	4									
46		5			6				9		4					11				
Round																				
3	1			4	6	2	8	5	9	u	u		10			7				
4	1	u		4	6	2	7	5	9		s11			10		8				
4r	1	s5		4	6	2	7	5	9		s10			10		8				
Round																				
2(1)	1	2	3	4	5	6			9		8			10		7	11	s10	s11	
2(2)	1	2	3	4				5	9d		11			10	6	8	7			
Round																				
2	1	2						3	9	7	11		10			8				

Match	Clark	Robinson	Appleby	Askew	Roche	Watson SC	Stimson	Gaynor	Peacock	Mitchell	Moran	Neilson	Hunt	Elliott	Makel	Srnicek	Watson JJ	
1																		1
2																		2
3																		3
4																		4
5																		5
6																		6
7	s8	s11																7
8	s5	u																8
9	s7																	9
10	u																	10
11																		11
12	s4																	12
13	8		4	s9														13
14	7		u	4	s9													14
15	7				u	s11												15
16	7					u	5											16
17	u				u		3	7										17
18	s7				u		3	7	6									18
19							3	10	8									19
20							3	10	8									20
21	u						3											21
22							3		8									22
23	u					11	3		8									23
24						11	3		8	10								24
25	u					11	3			8								25
26						10	3		8									26
27						10	3		8									27
28						s11	3d		8		10							28
29						10	3		8									29
30							3		8									30
31						3			8			s2	s10					31
32						3			8			2	10	s11				32
33						2			8			3	7					33
						2	*3*		*8*				*u*					
34						2	3		8				s10					34
35						2	3		8				10					35
36						2	3		8				10					36
37	s7					2	3		8				s10					37
38	7	s10			4	2	3		8				10					38
39	7	s10			4	2	3		8				10		u			39
40	7				4	2	3		8				10			1		40
41	7				4	2	3		8				10			1		41
42	7					2			8				10	3	u	1		42
43	7				s7	2			8				10	3		1		43
44	7				11	2			8				10	3	s2	1		44
45	7				s3	2			8				10	3	11	1		45
46	7					2			8				10	3	s10	1	s3	46
Round																		**Round**
3						11	3											3
4						11	3											4
4r						11	3											4r
Round																		**Round**
2(1)																		2(1)
2(2)	u	s3																2(2)
Round																		**Round**
2			s8		4	6	5								s4			2

Ab Abandoned after 45 mins due to rain

DateLine ... 10 Nov: Steve Watson appears against Wolves and becomes United's youngest player at 16 years 7 months and 9 days old. **1 Dec:** Another astonishing fixture with Leicester, this time won 5-4 by City at Filbert Street. **1 April:** Ossie Ardiles selects his first United eleven for the game with Bristol Rovers, a 2-0 defeat.

NEWCASTLE UNITED

SEASON 1991-92

DIVISION 2

Close to the edge on and off the field

The slight frame of Ossie Ardiles had a huge burden. To develop a side from within and lacking funds to spend was difficult enough, then he had to cope without the goals of Mick Quinn, a long term injury victim. Unquestionably, like Smith before him, events in the Boardroom took its toll while his youth policy was destined to fail, although a few of the youngsters were to later flourish.

At the same time as the little Argentinean tried to halt the slide on the field, recently knighted, Sir John Hall was making substantial inroads into forcing a coup at St James' Park. Having purchased much of the limited shareholding for vast sums of money and after an earlier brief period on the Board, he was invited to rejoin the club's directors during November. Newcastle were then close to financial collapse, they needed Hall's business acumen and not least his money. Gradually the Tyneside businessman forced through what just about all supporters now wanted, a complete takeover. By the end of the season the club belonged to Cameron-Hall empire. The revolution had started in earnest.

Before that dramatic turn of events happened, the Hall camp was influential in a change in manager. Newcastle United could not afford to deteriorate any further. Demotion to the then Third Division was unthinkable – and would result in financial ruin and probable bankruptcy. With United in a relegation fight, Ardiles was sacked following a defeat at Oxford during February. In jetted a past hero, Special K, Kevin Keegan, on a short-term mission to save United from the drop. Newcastle United never looked back.

Without any managerial experience, Keegan stirred both players and supporters. There was a fanfare welcome and home victory over Bristol City, then a struggle for points before crucial victories over Portsmouth – with a brilliant David Kelly half-volley securing a late 1-0 win – and a do-or-die 2-1 success at Filbert Street against Leicester on the last day of the season. United had survived the most crucial stage in their long history.

Pavel Srnicek arrived as an untested 'keeper who eventually commanded popular backing.

Memorabilia CORNER

United's programme heralded the return of Kevin Keegan and Terry McDermott.

IN CHARGE

Chairman: George Forbes/Sir John Hall
Manager: Ossie Ardiles/Kevin Keegan
Captain: Kevin Scott
Trainer/Coach: Tony Galvin/Terry McDermott/Derek Fazackerly
Club Sponsor: Newcastle Breweries
Kit Supplier: Umbro

ST JAMES' PARK

Average Attendance
Lg 21,024 Lg & Cup 20,748

Ossie Ardiles (centre, front) with his squad at the start of the 1991-92 season. His period in charge was not to last long.

PLAYER FOCUS Gavin Peacock

Born Welling. Striker, 5'8"
1990 to 1993: 120 app 46 goals.

The son of Charlton Athletic stalwart and Tyneside-born Keith Peacock, United claimed the talented Bournemouth striker in November 1990 for £450,000. That deal proved a steal as Gavin showed he was a most effective forward. With talent on the ball and the football brain to think ahead and work with colleagues, Peacock was influential in United's black-and-white, first, as the club survived the drop into the third-tier in 1992, then as part of Keegan's new combination which lifted the Division One Championship crown a year later. Able to operate in midfield as well, Peacock was often the team's star individual, non-more so than during 90 minutes at Filbert Street at the end of the 1991-92 season when his performance played a vital part in United remaining in the Second Division. A past England schools and youth international, Peacock's twists and turns up front and clean strike of the ball were a feature of the Magpies eleven for three seasons. Heading back south to join Chelsea in July 1993 for a £1.25m fee due to family reasons, Gavin did well at Stamford Bridge playing in over 100 matches and reaching the FA Cup final. He concluded his career with the club he started at, Queens Park Rangers and retired from the game in 2002. With a religious belief, in 2008 he quit a prominent role in the football media to study theology and become a Christian minister.

SEASON REVIEW

Football League Div 2: P46 W13 D13 L20 F66 A84 Pts 52.
Position: 20th (Champions; Ipswich Town).
FA Cup: R3 (Winners; Liverpool).
FL Rumbelows Cup: R3 (Winners; Manchester United).

Appearances (52m): Peacock GK 51, Scott KW 50, O'Brien WF 46, Wright TJ 36, Brock KS 34 (4), Clark LR 31 (4), Hunt A 27 (6), Kelly DT 26, Stimson MN 25 (1), Watson SC 25 (5), Bradshaw DS 21 (2), Roche D 21 (9), Appleby MW 20 (3), Quinn M 20 (4), Neilson AB 19, Srnicek P 16, Howey SN 14 (12), Carr FA 13 (3), Sheedy KM 13, Thompson A 13 (2), Kilcline B 12, Elliott RJ 11, Bodin PJ 6, Makel LR 6 (4), Ranson R 5 (1), Maguire GT 3, Walker AF 3, McDonough DK 2 (1), Wilson T 2, Kristensen B 1 (1), Fashanu JS 0 (1), Garland PJ 0 (2), Gourlay AM 0 (1), Robinson DJ 0 (3).

Goals (79g): Peacock GK 21, Hunt A 12, Kelly DT 11, Quinn M 10, Clark LR 6, Brock KS 4, O'Brien WF 4, Carr FA 2, Howey SN 2, Makel LR 1, Neilson AB 1, Scott KW 1, Sheedy KM 1, Watson SC 1, own goals 2.

Dismissals: 5 players; Bradshaw, Thompson, O'Brien, Scott, Brock.

MAJOR SIGNINGS

David Kelly (Leicester City) £250,000
Kevin Sheedy (Everton) free
Brian Kilcline (Oldham Ath) £250,000
Franz Carr (Nottingham Forest) £250,000
Darron McDonough (Luton Town) £80,000

FROM THE RANKS

Alan Thompson (Newcastle sch, Es/Ey)

TEAM COLOURS Black & white striped shirts, black shorts (Change; canary yellow shirts with green trim, green shorts)

SEASON 1991-92

Match	Date	H/A	Opponent	Res	F	A	HT	Att	Pos	Scorers	Srnicek	Watson SC	Elliott	O'Brien	Scott	Bradshaw	Clark	Peacock	Quinn	Carr	Brock	Robinson	Roche	Hunt	Makel	Neilson	Howey	Stimson	Walker	Appleby MW	Maguire	Wright	Thompson	Gourlay	Gallacher	Bodin	Kelly	Wilson	Ranson	Kilcline	Sheedy	McDonough	Kristensen	Garland	Fashanu	Match
			FL Division 2 (Barclays)																																											
1	18 Aug	A	Charlton Athletic	L	1	2	(0 0)	9,322		Carr	1	2	3	4	5	6	7	8	9	10	11	s2	s11																							1
2	24 Aug	H	**Watford**	D	2	2	(1 1)	22,440	19	Hunt, Clark	1	2	3	4	5	6	7	8	9	10			u	11	u																					2
3	27 Aug	A	Middlesbrough	L	0	3	(0 1)	16,970	22		1	s11	3	4	5	6	7	8	9	10			s4	11		2																				3
4	31 Aug	A	Bristol Rovers	W	2	1	(1 0)	6,334	18	O'Brien, Quinn	1		3	4	5	6	7	8	9	10			11	u	s11	2																				4
5	04 Sep	H	**Plymouth Argyle**	D	2	2	(0 1)	19,543	17	Carr, Quinn	1		3	4	5	6	7	8	9	10			11	s8	s11	2																				5
6	07 Sep	A	Tranmere Rovers	L	2	3	(2 1)	11,465	19	O'Brien, Clark	1	2	3	4	5	6	7	8	9	10	11		s11	u																						6
7	14 Sep	H	**Wolverhampton Wanderers**	L	1	2	(0 0)	20,195	20	og (Madden)	1		3	4	5	6	7	2	9	10	8		u	11			u																			7
8	17 Sep	H	**Ipswich Town**	D	1	1	(0 1)	16,336	21	Quinn (pen)	1			4	5	6	7	2	9	10	8		s10	11			s11	3																		8
9	21 Sep	A	Millwall	L	1	2	(1 1)	9,156	22	Neilson	1			4	5	6	7	8	9		11		u	s10		2		3	10																	9
10	28 Sep	H	**Derby County**	D	2	2	(0 1)	17,581	23	Hunt, Quinn	1		3	4	5	6	7	8	9		11		s6	s10		2			10																	10
11	05 Oct	A	Portsmouth	L	1	3	(0 2)	10,175	24	Quinn	1			4	5	6d	7	8	9	s10			11	10		2		3		s11																11
12	12 Oct	H	**Leicester City**	W	2	0	(0 0)	16,966	22	Hunt, Clark	1			4	5		7	8		11	s9		9	10		2	s11	3			6															12
13	19 Oct	H	**Oxford United**	W	4	3	(2 1)	16,454	21	Hunt, Peacock 3				4	5		7	8			u	s10	11	10		2	9	3			6	1														13
14	26 Oct	A	Bristol City	D	1	1	(1 0)	8,613	20	Clark				4	5		7	8				s8	11	10	s2	2	9	3			6	1														14
15	02 Nov	A	Swindon Town	L	1	2	(0 1)	10,731	21	Peacock				4	5	2	7	8					11	10			9	3		6		1	s10	u												15
16	06 Nov	H	**Cambridge United**	D	1	1	(0 0)	13,077	21	Hunt				4	5	2	7	8			10		11	s10			9	3		6		1	s2													16
17	09 Nov	H	**Grimsby Town**	W	2	0	(2 0)	16,959	21	Hunt, Howey		s10		4	5			8			10		2	11			9	3		6		1	7		u											17
18	17 Nov	A	Sunderland	D	1	1	(0 1)	29,224	21	O'Brien		s2		4	5	2		8					7	11	s10		9	3		6		1	10													18
19	20 Nov	H	**Southend United**	W	3	2	(3 1)	14,740	15	Peacock 2 (1 pen), Hunt		2		4	5	s3		8			s10		7	10			9	3		6		1	11													19
20	23 Nov	H	**Blackburn Rovers**	D	0	0	(0 0)	23,639	16			2	3	4	5	u		8			s11		7	10			9			6		1	11													20
21	30 Nov	A	Barnsley	L	0	3	(0 3)	9,648	17			2		4	5	s6		8			s11		7	10			9	3		6		1	11													21
22	07 Dec	H	**Port Vale**	D	2	2	(1 1)	18,162	17	Makel, Peacock (pen)		u		4	5			8			11		2	10	7		u			6		1				3	9									22
23	14 Dec	A	Brighton & Hove Albion	D	2	2	(2 1)	7,658	18	Peacock, Kelly		s4		4	5			8			11		2	10	7		u			6		1				3	9									23
24	20 Dec	A	Plymouth Argyle	L	0	2	(0 1)	5,048	18			s2			5	2		8			11		4	10	7		s7			6		1				3	9									24
25	26 Dec	H	**Middlesbrough**	L	0	1	(0 0)	26,563	21			2			5		s4	8			11		4	10	7		s7			6		1				3	9									25
26	28 Dec	H	**Bristol Rovers**	W	2	1	(0 1)	19,329	18	Brock, Kelly		2			5		7	8			11			10	u		s10			6		1	4			3	9									26
27	01 Jan	A	Southend United	L	0	4	(0 2)	9,458	20			2			5	u	7	8						s9	11		10			6		1	4			3	9									27
28	11 Jan	A	Watford	D	2	2	(1 2)	9,811	22	Kelly, Hunt		2		4	5	3	7	8					10	s3			u			6		1	11				9									28
29	18 Jan	H	**Charlton Athletic**	L	3	4	(3 1)	15,663	23	Clark, Hunt, Brock		2		4	5		7	8			11		s10	10			s9			6		1	3				9									29
30	01 Feb	A	Oxford United	L	2	5	(0 1)	5,872	23	Scott, Peacock (pen)				4	5		7	8			11			10		2	s3	3		s10		1					9	6								30
31	08 Feb	H	**Bristol City**	W	3	0	(0 0)	29,263	22	Kelly 2, O'Brien		7		4	5		u	8			11		s10			6		3				1					9	10	2							31
32	15 Feb	A	Blackburn Rovers	L	1	3	(1 1)	19,511	22	Kelly		7		4		5	10	8		s2	11		u			6		3				1					9		2							32
33	22 Feb	H	**Barnsley**	D	1	1	(0 0)	27,670	22	Kelly		2		4			10	8		s10	11		s7			6		3				1					9			5	7					33
34	29 Feb	A	Port Vale	W	1	0	(1 0)	10,321	19	Watson		7		4	6		s10	8	10		11		u			2		3				1					9			5						34
35	07 Mar	H	**Brighton & Hove Albion**	L	0	1	(0 0)	24,597	21			7		4	6			8	s7		11					u		3		2		1					9			5	10					35
36	10 Mar	A	Cambridge United	W	2	0	(2 0)	8,254	19	Peacock, Kelly		2		4	6			8	7		11					u		u				1	3				9			5	10					36
37	14 Mar	H	**Swindon Town**	W	3	1	(1 0)	23,138	18	Kelly, Peacock, Quinn		2		4	6			8	7		11						u	s3				1	3				9			5	10					37
38	21 Mar	A	Grimsby Town	D	1	1	(1 1)	11,613	19	Sheedy		2			6			8	7		11						u	3				1					9		s4	5	10	4				38
39	29 Mar	H	**Sunderland**	W	1	0	(1 0)	30,306	17	Kelly		2		4	6		u	8	7		11							3				1					9			5	10	u				39
40	31 Mar	A	Wolverhampton Wanderers	L	2	6	(1 3)	14,480	18	Quinn, Peacock		2		4	6		u	8	7		11							3				1					9			5	10	s5				40
41	04 Apr	H	**Tranmere Rovers**	L	2	3	(1 2)	21,125	19	Brock 2	1	2			6		s4	8	7		11						5	3									9		u		10	4				41
42	11 Apr	A	Ipswich Town	L	2	3	(2 1)	20,673	19	Peacock 2				4	6		7	8	s7		11						5	3				1					9		2		10		s2			42
43	18 Apr	H	**Millwall**	L	0	1	(0 0)	23,821	21					4	6		7	8	s7		11						3					1					9			5	10		2	s2		43
44	20 Apr	A	Derby County	L	1	4	(0 2)	21,363	22	Peacock		2		4d	6d			8	u	7	11d						s7					1	3				9			5	10					44
45	25 Apr	H	**Portsmouth**	W	1	0	(0 0)	25,989	20	Kelly		u		4	6			8	s11	7	11					3						1					9		2	5	10					45
46	02 May	A	Leicester City	W	2	1	(1 0)	21,861	20	Peacock, og (Walsh)				4	6		s11	8		7	11					3						1					9		2	5	10			s3		46
Round			**FA Cup**																																											**Round**
3	04 Jan	A	AFC Bournemouth	D	0	0	(0 0)	10,651				2		4	5	3	7	8			11			10			s10			6		1	u				9									3
3r	14 Jan	H	**AFC Bournemouth**	Ab	0	0	(0 0)	20,348				2		4	5		7	8			u		11	10			u			6		1	3				9									3r
3r	22 Jan	H	**AFC Bournemouth**	Dep	2	2	(1 0)	25,954		Hunt 2		2		4	5		7	8			11		9	10	u		s9			6		1	3d													3rr
Round			**FL Cup (Rumbelows Cup)**																																											**Round**
2(1)	24 Sep	A	Crewe Alexandra	W	4	3	(2 3)	4,251		Hunt, Peacock 3	1		3	4	5	6	7	8	9				11	10		2	s10			s11																2(1)
2(2)	09 Oct	H	**Crewe Alexandra**	W	1	0	(0 0)	9,197		Howey	1			4	5		7	8		11			u	10		2	s9	3	9	6																2(2)
3	29 Oct	A	Peterborough United	L	0	1	(0 0)	10,382						4	5	2	7						11	10	8		9	3		6		1		s8											s10	3
Round			**Full Members Cup (Zenith Data Systems Cup)**																																											**Round**
1	01 Oct	A	Tranmere Rovers	Dep	6	6	(2 2)	4,056		Quinn 3 (1 pen), Peacock 2, Clark	1		3	4	5	6	7	8	9		11		s11	10		2			u																	1

Ab — Abandoned after 17 mins due to fog

Dep — Drawn after extra time, tie lost on penalties (3-4 v AFC Bournemouth) (2-3 v Tranmere Rovers)

DateLine ... 1 Oct: A bizarre Full Members Cup game at Tranmere ends level at 6-6, United losing on penalties. **23 Nov:** United field their youngest ever side at the time against Blackburn with an average age of just under 22 years old. **8 Feb:** Kevin Keegan's first game as he returns as boss, a 3-0 victory over Bristol City. **20 April:** The Magpies finish the match at Derby with eight men, having three players sent-off, and lose 4-1. **25 April:** A single goal triumph over Portsmouth gives Newcastle a lifeline in the relegation struggle. **2 May:** The Black'n'Whites survive on the last day of the programme with a 2-1 win at Leicester.

NEWCASTLE UNITED

Revolution brings instant impact

With the introduction of the glitzy Premier League, the old Second Division was relabelled the First Division and the historic Football League Championship trophy, became the prize for promotion to what developed into the millionaire's paradise of the Premiership. With a new found cash-mountain from satellite television, that enormous change came at the right time for Newcastle United. Revolution within the corridors of Gallowgate was relentless. Hall and his corporate team dramatically transformed the club off the pitch; while Keegan not surprisingly was given the full-time job to make sure the Magpies joined the rich elite of the Premiership. The roller-coaster of the new, modern Newcastle United was off and running at pace.

Keegan installed a new air of confidence in both his players and supporters. From a relegation rabble, United turned into stylish Champions overnight. He was the catalyst and once the bandwagon got underway, it was difficult to stop. United started the new season with a bang, winning their first ten League games – and by displaying a brand of football that had not been seen by a team wearing the famous black-and-white stripes for many a year. A victory over Sunderland recorded 11 wins out of 11 played.

They cruised to the Division One title, and in the process the manager was planning for next season. Keegan had already purchased men of quality in Barry Venison, John Beresford and Rob Lee, when towards the end of the campaign he smashed the club's transfer record by some way by paying £1.75m for young England Under-21 striker Andy Cole, this after trying to land exiled Geordie Alan Shearer. Newcastle secured promotion with a 2-0 victory on a stirring evening at Grimsby's Blundell Park during May. The season was rounded off with a truly magnificent home send-off; a 7-1 victory in the sun against Leicester City. The Premier League awaited the re-born Newcastle United.

Pictured above: David Kelly became the Magpies' focal point at centre-forward as United cruised to the title.

Memorabilia CORNER

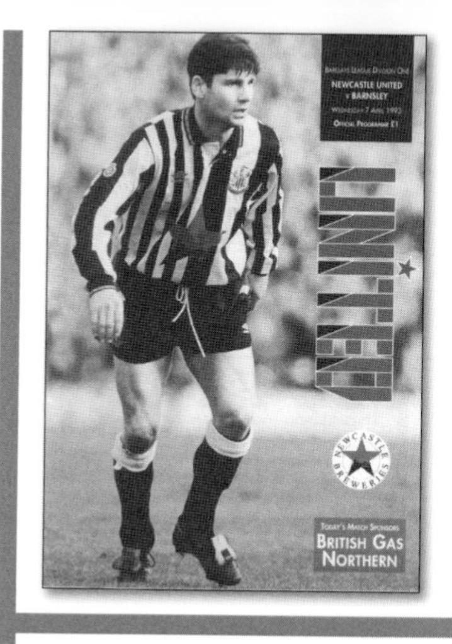

Paul Bracewe is pictured on the Barnsley programme, a 6-0 promotion extravaganza.

IN CHARGE

Chairman: Sir John Hall
Manager: Kevin Keegan
Captain: Brian Kilcline/Barry Venison
Trainer/Coach: Terry McDermott/Derek Fazackerly
Club Sponsor: Newcastle Breweries
Kit Supplier: Umbro

ST JAMES' PARK

Average Attendance
Lg 29,048 Lg & Cup 28,403

Kevin Keegan and assistant Terry McDermott (centre, front) at the beginning of the landmark 1992-93 Championship winning season.

PLAYER FOCUS Lee Clark

Born Wallsend. Midfield, 5'7"
1988 to 2007: 265 app 28 goals.

Raised supporting United and on the club's books since at school, Lee Clark was destined for a career in football even before he signed apprentice forms in the close-season of 1988. An England schoolboy star, he made his debut for Newcastle in season 1990-91 as a 17-year-old and with shaven-head became something of a local favourite as United secured promotion and the Division One title in 1993. He was an ever-present in that success story, a midfielder with foresight and consistently accurate with short and long balls. A regular for the England Under-21 team, he was unable to command a regular place in Keegan's side of internationals afterwards and Lee reluctantly moved to Sunderland in June 1997 where he again helped his club to promotion, as he did at his next stop, Fulham. Clark never lost his passion for everything black-and-white, and even made headlines by wearing a now infamous anti-Sunderland t-shirt at the Magpies' 1999 FA Cup final. That ended his Wearside career and made him even more of a cult hero to Toon supporters. Clark made a popular return to Gallowgate in August 2005, joining the coaching staff although he was also registered as a player going onto pull on the Magpie shirt once more on 25 occasions in season 2005-06. He moved to Norwich as coach in November 2007 after almost 500 senior games and then became boss of Huddersfield Town two years later. Lee picked up the nickname of Gnasher in United's dressing-room while he reached the England squad at full international level without gaining a first cap.

SEASON REVIEW

Football League Div 1: P46 W29 D9 L8 F92 A38 Pts 96.
Position: 1st, Champions.
FA Cup: R5 (Winners; Arsenal).
FL Coca-Cola Cup: R3 (Winners; Arsenal).

Appearances (61m): Clark LR 58, Kelly DT 57, Scott KW 56, Venison B 55, Howey SN 53, Beresford J 52, Lee RM 43, O'Brien WF 43, Srnicek P 41, Peacock GK 39 (3), Sheedy KM 33 (2), Bracewell PW 23 (8), Wright TJ 20, Kilcline B 15 (14), Sellars S 13, Carr FA 12 (5), Cole AA 11 (1), Brock KS 8 (4), Quinn M 8 (4), Neilson AB 6 (1), Ranson R 4 (1), Thompson A 4 (1), Kristensen B 3 (1), Stimson MN 3 (1), Watson SC 3 (2), Appleby MW 2 (1), Appleby RD 2, Hunt A 2, Robinson MJ 2 (7), Garland PJ 0 (1), Roche D 0 (1), Watson JI 0 (1).

Goals (114g): Kelly DT 28, Peacock GK 18, Lee RM 13, Cole AA 12, Clark LR 10, O'Brien WF 7, Quinn M 5, Sheedy KM 5, Bracewell PW 2, Brock KS 2, Howey SN 2, Scott KW 2, Sellars S 2, Beresford J 1, Carr FA 1, Kristensen B 1, own goals 3.

Dismissals: 2 players; Sheedy, Kelly.

MAJOR SIGNINGS

Robert Lee (Charlton Ath) £700,000
Scott Sellars (Leeds Utd) £600,000
Paul Bracewell (Sunderland) £250,000
John Beresford (Portsmouth) £650,000
Barry Venison (Liverpool) £250,000
Mark Robinson (Barnsley) £450,000
Andy Cole (Bristol City) £1.75m club record fee

FROM THE RANKS

None

TEAM COLOURS Black & white striped shirts, black shorts (Change; canary yellow shirts with green trim, green shorts)

SEASON 1992-93

Match			FL Division 1 (Barclays)					Posn		Wright	Venison	Beresford	Bracewell	Kilcline	Howey	Watson SC	Peacock	Kelly	Clark	Sheedy	Quinn	Stimson	Scott	Carr	Ranson	O'Brien	Brock	Thompson	Lee	Neilson	Srnicek	Kristensen	Robinson	Sellars	Cole	McDonough	Garland	Appleby MW	Hunt	Appleby RD	Watson JI	Roche	Murray	Cormack	Match
1	15 Aug	H	**Southend United**	W	3 2	(2 0)	28,545		Bracewell, og (Prior), Clark	1	2	3	4	5	6	7	8	9	10	11	u	u																							1
2	22 Aug	A	Derby County	W	2 1	(0 0)	17,522	4	Peacock, Clark	1	2	3		5	4		8	9	10	11	u		6	7	u																				2
3	29 Aug	H	**West Ham United**	W	2 0	(2 0)	29,855	4	Peacock, Kelly	1	2				6		8	9	10	11	u		5	7	3	4	u																		3
4	02 Sep	H	**Luton Town**	W	2 0	(2 0)	27,054	2	Clark, Kelly	1	2				6		8	9	10	11	u		5	7	3	4	u																		4
5	05 Sep	A	Bristol Rovers	W	2 1	(1 1)	7,487	2	Sheedy, O'Brien	1	2		s8	ss8	6		8	9	10	11			5	7	3	4																			5
6	12 Sep	H	**Portsmouth**	W	3 1	(2 0)	29,885	1	Quinn 2, Kelly	1	2	3		u	6			9	10	11	8		5	7		4		s9																	6
7	19 Sep	H	**Bristol City**	W	5 0	(2 0)	29,465	1	O'Brien, Peacock 2 (2 pens), Carr, Brock	1	2	3			6		8	9	10	11	s7		5	7		4	s11																		7
8	26 Sep	A	Peterborough United	W	1 0	(0 0)	14,487	1	Sheedy	1	2	3		u	6			9	10	11	8		5			4	s8		7																8
9	04 Oct	A	Brentford	W	2 1	(1 0)	10,131	1	Kelly, Peacock	1	2	3		u	6		8	9	10	11	u		5			4			7																9
10	10 Oct	H	**Tranmere Rovers**	W	1 0	(1 0)	30,137	1	Kelly	1	2	3			6		8	9	10		11	u	5	u		4			7																10
11	18 Oct	A	Sunderland	W	2 1	(1 0)	28,098	1	og (Owers), O'Brien	1	2	3		u	6		8	9	10		u		5			4	11		7																11
12	24 Oct	H	**Grimsby Town**	L	0 1	(0 0)	30,088	1		1	2	3	s11	s2	6		8		10		9		5			4	11		7																12
13	31 Oct	A	Leicester City	L	1 2	(0 2)	19,687	1	O'Brien	1		3	u	s7	6		8	9	10	11d			5			4	7			2															13
14	04 Nov	A	Birmingham City	W	3 2	(3 2)	14,376	1	Peacock, Scott, og (Matthewson)	1	2	3		s11	6		8	9	10	11			5	7		4	s1																		14
15	08 Nov	H	**Swindon Town**	D	0 0	(0 0)	28,091	1			2	3		u	6		8	9	10	11	u		5	7		4					1														15
16	14 Nov	A	Charlton Athletic	W	3 1	(2 0)	12,945	1	Peacock 2, Howey		2	3	11	u	6		8	9	10				5	u		4			7		1														16
17	21 Nov	H	**Watford**	W	2 0	(0 0)	28,871	1	Peacock, Lee		2	3	11	s6	6		8	9	10				5	s7		4			7		1														17
18	28 Nov	H	**Cambridge United**	W	4 1	(1 0)	27,991	1	Kelly 3 (1 pen), Peacock		2	3		6			8	9	10				5	u		4		11	7	u	1														18
19	05 Dec	A	Notts County	W	2 0	(0 0)	14,840	1	Sheedy, Peacock		2	3		u	6		8	9	10	11			5	u		4			7		1														19
20	13 Dec	A	Barnsley	L	0 1	(0 0)	13,263	1			2	3	u	u	6		8	9	10	11			5			4			7		1														20
21	20 Dec	H	**Millwall**	D	1 1	(0 1)	26,089	1	Kelly (pen)		2	3	8	s3	6			9	10	11			5	s11		4			7		1														21
22	26 Dec	H	**Wolverhampton Wanderers**	W	2 1	(1 1)	30,137	1	Kelly 2		2		u		6		8	9	10	11			5	u		4			7	3	1														22
23	28 Dec	A	Oxford United	L	2 4	(2 3)	9,293	1	O'Brien, Clark		2	3	u	s8	6		8	9	10	11			5			4			7		1														23
24	09 Jan	A	Bristol City	W	2 1	(2 1)	15,446	1	Kelly, Scott		2	3	s11	u	6		8	9	10	11			5			4			7		1														24
25	16 Jan	H	**Peterborough United**	W	3 0	(1 0)	29,155	1	Lee 2, Kelly		2	3	s11	u	6		8	9	10	11			5			4			7		1														25
26	20 Jan	A	Southend United	D	1 1	(1 1)	8,246	1	Peacock		2	3		u	6		8	9	10				5			4	11		7		1	u													26
27	27 Jan	A	Luton Town	D	0 0	(0 0)	10,237	1			2	3	11	u	6		8	9	10	u			5			4			7		1														27
28	31 Jan	H	**Derby County**	D	1 1	(0 1)	27,285	1	O'Brien		2	3	s11	s9	6		8	9	10	11			5			4			7		1														28
29	09 Feb	A	Portsmouth	L	0 2	(0 2)	21,028	1			2	3	11	5			8	9	10	s11			6			4			7	u	1														29
30	21 Feb	A	West Ham United	D	0 0	(0 0)	24,159	1			2	3	u	u	6		8	9	10	11			5			4			7		1														30
31	24 Feb	H	**Bristol Rovers**	D	0 0	(0 0)	29,372	1			2	3	u	6		s11	8	9	10	11			5			4			7		1														31
32	28 Feb	A	Tranmere Rovers	W	3 0	(2 0)	13,082	1	Lee 2, Kelly		2	3	ss5	s5	6		8	9	10	11			5			4			7		1														32
33	06 Mar	H	**Brentford**	W	5 1	(1 0)	30,006	1	Kelly, Bracewell, Clark 2, Lee		2	3	8		6			9	10			11	5			4	u		7	s6	1														33
34	10 Mar	H	**Charlton Athletic**	D	2 2	(2 1)	29,582	1	Lee, Kelly			3	8		6			9	10			s11	5			4			7	u	1		2	11											34
35	13 Mar	A	Swindon Town	L	1 2	(1 0)	17,574	1	Kelly		2	3	8		6			9	10				5			4			7		1		u	11	s4										35
36	20 Mar	H	**Notts County**	W	4 0	(1 0)	30,029	1	Lee, Kelly 2, Cole		2	3	4		6		s10	9	10				5						7		1		s5	11	8										36
37	23 Mar	A	Watford	L	0 1	(0 0)	11,634	1			2	3	4	u	6			9	10				5						7		1		s11	11	8										37
38	28 Mar	H	**Birmingham City**	D	2 2	(0 2)	27,087	1	Cole, Lee		2	3	4	u	6			9	10				5						7		1		u	11	8										38
39	03 Apr	A	Cambridge United	W	3 0	(1 0)	7,925	1	Howey, Kelly, Cole		2	3	4	u	6			9	10				5						7		1		s4	11	8										39
40	07 Apr	H	**Barnsley**	W	6 0	(2 0)	29,460	1	Cole 3, Clark, Beresford (pen), Sellars		2	3	4	s6	6			9	10				5						7		1		s4	11	8										40
41	10 Apr	A	Wolverhampton Wanderers	L	0 1	(0 0)	17,244	1			2	3	4	s9	6			9	10				5						7		1		s11	11	8										41
42	17 Apr	A	Millwall	W	2 1	(0 1)	14,262	1	Clark, Cole		2	3	4	6				9	10				5				u		7		1		s8	11	8										42
43	25 Apr	H	**Sunderland**	W	1 0	(1 0)	30,364	1	Sellars		2	3	4	u	6			9	10				5						7		1		u	11	8										43
44	04 May	A	Grimsby Town	W	2 0	(0 0)	14,402	1	Cole, Kelly		2	3	4	u	6		u	9	10				5						7		1			11	8										44
45	06 May	H	**Oxford United**	W	2 1	(0 0)	29,438	1	Clark, Cole		2	3	4	6			s4	9	10				5						7		1		s7	11	8										45
46	09 May	H	**Leicester City**	W	7 1	(6 0)	30,129	1	Cole 3, Lee, Kelly 3		2	3		s6	6		s3	9	10				5						7		1		4	11	8										46
Round			FA Cup																																										Round
3	02 Jan	H	**Port Vale**	W	4 0	(0 0)	29,873		Lee, Peacock 2, Sheedy		2	3	s9	s5	6		8	9	10	11			5			4			7		1														3
4	23 Jan	A	Rotherham United	D	1 1	(1 0)	13,405		Lee		2	3	11	u	6		8	9	10				5			4	u		7		1														4
4r	03 Feb	H	**Rotherham United**	W	2 0	(0 0)	29,005		Kelly, Clark		2	3	11	s6	6		8	9	10	s8			5			4			7		1														4r
5	13 Feb	A	Blackburn Rovers	L	0 1	(0 0)	19,972				2	3	s11	6			8	9	10	11			5			4			7	u	1														5
Round			FL Cup (Coca-Cola Cup)																																										Round
1(1)	19 Aug	H	**Mansfield Town**	W	2 1	(1 0)	14,083		Peacock 2	1	2	3		5	4		8	9	10	11	s9		6	s7			7																		1(1)
1(2)	25 Aug	A	Mansfield Town	D	0 0	(0 0)	6,725			1	2			5	4		8	9	10	11	u		6	7	3		u																		1(2)
2(1)	23 Sep	H	**Middlesbrough**	D	0 0	(0 0)	25,814			1	2	3			6			9	10	11	8		5	s7		4	u		7																2(1)
2(2)	07 Oct	A	Middlesbrough	W	3 1	(1 0)	24,390		O'Brien, Kelly 2	1	2	3		u	6		8	9	10	11	s11		5			4			7																2(2)
3	28 Oct	A	Chelsea	L	1 2	(0 0)	30,193		Lee	1		3	u	u	6		8		10		9		5			4	11		7	2															3
Round			Anglo-Italian Cup																																										Round
P	16 Sep	A	Grimsby Town	D	2 2	(2 1)	2,159		Quinn, Kelly		2	3		4	6			9	10		8		5	u			11				1	7				u									P
P	30 Sep	H	**Leicester City**	W	4 0	(2 0)	14,046		Brock, Quinn 2 (1 pen), Sheedy					5				9		11	8	3				4	7	10		6	1	2					s4	s9							P
Gp A	11 Nov	A	AS Lucchese	D	1 1	(0 1)	744		Kristensen		2	3	4	5	6	u	8		10	11	s7			7			s9	u			1	9													Gp A
Gp A	24 Nov	H	**Ascoli**	L	0 1	(0 0)	9,789				2			5		7		9d		11			6	s7	s8	4		10		3	1						u		8				u		Gp A
Gp A	08 Dec	A	AS Bari	L	0 3	(0 2)	1,229							5	6	4				11		3	u	7				10			1							2	9	8	s9	s11		u	Gp A
Gp A	16 Dec	H	**AC Cesena**	D	2 2	(1 1)	4,609		Peacock 2	1			5		6	s11	8	9	10					7	u	4				3		s6						2		11			u		Gp A

DateLine ... 18 Oct: United register a club record 11 successive victories from the start of the season with a derby win over Sunderland. **11 Nov:** An attendance of only 744 at Italian club Luchesse is the lowest to watch a competitive match since pioneer days. **4 May:** Promotion is assured with a 2-0 victory at Blundell Park, Grimsby.
9 May: The Magpies end the season as Champions with a sparkling 7-1 display against Leicester, being 6-0 up at the interval.

SEASON 1993-94

PREMIER LEAGUE

The Entertainers are born

With around £25m spent on totally transforming St James' Park, United's historic home was almost complete for the first game of the Premier League era, an attractive fixture with Tottenham Hotspur – ironically managed by Ossie Ardiles. United's former boss spoilt the party somewhat by guiding his Spurs eleven to victory. Matches were virtually a sell-out and a huge waiting list began to grow for season-tickets. Although losing that opener by a single goal, Newcastle soon came to terms with a competition that was quickly developing into Europe's elite league. With old favourite Peter Beardsley returning and becoming a focal point in the club's rebirth, the Magpies were amongst the top placings, in third spot by December. They had routed Liverpool 3-0 at Gallowgate – and completed a double over the Reds with a 2-0 success at Anfield later in the season. By then Keegan's trademark football – with slick, fast attacking moves – saw the Magpies branded as The Entertainers, fast becoming the most popular side in the country.

United demolished Notts County 11-2 over two legs in the League Cup but then went out to Wimbledon. Along with a FA Cup exit to Luton, they were the only low points of the season. In League action it was a different story. Six wins on the trot as spring approached showed that the new United meant business. The Magpies set about Swindon and scored seven goals to record the Premier League's highest score, while new centre-forward hero Andy Cole went from strength to strength. He hit the 40-goal barrier for the club with a strike in resounding triumph over Aston Villa – another terrific end-to-end contest that finished 5-1 to the Magpies.

The Black'n'Whites went onto claim a UEFA Cup place for the first time since 1977. It was a more than satisfying return to the top level. To finish in third place and qualify for Europe was a wonderful start to their Premier League life.

Pictured above: Liverpool full-back Barry Venison was an important addition to United's line-up.

Memorabilia CORNER

A busy programme cover for season 1993-94, Steve Howey is profiled.

IN CHARGE

Chairman: Sir John Hall
Manager: Kevin Keegan
Captain: Peter Beardsley
Trainer/Coach: Terry McDermott/Derek Fazackerly
Club Sponsor: Newcastle Breweries
Kit Supplier: Ascis

ST JAMES' PARK

Average Attendance
Lg 33,787 Lg & Cup 33,462

The Football League title silverware makes a return to St James' Park after 66 years as United start life in the new Premier League.

SEASON REVIEW

Premier League: P42 W23 D8 L11 F82 A41 Pts 77.
Position: 3rd (Champions; Manchester United).
FA Cup: R4 (Winners; Manchester United).
FL Coca-Cola Cup: R3 (Winners; Aston Villa).

Appearances (48m): Lee RM 47, Cole AA 45, Venison B 41 (1), Beardsley PA 41, Beresford J 40, Bracewell PW 36, Clark LR 34, Watson SC 34 (4), Sellars S 33 (2), Hooper MD 24, Srnicek P 22, Scott KW 21, Howey SN 16 (1), Elliott RJ 15 (2), Fox RA 14, Robinson MJ 13 (4), Allen M 12, Neilson AB 10 (4), Peacock D 9, Papavasiliou N 7, O'Brien WF 4 (2), Holland CJ 2 (1), Jeffrey MR 2, Kilcline B 2 (2), Wright TJ 2 (1), Appleby MW 1, Mathie AM 1 (16).

Goals (97g): Cole AA 41, Beardsley PA 24, Lee RM 8, Allen M 7, Sellars S 4, Mathie AM 3, Bracewell PW 2, Clark LR 2, Fox RA 2, Watson SC 2, own goals 2.

Dismissals: 1 player; Srnicek.

MAJOR SIGNINGS

Peter Beardsley (Everton) £1.5m
Mike Hooper (Liverpool) £550,000
Alex Mathie (Morton) £275,000
Niki Papavasiliou (OFI) £125,000
Ruel Fox (Norwich City) £2.25m club record fee
Darren Peacock (QPR) £2.7m club record fee

FROM THE RANKS

None

PLAYER FOCUS Andy Cole

Born Nottingham. Centre-forward, 5'11"
1993 to 1995: 84 app 68 goals.

When Kevin Keegan smashed the club record by paying a £1.75m fee for Bristol City's Andy Cole in March 1993, eyebrows were raised. Few knew much about the sleek and fast striker who had started in Arsenal's junior ranks. But 21-year-old Cole was a star in the making. He made a colossal impact on Tyneside, and very quickly on the Premiership. As a youngster at Highbury, he found it impossible to break through and moved to Ashton Gate. With only a season of first-team football behind him, Cole was thrown into the United attack and was an immediate success. He helped win the Division One title with a late rally, then smashed Newcastle's longstanding goals record by striking 41 in only 45 outings in season 1993-94 – his first in the Premier League. Having played for England schools, youth, Under-21 and B sides, a full call-up beckoned. Sensationally Andy was then sold for a then reported British record of £7m to Manchester United in January 1995. Magpie fans were stunned. Thereafter Cole matured and became a Reds' legend winning trophy after trophy, including the Champions League in 1999 while he also earned that England chance too. With formidable positional sense and pace to burn, he was a lethal hot-shot in the box, Andy totalling 270 senior goals in his career. Following a near seven year stay at Old Trafford, Cole appeared for Blackburn and in short spells at Fulham, Manchester City and Portsmouth, as well as Birmingham City, Sunderland, Burnley and Nottingham Forest. He retired in 2008 and entered coaching.

TEAM COLOURS Black & white striped shirts, black shorts (Change; all blue shirts & shorts with black trim)

SEASON 1993–94

Match	Date	Venue	Premiership (Carling)	Result	Score (HT)	Att	Posn	Scorers	Srnicek	Venison	Beresford	Bracewell	Scott	Howey	Lee	Allen	Cole	Clark	Papavasiliou	Watson SC	O'Brien	Burridge	Wright	Appleby MW	Neilson	Mathie	Beardsley	Kilcline	Hooper	Sellars	Elliott	Jeffrey	Robinson	Fox	Holland	Peacock	Reid	Match
								Squad numbers	1	2	3	4	5	6	7	21	9	10	17	19	16	29	13	24	20	14	8	15	30	11	26	31	12	5	23	15	29	
1	14 Aug	H	**Tottenham Hotspur**	L	0 1 (0 1)	35,216	15		1	2	3	4	5	6	7	8	9	10	11	s8	s11	u																1
2	18 Aug	A	Coventry City	L	1 2 (1 0)	15,763	18	og (Atherton)	1d	2	3	4	5		7	u	9	10	11	8	6		s11	u														2
3	21 Aug	A	Manchester United	D	1 1 (0 1)	41,829	17	Cole	1	2	3	4	5		7	u	9	10	11	8	6		u	u														3
4	25 Aug	H	**Everton**	W	1 0 (1 0)	34,833	14	Allen	1	2	3	4	5			8	9	10	11	7	6		u	u	u													4
5	29 Aug	H	**Blackburn Rovers**	D	1 1 (0 0)	34,272	15	Cole	1	2	3	4	5		7	u	9	10	11	8	6		u		u													5
6	31 Aug	A	Ipswich Town	D	1 1 (0 0)	19,126	16	Cole	1	2	3	4	5		7	8	9	10	11	6	s10		u		s11													6
7	13 Sep	H	**Sheffield Wednesday**	W	4 2 (1 1)	33,890	13	Cole 2, Mathie, Allen		2	3	4	5		7	8	9	10	11	6	u	u	1			s11												7
8	18 Sep	A	Swindon Town	D	2 2 (2 0)	15,015	13	Clark, Allen (pen)	u	2	3	4	5		7	11	9	10		6			1			u	8	u										8
9	25 Sep	H	**West Ham United**	W	2 0 (0 0)	34,366	11	Cole 2	u	2	3	4	5		7	11	9	10		6						u	8	u	1									9
10	02 Oct	A	Aston Villa	W	2 0 (0 0)	37,366	6	Allen (pen), Cole	u	2	3	4	5		7	11	9	10		6							8	u	1	u								10
11	16 Oct	H	**Queens Park Rangers**	L	1 2 (0 1)	33,926	11	Allen	u	2	3	4	5		7	11	9	10		6							8	u	1	u								11
12	24 Oct	A	Southampton	L	1 2 (0 0)	13,804	11	Cole	u	2	3	4	5		7	11	9	10		6						s11	8		1	s10								12
13	30 Oct	H	**Wimbledon**	W	4 0 (1 0)	33,371	9	Beardsley 3 (1 pen), Cole	u	2	3	4	5		7		9	10		6						u	8	u	1	11								13
14	08 Nov	A	Oldham Athletic	W	3 1 (0 1)	13,821	9	Cole 2, Beardsley	u	2		4	5		7		9	10		6					u	u	8		1	11	3							14
15	21 Nov	H	**Liverpool**	W	3 0 (3 0)	36,374	8	Cole 3	u	2		4	5		7	u	9	10		6						u	8		1	11	3							15
16	24 Nov	H	**Sheffield United**	W	4 0 (2 0)	35,101	4	og (Ward), Beardsley 2 (1 pen), Cole	u	2		4	5		7		9	10		6						s4	8	u	1	11	3							16
17	27 Nov	A	Arsenal	L	1 2 (0 1)	36,091	6	Beardsley	u	2		4	5	s3	7		9	10		6						s10	8		1	11	3							17
18	04 Dec	A	Tottenham Hotspur	W	2 1 (0 0)	30,780	3	Beardsley 2	u	2		4		5	7		9	10		6	u						8	u	1		3	11						18
19	11 Dec	H	**Manchester United**	D	1 1 (0 0)	36,388	4	Cole	u	2		4		5	7	u	9	10		6	u						8		1	11	3							19
20	18 Dec	A	Everton	W	2 0 (1 0)	25,189	4	Cole, Beardsley	u	2	3	4		5	7		9	10		6						u	8		1	11	s3							20
21	22 Dec	H	**Leeds United**	D	1 1 (0 0)	36,388	4	Cole	u	2	3	4		5	7		9	10		6						s10	8		1	11	u							21
22	28 Dec	A	Chelsea	L	0 1 (0 1)	23,133	5		u	2	3	4		5	7		9	10		6						s10	8		1	11			s6					22
23	01 Jan	H	**Manchester City**	W	2 0 (2 0)	35,585	5	Cole 2	u		3	4		6	7		9	10		s4						s2	8	5	1	11			2					23
24	04 Jan	A	Norwich City	W	2 1 (1 1)	19,564	4	Beardsley, Cole	u		3		5	6	7		9	10		u							8	u	1	11	4		2					24
25	16 Jan	A	Queens Park Rangers	W	2 1 (1 1)	15,774	3	Clark, Beardsley	u	2	3	4	u	6	7		9	10									8		1	11	u		5					25
26	22 Jan	H	**Southampton**	L	1 2 (1 1)	32,067	4	Cole	u	2	3	4	u	6	7		9	10								u	8		1	11			5					26
27	12 Feb	A	Wimbledon	L	2 4 (0 2)	13,358	4	Beardsley 2 (2 pens)	u	2	3			5	9			10		6						s9	8		1	11	4		u	7				27
28	19 Feb	A	Blackburn Rovers	L	0 1 (0 0)	21,269	5		1	2	3			5	9			10		6					u	u	8		u	11	4			7				28
29	23 Feb	H	**Coventry City**	W	4 0 (0 0)	32,210	3	Cole 3, Mathie	1						7		9	10		2				4	5	s11	8		u	11	3		s7	6				29
30	05 Mar	A	Sheffield Wednesday	W	1 0 (0 0)	33,153	4	Cole	1		3			4	7		9			6					5	u	8		u	11	s4		2	10				30
31	12 Mar	H	**Swindon Town**	W	7 1 (2 0)	32,219	3	Beardsley 2 (1 pen), Lee 2, Watson 2, Fox	1	4	3				7		9			6					u	u	8		u	11	5		2	10				31
32	19 Mar	A	West Ham United	W	4 2 (1 0)	23,132	3	Lee 2, Cole, Mathie	1	4	3				7		9			6					s6	s10	8		u	11	5		2	10				32
33	23 Mar	H	**Ipswich Town**	W	2 0 (1 0)	32,234	3	Sellars, Cole	1	4	3				7		9			6					s5	s6	8		u	11	5		2		10			33
34	29 Mar	H	**Norwich City**	W	3 0 (1 0)	32,228	3	Cole, Lee, Beardsley	1		3	4			7		9								6	s10	8		u	11			2	10	s4	5		34
35	01 Apr	A	Leeds United	D	1 1 (1 0)	40,005	3	Cole	1	s7	3	4			7		9								6	u	8		u	11			2	10		5		35
36	04 Apr	H	**Chelsea**	D	0 0 (0 0)	32,218	3		1	6	3	4			7		9								s3	s10	8		u	11			2		10	5		36
37	09 Apr	A	Manchester City	L	1 2 (1 1)	33,774	3	Sellars	1	3					7		9								6	s10	8		u	11		10	2	4		5	u	37
38	16 Apr	A	Liverpool	W	2 0 (1 0)	44,601	3	Lee, Cole	1	2	3	4			7		9								6	s8	8		u	11			s2	10		5		38
39	23 Apr	H	**Oldham Athletic**	W	3 2 (1 1)	32,214	3	Fox, Beardsley, Lee	1	2	3	4			7		9								6	u	8		u	11			u	10		5		39
40	27 Apr	H	**Aston Villa**	W	5 1 (3 1)	32,217	3	Bracewell, Beardsley 2 (1 pen), Cole, Sellars	1	2	3	4			7		9			s4					6	s9	8		u	11				10		5		40
41	30 Apr	A	Sheffield United	L	0 2 (0 0)	29,013	3		1	2	3	4			7		9			u					6	u	8		u	11				10		5		41
42	07 May	H	**Arsenal**	W	2 0 (0 0)	32,216	3	Cole, Beardsley (pen)	1	2	3				7		9			4					6		8		u	11		u	s4	10		5		42
Round			FA Cup																																			Round
3	08 Jan	H	**Coventry City**	W	2 0 (1 0)	35,444		Cole, Beardsley	u		3		5	6	7		9	10		s11							8	u	1	11	4		2					3
4	29 Jan	H	**Luton Town**	D	1 1 (0 1)	32,216		Beardsley (pen)	u	2	3	4	u	6	7		9	10		5						u	8		1	11								4
4r	09 Feb	A	Luton Town	L	0 2 (0 1)	12,503			u	2	3			5	7		9	10		6					u		8		1	11	4		u					4r
Round			FL Cup (Coca-Cola Cup)																																			Round
2(1)	22 Sep	H	**Notts County**	W	4 1 (1 1)	25,887		Cole 3, Bracewell	1	2	3	4			7	11	9	10	u	6		u				u	8	5										2(1)
2(2)	05 Oct	A	Notts County	W	7 1 (3 0)	6,068		Cole 3, Allen 2 (1 pen), Beardsley, Lee	u	2	3	4	5		7	11	9	10		6							8	s2	1	s4								2(2)
3	27 Oct	A	Wimbledon	L	1 2 (1 1)	11,531		Sellars	u	2	3	4	5		7	10				6					u	9	8	s10	1	11								3

DateLine ... 14 Aug: The new Leazes and upgraded Milburn Stands are opened for the first Premiership fixture with Tottenham. **21 Nov:** Newcastle field a rare all-English line-up in the fixture against Liverpool. **27 April:** Andy Cole sets a new goalscoring record for the club when he breaks the 40-goal barrier against Aston Villa.

NEWCASTLE UNITED

SEASON
1994-95
PREMIER LEAGUE

The rollercoaster gathers pace

The revitalised Newcastle United now had ambition. No-one could criticise the club at that time for a lack of drive and determination. And Keegan had plenty of money to spend to take United to the next level – to challenge for trophies. He brought in foreign World Cup stars from the summers' tournament, Philippe Albert and Marc Hottiger, the club now becoming more and more a cosmopolitan organisation like most of top football in England. Those two deals were the first of many which saw international players from all over the world end up on Tyneside.

Back on the European stage after a 17 year absence, the Magpies made their mark by demolishing Royal Antwerp in the opening round of the UEFA Cup by all of 10-2 on aggregate. Newcastle should have progressed further in the competition, but naivety in the home leg with Athletic Bilbao – conceding two away goals – was their downfall. But the European experience was welcome, the club becoming regular campaigners on the Continent over the next ten years.

As was to be Newcastle's unique way in this era, they made plenty of headlines. Although knocked out in the League Cup by Manchester City, Newcastle progressed to the quarter-final of the FA Cup in 1994-95, before losing by a single goal to Everton at Goodison Park. United's Premier League progress had a set-back, finishing in sixth place after leading the table during November. They missed European qualification while goalscoring sensation Andy Cole was sensationally sold for a record fee of £7m to the club the Magpies aspired to most, Manchester United. It was a bombshell and boss Keegan had to placate the fans who openly questioned the decision. But the manager had a longer term strategy and used the funds – and more on top – to revitalise his squad for the better in the summer.

Pictured above: Keith Gillespie was fast and direct on the wing as United's attack gelled.

Memorabilia CORNER

A European edition of United's magazine for the visit of Athletic Bilbao picturing Rob Lee.

IN CHARGE

Chairman: Sir John Hall
Manager: Kevin Keegan
Captain: Peter Beardsley
Trainer/Coach: Terry McDermott/Derek Fazackerly
Club Sponsor: Newcastle Breweries
Kit Supplier: Asics

ST JAMES' PARK

Average Attendance
Lg 34,692 Lg & Cup 33,894

United's Premier League first-team squad comprised 27 players. Arthur Cox makes a return to join Keegan and McDermott as the club's managerial team (front, centre).

PLAYER FOCUS Philippe Albert

Born Bouillon. Centre-half, 6'3"
1994 to 1999: 138 app 12 goals.

An automatic choice for the Belgian national side and a player who starred in the 1994 World Cup, Philippe Albert joined United in a £2.65m deal from RSC Anderlecht during August 1994 in readiness for United's second season in the Premier League. Tall, commanding and classy with the ball, Albert was a footballing centre-back who characterised Newcastle's Entertainers eleven. Philippe possessed a quality left-foot and always wanted to stride forward to both start, and take part in, the attack. Indeed, he scored several memorable goals, none more so that his precise and delightful 25-yard chip past Manchester United's Peter Schmeichel in 1996. Yet, the Belgian could be a competitor in defence as well, being tough and strong. Having won two Championship titles in his native country, he was an experienced and model professional to United for just over four seasons. Albert suffered two long term injury set-backs on Tyneside and underwent seven operations on his knee. Philippe headed to Fulham on loan in season 1998-99 before moving back to his local club in Belgium, Charleroi where he had began his senior career. Afterwards Philippe lived in his native Ardennes often a Belgian TV pundit and regularly to arrive back on Tyneside where he remains a popular character. Albert won 41 caps for his country and also took part in the 1990 World Cup tournament. He was Belgian Player of the Year in 1992.

SEASON REVIEW

Premier League: P42 W20 D12 L10 F67 A47 Pts 72.
Position: 6th (Champions; Blackburn Rovers).
FA Cup: R6 (Winners; Everton).
FL Coca-Cola Cup: R4 (Winners; Liverpool).
UEFA Cup: R2 (Winners; Parma AC).

Appearances (56m): Srnicek P 52, Fox RA 51, Hottiger M 51, Peacock D 48, Beresford J 46, Beardsley PA 44, Lee RM 44, Howey SN 39 (1), Venison B 36, Kitson P 31 (3), Cole AA 27, Watson SC 26 (9), Albert P 25, Sellars S 19, Gillespie KR 18 (2), Bracewell PW 16 (4), Clark LR 15 (12), Elliott RJ 13 (5), Neilson AB 6 (1), Hooper MD 4 (2), Mathie AM 4 (8), Jeffrey MR 1 (2), Allen M 0 (1), Guppy SA 0 (1).

Goals (95g): Beardsley PA 15, Cole AA 15, Lee RM 14, Fox RA 12, Kitson P 12, Watson SC 5, Gillespie KR 4, Albert P 3, Clark LR 2, Elliott RJ 2, Hottiger M 2, Beresford J 1, Howey SN 1, Jeffrey MR 1, Mathie AM 1, Peacock D 1, Sellars S 1, Venison B 1, own goals 2.

Dismissals: 4 players; Srnicek (2), Albert, Lee.

MAJOR SIGNINGS

Philippe Albert (RSC Anderlecht) £2.65m
Marc Hottiger (FC Sion) £520,000
Paul Kitson (Derby County) £2.25m
Keith Gillespie (Manchester Utd) exchange

FROM THE RANKS

None

TEAM COLOURS Black & white striped shirts, black shorts (Change; all blue shirts & shorts with black trim/green with blue pin-stripe shirts, green shorts)

SEASON 1994-95

Match	Date		Premiership (Carling)						Att	Posn	Scorers
1	21 Aug	A	Leicester City	W	3	1	(0	0)	20,048	3	Cole, Beardsley, Elliott
2	24 Aug	H	**Coventry City**	W	4	0	(3	0)	34,163	1	Lee 2, Watson, Cole
3	27 Aug	H	**Southampton**	W	5	1	(3	0)	34,182	1	Watson 2, Cole 2, Lee
4	31 Aug	A	West Ham United	W	3	1	(2	0)	18,580	1	og (Potts), Lee, Mathie
5	10 Sep	H	**Chelsea**	W	4	2	(2	2)	34,435	1	Cole 2, Fox, Lee
6	18 Sep	A	Arsenal	W	3	2	(2	1)	36,819	1	Beardsley 2 (1 pen), Fox
7	24 Sep	H	**Liverpool**	D	1	1	(0	0)	34,435	1	Lee
8	01 Oct	A	Aston Villa	W	2	0	(0	0)	29,960	1	Lee, Cole
9	09 Oct	H	**Blackburn Rovers**	D	1	1	(0	0)	34,344	1	og (Flowers)
10	15 Oct	A	Crystal Palace	W	1	0	(0	0)	17,760	1	Beardsley
11	22 Oct	H	**Sheffield Wednesday**	W	2	1	(2	0)	34,408	1	Watson, Cole
12	29 Oct	A	Manchester United	L	0	2	(0	1)	43,795	1	
13	05 Nov	H	**Queens Park Rangers**	W	2	1	(0	1)	34,278	1	Kitson, Beardsley
14	07 Nov	A	Nottingham Forest	D	0	0	(0	0)	22,102	1	
15	19 Nov	A	Wimbledon	L	2	3	(2	3)	14,203	3	Beardsley, Kitson
16	26 Nov	H	**Ipswich Town**	D	1	1	(0	0)	34,459	3	Cole
17	03 Dec	A	Tottenham Hotspur	L	2	4	(2	2)	28,002	3	Fox 2
18	10 Dec	H	**Leicester City**	W	3	1	(1	0)	34,400	3	Albert 2, Howey
19	17 Dec	A	Coventry City	D	0	0	(0	0)	17,237	3	
20	26 Dec	A	Leeds United	D	0	0	(0	0)	39,337	3	
21	31 Dec	A	Norwich City	L	1	2	(1	2)	21,172	4	Fox (pen)
22	02 Jan	H	**Manchester City**	D	0	0	(0	0)	34,437	5	
23	15 Jan	H	**Manchester United**	D	1	1	(0	1)	34,471	5	Kitson
24	21 Jan	A	Sheffield Wednesday	D	0	0	(0	0)	31,215	4	
25	25 Jan	H	**Wimbledon**	W	2	1	(1	0)	34,374	4	Fox, Kitson
26	01 Feb	H	**Everton**	W	2	0	(0	0)	34,465	3	Fox, Beardsley (pen)
27	04 Feb	A	Queens Park Rangers	L	0	3	(0	3)	16,576	3	
28	11 Feb	H	**Nottingham Forest**	W	2	1	(0	0)	34,471	3	Fox, Lee
29	25 Feb	H	**Aston Villa**	W	3	1	(1	1)	34,637	3	Venison, Beardsley 2
30	28 Feb	A	Ipswich Town	W	2	0	(2	0)	18,639	3	Fox, Kitson
31	04 Mar	A	Liverpool	L	0	2	(0	0)	39,300	3	
32	08 Mar	H	**West Ham United**	W	2	0	(1	0)	34,595	3	Clark, Kitson
33	19 Mar	H	**Arsenal**	W	1	0	(0	0)	35,611	3	Beardsley
34	22 Mar	A	Southampton	L	1	3	(1	0)	14,666	3	Kitson
35	01 Apr	A	Chelsea	D	1	1	(0	1)	22,987	3	Hottiger
36	08 Apr	H	**Norwich City**	W	3	0	(2	0)	35,518	3	Beardsley 2 (1 pen), Kitson
37	14 Apr	A	Everton	L	0	2	(0	1)	34,811	4	
38	17 Apr	H	**Leeds United**	L	1	2	(1	2)	35,626	5	Elliott
39	29 Apr	A	Manchester City	D	0	0	(0	0)	27,389	5	
40	03 May	H	**Tottenham Hotspur**	D	3	3	(2	3)	35,603	5	Gillespie, Peacock, Beardsley
41	08 May	A	Blackburn Rovers	L	0	1	(0	1)	30,545	5	
42	14 May	H	**Crystal Palace**	W	3	2	(3	0)	35,626	6	Fox, Lee, Gillespie
Round			**FA Cup (Littlewoods)**								
3	08 Jan	H	**Blackburn Rovers**	D	1	1	(0	1)	31,721		Lee
3r	18 Jan	A	Blackburn Rovers	W	2	1	(0	0)	22,658		Hottiger, Clark
4	28 Jan	H	**Swansea City**	W	3	0	(1	0)	34,372		Kitson 3
5	19 Feb	H	**Manchester City**	W	3	1	(1	1)	33,219		Gillespie 2, Beresford
6	12 Mar	A	Everton	L	0	1	(0	0)	35,203		
Round			**FL Cup (Coca-Cola Cup)**								
2(1)	21 Sep	H	**Barnsley**	W	2	1	(1	1)	27,208		Fox, Cole
2(2)	05 Oct	A	Barnsley	W	1	0	(1	0)	10,992		Cole
3	26 Oct	H	**Manchester United**	W	2	0	(0	0)	34,178		Albert, Kitson
4	30 Nov	A	Manchester City	D	1	1	(1	0)	25,162		Jeffrey
4r	21 Dec	H	**Manchester City**	L	0	2	(0	1)	30,156		
Round			**UEFA Cup**								
1(1)	13 Sep	A	Royal Antwerp (Bel)	W	5	0	(3	0)	19,700		Lee 3, Sellars, Watson
1(2)	27 Sep	H	**Royal Antwerp (Bel)**	W	5	2	(4	0)	31,383		Cole 3, Beardsley (pen), Lee
2(1)	18 Oct	H	**Athletic Bilbao (Sp)**	W	3	2	(2	0)	32,140		Cole, Beardsley (pen), Fox
2(2)	01 Nov	A	Athletic Bilbao (Sp)	La	0	1	(0	0)	47,000		

Match	Srnicek	Hottiger	Beresford	Venison	Peacock	Albert	Lee	Beardsley	Cole	Fox	Sellars	Mathie	Elliott	Hooper	Watson	Howey	Burridge	Kitson	Clark	Neilson	Drysdale	Jeffrey	Bracewell	Gillespie	Harper	Allen	Guppy	Holland
Squad numbers	1	12	3	2	15	27	7	8	9	5	11	14	26	30	19	6	29	28	10	20	16	31	4	18	32	21	18	23
1	1d	2	3	4	5	6	7	8	9	10	11	s8	s11	ss8														
2	1	2	3	4	5	6	7		9	10	11	s8	s11	u	8													
3	1	2	3	4	5	6	7		9	10	11	s10	s11	u	8													
4	1	2	3	4	5	6	7		9		11	10	s7	u	8	u												
5		2	3	4	5	6	7		9	10	11	u		1	8	u	u											
6	1	2	3		5	6	7	8	9	10	11	u		u	u	4												
7	1	2	3	4	5	6d	7	8	9	10	11			u	s11	s4												
8	1	2	3		5	6	7	8	9	10	11			u	u	4		s8										
9	1	2	3		5		7	8	9	10	11			u	6	4		s7	u									
10	1		3			6		8	9	10	11			u	5	4		7	u	2	u							
11	1	2	3		5	6		8	9	10	11	u		u	4			7	s7									
12	1	2	3		5	6	9	8		10	11	s10		u	7	4			s2									
13	1	2	3		5	6	9	8		10				u	7	4		11	u	u								
14	1	2	3		5	6	9	8		10		u		u	7			11	4	u								
15	1	2	3	7	5	6	9	8		10				u	s11	4		11	s5									
16	1	2	3	4		6	7	8	9	10		s7		u	11				s6	5								
17	1	2	3	4				8	9	10		7		u	6				11	5	u	u						
18	1	2	11	4	5	3		8	9	10		u		u	7	6			u									
19	1	2	3	4	5			8	9	10				u	7	6		11	s8				u					
20	1		3	2	u	6	7		9	10				u	4	5		11	u				8					
21	1	u	3	2	5		7		9	10				u	6	4		11	s6				8					
22	1	u	3	2	5		7	8	9	10				u		6		11	u				4					
23	1	2	3	4	5		7			10		u	11	u	u	6		9	8									
24	1	2	3	4	5		7	8		10				u		6		9	11				u	s7				
25	1	2		4	5			8		10			3	u	u	6		9	u				7	11				
26		2		4			7	8		10		9	3	1	u				s3	5			6	11	u			
27		2					7	8				s9	3	1	4			9	10	5	u		6	11	u			
28	1	2	3	4	5		7	8		10				u	u	6		9					s11	11				
29	1	2	3	4	5		7	8		10				u	u	6		9					u	11				
30	1	2	3	4	5		7	8		10				u	u	6		9					u	11				
31	1	2	3	4	5		7	8		10				u	s8	6		9					s10	11				
32	1	2	3	4	5		7			10				u	s9	6		9	8				s6	11				
33	1	2		4	5		7	8		10			3	u	u			9	s7				6	11				
34	1	2		4	5		7	8		10			3	u	u	6		9					u	11				
35	1	2		4	5		7	8		10			3	u	s9	6		9	s7				11					
36	1	2		4	5		7	8		10			3	u	u	6		9		u			11					
37		2		4	5		7d	8		10			3	1		6		9	s2				11	s10	u			
38	1	2					7	8		10			3	u	5	6		9	u	s3			4	11				
39	1	2	3		5			8		10				u	4	6			11	u			7	9		u		
40	1d	2	3		5		7	8		10				s10	11	6			u				4	9		s4		
41	1	2	3		5		7	8		10				u	4	6			11	u				9		u		
42	1	2	3		5		7	8		10				u	4	6			11	u				9		u		
Round																												
3	1		3	2	5		7	8	9	11			10	u	u	6		s10					4					
3r	1	2	3	4	5		7			11			10	u	u	6		9	8				u					
4	1	2		4	5			8		10		u	3	u	u	6		9					7	11				
5	1	2	3	4	5		7	8		10				u	u	6		9					u	11				
6	1	2	3	4	5		7			10			s3	u	s2			9	8				6	11				
Round																												
2(1)	1	2	3		5	6	7	8	9	10	11	s6		u	s11	4												
2(2)	1	2	3		5	6	7		9		11	s10		u	u	4		10	8									
3	1	2	3		5	6		8	9		11			u	7	4		10	u								s9	
4	1	2	3	4				8	9			7		u	6				10	5	u	11						u
4r	1	2	3	4	5	6			9	10				u	7			11	8	u			s2					
Round																												
1(1)	1	2	3	4	5	6	7	8	9	10	11		u	u	s8	u						s9						
1(2)	1	2	3		5	6	7	8	9	10	11			u	s7	4			s8								u	u
2(1)	1	2	3		5	6		8	9	10	11			u	u	4			7		u	u					u	
2(2)	1	2	3		5	6	9	8		10	11			u	7	4			s11		u	s10					u	

La — Tie lost on away goals

Match 6 — One of Beardsley's goals is recorded by some sources as a Keown og

DateLine ... 13 Sept: United return to European action and register their best ever scoreline, 5-0 in Antwerp. **18 Sept:** Newcastle record their sixth League win in a row and maintain top position with a 3-2 victory over Arsenal. **19 Nov:** A 3-2 defeat at Wimbledon knocks United from the head of the table. **15 Jan:** United line up without Andy Cole after a record £7m sale to opponents Manchester United. **28 Jan:** Paul Kitson grabs a FA Cup hat-trick in a 3-0 success over Swansea City.

SEASON
1995-96
PREMIER LEAGUE

So close to the Premiership crown

In the summer of 1995 Newcastle were big spenders as a mountain of cash was handed to Keegan to continue his team building – and replace the huge gap left by Andy Cole's sale. In the space of a week United spent £14m. QPR and England leader Les Ferdinand led the way, along with Warren Barton, goalkeeper Shaka Hislop and French star David Ginola. Another £11m was soon to be spent on David Batty and Tino Asprilla. Keegan's revamped side clicked from the off with a brand of attractive football that captured the public's imagination – and not only on Tyneside. Newcastle stormed to the top of the Premiership winning nine of their opening 10 fixtures and looked a cert to lift their first League title since 1927 – all of 69 long years. At one stage by the end of December they were 10 points clear of rivals Manchester United, with that lead set to extend further.

A clash with the Reds at Old Trafford though saw Alex Ferguson's men win 2-0 and then in the return meeting at St James' Park during March they won again, by a single goal – although the Magpies were by far the better side. The gap was closing. Crucial away fixtures were United's downfall – on each occasion conceding late goals. They lost 4-3 in an absorbing contest against Liverpool at Anfield – this after being 3-1 ahead – then lost again in a more vital fixture at Blackburn when they were again in front. At the City Ground against Nottingham Forest the Geordies were once more a goal up but again let vital points slip away by drawing 1-1. The upshot was that Manchester United step by step caught the Magpies and secured the trophy by four points. All Toon followers were disconsolate. The Black'n'Whites had thrown away a genuine prospect of bringing the topmost trophy back to Tyneside. Without doubt, they could have been, and should have been, Premier League Champions.

Pictured above: Steve Howey was one of several United's stars to claim international recognition

Memorabilia CORNER

David Batty shows off the Newcastle Brown Ale logo on United's shirt, a most popular design.

IN CHARGE

Chairman: Sir John Hall
Manager: Kevin Keegan
Captain: Peter Beardsley.
Trainer/Coach: Terry McDermott/Derek Fazackerly/Chris McMenemy
Club Sponsor: Newcastle Breweries
Kit Supplier: Adidas

ST JAMES' PARK

Average Attendance
Lg 36,505 Lg & Cup 36,499

United were set to make a serious bid for the Premier League title. Back row, left to right: Srnicek, Watson, Elliott, Howey, Kitson, Albert, Peacock, Ginola, Hislop. Sitting: Sellars, Barton, Gillespie, Beresford, Lee, Beardsley, Clark, Hottiger, Huckerby, Ferdinand.

PLAYER FOCUS David Ginola

Born Gassin. Midfield, 5'11"
1995 to 1997: 76 app 7 goals.

The purchase of David Ginola in July 1995 saw United move onto a different level – onto the European stage – being recognised as a major force in the game. Ginola was one of the Continent's finest players, a French pin-up star with style and match-winning ability. His very persona knitted with United's vision of being a club with razzmatazz. Highly skilled and mesmerising with it, the tall, elegant international winger-cum-midfielder cost £2.5m from Paris St-Germain. His flair and direct running had an eye-catching impact on the Premiership as he week after week sent defenders in a spin. The only way they could stop him was by foul means or hunting in packs to swamp his artistry. Although not one to track back often into a defensive role, he was a match-winner and Ginola went onto play an important part in the Magpies almost securing the Championship title. Having a rapport with manager Kevin Keegan, the Frenchman did not have the same good relationship with his replacement. The arrival of Kenny Dalglish saw David join Tottenham in July 1997 for £2.5m where he continued to shine, lifting a rare double of the Player of the Year and Footballer of the Year awards in 1998-99. He later moved to Aston Villa and Everton at the end of his career in England. Charming and articulate, Ginola was frequently in the limelight, at times a fashion model and later to enter the world of cinema as well as wine production. He is often to be seen as part of the football media and was known as Il Magnifique in his prime.

SEASON REVIEW

Premier League: P38 W24 D6 L8 F66 A37 Pts 78.
Position: 2nd (Champions; Manchester United).
FA Cup: R3 (Winners; Manchester United).
FL Coca-Cola Cup: QF (Winners; Aston Villa).

Appearances (45m): Ferdinand L 44, Lee RM 41, Beardsley PA 40, Ginola DDM 40, Peacock D 40 (1), Barton WD 37 (1), Beresford J 35 (1), Howey SN 33, Gillespie KR 30 (2), Hislop NS 28, Clark LR 26 (7), Albert P 23 (5), Watson SC 18 (11), Srnicek P 17 (2), Asprilla FHH 11 (3), Batty D 11, Elliott RJ 8 (2), Kitson P 4 (5), Sellars S 4 (4), Fox RA 3 (2), Brayson P 1, Hottiger M 1 (2), Crawford J 0 (1), Holland CJ 0 (1), Huckerby DC 0 (2).

Goals (82g): Ferdinand L 29, Beardsley PA 11, Lee RM 9, Albert P 6, Gillespie KR 5, Ginola DDM 5, Watson SC 4, Asprilla FHH 3, Clark LR 2, Kitson P 2, Peacock D 2, Barton WD 1, Batty D 1, Howey SN 1, Sellars S 1.

Dismissals: 3 players; Beresford, Ginola, Peacock.

MAJOR SIGNINGS

David Ginola (PSG) £2.5m
Shaka Hislop (Reading) £1.575m
Warren Barton (Wimbledon) £4m club record fee
Les Ferdinand (QPR) £6m club record fee
David Batty (Blackburn Rvs) £3.5m
Tino Asprilla (Parma AC) £7.5m club record fee

FROM THE RANKS

Paul Brayson (Walker Celtic)

TEAM COLOURS Black & white striped shirts, black shorts (Change; maroon & navy-blue hooped shirts, cream shorts)

SEASON 1995–96

Match	Date		Premiership (Carling)	Res	F	A	HT	Att	Posn	Scorers	Hislop	Barton	Beresford	Clark	Peacock	Howey	Lee	Beardsley	Ferdinand	Ginola	Gillespie	Fox	Elliott	Watson	Kitson	Srnicek	Hottiger	Sellars	Albert	Huckerby	Holland	Brayson	Asprilla	Batty	Crawford	Keen	Match
										Squad numbers	15	2	3	10	4	6	7	8	9	14	18	5	26	19	28	1	12	11	27	16	23	25	11	22	17	33	
1	19-Aug	H	**Coventry City**	W	3	0	(1 0)	36,485	1	Lee, Beardsley (pen), Ferdinand	1	2	3	4	5	6	7	8	9	10	11	s10	u	u													1
2	22-Aug	A	Bolton Wanderers	W	3	1	(1 0)	20,243	1	Ferdinand 2, Lee	1	2	3	4	5	6	7	8	9	10	11	u	u	u													2
3	27-Aug	A	Sheffield Wednesday	W	2	0	(0 0)	24,815	1	Ginola, Beardsley	1	2	3	4	5	6	7	8	9	10	11			u	u	u											3
4	30-Aug	H	**Middlesbrough**	W	1	0	(0 0)	36,483	1	Ferdinand	1	2	3	4	5	6	7	8	9	10	11	u				u	u										4
5	9-Sep	A	Southampton	L	0	1	(0 0)	15,237	1		1	2	3	4	5	6	7		9	10	11	8	u		s8	u											5
6	16-Sep	H	**Manchester City**	W	3	1	(2 0)	36,501	1	Beardsley (pen), Ferdinand 2	1	2	3	4	5	6	7	8	9	10	11	s8		s2				s3									6
7	24-Sep	H	**Chelsea**	W	2	0	(1 0)	36,225	1	Ferdinand 2	1	2	3	4	5	6	7		9	10	11	8		s2		u		s10									7
8	1-Oct	A	Everton	W	3	1	(1 0)	33,080	1	Ferdinand, Lee (pen), Kitson	1	2	3	4	5	6	7		9	10	8			s8	s10	u		11									8
9	14-Oct	A	Queens Park Rangers	W	3	2	(0 1)	18,254	1	Gillespie 2, Ferdinand	1	2	3	4	5	6	7	8	9	10	11			u		u		s10									9
10	21-Oct	H	**Wimbledon**	W	6	1	(3 0)	36,434	1	Howey, Ferdinand 3, Clark, Albert	1	2	3	4	5	6	7	8	9	10	11						s7	s4	s6								10
11	29-Oct	A	Tottenham Hotspur	D	1	1	(0 1)	32,279	1	Ginola	1	2	3		5	6	7	8	9	4	10			u		u		11	u								11
12	4-Nov	H	**Liverpool**	W	2	1	(1 1)	36,547	1	Ferdinand, Watson	1	2	3		5	6	7	8	9	10	11			4		u		u	s11								12
13	8-Nov	H	**Blackburn Rovers**	W	1	0	(1 0)	36,463	1	Lee	1	2	3		5	6	7	8	9	10	11		u	4		u			u								13
14	18-Nov	A	Aston Villa	D	1	1	(0 1)	39,167	1	Ferdinand	1	2	3	s4	5	6	7	8	9	10	11			4		u			s9								14
15	25-Nov	H	**Leeds United**	W	2	1	(0 1)	36,572	1	Lee, Beardsley	1	2	3	4	5	6	7	8	9	10	11			u				u	u								15
16	3-Dec	A	Wimbledon	D	3	3	(3 2)	18,002	1	Ferdinand 2, Gillespie	1	2	3	4	5	6	7	8	9	10	11			u		u			u								16
17	9-Dec	A	Chelsea	L	0	1	(0 1)	31,098	1		1	2	3	4	5	6	7	8	9	10	11			u		s1			u								17
18	16-Dec	H	**Everton**	W	1	0	(1 0)	36,557	1	Ferdinand		2	3d	4	5	6	7	8	9	10	11			u		1			s11	u							18
19	23-Dec	H	**Nottingham Forest**	W	3	1	(2 1)	36,531	1	Lee 2, Ginola		2	s3	4	5	6	7	8	9	10	11			s11	u	1			3								19
20	27-Dec	A	Manchester United	L	0	2	(0 1)	42,024	1			2	3	4	5	6	7	8	9	10	11		u	s11	s4	1											20
21	2-Jan	H	**Arsenal**	W	2	0	(1 0)	36,530	1	Ginola, Ferdinand		2		s7	5	6	7	8	9	10			4	s11	11	1	u		3								21
22	14-Jan	A	Coventry City	W	1	0	(1 0)	20,547	1	Watson		2	3	4	5		7	8	9	10			u	11	u	1			6		u						22
23	20-Jan	H	**Bolton Wanderers**	W	2	1	(2 1)	36,543	1	Kitson, Beardsley		2	3	4	5		7	8		10			u	11	9	1			6	s9	u						23
24	3-Feb	H	**Sheffield Wednesday**	W	2	0	(0 0)	36,567	1	Ferdinand, Clark		2	3	4		6	7	8	9		11		u	10	s11	1			5			u					24
25	10-Feb	A	Middlesbrough	W	2	1	(0 1)	30,011	1	Watson, Ferdinand		2	3	4	5		7	8	9		11		u	10	u	1			6				s11				25
26	21-Feb	A	West Ham United	L	0	2	(0 1)	23,843	1		u	2	3	10	5	6		8	9		11		u		s11	1			4				7				26
27	24-Feb	A	Manchester City	D	3	3	(1 1)	31,115	1	Albert 2, Asprilla	u	2	3	11	5	6		8	9	10	u		u			1			4				7				27
28	4-Mar	H	**Manchester United**	L	0	1	(0 0)	36,584	1		u	2	3	u		6	7	8	9	10				u		1			5				11	4			28
29	18-Mar	H	**West Ham United**	W	3	0	(1 0)	36,331	1	Albert, Asprilla, Ferdinand		2	3		u	6	7	8	9	10	u			s2		1			5				11	4			29
30	23-Mar	A	Arsenal	L	0	2	(0 2)	38,271	2			2	3		u	6	7	8	9	10	u			s2		1			5				11	4			30
31	3-Apr	A	Liverpool	L	3	4	(2 1)	40,702	2	Ferdinand, Ginola, Asprilla			3	u	s6	6	7	8	9	10	u			2		1			5				11	4			31
32	6-Apr	H	**Queens Park Rangers**	W	2	1	(0 0)	36,583	2	Beardsley 2	1		3	u	5		7	8	9	10	s7		u	2					6				11	4			32
33	8-Apr	A	Blackburn Rovers	L	1	2	(0 0)	30,717	2	Batty	1		3		5		7	8	9	10	s11		u	2	u				6				11	4			33
34	14-Apr	H	**Aston Villa**	W	1	0	(0 0)	36,510	2	Ferdinand	1	u	3	u	5		7	8	9	10			s3	2					6				11	4			34
35	17-Apr	H	**Southampton**	W	1	0	(1 0)	36,554	2	Lee	1	u	u	s11	5		7	8	9	10			3	2					6				11	4			35
36	29-Apr	A	Leeds United	W	1	0	(1 0)	38,562	2	Gillespie	1	s11		s10	5		7	8	9		11		3	2		u			6				10	4			36
37	2-May	A	Nottingham Forest	D	1	1	(1 0)	28,280	2	Beardsley	1	u		s10	5		7	8	9	10	11		3	2					6				s11	4			37
38	5-May	H	**Tottenham Hotspur**	D	1	1	(0 0)	36,589	2	Ferdinand	1	u		s11	5		7	8	9	10	11		3	2					6				s8	4			38
Round			FA Cup (Littlewoods)																																		Round
3	7-Jan	A	Chelsea	D	1	1	(0 1)	25,151		Ferdinand		2	u	s7	5	6	7	8	9	10			3	u	11	1			4								3
3r	17-Jan	H	**Chelsea**	Dep	2	2	(1 0)	36,535		Beardsley (pen), Albert		2	3	4	5d			8	9	10			s11	7	11	1			6	s9	u						3r
Round			FL Cup (Coca-Cola)																																		Round
2(1)	19-Sep	A	Bristol City	W	5	0	(3 0)	15,592		Peacock, Lee, Ferdinand, Sellars, Gillespie	1	2			5	6	7		9	10	8	4	3	s8		s1	s2	11									2(1)
2(2)	4-Oct	H	**Bristol City**	W	3	1	(0 1)	36,357		Ferdinand, Albert, Barton	1	7		4	5				9		10			6			2	11	3		s11	8			s8	u	2(2)
3	25-Oct	A	Stoke City	W	4	0	(2 0)	23,000		Peacock, Beardsley 2, Ferdinand	1	2		4	5	6	7	8	9	10	11		3	s7		u			s6								3
4	29-Nov	A	Liverpool	W	1	0	(0 0)	40,077		Watson	1	2	3	4	5	6	7	8	9	10	11			s9				u	u								4
5	10-Jan	A	Arsenal	L	0	2	(0 1)	37,857				2	3	u	5	6	7	8	9	10d			u	11	u	1			4								5

Dep — Drawn after extra time, tie lost on penalties (2-4)

DateLine ... 19 Aug: A remodelled St James' Park is completed for the fixture with Coventry City. **20 Jan:** United pick up three points against Bolton and are 12 ahead in the race for the title trophy. **3 April:** United lose a crucial Premier League game at Liverpool by 4-3 after being ahead by 3-2. **2 May:** Newcastle's title challenge falters when an Ian Woan equaliser levels the game at Forest. **10 June:** St James' Park hosts the European Championship meeting between France and Romania, the first of three fixtures.

SEASON 1996-97

PREMIER LEAGUE

Runners-up again to The Reds

Newcastle United were even more determined to secure the Premiership crown after the previous season's disappointment. That was made perfectly clear to all – including rivals Manchester United – when they won the chase with the Reds to land the country's top striker, Geordie-born Alan Shearer in a world record £15m-plus deal just before the new season started.

With Shearer paired with Ferdinand up front, Newcastle had an awesome cutting edge. And once they had settled into a new playing style, so it proved, the pair hitting the net at will. United began to click with a 2-1 victory over Sunderland at Roker Park, and by the time the Magpies faced Alex Ferguson's men in a Premier League clash at Gallowgate during October, Newcastle were leaders. And their emphatic and exhilarating 5-0 demolition of their closest rivals for League silverware saw the bookies make the Tynesiders firm favourites to lift the trophy.

Newcastle were well fancied in the UEFA Cup too, yet as Newcastle's way, the club – not for the first time, or the last – contributed to its own downfall. With football's corporate boom continuing, the focus was on becoming a public liability company. That brought conflict with manager Kevin Keegan which resulted in his shock resignation in January shortly after a 7-1 demolition job on Tottenham and a 3-0 triumph over Leeds at St James' Park.

In came another football icon, Kenny Dalglish. He had little time to settle. By then injuries to both Shearer and Ferdinand saw the Magpies slip in the Premiership chase, lose to Monaco in Europe as well as exit the FA Cup. But the Scot guided United to another runners-up spot in the table for a second year running behind Manchester United. A 5-0 end-of-season win over Nottingham Forest gave the Black'n'Whites a place in the new money-spinning world of the Champions League. However, Keegan's departure and Dalglish's arrival, was the start of a downward spiral for the Magpies, not halted until another formidable worthy arrived on Tyneside.

Pictured above: Long-haired, tough but thoughtful, Darren Peacock held one of the centre-back positions.

Memorabilia CORNER

By now Alan Shearer was United's talisman, pictured on the cover of the programme.

IN CHARGE

Chairman: Sir John Hall
Manager: Kevin Keegan/Kenny Dalglish
Captain: Peter Beardsley
Trainer/Coach: Terry McDermott/Chris McMenemy
Club Sponsor: Newcastle Breweries
Kit Supplier: Adidas

ST JAMES' PARK

Average Attendance
Lg 36,466 Lg & Cup 36,066

Newcastle's squad started to include stars from overseas. Pictured on this group in 1996 are Albert, Asprilla and Ginola. Also present was the world record purchase, Alan Shearer.

PLAYER FOCUS Les Ferdinand

Born London. Centre-forward, 5'11"
1995 to 1997: 84 app 50 goals.

The tall and powerful Les Ferdinand was one of the most effective strikers in the Premiership – being fast, having a ferocious shot, as well as supreme authority in the air. Settling on Tyneside in club record deal of £6m in June 1995 from Queens Park Rangers as a replacement for Andy Cole, Newcastle's new No. 9 made an immediate impact, the spearhead to a United side bursting with attacking talent. Known as Sir Les and capped by England, he grabbed 29 goals as United just missed the Premiership crown with the striker receiving the PFA Player of the Year award at the end of that campaign – the first Newcastle star to be awarded that prestigious honour. Immensely popular on Tyneside, Ferdinand then found himself partnered by Alan Shearer for season 1996-97 and the £21m strike force showed they were the best in the business. Despite being a huge success, United controversially sold him when a £6m bid from Spurs arrived for the now 30-year-old in the summer of 1997. Les spent over five years at White Hart Lane later appearing for West Ham United, Leicester, Bolton and Reading. During the early part of his career, Les had a successful spell in Turkey with Besiktas. He played on until nearing 40 years old, subsequently the Londoner worked in the media as well as being attached to his boyhood favourites Spurs as a coach. He is a cousin of Rio and Anton Ferdinand while along with other United strikers Cole, Owen and Shearer, is one of the Premier League's top goal scorers of all time. He was awarded the MBE in 2005.

SEASON REVIEW

Premier League: P38 W19 D11 L8 F73 A40 Pts 68.
Position: 2nd (Champions; Manchester United).
FA Cup: R4 (Winners; Chelsea).
FL Coca-Cola Cup: R4 (Winners; Leicester City).
UEFA Cup: QF (Winners; Schalke 04).

Appearances (52m): Peacock D 49, Batty D 45, Lee RM 44 (1), Shearer A 40, Watson SC 40 (6), Albert P 39 (1), Ferdinand L 38 (2), Elliott RJ 36 (2), Beardsley PA 34 (3), Gillespie KR 31 (13), Ginola DDM 31 (5), Srnicek P 30, Asprilla FHH 25 (8), Beresford J 25 (2), Hislop NS 22, Barton WD 20 (7), Clark LR 14 (20), Howey SN 9, Kitson P 0 (6), Crawford J 0 (2).

Goals (93g): Shearer A 28, Ferdinand L 21, Asprilla FHH 9, Beardsley PA 8, Elliott RJ 7, Lee RM 6, Albert P 3, Clark LR 3, Ginola DDM 2, Barton WD 1, Batty D 1, Gillespie KR 1, Howey SN 1, Peacock D 1, Watson SC 1.

Dismissals: 2 players; Batty, Gillespie.

MAJOR SIGNINGS

Derrik Hamilton (Bradford City) £1.375m

Alan Shearer (Blackburn Rvs) £15m club, national & world record fee

FROM THE RANKS

None

TEAM COLOURS Black & white striped shirts, black shorts (Change; all gorge-blue shirts & shorts with black & white trim)

SEASON 1996–97

Match	Date	Venue	Premiership (Carling)	Result	Score	HT	Att	Posn	Scorers
1	17 Aug	A	Everton	L	0 2	(0 2)	40,117	17	
2	21 Aug	H	**Wimbledon**	W	2 0	(1 0)	36,385	12	Batty, Shearer
3	24 Aug	H	**Sheffield Wednesday**	L	1 2	(1 1)	36,452	13	Shearer (pen)
4	04 Sep	A	Sunderland	W	2 1	(0 1)	22,037	8	Beardsley, Ferdinand
5	07 Sep	A	Tottenham Hotspur	W	2 1	(1 1)	32,535	6	Ferdinand 2
6	14 Sep	H	**Blackburn Rovers**	W	2 1	(1 0)	36,424	5	Shearer (pen), Ferdinand
7	21 Sep	A	Leeds United	W	1 0	(0 0)	36,070	2	Shearer
8	30 Sep	H	**Aston Villa**	W	4 3	(3 1)	36,400	2	Ferdinand 2, Shearer, Howey
9	12 Oct	A	Derby County	W	1 0	(0 0)	18,092	1	Shearer
10	20 Oct	H	**Manchester United**	W	5 0	(2 0)	36,579	1	Peacock, Ginola, Ferdinand, Shearer, Albert
11	26 Oct	A	Leicester City	L	0 2	(0 1)	21,134	2	
12	03 Nov	H	**Middlesbrough**	W	3 1	(1 0)	36,577	1	Beardsley 2 (1 pen), Lee
13	16 Nov	H	**West Ham United**	D	1 1	(0 1)	36,552	1	Beardsley
14	23 Nov	A	Chelsea	D	1 1	(1 1)	28,401	1	Shearer
15	30 Nov	H	**Arsenal**	L	1 2	(1 1)	36,565	2	Shearer
16	09 Dec	A	Nottingham Forest	D	0 0	(0 0)	25,762	4	
17	17 Dec	A	Coventry City	L	1 2	(0 2)	21,538	4	Shearer
18	23 Dec	H	**Liverpool**	D	1 1	(1 1)	36,570	6	Shearer
19	26 Dec	A	Blackburn Rovers	L	0 1	(0 0)	30,398	6	
20	28 Dec	H	**Tottenham Hotspur**	W	7 1	(2 0)	36,308	5	Shearer 2, Ferdinand 2, Lee 2, Albert
21	01 Jan	H	**Leeds United**	W	3 0	(1 0)	36,489	4	Shearer 2, Ferdinand
22	11 Jan	A	Aston Villa	D	2 2	(2 1)	39,339	4	Shearer, Clark
23	18 Jan	A	Southampton	D	2 2	(1 0)	15,251	4	Ferdinand, Clark
24	29 Jan	H	**Everton**	W	4 1	(0 1)	36,143	4	Ferdinand, Lee, Shearer (pen), Elliott R
25	02 Feb	H	**Leicester City**	W	4 3	(1 0)	36,396	4	Elliott R, Shearer 3
26	22 Feb	A	Middlesbrough	W	1 0	(1 0)	30,063	3	Ferdinand
27	01 Mar	H	**Southampton**	L	0 1	(0 0)	36,446	4	
28	10 Mar	A	Liverpool	L	3 4	(0 3)	40,751	4	Gillespie, Asprilla, Barton
29	15 Mar	H	**Coventry City**	W	4 0	(2 0)	36,571	4	Watson, Lee, Beardsley (pen), Elliott R
30	23 Mar	A	Wimbledon	D	1 1	(0 1)	23,175	4	Asprilla
31	05 Apr	H	**Sunderland**	D	1 1	(0 1)	36,582	4	Shearer
32	13 Apr	A	Sheffield Wednesday	D	1 1	(1 0)	33,798	5	Elliott R
33	16 Apr	H	**Chelsea**	W	3 1	(3 0)	36,320	4	Shearer 2, Asprilla
34	19 Apr	H	**Derby County**	W	3 1	(1 1)	36,550	4	Elliott R, Ferdinand, Shearer
35	03 May	A	Arsenal	W	1 0	(1 0)	38,179	4	Elliott R
36	06 May	A	West Ham United	D	0 0	(0 0)	24,617	4	
37	08 May	A	Manchester United	D	0 0	(0 0)	55,236	3	
38	11 May	H	**Nottingham Forest**	W	5 0	(4 0)	36,544	2	Asprilla, Ferdinand 2, Shearer, Elliott R
Round			FA Cup (Littlewoods)						
3	05 Jan	A	Charlton Athletic	D	1 1	(1 0)	14,980		Lee
3r	15 Jan	H	**Charlton Athletic**	We	2 1	(1 0)	36,398		Shearer, Clark
4	26 Jan	H	**Nottingham Forest**	L	1 2	(0 0)	36,434		Ferdinand
Round			FL Cup (Coca-Cola Cup)						
3	23 Oct	H	**Oldham Athletic**	W	1 0	(1 0)	36,314		Beardsley (pen)
4	27 Nov	A	Middlesbrough	L	1 3	(1 1)	29,831		Shearer
Round			UEFA Cup						
1(1)	10 Sep	H	**Halmstads BK (Se)**	W	4 0	(2 0)	28,124		Beardsley, Albert, Asprilla, Ferdinand
1(2)	24 Sep	A	Halmstads BK (Se)	L	1 2	(1 0)	7,847		Ferdinand
2(1)	15 Oct	A	Ferencvaros TC (H)	L	2 3	(2 2)	18,000		Shearer, Ferdinand
2(2)	29 Oct	H	**Ferencvaros TC (H)**	W	4 0	(1 0)	35,740		Asprilla 2, Ferdinand, Ginola
3(1)	19 Nov	A	FC Metz (F)	D	1 1	(1 0)	23,000		Beardsley (pen)
3(2)	03 Dec	H	**FC Metz (F)**	W	2 0	(0 0)	35,641		Asprilla 2
4(1)	04 Mar	H	**AS Monaco (F)**	L	0 1	(0 0)	36,215		
4(2)	18 Mar	A	AS Monaco (F)	L	0 3	(0 1)	18,500		
			FA Charity Shield						
	11 Aug	N	Manchester United	L	0 4	(0 2)	73,214		

Match	Hislop	Watson	Beresford	Batty	Howey	Albert	Lee	Gillespie	Shearer	Ferdinand	Ginola	Beardsley	Barton	Clark	Peacock	Srnicek	Elliott RJ	Asprilla	Kitson	Brayson	Crawford	Elliott ST	Hughes	Hamilton	Barrett
Squad numbers	15	19	3	4	6	27	7	18	9	10	14	8	2	20	5	1	26	11	28	25	17	33	30	22	29
1	1	2	3	4	5	6	7	8	9	10	11	s11	u	u	u	u									
2	u	2		4	5	6	7	u	9	10	11	u		s8	u	1	3	8							
3	u	2		4	5	6	7	s8	9	10	11	u		s7	u	1	3	8							
4	u	2		4	6	u	7	u	9	10	11	8		s10	5	1	3	u							
5	u	2			6	u	7	u	9	10	11	8	u	4	5	1	3	u							
6	u	2	3	4	6	u	7	s8	9	10	11	8		s7	5	1		s10							
7	u	2	3	4	6	u	7	s11	9		11	8		s8	5	1	u	10							
8	u	2	3	4	6	u	7	8	9	10	11				5	1	u	s11	u						
9	u	2	3	4		6	7	11	9	10	u	8		u	5	1	u		u						
10	u	2	3	4		6	7	u	9	10	11	8	s2	s7	5	1		u							
11	u	2	3	4		6	7			9	11	8	u	10	5	1	u	s2	s10						
12	u	u	u	4		6	7	2		9	11	8	s2	u	5	1	3	10							
13	u	s2	s3	4		6	7	2		9	11	8	u	s9	5	1	3	10							
14	u	s11		4d		6	7	2	9		11	8	u	s10	5	1	3	10	u						
15	u	s7	u	4		6	7	2	9		11	8		u	5	1	3	10	s10						
16	u	2				6	7	4	9	10	11	8	u	u	5	1	3		u	u					
17	u	2				6	7	4	9	10	11	8	u	u	5	1	3		u	u					
18	u	2				6	7	4	9	10	11	8	s4	s11	5	1	3		s10	u					
19	u	2		4		6	7	11	9	10		8		u	5	1	3		u	u	u				
20	1	2	3	4		6	7	11	9	10		8		s11	5	u	u		u		u				
21	1	2	3	4		6	7	u	9	10		8	u	11	5	u	u		u						
22	1	2	3	4		6		7	9	u		8	u	10	5	u	11		u		u				
23	1	u	3	4			s7	7	9	10	u	8	2	6	5	u	11					u			
24	1	2		4		6	7	11	9	10	u	8	s11	u	5	u	3	s8							
25	1	2		4		6	7	11	9	10	s11	u	u	s8	5	u	3	8							
26	1	4				6	7	8	9	10	u	u	2	11	5	u	3	u			u				
27	1	4				6	7	11		10	s10	s8	2	8	5	u	3	9			u		u		
28	1	2	u	4		6		7		s8	s10	8	11	10	5	u	3	9			ss8				
29	1	2		4		6	7	s9			11	8	10	s7	5	u	3	9			s11				
30	1	2	u	4		6	7	8			11	u	10	u	5	u	3	9			u				
31	1	6	u	4			7	8	9	10	11	u	2	s7	5	u	3	s10							
32	1	6	3	4			7	8	9	10	u	u	2	u	5	u	11	s9							
33	1	6	3	4			7	s8	9	10	ss8	u	2	s10	5	u	11	8							
34	1	6	3	4			7	s8	9	10	u	u	2	u	5	u	11	8							
35	u	6	3	4			7	s8d	9	10	u	u	2	s7	5	1	11	8							
36	u	2	3	4	u	6		s10	9			u	8	7	5	1	11	10						u	
37	u	2	3	4		6		7	9	10		u	8	u	5	1	11	s10						u	
38	u	2	3	4		6		s6	9	10		s4	8	s7	5	1	11	7						u	
Round																									
3	1	2	3	4		6	7		9	10		8	u	11	5		u		u						
3r	1	2	3	4		6		7	9	s11	11	8	s2	10	5		s6								
4	1	s3	3	4			7	s11	9	10	11	8	2	s2	5		6								
Round																									
3	1	u		4		6				9	11	8	2	10	5	u	3	7	s7						
4		s2		4		6	7	2	9		11	8		u	5	1	3	10	s10						
Round																									
1(1)	u	3			2	s2	6	s6	9	10	11	8	s3	4	5	1	u	7							
1(2)	u	u	3	4		6	7	11	9	10			2	s4	5	1	u	8	s8						
2(1)	u	2	3	4		6	7	11	9	10	s11	8		u	5	1	u	u							
2(2)	u	u		4		6	7	2		9	11	8	s2	u	5	1	3	10	u						
3(1)	u	u	3	4		6	7	11			10	8	2	u	5	1	s3	9	u						
3(2)	u	s11	u	4		6	7	2	9		11	8		s10	5	1	3	10	u						
4(1)	1	4	u	8		6	7	11			9	u	2	10	5	u	3				u				u
4(2)	1	2	s5	4		6	7	s8			11	8	10	s10	5	u	3	9			u				
CS		2	3	4		6	7	s11	9	10	11	8			5	1		s8							

N Played at Wembley Stadium, London

We Won after extra time

DateLine ... 21 Aug: Alan Shearer's first senior goal in a black-and-white shirt against Wimbledon. **20 Oct:** Against Manchester United, the Magpies show they are set for another title race by demolishing the Champions 5-0. **5 Jan:** Kevin Keegan resigns following the FA Cup-tie with Charlton at The Valley. **18 Jan:** Kenny Dalglish steps into the vacant manager's job and is in full control against Southampton. **11 May:** United qualify for the Champions League after a 5–0 demolition of Nottingham Forest.

SEASON
1997-98
PREMIER LEAGUE

Champions League adventure

The long haul pursuit of the Championship trophy was on hold as United focussed on first qualifying for the Champions League – which they did in dramatic fashion against Croatia Zagreb in the dying minutes of extra-time – then remodelling the side and concentrating on a FA Cup run. Without the injured Shearer, the first half of the season saw the Champions League take centre-stage. Opening at St James' Park against no other than Barcelona, United roared to a 3-0 lead thanks to a superb hat-trick by Tino Asprilla. Until the latter stages of the contest United had the Catalan giants on the rack, and although they conceded two late goals, United still took the points and made headlines throughout Europe. But after that the Magpies found it tough going. With a depleted side, they twice fell to PSV and had little chance of progressing further. Newcastle also slid down the Premier League table.

With Shearer back for the FA Cup, United needed the boost he gave the side. United's No. 9 was the driving force as the Magpies reached Wembley, scoring five goals including the close-in strike that defeated Sheffield United in the semi-final. United's display in the final against Arsenal though was abject. And the man in charge, Kenny Dalglish never recovered from that sun-drenched day in front the twin-towers. United supporters were split over his leadership.

By the end of another eventful season Keegan's Entertainers had all been dismantled. A new look Magpies were on show as a different group of players were unveiled, a mix of largely foreign unknowns like Andreas Andersson and Temuri Ketsbaia as well as veterans of bygone years such as Ian Rush and John Barnes. Many though were inferior in quality, mediocre on the eye, or past their best. Newcastle still had a fit again Shearer banging in the goals, but no longer could they be considered as second only to Manchester United in English football.

Pictured above: Tino Asprilla infuriated many, but had ability to become a match-winner in attack.

Memorabilia CORNER

The Black'n'Whi[tes] had no easy task [to] topple Arsenal in the FA Cup final.

IN CHARGE

Chairman: Sir John Hall/Freddy Shepherd
Manager: Kenny Dalglish
Captain: Robert Lee
Trainer/Coach: Terry McDermott/Tommy Burns
Club Sponsor: Newcastle Breweries
Kit Supplier: Adidas

ST JAMES' PARK

Average Attendance
Lg 36,672 Lg & Cup 36,234

PLAYER FOCUS John Beresford

Born Sheffield. Left-back, 5'6"
1992 to 1998: 232 app 8 goals.

Making the long trip from Portsmouth to Tyneside in June 1992 for a £650,000 fee John Beresford quickly became one of the Magpies' most consistent players. With an attacking flair from the left-back position, he immediately was a hit with the Geordie crowd as the Black'n'Whites lifted the Division One trophy in 1993. A Yorkshireman, John initially made an impact at Barnsley after being shown the door at Manchester City as a youngster. A former England youth skipper, he was included in his country's full squad when on the Gallowgate staff and was on the fringe of a full cap, on the bench as a substitute in 1995, while Bez also played for the England B side. A gutsy defender with a cultured left-foot, Beresford was always comfortable on the ball and committed to United's cause, having an important role down the left touchline as the Magpies' finished as runners-up in the Premier League in two consecutive years. John's father appeared for Notts County and Chesterfield while his cousin, Mick Ward played for Sheffield United and Everton. Joining Southampton in February 1998, after being forced to quit the game at The Dell due to a knee injury, John played on in non-league circles for a period totalling over 500 senior games. He entered the media too and also became a matchday host at St James' Park.

By the start of the 1997-98 season new boss Kenny Dalglish was starting to fashion his own squad.

SEASON REVIEW

Premier League: P38 W11 D11 L16 F35 A44 Pts 44.
Position: 13th (Champions; Arsenal).
FA Cup: Finalist (Winners; Arsenal).
FL Coca-Cola Cup: QF (Winners; Chelsea).
UEFA Champions League: Group (Winners; Real Madrid).

Appearances (56m): Batty D 47, Lee RM 40 (2), Watson SC 40 (4), Pistone A 39, Gillespie KR 37 (6), Pearce S 35 (1), Albert P 34 (4), Given SJJ 34, Barnes JCB 33 (6), Beresford J 29 (2), Barton WD 28 (7), Tomasson JD 27 (8), Peacock D 26 (3), Ketsbaia T 22 (25), Hislop NS 21, Shearer A 21 (2), Howey SN 18 (5), Speed GA 17, Asprilla FHH 14 (2), Andersson AC 12 (3), Dabizas N 12 (1), Hamilton DV 11 (6), Rush IJ 9 (5), Hughes AW 5 (3), Griffin A 4, Srnicek P 1, Brayson P 0 (1).

Goals (58g): Barnes JCB 7, Shearer A 7, Asprilla FHH 6, Beresford J 6, Ketsbaia T 5, Gillespie KR 4, Lee RM 4, Tomasson JD 4, Barton WD 3, Andersson AC 2, Batty D 2, Rush IJ 2, Speed GA 2, Dabizas N 1, Hamilton DV 1, Pearce S 1, Watson SC 1.

Dismissals: 3 players; Batty (3).

MAJOR SIGNINGS

John Barnes (Liverpool) free
Stuart Pearce (Nottingham Forest) free
Ian Rush (Leeds Utd) free
Alessandro Pistone (Inter) £4.3m
Gary Speed (Everton) £5.5m
Andreas Andersson (AC Milan) £3.6m
Nikos Dabizas (Olympiacos CFP) £2.1m
Andy Griffin (Stoke City) £1.5m
Paul Dalglish (Liverpool) free
Shay Given (Blackburn Rovers) £1.5m
Temuri Ketsbaia (AEK) free
Paul Robinson & James Coppinger (Darlington) £500,000 joint
Jon Tomasson (SC Heerenveen) £2.2m

FROM THE RANKS

Aaron Hughes (Irish BB, NIy)

TEAM COLOURS Black & white striped shirts, black shorts
(Change; dark blue shirts with a green & orange stripe, green shorts/navy-blue & grey shirts, navy-blue shorts)

SEASON 1997-98

Match	Date		Premiership (Carling)	Result	Att	Posn	Scorers	Given	Watson	Beresford	Albert	Pistone	Pearce	Lee	Batty	Asprilla	Ketsbaia	Tomasson	Beardsley	Howey	Hughes	Pinas	Srnicek	Rush	Gillespie	Barton	Elliott ST	Hislop	Barnes	Peacock	Hamilton	Brayson	Crawford	Keidel	Shearer	Terrier	Andersson	Griffin	Speed	Dabizas
							Squad numbers	1	19	3	27	23	12	7	4	11	14	16	8	6	28	24	21	8	18	2	31	15	10	5	22	25	17	32	9	33	40	38	11	34
1	09 Aug	H	**Sheffield Wednesday**	W 2 1 (1 1)	36,711	4	Asprilla 2	1	2	3	4	5	6	7	8	9	10	11	u	u	u	u	u																	
2	23 Aug	H	**Aston Villa**	W 1 0 (1 0)	36,783	6	Beresford	1	2	3	4	5	6	7	8d		11	s9		u				9	10	s11	u	u												
3	13 Sep	H	**Wimbledon**	L 1 3 (1 1)	36,526	12	Barton	1	2	3	4	5		7		s8	s6	11			u			9	8	6		u	10	u										
4	20 Sep	A	West Ham United	W 1 0 (1 0)	25,884	8	Barnes	1	2	3	6			7	8	9	u	u		s10				u	11	4		u	10	5										
5	24 Sep	H	**Everton**	W 1 0 (0 0)	36,705	7	Lee	1	2	s7	6	3		7	4	9		11		u				s11	8	s8		u	10	5										
6	27 Sep	A	Chelsea	L 0 1 (0 0)	31,563	10		1	2	3	4	5			8		s11	11		s3				9	s10	7		u	10	6	u									
7	04 Oct	H	**Tottenham Hotspur**	W 1 0 (0 0)	36,708	7	Barton	1	2	3	u				4		7	11		6		u	u	9	u	8			10	5	u									
8	18 Oct	A	Leeds United	L 1 4 (0 3)	39,834	10	Gillespie	1	4	3	u			7	8		11	s11		6			u	9	s10	2			10	5	u									
9	25 Oct	H	**Blackburn Rovers**	D 1 1 (1 0)	36,716	10	Gillespie		2	3	6			s7	4		11	9		s8	u		1		8			u	10	5	7	u								
10	01 Nov	H	**Leicester City**	D 3 3 (2 2)	36,754	9	Barnes (pen), Tomasson, Beresford	1	2	3	4			7	8		11	9		6	u			s9				u	10	5	s6		u							
11	08 Nov	A	Coventry City	D 2 2 (1 1)	22,679	9	Barnes, Lee	1	2	3	4	5		7	8		9	u							11	s8		u	10	6	u		u							
12	22 Nov	H	**Southampton**	W 2 1 (0 1)	36,769	9	Barnes 2		2		6	3	u	7	4		8	9			u		u		11		u	1	10	5	u									
13	29 Nov	A	Crystal Palace	W 2 1 (1 0)	26,085	8	Ketsbaia, Tomasson		2		u	5	3	s10	4		8	9			u		u		11			1	10	6	7		u							
14	01 Dec	A	Bolton Wanderers	L 0 1 (0 1)	24,494	8		u	2		u	5	3	7	4		9	10			u				11			1	s8	6	8		u							
15	06 Dec	H	**Arsenal**	L 0 1 (0 1)	36,751	9		u	2		s9	5	3	7	4	9	s8	8		u					11			1	10	6	u									
16	13 Dec	A	Barnsley	D 2 2 (1 1)	18,687	9	Gillespie 2	u	2		4	5	3	7	8	9	u	s9			u				11			1	10	6	u									
17	17 Dec	H	**Derby County**	D 0 0 (0 0)	36,289	9		u	2		6	5	3		4	9	8	11			u			s9	7	u		1	10	u										
18	21 Dec	H	**Manchester United**	L 0 1 (0 0)	36,767	9		u	2	11	4	3	6		8	9	s11	u						u	7	s4		1	10	5										
19	26 Dec	A	Derby County	L 0 1 (0 1)	30,232	10		u	2	11		3	6		4d	s9	s10	10		5	u			9	7			1	s5		8									
20	28 Dec	H	**Liverpool**	L 1 2 (1 2)	36,702	11	Watson	u	4	3		5	6	7	8	9	u	u						u	11	2		1	10		s2									
21	10 Jan	A	Sheffield Wednesday	L 1 2 (1 1)	29,446	11	Tomasson	u	6	11				4			s2	9			3			s8	7	2	u	1	10	5	8			u						
22	17 Jan	H	**Bolton Wanderers**	W 2 1 (1 0)	36,767	10	Barnes, Ketsbaia	u	4	11		3	6	7			s9	9						u	8	2		1	10	5	u				s10					
23	20 Jan	A	Liverpool	L 0 1 (0 1)	42,791	10		u	4	11		3	6	7			s11	9			5			u	8	2		1	10						s10	u				
24	01 Feb	A	Aston Villa	W 1 0 (0 0)	38,266	10	Batty	u	2	3	u	4	6	7	8		u	s10		5					11			1							9		10	u		
25	07 Feb	H	**West Ham United**	L 0 1 (0 1)	36,736	10		1			u	2	6	7	4			s3						u	8			u	u	5					9		10	3	11	
26	22 Feb	H	**Leeds United**	D 1 1 (0 0)	36,511	13	Ketsbaia	1			s2	3	6	7	4		s8	u		5	2				8			u	u						9		10		11	
27	28 Feb	A	Everton	D 0 0 (0 0)	37,972	12		1			6		3	7	4		s8	u		5					8	2		u	u	u					9		10		11	
28	14 Mar	H	**Coventry City**	D 0 0 (0 0)	36,762	15		1			6	2	3	7	4		8	u		5						s6		u	u						9		10		11	s3
29	18 Mar	H	**Crystal Palace**	L 1 2 (0 2)	36,565	15	Shearer	1				3			4		8	s8		5					7	2		u	s10	s5					9		10	u	11	6
30	28 Mar	A	Southampton	L 1 2 (0 0)	15,251	15	Lee	1			u	3	6	7			s11	8			2		u	u	11				10	5	s7				9					4
31	31 Mar	A	Wimbledon	D 0 0 (0 0)	15,478	15		1	2		4		3				8						u		s6	s5			u	5	7				9		u	6	11	10
32	11 Apr	A	Arsenal	L 1 3 (0 1)	38,102	16	Barton	1			6		3		4		s8	u			u		u			7			10		8				9		s10	2	11	5
33	13 Apr	H	**Barnsley**	W 2 1 (1 0)	36,534	15	Andersson, Shearer	1	s10		6		3	7	4		s8	u							8	2		u	u						9		10		11	5
34	18 Apr	A	Manchester United	D 1 1 (1 1)	55,194	15	Andersson	1	u		4	3	6	7	8		s10	u					u		u	2									9		10		11	5
35	25 Apr	A	Tottenham Hotspur	L 0 2 (0 1)	35,847	15		1	2		4	3	6		8		ss4			u					s4	7		u	u						9		10		11	5
36	29 Apr	A	Leicester City	D 0 0 (0 0)	21,699	15		1	u			3	6	7	8		10			5						2		u	u		u				9		u		11	4
37	02 May	H	**Chelsea**	W 3 1 (2 0)	36,710	13	Dabizas, Lee, Speed	1	s5			3	6	7	8			u		5						2		u	s10		s7				9		10		11	4
38	10 May	A	Blackburn Rovers	L 0 1 (0 0)	29,300	13		1	4		6	3	u		8d		7							u				u	10		s7				9		s10	2	11	5
Round			FA Cup (Littlewoods)																																					
3	04 Jan	A	Everton	W 1 0 (0 0)	20,885		Rush	u	2	3		4	6	7		9	u	u			s10			s9	11			1	10	5	8									
4	25 Jan	A	Stevenage Borough	D 1 1 (1 1)	8,040		Shearer	u	2	11	s11	3	6	7	4		s10	u		5				u	8			1	10						9					
4r	04 Feb	H	**Stevenage Borough**	W 2 1 (1 0)	36,705		Shearer 2	u	2	s5	4	3	6	7	8		s10	10		5				u	11	s2		1							9					
5	14 Feb	H	**Tranmere Rovers**	W 1 0 (1 0)	36,675		Shearer	1				3	6	7	4		s10	10		5				u	8	2		u	s11	u					9				11	
6	08 Mar	H	**Barnsley**	W 3 1 (2 0)	36,695		Ketsbaia, Speed, Batty	1			6		3	7	4		8	u		5						2		u	u	u	u				9		10		11	
SF	05 Apr	N1	Sheffield United	W 1 0 (0 0)	53,452		Shearer	1			6		3		4		s8	u			u			u	7	2		u	10						9		8		11	5
F	16 May	N2	Arsenal	L 0 2 (0 1)	79,183			1	s8		u	2	3	7	4		10			6						8		u	s10						9		s3		11	5
Round			FL Cup (Coca-Cola Cup)																																					
3	15 Oct	H	**Hull City**	W 2 0 (0 0)	35,856		Hamilton, Rush		s3	3	4						8	11		6	u			9		2		1	10	5	7	s7								
4	18 Nov	A	Derby County	W 1 0 (0 0)	27,364		Tomasson		4	3	6	5		7	8		u	9							11	2		1	10	s2	s3									
5	07 Jan	H	**Liverpool**	Le 0 2 (0 0)	33,207			u	2	3	4			7	6		s8	s4			11			9	8			1	10	5										
Round			UEFA Champions League																																					
2Q(1)	13 Aug	H	**NK Croatia Zagreb (Cr)**	W 2 1 (1 0)	34,465		Beresford 2	1	2	3	4	5	6	7	8	9	11	10	u	s4	u	u	u		s10								u							
2Q(2)	27 Aug	A	NK Croatia Zagreb (Cr)	De 2 2 (1 0)	34,000		Asprilla (pen), Ketsbaia	1	2	3	4	5	6	7	8	9	s10	10		s6	u		u		s3	11	u						u							
1GpC	17 Sep	H	**FC Barcelona (Sp)**	W 3 2 (2 0)	35,274		Asprilla 3 (1 pen)	1	2	3	5			7	4	9	s10	11		u	u	u	u	u	8	6			10	s11										
1GpC	01 Oct	A*	Dynamo Kyiv (U)	D 2 2 (0 2)	98,000		Beresford 2	1	2	3	6			7	4	9	s7	s9		u	u			u	11	8		u	10	5	u									
1GpC	22 Oct	A	PSV Eindhoven (N)	L 0 1 (0 1)	29,200			1	3	11	s2			7	4		s11	10		6	u			9	8	2		u	u	5	u	u								
1GpC	05 Nov	H	**PSV Eindhoven (N)**	L 0 2 (0 1)	35,214			1	2	3	6	5					8	9			u				11	4		u	10	u	7		u							
1GpC	26 Nov	A	FC Barcelona (Sp)	L 0 1 (0 1)	26,000				2	3	4	6	s5		8		11	9			s4	u	u				u	1	10	5	7		u							
1GpC	10 Dec	H	**Dynamo Kyiv (U)**	W 2 0 (2 0)	33,694		Barnes, Pearce	u	2		4	6	3	7	8	9	s9	u			s6			u	11		u	1	10	5	u									

N1 Played at Old Trafford, Manchester
N2 Played at Wembley Stadium, London
A* Played at Olympiyski Stadium, Kyiv

De Drawn after extra time
Le Lost after extra time

01 Oct Some sources record the attendance as 100,000

DateLine ... 9 Aug: Shay Given's debut against Sheffield Wednesday at St James' Park. **17 Sept:** Newcastle's debut in the Champions League Proper is an epic, a 3-2 victory over Barcelona with a Tino Asprilla hat-trick. **1 Oct:** A reported crowd of almost 100,000 at the Champions League clash in Kiev, the biggest gate to watch United other than in a Cup final. **28 Feb:** Newcastle select an all-international side for the first time against Everton. **5 April:** An Alan Shearer goal in the FA Cup semi-final with Sheffield United sends United to Wembley. **16 May:** The Magpies are overwhelmed by Arsenal in the FA Cup final and fall by 2-0.

Another Wembley let-down

There was much speculation over Kenny Dalglish's position as manager in the aftermath of the Wembley defeat by Arsenal. He initially spent big, Didi Hamann arriving from Bayern Munich while the purchase of a new striker in French World Cup winner Stephane Guivarc'h for £3.5m did not help, as he was the one star of a flamboyant Les Bleus line-up who had not impressed in the summer's cavalcade of football. United stuttered, and within days of the new 1998-99 season the Scot was gone, and another high profile boss was in charge, this time the celebrated Dutchman Ruud Gullit. United's style and playing staff changed yet again, as the ex-Milan star quickly dispensed with many of Dalglish's men, including the expensive Guivarc'h.

In the process of this makeover Newcastle struggled in League action again, at one point as low as 15th in the table during December and quickly dropped out of the League Cup as well as the UEFA Cup Winners Cup in a hostile Belgrade against Partizan. But once more the Magpies found the FA Cup to their liking as the Third Round arrived in January. Another rousing campaign was served up, United having good fortune with home advantage, while Alan Shearer was again the Toon's champion. With five goals in the Cup run, he banged home a double in the semi-final against Ginola and Ferdinand's Tottenham – both in extra-time, a penalty and a killer strike, a controlled drive into the top corner.

Back to Wembley it was, this time facing a Manchester United side not only aiming for the double – but for a unique treble of League, FA Cup and European Cup. The sun shone again at Wembley and once more Newcastle flopped, although they did put up something of a fight this time against the Reds. But the result was the same, a convincing 2-0 stroll for the opposition.

Pictured above: As Continental stars flocked to St James' Park, Temuri Ketsbaia became a big character.

Memorabilia Corner

The Magpies quickly returned to Wembley, yet the outcome was the same...this time against Manchester United.

IN CHARGE

Chairman: Freddy Shepherd
Manager: Kenny Dalglish/Ruud Gullit
Captain: Robert Lee
Trainer/Coach: Steve Clarke/John Carver
Club Sponsor: Newcastle Breweries
Kit Supplier: Adidas

ST JAMES' PARK

Average Attendance
Lg 36,692 Lg & Cup 36,182

Now that sponsors had become hugely important to clubs, their product brand was always prominent – here Newcastle Brown Ale.

PLAYER FOCUS David Batty

Born Leeds. Midfield, 5'7"
1996 to 1998: 114 app 4 goals.

The battling yet composed qualities of ex-Leeds star David Batty were added to United's squad in February 1996 after a £3.5m move from Blackburn Rovers. The England player immediately slipped into the central anchor role, operating just in front of Newcastle's defence. David was an instant hit, both with his manager and the fans who warmed to his competitive edge, unselfish play and immaculate distribution of the ball. David had been in the first-team at Elland Road by the time he was 18 years old and quickly became a big personality with the Tykes, helping the Yorkshire side to promotion and then to the Football League title in 1991-92. Batty was controversially sold to Blackburn in a deal that angered Leeds' support, then an ankle injury robbed Batty of a second Championship medal in 1994-95 with Rovers when he made only five appearances, in the squad alongside Alan Shearer. David settled on Tyneside, being intelligent with the ball in midfield. He soon was involved in the hunt for the title again with the Magpies during the next two seasons, both to end as runners-up. Then David reached the FA Cup final with United – once more as runner-up – before a change in manager at St James' Park led to a move when Ruud Gullit was in control. Batty headed back to Leeds during December 1998 for £4.4m where he concluded his career in 2004. Batty won 42 caps for England and also appeared for the Under-21 and B sides. He appeared in the 1998 World Cup finals.

SEASON REVIEW

Premier League: P38 W11 D13 L14 F48 A54 Pts 46.
Position: 13th (Champions; Manchester United).
FA Cup: Finalist (Winners; Manchester United).
FL Worthington Cup: R4 (Winners; Tottenham Hotspur).
UEFA Cup Winners Cup: R1 (Winners; SS Lazio).

Appearances (49m): Speed GA 43 (5), Given SJJ 41, Shearer A 39 (1), Charvet LJ 38 (1), Dabizas N 35 (5), Solano NAT 33 (6), Hamann D 30 (1), Glass S 24 (6), Lee RM 24 (6), Barton WD 23 (7), Ketsbaia T 22 (12), Griffin A 19, Domi D 18, Howey SN 18, Pearce S 16, Hughes AW 14 (3), Andersson AC 13 (4), Maric S 10 (3), Batty D 9 (2), Dalglish PK 8 (5), Georgiadis G 8 (5), Harper SA 8 (2), Watson SC 8, Ferguson DC 7 (2), Saha LL 6 (6), Brady G 5 (7), Gillespie KR 5 (3), Beharall DA 4, Albert P 3 (4), Serrant C 3 (1), Guivarc'h S 2 (2), Pistone A 2 (1), McClen JD 1, Barnes JCB 0 (1).

Goals (64g): Shearer A 21, Ketsbaia T 8, Solano NAT 6, Hamann D 5, Speed GA 5, Dabizas N 4, Glass S 3, Andersson AC 2, Dalglish PK 2, Ferguson DC 2, Saha LL 2, Charvet LJ 1, Georgiadis G 1, Guivarc'h S 1, own goal 1.

Dismissals: 5 players; Dabizas (2), Hamann, Given, Pearce.

MAJOR SIGNINGS

Duncan Ferguson (Everton) £8m
Stephane Guivarc'h (AJ Auxerre) £3.5m
Didi Hamann (Bayern) £4.5m
Silvio Maric (NK Croatia Zagreb) £3.5m
Nobby Solano (CA Boca Jnrs) £2.7m
Garry Brady (Tottenham Hot) £650,000
Laurent Charvet (AS Cannes) £515,000
Didier Domi (PSG) £3.25m
Stephen Glass (Aberdeen) £650,000
George Georgiadis (Panathinaikos) £493,000
Carl Serrant (Oldham Ath) £500,000
Louis Saha (FC Metz) loan

FROM THE RANKS

David Beharall (Walker Central Jnrs)
Steve Harper (Seaham Red Star)
Jamie McClen (Cramlington Jnrs)

TEAM COLOURS Black & white striped shirts, black shorts (Change; all Italian blue shirts & shorts with yellow trim)

SEASON 1998-99

Match	Date	Venue	Premiership (Carling)	Res	F	A	HT	Att	Posn	Scorers	Given	Watson	Pistone	Dabizas	Charvet	Pearce	Lee	Hamann	Shearer	Andersson	Speed	Barnes	Ketsbaia	Barton	Albert	Perez	Solano	Howey	Serrant	Guivarc'h	Glass
										Squad numbers	1	19	5	34	16	3	7	12	9	40	11	10	14	2	27	23	24	6	21	8	17
1	15 Aug	H	**Charlton Athletic**	D	0	0	(0 0)	36,719	13		1	2	3	4	5	6	7	8	9	10	11	s4	s10	ss4	u	u					
2	22 Aug	A	Chelsea	D	1	1	(1 1)	34,795	12	Andersson	1	2	3	4	5	6	7	8	9	10	11		u		s3	u	s10	u			
3	30 Aug	H	**Liverpool**	L	1	4	(1 4)	36,740	16	Guivarc'h	1	2		s2	5	6	7	8	9		11			s3	4	u			3	10	s8
4	09 Sep	A	Aston Villa	L	0	1	(0 0)	39,241	19		1	2	u		5	3	7		9	10	11		s10	u	6	u	4			s4	8
5	12 Sep	H	**Southampton**	W	4	0	(2 0)	36,454	14	Shearer 2 (1 pen), og (Marshall), Ketsbaia	1	2	u		5	3	7		9	10	11		8	s11	6	u				u	4
6	19 Sep	A	Coventry City	W	5	1	(3 1)	22,656	9	Dabizas, Shearer 2, Speed, Glass	1	2		4	5	3	7		9		s8			s11	u	u	8			10	6
7	26 Sep	H	**Nottingham Forest**	W	2	0	(1 0)	36,760	4	Shearer 2 (1 pen)	1	2		4	5	3	7		9		11		10	s2	u	u	8				6
8	04 Oct	A	Arsenal	L	0	3	(0 2)	38,102	10		1			4d	5	3			9		11		10	u	s6	u	8				6
9	17 Oct	H	**Derby County**	W	2	1	(2 0)	36,750	6	Dabizas, Glass	1			4	5	3	7		9		s10		s11	u	u	u	10				6
10	24 Oct	A	Tottenham Hotspur	L	0	2	(0 1)	36,047	7		1				5	6	7		9		s11			u		u	8		3	s10	11
11	31 Oct	H	**West Ham United**	L	0	3	(0 0)	36,744	11		1		s6	4	5	3d			9		11		s10	u			10				6
12	08 Nov	A	Manchester United	D	0	0	(0 0)	55,174	13		1			4	5	u		6	9		s6			u			u				11
13	14 Nov	H	**Sheffield Wednesday**	D	1	1	(1 0)	36,698	13	Dalglish	1				5		7	4	9	s9	11			2			u		s3		
14	23 Nov	A	Everton	L	0	1	(0 1)	30,357	14		1			4	5		7	s2		9	11			2	s3		u		3		
15	28 Nov	H	**Wimbledon**	W	3	1	(1 1)	36,623	11	Solano, Ferguson 2	1				5			8		9	11		u	2			s6	4			6
16	06 Dec	A	Middlesbrough	D	2	2	(1 1)	34,629	13	Charvet, Dabizas				s2	5		7	u		10	11			2		u	6	4			s6
17	12 Dec	A	Blackburn Rovers	D	0	0	(0 0)	27,569	15					s3	5			8		10	11	u	s10	2			6	4			7
18	19 Dec	H	**Leicester City**	W	1	0	(0 0)	36,718	10	Glass	1			4	3		7	u	s10	9	11		10	2			u	5			6
19	26 Dec	H	**Leeds United**	L	0	3	(0 1)	36,783	12		1			4	3		7	u	9		11		s8	2			u	5			6
20	28 Dec	A	Liverpool	L	2	4	(1 0)	44,605	13	Solano, Andersson	1			s6	2	3		8d	9	s10	11	u					6	5			7
21	09 Jan	H	**Chelsea**	L	0	1	(0 1)	36,711	13		1			u	2		s6	8	9	10	11			u			6	5			7
22	17 Jan	A	Charlton Athletic	D	2	2	(1 0)	20,043	14	Ketsbaia, Solano				4d	s7				9		11	u	10	2		u	6	5			
23	30 Jan	H	**Aston Villa**	W	2	1	(2 0)	36,766	13	Shearer, Ketsbaia	1			4		u		8	9	s10	11		10	2			6	5			7
24	06 Feb	A	Leeds United	W	1	0	(0 0)	40,202	12	Solano	1				4			8		s9	11		10	2			6	5			7
25	17 Feb	H	**Coventry City**	W	4	1	(1 1)	36,352	10	Shearer 2, Speed, Saha	1			4	2			8	9		11		s10	s11			6	5			7
26	20 Feb	A	Southampton	L	1	2	(0 2)	15,244	10	Hamann	1			4	2		s6	8	9		11		10	u			6	5			
27	28 Feb	H	**Arsenal**	D	1	1	(0 1)	36,708	11	Hamann	1			4	2		s7	8	9		11		s6	u			6	5			
28	10 Mar	A	Nottingham Forest	W	2	1	(1 1)	22,852	10	Shearer (pen), Hamann	1			s5	4		s11	8	9		11		s10	2			u	5			
29	13 Mar	H	**Manchester United**	L	1	2	(1 1)	36,776	11	Solano	1			4	5		s7	8	9		11		10	2			6				
30	20 Mar	A	West Ham United	L	0	2	(0 1)	25,997	12		1			4	5		s8		9		11		s7	u			6				
31	03 Apr	A	Derby County	W	4	3	(3 2)	32,039	9	Speed 2, Ketsbaia, Solano	1			4	5		7			u	8		10				6				
32	05 Apr	H	**Tottenham Hotspur**	D	1	1	(0 0)	36,655	10	Ketsbaia	1			4	5						8		10	s3			6				
33	17 Apr	H	**Everton**	L	1	3	(0 2)	36,775	11	Shearer (pen)	1					u	7	4	9	u	11		10	3			s10				
34	21 Apr	A	Sheffield Wednesday	D	1	1	(1 0)	21,545	11	Shearer (pen)	u			4			7	6	9	u	11		10	3			s9				
35	24 Apr	A	Wimbledon	D	1	1	(1 1)	21,172	12	Shearer	1			4				8	9	10	11			u			6				
36	01 May	H	**Middlesbrough**	D	1	1	(0 0)	36,784	12	Shearer (pen)	u			4			7	6	9		11		s10	2			s8				
37	08 May	A	Leicester City	L	0	2	(0 2)	21,125	12		u			4			7	8	9		11		s10	2			6				s6
38	16 May	H	**Blackburn Rovers**	D	1	1	(0 1)	36,623	13	Hamann	u			4			7	8			11		10	3			6				s7
Round			**FA Cup (AXA)**																												
3	02 Jan	H	**Crystal Palace**	W	2	1	(0 1)	36,536		Shearer, Speed	1d			4	2	u		8	9	10	11		u	3			6				7
4	23 Jan	H	**Bradford City**	W	3	0	(1 0)	36,698		Shearer, Ketsbaia, Hamann	1			4	5			8	9	u	11		10	u			6				s6
5	14 Feb	H	**Blackburn Rovers**	D	0	0	(0 0)	36,295			1				4			8	9		11		10	2			6	5			7
5r	24 Feb	A	Blackburn Rovers	W	1	0	(1 0)	27,483		Saha	1			4	2		u	8			11		10	3			6	5			
6	07 Mar	H	**Everton**	W	4	1	(1 0)	36,584		Shearer, Ketsbaia 2, Georgiadis	1			4	u		7	8	9				10	2			6	5			
SF	11 Apr	N1	Tottenham Hotspur	We	2	0	(0 0)	53,609		Shearer 2 (1 pen)	1			4			7	8	9		11		10	3			6	5			
F	22 May	N2	Manchester United	L	0	2	(0 1)	79,101			u			4	5		7	8	9		11		10	u			6				s10
Round			**FL Cup (Worthington Cup)**																												
3	27 Oct	A	Tranmere Rovers	W	1	0	(1 0)	12,017		Dalglish	1			4	5	3			9		11			u			10				6
4	11 Nov	H	**Blackburn Rovers**	Dep	1	1	(1 1)	34,702		Shearer	1			4	u	3		10	9		s6	u		2					u		6
Round			**UEFA Cup Winners Cup**																												
1(1)	17 Sep	H	**FK Partizan (Sb)**	W	2	1	(1 0)	26,599		Shearer, Dabizas	1	2	u	6	5	3	7		9	8	11		10	u	u	u	s8			u	4
1(2)	01 Oct	A	FK Partizan (Sb)	La	0	1	(0 0)	41,008			1			6	5	3			9		11		10	u	s2	u	8	u			7

Match	Dalglish	Gillespie	Batty	Griffin	Hughes	Harper	Georgiadis	Brady	Ferguson	Beharall	Keen	Domi	Saha	Maric	Caldwell S	McClen	Match
Squad numbers	25	18	4	38	28	13	15	29	20	33	39	4	18	10	37	36	
1																	1
2																	2
3	u																3
4																	4
5		s10															5
6	s10	11															6
7	s10		s8														7
8	s10	u	7	2													8
9	11		8	2													9
10	10		4	2	u												10
11	7	s7	8	2		u											11
12	10		8	3	2	u	7										12
13	10	8	s4	3	6	u											13
14	10	8	6			u		s10									14
15	u	7			3	s1			10	u							15
16	s10	8			3	1			9								16
17					3	1	s7		9		u						17
18					u	u	8										18
19					s2	u	8		10								19
20					4	u	s7		10								20
21					4	u						3	s10				21
22	s10				s6	1	8	7				3					22
23					u	u		s6				3					23
24				3	u	u	u	s7					9				24
25					u	u		s7				3	10				25
26					u	u	u	7				3					26
27				u		u		7				3	10				27
28						u	6					3	10	7			28
29				u		u	7					3	s10	s2			29
30				2	u	u	8					3	10	7			30
31				3	2	u		s6				11	s9	9	u		31
32				3	2	u	s7	u				11	s9	9		7	32
33				2	5	u				6			s8	8			33
34				2	5	1		s7		u				8			34
35				2	u	u		u		5		3		7		u	35
36					u	1			10	5		3		8		u	36
37					u	1		u	10	5		3					37
38				2	5	1				u			s10	9		u	38
Round																	Round
3					5	s7	s3	u									3
4				2	u	u		7				3					4
5				u	u	u		s11				3	u				5
5r	u			u	u	u		7					9				5r
6						u	s11	u				3	u	11			6
SF				2	s5	u			s6				u	s10			SF
F				2		1			s8			3		s6			F
Round																	Round
3	7	s6	8	2	u	u	u										3
4	11		8		5	u	7										4
Round																	Round
1(1)		u															1(1)
1(2)		u	4	2		u	u										1(2)

N1 Played at Old Trafford, Manchester
N2 Played at Wembley Stadium, London

We Won after extra time
Dep Drawn after extra time, tie lost on penalties (2-4)
La Tie lost on away goals

DateLine ... 30 Aug: With Kenny Dalglish departing, Liverpool give United a lesson at Gallowgate by winning 4-1. **9 Sept:** Ruud Gullit replaces Dalglish as boss and takes full charge against Aston Villa. **11 April:** Alan Shearer's double strike in the semi-final with Tottenham takes United back to Wembley in the FA Cup. **22 May:** The Geordies fail again in the FA Cup final, this time crushed 2-0 by Manchester United.

SEASON 1999-2000
PREMIER LEAGUE

Wor Bobby returns to his roots

Ruud Gullit's first full season in charge began with an under-current of disharmony in the camp. It became clear that the boss was at odds with several of his senior players, including Alan Shearer, Rob Lee, Greek centre-back Nikos Dabizas and big signing Duncan Ferguson. When the first high profile game of the season arrived, a local derby with Sunderland at St James' Park, rumours were rampant on Tyneside that there had been a dramatic bust-up. Shearer and Ferguson were on the bench and Lee in the stand for the Tyne versus Wear confrontation. And with their arch rivals winning 2-1 in a rainstorm, mayhem reigned. Gullit resigned and United were back to square one. Again the club's Board acted quickly and this time found the man they really wanted as boss, a local hero in former England supremo Bobby Robson.

Newcastle were in a relegation fight by then. Robson had to inspire all and get United firstly out of trouble and then back on course. In his first game on Tyneside, United won 8-0 – with the recalled Shearer bagging five of the goals. Robson steadily made an improvement with the Black'n'Whites moving up the table. By the turn of the year, the Magpies were comfortably positioned and a fine 3-0 triumph over Manchester United confirmed the Toon's recovery. With a Shearer and Ferguson partnership proving fruitful when in tandem, and with solid pros like Gary Speed, Rob Lee, Nobby Solano and Shay Given in the ranks, Robson had something to build on for the future.

Although Roma knocked United out of the UEFA Cup by a single goal in December, United claimed a hat-trick of Wembley appearances. The tournament started early that season, before Christmas, and the Geordies got off to a flier, with a 6-1 rout of Tottenham at St James' Park. United carried on to the semi-final played at Wembley where they only narrowly lost to Chelsea – a performance that many considered warranted victory.

Pictured above: Although often sidelined with injury, Duncan Ferguson showed he was a first rate striker.

Memorabilia CORNER

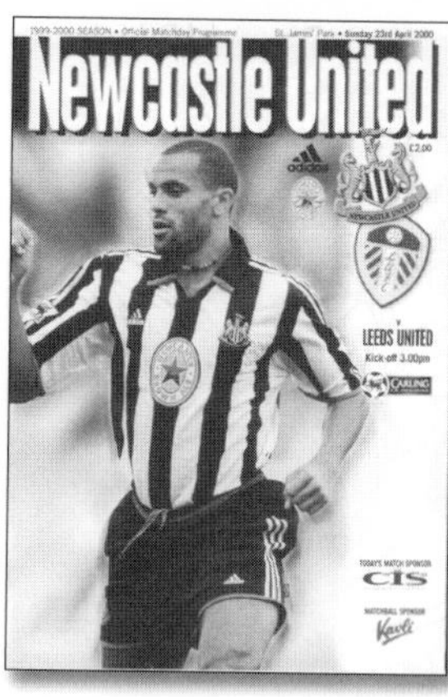

Programmes had by now reached £2, but were packed with features. Alain Goma is pictured

IN CHARGE

Chairman: Freddy Shepherd
Manager: Ruud Gullit/Bobby Robson
Captain: Alan Shearer
Trainer/Coach: Steve Clarke/Mick Wadsworth/John Carver
Club Sponsor: Newcastle Breweries
Kit Supplier: Adidas

ST JAMES' PARK

Average Attendance
Lg 36,312 Lg & Cup 36,168

Ruud Gullit was in charge for the start of the 1999-2000 season, pictured in United's white change kit (centre, front).

PLAYER FOCUS Robert Lee

Born London. Midfield, 5'11"
1992 to 2002: 381 app 56 goals.

During United's period of dramatic resurgence in the 1990s one player stood out as an influential figure, Robert Lee. Joining the Gallowgate set-up during September 1992, Lee contributed hugely in the whole success story. And at £700,000, the Londoner proved to be perhaps United's best value-for-money signing in that era. For several years and in over 300 games Lee was recognised as a committed and goalscoring winger with Charlton Athletic, often tipped for a move to a bigger stage. With United, Rob became a vital player as the Magpies lifted the First Division trophy, a raiding outside-right able to hit goals. Then in the Premier League he moved into midfield from the flank and Lee flourished. His stamina, strong-running from box to box, made him into one of the best competitors around. He was sturdy in possession and could score goals too. England recognition justly followed, eventually appearing 21 times for his country. Runner-up twice in the Premier League, Rob became captain of the Magpies, while later in his near ten-year Gallowgate career, Lee switched into an anchor role in midfield. He appeared in two Wembley FA Cup finals, in 1998 (as skipper) and 1999 before moving to Derby County during February 2002 and then to West Ham United. He ended playing with Wycombe Wanderers in 2006, the Londoner was often afterwards to be seen in the television media as an expert summariser. Lee registered United's first ever hat-trick in European competition against Royal Antwerp while his sons Oliver and Elliot started their careers in the game at West Ham.

SEASON REVIEW

Premier League: P38 W14 D10 L14 F63 A54 Pts 52.
Position: 11th (Champions; Manchester United).
FA Cup: SF (Winners; Chelsea).
FL Worthington Cup: R3 (Winners; Leicester City).
UEFA Cup: R3 (Winners; Galatasaray SK).

Appearances (51m): Shearer A 49 (1), Speed GA 49, Barton WD 45 (1), Dabizas N 42, Lee RM 41, Solano NAT 39 (1), Dyer KC 35 (4), Harper SA 29, Hughes AW 27 (7), Domi D 25 (11), Ferguson DC 25 (7), Pistone A 20 (1), Gallacher KW 19 (6), Goma A 17, Given SJJ 16 (1), Ketsbaia T 13 (15), Marcelino ES 13 (2), Helder 12, Howey SN 8 (2), Dumas F 7, Maric S 7 (11), Charvet LJ 4 (1), Karelse 3, McClen JD 3 (9), Wright TJ 3, Gavilan DAZ 2 (4), Glass S 2 (10), Robinson PD 2 (14), Serrant C 2 (1), Fumaca 1 (5), Griffin A 1 (2), Beharall DA 0 (2), Hamilton DV 0 (1).

Goals (89g): Shearer A 30, Speed GA 13, Ferguson DC 10, Dabizas N 5, Domi D 4, Dyer KC 4, Solano NAT 4, Gallacher KW 3, Hughes AW 2, Maric S 2, Gavilan DAZ 1, Glass S 1, Griffin A 1, Helder 1, Ketsbaia T 1, Lee RM 1, Pistone A 1, Robinson PD 1, own goals 4.

Dismissals: 4 players; Shearer, Dabizas, Harper, Barton.

MAJOR SIGNINGS

Kieron Dyer (Ipswich Town) £7m
Marcelino (RCD Mallorca) £5m
Alain Goma (PSG) £4.75m
Franck Dumas (AS Monaco) £500,000
Kevin Gallacher (Blackburn Rvs) £700,000
Diego Gavilan (Cerro Porteno) £2m
John Karelse (NAC Breda) £750,000
Helder (Deportivo La Coruna) loan

FROM THE RANKS

None

TEAM COLOURS Black & white striped shirts, black shorts (Change; all white shirts & shorts with black-blue-green trim)

SEASON 1999-2000

Match	Date		Premiership (Carling)					Posn		Harper	Barton	Domi	Marcelino	Goma	Dumas	Solano	Serrant	Shearer	Ketsbaia	Speed	Dyer	Robinson	Maric	Charvet	Perez	Hughes	Caldwell G	Karelse	McClen	Beharall	Ferguson	Kerr	Wright	Dabizas	Green	Lee	Glass	Gallacher	Given	Pistone	Fumaca	Helder	Gavilan	Howey	Griffin	Hamilton	Match
									Squad numbers	13	2	4	3	5	8	15	21	9	14	11	7	28	10	16	23	18	22	29	19	27	20	25	32	34	31	37	17	32	1	36	38	39	8	6	12	33	
1	07 Aug	H	**Aston Villa**	L	0 1	(0 0)	36,376	18		1	2	3	4	5	6	7	8	9d	10	11	s4	s7	s8	u	u																						1
2	09 Aug	A	Tottenham Hotspur	L	1 3	(1 2)	28,701	19	Solano	1	2	3		5	6	8	u	9	10	11	7	s6	s4		u	4	u																				2
3	15 Aug	A	Southampton	L	2 4	(1 0)	15,030	20	Shearer (pen), Speed,	u	2	3		5		8	6	9	10	11	7	ss6	s6			4	u	1	u																		3
4	21 Aug	H	**Wimbledon**	D	3 3	(2 1)	35,809	18	Speed, Domi, Solano (pen)	u	2	3	4	5		8			10	11	7	9				u		1	6	s5	s10	u															4
5	25 Aug	H	**Sunderland**	L	1 2	(1 0)	36,420	19	Dyer	u	2	3		5		8		s10		11	7	9	10			u			6		s9		1	4	u												5
6	30 Aug	A	Manchester United	L	1 5	(1 1)	55,190	19	og (Berg)	u	2			5		8		9		11	7	s10	u			3			s6	s8	10		1	4d		6											6
7	11 Sep	A	Chelsea	L	0 1	(0 1)	35,092	19		u	2	3		5		8		9		11	7	s10	s6			s8			u		10		1	4		6											7
8	19 Sep	H	**Sheffield Wednesday**	W	8 0	(4 0)	36,619	19	Hughes, Shearer 5 (2 pens), Dyer, Speed	1	2	3		5		8		9	10	11	7	s7				4			s10	u			u			6	s3										8
9	25 Sep	A	Leeds United	L	2 3	(1 2)	40,192	19	Shearer 2	1	2	3	4	5		8		9	10	11	7	s10		s6		u			6				u				u										9
10	03 Oct	H	**Middlesbrough**	W	2 1	(2 0)	36,421	19	Shearer 2	1	2	3	u	5		8		9		11	7	s10				u		u						4		6	s8	10									10
11	16 Oct	A	Coventry City	L	1 4	(0 3)	23,031	19	Domi	u	2d	3				8		9		11	7		u			5			u					4		6	u	10	1	u							11
12	25 Oct	H	**Derby County**	W	2 0	(1 0)	35,614	17	og (Eranio), Shearer	u	2		5			8		9		11	7		s7			s2			u		s10			4		6		10	1	3							12
13	30 Oct	A	Arsenal	D	0 0	(0 0)	38,106	17				3	5		6	8		9		11			u	u	u	u		1			s8			4		7		10		2							13
14	07 Nov	H	**Everton**	D	1 1	(0 0)	36,164	16	Shearer (pen)	1		3	u		5	7		9		11			s10			u		u			10			4		6	u	8		2							14
15	20 Nov	A	Watford	D	1 1	(0 0)	19,539	16	Dabizas	1			5		2	u		9	s10	11			8			6		u						4		7	s8	10		3	u						15
16	28 Nov	H	**Tottenham Hotspur**	W	2 1	(1 1)	36,454	15	Glass, Dabizas	1						7		9	10				s7	2		3			s8	u	s10			4		6	11		u		8	5					16
17	04 Dec	A	Aston Villa	W	1 0	(0 0)	34,531	14	Ferguson	1	s7				2	7		9	10	11			8			s10					s8			4		6	u		u	3		5					17
18	18 Dec	A	Bradford City	L	0 2	(0 0)	18,276	15		1	2					7		9	u	11	s7					4					10					6	s8	8	u	3	s6	5					18
19	26 Dec	H	**Liverpool**	D	2 2	(1 1)	36,445	15	Shearer, Ferguson	1	2		u			8		9	s10	11	7					5					10			4		6	s7	s8	u	3							19
20	28 Dec	A	Leicester City	W	2 1	(1 0)	21,225	14	Ferguson, Shearer	1	2		5			7		9	u	11						u					10			4		6	u	8	u	3	u						20
21	03 Jan	H	**West Ham United**	D	2 2	(1 0)	36,314	15	Dabizas, Speed	1	2		5			7		9	s10	11						u					10			4		6	s8	8	u	3	s6						21
22	16 Jan	H	**Southampton**	W	5 0	(4 0)	35,623	13	Ferguson 2, Solano, og 2 (Monk, Dryden)	1	2	s8	5			7		9	s7	11	6					s2					10			4				8	u	3	u						22
23	22 Jan	A	Wimbledon	L	0 2	(0 0)	22,118	15		1	2	s8	5			7		9	u	11	6					u					10			4				8	u	3		u					23
24	05 Feb	A	Sunderland	D	2 2	(2 1)	42,192	13	Domi, Helder	1	2	6						9		11	7					s3					10			4		8		s6	u	3	u	5	s8				24
25	12 Feb	H	**Manchester United**	W	3 0	(1 0)	36,470	13	Ferguson, Shearer 2	1	2	s8						9	s10	11	7					3					10			4		6		8	u		u	5	s7				25
26	26 Feb	A	Sheffield Wednesday	W	2 0	(1 0)	29,212	12	Gallacher, Shearer		2	s8						9	s10	11	7					3		u			10			4		6		8	1			5	u	s5			26
27	04 Mar	H	**Chelsea**	L	0 1	(0 1)	36,448	12		u	2	6				s6		9	s8	11	7					3					10			4		8			1		u		u	5			27
28	11 Mar	H	**Watford**	W	1 0	(0 0)	36,433	12	Gallacher	u	2	s3				7		9	u	11						3					10			4		6		8	1		u		u	5			28
29	19 Mar	A	Everton	W	2 0	(0 0)	32,512	11	Hughes, Dyer	u	2	s8		u		7		9	u	11	s7					3					10			4		6		8	1					5			29
30	25 Mar	A	Liverpool	L	1 2	(0 0)	44,743	11	Shearer	u	2	s6		6				9	u	11	7					3					10			4		8		s8	1		u			5			30
31	01 Apr	H	**Bradford City**	W	2 0	(1 0)	36,572	11	Speed, Shearer	1	2	6	u	5				9	s7	11	7		u			3					10					8			u		u	4					31
32	12 Apr	A	West Ham United	L	1 2	(0 0)	25,817	10	Speed	u	2	6		5		7		9	s10	11	10					3								4		8			1		u		u	s4			32
33	15 Apr	H	**Leicester City**	L	0 2	(0 1)	36,426	11		u	2	6		5		7		9		11	10	s3				3										8			1		s10		s7	4	u		33
34	23 Apr	H	**Leeds United**	D	2 2	(1 2)	36,460	12	Shearer 2	u	2	11	s6					9			7		s7			3			u					4		10			1		s8	6	8	5			34
35	29 Apr	H	**Coventry City**	W	2 0	(0 0)	36,408	12	Shearer (pen), Gavilan	u	2	6						9	s6	11	7		u			5			s10					4		10			1	3			8		s8		35
36	02 May	A	Middlesbrough	D	2 2	(2 1)	34,744	12	Speed, Pistone	u	2					7		9	10	11	8		s10			5			s8					4		6			1	3			u		s7		36
37	06 May	A	Derby County	D	0 0	(0 0)	32,724	12			2	s3				7		9	10	11	8		u			5		u						4		6		s7	1	3			s10				37
38	14 May	H	**Arsenal**	W	4 2	(2 1)	36,450	11	Speed 2, Shearer, Griffin		3			u		7		9	10	11	8		s7		u				s6					4		6		s10	1					5	2		38
Round			FA Cup (AXA)																																												Round
3	12 Dec	A	Tottenham Hotspur	D	1 1	(0 0)	33,116		Speed	1	2							9	s7	11	7			6		u					10			4		8	s5	s10	u	3		5					3
3r	22 Dec	H	**Tottenham Hotspur**	W	6 1	(3 1)	35,415		Speed, Dabizas, Ferguson, Dyer, Shearer 2 (1 pen)	1	2		s5			7		9	s10	11	s8					3					10			4		6	u	8	u			5					3r
4	08 Jan	H	**Sheffield United**	W	4 1	(1 1)	36,220		Shearer, Dabizas, Ferguson, Gallacher	1	2	s3	5			6		9	s8	11	7					u					10			4				8	u	3	s7						4
5	31 Jan	A	Blackburn Rovers	W	2 1	(1 1)	29,946		Shearer 2	1	2	s8						9		11	7		s7			s5					10			4		6		8	u	3	u	5					5
6	20 Feb	A	Tranmere Rovers	W	3 2	(2 1)	15,776		Speed, Domi, Ferguson		2	6						9	u	11	7					3		u			10			4			u	8	1		u	5		u			6
SF	09 Apr	N	Chelsea	L	1 2	(0 1)	73,876		Lee	u	2	s10		u		7		9	s3	11	8					3					10			4		6			1				u	5			SF
Round			FL Cup (Worthington Cup)																																												Round
3	12 Oct	A	Birmingham City	L	0 2	(0 1)	19,795			1d	2	3		5		7	u	9		10		s9	8						u					4		6	11		s7	s6							3
Round			UEFA Cup																																												Round
1(1)	16 Sep	A	CSKA Sofia (Bul)	W	2 0	(0 0)	20,260		Solano, Ketsbaia	1	2	3		5		8		9	s10	11	7	u				u		u	u	u	10			4		6										s8	1(1)
1(2)	30 Sep	H	**CSKA Sofia (Bul)**	D	2 2	(1 1)	36,228		Shearer, Robinson	1	2	3	4	5		7		9		11		s10	10	u		u		u	s8					6		8	s9			u							1(2)
2(1)	21 Oct	A	FC Zurich (Sw)	W	2 1	(0 0)	9,600		Shearer, Maric	1	2	3	u			8	s7	9		11	7	s10	10			5			s8			u		4		6			u	u							2(1)
2(2)	04 Nov	H	**FC Zurich (Sw)**	W	3 1	(1 1)	34,502		Maric, Speed, Ferguson	1	2	3	5			7		9		11		s10	8	u		u		u	s6		10			4		6	s8			u							2(2)
3(1)	25 Nov	A	AS Roma (I)	L	0 1	(0 0)	45,655			1	2					7	u	9	10	11		s10	u	6		5	u	u	u					4		8	u			3							3(1)
3(2)	09 Dec	H	**AS Roma (I)**	D	0 0	(0 0)	35,739			1	u				5	8		9	10	11	7		u	2		s5			u		s7			4		6	s10		u	3							3(2)

N Played at Wembley Stadium, London

DateLine ... 11 Sept: Bobby Robson returns to the North East and takes control of Newcastle United against Chelsea. **19 Sept:** Robson's first home game in charge results in an amazing 8-0 win over Sheffield Wednesday, United's best Premier League result. **19 Sept:** Alan Shearer nets five goals against Sheffield Wednesday. **9 April:** Chelsea narrowly topple the Magpies 2-1 in the FA Cup semi-final at Wembley. **14 May:** Alan Shearer nets his 30th goal of the season in the match with Arsenal.

SEASON
2000-01
PREMIER LEAGUE

Recovery plan on track

With Premiership security achieved, Bobby Robson now looked to fashion a squad which could again challenge at the right end of the Premier League table.

After such a period of high spending, finances were such that funds were limited due to ground enlargement expenditure, but the manager did bring in striker Carl Cort for a substantial £7m fee as well as experienced South Americans Bassedas, Cordone and Acuna. However, this round of transfer activity was to be far from successful.

The redeveloped St James' Park with a capacity much increased to over 52,000 was unveiled for the opening home fixture of the season with Derby County. United got off to a winning start – with a 3-2 victory – at their new surroundings while for the next decade rarely did attendances drop below the 50,000 mark for Premier League contests. Only Manchester United – and Arsenal in future years – could match the Geordie support. Following that opener with the Rams, six more points were secured with follow-up victories against Tottenham and Coventry. Robson's men led the table, but consistency was lacking after that. Mixed results saw the Tynesiders gradually slide down the ranking.

With Alan Shearer injured in December and out for much of the following six months, the season was very much a rebuilding campaign for Robson. Now in mid-table, Newcastle disappointed in both the League Cup and FA Cup. They went out to Midland clubs in both competitions, to Birmingham City in the League Cup at St Andrews, then to Aston Villa after a replay in the FA Cup. With the season ending on a high as Shearer was on the road to fitness, something of a revenge 3-0 victory over Aston Villa was recorded on the last day of the campaign. Robson was determined his next spending spree was to bring a much better dividend.

Pictured above: Londoner Warren Barton flourished in the North East, a dedicated and solid professional.

Memorabilia CORNER

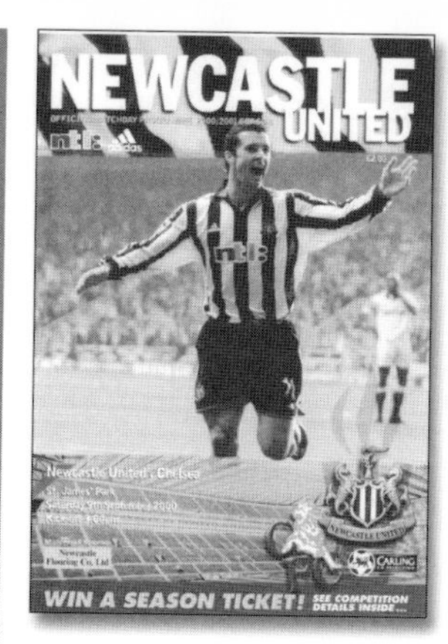

The enlarged St James' Park is featured on the cover of the programme, along with Gary Speed.

IN CHARGE

Chairman: Freddy Shepherd
Manager: Bobby Robson
Captain: Alan Shearer
Trainer/Coach: Mick Wadsworth
Club Sponsor: NTL
Kit Supplier: Adidas

ST JAMES' PARK

Average Attendance
Lg 51,299 Lg & Cup 49,613

Another change in manager brought Bobby Robson back to his native North East (front, centre) flanked by Alan Shearer (right) and Carl Cort (left).

PLAYER FOCUS Steve Watson

Born North Shields. Right-back, 6'0"
1989 to 1998: 263 app 14 goals.

Alongside Lee Clark, fellow Tynesider Steve Watson developed through the ranks at Gallowgate, first attached to the club as a schoolboy in 1989 when at Wallsend Boy's Club. He was proud to wear the black-and-white shirt, forever a United supporter. Steve became the Magpies' youngest ever debutant being aged 16 years 223 days in November 1990 and was quickly part of the first-team squad claiming 100 games before he was 20 years old. Although often in and out of the Newcastle line-up, Steve was able to operate in a number of roles – at full-back, centre-back, midfield and even as a striker, scoring one memorable goal when up front against Liverpool. Perhaps that versatility was an obstacle to Watson claiming a settled place in the side, yet the Tynesider more than held his own in United's team of internationals. Tall and able to take knocks, Steve could also call on delightful ball skills with ability to go past opponents. He moved to Aston Villa in October 1998 for £3.75m as Ruud Gullit started a rebuilding strategy on Tyneside. Watson then enjoyed successful periods with Everton, West Bromwich Albion and finally Sheffield Wednesday before a hip injury forced his retirement in 2009. He afterwards began coaching as part of the Huddersfield Town staff. Steve was a regular for the England youth and Under-21 line-ups while he also claimed a B cap and was called into the full squad during 1997-98.

SEASON REVIEW

Premier League: P38 W14 D9 L15 F44 A50 Pts 51.
Position: 11th (Champions; Manchester United).
FA Cup: R3 (Winners; Liverpool).
FL Worthington Cup: R4 (Winners; Liverpool).

Appearances (44m): Speed GA 41, Hughes AW 39 (1), Given SJJ 35, Solano NAT 35 (3), Dyer KC 30 (1), Barton WD 29 (3), Acuna CWD 26 (3), Lee RM 24 (2), Goma A 23 (1), Shearer A 23, Bassedas CG 20 (6), Griffin A 20 (5), Cort CER 15, Gallacher KW 15 (7), Ameobi F 14 (8), Quinn WR 14 (1), Cordone CD 13 (14), Domi D 12 (4), Dabizas N 9, Harper SA 9 (1), O'Brien AJ 9, Charvet LJ 8 (1), Caldwell S 6 (4), Glass S 6 (10), Marcelino ES 6 (1), LuaLua LT 3 (20), Coppinger J 0 (1), Gavilan DAZ 0 (2), Kerr B 0 (1).

Goals (53g): Cort CER 7, Shearer A 7, Solano NAT 7, Dyer KC 6, Speed GA 6, Acuna CWD 3, Cordone CD 3, Gallacher KW 3, Glass S 3, Ameobi F 2, Bassedas CG 1, Caldwell S 1, Goma A 1, O'Brien AJ 1, own goals 2.

Dismissals: 5 players; Barton, Solano (2), Dyer, Speed.

MAJOR SIGNINGS

Christian Bassedas (CA Velez Sarsfield) £3.5m
Carl Cort (Wimbledon) £7m
Andy O'Brien (Bradford City) £2m
Clarence Acuna (CF Universidad de Chile) £954,000
Lomana LuaLua (Colchester Utd) £2.25m
Daniel Cordone (Racing Club) £500,000
Wayne Quinn (Sheffield Utd) £1m

FROM THE RANKS

Shola Ameobi (Walker Central BC)
Stephen Caldwell (Stirling sch, Sy)
Brian Kerr (Scotland sch, Ss/Sy)

TEAM COLOURS Black & white striped shirts, black shorts (Change; all black shirts & shorts with white-blue trim)

SEASON 2000-01

Match	Date		Premiership (Carling)						Posn		Given	Barton	Hughes	Dabizas	Goma	Marcelino	Lee	Cort	Shearer	Cordone	Speed	Dyer	Solano	Charvet	Domi	Harper	Glass	Kerr	Coppinger	Griffin	Gavilan	Gallacher	Ameobi	McClen	Hamilton	LuaLua	Karelse	Caldwell S	Bassedas	Acuna	Quinn	O'Brien	Match
										Squad numbers	1	2	18	34	5	3	7	16	9	17	11	8	15	37	4	13	19	25	26	12	21	32	23	22	33	20	29	30	10	6	14	5	
1	20 Aug	A	Manchester United	L	0	2	(0 1)	67,477	18		1	2	3	4	5	6	7	8	9	10	11	s5	s7	u	u	u																	1
2	23 Aug	H	**Derby County**	W	3	2	(1 1)	51,327	12	Cort, Cordone, Glass	1	2d	5	4	s4			8	9	10	11	6	7	s7	3	u	s8	u															2
3	26 Aug	H	**Tottenham Hotspur**	W	2	0	(1 0)	51,573	3	Speed, Cordone	1	2	6		5				9	8	10	4	7	u	3	u	11		s8	s11	u													3
4	06 Sep	A	Coventry City	W	2	0	(1 0)	22,109	1	Shearer (pen), Gallacher	1		6		5		4		9	8	10	7		2	3	u	11	s8		s3	u	s11											4
5	09 Sep	H	**Chelsea**	D	0	0	(0 0)	51,687	3		1	3	6		5				9	10	11	4	7	2		u				u	s7	8	s8	u									5
6	16 Sep	A	Southampton	L	0	2	(0 0)	15,221	6		1		6		5				9	10	11	4	7	2	3	u		u		s3		8	s8		u								6
7	23 Sep	H	**Charlton Athletic**	L	0	1	(0 1)	50,866	7		1		6		5		s10	8	9	10	11	4	7	2	s2					3		u				s7	u						7
8	30 Sep	A	Manchester City	W	1	0	(0 0)	34,497	3	Shearer	1		6				4		9	10	11	7	s7	5	3					2		8			u	s10	u	s2				8
9	16 Oct	A	Middlesbrough	W	3	1	(1 0)	31,436	3	Shearer, Goma, Dyer	1		6		5	u	4		9	10	11	8	7	2	3	u						u				s10			u				9
10	21 Oct	H	**Everton**	L	0	1	(0 0)	51,625	4		1	2	6		5		4		9	10	11	8	7		3	u						s2				s10		u	u				10
11	28 Oct	A	West Ham United	L	0	1	(0 0)	26,044	8		1		6		5		4		9	s8	11	7	2			u	s4			3							8		u	u	10			11
12	04 Nov	H	**Ipswich Town**	W	2	1	(1 1)	50,922	5	Shearer 2 (1 pen)	1		6		5		4		9	10	11	7	2		3	u	u										s10		s2	s8	8			12
13	11 Nov	A	Leicester City	D	1	1	(0 0)	21,406	7	Speed	1		6		5		4		9	s4	11	7			3	u		u		2			u						u	10	8			13
14	18 Nov	H	**Sunderland**	L	1	2	(1 0)	52,030	8	Speed	1	s8	6				4		9	u	11	7	2		3	u				u						s10		5	10	8			14
15	26 Nov	H	**Liverpool**	W	2	1	(1 0)	51,949	7	Solano, Dyer	1	5	6				4		9	u	11	8	7		3	u				2						u		u	10	s10			15
16	02 Dec	A	Aston Villa	D	1	1	(0 1)	34,255	8	Solano	1	2	6		5		4			9	11	8	7		s5	u				3						s4		s6	u	10			16
17	09 Dec	A	Arsenal	L	0	5	(0 2)	38,052	10		1	2	6				4			s8	11	8	7		s3	u	s4			3						9		5	u	10			17
18	16 Dec	H	**Bradford City**	W	2	1	(1 0)	50,470	7	Speed, Dyer	1	2	6			5	4		9	u	11	8	7			u	u			3						u			10	s10			18
19	23 Dec	A	Derby County	L	0	2	(0 1)	29,978	8		1	2	6			5	7		9	s7		8				s1	s4			3	u					u		4	10	11			19
20	26 Dec	H	**Leeds United**	W	2	1	(2 1)	52,118	7	Solano, Acuna		2	6			5				u	11	8	7			1	u			3			9			u	u	u	10	4			20
21	30 Dec	H	**Manchester United**	D	1	1	(0 1)	52,134	7	Glass	u	2	6		5					s9	11	8	7			1	s4			3			9			s10		u	10	4			21
22	02 Jan	A	Tottenham Hotspur	L	2	4	(1 3)	34,323	8	Solano, Dyer (pen)	u	2	6		5					u	11	8d	7d			1	s3			3			9			s9		u	10	4			22
23	13 Jan	H	**Coventry City**	W	3	1	(1 0)	50,159	7	Speed, Ameobi, Dyer	u	2	6		5	u				u	11	8	7			1	s10						9			u			10	4	3		23
24	20 Jan	A	Leeds United	W	3	1	(2 1)	40,005	6	Solano (pen), Acuna, Ameobi	1	2	6		5	s9	8			u	11		7									10	9			s10	u		s8	4	3		24
25	31 Jan	A	Chelsea	L	1	3	(1 1)	35,108	7	Bassedas	1	2	6		5	u				s9	11	8	7							u			9			s8	u		10	4	3		25
26	11 Feb	A	Charlton Athletic	L	0	2	(0 2)	20,043	10		1	2	6			5	10				11	8	7			u			u		s4	9			s7			s10	4	3		26
27	24 Feb	H	**Manchester City**	L	0	1	(0 0)	51,981	11		1	s4	6		5				9	u		8	7			u	s11			2		11	10			s10				4	3		27
28	03 Mar	A	Everton	D	1	1	(0 0)	35,779	11	og (Unsworth)	1		6				8		9	s7			7			u	s11			2		s10	10	u				5	11	4	3		28
29	17 Mar	H	**Middlesbrough**	L	1	2	(0 2)	51,751	13	Cort	1	2	6				4	9		s8	11		7			u			s2		s10	10					5	u	8	3		29
30	31 Mar	A	Bradford City	D	2	2	(1 2)	20,160	13	Cort, Acuna	1	2	6				8	9		u	11		7			u			u		s7	10						s4	4	3	5	30
31	14 Apr	A	Ipswich Town	L	0	1	(0 0)	24,026	14		1	2	6				8	9			11		7d			u						s10	10			s8		u	u	4	3	5	31
32	16 Apr	H	**West Ham United**	W	2	1	(1 0)	51,107	13	Cort, Solano (pen)	1	2		6			4	9		u	11		7			u						10				s10		s2	8	s4	3	5	32
33	21 Apr	A	Sunderland	D	1	1	(0 0)	48,277	13	O'Brien	1	2	u	6				9		s10	11		7			u				s4		10	s7						8	4	3	5	33
34	28 Apr	H	**Leicester City**	W	1	0	(0 0)	50,501	10	Cort	1	2	u	6				9		u	10					u	11						8	s8			s7			7	4	3	5	34
35	01 May	H	**Southampton**	D	1	1	(1 0)	50,439	10	Gallacher	1	2	s10	6				9		u	11					u						8	s8			7		u	10	4	3	5	35
36	05 May	A	Liverpool	L	0	3	(0 1)	44,363	11		1	2	3	6				9			10		7			u						8	s9			s8		u	s4	4	11	5	36
37	15 May	H	**Arsenal**	D	0	0	(0 0)	50,729	11		1	2	3	6				9			10		7			u	11					8	s8	u		u			4		u	5	37
38	19 May	H	**Aston Villa**	W	3	0	(2 0)	51,306	11	Glass, Cort, og (Delaney)	1	2	3	6				9			10d		7			u	11					8	s8	u		s7			4		s11	5	38
Round			FA Cup (AXA)																																							Round
3	07 Jan	H	**Aston Villa**	D	1	1	(0 0)	37,682		Solano	u	2	6		5	u				s11	11	8	7			1	s2			3			9			s9			10	4			3
3r	17 Jan	A	Aston Villa	L	0	1	(0 0)	25,387			u	s10	3		5	6				s8	10					1	11			2	u	8	9			s11			7	4			3r
Round			FL Cup (Worthington Cup)																																							Round
2(1)	20 Sep	H	**Leyton Orient**	W	2	0	(1 0)	37,284		Cort, Speed	u		6		5		s7	10	9	s8	11	4	7	2	u	1				3	s10	8											2(1)
2(2)	26 Sep	A	Leyton Orient	D	1	1	(1 1)	9,522		Gallacher	1		6				4	8	9	s8	11	7	s10	5	3					2	u	10					u	u					2(2)
3	01 Nov	H	**Bradford City**	W	4	3	(3 1)	41,847		Shearer 2, Cordone, Caldwell	u				5		4		9	10	11	7	2		s3	1	u			3			u					6	s10	8			3
4	29 Nov	A	Birmingham City	L	1	2	(1 1)	18,520		Dyer	u	2	6		5		4		9	s10	11	8	7		u	1				3								u	10	u			4

NEWCASTLE UNITED

DateLine ... 23 Aug: An enlarged St James' Park is unvielled against Derby County with a new capacity of 52,243. **9 Sept:** Record gate receipts established of £1.251m for the visit of Chelsea. **2 Jan:** Nobby Solano and Kieron Dyer both sent-off against Tottenham.

SEASON
2001-02
PREMIER LEAGUE

Title challenge once more

With funds replenished, Robson was handed a transfer kitty which saw potent winger Laurent Robert arrive on Tyneside with Craig Bellamy, a tigerish and pacey striker. And this time the new men were a roaring success. The Frenchman made a difference giving all-important service to Shearer, while Welshman Bellamy formed a productive strike-force with England's skipper. The result was that Robson's refreshed line-up challenged at the top of the table again.

As the season got underway United won 4-1 at Middlesbrough and then followed that Tyne-Tees derby victory with an absorbing end-to-end triumph over Manchester United – the Geordies grabbing the winner in a 4-3 victory. As Christmas approached, a 3-1 win over Arsenal at Highbury put the Magpies at the head of the Premier League. They stayed there with another fine away success, again by 4-3, on this occasion at Leeds.

Robson's growing status as a Geordie icon was reinforced with three points at Sunderland during February when United's title aspirations were confirmed. But defeats to Arsenal and Liverpool in quick succession saw United drop to fourth place – where they stayed for the remainder of the programme.

Apart from a good League showing, United also had two decent cup runs, but received no luck in the draw. Their League Cup journey was halted in the Fifth Round when paired against Chelsea at Stamford Bridge, while in the FA Cup quarter-final, the Black'n'Whites fell to Arsenal, also in the capital.

At the beginning of the season, indeed during mid-July, the club tasted the Intertoto Cup for the first time, in a bid to qualify for the UEFA Cup. United reached the so-called final but lost on away goals in an extraordinary deciding leg on Tyneside with Troyes. After being down 4-1, Newcastle hit back to claim a 4-4 draw and very nearly grabbed a dramatic winner. All that had been forgotten by the time United squeezed into the qualifying round of the Champions League at the end of the season. Serious European competition was now for the taking.

Pictured above: When fit, Kieron Dyer possessed a cutting edge from midfield to give United a special quality.

Memorabilia CORNER

By now sponsors NTL were associated with the club. Rob Lee and Alan Shearer are pictured.

IN CHARGE

Chairman: Freddy Shepherd
Manager: Bobby Robson
Captain: Alan Shearer
Trainer/Coach: John Carver
Club Sponsor: NTL
Kit Supplier: Adidas

ST JAMES' PARK

Average Attendance
Lg 51,373 Lg & Cup 47,284

The photographic symmetry of United's photo-call by now was first-class, matching anything from the club's pre-war years.

PLAYER FOCUS Gary Speed

Born Mancot. Midfield, 5'11"
1998 to 2004: 285 app 40 goals.

When Welsh international Gary Speed joined the Magpies, it took the commanding midfield player several months to settle and display the form that had earned him the reputation of being one of the best all-round competitors in the business. Initially given an unfamiliar role on the left of midfield, when Gary was pushed into the heart of the action – and a central role – Newcastle fans saw the real Gary Speed. Powerful in the air and always a threat in the opponent's box, he began his career at Elland Road. Speed helped Leeds to promotion and to the League Championship in 1992 before moving to Everton four years later. At Goodison Park, the Welshman never quite took root on Merseyside and he made a somewhat controversial move to Tyneside for a £5.5m fee during February 1998. Appearing in two FA Cup finals for the Black'n'Whites, Speed became an important cog in Sir Bobby Robson's Magpie eleven, giving the side balance in midfield with his all-action, combative style. After seven seasons of worthy service, Gary joined Bolton Wanderers in July 2004 when 34-years-old, later becoming player-coach briefly. Speed moved to Sheffield United where he also resurrected his career on the sidelines as well as playing on until 2010 when he was over 40. He became the Blades' manager as the 2010-11 season got underway then took charge of Wales. Captain of his country with 85 caps, only a handful of players have appeared more for the Welsh, while Speed clocked up over 800 senior appearances and also held for a period the record for most games played in the Premiership (535). Gary was awarded the MBE in 2010.

SEASON REVIEW

Premier League: P38 W21 D8 L9 F74 A52 Pts 71.
Position: 4th (Champions; Arsenal).
FA Cup: QF (Winners; Arsenal).
FL Worthington Cup: QF (Winners; Blackburn Rovers).
Intertoto Cup: Finalist (Winners; Troyes-Aube Champagne).

Appearances (53m): Solano NAT 52, Given SJJ 50, Hughes AW 48, Shearer A 45 (1), Dabizas N 44 (2), Robert L 40 (2), Speed GA 39 (1), O'Brien AJ 38 (6) Bellamy CD 37 (2), Elliott RJ 37 (3), Distin S 27 (8), Lee RM 21 (1), Dyer KC 17 (4), Acuna CWD 14 (10), Ameobi F 12 (13), Barton WD 11 (1), Bernard OJW 8 (15), Cort CER 8 (2), Quinn WR 7 (1), Jenas JA 6 (6), McClen JD 6 (2), Bassedas CG 5 (2), Griffin A 4 (1), LuaLua LT 4 (28), Harper SA 3, Caldwell S 0 (3), Kerr B 0 (2).

Goals (106g): Shearer A 27, Bellamy CD 14, Solano NAT 12, Robert L 10, Speed GA 7, Ameobi F 5, LuaLua LT 5, Acuna CWD 4, Bernard OJW 3, Dabizas N 3, Dyer KC 3, O'Brien AJ 3, Elliott RJ 2, Hughes AW 2, Cort CER 1, Lee RM 1, McClen JD 1, Quinn WR 1, own goals 2.

Dismissals: 2 players; Shearer, Bellamy (both red cards later withdrawn).

MAJOR SIGNINGS

Craig Bellamy (Coventry City) £6.5m
Laurent Robert (PSG) £9.2m
Jermaine Jenas (Nottingham Forest) £5m
Sylvain Distin (PSG) loan

FROM THE RANKS

Olivier Bernard (Olympique Lyonnais)

TEAM COLOURS Black & white striped shirts, black shorts (Change; all blue shirts & shorts with white-grey trim)

SEASON 2001-02

Match	Date		Premiership (Barclaycard)	Result	Att	Posn	Scorers	Given	Barton	Elliott	Acuna	Dabizas	Hughes	Lee	Bassedas	Ameobi	Bellamy	Robert	O'Brien	Griffin	LuaLua	Harper	Quinn	Solano	Speed	Shearer	Distin	Bernard	Dyer	McClen	Kerr	Jenas	Caldwell S	Cort	Gavilan	Green	Match
							Squad numbers	1	2	3	6	34	18	7	10	23	17	32	5	12	20	13	14	4	11	9	24	35	8	22	25	7	30	16	21	31	
1	19 Aug	A	Chelsea	D 1 1 (0 1)	40,124	10	Acuna	1	2	3	4	5	6	7	8	9	10	11	s4	s8	s9	u	u														1
2	26 Aug	H	**Sunderland**	D 1 1 (1 1)	52,021	14	Bellamy	1	2	3	s10	5	6	4		9	8	11	s3		u	u		7	10	s9											2
3	08 Sep	A	Middlesbrough	W 4 1 (1 1)	30,004	7	Shearer 2 (1 pen), Dabizas, Robert	1	2	3	4	5	6	8	u	s9	10	11	s2		s10	u		7		9											3
4	15 Sep	H	**Manchester United**	W 4 3 (2 1)	52,056	3	Robert, Lee, Dabizas, og (Brown)	1	s8	3	4	5		8		u	10	11	6	2	u	u		7		9	s10										4
5	23 Sep	A	West Ham United	L 0 3 (0 1)	24,840	9		1	2	3	4	5		8	u	s7	10	11	6		u	u		7		9	s2										5
6	26 Sep	H	**Leicester City**	W 1 0 (1 0)	49,185	5	Solano	1		3	4	5		8	u	s9	10	11	6	2	u	u		7		9	u										6
7	30 Sep	H	**Liverpool**	L 0 2 (0 1)	52,095	8		1		3	4	5		8		s7	10	11	6	2	u	u		7	s4	9	u										7
8	13 Oct	A	Bolton Wanderers	W 4 0 (1 0)	25,631	4	Solano, Robert, Shearer, Bellamy	1		3	s10	5	2	4		s8	8	11	6			u		7	10	9	s5	u									8
9	21 Oct	H	**Tottenham Hotspur**	L 0 2 (0 2)	50,593	10		1		u	4	5	2		s4	s2	8	11	6		s7	u		7	10	9	3										9
10	27 Oct	A	Everton	W 3 1 (1 0)	37,524	6	Bellamy, Solano, Acuna	1		3	4	5	2		u	u	8	11	6		s7	u		7	10	9	u										10
11	03 Nov	H	**Aston Villa**	W 3 0 (1 0)	51,057	3	Bellamy 2, Shearer	1		3	u	5	2	4			8	11	6		u	u		7	10	9	u	s11									11
12	17 Nov	A	Fulham	L 1 3 (0 2)	21,159	6	Speed	1		3	u	5	2	4		s4	8	11	6		s7	u		7	10	9	s5										12
13	24 Nov	H	**Derby County**	W 1 0 (1 0)	50,070	3	Shearer (pen)	1		3	u	5	2	4		u	8	11	6		s11	u		7	10	9	u										13
14	01 Dec	A	Charlton Athletic	D 1 1 (0 0)	24,151	4	Speed	1		3	u	5	2	4		s8	8	11	6		s11	u		7	10	9d	u										14
15	09 Dec	A	Ipswich Town	W 1 0 (1 0)	24,749	4	Solano	1		3		5	2	4		u	8	11	6			u		7	10	9	u	s11	s7								15
16	15 Dec	H	**Blackburn Rovers**	W 2 1 (0 1)	50,064	3	Bernard, Speed	1		3		u	2	4		8			6	u	s8	u		7	10	9	5	11	s4								16
17	18 Dec	A	Arsenal	W 3 1 (0 1)	38,012	1	O'Brien, Shearer (pen), Robert	1		3		5	2				8d	s3	6		s7	u		7	10	9	s4	11	4	u							17
18	22 Dec	A	Leeds United	W 4 3 (1 1)	40,287	1	Bellamy, Elliott, Shearer (pen), Solano	1		3	u	5	2				8	11	6		s8	u		7	10	9	s5	s11	4								18
19	26 Dec	H	**Middlesbrough**	W 3 0 (1 0)	52,127	1	Shearer, Speed, Bernard	1	u	3			2	s7			8	11	6		s4	u		7	10	9	5	s11	4								19
20	29 Dec	H	**Chelsea**	L 1 2 (1 2)	52,123	2	Shearer	1		3		u	2	u			8	11	6		s7	u		7	10	9	5	s3	4								20
21	02 Jan	A	Manchester United	L 1 3 (0 1)	67,646	4	Shearer	1		3		5	2	4		s8	8		u		u	u		7	10	9	6	s7	11								21
22	12 Jan	H	**Leeds United**	W 3 1 (1 1)	52,130	1	og (Duberry), Dyer, Bellamy	1		3	u	5	2				8	11	6		u	u		7	10	9	s6	u	4								22
23	19 Jan	A	Leicester City	D 0 0 (0 0)	21,354	2		1		3	u	5	2			u	8	11	u			u		7	10	9	6	u	4								23
24	30 Jan	A	Tottenham Hotspur	W 3 1 (0 1)	35,798	3	Acuna, Shearer, Bellamy	1	u	3	10	5	4			u	8	s3	2			u		7		9	6			11	u						24
25	02 Feb	H	**Bolton Wanderers**	W 3 2 (2 2)	52,094	2	Shearer 2, Bellamy	1		u	s4	5	2			u	8	11	6			u		7	10	9	3	u		4							25
26	09 Feb	H	**Southampton**	W 3 1 (3 1)	51,857	2	Robert, Shearer 2 (1 pen)	1		s3	u	5	2			u	8	11	6			u		7	10	9	3			4		s4					26
27	24 Feb	A	Sunderland	W 1 0 (0 0)	48,290	2	Dabizas	1		u	u	5	2			s11	8	11	6		u	u		7	10	9	3					4					27
28	02 Mar	H	**Arsenal**	L 0 2 (0 2)	52,067	4		1		u	u	5	2			8		11	6		s8	u		7	10	9	3					4		s2			28
29	06 Mar	A	Liverpool	L 0 3 (0 1)	44,204	4		1		u	s10	5	2			u		11	6			u		7	10	9	3	s8				4		8			29
30	16 Mar	H	**Ipswich Town**	D 2 2 (0 0)	51,115	4	Robert, Shearer	1		u	4	5	2			s10		11	6		s7	u		7		9	3		s8			8		10			30
31	29 Mar	H	**Everton**	W 6 2 (2 2)	51,921	4	Shearer, Cort, O'Brien, Solano 2, Bernard	1		u	s8	5	2					11	6		s10	u		7		9	3	s11	8			4		10			31
32	02 Apr	A	Aston Villa	D 1 1 (1 1)	36,597	4	Shearer	1		u	s10	5	2					11	6		u	u		7		9	3	s11	8			4		10			32
33	08 Apr	H	**Fulham**	D 1 1 (1 0)	50,017	4	Dyer	1		3		s5	2					11	5		u	u		7	10	9	6	u	4			s8		8			33
34	13 Apr	A	Derby County	W 3 2 (0 0)	31,031	4	Robert, Dyer, LuaLua	1		u		5	2					11	6		s8	u		7	10	9	3	s6	4			s9		8			34
35	20 Apr	H	**Charlton Athletic**	W 3 0 (1 0)	51,360	4	Speed, LuaLua, Shearer	1		3		s5	2				u	11	5		8	u		7	10	9	6	s11	4			s7					35
36	23 Apr	A	Blackburn Rovers	D 2 2 (0 1)	26,712	4	Shearer 2	1		3		5	2				s8	11	u		8	u		7	10	9	6	s3	4			u					36
37	27 Apr	H	**West Ham United**	W 3 1 (1 1)	52,127	4	Shearer, LuaLua, Robert	1				5	2					11	6		8	u		7	10	9	s6	3	4		u	s4		s8			37
38	11 May	A	Southampton	L 1 3 (0 2)	31,973	4	Shearer	1				5	2					11	u		8	u		7	10	9	6	3	4		u	s4		u			38
Round			FA Cup (AXA)																																		Round
3	05 Jan	H	**Crystal Palace**	W 2 0 (1 0)	38,089		Shearer, Acuna	1		3	s10	5	2			u	8		s4		s7	u		7	10	9	6	11	4								3
4	27 Jan	A	Peterborough United	W 4 2 (2 0)	13,841		O'Brien, McClen, Shearer (pen), Hughes	1		3	4		2			u	8		5	u		u	s11	7		9	6	11		10	s10						4
5	17 Feb	H	**Manchester City**	W 1 0 (0 0)	51,020		Solano	1		3	s4	u	2			u	8	11	6		s11	u		7	10	9	5			4							5
6	09 Mar	H	**Arsenal**	D 1 1 (0 1)	51,027		Robert	1		u	4	5	2			s8		11	6		u	u		7		9	3	u		10				8			6
6	23 Mar	A	Arsenal	L 0 3 (0 2)	38,073			1		s3	4	5	2					11	6		s10	u		7		9	3	u	8		s4			10			6
Round			FL Cup (Worthington Cup)																																		Round
2	12 Sep	H	**Brentford**	We 4 1 (0 1)	25,633		Ameobi, Bellamy 3	u		s6	4		6		8	10	s3	11	5	2	s5	1	3	7		9				u							2
3	09 Oct	A	Barnsley	W 1 0 (0 0)	14,493		Bellamy	u	2		u		u	4		u	8	11	6		u	1		7	10	9	5	3									3
4	27 Nov	H	**Ipswich Town**	W 4 1 (4 0)	32,576		Robert, Ameobi, Shearer 2	u		3	s4	5	2	4	u	8		11	s2		s11	1		7	10	9	6										4
5	12 Dec	A	Chelsea	L 0 1 (0 0)	27,613			1		3		5	2	4		s4	8		6		s7	u		7	10	9	u	11	s11								5
Round			Intertoto Cup																																		Round
3(1)	14 Jul	A	Sporting Lokeren SNW (Bel)	W 4 0 (3 0)	2,425		Quinn, Ameobi 2, LuaLua	1	2	3		5	4		8	9	10				s9	u	6	7	11			u		s8			s4		u	u	3(1)
3(2)	21 Jul	H	**Sporting Lokeren SNW (Bel)**	W 1 0 (0 0)	29,021		Bellamy	1	2	3		5	4		8	9	10			u	s10	u	6	7	11			s6		s8			u		u		3(2)
SF(1)	25 Jul	A	TSV 1860 Munich (G)	W 3 2 (1 0)	15,000		Solano 2 (1 pen), Hughes	1	2	3		5	4		8	9	10			u	s9	u	6	7	11			s6		u			s8		u		SF(1)
SF(2)	01 Aug	H	**TSV 1860 Munich (G)**	W 3 1 (1 1)	36,635		Speed, LuaLua, Solano (pen)	1	2	3	s11	5	4	8	u	9	10			u	s10	u	6	7	11			u					s8				SF(2)
F(1)	07 Aug	A	Troyes-Aube Champagne (F)	D 0 0 (0 0)	10,414			1	2	3	u	5	4	8	s9	9	10			u	s10	u	6	7	11			u					u				F(1)
F(2)	21 Aug	H	**Troyes-Aube Champagne (F)**	Da 4 4 (1 2)	36,577		Solano, Ameobi, Speed (pen), Elliott	1	2	3	u	5	6	4	u	9	8		s2		s7	u	11	7	10			s11							u		F(2)

We — Won after extra time
Da — Tie lost on away goals

Match 14 — Shearer's red card later revoked
Match 17 — Bellamy's red card rescinded on appeal

DateLine ... 5 Sept: United's Gallowgate arena hosts the World Cup qualifier between England and Albania. **21 Aug:** United fail to qualify for the UEFA Cup after an Intertoto Cup final with Troyes. **12 Sept:** Craig Bellamy scores an extra-time League Cup hat-trick from the bench against Brentford. **15 Sept:** A classic encounter with Manchester United ends in a 4-3 Magpie win.

SEASON 2002-03

PREMER LEAGUE

Champions League drama

Following a comfortable qualifying stage, Newcastle's second taste of the Champions League was a dramatic affair. Being almost down and out early on, the Magpies remarkably recovered and edged into the second stage of the glittering competition. Losing their first three matches, United then defeated Juventus and Dynamo Kyiv in return meetings, and had to get something against Feyenoord in the final group match at the De Kuip arena in Rotterdam. Newcastle were brilliant from the off and raced to a 2-0 lead, only to allow the Dutch to level the contest at 2-2 with time running out. United were out, or so it seemed. Then dramatically Craig Bellamy rifled the ball home in the dying seconds of injury time to earn a 3-2 victory and a place in the next stage.

United again started badly, but recovered once more to show they could match the very best in Europe, deserving a victory instead of a 2-2 draw in the San Siro when Alan Shearer led the charge against Internazionale. This time there was to be no late rally; defeat by Barcelona on Tyneside ended the Magpie's European dream.

While Continental action took the spotlight, Newcastle also did well on the League front. They challenged again for the top places in the Premier League, at one point having an outside chance of lifting silverware. Now rated again as one of the best sides in the country alongside Manchester United and Arsenal, by the start of December they won eight games out of 11 played – starting with three points in a clash with Sunderland – and climbed the table after a slow start. By January they were in contention at the top, reaching second spot and being unbeaten in nine Premier League fixtures. As April began though Robson's men lost three in a row, to Everton, crucially to Manchester United – 6-2 at Gallowgate – and then Fulham, defeats which meant Newcastle's title bid was over.

Pictured above: Aaron Hughes developed into an honest defender at the highest level, for both club and country.

Memorabilia CORNER

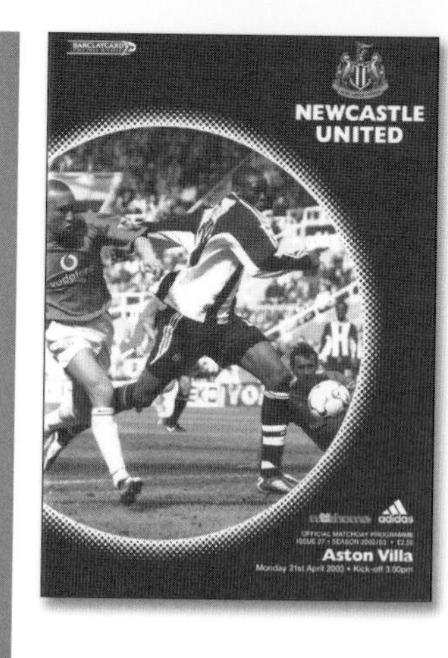

One of the club's finest programmes, with a striking cover featuring Shola Ameobi.

IN CHARGE

Chairman: Freddy Shepherd
Manager: Sir Bobby Robson
Captain: Alan Shearer
Trainer/Coach: John Carver
Club Sponsor: NTL
Kit Supplier: Adidas

ST JAMES' PARK

Average Attendance
Lg 51,920 Lg & Cup 49,138

With kit manufacturers part of the club's sponsor team, Newcastle's shirts changed usually every two years. Adidas produced a range of inventive black-and-white designs during their lengthy period associated with the Magpies.

PLAYER FOCUS Nobby Solano

Born Callao. Midfield, 5'9"
1998 to 2007: 315 app 48 goals.

The first player from Peru to make a big impact in England, Nolberto Solano was an experienced player in South America by the time he found his way to Gallowgate. Having won Championship titles in his native Peru, he joined Newcastle as a 23-year-old in August 1998 from Argentinean giants Boca Juniors where he played alongside Diego Maradona. Known as Nobby and costing £2.76m, the talented midfielder took a year to settle then quickly developed as one of the best creative players in the Premier League. Although he often played at right-back for Peru, with an exquisite right-boot, Nobby could place the ball in the danger area with precision and was always on hand to grab goals himself, notably from free-kicks or fierce drives. Skipper of his country, he appeared in the 1999 FA Cup final for United but the immensely popular Solano was controversially sold to Aston Villa in January 2004 only to return less than two years later during August 2005 in a £1.5m deal for a second spell on Tyneside. Aged 32, he moved to London during August 2007 and ran down his long career with West Ham United, then in Greece with Larissa, as well as back in Chile with Universitario before settling again in England with Leicester City, Hull City and Hartlepool. Winning several titles in South America, he is one of the most celebrated Peruvian sportsmen. Nobby won almost a century of caps for his country.

SEASON REVIEW

Premier League: P38 W21 D6 L11 F63 A48 Pts 69.
Position: 3rd (Champions; Manchester United).
FA Cup: R3 (Winners; Arsenal).
FL Worthington Cup: R3 (Winners; Liverpool).
UEFA Champions League: Group, Phase 2 (Winners; AC Milan).

Appearances (54m): Given SJJ 51, Shearer A 48, Hughes AW 47 (1), Dyer KC 45 (3), Solano NAT 40 (5), O'Brien AJ 38 (1), Griffin A 35 (5), Robert L 35 (5), Speed GA 35 (1), Bellamy CD 34 (2), Bernard OJW 34 (8), Jenas JA 32 (9), Bramble TM 21 (3), Dabizas N 21 (5), Viana HMF 17 (17), Caldwell S 14 (3), Ameobi F 12 (27), LuaLua LT 11 (11), Woodgate JS 10, Kerr B 5 (5), Acuna CWD 4 (2), Harper SA 3, Cort CER 1 (2), Elliott RJ 1 (3), Ambrose DPF 0 (1), Chopra MR 0 (4), McClen JD 0 (1), Quinn WR 0 (1).

Goals (89g): Shearer A 25, Bellamy CD 9, Ameobi F 8, Solano NAT 8, Jenas JA 7, Dyer KC 6, Robert L 5, LuaLua LT 4, Viana HMF 4, Speed GA 3, Bernard OJW 2, Griffin A 2, Caldwell S 1, Hughes AW 1, own goals 4.

Dismissals: 5 players; Dabizas, Caldwell, Bellamy, Robert, Griffin.

MAJOR SIGNINGS

Hugo Viana (Sporting Clube de Portugal) £8.2m
Titus Bramble (Ipswich Town) £5m
Jonathan Woodgate (Leeds Utd) £8m
Darren Ambrose (Ipswich Town) £2m

FROM THE RANKS

Michael Chopra
(Montague BC, Es/Ey)

TEAM COLOURS Black & white striped shirts, black shorts
(Change; marine & opal shirts, dark marine shorts/all silver-grey/navy-blue & grey shirts, navy-blue shorts)

SEASON 2002–03

Match	Date	Venue	Opponent	Res	F	A	HT	Att	Posn	Scorers	Given	Hughes	Bernard	Jenas	Bramble	Dabizas	Solano	Dyer	Shearer	LuaLua	Viana	McClen	Ameobi	Elliott	Griffin	Harper	Speed	O'Brien	Bellamy	Robert	Chopra	Caldwell S	Acuna	Kerr	Cort	Caig	Woodgate	Ambrose	Quinn	Bassedas	Match
Match			**Premiership (Barclaycard)**						Posn	Squad numbers	1	18	35	7	19	34	4	8	9	20	45	22	23	3	12	13	11	5	10	32	28	30	6	25	16	24	27	17	14	17	Match
1	19 Aug	H	**West Ham United**	W	4	0	(0 0)	51,072	1	LuaLua 2, Shearer, Solano	1	2	3	4	5	6	7	8	9	10	11	s7	s10	s11	u	u															1
2	24 Aug	A	Manchester City	L	0	1	(0 1)	34,776	10		1	2	3	4	5	6	7	8	9	10	s11		s10		s3	u	11	u													2
3	02 Sep	A	Liverpool	D	2	2	(0 0)	43,241	13	Speed, Shearer	1	2	3	s7	5	6	7	4	9	8	11					u	10	u	s8	s11											3
4	11 Sep	H	**Leeds United**	L	0	2	(0 1)	51,730	19		1	2	3	u	5		7	4	9		s10		8		s6	u	10	6	s8	11											4
5	14 Sep	A	Chelsea	L	0	3	(0 2)	39,746	19		1	2	3	s7	u	5	7	4	9		s11		s8			u	10	6	8	11											5
6	21 Sep	H	**Sunderland**	W	2	0	(2 0)	52,181	13	Bellamy, Shearer	1	3		s7	u	5	7	4	9		s11		s8		2	u	10	6	8	11											6
7	28 Sep	A	Birmingham City	W	2	0	(1 0)	29,072	10	Solano, Ameobi	1	3		s7	u	5	7	4	9	8	s11		s8		2	u	10	6		11											7
8	05 Oct	H	**West Bromwich Albion**	W	2	1	(1 1)	52,142	6	Shearer 2	1	3	s11	s7		5	7	4	9	s8			u		2	u	10	6	8	11											8
9	19 Oct	A	Blackburn Rovers	L	2	5	(1 2)	27,307	11	Shearer 2 (1 pen)	1	3	s3	4	s2	5d	7		9		s11		u		2	u	10	6	8	11											9
10	26 Oct	H	**Charlton Athletic**	W	2	1	(1 1)	51,607	8	Griffin, Robert	1	3	s11	4	5	u	7		9		s7		8		2	u	10	6		11	u										10
11	04 Nov	H	**Middlesbrough**	W	2	0	(1 0)	51,558	8	Ameobi, Caldwell S	1	6	3	4			7	s7	9	u	s11		8	u	2	u	10			11		5									11
12	09 Nov	A	Arsenal	L	0	1	(0 1)	38,121	9		1	3	s11	4		6	7	8	9	u	11		s7		2	u	10	5				u									12
13	16 Nov	H	**Southampton**	W	2	1	(1 1)	51,812	6	Ameobi, Hughes	1	3	s11	4		s5	u	7	9	u	11		8		2	u	10	5				6									13
14	23 Nov	A	Manchester United	L	3	5	(1 3)	67,619	7	Bernard, Shearer, Bellamy	1	3	11	4		6	s11	7	9				u	u	2	u	10	5	8				u								14
15	01 Dec	H	**Everton**	W	2	1	(0 1)	51,607	6	Shearer, og (Li Tie)	1		3	u		u	7	4	9		s10		s5		2	u	10	6	8	11		5									15
16	07 Dec	A	Aston Villa	W	1	0	(0 0)	33,446	6	Shearer	1	6	3	4			7	8	9	u			u		2	u		5	10	11		u	u								16
17	14 Dec	A	Southampton	D	1	1	(0 0)	32,061	6	Bellamy	1	3		4		u		7	9	u			u		2	u	10	6	8	11		5	u								17
18	21 Dec	H	**Fulham**	W	2	0	(1 0)	51,576	4	Solano, Bellamy	1	3		s4		u	7	4	9				s7		2	u	10	6	8	11		5	s10								18
19	26 Dec	A	Bolton Wanderers	L	3	4	(1 3)	27,314	6	Shearer 2, Ameobi	1	3		s7		u	7	4	9	s8			8		2	u	10	6	u	11		5									19
20	29 Dec	H	**Tottenham Hotspur**	W	2	1	(1 0)	52,145	4	Speed, Shearer	1	2	3	s10		s7	7	4	9	s4			u			u	10	6	8	11		5									20
21	01 Jan	H	**Liverpool**	W	1	0	(1 0)	52,147	4	Robert	1	5	3	10		u			9	u			s7	s4	2	u		6	8	11			4	7							21
22	11 Jan	A	West Ham United	D	2	2	(1 2)	35,048	4	Bellamy, Jenas	1	6	3	10		u	u	7		s4			9		2	u			8	11		5	4		s9						22
23	18 Jan	H	**Manchester City**	W	2	0	(1 0)	52,152	3	Shearer, Bellamy	1	2	3	4		6	7	8	9	u			u	u		u			10	11		5		s7							23
24	22 Jan	H	**Bolton Wanderers**	W	1	0	(1 0)	52,005	3	Jenas	1	2	3	4		6	7	8	9	u			u	u		u			10	11		5		s7							24
25	29 Jan	A	Tottenham Hotspur	W	1	0	(0 0)	36,084	2	Jenas	1		3	4	5	6	s7	8	9	u			u	u		u		2	10	11				7							25
26	09 Feb	H	**Arsenal**	D	1	1	(0 1)	52,157	3	Robert	1	2	3	4	5	u	7	8	9	u			s9				s7	6	10	11d						u					26
27	22 Feb	A	Leeds United	W	3	0	(1 0)	40,025	3	Dyer 2, Shearer	1	3			5	s2		7	9				s4		2		10	6	8	11	u		s7	4		u					27
28	01 Mar	H	**Chelsea**	W	2	1	(1 1)	52,157	3	og (Hasselbaink), Bernard	1	2	3		s11		7	4	9	u	11		s4		s7		10	6	8							u	5				28
29	05 Mar	A	Middlesbrough	L	0	1	(0 0)	34,814	3		1	2	3	4	6		u	7	9		s10		s11			u	10	u	8	11							5				29
30	15 Mar	A	Charlton Athletic	W	2	0	(1 0)	26,728	3	Shearer (pen), Solano	1	2	3	4	6		7	s10	9	u	11		s7		s11	u	10		8								5				30
31	22 Mar	H	**Blackburn Rovers**	W	5	1	(1 0)	52,106	3	Solano, Robert, Jenas, og (Gresko), Bellamy	1	3		s7	6		7	4	9		s11		s9		2	u	10	u	8	11							5				31
32	06 Apr	A	Everton	L	1	2	(1 1)	40,031	3	Robert	1	u	3	4	6			8	9	u			s7		s2	u		2	10	11				7			5				32
33	12 Apr	H	**Manchester United**	L	2	6	(1 4)	52,164	3	Jenas, Ameobi	1	2	3	4	6		7	8	9	ss11	s11		s7		u	u			10	11							5				33
34	19 Apr	A	Fulham	L	1	2	(1 0)	17,900	3	Shearer	1	4	3				7	8	9	u	11		s11		2d	u		6	10			s7	u				5				34
35	21 Apr	H	**Aston Villa**	D	1	1	(1 0)	52,015	4	Solano	1	3	11		s5		7	8	9	s11	4		s9		2	u		6	10				u				5				35
36	26 Apr	A	Sunderland	W	1	0	(1 0)	45,067	3	Solano (pen)	1	3	s11	4			7	8	9	u	11		s9		2	u		6	10			s6					5				36
37	03 May	H	**Birmingham City**	W	1	0	(1 0)	52,146	3	Viana	1	2	3	4	u		7	8		u	11		9			u			10	s11		6		s7			5				37
38	11 May	A	West Bromwich Albion	D	2	2	(1 0)	27,036	3	Jenas, Viana	1	3		4	u		7	8		10	11		9		2	u		5			s10	6		s8				s7			38
Round			**FA Cup**																																						Round
3	05 Jan	A	Wolverhampton Wanderers	L	2	3	(2 2)	27,316		Jenas, Shearer (pen)	1	5	3	10		s6	7		9	s7			s4		2	u		6	8	11			4	u							3
Round			**FL Cup (Worthington Cup)**																																						Round
3	06 Nov	H	**Everton**	Dep	3	3	(0 1)	34,584		Dyer 2, og (Pistone)	u	u	11			6	s4	7		8	10			3	2	1				s11	s8	5d	4		9						3
Round			**UEFA Champions League**																																						Round
3Q(1)	14 Aug	A*	NK Zeljeznicar (BH)	W	1	0	(0 0)	36,000		Dyer	1	2	3	4	5	6	7	8	9	10	11		s10	s11	u	u		u											s3	u	3Q(1)
3Q(2)	28 Aug	H	**NK Zeljeznicar (BH)**	W	4	0	(2 0)	34,067		Dyer, LuaLua, Viana, Shearer	1	2	3	u	5	6	7	4	9	8	11		s8	u	u	u	10	s6						s7							3Q(2)
1GpE	18 Sep	A**	Dynamo Kyiv (U)	L	0	2	(0 1)	42,500			1	4	3	u	u	5	s4	7	9	u	11		s9		2	u	10	6	8	s3											1GpE
1GpE	24 Sep	H	**Feyenoord (N)**	L	0	1	(0 1)	40,540			1	3	u	u	u	5	7	4	9	s8	u		u		2	u	10	6	8	11											1GpE
1GpE	01 Oct	A	Juventus (I)	L	0	2	(0 0)	41,424			1	3	u	4	u	5	7	8	9	s4	s7		s2	u	2	u	10	6		11											1GpE
1GpE	23 Oct	H	**Juventus (I)**	W	1	0	(0 0)	48,370		Griffin	u	3	u	4	5		7		9	8	s11		s8	u	2	1	10	6		11			u	u							1GpE
1GpE	29 Oct	H	**Dynamo Kyiv (U)**	W	2	1	(0 0)	40,185		Speed, Shearer (pen)	u	3	s6	4	5	s5	7	s7	9	u	u		8		2	1	10	6		11			u								1GpE
1GpE	13 Nov	A	Feyenoord (N)	W	3	2	(1 0)	44,500		Bellamy 2, Viana	1	3	s11	4		6	u	7	9	u	11		u		2	u	10	5	8			u	u								1GpE
2GpA	27 Nov	H	**Internazionale Milano (I)**	L	1	4	(0 3)	50,108		Solano	1	3		u		6	7	4	9	u	11		u		2	u	10	5	8d	s11		s3	u								2GpA
2GpA	11 Dec	A	FC Barcelona (Sp)	L	1	3	(1 2)	45,100		Ameobi	1	6	3	u		u	7	4		8			9		2	u	10	5		11	s8	u	u		u						2GpA
2GpA	18 Feb	A	Bayer 04 Leverkusen (G)	W	3	1	(3 1)	22,500		Ameobi 2, LuaLua	1	2	3	4	5			8		7			9		u	u	10	6		11	s7	u	u	u	s9						2GpA
2GpA	26 Feb	H	**Bayer 04 Leverkusen (G)**	W	3	1	(3 0)	40,508		Shearer 3 (1 pen)	1	u	3		5		s7	7	9	s9	s4		8		2	u	10	u		11		6		4	u						2GpA
2GpA	11 Mar	A	Internazionale Milano (I)	D	2	2	(1 0)	53,459		Shearer 2	1	s5	3	4	6		7		9	s7	s11		u		2	u	10	5	8	11		u		u							2GpA
2GpA	19 Mar	H	**FC Barcelona (Sp)**	L	0	2	(0 0)	51,883			1	u	3	4	6		7	10	9	u	s11		s7		2	u		5	8	11		u		u							2GpA

A* Played at Kosevo Olimpijski Stadion, Sarajevo
A** Played at Olympiyski Stadium, Kyiv

Dep Drawn after extra time, tie lost on penalties (2-3)

23 Oct Griffin's goal recorded by some sources as a Buffon og

DateLine ... 7 Aug: A pre-season friendly with Barcelona attracts 51,257 to Gallowgate, a record home friendly crowd. **19 Oct:** Nicos Dabizas sent-off for handball after only four minutes of the game with Blackburn. **13 Nov:** United qualify for the second stage of the Champions League with a dramatic 3-2 victory over Feyenoord. **18 Jan:** Alan Shearer scores after only 10 seconds against Manchester City at St James' Park.

Trophy bid ends in Provence

More European deeds were in store for United's rapidly cosmopolitan Geordie following. But there was to be no Champions League, Newcastle failing in the qualifying stage after doing all the hard work against Partizan in Belgrade, with a 1-0 victory. In the return leg, United never got going, conceded a goal and went into extra-time then a penalty shoot-out. The stakes were high. With a price tag of around £15m, United's spot-kicks were appalling, Partizan's good. That miserable evening took several weeks to recover from – in Premier League action the Magpies didn't win until their seventh game – but once the disappointment had been buried, the UEFA Cup became the focus as the Black'n'Whites almost went all the way to the final in Gothenburg.

Newcastle were one of the favourites on what was to be a long road. But for injury at the vital stage – in the semi-final – United could well have reached a European final for the first time in 35 years.

After 10 games in European action since the Champions League qualifier, French club Marseille arrived on Tyneside in the first leg of the semi-final. With Didier Drogba leading the visitor's attack, fast becoming hot property, they held United to a 0-0 draw. Going well in the Premier League too, in fourth place by April, injury wrecked United's hopes. For the crucial return leg in Marseille, United missed several regulars. And Drogba was the difference. He netted twice to secure a 2-0 victory in front of over 57,000 in the Stade Velodrome.

Those injuries also stopped United climbing any higher in the table, the Magpies finished in fifth place in the Premier League, just missing out on another chance at the Champions League. But Robson's second stage recovery had been achieved. Now he needed to lead United to a trophy.

Pictured above: Jonathan Woodgate was Newcastle's answer to a leaky defence, when fit he looked the part.

Memorabilia CORNER

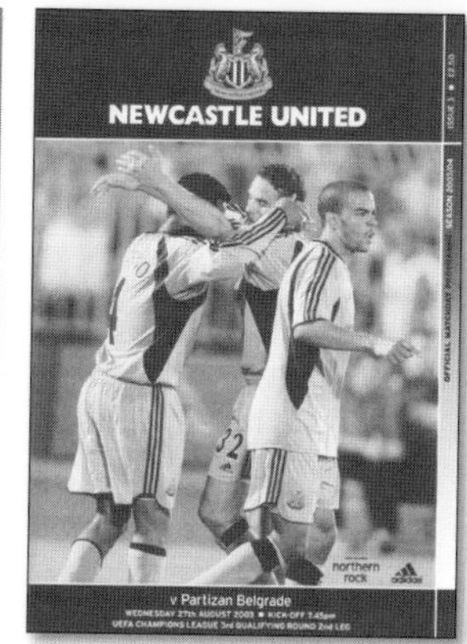

In the new Millennium the programme was a first-class publication, this issue a Champions League edition.

IN CHARGE

Chairman: Freddy Shepherd
Manager: Sir Bobby Robson
Captain: Alan Shearer
Trainer/Coach: John Carver
Club Sponsor: Northern Rock
Kit Supplier: Adidas

ST JAMES' PARK

Average Attendance
Lg 51,966 Lg & Cup 49,134

United line-up before a European fixture. Back row, left to right: Solano, Dyer, Bernard, Hughes, O'Brien, Woodgate, Ameobi. Front: Shearer, Given, Viana, Speed.

PLAYER FOCUS Laurent Robert

Born Saint-Benoit. Outside-left, 5'8"
2001 to 2005: 181 app 32 goals.

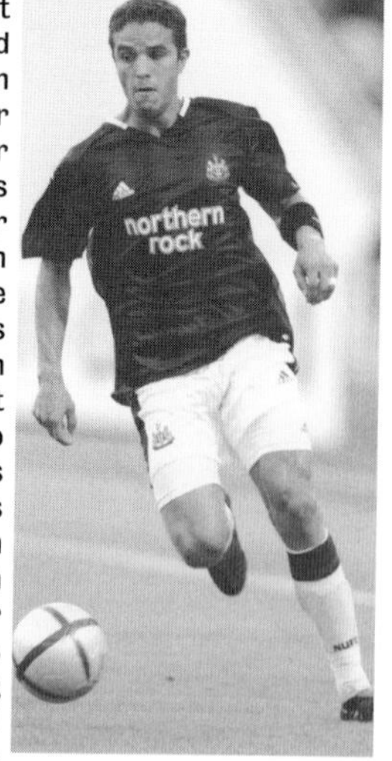

Born on the French Pacific island of La Reunion, Laurent Robert was purchased from Paris St-Germain during August 2001 for a hefty £9.2m transfer fee, one of Newcastle's biggest ever acquisitions. A French international with nine appearances to his name, his play down the left wing was at times a delight, able to skip past defenders and whip in a vicious cross – often capitalised on by Alan Shearer. Part of Sir Bobby Robson's outstanding United side which did well in the Champions League of 2002-03, he struck the ball true and hard, and with swerve. Laurent scored several spectacular goals from outside the box much recalled by Toon supporters and he was always a danger from dead-balls too. Yet Robert in the end enjoyed an enigmatic four-year stay on Tyneside. Often temperamental, he had the talent to have joined the elite, but too often was inconsistent and moody. After a fall-out with new boss Graeme Souness, Laurent moved south during June 2005 to join Portsmouth on a year-long loan deal then permanently with Benfica. Robert had a brief spell back in England with Derby County then he played in Spain, North America and in Greece. His early career saw him appear for Montpellier while he developed through the highly rated French national coaching system, appearing at youth and under-21 level before reaching the B and full sides. The Frenchman appeared in the Champions League for three different clubs; United, PSG and Benfica.

SEASON REVIEW

Premier League: P38 W13 D17 L8 F52 A40 Pts 56.
Position: 5th (Champions; Arsenal).
FA Cup: R4 (Winners; Manchester United).
FL Carling Cup: R3 (Winners; Middlesbrough).
UEFA Cup: SF (Winners; Valencia CF).

Appearances (55m): Given SJJ 53, Speed GA 52 (2), Bernard OJW 51, Shearer A 51 (1), Hughes AW 47, Robert L 46 (6), Bramble TM 40 (2), O'Brien AJ 40 (2), Jenas JA 39 (7), Dyer KC 33 (1), Ameobi F 27 (14), Woodgate JS 27, Bellamy CD 20 (4), Bowyer LD 17 (8), Ambrose DPF 16 (21), Solano NAT 15 (5), Viana HMF 11 (16), Griffin A 8, Caldwell S 4 (3), LuaLua LT 3 (8), Harper SA 2, Bridges M 1 (8), Chopra MR 1 (5), Taylor SV 1 (1), Brittain M 0 (2).

Goals (82g): Shearer A 28, Robert L 12, Ameobi F 10, Bellamy CD 9, Speed GA 4, Ambrose DP 3, Bramble TM 3, Dyer KC 3, Jenas JA 3, Bowyer LD 2, Bernard OJW 1, O'Brien AJ 1, Solano NAT 1, own goals 2.

Dismissals: 3 players; Robert, O'Brien (2).

MAJOR SIGNINGS

Lee Bowyer (West Ham Utd) free
Michael Bridges (Leeds Utd) loan

FROM THE RANKS

Steven Taylor (Wallsend BC, Es/Ey)
Martin Brittain (Cramlington sch)

TEAM COLOURS Black & white striped shirts, black shorts (Change; all black shirts & shorts with white trim/ all silver-grey shirts & shorts with black trim/navy-blue & grey shirts, navy-blue shorts)

SEASON 2003-04

Match	Date		Premiership (Barclaycard)		Score	HT	Att	Posn	Scorers
1	17 Aug	A	Leeds United	D	2 2	(1 1)	36,766	11	Shearer 2 (1 pen)
2	23 Aug	H	**Manchester United**	L	1 2	(1 0)	52,165	15	Shearer
3	30 Aug	H	**Birmingham City**	L	0 1	(0 0)	52,006	18	
4	13 Sep	A	Everton	D	2 2	(0 0)	40,228	17	Shearer 2 (2 pens)
5	20 Sep	H	**Bolton Wanderers**	D	0 0	(0 0)	52,014	18	
6	26 Sep	A	Arsenal	L	2 3	(1 1)	38,112	19	Robert, Bernard
7	04 Oct	H	**Southampton**	W	1 0	(1 0)	52,127	18	Shearer
8	18 Oct	A	Middlesbrough	W	1 0	(1 0)	34,081	11	Ameobi
9	21 Oct	A	Fulham	W	3 2	(1 2)	16,506	10	Robert, Shearer 2 (1 pen)
10	25 Oct	H	**Portsmouth**	W	3 0	(2 0)	52,161	8	Speed, Shearer (pen), Ameobi
11	01 Nov	H	**Aston Villa**	D	1 1	(1 1)	51,975	7	Robert
12	09 Nov	A	Chelsea	L	0 5	(0 3)	41,332	10	
13	22 Nov	H	**Manchester City**	W	3 0	(0 0)	52,159	6	Ameobi, Shearer 2
14	29 Nov	A	Wolverhampton Wanderers	D	1 1	(1 1)	29,344	6	Shearer
15	06 Dec	H	**Liverpool**	D	1 1	(0 1)	52,151	7	Shearer (pen)
16	13 Dec	H	**Tottenham Hotspur**	W	4 0	(1 0)	52,139	5	Robert 2, Shearer 2
17	20 Dec	A	Charlton Athletic	D	0 0	(0 0)	26,508	5	
18	26 Dec	A	Leicester City	D	1 1	(0 0)	32,148	6	Ambrose
19	28 Dec	H	**Blackburn Rovers**	L	0 1	(0 0)	51,648	7	
20	07 Jan	H	**Leeds United**	W	1 0	(1 0)	52,130	6	Shearer
21	11 Jan	A	Manchester United	D	0 0	(0 0)	67,622	7	
22	19 Jan	H	**Fulham**	W	3 1	(2 0)	50,104	5	O'Brien, Speed, Robert
23	31 Jan	A	Birmingham City	D	1 1	(1 0)	29,513	6	Speed
24	07 Feb	H	**Leicester City**	W	3 1	(2 0)	52,125	4	Ameobi, og (Taggart), Jenas
25	11 Feb	A	Blackburn Rovers	D	1 1	(0 0)	23,459	4	Bellamy
26	21 Feb	H	**Middlesbrough**	W	2 1	(0 1)	52,156	4	Bellamy, Shearer (pen)
27	29 Feb	A	Portsmouth	D	1 1	(1 0)	20,140	4	Bellamy
28	14 Mar	A	Tottenham Hotspur	L	0 1	(0 0)	36,083	5	
29	20 Mar	H	**Charlton Athletic**	W	3 1	(2 0)	51,847	5	Shearer 2, Jenas
30	28 Mar	A	Bolton Wanderers	L	0 1	(0 1)	27,360	5	
31	03 Apr	H	**Everton**	W	4 2	(2 1)	52,155	4	Bellamy, Dyer, Shearer 2
32	11 Apr	H	**Arsenal**	D	0 0	(0 0)	52,141	5	
33	18 Apr	A	Aston Villa	D	0 0	(0 0)	40,786	5	
34	25 Apr	H	**Chelsea**	W	2 1	(1 1)	52,016	5	Ameobi, Shearer
35	01 May	A	Manchester City	L	0 1	(0 0)	47,226	5	
36	09 May	H	**Wolverhampton Wanderers**	D	1 1	(1 0)	52,139	6	Bowyer
37	12 May	A	Southampton	D	3 3	(2 2)	31,815	6	Ameobi, Bowyer, Ambrose
38	15 May	A	Liverpool	D	1 1	(1 0)	44,172	5	Ameobi
Round			**FA Cup**						
3	03 Jan	A	Southampton	W	3 0	(2 0)	28,456		Dyer 2, Robert
4	24 Jan	A	Liverpool	L	1 2	(1 1)	41,365		Robert
Round			**FL Cup (Carling Cup)**						
3	29 Oct	H	**West Bromwich Albion**	Le	1 2	(0 1)	46,932		Robert
Round			**UEFA Champions League**						
3Q(1)	13 Aug	A	FK Partizan (Sb)	W	1 0	(1 0)	32,500		Solano
3Q(2)	27 Aug	H	**FK Partizan (Sb)**	Lep	0 1	(0 0)	37,293		
Round			**UEFA Cup**						
1(1)	24 Sep	H	**NAC Breda (N)**	W	5 0	(2 0)	36,007		Bellamy 2, Bramble, Shearer, Ambrose
1(2)	15 Oct	A	NAC Breda (N)	W	1 0	(0 0)	15,564		Robert
2(1)	06 Nov	A	FC Basel (Sw)	W	3 2	(2 2)	30,000		Robert, Bramble, Ameobi
2(2)	27 Nov	H	**FC Basel (Sw)**	W	1 0	(1 0)	40,395		og (Smiljanic)
3(1)	26 Feb	A*	Valerenga IF (Nw)	D	1 1	(1 0)	17,039		Bellamy
3(2)	03 Mar	H	**Valerenga IF (Nw)**	W	3 1	(1 1)	38,531		Shearer, Ameobi 2
4(1)	11 Mar	H	**RCD Mallorca (Sp)**	W	4 1	(0 0)	38,012		Bellamy, Shearer, Robert, Bramble
4(2)	25 Mar	A	RCD Mallorca (Sp)	W	3 0	(0 0)	11,500		Shearer 2, Bellamy
5(1)	08 Apr	A	PSV Eindhoven (N)	D	1 1	(1 1)	32,500		Jenas
5(2)	14 Apr	H	**PSV Eindhoven (N)**	W	2 1	(1 0)	50,083		Shearer, Speed
SF(1)	22 Apr	H	**Olympique de Marseille (F)**	D	0 0	(0 0)	52,004		
SF(2)	06 May	A	Olympique de Marseille (F)	L	0 2	(0 1)	57,500		

Match	Given	Hughes	Bernard	Bowyer	Woodgate	O'Brien	Dyer	Bellamy	Shearer	Speed	Robert	Jenas	Ameobi	Solano	Griffin	Harper	Bramble	Chopra	Viana	Caig	Ambrose	LuaLua	Caldwell S	Dabizas	Bridges	Elliott	Taylor	Brittain	Orr
Squad numbers	1	18	35	29	27	5	8	10	9	11	32	7	23	4	2	12	19	28	45	24	17	20	30	34	14	3	38	39	40
1	1	2	3	4	5	6	7	8	9	10	11	s3	s4	s11	u	u													
2	1	3	u	4		6	7		9	10	11	s4	8		2	u	5	s8	s11										
3	1	u		s7		6	8		9	3	s11	4	10	7	2	u	5	s10	11										
4	1	u	3	4		6	7	8	9	10	11d	s10	u		2		5		u	u									
5	1	u	3	u	5		4	8	9	10	11	s10	s7	7	2		6			u									
6	1	2	3	10		5	7	8	9	s10	11	4	s4		u		6			u	s11								
7	1	2	3	10		5	7	8	9	11		4	u		u	u	6		u		u								
8	1	2	3	4		5	7		9	11	s4	8	10		u	u	6		u			u							
9	1	2	3	4		5			9	10	11	7	8			u	6		u		s11	u	u						
10	1	2	3	7		5			9	10	11	4	8			u	6		s11		s7	s8	u						
11	1	2	3	7					9	10	11	4	8	u		u	6				u	u	5	u					
12	1	2	3	7		5d				10	11	4	9	u		u	6	u	8			s11	s8						
13	1	2	3	s7	5		7		9	10	11	4	8			u	6				s11	s8	u						
14	1	2	3	8	5		7		9	10		4	s11	s8		u	6		u			11	u						
15	1	2	3		5	u	7		9	10	11	4	8	s2		u	6				u	u							
16	1	2	3		5	s5	7		9	10	11	4	8	s10		u	6				s11	u							
17	1	6	3			5	7		9	10	11	4	8	2		u			u		s11	s8	u						
18	1	2	3		u	5			9	10	11	4		7		u	6	s8	u		s2	8							
19	1	2	3		u	5			9	10	11	4		7		u	6	8	s10		s7	s8							
20	1	2	3		5	u	8		9	10	11	4		7		u	6		s11		s7	u							
21	1	2	3		5	6	8		9	10	11	4		7	u	u		u	u		s7								
22	1	2	3		5	6	8		9	10	11	4	s9	7		u	u		s11		s7								
23	1	2	3		5	6	8	s7	9	10	11	4	u		u	u			s11		7								
24	1	2	3		5	6	7	s8	9	10		4	8			u	u		11		s7				s9				
25	1	2	3			6	7	8	9	10	11	4	u			u	5		u		u					u			
26	1	2	3	s4		5	7	8	9	10	11		u			u	6		u		4					u			
27	1	2	3	4	u	5	7	8	9	10	11	s7				u	6		s11						s4				
28	1	2	3	7	5	6		8	9	10	11	4	s2			u			u		s7					u			
29	1	2	3	s7	5	6			9	10	11	4	8			u	s2	u	u		7								
30	1		3	7	5			8	9	10	11	4	s11			u	6		s4		s7					u	2		
31	1	2	3	s4	5		7	8	9	10	11		s11			u	6		u		4						u		
32	1	2	3	s7	5	6		8	9	10	11	4	u			u	u		s11		7								
33	1	2	3	s11	5	6d	7	8	9	10	11	4				u			s4						s8	u			
34	1	2	3		5	6			9	10	11		8			u	s5	u	7		4				s8			u	
35	1	2	3			6			9	10	11		8			u	5	s4	7		4				s8		u	s11	
36	1	2	3	7					9	10	11		8		u	u	5	s4	s11		4		6		u				
37	1	2	3	7			11		9	10	s11		8		u	u	5		u		4		6		s5				
38	1	3		7		6	11	s8	9	10	s4		8		2	u	5		u		4		s2						
Round																													
3	1	2	3		5	u	8		9	10	11	4		7		u	6		s11		s7	s8							
4	1	2	3		5	6	8		9	10	11	4	s7	7		u	u		u		u								
Round																													
3	u	u	3						s11	s10	11	4	9	7	2	1	6		10		s7	8	5						
Round																													
3Q(1)	1	u	3		5	6	4	8	9	10	11	s7	s11	7	2	u	u	u								u			
3Q(2)	1	2	3		5	6	4		9	10	s11	s10	8	7	u	u	u	u	11			s7							
Round																													
1(1)	1	2	3			5	7	8	9	10	11	4	s8		u		6		s3	u	s7	u	u						
1(2)	u	u	3			5	8		u	u	11	4	9	7	2	1	6		10		s7	s8	s6						
2(1)	1	2	3			5			9	10	11	4	8	7		u	6	u	s11		s7	u	u	u					
2(2)	1	2	3		u	5	7		9	10	11	4	8	s7		u	6		u		s11	u	u						
3(1)	1	2	3			5	s7	8	u	10	s11	4	9			u	6		11		7				s9	u	u		
3(2)	1	3			5	2		8	9	10	11	4	s8			u	6		u						7	u	u	s7	u
4(1)	1	2	3		u	5	7	8	9	10	11	4	u				6		u	u	s7				u	u			
4(2)	1		3		5	2		s10	9	10	11	4	8			u	6	u	s11		7					u	s2		u
5(1)	1	2	3		5	u		8	9	10	11	4	s9			u	6		u		7				u	u		u	
5(2)	1	2	3		5	s6	u	8	9	10	11	4	s7			u	6		s11		7				u	u			
SF(1)	1	2	3		5	6			9	10	11		8			u	u	u	7		4				s8	u		u	u
SF(2)	1	2	3	s7		6			9	10	11		8			u	5	u	7		4		u		u	u		u	

A* Played at Ulleval Stadion, Oslo

Le Lost after extra time

Lep Lost after extra time, tie lost on penalties (3-4)

DateLine ... 27 Aug: United lose on penalties in the Champions League qualifier with Partizan on Tyneside. **21 Feb:** A 2-1 defeat of Middlesbrough puts United in fourth spot in the table and challenging for the title. **6 May:** The UEFA Cup semi-final decider goes the way of Marseille after two goals from Didier Drogba.

SEASON 2004-05

PREMIER LEAGUE

St James' Park merry-go-round

United's record under Bobby Robson had been first-class. Finishing fourth, third and fifth in the Premier League in his last three seasons, and reaching the Champions League as well as semi-finals of the FA Cup and UEFA Cup.

It was, apart from winning silverware, as good as it gets. Yet Newcastle's hierarchy wanted that trophy and as United struggled in the opening weeks of the 2004-05 campaign with Robson changing a successful line-up, the manager became increasingly under huge pressure. And he paid the price with his job. Did he deserve the axe as the Magpies started badly? Most reckoned he did not, but football is a strange business. Following a 4-2 defeat at Aston Villa in August, Sir Bobby, the game's doyen was dismissed. He was replaced by Blackburn Rovers' boss Graeme Souness, another odd move. United's decision making led to prolonged instability and ultimate collapse as the decade continued.

With United in mid-table, Souness made sure of safety while the Scot also guided United to a UEFA Cup quarter-final and to the club's 17th FA Cup semi-final. But the Magpies went out in both tournaments in disastrous circumstances; to Sporting Clube de Portugal in Europe, and Manchester United at the Millennium Stadium in the FA Cup. Along the way a tricky David versus Goliath tie with non-leaguers Yeading was overcome before the Magpies proved their worth by disposing of both Tottenham and Chelsea. In Europe the Geordies started in the football outpost of Israel, recorded their century of fixtures in competitive action with a 4-0 win against Olympiacos during March before meeting old foes from 1968, Lisbon's Sporting Clube. United had been cruising to another European semi-final in the newly constructed Estadio Jose Alvalade, 2-0 ahead on aggregate, before they capitulated to a late Portuguese onslaught. Then in Cardiff against the Reds of Manchester, the Black'n'Whites surrendered meekly without a fight, conceding four goals. And all within the same week during April.

Pictured above: Superstar Patrick Kluivert arrived at Gallowgate at the end of his career and showed quality on occasion.

Memorabilia CORNER

Another stunning programme cover design, now renamed the Black'n'White and costing £3.

IN CHARGE

Chairman: Freddy Shepherd
Manager: Sir Bobby Robson/Graeme Souness
Captain: Alan Shearer
Trainer/Coach: John Carver/ Alan Murray/Dean Saunders
Club Sponsor: Northern Rock
Kit Supplier: Adidas

ST JAMES' PARK

Average Attendance
Lg 51,844 Lg & Cup 46,229

The Magpies pictured in Israel before a European tie. Back row, left to right: Hughes, O'Brien, Bowyer, Bernard, Robert, Kluivert. Front: Jenas, Shearer, Given Carr, Bellamy.

PLAYER FOCUS Craig Bellamy

Born Cardiff. Striker, 5'8"
2001 to 2005: 128 app 42 goals.

Much travelled and on occasion controversial, Craig Bellamy nevertheless was a lightning fast and match-winning forward who formed a telling partnership with Alan Shearer for a period – one of the best pairings in Europe. The Welshman started with Norwich City and joined United from Coventry City for a £6.5m fee in July 2001. Soon winning the PFA Young Player of the Year award when at St James' Park, he was often at odds with referees, fellow teammates, managers and at times supporters. Craig had a volatile temperament but the ability to secure victory with devastating pace in attack. Over four seasons the pairing of Bellamy and Shearer – a pace and power combination – saw United compete at the top of the table and on the European stage in both the Champions League and UEFA Cup. Frequently on the sidelines at times with knee injuries, during season 2004-05 he was at odds with manager Graeme Souness and several dressing-room colleagues. He left Tyneside amidst controversy on a loan deal to Celtic in January of that season. Then Bellamy moved on again, to Blackburn Rovers in summer of 2005 and thereafter pulled on the colours of Liverpool, West Ham United and Manchester City, all after big moves. And at each stadium he showed the cutting edge and goalscoring ability to be the difference. Craig moved back to his home city of Cardiff in 2010 joining the Bluebirds on a season-long loan deal. He won over 60 caps for Wales, also being captain of his country on occasion.

SEASON REVIEW

Premier League: P38 W10 D14 L14 F47 A57 Pts 44.
Position: 14th (Champions; Chelsea).
FA Cup: SF (Winners; Arsenal).
FL Carling Cup: R4 (Winners; Chelsea).
UEFA Cup: QF (Winners; CSKA Moscow).

Appearances (57m): Given SJJ 52, Jenas JA 42 (6), Shearer A 40 (2), Carr S 39, Bowyer LD 36 (3), Robert L 34 (13), O'Brien AJ 32 (6), Bramble TM 30 (2), Dyer KC 29 (5), Hughes AW 29 (7), Bellamy CD 28 (1), Ameobi F 27 (18), Bernard OJW 26 (3), Kluivert PS 25 (12), Butt N 23 (3), Elliott RJ 20 (2), Boumsong J-AS 18, Milner JP 18 (23), Taylor SV 17 (5), Faye AM 16 (1), Babayaro CH 13, Ambrose DPF 11 (7), N'Zogbia CJ 10 (9), Harper SA 5 (2), Johnsen JR 5, Ramage PI 2 (3), Chopra MR 0 (1), Guy LB 0 (1).

Goals (85g): Shearer A 19, Kluivert PS 13, Bellamy CD 10, Ameobi F 7, Bowyer LD 7, Dyer KC 6, Robert L 5, Ambrose DP 3, Jenas JA 2, O'Brien AJ 2, Babayaro CH 1, Bramble TM 1, Butt N 1, Carr S 1, Elliott RJ 1, Hughes AW 1, Milner JP 1, own goals 4.

Dismissals: 7 players; Butt, Bowyer (3), Dyer, Taylor, Ameobi.

MAJOR SIGNINGS

James Milner (Leeds Utd) £3.5m
Patrick Kluivert (FC Barcelona) free
Nicky Butt (Manchester Utd) £2m
Jean-Alain Boumsong (Rangers) £8m
Stephen Carr (Tottenham Hot) £1.5m
Amdy Faye (Portsmouth) £2m
Ronny Johnsen (Aston Villa) free
Celestine Babayaro (Chelsea) free

FROM THE RANKS

Charles N'Zogbia (Le Havre AC)
Peter Ramage (Northb sch)
Lewis Guy (sch, Ey)

TEAM COLOURS Black & white striped shirts, black shorts
(Change; marine & Atlantic blue shirts, white shorts/yellow shirts with black trim, black shorts/blue striped shirts, white shorts)

SEASON 2004-05

Match	Date		Premiership (Barclays)					Posn		Given	Carr	Bernard	Jenas	Hughes	Elliott	Milner	Butt	Shearer	Bellamy	Robert	Dyer	Kluivert	Ameobi	Harper	Ramage	O'Brien	Bowyer	N'Zogbia	Ambrose	Bramble	Caig	Johnsen	Taylor	Brittain	Babayaro	Boumsong	Faye	McClen	Chopra	Guy	Match
									Squad numbers	1	2	35	7	18	3	16	4	9	10	32	8	11	23	12	42	5	29	14	17	19	24	25	27	39	33	6	15	22	28	40	
1	14 Aug	A	Middlesbrough	D	2 2	(1 0)	34,268	3	Bellamy, Shearer (pen)	1	2	3	4	5	6	7	8	9	10	11	s7	s9	s11	u	u																1
2	21 Aug	H	**Tottenham Hotspur**	L	0 1	(0 0)	52,185	16		1	2	3	4	5	u	7	8	9	10	11	s4	s7	s11	u		6															2
3	25 Aug	H	**Norwich City**	D	2 2	(1 0)	51,574	15	Bellamy, Hughes	1	2	3		5	u	7	4	9	10	11	8	u	s7	u		6	s8														3
4	28 Aug	A	Aston Villa	L	2 4	(2 1)	36,305	16	Kluivert, O'Brien	1	2	3	8	5	s3	u	4	s9	10	11		9	s7	u		6	7														4
5	11 Sep	H	**Blackburn Rovers**	W	3 0	(2 0)	52,015	12	og (Flitcroft), Shearer, O'Brien	1	2		4	3	6	s7		9	10	11	7	u	s10	u		5	8	s11													5
6	19 Sep	A	Southampton	W	2 1	(1 0)	30,709	8	og (Prutton), Carr	1	2	3	11	u	6	s10	4	9	7	u		10		u		5	8		u												6
7	25 Sep	H	**West Bromwich Albion**	W	3 1	(0 0)	52,308	6	Kluivert, Milner, Shearer	1	2	3	7	u	6	s10	4	9	11	s11		10		u		5	8		u												7
8	03 Oct	A	Birmingham City	D	2 2	(1 1)	29,021	6	Jenas, Butt	1	2	3	7	s8	6	s10	4	9	11	s3		10		u		5	8		u												8
9	17 Oct	A	Charlton Athletic	D	1 1	(1 0)	26,553	8	Bellamy	1	2	3	7	u	6	s4	4	9	10	s11			s10	u		5	8		11												9
10	24 Oct	H	**Manchester City**	W	4 3	(0 0)	52,316	7	Robert, Shearer (pen), Elliott, Bellamy	1	2	3	7	s2	6	s11	4	9	10	11			s10	u		5	8		u												10
11	31 Oct	A	Bolton Wanderers	L	1 2	(0 0)	27,196	8	Ambrose	1	2	s2		3	6		4	9	8	s10		10	s7	u		5	11		7	u											11
12	07 Nov	H	**Fulham**	L	1 4	(0 1)	51,118	9	Bellamy			3	7	2	6		4	9	11	s2		10	s3	1		5	8			u	u	u									12
13	14 Nov	H	**Manchester United**	L	1 3	(0 1)	52,320	10	Shearer	1	2	3	7				4	9	11	s10	s8	10	u	u		s2	8			5		6									13
14	20 Nov	A	Crystal Palace	W	2 0	(0 0)	22,937	9	Kluivert, Bellamy	1		3	4	2	s6	s8			10	11	7	9	u				8		u	5	u	6									14
15	28 Nov	H	**Everton**	D	1 1	(1 0)	51,247	10	Bellamy	1		3	4	6		u			10	11	7	9	s8	u			8		u	5			2	u							15
16	04 Dec	A	Chelsea	L	0 4	(0 0)	42,328	11		1			4	3	u	u			10	11	7	9	s11	u			8		u	5		6	2								16
17	11 Dec	H	**Portsmouth**	D	1 1	(1 1)	51,480	12	Bowyer	1		3	4	6	u	11			10	s11	8		9	u		u	7		s7	5			2								17
18	19 Dec	A	Liverpool	L	1 3	(1 2)	43,856	13	Kluivert	1		3	4		6	11				s10	7	10	9	u		2	8d	s11	s7	5											18
19	26 Dec	A	Blackburn Rovers	D	2 2	(2 1)	29,271	14	Dyer, Robert	1		s7	4	6	3	7			10	11	8	9	s9	u		5		u		s3			2								19
20	29 Dec	H	**Arsenal**	L	0 1	(0 1)	52,320	14		1		3	4	6		u			7	11	8		9	u	u		10	s3		5			2	u							20
21	01 Jan	H	**Birmingham City**	W	2 1	(2 0)	52,222	13	Ameobi, Bowyer	1		3	4	6		s11			10	11	7		9	u		u	8	s10	u	5			2								21
22	03 Jan	A	West Bromwich Albion	D	0 0	(0 0)	25,259	13		1		3	4	6		s10				11	7		9	u		u	8	10	u	5			2	u							22
23	15 Jan	H	**Southampton**	W	2 1	(2 1)	51,266	12	Shearer (pen), Bramble	1			4	s3		s11		9	11	u	7	s9	10	u			8			6			2		3	5					23
24	23 Jan	A	Arsenal	L	0 1	(0 1)	38,137	12		1		3	4	s2				9		11	8	u	10	u		s5	7	s11		6			2			5					24
25	02 Feb	A	Manchester City	D	1 1	(1 0)	45,752	12	Shearer	1	2		11	u			s8	9		u	8	s10	10	u		5	7			6					3		4				25
26	05 Feb	H	**Charlton Athletic**	D	1 1	(0 0)	51,114	12	Dyer	1	2		11	u			u	9		s7	8	s10	10	u		5	7			6					3		4				26
27	27 Feb	H	**Bolton Wanderers**	W	2 1	(1 1)	50,430	11	Bowyer, Dyer	1	2		s11	u		u	u	9		11	7		10	u			8			6					3	5	4				27
28	05 Mar	H	**Liverpool**	W	1 0	(0 0)	52,323	11	Robert	1	2		s8	3			s7	9		11	7	s10	10	u			8			6			u			5	4				28
29	19 Mar	A	Portsmouth	D	1 1	(1 1)	20,165	11	Dyer	1	2		s4	3		s11	8	9		11	10	s8		u		6	7						u			5	4				29
30	02 Apr	H	**Aston Villa**	L	0 3	(0 1)	52,306	11		1	2		7	3		u	4	9		11	10d		s7	u		6	8d						s6d			5	s11				30
31	10 Apr	A	Tottenham Hotspur	L	0 1	(0 1)	35,885	12			2		7	u		s9	8	9		11			10	1		6		s11	s8		u				3	5	4				31
32	20 Apr	A	Norwich City	L	1 2	(0 0)	25,503	14	Kluivert	1	2				3	7	4	9		11		s8	8	u	u	6		10	s7							5					32
33	24 Apr	A	Manchester United	L	1 2	(1 0)	67,845	14	Ambrose	1	4				3	11		9		s2		s9	8	u	2	6		10	7					u		5		u			33
34	27 Apr	H	**Middlesbrough**	D	0 0	(0 0)	52,047	14		1	4				3	11		9		u	7	u	s7	u	2	6		10	8					u		5					34
35	30 Apr	H	**Crystal Palace**	D	0 0	(0 0)	52,123	14		1	2				3	11		9		s8		s7	8	u	s3	u		10	7				6			5	4				35
36	04 May	A	Fulham	W	3 1	(1 0)	19,003	12	Ambrose, Kluivert, Ameobi	1	2					11				u		9	8	u	u	u		10	7	6			3	u		5	4				36
37	07 May	A	Everton	L	0 2	(0 1)	40,438	12		1	2		4			11		s11		u		9	8d	u	s2	u		10	7	6					3	5					37
38	15 May	H	**Chelsea**	D	1 1	(1 1)	52,326	14	og (Geremi)	1	2		4			7		9		u		10		u		u		11	8	6			s2		3	5			s10		38
Round			FA Cup																																						Round
3	09 Jan	A*	Yeading	W	2 0	(0 0)	10,824		Bowyer, Ameobi	u			4	u		s11			8	11			9	1		s6	7	10	s10	6			2		3	5					3
4	29 Jan	H	**Coventry City**	W	3 1	(2 1)	44,044		Shearer, Ameobi, Babayaro	u	2		8	s4		u		9		u	7	11	10	1		5				6			u		3		4				4
5	20 Feb	H	**Chelsea**	W	1 0	(1 0)	45,740		Kluivert	1	2		8	u		s7	4	9		11	7	10	s9					u		6	u				3	5					5
6	13 Mar	H	**Tottenham Hotspur**	W	1 0	(1 0)	51,307		Kluivert	1	2		s6	3		s11	u	9		11	7	10	s10	u			8			6						5	4				6
SF	17 Apr	N	Manchester United	L	1 4	(0 2)	69,280		Ameobi	1	2					7	8	9		11		s7	10	u		s3		s4	u				6		3	5	4				SF
Round			FL Cup (Carling Cup)																																						Round
3	27 Oct	H	**Norwich City**	W	2 1	(2 0)	42,153		Jenas, Ameobi (pen)	u		3	4	2		7		u	s11	11		10	9	1		u	s9		8	6		5									3
4	10 Nov	H	**Chelsea**	Le	0 2	(0 0)	38,055			1		3	8	s3			4	9	7	11	s4	10	s10	u		2	u			5		6									4
Round			UEFA Cup																																						Round
1(1)	16 Sep	H	**Hapoel Bnei Sakhnin (Is)**	W	2 0	(2 0)	30,221		Kluivert 2	1	2	s3	4	3	6	s10	s7d	u	u	11	7	9	10	u		5	8		u												1(1)
1(2)	30 Sep	A**	Hapoel Bnei Sakhnin (Is)	W	5 1	(3 1)	14,000		Kluivert 2, Shearer 3 (1 pen)	1	2	3	7	6	u	s10		9	8	11		10		s1	u	5	4		s11				u	u							1(2)
GpD1	21 Oct	A	Panionios (Gr)	W	1 0	(0 0)	8,000	2	Shearer (pen)	1	2	3	4	u	6	7		9	10	11			s7	u		5	8		u	u			u	u							GpD1
GpD2	04 Nov	H	**Dinamo Tbilisi (Ge)**	W	2 0	(1 0)	27,218	1	Shearer, Bellamy	1		3	4	2	6	s9		9	7	11		10	u	u		5	8		s8	s6			u	u							GpD2
GpD3	25 Nov	A	FC Sochaux-Montbeliard (F)	W	4 0	(1 0)	15,173	1	Bowyer, Ameobi, Bellamy, Robert	1		3	u	2	6	11	4		10	s11	s8	u	9	u			8		7	5			s7	u							GpD3
GpD4	16 Dec	H	**Sporting Clube de Portugal (P)**	D	1 1	(1 1)	28,017	1	Bellamy	1		11	4	6	3	7			10				9	u	u	s2			8	5			2	u						s10	GpD4
32(1)	17 Feb	A	SC Heerenveen (N)	W	2 1	(0 1)	19,500		Shearer, Bowyer	1	2		11	s3		u		9		s10		8	10			5	7d	u	u	6	u		s9		3		4				32(1)
32(2)	24 Feb	H	**SC Heerenveen (N)**	W	2 1	(2 0)	26,156		og (Breuer), Shearer	1	2		s7	3		s9	8	9		11	7		10		u	5		u	u	6	u		s5				4				32(2)
16(1)	10 Mar	A	Olympiacos CFP (Gr)	W	3 1	(2 1)	30,595		Shearer (pen), Robert, Kluivert	1	2		s7	3		s11	8	9		11	7	10	u	u		5	u	s4		6			u				4				16(1)
16(2)	16 Mar	H	**Olympiacos CFP (Gr)**	W	4 0	(2 0)	32,163		Dyer, Shearer 2, Bowyer	1	2		7	6		s10	4	9		11	10			u	s2	5	8	s11	u				3				u				16(2)
8(1)	07 Apr	H	**Sporting Clube de Portugal (P)**	W	1 0	(1 0)	36,753		Shearer	1	2		8	3	u	s11	u	9		11	7		10	s1		5	s7	u	u				6				4				8(1)
8(2)	14 Apr	A	Sporting Clube de Portugal (P)	L	1 4	(1 1)	33,309		Dyer	1	2		7			s7	u	9			10	s10	u	u		s6	8	11	u	6			5		3		4				8(2)

N Played at Millennium Stadium, Cardiff
A* Played at Loftus Road, London
A** Played at Ramat Gan Stadium, Tel Aviv

Le Lost after extra time

DateLine ... 28 Aug: A 4-2 defeat at Aston Villa signals the end of Sir Bobby Robson's time at St James' Park. **16 Sept:** New boss Graeme Souness takes the hot seat for the European trip to face Hapoel. **16 March:** United's 100th competitive fixture in Europe is recorded with the return leg against Olympiakos. **30 March:** England beat Azerbaijan at St James' Park in a World Cup qualifier. **2 April:** The Magpies concede two penalties and have three men sent-off, including Dyer and Bowyer for fighting each other, in a home defeat by Aston Villa. **17 April:** United concede four goals to Manchester United in the semi-final of the FA Cup in Cardiff.

SEASON 2005-06

PREMIER LEAGUE

Shearer signs off in style

Newcastle started the 2005-06 season in an accustomed fashion, by making headlines. The club splashed out a record fee of £16m to bring England icon Michael Owen to Tyneside from Real Madrid. Teaming up with his international colleague up front, Alan Shearer, United's officials and supporters drooled at the prospect. Another £11m-plus was spent on Spaniard Albert Luque. But money alone never could buy success and in the final analysis the trophy signings were to be a failure which pushed the club into substantial debt.

Newcastle's season began during July, another early qualification test in the Intertoto Cup, to end in elimination by Deportivo La Coruna. With Shearer and Owen together up front, United looked the part, but after a hat-trick against West Ham United during December, the Toon's expensive signing was often on the sidelines. United were mediocre in the League's safe zone and with Souness struggling to show noticeable progress, the axe fell once more, with ex-captain and Academy Manager Glenn Roeder taking charge on a temporary basis in February. Roeder improved results, taking United to the quarter-final of the FA Cup before losing to Chelsea at Stamford Bridge, while he guided the Magpies to seventh place after a late season rally with six wins out of seven played. With that good run came a chance to qualify for the UEFA Cup again, if they got through another Intertoto examination.

The highlight of a lacklustre season was superstar Alan Shearer's farewell. First he equalled Jackie Milburn's longstanding aggregate goals total for the club of 200 with a strike in a FA Cup victory over Mansfield Town, then passed it with a huge fanfare at St James' Park against Portsmouth. Appropriately maybe, his final goal was in a 4-1 drubbing of Sunderland on Wearside, a day as it happened he also picked up another bad injury. He signed off in a spectacular goodbye to a capacity crowd and live television audience against Celtic during May.

Pictured above: To have two spells with United, Robbie Elliott held his own in a team of internationals.

Memorabilia CORNER

England duo Shearer and Owen in celebration on the cover against Manchester City.

IN CHARGE

Chairman: Freddy Shepherd
Manager: Graeme Souness/Glenn Roeder
Captain: Alan Shearer
Trainer/Coach: Alan Murray/Dean Saunders/Terry McDermott/Tommy Craig
Club Sponsor: Northern Rock
Kit Supplier: Adidas

ST JAMES' PARK

Average Attendance
Lg 52,032 Lg & Cup 49,148

Another former Liverpool icon was in charge of the Black'n'Whites for 2005-06, Graeme Souness (front, centre).

PLAYER FOCUS Alan Shearer

Born Newcastle upon Tyne. Centre-forward, 6'0"
1996 to 2006: 405 app 206 goals.

One of the finest centre-forwards of all time, Alan Shearer's record of over 400 senior goals speaks for itself. He returned home to Tyneside for a sensational world record £15m-plus at the end of July 1996 and over the next ten seasons he became Newcastle's talisman, ultimately the club's all-time record goalscorer with 206 goals. Voted the Premier League's Player of the Decade, he is also the competition's goal-king with 260 goals. And all this despite several bad injuries which both kept him out of action and threatened his career. United in fact tried to sign him as an emerging player at Southampton in 1992, but lost out to Blackburn Rovers who claimed his signature in a record deal. Shearer then spearheaded Rovers to the Premier League crown in 1995 before joining the Magpies. Alan was perhaps the perfect old-fashioned No. 9; a tough competitor, able to hold the ball, bring colleagues into play, was deadly in the air, clinical in the box and possessed a stunning long-range shot. Shearer was a runner-up in the Premier League with United, reached two FA Cup finals and led the charge on the Champions League. Alan is one of only three players in both United's top-ten appearances and top-ten goals charts while he is, along with Jack Milburn, the only player to total over 400 games and reach 200 goals for the club. Capped on 63 occasions (30 goals), he was also England and United skipper for much of his stay at St James' Park. Shearer collected the Footballer of Year and Player of the Year awards on three occasions and after he retired at the end of the 2005-06 season became one of the BBC's resident experts while he had a brief spell as United's boss when the club were in relegation trouble from April to May 2009. The Tynesider was honoured with the Freedom of the City and OBE in 2001. His testimonial match in 2006 raised £1.64m for charity.

SEASON REVIEW

Premier League: P38 W17 D7 L14 F47 A42 Pts 58.
Position: 7th (Champions; Chelsea).
FA Cup: R6 (Winners; Liverpool).
FL Carling Cup: R4 (Winners; Manchester United).
Intertoto Cup: SF (Winners; Hamburger SV, RC Lens, Olympique Marseille).

Appearances (48m): Given SJJ 47, Shearer A 40 (1), Boumsong J-AS 38 (3), N'Zogbia CJ 34 (7), Babayaro CH 33 (2), Solano NAT 33 (2), Parker SM 32, Ameobi F 28 (6), Ramage PI 28 (1), Bramble TM 25 (3), Carr S 24, Bowyer LD 23 (11), Emre B 22 (3), Elliott RJ 19 (3), Faye AM 19 (9), Taylor SV 17, Clark LR 10 (15), Owen MJ 10 (1), Chopra MR 9 (11), Luque AM 8 (10), Moore CA 8 (1), Dyer KC 6 (7), Milner JP 5 (2), Jenas JA 4 (1), Butt N 2, Pattison MJ 2 (1), Brittain M 1 (5), Harper SA 1, O'Brien A 0 (4).

Goals (59g): Shearer A 14, Ameobi F 9, Owen MJ 7, N'Zogbia CJ 6, Solano NAT 6, Chopra MR 3, Bowyer LD 2, Bramble TM 2, Emre B 2, Milner JP 2, Parker SM 2, Clark LR 1, Dyer KC 1, Luque AM 1, own goal 1.

Dismissals: 9 players; Babayaro, Parker, Taylor, Bowyer, Boumsong, Elliott, Carr (2), Jenas (one of Carr's dismissals was later rescinded, while both Parker and Jenas also had red cards adjusted).

MAJOR SIGNINGS

Scott Parker (Chelsea) £6.5m
Emre (Inter) £3.8m
Albert Luque (Deportivo La Coruna) £11.4m
Craig Moore (Borussia Moench) free
Michael Owen (Real Madrid) £16m club record fee

FROM THE RANKS

Matty Pattison (Redheugh BC)
Alan O'Brien (Dublin sch, RoIs/y)

TEAM COLOURS Black & white striped shirts, black shorts
(Change; cypress green striped shirts, white shorts/all blue shirts & shorts with white trim/all sky-blue shirts & shorts with black trim)

SEASON 2005–06

Match	Date		Premiership (Barclays)	Result	Score	(HT)	Att	Posn	Goalscorers
1	14 Aug	A	Arsenal	L	0 2	(0 0)	38,072	19	
2	20 Aug	H	**West Ham United**	D	0 0	(0 0)	51,620	16	
3	24 Aug	A	Bolton Wanderers	L	0 2	(0 1)	29,504	18	
4	28 Aug	H	**Manchester United**	L	0 2	(0 0)	52,327	19	
5	10 Sep	H	**Fulham**	D	1 1	(0 1)	52,208	19	N'Zogbia
6	18 Sep	A	Blackburn Rovers	W	3 0	(0 0)	20,725	14	Shearer, Owen, N'Zogbia
7	24 Sep	H	**Manchester City**	W	1 0	(1 0)	52,280	11	Owen
8	01 Oct	A	Portsmouth	D	0 0	(0 0)	20,220	11	
9	15 Oct	A	Wigan Athletic	L	0 1	(0 1)	22,374	13	
10	23 Oct	H	**Sunderland**	W	3 2	(2 2)	52,302	11	Ameobi 2, Emre
11	30 Oct	A	West Bromwich Albion	W	3 0	(0 0)	26,216	10	Owen 2, Shearer
12	05 Nov	H	**Birmingham City**	W	1 0	(0 0)	52,191	10	Emre
13	19 Nov	A	Chelsea	L	0 3	(0 0)	42,268	12	
14	27 Nov	A	Everton	L	0 1	(0 0)	36,207	12	
15	03 Dec	H	**Aston Villa**	D	1 1	(1 0)	52,267	12	Shearer (pen)
16	10 Dec	H	**Arsenal**	W	1 0	(0 0)	52,297	10	Solano
17	17 Dec	A	West Ham United	W	4 2	(2 1)	34,836	10	Owen 3, Shearer
18	26 Dec	A	Liverpool	L	0 2	(0 2)	44,197	10	
19	31 Dec	A	Tottenham Hotspur	L	0 2	(0 1)	36,246	11	
20	02 Jan	H	**Middlesbrough**	D	2 2	(1 0)	52,302	11	Solano, Clark
21	14 Jan	A	Fulham	L	0 1	(0 0)	21,974	13	
22	21 Jan	H	**Blackburn Rovers**	L	0 1	(0 0)	51,323	14	
23	01 Feb	A	Manchester City	L	0 3	(0 2)	42,413	15	
24	04 Feb	H	**Portsmouth**	W	2 0	(1 0)	51,627	15	N'Zogbia, Shearer
25	11 Feb	A	Aston Villa	W	2 1	(2 1)	37,140	14	Ameobi, N'Zogbia
26	22 Feb	H	**Charlton Athletic**	D	0 0	(0 0)	50,451	13	
27	25 Feb	H	**Everton**	W	2 0	(0 0)	51,916	11	Solano 2
28	04 Mar	H	**Bolton Wanderers**	W	3 1	(2 0)	52,012	10	Solano, Shearer, Ameobi
29	12 Mar	A	Manchester United	L	0 2	(0 2)	67,858	12	
30	19 Mar	H	**Liverpool**	L	1 3	(1 2)	52,302	12	Ameobi
31	26 Mar	A	Charlton Athletic	L	1 3	(1 2)	27,019	13	Parker
32	01 Apr	H	**Tottenham Hotspur**	W	3 1	(3 1)	52,301	12	Bowyer, Ameobi, Shearer (pen)
33	09 Apr	A	Middlesbrough	W	2 1	(2 0)	31,202	10	og (Boateng), Ameobi
34	15 Apr	H	**Wigan Athletic**	W	3 1	(2 1)	52,302	9	Shearer 2 (1 pen), Bramble
35	17 Apr	A	Sunderland	W	4 1	(0 1)	40,032	7	Chopra, Shearer (pen), N'Zogbia, Luque
36	22 Apr	H	**West Bromwich Albion**	W	3 0	(2 0)	52,272	6	Solano, Ameobi 2 (1 pen)
37	29 Apr	A	Birmingham City	D	0 0	(0 0)	28,331	7	
38	07 May	H	**Chelsea**	W	1 0	(0 0)	52,309	7	Bramble
Round			FA Cup						
3	07 Jan	H	**Mansfield Town**	W	1 0	(0 0)	41,459		Shearer
4	28 Jan	A	Cheltenham Town	W	2 0	(2 0)	7,022		Chopra, Parker
5	18 Feb	H	**Southampton**	W	1 0	(0 0)	40,975		Dyer
6	22 Mar	A	Chelsea	L	0 1	(0 1)	42,279		
Round			FL Cup (Carling Cup)						
3	26 Oct	A	Grimsby Town	W	1 0	(0 0)	9,311		Shearer
4	30 Nov	A	Wigan Athletic	L	0 1	(0 0)	11,574		
Round			Intertoto Cup						
3(1)	17 Jul	A	FK ZTS Dubnica (Sv)	W	3 1	(2 1)	6,200		Chopra, N'Zogbia, Milner
3(2)	23 Jul	H	**FK ZTS Dubnica (Sv)**	W	2 0	(0 0)	25,135		Shearer 2
SF(1)	27 Jul	A	RC Deportivo La Coruna (Sp)	L	1 2	(0 1)	16,000		Bowyer
SF(2)	03 Aug	H	**RC Deportivo La Coruna (Sp)**	L	1 2	(1 1)	34,215		Milner

Match	Given	Carr	Babayaro	Jenas	Boumsong	Taylor	Dyer	Parker	Shearer	Bowyer	Emre	N'Zogbia	Faye	Milner	Elliott	Harper	Clark	Brittain	Ameobi	Luque	Bramble	Owen	O'Brien	Moore	Chopra	Ramage	Solano	Caig	Gate	Pattison	Butt	Huntington
Squad numbers	1	2	33	7	6	27	8	17	9	11	5	14	15	16	3	12	21	39	23	20	19	10	37	18	28	26	4	24	36	35	4	
1	1	2	3	4d	5	6	7	8	9	10	11	s7	s8	s9	u	u																
2	1	2	3	4	5	6		8	9	10		11	u	7	u	u	s11	u														
3	1	2	3	11	5	6		8	9	7		u	4	s7	u	u	s4		10													
4	1	2	3	s10	5	6	7	8	9	4	10		s4		u	u			s7	11												
5	1	4	3		6	2		8d	9	s2		s11	7		u	u	s7			11	5	10										
6	1	2	3		5	6d			9	8		11	4		u	u	7	u			s9	10	u									
7	1	2	3		5			8	9	4		11	s4		u	u	7		s9		6	10		u								
8	1	2	3		5	6		8	9	4		11	s7		s3	u	7	u	10						u							
9	1	2			5	6		8	9	7	s4	11	4		3	u	s3		s7			10				u						
10	1	2d			5	6		8	9		4	11	s4				s7	u	10						s10	3	7	u				
11	1		3		5	6	s11	8	s9		4	11	u			u			9		s5	10				2	7					
12	1		3			5		8	9		4	11	u		u	u	s7		s11		6	10				2	7					
13	1		3		5			8		4	10	11	u			u	u	u	9		6				s7	2	7					
14	1		3		5			8	9	s7	4	11	u			u	u		10	s3	6					2	7					
15	1				5			8	9	s7			4		3	u	u	u	11	s10	6				10	2	7					
16	1				5			8	9	s8			4		3	u		u	11	u	6	10			s10	2	7					
17	1				5			8	9	s7			4		3	u			11	u	6	10			u	2	7		u			
18	1		3		5	6			9	8d		7	4		u	u			s11	11	s6	10				2	s7					
19	1		s2		5			8	9	u		s7	4		3	u			11	s10	6	10				2	7					
20	1		s3		5				9			s10	4		3	u	8	u	10	11	6				u	2	7					
21	1	2	3		5				9	4		11			s2	u	8	u		10			s10		s11	6	7					
22	1		3		5				9	4		u			u	u	8	u		11	6		s11		10	2	7					
23	1		3		5			8	9		11	7			u	u	4			s10	6		s11		10	2	s7					
24	1		3		5		s7	4	9	s10	10	11			u	u	s4		8		6					2	7					
25	1		3d		5		s8	4	9	s11	10	11			s7	u	u		8		6					2	7					
26	1				5			4		8	10	11	u		3	u	u		9	s6	6				u	2	7					
27	1		3		5			4		8	10	11	u		6	u	s10		9						u	2	7			s11		
28	1		3		5			4	9	s10	10	11	u		6	u	u		8	s8						2	7					
29	1		3		5		s7	4	9	s8	10	11			6	u	u		8	s11						2	7					
30	1		3		5d		s8	4	9	s11	10	11			6	u	s10		8					u		2	7					
31	1	2			5		s7	4	9	10	11	s8	u			u	u		8					6		3	7					
32	1	2			u				9	4	10	11	s7		3	u	s10		8					6	s11	5	7					
33	1	2					s7		9	4	10	11	s10		3	u	u		8		5			6		u	7					
34	1	2					10		9	4		11	s4		3	u	s10		8		5			6	s8	u	7					
35	1	2	3		s11		8		9			11	4			u	10			s9	5			6	s10	u	7					
36	1	2	3		u							11	4		u	u	s8		9	u	5			6	10		7			8		
37	1	2	3		s4							11	4		u	u	s8		9		5	s10		6	10		7			8		
38	1	2d	3		s7						8	11	4		u	u	s10		9		5			6	10		7			u		
Round																																
3	1	2	3		5				9			11			u	u	8	4		10	6		s10		s4	s2	7					
4	1		3		5			8	9		s7	s10			u	u	4		11	s8	6				10	2	7					
5	1				5		8	4		s8	10	11	u		3	u	u		9	s9	6					2	7					
6	1	2	3				11	4	9	10	s7		u		6d	u	u		8					s3		5	7					
Round																																
3	1		3		u	5		8	9			11	4		u		s7	s4			6				10	2	7	u				
4	1				5			8	9	4	10	3	s10		6	u	u	s4		11					s11	2	7					
Round																																
3(1)	u		3		6	2			9			11	4	7	5	1		s10							10	u					8	u
3(2)	1	2	3	10	5	6			9	8		11	4	7	u	u		ss10							s10	u					u	
SF(1)	1	2	3		5	6			9	8		11	4	7	u	u		u							s7	u					10	u
SF(2)	1	2			5	6		8	9	10	11	s7	4	7	3	u		s11	s4						u	u						

Match 1 Jenas's red card later downgraded to yellow
Match 10 Carr given a red card after the game following adjustment of a yellow card to Parker
Match 38 Carr's red card later rescinded

DateLine ... 17 Dec: A hat-trick for £16m signing Michael Owen as the black-and-whites win 4-2 at West Ham. **4 Feb:** Glenn Roeder's first game as permanent boss against Portsmouth. **4 Feb:** Jack Milburn's record goals tally of 200 is broken by Alan Shearer with a strike against Portsmouth. **17 April:** Alan Shearer nets his final goal in the 4-1 derby victory on Wearside against Sunderland and then is carried off injured. The match proves to be his last for the Magpies. **11 May:** A crowd of 52,275 pack St James' Park to bid farewell to Alan Shearer in a televised spectacular against Glasgow Celtic.

SEASON 2006-07

PREMIER LEAGUE

A long road to mediocrity

Glenn Roeder had done enough to earn the permanent post of manager following his few months in charge of the Magpies but the newly appointed boss was unlucky that he had to now select a side without his two main players; Shearer – retired – and Owen – again injured, this time on England duty and to be out until the latter weeks of the season. United not surprisingly struggled and slipped into mediocrity. They were a long way from the heady days of challenging for the Premier League and eyeing Champions League football under Keegan and Robson. And that was not good enough for a club which spent big and paid top wages.

Newcastle only claimed two victories in the opening two months of Premier League action and dropped to 18th in the table. Goals were at a premium until new centre-forward Oba Martins started to show his talent with a flurry of good performances. United climbed to mid-table and into ninth spot after defeating Liverpool 2-1 during February. After recording their very first senior penalty shoot-out success at the seventh attempt in a League Cup clash with Watford, United fell to Chelsea. That was no surprise, but the 5-1 home defeat by Birmingham City in the Third Round of the FA Cup – equalling the club's worst ever result in the competition at Gallowgate – was a huge shock. The Blues were a division lower than the Magpies and made the black-and-whites look distinctly second-rate in every department.

Only the UEFA Cup provided a degree of comfort although before losing to AZ of Alkmaar in the last 16 they were still some way from the final. It had been a long road of 14 European games. Included were trips for United's keen European travelling support to Estonia, Latvia, Italy, Germany, Belgium and Holland. It was however to be the end of those enjoyable visits to all points on the Continent for some while. United were heading no-where fast and before the end of the season United again were looking for a new boss as Glenn Roeder departed.

Pictured above: Obafemi Martins took over the No. 9 shirt and occasionally showed menace up front.

Memorabilia CORNER

Charles N'Zogbia is prominent on the cover of the programme for the visit of Wigan Athletic.

IN CHARGE

Chairman: Freddy Shepherd/Chris Mort
Manager: Glenn Roeder
Captain: Scott Parker
Trainer/Coach: Kevin Bond/Nigel Pearson
Club Sponsor: Northern Rock
Kit Supplier: Adidas

ST JAMES' PARK

Average Attendance
Lg 50,686 Lg & Cup 43,234

Glenn Roeder's 28 player squad for 2006-07, now sponsored by Northern Rock.

PLAYER FOCUS Shay Given

Born Lifford. Goalkeeper, 6'0"
1997 to 2009: 463 app 0 goals.

Starting his senior career with Glasgow Celtic as a teenager, Shay Given was an emerging goalkeeper at Blackburn Rovers when Kenny Dalglish was boss at Ewood Park. He was brought to Tyneside during June 1997 for £1.5m once his manager moved to Gallowgate. Having showed his potential following successful loan spells with first Swindon, then Sunderland where he helped win promotion, Given was soon making an impression and he became United's regular 'keeper for all of 12 seasons – with only the odd period exchanged with his long term rival Steve Harper. Always able to produce breathtaking saves, Shay developed into one of the Premier League's finest custodians. He took part in two FA Cup finals – one on the bench – and was just as much a match-winner as his forward colleagues on many occasions. The Irishman also featured in a succession of European ties with Newcastle, including Champions League action. Becoming hugely popular with supporters, he was on course to overtake Edwardian star Jimmy Lawrence's all-time appearance record for United before moving to Manchester City in February 2009 for a reported £5.9m after the decline and managerial upheaval at the club. Shay is recognised as one of the best stoppers in world football, able to pull-off incredible saves and in a consistent manner too. Winning over a century of caps for the Republic of Ireland, he became one of the most respected footballers in the game. No other player has appeared more for United in post-war League and Cup football.

SEASON REVIEW

Premier League: P38 W11 D10 L17 F38 A47 Pts 43.
Position: 13th (Champions; Manchester United).
FA Cup: R3 (Winners; Chelsea).
FL Carling Cup: QF (Winners; Chelsea).
UEFA Cup: R4 (Winners; Sevilla).

Appearances (57m): Milner JP 46 (7), Martins OA 43 (3), Taylor SV 43 (1), Butt N 40 (7), Solano NAT 39 (5), Parker SM 38 (3), Emre B 33 (5), Given SJJ 33, Carr S 32, Bramble TM 31, Duff DA 29 (4), Ramage PI 29 (3), Dyer KC 27 (3), Sibierski AC 25 (14), Harper SA 22 (3), Moore CA 21 (1), Babayaro CH 20, N'Zogbia CJ 20 (15), Huntington PD 14 (2), Ameobi F 11 (5), Onyewu OC 7 (4), Luque AM 6 (10), Rossi G 5 (8), Pattison MJ 4 (8), Edgar DE 3 (1), Owen MJ 3, Krul TM 1, O'Brien A 1 (4), Srnicek P 1 (1), Carroll AT 0 (7).

Goals (66g): Martins OA 17, Sibierski AC 8, Dyer KC 7, Ameobi F 5, Milner JP 4, Parker SM 4, Solano NAT 4, Taylor SV 4, Emre B 3, Luque AM 2, Bramble TM 1, Butt N 1, Duff DA 1, Edgar DE 1, Huntington PD 1, Rossi G 1, own goals 2.

Dismissals: 2 players; Bramble, Taylor.

MAJOR SIGNINGS

Damien Duff (Chelsea) £5m
Obafemi Martins (Inter) £10.1m
Giuseppe Rossi (Manchester Utd) loan
Antoine Sibierski (Manchester City) free
Oguchi Onyewu (Standard Liege) loan

FROM THE RANKS

Paul Huntington (Yewdale Pegasus BC, Ey)
Tim Krul (ADO Den Haag, Ny)
Andy Carroll (Low Fell Jnrs, Ey)
Dave Edgar (Canada sch, Cy)

TEAM COLOURS Black & white striped shirts, black shorts
(Change; cardinal & navy-blue shirts, navy-blue shorts/all sky-blue shirts & shorts with black trim)

SEASON 2006-07

Match	Date		Premiership (Barclays)				Att	Posn	Scorers
1	19 Aug	H	**Wigan Athletic**	W	2 1	(1 0)	51,569	6	Parker, Ameobi
2	27 Aug	A	Aston Villa	L	0 2	(0 2)	35,141	14	
3	09 Sep	H	**Fulham**	L	1 2	(0 0)	50,365	14	Parker
4	17 Sep	A	West Ham United	W	2 0	(0 0)	34,938	9	Duff, Martins
5	20 Sep	A	Liverpool	L	0 2	(0 1)	43,754	10	
6	24 Sep	H	**Everton**	D	1 1	(1 1)	50,107	12	Ameobi
7	01 Oct	A	Manchester United	L	0 2	(0 1)	75,664	13	
8	15 Oct	H	**Bolton Wanderers**	L	1 2	(1 0)	48,145	15	Ameobi (pen)
9	22 Oct	A	Middlesbrough	L	0 1	(0 0)	30,060	16	
10	28 Oct	H	**Charlton Athletic**	D	0 0	(0 0)	48,642	16	
11	04 Nov	H	**Sheffield United**	L	0 1	(0 0)	50,188	19	
12	11 Nov	A	Manchester City	D	0 0	(0 0)	40,571	18	
13	18 Nov	A	Arsenal	D	1 1	(1 0)	60,058	17	Dyer
14	26 Nov	H	**Portsmouth**	W	1 0	(0 0)	48,743	17	Sibierski
15	06 Dec	H	**Reading**	W	3 2	(1 2)	48,182	15	Sibierski, Martins (pen), Emre
16	09 Dec	A	Blackburn Rovers	W	3 1	(2 0)	19,225	14	Martins 2, Taylor
17	13 Dec	A	Chelsea	L	0 1	(0 0)	41,945	14	
18	16 Dec	H	**Watford**	W	2 1	(0 0)	49,231	12	Martins 2
19	23 Dec	H	**Tottenham Hotspur**	W	3 1	(3 1)	52,079	11	Dyer, Martins, Parker
20	26 Dec	A	Bolton Wanderers	L	1 2	(1 1)	26,437	11	Dyer
21	30 Dec	A	Everton	L	0 3	(0 1)	38,682	13	
22	01 Jan	H	**Manchester United**	D	2 2	(1 1)	52,302	13	Milner, Edgar
23	14 Jan	A	Tottenham Hotspur	W	3 2	(1 1)	35,942	11	Huntington, Martins, Butt
24	20 Jan	H	**West Ham United**	D	2 2	(1 2)	52,095	12	Milner, Solano (pen)
25	31 Jan	H	**Aston Villa**	W	3 1	(2 1)	49,201	9	Milner, Dyer, Sibierski
26	03 Feb	A	Fulham	L	1 2	(0 0)	24,340	10	Martins
27	10 Feb	H	**Liverpool**	W	2 1	(1 1)	52,305	9	Martins, Solano (pen)
28	25 Feb	A	Wigan Athletic	L	0 1	(0 1)	21,179	11	
29	03 Mar	H	**Middlesbrough**	D	0 0	(0 0)	52,303	10	
30	18 Mar	A	Charlton Athletic	L	0 2	(0 0)	27,028	11	
31	31 Mar	H	**Manchester City**	L	0 1	(0 0)	52,004	11	
32	07 Apr	A	Sheffield United	W	2 1	(1 0)	32,572	10	Martins, Taylor
33	09 Apr	H	**Arsenal**	D	0 0	(0 0)	52,293	10	
34	14 Apr	A	Portsmouth	L	1 2	(0 1)	20,165	11	Emre (pen)
35	22 Apr	H	**Chelsea**	D	0 0	(0 0)	52,056	12	
36	30 Apr	A	Reading	L	0 1	(0 0)	24,109	12	
37	05 May	H	**Blackburn Rovers**	L	0 2	(0 1)	51,226	13	
38	13 May	A	Watford	D	1 1	(1 0)	19,830	13	Dyer
Round			**FA Cup (E.ON)**						
3	06 Jan	A	Birmingham City	D	2 2	(1 1)	16,444		Taylor, Dyer
3r	17 Jan	H	**Birmingham City**	L	1 5	(0 2)	26,099		Milner
Round			**FL Cup (Carling Cup)**						
3	25 Oct	H	**Portsmouth**	W	3 0	(0 0)	25,028		Rossi, Solano 2
4	07 Nov	A	Watford	Dep	2 2	(1 0)	16,791		Sibierski, Parker
5	20 Dec	H	**Chelsea**	L	0 1	(0 0)	37,406		
Round			**Intertoto Cup**						
3(1)	15 Jul	H	**Lillestrom SK (Nw)**	D	1 1	(0 1)	31,059		Luque
3(2)	22 Jul	A	Lillestrom SK (Nw)	W	3 0	(2 0)	8,742		Ameobi 2, Emre
Round			**UEFA Cup**						
2Q(1)	10 Aug	A*	FK Ventspils (L)	W	1 0	(0 0)	6,000		Bramble
2Q(2)	24 Aug	H	**FK Ventspils (L)**	D	0 0	(0 0)	30,498		
1(1)	14 Sep	A	Levadia Tallinn (Es)	W	1 0	(1 0)	7,917		Sibierski
1(2)	28 Sep	H	**Levadia Tallinn (Es)**	W	2 1	(0 0)	27,012		Martins 2
GpH1	19 Oct	H	**Fenerbahce SK (H)**	W	1 0	(0 0)	30,035	2	Sibierski
GpH2	02 Nov	A	Palermo (I)	W	1 0	(1 0)	16,904	1	Luque
GpH3	23 Nov	H	**Real Club Celta de Vigo (Sp)**	W	2 1	(1 1)	25,079	1	Sibierski, Taylor
GpH4	30 Nov	A	Eintracht Frankfurt (G)	D	0 0	(0 0)	47,000	1	
32(1)	15 Feb	A**	SV Zulte Waregem (Bel)	W	3 1	(0 0)	8,015		og (Dindeleux), Martins (pen), Sibierski
32(2)	22 Feb	H	**SV Zulte Waregem (Bel)**	W	1 0	(0 0)	30,083		Martins
16(1)	08 Mar	H	**AZ (Alkmaar) (N)**	W	4 2	(4 1)	28,452		og (Steinsson), Dyer, Martins 2
16(2)	15 Mar	A	AZ (Alkmaar) (N)	La	0 2	(0 1)	16,401		

Match	Given	Carr	Babayaro	Parker	Moore	Bramble	Solano	Butt	Ameobi	Emre	Duff	Taylor	N'Zogbia	Luque	Harper	Milner	Martins	Ramage	Rossi	Sibierski	Krul	Pattison	Smicek	Dyer	Huntington	Edgar	O'Brien A	Carroll	Troisi	Onyewu	Owen	LuaLua	Faye	Bernard	Forster
Squad numbers	1	2	33	17	18	19	4	22	23	5	11	27	14	7	12	16	9	26	15	20	40	35	24	8	32	30	37	39	42	15	10	43	15	34	41
1	1	2	3	4	5	6	7	8	9	10	11	s5	s8	s9	u	u																			
2	1	2	3	4	5	6	7	s10		10	11	u	s7	s3	u	8	9																		
3	1	2		4	5	6	u	s4	8	10	7		11		u		9	3	s9	u															
4	1	2	3	4	5			s10	8	10	11		u		s1	7	9	6	u	s8															
5		2	3	4	5			u	8	10	11		s7		1	7	9	6	s9	s8	u														
6		2		4	5	6d		u	8	10		u	11		1	7	9	3	s9	s8	u														
7		2		4	5			8	9	10	11	6	s7	u	1	7	s8	3			u	s10													
8		2		4	5	6	7		8	10	11	u	s7		1		9	3	s10	u			u												
9		2		4	6	u		8	s10		11	5	s7		1	7	9	3	u	10			u												
10		2	3	4	5	6	7	8			11	u	10	u	1	s7		u	9				u												
11		2	3	4	5	6	s11	8		s8	7		11	s10	1	10		u	9				u												
12		2		4	6		s2	u	9	10	11	5	s11		1	7		3		8			u	s9											
13	1			4	5	6	7	8			11	2	s11		u	s7	9	3	u	s5				10											
14	1			4		6	2	s4		10		5	11	s11		7	9	3		s7			u	8	u										
15	1		3				2	4		10		5	11	u		7	9	6	s9	8		u	u		u										
16	1		3				2	4		10		5	11	u		7	9	6	s2	8		s10	u		s8										
17	1		3					4				5	11	s8		7	9	6	10	8		s11	u		2	u	u								
18	1		3	s4				4		10	s10	5				11	9	6	u	8		u	u	7	2										
19	1			4			2	8		10		5		u		11	9	6	s7	s10			s1	7	3	u									
20				4				8		s7		5		u		11	9	6	s11	10	u	u	1	7	3	2									
21	1			4			2	8		10		5				11	9	6	u	s6		s7	u	7	3	u									
22	1			4			2			10		5		u		11	9			8		s10	u	7	6	3	u	u							
23	1						2	8				5			u	11	9	6		10		4		7	3	u	u	u	u						
24	1	3		4			2	8						u	s1	7	9	6				u		10	5	s6	11	u							
25		2		4		6		10			11	5			1	7	9			s10			u	8	3	u	u	u							
26		3		4		6	s8	10			11	2			1	7	9			s11			u	8	u		u			5					
27			3	4		6	7	10			s7	2		u	1	11	9			s8			u	8	u					5					
28	1			4		6	7	8			11	2	s11		u	s7	9			10					3	u		s3		5					
29	1			4		6	2	10				3	11		u	7	9			s7				8	u		u	u		5					
30	1			4	5	u	2			10	3		s7		u	11	9			8				7	u			u		6					
31	1	2	3	4	6		7	10		u	11	5			u	s7	9			s8				8						s6					
32	1	3	u	4	6		2	8		s4	11	5			u	7	9			10				s10						s2					
33	1	3				u	2	4		10	11	5	s8	s10	s1	7	9	u						8						6					
34		3	u		6		2	4		10	11	5	7	s11	1	8	9						u					s7		s6					
35		3	u			6	2	4		10		5	u		1	11	9	u		8			u	7				s8							
36		3				6	2		s8	11		5	s11		1	4	9			8			u	7				u		u	10				
37		3		4		6	2	8	s11				u		1	7	9	s6					u	11				u		5	10				
38	1	3					2	4	9			5			u	7		6				8		11	u		s10	s9		s2	10				
Round																																			
3	1						2	8				5		u		11	9			10		4	u	7	6	3	s10	u				u			
3r	1						2	8				5d			u	11	9	6		10		4		7	3	u	s4	s10				u			
Round																																			
3			3		5	6	7	4			s9	2	11	u	1	8	9	s2	10				u	s4											
4		2	3	4			s9			10	11	5	s8	u	1	7		6	9	8			u		u										
5	1			4			2	8		10		5		u		11	9	6	u	s11			u	7	3	u									
Round																																			
3(1)	1	2	3	4		6	7	u	s8	10		5	11	9	u	8		u									s9						u		
3(2)	1	2	3	4	s3	6	7	s9	9	10		5	11		u	8		u				s11					u						u		
Round																																			
2Q(1)	1	2	3	4	5	6	7	8	9	10	11	u	s10	u	u	s7		s3									u								
2Q(2)		2	3	4		6	u	u		10	7	5	11	9	1	8		u			u	u			u		u								
1(1)	1	2		4	5	6		s11		10	7		11	s8	u	s6	9	3		8		u			u									u	
1(2)		2		s10	u	6		4	u	10	s11	5	11	s9	1	7	9	3		8	u	u													
GpH1		2		4	u	u	s11	s10	s9	10	3	5	11	u	1	7	9	6		8	u														
GpH2					5	6	7	4		10		2	11	9	u	8		3		s11	1	s9			u			s7	u					u	
GpH3	1			s4		6	2	4		10		5	11	9	u	7	s10	3		8					u	u		u	u						
GpH4	1					6	2	4		10		5	11	9		7	s9	3		8		u			u	u		u	u						u
32(1)			3			6	2	4			11	5		s9	1	7	9			10		u	u	8	u	u		u	u						
32(2)			3			6	2	4			11	5		10	1	7	9					s4	u	8	s3	u	u	s10				u			
16(1)	1	3		4		6	2	8		s11	11	5	u	u	u	s10	9			10				7	u			u							
16(2)	1			4	u	6	2	8		s11	11	5	s3	u	u	u	9			10				7	3			u							

A* Played at Skonto Stadium, Riga
A** Played at Jules Ottenstadion, Ghent

Dep Drawn after extra time, tie won on penalties (5-4)
La Tie lost on away goals

DateLine ... 7 Nov: United defeat Watford 5-4 on penalties in the League Cup, the club's first senior success in a shoot-out. **30 Nov:** United finish top of their UEFA Cup Group and move into the knock-out stage after a 0-0 draw with Eintracht Frankfurt. **17 Jan:** Birmingham win 5-1 on Tyneside in a FA Cup replay, one of the worst home defeats on record.

NEWCASTLE UNITED

SEASON 2007-08

PREMIER LEAGUE

Upheaval at Gallowgate

Heralded by many in the game, Bolton's Sam Allardyce landed the hot-seat of St James' Park before the season began. Yet it was to be one of the shortest stays on record at Gallowgate. Allardyce brought with him to Tyneside an array of backroom staff and had funds to spend. He had a wonderful start – a 3-1 victory at his old haunt of the Reebok Stadium in Bolton. Michael Owen gave the Magpies better service this time round, yet United still were also-rans in League action while they were knocked out of the cup tournaments, twice by Arsenal at the hands of their eager-to-impress kids.

Once a regular at the top end of the Premier League, United were now locked in mid-table, a run-of-the-mill club. Newcastle's sagging status was difficult to reverse. Allardyce could not do it and with the Sir John Hall family bowing out, selling their majority stake in Newcastle United to London businessman Mike Ashley during June 2007, things were bound to change at St James' Park. Chairman Freddy Shepherd was forced to sell up soon after and Allardyce was a casualty when he was replaced with an old favourite. Following a dreadful showing at Old Trafford in January – United conceding six goals in the second period – Kevin Keegan arrived for a third period at St James' Park.

While the old razzmatazz was still evident, it was not quite the same as before and there was to be no instant impact. Yet after a stuttering start that saw United unable to get a win for nine games, Special K gained enough points to make sure he could rebuild and start from scratch in the summer. But the new style management regime on Tyneside brought with it conflict between manager and owner. Things were going to get a lot worse within the corridors of Gallowgate before they got better.

Pictured above: Joey Barton became an influential player in United's midfield battleground.

Memorabilia CORNER

Turkish international Emre is profiled in the programme for the clash with Portsmouth.

IN CHARGE

Chairman: Chris Mort/Derek Llambias (MD)
Manager: Sam Allardyce/Kevin Keegan
Captain: Alan Smith/Michael Owen
Trainer/Coach: Nigel Pearson/Steve Round
Club Sponsor: Northern Rock
Kit Supplier: Adidas

ST JAMES' PARK

Average Attendance
Lg 51,321 Lg & Cup 49,558

Sam Allardyce was in charge at St James' Park only briefly, pictured (front, centre) at the start of the 2007-08 season.

PLAYER FOCUS Steven Taylor

Born Greenwich. Centre-half, 6'2"
1995 to date: 187 app 13 goals.

Although born in London, Steven Taylor settled on Tyneside within weeks of his birth and was brought up in Whitley Bay, very much as a Geordie. As a schoolboy he was soon part of the club's junior ranks, signing professional in January 2003 and making his teenage debut in season 2003-04 against Real Mallorca in the UEFA Cup. A strapping 6'2" centre-back, positive in the air and in the tackle, Taylor became a regular for the England school and youth sides, then also the Under-21 eleven winning 29 caps all told, skipper of the Three Lions on occasion. Gaining a regular slot in United's line-up in 2004-05, he also got into his country's B team during 2007 and was tipped for a full call-up. However, injury and then relegation halted his bright progress. Also to operate occasionally at right-back, Taylor missed a large slice of the Championship title winning campaign in 2009-10 due to further injury then was out of action again before United's start back in the Premier League. He returned to the side in December 2010 and started to recapture the form that had him in contention for full international recognition. Steven played with both Cramlington and Whitley Bay Juniors as well as Wallsend Boy's Club, three notable local nursery sides. He also had a spell at Wycombe Wanderers on loan under the guidance of Tony Adams during the early part of his career in season 2003-04 when he made his Football League bow as a teenager.

SEASON REVIEW

Premier League: P38 W11 D10 L17 F45 A65 Pts 43.
Position: 12th (Champions; Manchester United).
FA Cup: R4 (Winners; Portsmouth).
FL Carling Cup: R3 (Winners; Tottenham Hotspur).

Appearances (43m): Butt N 37 (2), Taylor SV 34 (2), N'Zogbia CJ 32 (5), Smith Alan 30 (7), Beye H 28 (2), Milner JP 28 (4), Owen MJ 28 (5), Geremi 25 (3), Given SJJ 24, Martins OA 24 (9), Enrique JSD 23 (5), Diagne-Faye A 22 (2), Viduka MA 21 (7), Barton JA 20 (3), Cacapa 19 (3), Harper SA 19 (2), Rozehnal DS 18 (7), Duff DA 15 (4), Carr S 10 (2), Emre B 8 (9), Ameobi F 4 (4), Edgar DE 2 (4), Carroll AT 1 (5), Solano NAT 1 (1), Diatta L 0 (2), LuaLua K 0 (5), Ramage PI 0 (3).

Goals (51g): Owen MJ 13, Martins OA 10, Viduka MA 7, Butt N 3, Milner JP 3, N'Zogbia CJ 3, Cacapa 2, Barton JA 1, Beye H 1, Duff DA 1, Emre B 1, Diagne-Faye A 1, Geremi 1, Taylor SV 1, own goals 3.

Dismissals: 2 players; Smith, Emre.

MAJOR SIGNINGS

Joey Barton (Manchester City) £5.8m
Mark Viduka (Middlesbrough) free
Alan Smith (Manchester Utd) £6m
Jose Enrique (Villareal CF) £6.3m
David Rozehnal (PSG) £2.9m
Geremi (Chelsea) free
Habib Baye (Olympique Marseille) £2m
Abdoulaye Faye (Bolton Wand) £2m
Cacapa (Olympique Lyonnais) free

FROM THE RANKS

Kazenga LuaLua (sch)

TEAM COLOURS Black & white striped shirts, black shorts
(Change; all sky-blue shirts & shorts with black trim/white-grey-blue shirts, white shorts)

SEASON 2007-08

Match	Date		Premier League (Barclays)	Result	Att	Posn	Scorers	Harper	Carr	N'Zogbia	Geremi	Taylor	Rozehnal	Milner	Butt	Martins	Viduka	Smith	Ramage	Solano	Ameobi	Cacapa	Forster	Owen	Given	Edgar	Pattison	Beye	Diagne-Faye	Enrique	Emre	Barton	Duff	LuaLua	Carroll	Troisi	Diatta	Tozer	Huntington	Match
							Squad numbers	13	2	14	20	27	4	16	22	9	36	17	26	15	23	6	34	10	1	30	35	21	25	3	5	7	11	38	39	37	15	35	32	
1	11 Aug	A	Bolton Wanderers	W 3 1 (3 0)	25,414	1	N'Zogbia, Martins 2	1	2	3	4	5	6	7	8	9	10	11	s7	s9	s10	u	u																	1
2	18 Aug	H	Aston Villa	D 0 0 (0 0)	51,049	6		1	2	3	4	5	6	7	8	9	10	11	u		s10	s4	u	s9																2
3	26 Aug	A	Middlesbrough	D 2 2 (1 1)	28,875	7	N'Zogbia, Viduka	1	2	3	4	5	6	7	8	9	10	11	s2		u	ss2		s9	u															3
4	01 Sep	H	Wigan Athletic	W 1 0 (0 0)	50,461	5	Owen	1		3	4	2	5	7	8	s11	9	11			s9	6		10	u	u	u													4
5	17 Sep	A	Derby County	L 0 1 (0 1)	33,016	10		1		3	4	2	5	7	8	s10		11			9	6		10	u		u	s2	s4											5
6	23 Sep	H	West Ham United	W 3 1 (2 1)	50,104	5	Viduka 2, N'Zogbia	1		3	4	s6	5	7	8	s10	9	11				6		10	u			2	u	s9										6
7	29 Sep	A	Manchester City	L 1 3 (1 1)	40,606	8	Martins	u		3	4	5	6	7	8	9	10	11							1		u	2	s5	s4	s10									7
8	07 Oct	H	Everton	W 3 2 (1 0)	50,152	9	Butt, Emre, Owen	u		11	4	u	s4	7	8	9		10				6		s9	1			2	5	3	s7									8
9	22 Oct	H	Tottenham Hotspur	W 3 1 (1 0)	51,411	8	Martins, Cacapa, Milner	u		7	4		s10	s7	8	9					u	6		10	1			2	5	3	11	s11								9
10	27 Oct	A	Reading	L 1 2 (0 0)	24,119	8	og (Duberry)	u		s8	4		u	s5	8	9		s9				6		10	1			2	5	3	11	7								10
11	03 Nov	H	Portsmouth	L 1 4 (1 3)	51,490	10	og (Campbell)	1		11	u	2	s6	7	8	s3		9				6	u	10					5	3	s7	4								11
12	10 Nov	A	Sunderland	D 1 1 (0 0)	47,701	11	Milner	1		3	s11	2	6	7		s10	9	4					u	10				s5	5	u	11	8								12
13	24 Nov	H	Liverpool	L 0 3 (0 1)	52,307	11		u	s3	7	2		6	s7	8	9	10	4							1	u		5		3	11	s11								13
14	01 Dec	A	Blackburn Rovers	L 1 3 (0 0)	27,477	11	Martins	u	s5	3	4		6	7	8	9	ss5	10							1			2	5	u	u	11								14
15	05 Dec	H	Arsenal	D 1 1 (0 1)	50,305	11	Taylor	u		3	4	5	6	7	8	9	s4	10							1	u		2		u	u	11								15
16	08 Dec	H	Birmingham City	W 2 1 (1 1)	49,948	10	Martins (pen), Beye	u		3	4	5	6	7	8	9	s8	10							1	u		2		s9	s4	11								16
17	15 Dec	A	Fulham	W 1 0 (0 0)	24,959	10	Barton (pen)	u		3	4		5	7	8	9	s9	10				6			1	u		2		u	s4	11								17
18	23 Dec	H	Derby County	D 2 2 (1 1)	51,386	9	Viduka 2	u		3	u	s5	5	7	8	9	10	4				6			1			2			s11	11	s8							18
19	26 Dec	A	Wigan Athletic	L 0 1 (0 0)	20,304	11		u		3	4	5		7	u	s4	9	8				u			1			2	6	s11	10		11							19
20	29 Dec	A	Chelsea	L 1 2 (0 1)	41,751	11	Butt	u		3		5	s4	7	8	9	s11	4				6		s9	1			2	10		u		11							20
21	02 Jan	H	Manchester City	L 0 2 (0 1)	50,956	11		u		3		5	u	7	8	9	10					6		s9	1			2	4	s11	s4		11							21
22	12 Jan	A	Manchester United	L 0 6 (0 0)	75,965	11		u	2	7		5	s10	4	8		s4	9d				6		10	1					3	u		11	u						22
23	19 Jan	H	Bolton Wanderers	D 0 0 (0 0)	52,250	12		u	2	7		5	4	8							9	6		10	1	u				3			11	s11	u	u				23
24	29 Jan	A	Arsenal	L 0 3 (0 1)	60,127	12		u	2	3		5	4	7	8			9			s7	6		10	1	u						s4	11	u						24
25	03 Feb	H	Middlesbrough	D 1 1 (0 0)	51,105	12	Owen		2	3		5		s8	7		s9	9			u	6	u	10	1	u					8	4	11							25
26	09 Feb	A	Aston Villa	L 1 4 (1 0)	42,640	13	Owen	s1	3			5		7	8		u	9				6		10	1			2	u	u	s4	4	11							26
27	23 Feb	H	Manchester United	L 1 5 (0 2)	52,291	13	Faye	s1		3	s7	5		7	8			9			u	u		10	1			2	6			4	11		s4					27
28	01 Mar	H	Blackburn Rovers	L 0 1 (0 0)	50,796	13		1		s11		5		7	8	s8		9				u	u	10				2	6	3		4	11		u					28
29	08 Mar	A	Liverpool	L 0 3 (0 2)	44,031	14		1		7	s8	5		8	4	s11		9				u	u	10				2	6	3			11		u					29
30	17 Mar	A	Birmingham City	D 1 1 (0 1)	25,777	14	Owen	1		s9	4	5			8	9	11	u				u	u	10				2	6	3		7			u					30
31	22 Mar	H	Fulham	W 2 0 (1 0)	52,293	13	Viduka, Owen	1		s9	4	5			8	9	11	s11					u	10		s2		2	6	3		7			u					31
32	30 Mar	A	Tottenham Hotspur	W 4 1 (1 1)	36,067	12	Butt, Geremi, Owen, Martins	1			4	5			8	9	11	s11					u	10		s4		2	6	3		7	u		s10					32
33	05 Apr	H	Reading	W 3 0 (2 0)	52,179	12	Martins, Owen, Viduka	1			4				8	9	11	s8					u	10		5		2	6	3		7	s11		u		s6			33
34	12 Apr	A	Portsmouth	D 0 0 (0 0)	20,507	12		1			4	5			8	9	11	s11					u	10		u		2	6	3		7	u		u					34
35	20 Apr	H	Sunderland	W 2 0 (2 0)	52,305	12	Owen 2 (1 pen)	1			4	5			8	9	11	u					u	10		s3		2	6	3		7	s9		s11					35
36	26 Apr	A	West Ham United	D 2 2 (2 2)	34,980	12	Martins, og (McCartney)	1			4	5			8	9	11	s11					u	10		6		2		3		7	u		u		s6			36
37	05 May	H	Chelsea	L 0 2 (0 0)	52,305	12		1		s3	4	5			8	9	11	s11				u	u	10				2	6	3		7	s4							37
38	11 May	A	Everton	L 1 3 (0 1)	39,952	12	Owen (pen)	1		11		5			8			4	s5			s6	u	10				2	6	3			7	s3	9			u		38
Round			FA Cup (E.ON)																																					Round
3	06 Jan	A	Stoke City	D 0 0 (0 0)	22,861			u		11		5	2		8		9	4				u		10	1	u			6	3			7	s7	s9					3
3r	16 Jan	H	Stoke City	W 4 1 (2 0)	35,108		Owen, Cacapa, Milner, Duff	u	2	7		5	s6	4			9					6		10	1	u				3	8d		11	s7	s9					3r
4	26 Jan	A	Arsenal	L 0 3 (0 0)	60,046			u	2	7		5	s3	8	4			9				6		10	1	u				3			11	s11	u					4
Round			FL Cup (Carling Cup)																																					Round
2	29 Aug	H	Barnsley	W 2 0 (0 0)	30,523		Owen, Martins	u		11	4	5			s8	s10		7		2	9	6		10	1	s7				3	8								u	2
3	25 Sep	A	Arsenal	L 0 2 (0 0)	60,004				11	u	5	6	7	s7	9		8			10		u		1	u		2	4	3	s10									3

DateLine ... 11 Aug: Sam Allardyce selects his first United eleven against his ex-club Bolton. **3 Nov:** The Magpies concede three goals in the first 11 minutes on Tyneside against Portsmouth and lose 4–1. **12 Jan:** At Old Trafford, Manchester United hit the Black'n'Whites for six second-half goals as they win 6–0. **19 Jan:** Kevin Keegan returns to Tyneside and takes control for the game with Bolton. **23 Feb:** Manchester United inflict another heavy defeat on the Geordies, winning 5–1 on Tyneside. **20 April:** Michael Owen strikes a brace to demolish Sunderland at Gallowgate.

NEWCASTLE UNITED

SEASON 2008-09

PREMIER LEAGUE

A Third Coming and relegation shock

United started the new Keegan-era in good shape. On the opening day the Black'n'Whites headed to face Manchester United at Old Trafford and matched the Champions, stealing a point in a 1-1 draw. There was much optimism, yet there was discord behind the scenes to result in the Tyneside icon's surprise departure during September after only seven months in charge. Newcastle were in disarray – yet again. As a temporary appointment, Joe Kinnear arrived, out of football for over three years and thrust into the limelight. Unrest affected the players, disorder was evident from supporters and United stumbled through the season. They dropped into the relegation places during October, recovered to 12th spot by Christmas, then slipped into the mire again.

Kinnear, with previous heart problems, suffered a further health complaint just before a fixture at West Bromwich Albion. United's hierarchy were now under intense pressure to find someone to inspire and guide the Magpies to safety. Eventually, they turned to the man who had replaced Keegan as the Geordies hero, Alan Shearer. Without managerial experience, Shearer had little time to do anything. Newcastle were 18th with eight games left. The Magpies needed points desperately. But Shearer found it hard to motivate a dressing-room filled with discontent. United won only one game, a Tyne-Tees derby with Middlesbrough. By then two matches remained to survive the drop. A home defeat by Fulham was the killer blow. Another defeat followed on the final, desperate day of the season, at Villa Park. A point would have meant survival, but a spineless performance when a draw was for the taking incensed all.

Relegation after 16 seasons at the top was a colossal shock. United's new owner experienced an uncomfortable introduction to the world of football. And more than once the club was offered for sale. With finances now in free-fall as the high spending and high wages of the past came home to roost, to Ashley's credit he protected his investment and steadied the once fortress of St James' Park. A rapid turnaround in the club's fortunes was needed. They could not afford a prolonged period in the much different world of the Football League's Championship.

Pictured above: Kevin Nolan soon became an influential figure at St James' Park, regularly able to hit the net.

Memorabilia CORNER

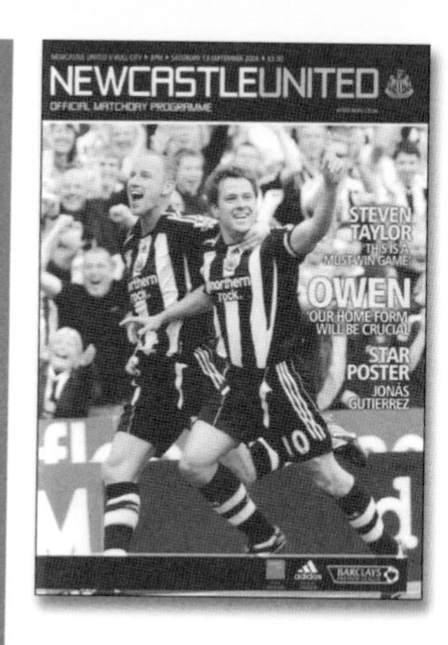

Owen celebrates again, this time with Nicky Butt on the cover for the game with Hull City.

IN CHARGE

Managing Director; Derek Llambias
Manager: Kevin Keegan/Joe Kinnear/ Alan Shearer
Captain: Michael Owen/Nicky Butt
Trainer/Coach: Chris Hughton/Iain Dowie
Club Sponsor: Northern Rock
Kit Supplier: Adidas

ST JAMES' PARK

Average Attendance
Lg 48,750 Lg & Cup 46,581

It was a period a much change at Gallowgate. Joe Kinnear (centre, front) is featured in control of United's first-team squad.

PLAYER FOCUS Michael Owen

Born Chester. Striker, 5'9"
2005 to 2009: 79 app 30 goals.

One of world football's biggest names of recent times, Michael Owen sensationally joined United at the end of August 2005 from Real Madrid for a club record £16m fee, and a substantial wage. A graduate of the FA's Lilleshall centre and a teenage star with Liverpool and England, he scored almost 200 goals before a headlining transfer to the Bernabeu in 2004. Small and quick to get away from the last line of defence, Owen though was often sidelined with injury. After impressing in a Toon shirt alongside his former England colleague Alan Shearer, he was missing with a broken metatarsal then suffered a bad cruciate injury playing for his country and out of action for over 12 months, only to return and end up on the treatment table again. All told, Owen's expensive stay on Tyneside was a letdown and he departed on the Magpies' relegation joining Manchester United on a free transfer in July 2009 where he was once more often in the hands of the medical team. When fit and on his day though Michael was up there with the best as his scoring record more than demonstrates; over 250 senior goals including 40 for England in 89 appearances. Winning FA Cup, League Cup and UEFA Cup medals, he occasionally skippered his country and became one of England's youngest players when he made his debut during 1998 as an 18-year-old, the year he became the BBC's Sports Personality of the Year. Owen is also involved in horse racing, owning a stable complex in his native Cheshire while Michael's father Terry Owen appeared for Everton and Chester.

SEASON REVIEW

Premier League: P38 W7 D13 L18 F40 A59 Pts 34.
Position: 18th, Relegated (Champions; Manchester United).
FA Cup: R3 (Winners; Chelsea).
FL Carling Cup: R3 (Winners; Manchester United).

Appearances (42m): Coloccini F 38, Butt N 37, Duff DA 31 (2), Bassong SA 30 (4), Taylor SV 27 (2), Enrique JSD 26 (2), Given SJJ 26, Gutierrez JM 25 (8), Guthrie DS 24 (3), Owen MJ 24 (8), Beye H 23 (1), Martins OA 22 (3), N'Zogbia CJ 18 (4), Harper SA 16, Ameobi F 14 (8), Geremi 13 (4), Nolan KAJ 10 (1), Edgar DE 8 (5), Lovenkrands PR 8 (4), Taylor RA 8 (2), Barton JA 6 (3), Carroll AT 6 (10), Viduka MA 6 (6), Cacapa 5 (2), Smith Alan 4 (2), Xisco 4 (3), Milner JP 3, Gonzalez IMG 0 (2), LuaLua K 0 (4).

Goals (44g): Owen MJ 10, Martins OA 8, Ameobi F 4, Taylor SV 4, Carroll AT 3, Duff DA 3, Lovenkrands PR 3, Guthrie DS 2, N'Zogbia CJ 2, Barton JA 1, Edgar DE 1, Milner JP 1, Xisco 1, own goal 1.

Dismissals: 8 players; Guthrie, Beye, Bassong (2), Butt, Nolan, Barton, Edgar.
(Beye's red card was later rescinded)

MAJOR SIGNINGS

Fabricio Coloccini (Deportivo La Coruna) £10m
Jonas Gutierrez (RCD Mallorca) £5m
Xisco (Deportivo La Coruna) £5.7m
Peter Lovenkrands (Schalke 04) free
Kevin Nolan (Bolton Wand) £4m
Danny Guthrie (Liverpool) £2.5m
Ryan Taylor (Wigan Ath) £2m
Sebastien Bassong (FC Metz) £1.5m
Gonzalez (Valencia CF) loan

FROM THE RANKS

None

TEAM COLOURS Black & white striped shirts, black shorts
(Change; all blue-purple shirts & shorts with white trim/white-grey-blue shirts, white shorts)

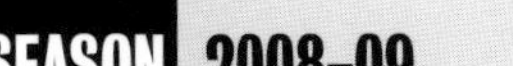

SEASON 2008-09

Match	Date		Premier League (Barclays)				Att	Posn	Scorers
1	17 Aug	A	Manchester United	D	1 1	(1 1)	75,512	11	Martins
2	23 Aug	H	**Bolton Wanderers**	W	1 0	(0 0)	47,711	4	Owen
3	30 Aug	A	Arsenal	L	0 3	(0 2)	60,067	9	
4	13 Sep	H	**Hull City**	L	1 2	(0 1)	50,242	15	Xisco
5	20 Sep	A	West Ham United	L	1 3	(0 2)	34,743	19	Owen
6	27 Sep	H	**Blackburn Rovers**	L	1 2	(0 2)	44,935	19	Owen (pen)
7	05 Oct	A	Everton	D	2 2	(1 2)	33,805	18	Taylor S, Duff
8	20 Oct	H	**Manchester City**	D	2 2	(1 1)	45,908	19	Ameobi, og (Dunne)
9	25 Oct	A	Sunderland	L	1 2	(1 1)	47,936	19	Ameobi
10	28 Oct	H	**West Bromwich Albion**	W	2 1	(2 0)	45,801	15	Barton (pen), Martins
11	03 Nov	H	**Aston Villa**	W	2 0	(0 0)	44,567	14	Martins 2
12	09 Nov	A	Fulham	L	1 2	(0 1)	24,740	18	Ameobi
13	15 Nov	H	**Wigan Athletic**	D	2 2	(0 1)	47,657	17	Owen, Martins
14	22 Nov	A	Chelsea	D	0 0	(0 0)	41,660	15	
15	29 Nov	A	Middlesbrough	D	0 0	(0 0)	32,160	17	
16	06 Dec	H	**Stoke City**	D	2 2	(2 0)	47,422	16	Owen 2
17	14 Dec	A	Portsmouth	W	3 0	(0 0)	19,416	14	Owen, Martins, Guthrie
18	21 Dec	H	**Tottenham Hotspur**	W	2 1	(1 1)	47,982	12	N'Zogbia, Duff
19	26 Dec	A	Wigan Athletic	L	1 2	(0 1)	20,266	12	Guthrie (pen)
20	28 Dec	H	**Liverpool**	L	1 5	(1 2)	52,114	14	Edgar
21	10 Jan	H	**West Ham United**	D	2 2	(1 1)	47,571	11	Owen, Carroll
22	17 Jan	A	Blackburn Rovers	L	0 3	(0 0)	25,583	14	
23	28 Jan	A	Manchester City	L	1 2	(0 1)	42,280	16	Carroll
24	01 Feb	H	**Sunderland**	D	1 1	(0 1)	52,084	15	Ameobi (pen)
25	07 Feb	A	West Bromwich Albion	W	3 2	(3 1)	25,817	13	Duff, Lovenkrands, Taylor S
26	22 Feb	H	**Everton**	D	0 0	(0 0)	47,683	14	
27	01 Mar	A	Bolton Wanderers	L	0 1	(0 0)	20,763	15	
28	04 Mar	H	**Manchester United**	L	1 2	(1 1)	51,636	16	Lovenkrands
29	14 Mar	A	Hull City	D	1 1	(1 1)	24,914	16	Taylor S
30	21 Mar	H	**Arsenal**	L	1 3	(0 0)	49,972	18	Martins
31	04 Apr	H	**Chelsea**	L	0 2	(0 0)	52,112	18	
32	11 Apr	A	Stoke City	D	1 1	(0 1)	27,382	18	Carroll
33	19 Apr	A	Tottenham Hotspur	L	0 1	(0 1)	35,850	19	
34	27 Apr	H	**Portsmouth**	D	0 0	(0 0)	47,481	18	
35	03 May	A	Liverpool	L	0 3	(0 2)	44,121	18	
36	11 May	H	**Middlesbrough**	W	3 1	(1 1)	51,252	17	Taylor S, Martins, Lovenkrands
37	16 May	H	**Fulham**	L	0 1	(0 1)	52,114	18	
38	24 May	A	Aston Villa	L	0 1	(0 1)	42,585	18	
Round			**FA Cup (E.ON)**						
3	03 Jan	A	Hull City	D	0 0	(0 0)	20,557		
3r	14 Jan	H	**Hull City**	L	0 1	(0 0)	31,380		
Round			**FL Cup (Carling Cup)**						
2	26 Aug	A	Coventry City	We	3 2	(2 1)	19,249		N'Zogbia, Milner, Owen
3	24 Sep	H	**Tottenham Hotspur**	L	1 2	(0 0)	20,577		Owen

Match	Given	Beye	N'Zogbia	Butt	Taylor SV	Coloccini	Duff	Guthrie	Martins	Milner	Gutierrez	Bassong	Donaldson	Edgar	Enrique	Geremi	Harper	Smith	Owen	Ameobi	Barton
Squad numbers	1	21	14	22	27	2	11	8	9	16	18	12	42	30	3	20	13	17	10	23	7
1	1	2	3	4	5	6	7	8	9	10	11	u	u	u	u	u	u	u			
2	1	2	3	4	5	6	7	8	9	10	11	u		u	u	s7	u	u	s9		
3	1	2	7	4	5	6		8			11	s3	u	s2	3		u		10	9	s11
4	1		3	8	5	6		7d				s2	u	2		4	u		10	9	
5	1		3	8	5	6	11					s2	u	2		7	u		10	u	
6	1		11	8	5	6	7					3	u	s11		2	u		10	s2	
7	1		11	8	5	6	9	7				s3	u	u	3	2	u		10	s2	
8	1	2d	s9	8	5	6	11	7	9			3		u	u	4	u			10	
9	1	2	u	8	5	6	11	7	9		s4	3			s3	4	u			10	s8
10	1	2	u		5	6	7	8	9		11	u		u	3	s11	u			10	4
11	1	2	u	8	5	6	7	u	9		11	u			3	u	u		s10	10	4
12	1	2	u	8		6	7	u	9		11	u			3	u	u		s11	10	4
13	1	2	s3	8		6	7	s4	9		11	5			3	u	u		s11	10	4
14	1	2	s11	8		6	7	4	9		11	5		u	3		u		10	s9	
15	1	2	11	8	u	6		4	9		7	5		u	3	u	u		10		
16	1	2	11		s8	6		8	9		7	5		u	3	4	u		10		
17	1	2	11	8	u	6	u	4	9		7	5			3	u	u		10	s9	
18	1	2	11	8	u	6	s3	4			7	5		u	3	u	u		10	9	
19	1	2	3	8	s2	6	11	4			7	5d		s10		u	u		10		
20	1		11	8	5	6	9	4			7			2	3	s8	u		10	s3	
21	1		s4		2	6	11	8			7	5	u	u	3	4	u		10		
22	1		11	8d	u	6	7	4			s7	5		2	3		u		10		s11
23					5	4	11				s10	6	u	2	3	7	1		10		8
24				8	2	6	7				11	5	u	s6	3	u	1			10	
25				8	5	2	11					6		u	3	u	1	u		9	
26				8	2	6	11		s9		s11	5			3	u	1	s10		9	
27				8	2	6			9		11	5		u	3	s8	1	u		10	
28				u	2	6			9		11	5		u	3	4	1	8		u	
29				8	2	6	u		9		11	5		u	3	4	1	7	10	s10	
30		s5		8	2	6	11		9		u	5			3	u	1	u	s2	s10	
31		5		8		6	s11	s4	9		7			u	3	u	1	u	10		
32		2		8		u	11	7			s7	5		6		u	1	u	10	9	
33		2		8	5		11	u	s9		7	6		u			1	s5	10	u	
34		2		8		6	7	s3	9		s8	5		u	3		1	4	10		u
35		2		8		6	3	u	9		s11	5		u			1	4	s9		7d
36		2		8	5	u	3	7	s10		11	6					1		10		
37		2		8	5	u	3	7	9		11	6d					1	u		u	
38				8	5	2	3	7	9		u			6d	s11		1	u	s4	s10	
Round																					
3	1		11	8	5	6	7	4			s11	2		u	3	u	u		10		
3r	1		3	8	u	6	7	4			11	5	u	2			u		10		
Round																					
2	1	2	7	10	u	6		8		9	11	5	u	u	3	4	u		s4		
3	1		11	8	2	6	7		9			3	u	s5		4	u		10	u	

Match	Ranger	Tozer	Xisco	Gonzalez	Cacapa	Danquah	Doninger	Carroll	LuaLua	Viduka	Kadar	Lovenkrands	Forster	Inman	Nolan	Krul	Taylor RA
Squad numbers	46	35	19	15	6	31	41	39	38	36	28	24	34		4	40	16
1																	
2																	
3	u	u															
4			11	s9	u	u	u										
5		u	9	s4	4		u										
6	u	u	9		4		u										
7			u		4		u										
8			u		u			s10									
9			u		u												
10			s9					s10									
11					s9												
12					5			u									
13					u			u									
14					u			u	u								
15					u			u		s9							
16			u		s4			u		s9							
17					u					u							
18								u		s9							
19			u					s9	u	9							
20			u					u	s10		u						
21			u					9	u		u						
22			u					9	u		u						
23			u					9	s7			s8	u	u			
24			u					9	u			s9			4	u	
25			s10		u					s9		10	u		4		7
26					u					u		10			4d	u	7
27					u			u		s9		7	u				4
28					u			s7	s8			10				u	7
29								u				u	u				s7
30												10			4	u	7
31								s9				11	u		4		2
32	u							s9							4	u	3
33								9		s4					4	u	3
34								s11		11		u				u	
35								u		10		11			s10	u	
36								s9	u	9		s11			4	u	u
37								s10		10		s11			4	u	s7
38										10		11			4	u	u
Round																	
3			u					9	u		u						
3r	u		9					s9	s11		u						
Round																	
2	u	u															
3		u	s7		5		u										

We — Won after extra time

Match 8 — Beye's red card later rescinded

26 Aug — N'Zogbia's goal recorded by some sources as Dann og

DateLine ... 27 Sept: Ex-Wimbledon boss Joe Kinnear arrives to take charge of United against Blackburn. **28 Dec:** Liverpool inflict a 5-1 defeat on United at Gallowgate as Dave Edgar nets on his full debut. **7 Feb:** Boss Joe Kinnear is taken ill before the game at The Hawthorns, his last in charge of United. **4 April:** Alan Shearer takes over in a bid to halt a slide and selects the team against Chelsea. **24 May:** A lack-lustre performance and 1-0 defeat at Aston Villa confirms relegation after 16 years in the Premier League.

SEASON 2009-10
CHAMPIONSHIP

Stability amidst the unrest

Experienced coach and three times caretaker boss, Chris Hughton was appointed manager, remarkably United's 10th in only a dozen years. Apart from a quick return to the glamour world of the Premier League, Newcastle United needed a lengthy period of stability after much volatility at St James' Park. Thankfully one thing was in United's favour; Premier League acumen. Having let several big names depart, they still retained a core of experienced players; several internationals included and enjoyed the emergence of local youngster Andy Carroll at centre-forward. And the gulf between Premier League football and the Championship second-tier was vast. Newcastle looked a class apart from start to finish. As a consequence of results on the pitch, stability returned to Gallowgate – and so did the feel-good factor.

Alongside United, West Bromwich Albion – relegated with the Magpies – dominated the top placings. Nottingham Forest joined the race and it was clear from an early point in the campaign that the two automatic promotion slots would be taken from the trio. Winning five of the first six matches, the Tynesiders led the table more often than not and by October were the pacesetters at the head of the division. With both the League Cup and FA Cup sacrificed for the greater goal, by the time they demolished Barnsley 6-1 during March, United were on the home straight.

They took care of rivals Nottingham Forest by 2-0, one of a sequence of seven straight victories, an undefeated run of 17 games which ensured promotion. United sealed a quick return to the Premier League before getting onto the pitch against Sheffield United during April when rivals Nottingham Forest failed to collect three points. The long trek to face Plymouth Argyle followed, a 2-0 triumph, and saw United confirmed as worthy Champions. They remained undefeated at home, winning 18 of the 23 Championship fixtures – equalling statistics from way back in 1906-07 – while they totalled 102 points, a club record.

The trophy was presented against Ipswich Town on the last home day of the season. Smiles returned to players and officials, and to supporters. The rift between fans and club, while not totally healed, was on the mend.

Pictured above: Fabricio Coloccini had an uneasy start in England, but soon showed he was a top defender.

Memorabilia CORNER

A goal for Shola Ameobi, congratulated by Kevin Nolan.

IN CHARGE

Managing Director: Derek Llambias
Manager: Chris Hughton
Captain: Nicky Butt/Alan Smith
Trainer/Coach: Colin Calderwood
Club Sponsor: Northern Rock
Kit Supplier: Adidas

ST JAMES' PARK

Average Attendance
Lg 43,388 Lg & Cup 41,501

Chris Hughton (centre, front) moved into the manager's room to take over as boss for the 2009-10 Championship campaign. It was to be a trophy winning season.

PLAYER FOCUS Steve Harper

Born Easington. Goalkeeper, 6'2"
1993 to date: 190 app 0 goals.

United's longest serving player of all time, Steve Harper first donned the Newcastle goalkeeper's jersey for a Northern Intermediate League fixture during December 1991 at a time when he also played for Seaham Red Star. A County Durham lad, he signed forms in July 1993 and has served the club for almost 20 years all-told, many as reserve custodian, being a patient substitute and on the bench in over 380 matches. Having periods on loan with Bradford City, Gateshead, Stockport, Hartlepool and Huddersfield Town, Steve made his Toon debut against Wimbledon during November 1998 and was first choice for the Magpies in that season when he also reached the FA Cup final against Manchester United. It was ten years later by the time he took over between the posts again on a regular basis, for the remainder of season 2008-09 on Shay Given's departure in January. Tall and able to pull off the unbelievable save, when 35 years of age Harper was a safe pair of hands as the Black'n'Whites lifted the Championship trophy the following campaign. He recorded a new club record of keeping 21 clean sheets in that season. Extremely popular with supporters who acknowledged his undoubted loyalty to the club, Harper has taken part in nearly 600 senior matches – either on the bench or on the pitch – for Newcastle, more than anyone else. Steve has also trained to be a referee, holding an FA licence, while he also earned an Open University degree in social sciences. He is related to pre-war United striker Jonathan Wilkinson.

SEASON REVIEW

Football League Championship: P46 W30 D12 L4 F90 A35 Pts 102.
Position: 1st, Champions.
FA Cup: R4 (Winners; Chelsea).
FL Carling Cup: R3 (Winners; Manchester United).

Appearances (51m): Nolan KAJ 47 (1), Harper SA 45, Simpson DP 41, Coloccini F 40, Guthrie DS 40 (3), Enrique JSD 36 (1), Gutierrez JM 36 (5), Carroll AT 35 (7), Smith Alan 33 (2), Taylor RA 24 (12), Taylor SV 23, Lovenkrands PR 21 (11), Williamson MJ 16, Routledge WNA 15 (2), Butt N 13 (7), Ameobi F 12 (9), Harewood MA 9 (6), Kadar T 9 (7), Barton JA 8 (7), Pancrate F 8 (11), Hall FB 7, Ranger N 7 (23), van Aanholt PJM 7, Best LJB 6 (7), Khizanishvili Z 6 (1), Krul TM 6 (2), Geremi 4 (5), LuaLua K 2 (1), Donaldson RM 1 (4), Duff DA 1, Tavernier JH 1, Tozer BPA 1 (1), Vuckic H 1 (3), Xisco 0 (2).

Goals (99g): Carroll AT 19, Nolan KAJ 18, Lovenkrands PR 16, Ameobi F 11, Guthrie DS 5, Harewood MA 5, Gutierrez JM 4, Taylor RA 4, Routledge WNA 3, Coloccini F 2, Ranger N 2, Barton JA 1, Duff DA 1, Enrique JSD 1, Geremi 1, Pancrate F 1, Simpson DP 1, Taylor SV 1, own goals 3.

Dismissals: 5 players; Smith, Guthrie, Khizanishvili, Nolan, Taylor RA.

MAJOR SIGNINGS

Mike Williamson (Portsmouth) u-fee
Wayne Routledge (QPR) u-fee
Leon Best (Coventry City) u-fee
Danny Simpson (Man Utd) £500,000
Fabrice Pancrate (PSG) free
Zurab Khizanishvili (Blackburn Rvs) loan
Marlon Harewood (Aston Villa) loan
Fitz Hall (QPR) loan
Patrick van Aanholt (Chelsea) loan

FROM THE RANKS

Tamas Kadar (Zalaegerszegi TE, Hy)
Nile Ranger (Southampton, Ey)
Ryan Donaldson (Newcastle sch, Ey)
James Tavernier
(Newcastle sch/Leeds Utd)

TEAM COLOURS Black & white striped shirts, black shorts (Change; yellow striped shirts, yellow shorts/blue & black striped shirts, black shorts)

SEASON 2009-10

Match	Date		FL Championship (Coca-Cola)					Posn		Harper	Taylor RA	Enrique	Nolan	Taylor SV	Coloccini	Duff	Smith	Carroll	Ameobi	Gutierrez	Krul	Barton	Ranger	Geremi	Kadar	LuaLua	Xisco	Donaldson	Simpson	Guthrie	Butt	Vuckic	Ngo Baheng	Tozer	Lovenkrands	Khizanishvili	Harewood	Pancrate	Williamson	Routledge	van Aanholt	Hall	Best	Ferguson	Tavernier	Inman	Soderberg	Match
									Squad numbers	1	16	3	4	27	2	11	17	24	23	18	26	7	30	20	28	25	19	42	12	8	22	46	32	35	11	13	10	21	6	10	14	5	20	41	44	47	33	
1	08 Aug	A	West Bromwich Albion	D	1 1	(0 1)	23,502	10	Duff	1	2	3	4	5	6	7	8	9	10	11	s1	s9	s10	u	u	u	u																					1
2	15 Aug	H	**Reading**	W	3 0	(1 0)	36,944	3	Ameobi 3 (1 pen)	1	2	3	4	5	6		8	9	10	11	u	7	u	s8	u	s7	s10	u																				2
3	19 Aug	H	**Sheffield Wednesday**	W	1 0	(1 0)	43,904	3	Ameobi	1	7	3	4	5	6		8	9	10	11	u		s10	u	u	u	s9		2	s7																		3
4	22 Aug	A	Crystal Palace	W	2 0	(2 0)	20,643	2	Nolan, Taylor R	1	7	3	4	5	6		8		9	11	u		s10	s11	u	u	u		2	10	s7																	4
5	31 Aug	H	**Leicester City**	W	1 0	(0 0)	38,813	1	Guthrie	1	2	3	8	5			10				u	7	9	4	s7	u		s11	6	11		s9	u	u														5
6	13 Sep	A	Cardiff City	W	1 0	(1 0)	25,630	1	Coloccini	1	4	3	8	5	6		10d				u	11	9	s11	u	u		u	2	7	s4				s7													6
7	16 Sep	A	Blackpool	L	1 2	(1 1)	9,647	3	Carroll	1	4	3	8	5	6			9			u	7	s7	s4	u	u		u	2	11	10				s11													7
8	19 Sep	H	**Plymouth Argyle**	W	3 1	(1 0)	42,898	2	Taylor S, Nolan, Carroll	1	s2	3	10	5	6		8	9			u	7	s11	4		u			2	s7	u				11	u												8
9	26 Sep	A	Ipswich Town	W	4 0	(3 0)	27,059	1	Nolan 3, Taylor R	1	4	3	7	5	6		10	9			u		11					s4			8	u	u	u	s6	2	s11											9
10	30 Sep	H	**Queens Park Rangers**	D	1 1	(0 1)	38,923	1	Harewood	1		3	10	5			4	9		s8	u		11	u	u			u	2	7	8				s7	6	s11											10
11	03 Oct	H	**Bristol City**	D	0 0	(0 0)	43,326	1		1	3		8	5			4	s11		11	u		s10	u	u			u	2	10	u				7	6	9											11
12	17 Oct	A	Nottingham Forest	L	0 1	(0 1)	29,155	2		1	2	3	8				4	9		s11	u		s10	u	u			u	6	7	u				11	5	10											12
13	20 Oct	A	Scunthorpe United	L	1 2	(0 0)	8,921	2	Nolan	1	2	3	8				4	9		11	u		s10	7	u			u	6	10				u	u	5	s7											13
14	24 Oct	H	**Doncaster Rovers**	W	2 1	(0 1)	43,949	1	Carroll, Nolan	1	2	3	8					9		11	u		s10	u	6			u		7	4		u	s11	u	5d	10											14
15	02 Nov	A	Sheffield United	W	1 0	(0 0)	26,536	1	og (Morgan)	1	4	3	10		6		8	9		11	u		s2	u	5			u	2	u	7			u			s11											15
16	07 Nov	H	**Peterborough United**	W	3 1	(2 0)	43,067	1	Gutierrez, Carroll, Simpson	1	s11	3	8	5	6		4	9		11	u		s10	u	u				2	7	u				s9		10											16
17	23 Nov	A	Preston North End	W	1 0	(0 0)	16,924	1	Nolan	1		3	8	5	6		4	9		11	u		s9	u	s2			u	2	7					s7		10	u										17
18	28 Nov	H	**Swansea City**	W	3 0	(3 0)	42,616	1	Harewood 2, Lovenkrands	1	u	3	8	5	6		4			11	s1		s9		u	u			2	7					10	u	9	s7										18
19	05 Dec	H	**Watford**	W	2 0	(1 0)	43,050	1	Lovenkrands, Pancrate	1	u	3	8d	5	6		4	s9		11	u		u						2	7	s10				10	u	9	s7										19
20	09 Dec	A	Coventry City	W	2 0	(1 0)	21,688	1	Ameobi, Ranger	1	s7	3		5	6		4		9	11	u		s10		u				2	u	8				10	u	s9	7										20
21	12 Dec	A	Barnsley	D	2 2	(1 0)	20,079	1	Nolan, Harewood	1	2	3	10	5	6		4	9	u	11	u		s7						u		8				u	s3	s11	7										21
22	20 Dec	H	**Middlesbrough**	W	2 0	(1 0)	49,644	1	Harewood, Ameobi	1	u	3	8	5	6		4		10	11	u		s9		u				2	7	s4				u		9	s10										22
23	26 Dec	A	Sheffield Wednesday	D	2 2	(2 1)	30,030	1	Nolan, Ameobi	1	u	3	8	5	6			s10	10	11	u		u		u				2	7	4				s9		9	s11										23
24	28 Dec	H	**Derby County**	D	0 0	(0 0)	47,505	1		1	7	3	8	5	6		4	9	s9	11	u		s10		u				2	u	u				10			s7										24
25	18 Jan	H	**West Bromwich Albion**	D	2 2	(1 1)	39,291	1	Guthrie, Lovenkrands	1	s2	3	8	5	6		4	s9	9	11	u		u		u				2	7	u				10			u										25
26	27 Jan	H	**Crystal Palace**	W	2 0	(1 0)	37,886	1	og (Derry), Ranger	1		3	8		6		4	9		11	u		s11		2			u		7	u			u	10			s3	5	s10								26
27	30 Jan	A	Leicester City	D	0 0	(0 0)	29,067	1		1	2		10		6		4	9		u	u		s4		u					11	8				u			s10	5	7	3	u						27
28	05 Feb	H	**Cardiff City**	W	5 1	(3 0)	44,028	1	Carroll 2, og (Gyepas), Lovenkrands 2	1	s11		4					9	u	11	u		u		s6				2	8					s10			u	5	7	3	6	10					28
29	09 Feb	A	Derby County	L	0 3	(0 1)	28,607	2		1			4				s3	9	s9	11	u				u			u	2	8					s10			u	5	7	3	6	10					29
30	13 Feb	A	Swansea City	D	1 1	(0 0)	15,188	1	Carroll	1	u		10		6		4	9			u		u		u				2	8					11			u	u	7	3	5	s11					30
31	17 Feb	H	**Coventry City**	W	4 1	(1 1)	39,334	1	Routledge, Carroll, Lovenkrands (pen), Taylor R	1	s7		4		6		u	9		11	u		u						2	8					10			s11	5	7	3	u	s10					31
32	20 Feb	H	**Preston North End**	W	3 0	(1 0)	45,525	1	Lovenkrands, Nolan, Taylor R	1	s11		8		6		4	9		11	u		u		u				2	7					10			s7	5		3	u	s10					32
33	27 Feb	A	Watford	W	2 1	(1 0)	17,120	1	Coloccini, Carroll	1	s11		8		6		4	9		11	u		s10		u			u	2	7								s7	5		3	u	10					33
34	06 Mar	H	**Barnsley**	W	6 1	(1 0)	44,464	1	Lovenkrands 2 (1 pen), Guthrie 2, Gutierrez, Nolan	1	s4	3	4		6			9		11	u		u		s3				2	8	u				10			7	5			u	s9					34
35	13 Mar	A	Middlesbrough	D	2 2	(1 1)	27,342	1	Lovenkrands, Carroll	1	s6	u	4		6			9		11	u		u		3				2	8	s10				10			7		u		5	s7					35
36	17 Mar	H	**Scunthorpe United**	W	3 0	(2 0)	39,301	1	Carroll 2, Lovenkrands	1	u	3	4		6			9		11	u		s10		s3				2	8	u				10			u		7		5	s9					36
37	20 Mar	A	Bristol City	D	2 2	(0 2)	19,144	1	Gutierrez, Carroll	1	u	3	4		6			9		11	u		u		s5			u	2	8	u							u		7		5	10					37
38	23 Mar	A	Doncaster Rovers	W	1 0	(0 0)	14,850	1	Carroll	1	2	u	4		5			9		11	u	s8	u		6				3	8	10			u				s7		7			u					38
39	29 Mar	H	**Nottingham Forest**	W	2 0	(0 0)	45,987	1	Ameobi, Enrique	1	u	3	4		6			9	s9	11	u	s10			u				2	8	u				10				5	7			u					39
40	03 Apr	A	Peterborough United	W	3 2	(1 1)	12,877	1	Nolan, Barton, Ameobi	1	u	3	8		6		4		9	s11	u	11			u				2		s9				u			7	5	s7			10					40
41	05 Apr	H	**Sheffield United**	W	2 1	(1 1)	48,270	1	Lovenkrands (pen), Nolan	1	s7	3	4		6			9	s10	11	u	s8			u				2	8	u				10				5	7			u					41
42	10 Apr	H	**Blackpool**	W	4 1	(2 0)	47,010	1	Gutierrez, Carroll, Nolan, Routledge	1	s3		4		6		u	9	s2	11	u	s4			3				2	8					10			u	5	7			u					42
43	13 Apr	A	Reading	W	2 1	(2 0)	23,163	1	Nolan 2	1	2	s6	10		6		4	s8	9	11	u	s7							3	8					u			u	5	7			u					43
44	19 Apr	A	Plymouth Argyle	W	2 0	(2 0)	13,111	1	Carroll, Routledge	1	u	3	10				4	9	s9		u	11			s6				2	8					u			u	5	7		6	s10					44
45	24 Apr	H	**Ipswich Town**	D	2 2	(1 1)	52,181	1	Carroll, Ameobi (pen)	1	u	3	4		6		u	9	s10	11	u	s8							2	8	s4				10				5	7			u					45
46	02 May	A	Queens Park Rangers	W	1 0	(0 0)	16,819	1	Lovenkrands	u	2		u		6		4	s9	9		1	7						u	3	8		s8			s10			u	5	11			10					46
Round			FA Cup (E.ON)																																													Round
3	02 Jan	A	Plymouth Argyle	D	0 0	(0 0)	16,451			u	2	u			6		4	s9	10	s4	1		9		5			u	3	7	8			u	s11			11										3
3r	13 Jan	H	**Plymouth Argyle**	W	3 0	(2 0)	15,805		Lovenkrands 3	u	2	3	8	5	6			9	u	11	1		s4					s10		s7	4			u	10			7						u				3r
4	23 Jan	A	West Bromwich Albion	L	2 4	(0 2)	16,102		Carroll 2	u	2d	3	10		6		4	9	s7	11	1		ss7		5	u		s8		8				u				7						u				4
Round			FL Cup (Carling Cup)																																													Round
2	26 Aug	H	**Huddersfield Town**	W	4 3	(1 2)	23,815		Guthrie, Geremi, Ameobi (pen), Nolan	u	2	3	8				u		s10	s11	1		9	4	5	11		u	6	7	10	ss10		u														2
3	22 Sep	A	Peterborough United	L	0 2	(0 2)	10,298				3		s8	5			s7				1		9	s10		7		10		4d		8	u	6	11									u	2	u	u	3

DateLine ... 8 Aug: Chris Hughton's first game as boss, a 1-1 draw with promotion rivals West Bromwich Albion. **22 Sept:** The side against Peterborough in the League Cup is the club's youngest ever at 21 years 51 days. **20 Dec:** Nearly 50,000 see the second-tier Tyne-Tees derby with Middlesbrough, a 2-0 win. **6 March:** A 6-1 victory over Barnsley sets Newcastle on a promotion run-in. **29 March:** Promotion back to the Premier League is assured with eight games to spare before the game with Forest. **19 April:** United clinch the Championship title with a 2-0 victory at Plymouth. **2 May:** The Magpies win at QPR and reach 102 points, a club record.

SEASON 2010-11

PREMIER LEAGUE

A new beginning 130 years on

United were delighted to be back in the Premier League after just one season's absence. It was in many ways a new beginning for the club. The Black'n'Whites were now a very different club to before. New ownership still wanted success, but had a much changed thinking on how to get there. Gone was the big spending, and so was the arrival of trophy signings.

Veteran England defender Sol Campbell was an experienced addition to the squad while United also brought in Cheik Tiote and the exciting Marseille and French international Hatem Ben Arfa. The winger scored a stunning goal on his debut but then broke his leg against Manchester City. He was to be out of action for most of the season. Newcastle started well and United crushed manageress Aston Villa by 6-0 in their first match at St James' Park, Andy Carroll celebrating wearing the famous No. 9 shirt with a marvellous hat-trick. The robust striker was to shine and reach the England side. After that fantastic opening though Newcastle's home form let them down. Winnable games on Tyneside saw United fail to pick up points. But a satisfactory away record saw United in mid-table and a 5-1 demolition of Sunderland on Tyneside put the Magpies in a comfortable position. However, Newcastle's record at Gallowgate continued to be disappointing, and they loitered close to being sucked into the relegation battle as the climax of the season unfolded. But wins over Wolves and Birmingham gave United a mid-table finish, in the end, a satisfactory return to the top flight.

Newcastle had a good opportunity to reach the latter stages of the League Cup after beating Accrington Stanley and a Chelsea line-up at Stamford Bridge in a thrilling 5-4 victory in which both sides rested noted players; it was perhaps the best ever 'reserve' fixture on record. However, against Arsenal at St James' Park a whole start-studded eleven was again left on both benches and United's second-string were no match for the Gunners, losing by four goals. In the FA Cup another shock was added to the record book, a 3-1 defeat to League newcomers Stevenage.

There were more shocks in the season too. Firstly, Chris Hughton was sacked in December with Alan Pardew appointed as United's boss then new local hero, Andy Carroll was sold to Liverpool for a huge £35m fee, the most expensive British player of all time.

Pictured above: Recovering from a broken leg, Hatem Ben Arfa gave United quality and match-winning class.

Memorabilia CORNER

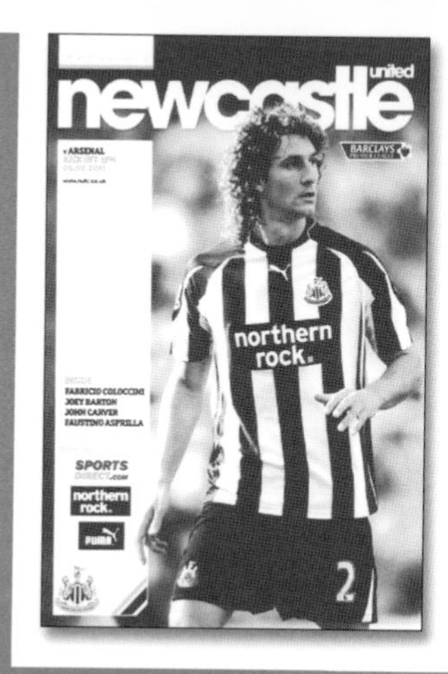

United's magazin in 2011 featuring Fabricio Coloccin comprised 86 pages, compared t the single-sheet of the Victorian era.

IN CHARGE

Managing Director: Derek Llambias.
Manager: Chris Hughton/Alan Pardew.
Captain: Kevin Nolan.
Trainer/Coach: Colin Calderwood/Steve Stone/Willie Donachie/John Carver.
Club Sponsor: Northern Rock.
Kit Supplier: Puma.

ST JAMES' PARK

Average Attendance
Lg 47,718 Lg & Cup 46,990

Pictured at the Little Benton training complex, United are back in the Premier League and custodians of the historic Football League Championship trophy once more.

PLAYER FOCUS Shola Ameobi

Born Zaria. Striker, 6'3"
1995 to date*: 303 app 70 goals.

Although born in Nigeria, Foluwashola Ameobi – Shola to all – was raised in Newcastle from the age of five and was soon in United's sights as a footballer, part of the Academy set-up as a 13-year-old when still with Walker Boy's Club. Tall, leggy and with skill on the ball, he made his senior debut in season 2000-01 and soon was an England Under-21 regular. He had a bright future, tipped to go to the very top. Although his laid back style and inconsistency frustrates many, Ameobi has served the Black'n'Whites for his whole career and on occasion has displayed the special qualities which some thought would bring him full international recognition for England. Under Sir Bobby Robson's guidance, his ability to cause problems in the box was evident in not only domestic football, but also in the Champions League and UEFA Cup. He netted 34 goals over a four season period between 2002 and 2006 and was destined to become, if not Alan Shearer's replacement, a first-rate support striker for the Magpies. He survived several managerial changes at Gallowgate and while he has been constantly in and out of the first choice line-up due to injury and that inconsistency, Shola has remained a popular character on Tyneside claiming his 300th appearance for the club and reaching full international contention for Nigeria. Two younger brothers have been in the ranks at St James' Park as well; Sammy and Tomi Ameobi, Sammy appearing in the same Premier League line-up as Shola in 2010-11.

SEASON REVIEW

Premier League: P38 W11 D13 L14 F56 A57 Pts 46.
Position: 12th (Champions; Manchester United).
FA Cup: R3 (Winners; Manchester City).
FL Carling Cup: R4 (Winners; Birmingham City).

Appearances (42m): Coloccini F 37, Enrique JSD 36, Gutierrez JM 35 (4), Barton JA 33 (2), Nolan KAJ 31 (1), Simpson DP 31, Williamson MJ 30 (2), Tiote CI 26 (2), Krul TM 24 (1), Ameobi F 23 (7), Lovenkrands PR 22 (7), Carroll AT 18 (2), Harper SA 18, Routledge WNA 12 (7), Guthrie DS 12 (3), Taylor SV 12 (2), Perch JR 11 (4), Smith Alan 10 (4), Best LJB 10 (2), Taylor RA 6 (2), Ferguson SK 5 (4), Campbell SJ 5 (3), Ranger N 4 (24), Ben Arfa H 3 (1), Vuckic H 3, Kadar T 2, LuaLua K 1 (2), Donaldson RM 1, Tavernier JH 1, Kuqi S (6), Ireland SJ (2), Xisco (2), Airey PJ (1), Ameobi SOJ (1). Gosling D (1).

Goals (64g): Nolan KAJ 12, Carroll AT 11, Ameobi F 9, Lovenkrands PR 7, Best LJB 6, Barton JA 5, Gutierrez JM 3, Taylor SV 3, Coloccini F 2, Taylor RA 2, Ben Arfa H 1, Ranger N 1, Tiote CI 1, og 1.

Dismissals: 5 players; Barton, Coloccini,Taylor (R),Tiote, Williamson.

MAJOR SIGNINGS

James Perch (Nottingham Forest) u-fee
Hatem Ben Arfa (Olympique Marseille) £5.1m
Dan Gosling (Everton) free
Cheik Tiote (FC Twente) £3.5m
Sol Campbell (Unattached) free
Stephen Ireland (Aston Villa) loan
Shefki Kuqi (Unattached) free

FROM THE RANKS

Shane Ferguson (Limavady schools, NIy)
Haris Vuckic (NK Domzale, Sly)
Kazenga LuaLua (Tyneside sch)
Phil Airey (Northb sch)

TEAM COLOURS Black & white striped shirts, black shorts (Change; blue shirts & blue shorts with white trim/white shirts & white shorts with blue trim)

SEASON 2010-11

Match	Date	H/A	Premier League (Barclays)	Result	Att	Posn	Scorers	Harper	Perch	Enrique	Smith	Williamson	Coloccini	Routledge	Barton	Carroll	Nolan	Gutierrez	Ameobi F	Xisco	Krul	Ranger	Tavernier	Taylor RA	Vuckic	Lovenkrands	Kadar	Ben Arfa	Campbell	Tiote	Soderberg	Guthrie	Simpson	Taylor SV	Best	Ferguson	Gosling	Richardson	Kuqi	Donaldson	Ireland	LuaLua	Ameobi SOJ	Airey	Match
							Squad numbers	1	14	3	17	6	2	10	7	9	4	18	23	19	26	30	34	16	29	11	28	37	5	24	33	8	12	27	20	31	15	40	42	32	22	25	44	38	Match
1	16 Aug	A	Manchester United	L 0 3 (0 2)	75,221	17		1	2	3	4	5	6	7	8	9	10	11	s10	s11	u	u	u	u	u																				1
2	22 Aug	H	**Aston Villa**	W 6 0 (3 0)	43,546	8	Barton, Nolan 2, Carroll 3	1	2	3	4	5	6	7	8	9	10	11	s7	s11	u		u	s4	u	u																			2
3	28 Aug	A	Wolverhampton Wanderers	D 1 1 (0 1)	27,745	5	Carroll	1	2	3	4	5	6	7	8	9	10	11	s9		u	u		u	u	u	u																		3
4	11 Sep	H	**Blackpool**	L 0 2 (0 1)	49,597	13		1	2	3	4	5	6	7	8	9	10	11	s7		u			u		s4		s11	u	u															4
5	18 Sep	A	Everton	W 1 0 (1 0)	38,019	5	Ben Arfa	1	2	3	u	5	6	7	8	9	10	s11	u		s1			u		u		11	u	4															5
6	26 Sep	H	**Stoke City**	L 1 2 (1 0)	41,915	10	Nolan (pen)		2	3	u	5	6	7	8	9	10	s11	s4		1	u		u		u		11		4	u														6
7	03 Oct	A	Manchester City	L 1 2 (1 1)	46,067	15	Gutierrez		2	3	u	5	6	s7	8	s10	10	11	9		1			u		u		7	s6	4	u														7
8	16 Oct	H	**Wigan Athletic**	D 2 2 (0 2)	44,415	15	Ameobi F, Coloccini		2	3	u	5	6	s7	8	9		11	s10		1	s2		u		10	u			4	u	7													8
9	23 Oct	A	West Ham United	W 2 1 (1 1)	34,486	9	Nolan, Carroll		u	3	u	5	6	u	7	9	8	11	10		1			u		u				4	u	u	2												9
10	31 Oct	H	**Sunderland**	W 5 1 (3 0)	51,988	7	Nolan 3, Ameobi F 2 (1 pen)		u	3	u	5	6	u	7	9	8	11	10		1	s10				u				4	u		2	u											10
11	07 Nov	A	Arsenal	W 1 0 (1 0)	60,059	5	Carroll			3	u	5	6	u	7	9	8	11	10		1	s10				u			u	4	u		2	u											11
12	10 Nov	H	**Blackburn Rovers**	L 1 2 (0 1)	41,053	5	Carroll			3	u	5	6	s4	7d	9	8	11	10		1	s10				u			u	4	u		2	u											12
13	13 Nov	H	**Fulham**	D 0 0 (0 0)	44,686	7				3	u	5	6	s7		9	8	11		u	1	s10				10			u	4	u	7	2	u											13
14	20 Nov	A	Bolton Wanderers	L 1 5 (0 2)	22,203	10	Carroll		u	3	4	5d	6d	s7		9	8	11	10		1	u				s10			s11		u	7	2	u											14
15	28 Nov	H	**Chelsea**	D 1 1 (1 1)	46,469	9	Carroll		u	3	u			7		9		11	10		1	s10				u	u		5	4	u	8	2	6	u										15
16	05 Dec	A	West Bromwich Albion	L 1 3 (0 1)	23,486	11	Lovenkrands		u	3	s8			7		9		11	10		1	s7				s10	u		5	4	u	8	2	6	u										16
17	11 Dec	H	**Liverpool**	W 3 1 (1 0)	50,137	8	Nolan, Barton, Carroll	u	u	3	s8			s7	7	9	8	11	10		1	s10				u			5	4		u	2	6											17
18	26 Dec	H	**Manchester City**	L 1 3 (0 2)	51,635	9	Carroll	u	u	3	u	u	5	7	8	9	10	11			1	s7								4		u	2	6	u										18
19	28 Dec	A	Tottenham Hotspur	L 0 2 (0 0)	35,927	13		u	3		10	u	5	7	8	9		11		u	1	s11				s4	u			4			2	6	u										19
20	02 Jan	A	Wigan Athletic	W 1 0 (1 0)	15,277	10	Ameobi F	1	u	3	s8	u	5	s10	7		8	11	9		u	u				10				4			2	6	s9										20
21	05 Jan	H	**West Ham United**	W 5 0 (3 0)	42,387	8	Best 3, Nolan, Lovenkrands	1	u	3		s6	5	u	7		8	11			u	s9				10				4		u	2	6	9	s11									21
22	16 Jan	A	Sunderland	D 1 1 (0 0)	47,864	9	Nolan	1	u	3	4	6	5	u	7		8	11	10		u	u				s9						s4	2		9		s11								22
23	22 Jan	H	**Tottenham Hotspur**	D 1 1 (0 0)	51,010	7	Coloccini	1	s4	3		6	5		7		8	11	10	u	u	s10				s9			u			4	2		9	u									23
24	02 Feb	A	Fulham	L 0 1 (0 0)	25,620	10		1	u	3		6	5		7		8	11	10		u	s10				s9			u			4	2		9	u		u							24
25	05 Feb	H	**Arsenal**	D 4 4 (0 4)	51,561	10	Barton 2 (2 pens), Best, Tiote	1	u	3		6	5		7		8	11			u	s10				10			u	4		s9	2		9	u		u							25
26	12 Feb	A	Blackburn Rovers	D 0 0 (0 0)	26,781	10		1	s2	3		6	5		7		8	11			u	s10				10			u	4		u	2		9	u			s9						26
27	15 Feb	A	Birmingham City	W 2 0 (1 0)	28,270	9	Lovenkrands, Best	1	u	3		6	5		7		8	11			u	s10				10			s11	4		s9	2		9	u			u						27
28	26 Feb	H	**Bolton Wanderers**	D 1 1 (1 1)	48,062	9	Nolan	1	u	3		6	5				8	11			u	s10		7d		10			u	4			2	s11	9	u			s9						28
29	05 Mar	H	**Everton**	L 1 2 (1 2)	50,128	9	Best	1	u	3		6	5				8	11	s3		u					10				4		u	7	2	9	s2		u	s9						29
30	19 Mar	A	Stoke City	L 0 4 (0 1)	27,505	11		1		3		6	4		7		8	s5	9		u	s11				11			5	10		u	2	u		s3			u						30
31	02 Apr	H	**Wolverhampton Wanderers**	W 4 1 (2 0)	49,939	9	Nolan, Ameobi F, Lovenkrands, Gutierrez	1	s3			6	5		7		8	11	9		u	s10	u			10			u			4	2	s7		3			u						31
32	10 Apr	A	Aston Villa	L 0 1 (0 1)	37,090	9		1		3		6	4		7			11			u	9	u	s5		10						8	2	5		u		u	s9	u					32
33	19 Apr	H	**Manchester United**	D 0 0 (0 0)	49,025	9			u	3		6	5		7			11	9		1	s9		u		10				4	u	8	2	u					u		s10				33
34	23 Apr	A	Blackpool	D 1 1 (1 1)	16,003	9	Lovenkrands		s8	3		6	5		7		8	11	9		1	u		u		10				4	u		2	u					s9		s10				34
35	01 May	A	Liverpool	L 0 3 (0 1)	44,923	12		u		3		6	5		7		8	11	9		1	s10	u	u		10				4			2	u		s3			s9						35
36	07 May	H	**Birmingham City**	W 2 1 (2 1)	47,409	10	Ameobi F (pen), Taylor S	u		3			5		7		8	11	9		1	s10	u	u		10				4			2	6		u			u	u					36
37	15 May	A	Chelsea	D 2 2 (1 1)	41,739	12	Gutierrez, Taylor S			3	u		5		8			10	9		1	s10	u	4		7					u		2	6		11			u			s11	s7		37
38	22 May	H	**West Bromwich Albion**	D 3 3 (2 0)	51,678	12	Lovenkrands, Taylor S, og (Olsson)			3	s8		5		7				9		1	u	u	4		10					u	8	2	6	s10	11			u			s11			38
Round			**FA Cup (E.ON)**																																									**Round**
3	08 Jan	A	Stevenage	L 1 3 (0 0)	6,644		Barton		3		4	6	5	7	11		8				1	s9				10	u			s4d	u	u	2		9	u								s10	3
Round			**FL Cup (Carling Cup)**																																									**Round**
2	25 Aug	A	Accrington Stanley	W 3 2 (1 1)	4,098		Taylor R, Ameobi F, Lovenkrands		u		u	u		u	u		s8		9		1	7	5	2	8	10	6				u					3				4		11			2
3	22 Sep	A	Chelsea	W 4 3 (2 1)	41,511		Ranger, Taylor R, Ameobi F 2				4	s6	6		s3	u	u	11	9		1	7		2	8	10		u	5	s2	u					3									3
4	27 Oct	H	**Arsenal**	L 0 4 (0 1)	33,157					6	u	4	5	u	7	s4	s10		s7			1	9		2	11	10	3			u	u	8													4

Match 12 Barton given red card after the game following video evidence
Match 14 Williamson given red card after the game following video evidence

DateLine ... 22 Aug: United announce their return to the big stage with a six goal victory over Aston Villa. **3 Oct:** Star signing Hatem Ben Arfa breaks his leg in contest with Manchester City. **31 Oct:** Newcastle thrash Sunderland at Gallowgate by 5-1 with Kevin Nolan claiming a hat-trick. **11 Dec:** Alan Pardew takes over from Chris Hughton and is in charge against Liverpool. **8 Jan:** The Magpies crash out of the FA Cup at the hands of League newcomers Stevenage. **5 Feb:** Arsenal lead 4-0 at half-time on Tyneside, yet United make a remarkable recovery to draw 4-4.

NEWCASTLE UNITED

- Wartime football; League & Cup fixtures 1918-19, 1939-40 to 1945-46.
- Other first-eleven fixtures including all friendlies, testimonials, & sundry charity, benefit or invitation tournaments.
- Northumberland & Durham Challenge Cup & Northumberland Challenge Cup fixtures 1882-83 to 1889-90.
- Reserve & Junior teams; summary, background & victorious seasons.

United in wartime

With Government backing wartime football provided a boost to the public in difficult times, and while the standard of the football was some way below normal, a competitive structure was put in place although restrictions were at times imposed on attendances. Both league and cup tournaments were arranged while clubs were also allowed to field 'guest players' due to the unavailability of their own stars.

World War One: Following the closure of Football League action at the end of the 1914-15 programme, Newcastle United took little part in the game during the First World War. They did not enter an organised competition in 1915-16, despite the existence of regionalised competitions in other parts of the country. The North East was left with only friendly games between a handful of clubs. No club sides were fielded by United during 1916-17 either, although unofficial elevens were put together by Newcastle players such as Bill McCracken and Bob Hewison.

For seasons 1917-18 and 1918-19 the club entered a team in the local Newcastle & District United League which comprised of local clubs like Benton Square and Pandon Temperance. In no way could this United team be recognised as a senior eleven, more a reserve combination with the odd appearance by a first-teamer. A few friendlies were also arranged. United continued in this wartime competition until during January 1919 when the Northern Victory League was formed to celebrate the Armistice and end of the Great War.

World War Two: The Football League programme of 1939-40 was only three games old when war was declared and the competition terminated. Friendly matches were quickly organised until a regional league system was introduced around the country, initially into 13 localised areas. Newcastle took part in all competitions, including the Football League War Cup which was competed on a north and south basis, with a regional and combined final, the knock-out tournament including a qualification system linked to league results. A Football League North and Football League South soon developed, while there were also local cup tournaments such as the Tyne-Wear-Tees Cup. These results all counted in the overall league tally, a somewhat complicated process split into First and Second Championships.

In season 1945-46, with peace restored, wartime competition was structured back to a more familiar 42-match programme in preparation for the return to a normal Football League action for season 1946-47, although still split North and South. In the same season the FA Cup returned, but on a home and away two-legged format up to and including the quarter-final stage.

Details of United's fixtures during wartime cover first-eleven fixtures and include the abandoned 1939-40 Football League programme. Match details for these wartime fixtures were reported in the local press but, unsurprisingly, not in a comprehensive manner during those troubled years. There are several differences and gaps contained in the various newspapers, however Newcastle United's staff did keep comprehensive records of all matches played and thankfully these ledgers survive intact and provide a valuable source of information. Where discrepancies exist in team line-ups, the club's record has been taken as the deciding factor.

Other fixtures

Full match details of FA Charity/Community Shield (and its forerunner, the Sheriff of London Charity Shield), Texaco Cup, Anglo-Scottish Cup as well as Anglo-Italian Cup, Full Members Cup (and later sponsored tournaments) and the wider Mercantile Credit Centenary competition are all included on the season by season data sheets. These games are considered to be first-class competitive matches.

Other semi-competitive games including local tournaments like the Newcastle & Sunderland Hospitals Cup as well as invitation events such as the Japan Cup or Cumberland Cup are not treated as first-class competitive fixtures and are included along with the friendly and miscellaneous games as 'Other Fixtures'.

Also included are competitions not fully sanctioned by the game's authorities such as the Anglo-French-Scottish Friendship Cup and the Anglo-Scottish Floodlit League as well as the local Cock O' The North League, all being played out in the early years of floodlit football during the late-1950s and early-1960s. Earlier competitions such as the North East Counties Cup are also shown.

Included are the miscellaneous tournaments United have taken part in, usually either pre-season warm-up matches, or organised events as part of an overseas tour. These have taken place since pre-war years, more commonly in modern football when sponsors have been attracted to televised mini-competitions around the world. Newcastle have contested games during the 1920s for the Copa Barcelona and Paris Sporting Cup, while they have been invited twice to take part in Spain's historic Trefeo Teresa Herrera in La Coruna and were the opposition for the Coppa del Centenario when Juventus celebrated their centenary. Recent competitions such as the Umbro Cup, Ibrox International Trophy and Asia Cup have taken place. All are recorded.

When the club have embarked on pre-season or end-of-season tours abroad these are highlighted as an 'Overseas Tour'. For many years before World War Two these were of high-status, exhibition events when much of the rest of Europe was still learning the game. Newcastle's first tour was to Denmark in 1904 and subsequently many extensive visits took place around the Continent. In the years shortly after 1945 United also went further afield for the first time, and lengthy tours to North America and South Africa took place.

Several of the games classified as 'Other Fixtures' have been prominent contests with substantial attendances. Included is the 1953 Coronation Cup which consisted of the top eight ranked clubs from England and Scotland gathering north of the border to celebrate HM Queen Elizabeth II's ascent to the throne. There have been Anglo-Scottish Cup winners challenge matches, an unofficial 'British Cup' in both 1932 and 1951, while during the pioneering days, East End took part in the Inter County Cup Challenge when the successful clubs of the regions local Challenge Cup – from Northumberland and Durham – competed for the prize of top-dog of the North East.

National events such as the Festival of Britain in 1951 and Football League Jubilee just before the Second World War, saw matches staged around the country, these are included also, as is the occasional fixture which saw Newcastle field a first-eleven in reserve competition (the North Eastern League). Games in aid of charity have been often staged over the years, to boost the funds of local hospitals and other health organisations. During the two wars, matches in aid of various war funds were also scheduled, as were games to support occasional disasters, be it the Ibrox disaster of 1902 or colliery tragedies. In the years before the Welfare State these games were hugely important. In addition, matches have been played in support of the fledgling Players' Union, Newcastle's footballers being committed to the development of the new organisation.

Throughout United's history, the club has taken part in benefit or testimonial fixtures, either for their own players, or by providing the opposition at other clubs. More often than not these benefits or testimonials have been earned for long service, or if a player has been forced to quit the game due to injury. During pre-war years players on occasion were allocated part of the proceeds from Football League matches, later all such games becoming stand-alone fixtures. In more recent times some high-profile testimonials have been in aid of charity, Alan Shearer's glitzy farewell in 2006 raising around £1.6m. Within the match data the beneficiary of these matches is named, a past United personality (indicated by*), an opposition player or, in certain circumstances, the dependants of ex-players.

The multitude of 'Other Fixtures' arranged since 1881 are scheduled season by season and include matches when United's first-team was fielded. For several games over the years a Newcastle United XI opposed certain teams, with the make-up of the side being far from the regular senior eleven. A judgement has been taken to classify these matches into either 'first-eleven' or 'reserve' fixtures, dependent on the number of first-teamers included. A schedule is also included of marginal games, when only a handful of the club's senior men played. Additionally, a few Newcastle XI matches are included in the match charts, when strictly a non-official Newcastle United side was fielded for a handful of Testimonial matches. In these instances the Newcastle side contained certain guest players. Such matches are highlighted in the data.

Northumberland & Durham Challenge Cup
Northumberland Challenge Cup

In the formative years of Newcastle United the principal tournament was the local Challenge Cup which began in a joint Northumberland and Durham format for season 1880-81. By the summer of 1890, the club decided to enter their reserve combination for the Northumberland Challenge Cup. Games prior to this are included in the following summary while matches afterwards, are classed as 'reserve' fixtures.

Reserve & Juniors teams

For the first time a summary of United's Reserve and Junior sides has been completed. The development of the club's various subsidiary teams from Victorian times to the present day is included. In past eras United fielded at times up to five or six different teams in a mix of various league and cup competitions. Apart from the first-eleven, the modern Newcastle United now only fields two other primary sides; during season 2010-11 being the Reserve team in the Premier League Northern Section A and the senior Academy side in the Premier Academy League.

Jackie Milburn meets HRH Duke of Edinburgh before the 1955 FA Cup final.

SEASON 1918-19

NORTHERN VICTORY LEAGUE

Victory joy in the North East

For two-and-a-half years since the 1915 closedown, Newcastle United had largely gone into mothballs. There had been occasional matches arranged by senior players, such as under the title of Bill McCracken's XI, and the club did join the local Newcastle & District United League with a scratch squad for season 1917-18, neither though could be classed in any way as a senior Magpie eleven. It was not until the Armistice was signed in November 1918 and the Great War came to an end that the club's officials began to clear the cobwebs away and start to resurrect what was Newcastle United. To celebrate peace the Northern Victory League was created as part of a series of 'Victory' competitions around the country. During January 1919 matches kicked off with United facing Hartlepools United at St James' Park then a short trip for a local derby with Scotswood alongside the Tyne.

The Magpies hardly fielded a full strength eleven with many players still not back home. A largely unrecognisable team was fielded with a sprinkling of pre-war stars mixed with local youngsters. Jimmy Lawrence, Bill McCracken and Frank Hudspeth were seen back in action as was Wilf Low. They guided the likes of Charles Farrier and George Fulthorpe in their first taste of what could be called senior action. Newcastle finished the Victory League in fifth place, well behind Champions Middlesbrough. Crowds were healthy with 38,000 witnessing the Tyneside clash with South Shields in April, a 1-1 draw.

Pictured above: From Gateshead, Curtis Booth was top scorer in the Northern Victory League.

Memorabilia CORNER

A marvellously designed letterhead displayed on this hand-written note of January 1919.

IN CHARGE

Chairman: John Graham/John Oliver
Manager: Director Committee
Captain: Bill McCracken
Trainer/Coach: James McPherson

ST JAMES' PARK

Average Attendance
Lg 20,143 Lg & Cup 20,143

United just as World War One has ended, in change shirts. Left to right: Mitchell, Scott, Wilson, Hall, Phillipson, Bradley, Ramsay, unknown, Cooper, Russell, Wake.

PLAYER FOCUS Tom Curry

Born South Shields. Wing-half, 5'8"
1912 to 1929: 248 app 5 goals.

Locally developed with South Shields based non-league clubs in the Northern Alliance, as a youngster Tom Curry joined United in April 1912 for all of £20 and was one of several North East products the club relied on immediately after the First World War. A good all round player, versatile in midfield, Curry spent all of 12 seasons in United's squad. Good enough to represent the Football League combination in 1919-20, he unluckily missed out on Newcastle's 1924 FA Cup triumph after appearing in several of the ties on the way to Wembley. Rivalling Willie Gibson at left-half and Ed Mooney at right-half, Curry ended up second choice to both in midfield. Tom was again on the sidelines for much of the 1927 Championship success, playing in only five games of the successful campaign. When aged 34 years old, Curry moved on to join Stockport County in January 1929 where he came to the end of his playing days. Tom then moved into coaching as Carlisle United's trainer before starting a long career with Manchester United in 1934. He was after the Second World War a respected back-stage aide to Matt Busby, sadly one of the victims of the Munich Air Disaster in 1958 when the Manchester United squad's aircraft crashed on take-off en-route home from a European Cup match in Belgrade. Curry looked after the British Olympic side during the 1948 Games in London.

SEASON REVIEW

Northern Victory League: P14 W5 D4 L5 F21 A23 Pts 14.
Position: 5th (Champions; Middlesbrough).
FA Cup: no competition.

Appearances (14m): Curry T 13, Finlay J 12, Low WL 11, Cooper E 10, Hudspeth FC 10, McCracken WR 10, Lawrence J 9, Booth CT 8, Dixon ES 8, Farrier C 7, Fulthorpe G 6, Donnelly JW 5, Ramsay AP 5, Bradley W 4, Doran JF 4, Hagan A 4, Hibbert W 4, Little R 4, Bell GW 3, Reed FTW 2, Wilson JT 2, Wilson WA 2, Best J 1, Brown J 1, Cook J 1, Cummings H 1, Gibson RJ 1, Hunter I 1, Hutchinson R 1, Mellor WG 1, Smith S 1, Wake HW 1, Wall GH 1.

Goals (21g): Booth CT 5, Cooper E 2, Ramsay AP 2, Brown J 1, Donnelly JW 1, Doran JF 1, Finlay J 1, Fulthorpe G 1, Hagan A 1, Hibbert W 1, Hudspeth FC 1, Little R 1, Wilson JT 1, own goals 2.

Dismissals: 0 players

MAJOR SIGNINGS

None

FROM THE RANKS

Tom Curry (South Shields Parkside)
Charles Farrier (Newcastle sch)
Alf Hagen (Washington CW)
Alex Ramsay (Swalwell)
John Donnelly (Newcastle sch)
George Fulthorpe (Newcastle sch)
George Wall (Chester-le-Street sch, Es)

TEAM COLOURS Black & white striped shirts, black shorts (Change; white shirts with broad black diamond stripe, black shorts)

Lest We Forget

Newcastle United unveiled a Roll of Honour memorial bronze plaque to commemorate those players, officials and staff to serve and lose their life in the Great War when with the club. For many years this was stored in a dusty corner of St James' Park but was latterly restored and placed on view in the Club Museum. It can now be seen in the Milburn Stand 'tunnel' walkway.

Five players are recorded killed in action: Tommy Goodwill, Dan Dunglinson, George Rivers, Richard McGough and Thomas Cairns. Certain other ex-United players also lost their life including James Fleming, Tom Hughes, Tom Rowlandson and Donald Bell. Several footballers returned home with injury or the effects of war. Stan Hardy was badly gassed while James Esther was wounded. Both had to give up their professional career in the game.

Serving Their Country

Several celebrated names served their country during World War One especially in the local Northumberland Fusiliers and Durham Light Infantry. Frank Hudspeth was in the Royal Navy, John King in the Scottish Rifles and Alex Ramsay in the Machine Gun Corps. Colin Veitch (left) rose to the rank of Second Lieutenant and served in France. He is pictured when in the armed services.

Certain players were awarded medals of bravery during the conflict including Tom Rowlandson (Military Cross) and James Esther (Military Medal) while Sandy Higgins also earned the same high decoration. Ex-United inside-forward Jack Thomas (right) was captured at Ypres. He escaped and was later attached to the Intelligence Corps as an undercover agent on the Continent, winning the Meritorious Service Medal.

WW1

Donald Bell VC

Only a handful of footballers have been awarded the country's most prestigious honour, the Victoria Cross. Donald Bell was a reserve full-back on the St James' Park staff in 1911 and 1912. As Second Lieutenant Bell of the Green Howards he became one of the nation's heroes. During the dreadful Battle of the Somme in 1916, Bell's company came under heavy fire and he led a courageous head-on charge on a German machine-gun post, killing several of the enemy. Not long after that he was killed in similar circumstances at Contalmaison village. Bell was awarded the VC for his brave deeds and a memorial now stands to his honour in France.

SEASON 1918-19

Match	Date		Northern Victory League	Result		Att	Posn	Scorers	1	2	3	4	5	6	7	8	9	10	11	Match
1	11 Jan	H	**Hartlepools United**	D 0 0	(0 0)	15,000	4		Lawrence	McCracken	Hudspeth	Wake	Finlay	Hunter	Farrier	Dixon	Cooper	Booth	Best	1
2	18 Jan	A	Scotswood	W 3 2	(2 2)	10,000	1	Donnelly, Fulthorpe, Brown	Lawrence	McCracken	Hudspeth	Curry	Low	Finlay	Farrier	Cooper	Brown	Fulthorpe	Donnelly	2
3	25 Jan	H	**Sunderland**	W 4 3	(2 3)	18,000	2	Hudspeth (pen), Booth 2, Finlay	Lawrence	McCracken	Hudspeth	Curry	Reed	Finlay	Farrier	Dixon	Booth	Fulthorpe	Donnelly	3
4	01 Feb	A	Durham City	W 2 0	(0 0)	10,000	1	Booth 2	Lawrence	McCracken	Hudspeth	Curry	Reed	Finlay	Farrier	Dixon	Booth	Fulthorpe	Donnelly	4
5	08 Feb	A	Middlesbrough	L 0 3	(0 0)	20,000	2		Lawrence	McCracken	Hudspeth	Curry	Low	Finlay	Farrier	Wall	Booth	Fulthorpe	Donnelly	5
6	22 Feb	A	South Shields	D 1 1	(1 0)	10,000	3	Cooper	Lawrence	McCracken	Hudspeth	Curry	Low	Finlay	Farrier	Dixon	Booth	Fulthorpe	Cooper	6
7	01 Mar	H	**Darlington Forge Albion**	L 0 2	(0 1)	8,000	3		Lawrence	McCracken	Hudspeth	Curry	Low	Finlay	Farrier	Dixon	Booth	Fulthorpe	Smith	7
8	15 Mar	H	**Scotswood**	D 2 2	(2 1)	12,000	5	Booth, Cooper	Lawrence	McCracken	Little	Curry	Low	Finlay	Gibson	Hutchinson	Cooper	Booth	Wilson WA	8
9	22 Mar	A	Sunderland	L 1 2	(1 1)	20,000	5	Doran	Lawrence	Hudspeth	Bell	Curry	Low	Finlay	Cooper	Dixon	Doran	Booth	Cummings	9
10	29 Mar	H	**Middlesbrough**	L 0 1	(0 1)	35,000	5		Bradley	McCracken	Hudspeth	Curry	Low	Wilson WA	Cooper	Dixon	Doran	Cook	Ramsay	10
11	12 Apr	H	**Durham City**	W 2 0	(1 0)	15,000	5	Hagan, og (Musgrove)	Mellor	McCracken	Hudspeth	Curry	Low	Finlay	Cooper	Hagan	Doran	Hibbert	Ramsay	11
12	19 Apr	H	**South Shields**	D 1 1	(1 0)	38,000	5	Little (pen)	Bradley	Little	Bell	Dixon	Low	Curry	Cooper	Hagan	Doran	Hibbert	Ramsay	12
13	21 Apr	A*	Hartlepools United	L 1 6	(0 3)	5,000	5	Hibbert	Bradley	Little	Bell	Curry	Low	Finlay	Cooper	Hagan	Wilson JT	Hibbert	Ramsay	13
14	26 Apr	A	Darlington Forge Albion	W 4 0	(3 0)	4,000	5	Ramsay 2, Wilson J, og (Cook)	Bradley	Little	Donnelly	Curry	Low	Finlay	Cooper	Hagan	Wilson JT	Hibbert	Ramsay	14

A* Played at Foggy Furze (West Hartlepool Expansion FC)

Note In the local press 3 of Doran's appearances are noted as Johnson. No record of this player exists in NUFC's contemporary ledgers and Doran is recorded as playing. Johnson may have been a pseudonym.

DateLine ... 18 Jan: A derby with a difference on Tyneside; a 3-2 success over neighbours Scotswood. **25 Jan:** A Northern Victory League Tyne and Wear clash ends 4-3 to the Black'n'Whites. **19 April:** Newcastle entertain South Shields in front of 38,000, the game ending all level at 1-1. **21 April:** Hartlepools beat the Magpies 6-1 at their wartime home of Foggy Furze.

SEASON
1939-40

WAR NORTH EAST LEAGUE

An eight goal sign-off

With only three games of the 1939-40 season completed, Prime Minister Neville Chamberlain declared war on Hitler's Germany and senior football all but closed down for seven years. Less than 24-hours before, United had recorded an emphatic 8-1 home victory over Swansea Town, with the Magpies netting six goals in a second-half spree. Ray Bowden grabbed a hat-trick on what was his last first-class match. Football's authorities wiped clean the record book, disregarding all matches played and mothballed the fixture list until peace was restored again. Players also had their contracts cancelled.

The government wanted the game to continue in some form although there were severe restrictions on crowd numbers attending any sporting event. To fill the gap a wartime structure was put in place of initially 10 regional leagues, and still to include a national knock-out cup. It took a season to really develop and clubs organised many friendly matches in between competitive action.

Unlike during World War One, the Black'n'Whites operated throughout the hostilities and did well in the coming months and years. In the 1939-40 wartime Football League North East, United were at the top-of-the-table alongside Leeds United, winning five games in a row as 1940 opened, but they fell out of the race as the season developed and finished a long way behind eventual Champions Huddersfield Town.

Newcastle almost went all the way to Wembley in the War Cup, reaching the semi-final. In matches with a two-legged format, the Black'n'Whites narrowly defeated Bradford Park Avenue 3-2 on aggregate in the opening round then a Tyne-Tees derby with Boro saw the Magpies again progress after a close call, this time 4-3 on aggregate. More customary knock-out ties followed with Bristol Rovers and Blackpool and at the beginning of June they faced Blackburn Rovers in the semi-final. But in the one-off contest, Rovers were handed home advantage at Ewood Park and the Geordies fell by a single goal after a goalkeeping mishap from Tom Swinburne.

Pictured above: England inside-forward Ray Bowden joined United from team of the era, Arsenal.

Programme from the 'North East Regional League' clash with Huddersfield Town

A caricature view of United's first-team as the Second World War began.

IN CHARGE

Chairman: James Lunn
Manager: Tom Mather/Director Committee
Captain: Jimmy Denmark
Trainer/Coach: Norman Smith

ST JAMES' PARK

Average Attendance
Lg 4,810 Lg & Cup 6,438

PLAYER FOCUS Benny Craig

Born Leadgate. Full-back, 5'7"
1938 to 1950: 119 app 0 goals.

Like Joe Richardson, full-back colleague on the field for many a game, Benny Craig also became one of the characters in the inner-corridors of St James' Park and served the club for over 43 years. Locally produced in Durham football and having trials with both Sunderland and Arsenal as a teenager, Craig joined Huddersfield Town as 1934 began and reached the FA Cup final with the Terriers in 1938. A runner-up at Wembley against Preston, shortly afterwards Craig made the move back to the North East to join the Gallowgate staff during November of that year in a £4,000 deal. Versatile on either the right or left of defence, Benny was a shrewd full-back and respected in the professional game. Although much of his football career was lost to the war as he served in the Royal Artillery, Benny returned to the fold and assisted in rebuilding the club, part of the Magpies' promotion side in 1948 when over 30 years old. He played on until the end of the 1949-50 season when he moved into the trainer's room at St James' Park. There he stayed for the next three decades, notably coaching United's kids to a FA Youth Cup triumph in 1962, the Magpies' first success in the competition. With Richardson, the pair formed a likable and experienced double-act to be remembered by all who came into contact with them; witty, knowledgeable and steeped in Newcastle United tradition.

SEASON REVIEW

Football League Div 2: P3 W1 D0 L2 F8 A6 Pts 2.
Position: Competition annulled after 3 games.
Football League North East: P20 W12 L7 D1 F58 A39 Pts 25.
Position: 2nd (Champions; Huddersfield Town)
Football League War Cup: SF (Winners; West Ham United).

Annulled Football League fixtures

Appearances (3m): Ancell RFD 3, Bowden ER 3, Craig B 3, Denmark J 3, Scott W 3, Swinburne TA 3, Woodburn J 3, Cairns WH 2, Hamilton DS 2, Pearson TU 2, Wright JD 2, Birkett RJE 1, Gordon J 1, Mooney T 1, Stubbins A 1.

Goals (8g): Bowden ER 3, Pearson TU 2, Cairns WH 1, Hamilton DS 1, Scott W 1.

Wartime fixtures

Appearances (27m): Craig B 26, Pearson TU 26, Swinburne TA 25, Gordon J 24, Ancell RFD 21, Clifton H 21, Stubbins A 19, Cairns WH 18, Denmark J 18, Bradley GJ 12, Park JB 12, Kelly D 8, Moses G 8, Duns L 7, Wright JD 7, Woodburn J 6, Richardson J 5, Scott W 5, Price A 3, Dodgin N 2, Green S 2, Hamilton DS 2, Birkett RJE 1, Blackburn M 1, Gallacher P 1, Gilholme AG 1, Graham D 1, Gray R 1, Hart WR 1, Howe D 1, Hudson J 1, Law JA 1, Litchfield EB 1, McVay TL 1, Meek J 1, Nevins L 1, Robson R 1, Seymour CM 1, Taylor JD 1, Thompson M 1, Westwood RW 1, Yeats J 1.

Goals (68g): Cairns WH 13, Clifton H 11, Stubbins A 10, Howe D 5, Moses G 5, Pearson TU 5, Gordon J 3, Scott W 3, Westwood RW 3, Duns L 2, Park JB 2, Taylor JD 2, Blackburn M 1, Bradley GJ 1, Gilholme AG 1, Meek J 1.

Dismissals: 0 players.

MAJOR SIGNINGS

None

FROM THE RANKS

Alan Gilholme (Backworth)
Bill Hart (Willington Quay)
Dave Hamilton (Shawfield Jnrs)

NOTABLE GUESTS

Len Duns (Sunderland)
Patsy Gallacher (Stoke City)
Don Howe (Bolton Wand)
Ray Westwood (Bolton Wand)

TEAM COLOURS Black & white striped shirts, black shorts (Change; white shirts, black shorts)

SEASON 1939–40

Match	Date		FL Division 2						Posn		1	2	3	4	5	6	7	8	9	10	11	Match
1	26 Aug	A	Millwall	L*	0	3	(0 2)	28,114			*Swinburne*	*Craig*	*Ancell*	*Woodburn*	*Denmark*	*Wright*	*Birkett*	*Bowden*	*Cairns*	*Scott*	*Mooney*	1
2	31 Aug	A	Nottingham Forest	L*	0	2	(0 2)	12,450	21		*Swinburne*	*Craig*	*Ancell*	*Gordon*	*Denmark*	*Woodburn*	*Hamilton*	*Bowden*	*Scott*	*Stubbins*	*Pearson TU*	2
3	02 Sep	H	**Swansea Town**	W*	8	1	(2 1)	17,480	14	*Bowden 3, Pearson T 2, Hamilton, Scott, Cairns*	*Swinburne*	*Craig*	*Ancell*	*Woodburn*	*Denmark*	*Wright*	*Hamilton*	*Bowden*	*Scott*	*Cairns*	*Pearson TU*	3
			FL North East																			
4	21 Oct	A	Hartlepools United	W	2	1	(1 1)	4,000		Pearson T (pen), Meek	Swinburne	Richardson	Craig	Gordon	Kelly	Bradley	Duns	Clifton	Meek	Gallacher	Pearson TU	4
5	28 Oct	H	**York City**	W	9	2	(1 1)	5,300	1	Howe 5, Westwood 3, Clifton	Swinburne	Richardson	Craig	Gordon	Kelly	Bradley	Duns	Clifton	Howe	Westwood	Pearson TU	5
6	04 Nov	A	Darlington	W	2	1	(0 0)	5,377	1	Moses, Pearson T	Swinburne	Richardson	Craig	Gordon	Kelly	Bradley	Duns	Clifton	Moses	Cairns	Pearson TU	6
7	11 Nov	A	Huddersfield Town	L	0	2	(0 2)	4,931	2		Swinburne	Craig	Ancell	Gordon	Kelly	Bradley	Litchfield	Woodburn	Moses	Cairns	Pearson TU	7
8	18 Nov	H	**Bradford Park Avenue**	L	2	3	(1 1)	5,691	4	Stubbins, Pearson T	Swinburne	Craig	Ancell	Gordon	Kelly	Bradley	Duns	Clifton	Scott	Stubbins	Pearson TU	8
9	25 Nov	A	Middlesbrough	W	2	1	(1 0)	3,537	2	Stubbins, Clifton	Swinburne	Craig	Ancell	Gordon	Kelly	Woodburn	Birkett	Clifton	Moses	Stubbins	Pearson TU	9
10	09 Dec	H	**Hull City**	W	3	0	(0 0)	2,500	2	Cairns, Clifton, Duns	Swinburne	Craig	Ancell	Gordon	Kelly	Bradley	Duns	Stubbins	Cairns	Clifton	Pearson TU	10
11	23 Dec	A	Halifax Town	W	4	3	(2 2)	5,000	2	Clifton 2, Cairns, Duns	Swinburne	Craig	Ancell	Gordon	Kelly	Bradley	Duns	Clifton	Cairns	Stubbins	Pearson TU	11
12	06 Jan	H	**Leeds United**	W	3	0	(1 0)	6,089	1	Moses, Gordon, Park	Swinburne	Richardson	Craig	Gordon	Denmark	Woodburn	Park	Duns	Moses	Cairns	Pearson TU	12
13	10 Feb	H	**Hartlepools United**	W	3	0	(1 0)	4,333	1	Stubbins 2, Pearson T	Swinburne	Craig	Ancell	Gordon	Denmark	Wright	Hamilton	Clifton	Scott	Stubbins	Pearson TU	13
14	09 Mar	H	**Huddersfield Town**	L	3	5	(1 2)	6,000	1	Scott, Moses, Pearson T (pen)	Swinburne	Craig	Ancell	Gordon	Denmark	Wright	Moses	Clifton	Scott	Stubbins	Pearson TU	14
15	16 Mar	A	Bradford Park Avenue	L	1	2	(1 1)	3,000	2	Moses	Swinburne	Craig	Ancell	Gordon	Denmark	Clifton	Hamilton	Cairns	Moses	Stubbins	Pearson TU	15
16	22 Mar	H	**Darlington**	W	3	0	(1 0)	6,000	1	Stubbins 2, Scott	Swinburne	Craig	Ancell	Gordon	Denmark	Wright	Park	Clifton	Scott	Stubbins	Pearson TU	16
17	23 Mar	H	**Middlesbrough**	L	3	5	(0 3)	9,410	2	Park, Scott, Gordon	Swinburne	Craig	Ancell	Gordon	Denmark	Wright	Park	Clifton	Scott	Stubbins	Pearson TU	17
18	26 Mar	A	Bradford City	L	1	3	(0 2)	5,950	2	Moses	Swinburne	Craig	Ancell	Gordon	Denmark	Wright	Park	Clifton	Moses	Cairns	Pearson TU	18
19	06 Apr	A	Hull City	L	1	3	(1 1)	6,000	4	Cairns	Swinburne	Craig	Ancell	Gordon	Denmark	Wright	Park	Clifton	Cairns	Stubbins	Pearson TU	19
20	17 Apr	A	York City	W	4	2	(3 2)	3,000	2	Cairns 3, Stubbins	Swinburne	Craig	Law	Gordon	Denmark	Dodgin	Clifton	Green	Cairns	Stubbins	Pearson TU	20
21	29 May	H	**Halifax Town**	W	6	1	(2 1)	1,279		Cairns 5 (1 pen), Stubbins	Swinburne	Craig	Ancell	Gordon	Denmark	Price	Hudson	Stubbins	Cairns	Seymour	Pearson TU	21
22	08 Jun	A	Leeds United	W	3	1	(2 1)	2,000		Blackburn, Bradley, Gilholme	McVay	Craig	Ancell	Dodgin	Denmark	Bradley	Moses	Gilholme	Cairns	Blackburn	Pearson TU	22
23	08 Jun	H	**Bradford City**	L	3	4	(1 2)	1,500	2	Taylor J 2, Stubbins	Gray R	Richardson	Graham	Hart	Yeats	Price	Thompson	Stubbins	Taylor JD	Robson	Nevins	23
Round			**FL War Cup**																			**Round**
1(1)	20 Apr	A	Bradford Park Avenue	L	0	2	(0 0)	5,208			Swinburne	Craig	Ancell	Gordon	Denmark	Wright	Park	Clifton	Cairns	Stubbins	Pearson TU	1(1)
1(2)	27 Apr	H	**Bradford Park Avenue**	W	3	0	(1 0)	9,470		Clifton 3	Swinburne	Craig	Ancell	Gordon	Denmark	Bradley	Park	Clifton	Cairns	Stubbins	Pearson TU	1(2)
2(1)	04 May	A	Middlesbrough	D	2	2	(1 1)	10,229		Stubbins, Clifton	Swinburne	Craig	Ancell	Gordon	Denmark	Bradley	Park	Clifton	Cairns	Stubbins	Pearson TU	2(1)
2(2)	11 May	H	**Middlesbrough**	W	2	1	(1 1)	14,551		Clifton 2	Swinburne	Craig	Ancell	Green	Denmark	Price	Park	Clifton	Cairns	Stubbins	Pearson TU	2(2)
3	18 May	H	**Bristol Rovers**	W	1	0	(0 0)	11,573		Cairns	Swinburne	Craig	Ancell	Gordon	Denmark	Woodburn	Park	Stubbins	Cairns	Clifton	Pearson TU	3
4	25 May	A	Blackpool	W	2	0	(1 0)	7,800		Cairns, Gordon	Swinburne	Craig	Ancell	Gordon	Denmark	Bradley	Park	Woodburn	Cairns	Clifton	Pearson TU	4
SF	01 Jun	A	Blackburn Rovers	L	0	1	(0 0)	14,238			Swinburne	Craig	Ancell	Gordon	Denmark	Bradley	Park	Woodburn	Cairns	Stubbins	Pearson TU	SF

W*, L*	Matches declared void because of WWII
Match 13	One of Stubbins' goals also credited to Scott by some reports
Match 22 & 23	United played two fixtures on the same day
Match 23	The result was disputed, certain reports noting a 4-4 draw with Stubbins claiming an equaliser with a shot through a hole in the net

DateLine ... 26 Aug: Billy Cairns wears the No. 9 shirt as United use numbers for the first time against Millwall. **2 Sept:** United's last game before World War Two, a resounding 8-1 triumph over Swansea. **2 Dec:** St James' Park hosts a wartime international, a 2-1 victory for England over Scotland. **1 June:** Blackburn win the War Cup semi-final clash with the Magpies by a single goal. **8 June:** Newcastle play two first-team matches on the same day against Leeds and Bradford City. **8 June:** Bob Gray becomes United's youngest player in competitive action against Bradford City at 16 years 5 months and 25 days old.

SEASON
1940-41
WAR LEAGUE NORTH

War Cup challenge again

Wartime football was expanded somewhat for 1940-41, with a wider league structure and results acting as a qualifying competition for the War Cup. Regional leagues were thrown together into one consolidated table with a somewhat complicated tallying procedure based on goal-average. Football was not quite as it was and at the same time hardly of the standard of normal peacetime action. Yet the aim was to give the increasingly war-torn public some sort of entertainment and distraction from other events. And entertain the wartime game certainly did through a cascade of goals. It was normal for matches to record four or five goals, and often many more. During January and February United hit Sheffield Wednesday for seven, and followed that with six more goals against Middlesbrough. Then they lost narrowly by 4-3 in the return match on Teesside.

Newcastle again threatened to reach the War Cup final and earn a place at Wembley. With all matches this time played over two legs, Rochdale and York City were taken care of, then another meeting with Middlesbrough was played out during March. Newcastle won convincingly this time, 4-0 on aggregate. They secured a semi-final place for the second year running by toppling Sheffield United over two legs. The Blades were one of the best around in wartime football and following a two goal reverse in Yorkshire, Newcastle hammered four goals into the net at Gallowgate.

Newcastle were paired with Preston North End, one of the pre-war 1930s elite. In the semi-final, United lost 2-0 at Deepdale and were unable to turn the deficit around on home soil. At Gallowgate a substantial crowd of nearly 30,000 was in attendance with restrictions on public gatherings in wartime being eased to allow such a gathering. Preston held a firm defence and stopped United's attack for the full 90 minutes. The 0-0 draw was enough to take them to the final and land a rare wartime double victory in both competitions.

Pictured above: Jimmy Denmark held the defensive pivot's role as the Second World War approached.

Memorabilia CORNER

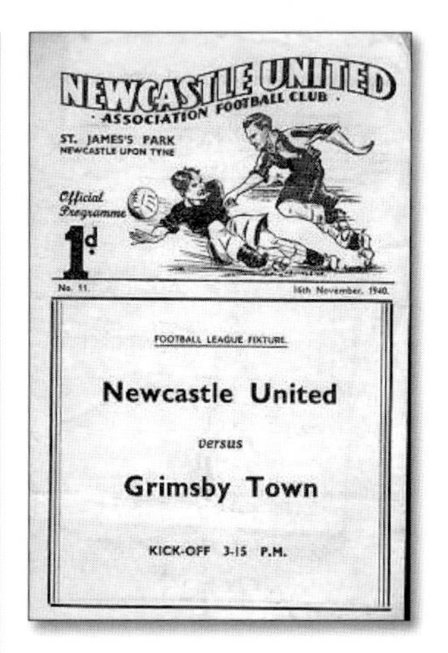
NEWCASTLE UNITED
ASSOCIATION FOOTBALL CLUB
ST. JAMES'S PARK
NEWCASTLE UPON TYNE
Official Programme
1d
No. 11. 16th November, 1940.
FOOTBALL LEAGUE FIXTURE
Newcastle United
versus
Grimsby Town
KICK-OFF 3-15 P.M.

Described as a 'Football League Fixture' this game with Grimsby Town was in the Northern Section.

IN CHARGE

Chairman: James Lunn/George Rutherford
Manager: Director Committee
Captain: Jimmy Denmark
Trainer/Coach: Norman Smith

ST JAMES' PARK

Average Attendance
Lg 3,935 Lg & Cup 6,778

1 Cam Theaker

2 Benny Craig

3 Bobby Ancell

4 Jimmy Gordon

5 James Denmark

6 Norman Dodgin

7 Ralph Birkett

8 Alex Herd

9 Albert Stubbins

10 Alan Gilholme

11 Len Duns

PLAYER FOCUS Bobby Ancell

Born Dumfries. Left-back, 5'10"
1936 to 1944: 152 app 1 goal.

A headline signing in August 1936 from St Mirren, Scottish international left-back Bobby Ancell was described as being a cultured defender, slimly built with vision and the tactical know-how at the back. He cost United £2,750 and soon became a favourite of the Gallowgate crowd during the years before war was declared in 1939. Contesting the left-back role with Dave Fairhurst, Bobby always aimed to play football from the back and was likened in style to the great Warney Cresswell of Everton and England fame. Bobby guested for a number of clubs around the country during wartime football and appeared for his country during that period too. He moved back across the border in July 1944 joining Dundee then headed to Aberdeen, both as player and trainer. Ancell then entered the managerial side of the game at Berwick Rangers, becoming a noted boss in Scotland, later guiding Dunfermline and Motherwell before a stint back at Dundee. He is especially remembered for his near decade in charge at Fir Park where Bobby built an attractive side dubbed the Ancell Babes which included many talented players such as Ian St John. When he joined United, negotiations took place on the platform of Dumfries railway station, Newcastle boss Tom Mather eventually concluding the deal amidst the steam and noise of passing trains.

SEASON REVIEW

Football League North: P23 W12 L11 D0 F49 A41 Av 1.195.
Position: 10th (Champions; Preston North End).
Football League War Cup: SF (Winners; Preston North End).

Appearances (33m): Theaker CA 31, Nevins L 30, Ancell RFD 28, Dodgin N 28, Denmark J 26, Birkett RJE 23, Craig B 20, Gordon J 20, Stubbins A 19, Gilholme AG 17, English A 16, Price A 14, Duns L 12, Richardson J 12, Blackburn M 11, Graham D 9, Billington HJR 4, Herd A 4, Short JD 4, Woodburn J 4, Cairns WH 3, Hutton TO 3, McIntosh A 3, Bradley GJ 2, Hudson J 2, Pearson TU 2, Swinburne TA 2, Yeats J 2, Anderson RJ 1, Clifton H 1, Deswart WP 1, Hart WR 1, Lockie AJ 1, Milburn JN 1, Myers J 1, Osborne F 1, Salthouse W 1, Smirk AH 1, Thompson M 1, Thompson WN 1.

Goals (66g): Stubbins A 21, Birkett RJE 9, Duns L 6, Gordon J 6, Nevins L 5, English A 4, Billington HJR 3, Herd A 3, Gilholme AG 2, McIntosh A 2, Short JD 2, Dodgin N 1, Graham D 1, Myers J 1.

Dismissals: 0 players.

MAJOR SIGNINGS

None

FROM THE RANKS

Doug Graham (Barrington Utd)
Norman Dodgin (Whitehall Jnrs)
Andrew English (Coxlodge Jnrs)
Laurie Nevins (Tyneside sch)
Arthur Price (Spen Jnrs)

NOTABLE GUESTS

Hugh Billington (Luton Town)
Alex Herd (Manchester City)
John Short (Leeds Utd)

TEAM COLOURS Black & white striped shirts, black shorts (Change; white shirts, black shorts)

SEASON 1940-41

Match	Date	Venue	FL North	Res	F	A	HT F	HT A	Att	Posn	Scorers	1	2	3	4	5	6	7	8	9	10	11	Match
1	31 Aug	H	**Bradford Park Avenue**	L	0	2	0	1	4,500			Swinburne	Craig	Graham	Gordon	Yeats	Price	Hudson	Stubbins	Cairns	Blackburn	Nevins	1
2	07 Sep	H	**Leeds United**	W	1	0	1	0	4,700		Dodgin	Swinburne	Craig	Ancell	Gordon	Denmark	Dodgin	Birkett	Stubbins	English	Clifton	Nevins	2
3	14 Sep	H	**Middlesbrough**	W	3	0	1	0	5,700		Birkett 2, Nevins	Theaker	Craig	Graham	Gordon	Richardson	Dodgin	Birkett	Stubbins	English	Cairns	Nevins	3
4	21 Sep	A	Middlesbrough	L	2	3	1	1	3,300		English 2	Theaker	Craig	Ancell	Gordon	Denmark	Dodgin	Birkett	Stubbins	English	Blackburn	Nevins	4
5	28 Sep	H	**Barnsley**	W	1	0	0	0	3,500		Birkett	Theaker	Craig	Ancell	Gordon	Denmark	Dodgin	Birkett	Stubbins	English	Blackburn	Nevins	5
6	05 Oct	A	Barnsley	L	0	1	0	0	2,000	14		Theaker	Craig	Ancell	Gordon	Denmark	Dodgin	Thompson WN	Gilholme	English	Blackburn	Nevins	6
7	12 Oct	H	**Chesterfield**	W	3	0	0	0	5,000	7	Short, Nevins, Gordon (pen)	Theaker	Craig	Ancell	Gordon	Denmark	Dodgin	Smirk	Short	English	Stubbins	Nevins	7
8	19 Oct	A	Hull City	L	1	2	0	1	3,000	10	Gilholme	Theaker	Craig	Ancell	Gordon	Denmark	Dodgin	Duns	Blackburn	English	Gilholme	Nevins	8
9	26 Oct	A	Bradford Park Avenue	W	1	0	0	0	1,571	6	Billington	Theaker	Craig	Ancell	Gordon	Denmark	Dodgin	English	Blackburn	Billington	Gilholme	Nevins	9
10	02 Nov	A	Chesterfield	L	1	5	1	5	1,781	17	Graham	Theaker	Craig	Ancell	Gordon	Denmark	Dodgin	English	Blackburn	Graham	Gilholme	Nevins	10
11	09 Nov	H	**York City**	W	3	0	2	0	3,000	9	Nevins, Stubbins, Gordon (pen)	Theaker	Craig	Ancell	Gordon	Denmark	Dodgin	English	Blackburn	Stubbins	Gilholme	Nevins	11
12	16 Nov	H*	**Grimsby Town**	W	3	1	2	0	4,000	9	English 2, Nevins	Theaker	Craig	Ancell	Gordon	Denmark	Dodgin	Birkett	Stubbins	English	Gilholme	Nevins	12
13	23 Nov	A	York City	L	0	3	0	3	2,000	14		Theaker	Ancell	Graham	Gordon	Lockie	Dodgin	Hudson	Stubbins	English	Gilholme	Nevins	13
14	30 Nov	A	Leeds United	L	2	3	1	2	3,000	15	Billington, Gordon (pen)	Theaker	Craig	Ancell	Gordon	Denmark	Dodgin	Birkett	Blackburn	Billington	Gilholme	Nevins	14
15	07 Dec	H	**Hull City**	W	3	1	2	1	2,415	12	Nevins, Stubbins 2	Theaker	Craig	Ancell	Gordon	Denmark	Dodgin	Birkett	Stubbins	English	Blackburn	Nevins	15
16	25 Dec	H	**Middlesbrough**	L	1	3	1	2	4,500	17	Stubbins	Theaker	Craig	Ancell	Gordon	Hutton	Dodgin	Birkett	Stubbins	Billington	Osborne	Salthouse	16
17	28 Dec	H	**Grimsby Town**	W	5	2	2	1	3,654	11	Gordon 2 (1 pen), Birkett, Billington, Herd	Theaker	Craig	Ancell	Gordon	Hutton	Dodgin	Birkett	Stubbins	Billington	Herd	Milburn JN	17
18	11 Jan	A*	Grimsby Town	L	0	4	0	1	3,500	21		Theaker	Craig	Ancell	Deswart	Denmark	Dodgin	Birkett	Blackburn	Gordon	Gilholme	Nevins	18
19	25 Jan	H	**Sheffield Wednesday**	W	7	1	6	0	2,500	11	Herd, Birkett, Stubbins 4, Gordon	Theaker	Craig	Ancell	Gordon	Denmark	Dodgin	Birkett	Herd	Stubbins	Woodburn	Duns	19
20	01 Feb	H	**Middlesbrough**	W	6	2	3	2	4,500	8	Duns, Herd, Birkett, Stubbins 3	Theaker	Craig	Ancell	Gordon	Denmark	Price	Birkett	Herd	Stubbins	Duns	Nevins	20
21	08 Feb	A	Middlesbrough	L	3	4	1	3	1,700	8	Stubbins 3	Theaker	Herd	Ancell	Hart	Denmark	Price	Duns	Thompson M	Stubbins	Gilholme	Nevins	21
22	15 Mar	A	Sheffield Wednesday	L	0	2	0	0	1,371			Theaker	Richardson	Graham	Price	Yeats	Bradley	Birkett	Duns	English	Gilholme	Nevins	22
23	03 May	H	**Leeds United**	W	3	2	2	1	3,187	10	Stubbins 2, Myers	Theaker	Graham	Ancell	Price	Denmark	Dodgin	Birkett	Myers	Stubbins	Gilholme	Nevins	23
Round			**FL War Cup**																				**Round**
1(1)	15 Feb	H	**Rochdale**	L	1	2	0	0	4,385		McIntosh	Theaker	Richardson	Ancell	Dodgin	Hutton	Price	Pearson TU	McIntosh	English	Woodburn	Nevins	1(1)
1(2)	22 Feb	A	Rochdale	W	3	1	2	1	3,000		Stubbins 3	Theaker	Richardson	Ancell	Dodgin	Denmark	Price	Birkett	Duns	Stubbins	Woodburn	Nevins	1(2)
2(1)	01 Mar	A	York City	D	1	1	0	0	4,935		Duns	Theaker	Craig	Ancell	Richardson	Denmark	Dodgin	Birkett	McIntosh	Duns	Gilholme	Nevins	2(1)
2(2)	08 Mar	H	**York City**	W	4	1	2	1	6,391		Stubbins 2, Birkett, McIntosh	Theaker	Richardson	Ancell	Price	Denmark	Bradley	Birkett	Duns	Stubbins	McIntosh	Nevins	2(2)
3(1)	22 Mar	A	Middlesbrough	W	1	0	1	0	12,799		Duns	Theaker	Richardson	Graham	Price	Denmark	Dodgin	Birkett	Woodburn	Duns	Gilholme	Nevins	3(1)
3(2)	29 Mar	H	**Middlesbrough**	W	3	0	0	0	12,397		Birkett, Duns, Gilholme	Theaker	Richardson	Graham	Price	Denmark	Dodgin	Birkett	Anderson	Duns	Gilholme	Nevins	3(2)
4(1)	05 Apr	A	Sheffield United	L	0	2	0	1	5,745			Theaker	Richardson	Graham	Price	Denmark	Dodgin	Birkett	Ancell	English	Gilholme	Nevins	4(1)
4(2)	12 Apr	H	**Sheffield United**	W	4	0	0	0	17,747		Short, Duns 2 (1 pen), Birkett	Theaker	Richardson	Ancell	Price	Denmark	Dodgin	Birkett	Duns	Cairns	Short	Nevins	4(2)
SF(1)	19 Apr	A	Preston North End	L	0	2	0	0	23,000			Theaker	Richardson	Ancell	Price	Denmark	Dodgin	Birkett	Short	Duns	Gilholme	Nevins	SF(1)
SF(2)	26 Apr	H	**Preston North End**	D	0	0	0	0	29,931			Theaker	Richardson	Ancell	Price	Denmark	Dodgin	Birkett	Short	Stubbins	Pearson TU	Nevins	SF(2)

H* Scheduled for Grimsby but played at Newcastle by agreement
A* Played at Old Showground, Scunthorpe

DateLine ... 8 Feb: Scotland defeat England 3-2 in the wartime international at Gallowgate. **22 Feb:** Albert Stubbins strikes his fourth consecutive hat-trick for United against Rochdale. **8 March:** Stubbins nearly makes it five hat-tricks in a row with two goals against York City. **26 April:** United are eliminated in the semi-final of the War Cup by Preston, 2-0 on aggregate.

SEASON **1941-42**

WAR LEAGUE NORTH

Stubbins leads the line

The complicated league structure continued with all of England's participating clubs being rolled together with the league championship being split as the 'First' and 'Second' competitions, before and after Christmas. With United's peacetime squad by now decimated with players entering the armed services or back in their native areas on essential war work, the club relied heavily on local talent from around Tyneside. One pre-war youngster came to the forefront, Albert Stubbins who had been recognised as a promising starlet before war, and since employed as a draughtsman, an essential occupation in the Tyne and Wear shipyards. He started to rattle in the goals during season 1941-42, claiming 33, but that was just the start of over 200 goals for the Black'n'Whites in wartime football.

High scoring matches continued with Middlesbrough suffering two seven goal defeats by the Magpies in the space of two weekends during December. Stubbins was to hit five goals at Ayresome Park and then struck another five goal haul against Gateshead at the end of the season in May.

Wartime football did bring the benefit of competitive fixtures against Newcastle's closest neighbours, Gateshead, for the first time. The Redheugh Park club were a Football League side at the time, members of the Third Division North and had even tasted Second Division football. Entering wartime action for season 1941-42, the Magpies met Gateshead on 24 occasions during those years, a local Tyne derby which has never been repeated except for the occasional friendly match.

United had an ordinary 'First' championship, finishing in 15th place, and did not improve for the 'Second' competition which ran from 27th December to 30th May. The first 22 clubs in the table qualified for the War Cup, but the Magpies did not get anywhere near the knock-out stage of the tournament.

Pictured above: Although never reaching the League side, at outside-left Charlie Woollett shined in wartime.

Memorabilia CORNER

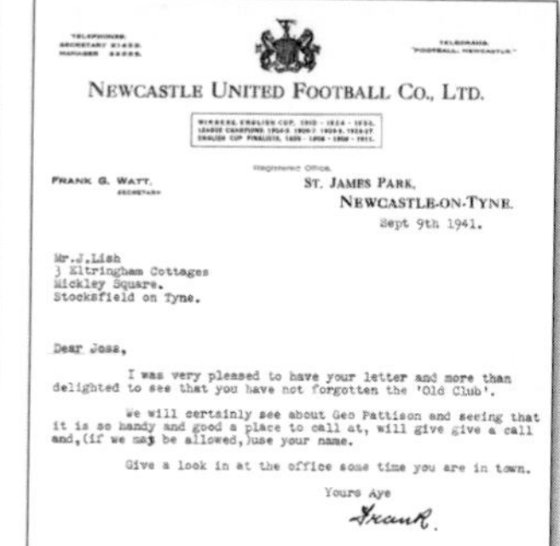

NEWCASTLE UNITED FOOTBALL CO., LTD.

FRANK G. WATT, SECRETARY

Registered Office, ST. JAMES PARK, NEWCASTLE-ON-TYNE.

Sept 9th 1941.

Mr.J.Lish
3 Eltringham Cottages
Mickley Square.
Stocksfield on Tyne.

Dear Joss,

I was very pleased to have your letter and more than delighted to see that you have not forgotten the 'Old Club'.

We will certainly see about Geo Pattison and seeing that it is so handy and good a place to call at, will give give a call and,(if we may be allowed,)use your name.

Give a look in at the office some time you are in town.

Yours Aye

Frank.

By 1941 correspondence was typed, not hand-written, in this note to a local scout.

IN CHARGE

Chairman: George Rutherford
Manager: Director Committee
Captain: Joe Richardson
Trainer/Coach: Norman Smith

ST JAMES' PARK

Average Attendance
Lg 7,595 Lg & Cup 8,762

PLAYER FOCUS Doug Graham

Born Ashington. Left-back, 5'10"
1940 to 1950: 164 app 1 goal.

Nicknamed The Duke when he was at St James' Park for his smart and trendy attire, Doug Graham like many of this era was unlucky to lose his prime footballing years to the Second World War. From a coal mining background, he joined United from Barrington United in August 1940 and was a promising youngster as the hostilities developed. Doug was one of United's mainstays during wartime football, appearing on 90 occasions for the Black'n'Whites during the conflict. He was on the field during some remarkable games, a 9-0 victory over Leeds United included. A versatile player, operating in both full-back roles and at half-back too, Graham was a stylish, upright footballer. As United pushed to gain their top-tier status in 1947-48, he was a solid performer and claimed a regular place at left-back until injury put him on the sidelines before Christmas, losing his place to the experienced Benny Craig. Graham moved to Deepdale in November 1950 when he joined Preston for a sizable £8,000 fee but he failed to claim a place and afterwards assisted Lincoln City for almost six years. Skipper of the Imps, Doug totalled over 200 games for Lincoln where he also experienced the success of promotion at Sincil Bank in 1951-52 as Third Division North Champions. Graham then turned to coaching, firstly in Switzerland then back on Tyneside with Gateshead. He married the daughter of United's long-time trainer Norman Smith.

1 Cam Theaker

2 Joe Richardson

3 Doug Graham

4 James Denmark

5 Phil Taylor

6 Frank Soo

7 Tommy Walker

8 Johnny Dixon

9 Albert Stubbins

10 Stan Pearson

11 Walter Boyes

SEASON REVIEW

Football League North: First Champ; P18 W7 D6 L5 F46 A39 Pts 20.
Second Champ; P17 W5 D6 L6 F33 A40 Pts 16.
Position: First Champ, 15th (Champions; Blackpool).
Second Champ, did not qualify (Champions; Manchester United).
Football League War Cup: Did not qualify (Winners; Wolverhampton Wanderers).

Appearances (35m): Graham D 35, Theaker CA 34, Smith T 30, Stubbins A 26, Richardson J 24, Price A 23, Hart WR 22, Short JD 20, Birkett RJE 15, Walker TJ 15, Dodgin N 14, Woollett C 13, Wayman C 12, Hunter JB 8, Denmark J 7, Howdon S 7, Taylor PH 7, Balmer J 6, Donaldson RS 5, Pearson SC 5, Dixon JT 4, Robson R 4, Walshaw K 4, Gilholme AG 3, Spike S 3, Anderson RJ 2, Boyes WE 2, Craig B 2, Gordon J 2, Kinghorn WJD 2, McKerrell D 2, Nevins L 2, Peppitt S 2, Simpson TG 2, Soo F 2, Surtees J 2, Watters J 2, Duns L 1, Eastham H 1, Hubble L 1, King R 1, McInnes JS 1, McQuade G 1, Meek J 1, Pearson TU 1, Robinson JA 1, Steel W 1, Varty TH 1, Watson JF 1, Willitts J 1, Woodburn J 1, Yeats J 1.

Goals (79g): Stubbins A 33, Short JD 17, Woollett C 5, Wayman C 4, Birkett RJE 3, Dixon JT 2, Surtees J 2, Woodburn J 2, Anderson RJ 1, Balmer J 1, Donaldson RS 1, Hart WR 1, Howdon S 1, Meek J 1, Price A 1, Robson R 1, Walker TJ 1, Watters J 1, own goal 1.

Dismissals: 0 players.

MAJOR SIGNINGS

None

FROM THE RANKS

Ray King (Amble)
Tom Smith (Horden CW)
Tommy Walker (Netherton Jnrs)
Johnny Dixon (Reyrolles)
Charlie Woollett (Eppleton CW)

NOTABLE GUESTS

Eddie Carr (Arsenal)
Wally Boyes (Everton)
Stan Pearson (Manchester Utd)
Jackie Robinson (Sheffield Wed)
Frank Soo (Stoke City)
Jack Balmer, Harry Eastham & Phil Taylor (all Liverpool)

TEAM COLOURS Black & white striped shirts, black shorts (Change; white shirts, black shorts)

Match	Date		Opponent	Res			HT	Att	Posn	Scorers	1	2	3	4	5	6	7	8	9	10	11	Match
			FL North (First Championship)																			
1	30 Aug	H	**Bradford City**	D	1	1	(0 1)	6,046		Birkett	Theaker	Richardson	Graham	Price	Denmark	Dodgin	Birkett	Howdon	Stubbins	Gilholme	Hunter	1
2	06 Sep	A	Bradford City	D	1	1	(0 1)	2,106		Anderson	Theaker	Spike	Graham	Price	Smith	Soo	Birkett	Howdon	Anderson	Gilholme	McKerrell	2
3	13 Sep	A	Huddersfield Town	L	0	5	(0 2)	6,991			Theaker	Spike	Graham	Price	Smith	Soo	Hunter	Taylor PH	Anderson	Gilholme	Steel	3
4	20 Sep	H	**Huddersfield Town**	W	3	1	(2 1)	5,500		Stubbins 2, Price	Theaker	Richardson	Graham	Price	Smith	Dodgin	Hunter	Gordon	Stubbins	Wayman	Robson	4
5	27 Sep	H	**York City**	W	5	3	(3 1)	7,900		Stubbins 3 (2 pens), Watters, Birkett	Theaker	Richardson	Graham	Price	Smith	Dodgin	Birkett	Stubbins	Watters	Wayman	Hunter	5
6	04 Oct	A	York City	D	2	2	(0 1)	4,500		Stubbins 2 (1 pen)	Theaker	Richardson	Graham	Price	Smith	Dodgin	Birkett	Stubbins	Watters	Wayman	Hunter	6
7	11 Oct	A	Gateshead	D	1	1	(0 0)	12,000		Stubbins	Theaker	Richardson	Graham	Price	Smith	Dodgin	Hunter	Short	Stubbins	Wayman	McKerrell	7
8	18 Oct	H	**Gateshead**	W	3	1	(3 0)	12,000		Stubbins 2, Wayman	Theaker	Richardson	Graham	Price	Smith	Dodgin	Hunter	Short	Stubbins	Wayman	Pearson TU	8
9	25 Oct	H	**Sunderland**	D	1	1	(1 0)	22,000		Wayman	Theaker	Richardson	Graham	Price	Smith	Dodgin	Birkett	Short	Stubbins	Wayman	Peppitt	9
10	01 Nov	A	Sunderland	L	2	3	(0 1)	12,000		Short, Stubbins	Theaker	Richardson	Graham	Hart	Smith	Price	Birkett	Short	Stubbins	Wayman	Peppitt	10
11	08 Nov	A	Bradford Park Avenue	D	0	0	(0 0)	4,700			Theaker	Richardson	Graham	Denmark	Smith	Price	Hunter	Watson	Walshaw	Wayman	Robson	11
12	15 Nov	H	**Bradford Park Avenue**	W	3	1	(2 1)	5,000	13	Short, Stubbins, Birkett	Theaker	Richardson	Graham	Denmark	Smith	Dodgin	Birkett	Short	Stubbins	Wayman	Robson	12
13	22 Nov	H	**Leeds United**	W	4	2	(2 2)	4,500		Meek (pen), Wayman 2, og (Daniels)	Theaker	Richardson	Graham	Denmark	Smith	Dodgin	Birkett	Meek	Walshaw	Wayman	Nevins	13
14	29 Nov	A	Leeds United	L	2	5	(1 1)	3,000	14	Surtees 2 (1 pen)	Theaker	Richardson	Graham	Denmark	Smith	Dodgin	Birkett	Surtees	Walshaw	Wayman	Varty	14
15	06 Dec	A	Middlesbrough	W	7	0	(5 0)	3,000	13	Stubbins 5, Short, Woollett	Theaker	Craig	Graham	Hart	Smith	Dodgin	Walker	Short	Stubbins	Wayman	Woollett	15
16	13 Dec	H	**Middlesbrough**	W	7	4	(2 3)	8,920	10	Short 4, Woodburn 2, Stubbins	Theaker	Richardson	Graham	Hart	Smith	Dodgin	Walker	Short	Stubbins	Woodburn	Woollett	16
17	20 Dec	A	Sheffield Wednesday	L	2	4	(1 3)	4,000	11	Dixon 2	Theaker	Willitts	Graham	Hart	Smith	Price	Walker	Dixon	Walshaw	Pearson SC	Nevins	17
18	25 Dec	H	**Sheffield Wednesday**	L	2	4	(1 2)	10,000	15	Stubbins 2 (1 pen)	Theaker	Graham	Hubble	Hart	Yeats	McInnes	Walker	Short	Stubbins	Balmer	Woollett	18
			FL North (Second Championship) & FL War Cup (Qualifying)																			
19	27 Dec	A	Gateshead	D	2	2	(0 0)	10,000		Stubbins 2 (1 pen)	Theaker	Gordon	Graham	Hart	Taylor PH	Price	Birkett	Short	Stubbins	Pearson SC	Woollett	19
20	03 Jan	H	**Gateshead**	W	4	2	(2 0)	17,218		Balmer, Woollett, Stubbins, Short	Theaker	Richardson	Graham	Hart	Taylor PH	Dodgin	Birkett	Short	Stubbins	Balmer	Woollett	20
21	10 Jan	A	Sunderland	D	2	2	(2 0)	10,459		Stubbins, Short	Theaker	Richardson	Graham	Hart	Taylor PH	Dodgin	Birkett	Short	Stubbins	Balmer	Woollett	21
22	17 Jan	H	**Sunderland**	W	2	1	(0 1)	19,728	10	Stubbins, Short	Theaker	Richardson	Graham	Taylor PH	Smith	Hart	Birkett	Short	Stubbins	Balmer	Eastham	22
23	07 Feb	A	Rotherham United	L	1	2	(1 1)	3,000		Robson	Theaker	Richardson	Graham	Price	Smith	Hart	Walker	Dixon	Simpson	Surtees	Robson	23
24	14 Feb	H	**Rotherham United**	L	1	3	(0 1)	6,200	23	Woollett	Theaker	Richardson	Graham	Taylor PH	Smith	Hart	Birkett	Short	Stubbins	Balmer	Woollett	24
25	21 Feb	A	Middlesbrough	L	1	4	(1 4)	3,000		Short	Theaker	Spike	Graham	Price	Smith	Hart	Walker	Short	Stubbins	Pearson SC	Woollett	25
26	28 Feb	H	**Middlesbrough**	D	1	1	(0 1)	8,000	31	Short	Theaker	Craig	Graham	Price	Smith	Hart	Walker	Short	Stubbins	Robinson	Boyes	26
27	14 Mar	A	Sheffield United	D	0	0	(0 0)	8,019			Theaker	Smith	Graham	Price	Denmark	Hart	Walker	Short	Simpson	Pearson SC	Kinghorn	27
28	28 Mar	H	**Sheffield United**	L	1	6	(1 2)	9,000	38	Stubbins	Theaker	Smith	Graham	Price	Taylor PH	Hart	Birkett	Duns	Stubbins	Pearson SC	Boyes	28
			FL North (Second Championship)																			
29	21 Mar	H	**Preston North End**	D	4	4	(2 1)	7,918		Short 3, Stubbins	Theaker	Smith	Graham	Price	Denmark	Hart	Walker	Stubbins	Short	Balmer	Kinghorn	29
30	04 Apr	A	Gateshead	L	0	4	(0 2)	2,774			Theaker	Richardson	Graham	Donaldson RS	Smith	Hart	Walker	Dixon	Stubbins	Short	Woollett	30
31	06 Apr	H	**Gateshead**	L	0	2	(0 1)	4,658			Theaker	Richardson	Graham	Donaldson RS	Smith	Hart	Walker	Dixon	Stubbins	Howdon	Woollett	31
32	11 Apr	A	Middlesbrough	W	3	2	(2 0)	2,500		Woollett, Howdon, Hart	Theaker	Richardson	Graham	Price	Smith	Hart	Walker	Donaldson RS	Stubbins	Howdon	Woollett	32
33	18 Apr	H	**Middlesbrough**	W	3	1	(1 0)	4,888		Woollett, Stubbins, Short	Theaker	Richardson	Graham	Price	Smith	Hart	Walker	Short	Stubbins	Howdon	Woollett	33
34	09 May	H	**Gateshead**	W	6	2	(2 1)	3,500		Stubbins 5, Donaldson RS	Theaker	Richardson	Graham	Price	Smith	Hart	Walker	Donaldson RS	Stubbins	Howdon	Woollett	34
35	25 May	H	**Sunderland**	D	2	2	(1 1)	3,500	37	Short (pen), Walker	King	Richardson	Graham	Price	Smith	Hart	Walker	Donaldson RS	Short	Howdon	McQuade	35

Match 10 Some reports note that Dodgin played instead of Price

DateLine ... 6 Dec: Albert Stubbins records a five goal haul in the 7–0 victory over Boro. **13 Dec:** United hit seven goals against Middlesbrough for the second time in the space of a week. **28 March:** Sheffield United inflict a shock 6–1 defeat on the Magpies at St James' Park. **9 May:** Stubbins registers another five goals in a 6–2 win over Gateshead.

Guest players make their mark

A similar format of football continued, and United improved in season 1942-43 with goals by the bagful being scored – some 113 in total during the campaign. Albert Stubbins was now on fire claiming 42 goals in the season. He was joined by several new faces as United took advantage of the introduced 'Guest' system of player registration which allowed clubs to field any footballer who was temporarily in their region, either in war employment, in the services or back at their home. Several famous names pulled on the black-and-white shirts as a consequence; pre-war stars like Alex Herd and Ray Westwood and icons of the Fifties such as Tom Finney and Stan Mortensen. Other North East raised guests made a big impact at Gallowgate, notably Eddie Carr and John Short.

After the split in championships, United this time qualified for the War Cup, and went into a preliminary regional league, another test to see which clubs could make the grade to the actual knock-out stage of the competition. The Magpies finished in 12th spot and squeezed into the knock-out draw. They faced York City but lost 4-3 on aggregate and went out at the first serious hurdle.

As a result of the more locally based football, the Tynesiders met neighbouring clubs on several occasions during the season. Apart from Gateshead and the likes of York City, what could be termed derby matches were soon to be scheduled against Hartlepools United and Darlington, a club which fielded a strong line-up made up of many guest footballers stationed in the North Yorkshire camps. During 1942-43 United met Leeds on six occasions and scored an incredible 28 goals against the Tykes. In the final match of the sequence the Magpies led by four goals with 20 minutes left on the referee's watch, only to lose by 5-4!

Pictured above: Tom Finney (left) and Stan Mortensen, two United guest players to become huge post-war stars.

Memorabilia CORNER

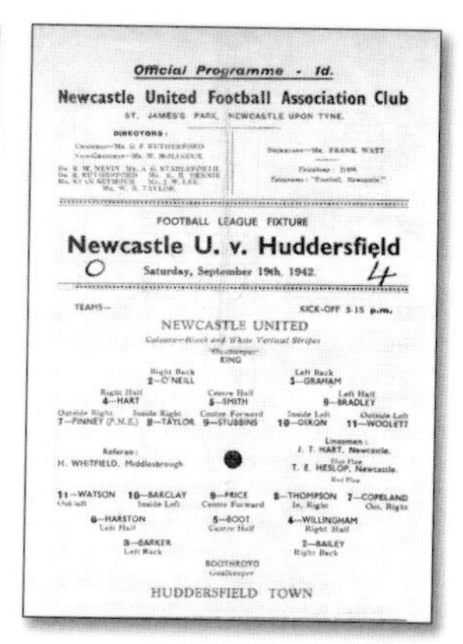
Official Programme - 1d.
Newcastle United Football Association Club
ST. JAMES'S PARK, NEWCASTLE UPON TYNE.
FOOTBALL LEAGUE FIXTURE
Newcastle U. v. Huddersfield
Saturday, September 19th, 1942.
NEWCASTLE UNITED
KING
2—O'NEILL 3—GRAHAM
4—HART 5—SMITH 6—BRADLEY
7—FINNEY (P.N.E.) 8—TAYLOR 9—STUBBINS 10—DIXON 11—WOOLETT
11—WATSON 10—BARCLAY 9—PRICE 8—THOMPSON 7—COPELAND
6—HARSTON 5—BOOT 4—WILLINGHAM
3—BARKER 2—BAILEY
BOOTHROYD
HUDDERSFIELD TOWN

With war rationing, programmes were reduced to a single-sheet displaying little more than the proposed teams.

IN CHARGE

Chairman: George Rutherford
Manager: Director Committee
Captain: Joe Richardson
Trainer/Coach: Norman Smith

ST JAMES' PARK

Average Attendance
Lg 8,866 Lg & Cup 10,608

PLAYER FOCUS Jimmy Gordon

Born Fauldhouse. Right-half, 5'7"
1935 to 1945: 253 app 21 goals.

United's wartime line-up contained a mix of youngsters, big-name signings and experienced pre-war veterans. A Scot from West Lothian, Jimmy Gordon was one of the latter, a tried and tested midfielder who had served the Magpies in four seasons before senior football closed its doors. He had settled on Tyneside from Wishaw Juniors as a 19-year-old during April 1935 having impressed boss Andy Cunningham playing in the Scottish Junior Cup. A polished footballer in the thick of the action, Jimmy broke into United's line-up during season 1935-36 and was tipped for a Scottish cap before war erupted, yet unluckily was injured when a certainty to pull on his country's blue jersey. A fixture for the Magpies in wartime football, he was dogged in winning the ball and rarely flustered. Gordon also had a mighty throw which he used to good effect. He was over 30 years of age when Football League action resumed in 1946 and by then Jimmy moved down the North East coast to join Middlesbrough, signing for a £3,500 fee in November 1945. Gordon continued playing in 253 games for Boro when past his 30th year. He entered coaching at Ayresome Park in 1955 and soon tutored a young and enterprising Brian Clough, then later assisted him at both Derby and Nottingham Forest, part of the managerial team that lifted a string of trophies, including the European Cup. Jimmy once led out Forest at Wembley in the League Cup final and didn't retire from the game until 1981.

1 Ray King *2 Joe Richardson* *3 John Connor* *4 Jimmy Woodburn* *5 Allenby Chilton* *6 Bob Batey*

7 Tom Finney *8 John Short* *9 Albert Stubbins* *10 Eddie Carr* *11 Jimmy Mullen*

SEASON REVIEW

Football League North: First Champ; P18 W6 D4 L8 F51 A52 Pts 16.
Second Champ; P19 W10 D3 L6 F62 A42 Pts 23.
Position: First Champ, 26th (Champions; Blackpool).
Second Champ, 14th (Champions; Liverpool).
Football League North War Cup: Qualifying competition, position 12th; P9 W6 D1 L2 F37 A21 Pts 13, then R1 (Winners; Blackpool).

Appearances (37m): Carr EM 31, Richardson J 29, Stubbins A 29, Sales RD 25, Graham D 23, Woollett C 22, Short JD 19, Gordon J 18, Rutherford TV 17, Hart WR 14, Donaldson RS 12, Mullen J 11, Smith T 11, Woodburn J 11, Dixon JT 10, Tapken NH 9, Taylor E 9, Batey R 8, King R 8, Coyde N 7, English A 7, Finney T 6, Hindmarsh E 6, Porter W 6, Wright JD 5, Hamilton DS 4, Walker TJ 4, Bradley GJ 3, Forster LJ 3, Highmoor GW 3, Nicholson WE 3, Bell W 2, Chilton AC 2, Connor J 2, Fagan W 2, Howdon S 2, Hughes Jos 2, McCormack JH 2, Scarr R 2, Seymour CM 2, Simpson TG 2, Smallwood F 2, Ancell RFD 1, Broady PK 1, Calder NA 1, Dimond S 1, Dodgin N 1, Garnham A 1, Litchfield EB 1, Mortensen SH 1, Moses G 1, O'Neil TH 1, Price A 1, Wallace JL 1.

Goals (113g): Stubbins A 42, Carr EM 28, Short JD 16, Dixon JT 4, Mullen J 4, Finney T 3, Taylor E 3, English A 2, Mortensen SH 2, Coyde N 1, Dimond S 1, Gordon J 1, McCormack JH 1, Moses G 1, Walker TJ 1, Woollett C 1, own goals 2.

Dismissals: 0 players.

MAJOR SIGNINGS

None

FROM THE RANKS

Ernie Taylor (Hylton CW)
Tom Rutherford (Scotswood)
Ron Sales (Reyrolles)
Bobby Donaldson (South Shields ex-sch)

NOTABLE GUESTS

Allenby Chilton (Manchester Utd)
Bill Fagan (Liverpool)
Tom Finney (Preston NE)
Stan Mortensen (Blackpool)
Jimmy Mullen (Wolves)
Bill Nicholson (Tottenham Hot)

TEAM COLOURS Black & white striped shirts, black shorts (Change; white shirts, black shorts)

Match	Date		FL North (First Championship)						Posn		1	2	3	4	5	6	7	8	9	10	11	Match
1	29 Aug	H	**Bradford Park Avenue**	L	1	4	(0 1)	7,500		Short	Tapken	Hughes	Graham	Donaldson RS	Smith	Hart	Simpson	Fagan	Stubbins	Short	Woollett	1
2	05 Sep	A	Bradford Park Avenue	D	0	0	(0 0)	3,500			Tapken	Hughes	Graham	Hart	Smith	Bradley	Finney	Fagan	Simpson	Howdon	Woollett	2
3	12 Sep	A	Huddersfield Town	L	0	4	(0 3)	2,475			Tapken	Sales	Graham	Hart	Smith	Bradley	Finney	Donaldson RS	Wallace	Howdon	Woollett	3
4	19 Sep	H	**Huddersfield Town**	L	0	4	(0 0)	7,542			King	O'Neil	Graham	Price	Smith	Hart	Finney	Taylor E	Stubbins	Dixon	Woollett	4
5	26 Sep	H	**Leeds United**	L	3	5	(2 3)	6,000		Moses, Stubbins, Carr	King	Porter W	Graham	Hindmarsh	Smith	Dodgin	Moses	Dixon	Stubbins	Carr	Woollett	5
6	03 Oct	A	Leeds United	W	7	1	(3 0)	3,000		Carr 3, Dixon, Taylor E 3	King	Richardson	Porter W	Gordon	Smith	Hindmarsh	Finney	Taylor E	Carr	Dixon	Woollett	6
7	10 Oct	A	York City	L	3	4	(2 2)	4,460		Carr 3	King	Richardson	Porter W	Gordon	Smith	Hindmarsh	Finney	Taylor E	Carr	Dixon	Woollett	7
8	17 Oct	H	**York City**	D	3	3	(0 2)	5,967		Carr, Stubbins, McCormack	King	Richardson	Graham	Woodburn	Smith	Hindmarsh	McCormack	Taylor E	Carr	Stubbins	Woollett	8
9	24 Oct	H	**Bradford City**	W	1	0	(1 0)	5,497		Stubbins (pen)	King	Richardson	Graham	Woodburn	Sales	Hindmarsh	Highmoor	Taylor E	Carr	Stubbins	Woollett	9
10	31 Oct	A	Bradford City	L	1	3	(1 2)	3,091		Carr	King	Richardson	Graham	Hart	Sales	Bradley	Highmoor	Taylor E	Carr	Seymour	Woollett	10
11	07 Nov	A	Gateshead	L	1	4	(0 3)	6,644	43	Stubbins (pen)	King	Richardson	Connor	Gordon	Sales	Hart	Highmoor	Short	Carr	Stubbins	Seymour	11
12	14 Nov	H	**Gateshead**	W	7	4	(1 3)	10,000		Finney 3, Stubbins 2, Short 2	Tapken	Richardson	Connor	Gordon	Sales	Woodburn	Finney	Short	Stubbins	Carr	Woollett	12
13	21 Nov	H	**Middlesbrough**	W	3	0	(3 0)	6,459	33	Gordon, Stubbins, Carr	Tapken	Richardson	Graham	Gordon	Sales	Woodburn	Coyde	Short	Stubbins	Carr	Woollett	13
14	28 Nov	A	Middlesbrough	W	6	1	(3 0)	3,500	23	Carr, Short 2, Stubbins 3 (1 pen)	Tapken	Richardson	Graham	Hart	Sales	Wright	Coyde	Short	Stubbins	Carr	Walker	14
15	05 Dec	A	Sunderland	W	5	3	(2 2)	7,000	27	Walker, Stubbins 4	Tapken	Richardson	Graham	Gordon	Sales	Hart	Walker	Short	Stubbins	Carr	Mullen	15
16	12 Dec	H	**Sunderland**	D	3	3	(1 2)	15,115		Carr, Stubbins 2	Tapken	Richardson	Graham	Gordon	Sales	Hart	Coyde	Short	Stubbins	Carr	Mullen	16
17	19 Dec	A	Gateshead	L	1	3	(1 1)	5,300	28	Short	Tapken	Richardson	Graham	Donaldson RS	Sales	Hart	Coyde	Short	Stubbins	Carr	Woollett	17
18	25 Dec	H	**Gateshead**	D	6	6	(4 2)	15,000	26	Coyde, Short 2, Stubbins 3	Rutherford TV	Gordon	Porter W	Woodburn	Sales	Wright	Coyde	Taylor E	Stubbins	Short	Woollett	18
			FL North (Second Championship) & FL War Cup (Qualifying)																			
19	26 Dec	H	**Middlesbrough**	W	3	2	(0 0)	13,300		Short, Woollett, og (Dawson)	Rutherford TV	Gordon	Porter W	Woodburn	Sales	Wright	Coyde	Taylor E	Stubbins	Short	Woollett	19
20	02 Jan	A	Middlesbrough	W	7	3	(4 1)	3,000		Stubbins 3, Short 2, Carr, Mullen	Rutherford TV	Gordon	Richardson	Donaldson RS	Sales	Wright	Coyde	Short	Stubbins	Carr	Mullen	20
21	16 Jan	H	**York City**	W	3	1	(2 0)	5,203		Carr 2, English	Rutherford TV	Richardson	Graham	Gordon	Sales	Donaldson RS	English	Short	Stubbins	Carr	Mullen	21
22	23 Jan	H	**Leeds United**	W	9	0	(3 0)	10,200	7	English, Mullen 2, Carr, Stubbins 3, Mortensen 2	Rutherford TV	Richardson	Graham	Gordon	Sales	Donaldson RS	English	Mortensen	Stubbins	Carr	Mullen	22
23	30 Jan	A	Leeds United	L	2	7	(2 2)	2,000	12	Mullen, Carr	Calder	Richardson	Woodburn	Hindmarsh	Sales	Hart	Hamilton	Taylor E	English	Carr	Mullen	23
24	06 Feb	A	Sunderland	D	3	3	(2 2)	12,000	13	Carr, Short, Stubbins (pen)	Rutherford TV	Richardson	Graham	Gordon	Sales	Woodburn	Hamilton	Short	Stubbins	Carr	Mullen	24
25	13 Feb	H	**Sunderland**	L	2	3	(1 2)	20,500	21	Stubbins, Short	Rutherford TV	Richardson	Ancell	Woodburn	Sales	Donaldson RS	Hamilton	Short	Stubbins	Carr	Mullen	25
26	20 Feb	H	**Gateshead**	W	2	0	(1 0)	17,100	13	Short 2	Bell	Richardson	Graham	Gordon	Sales	Wright	Hamilton	Short	Stubbins	Carr	Woollett	26
27	27 Feb	A	Gateshead	W	6	2	(3 1)	9,500	12	Carr 2, Stubbins 4 (1 pen)	Rutherford TV	Gordon	Richardson	Hart	Sales	Donaldson RS	Walker	Short	Stubbins	Carr	Mullen	27
Round			FL War Cup (Proper)																			**Round**
1(1)	06 Mar	H	**York City**	W	3	2	(2 2)	19,989		Short, Stubbins, Carr	Rutherford TV	Richardson	Graham	Gordon	Sales	Woodburn	Walker	Short	Stubbins	Carr	Smallwood	1(1)
1(2)	13 Mar	A	York City	L	0	2	(0 2)	11,385			Rutherford TV	Richardson	Graham	Gordon	Sales	Donaldson RS	Forster	Short	Stubbins	Carr	Smallwood	1(2)
Match			FL North (Second Championship)																			**Match**
28	20 Mar	A	Leeds United	W	3	1	(1 0)	2,500		Carr 2, Dixon	Bell	Richardson	Graham	Gordon	Sales	Batey	English	Dixon	Carr	Scarr	Woollett	28
29	27 Mar	H	**Leeds United**	L	4	5	(2 0)	8,403		Dimond, og (Warren), Stubbins 2	Rutherford TV	Richardson	Batey	Hart	Sales	Donaldson RS	McCormack	Stubbins	Dimond	Carr	Woollett	29
30	03 Apr	A	Middlesbrough	L	1	2	(1 2)	3,000		Stubbins	Rutherford TV	Richardson	Batey	Hart	Sales	Donaldson RS	English	Dixon	Stubbins	Carr	Woollett	30
31	10 Apr	H	**Middlesbrough**	W	4	0	(1 0)	8,811		Dixon, Carr, Stubbins 2	Rutherford TV	Nicholson	Graham	Woodburn	Smith	Batey	Litchfield	Dixon	Stubbins	Carr	Mullen	31
32	17 Apr	A	Huddersfield Town	L	0	1	(0 0)	2,835			Rutherford TV	Nicholson	Richardson	Donaldson RS	Smith	Batey	Forster	Short	English	Carr	Mullen	32
33	24 Apr	H	**Huddersfield Town**	D	2	2	(1 0)	14,820		Carr, Stubbins	Rutherford TV	Nicholson	Richardson	Garnham	Smith	Batey	Forster	Dixon	Stubbins	Carr	Woollett	33
34	26 Apr	H	**Gateshead**	W	3	1	(1 1)	4,148		Stubbins, Carr 2	Rutherford TV	Richardson	Graham	Porter W	Chilton	Batey	Scarr	Dixon	Stubbins	Carr	Woollett	34
35	01 May	A	York City	D	5	5	(4 2)	2,308	14	Stubbins 3, Carr, Dixon	Rutherford TV	Richardson	Graham	Broady	Chilton	Batey	English	Dixon	Stubbins	Carr	Woollett	35

Matches 28 to 33 — Also counted towards the West Riding FA Combined Counties Cup, United losing on aggregate to Huddersfield Town in the semi-final

Match 34 — Some reports have Short playing instead of Scarr

DateLine ... 3 Oct: Ernie Taylor scores a hat-trick against Leeds aged 17 years 31 days old, United's youngest ever scorer. **14 Nov:** Tom Finney nets a hat-trick for United in a 7-4 success over Gateshead. **23 Jan:** Stan Mortensen is among the scorers as United wallop Leeds 9-0. **1 May:** Albert Stubbins grabs his 42nd goal of the season against York with another hat-trick.

SEASON
1943-44

WAR LEAGUE NORTH

Fire-power up front

There were some unusual teams in senior wartime football. Included in the overall league table – although not to face the Magpies due to regional separation – were Bath City, Lovell's Athletic and Aberaman. Indeed, Bath came out on top of the pile when the 'Second' Championship was finalised, United finishing in a decent 11th place. With fire-power up front Newcastle were a real threat in attack. Stubbins grabbed 43 goals while a fresh-faced youngster often played in the forward line, Jack Milburn. Yet it was not all plain sailing for United. Darlington were 5-0 up at half-time in a contest during February and ended up winning 8-2!

Newcastle reached the knock-out stage of the War Cup again, disposing of Hartlepools and Darlington before meeting Sheffield United. Over two legs the Black'n'Whites only just lost out. In the first meeting in Yorkshire, United received a hammering, losing 4-0 to the Blades. There was much to do in the deciding leg at Gallowgate a week later. With restrictions eased, a terrific crowd of almost 53,000 saw the Magpies give it a go, and goals from Stubbins, Spulher and Dixon put the tie in the balance. But the Tykes struck back through Colin Collindridge to give them the tie 5-3 on aggregate.

Out of the big stage, Newcastle then took part in what was labelled the Tyne-Wear-Tees Cup, a secondary competition running alongside the normal league results (with the same results acting for both), to see who was top-dog in the North East. United secured the title and in novel circumstances. Having reached the final to play Darlington over two legs, in the deciding contest at St James' Park during May, all was square at 3-3 on aggregate after extra-time. It was decided by the two teams to settle the contest by playing on until the first team scored – an early 'Golden Goal'. After 32 minutes over extra-time and some 140-odd minutes of action on the day, Jackie Milburn netted the winning goal.

Pictured above: Ernie Taylor was one of several United youngsters to reach the top in peacetime football.

Memorabilia CORNER

Programme from the local meeting with Hartlepools United who featured all of 11 guest players.

IN CHARGE

Chairman: George Rutherford
Manager: Director Committee
Captain: Joe Richardson
Trainer/Coach: Norman Smith

ST JAMES' PARK

Average Attendance
Lg 12,257 Lg & Cup 17,429

1 Dave Cumming

2 Bobby Cowell

3 Bobby Corbett

4 Jimmy Gordon

5 Tom Smith

6 Pat Woods

7 Eddie Copeland

8 Johnny Dixon

9 Andy Donaldson

10 Jack Milburn

11 Charlie Woollett

PLAYER FOCUS Albert Stubbins

Born Wallsend. Centre-forward, 5'11"
1936 to 1946: 217 app 237 goals.

From Wallsend, although as a kid he was raised in the United States, Albert Stubbins started his career with United in March 1936. A teenage inside-forward, he soon demonstrated pace and the ability to get into the box. He quickly flourished when Albert was switched to the leader's role as war broke out. Tall and leggy, Stubbins had a terrific turn of pace and loved to run at defenders and such was his development that he was very soon championed for an England place during 1938-39. He packed a ferocious shot in his size 11 boots and during the war years smashed goals from every angle. Stubbins was the country's best striker, hitting a truly remarkable 231 goals in the five war seasons, four times claiming 40 or more in a campaign. Tyneside fans treasured him, but were stunned when he decided to move to Liverpool for a record £12,500 fee in September 1946 in search of First Division football. At Anfield Stubbins was equally worshipped as he scored plenty more goals – 83 – helping the Reds to the title in 1947 and to the FA Cup final in 1950. Capped by England during the war and in Victory internationals, Albert retired in 1954 and returned to Tyneside becoming a respected journalist. A gentleman of the game, he was nicknamed The Smiling Assassin at his peak and is featured as one of the faces on the legendary Beatle's album cover Sergeant Pepper's Lonely Hearts Club Band. In 1942 Albert appeared in the War Cup final as a guest for Sunderland.

SEASON REVIEW

Football League North: First Champ; P18 W5 D4 L9 F32 A37 Pts 14.
Second Champ; P20 W13 D0 L7 F47 A36 Pts 26.
Position: First Champ, 39th (Champions; Blackpool).
Second Champ, 11th (Bath City).
Football League North War Cup: Qualifying competition, position 12th, P10 W7 D0 L3 F25 A20 Pts 14, then R3 (Winners; Aston Villa).

Appearances (38m): Smith T 32, Stubbins A 32, Donaldson RS 30, Richardson J 30, Cumming DS 25, Dixon JT 24, Milburn JET 24, Woollett C 24, Copeland E 20, Cowell RG 18, Gordon J 17, Nicholson WE 16, Rutherford R 14, Woodburn J 11, Lightfoot L 10, Woods PB 10, Rutherford TV 8, Taylor E 7, Walker TJ 7, Corbett R 6, Sales RD 6, Henderson HB 5, Scarr R 5, Donaldson A 4, Mullen J 4, Bradley GJ 3, King R 3, Porter L 3, Glassey JR 2, Graham D 2, Lee R 2, Price A 2, Spuhler JO 2, Stewart AV 2, Wright JD 2, Bainbridge R 1, Hope G 1, Howdon S 1, Juliussen AL 1, Lewis DJ 1, Parr J 1.

Goals (80g): Stubbins A 43, Milburn JET 12, Dixon JT 7, Woollett C 4, Copeland E 3, Rutherford R 2, Taylor E 2, Donaldson RS 1, Porter L 1, Spuhler JO 1, Woodburn J 1, own goals 3. (includes Milburn's 'Golden Goal' v Darlington, 6 May)

Dismissals: 1 player; Stubbins.

MAJOR SIGNINGS

None

FROM THE RANKS

Bobby Corbett (Throckley CW)
Bobby Cowell (Blackhall CW)
Andy Donaldson (Vickers Armstrong)
Pat Woods (Bedewell)
Bobby Rutherford (Wallsend St Lukes)
Jack Milburn (Ashington ATC)

NOTABLE GUESTS

Dave Cumming (Middlesbrough)
Albert Juliussen (Huddersfield Town)

TEAM COLOURS Black & white striped shirts, black shorts (Change; white shirts, black shorts)

Match	Date		FL North (First Championship)					Posn		1	2	3	4	5	6	7	8	9	10	11	Match
1	28 Aug	A	Bradford City	L	1 2	(0 1)	3,038		Dixon	Rutherford TV	Richardson	Nicholson	Gordon	Smith	Bradley	Walker	Dixon	Howdon	Milburn JET	Mullen	1
2	04 Sep	H	**Bradford City**	W	3 2	(2 0)	10,695		Stubbins, Milburn JET, Dixon	Rutherford TV	Richardson	Nicholson	Gordon	Smith	Donaldson RS	Walker	Dixon	Stubbins	Milburn JET	Mullen	2
3	11 Sep	A	Bradford Park Avenue	L	0 1	(0 0)	2,763	32		Rutherford TV	Cowell	Nicholson	Woodburn	Smith	Bradley	Lightfoot	Dixon	Bainbridge	Milburn JET	Woollett	3
4	18 Sep	H	**Bradford Park Avenue**	W	2 1	(1 0)	9,896	29	Stubbins, Dixon	Rutherford TV	Richardson	Nicholson	Gordon	Smith	Woodburn	Copeland	Dixon	Stubbins	Milburn JET	Mullen	4
5	25 Sep	A	York City	L	0 2	(0 2)	5,938	35		Rutherford TV	Richardson	Nicholson	Gordon	Smith	Donaldson RS	Copeland	Dixon	Stubbins	Milburn JET	Lightfoot	5
6	02 Oct	H	**York City**	D	1 1	(1 0)	9,877	31	Milburn JET	Rutherford TV	Richardson	Nicholson	Donaldson RS	Smith	Bradley	Copeland	Dixon	Stubbins	Milburn JET	Lightfoot	6
7	09 Oct	H	**Huddersfield Town**	W	5 2	(4 1)	10,400	22	Stubbins 2, Milburn JET 2, Woollett	King	Richardson	Corbett	Donaldson RS	Smith	Woodburn	Copeland	Dixon	Stubbins	Milburn JET	Woollett	7
8	16 Oct	A	Huddersfield Town	D	1 1	(1 1)	4,268	21	Milburn JET	Rutherford TV	Richardson	Nicholson	Gordon	Smith	Donaldson RS	Copeland	Dixon	Donaldson A	Milburn JET	Woollett	8
9	23 Oct	H	**Hartlepools United**	L	0 1	(0 1)	10,065	29		King	Cowell	Graham	Price	Smith	Donaldson RS	Copeland	Hope	Stubbins	Milburn JET	Henderson	9
10	30 Oct	A	Hartlepools United	L	4 5	(1 2)	7,472	33	Stubbins 3, Milburn JET	Lee	Cowell	Graham	Price	Smith	Donaldson RS	Copeland	Dixon	Stubbins	Milburn JET	Lightfoot	10
11	06 Nov	A	Sunderland	L	2 4	(1 2)	16,000		Stubbins 2	Rutherford TV	Cowell	Nicholson	Woodburn	Smith	Donaldson RS	Copeland	Dixon	Stubbins	Milburn JET	Lightfoot	11
12	13 Nov	H	**Sunderland**	W	3 1	(2 1)	24,241	36	Stubbins, Milburn JET, Taylor E	King	Richardson	Cowell	Donaldson RS	Smith	Woods	Copeland	Taylor E	Stubbins d	Milburn JET	Lightfoot	12
13	20 Nov	A	Darlington	L	1 4	(0 4)	7,838	37	Stubbins	Cumming	Richardson	Cowell	Wright	Smith	Woods	Copeland	Taylor E	Stubbins	Milburn JET	Lightfoot	13
14	27 Nov	H	**Darlington**	L	4 5	(2 1)	8,672	39	Stubbins 2, Donaldson R, Taylor E	Cumming	Gordon	Cowell	Donaldson RS	Smith	Wright	Copeland	Taylor E	Stubbins	Rutherford R	Mullen	14
15	04 Dec	A	Middlesbrough	D	1 1	(0 0)	3,500	40	Stubbins	Cumming	Cowell	Corbett	Gordon	Smith	Woods	Copeland	Taylor E	Stubbins	Rutherford R	Lightfoot	15
16	11 Dec	H	**Middlesbrough**	D	1 1	(1 0)	8,845	38	Dixon	Cumming	Richardson	Nicholson	Donaldson RS	Smith	Woods	Walker	Dixon	Donaldson A	Stubbins	Lightfoot	16
17	18 Dec	A	Gateshead	W	3 1	(2 0)	6,000		Copeland 2, Dixon	Cumming	Richardson	Cowell	Donaldson RS	Sales	Woods	Copeland	Dixon	Donaldson A	Scarr	Lightfoot	17
18	25 Dec	H	**Gateshead**	L	0 2	(0 0)	15,635	39		Cumming	Richardson	Cowell	Donaldson RS	Sales	Woodburn	Copeland	Dixon	Donaldson A	Scarr	Woollett	18
			FL North (Second Championship) & FL War Cup (Qualifying)																		
19	27 Dec	H	**Sunderland**	W	4 2	(2 2)	26,272		Stubbins 2, Woollett, og (Lockie)	Cumming	Richardson	Nicholson	Donaldson RS	Sales	Woodburn	Copeland	Dixon	Stubbins	Milburn JET	Woollett	19
20	01 Jan	A	Sunderland	L	0 3	(0 1)	20,000	32		Cumming	Richardson	Nicholson	Donaldson RS	Sales	Woods	Copeland	Dixon	Stubbins	Taylor E	Woollett	20
21	08 Jan	A	Hartlepools United	W	2 1	(1 0)	6,326	20	Stubbins 2	Cumming	Richardson	Cowell	Donaldson RS	Smith	Scarr	Copeland	Dixon	Stubbins	Milburn JET	Woollett	21
22	15 Jan	H	**Hartlepools United**	W	5 1	(2 1)	13,835		Milburn JET, Stubbins 3 (1 pen), Dixon	Cumming	Richardson	Cowell	Gordon	Smith	Donaldson RS	Copeland	Dixon	Stubbins	Milburn JET	Woollett	22
23	22 Jan	H	**Gateshead**	W	2 1	(1 1)	13,681	7	Milburn JET, Stubbins	Cumming	Richardson	Cowell	Donaldson RS	Smith	Woods	Copeland	Dixon	Stubbins	Milburn JET	Woollett	23
24	29 Jan	A	Gateshead	W	3 1	(1 1)	8,859	5	Woollett, Stubbins, Milburn JET	Cumming	Richardson	Nicholson	Gordon	Smith	Donaldson RS	Lewis	Taylor E	Stubbins	Milburn JET	Woollett	24
25	05 Feb	A	Middlesbrough	L	1 2	(0 1)	5,000	13	Copeland	Cumming	Richardson	Corbett	Donaldson RS	Smith	Woodburn	Copeland	Dixon	Milburn JET	Taylor E	Woollett	25
26	12 Feb	H	**Middlesbrough**	W	4 1	(1 0)	14,857	7	Stubbins 3, og (Martin)	Cumming	Nicholson	Corbett	Donaldson RS	Smith	Woodburn	Henderson	Dixon	Stubbins	Milburn JET	Woollett	26
27	19 Feb	H	**Darlington**	W	2 0	(0 0)	12,500	6	Stubbins 2 (1 pen)	Cumming	Richardson	Nicholson	Donaldson RS	Smith	Woods	Henderson	Dixon	Stubbins	Rutherford R	Woollett	27
28	26 Feb	A	Darlington	L	2 8	(0 5)	5,482	12	Stubbins 2	Lee	Richardson	Corbett	Donaldson RS	Smith	Woods	Henderson	Dixon	Stubbins	Rutherford R	Woollett	28
Round			FL War Cup (Proper)																		**Round**
1(1)	04 Mar	A	Hartlepools United	L	1 3	(0 1)	8,432		Woollett	Cumming	Richardson	Corbett	Donaldson RS	Smith	Woods	Walker	Dixon	Stubbins	Rutherford R	Woollett	1(1)
1(2)	11 Mar	H	**Hartlepools United**	W	3 0	(1 0)	26,110		Stubbins 2 (1 pen), Woodburn	Cumming	Richardson	Nicholson	Gordon	Sales	Woodburn	Walker	Juliussen	Stubbins	Rutherford R	Woollett	1(2)
2(1)	18 Mar	A	Darlington	L	0 2	(0 0)	12,835			Cumming	Richardson	Stewart	Gordon	Sales	Woodburn	Walker	Scarr	Stubbins	Rutherford R	Woollett	2(1)
2(2)	25 Mar	H	**Darlington**	W	4 1	(3 0)	36,237		Stubbins 4	Cumming	Cowell	Stewart	Gordon	Smith	Donaldson RS	Walker	Glassey	Stubbins	Rutherford R	Woollett	2(2)
3(1)	01 Apr	A	Sheffield United	L	0 4	(0 1)	30,567			Cumming	Richardson	Parr	Gordon	Smith	Woodburn	Spuhler	Glassey	Stubbins	Rutherford R	Woollett	3(1)
3(2)	08 Apr	H	**Sheffield United**	W	3 1	(1 0)	52,836		Stubbins (pen), Dixon, Spuhler	Cumming	Richardson	Nicholson	Gordon	Smith	Donaldson RS	Spuhler	Dixon	Stubbins	Rutherford R	Woollett	3(2)
Match			FL North (Second Championship)																		**Match**
29	15 Apr	A	Sunderland	W	3 0	(1 0)	7,000		Rutherford R 2, Stubbins	Cumming	Richardson	Cowell	Donaldson RS	Smith	Scarr	Henderson	Milburn JET	Stubbins	Rutherford R	Woollett	29
30	22 Apr	H	**Sunderland**	W	5 2	(2 1)	12,106		Stubbins 3, Milburn JET, og (Eves)	Cumming	Richardson	Cowell	Gordon	Smith	Donaldson RS	Porter L	Milburn JET	Stubbins	Rutherford R	Woollett	30
31	29 Apr	A	Darlington	W	3 2	(0 0)	7,660		Stubbins 2, Porter L	Cumming	Richardson	Cowell	Gordon	Smith	Donaldson RS	Porter L	Milburn JET	Stubbins	Rutherford R	Woollett	31
32	06 May	H	**Darlington**	L	0 1	(0 0)	14,400	11		Cumming	Richardson	Cowell	Gordon	Smith	Donaldson RS	Porter L	Milburn JET	Stubbins	Rutherford R	Woollett	32

Matches 29 to 32 — Also counted towards the Tyne-Tees-Wear Cup, United reaching the final with Darlington

Match 32 — The fixture with Darlington ended 0-1 in terms of the League Competition, but the match was also the deciding leg of the Tyne-Tees-Wear Cup final. Extra-time was played and the aggregate scores were still level so it was agreed that the two sides would play on with the first team to score being the winners. Jack Milburn scored after around 143 mins of action.

DateLine ... 28 Aug: Jackie Milburn's first game in United's first eleven, against Bradford City. **26 Feb:** Darlington inflict an 8-2 defeat on the Magpies at Feethams.
29 April: Albert Stubbins scores his 43rd goal of the campaign against Darlington. **6 May:** A 'Golden Goal' by Jack Milburn in extra-time secures the Tyne-Wear-Tees Cup against Darlington.

SEASON 1944-45

WAR LEAGUE NORTH

Goals entertain the crowds

The order of the day was attack-minded football as the Second World War drew to a close. Newcastle were among the very best in the country in front of goal, hitting 122 goals in the season as the St James' Park crowd were treated to another feast of goalmouth action. For the third season running Stubbins scored more than 40 goals in the campaign, and Eddie Carr netted another 29. During November, Bradford City were on the receiving end of a 11-0 hammering, immediately after United had given Hull City a hiding in back-to-back victories; 7-0 and 6-3.

United ended the 'Second' Championship in fifth spot and went onto reach the War Cup proper. The Magpies eliminated Darlington and Bradford City comfortably, 5-1 and 7-2 on aggregate, then faced Bolton Wanderers in an epic tussle. Government restrictions on crowds had been eased since the early years of wartime football, and over 43,000 saw the second leg of the tie at St James' Park – indication that football was slowly getting back to a degree of normality. United needed to turn-around a 3-0 first leg defeat. That was a tough ask, but thanks to the dynamic qualities of Albert Stubbins they very nearly did so. The tall Tynesider ripped Bolton apart and struck a brilliant hat-trick, but in extra-time the visitors – and eventual Cup winners – had the edge, winning in the end 4-2.

By the mid-point of the 1944-45 season indications of an end to the world conflict was in sight as a trickle of United players started to leave the forces and return to Gallowgate. And as shown by the headlining crowd against Bolton, supporters began to flock back to football. Newcastle's home gates during 1945 were sizable with 40,000-plus watching the game with Sunderland, over 30,000 in the ground for the tie with Bradford City and almost 28,000 at the contest with Darlington. Attendances would soon reach boom proportions in the coming seasons.

Pictured above: Locally born, Tom Smith was an uncompromising centre-half in the style of the day.

Memorabilia CORNER

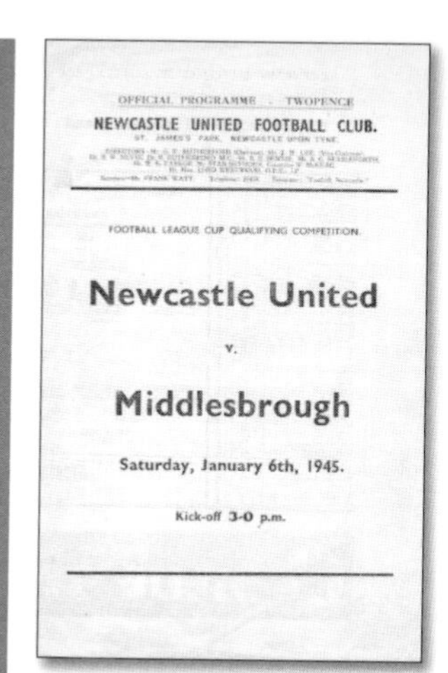

OFFICIAL PROGRAMME . TWOPENCE

NEWCASTLE UNITED FOOTBALL CLUB.

FOOTBALL LEAGUE CUP QUALIFYING COMPETITION.

Newcastle United

v.

Middlesbrough

Saturday, January 6th, 1945.

Kick-off 3-0 p.m.

A Football League War Cup Qualifying clash with Boro, a 5-1 victory.

IN CHARGE

Chairman: George Rutherford
Manager: Director Committee
Captain: Harry Clifton
Trainer/Coach: Norman Smith

ST JAMES' PARK

Average Attendance
Lg 14,787 Lg & Cup 18,959

Newcastle line-up before a wartime fixture.
Left to right: Clifton, Stubbins, Corbett, Swinburne, Smith, Donaldson (R), Gordon, Hair, Cowell, Wayman, Milburn.

PLAYER FOCUS Eddie Carr

Born Wheatley Hill. Centre-forward, 5'6"
1942 to 1945: 70 app 57 goals.

One of several locally born footballers to return to the region during the war years, Arsenal's Eddie Carr was a worthy goal-getter for United over two seasons as a guest forward when he worked down one of the local pits. Born in County Durham and a nimble and quick-footed striker, he had moved south from his local colliery side to join the team of the Thirties, Arsenal in 1935. Although never a regular in the Londoner's star-studded line-up being a deputy in the main to Ted Drake, Carr had showed at times he could become a top goal-poacher before injury halted his bright progress and threatened his career. A little'un at only 5'6" tall but sturdy with it, Eddie teamed up with Albert Stubbins on many occasions in a Magpie shirt and plundered plenty of goals for the Black'n'Whites – almost a goal a game for the club. He once netted all of six goals in a match against Bradford City. On peacetime, he could not find a place in the Gunners' ranks and moved to Huddersfield Town in 1945 later pulling on the colours of Newport County and Bradford City. He eventually returned to his native North East, briefly playing for Darlington before turning to coaching then management at Feethams and afterwards on the local non-league scene. He was also a United scout for a period. Eddie netted over 175 goals in senior and wartime football

SEASON REVIEW

Football League North: First Champ; P18 W7 D1 L10 F51 A38 Pts 15.
Second Champ; P23 W15 D1 L7 F71 A38 Pts 31.
Position: First Champ, 35th (Champions; Huddersfield Town).
Second Champ, 5th (Champions; Derby County).
Football League War Cup: Qualifying competition, position 17th, P10 W6 D0 L4 F30 A21 Pts 12, then R3 (Winners; Bolton Wanderers).

Appearances (41m): Cowell RG 41, Carr EM 39, Smith T 38, Donaldson RS 35, Milburn JET 32, Cumming DS 31, Stubbins A 31, Wayman C 29, Corbett R 21, Duffy RMD 21, Gordon J 21, Hair G 16, Woollett C 16, Richardson J 14, Pearson TU 9, Harnby DR 7, Porter L 7, Scott FH 6, Rutherford R 5, Wood GA 5, Woods PB 5, Donaldson A 4, Sloan J 4, Sales RD 3, Golding W 2, Taylor E 2, Barron J 1, Crowe CA 1, Gray R 1, Gray TD 1, King R 1, McCormack CJ 1, Whittle E 1.

Goals (122g): Stubbins A 43, Carr EM 29, Wayman C 17, Milburn JET 12, Gordon J 8, Hair G 4, Woollett C 3, Donaldson A 2, Pearson TU 1, Porter L 1, Scott FH 1, Taylor E 1.

Dismissals: 0 players.

MAJOR SIGNINGS

None

FROM THE RANKS

Charlie Crowe (Heaton & Byker YC)
George Hair (Spen Jnrs)
Charlie Wayman (Spennymoor Utd)

NOTABLE GUESTS

Cec McCormack (Gateshead)

TEAM COLOURS Black & white striped shirts, black shorts (Change; white shirts, black shorts)

SEASON 1944-45

Match	Date		Opponent	Res	F	A	HT	Att	Posn	Scorers	1	2	3	4	5	6	7	8	9	10	11	Match
			FL North (First Championship)																			
1	26 Aug	A	Gateshead	D	2	2	(0 0)	8,109		Stubbins, Carr	Cumming	Hamby	Cowell	Gordon	Smith	Donaldson RS	Porter L	Carr	Stubbins	Rutherford R	Woollett	1
2	02 Sep	H	**Gateshead**	W	3	1	(0 0)	3,320		Stubbins, Porter L, Carr	Cumming	Hamby	Cowell	Woods	Smith	Donaldson RS	Porter L	Carr	Stubbins	Rutherford R	Woollett	2
3	09 Sep	H	**Bradford Park Avenue**	L	0	2	(0 1)	16,112			Cumming	Hamby	Cowell	Woods	Smith	Donaldson RS	Porter L	Carr	Stubbins	Milburn JET	Hair	3
4	16 Sep	A	Bradford Park Avenue	L	0	1	(0 1)	8,309			Cumming	Hamby	Cowell	Gordon	Smith	Donaldson RS	Porter L	Milburn JET	Carr	Rutherford R	Woollett	4
5	23 Sep	A	Sunderland	L	0	2	(0 0)	18,000			Cumming	Hamby	Cowell	Gordon	Smith	Donaldson RS	Porter L	Milburn JET	Stubbins	Carr	Woollett	5
6	30 Sep	H	**Sunderland**	L	1	5	(1 1)	28,693	52	Milburn JET	Cumming	Hamby	Cowell	Gordon	Smith	Donaldson RS	Porter L	Milburn JET	Stubbins	Carr	Woollett	6
7	07 Oct	H	**Middlesbrough**	L	0	1	(0 1)	13,366	53		Cumming	Richardson	Cowell	Donaldson RS	Smith	Crowe	Porter L	Carr	Milburn JET	Rutherford R	Woollett	7
8	14 Oct	A	Middlesbrough	W	8	2	(4 2)	5,000	45	Carr 3, Milburn JET 2, Wayman 2, Gordon	Golding	Richardson	Cowell	Gordon	Smith	Donaldson RS	Milburn JET	Taylor E	Carr	Wayman	Hair	8
9	21 Oct	A	Leeds United	L	1	2	(1 2)	8,000	48	Donaldson A	Cumming	Hamby	Cowell	Donaldson RS	Smith	Woods	Milburn JET	Carr	Donaldson A	Rutherford R	Woollett	9
10	28 Oct	H	**Leeds United**	L	2	4	(0 2)	18,040	50	Wayman 2	Cumming	Richardson	Cowell	Donaldson RS	Smith	Woods	Milburn JET	Carr	Donaldson A	Wayman	Pearson TU	10
11	04 Nov	H	**Hull City**	W	7	0	(1 0)	9,408	47	Wayman, Woollett, Stubbins, Carr 2, Gordon 2	Cumming	Cowell	Corbett	Stubbins	Smith	Duffy	Milburn JET	Gordon	Carr	Wayman	Woollett	11
12	11 Nov	A*	Hull City	W	6	3	(2 2)	3,000		Stubbins 3, Gordon 2, Carr	Cumming	Cowell	Corbett	Donaldson RS	Smith	Duffy	Milburn JET	Gordon	Stubbins	Carr	Woollett	12
13	18 Nov	H	**Bradford City**	W	11	0	(4 0)	15,642	39	Carr 6, Gordon, Stubbins 2, Woollett 2	King	Cowell	Corbett	Donaldson RS	Smith	Duffy	Milburn JET	Gordon	Stubbins	Carr	Woollett	13
14	25 Nov	A	Bradford City	L	2	5	(1 3)	5,500	41	Wayman, Gordon	Golding	Richardson	Cowell	Donaldson RS	Smith	Duffy	Milburn JET	Gordon	Carr	Wayman	Woollett	14
15	02 Dec	A	Hartlepools United	W	3	2	(1 1)	7,204		Stubbins 2, Wayman	Cumming	Richardson	Cowell	Gordon	Smith	Duffy	Milburn JET	Wayman	Stubbins	Carr	Pearson TU	15
16	09 Dec	H	**Hartlepools United**	W	3	0	(1 0)	12,000	31	Stubbins 2, Milburn JET	Cumming	Richardson	Cowell	Gordon	Sales	Duffy	Milburn JET	Wayman	Stubbins	Carr	Pearson TU	16
17	16 Dec	H	**Huddersfield Town**	L	1	2	(0 2)	22,637	33	Milburn JET	Cumming	Richardson	Cowell	Donaldson RS	Smith	Duffy	Milburn JET	Carr	Stubbins	Wayman	Pearson TU	17
18	23 Dec	A	Huddersfield Town	L	1	4	(0 1)	17,253	35	Donaldson A	Barron	Richardson	Cowell	Donaldson RS	Smith	Duffy	Milburn JET	Carr	Donaldson A	Wayman	Pearson TU	18
			FL North (Second Championship) & FL War Cup (Qualifying)																			
19	26 Dec	H	**Sunderland**	W	3	1	(2 0)	40,311		Stubbins 2, Wayman	Cumming	Richardson	Cowell	Gray TD	Smith	Duffy	Milburn JET	Carr	Stubbins	Wayman	Pearson TU	19
20	30 Dec	A	Sunderland	L	3	4	(1 1)	19,000		Stubbins 2 (1 pen), Wayman	Cumming	Richardson	Cowell	Donaldson RS	Sales	Duffy	Milburn JET	Carr	Stubbins	Wayman	Pearson TU	20
21	06 Jan	H	**Middlesbrough**	W	5	1	(1 1)	17,000	14	Carr 4, Stubbins	Cumming	Richardson	Cowell	Gordon	Smith	Duffy	Milburn JET	Carr	Stubbins	Wayman	Woollett	21
22	13 Jan	A	Middlesbrough	L	3	5	(3 2)	5,000	17	Wayman 2, Milburn JET	Cumming	Richardson	Cowell	Gordon	Smith	Duffy	Milburn JET	Carr	Sloan	Wayman	Pearson TU	22
23	20 Jan	H	**Gateshead**	L	2	4	(0 1)	11,688	32	Carr, Milburn JET	Cumming	Richardson	Cowell	Donaldson RS	Smith	Duffy	Milburn JET	Carr	Stubbins	Wayman	Woollett	23
24	10 Feb	H	**Hartlepools United**	W	4	1	(4 1)	15,467	36	Stubbins 4	Cumming	Cowell	Corbett	Donaldson RS	Smith	Duffy	Milburn JET	Carr	Stubbins	Whittle	Woollett	24
25	17 Feb	H	**Darlington**	W	3	1	(1 0)	19,899		Taylor E, Pearson T, Stubbins	Cumming	Cowell	Corbett	Donaldson RS	Smith	Duffy	Milburn JET	Taylor E	Stubbins	Carr	Pearson TU	25
26	24 Feb	A	Darlington	W	3	2	(1 0)	8,920	24	Stubbins, Carr 2	Cumming	Cowell	Corbett	Donaldson RS	Smith	Duffy	Milburn JET	Carr	Stubbins	Wayman	Woollett	26
27	03 Mar	A	Hartlepools United	L	1	2	(0 1)	9,523	26	Carr	Cumming	Cowell	Corbett	Donaldson RS	Smith	Duffy	Milburn JET	Carr	Stubbins	Wayman	Woollett	27
28	17 Mar	A	Gateshead	W	3	0	(1 0)	14,300	17	Stubbins 3	Cumming	Cowell	Corbett	Gordon	Smith	Donaldson RS	Scott	Carr	Stubbins	Wayman	Hair	28
Round			**FL War Cup (Proper)**																			**Round**
1(1)	24 Mar	H	**Darlington**	W	2	1	(0 0)	27,991		Hair, Stubbins	Gray R	Cowell	Corbett	Donaldson RS	Smith	Duffy	Scott	Carr	Stubbins	Wayman	Hair	1(1)
1(2)	31 Mar	A	Darlington	W	3	0	(2 0)	15,796		Wayman, Carr 2	Cumming	Cowell	Corbett	Gordon	Smith	Donaldson RS	Scott	Carr	Stubbins	Wayman	Hair	1(2)
2(1)	07 Apr	H	**Bradford City**	W	6	2	(2 2)	30,093		Scott, Wayman 2, Stubbins 2 (1 pen), Carr	Cumming	Cowell	Corbett	Gordon	Smith	Donaldson RS	Scott	Carr	Stubbins	Wayman	Hair	2(1)
2(2)	14 Apr	A	Bradford City	W	1	0	(0 0)	10,000		Hair	Cumming	Cowell	Corbett	Gordon	Smith	Donaldson RS	Scott	Carr	Stubbins	Wayman	Hair	2(2)
3(1)	21 Apr	A	Bolton Wanderers	L	0	3	(0 2)	25,974			Cumming	Cowell	Corbett	Donaldson RS	Smith	Duffy	Scott	Carr	McCormack	Wayman	Hair	3(1)
3(2)	28 Apr	H	**Bolton Wanderers**	We	4	2	(3 0)	43,453		Stubbins 3, Milburn JET	Cumming	Cowell	Corbett	Gordon	Smith	Donaldson RS	Milburn JET	Carr	Stubbins	Wayman	Hair	3(2)
Match			**FL North (Second Championship)**																			**Match**
29	10 Mar	A	Middlesbrough	W	5	1	(1 1)	5,000		Stubbins 4, Carr	Cumming	Cowell	Corbett	Donaldson RS	Sales	Smith	Sloan	Carr	Stubbins	Wayman	Hair	29
30	02 Apr	H	**Sunderland**	L	0	3	(0 0)	13,000			Wood	Cowell	Corbett	Woods	Richardson	Donaldson RS	Sloan	Milburn JET	Donaldson A	Wayman	Hair	30
31	05 May	A	Middlesbrough	D	1	1	(1 1)	4,000		Milburn JET	Cumming	Cowell	Corbett	Gordon	Smith	Donaldson RS	Milburn JET	Sloan	Stubbins	Wayman	Hair	31
32	09 May	H	**Sunderland**	W	5	0	(3 0)	10,217		Wayman 3, Milburn JET, Stubbins	Wood	Cowell	Corbett	Gordon	Smith	Donaldson RS	Milburn JET	Carr	Stubbins	Wayman	Hair	32
33	12 May	H	**Middlesbrough**	W	11	0	(4 0)	11,800		Gordon, Hair 2, Stubbins 5, Carr 2, Milburn JET	Wood	Cowell	Corbett	Gordon	Smith	Donaldson RS	Milburn JET	Carr	Stubbins	Wayman	Hair	33
34	19 May	A	Gateshead	L	0	3	(0 0)	9,977			Wood	Cowell	Corbett	Donaldson RS	Smith	Duffy	Milburn JET	Carr	Stubbins	Wayman	Hair	34
35	21 May	H	**Gateshead**	W	3	1	(0 0)	18,000	5	Stubbins, Milburn JET, Carr	Wood	Cowell	Corbett	Donaldson RS	Smith	Duffy	Milburn JET	Carr	Stubbins	Wayman	Hair	35

A* — Played at Bootham Crescent, York
We — Won after extra time, tie lost on aggregate

Match 32 — This fixture was labelled as a "Victory Game" celebrating the end of WWII

Matches 31 & 33 to 35 — Also counted towards the Tyne-Tees-Wear Cup, United reaching the semi-final

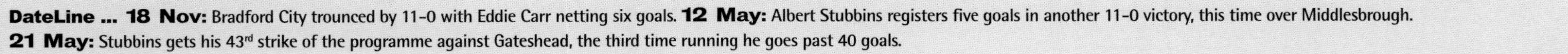

DateLine ... 18 Nov: Bradford City trounced by 11-0 with Eddie Carr netting six goals. **12 May:** Albert Stubbins registers five goals in another 11-0 victory, this time over Middlesbrough. **21 May:** Stubbins gets his 43rd strike of the programme against Gateshead, the third time running he goes past 40 goals.

SEASON
1945-46
WAR LEAGUE NORTH

Peace and a resurgent United

With the Second World War over apart from the repercussion, the national game returned to a semblance of familiarity in 1945-46. Regional leagues continued, but now two divisions – North and South – with a normal 42 match home and away programme. The FA Cup returned too – albeit a two-legged arrangement was tried in the early ties for the first time. Everybody was focussed in getting the game back to its customary structure for the following season.

Crowds massed back to stadiums around the country and few places more so than at United's base on Barrack Road. Newcastle's average gate was almost 40,000, and that was to increase dramatically as normal action resumed. United hit a century of goals once more, 106 in League action this time, second only to the North Champions Sheffield United. Stubbins again was the focal point with another 40 goals, and he led the charge as the Magpies recorded some noted scorelines; 9-1 against Stoke City and 8-1 when Blackburn Rovers arrived on Tyneside. Newcastle had opened the new season with an impressive 6-0 demolition of Sheffield United at St James' Park – by the end of the season the best side in the competition. Soon afterwards they crushed Middlesbrough by the same scoreline at Ayresome Park. The Magpies registered four or more goals on 12 occasions in the season.

The glory of the FA Cup returned in January and served up an enthralling clash with Barnsley, won narrowly by the Tykes 5-4 on aggregate. The Reds' main striker, Chilean George Robledo, made a big impression on United supremo Stan Seymour. The powerful South American was soon to be heading to Tyneside. But it appeared Seymour and the rest of the Board had no plans to appoint a new boss at St James' Park. Tom Mather had long since returned to the Potteries.

Pictured above: In England's reckoning before war, Harry Clifton skippered United as the fighting came to an end.

Memorabilia CORNER

Football was nearly back to normal by the time of Everton's visit, almost 50,000 saw the clash.

IN CHARGE

Chairman: George Rutherford
Manager: Director Committee
Captain: Joe Harvey
Trainer/Coach: Norman Smith

ST JAMES' PARK

Average Attendance
Lg 38,628 Lg & Cup 39,612

United during their visit to Scandinavia just after World War Two. Left to right: Harvey, Smith, Wright, Swinburne, Stubbins, Milburn, Craig, Woodburn, Wayman (looking away), Graham, Pearson.

PLAYER FOCUS Charlie Crowe

Born Newcastle upon Tyne. Left-half, 5'8"
1944 to 1957: 216 app 7 goals.

Charlie Crowe was one of several local youngsters groomed during the war years to quickly develop on peace being restored and then make a name for himself at the top level of the game. Tyneside born and bred, Crowe was a tenacious wing-half who did the foraging and tackling in midfield. He wasn't big or well-built, yet his aggressive tactics were hugely important to United's FA Cup winning side in 1951. Joining the Magpies in October 1944 alongside Jack Milburn, he earned a debut in the wartime leagues and Crowe went on to spend all of 13 seasons in United's squad. After making his mark in season 1945-46, he was in and out of the side during the immediate post-war years. But Charlie was a regular midfielder in 1949-50 and during the first of United's treble of Wembley victories in the Fifties when he pulled on the number six shirt with distinction. He unluckily missed the 1955 final due to a late ankle injury when due to face Manchester City on the big day. Crowe spent the majority of his career at St James' Park, departing in February 1957 when he joined Mansfield Town for a brief period. Afterwards he was back on Tyneside for the rest of his life always an admired and genial character, ever willing to reminisce about his footballing days. An FA coach, he was for a period in charge of Whitley Bay.

SEASON REVIEW

Football League North: P42 W21 D5 L16 F106 A70 Pts 47.
Position: 6th (Champions; Sheffield United).
FA Cup: R3 (Winners; Derby County).

Appearances (44m): Milburn JET 41, Corbett R 37, Hair G 37, Smith T 36, Harvey Jos 35, Stubbins A 33, Wayman C 31, Crowe CA 25, Cowell RG 24, Clifton H 22, Swinburne TA 21, Graham D 20, King R 20, Brown EC 12, Woodburn J 12, Pearson TU 11, Taylor E 9, Wright JD 9, Gordon J 8, Sales RD 8, Donaldson RS 5, Craig B 4, Donaldson A 4, Sloan J 3, Walker TJ 3, Hamilton DS 2, Scott W 2, Wood GA 2, Batty RR 1, Dodgin N 1, Garbutt EJE 1, Harnby DR 1, Hubble L 1, Porter L 1, Rushton G 1, Woods PB 1.

Goals (110g): Stubbins A 40, Clifton H 16, Milburn JET 16, Wayman C 14, Hair G 11, Brown EC 4, Pearson TU 2, Crowe CA 1, Donaldson A 1, Hamilton DS 1, Harvey Jos 1, Taylor E 1, Woodburn J 1, own goal 1.

Dismissals: 0 players.

MAJOR SIGNINGS

Joe Harvey (Bradford City) £4,250

FROM THE RANKS

Eric Garbutt (Billingham)

TEAM COLOURS Black & white striped shirts, black shorts (Change; white shirts, black shorts)

SEASON 1945–46

Match	Date		FL North	Result	Score	HT	Att	Posn	Scorers	1	2	3	4	5	6	7	8	9	10	11	Match
1	25 Aug	H	**Sheffield United**	W	6 0	(1 0)	31,391		Milburn JET, Clifton, Stubbins 3, Wayman	Garbutt	Cowell	Corbett	Woods	Smith	Donaldson RS	Milburn JET	Clifton	Stubbins	Wayman	Hair	1
2	01 Sep	A	Sheffield United	L	0 3	(0 0)	16,647			Swinburne	Cowell	Corbett	Sales	Smith	Donaldson RS	Walker	Clifton	Stubbins	Wayman	Hair	2
3	08 Sep	A	Middlesbrough	W	6 0	(0 0)	16,419		Clifton 3, Stubbins 2, Milburn JET	Swinburne	Cowell	Corbett	Gordon	Smith	Donaldson RS	Milburn JET	Clifton	Stubbins	Wayman	Hair	3
4	12 Sep	H	**Burnley**	L	0 1	(0 1)	27,660			Swinburne	Cowell	Corbett	Gordon	Smith	Donaldson RS	Milburn JET	Scott	Stubbins	Wayman	Hair	4
5	15 Sep	H	**Middlesbrough**	D	1 1	(1 1)	32,211	10	Wayman	Swinburne	Cowell	Hubble	Gordon	Smith	Donaldson RS	Milburn JET	Clifton	Taylor E	Wayman	Hair	5
6	22 Sep	H	**Stoke City**	W	9 1	(3 1)	46,349	12	Hair, Wayman, Stubbins 5, Clifton 2	Swinburne	Cowell	Corbett	Gordon	Smith	Crowe	Milburn JET	Clifton	Stubbins	Wayman	Hair	6
7	29 Sep	A	Stoke City	L	1 3	(1 1)	20,229	13	Stubbins	Wood	Cowell	Corbett	Gordon	Smith	Crowe	Milburn JET	Clifton	Stubbins	Wayman	Hair	7
8	06 Oct	A	Grimsby Town	W	2 0	(0 0)	12,560	9	Woodburn, Stubbins	Swinburne	Cowell	Corbett	Gordon	Smith	Crowe	Milburn JET	Clifton	Stubbins	Woodburn	Hair	8
9	13 Oct	H	**Grimsby Town**	W	6 2	(1 2)	46,568	9	Stubbins 2, Crowe, Hair, Milburn JET 2	Swinburne	Cowell	Corbett	Dodgin	Smith	Crowe	Milburn JET	Clifton	Stubbins	Gordon	Hair	9
10	20 Oct	H	**Blackpool**	D	2 2	(2 2)	35,299	8	Wayman, Clifton	Swinburne	Cowell	Corbett	Harvey	Smith	Crowe	Milburn JET	Clifton	Donaldson A	Wayman	Hair	10
11	27 Oct	A	Blackpool	D	1 1	(1 1)	14,910	9	Clifton	Wood	Cowell	Corbett	Gordon	Smith	Harvey	Milburn JET	Clifton	Stubbins	Crowe	Hair	11
12	03 Nov	A	Liverpool	L	0 3	(0 2)	33,818	12		Swinburne	Cowell	Corbett	Harvey	Smith	Porter L	Milburn JET	Clifton	Sloan	Graham	Hair	12
13	10 Nov	H	**Liverpool**	W	6 2	(3 0)	50,833	9	Stubbins, Clifton 3, Wayman, Hair	Swinburne	Cowell	Corbett	Harvey	Smith	Crowe	Milburn JET	Clifton	Stubbins	Wayman	Hair	13
14	17 Nov	H	**Bury**	W	4 2	(1 2)	43,082	7	Hair, Clifton, Stubbins 2	Swinburne	Cowell	Corbett	Harvey	Smith	Crowe	Milburn JET	Clifton	Stubbins	Wayman	Hair	14
15	24 Nov	A	Bury	L	1 2	(1 2)	11,264	8	Harvey	King	Cowell	Corbett	Harvey	Smith	Crowe	Milburn JET	Clifton	Stubbins	Wayman	Hair	15
16	01 Dec	A	Blackburn Rovers	W	2 1	(2 1)	10,625	7	Stubbins 2	King	Cowell	Corbett	Harvey	Smith	Crowe	Rushton	Taylor E	Stubbins	Wayman	Hair	16
17	08 Dec	H	**Blackburn Rovers**	W	8 1	(2 0)	33,092	5	Stubbins 5, Wayman 2, Hair	King	Cowell	Corbett	Harvey	Sales	Crowe	Milburn JET	Clifton	Stubbins	Wayman	Hair	17
18	15 Dec	H	**Bradford Park Avenue**	W	4 0	(0 0)	38,871	5	Stubbins 2 (1 pen), Clifton 2	King	Cowell	Corbett	Harvey	Smith	Crowe	Milburn JET	Clifton	Stubbins	Wayman	Hair	18
19	25 Dec	A	Manchester City	L	3 4	(1 3)	29,408		Clifton 2, Donaldson A	King	Cowell	Corbett	Harvey	Smith	Crowe	Milburn JET	Clifton	Donaldson A	Wayman	Hair	19
20	26 Dec	H	**Manchester City**	D	1 1	(0 0)	54,954		Milburn JET	King	Cowell	Corbett	Harvey	Smith	Crowe	Milburn JET	Clifton	Donaldson A	Wayman	Hair	20
21	29 Dec	A	Burnley	L	2 3	(1 1)	16,877	8	Hair, Wayman	King	Hamby	Corbett	Harvey	Smith	Crowe	Milburn JET	Clifton	Donaldson A	Wayman	Hair	21
22	01 Jan	H	**Sheffield Wednesday**	W	2 0	(0 0)	47,228		Hair, Wayman	King	Graham	Corbett	Harvey	Smith	Crowe	Milburn JET	Taylor E	Wayman	Clifton	Hair	22
23	12 Jan	A	Huddersfield Town	W	4 1	(2 0)	11,423	6	Hair, Stubbins 2, Taylor E	King	Graham	Corbett	Harvey	Smith	Crowe	Milburn JET	Taylor E	Stubbins	Woodburn	Hair	23
24	19 Jan	H	**Huddersfield Town**	W	4 1	(3 0)	34,777	5	Stubbins 3, Milburn JET	King	Graham	Corbett	Harvey	Smith	Crowe	Milburn JET	Taylor E	Stubbins	Wayman	Hair	24
25	26 Jan	H	**Chesterfield**	W	3 2	(2 0)	45,995	4	Stubbins 2, Milburn JET	King	Graham	Corbett	Harvey	Smith	Crowe	Milburn JET	Taylor E	Stubbins	Wayman	Hair	25
26	02 Feb	A	Chesterfield	L	0 2	(0 2)	11,604	5		King	Cowell	Corbett	Harvey	Smith	Crowe	Milburn JET	Taylor E	Stubbins	Sloan	Hair	26
27	16 Feb	A	Barnsley	W	3 1	(1 0)	17,071	4	Wayman, Hair, Milburn JET	King	Graham	Corbett	Harvey	Smith	Crowe	Milburn JET	Woodburn	Stubbins	Wayman	Hair	27
28	23 Feb	H	**Everton**	L	1 3	(1 2)	49,660	6	Hair	King	Cowell	Corbett	Harvey	Smith	Crowe	Milburn JET	Woodburn	Stubbins	Wayman	Hair	28
29	02 Mar	A	Everton	L	1 4	(0 3)	54,186	6	Milburn JET	King	Graham	Corbett	Harvey	Smith	Woodburn	Milburn JET	Brown	Stubbins	Crowe	Hair	29
30	16 Mar	H	**Bolton Wanderers**	L	3 4	(2 3)	38,517	8	Stubbins 2, Wayman	King	Graham	Corbett	Harvey	Smith	Wright	Milburn JET	Brown	Stubbins	Wayman	Hair	30
31	23 Mar	H	**Preston North End**	W	2 1	(1 1)	34,486	6	Milburn JET, og (Williams)	King	Graham	Corbett	Harvey	Sales	Wright	Milburn JET	Brown	Stubbins	Pearson TU	Hair	31
32	27 Mar	A	Bradford Park Avenue	L	3 5	(2 2)	9,397		Stubbins 2 (1 pen), Milburn JET	King	Batty	Graham	Harvey	Sales	Wright	Milburn JET	Hamilton	Stubbins	Pearson TU	Hair	32
33	30 Mar	A	Preston North End	L	1 3	(0 0)	10,000	10	Hamilton	Swinburne	Woodburn	Graham	Harvey	Sales	Wright	Hamilton	Brown	Stubbins	Pearson TU	Hair	33
34	06 Apr	A	Leeds United	W	3 0	(1 0)	16,500	10	Brown 2, Wayman	Swinburne	Craig	Graham	Woodburn	Sales	Wright	Milburn JET	Harvey	Wayman	Brown	Pearson TU	34
35	10 Apr	A	Bolton Wanderers	W	1 0	(1 0)	9,386		Pearson T	Swinburne	Craig	Graham	Harvey	Sales	Wright	Walker	Milburn JET	Scott	Brown	Pearson TU	35
36	13 Apr	H	**Leeds United**	D	1 1	(0 1)	22,991		Milburn JET	Swinburne	Craig	Graham	Harvey	Woodburn	Wright	Milburn JET	Brown	Sloan	Wayman	Pearson TU	36
37	19 Apr	H	**Manchester United**	L	0 1	(0 0)	47,493			Swinburne	Craig	Graham	Harvey	Sales	Wright	Walker	Taylor E	Stubbins	Milburn JET	Pearson TU	37
38	20 Apr	A	Sunderland	L	0 1	(0 1)	37,000			Swinburne	Graham	Corbett	Harvey	Smith	Wright	Milburn JET	Brown	Stubbins	Wayman	Hair	38
39	22 Apr	A*	Manchester United	L	1 4	(1 1)	39,173		Wayman	Swinburne	Graham	Corbett	Harvey	Smith	Woodburn	Milburn JET	Brown	Wayman	Pearson TU	Hair	39
40	27 Apr	H	**Sunderland**	W	4 1	(1 0)	29,564		Milburn JET, Brown, Pearson T, Stubbins	Swinburne	Graham	Corbett	Harvey	Smith	Woodburn	Milburn JET	Brown	Stubbins	Wayman	Pearson TU	40
41	01 May	H	**Barnsley**	W	1 0	(0 0)	20,158		Milburn JET	Swinburne	Graham	Corbett	Harvey	Smith	Woodburn	Milburn JET	Brown	Stubbins	Wayman	Pearson TU	41
42	04 May	A	Sheffield Wednesday	W	3 2	(2 0)	20,000	6	Brown, Wayman, Stubbins	Swinburne	Graham	Corbett	Harvey	Smith	Woodburn	Milburn JET	Brown	Stubbins	Wayman	Pearson TU	42
Round			**FA Cup**																		**Round**
3(1)	05 Jan	H	**Barnsley**	W	4 2	(2 2)	60,284		Hair, Stubbins, Milburn JET 2	King	Cowell	Corbett	Harvey	Smith	Crowe	Milburn JET	Clifton	Stubbins	Wayman	Hair	3(1)
3(2)	09 Jan	A	Barnsley	L	0 3	(0 2)	27,000			King	Cowell	Corbett	Harvey	Smith	Crowe	Milburn JET	Taylor E	Stubbins	Clifton	Hair	3(2)

A* Played at Maine Road, Manchester

DateLine ... 22 Sept: Stoke are humbled 9-1 on Tyneside, United scoring 22 goals in the opening six games. **5 Jan:** Over 60,000 see the FA Cup first-leg meeting with Barnsley end 4-2. **27 April:** Newcastle score their 100th goal of the season in a 4-1 victory over Sunderland.

Other Matches

Senior fixtures 1881 to date

Senior 'non first-class' fixtures comprising: friendlies, tour games, invitation cups, unofficial leagues, testimonials and the like are scheduled below. A judgement has been made where a club squad game has taken place. In such cases where sufficient first-team regulars played, the match has been classified as a senior 'Other Match' and included here, while marginal fixtures are scheduled under the label of *Newcastle United XI* contests. Remaining games are classed as reserve fixtures and not included.

Prior to joining the Football League in the close-season of 1893, the club played in the Northern League (1888-93). But in the main the programme of fixtures consisted of friendly challenge matches with either other local sides or visits to the region by teams from Scotland or the rest of England, often clubs advanced in development. There were several big-names fixtures on Tyneside such as the appearance of West Bromwich Albion, Preston North End as well as Blackburn Rovers, Wolves, Derby County, and Renton from north of the border. As a consequence, the register for this early period is extensive. Also included in these pioneer years are historic fixtures; the very first game played against Elswick Leather Works in November 1881 as well as the first match under the title of Newcastle United when Middlesbrough arrived at St James' Park during December 1892 and also the club's highest ever scoreline, 19-0 versus Point Pleasant in a 1888 Northumberland Challenge Cup meeting.

It has been difficult at times to piece together many of the details of Victorian matches and the club's overseas fixtures. Many of the games have been scantily recorded, either in the club's own archive, or by newspapers. This is even the case for relatively modern tours abroad. Various points of research have been used to gather information, from club Minute books, official documents such as those housed at FC Barcelona's museum, to original correspondence including those from the Hungarian FA relating to the somewhat notorious 1929 tour, as well as match programmes, contemporary magazines and newspapers from throughout the Continent. Much new data has been collected to give a fuller picture of Newcastle's trips abroad, especially so in pre-war years. Fortunately the Magpies lengthy tours to North America and South Africa soon after World War Two are well recorded with extensive 'scrapbooks' being kept by the club. However, certain early Continental voyages, notably to Denmark (1904) and Central Europe (1905) remain something of a mystery.

A review of all these matches includes ascertaining which club United actually played. Information has been limited for many games and in several instances the opponents faced is open to conjecture. On occasion brief reports noted that United, for example, played a team from Berlin or Vienna. But which club was it? Newcastle also faced several combination elevens comprising local teams or districts. Language was also something of a quandary at times. Apart from inaccuracies in translation, certain tours, notably those to Scandinavia, have also caused problems where towns or cities are often different from the football club names. It was reported that the Black'n'Whites faced Orebro in 1991, but the club actually faced was Rynninge IK who are based in the Swedish town. Most of these club title questions have been resolved, although some inconsistencies remain.

Fixture classification & abbreviations:

AC = Asia Cup, **ASL** = Anglo-Scottish unofficial league, **BC** = Budapest Cup, **CB** = Copa Barcelona, **CC** = Counties Cup, **CdC** = Coppa del Centenario, **Cent** = Centenary celebration fixture, **CrC** = Coronation Cup, **Ch** = Charity fixture, **CoN** = Cock of the North unofficial league, **CwC** = England v Scotland Cup winners challenge, **DF** = Disaster Fund, **DIT** = Dublin International Tournament (Irish International Club Soccer Tournament), **FoB** = Festival of Britain, **FF** = Franco-Anglo-Scottish Friendship unofficial tournament, **FLJ** = Football League Jubilee, **Fr** = Friendly match, **HC** = Hospitals Cup, **HCf** = Hospitals Cup final, **ICC** = Inter County Cup winners challenge, **IMC** = Isle of Man Cup, **ICT** = Ibrox International Challenge Trophy, **JC** = Japan Cup, **JDC** = JD Sports Cup, **Jub** = Jubilee celebration fixture, **wFr** = Wartime friendly, **MCT** = Mercantile Centenary Credit Trophy (Football League Centenary Tournament), **MSC** = Mallorca Summer Cup, **MT** = Madeira Tournament, **NCC** = Northumberland County Championship, **NCS** = Northumberland Charity Shield, **NEL** = North Eastern League, **NES** = Newcastle Exhibition Superchallenge Cup, **NGC** = Newcastle Gateshead Cup, **Ot** = Overseas tour match, **PSC** = Paris Sporting Cup, **PU** = Player's Union fund fixture, **SF** = Social, Unemployed or Distress Fund, **TCS** = Tyne Charity Shield, **TDS** = Torneo Costa Del Sol, **Test** *or* **Ben** = Testimonial or Benefit match, with beneficiary named (*indicating a United personality), **TTH** = Trofeo Teresa Herrera, **TF** = Temperance Festival, **UCC** = United Christian Medical Service Charity Cup, **UT** = Umbro Tournament, **WF** = War Fund, **WCh** = War charity.

Note:

Where attendances or half-times are left bank, the details are untraced. Where goalscorers have not been verified, these are also left blank or *ano* (another) inserted, or noted as *(Scorers untraced)*.

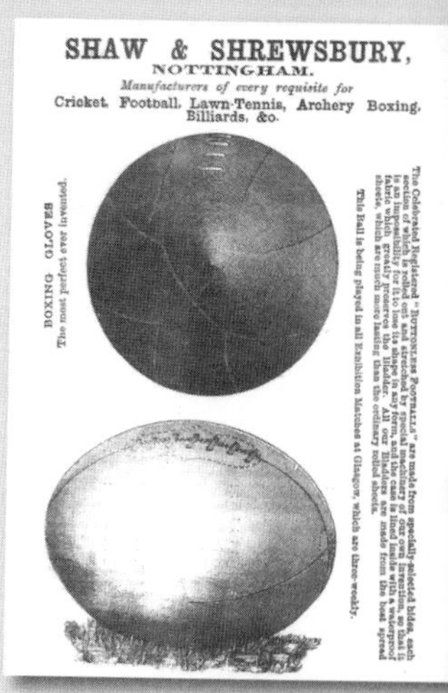

A Victorian advert for both types of 'football'; the round 'Association Code' ball, and the oval 'Rugby Code' version.

Local outfitter Murton's was used by almost every football club in the North East. They were based on Grainger Street.

1881-82 (as Stanley FC)

26 Nov	Elswick Leather Works 2nd XI	Fr	(h)	W	5-0	(0-0)	McKenzie, Dixon 2, Coulson, Findlay (W) (Newcastle United's first ever fixture)
10 Dec	North Eastern 2nd XI	Fr	(a)	W	3-1		(One of Stanley's goals disputed)
17 Dec	Newcastle FA 2nd XI	Fr	(a)	D	0-0	(0-0)	
21 Jan	Elswick Leather Works 2nd XI	Fr	(a)	W	2-0		
4 Feb	Newcastle FA 2nd XI	Fr	(h)	W	7-0		(Two goals disputed)
11 Feb	Derwent Rovers	Fr	(a)	L	2-3		
11 March	Rangers 2nd XI	Fr	(h)	W	2-1	(1-0)	(One of Stanley's goals disputed)
18 March	Burnopfield	Fr	(h)	W	2-0		
25 March	Derwent Rovers	Fr	(h)	L	0-2		(One goal disputed)
1 April	Burnopfield 2nd XI	Fr	(h)	W	2-0	(0-0)	
8 April	Burnopfield	Fr	(a)	L	0-2		

1882-83 (as East End FC)

7 Oct	Hamsterley Rangers	Fr	(h)	W	1-0		Gardner
11 Nov	Hamsterley Rangers	Fr	(a)	L	0-4		
25 Nov	Birtley	Fr	(h)	W	2-1		(Birtley's goal disputed)
23 Dec	All Saints	Fr	(h)	W	4-0		
1 Jan	North Eastern	Fr	(a)	L	1-2		
10 Feb	Heaton Association	Fr	(a)	D	0-0	(0-0)	
17 March	Tyne Association	Fr	(a)	L	0-8		
7 April	Newton	Fr	(h)	L	0-2		
8 June	Bedlington Burdon	TF	(a)	L	0-2		

1883-84

13 Oct	Prudhoe Rovers	Fr	(h)	W	1-0		
20 Oct	Birtley	Fr	(a)	W	1-0	(0-0)	(Goal disputed)
27 Oct	Tantobie	Fr	(h)	W	3-0		
3 Nov	Sunderland 'A'	Fr	(h)	L	0-3	(0-0)	(Newcastle United's first fixture with Sunderland)
10 Nov	Newcastle West End	Fr	(h)	D	1-1		
17 Nov	Jarrow	Fr	(h)	W	4-2		Findlay (R) 2, Armstrong, Fenwick
24 Nov	Whitburn	Fr	(a)	W	1-0		
1 Jan	All Saints	Fr	(a)	W	4-1		Findlay (R) 2, Speight, Cook
2 Jan	Newcastle FA	Fr	(a)	L	0-2		
19 Jan	St Cuthberts	Fr	(h)	W	3-0	(0-0)	
2 Feb	City Harriers	Fr	(a)	W	8-0		
16 Feb	Rosehill	Fr	(a)	W	2-0		
23 Feb	Whitburn	Fr	(h)	W	2-0		
8 March	Prudhoe Rovers	Fr	(a)	L	1-4		
22 March	Newcastle West End	Fr	(a)	L	0-2		(One goal disputed)
29 March	North Eastern	Fr	(a)	W	4-3	(2-2)	Hiscock (E), Cook 3 (One of NE's goals disputed)
19 April	Newton	Fr	(a)	W	2-1		
14 June	Newcastle West End	TF	(n)	W	2-0		
25 June	North Eastern	TF	(n)	W	2-0		
25 June	Sunderland	TF	(n)	L	1-3		

East End faced Sunderland for the very first time in 1883.

1884-85

27 Sept	Hibernia	Fr	(h)	W	4-0			
4 Oct	Sleekburn Wanderers	Fr	(h)	D	2-2			
25 Oct	North Eastern	Fr	(a)	W	5-2	(2-2)	Cook 2, Hoban, Armstrong, Fenwick	
22 Nov	Whitburn	Fr	(h)	W	1-0			
13 Dec	Hibernia	Fr	(a)	W	9-0		Hiscock (E) 4, Cook 2, Hoban 2, Speight	
20 Dec	Morpeth Harriers	Fr	(a)	W	2-0		Cook, Hiscock (E)	
1 Jan	Rosehill	Fr	(a)	D	1-1		Cook	
10 Jan	North Eastern	Fr	(h)	W	1-0			
17 Jan	Newcastle FA 'B'	Fr	(a)	W	7-1		(4 of the goals were disputed, 3 for East End)	
31 Jan	Morpeth Harriers	Fr	(h)	W	1-0		Cook	
21 Feb	Whitburn	Fr	(a)	L	4-6		(1 of Whitburn's goals disputed)	
11 April	Sleekburn Wanderers	NCS	(n)	W	6-0	(3-0)	Gorman 2, Hiscock (E) 2, Gray, Hoban	500
18 April	Newcastle FA	NCS	(n)	W	10-0	(5-0)	Hiscock (E) 3, Hoban 3, Gorman, White, Armstrong, Blackett	600
25 April	Darlington	ICC	(a)	L	0-1	(0-0)		
13 June	Shankhouse Albion	TF	(n)	L	1-2			

Pioneer clubs were located throughout the region. One of the strongest were Darlington. They faced East End in the Inter County Challenge match in 1885.

1885-86

19 Sept	Elswick Ordnance Works	TF	(n)	L	0-3		(Elswick had 2 goals start, 7-a-side match)	
26 Sept	Bishop Auckland CI	Fr	(h)	W	3-0	(2-0)	Scott, Cook, ano	
17 Oct	Sleekburn Wanderers	Fr	(a)	L	2-3	(0-1)		300
31 Oct	Berwick Rangers	Fr	(h)	D	0-0	(0-0)		
7 Nov	Sunderland	Fr	(h)	L	0-1	(0-1)		
14 Nov	Newcastle West End	Fr	(a)	W	6-1			
28 Nov	Newcastle FA	Fr	(h)	W	1-0	(0-0)		
5 Dec	Tyne Association	Fr	(h)	D	1-1	(1-0)	Muir (W)	
19 Dec	Gateshead Casuals	Fr	(h)	W	1-0	(0-0)		
26 Dec	Newcastle West End	Fr	(h)	D	2-2	(2-1)	Hoban, Gray	
2 Jan	Dumbarton Athletic	Fr	(h)	L	1-4	(0-3)	Hoban	
16 Jan	Wearmouth	Fr	(a)	W	5-0	(1-0)	Scott 2, Muir (W), O'Brien, Hoban	
6 Feb	Heaton Association	Fr	(a)	W	9-0			
13 Feb	Bishop Auckland CI	Fr	(a)	L	3-6	(0-4)	Muir (W) 2, White	
20 Feb	Sunderland	Fr	(a)	D	1-1	(1-0)	Muir (W)	
10 April	Elswick Leather Works	NCS	(n)	W	4-1	(1-1)	Scott, Hoban, O'Brien, Muir (W)	
17 April	Shankhouse Black Watch	NCS	(n)	D	1-1	(0-1)	Hoban	
1 May	Morpeth Harriers	NCS	(n)	W	2-1	(1-0)	Hiscock (E), Scott	

1886-87

25 Sept	Morpeth Harriers	Fr	(a)	L	2-3	(1-1)	Hiscock (E), ano	
2 Oct	Newcastle West End	Fr	(a)	L	2-3	(0-2)	O'Brien, Muir (W)	2,000
9 Oct	Gateshead Association	Fr	(a)	W	7-1	(3-1)	Hiscock(E) 3, White, Muir (W), O'Brien, og (Douglas)	
16 Oct	Durham Training College	Fr	(a)	L	1-3	(1-2)	Hiscock (E)	
23 Oct	Darlington St Augustine's	Fr	(h)	D	2-2	(1-1)	Muir (W), Hoban	
20 Nov	Newcastle FA	Fr	(h)	W	6-0	(5-0)	Hiscock (E), Scott, ano 4	
27 Nov	Newcastle FA	Fr	(a)	W	4-0			
4 Dec	Sunderland	Fr	(a)	D	1-1	(1-0)	O'Brien	
11 Dec	Rendel	Fr	(h)	W	2-1	(1-1)	Muir (W) 2	400
18 Dec	Elswick Rangers	Fr	(a)	D	0-0	(0-0)		
25 Dec	Darlington St Augustine's	Fr	(h)	D	1-1	(1-0)	Muir (W)	
1 Jan	Elswick Rangers	Fr	(h)	L	0-2	(0-2)	(Unofficial game)	
15 Jan	Shankhouse Black Watch	Fr	(a)	L	0-3	(0-3)		
12 Feb	Bishop Auckland CI	Fr	(h)	W	2-0	(0-0)	Hiscock (E), Hoban	
26 Feb	Durham University	Fr	(h)	D	2-2	(2-1)	Scott, ano	
5 March	Elswick Rangers	Fr	(a)	D	0-0	(0-0)		
26 March	Bishop Auckland	Fr	(a)	W	2-1	(0-1)	og (Strachan), ano	2,000
2 April	Elswick Leather Works	Fr	(h)	W	5-0	(2-0)	Hiscock (E) 4, Muir (W)	
8 April	Shankhouse Black Watch	Fr	(h)	W	4-1	(1-0)		
11 April	Medomsley	Fr	(a)	L	2-4	(1-2)		
16 April	Darlington St Augustine's	Fr	(h)	D	1-1	(1-0)	White	1,000
30 April	Morpeth Harriers	Fr	(h)	W	3-1	(2-1)	Muir (W), Hoban, O'Brien	
21 May	Elswick Rangers (J McCallum)	Ben	(h)	L	0-1	(0-0)		
11 June	Hebburn	TF	(h)	W	6-0			
18 June	Morpeth Harriers	TF	(a)	W	2-1	(0-0)	Hoban, Roche	
29 June	Elswick Rangers	TF	(n)	L	2-3		aet (1-1 after normal time)	5,500

East End's great rivals were not from Wearside, rather neighbours Newcastle West End as featurd on this Baines collector card.

1887-88

23 July	Elswick Rangers (John Blackett)	Ben					(Result untraced)	
17 Sept	Elswick Rangers	Fr	(h)	D	0-0	(0-0)		
24 Sept	Rendel	Fr	(a)	W	2-1	(1-0)	Jenkins, Roche	
1 Oct	Darlington St Augustine's	Fr	(a)	L	2-4	(1-2)	Hoban, Hiscock (E)	
8 Oct	Morpeth Harriers	Fr	(h)	W	3-1	(3-1)	Scott 2, Muir (A)	
22 Oct	Newcastle West End	Fr	(a)	D	0-0	(0-0)		
29 Oct	Bede College	Fr	(a)	L	2-3	(2-1)	Scott, Hoban	
5 Nov	Morpeth Harriers	Fr	(a)	W	3-2	(2-1)	Hiscock (E), Muir, og (Donaldson)	
12 Nov	Rendel	Fr	(h)	W	1-0	(1-0)	og	
19 Nov	Whitburn	Fr	(a)	D	1-1	(1-1)	Mulvey	
26 Nov	Gateshead Association	Fr	(h)	W	3-0	(1-0)	Hiscock (E), Purvis 2	
3 Dec	Shankhouse Black Watch	Fr	(h)	L	0-1	(0-1)		
10 Dec	Bishop Auckland CI	Fr	(a)	W	2-0	(1-0)	Hoban, Hiscock (E)	
26 Dec	South Bank	Fr	(h)	D	2-2	(0-2)		
27 Dec	Darlington	Fr	(a)	L	2-5	(1-3)	Hoban, Scott	
31 Dec	Abercorn (Paisley)	Fr	(h)	L	1-7	(0-3)	Mulvey	
2 Jan	Partick Thistle	Fr	(h)	L	1-3	(0-0)	Scott	
14 Jan	Elswick Rangers	Fr	(a)	D	0-0	(0-0)		
28 Jan	Newcastle West End	Fr	(h)	L	0-3	(0-1)		
4 Feb	Middlesbrough	Fr	(h)	L	0-6	(0-3)		
11 Feb	Gateshead Association	Fr	(h)	W	4-2	(3-1)	Scott 2, Mulvey, Hetherington	
18 Feb	Hebburn	Fr	(a)	W	5-1	(4-0)	Hetherington, White 2, Scott, Hoban	
24 March	Middlesbrough	Fr	(a)	L	1-3	(0-0)	Muir (W)	
31 March	Rendel	Fr	(h)	W	3-1	(2-1)	Mulvey 2, Scott (1 of Mulvey's goals disputed)	
2 April	Port Clarence	Fr	(h)	W	2-1	(0-1)	Scott, Hoban	
7 April	Newcastle West End	NCS	(h)	L	0-2	(0-2)		
14 April	Medomsley	Fr	(h)	W	3-2			
21 April	Elswick Rangers	Fr	(a)	L	1-4			

Shankhouse Black Watch often faced East End. A noted side, they are pictured with the Northumberland Senior Cup.

1888-89

Date	Opponent	Comp	Venue	Res	Score	HT	Scorers	Att
18 Aug	Elswick Rangers (John Blackett)	Ben	(h)	L	0-4			
1 Sept	Ashington	Fr	(a)	L	1-2	(0-1)	Smith	
8 Sept	Sheffield Park Grange	Fr	(h)	W	3-2	(1-2)	Muir (A), ano 2	
15 Sept	Gateshead Association	Fr	(h)	W	3-1	(2-1)	Muir (A), Hoban 2	
22 Sept	Middlesbrough	Fr	(a)	L	2-3	(0-2)	Coupe, Shaw	3,000
29 Sept	West Hartlepool	Fr	(a)	W	5-0		Collins, White 2, ano 2	
13 Oct	North Sands Rovers	Fr	(a)	W	2-0	(1-0)		
20 Oct	Ashington	Fr	(a)	W	1-0	(0-0)	Hoban	
3 Nov	Elswick Rangers	Fr	(a)	L	2-4	(0-1)	Samson, Muir (A)	
10 Nov	North Sands Rovers	Fr	(h)	W	2-0	(1-0)	White, Hoban	
24 Nov	Bishop Auckland	Fr	(a)	D	2-2	(2-0)	McCrinnon, Theakstone	
1 Dec	Elswick Rangers	Fr	(h)	W	2-0	(0-0)	Hoban, Collins	1,500
8 Dec	Birtley	Fr	(h)	D	1-1	(0-1)	Blackett	
15 Dec	Birtley	Fr	(h)	W	5-0	(4-0)	Blackett 2, Hoban, Mack, Mulvey	
22 Dec	Sunderland	Fr	(h)	D	1-1	(1-1)	Mack	3,000
25 Dec	Newcastle West End	Fr	(a)	L	1-4	(0-2)	Blackett	5,000
26 Dec	Port Clarence	Fr	(h)	W	5-1	(2-0)	Mulvey 2, Mack, Collins, Young	
29 Dec	Mossend Swifts	Fr	(h)	L	1-3	(0-1)	Richardson	
31 Dec	Renton	Fr	(h)	D	2-2	(0-1)	Collins, Mulvey	4,000
1 Jan	Airdrieonians	Fr	(h)	D	0-0	(0-0)		
12 Jan	Edinburgh University	Fr	(h)	W	2-1	(1-0)	Mack, Smith	
19 Jan	Rendel	Fr	(h)	W	2-0	(1-0)	Mack 2	
26 Jan	Morpeth Harriers	Fr	(a)	W	4-2	(3-1)	Mulvey 2, McKane, ano	
2 Feb	Newcastle West End	Fr	(h)	W	2-1	(0-1)	Mack, Smith	3,000
16 Feb	Middlesbrough	Fr	(h)	D	1-1	(1-1)	Mack	1,000
23 Feb	Birtley	Fr	(a)	W	1-0	(1-0)	og (Kennedy)	
5 March	Sunderland Albion	Fr	(a)	L	1-4	(1-0)	Mulvey	2,000
9 March	Port Clarence	Fr	(a)	D	2-2	(1-2)	Mack, Mulvey	
16 March	Rendel	Fr	(h)	W	4-0	(2-0)	Mack 2, Smith, Creilly	
30 March	Rendel	TCS	(h)	W	3-0	(2-0)	Mulvey, Mack, Collins	
April	Elswick Rangers	TCS	(n)	W	w/o		(Rangers refused to play)	
19 April	Gateshead NE	Fr	(h)	D	0-0	(0-0)		
20 April	Mossend Swifts	Fr	(a)	L	1-3	(1-0)	Collins	
22 April	Glasgow Thistle	Fr	(a)	W	2-1	(1-1)	Mulvey, White	4,000
23 April	Hurlford	Fr	(a)	L	1-4		(scorer untraced)	
27 April	Rendel	Fr	(a)	L	0-2	(0-0)		
30 April	Preston North End	Fr	(h)	L	1-4	(0-3)	Collins	3,000
11 May	Shankhouse Black Watch	NCC	(h)	W	1-0	(1-0)	Collins	
13 May	Wolverhampton Wanderers	Fr	(h)	L	2-3	(2-0)	Collins, Smith	3,000
15 May	East End Swifts	Fr	(n)	W	8-1	(2-0)	Barker 2, Mulvey 2, Miller (Jas), McCurdie, ano 2	
18 May	Darlington St Augustine's	Fr	(h)	W	2-0	(2-0)	Mulvey, Gibbon	
23 May	Sunderland Albion	ICC	(a)	W	1-0	(0-0)	Mulvey	
30 May	Sunderland Albion	Fr	(h)	W	1-0	(1-0)	Barker	2,000

1889-90

Date	Opponent	Comp	Venue	Res	Score	HT	Scorers	Att
3 Sept	Blackburn Rovers	Fr	(h)	L	1-2	(0-0)	Collins	
4 Sept	Sunderland Albion	Fr	(a)	W	2-1	(1-0)	Mulvey 2	3,000
5 Sept	Alnwick Working Men	Fr	(a)	W	6-1	(3-1)	(scorers untraced)	
2 Nov	Morpeth Harriers	Fr	(h)	W	3-1	(1-0)	Watson, Collins, Miller	
16 Nov	Sunderland	Fr	(h)	L	0-4	(0-3)		6,500
30 Nov	Morpeth Harriers	Fr	(a)	W	2-1	(2-1)	Nugent, McLaughlan	
7 Dec	Notts Rangers	Fr	(h)	D	1-1	(1-1)	Gibbon	
25 Dec	Newcastle West End	Fr	(a)	L	0-3	(0-2)		6,000
1 Jan	London Casuals	Fr	(h)	L	0-2	(0-2)		1,200
2 Jan	Abercorn (Paisley)	Fr	(h)	L	2-4	(2-1)	Thompson, McInnes	1,500
3 Jan	Shankhouse Black Watch	Fr	(h)	L	1-2	(1-2)	Collins	
1 Feb	Middlesbrough Ironopolis	Fr	(a)	W	2-1	(0-0)	Thompson, McLaughlan	3,000
29 March	Grimsby Town	Fr	(a)	L	0-2	(0-0)		5,000
4 April	Sunderland Albion	Fr	(a)	D	1-1	(0-0)	(scorer untraced)	10,000
5 April	Newcastle West End	Fr	(a)	D	0-0	(0-0)		3,000
7 April	Edinburgh University	Fr	(h)	W	6-1	(0-1)	McInnes 4, Thompson, ano	
8 April	Darlington St Augustine's	Fr	(a)	L	1-2	(0-2)	McInnes	
19 April	Sheffield United	Fr	(h)	W	2-0	(2-0)	Collins, Thompson	1,000
22 April	Notts County (at Jesmond)	Fr	(h)	D	1-1	(0-0)	McInnes	
24 April	Rendel	TCS	(n)	W	6-0	(2-0)	McInnes 2, White 2, Collins, Mulvey	
26 April	Sunderland Albion	Fr	(a)	L	1-3	(1-1)	Collins	6,000
3 May	Elswick Rangers	Fr	(h)	W	5-0	(0-0)	McInnes, Mulvey 2, McKane, McCurdie	1,000
10 May	Elswick Rangers	TCS	(n)	W	6-2	(4-2)	White, McInnes, Mulvey, Thompson, McCurdie, og (Simm)	3,000
26 May	Sunderland Albion	Fr	(h)	W	3-1	(1-0)	Thompson, Smith, ano	2,000

1890-91

Date	Opponent	Comp	Venue	Res	Score	HT	Scorers	Att
1 Sept	Sheffield Wednesday	Fr	(h)	D	1-1	(0-1)	McInnes	1,500
6 Sept	West Hartlepool NER	Fr	(a)	W	5-1	(4-1)	Mulvey, Creilly, 3 ano	
4 Oct	South Bank	Fr	(h)	W	3-1	(1-0)	Young, McInnes, Collins	1,200
11 Oct	Elswick Rangers	Fr	(h)	W	9-1	(7-0)	Mulvey, McInnes 3, Collins, Thompson 4	
18 Oct	South Bank	Fr	(a)	W	2-1	(1-1)	Penny, Creilly	1,600
13 Dec	Newmilns	Fr	(h)	W	3-1	(1-0)	McInnes, Creilly, Thompson	1,500
25 Dec	Newcastle West End	Fr	(a)	W	5-0	(3-0)	Creilly 2, McInnes, Thompson, Collins	6,000
31 Dec	Burnley	Fr	(h)	W	4-1	(2-0)	Wallace 2, McInnes, Collins	
1 Jan	Glasgow Northern	Fr	(h)	D	3-3	(0-3)	McInnes, Thompson, ano	2,000
2 Jan	Rendel	Fr	(h)	W	3-2	(2-2)	Thompson 2, McCurdie	1,000
7 Feb	Sheffield United	Fr	(h)	W	4-0	(1-0)	McInnes 2, Thompson, Sorley	2,000
14 Feb	Middlesbrough	DF	(a)	L	0-4	(0-2)		3,000
21 Feb	Rendel	Fr	(h)	W	6-1	(3-1)	Sorley, Creilly, Collins 2, McInnes, Mulvey	
28 Feb	Sunderland Albion	Fr	(a)	L	0-1	(0-0)		4,000
27 March	Newcastle West End	Fr	(h)	W	4-0	(4-0)	Sorley 2, Wilson, Mulvey	4,000
28 March	Nottingham Forest	Fr	(h)	L	1-2	(1-0)	Sorley	3,000
30 March	Derby County	Fr	(h)	L	0-5	(0-1)		2,000
11 April	Sheffield United	Fr	(a)	D	2-2	(2-0)	Mulvey, McInnes	3,000
30 April	Sunderland	Fr	(h)	L	0-3	(0-1)		3,000
2 May	Science & Art	TCS	(h)	D	0-0	(0-0)		
5 May	Science & Art	TCS	(n)	W	4-3	(2-2)	Collins 2, Sorley, ano	
7 May	Willington Athletic	TCS	(n)	L	0-1	(0-1)		

Newcastle upon Tyne boasted several strong clubs in the early days of the game. Rendel were based near to the West Road and faced the East Enders many times.

Tyneside fans had two clubs from Wearside to get excited about. Sunderland Albion faced East End on several occasions.

John Barker appeared with distinction for both West End and East End. He netted twice in the contest with East End Swifts in 1889.

1891-92

5 Sept	London Casuals	Fr	(h)	W	4-0	(2-0)	Sorley 2, Crate, Connolly	3,000
7 Sept	Sunderland	Fr	(h)	W	2-0	(2-0)	Spence, Crate (Abandoned 60m, darkness)	4,000
12 Sept	Queen of the South Wanderers	Fr	(h)	W	6-3	(4-0)	Connolly 4, Reay, Thompson	3,000
26 Sept	Sunderland	Fr	(a)	L	0-2	(0-0)		5,000
30 Sept	Victoria Wednesday	Fr	(h)	W	3-1	(3-1)	Thompson 2, Sorley	
28 Nov	Edinburgh University	Fr	(h)	W	8-1	(4-1)	Sorley, Wallace 2, McKane, Reay, Thompson 2, Gardner	
12 Dec	Middlesbrough	Fr	(h)	L	0-1	(0-0)		2,500
25 Dec	Newcastle West End	Fr	(a)	W	3-0	(2-0)	Thompson, Wallace, ano	5,000
1 Jan	Annbank	Fr	(h)	W	4-2	(1-2)	Barker, Sorley, Reay, Thompson	2,000
2 Jan	Sunderland Albion	Fr	(h)	W	3-1	(2-1)	Sorley, Thompson, Crate	3,000
9 Jan	Sunderland	Fr	(h)	L	4-6	(4-1)	Thompson 2, Crate, Reay	5,000
23 Jan	Middlesbrough	Fr	(a)	W	1-0	(0-0)	Thompson (p)	2,500
13 Feb	Blackburn Rovers	Fr	(h)	L	1-3	(0-3)	Sorley	5,803
12 March	Long Eaton Rangers	Fr	(h)	W	7-1	(5-0)	Sorley 3, Barker 2, Reay, Wallace	
19 March	Wolverhampton Wanderers	Fr	(h)	W	3-0	(1-0)	Barker 3	5,000
26 March	Stoke	Fr	(h)	W	2-0	(0-0)	Barker, Crate	4,000
30 March	Newcastle West End	Fr	(h)	W	4-0	(3-0)	Thompson, Reay, Sorley 2	1,300
9 April	Burnley	Fr	(h)	L	1-2	(0-1)	Wallace	
11 April	Sunderland	Fr	(h)	L	1-4	(0-2)	Barker	3,500
15 April	Stoke	Fr	(h)	L	2-3	(1-2)	Reay, Sorley	5,000
18 April	London Casuals	Fr	(h)	W	2-0	(0-0)	Sorley 2	2,000
21 April	Shankhouse Black Watch (William Bayles*)	Test	(h)	W	1-0	(1-0)	Thompson	
23 April	Derby County	Fr	(h)	W	4-1	(1-1)	Thompson, Wallace, Crate, og (Roberts)	2,500
25 April	Shankhouse Black Watch	Ben	(a)	L	0-5	(0-2)		1,000
28 April	Preston North End	Fr	(h)	L	0-2	(0-1)		2,000

A rare West End team group, the club's great rivals, pictured at their base of St James' Park, soon to be the new home of the East Enders.

1892-93 (as East End/Newcastle Utd)

3 Sept	Glasgow Celtic	Fr	(h)	L	0-1	(0-1)	(First East End fixture at St James' Park)	7,000
7 Sept	Sunderland	Fr	(h)	D	2-2	(2-2)	Crate, Wallace	6,000
10 Sept	Middlesbrough Ironopolis	Fr	(h)	W	4-1	(2-0)	Thompson 2, Collins, og (Oliver)	4,000
17 Sept	Middlesbrough Ironopolis	Fr	(a)	W	2-1	(1-0)	Sorley, Collins	4,000
6 Oct	Stockton	Fr	(a)	L	1-3	(0-0)	Collins	3,500
8 Oct	Middlesbrough	Fr	(a)	W	1-0	(1-0)	Collins	3,000
15 Oct	South of Ayrshire	Fr	(h)	W	7-0	(4-0)	Reay, Creilly, Collins 3, Crate 2	3.000
22 Oct	Heart of Midlothian	Fr	(h)	W	2-0	(1-0)	Reay 2	3,000
29 Oct	Mossend Swifts	Fr	(h)	W	4-1	(3-1)	Sorley 3, ano	1,500
5 Nov	Sheffield United	Fr	(h)	D	2-2	(1-2)	Reay, Sorley	4,500
24 Dec	Middlesbrough	Fr	(h)	W	2-1	(1-0)	McIntosh, Reay (First fixture under the title of Newcastle United)	1,500
26 Dec	Sheffield Wednesday	Fr	(a)	L	0-1	(0-1)		6,000
31 Dec	Corinthians	Fr	(h)	W	8-1	(3-1)	McKane, Sorley, McIntosh, Thompson 3, Reay 2	1,500
2 Jan	Everton	Fr	(h)	W	4-2	(3-0)	Thompson 2, Sorley, Reay	3,000
3 Jan	Glasgow Rangers	Fr	(h)	W	4-0	(2-0)	Reay, Creilly, Thompson, Sorley	3,000
7 Jan	Bolton Wanderers	Fr	(h)	W	3-1	(2-1)	Reay 2, Thompson	2,000
28 Jan	Stockton	Fr	(a)	L	2-3	(0-1)	Sorley 2	2,000
4 Feb	Stockton	Fr	(h)	W	3-1	(2-0)	Reay, Crate, ano	1,500
15 Feb	Bedlington Wednesday	Fr	(a)	W	9-1	(5-0)	Crate 3, Creilly, Miller, Reay, Wallace, ano 2 (Some records show score as 8-1)	1,000
18 Feb	Notts County	Fr	(h)	W	3-2	(3-2)	Thompson, Sorley 2	3,000
25 Feb	Sunderland	Fr	(h)	L	1-6	(0-3)	Graham	7,000
4 March	Stoke	Fr	(h)	L	3-4	(2-1)	Graham, Reay, Wallace	4,000
11 March	Annbank	Fr	(h)	W	6-1	(4-1)	Reay 5, Thompson	2,000
18 March	Derby County	Fr	(h)	W	3-1	(1-1)	Collins, og (Methven), ano	3,000
25 March	Nottingham Forest	Fr	(h)	W	4-1	(3-0)	Sorley 2 (1p), Reay 2	3,000
31 March	Blyth	Fr	(a)	W	3-2	(1-1)	Reay 2, Sorley (p)	3,000
1 April	London Casuals	Fr	(h)	W	5-0	(0-0)	Pattinson, Collins 3, Crate	2,000
3 April	Stockton	Fr	(a)	D	3-3	(3-2)	Crate, Graham, Collins	
8 April	Liverpool	Fr	(h)	D	0-0	(0-0)		2,500
12 April	Sunderland	Fr	(h)	L	0-4	(0-3)		3,000
15 April	West Bromwich Albion	Fr	(h)	W	7-2	(1-2)	Sorley 4, Crate, Wallace, Reay	2,000
17 April	Everton	Fr	(a)	L	2-5	(0-4)	Collins, Crate	
22 April	Accrington XI	Fr	(h)	W	5-0	(3-0)	Crate, Pattinson, Collins 3	2,000
26 April	Middlesbrough Ironopolis	Fr	(h)	W	1-0	(0-0)	Collins	2,000
28 April	District XI (Alec McCurdie*)	Test	(n)	W	5-3	(4-1)	(scorers untraced)	
29 April	Preston North End	Fr	(h)	W	5-0	(3-0)	Sorley 2, Collins 2, Crate	2,000

Harry Reay was a prominent local footballer, joining East End from Shankhouse. He scored five goals against Annbank in 1893.

1893-94

4 Sept	Trafalgar	Fr	(a)	W	2-0	(2-0)	Pattinson, Thompson	800
6 Sept	Sunderland	Fr	(h)	L	1-3	(0-3)	Thompson	2,800
9 Sept	Middlesbrough	Fr	(a)	D	2-2	(0-1)	Creilly, Crate	1,400
11 Nov	Sheffield United	Fr	(h)	W	5-1	(1-1)	Crate 2, Thompson 2, Milne	4,000
2 Dec	Dipton Wanderers	Fr	(a)	W	2-0	(2-0)	Thompson, Quinn	500
23 Dec	Royal Scots Regiment	Fr	(h)	W	3-0	(1-0)	Crate 2, Willis	2,000
17 March	Burslem Port Vale	Fr	(h)	W	6-1	(4-0)	Quinn, Willis 3, Thompson, Wallace	1,500
26 March	Leicester Fosse	Fr	(a)	L	0-2	(0-0)		10,000
31 March	Middlesbrough Ironopolis	Fr	(h)	W	3-0	(0-0)	Crate, Wallace, Law	1,000
5 April	Sunderland	Fr	(h)	L	1-2	(0-2)	Graham (p)	5,000
7 April	Dundee	Fr	(a)	L	2-8	(2-2)	MacFarlane, Willis	2,000
21 April	Sunderland	Fr	(h)	W	4-1	(1-1)	Quinn, Crate, Campbell, Willis	7,500
23 April	Willington Athletic (W Steele)	Ben	(a)	W	2-0	(2-0)	Law, ano	
25 April	Shankhouse (G Matthews widow)	Ben	(a)	D	1-1	(1-1)	Crate	
28 April	Middlesbrough Ironopolis	Fr	(a)	D	0-0	(0-0)		2,000
30 April	Sunderland	Fr	(h)	L	1-3	(0-2)	Crate	6,000

John Law was one of many Scots to land on Tyneside as football developed. The winger scored against Willington Athletic in 1894.

1894-95

5 Sept	Sunderland	Fr	(h)	L	1-4	(0-2)	Smith	4,500
12 Sept	Hibernian	Fr	(h)	L	1-3	(0-2)	Campbell	1,500
5 Dec	Bedlington Turks	Fr	(a)	W	4-2	(1-2)	Thompson, og (Burton), McNee, ano	1,200
19 Jan	Sunderland	Fr	(h)	L	1-4	(1-3)	Smith	8,000
26 Jan	Hurlford	Fr	(h)	W	5-1	(1-1)	Thompson 2, og, McNee 2	4,000
23 Feb	Blyth	Fr	(a)	D	2-2	(2-1)	Wallace, Graham (p)	3,000
2 March	East Stirlingshire	Fr	(h)	W	6-1	(5-0)	Dickson 2, Thompson 2, Smith, Milne	1,000
30 March	Glasgow Rangers	Fr	(h)	L	2-5	(1-5)	Milne, Wallace	2,000
16 April	Bolton Wanderers	Fr	(h)	L	1-6	(0-3)	McNee	4,000
22 April	Sunderland	Fr	(h)	W	1-0	(0-0)	Thompson	4,000
27 April	Preston North End	Fr	(h)	W	5-3	(2-1)	Wright 2, Dickson 2, Thompson	4,000
30 April	Jarrow	Fr	(a)	W	1-0	(1-0)	Thompson	2,500

1895-96

Date	Opponent	Comp	Venue	Res	Score	HT	Scorers	Att
2 Sept	Hibernian	Fr	(h)	L	1-2	(0-1)	McKay	7,000
4 Sept	Glasgow Celtic	Fr	(h)	W	3-0	(1-0)	Logan 2, Milne	5,500
11 Sept	Sunderland	Fr	(a)	L	3-5	(2-2)	McKay, Graham, ano	5,000
30 Nov	Sunderland	Fr	(h)	L	0-4	(0-1)		11,000
29 Feb	Sunderland	Fr	(h)	D	2-2	(2-2)	Lennox, Aitken	6,000
11 April	Clyde	Fr	(h)	D	0-0	(0-0)		2,000
15 April	Newcastle East End	Fr	(h)	D	3-3	(0-2)	Lennox 2, Wardrope	200
18 April	Sheffield United	Fr	(h)	W	3-1	(2-1)	Wardrope 2, Lennox	6,000
22 April	Aston Villa	Fr	(h)	D	1-1	(1-1)	Lennox	7,000
25 April	Derby County	Fr	(h)	W	4-2	(2-2)	Stott 2, Lennox, Collins	8,000
27 April	Sheffield Wednesday	Fr	(h)	L	1-4	(1-1)	Aitken (p)	3,000
30 April	Sunderland	Fr	(h)	D	3-3	(3-0)	Thompson, Aitken, Collins	4,000

1896-97

Date	Opponent	Comp	Venue	Res	Score	HT	Scorers	Att
1 Sept	Hibernian	Fr	(h)	D	1-1	(1-1)	Thompson	6,000
2 Sept	Sunderland	Fr	(h)	D	2-2	(0-2)	Aitken 2	8,000
7 Sept	Edinburgh St Bernards	Fr	(h)	L	0-3	(0-1)		4,500
10 Sept	Leadgate Exiles	Fr	(a)	D	1-1	(0-1)	Graham	800
23 Sept	Sunderland (John Campbell*)	Test	(a)	D	1-1	(1-0)	Wardrope	3,000
31 Oct	Burnley	Fr	(h)	W	4-1	(1-1)	Auld, Wardrope, Smellie 2	8,000
16 Nov	Darlington	Fr	(a)	L	1-2	(1-0)	Wardrope	2,000
21 Nov	Leith Athletic	Fr	(a)	W	2-1	(1-1)	Aitken, Smellie	1,200
25 Dec	Dundee	Fr	(h)	W	3-1	(2-0)	Wardrope, Thompson, Milne	10,000
4 Jan	Stockton	Fr	(h)	W	3-2	(1-2)	Lennox 2, Smellie	1,000
13 Feb	Grimsby Town	Fr	(h)	W	4-0	(1-0)	Aitken 2, Connell, Lennox	4,000
27 Feb	Leith Athletic	Fr	(h)	W	5-0	(2-0)	Connell 2, Aitken 2, Lennox	3,500
31 March	Sunderland (Willie Graham* & Willie Thompson*)	Test	(h)	W	5-2	(3-0)	Lennox 2, Aitken, Thompson 2 (1p)	3,000
17 April	Heart of Midlothian	Fr	(h)	W	3-0	(1-0)	Blyth, Aitken 2	3,000
20 April	St Mirren	Fr	(h)	W	3-0	(2-0)	Stewart, Smellie, Aitken	2,000
24 April	Glasgow Rangers	Fr	(h)	W	3-1	(0-1)	Connell, Lennox, Smellie	7,000
26 April	Third Lanark	Fr	(h)	W	1-0	(1-0)	Aitken	1,000
28 April	Sunderland	Fr	(h)	W	3-0	(2-0)	Aitken 2, Ostler	5,000
30 April	Hibernian	Fr	(h)	L	0-3	(0-2)		1,000

1897-98

Date	Opponent	Comp	Venue	Res	Score	HT	Scorers	Att
1 Sept	Sunderland	Fr	(h)	L	1-3	(0-1)	Ghee	11,000
6 Sept	Hibernian	Fr	(h)	D	1-1	(1-0)	(scorer untraced)	4,000
4 Jan	South Shields	Fr	(a)	W	6-2	(3-1)	Peddie 4, Campbell, Harvey	2,000
5 Feb	Derby County	Fr	(h)	D	4-4	(2-4)	Aitken, Peddie, Ostler, Allan	7,000
19 March	Sunderland	Fr	(h)	D	1-1	(1-1)	Wardrope	16,000
16 April	West Bromwich Albion	Fr	(h)	D	1-1	(1-0)	Blyth	10,000

1898-99

Date	Opponent	Comp	Venue	Res	Score	HT	Scorers	Att
1 Sept	Sunderland	Fr	(h)	D	1-1	(0-1)	Peddie	15,000
7 Sept	Grimsby Town	Fr	(h)	W	6-2	(2-1)	Milne 2, Niblo 2, Peddie, Aitken	4,000
15 Sept	Grimsby Town	Fr	(a)	D	4-4	(1-1)	Smith 2, Birnie, Harvey	1,000
27 Dec	Coventry City	Fr	(a)	W	2-0	(2-0)	Wardrope, Stevenson	2,000
2 Jan	Burnley	Fr	(h)	L	1-4	(1-2)	Stevenson	9,000
3 Jan	Heart of Midlothian	Fr	(h)	W	4-1	(2-0)	MacFarlane 3, Rogers	4,000
14 Feb	Sunderland	Fr	(a)	W	4-3	(1-2)	Peddie 2, Niblo, Stevenson	5,000
2 March	Brampton Athletic	Fr	(a)	W	12-2	(6-0)	Harvey 2, Stevenson, Ghee, Peddie, Niblo, Higgins, Lindsay, Ostler, Stott, Kingsley, MacFarlane	1,000
4 March	Liverpool	Fr	(h)	L	1-3	(1-2)	MacFarlane	4,000
31 March	Everton	Fr	(h)	W	2-1	(1-1)	Rogers, Aitken (p)	2,000
17 April	Hibernian	Fr	(a)	L	0-2	(0-0)		3,000
24 April	Hibernian	Fr	(h)	D	2-2	(0-1)	Aitken, MacFarlane	2,000
29 April	Derby County	Fr	(h)	W	4-1	(3-0)	Aitken, Stevenson, Wardrope, Peddie	2,000

1899-00

Date	Opponent	Comp	Venue	Res	Score	HT	Scorers	Att
5 Sept	Kaffirs (SA)	Fr	(h)	W	6-3	(3-2)	Ghee, Wardrope, Stevenson, Niblo 2, og (Bothloko) (First foreign side to oppose Newcastle Utd)	6,000
9 Dec	Dundee	Fr	(h)	D	2-2	(1-1)	Peddie, Stevenson	2,000
25 Dec	Kilmarnock	Fr	(h)	W	4-1	(3-1)	Fraser, Rogers 2, Wardrope	1,200
26 Dec	Third Lanark	Fr	(h)	D	1-1	(0-1)	Peddie	1,000
17 April	Coventry City	Fr	(a)	W	5-1	(1-0)	Peddie 3, Rogers, Kingsley (p)	1,000

1900-01

Date	Opponent	Comp	Venue	Res	Score	HT	Scorers	Att
5 Sept	Middlesbrough	Fr	(a)	W	2-1	(1-1)	Gardner (A), Laidlaw	4,000
8 Oct	Dundee	Fr	(a)	L	3-4	(2-2)	MacFarlane 2, Burgess	3,000
25 Dec	Glasgow Rangers	Fr	(h)	W	4-1	(3-0)	Niblo 2, MacFarlane, Peddie	5,000
26 Dec	Woolwich Arsenal	Fr	(a)	D	1-1	(1-1)	Niblo	8,000
1 Jan	Woolwich Arsenal	Fr	(h)	W	5-1	(1-1)	Niblo 2, Fraser (p), Laidlaw, MacFarlane	6,000
23 Feb	Derby County	Fr	(h)	W	2-1	(0-1)	MacFarlane, Fraser	6,000
23 March	Everton	Fr	(h)	W	2-1	(1-0)	Heywood, Peddie	4,000
9 April	Belfast Distillery	Fr	(a)	W	4-1	(0-1)	Peddie 3, Aitken	5,000
29 April	Glasgow Rangers	Fr	(a)	L	1-3	(0-2)	MacFarlane	3,000
30 April	Heart of Midlothian	Fr	(a)	L	0-2	(0-2)		3,000

1901-02

Date	Opponent	Comp	Venue	Res	Score	HT	Scorers	Att
2 Sept	Middlesbrough	Fr	(a)	L	1-2	(0-0)	Orr	8,000
14 Oct	Dundee	Fr	(a)	D	2-2	(1-0)	Roberts 2	2,000
23 Oct	Middlesbrough	DF	(h)	W	4-1	(1-1)	Roberts 2, Niblo, Birnie	3,000
25 Dec	Dundee	Fr	(h)	D	1-1	(1-0)	Graham	1,000
1 Jan	Third Lanark	Fr	(h)	W	2-1	(1-1)	Ghee, Veitch (p)	5,000
2 Jan	Corinthians	Fr	(h)	D	2-2	(1-1)	Roberts, Veitch	6,000
5 March	Alnwick St James	Fr	(a)	W	4-0	(0-0)	Peddie, Aitken, Gardner (A), Roberts	
13 March	Glasgow Celtic (in Berwick)	Fr	(n)	L	2-4	(1-1)	Rutherford, Heywood	2,000
23 April	Middlesbrough	DF	(h)	W	2-1	(1-0)	Rutherford, Orr	2,000
28 April	Workington Black Diamond	Fr	(a)	D	1-1	(1-0)	Harvey	5,000
29 April	Glasgow Rangers (at Third Lanark FC)	DF	(n)	W	5-0	(1-0)	Peddie 2, McColl 2, Orr	4,500
30 April	St Mirren	DF	(a)	W	2-1	(0-1)	Stewart, Harvey	4,000
1 May	Kilmarnock	DF	(a)	L	0-2	(0-1)		3,000

John Harvey (Hernie, sic) featured on a cigarette card of the day, a star of Sunderland's famous 'Team of all the Talents' before he moved to Tyneside.

Jock Peddie made an impression facing the Black'n'Whites in a friendly for Third Lanark in 1897. He was soon banging home the goals for United.

Newcastle faced South African tourists, The Kaffirs in 1899. The coloured visitors caused quite a stir in England at the time.

Joe Rogers was a talented forward, capped in unofficial matches for England on tour to Germany. He scored against Hearts in 1899.

1902-03

1 Sept	Glasgow Rangers	Fr	(h)	W	3-1	(3-1)	Rutherford, Orr, McColl	7,000
13 Oct	Dundee	Fr	(a)	W	2-1	(2-1)	Roberts, Carr	9,000
19 Nov	Middlesbrough	Ch	(a)	W	3-1	(0-1)	Gardner (Andw), Graham, ano	1,000
1 Dec	Aberaman	Fr	(a)	D	1-1	(1-1)	Stenhouse	
25 Dec	Hibernian	Fr	(h)	W	1-0	(1-0)	Stenhouse	3,000
26 Dec	Dundee	Fr	(h)	D	1-1	(0-0)	Rutherford	3,000
1 Jan	Third Lanark	Fr	(h)	W	4-0	(1-0)	Veitch, Carr, Gardner (Andw), og (Thompson)	2,500
5 Jan	Glasgow Rangers	Fr	(a)	L	1-3	(0-2)	McColl	10,000
6 Jan	Moffat	Fr	(a)	W	7-0	(2-0)	McColl 4, Stenhouse, Caie, McWilliam	1,000
21 Feb	Sunderland	Fr	(h)	W	1-0	(1-0)	Rutherford	4,000
27 April	Workington Black Diamond	Fr	(a)	L	2-3	(2-0)	Graham, Appleyard	
28 April	Kilmarnock	Fr	(a)	W	2-0	(2-0)	Carr, Appleyard	4,500
29 April	Glasgow Rangers	Fr	(a)	D	2-2	(1-1)	Rutherford, Templeton	3,000
30 April	St Mirren	Fr	(a)	L	0-1	(0-1)		3,000

1903-04

30 Dec	Corinthians	Fr	(h)	W	4-2	(1-2)	Fraser 2, Birnie, Graham	7,000
16 Feb	Bradford City	Fr	(a)	D	2-2	(1-0)	Fraser 2	6,000
20 Feb	Everton	Fr	(h)	W	2-0	(0-0)	Rutherford, McWilliam	4,500
5 March	St Mirren	Fr	(h)	W	5-2	(2-0)	McClarence 4, Rutherford	3,000
4 April	Queen's Park	Fr	(h)	W	2-1	(1-0)	Orr 2	5,000
5 April	Belfast Distillery	Fr	(a)	W	5-4	(2-3)	Orr 2, Aitken, Rutherford, Appleyard (p)	4,000
14 April	Shaddongate United	Fr	(a)	W	4-1	(1-1)	Fraser 3, Finlay	3,000
23 April	Sunderland	Fr	(a)	L	0-3	(0-1)		3,000
25 April	Heart of Midlothian	Fr	(a)	W	3-2	(0-0)	Appleyard 2, Orr	6,000
26 April	St Mirren	Fr	(a)	W	2-1	(0-1)	McClarence, Howie	2,500
27 April	Glasgow Rangers	Fr	(a)	L	0-2	(0-1)		8,000
28 April	Kilmarnock	Fr	(a)	L	1-4	(1-2)	Aitken	3,000
30 April	Aberdeen	Fr	(a)	W	7-1	(2-0)	McClarence 2, Templeton, Orr 2, McColl, Gardner (A)	5,000
7 May	Copenhagen XI (D)	Ot	(a)	W	6-1		(Scorers untraced)	
8 May	Copenhagen XI (D)	Ot	(a)	W	6-2		(Scorers untraced)	
10 May	Southampton (in Copenhagen)	Ot	(n)	W	4-0		(Scorers untraced)	
12 May	Danish Rep XI (D)	Ot	(a)	W	3-1		(Scorers untraced)	

1904-05

1 Sept	Club Athletique Parisien (F)	Fr	(h)	W	11-2	(4-0)	Appleyard 5, Howie 2, Orr 2, Templeton, Rutherford	3,500
7 Sept	Middlesbrough	Fr	(a)	L	1-2	(1-1)	Appleyard	2,000
27 Sept	Sunderland	Fr	(h)	L	1-2	(1-1)	Appleyard	18,761
12 Oct	Alnwick St James	Fr	(a)	W	6-1	(2-0)	Orr 2, Aitken 2, Appleyard 2 (Abandoned after 75m, bad light)	1,000
3 Jan	Corinthians	Fr	(h)	L	1-2	(0-1)	McWilliam	5,000
11 May	Austria XI	Ot	(a)	W	8-0		(Scorers untraced)	
15 May	Austria XI	Ot	(a)	W	11-0		(Scorers untraced)	
16 May	Austria XI	Ot	(a)	W	4-0		(Scorers untraced)	
17 May	Bohemia Spartans (B)	Ot	(a)	W	3-2		(Scorers untraced)	
21 May	Berlin Britannia (G)	Ot	(a)	W	10-1		(Scorers untraced)	

1905-06

18 Sept	Edinburgh St Bernards	Fr	(a)	D	2-2	(0-1)	Hardinge 2	2,000
9 Oct	Dundee	Fr	(a)	D	1-1	(0-0)	Gosnell	7,000
14 Oct	Belfast Distillery	Fr	(h)	W	5-0	(3-0)	Orr, Howie, Rutherford, McWilliam, McIntyre	2,800
25 Oct	Darlington	Fr	(a)	W	7-2	(4-0)	Orr 3, Howie 2, Appleyard, Gosnell	2,000
8 Nov	Blyth Spartans	DF	(a)	W	7-1	(4-0)	Howie 2, Carr 2, Rutherford, Bolton, og (Fairhurst)	1,000
2 Jan	Corinthians	Fr	(h)	L	5-7	(2-3)	Orr 2, Higgins, Hardinge, og (Norris)	3,000
13 May	Vienna XI (A)	Ot	(a)	W	7-1		Gosnell 2, Orr 3, Aitken, Higgins	4,000
16 May	Vienna/Austria XI	Ot	(a)	W	7-0		Gardner 3, Higgins 3, Orr	3,500
20 May	Vienna Cricket & Sport Club (A)	Ot	(a)	W	4-0	(4-0)	Higgins 4	
23 May	Vienna Ath Sports (A)	Ot	(a)	W	4-0	(0-0)	Veitch, Gosnell, Orr, Gardner	
26 May	German Sport XI (in Prague)	Ot	(n)	W	4-1		Orr, Carr, Gardner 2	4,000
29 May	Prague XI (B)	Ot	(a)	W	9-1		Gardner 2, Higgins, Veitch 3, Orr 3	
30 May	Glasgow Celtic (in Prague)	Ot	(n)	D	2-2		(Scorers untraced)	
3 June	Berlin XI/ Prussian FC (G)	Ot	(a)	W	6-0		(Scorers untraced)	

1906-07

2 Jan	Corinthians	Fr	(h)	W	3-0	(2-0)	McClarence 2, Orr	5,000
11 March	Maidstone United	Fr	(a)	W	5-2	(2-2)	Appleyard 2, Hardinge, Gosnell, Orr	5,000
23 April	Leith Athletic (Willie Walker's widow) (at Hibernian FC)	Ben	(n)	L	0-1	(0-1)		6,000
24 April	Glasgow Rangers	Fr	(a)	L	0-3	(0-0)		10,000
27 April	Aberdeen	Fr	(a)	L	2-4		Dodds, Court	3,000
29 April	Fulham	Fr	(h)	D	1-1	(1-1)	Hall	10,000
5 May	Frankfurt (G)	Ot	(a)	W	6-2		Hall 3, Blackburn, McWilliam, Brown	
7 May	Mannheim (G)	Ot	(a)	W	5-0		Howie 2, Hall 2, McWilliam	
9 May	SC Freiburg (G)	Ot	(a)	W	8-1		Hall 5, Dodds 2, Higgins	
13 May	Karlsruher (G)	Ot	(a)	W	7-0		(Scorers untraced)	

1907-08

25 Sept	Chester-le-Street & District Select (in Pelton Fell)	Fr	(a)	W	4-0	(3-0)	Appleyard 3 (1p), Howie	4,500
9 Oct	Sunderland (in West Stanley)	SF	(n)	W	2-0	(1-0)	Soye, Hedley	10,000
31 Oct	Berwick Rangers	Fr	(a)	W	5-1	(1-1)	Appleyard 3, Hardinge 2	2,000
5 Feb	Beaumaris	Fr	(a)	W	14-1		Appleyard 9, Howie 2, Higgins, Speedie, ano	
13 Feb	Rhyl	Fr	(a)	W	5-1	(0-0)	Appleyard, Howie, Veitch. Orr, og (Jones J)	
29 April	Manchester United	PU	(a)	L	1-4	(0-2)	Ridley	8,000

1908-09

24 Sept	Carlisle United	HC	(a)	L	3-4	(1-4)	Allan 3	7,000
30 Sept	Glasgow Rangers	SF	(h)	W	4-1	(2-0)	Higgins 4	8,000
7 Oct	Glasgow Rangers	SF	(a)	W	4-2	(2-1)	Duncan, Veitch, Higgins, Howie	10,000
18 Nov	Middlesbrough	Ch	(h)	W	5-1	(2-0)	Stewart 3, Higgins, Wilson	3,000
16 Dec	Middlesbrough	SF	(a)	W	2-1	(1-0)	Stewart, Liddell (p)	800
16 May	Copenhagen XI (D)	Ot	(a)	D	1-1		(Scorer untraced)	
18 May	West Bromwich Albion (in Copenhagen)	Ot	(n)	W	3-0	(2-0)	Shepherd 2, Anderson	5,000
20 May	Danish XI (in Copenhagen)	Ot	(a)	W	2-1		(Scorers untraced)	
23 May	Danish XI (in Copenhagen)	Ot	(a)	W	3-1		(Scorers untraced)	
25 May	Prossen (G)	Ot	(a)	W	2-1		(Scorers untraced)	

1909-10

16 March	Darlington	Ben	(a)	L	0-1	(0-1)		3,000

Andy Aitken led United to their first tour abroad in 1905, featured on this 'Three Nuns Tobacco' cigarette card.

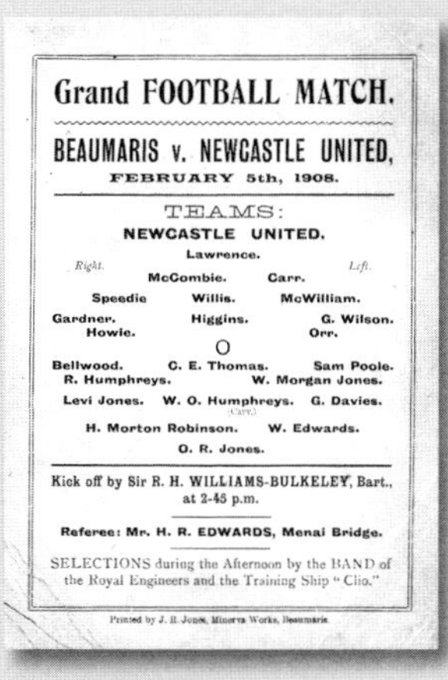
Grand FOOTBALL MATCH.

BEAUMARIS v. NEWCASTLE UNITED,

FEBRUARY 5th, 1908.

TEAMS:

NEWCASTLE UNITED.

Lawrence.

Right. McCombie. Carr. Left.

Speedie Willis. McWilliam.

Gardner. Higgins. G. Wilson.

Howie. Orr.

O

Bellwood. C. E. Thomas. Sam Poole.

R. Humphreys. W. Morgan Jones.

Levi Jones. W. O. Humphreys. (Capt.) G. Davies.

H. Morton Robinson. W. Edwards.

O. R. Jones.

Kick off by Sir R. H. WILLIAMS-BULKELEY, Bart., at 2-45 p.m.

Referee: Mr. H. R. EDWARDS, Menai Bridge.

SELECTIONS during the Afternoon by the BAND of the Royal Engineers and the Training Ship "Clio."

Printed by J. R. Jones, Minerva Works, Beaumaris

When Newcastle spent a training break in North Wales during 1908 they faced local club Beaumaris and racked up a remarkable 14-1 victory.

Bill Appleyard was a forceful striker; he netted nine goals against little Beaumaris.

1910-11

19 Sept	Norwich City	HC	(a)	D	1-1	(1-0)	Veitch	13,473
11 Oct	Hull City	Fr	(a)	W	3-1	(1-0)	Higgins 2, Shepherd	12,000
23 Nov	Norwich City	HC	(h)	W	3-0	(1-0)	Shepherd 3	5,944
7 May	Koln 1899 (G)	Ot	(a)	W	5-0		Fleming 4, Kelly	
9 May	Dusseldorfer FC 1899 (G)	Ot	(a)	W	7-0	(4-0)	(Scorers untraced)	
11 May	Pforzheim (G)	Ot	(a)	W	5-2		(Scorers untraced)	
14 May	Stuttgarter Kickers (G)	Ot	(a)	W	6-1	(2-1)	Higgins 2, Kelly 2, Anderson 2	
16 May	Furth (G)	Ot	(a)	W	2-1		(Scorers untraced)	
21 May	FC Basle (Sw)	Ot	(a)	W	7-0		(Scorers untraced – Swiss archives show 7-1)	5,000

1911-12

13 Sept	Saltburn	Fr	(a)	W	6-2	(5-1)	Kelly 3, Wilson 3	1,000
18 Sept	Northampton Town	HC	(a)	W	2-1	(1-1)	Kelly, Stewart	10,000
25 Oct	Sunderland	HC	(h)	W	1-0	(0-0)	Stewart	11,372
15 April	Hibernian	Fr	(a)	W	4-2	(1-2)	Fleming 2, Wilson, Hibbert	8,000
22 April	Norwich City	HC	(a)	D	0-0	(0-0)	(aet)	8,307
29 April	Aberdeen	Fr	(a)	W	1-0	(0-0)	Hudspeth (p)	6,000
30 April	Inverness XI	Fr	(a)	D	3-3	(1-1)	Higgins, Duncan, Hudspeth (p)	5,000

1912-13

2 Oct	South Shields	Fr	(a)	W	6-2	(2-1)	Lowes 4, Hughes, Duncan	5,000
23 Oct	Sunderland	HC	(h)	L	0-1	(0-0)		7,000
12 May	Danish XI (in Copenhagen)	Ot	(a)	W	4-1		Hall 2, Hewison, Finlay	
15 May	Danish XI (in Copenhagen)	Ot	(a)	W	3-2		(Scorers untraced)	
18 May	Danish XI (in Copenhagen)	Ot	(a)	D	1-1		Higgins	

1913-14

10 Sept	Players Union XI	PU	(h)	L	1-3	(0-1)	Higgins	7,000
15 Oct	Sunderland	HC	(a)	L	0-1	(0-0)		6,500
28 March	Glasgow Rangers	Fr	(h)	D	1-1	(0-1)	Dixon	15,000

1914-15

23 Sept	Sunderland	HC	(h)	L	0-1	(0-0)		6,738

1915-16

4 Sept	English & Southern League XI (at Brough Pk, Newcastle)	WCh	(n)	D	2-2	(1-1)	Hudspeth (p), Hibbert	6,000
13 Nov	South Shields	WCh	(a)	D	3-3	(2-1)	Gosnell, Higgins, Hogg	2,000
21 April	Blackburn Rovers	WCh	(h)	L	0-4	(0-2)		16,000
22 April	Blackburn Rovers	WCh	(a)	W	5-4	(2-2)	Hibbert, Booth, Hall, Rutherford 2	12,000
6 May	Sunderland	WCh	(h)	D	1-1	(0-1)	Low	3,299

1916-17

No matches arranged

1917-18

13 Oct	South Shields	HC	(h)	W	4-1	(1-1)	Hall 2, Dixon (p), Holford	2,000
27 Oct	South Shields	Ch	(a)	W	2-1	(1-1)	Hall 2	3,000
4 May	Sunderland	WF	(h)	L	1-3	(0-2)	Phillipson	6,000
11 May	Middlesbrough	WF	(h)	D	3-3	(1-2)	Chambers 2 (1p), Low	4,000

1918-19

31 Aug	Sunderland	WF	(h)	L	0-4	(0-1)		5,000
21 Dec	Sunderland	WCh	(h)	W	4-0	(0-0)	Cooper 2, Clark, Bloomer	19,000
26 Dec	Sunderland	Fr	(a)	L	0-1	(0-1)		18,000
5 April	Middlesbrough	Fr	(a)	L	1-4	(1-1)	Hudspeth (p)	6,000
18 April	Scotswood	Fr	(h)	W	1-0	(1-0)	Low	30,000
29 April	South Shields	Fr	(a)	W	1-0	(1-0)	Hibbert	5,000
30 April	Wallsend	Fr	(a)	W	2-0	(1-0)	Hibbert, Johnson	3,000
3 May	Middlesbrough	WF	(h)	D	2-2	(1-0)	Cox, Hagan	18,000
17 May	Sunderland	WF	(a)	L	2-3	(0-2)	Hagan 2	16,000

1919-20

26 July	South Shields	Fr	(h)	L	0-1	(0-0)		15,000
27 Oct	Alnwick Ex-Servicemen XI	Fr	(a)	W	8-1	(7-0)	Hall 5, Hibbert 2, Carr	
10 April	Edinburgh St Bernards	Fr	(h)	W	5-0	(4-0)	Pyke 4, Dark	4,000
13 April	Partick Thistle	Fr	(a)	L	2-3	(1-2)	Smailes, Curry	7,000
21 April	Middlesbrough	CC	(a)	L	1-2	(1-0)	Smailes	10,000

1920-21

13 Sept	South Shields (Tom Ghee*)	Test	(h)	W	1-0	(1-0)	Hudspeth (p)	4,000
20 April	Middlesbrough	CC	(a)	L	1-2	(0-0)	King	12,000
26 April	Glasgow Rangers (Tommy Cairns)	Test	(a)	D	0-0	(0-0)		25,000
15 May	FC Barcelona (Sp)	Ot	(a)	W	3-2		McDonald 2, Pyke	
17 May	FC Barcelona (Sp)	Ot	(a)	L	2-3		(Scorers untraced)	
22 May	San Sebastian (Sp)	Ot	(a)	W	3-0		Smailes 2, McDonald	
28 May	Gallia (F) (in Paris)	PSC	(a)	W	4-1		Aitken 3, McDonald	
29 May	Glasgow Celtic (in Paris)	PSC	(n)	L	0-3			

1921-22

14 Sept	Glasgow Rangers	Fr	(h)	W	2-1	(1-0)	Harris, Hudspeth	15,000
26 Oct	George Robey's XI	SF	(h)	L	4-7	(3-4)	Harris 2 (1p), Smailes, Russell	16,000
14 Dec	South Shields	HCf	(a)	L	0-3	(0-3)		10,000
28 Dec	Corinthians	Fr	(h)	W	5-4	(4-1)	Dixon, Paton 2, McDonald 2 (Abandoned after 80m, snow)	5,000
10 April	Newport County	Fr	(a)	W	5-1	(4-1)	Smailes 2, McDonald 3	10,000
25 April	Glasgow Rangers (Andy Cunningham*)	Test	(a)	D	1-1	(1-0)	Harris	20,000
3 May	Rest of League XI (Jack Carr*)	Test	(h)	L	2-3	(1-1)	Hagan, Smailes	7,000
10 May	South Shields	HCf	(h)	W	3-2	(1-1)	Hudspeth (p), Aitken, Swan	12,000
15 May	Frigg SK (Oslo) (Nw)	Ot	(a)	W	5-0	(0-0)	Smailes 2, McDonald, Dixon, og (Finstad)	
17 May	Christiania XI (Oslo) (Nw)	Ot	(a)	W	1-0	(1-0)	Smailes	
21 May	GAIS (Goteborg) (Se)	Ot	(a)	W	3-1	(1-0)	Smailes, McDonald, Dixon	4,248
23 May	IFK Goteborg (Se)	Ot	(a)	W	4-0	(1-0)	McDonald 2, og 2	6,000
28 May	Copenhagen XI (D)	Ot	(a)	W	2-1	(1-0)	Dixon, McDonald	15,000
30 May	Copenhagen XI (D)	Ot	(a)	W	1-0	(0-0)	Mitchell	10,000

United were occasionally invited t take part in charity matches aroun the country to raise funds. They face Norwich in 1910-11 and lifted the Hospital Cup trophy.

The Magpies visited Spain and France in the close season of 1921. United's tour group is pictured in jovial mood.

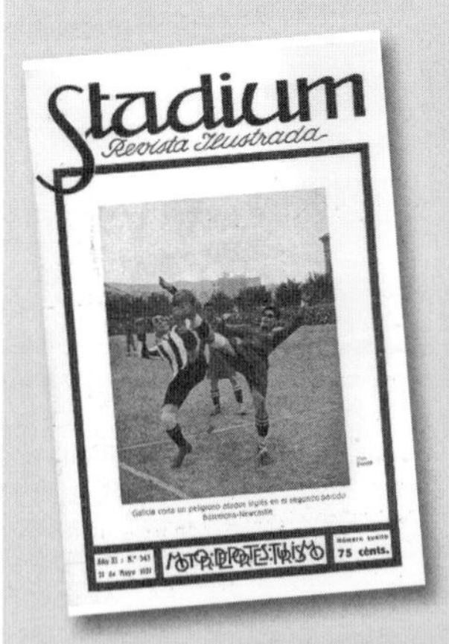

Spanish magazines from the club's visit to Barcelona during May 1921 featuring the Magpies on the cover.

1922-23

20 Sept	Glasgow Rangers	Fr	(h)	W	4-1	(1-1)	Harris 3, McDonald (p)	10,000
27 Sept	Glasgow Celtic	Fr	(h)	D	1-1	(0-0)	Harris	8,000
2 Oct	Cardiff City (in Wigan)	DF	(n)	L	0-4	(0-3)		15,000
3 Jan	Corinthians	Fr	(h)	W	3-0	(3-0)	Dixon 2, Clark	2,000
24 March	Hull City	Fr	(h)	W	3-2	(2-1)	Scott 2, McDonald	5,000
18 April	South Shields	HCf	(a)	W	1-0	(0-0)	McDonald	
2 May	South Shields	HCf	(h)	D	0-0	(0-0)		4,000

1923-24

3 May	West Stanley	NEL	(a)	W	2-1	(2-0)	Seymour 2 (NE League fixture in which United fielded their entire FA Cup winning XI)	15,000
9 May	Real Sociedad (Sp)	Ot	(a)	W	3-0	(3-0)	Keating 2, Cowan	
12 May	Spanish Select XI (in Bilbao)	Ot	(a)	L	0-1			
15 May	Real Sociedad (Sp) (in Madrid)	Ot	(a)				(Result untraced)	
17 May	Real Madrid CF (Sp)	Ot	(a)	L	2-3		(Scorers untraced) (Real Madrid stadium opening)	15,000
18 May	Spanish Select XI (at Real Madrid CF)	Ot	(a)	L	0-2			
21 May	Everton (at FC Barcelona)	CB	(n)	L	2-3		Cowan, Keating	
22 May	Real Madrid CF (Sp)	Ot	(a)	L	1-2		(Scorers untraced)	
24 May	FC Barcelona (Sp)	Ot	(a)	W	2-0		Keating, Hudspeth (p)	
25 May	FC Barcelona (Sp)	Ot	(a)	W	1-0		Keating	

1924-25

22 Oct	South Shields	HCf	(h)	L	1-2	(1-1)	Mooney	2,000
5 Nov	South Shields	HCf	(a)	D	2-2	(2-0)	Clark, Keating	3,000
27 April	Glasgow Rangers (James Walls)	Ben	(a)	L	0-1	(0-1)		4,000
29 April	Hibernian	Fr	(a)	L	1-3	(1-2)	Low	10,000

1925-26

31 Aug	Real Madrid CF (Sp)	Fr	(h)	W	6-1	(1-1)	McDonald, Curry, Urwin, Clark, MacKenzie, Cowan	10,000
2 Sept	Glasgow Rangers	Fr	(h)	L	0-2	(0-1)		10,000
5 Oct	Raith Rovers (Dave Morris)	Test	(a)	W	6-1	(2-1)	Clark 3, Mitchell, McDonald, Cowan	3,000

1926-27

25 April	Hull City	HC	(a)	L	0-3	(0-1)		6,000
4 May	Middlesbrough (Charlie Cole)	Test	(a)	D	0-0	(0-0)		21,000
15 May	Dutch Olympic XI (in Amsterdam)	Ot	(a)	L	0-4	(0-1)		25,000
18 May	Dutch Olympic XI (in Rotterdam)	Ot	(a)	W	2-0	(1-0)	Gallacher, McDonald	16,000
22 May	Dutch Olympic XI (in Deventer)	Ot	(a)	W	4-1	(2-0)	McDonald (p), Clark, MacKenzie, Harris	12,000
24 May	Ajax Amsterdam (N)	Ot	(a)	W	3-0	(2-0)	McDonald 2, Seymour	10,000
26 May	Dutch Olympic XI (in Eindhoven)	Ot	(a)	W	4-2	(4-1)	Gallacher 4	
29 May	Dutch Olympic XI (in Groningen)	Ot	(a)	W	5-0		(Scorers untraced)	

1927-28

29 Aug	South Shields (in Wallsend)	Ch	(n)	W	4-2	(3-1)	McDonald 2, Lang, McKay	2,500
19 Oct	Middlesbrough (James McPherson*)	Test	(h)	L	2-5	(2-3)	Gallacher, McDonald	3,550

1928-29

10 Oct	Heart of Midlothian	Fr	(h)	L	0-1	(0-0)		20,000
9 April	Heart of Midlothian (John Johnston)	Test	(a)	D	3-3	(1-1)	Chalmers 2, Boyd	15,000
19 May	AC Ambrosiana (Milan) (I)	Ot	(a)	W	1-0	(1-0)	Chalmers	30,000
23 May	WAC Vienna (A)	Ot	(a)	L	0-2			
26 May	CSK Bratislava (Cz)	Ot	(a)	L	1-8	(1-2)	Gallacher	6,000
28 May	SK Slavia (Prague) (Cz)	Ot	(a)	D	1-1	(0-0)	Chalmers	12,000
30 May	Hungarian Professional XI (in Budapest)	Ot	(a)	L	1-4		Gallacher (p)	4,000

1929-30

1 Jan	Corinthians	Fr	(h)	D	4-4	(3-0)	Hutchison 2, Richardson (JR), McCurley	4,000

1930-31

24 Sept	Heart of Midlothian (Andy McCombie*)	Test	(h)	L	2-3	(1-1)	Chalmers, Devine	5,000
30 April	Yeovil & Petters United	Fr	(a)	W	3-2	(2-0)	Boyd, Starling 2	7,000

1931-32

28 Sept	Heart of Midlothian (Robert King)	Test	(a)	W	2-1	(1-0)	Ford 2	1,998
22 May	Red Star Olympique/ Racing Club de Paris XI (F) (in Paris)	Ot	(a)	L	1-3	(1-1)	Weaver (p)	
29 May	German XI (in Frankfurt)	Ot	(a)	W	6-3	(3-1)	Richardson (JR) 2, McMenemy, Lang, Boyd, Cape	15,000

1932-33

14 Sept	Glasgow Rangers	CwC	(a)	L	1-4	(1-3)	Weaver	31,000
21 Sept	Glasgow Rangers	CwC	(h)	W	5-0	(2-0)	Murray 2, Allen 2, McMenemy	20,000
18 March	Inverness Thistle XI	Fr	(a)	W	5-3	(1-1)	Richardson (JR) 3, Lang, McMenemy	5,000

1933-34

11 Oct	Peru & Chile FA XI	Fr	(h)	W	6-1	(3-1)	Cape 2, Murray, Pearson, Richardson (JR), og (Astengo)	2,000
17 Feb	Manchester United	Fr	(a)	W	4-3	(3-2)	Williams 2, Richardson (JR), Weaver (p)	10,000
30 April	Bohemians (Dublin)	Fr	(a)	W	3-1	(2-1)	Williams , Richardson (JR) 2	5,000

1934-35

10 Oct	Army XI (in Catterick)	Fr	(a)	W	5-2	(5-0)	Kelly 2, Cairns 2, Leighton	
17 Oct	Middlesbrough	DF	(h)	W	3-2	(2-1)	Boyd, Smith, Lang	3,200

1935-36

No matches arranged

1936-37

19 April	Ipswich Town	Fr	(a)	W	4-1	(1-0)	Smith 2, Docking, Pearson	10,500
28 April	Third Lanark	Fr	(h)	L	1-3	(0-3)	Smith	4,000
28 April	Queen of the South (Jock Smith)	Test	(a)	W	4-2	(0-0)	Cairns 2, McMenemy, Ware (United played 2 fixtures on the same day using a mix of first-team and reserves)	3,500

1937-38

22 Jan	Grimsby Town	Fr	(h)	D	3-3	(0-2)	Imrie 2, Cairns	19,000

Newcastle were back in Spain during 1924 and were a big draw as FA Cup winners. They faced Real Madrid at the opening of their new stadium at Chamartin, now the Bernabeau.

United and fellow tourists Everton contested the Barcelona Cup in 1924, a narrow victory for the Merseysiders.

United twice faced Barcelona in action. Pictured is Bert Keating hitting one of his two goals.

United faced a German XI in Frankfurt during 1932. Goalkeeper Albert McInroy collects the ball safely.

1938-39

20 Aug	Gateshead	FLJ	(h)	W	2-1	(1-1)	Cairns, Birkett	30,500
12 Oct	Gateshead (George Neilson & Joe Inskip)	Test	(a)	L	2-3	(0-1)	Park, Dobson	1,700
1 May	York City (Ted Wass)	Test	(a)	W	3-1	(2-1)	Cairns, Isaac, og (Wass)	5,000
6 May	Barnsley (Beaumont Asquith)	Test	(a)	L	1-4	(1-4)	Clifton	7,500
8 May	Grimsby Town	HC	(a)	L	2-3	(2-1)	Clifton, Cairns	10,000

1939-40

19 Aug	Gateshead	FLJ	(h)	W	3-0	(1-0)	Bowden, Cairns, og (Dudgeon)	18,092
23 Sept	Leeds United	Fr	(h)	D	2-2	(1-1)	Scott (W), Pearson (p)	4,300
30 Sept	Barnsley	Fr	(h)	L	1-2	(0-1)	Stubbins	5,041
7 Oct	Middlesbrough	Fr	(h)	W	3-2	(1-2)	Clifton, Scott (WR), Scott (W)	7,316
14 Oct	Preston North End	Fr	(a)	L	0-4	(0-3)		7,000
16 Dec	Carlisle United	Fr	(a)	W	5-2	(5-1)	Cairns 2, Moses 2, Pearson	1,700
25 Dec	Gateshead	Fr	(h)	D	1-1	(0-0)	Cairns	5,071
26 Dec	Middlesbrough	Fr	(h)	D	1-1	(0-0)	Clifton	6,500
30 Dec	Darlington	Fr	(a)	W	2-1	(0-1)	Stubbins, Pearson (p)	2,089
1 Jan	Middlesbrough	Fr	(a)	L	2-5	(2-3)	Duns 2	2,400
3 Jan	Falkirk	Fr	(a)	L	1-2	(1-2)	Duns	5,000
13 Jan	Gateshead	Fr	(h)	W	3-1	(0-1)	Stubbins, Clifton, Moses	1,890
17 Feb	Preston North End	Fr	(h)	W	4-1	(2-0)	Pearson, Stubbins, Hamilton, Scott	3,167
2 March	Blackpool	Fr	(a)	L	0-1	(0-0)		2,000
25 March	Sheffield United	Fr	(h)	W	2-1	(0-1)	Denmark, Gordon	4,648
30 March	Sunderland	WF	(h)	W	2-0	(0-0)	Scott (W) 2	15,000
13 April	Sunderland	WF	(h)	W	3-2	(2-0)	Stubbins 3	8,666

1940-41

21 Dec	Sunderland	Fr	(h)	W	3-1	(0-0)	Billington, Stubbins, Birkett	3,226
14 April	Sunderland	Fr	(h)	L	3-4	(1-3)	Short, Nevins, Dodgin	4,700
24 May	Army & RAF XI	Fr	(h)	L	0-4	(0-3)		4,217

1941-42

25 April	Heart of Midlothian	Fr	(h)	W	2-0	(1-0)	Woollett, Stubbins	8,000
9 May	Gateshead	Fr	(h)	W	6-2		Stubbins 5, Donaldson (RS)	
30 May	Aberdeen	Fr	(h)	D	1-1	(0-0)	Stubbins	3,500

1942-43

15 Aug	Sunderland	Fr	(h)	L	2-4	(0-1)	Walker, Stubbins	2,000
16 Sept	Northumberland Army	Fr	(h)	L	0-2	(0-1)		
28 Sept	Aberdeen	Fr	(a)	D	0-0	(0-0)		7,000

1943-44

10 April	Preston North End	Fr	(h)	D	2-2	(2-1)	Stubbins (p), Rutherford	2,000
13 May	North East Select XI (Widow of Wilf Gillow)	Ben	(h)	D	3-3	(1-0)	Stubbins 2, Woodburn	11,270

1944-45

No matches arranged

1945-46

25 Sept	Glasgow Rangers	Ch	(a)	L	2-3	(1-2)	Milburn, Wayman	50,000
9 Feb	Huddersfield Town	Fr	(h)	L	2-3	(1-0)	Stubbins, Wayman	19,651
9 March	Millwall	Fr	(a)	W	7-1	(2-1)	Stubbins 2, Brown 2, Wayman 2, Milburn	17,000
3 April	Blackpool (at Workington FC)	CC	(n)	L	0-1	(0-0)		9,000
14 May	SK Brann (Bergen) (Nw)	Ot	(a)	W	7-0	(4-0)	Milburn 2, Wayman 2, Stubbins 3	10,500
17 May	Frigg SK (Oslo) (Nw)	Ot	(a)	W	6-0	(1-0)	Stubbins 2, Wayman 4	12,000
21 May	IFK Norrkoping (Se)	Ot	(a)	L	0-5	(0-0)		20,000
22 May	Hammarby IF XI (Se)	Ot	(a)	L	0-1			2,000
24 May	BK Kenty (Linkoping) (Se)	Ot	(a)	L	0-1	(0-0)		6,700

1946-47

6 Nov	IFK Norrkoping (Se)	Fr	(h)	L	2-3	(1-3)	Milburn 2	46,124
21 May	Blackburn Rovers (at Workington FC)	CC	(n)	W	1-0	(0-0)	Hair	9,000

1947-48

7 Feb	Aston Villa	Fr	(a)	W	2-1	(1-0)	McCall, Taylor	25,000
14 Feb	Liverpool	Fr	(h)	L	0-3	(0-1)		44,830
5 May	Linfield XI	Fr	(a)	W	6-0	(4-0)	Milburn 4, Stobbart, Taylor	
8 May	Ballymena XI	Fr	(a)	W	3-2	(1-1)	Sibley, Stobbart 2	
10 May	Shelbourne Select	Fr	(a)	W	6-0	(3-0)	Sibley, Stobbart, Milburn 3, Taylor	
15 May	Cork XI	Fr	(a)	D	2-2	(2-2)	Stobbart, Milburn	10,000

1948-49

29 Jan	Bristol Rovers	Fr	(a)	D	1-1	(1-0)	Taylor (Abandoned after 65m, fog)	25,885
12 Feb	Middlesbrough	Fr	(a)	D	3-3	(0-1)	Stobbart 2, Robledo (G)	36,000
26 Feb	Liverpool	Fr	(h)	D	1-1	(1-0)	Milburn	29,980
19 May	Montreal All Stars (Ca)	Ot	(a)	W	4-1	(0-0)	Milburn 2, Robledo (G), Taylor	15,000
24 May	Ontario All Stars (Ca) (in Toronto)	Ot	(a)	W	8-2	(1-2)	Milburn 4, Mitchell, Robledo (G) 2, Walker	17,000
28 May	Saskatchewan All Stars (Ca) (in Saskatoon)	Ot	(a)	W	13-2	(7-0)	Robledo (G) 4, Thompson 2, Walker 2, Milburn, Dodgin, Houghton, Mitchell, og (Greyeyes)	7,000
1 June	Alberta FA All Stars (Ca) (in Edmonton)	Ot	(a)	W	16-2	(5-0)	Milburn 6, Robledo (G) 5, Mitchell 2, Harvey 2, Walker	5,000
4 June	British Columbia All Stars (Ca) (in Vancouver)	Ot	(a)	W	5-2	(2-1)	Milburn 2, Walker 2, Mitchell	7,408
5 June	Washington State FA (USA) (in Seattle)	Ot	(a)	W	10-1	(6-0)	Milburn 4, Robledo (G) 3, Taylor 2, Walker	8,000
7 June	British Columbia All Stars (Ca) (in Vancouver)	Ot	(a)	W	8-1	(3-1)	Milburn 5, Robledo (G) 2, Walker	8,815
11 June	Winnipeg All Stars (Ca)	Ot	(a)	W	7-4	(6-3)	Milburn 2, Taylor 2, Robledo (G) 2, Walker	6,000
15 June	IFK Goteborg (Se) (in Toronto)	Ot	(n)	W	4-0	(2-0)	Millburn 3, Mitchell	22,105
19 June	IFK Goteborg (Se) (in New York)	Ot	(n)	W	3-0	(1-0)	Milburn 2, Mitchell	18,000

1949-50

11 Feb	Middlesbrough	Fr	(h)	W	3-2	(1-2)	Milburn 2, Taylor	17,000
26 April	Dundee	Fr	(h)	L	2-3	(1-0)	Robledo (G), Taylor	16,490
10 May	Ayr United (at Ashington FC)	Fr	(n)	W	2-1	(1-0)	Mitchell 2	10,000

NEWCASTLE UNITED
ST. JAMES'S PARK, NEWCASTLE UPON TYNE
OFFICIAL PROGRAMME - 2d. No. 13.
You can obtain an Excellent Meal at a Moderate Price at any of Carricks Cafes
The Big Five — NEWCASTLE JOURNAL, EVENING CHRONICLE, SUNDAY SUN, WEEKLY CHRONICLE, SPORTING MAN
NEWCASTLE UNITED versus NORRKOPING
KICK-OFF 2-30 P.M.
OXO

Swedish s IFK Norrk had a note up immedi after Worl Two. Their to Tyneside 1946 was attraction.

Jackie Millburn in action on the extensiv tour of North America during the summe of 1949.

ALBERTA FOOTBALL ASSOCIATION
Souvenir Programme
EXHIBITION FOOTBALL GAME
Newcastle United Football Club Ltd.
and
The Alberta Football Association All-Stars
CLARKE STADIUM — EDMONTON, ALBERTA

Match programm from the exhibition match wit Alberta Al Stars on t tour of No America. United wo all of 16-2

Skipper Joe Harvey leads out the Magpies with his Swedish counterpart, captain of IFK Goteborg.

1950-51

5 Aug	Edinburgh Select XI (at Hearts FC)	Ch	(a)	D	1-1	(0-1)	Milburn	50,000
9 May	Stade Rennais (F)	FoB	(h)	D	1-1	(1-0)	Robledo (G)	12,222
19 May	Cumberland XI (at Workington FC)	CC	(a)	W	6-5	(3-1)	Stokoe 2, Hannah 2, Cameron, og (Buchanan)	10,000
26 May	RSC Anderlecht (Bel)	Fr	(a)	W	6-0	(2-0)	Milburn 2, Taylor 2, Robledo (G), og (Matthys)	

1951-52

12 Sept	Glasgow Celtic	CwC	(a)	D	3-3	(1-1)	Robledo (G), Mitchell, Taylor (Highest attendance for a friendly fixture)	61,300
10 Dec	Merthyr Tydfil	Fr	(a)	W	6-4	(1-2)	Davies, Cowell, Foulkes 2, Duncan 2	5,200
17 May	Southern Transvaal (SA) (in Johannesburg)	Ot	(a)	W	3-2	(2-0)	Robledo (G) 2, Hannah	25,000
21 May	Natal (SA) (in Pietermartzburg)	Ot	(a)	W	6-2	(5-0)	Robledo (G) 4, Harvey, Davies	8,000
24 May	Natal (SA) (in Durban)	Ot	(a)	W	4-0	(2-0)	Davies 3, Mitchell (p)	30,000
31 May	Western Province (SA) (in Cape Town)	Ot	(a)	W	8-0	(1-0)	Davies 3, Milburn 3, Robledo (G), Mitchell (p)	13,000
4 June	Griqualand West (SA) (in Kimberley)	Ot	(a)	W	3-0	(1-0)	Robledo (G), Robledo (E), Milburn	8,000
7 June	Northern Transvaal (SA) (in Pretoria)	Ot	(a)	W	2-1	(1-1)	Milburn, Hannah	
10 June	Lourenco Marques (PEA)	Ot	(a)	W	5-0	(3-0)	Mitchell 2 (1p), Davies, Robledo (G), Crowe	9,000
14 June	Northern Rhodesia (Rh) (in Nkana)	Ot	(a)	W	6-1	(3-0)	Walker 2, Robledo (G), Crowe, Harvey, Cowell (p)	
18 June	Southern Rhodesia (Rh) (in Salisbury)	Ot	(a)	W	4-2	(2-0)	Robledo (G) 3, Harvey	
21 June	Eastern Transvaal (SA) (in Benoni)	Ot	(a)	W	2-0	(0-0)	Mitchell, Brennan	13,000
25 June	Orange Free State (SA) (in Bloemfontein)	Ot	(a)	W	3-0	(2-0)	Foulkes 2, Mitchell	
28 June	South Africa (in Durban)	Ot	(a)	W	3-0	(2-0)	Davies 2, Milburn	20,000
2 July	Border Province (SA) (in East London)	Ot	(a)	W	10-0	(5-0)	Robledo (G) 7, Davies, Foulkes, Crowe (p)	4,000
5 July	Eastern Province (SA) (in Port Elizabeth)	Ot	(a)	W	5-1	(1-0)	Davies 3, Robledo (G), Mitchell	
12 July	South Africa (in Johannesburg)	Ot	(a)	L	3-5	(2-2)	Milburn, Mitchell, Davies	25,000
16 July	Southern Transvaal (SA) (in Johannesburg)	Ot	(a)	W	6-4	(3-2)	Foulkes 2, Crowe, Walker, Mitchell, Davies	10,000

1952-53

25 Feb	Glasgow Celtic	Fr	(h)	W	2-0	(1-0)	Robledo (G) 2 (St James' Park floodlights opening)	41,888
25 March	Airdrieonians	Fr	(h)	W	5-1	(3-1)	Foulkes, Davies 2, Hannah, Robledo (G)	38,800
15 April	East Fife	Fr	(h)	W	4-1	(1-0)	Mitchell 2, Mulgrew, Hannah	18,600
27 April	Berwick Rangers	Ben	(a)	D	1-1	(0-1)	Robledo (G) (Abandoned 80m, rainstorm)	3,000
13 May	Aberdeen (at Glasgow Rangers FC)	CrC	(n)	W	4-0	(2-0)	White, Hannah, Milburn, og (Young)	16,000
16 May	Hibernian (at Glasgow Rangers FC)	CrC	(n)	L	0-4	(0-2)		48,876

1953-54

7 Oct	Heart of Midlothian	Fr	(h)	D	2-2	(1-0)	Milburn, Davies	38,201
20 Oct	Falkirk	Fr	(a)	L	2-3	(2-1)	Milburn, og (Black)	11,000
28 Oct	South Africa XI	Fr	(h)	W	3-1	(3-1)	Milburn, Hannah, Mitchell	17,460
30 Nov	Portsmouth (Jack Eden)	Ben	(a)	D	1-1	(0-1)	Mitchell	14,533
5 April	Millwall	Fr	(a)	L	1-4	(1-2)	Foulkes	12,507
26 April	Reading (George Marks & Bill Livingstone)	Test	(a)	D	2-2	(1-1)	Milburn, Davies	8,428
28 April	Hartlepools United (Ray Thompson & Jack Newton)	Test	(a)	D	1-1	(1-0)	og (Stamper)	9,635

1954-55

4 Oct	Plymouth Argyle	Fr	(a)	L	2-3	(1-0)	Milburn, White	11,679
13 Oct	Heart of Midlothian	Fr	(h)	L	2-3	(0-3)	Milburn 2 (1p)	22,594
18 Oct	Doncaster Rovers	Fr	(a)	L	2-7	(1-5)	White, Milburn	16,479
27 Oct	Hibernian	Fr	(a)	D	1-1	(0-0)	Crowe	21,000
10 Nov	SK Admira Wien (A)	Fr	(h)	W	3-1	(0-0)	Broadis, Mitchell, Milburn	18,834
25 May	SC Wacker 04 Berlin & Hertha Berliner SC XI (WG)	Ot	(a)	W	3-2	(2-1)	Milburn 2, Keeble	15,000
28 May	Nuremburg (WG)	Ot	(a)	L	0-1	(0-0)		
1 June	Munich Combined/Bavarian Select XI (WG)	Ot	(a)	L	1-2	(0-2)	Mitchell	
5 June	Karlsruher FV (WG)	Ot	(a)	W	4-2	(2-1)	Hannah, Keeble, Milburn, White	

1955-56

6 Aug	Edinburgh Select XI (at Hibernian FC)	Ch	(a)	D	1-1	(0-1)	Keeble	50,000
21 Sept	Hartlepools United (Joe Willitts* & Wally Moore)	Test	(a)	W	5-0	(3-0)	Mitchell 3 (1p), Milburn 2	5,435
10 Oct	Heart of Midlothian	ASL	(h)	D	2-2	(0-0)	Keeble, Mitchell	22,542
19 Oct	Hibernian	ASL	(h)	L	1-2	(0-1)	White	17,992
7 Nov	Heart of Midlothian (at Hibernian FC)	ASL	(a)	W	6-4	(3-1)	Keeble 3, Hannah 2, Davies	12,500
16 Nov	Hibernian	ASL	(a)	L	0-2	(0-1)	(Abandoned after 70m, fog, result stood)	20,000
12 March	Partick Thistle	ASL	(h)	D	1-1	(0-0)	Taylor	13,735
9 April	Partick Thistle	ASL	(a)	D	1-1	(1-1)	Milburn	18,000
16 April	All Star XI (Bobby Cowell*)	Test	(h)	W	5-0	(1-0)	White 2, Curry, Keeble, Milburn	36,240
19 April	Barrow (Willie Buchanan & Billy Gordon)	Test	(a)	W	4-3	(1-1)	White 3, Curry	7,098
25 April	Hartlepools United (Tommy McGuigan & Frank Stamper)	Test	(a)	L	3-6	(0-5)	Keeble, Mitchell (p), Cummings	7,206
29 April	Atletico Madrid (Sp)	Ot	(a)	L	1-4	(0-1)	Curry	60,000
3 May	Altona & St Pauli XI (Hamburg) (WG)	Ot	(a)	D	1-1	(1-0)	Keeble	18,000
6 May	Frankfurt Combined XI (WG)	Ot	(a)	W	2-1	(0-0)	Keeble, Davies	16,000
9 May	Augsburg Combined XI (WG)	Ot	(a)	W	4-2	(2-1)	Hannah, Keeble, White 2	26,000

1956-57

10 Sept	Greenock Morton XI (Tommy Orr)	Test	(a)	W	3-1	(2-0)	Milburn 2, Davies	6,000
19 Sept	Heart of Midlothian	ASL	(h)	L	1-2	(1-1)	Keeble	23,780
3 Oct	Hibernian	ASL	(h)	W	2-1	(0-1)	Milburn, Hannah	16,668
10 Oct	Linfield	Fr	(a)	W	4-1	(2-0)	Milburn, Mitchell, Hannah 2	25,000
17 Oct	Partick Thistle	ASL	(a)	L	1-4	(1-3)	Milburn	15,000
22 Oct	British Olympic XI	Fr	(h)	W	5-0	(3-0)	Curry 5	8,860
29 Oct	Reading	Fr	(a)	W	3-2	(1-0)	Curry, Eastham, White	7,023
5 Nov	Heart of Midlothian	ASL	(a)	D	0-0	(0-0)		18,000
14 Nov	Partick Thistle	ASL	(h)	W	5-0	(2-0)	Keeble 2, Milburn, Keery, Spears	8,880
26 Nov	Hibernian	ASL	(a)	W	3-1	(1-0)	Millburn 2, White	8,000
19 Feb	OS Belenenses (P)	Fr	(a)	L	1-2	(0-2)	Mitchell (p)	
10 April	FC Nancy (F)	Fr	(h)	D	2-2	(0-2)	White, Hannah	15,224
27 April	Barrow (Peter Wilson & Jackie Keen)	Test	(a)	W	8-0	(4-0)	Milburn 4, Franks, Davies, Tait, Hughes	6,000
1 May	Lincoln City (Doug Graham*)	Test	(a)	D	2-2	(1-1)	Hannah, Hale	5,600

Newcastle took the FA Cup on tour of South Africa in the summer of 1952. Match programme from the challenge contest with Southern Rhodesia in Salisbury.

As one of the country's top line-ups, United were invited to complete for the Coronation Cup trophy at the end of the 1952-53 season.

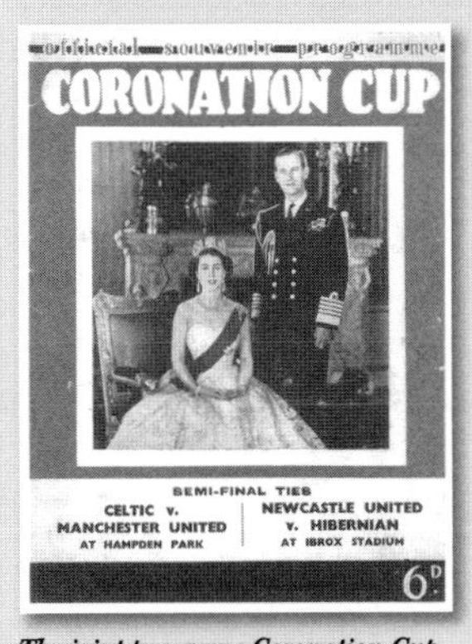

The joint two-game Coronation Cup semi-final programme. Newcastle faced Hibs at Ibrox but lost by four goals.

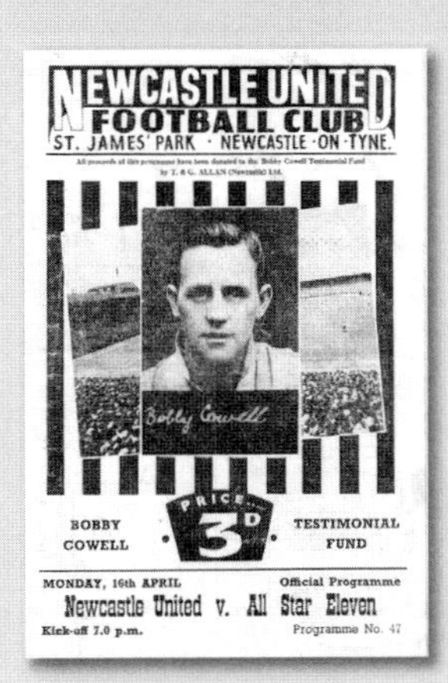

After more than 400 games for United, Bobby Cowell was injured on tour in Germany. He earned a Testimonial in 1956.

1957-58

30 Oct	Middlesbrough	Fr	(a)	L	0-3	(0-1)		27,056
6 Nov	Gwardia Warsaw (Pol)	Fr	(h)	L	1-3	(1-1)	Punton	17,883
20 Nov	Heart of Midlothian	ASL	(a)	D	2-2	(1-2)	Bell, White	14,500
27 Nov	Heart of Midlothian	ASL	(h)	W	2-0	(2-0)	White, Eastham	10,260
11 May	FC Barcelona (Sp)	Ot	(a)	L	2-3	(1-1)	Mitchell (p), Davies	50,000
22 May	Progresul Bucharest (R)	Ot	(a)	D	1-1	(1-0)	Mitchell	40,000
24 May	Dinamo Bucharest (R)	Ot	(a)	L	2-3	(1-0)	Eastham, Scoular	
31 May	Petrolul Ploiesti (R)	Ot	(a)	L	2-3	(0-0)	White 2	

1958-59

1 Oct	Bela Vista (Br)	Fr	(h)	W	12-1	(4-1)	White 5, Bottom 5, Evans, Davies	25,395
21 Oct	TSV 1860 Munich (WG)	Fr	(h)	W	3-0	(2-0)	Allchurch, Eastham, Hughes	21,530
17 Nov	Orgryte IS (Se)	Fr	(h)	W	5-2	(1-1)	Allchurch 2, White, Eastham, Curry	18,356
3 Dec	Bucharest XI (R)	Fr	(h)	W	4-1	(2-0)	Curry, Allchurch, Eastham, Hughes	20,862
24 Jan	Liverpool	Fr	(a)	D	2-2	(2-1)	White, Allchurch	18,449
13 Feb	Wiener Sportklub (A)	Fr	(h)	D	1-1	(0-0)	McGuigan	25,370
23 Feb	Linfield	Fr	(a)	D	3-3	(2-1)	Taylor, Allchurch, White	12,000
2 March	All Stars XI (Northumberland CCC)	Ben	(h)	L	2-4	(0-1)	Allchurch 2	15,662
4 April	Halmstads BK (Se)	Fr	(h)	W	3-1	(2-0)	Taylor, Eastham, Gibson	10,696
1 May	Brighton & Hove Albion	Fr	(a)	D	1-1	(0-0)	Hughes	6,682
4 May	Peterborough United (Ellis Stafford, Dennis Emry & Andy Donaldson*)	Test	(a)	W	5-3	(4-3)	Eastham 2, Curry 2, Mitchell	11,000
6 May	Drumcondra Select	Fr	(a)	W	6-3	(1-0)	White 4, Allchurch, Mitten (C)	7,000
8 May	Evergreen United Select (John Coughlan)	Test	(a)	W	4-2	(0-1)	Allchurch 2, White, Eastham	5,000
11 May	Glentoran	Fr	(a)	D	3-3	(2-1)	Eastham 2, White	7,500

1959-60

1 Aug	Edinburgh Select XI (at Hibernian FC)	Ch	(a)	L	3-4	(1-1)	McGuigan, White, Eastham	26,239
14 Aug	RCD Mallorca (Sp)	Ot	(a)	D	1-1	(1-1)	White	
16 Aug	Olympic Club de Charleroi (Bel) (at RCD Mallorca)	Ot	(n)	W	5-1	(2-0)	White 3, Allchurch, Eastham	
28 Sept	Aberdeen	Fr	(a)	D	3-3	(1-1)	Scott 2, Eastham	10,100
5 Oct	Dundee United	Fr	(a)	W	9-2	(4-1)	White 3, Eastham 2, Scott 2, Hale, Scoular	8,500
14 Oct	All Star XI (Norman Smith*)	Test	(h)	W	11-4	(5-1)	Eastham 3, White 3, Mitchell 2, Hale 2, Hughes	14,467
28 Oct	York City	Fr	(a)	W	8-2	(5-0)	White 3, Allchurch 2, Eastham, Mitchell, Gilfillan	9,414
19 Nov	Torpedo Moscow (USSR)	Fr	(h)	D	4-4	(2-2)	White 2, Allchurch, Eastham (p)	7,921
3 May	Shamrock Rovers (Liam Hennessey & Liam Tuohy*)	Test	(a)	W	3-0	(2-0)	White 2, Allchurch	20,000
6 May	Southend United (Arthur Williamson, Sandy Anderson & Sam McCrory)	Test	(a)	W	6-3	(5-1)	McGuigan, White 2, Allchurch, Hughes, og (Williamson)	10,000
14 May	FC Schalke 04 (WG)	Ot	(a)	W	3-0	(1-0)	White 2, McGuigan	10,000
17 May	NK Dinamo Zagreb (Y)	Ot	(a)	W	3-1	(2-1)	McGuigan, Allchurch, Hughes	
22 May	NK Hadjuk Split (Y)	Ot	(a)	L	2-3	(0-1)	White, Stokoe (p)	
25 May	RCD Espanyol (Sp)	Ot	(a)	W	5-2	(4-1)	White 2, Allchurch 2, Eastham	40,000
29 May	Sevilla (Sp) (in La Coruna)	TTH	(a)	L	1-2	(0-1)	Eastham	

1960-61

10 Aug	Racing Club de Paris (F)	FF	(a)	W	3-2	(2-1)	White, Allchurch, Stokoe (p)	3,000
29 Aug	FC Barcelona (Sp)	Fr	(h)	L	3-4	(3-0)	Tuohy, Allchurch, Woods	31,361
28 Sept	Racing Club de Paris (F)	FF	(h)	W	2-1	(1-0)	Mitchell, White	9,077

1961-62

9 Aug	Aarhus GF (D)	Ch	(h)	W	6-0	(3-0)	Leek 3, Neale, Allchurch, Tuohy	13,667
12 Aug	Odense (D)	Fr	(h)	W	2-0	(2-0)	Allchurch 2	9,869
6 Sept	Sunderland	CoN	(a)	W	1-0	(1-0)	Leek	18,239
9 Oct	Bobby Mitchell XI (Bobby Mitchell*)	Test	(h)	L	2-3	(0-2)	Allchurch, Tuohy	40,993
16 Oct	Middlesbrough	CoN	(h)	L	2-3	(2-1)	Leek, Hale	10,154
25 Oct	Sunderland	CoN	(h)	W	2-1	(1-1)	White 2	12,230
8 Nov	Middlesbrough	CoN	(a)	L	3-4	(1-1)	McGuigan, Hughes, Woods	5,221

1962-63

No matches arranged

1963-64

17 Aug	Huddersfield Town	Fr	(h)	W	5-1	(3-0)	Taylor 3, Hilley, McGarry	12,622
21 Oct	Alf McMichael's XI (Alf McMichael*)	Test	(h)	L	4-5	(3-2)	Taylor 2, Kirkman, Cummings	24,175
9 Dec	Dunfermline Ath (Willie Cunningham & John Williamson)	Test	(a)	L	0-2	(0-2)		10,000
25 Jan	Middlesbrough	Fr	(h)	W	4-3	(3-3)	Mahon, Thomas, Burton, McGarry	14,455
15 Feb	St Johnstone	Fr	(a)	W	3-1	(0-1)	Burton, Cummings, Hilley	7,000

1964-65

8 Aug	Burnley	Fr	(h)	D	1-1	(0-0)	McGrath	14,800
15 Aug	Burnley	Fr	(a)	W	1-0	(0-0)	Iley	6,070
5 May	HfS Horsens SK (D)	Ot	(a)	W	5-3	(2-1)	Hilley, Penman, Anderson, Cummings 2 (1p)	3,300
8 May	SV Gottingen (WG)	Ot	(a)	W	2-0	(1-0)	Cummings, Penman	5,000
12 May	VfL Wolfsburg EV (WG)	Ot	(a)	W	3-1	(0-1)	Cummings, Penman 2	3,000
14 May	KSV Holstein Kiel (WG)	Ot	(a)	D	1-1	(0-1)	Anderson	4,000
17 May	Aalborg BK (D)	Ot	(a)	W	2-1	(2-0)	Cummings, Robson	3,000

1965-66

10 Aug	Middlesbrough	Fr	(a)	D	0-2	(0-0)		12,590
14 Aug	Middlesbrough	Fr	(h)	W	3-2	(3-2)	Hockey, Cummings, og (Jones)	13,534
11 Oct	Heart of Midlothian	Fr	(a)	L	1-2	(0-1)	Moncur	5,683
27 Oct	Sunderland (Brian Clough)	Test	(a)	W	6-2	(1-1)	Eastham, Burton, Hateley, Dobson (p), Iley, St John (Newcastle Utd Select XI)	31,898
22 Nov	Dynamo Moscow (USSR)	Fr	(h)	L	1-4	(1-3)	Moncur	11,130

Newcastle faced Brazilian opposition for the first time in 1958 when Bela Vista arrived on Tyneside. They were no match for the Magpies losing by 12-1.

Along with Len White, striker Arthur Bottom (above) ravaged the Brazilians. Both players grabbed five goals.

Newcastle faced Sevilla for the Trofeo Teresa Herrera during 1960 in the Estadio De Riazor. A match poster survives.

During the late 1950s United started to play floodlit friendlies against foreign opposition including Racing Club de Paris.

1966-67

6 Aug	Aalborg BK (D)	Fr	(h)	D	1-1	(0-1)	Suddick	7,734
10 Aug	Carlisle United	Fr	(h)	D	2-2	(0-1)	Robson (B), Suddick	6,007
15 Aug	Carlisle United	Fr	(a)	L	2-4	(1-2)	Robson (B) 2	10,000
19 Sept	Linfield	Fr	(h)	W	7-2	(4-0)	McGarry 2 (1p), Robson (B) 2, Burton, Guthrie, Suddick	4,224
26 Sept	Heart of Midlothian	Fr	(h)	L	2-7	(1-5)	Robson (B), Noble	5,256
10 May	International XI (Jackie Milburn*)	Test	(h)	L	1-3	(1-1)	Milburn (Abandoned 70m rain) (Newcastle Utd & Sunderland Select XI)	45,404
17 May	Bournemouth (Dick Keith* Fund)	Test	(a)	W	4-1	(3-0)	Bennett 2, Davies, Robson (B)	4,039
19 May	Chelmsford City	Fr	(a)	W	2-0	(2-0)	Allen, Bennett	2,210

1967-68

8 Aug	Middlesbrough	CoN	(a)	L	2-3	(2-2)	Hilley, Robson (B)	15,008
12 Aug	Middlesbrough	CoN	(h)	W	2-0	(0-0)	Hilley, Davies	13,850
20 Oct	Glentoran	Fr	(a)	L	1-2	(0-1)	og (Creighton)	8,000
17 Feb	Glasgow Celtic	Fr	(h)	W	1-0	(0-0)	Scott	38,836
8 March	Glasgow Celtic	Fr	(a)	W	3-2	(1-0)	Davies, Scott, Robson (T)	42,000
30 March	Hibernian	Fr	(h)	W	2-1	(1-1)	Scott, McNamee	14,650

1968-69

3 Aug	Hibernian	Fr	(a)	W	2-1	(1-0)	Davies, og (Shevlane)	14,737
5 Aug	Aberdeen	Fr	(h)	W	1-0	(1-0)	Bennett	16,000
26 Nov	Barnsley (Barrie Thomas*)	Test	(a)	L	1-5	(1-3)	Hindson	10,000

1969-70

30 July	Heart of Midlothian	Fr	(h)	W	1-0	(1-0)	Robson (B)	21,000
2 Aug	Hull City	Fr	(a)	L	0-1	(0-0)		8,559
5 Aug	Hibernian	Fr	(a)	D	0-0	(0-0)		15,309
12 Nov	Sunderland (Len Ashurst)	Test	(a)	L	2-4	(1-1)	Moncur, Scott (Newcastle Utd Select XI)	6,470
7 Dec	British XI (in Horden)	DF	(a)	D	5-5	(3-1)	Harris 2, Clark, Foggon, og (McFarland) (Newcastle Utd & Sunderland Select XI)	8,000
20 Feb	Dundee United	Fr	(h)	W	3-2	(1-0)	Moncur, Robson(B), Dyson	8,685
2 May	Aberdeen	Fr	(h)	L	0-1	(0-1)		10,300
8 May	Chicago (USA)	Ot	(a)	W	5-0	(2-0)	Robson (B) 3 (1p), Dyson 2	3,000
10 May	Victoria Royals (Ca) (in Nanaimo)	Ot	(a)	W	3-0	(2-0)	Gibb, Robson(B) (p), Smith	1,800
16 May	Victoria Royals (Ca) (in Victoria)	Ot	(a)	W	2-1	(1-1)	Robson (B), Foggon	2,335
18 May	Vancouver Spartans (Ca)	Ot	(a)	W	4-3	(2-1)	Robson (B) 2, Dyson, Young	6,000
24 May	Seattle Seatacs (USA)	Ot	(a)	W	2-1	(1-1)	Young, Craig	2,900
27 May	Vancouver Spartans (Ca)	Ot	(a)	W	3-0	(2-0)	Robson (B), Dyson, McGovern	2,847
30 May	Eintracht Frankfurt (WG) (in Toronto)	Ot	(n)	W	4-0	(3-0)	Robson (B) 2, Foggon, Craig	6,000

1970-71

1 Aug	Dundee United	Fr	(a)	W	2-1	(1-0)	Smith, Davies	7,000
5 Aug	Dundee United	Fr	(h)	W	1-0	(0-0)	Davies	15,000
8 Aug	Bolton Wanderers	Fr	(h)	W	3-0	(0-0)	Gibb, Moncur, Foggon	9,900
18 Nov	Ayr United	Fr	(a)	L	0-2	(0-0)		5,000
23 Jan	Sunderland	Fr	(h)	D	1-1	(0-0)	Moncur	16,650
5 May	All Star XI (Geoff Allen*)	Test	(h)	W	6-5	(1-0)	McNamee 2, Craggs 2, Dyson, Craig	10,000

1971-72

30 July	AS Saint-Etienne (F)	Fr	(a)	L	1-2	(0-2)	Macdonald	8,000
7 Aug	SL Benfica (P)	Fr	(h)	W	1-0	(1-0)	Gibb	27,630
10 Aug	Aberdeen	Fr	(a)	L	2-3	(0-1)	Tudor, Cassidy	17,000
31 May	Rajpracha Nukrow (Th) (in Bangkok)	Ot	(a)	W	3-1		Tudor 3	
2 June	Thailand Select XI (in Bangkok)	Ot	(a)	D	2-2	(0-2)	Tudor 2	8,000
4 June	Santos (Br) (in Hong Kong)	Ot	(n)	L	2-4	(2-1)	Green, Tudor	
9 June	Javanan (Ir) (in Hong Kong)	Ot	(n)	D	1-1	(1-1)	Tudor	

1972-73

29 July	St Johnstone	Fr	(a)	W	7-3	(4-1)	Macdonald 3, Tudor 3, Hibbitt	4,600
31 July	Partick Thistle	Fr	(a)	D	2-2	(1-1)	Macdonald, Gibb	7,012
5 Aug	Greenock Morton	Fr	(a)	D	1-1	(0-0)	Howard	4,061
5 March	League of Ireland (in Dublin)	Fr	(a)	D	0-0	(0-0)		6,000
14 May	Sunderland (Ollie Burton*)	Test	(h)	W	2-1	(1-0)	Cassidy, Tudor	35,873

1973-74

11 Aug	Middlesbrough	Fr	(a)	W	3-1	(2-1)	Cassidy 2, Howard	12,272
14 Aug	Workington	Fr	(a)	W	4-1	(1-1)	Hodgson 2, Gibb, McDermott	1,000
18 Aug	Blackpool	Fr	(a)	W	1-0	(1-0)	Hibbitt	6,297
10 May	Middlesbrough (Tony Green*)	Test	(h)	W	5-3	(2-1)	Tudor 3, Bruce, og (Craggs)	27,938
13 May	Sunderland (Jim Montgomery)	Test	(a)	W	3-2	(2-1)	McDermott 2 (1p), Bruce	29,625

1974-75

29 July	Queen of the South	Fr	(a)	W	2-0	(1-0)	Macdonald, McDermott (p)	3,411
8 March	SC Internacional (Br)	Fr	(h)	L	0-3	(0-2)		23,475
28 April	Sunderland (Martin Harvey)	Test	(a)	L	2-3	(1-2)	Gibb, Burns	13,654
30 April	Sunderland (David Craig*)	Test	(h)	W	5-3	(2-0)	Macdonald 2, Tudor, Burns, Kennedy	21,280
10 May	Heart of Midlothian	Fr	(a)	D	2-2	(1-0)	Tudor, Burns	8,500

1975-76

24 July	Jersey Select XI	Fr	(a)	W	6-0	(4-0)	Burns 2, Bruce, Nulty, Macdonald, Keeley	2,000
21 Oct	SK Brann (Bergen) (Nw)	Fr	(a)	D	1-1	(0-0)	Macdonald	10,000
28 April	Sunderland (Frank Clark*)	Test	(h)	W	6-3	(2-3)	Kennedy 2, Burns 2, Macdonald, Guy	19,974
3 May	Leeds Utd (Paul Reaney)	Test	(a)	W	5-4	(2-2)	Macdonald 2, Gowling, Kennedy, Burns	16,000
5 May	IK Start (Nw)	Ot	(a)	W	3-1	(2-0)	Macdonald, Burns, Kennedy	3,000
6 May	Fredrikstad FK (Nw)	Ot	(a)	W	4-2	(2-0)	Burns, Gowling, Nattrass, Kennedy	2,000
17 May	North Shields	Ch	(a)	L	2-4	(2-2)	Burns 2	3,000

1976-77

4 Aug	Southend United	Fr	(a)	W	2-1		Nattrass, Gowling	5,000
9 Oct	Hibernian	Fr	(h)	W	2-1	(0-1)	Cannell, Gowling	10,284
9 May	Don Revie International XI (Joe Harvey*)	Test	(h)	L	2-5	(0-3)	Burns, Craig (T) (p)	14,000
26 May	Bradford City (Ian Cooper)	Test	(a)	W	4-3	(2-0)	Burns 2, Callachan, Barrowclough	3,292
30 May	Sliema Wanderers (M)	Ot	(a)	W	4-0	(1-0)	Cannell, Kennedy, Barrowclough, Nulty	2,000
2 June	Floriana (M)	Ot	(a)	D	1-1	(1-0)	Gowling	3,156

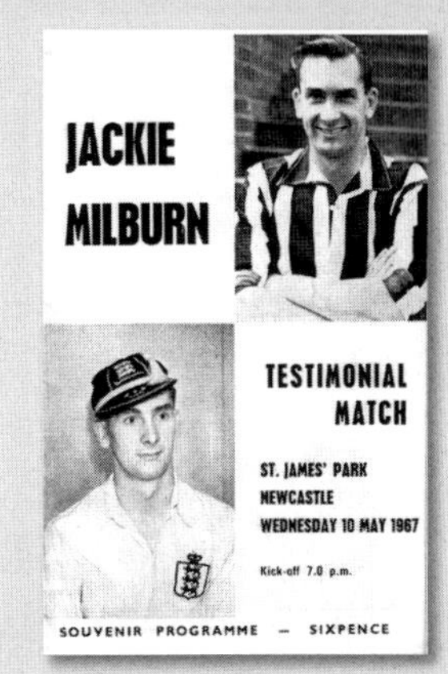

Belatedly Jackie Milburn was awarded a Testimonial game in 1967. A crowd of over 45,000 gave him an official farewell, 10 years after he last played for United.

Geoff Allen proved to be a bright prospect on the wing for United, but his career was wrecked by injury. His Testimonial took place in 1971.

In a friendly match with St Johnstone, Malcolm Macdonald netted one of the quickest goals on record, direct from the kick-off. It was timed at around 4 seconds.

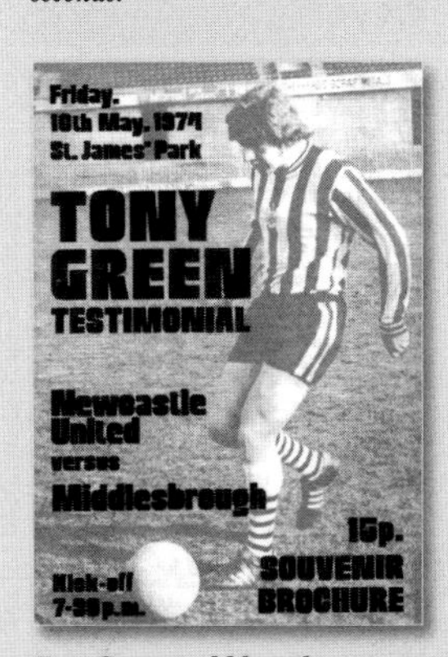

Tony Green could have become one of United's greatest ever players – yet the Scot was another who was forced to retire due to injury. His Testimonial was against Boro in 1974.

1977-78								
1 Aug	Telstar (Velsen) (N)	Ot	(a)	L	1-2	(1-1)	Burns	
3 Aug	Sparta Rotterdam (N)	Ot	(a)	D	2-2	(1-1)	Burns 2	
6 Aug	FC Volendam (N)	Ot	(a)	L	1-2	(1-0)	Callachan	
8 Aug	Chesterfield	Fr	(a)	W	4-2	(1-1)	Gowling 2, Craig (D), Craig (T)	2,201
10 Aug	Carlisle Utd (Dick Young)	Test	(a)	D	1-1	(0-1)	og (Carr)	5,413
6 Sept	Hibernian	Fr	(a)	L	0-3	(0-0)		5,000
2 May	Chelmsford City	Fr	(a)	W	2-1	(1-0)	Larnach 2	1,500
8 May	Jim Smith XI (Jim Smith*)	Test	(h)	L	3-6	(2-2)	McGhee, Burns, Barton	17,428

1978-79								
23 July	Trollhattans (Se)	Ot	(a)	W	2-1		Kennedy, Bird	
25 July	Tidaholms GIF (Se)	Ot	(a)	W	2-1	(0-1)	McGhee, Mitchell	
26 July	Gislaveds IS (Se)	Ot	(a)	D	0-0	(0-0)		
29 July	Ockero IF (Se)	Ot	(a)	W	2-0	(0-0)	Parkinson, McGhee	
30 July	Satila SK (Se)	Ot	(a)	W	3-2		Connolly, Kennedy, Walker	
7 Aug	Hull City	Fr	(a)	D	0-0	(0-0)		2,960
10 Aug	Gateshead	Fr	(a)	W	1-0	(0-0)	Callachan	3,000
15 Aug	Arbroath	Cent	(a)	D	0-0	(0-0)		1,736
9 May	Cognac (F)	Fr	(a)	W	2-1	(1-0)	Withe, Shoulder	1,500

1979-80								
26 July	Bath City	Fr	(a)	D	1-1	(0-0)	Shoulder	2,146
28 July	Plymouth Argyle	Fr	(a)	W	3-0	(1-0)	Martin, Shoulder, Withe	2,397
1 Aug	Torquay United	Fr	(a)	W	3-2	(2-2)	Shoulder, Walker, Mitchell	2,450
3 Aug	Exeter City	Fr	(a)	L	2-3	(2-1)	Withe, Brownlie	1,829
9 Aug	Blyth Spartans (Eddie Alder & Ron Scott)	Test	(a)	D	1-1	(1-1)	Shoulder	2,398
11 Aug	Sparta Rotterdam (N)	Fr	(h)	L	0-1	(0-1)		7,596
13 Nov	Manchester City (Willie McFaul*)	Test	(h)	W	4-1	(2-1)	Macdonald, Withe, Connolly, McDermott	14,995
3 Dec	North Shields	Fr	(a)	W	4-1	(1-0)	Rafferty, Martin 2, Withe	1,029
15 Feb	Dundee	Fr	(a)	W	3-1	(0-0)	Mitchell, Withe, Rafferty	3,596

1980-81								
20 July	Solvesborg Mjallby (Se)	Ot	(a)	D	0-0	(0-0)		1,500
22 July	Oskarshams AIK (Se)	Ot	(a)	W	3-0	(2-0)	Clarke, Rafferty, Davies	2,000
24 July	Trelleborgs FF (Se)	Ot	(a)	D	1-1		Shinton	1,000
26 July	Hoor IS (Se)	Ot	(a)	L	1-2		Brownlie	1,000
28 July	Tomelilla IF/IFK Ystad XI (Se)	Ot	(a)	W	3-0		Cartwright, Rafferty, Montgomerie	2,000
4 Aug	Heart of Midlothian	Fr	(a)	D	1-1	(1-0)	Shinton	3,334
9 Aug	Leeds United	Fr	(h)	D	2-2	(1-1)	Davies (p), Rafferty	7,448

1981-82								
14 Aug	West Bromwich Albion	Fr	(h)	L	0-2	(0-1)		6,843
18 Aug	Sunderland	Fr	(h)	D	1-1	(1-1)	Shinton	9,982
22 Aug	Sunderland	Fr	(a)	L	1-2	(1-1)	Shoulder	10,032
3 Nov	Berwick Rangers	Fr	(a)	W	3-2	(3-0)	Trewick 2, Wharton	1,167
18 May	Hartlepool United	Fr	(a)	W	6-2	(3-0)	Varadi 5, Wharton	1,037

1982-83								
7 Aug	Greenock Morton	Fr	(a)	W	3-1	(2-1)	Todd, Doyle, Varadi	2,000
9 Aug	Kilmarnock	Fr	(a)	D	0-0	(0-0)		3,000
11 Aug	Partick Thistle	Fr	(a)	W	2-0	(2-0)	Varadi 2	1,500
19 Aug	CD Nacional (P) (in Funchal)	MT	(a)	D	0-0	(0-0)	(Lost on pens)	1,000
21 Aug	CS Maritimo (P) (in Funchal)	MT	(a)	W	1-0	(1-0)	Waddle	1,000
23 Nov	Dynamo Kyiv (USSR)	Fr	(h)	W	2-1	(0-1)	Waddle, Varadi	13,824
9 May	Hull City	Fr	(a)	L	2-3	(1-3)	Varadi 2	5,431
18 May	Malaysia Select XI (in Kuala Lumpar)	Ot	(a)	W	5-2	(0-2)	Keegan 3, Carney, Varadi	
20 May	Malaysia Select XI (in Kuala Lumpar)	Ot	(a)	W	1-0	(1-0)	Varadi	
22 May	Thailand Select XI (in Bangkok)	Ot	(a)	W	1-0	(1-0)	McDermott	25,000
25 May	Thailand & Lopburi Select XI (in Bangkok)	Ot	(a)	W	3-0		McDermott 2, Keegan	10,000
29 May	Japan XI (in Tokyo)	JC	(a)	W	4-0	(3-0)	Waddle 2, Keegan, Clarke	
31 May	Syria XI (in Okayama)	JC	(n)	D	1-1	(1-0)	McCreery	
4 June	Yamaha (J) (in Nagoya)	JC	(a)	W	1-0	(1-0)	Waddle	
7 June	Botafogo (Br) (in Tokyo)	JC	(n)	D	0-0	(0-0)		30,000

1983-84								
10 Aug	Altona 93 (WG)	Ot	(a)	W	6-1	(3-1)	Anderson 3, Ryan, Keegan, Wharton	4,500
11 Aug	SC Drochtersen (WG)	Ot	(a)	W	5-0	(2-0)	Varadi, Waddle, Trewick, Wharton, Ferris	3,000
17 Aug	AEK (Athens) (Gr)	Ot	(a)	D	0-0	(0-0)		15,000
20 Aug	League of Ireland	Fr	(h)	W	3-0	(1-0)	Waddle 2, Keegan	7,739
6 Dec	Bristol Rovers	Cent	(a)	L	4-5	(2-3)	Waddle, Trewick, McDermott, Mills	4,107
13 May	Darlington (David Barton*)	Test	(a)	W	3-0	(0-0)	Keegan (p), Clarke, Wharton	5,500
17 May	Liverpool (Kevin Keegan*)	Test	(h)	D	2-2	(1-2)	Keegan (p), McDermott	36,722

1984-85								
4 Aug	Queen of the South	Fr	(a)	D	1-1	(0-1)	Beardsley	2,000
5 Aug	Hibernian (Jack McNamara)	Test	(a)	W	3-0	(2-0)	Beardsley, Wharton 2	6,000
7 Aug	Berwick Rangers	Fr	(a)	W	3-1	(2-0)	Beardsley, Wharton, Waddle	2,000
14 Aug	Hartlepool United	Fr	(a)	W	4-2	(2-1)	Wharton 3, Roeder	2,084
18 Aug	Middlesbrough	Fr	(h)	D	2-2	(1-2)	Waddle 2	6,867
20 Aug	Gateshead XI (Bob Topping & Terry Hibbitt*)	Test	(a)	W	7-1	(2-0)	Wharton 4, Ryan, Waddle, Beardsley	5,200
24 Oct	New Zealand FA	Fr	(h)	W	3-0	(3-0)	Wharton, Waddle, Heard	3,486
18 May	New Zealand FA (in Christchurch)	Ot	(a)	W	2-1	(0-0)	Anderson, McDonald	5,000
19 May	New Zealand FA (in Wellington)	Ot	(a)	D	2-2	(0-0)	Beardsley 2 (1p)	4,000
22 May	New Zealand FA (in Napier)	Ot	(a)	W	4-0	(3-0)	Reilly 2, Beardsley, Gascoigne	6,500
25 May	New Zealand FA (in Auckland)	Ot	(a)	W	3-2		Reilly, McDonald 2	4,400
26 May	Fiji FA (in Nadi)	Ot	(a)	L	0-3			4,800
28 May	Fiji FA (in Suva)	Ot	(a)	W	2-0		Gascoigne, Anderson	12,000

1985-86								
28 July	Leicester City (in Douglas)	IMC	(n)	L	2-3	(2-0)	Beardsley, Reilly	3,000
30 July	Blackburn Rovers (in Ramsay)	IMC	(n)	L	1-2	(0-0)	Gascoigne	5,000
1 Aug	Wigan Athletic (in Castletown)	IMC	(n)	W	4-1	(1-0)	McDonald 2, Beardsley, Roeder	3,000
7 Aug	Carlisle United	Fr	(a)	D	0-0	(0-0)		2,297
10 Aug	Sheffield United	Fr	(h)	D	1-1	(0-0)	Cunningham	4,952
24 Jan	Nottingham Forest (in Bermuda)	Fr	(n)	L	0-3	(0-3)		4,000
28 April	Middlesbrough (David Mills*)	Test	(a)	L	1-2	(1-0)	Cunningham	3,500

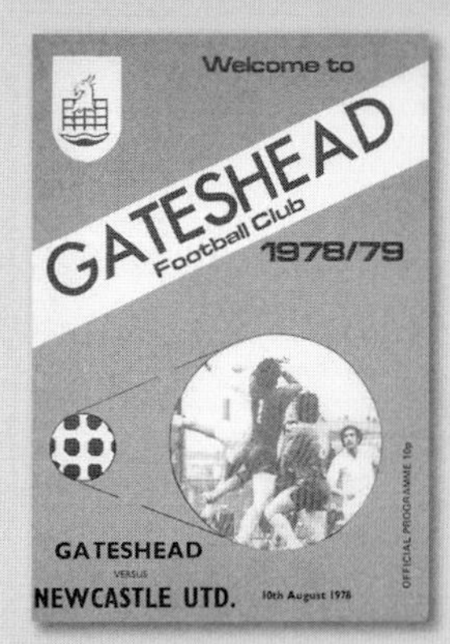

United often supported local clubs in pre-season matches. Newcastle faced Gateshead in 1978.

With Kevin Keegan in the line-up, United were invited to take part in the Japan Cup tournament during 1983. The Black'n'Whites lifted the trophy – a jade vase.

Another lengthy tour took place in the close-season of 1985, this time to New Zealand. The tour programme is illustrated.

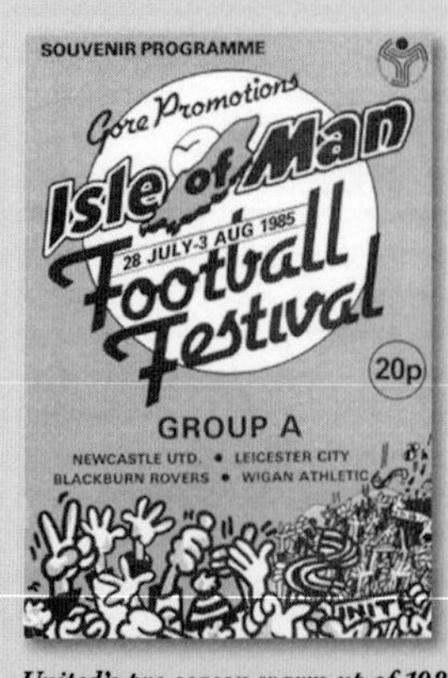

United's pre-season warm-up of 1985-86 largely took place on the Isle of Man, competing in a football festival.

1986-87

Date	Opponent	Comp	Venue	Res	Score	HT	Scorers	Att
27 July	Blackburn Rovers (in Douglas)	IMC	(n)	D	2-2	(1-1)	Gascoigne, McDonald	1,000
29 July	Portsmouth (in Castletown)	IMC	(n)	D	2-2	(0-0)	McDonald, Allon	2,500
30 July	Isle of Man XI (in Castletown)	IMC	(n)	W	5-1	(3-0)	Stewart, Beardsley, Allon 2, Ferris	3,000
5 Aug	Linfield	Fr	(a)	W	3-2	(2-1)	Whitehurst 2, Allon	5,000
7 Aug	Coleraine	Fr	(a)	D	0-0	(0-0)		2,000
11 Aug	Carlisle United	Fr	(a)	L	2-3	(1-1)	Allon 2	3,500
15 Aug	Durham City (Paul Main)	Ben	(a)	W	8-0	(4-0)	Allon 2, Davies, Bogie, McDonald (p), Anderson, Whitehurst, McCreery	1,000
18 Aug	Monterrey CF (Mex)	Fr	(h)	D	1-1	(1-0)	og (Campa)	8,417

1987-88

Date	Opponent	Comp	Venue	Res	Score	HT	Scorers	Att
1 Aug	Brondby IF (D)	Fr	(a)	L	1-2	(0-1)	Goddard	1,452
3 Aug	Heart of Midlothian	Fr	(a)	W	1-0	(0-0)	Gascoigne	10,113
6 Aug	Scarborough	Fr	(a)	D	2-2	(0-1)	Gascoigne, McDonald	3,000
19 Oct	Blyth Spartans (Dave Clarke*)	Test	(a)	L	0-3	(0-2)		4,000
18 Jan	Queen of the South	Fr	(a)	W	4-0	(2-0)	Goddard 2, Lormor, Jackson (P)	2,500
10 Feb	AS Monaco (F/PoM)	Fr	(h)	L	1-2	(1-1)	Gascoigne	8,003
10 March	Greenock Morton	Fr	(a)	W	1-0	(1-0)	Gascoigne (p)	2,000
14 March	Alnwick Town	Fr	(a)	W	6-1	(4-1)	Jackson (D), Anderson, O'Neill, Bogie, Robinson 2	1,500
16 April	Liverpool (at Wembley)	MCT R1	(n)	D	0-0	(0-0)	(Won on sudden-death pens, 1-0) (Contest of 40m)	27,000
16 April	Tranmere Rovers (at Wembley)	MCT QF	(n)	L	0-2	(0-2)	(Contest of 40m)	27,000
9 May	Whitley Bay	Fr	(a)	W	1-1	(1-1)	Lormor	1,200
17 May	Trinidad & Tobago (in Port of Spain)	Ot	(a)	L	0-1	(0-1)		8,000
22 May	Jamaica (in Kingston)	Ot	(a)	D	1-1	(0-0)	og	1,000

1988-89

Date	Opponent	Comp	Venue	Res	Score	HT	Scorers	Att
25 July	Hestra SSK (Se)	Ot	(a)	W	6-0		Stephenson 2, Robertson, Mirandinha, Robinson 2	1,000
27 July	Oskarshamns AIK (Se)	Ot	(a)	W	6-2	(3-1)	Roeder, Mirandinha 3, Robinson 2	1,500
28 July	Nykvarns SK (Se)	Ot	(a)	W	4-0	(2-0)	Robinson 2, Jackson (D), Mirandinha	1,000
1 Aug	Varmbols GoIF (Katrineholm) (Se)	Ot	(a)	W	4-0	(0-0)	Mirandinha, Hendrie, Robertson, O'Neill	1,000
2 Aug	Gullringens GoIF (Se)	Ot	(a)	D	0-0	(0-0)		1,000
4 Aug	TFK/TBIS Combined XI (Trollhattan) (Se)	Ot	(a)	W	2-1		Mirandinha, Jackson (D)	1,500
8 Aug	Dundee	Fr	(a)	L	0-2	(0-0)		3,000
13 Aug	Whitby Town	Fr	(a)	W	5-1	(2-1)	Robertson, Mirandinha, O'Neill, Thorn, og (Burton)	1,500
16 Aug	Peterborough United	Fr	(a)	W	7-0	(1-0)	Mirandinha 4, O'Neill, Robertson, Wharton	4,000
19 Aug	Blackburn Rovers (Simon Garner)	Test	(a)	D	2-2	(1-2)	Mirandinha, Hendrie	9,000
18 Feb	Boston United	Fr	(a)	W	1-0	(0-0)	Pingel	3,588
4 March	Brondby IF (D)	Fr	(h)	W	2-0	(1-0)	O'Brien, Brazil	3,338
3 April	Kevin Keegan XI (Kenny Wharton*)	Test	(h)	D	2-2	(1-1)	Pingel, Mirandinha	20,899

1989-90

Date	Opponent	Comp	Venue	Res	Score	HT	Scorers	Att
26 July	Nybro IF (Se)	Ot	(a)	W	2-1	(0-0)	Brazil, McGhee	1,000
29 July	Askeroda IF (Se)	Ot	(a)	D	0-0	(0-0)		1,000
30 July	Rydobruk (Se)	Ot	(a)	W	1-0	(0-0)	McGhee	1,000
1 Aug	Mjallby AIF (Se)	Ot	(a)	W	3-0	(1-0)	Quinn, McGhee, Brazil	1,000
2 Aug	Falkenbergs FF (Se)	Ot	(a)	D	1-1	(0-1)	Kristensen	1,500
8 Aug	Raith Rovers	Fr	(a)	W	4-0	(3-0)	Quinn 2 (1p), Brazil (p), og (Glennie)	1,959
10 Aug	Carlisle United	Fr	(a)	L	1-2	(0-1)	Brazil (p)	2,994
14 Aug	Scarborough	Fr	(a)	W	1-0	(0-0)	McGhee	3,000
8 May	Derry City (Liam Coyle)	Test	(a)	D	1-1	(1-1)	O'Brien	2,000
20 May	NE Non-League XI (Jackie Bell*) (at Evenwood FC)	Test	(a)	L	2-4		(Scorers untraced)	1,000

1990-91

Date	Opponent	Comp	Venue	Res	Score	HT	Scorers	Att
1 Aug	Oadby Town	Fr	(a)	W	3-0	(1-0)	Gallacher, O'Brien, og (Kirby)	980
4 Aug	Yeovil Town	Fr	(a)	W	2-1	(1-0)	McGhee, Anderson	5,093
7 Aug	Gloucester City	Fr	(a)	W	2-0	(1-0)	Quinn, Robinson	500
10 Aug	Videoton (H) (in Budapest)	BC	(n)	L	1-2	(0-2)	McGhee (p)	8,000
11 Aug	Cercle Brugge KSV (Bel) (in Budapest)	BC	(n)	W	2-0	(0-0)	Stimson, O'Brien	5,000
15 Aug	St Johnstone	Fr	(a)	W	3-1	(1-1)	Quinn, McGhee, O'Brien	4,665
17 Aug	Dunfermline Athletic (Norrie McCathie)	Test	(a)	D	0-0	(0-0)		5,000
19 Aug	Scarborough	Fr	(a)	D	1-1	(0-0)	Brazil (p)	1,488

1991-92

Date	Opponent	Comp	Venue	Res	Score	HT	Scorers	Att
22 July	Mjolby Sodra IF (Se)	Ot	(a)	W	7-0		Hunt 2, Quinn, Robinson, O'Brien, Clark, Makel	1,000
23 July	Rynninge IK (Orebro) (Se)	Ot	(a)	W	8-2	(6-2)	Quinn 4, Elliott, Clark, Robinson, Peacock	1,000
25 July	IF Sylvia (Norrkoping) (Se)	Ot	(a)	W	3-0		Peacock 2, Scott	1,000
27 July	Hille IF (Se)	Ot	(a)	W	11-1	(5-0)	Robinson 4, Quinn 2, Clark 2, O'Brien, Makel, Hunt	1,000
29 July	Nykopings BIS (Se)	Ot	(a)	L	0-1	(0-0)		2,000
30 July	IF Rimbo (Se)	Ot	(a)	W	6-2	(1-1)	Quinn 3, Hunt 3	1,000
3 Aug	Greenock Morton	Fr	(a)	W	4-1	(0-1)	Quinn 2, Peacock 2	1,284
7 Aug	Darlington	Fr	(a)	W	2-1	(1-1)	O'Brien, Bradshaw	3,027
10 Aug	Ujpesti Dozsa (H)	Fr	(h)	W	3-0	(2-0)	Quinn 3 (2p)	10,000
18 Feb	New Zealand	Fr	(h)	W	2-1	(1-0)	Makel, og (Rufer)	5,436
28 April	John Anderson All Stars (John Anderson*)	Test	(h)	W	3-2	(2-1)	Clark 2, Watson	13,780

1992-93

Date	Opponent	Comp	Venue	Res	Score	HT	Scorers	Att
27 July	Heart of Midlothian (John Robertson*)	Test	(a)	L	0-1	(0-0)		11,105
29 July	Gateshead	Fr	(a)	W	3-0	(2-0)	Carr 2, Watson	3,500
1 Aug	York City	Fr	(a)	W	3-1	(1-0)	Carr, Peacock, Sheedy	3,424
4 Aug	Doncaster Rovers	Fr	(a)	D	1-1	(0-0)	O'Brien	3,951
8 Aug	Middlesbrough	NES	(h)	W	1-0	(1-0)	Peacock (p)	8,548
9 Aug	Sporting Clube de Portugal	NES	(h)	L	3-5	(3-0)	Peacock 2, Clark	7,764

1993-94

Date	Opponent	Comp	Venue	Res	Score	HT	Scorers	Att
24 July	Hartlepool United	Fr	(a)	W	2-0	(2-0)	Beardsley, Sellars	6,000
31 July	Berwick Rangers	Fr	(a)	W	3-0	(1-0)	Papavasiliou, Cole, Mathie	2,500
3 Aug	Glasgow Rangers (Ally McCoist)	Test	(a)	W	2-1	(0-0)	Cole, Sellars	42,623
5 Aug	Gateshead (Derek Bell*)	Test	(a)	W	3-0	(3-0)	Mathie 2, O'Brien	4,500
7 Aug	Scunthorpe United	Fr	(a)	D	1-1	(0-1)	Watson	3,975
9 Aug	Liverpool (Ronnie Whelan)	Test	(a)	L	0-1	(0-1)		21,757

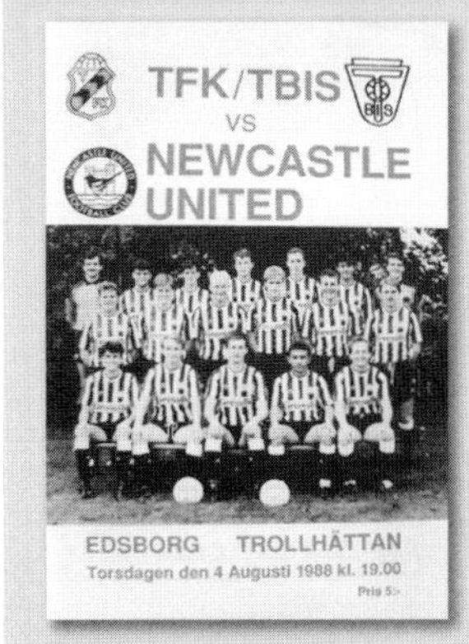

The Magpies have made several visits to Scandinavia over the years. The 1988 meeting with a combined TFK and TBIS side was part of a pre-season training camp in Sweden.

Newcastle were often a big attraction to smaller clubs. Boston United faced the Magpies in 1989 and Mirandinha was featured on the programme cover.

Popular full-back John Anderson staged his Testimonial in 1992 at St James' Park.

Scott Sellars was a most effective midfielder, he scored in the Ally McCoist Testimonial in Glasgow during 1993.

1994-95

27 July	MyPa-47 (Fn)	Ot	(a)	L	1-2	(0-1)	Cole	1,000
28 July	Visan Pallo (Fn)	Ot	(a)	W	2-0	(1-0)	Lee, Mathie	2,500
1 Aug	Wrexham (Dixie McNeil)	Test	(a)	L	3-4	(1-1)	Mathie 2, og (Hunter)	5,842
5 Aug	Manchester United (at Rangers FC)	ICT	(n)	D	1-1	(1-1)	Fox (Won 6-5 on pens)	27,282
6 Aug	UC Sampdoria (I) (at Rangers FC)	ICT	(n)	L	1-3	(1-1)	Cole	30,186
12 Aug	Northern Ireland XI (Billy Bingham) (at Linfield FC)	Test	(a)	W	5-2	(3-1)	Cole, Fox, Lee, Mathie, Elliott	7,000

Alex Mathie arrived at Gallowgate from Morton and was used as a more than useful substitute striker. He netted twice against Wrexham in 1994.

1995-96

22 July	Hartlepool 1991 XI (Brian Honour)	Test	(a)	W	4-0	(2-0)	Kitson, Allen 2, Brayson	5,033
26 July	Rushden & Diamonds	Fr	(a)	W	3-1	(1-0)	Ferdinand 2, Brayson	4,600
2 Aug	Bishop Auckland	Fr	(a)	W	4-3	(3-0)	Kitson 2, Brayson, Burt	
5 Aug	Glasgow Celtic	Fr	(a)	D	1-1	(0-1)	Ferdinand	31,000
7 Aug	Gateshead	Fr	(a)	W	4-0	(3-0)	Ferdinand 2, Beardsley (p), Gillespie	11,750
9 Aug	Heart of Midlothian	Fr	(a)	W	1-0	(0-0)	Beardsley	13,337
12 Aug	Tottenham Hotspur (Gary Mabbutt)	Test	(a)	W	2-0	(1-0)	Ferdinand, Sellars	17,288
8 May	Nottingham Forest (Stuart Pearce*)	Test	(a)	L	5-6	(1-2)	Barton, Ferdinand 2, Keegan, Guinan	23,818

1996-97

24 July	Gateshead/Blyth Spartans	Fr	(h)	W	6-0	(2-0)	Kitson 2, Ferdinand 2, Lee 2 (45m v each team; 2-0 v Gateshead, 4-0 v Blyth)	13,000
30 July	Thailand (in Bangkok)	Ot	(a)	W	2-1	(1-1)	Lee, Asprilla	18,000
1 Aug	Singapore League All Stars (in Singapore)	Ot	(a)	W	5-0	(2-0)	Ginola 2 (1p), Ferdinand, Kitson 2	50,000
4 Aug	Gambia Osaka (J)	Ot	(a)	L	1-3	(0-2)	Ferdinand	6,949
9 Aug	Lincoln City	Fr	(a)	W	2-0	(1-0)	Shearer (p), Albert	10,069
13 Aug	RSC Anderlecht (Bel)	Fr	(a)	W	2-1	(1-0)	Asprilla, Ginola	18,000

Modern football has seen the development of many pre-season sponsored competitions. United took part in the Umbro Tournament at Goodison Park in 1997.

1997-98

15 July	PSV Eindhoven (N) (in Dublin)	DIT	(n)	W	3-2	(2-1)	Gillespie, Tomasson 2	18,000
16 July	Derry City (in Dublin)	DIT	(n)	W	2-0	(2-0)	Crawford, Beardsley	14,500
19 July	Birmingham City	Fr	(a)	W	3-2	(1-1)	Shearer, Tomasson, Beardsley	13,799
26 July	Chelsea (at Everton FC)	UT	(n)	D	1-1	(1-0)	Tomasson (Lost 1-3 on pens)	15,264
27 July	Ajax Amsterdam (N) (at Everton FC)	UT	(n)	L	0-3	(0-0)		10,289
30 July	Bradford City	Fr	(a)	W	3-0	(3-0)	Asprilla, Beardsley, Watson	8,470
3 Aug	Juventus (I) (in Cesena)	CdC	(a)	L	2-3	(0-3)	Asprilla 2 (1p)	22,511

1998-99

27 July	Bohemians (Dublin)	Fr	(a)	D	1-1	(0-0)	Keidel	4,200
1 Aug	SL Benfica (P) (at Middlesbrough FC)	JDC	(n)	D	0-0	(0-0)	(Lost 3-4 on pens)	5,430
2 Aug	Middlesbrough	JDC	(a)	D	1-1	(0-1)	Shearer (p) (Won 4-3 on pens)	5,230
5 Aug	Bray Wanderers	Fr	(a)	W	6-0	(3-0)	Shearer 3, Dalglish 2, Hamann	5,700
10 Aug	Juventus (I)	Fr	(h)	W	2-1	(2-0)	Hamann, Pearce	32,590
27 Jan	Glasgow Celtic (Peter Beardsley*)	Test	(h)	L	1-3	(0-2)	Beardsley (p) (P Beardsley Select XI)	36,733

1999-00

15 July	FC Den Bosch (N)	Ot	(a)	W	2-1	(1-1)	McClen, Coppinger (p)	1,700
16 July	SV Deurne (N)	Ot	(a)	W	4-0	(1-0)	Shearer (p), Barton, McClen, Coppinger	1,200
17 July	Helmond Sport (N)	Ot	(a)	W	2-1	(1-1)	Andersson, Ketsbaia	1,500
20 July	Livingston	Fr	(a)	L	1-2	(0-1)	Dyer	4,934
22 July	Dundee United	Fr	(a)	L	1-3	(0-2)	Robinson	7,987
24 July	Reading	Fr	(a)	D	2-2	(0-2)	Coppinger (p), Robinson	16,734
27 July	Glasgow Celtic	Fr	(a)	L	0-2	(0-0)		59,252
28 July	Stoke City	Fr	(a)	W	2-1	(1-1)	Dumas, Robinson	6,742
31 July	VfL Bochum (G)	Fr	(a)	L	2-3	(1-1)	Shearer 2	11,644
18 May	PFL All Stars (Tr) (in Port of Spain)	Ot	(a)	W	1-0	(0-0)	Gallacher	2,000
21 May	Tobago XI (in Roxborough)	Ot	(a)	W	4-2	(2-0)	Gallacher, Gavilan, Solano 2	4,000

Over 36,000 watched Peter Beardsley's farewell night in 1999 when Celtic were the opponents.

2000-01

22 July	DC United (USA) (in Washington)	Ot	(a)	L	1-3	(0-2)	Cordone	17,610
26 July	Columbus Crew (USA) (in Columbus, Ohio)	Ot	(a)	D	2-2	(1-0)	Cort 2	18,212
31 July	Burnley	Fr	(a)	W	1-0	(1-0)	Cort	11,441
5 Aug	Feyenoord (N)	Fr	(a)	L	1-2	(1-1)	Lee	32,340
13 Aug	RCD Espanyol (Sp)	Fr	(a)	L	1-2	(0-0)	Shearer	7,900
8 May	West Bromwich Albion (Daryl Burgess)	Test	(a)	W	3-0	(2-0)	Cordone 2, Bassedas	4,440
22 May	Exeter City	Fr	(a)	W	2-1	(1-1)	LuaLua, Quinn	4,702

2001-02

11 Aug	Athletic Bilbao (Sp) (Robert Lee*)	Test	(h)	L	0-1	(0-0)		18,189

2002-03

20 July	VV Capelle (N)	Ot	(a)	W	4-0	(1-0)	Robert, Ameobi, Solano, Griffin	2,500
22 July	De Tubanters Enschede (N)	Ot	(a)	W	9-0	(4-0)	Shearer 3, Robert 2, LuaLua, Marcelino, Bassedas, og (Bollen)	1,500
24 July	GVVV Veenendaal (N)	Ot	(a)	W	4-0	(4-0)	Dyer, Viana 2, Robert	1,400
26 July	Beter Bed UDI 90 (N)	Ot	(a)	W	5-0	(5-0)	LuaLua 3, Speed, Shearer	2,000
31 July	Nottingham Forest	Fr	(a)	L	1-3	(1-1)	Viana	19,191
3 Aug	Wolverhampton Wanderers	Fr	(a)	W	2-0	(1-0)	LuaLua 2	14,973
7 Aug	FC Barcelona (Sp)	Fr	(h)	L	0-3	(0-2)	(Record home friendly crowd)	51,257

2003-04

24 July	Birmingham City (in Kuala Lumpur)	AC	(n)	W	2-1	(1-0)	Shearer (p), Ameobi	14,600
27 July	Chelsea (in Kuala Lumpur)	AC	(n)	D	0-0	(0-0)	(Lost 4-5 on pens)	41,500
1 Aug	Sheffield Wednesday	Fr	(a)	L	3-4	(1-1)	Dyer, Ameobi, LuaLua	14,995
1 Aug	Hartlepool United	Fr	(a)	W	6-0	(4-0)	Shearer 3, Bellamy, Speed, Solano (2 first team games played on the same day)	4,712
4 Aug	Hull City	Fr	(a)	W	4-0	(2-0)	Chopra 2, Ameobi, Cort	15,206
5 Aug	Bayern Munich (G)	Fr	(h)	D	2-2	(1-0)	Shearer 2	33,277

United and England midfielder, Rob Lee's testimonial match was against Athletic Bilbao.

2004-05

14 July	Thailand XI (in Bangkok)	UCC	(a)	D	1-1	(0-1)	Bowyer (Lost 2-4 on pens)	30,000
18 July	FC Kitchee (HK)	UCC	(a)	D	1-1	(0-1)	Milner (Won 7-6 on pens)	13,131
28 July	Ipswich Town (Dale Roberts Memorial)	Ben	(a)	L	1-2	(1-1)	Robert	24,644
31 July	Glasgow Rangers	NGC	(h)	W	4-2	(3-1)	Shearer (p), Bellamy, Bernard, Dyer	31,554
1 Aug	Sporting Clube de Portugal	NGC	(h)	L	0-1	(0-1)		23,446
4 Aug	Glasgow Celtic	Fr	(a)	L	1-2	(0-0)	Bellamy	20,000

2005-06

6 Aug	Yeading	Fr	(h)	W	5-0	(1-0)	Moore, Milner, Emre, Ameobi 2	6,151
9 Aug	Bray Wanderers	Fr	(a)	W	7-1	(2-0)	Ameobi 2, N'Zogbia 2, Chopra, Milner, Dyer	3,500
11 May	Glasgow Celtic (Alan Shearer*)	Test	(h)	W	3-2	(0-0)	Luque, Shearer (p), og (Virgo) (Record home testimonial crowd)	52,275

The biggest crowd for a Testimonial fixture at St James' Park is the 52,275 to watch Alan Shearer's farewell in 2006. The superb matchday souvenir programme was sold out well before kick off. A reprinted Special Edition was produced immediately after the game to satisfy demand, which included match action, sold over 40,000 copies.

2006-07

26 July	Norwich City (Craig Fleming)	Test	(a)	W	2-1	(1-0)	Ramage, N'Zogbia	15,205
29 July	PSV Eindhoven (N)	Fr	(h)	L	2-3	(0-2)	Ameobi, Luque (p)	20,185
5 Aug	Villareal CF (Sp)	Fr	(h)	D	3-3	(1-2)	Ameobi, Butt 2	20,114

2007-08

17 July	Hartlepool United	Fr	(a)	W	3-1	(0-0)	Ameobi 2, Owen	6,030
21 July	Carlisle United	Fr	(a)	D	1-1	(0-0)	Solano	12,346
26 July	Glasgow Celtic	Fr	(h)	W	4-1	(3-0)	Martins, Luque 2, Milner	30,225
29 July	Juventus (I)	Fr	(h)	W	2-0	(2-0)	Luque (p), Carroll	34,016
5 Aug	UC Sampdoria (I)	Fr	(h)	W	1-0	(0-0)	Smith	23,078

2008-09

19 July	Hartlepool United	Fr	(a)	W	4-1	(1-1)	Duff 3, Guthrie	4,249
26 July	Doncaster Rovers	Fr	(a)	L	0-1	(0-0)		9,826
1 Aug	Hertha Berlin (G) (at RCD Mallorca)	MSC	(n)	L	0-1	(0-0)		2,000
3 Aug	RCD Mallorca (Sp)	MSC	(a)	L	0-1	(0-1)		2,000
6 Aug	PSV Eindhoven (N)	Fr	(h)	D	2-2	(2-1)	Taylor (S), Guthrie	13,477
9 Aug	Valencia CF (Sp)	Fr	(h)	W	2-1	(0-1)	Duff, Milner	31,494

Fans celebrate at the unforgettable night that was Alan Shearer's record-breaking Testimonial.

2009-10

11 July	Shamrock Rovers	Fr	(a)	W	3-0	(0-0)	Taylor (S), Ameobi, Ranger	5,200
18 July	Darlington	Fr	(a)	W	7-2	(4-1)	Ameobi 2, Duff, Nolan, Taylor (S), Carroll, Gutierrez	6,698
21 July	Huddersfield Town	Fr	(a)	W	1-0	(0-0)	Nolan	9,691
25 July	Leyton Orient	Fr	(a)	L	1-6	(1-2)	Barton (p)	3,615
29 July	Leeds United	Fr	(h)	D	0-0	(0-0)		16,945
2 Aug	Dundee United	Fr	(a)	D	1-1	(0-0)	Carroll	8,876

2010-11

17 July	Carlisle United	Cent	(a)	W	3-0	(0-0)	Best, Ranger, Vuckic	7,412
24 July	Norwich City	Fr	(a)	L	1-2	(0-1)	Ameobi	13,195
31 July	PSV Eindhoven (N)	Fr	(h)	D	2-2	(0-2)	Taylor (R), Best	16,118
3 Aug	Deportivo la Coruna (Sp)	TTH	(a)	D	0-0	(0-0)	(Won 5-3 on pens)	8,000
7 Aug	Glasgow Rangers	Fr	(a)	L	1-2	(0-1)	Lovenkrands	30,220

Newcastle United XI fixtures

Newcastle have frequently fielded teams under the 'Newcastle United' banner which, in fact, were often no more than reserve teams, with sometimes a mixture of junior players included. Occasionally, however, the line-up contained a number of first-teamers supplemented by reserve or squad players. These sides are not strong enough to be regarded strictly as senior fixtures, but may be classified as a Newcastle United XI game. The following matches relate to selected teams that are not fully first-team matches, but cannot either be labelled as a reserve fixture. In addition, included are two testimonial fixtures for Magpie stalwarts of the 1950s, Frank Brennan and Len White. Both games were played several years after they had retired, and both away from St James' Park, at Roker Park and Hillheads. A United XI was fielded in White's benefit match while the Brennan XI consisted of a substantially ex-Newcastle line-up.

1903-04

7 Sept	Darlington	Fr	(a)	W	2-1	(2-0)	Roberts, Graham	

1909-10

2 Sept	Carlisle United	Fr	(a)	W	2-0	(1-0)	Allan 2	3,000

1910-11

14 Sept	Heworth Cup Select	Fr	(a)	W	3-0	(1-0)	Metcalf 3	3,000
3 Oct	Annfield Plain Celtic	Fr	(a)	D	0-0	(0-0)		1,000

Joe Ford shined in reserve and friendly action. He scored twice against King's Park in 1932. A broken leg wrecked his career.

1912-13

20 Nov	Thackery's XI (in Chester-le-Street)	Ben	(a)	L	2-3	(2-3)	Fleming 2	

1924-25

10 Dec	Wallsend XI	Ch	(a)	W	6-0	(3-0)	Pigg 3, Keating, Mitchell, Dowsey	

1926-27

27 Sept	York City	Fr	(a)	W	3-2		Mordue 2, Nicholson	2,500

1929-30

24 April	Carlisle United (James Smiles)	Ben	(a)	D	1-1	(0-1)	Kean	3,700

1932-33

3 Dec	King's Park (Stirling)	Fr	(a)	W	2-1	(2-1)	Ford 2	3,700
8 May	Rest of Northumberland County	Jub	(h)	W	5-3	(3-0)	Kelly 4, Gallantree	598

1939-40

14 Oct	53rd Royal Field Artillery	Fr	(h)	L	0-1	(0-1)		
4 Nov	North Shields	Fr	(a)	D	2-2	(0-1)	Stubbins, Park	

1955-56

26 Sept	Annfield Plain (Ray Scarr*)	Ben	(a)	W	5-3		Brennan 5	

1956-57

9 March	Stirling Albion	Fr	(a)	W	5-2	(2-1)	Curry 3, Hughes, Hannah	
29 April	South Shields	Fr	(a)	W	6-1	(4-1)	Tait 3, Keery 2 (1 pen), Hannah	4,000

Alex Tait was always able to find the net, scoring a hat-trick against South Shields in 1957.

Date	Opponent	Type	Venue	Res	Score	HT	Scorers	Att
1958-59								
13 April	North Shields	Fr	(a)	L	0-1	(0-0)		
1961-62								
12 Aug	Hartlepools United	Fr	(a)	W	1-0	(1-0)	Bell (pen)	2,207
30 April	All Star XI (Frank Brennan*) (at Sunderland FC)	Test	(n)	W	6-3	(3-0)	Milburn 3, Allchurch, Stokoe, Chisholm (F Brennan Select XI)	13,983
1967-68								
13 May	Whitley Bay	Fr	(a)	W	6-2	(4-1)	Robson (B) 3, Moncur, Iley, Milburn (Newcastle XI with guest players)	
1977-78								
25 Jan	North Shields	Fr	(a)	D	1-1	(1-1)	Robinson	
1978-79								
5 Aug	Berwick Rangers	Fr	(a)	W	1-0	(0-0)	Blackhall	
1980-81								
2 Aug	Spennymoor United	Fr	(a)	W	6-1	(4-1)	Nicholson 2, Walker, Montgomerie 2, og (Robson)	
5 Aug	Consett	Fr	(a)	W	2-0		Waddle, Nicholson	
1982-83								
14 Aug	Workington	Fr	(a)	W	6-1	(1-0)	Wharton 2, Doyle, McNall, Barton, Hedworth	254
1984-85								
11 Aug	Ashington	Fr	(a)	W	7-0	(2-0)	Ferris 2, Ryan, McDonald, Carney, Allon, Dawes	1,000
1985-86								
13 Aug	Scarborough	Fr	(a)	W	4-3	(1-3)	Gascoigne, Scott, Allon 2	681
1987-88								
10 Aug	Worksop Town	Fr	(a)	D	2-2	(2-2)	Watson, Scott	
1989-90								
8 Oct	All Star XI (Len White*) (at Whitley Bay FC)	Test	(n)	D	0-0	(0-0)		1,500
1990-91								
21 Aug	Durham City	Fr	(a)	W	5-2	(3-1)	Howey, Appleby (M), Heron, Carter, Sloan	
5 May	Whitley Bay (Warren Teasdale*)	Test	(a)	D	1-1		(scorers untraced)	
1992-93								
31 July	Crook Town	Fr	(a)	W	8-1	(5-0)	Carr 2, Quinn 2 (2p), Brock 2, Kristensen, O'Brien	500
1999-00								
2 Aug	Hartlepool United	Fr	(a)	D	0-0	(0-0)		2,793
15 Feb	Blyth Spartans	Cent	(a)	W	3-0	(2-0)	Ketsbaia, Maric, Elliott	2,036
2002-03								
9 Aug	Gateshead	Fr	(a)	W	8-0	(5-0)	Shearer 2, Ameobi, Cort (pen), Griffin, Jenas 2, og (Morgan)	4,560
2005-06								
2 Sept	Malaga CF (Sp)	TDS	(a)	L	0-2	(0-0)		9,750
2007-08								
1 Aug	Hull City	Fr	(a)	L	0-1	(0-1)		14,000

Paul Ferris, netted two goals against Ashington in 1984. He became for a time the club's youngest ever debutant and later was assistant physio.

Practice & Trial Fixtures

During the period from the Victorian 1890s to the latter years of the 1950s, Newcastle United organised public-practice matches, also known as trial fixtures, usually scheduled prior to the start of the new season. Apart from being part of the fitness regime for the professional squad in the season's preparation, these games also gave the opportunity to either up-and-coming youngsters or players to have excelled in the non-league scene or, in later years, footballers from other clubs to have taken the eye of United's scouts. In addition for many years the proceeds of these games were given to local charities. During the Twenties receipts from a series of four pre-season practice games totalled £964 and was shared between 32 health based organisations, critical funding in an era before the Welfare State was introduced.

Often labelled as the Whites versus Stripes, games were frequently watched at St James' Park by large crowds over the decades. In the years up to World War One gates of 10,000 were often recorded, while between the wars attendances reached over 20,000 on occasion. In August 1921 The Stripes defeated The Whites by 5-2 in front of 21,350 at Gallowgate.

Several famous names earned a contract with Newcastle United after impressing in such trial games. Both Jack Milburn and Charlie Crowe took part in trial matches during 1943. When 19 years old Milburn answered an advert in The North Mail and was invited to St James' Park for a trial. He first appeared in the The Probables against The Rest and scored twice. He then scored six second-half goals in The Stripes versus The Blues follow up contest.

The last recorded pre-season public-practice match took place in 1963 when 8,672 fans turned up to see the Probables versus Possibles, a game that ended 1-1 with the goals coming from Ron McGarry and Charlie Younger respectively.

Behind Closed Doors Fixtures

A modern trend in football has seen the tendency for Behind Closed Doors fixtures to be organised, matches between clubs without public admission. Usually organised in order to keep players match-fit during a period of inactivity, or to allow certain players action after injury, several games have been played although some have lasted less than the normal 90 minutes.

The first recorded match appears to be during April 1958 when an 'unofficial' match took place against a combination from the Royal Northumberland Fusiliers. Not surprisingly, the Magpies won easily, by 10-0. During November 1959 a United XI faced the England Under-21 side in a match of 30 minutes each period. The Magpies won 2-1. Games with several clubs have taken place in the years that followed. United have faced the likes of Carlisle United, Workington, Walsall, York City, Doncaster Rovers and Middlesbrough as well as against Scottish clubs Glasgow Rangers and Gretna. In addition several matches have also taken place against local clubs such as Blyth Spartans and Whitley Bay. In many of these games, United have taken the opportunity to field fringe first-team players as well more junior colleagues alongside their more senior men to give the former valuable experience.

There have been an increasing number of reserve team friendly games played behind closed doors in the last few years. Indeed, recently, many scheduled reserve league fixtures have ended as closed matches with no public admittance.

The club's pre-season practice match between The Probables and The Possibles in 1960. Back row, left to right: Mitchell, McKinney, Scott, Harvey, Stokoe, Whitehead, Scoular, Franks, Keith, Simpson, McMichael, Bell. Front: Hughes, Neale, Tait, Marshall, Hale, Taylor, Eastham, White, Allchurch, McGuigan.

Northumberland & Durham FA Challenge Cup & Northumberland FA Challenge Cup fixtures 1881-1890

Fixtures relating to Newcastle United (as Newcastle East End) in the above competitions when fielding their first eleven side are detailed below. For season 1890-91 the club selected essentially a reserve eleven for the competition. From this season games are classified as reserve fixtures and not included. The combined Northumberland & Durham FA Challenge Cup ran from season 1880-81 to 1882-83. The two bodies split in the summer of 1883 and East End – and later as Newcastle United – have competed in the Northumberland FA Challenge Cup from 1883-84 to date, although there was a hiatus between 1935 and 1983 when the club either declined to enter the competition, or in later years, were debarred from doing so. More recently the tournament has been known as the Northumberland Senior Cup.

An important milestone in football development in the North East occurred when the Northumberland & Durham FA was formed in 1880 at the Turks Head Hotel on Grey Street (left).

1882-83

Date	Opponent	Rd	Venue	Res	Score	HT	Scorers	Att
13 Jan	Elswick Leather Works	R1	(h)	L	1-2	(1-1)	(scorers untraced)	

1883-84

Date	Opponent	Rd	Venue	Res	Score	HT	Scorers	Att
1 Dec	North Eastern	R1	(h)	L	2-3	(0-2)	(scorers untraced)	

1884-85

Date	Opponent	Rd	Venue	Res	Score	HT	Scorers	Att
24 Jan	Elswick Leather Works	R1	(h)	W	3-1	(0-1)	Gorman, Hiscock (E), Hoban	
7 Feb	Bye	R2						
28 Feb	Brunswick Villa Athletic	R3	(h)	W	8-1	(3-0)	Cook 2, Hoban 2, Parr 2, Armstrong, White	
7 March	Newcastle West End	SF	(h)	D	3-3	(3-1)	White 2, Armstrong	1,500
14 March	Newcastle West End	SFr	(n)	W	5-0	(2-0)	White 2, Cook, Scott, Hiscock (E)	600
21 March	Sleekburn Wanderers	F	(n)	W	1-0	(0-0)	Gorman	500

1885-86

Date	Opponent	Rd	Venue	Res	Score	HT	Scorers	Att
30 Jan	Newcastle West End	R2	(n)	L	1-2	(1-2)	Lightfoot	300

1886-87

Date	Opponent	Rd	Venue	Res	Score	HT	Scorers	Att
8 Jan	Brunswick Villa Athletic	R1	(h)	W	10-0	(3-0)	Hiscock (E) 3, Hoban 3, Lord 2, White, O'Brien	
29 Jan	Boundary	R2	(h)	W	5-0	(2-0)	Hoban 2, Hiscock (E) 2, Marshall	
5 Feb	Berwick Rangers	R3	(a)	W	5-2	(3-2)	O'Brien 2, Marshall 2, Hoban (East End's 5th goal disputed)	
19 Feb	Shankhouse Black Watch	SF	(n)	L	1-3	(1-1)	Hiscock (E)	3,000

1887-88

Date	Opponent	Rd	Venue	Res	Score	HT	Scorers	Att
7 Jan	Point Pleasant	R1	(h)	W	19-0	(6-0)	White 7, Muir (A) 5, Scott 3, Hiscock (E) 3, Wakefield (Newcastle United's record victory)	
21 Jan	Elswick Rangers	R2	(h)	L	1-3	(1-2)	Hoban	3,000

1888-89

Date	Opponent	Rd	Venue	Res	Score	HT	Scorers	Att
9 Feb	Ovingham	R3	(h)	W	9-1	(7-0)	Muir (A) 4, Smith, Mulvey, Young, White, Miller (Jas)	
16 Feb	Ashington	SF	(h)	W	5-0	(1-0)	Coupe, White 2, Hoban, Smith	1,000
23 March	Elswick Rangers	F	(n)	D	0-0	(0-0)		3,000
6 April	Elswick Rangers	Fr	(n)	L	1-2	(1-0)	Hiscock (E) (Match declared void and replayed)	4,000
13 April	Elswick Rangers	Fr	(n)	W	3-2	(2-0)	Mack, Collins, Hiscock (E)	5,000

1889-90

Date	Opponent	Rd	Venue	Res	Score	HT	Scorers	Att
15 Feb	Rendel	SF	(h)	D	1-1	(1-1)	McLaughlin	
15 March	Rendel	SFr	(n)	L	2-4	(2-0)	Mulvey, Miller (Jas)	

Note: 7 Jan 1888 v Point Pleasant. Various reports are in conflict regarding goalscorers with Alec White possibly scoring as many as nine or even 10 goals.

Newcastle United Reserve XI

The origins of Newcastle United's reserve team can be traced back almost to the inception of the club itself during its inaugural season as Stanley FC. Then termed 'Stanley Second XI', possibly reflecting the club's cricketing roots, the reserves' first appearance was a home contest in January 1882 against the local Tyne Pilgrims Junior team (a 0-1 defeat). This was a mere two months after the senior side's first ever fixture.

Thereafter the 'Second XI' continued to play other local junior and second teams in friendly matches, naturally becoming East End Second XI when the parent club changed its name.

They continued to perform throughout the 1880s and by the middle of the decade the club were fielding two elevens (a Second 'A' side and a Second 'B' team). They participated in the Northumberland Second Team Challenge Cup/Medals Competitions from 1883-84 onwards, later entering both the 'A' and the 'B' sides, the former reaching the final in 1886 before losing to Cramlington Union Jacks.

By the time that the club's reserve side first began to play league football in the Northern Alliance during the 1892-93 season, they took the field as East End 'A', subsequently changing their name to Newcastle United 'A' when the club adopted its new title.

It took a few years for the 'A' team to find their feet in the Northern Alliance although, from 1896 onwards, they began to dominate local league football. United never finished below second place during the following 16 seasons despite playing in different leagues. After winning three Northern Alliance titles in the five seasons up to 1902, they switched to the ostensibly stronger Northern League along with the likes of Sunderland 'A' and Middlesbrough 'A'. But their sojourn in the Northern League was brief and was terminated when that body decided to adopt amateur status. All three of the North East's senior clubs switched to the professional North Eastern League. At least Newcastle's four years in the Northern League had proved profitable with three titles and one runners-up spot coming their way.

United continued to prove themselves among the strongest in their new league, winning four more Championships in the nine seasons until the outbreak of the First World War. They resumed in the competition after the war but without the same dominance. However they still won two more titles and only twice finished below third place in the 14 seasons before eventually leaving the North Eastern League in 1933.

The club's second eleven also generally took part in the many of the local knock-out cup competitions once Newcastle East End and Newcastle United's first-team graduated to the national FA Cup tournament. After 1890 the club's reserve line-up started to represent Newcastle United in the Northumberland FA Challenge Cup, later known as the Northumberland Senior Cup, and still do so presently, winning the trophy on no fewer than 32 occasions, once as joint-holders with North Shields (1912). This is an impressive success ratio bearing in mind that for a number of years (1935 to 1983) the club either declined to enter for the competition or, in the later years, were debarred from doing so.

That period of inactivity in the competition was due arguably to the club's wish to concentrate on the stronger Central League. With United's absence, a conflict with the Northumberland FA ensued as a consequence of a substantial drop in revenue for the Association at the gate. Much later, when United decided to rejoin the Senior Cup, certain member clubs considered their chances of winning the trophy would be severely handicapped and therefore objected. United though were allowed to rejoin the fold in 1983.

It should also be noted that while it is recorded that United's first-eleven lifted various invitation trophies such as the Shields Ingham Cup or Hull Hospital Cup, the line-up usually contained several reserve players mixed with a few first-team regulars.

By the late 1920s, the club was determined to find a better standard of competition for their second string, preferring to face other senior clubs from outside the region rather than just local sides. The Central League, formed in 1911, was recognised as the country's strongest, but United's geographic location was a barrier to admittance. Newcastle thought that they had succeeded in gaining entry in 1929 when they were elected into that league but an appeal by Stockport County (whom Newcastle had replaced) on the grounds that the Magpies had offered "prejudicial inducements" to visiting clubs was sustained and United's application was ultimately rejected. The "inducements" were based on an undertaking by Newcastle to pay visiting clubs their return rail fares from Leeds and overnight expenses of up to £20 to cover the costs of visits to Tyneside.

Following this failure, United even tried (unsuccessfully) to join the Scottish Second Division when Bo'ness resigned their position in 1932. However, eventually, after almost a decade of trying (and following much lobbying) the club gained entry to the Central League. Newcastle first tasted arguably football's premier reserve tournament for season 1933-34 when, by a quirk of fate, they eventually replaced Stockport County. A crowd of 12,000 turned up for the reserve team's first home fixture against Blackburn Rovers, a 2-1 victory. Attendances were encouraging during that first season and peaked when an amazing 22,000 saw the home game against Aston Villa in November of that year.

Newcastle remained members of the Central League for well over 50 years although they only once won the title, in 1947-48. A second division of the competition was formed in 1983 and Newcastle suffered the ignominy of relegation to it four years later. They quickly won promotion only to go down once more after a further six years. Again they bounced back at the first time of asking, this time as Champions.

Just on a single occasion has the club not fielded a regular reserve line-up since Victorian years, that for season 1996-97 when manager Kevin Keegan somewhat controversially decided to scrap reserve football following a venue dispute. This decision saw Newcastle subsequently demoted to the lowest tier of the Central League – the third tier – when they returned to league action for 1997-98. Successive promotions quickly followed, as Champions again in 1999. But the club never returned to the top flight of the Central League, instead resigning from the competition in that year when the FA Premier League formed its own competition, Newcastle switching to the new set-up. They remained in that tournament for 10 years but lost membership when the first-team were relegated from the Premier League in 2009. A single season in the Totesport Central League followed before success for the senior side saw the reserves return to a radically restructured Premier Reserve League which was divided into small groups although many fixtures were against clubs nationwide, outside the league grouping. In addition, Newcastle decided to stage most of their home games behind closed doors, thus denying access to supporters.

Until relatively modern years United's reserve selection always included many seasoned campaigners – with a sprinkling of full international players – alongside up and coming youngsters. Recently though a trend of rarely selecting players from the first-team squad has developed, and normally the club's reserve line-up contains players on the fringe of a senior call-up, and usually in the age group of between 17 to 21 years old.

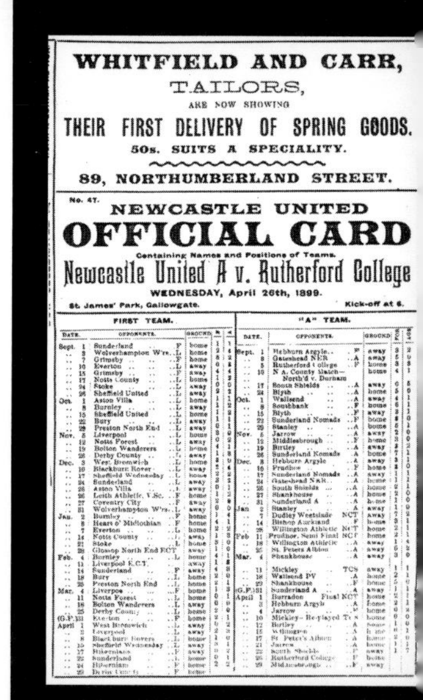

WHITFIELD AND CARR,
TAILORS,
ARE NOW SHOWING
THEIR FIRST DELIVERY OF SPRING GOODS.
50s. SUITS A SPECIALITY.
89, NORTHUMBERLAND STREET.

No. 47.
NEWCASTLE UNITED
OFFICIAL CARD
Containing Names and Positions of Teams.
Newcastle United A v. Rutherford College
WEDNESDAY, April 26th, 1899.
St. James' Park, Gallowgate. Kick-off at 6.

FIRST TEAM. "A" TEAM.

United's reserve programme from the Northern Alliance fixture against Rutherford College in September 1900.

Jack Patten appeared in the pioneer days the club then was secretary and manager the reserve line-up for a long period.

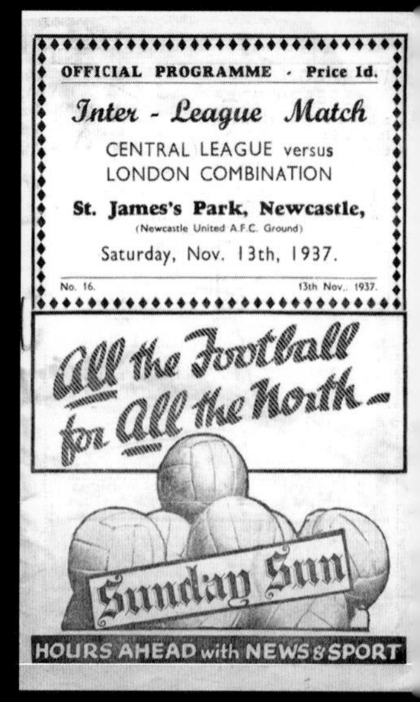

After several attempts, United eventually gained entry to the Central League, and in 1937 staged the Inter-League contest between the two strongest reserve competitions.

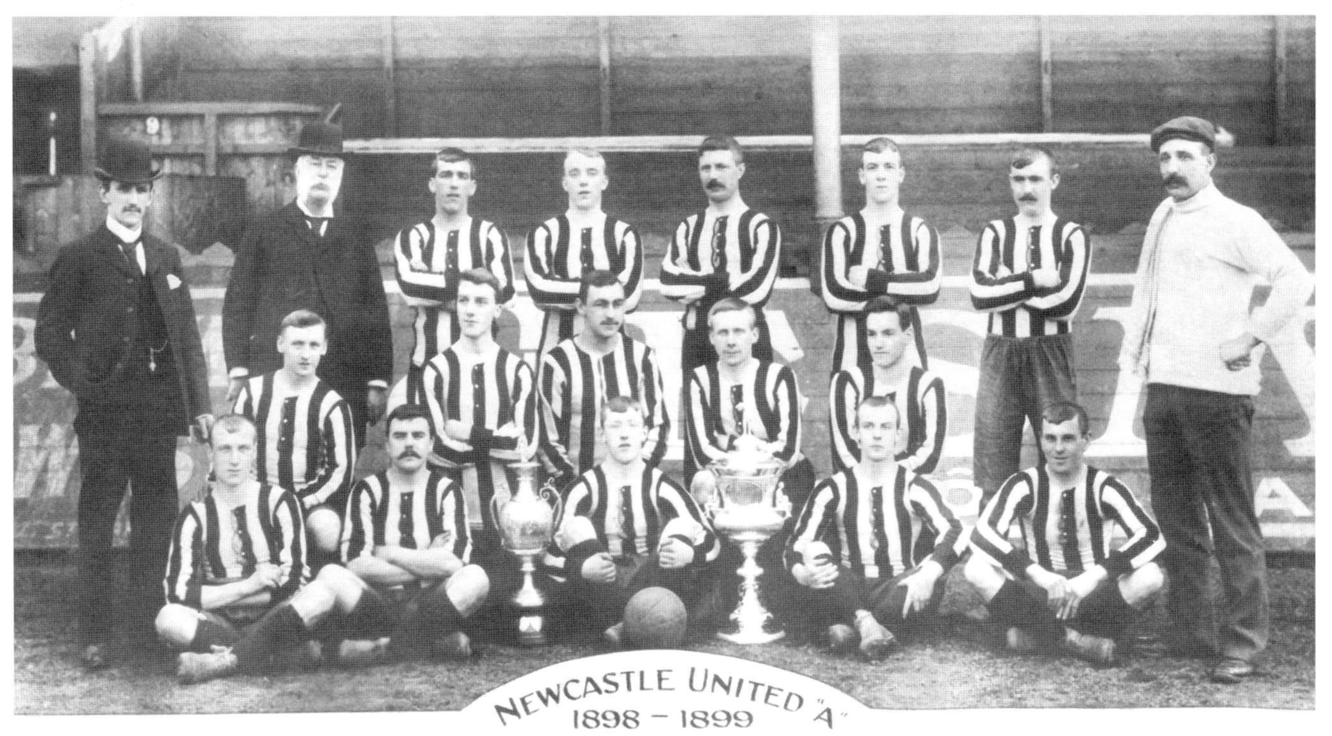
NEWCASTLE UNITED "A"
1898 – 1899
J. PATTEN. W. NEASHAM. T. BAMLETT. T. LACEY. C. WATTS. W. WILSON. R. HEDLEY.
J. BRUCE. ANDY STOKER. TED BIRNEY. W. INNERD. COLIN VEITCH. H. RYDER.
J. LAMB. G. COLLINS. E. McINTYRE. DAN PATTERSON. J. LITTLEFAIR.
NORTHUMBERLAND CUP NORTHERN ALLIANCE.

NEWCASTLE UTD RESERVES
1922 – 1923.
UNDEFEATED CHAMPIONS NORTH EASTERN LEAGUE WINNERS NORTHUMBERLAND AGED MINERS AND NEWCASTLE INFIRMARY CUPS
A. McCOMBIE. H. WOODS. S. DIXON. E. REED. J. FINLAY. C. W. SPENCER. R. ROXBURGH. W. J. AITKEN.
W. H. SCOTT. S. RUSSELL. H. W. WAKE. T. D. COULTHARD. W. LILBURN. R. MACKENZIE. J. F. KEEN. J. R. CLARK.
J. ARCHIBALD.

Reserve League Record

Northern Alliance

Season	P	W	D	L	F	A	Pts	Position
1892-93	P20	W6	D2	L12	F40	A55	14 Pts	Position 7th (season curtailed)
1893-94	P18	W5	D4	L9	F36	A45	14 Pts	Position 8th
1894-95	P22	W5	D5	L12	F35	A65	11 Pts	Position 11th (4 pts deducted)
1895-96	P26	W15	D5	L6	F74	A36	35 Pts	Position 4th
1896-97	P24	W17	D4	L3	F74	A22	38 Pts	Position 2nd
1897-98	P26	W21	D3	L2	F73	A23	45 Pts	**Champions**
1898-99	P24	W17	D4	L3	F56	A25	36 Pts	Position 2nd (2 pts deducted)
1899-00	P26	W16	D8	L2	F49	A17	40 Pts	Position 2nd
1900-01	P26	W20	D5	L1	F83	A23	45 Pts	**Champions**
1901-02	P26	W22	D3	L1	F84	A16	47 Pts	**Champions**

Northern League

Season	P	W	D	L	F	A	Pts	Position
1902-03	P24	W22	D0	L2	F100	A14	42 Pts	**Champions** (2 pts deducted)
1903-04	P24	W19	D1	L4	F97	A23	39 Pts	**Champions**
1904-05	P24	W22	D0	L2	F83	A12	44 Pts	**Champions**
1905-06	P26	W19	D4	L3	F92	A14	42 Pts	Position 2nd

North Eastern League

Season	P	W	D	L	F	A	Pts	Position
1906-07	P18	W12	D2	L4	F35	A20	26 Pts	**Champions**
1907-08	P24	W16	D2	L6	F90	A28	34 Pts	**Champions**
1908-09	P34	W26	D4	L4	F106	A48	56 Pts	**Champions**
1909-10	P32	W21	D6	L5	F134	A33	48 Pts	Position 2nd
1910-11	P34	W25	D4	L5	F88	A25	54 Pts	**Champions**
1911-12	P36	W28	D2	L6	F111	A33	58 Pts	Position 2nd
1912-13	P38	W24	D5	L9	F109	A47	53 Pts	Position 5th
1913-14	P38	W24	D5	L9	F91	A42	53 Pts	Position 3rd
1914-15	P38	W26	D6	L6	F132	A43	58 Pts	Position 3rd

World War One; Newcastle & District United League

Season	P	W	D	L	F	A	Pts	Position
1915-16								No reserve side competed
1916-17								No reserve side competed
1917-18	P27	W11	D7	L9	F44	A35	29 Pts	Position 5th (record incomplete)
1918-19	P28	W15	D4	L9	F69	A47	34 Pts	Position 5th

North Eastern League

Season	P	W	D	L	F	A	Pts	Position
1919-20	P34	W22	D5	L7	F82	A41	49 Pts	Position 3rd
1920-21	P38	W23	D7	L8	F96	A39	53 Pts	Position 3rd
1921-22	P38	W24	D7	L7	F80	A55	55 Pts	Position 2nd
1922-23	P38	W30	D8	L0	F109	A24	68 Pts	**Champions**
1923-24	P38	W26	D9	L3	F99	A44	61 Pts	Position 2nd
1924-25	P38	W24	D5	L9	F93	A35	53 Pts	Position 3rd
1925-26	P38	W31	D4	L3	F147	A43	66 Pts	**Champions**
1926-27	P38	W24	D6	L8	F99	A43	54 Pts	Position 2nd
1927-28	P38	W21	D4	L13	F101	A61	46 Pts	Position 6th
1928-29	P38	W20	D4	L14	F99	A67	44 Pts	Position 5th
1929-30	P38	W27	D2	L9	F111	A46	56 Pts	Position 2nd
1930-31	P42	W33	D6	L3	F159	A39	72 Pts	Position 2nd
1931-32	P42	W29	D6	L7	F139	A48	64 Pts	Position 2nd
1932-33	P38	W24	D7	L7	F91	A52	55 Pts	Position 2nd

Central League

Season	P	W	D	L	F	A	Pts	Position
1933-34	P42	W21	D11	L10	F85	A66	53 Pts	Position 5th
1934-35	P42	W12	D11	L19	F86	A81	35 Pts	Position 19th
1935-36	P42	W22	D9	L11	F105	A62	53 Pts	Position 2nd
1936-37	P42	W19	D11	L12	F92	A86	49 Pts	Position 5th
1937-38	P42	W17	D6	L19	F69	A72	40 Pts	Position 13th
1938-39	P42	W15	D10	L17	F80	A80	40 Pts	Position 13th
1939-40	P3	W2	D0	L1	F11	A6	4 Pts	Record expunged due to War

World War Two: Northumberland & Durham Wartime League (1940-41), Northern Combination League (1941-45)

Season	P	W	D	L	F	A	Pts	Position
1939-40								No competition
1940-41	P23	W7	D1	L15	F40	A63	15 pts	Position 8th (resigned from league)
1941-42	P26	W14	D4	L8	F97	A56	32 Pts	Position 7th
1942-43	P30	W14	D7	L9	F85	A70	35 Pts	Position 7th
1943-44	P30	W13	D5	L12	F95	A78	31 Pts	Position 10th (one result missing)
1944-45	P28	W21	D4	L3	F122	A36	46 Pts	**Champions**

Central League (From 1990-91 sponsored by Pontins)

Season	P	W	D	L	F	A	Pts	Position
1945-46	P40	W19	D10	L11	F93	A61	48 Pts	Position 6th
1946-47	P42	W16	D12	L14	F90	A77	44 Pts	Position 9th
1947-48	P42	W28	D5	L9	F95	A45	61 Pts	**Champions**
1948-49	P42	W18	D8	L16	F64	A54	44 Pts	Position 11th
1949-50	P42	W20	D9	L13	F62	A42	49 Pts	Position 6th
1950-51	P42	W14	D11	L17	F54	A69	39 Pts	Position 15th
1951-52	P42	W16	D5	L21	F68	A76	37 Pts	Position 19th
1952-53	P42	W10	D13	L19	F64	A81	33 Pts	Position 18th
1953-54	P42	W17	D4	L21	F61	A93	38 Pts	Position 16th
1954-55	P42	W19	D6	L17	F69	A64	44 Pts	Position 8th
1955-56	P42	W13	D9	L20	F72	A84	35 Pts	Position 16th
1956-57	P42	W20	D10	L12	F94	A75	50 Pts	Position 5th
1957-58	P42	W18	D1	L23	F70	A89	37 Pts	Position 15th
1958-59	P42	W17	D7	L18	F82	A94	41 Pts	Position 12th
1959-60	P42	W18	D12	L12	F94	A58	48 Pts	Position 8th
1960-61	P42	W17	D10	L15	F68	A69	44 Pts	Position 10th
1961-62	P42	W20	D7	L15	F82	A66	47 Pts	Position 6th
1962-63	P42	W19	D10	L13	F71	A59	48 Pts	Position 9th
1963-64	P42	W15	D11	L16	F48	A65	41 Pts	Position 12th
1964-65	P42	W20	D10	L12	F86	A63	50 Pts	Position 7th
1965-66	P42	W15	D5	L22	F75	A81	35 Pts	Position 18th
1966-67	P42	W22	D7	L13	F87	A61	51 Pts	Position 5th
1967-68	P42	W13	D17	L12	F59	A50	43 Pts	Position 12th
1968-69	P42	W22	D8	L12	F63	A46	52 Pts	Position 4th
1969-70	P42	W21	D10	L11	F59	A52	52 Pts	Position 6th
1970-71	P42	W12	D17	L13	F45	A43	41 Pts	Position 11th

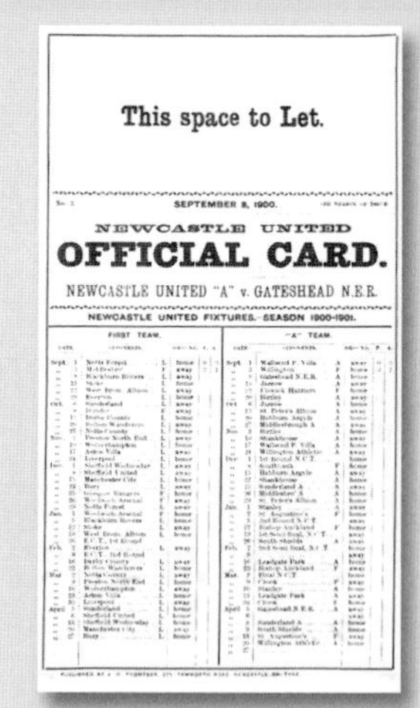
This space to Let.

SEPTEMBER 8, 1900.

NEWCASTLE UNITED

OFFICIAL CARD.

NEWCASTLE UNITED "A" v. GATESHEAD N.E.R.

NEWCASTLE UNITED FIXTURES. SEASON 1900-1901.

FIRST TEAM. "A" TEAM.

Match programme from the Northern Alliance fixture with Gateshead NER in April 1899.

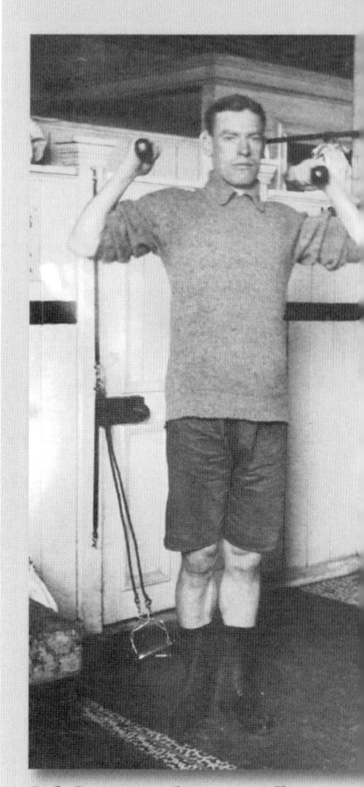
Jack Carr pictured in a marvellous fitness pose. He later became trainer to the second eleven.

Programme No. 11. Saturday 2nd October Central League

CENTRAL LEAGUE CHAMPIONS
(Newcastle United Reserves)
versus
THE REST
Kick off 3-15 p.m.

United lifted the Central League title in 1947-48 and staged the Champions v The Rest contest at the beginning of the following season.

1971-72	P42	W19	D13	L10	F68	A54	51 Pts	Position 5th	
1972-73	P42	W18	D8	L16	F70	A58	44 Pts	Position 9th	
1973-74	P42	W13	D14	L15	F55	A50	40 Pts	Position 14th	
1974-75	P42	W14	D10	L18	F43	A50	38 Pts	Position 15th	
1975-76	P42	W14	D11	L17	F53	A58	39 Pts	Position 14th	
1976-77	P42	W10	D15	L17	F50	A55	35 Pts	Position 17th	
1977-78	P42	W14	D12	L16	F51	A63	40 Pts	Position 13th	
1978-79	P42	W12	D8	L22	F44	A72	32 Pts	Position 19th	
1979-80	P42	W14	D10	L18	F41	A55	38 Pts	Position 16th	
1980-81	P42	W23	D9	L10	F74	A40	55 Pts	Position 3rd	
1981-82	P42	W19	D10	L13	F61	A57	48 Pts	Position 5th	
1982-83	P30	W12	D9	L9	F41	A34	33 Pts	Position 8th	
1983-84	P30	W14	D7	L9	F44	A37	49 Pts	Position 7th	Div One
1984-85	P34	W10	D9	L15	F45	A62	39 Pts	Position 12th	Div One
1985-86	P34	W13	D7	L14	F52	A61	46 Pts	Position 12th	Div One
1986-87	P34	W8	D5	L21	F38	A67	29 Pts	Position 16th	Div One (relegated)
1987-88	P34	W20	D7	L7	F81	A42	67 Pts	Position 2nd	Div Two (promoted)
1988-89	P34	W10	D10	L14	F51	A58	40 Pts	Position 14th	Div One
1989-90	P34	W15	D5	L14	F42	A50	50 Pts	Position 11th	Div One
1990-91	P34	W12	D5	L17	F46	A52	41 Pts	Position 13th	Div One
1991-92	P34	W12	D7	L15	F60	A43	43 Pts	Position 11th	Div One
1992-93	P34	W12	D7	L15	F36	A43	43 Pts	Position 12th	Div One
1993-94	P34	W10	D8	L16	F46	A53	38 Pts	Position 15th	Div One (relegated)
1994-95	P34	W22	D4	L8	F68	A38	70 Pts	**Champions**	Div Two (promoted)
1995-96	P34	W13	D6	L15	F55	A59	45 Pts	Position 10th	Div One
1996-97								Withdrew from league for this season	
1997-98	P18	W10	D5	L3	F24	A10	35 Pts	Position 2nd	Div Three (promoted)
1998-99	P24	W14	D6	L4	F46	A17	48 Pts	**Champions**	Div Two (promoted)

FA Premier Reserve League (North)

1999-00	P24	W11	D4	L9	F37	A35	37 Pts	Position 5th	
2000-01	P22	W8	D4	L10	F34	A35	28 Pts	Position 10th	
2001-02	P24	W13	D3	A8	F46	A28	42 Pts	Position 2nd	
2002-03	P28	W8	D9	L11	F44	A43	33 Pts	Position 12th	
2003-04	P26	W13	D4	L9	F50	A42	43 Pts	Position 4th	Also played in Pontins Lg (2nd)
2004-05	P28	W8	D7	L13	F30	A41	31 Pts	Position 12th	
2005-06	P28	W12	D8	L8	F45	A40	44 Pts	Position 5th	
2006-07	P18	W6	D5	L7	F29	A29	23 Pts	Position 18th	
2007-08	P18	W5	D7	L6	F31	A27	22 Pts	Position 6th	
2008-09	P20	W9	D5	L6	F34	A30	32 Pts	Position 4th	

Totesport.com League - East Division

2009-10	P18	W7	D4	L7	F31	A26	25 Pts	Position 5th

FA Premier Reserve League (North - Group)

2010-11	P19	W8	D4	L7	F40	A40	28 Pts	Position 4th

The Central League Championship winning medal awarded to United's players and officials in 1948.

Reserve XI: Principal Honours summary

Northern Alliance Champions: 1898, 1901, 1902.

Northern League Champions: 1903, 1904, 1905.

North Eastern League Champions: 1907, 1908, 1909, 1911, 1923, 1926.

Northern Combination League Champions: 1945.

Central League Champions: 1948.

Northumberland FA Challenge Cup (Senior Cup) Winners: 1885*, 1889*, 1898, 1899, 1901, 1904, 1905, 1907, 1909, 1910, 1911, 1912+, 1922, 1924, 1925, 1926, 1927, 1929, 1930, 1931, 1989, 1990, 1995, 1996, 1999, 2000, 2001, 2003, 2006, 2008, 2009, 2011.
** Prior to 1891, East End fielded their first team in the Northumberland Challenge Cup.*
+ In 1912, Newcastle United Reserves (known as 'A' team) shared the trophy with North Shields.

Northumberland FA Bowl Winners: 1894, 1898, 1903, 1910, 1912.

Northern Combination Cup Winners: 1942, 1944.

North East Exhibition Cup Winners: 1930.

Newcastle Infirmary Cup Winners: 1912, 1913, 1921, 1923, 1924, 1925, 1929, 1931.

Northumberland Aged Miners Cup Winners: 1921+, 1922, 1923, 1924, 1927, 1928, 1929, 1931, 1932, 1946, 1960.
+ In 1921 Newcastle United Reserves shared the trophy with Blyth Spartans.

RVI Cup Winners: 1907, 1911.

Tynemouth Hospital Cup Winners: 1907.

Winger George Hair was prominent in the title season of 1948.

Central League Championship winning details, 1947-48

Since the club's reserve eleven moved onto the national stage, only once have Newcastle United lifted the Championship title, that in season 1947-48. The Magpies' squad of senior players was first rate, the senior team also gaining success by winning promotion back to the top flight that season. United's second string saw off the challenge of Manchester United by three points to secure the Central League trophy. Mainstays of the success were Andy Donaldson at centre-forward – goal-getter in chief with 33 goals – captain Tot Smith at centre-half, future England player Tommy Thompson, raiding winger George Hair, as well as Ernie Taylor, Ron Batty and Charlie Crowe, all to soon win the FA Cup with United. Bobby Cowell was also in the side, he went on to win the FA Cup on three occasions for Newcastle. A top crowd of 19,824 saw the reserve clash with Bolton Wanderers during September. In the annual *Champions* versus *The Rest* challenge contest during October 1948, United drew 1-1 in front of a 15,000 gate.

Appearances (42m): Smith T 34, Donaldson A 30, Thompson T 28, Hair G 27, Cowell RG 25, Batty RR 24, Taylor E 24, Crowe CA 23, McNichol J 23, Woodburn J 18, Sibley A 17, Garbutt EJE 16, Craig B 15, Lowery J 15, Clark AH 14, Dodgin N 14, McCoy PJ 14, Fairbrother J 11, Porter L 11, Bentley RTF 9, Fraser R 9, Stobbart GC 9, Yates D 7, Walker TJ 6, Graver AM 6, Pearson TU 5, Corbett R 4, Stokoe R 4, King G 3, Milburn JET 3, Wayman C 3, Ramsay R 2, Rattray R 2, Shackleton LF 2, Boyle DW 1, Graham D 1, King A 1, Robinson C 1, Wood W 1.

Goals (95g): Donaldson A 33, Taylor E 10, Thompson T 10, Hair G 8, Sibley A 4, Woodburn J 4, Stobbart GC 3, Walker TJ 3, Crowe CA 2, Graver AM 2, Milburn JET 2, McNichol J 2, Pearson TU 2, Porter L 2, Yates D 2, Corbett R 1, Fraser R 1, King G 1, Wayman C 1, og 2.

Average attendance at St James' Park: 12,913

Ernie Taylor would blossom quickly after being a regular in the 1948 reserve line-up.

Other Newcastle United XIs

As already related, from almost its earliest existence, Newcastle United have fielded a number of teams below first-team level. As early as the 1882-83 season, East End selected a Juniors side formed from the nucleus of their young second string, in the Northumberland & Durham Junior Challenge Cup. They were eventually disqualified for fielding over-age players, 17 years of age being the qualifying limit.

Even in the club's East End days, up to six different sides were fielded although this figure has fluctuated over the years. By 1887, the club selected a second team, a third team, a Swifts' combination and a juniors' XI. The distinction between them was not always clear although towards the end of the decade it was the Swifts' team which contained the more senior players and thus became established as more of a 'reserve' side to the senior team.

After the club permanently adopted the reserve title for its second eleven, other United teams went under various labels; Newcastle United 'A', Newcastle United 'B', Newcastle United 'Swifts', Newcastle United 'Ns' to more modern titles such as Newcastle United Juniors, to the present-day line-ups from the Academy. Significantly, references to East End Juniors virtually disappear by 1886 although the name was resurrected for the 1887 Tyneside Temperance Festival when a junior team (Under-17s) was entered for the Junior Competition. They won it, defeating St Silas in the final and being rewarded with eleven silver medals to the value of £5 10s 0d (£5 50p).

After this, the Swifts went from strength to strength, defeating the East End 2nd team in the semi-final of the Northumberland FA Medals competition (Northumberland Second Team Cup) in 1888 before lifting the trophy in controversial circumstances against Shankhouse 'A' at Blyth. The Swifts were leading 1-0 (or 2-0 – the second goal being disputed) when a pitch invasion caused the match to be abandoned with only six minutes to go. The Northumberland FA ordered that the final few minutes should be played out at Newcastle. Shankhouse refused to travel and East End Swifts were awarded the trophy. They retained silverware the following year, defeating Science & Art but then surrendered it a year later, again in controversial circumstances, when they did not turn up for a semi-final tie against West End Reserves. West End kicked off, scored a goal and claimed the match!

By the following season of 1890-91 the Swifts had effectively ceased to exist under that name, becoming East End Reserves. The latter title did not last long either, being replaced by East End Amateurs. But they only survived a few months, withdrawing from the Northumberland Senior Cup and disbanding in January 1892. A few months later, an East End 'A' team was reformed from the remnants of West End Reserves whose parent club had folded. The new 'A' team was elected to the Northern Alliance in the summer of 1892 and changed its name to Newcastle United 'A' when the first team adopted their new title.

Newcastle United Swifts no longer existed but the name was temporarily used again during the First World War when Newcastle entered a team in the Newcastle & District United League. The name became dormant once more when peacetime football resumed. It was resurrected, yet again, in the summer of 1923, this time the brainchild of former star Colin Veitch. He persuaded United's hierarchy to create a properly structured youth and junior system as a stepped development from the club's previous 'junior' line-up which had been somewhat haphazard in various forms and age groups since the days of East End. Veitch was in charge of this new set-up for three years before the Swifts were again disbanded. Although reappearing for a brief period, it took a while for a similar youth system to be recreated.

In the meantime, the club's third and fourth teams were developed and began to play league football. The former were known as Newcastle United 'A' and started to play in the Tyneside League during 1933, graduating to the Northern Alliance four years later. There was a virtual hiatus at this level during the Second World War but the 'A' team resumed in the Alliance in 1947 and stayed there until the mid-1960s. The fourth team (Newcastle United 'B') was a later creation. Mainly comprising youngsters, they played in the Northern Combination throughout the 1950s.

It was at this time that the club had teams in six different leagues. The main junior team was the NNNNs (Northumberland, North Durham and Newcastle Nursery), created soon after World War Two although initially the link to the parent club was rather informal but was integrated fully for season 1948-49, soon with a shortened title of the 'Ns'. As the club developed a youth policy, the Ns became increasingly important, joining the Northern Intermediate League for 1950-51 to compete with the junior sides of other senior clubs. At an even lower level, there was another Ns team, often referred to as Ns Juniors, which played in the local Newcastle & District Junior League.

The lower level teams were gradually disbanded during the 1960s and the emphasis within the club was on the development of the Ns which evolved into Newcastle United Juniors during the early 1970s. They continued to play in the Northern Intermediate League winning the title on seven occasions.

The national FA Youth Cup was introduced for season 1952-53 and quickly became the foremost tournament for youth sides throughout the country. Newcastle have participated in the competition since its inception, winning it twice in 1962 and 1985.

Apart from local and regional league competitions and the FA Youth Cup, United's minor teams also competed in various local knock-out tournaments, as well as the Northern Intermediate League Challenge Cup which they won 11 times. The club's junior sides also were often invited to take part in both home and Continental youth competitions, frequently with success.

Centre of Excellence and Premier League Academy

The formation of the FA Premier League in 1992 saw youth development take on a high-profile and nationwide structure. The *Premier League Academy* is now the country's highest ranked youth development scheme, with the majority of Premier League clubs – and many in the Football League too – having such a facility. Being officially licensed, requirements of the Academies include high-quality facilities, qualified UEFA coaches while up-and-coming footballers must be registered and are restricted to only playing games for the club itself. There are several age groups from Under-9s upwards, and players can become professional from 17 years of age. A similar set-up has been formed under football's *Centre of Excellence*, the second highest tier of elite youth development.

Newcastle United first created a Centre of Excellence and then received an Academy Licence in 1999. The club purchased land at Darsley Park in North Tyneside during 2001 to construct a purpose-built Academy, on an adjoining site to a planned Newcastle United Training Centre which was unveiled in January 2002. The new Academy development was opened in February 2003 alongside the seniors' base, jointly making an impressive and vast 56 acre complex. Now it is one of the finest in the country.

Newcastle fielded Under-17 and Under-19 teams and enjoyed major success during the 2001-02 season when they won the national FA Academy Under-17 title. In 2004, the two age limit categories were combined and the FA Academy League became an Under-18 competition, thus bringing it more or less in line with the FA Youth Cup.

League Summary; principal competitions 1920 to date

1920s	
Newcastle United Swifts	Tyneside League
Newcastle United Juniors	Tyneside Combination League, East Tyne League
1930s	
Newcastle United 'A'	Tyneside League, Northern Alliance League
1940s	
Newcastle United Swifts/'Ns'	Northern Combination League
Newcastle United 'A'	Northern Alliance League, Northern Combination League
1950s	
Newcastle United 'A'	Northern Alliance League
Newcastle United 'B'	Northern Combination League
Newcastle United 'Ns'	Northern Intermediate League
Newcastle United 'Ns Juniors'	Newcastle & District Junior League
1960s	
Newcastle United 'A'	Northern Alliance League, Northern Combination League
Newcastle United 'Ns'	Northern Intermediate League
Newcastle United 'Ns Juniors'	Newcastle & District Junior League
1970s	
Newcastle United 'Ns'/'Juniors'	Northern Intermediate League
Newcastle United 'Ns Juniors'	East Northumberland League
1980s	
Newcastle United 'Juniors'	Northern Intermediate League
Newcastle United 'A'	Northern Alliance League
Newcastle United 'Schoolboys'	East Northumberland League
1990s/2000s	
Newcastle United 'Under-17'	FA Academy Under-17 League
Newcastle United 'Under-19'	FA Academy Under-19 League
2004-date	
Newcastle United 'Under-18'	FA Academy Under-18 League

FA Youth Cup Record

Season	Round	Opponent	Venue	Result	Score
1952-53	R1	Scarborough	(a)	W	9-0
	R2	Billingham Synth	(h)	W	8-3
	R3	Sunderland	(h)	W	3-2
	R4	Barnsley	(h)	L	1-2
1953-54	R1	Middlesbrough	(a)	W	4-0
	R2	Silksworth CW	(h)	W	11-1
	R3	Sunderland	(a)	L	1-2
1954-55	R1	Bye			
	R2	South Bank Jnrs	(h)	W	6-1
	R3	Leeds United	(h)	W	3-1
	R4	Blackburn Rovers	(h)	L	2-3
1955-56	R1	Seaton Delaval	(a)	D	1-1
	R1r	Seaton Delaval	(h)	W	6-1
	R2	Middlesbrough	(h)	W	2-1
	R3	North Shields	(h)	W	3-1
	R4	Manchester United	(a)	L	1-7
1956-57	R1	Seaton Delaval	(a)	L	0-1
1957-58	R1	Ashington Welfare	(a)	W	5-2
	R2	Seaton Delaval	(h)	W	6-5
	R3	South Bank	(h)	W	7-0
	R4	Manchester United	(a)	L	0-8
1958-59	R2	Billingham Synth	(a)	W	4-0
	R3	Middlesbrough	(a)	W	5-2
	R4	Blackburn Rovers	(a)	D	3-3
	R4r	Blackburn Rovers	(h)	L	1-3
1959-60	R1	Bye			
	R2	Whitehall Jnrs	(h)	W	9-2
	R3	Middlesbrough	(h)	L	2-3
1960-61	R1	Bye			
	R2	Middlesbrough	(h)	L	1-4
1961-62	R1	Seaton Delaval	(h)	W	14-0
	R2	Corinthians	(h)	W	3-0
	R3	Sunderland	(a)	W	3-1
	R4	Manchester United	(a)	W	2-1
	R5	North Shields	(h)	W	2-1
	SF1	Portsmouth	(a)	L	0-1
	SF2	Portsmouth	(h)	W	4-2
	F1	Wolverhampton W	(a)	D	1-1
	F2	Wolverhampton W	(h)	W	1-0
1962-63	R1	Bye			
	R2	Barrow	(h)	W	3-1
	R3	Bolton Wanderers	(h)	W	1-0
	R4	Manchester United	(a)	L	0-3
1963-64	R1	Bye			
	R2	Hull City	(h)	W	4-1
	R3	Middlesbrough	(a)	L	3-5
1964-65	R1	Bye			
	R2	Workington	(h)	W	3-1
	R3	Sunderland	(a)	L	1-3
1965-66	R1	Bye			
	R2	Middlesbrough	(a)	D	1-1
	R2r	Middlesbrough	(h)	L	1-4
1966-67	R1	Darlington	(a)	W	4-1
	R2	Sunderland	(a)	L	0-4
1967-68	R1	Hartlepools United	(a)	W	7-1
	R2	Darlington	(h)	W	2-1
	R3	Sunderland	(h)	L	0-1
1968-69	R1	Bye			
	R2	Hartlepool	(a)	D	0-0
	R2r	Hartlepool	(h)	L	1-2
1969-70	R1	Billingham Synth	(a)	W	5-1
	R2	Sunderland	(h)	L	0-2
1970-71	R1	North Shields	(h)	W	3-0
	R2	Sunderland	(h)	W	3-2
	R3	Gateshead	(h)	W	4-0
	R4	Hull City	(a)	L	0-2
1971-72	R1	Bye			
	R2	Sunderland	(a)	W	3-2
	R3	Middlesbrough	(a)	L	0-1
1972-73	R1	Bye			
	R2	Leeds United	(a)	W	1-0
	R3	Manchester United	(h)	D	1-1
	R3r	Manchester United	(a)	L	1-4
1973-74	R1	Bye			
	R2	Leeds United	(a)	L	0-1
1974-75	R1	Bye			
	R2	Consett	(a)	W	2-0
	R3	Manchester United	(h)	D	0-0
	R3r	Manchester United	(a)	L	0-2
1975-76	R1	Bye			
	R2	Barnsley	(h)	W	4-1
	R3	Middlesbrough	(a)	W	3-2
	R4	Newport County	(a)	W	2-1
	R5	Bristol City	(a)	D	1-1
	R5r	Bristol City	(h)	W	6-1
	SF1	Wolverhampton W	(h)	L	1-2
	SF2	Wolverhampton W	(a)	L	1-2
1976-77	R1	Bye			
	R2	Sunderland	(h)	L	0-3
1977-78	R1	Bye			
	R2	Sunderland	(a)	L	1-2
1978-79	R1	New Hartley Jnrs	(a)	W	6-2
	R2	Hull City	(a)	W	3-0
	R3	Manchester City	(h)	D	0-0
	R3r	Manchester City	(a)	L	0-3
1979-80	R1	Bradford City	(a)	W	1-0
	R2	Yorkshire Amateurs	(a)	W	3-2
	R3	Hartlepool United	(a)	L	0-3
1980-81	R1	Bye			
	R2	Blackburn Rovers	(a)	W	4-0
	R3	Burnley	(h)	W	2-0
	R4	Manchester City	(a)	L	2-5
1981-82	R1	Bye			
	R2	Doncaster Rovers	(a)	D	1-1
	R2r	Doncaster Rovers	(h)	W	2-0
	R3	Leeds United	(h)	D	2-2
	R3r	Leeds United	(a)	L	2-3
1982-83	R1	Bye			
	R2	Rotherham United	(h)	W	3-1
	R3	Wrexham	(a)	L	0-1
1983-84	R1	Bye			
	R2	Hull City	(h)	W	2-0
	R3	Leeds United	(h)	W	1-0
	R4	Southampton	(h)	W	3-2
	R5	Everton	(a)	L	1-2
1984-85	R1	Bye			
	R2	Everton	(h)	W	6-0
	R3	Leeds United	(h)	W	2-0
	R4	Manchester City	(h)	W	2-1
	R5	Coventry City	(h)	W	3-0
	SF1	Birmingham City	(h)	W	2-0
	SF2	Birmingham City	(a)	W	5-2
	F1	Watford	(h)	D	0-0
	F2	Watford	(a)	W	4-1
1985-86	R1	Bye			
	R2	Barnsley	(h)	W	3-1
	R3	Coventry City	(h)	L	1-4
1986-87	R1	Bye			
	R2	Barnsley	(h)	D	0-0
	R2r	Barnsley	(a)	W	3-1
	R3	Manchester City	(a)	L	1-2
1987-88	R1	Bye			
	R2	Burnley	(h)	W	2-0
	R3	Everton	(a)	L	2-4
1988-89	R1	Bye			
	R2	Blackpool	(a)	W	2-1
	R3	Walsall	(h)	W	4-3
	R4	Leicester City	(a)	W	3-1
	R5	Arsenal	(h)	W	1-0
	SF1	Manchester City	(a)	L	1-2
	SF2	Manchester City	(h)	L	0-1
1989-90	R2	Tranmere Rovers	(h)	D	1-1
	R2r	Tranmere Rovers	(a)	W	3-1
	R3	Liverpool	(a)	L	0-5
1990-91	R1	Bye			
	R2	Oldham Athletic	(h)	W	2-0
	R3	West Bromwich Albion	(h)	L	1-2

Geoff Allen was forced to retire from playing and became coach to the juniors and reserves.

After retirement Colin Suggett led the junior's set-up for a period.

Present-day Academy leader Joe Joyce, a former Barnsley defender.

FA Youth Cup Record (continued)

Season	Round	Opponent	Venue	Result	Score
1991-92	R1	Bye			
	R2	Middlesbrough	(a)	L	0-4
1992-93	R1	Bye			
	R2	York City	(a)	L	0-2
1993-94	R1	Burnley	(h)	D	1-1
	R1r	Burnley	(a)	L	0-3
1994-95	R1	Everton	(h)	L	0-2
1995-96	R1	Blackpool	(h)	W	3-1
	R2	Sheffield United	(a)	L	1-2
1996-97	R1	Burnley	(h)	L	1-2
1997-98	R1	Hull City	(h)	L	0-1
1998-99	R1	Bye			
	R2	Bye			
	R3	Bury	(a)	D	0-0
	R3r	Bury	(h)	W	3-1
	R4	Chelsea	(h)	D	0-0
	R4r	Chelsea	(a)	W	2-1
	R5	Middlesbrough	(h)	D	0-0
	R5r	Middlesbrough	(a)	W	5-0
	R6	Nottingham Forest	(a)	W	3-2
	SF1	Coventry City	(h)	L	0-4
	SF2	Coventry City	(a)	W	2-1
1999-00	R2	Bye			
	R3	Millwall	(h)	W	2-0
	R4	Wycombe Wanderers	(h)	W	1-0
	R5	Sunderland	(a)	D	1-1
	R5r	Sunderland	(h)	W	2-1
	R6	Middlesbrough	(a)	L	1-2
2000-01	R3	Crystal Palace	(h)	D	2-2
	R3r	Crystal Palace	(a)	L	1-4
2001-02	R3	Norwich City	(a)	L	1-2
2002-03	R3	Manchester United	(h)	L	1-3
2003-04	R3	Portsmouth	(a)	W	2-1
	R4	Stoke City	(a)	W	1-0
	R5	Middlesbrough	(a)	L	1-2
2004-05	R3	Blackpool	(h)	W	2-1
	R4	Watford	(a)	L	0-1
2005-06	R3	Stoke City (won 8-7 on pens)	(h)	D	0-0
	R4	Sheffield Wednesday	(a)	W	2-1
	R5	Brentford	(a)	W	2-1
	R6	Brighton (won 3-2 on pens)	(h)	D	0-0
	SF1	Manchester City	(h)	L	2-3
	SF2	Manchester City	(a)	D	1-1
2006-07	R3	Exeter City	(a)	W	4-0
	R4	Norwich City	(h)	W	3-1
	R5	Millwall	(h)	W	1-0
	R6	Swindon Town	(a)	W	2-1
	SF1	Liverpool	(h)	L	2-4
	SF2	Liverpool	(a)	L	1-3
2007-08	R3	Shrewsbury Town	(h)	L	0-1
2008-09	R3	Oldham Athletic	(h)	W	2-1
	R4	QPR	(a)	W	3-1
	R5	Manchester City	(a)	L	2-4
2009-10	R3	Doncaster Rovers	(a)	W	3-0
	R4	Reading	(a)	W	3-1
	R5	West Ham United	(a)	W	3-0
	R6	Crystal Palace	(h)	W	4-2
	SF1	Aston Villa	(a)	D	1-1
	SF2	Aston Villa	(h)	L	0-1
2010-11	R3	Dulwich Hamlet	(a)	W	6-2
	R4	Grimsby Town	(h)	W	2-1
	R5	Manchester United	(a)	L	0-1

Newcastle's 1962 FA Youth Cup winning line-up.

Back row, left to right: Hughes (staff), Chapman, Turner, Craig (David), Craig (Stan), Watkin, Gowland, Wilkinson, Craig (coach). Front: Markie, Suddick, Harvey (manager), Clish, Moncur, O'Neill.

In 1985 United again lifted the FA Youth Cup.

Back row, left to right: Suggett (coach), Kilford, Wrightson, Tinnion, Allon, Kelly, Forster, Scott, Nelson (asst coach). Front: Stephenson, Hayton, Harbach, Dickinson, Gascoigne, Bogie, Nesbit, McKenzie.

FA YOUTH CUP FINAL • 1962

v Wolverhampton Wanderers

Newcastle United won 2-1 on aggregate

With several stars of the future, the likes of Alan Suddick, Bob Moncur and David Craig, in United's side, the Black'n'Whites battled back from a goal behind at Molineux and grabbed a second-half equaliser through Clive Chapman. That set up the return leg on Tyneside perfectly for the Magpies. With playmaker Alan Suddick pulling the strings, United got the better of Wolves in a close encounter. The winning goal came in the 59th minute from the head of Bob Moncur, playing in his early role of inside-forward, following a Les O'Neil corner. Skipper Colin Clish lifted the trophy in front of a substantial gate which was just below United's average attendance for first-team fixtures that season.

First Leg:
17th April 1962 at Molineux
Wolves 1(1) Newcastle United 1(0)
United: Craig (Stan), Craig (David), Clish, Chapman, Markie, Turner, Gowland, Suddick, Watkin, Moncur, O'Neil.
Goals: Chapman. Attendance: 13,916

Second Leg:
2nd May 1962 at St James' Park
Newcastle United 1(0) Wolves 0(0)
United: Craig (Stan), Craig (David), Clish, Chapman, Markie, Turner, Gowland, Suddick, Watkin, Moncur, O'Neil.
Goals: Moncur. Attendance: 20,588

Coach; Ted Hughes/Benny Craig

FA YOUTH CUP FINAL • 1985

v Watford

Newcastle United won 4-1 on aggregate

Watford appeared to have the upper hand following a good display at Gallowgate and holding the free-scoring United line-up led by 37-goal Joe Allon and play-maker Paul Gascoigne. Indeed, the visitors could have left Tyneside with goals in hand, but a series of fine saves by 'keeper Gary Kelly kept United in the tie. Those saves were crucial as Newcastle found their rhythm and spark at Vicarage Road but not until they stormed back after being rocked by a Watford goal in the opening minutes. United equalised through skipper Gascoigne within three minutes, then the blossoming talent of Gazza took over. He controlled the match with Allon being a constant danger all evening. The pair shared the four goals which secured the trophy for Newcastle.

First Leg:
30th April 1985 at St James' Park
Newcastle United 0(0) Watford 0(0)
United: Kelly, Dickinson, Tinnion, Nesbit, Scott, Kilford, Hayton, Gascoigne, Allon, Forster, McKenzie (Wrightson).
Goals: none. Attendance: 5,774

Second Leg:
10th May 1985 at Vicarage Road
Watford 1(1) Newcastle United 4(1)
United: Kelly, Dickinson, Tinnion, Nesbit, Scott, Kilford, Hayton, Gascoigne, Allon, Forster, Wrightson.
Goals: Allon 2, Gascoigne 2.
Attendance: 7,087

Coach; Colin Suggett

FA ACADEMY UNDER-17 LEAGUE CHAMPIONS: PLAY-OFF • 2002

v Manchester United

Newcastle won 5-2 on aggregate

The early part of the competition was structured into four leagues consisting of 35 clubs in total. United won Group D, finishing three points ahead of Sunderland. The Magpies then entered a Play-Off format comprising initially of nine mini-leagues and the Black'n'Whites ended top of Group 7 with a 100% record, ahead of Crewe, Wimbledon and Fulham. That took the young Magpies into the knock-out stage of the tournament. In the quarter-final, United travelled to face Arsenal and won 2-1, then defeated Sheffield United in Yorkshire by 3-2, Steven Taylor grabbing two goals. Manchester United faced Newcastle in a two-legged final during May.

With Lewis Guy the main threat up front – he had scored over 30 goals in the season – Newcastle took the game to the Reds at Old Trafford from the off. Calvin Zola gave the Magpies the lead and Guy rattled home two more goals just before the interval. Manchester United hit back though after the break and goals from David Poole and Kieran Richardson reduced the deficit. The deciding clash at St James' Park saw Newcastle control much of the game and they increased their lead with goals from Calvin Zola and James Beaumont to secure the trophy by a convincing 5-2 aggregate scoreline.

First Leg: 4th May 2002 at Old Trafford.
Manchester United 2(0) Newcastle United 3(3)

United; Collin, Brittain, Gate, Webster, Carr, Taylor, McDermott, Beaumont, Guy, Zola Makongo, O'Brien (Howe). Subs (unused); Shanks, Bartlett, Jackson, Bates.

Goals: Zola Makongo, Guy 2. Attendance: 1,000

Second Leg: 13th May 2002 at St James' Park.
Newcastle United 2(0) Manchester United 0(0)

United; Collin, Brittain, Gate, Gardner, Carr, Taylor (Webster), McDermott, Beaumont (Shanks), Guy, Zola Makongo (Bates), O'Brien. Subs (unused); Bartlett, Howe.

Goals: Zola Makongo, Beaumont.
Attendance: 6,109

Coach; Alan Irvine.

2002

Match programme from the Under-17 Champions Play-off with Manchester United in 2002.

A young Steven Taylor who played in both legs of the victory over Manchester United.

Junior XIs: Principal Honours Summary

FA Youth Cup Winners: 1962, 1985.

Northern Combination League Champions: 1958.

Northern Alliance League Champions: 1939, 1958.

Northern Intermediate League Champions: 1957, 1960, 1968, 1971, 1988, 1995, 1998.

Northern Intermediate League Challenge Cup Winners: 1955, 1957, 1960, 1963, 1967, 1968, 1970, 1971, 1972, 1986, 1988.

FA Academy Under-17 Regional Group Champions: 1999, 2000, 2002.

FA Academy Under-17 National Play-Off Champions: 2002.

FA Academy Under-18 Divisional Group Champions: 2005.

Northern Alliance Cup Winners: 1956, 1960.

Northern Combination Cup Winners: 1947, 1952, 1959.

Northumberland FA Junior Cup Winners: 1949, 1950.

Northumberland FA Minor Cup Winners: 1903, 1930.

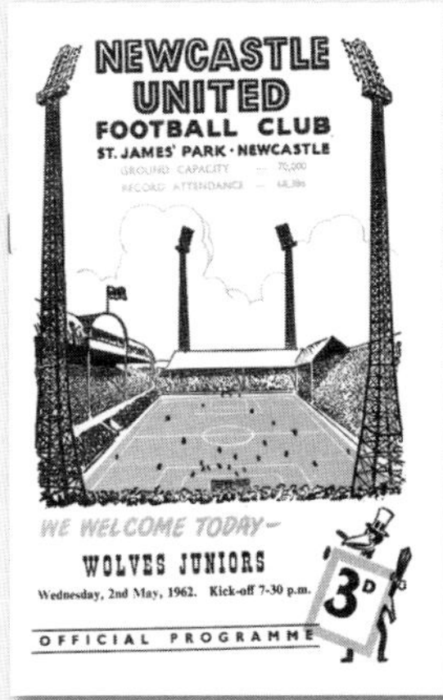

Programme for United's FA Youth Cup Final against Wolves in 1962.

Reserve & Junior Grounds

For decades the club's principal reserve side played the majority of their fixtures at St James' Park, games being scheduled in such a way that the second-string played on home turf when the seniors were on their travels. However, modern football has ensured protection of the pitch surface from overuse is paramount and a result has been that only the first-team are usually allowed to play their football on St James' Park.

As a consequence reserve matches have taken place at a variety of locations around Tyneside including the Gateshead International Stadium and the Falcons rugby ground in Kingston Park as well as Durham City's Archibald Stadium. The Blue Flames Sporting Club complex at Darsley Park has also been used as a venue. Matches are now played at the club's Training & Academy complex nearby in Benton. St James' Park still hosts the occasional reserve contest, usually a meeting against rivals Sunderland or top-level Premier League opponents.

Attendances for reserve fixtures over the years have been at times exceptional. In the era before 1930 crowds were often 10,000 and over. When the club joined the Central League for season 1933-34 gates increased with an average of around 17,000 recorded with a top crowd of 22,000 against Aston Villa. By far the highest crowd recorded for a reserve match was during May 1951 when Leeds United Reserves faced Newcastle United Reserves, just prior to the FA Cup being paraded around Gallowgate following victory at Wembley five days earlier. A reported crowd approaching 60,000 were at St James' Park for that game, or at least, towards the end of the contest.

Apart from that exceptional occasion, the best attendance since the 1930s was for the Central League match with Bolton Wanderers during 1947-48 when 19,824 came through the turnstiles. In that season the average gate was 12,913 and from that post-war high point reserve crowds gradually declined. The club's archive shows that during the early part of the 1950s decade the average stood at between 5,000 and 6,000, while by season 1961-62 it had dropped to 2,044. Although an increase was seen for season 1969-70 with an average of 3,176, in 1975-76 gates slumped and the norm was a mere 700. Now only around 500 attend reserve outings, although that rises substantially for a local Tyne-Wear derby or contests against the likes of Manchester United, Chelsea or Arsenal when gates can approach 5,000 at St James' Park.

The various Newcastle United teams below reserve level from era to era, third and fourth elevens, as well as a variety of junior sides, have all played at a number of different locations over time. On occasion St James' Park was used, but generally the club owned or leased other pitches at various stages in their past. The Magpies have played on a regular basis at Cowgate, in Wallsend and Scotswood as well as at Hunter's Moor, a short distance from St James' Park.

During the 1980s a training complex at Benwell was developed and used for junior matches and when that was sold an assortment of venues were used until the club's purpose built Academy was opened. United's junior sides played at Durham University's centre at Maiden Castle, the Riverside complex at Chester-le-Street, Hillheads, Ponteland Leisure Centre as well as Bullocksteads in Kenton Bank Foot, Killingworth and Darsley Park.

St. James' Park has been used for big-match junior fixtures such as FA Youth Cup finals and semi-finals, and certain other high-profile contests. The largest gate traced to watch a Newcastle United junior match is the 20,588 for the deciding leg of the 1962 FA Youth Cup final against Wolves.

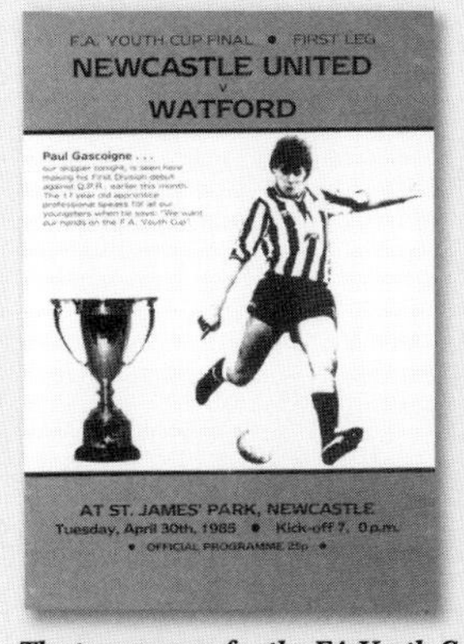

The programme for the FA Youth Cup Final with Watford in 1985 featuring a 17-year-old Paul Gascoigne.

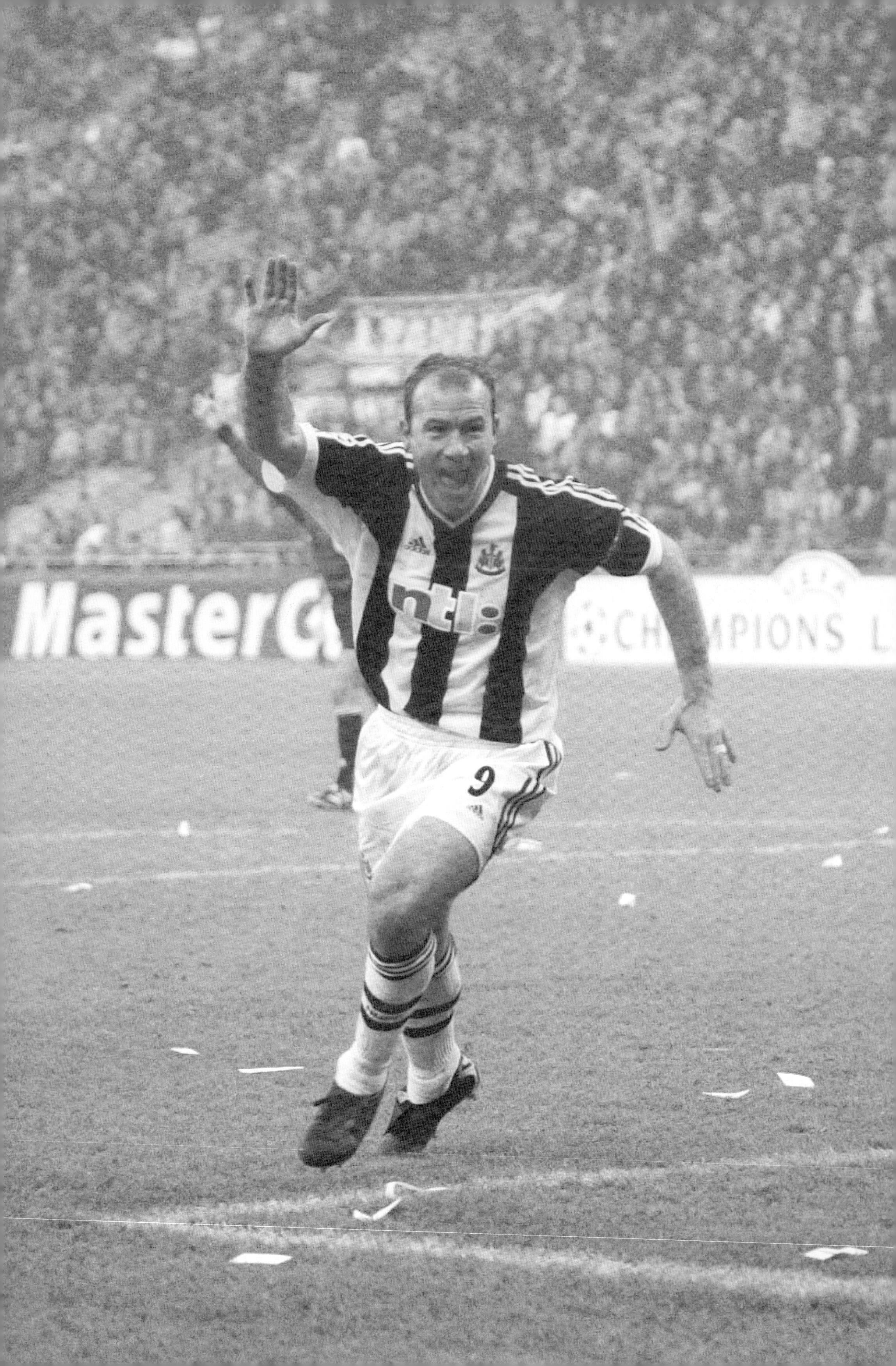

MasterC
CHAMPIONS L
ntl:
9

Section 3

The Men Who Made United 1881-2011

- Player by Player; appearances & goals for all first-team competitive fixtures 1881-82 to 2010-11
- Managers & Coaching staff 1881-82 to 2010-11
- Corporate Newcastle United 1881-82 to 2010-11
- Chairmen, Directors & Officials 1881-82 to 2010-11

Notes on the statistics

Player by Player Register

Appearances and Goals

The following register summarises in alphabetical order all those players to have appeared for the club in senior competitive football including substitute appearances. The totals are split into five categories as follows;

- League: Northern League (excluding void fixtures), Football League & Premier League, including Test Matches & Play-Offs.
- FA Cup, including qualifying matches, but excluding the 1973-74 annulled fixture with Nottingham Forest.
- Football League Cup.
- European competitions; UEFA Champions League, UEFA Cup, UEFA Cup Winners Cup, Inter Cities/European Fairs Cup & Intertoto Cup.
- Others: Sheriff of London Charity Shield, FA Charity Shield, Wartime League & Cup (excluding the 1939-40 aborted Football League season), Texaco Cup, Anglo-Italian Cup, Anglo-Scottish Cup, Full Members Cup (and later sponsored variations) and Mercantile Credit Centenary fixtures (but excluding the tournament at Wembley).

Appearances in all other matches, including abandoned games, are not included. Annulled and void match details are also not included, but shown at the end of the register.

Also at the end of the schedule a concise list is added of all those players who just missed out on making a senior appearance for the club; players who were on the first-eleven substitute bench without graduating to the senior team.

Players

In the pioneering Victorian era differences are evident in the reporting of player names. Many of United's earliest players are often identified with variances. For instance Sawyers is noted with the initial A or G, while Gibbons has P, PE or G! Even players changed their name. Jock Sorley arrived on Tyneside under the name of McSorland, while he also used McSorley, although his birth certificate notes Sorley. The use of the Scottish prefix of 'Mac' and 'Mc' causes problems too with the differing spelling of players names contained in many sources of information. Examples such as MacFarlane / Macfarlane / McFarlane or MacKenzie/Mackenzie/McKenzie are typical. It becomes almost impossible to determine the correct usage when the player's own autograph also uses the different spellings, as is the case with Roddie McKenzie/ MacKenzie.

Jack Doran appeared in the Northern Victory League.

There are a few instances where the true identity of a player has yet to be ascertained. These are restricted to a mere handful. In season 1894-95 two appearances were made by a player called Hynd or Haynes, which may be the same player or two different individuals. During wartime football in 1918-19 Jack Doran was at St James' Park, a player to later have a good career elsewhere. He is noted in the club's ledgers but in newspaper reports some of his four games are identified as a player called Johnson who is not recorded in the club's team line-up. It is possible that Doran played under a pseudonym as he may not have been properly registered at the time.

Anomalies also exist with certain birthplaces and birthdates, especially from earlier years. Often the player's birth would be registered and noted in a town or city several miles from his actual birthplace and home. Additionally on occasion birthdates are given as the baptism date, which could be a few days or even weeks later than his birth. Jackie Rutherford is one such player to have his birth and baptism dates mixed up, being a few days apart.

There are several players not to have appeared in first-class action for Newcastle, but who did make a debut for the club in one of the 'Other Matches' charted in Section 2. Certain guest players have also appeared for United in these matches, some famous names being on show; Steve Bloomer (1919) and Bobby Charlton (1974) included. Detailed biographies of all United's players, including 'Other' appearances as well as 'Guests' will be incorporated in the forthcoming updated *Newcastle United: The Ultimate Who's Who.*

Managers & Coaching Staff

Until 1930 and the arrival of Andy Cunningham as United's first manager, Newcastle United appointed a *Selection Committee* season by season to decide on playing matters; picking teams and as noted in the Club's Board Minutes, they also had the "power to transfer any player at their discretion". Usually the Committee was made up of three or four members of the Directorate. In 1920-21 Messrs Robert Oliver, Robert Mackenzie and John Graham decided on United's team affairs.

A detailed analysis of managerial appointments, including caretaker and short-term roles, is charted. Included also is a schedule of United's coaching staff from earliest times, identifying the senior trainer (as titled until the 1960s), then as senior coach, as well as assistant managers in the modern era. In addition, assistant coaches are recorded, individuals who looked after United's reserve and junior teams, and recently the United Academy. The position of club physiotherapist is noted too, from the point when a dedicated role started around 1957.

Robert Oliver, on United's Selection Committee.

Corporate Newcastle United

Included in this section is a summary of the club's ownership and company structure since Victorian times, as well as a précis of United's turnover since World War Two.

Chairmen, Directors & Officials

For the first time a comprehensive schedule of Newcastle United's Chairmen, directors and officials is charted season by season. All Board members who served the club during a particular season are recorded and are primarily taken from the club's issued Annual Reports. Prior to becoming a limited company in 1890, the club was run by committee, these individuals are also noted however certain seasons remain untraced.

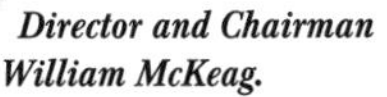

Director and Chairman William McKeag.

Alan Shearer turns away after netting in the San Siro against Internazionale in the UEFA Champions League.

Player by Player Register

Appearances and Goals

A-B

John Thompson

Arnold Woollard

Tom Wills

Billy Wilson

Bill Thompson

Craig Moore

John Gallacher

Tommy Thompson

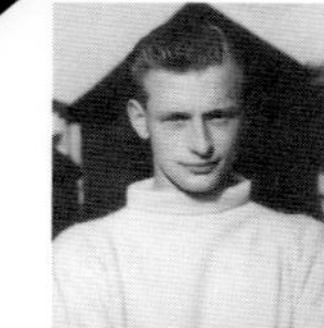
Roy Bentley

George Luke

Jonas Gutierrez

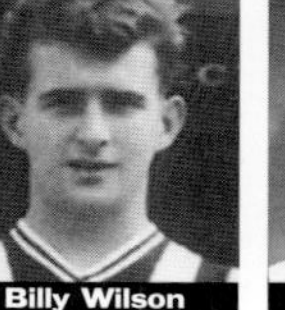

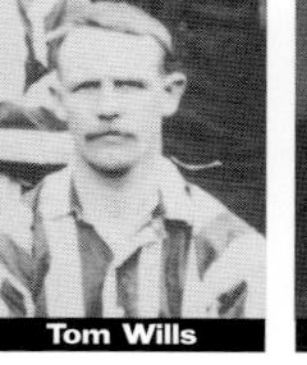

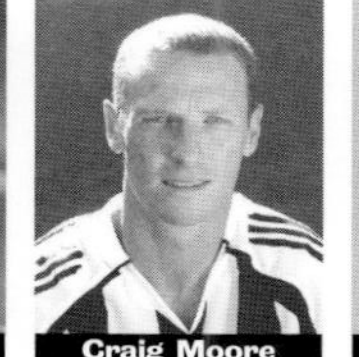

Notes

1. Where a player has more than a single period with the club, this is indicated by two or three-line entries with appearances and goals consolidated.
2. Players to have made a full international appearance for their country during their career are indicated in the 'Int' column with the country abbreviation noted.
3. Where players have also recorded additional appearances and/or goals in annulled or void fixtures, these are indicated by 'x' and details are contained at the end of the Register.

PLAYER	INT	JOINED FROM	YEAR	YEAR	LEFT TO	LEAGUE			FA CUP			FL CUP			EUROPE			TOTAL			OTHERS			GRAND TOTAL			
						APP	SUB	GL	APP	SUB	GL	APP	SUB	GL	APP	SUB	GL	APP	SUB	GL	APP	SUB	GL	APP	SUB	GL	
Acuna CWD	Ch	Universidad de Chile (Ch)	2000	2003	CA Rosario (Ag)	35	11	6	6	2	1	3	1	0		1	0	44	15	7				44	15	7	
Adams G		Kilmarnock	1896	1897	Hebburn Argyle	13		1										13		1				13		1	
Agnew WB	S	Kilmarnock	1902	1904	Middlesbrough	43		0	1		0							44		0				44		0	
Airey PJ		Juniors	2007	date						1	0								1	0					1	0	
Aitken A	S	Ayr Parkhouse	1895	1906	Middlesbrough	316		31	33		8							349		39				349		39	
Aitken RS	S	Glasgow Celtic	1990	1991	St Mirren	56		1	6		0	2		0				64		1	1		0	65		1	
Aitken WJ		Glasgow Rangers	1920	1924	Preston North End	104		10	6		0							110		10				110		10	
Albert P	Bel	RSC Anderlecht (Bel)	1994	1999	RSC Charleroi (Bel)	87	9	8	7	1	1	11	1	2	18	3	1	123	14	12	1		0	124	14	12	
Alderson JT	E	Shildon Athletic	1913	1919	Crystal Palace	1		0										1		0				1		0	
Alderson S		Evenwood Town	1965	1967	York City	3		0				1		0				4		0				4		0	
Allan R		Dundee	1897	1898	Bristol St George	24		4	5		0							29		4				29		4	
Allan SJE		Sunderland	1908	1911	West Bromwich Albion	15		5										15		5	1		1	16		6	
Allchurch IJ	W	Swansea Town	1958	1962	Cardiff City	143		46	8		4	3		1				154		51				154		51	
Allen E		Millwall Athletic	1900	1901	Dundee	4		0										4		0				4		0	
Allen GB		Juniors	1964	1970	*Retired, NU coach*	22		1	1		0	1		0	2		0	26		1				26		1	
Allen J		Bishop Auckland	1898	1901	Local	1		0										1		0				1		0	
Allen JWA		Sheffield Wednesday	1931	1934	Bristol Rovers	81		34	9		7							90		41	1		0	91		41	
Allen M	W	Millwall	1993	1995	*Retired*	9	1	5				3		2				12	1	7				12	1	7	
Allon JB		Juniors	1984	1987	Swansea City	9		2				1		0				10		2				10		2	
Ambrose DPF		Ipswich Town	2003	2005	Charlton Athletic	18	19	5		2	0	1	1	0	8	7	1	27	29	6				27	29	6	
Ameobi F		Walker Central BC	1995	date		141	95	48	9	6	3	8	3	7	26	15	12	184	119	70				184	119	70	
Ameobi SOJ		Juniors	2008	date			1	0											1	0					1	0	
Ancell RFD	S	St Mirren	1936	1944	Dundee	97		1	5		0							102		1	50		0	152		1	x
Anderson AL		St Mirren	1908	1912	Third Lanark	61		5	6		2							67		7	1		0	68		7	
Anderson JCP	RoI	Preston North End	1982	1992	*Retired*	285	16	14	14		0	17		1				316	16	15	4	1	0	320	17	15	
Anderson RJ		Bury	1941	1941	*War-time guest*																3		1	3		1	
Anderson S	E	Sunderland	1963	1965	Middlesbrough	81		13	2		1	1		0				84		14				84		14	
Anderson WR		Throckley CW	1946	1948	Annfield Plain	1		0										1		0				1		0	
Andersson AC	Se	AC Milan (I)	1998	1999	AIK (Solna) (Se)	21	6	4	3	1	0				1		0	25	7	4				25	7	4	
Appleby MW		Juniors	1989	1994	Darlington	18	2	0	2		0	2	1	0				22	3	0	2	2	0	24	5	0	
Appleby RD		Juniors	1991	1995	Ipswich Town																2		0	2		0	
Appleyard W		Grimsby Town	1903	1908	Oldham Athletic	128		71	17		16							145		87	1		1	146		88	
Archibald J		Edinburgh St Bernards	1922	1923	Grimsby Town	1		0										1		0				1		0	
Arentoft P	D	Morton	1969	1971	Blackburn Rovers	46	4	2	3		0				10	1	1	59	5	3				59	5	3	
Askew W		Hull City	1990	1992	Gateshead	7	1	0										7	1	0				7	1	0	
Asprilla FHH	Col	Parma AC (I)	1996	1998	Parma AC (I)	36	12	9	1		0	2		0	11		9	50	12	18		1	0	50	13	18	
Auld JR	S	Sunderland	1896	1897	*Retired, NU director*	14		3	1		0							15		3				15		3	
Babayaro CH	Ng	Chelsea	2005	2007	*Released*	45	2	0	7		1	3		0	11		0	66	2	1				66	2	1	
Bailey JA		Everton	1985	1988	Bristol City	39	1	0	1		0	1		0				41	1	0				41	1	0	
Bainbridge R		Grimsby Town	1943	1943	*War-time guest*																1		0	1		0	
Baird IJ		Southampton	1984	1985	Southampton	4	1	1										4	1	1				4	1	1	
Balmer J	Ewt	Liverpool	1941	1942	*War-time guest*																6		1	6		1	
Bamlett T		Kibblesworth	1901	1904	West Ham United	2		0										2		0				2		0	
Barber S		Wallsend	1925	1928	Bristol City	1		0										1		0				1		0	
Barker J		Newcastle West End	1891	1893	Trafalgar																6		2	6		2	
Barker MA		Juniors	1972	1979	Gillingham	21	2	0	4		0	1		0				26	2	0	1		0	27	2	0	
Barnes JCB	E	Liverpool	1997	1999	Charlton Athletic	22	5	6	3	2	0	3		0	5		1	33	7	7				33	7	7	
Barr JW		Grantham Rovers	1893	1894	Ashington	1		0										1		0				1		0	
Barron J		Blackburn Rovers	1944	1944	*War-time guest*																1		0	1		0	
Barrowclough SJ		Barnsley	1970	1978	Birmingham City	201	18	21	14	7	2	14	3	1	4		0	233	28	24	27		4	260	28	28	x
Bartlett T		Arthur's Hill	1893	1894	Willington Athletic	3		3										3		3				3		3	
		Willington Athletic	1896	1897	Hebburn Argyle																						
Barton D		Juniors	1975	1983	Darlington	101	1	5	2	1	0	5		1				108	2	6				108	2	6	
Barton JA	E	Manchester City	2007	date		66	13	7	1		1		2	0				67	15	8				67	15	8	
Barton WD	E	Wimbledon	1995	2002	Derby County	142	22	4	19	3	0	12		1	20	2	0	193	27	5				193	27	5	
Bassedas CG	Ag	CA Velez Sarsfield (Ag)	2000	2003	CA Newell's Old Boys (Ag)	18	6	1	2		0	2	1	0	3	1	0	25	8	1				25	8	1	
Bassong SA	Cm	FC Metz (F)	2008	2009	Tottenham Hotspur	26	4	0	2		0	2		0				30	4	0				30	4	0	
Batey R		Preston North End	1943	1943	*War-time guest*																8		0	8		0	
Batty D	E	Blackburn Rovers	1996	1998	Leeds United	81	2	3	9		1	6		0	15		0	111	2	4	1		0	112	2	4	
Batty RR		Quaking Houses	1945	1958	Gateshead	161		1	20		0							181		1	2		0	183		1	
Beardsley PA	E	Vancouver Whitecaps (Ca)	1983	1987	Liverpool	272	4	108	17		3	21		4	10		4	320	4	119	2		0	322	4	119	
		Everton	1993	1997	Bolton Wanderers																						
Beasant DJ	E	Wimbledon	1988	1989	Chelsea	20		0	2		0	2		0				24		0	3		0	27		0	
Bedford H	E	Derby County	1930	1932	Sunderland	30		17	2		1							32		18				32		18	
Beharall DA		Juniors	1997	2002	Oldham Athletic	4	2	0										4	2	0				4	2	0	
Bell AW		Juniors	1973	1975	North Shields	1		0										1		0	1		0	2		0	
Bell D		Wallyford Bluebell	1930	1934	Derby County	21		1	2		0							23		1	1		0	24		1	

PLAYER	INT	JOINED FROM	YEAR	YEAR	LEFT TO	LEAGUE			FA CUP			FL CUP			EUROPE			TOTAL			OTHERS			GRAND TOTAL			
						APP	SUB	GL	APP	SUB	GL	APP	SUB	GL	APP	SUB	GL	APP	SUB	GL	APP	SUB	GL	APP	SUB	GL	
Bell DS		Juniors	1981	1983	*Retired*	3	1	0										3	1	0				3	1	0	
Bell GW		Local	1918	1920																	3		0	3		0	
Bell JR		Evenwood Town	1956	1962	Norwich City	111		8	6		0							117		8				117		8	
Bell W		Kilmarnock	1943	1943	*War-time guest*																2		0	2		0	
Bellamy CD	W	Coventry City	2001	2005	Blackburn Rovers	87	6	27	5		0	3	2	4	24	1	11	119	9	42				119	9	42	
Ben Arfa H	F	Olympique de Marseille (F)	2010	date		3	1	1										3	1	1				3	1	1	
Bennett A		Rotherham United	1965	1969	Norwich City	85		22	1		0	3		1		1	0	89	1	23				89	1	23	
Bennie RB		St Mirren	1901	1904	*Retired*	33		0	4		0							37		0				37		0	
Benson RW	E	Swalwell	1902	1904	Southampton	1		0										1		0				1		0	
Bentley RTF	E	Bristol City	1946	1948	Chelsea	48		22	6		3							54		25				54		25	
Beresford J		Portsmouth	1992	1998	Southampton	176	3	3	17	1	1	17		0	14	1	4	224	5	8	3		0	227	5	8	
Bernard OJW		Olympique Lyonnais (F)	2000	2005	Southampton	82	20	6	5		0	6		0	26	6	0	119	26	6				119	26	6	
		Glasgow Rangers	2006	2007	*Released*																						
Bertram W		Durham City	1920	1921	Norwich City	3		0										3		0				3		0	
Best J		Mickley CW	1919	1920	Leeds United	2		0										2		0	1		0	3		0	
Best LJB	RoI	Coventry City	2010	date		15	9	6	1		0							16	9	6				16	9	6	
Betton A		Scarborough Town	1931	1934	Stockport County	61		1	2		0							63		1				63		1	
Beye H	Sg	Olympique de Marseille (F)	2007	2009	Aston Villa	49	3	1				2		0				51	3	1				51	3	1	
Billington HJR		Luton Town	1940	1941	*War-time guest*																4		3	4		3	
Bird JC		Preston North End	1975	1980	Hartlepool United	84	3	5	4		1	4		0	1	1	0	93	4	6	2		0	95	4	6	
Birkett RJE	E	Middlesbrough	1938	1941	*Retired*	23		3	3		0							26		3	39		12	65		15	x
Birnie EL		Seaburn	1898	1905	Crystal Palace	19		0	1		0							20		0				20		0	
Black N		Pegswood	1949	1953	Exeter City																1		0	1		0	
Blackburn M		Backworth	1939	1941																	12		1	12		1	
Blackburn R		Leith Athletic	1906	1908	Aberdeen	5		0										5		0				5		0	
Blackett F		Local	1883	1891																	2		0	2		0	
Blackett W		Local	1883	1891	Barrow				1		0							1		0	1		0	2		0	
Blackhall R		Juniors	1973	1978	Sheffield Wednesday	26	11	0	5	1	2		1	0	1		0	32	13	2	1	1	0	33	14	2	
Blackley JH	S	Hibernian	1977	1979	Preston North End	46		0	5		0	1		0				52		0				52		0	
Blake S		Whitley Athletic	1905	1906	Queens Park Rangers	14		0	1		0							15		0				15		0	
		North Shields Athletic	1909	1914	Coventry City																						
Blanthorne R		Grimsby Town	1908	1910	Hartlepools United	1		0										1		0				1		0	
Blyth TH		Durham University	1896	1898	*Retired*	1		1										1		1				1		1	
Boam SW		Middlesbrough	1979	1981	Mansfield Town	69		1	5		0	3		1				77		2				77		2	
Bodin PJ	W	Crystal Palace	1991	1992	Crystal Palace	6		0										6		0				6		0	
Bogie I		Wallsend BC	1985	1989	Preston North End	7	7	0	1	2	0		1	0				8	10	0	3	1	1	11	11	1	
Bolton H		Glasgow Athletic	1905	1906	Everton	1		0										1		0				1		0	
Booth CT		Wallsend Elm Villa	1913	1920	Norwich City	34		6										34		6	8		5	42		11	
Bott WE		Huddersfield Town	1934	1936	Queens Park Rangers	37		11	7		4							44		15				44		15	
Bottom AE		York City	1958	1958	Chesterfield	11		10										11		10				11		10	
Boumsong J-A S	F	Glasgow Rangers	2005	2006	Juventus (!)	44	3	0	7		0	1		0	4		0	56	3	0				56	3	0	
Bowden ER	E	Arsenal	1937	1939	*Retired*	48		6	4		0							52		6				52		6	x
Bowman J		Dundee East End	1893	1894		1		0										1		0				1		0	
Bowyer LD	E	West Ham United	2003	2006	West Ham United	61	18	6	3	1	1	1	1	0	11	2	4	76	22	11				76	22	11	
Boyd JM	S	Edinburgh St Bernards	1925	1935	Derby County	198		58	16		5							214		63	1		1	215		64	
Boyes WE	E	Everton	1942	1942	*War-time guest*																2		0	2		0	
Bracewell PW	E	Sunderland	1992	1995	Sunderland	64	9	3	6	2	0	3	1	1				73	12	4	2		0	75	12	4	
Bradley GJ		Rotherham United	1938	1946	Millwall	1		0										1		0	20		1	21		1	
Bradley R		Bishop Auckland	1927	1929	Fulham	1		0										1		0				1		0	
Bradley W		Portsmouth	1914	1927	Ashington	133		0	10		0							143		0	4		0	147		0	
Bradshaw DS		York City	1989	1992	Peterborough United	33	6	0	2	1	0	3		0				38	7	0	2		0	40	7	0	
Brady G		Tottenham Hotspur	1998	2001	Portsmouth	3	6	0	2	1	0							5	7	0				5	7	0	
Bramble TM		Ipswich Town	2002	2007	Wigan Athletic	96	9	3	8		0	5		0	38	1	4	147	10	7				147	10	7	
Brander GM		Raith Rovers	1952	1954	Stirling Albion	5		2										5		2				5		2	
Brayson P		Walker Central	1994	1998	Reading							1	1	0				1	1	0				1	1	0	
Brazil GN		Preston North End	1989	1990	Fulham	7	16	2		1	0	1	1	1				8	18	3		1	0	8	19	3	
Brennan F	S	Airdrieonians	1946	1956	North Shields	318		3	29		0							347		3	2		0	349		3	
Bridges M		Leeds United	2004	2004	Leeds United		6	0							1	2	0	1	8	0				1	8	0	
Brittain M		Juniors	2001	2006	Ipswich Town		1	0	1		0		2	0		4	0	1	7	0				1	7	0	
Broadis IA	E	Manchester City	1953	1955	Carlisle United	42		15	9		3							51		18				51		18	
Broady PK		Local	1942	1945																	1		0	1		0	
Brock KS		Queens Park Rangers	1988	1994	Stevenage Borough	137	10	14	11		1	7		1				155	10	16	7	1	1	162	11	17	
Broughton JR		Rosewood	1888	1890					2		0							2		0	3		0	5		0	
Brown A		Sunderland	1981	1982	Sunderland	5		3										5		3				5		3	
Brown EC		South Shields	1945	1947	Southend United																12		4	12		4	
Brown H		Southampton	1906	1907	Bradford Park Avenue	24		8										24		8	1		2	25		10	
Brown J		Local	1919	1919	Local																1		1	1		1	
Brown M		Huddersfield Town	1983	1985	Huddersfield Town	39		0	2		0	4		0				45		0				45		0	
Brown N		Local	1907	1908		1		0										1		0				1		0	
Brownlie JJ	S	Hibernian	1978	1982	Middlesbrough	124		2	7	1	1	4		0				135	1	3				135	1	3	
Bruce AR		Preston North End	1974	1975	Preston North End	16	4	3										16	4	3	4		1	20	4	4	
Bulloch HC		Portadown	1935	1936	New Brighton	5		0										5		0				5		0	
Burgess C		Millwall Athletic	1900	1901	Portsmouth	30		0	1		0							31		0				31		0	
Burke RJ		Blackpool	1946	1947	Carlisle United	15		0	2		0							17		0				17		0	
Burleigh MS		Willington	1968	1974	Darlington	11		0										11		0	4		0	15		0	
Burns ME		Blackpool	1974	1978	Cardiff City	143	2	39	17		5	14		4	4		0	178	2	48	11		3	189	2	51	
Burns MT		Chilton CW	1927	1936	Preston North End	104		0	3		0							107		0	1		0	108		0	
Burridge J		Southampton	1989	1991	Hibernian	69		0	7		0	4		0				80		0	4		0	84		0	
		Barrow	1993	1993	Scarborough																						
Burton AD	W	Norwich City	1963	1973	*Retired*	181	7	6	9		0	7	1	2	18	1	0	215	9	8	5		0	220	9	8	

B-C Player by Player Register

PLAYER	INT	JOINED FROM	YEAR	YEAR	LEFT TO	LEAGUE APP	LEAGUE SUB	LEAGUE GL	FA CUP APP	FA CUP SUB	FA CUP GL	FL CUP APP	FL CUP SUB	FL CUP GL	EUROPE APP	EUROPE SUB	EUROPE GL	TOTAL APP	TOTAL SUB	TOTAL GL	OTHERS APP	OTHERS SUB	OTHERS GL	GRAND TOTAL APP	GRAND TOTAL SUB	GRAND TOTAL GL	
Busby VD		Luton Town	1971	1972	Luton Town	4		2	1		0							5		2				5		2	
Butler JW		Juniors	1960	1965	Swindon Town	3		0				1		0				4		0				4		0	
Butt N	E	Manchester United	2004	2010	*Retired*	121	13	5	10		0	6	2	0	15	4	0	152	19	5				152	19	5	
"Cacapa", da Silva CR	Br	Olympique Lyonnais (F)	2007	2009	Cruzeiro EC (Br)	20	5	1	2		1	2		0				24	5	2				24	5	2	
Cahill T		Vale of Leven	1951	1955	Barrow	4		0										4		0				4		0	
Caie AS		Millwall Athletic	1901	1903	Brentford	31		1	4		0							35		1				35		1	
Cairns T		Newcastle City	1914	1916	*Demise*	1		0										1		0				1		0	
Cairns WH		Stargate Rovers	1933	1944	Gateshead	87		51	3		2							90		53	21		13	111		66	x
Calder H		Albion Rovers	1889	1890	Sunderland																9		0	9		0	
Calder NA		Ryton Jnrs	1942	1943																	1		0	1		0	
Caldwell S	S	Juniors	1997	2004	Sunderland	20	8	1				3		1	1	5	0	24	13	2				24	13	2	
Callachan R		Heart of Midlothian	1977	1978	Hibernian	9		0							2		0	11		0				11		0	
Cambell T		Boundary	1894	1895		2		0										2		0				2		0	
Cameron HG		Torquay United	1951	1952	Bury	2		0										2		0				2		0	
Campbell JM		Sunderland	1897	1898	*Retired*	26		10	3		2							29		12				29		12	
Campbell SJ	E	Arsenal	2010	2011	*Released*	4	3	0				1		0				5	3	0				5	3	0	
Cannell PA		Juniors	1972	1978	Washington Diplomats (USA)	47	1	13	5		0	7	1	4	3		1	62	2	18	5	1	2	67	3	20	
Cape JP		Carlisle United	1930	1934	Manchester United	51		18	2		2							53		20				53		20	
Carlton W		Washington CW	1926	1929	Merthyr Tydfil	5		1	1		0							6		1				6		1	
Carney S		Blyth Spartans	1979	1985	Darlington	125	9	1	9		0	6		0				140	9	1				140	9	1	
Carr EM		Arsenal	1942	1945	*War-time guest*																70		57	70		57	
Carr FA		Nottingham Forest	1991	1993	Sheffield United	20	5	3				2	2	0				22	7	3	3	1	0	25	8	3	
Carr J	E	Seaton Burn	1897	1912	*Retired, NU trainer*	252		5	25		0							277		5	1		0	278		5	
Carr JR		Science & Art	1894	1898	Kilmarnock	4		0										4		0				4		0	
Carr K		Juniors	1976	1985	Carlisle United	173		0	13		0	9		0				195		0				195		0	
Carr R		Hebburn Argyle	1890	1891																	1		0	1		0	
Carr S	RoI	Tottenham Hotspur	2004	2008	Birmingham City	76	2	1	8		0	1		0	20		0	105	2	1				105	2	1	
Carroll AT	E	Low Fell Jnrs	2004	2011	Liverpool	57	23	31	3	5	2		1	0		2	0	60	31	33				60	31	33	
Cartwright P		North Shields	1979	1983	Darlington	57	8	3	1		0		3	1				58	11	4				58	11	4	
Carver J		Blackburn Rovers	1936	1939	Bury	70		0	6		0							76		0				76		0	
Casey T	NI	Bournemouth & BA	1952	1958	Portsmouth	116		8	16		2							132		10	2		0	134		10	
Cassidy T	NI	Glentoran	1970	1980	Burnley	170	10	22	22	1	1	17	2	3	3		0	212	13	26	13	1	2	225	14	28	
Chalmers W		Glasgow Rangers	1928	1931	Grimsby Town	41		13	1		0							42		13				42		13	
Chambers C		Juniors	1975	1978	Whitley Bay																1		0	1		0	
Chandler A		Derby County	1925	1926	Sheffield United	33		0	3		0							36		0				36		0	
Channon MR	E	Caroline Hill (HK)	1982	1982	Bristol Rovers	4		1										4		1				4		1	
Chard W		Newcastle FA	1886	1889					1		0							1		0				1		0	
Charvet LJ		AS Cannes (F)	1998	2000	Manchester City	37	3	1	6		0	3		0	4		0	50	3	1				50	3	1	
Chilton AC	E	Manchester United	1943	1943	*War-time guest*																2		0	2		0	
Chopra MR		Montague BC	1993	2006	Cardiff City	7	14	1	1	1	1	1	2	0	1	4	1	10	21	3				10	21	3	
Clark AH		North Shields	1948	1949	North Shields	1		0										1		0				1		0	
Clark FA		Crook Town	1962	1975	Nottingham Forest	388	1	0	25		0	19		1	23		0	455	1	1	29	1	1	484	2	2	x
Clark JasR (James R)		Jarrow	1921	1924	Leeds United	11		2										11		2				11		2	x
Clark JnR (John R)		Prudhoe Castle	1923	1928	Liverpool	77		16										77		16				77		16	
Clark LR		Juniors	1988	1997	Sunderland	161	56	24	16	2	3	17	1	0	3	5	0	197	64	27	4		1	201	64	28	
		Fulham	2005	2006	*Retired, NU coach*																						
Clarke JD		Sunderland	1982	1987	MKE Ankaragucu (T)	124		4	5		0	5		1				134		5				134		5	
Clarke RC		Brighton & Hove Albion	1980	1981	*Retired*	14		2	4		1							18		3				18		3	
Clifton H	Ewt	Chesterfield	1938	1946	Grimsby Town	29		15	6		2							35		17	42		27	77		44	
Clish C		Juniors	1961	1963	Rotherham United	20		0	2		0	1		0				23		0				23		0	
Coldwell W		Cheviot	1887	1891					4		0							4		0	1		0	5		0	
Cole AA	E	Bristol City	1993	1995	Manchester United	69	1	55	4		1	7		8	3		4	83	1	68				83	1	68	
Collins J			1888	1891	Newcastle West End	34		8	16		3							50		11	41		7	91		18	x
		Nottingham Forest	1895	1897	Sheppey United																						
Coloccini F	Ag	Deportivo La Coruna (Sp)	2008	date		106		4	6		0	3		0				115		4				115		4	
Connell J		Galston	1896	1897		24		3	1		0							25		3				25		3	
Connelly EJ		Rosslyn Jnrs	1935	1938	Luton Town	25		8	5		1							30		9				30		9	
Connolly J1		Stockton	1891	1891	Newcastle West End																1		0	1		0	
Connolly J2	S	Birmingham City	1978	1980	Hibernian	42	7	10		1	0	1		0				43	8	10				43	8	10	
Connor J		Bolton Wanderers	1942	1942	*War-time guest*																2		0	2		0	
Cook J		Local	1918	1920	Scotswood																1		0	1		0	
Cooper E		Glossop North End	1913	1919	Rochdale	45		2	1		0							46		2	10		2	56		4	
Cooper J		Winlaton Mill	1952	1959	*Released*	6		0										6		0				6		0	
Copeland E		Easington Colliery	1939	1946	Hartlepools United																20		3	20		3	
Coppinger J		Darlington	1998	2002	Exeter City		1	0											1	0					1	0	
Corbett R		Throckley CW	1943	1951	Middlesbrough	46		1	14		0							60		1	62		0	122		1	
Cordone CD		Racing Club (B Aires) (Ag)	2000	2001	AA Argentinos Juniors (Ag)	12	9	2		2	0	1	3	1				13	14	3				13	14	3	
Cornwell JA		Leyton Orient	1987	1988	Swindon Town	28	5	1	1		0	3		0				32	5	1	4	1	0	36	6	1	
Cort CER		Wimbledon	2000	2004	Wolverhampton Wanderers	19	3	7	2		0	3		1		1	0	24	4	8				24	4	8	
Coulson WJ		North Shields	1971	1973	Southend United																1		0	1		0	
Coupe J		Blackburn Olympic	1888	1891					2		0							2		0	4		0	6		0	
Cowan J	NI	Crusaders	1967	1973	Drogheda United	6	3	0					1	0				6	4	0				6	4	0	
Cowan WD	S	Dundee	1923	1926	Manchester City	87		22	14		5							101		27				101		27	
Cowell RG		Blackhall CW	1943	1956	*Retired*	289		0	38		0							327		0	82		0	409		0	
Coyde N		Southend United	1942	1943	*War-time guest*																7		1	7		1	
Craggs JE		Juniors	1964	1971	Middlesbrough	60	4	1	2		0	1	1	0	5		0	68	5	1				68	5	1	
		Middlesbrough	1982	1983	Darlington																						
Craig AH		Hamilton Academicals	1987	1989	Dundee	6	4	0	1	1	0							7	5	0	2		0	9	5	0	
Craig B		Huddersfield Town	1938	1950	*Retired, NU trainer*	66		0	1		0							67		0	52		0	119		0	x
Craig DJ	NI	Boys Brigade	1960	1978	Blyth Spartans	346	5	8	21		2	17	1	1	21		0	405	6	11	23		1	428	6	12	x

PLAYER	INT	JOINED FROM	YEAR	YEAR	LEFT TO	LEAGUE APP	LEAGUE SUB	LEAGUE GL	FA CUP APP	FA CUP SUB	FA CUP GL	FL CUP APP	FL CUP SUB	FL CUP GL	EUROPE APP	EUROPE SUB	EUROPE GL	TOTAL APP	TOTAL SUB	TOTAL GL	OTHERS APP	OTHERS SUB	OTHERS GL	GRAND TOTAL APP	GRAND TOTAL SUB	GRAND TOTAL GL	
Craig DM		Juniors	1969	1975	San Jose Earthquakes (USA)							1		0				1		0	1		0	2		0	
Craig TB	S	Sheffield Wednesday	1974	1978	Aston Villa	122	2	22	13		3	11		2	4		2	150	2	29	5		0	155	2	29	
Crate T		New Cumnock	1891	1895	Hebburn Argyle	39		14	7		2							46		16	23		4	69		20	
Crawford J		Bohemians (Dublin)	1995	1998	Reading		2	0					1	0					3	0					3	0	
Creilly R		Dunmore	1889	1895	Hebburn Argyle	54		1	17		0							71		1	52		5	123		6	x
Cropley AJ	S	Aston Villa	1980	1980	Aston Villa	3		0										3		0				3		0	
Crosson D		Juniors	1972	1975	Darlington	6		0					1	0				6	1	0	3		0	9	1	0	
Crowe CA		Heaton & Byker YC	1944	1957	Mansfield Town	178		5	14		1							192		6	24		1	216		7	
Crown L		South Shields	1926	1927	Bury	2		0										2		0				2		0	
Crumley RJ		Lochee United	1903	1907	Dundee	4		0										4		0				4		0	
Cumming DS	S	Middlesbrough	1943	1945	*War-time guest*																56		0	56		0	
Cummings H		Local	1918	1919																	1		0	1		0	
Cummings RD		New Hartley	1954	1956	Ashington	43	1	14				1		0				44	1	14				44	1	14	
		Aberdeen	1963	1965	Darlington																						
Cunningham AE		Manchester City	1985	1987	Blackpool	37	10	4	1	1	0	2		2				40	11	6				40	11	6	
Cunningham AN	S	Glasgow Rangers	1929	1930	*Retired, NU manager*	12		2	3		0							15		2				15		2	
Curry T		South Shields Parkside	1912	1929	Stockport County	221		5	14		0							235		5	13		0	248		5	
Curry WM		Juniors	1953	1959	Brighton & Hove Albion	80		36	8		4							88		40				88		40	
Dabizas N	Gr	Olympiacos CFP (Gr)	1998	2004	Leicester City	119	11	10	17	1	2	6		0	21	1	1	163	13	13				163	13	13	
Dalglish PK		Liverpool	1997	1999	Norwich City	6	5	1				2		1				8	5	2				8	5	2	
Dalton G		Juniors	1958	1967	Brighton & Hove Albion	85		2	2		0	7		0				94		2				94		2	
Davidson DL		Liverpool	1930	1937	Hartlepools United	128		0	16		0							144		0	1		0	145		0	
Davidson T		Millwall Athletic	1901	1903	Brentford	38		0	5		0							43		0				43		0	
Davies A	W	Manchester United	1985	1987	Swansea City	20	1	1				2	1	0				22	2	1				22	2	1	
Davies ER	W	Southend United	1951	1958	Swansea Town	157		49	13		1							170		50	1		0	171		50	
Davies IC		Norwich City	1979	1982	Manchester City	74	1	3	1		0	6		1				81	1	4				81	1	4	
Davies RW	W	Bolton Wanderers	1966	1971	Manchester City	181		40	8		3	3		0	24		10	216		53				216		53	
Day W		Middlesbrough	1962	1963	Peterborough United	13		1				1		0				14		1				14		1	
Denmark J		Third Lanark	1937	1946	Queen of the South	51		0										51		0	51		0	102		0	x
Dennison RS		Radcliffe Welfare United	1929	1934	Nottingham Forest	11		2										11		2				11		2	
Deswart WP		Ouston Jnrs	1940	1941																	1		0	1		0	
Devine JC		Burnley	1930	1931	Sunderland	22		11										22		11				22		11	
Diatta L	Sg	Besiktas JK (T)	2008	2008	*Released*		2	0											2	0					2	0	
Dickson C		Preston North End	1894	1895	Loughborough	20		11	2		0							22		11				22		11	
Dillon KP		Portsmouth	1989	1991	Reading	62	1	0	6	1	0	3		0				71	2	0	3		0	74	2	0	
Dimond S		Manchester United	1943	1943	*War-time guest*																1		1	1		1	
Distin S		Paris St-Germain (F)	2001	2002	Paris St-Germain (F)	20	8	0	5		0	2		0				27	8	0				27	8	0	
Dixon ES		Barrington Albion	1914	1923	Blackburn Rovers	49		7	4		3							53		10	8		0	61		10	
Dixon JT		Reyrolles	1943	1944	Aston Villa																38		13	38		13	
Docking SH		Birtley	1934	1938	Tranmere Rovers	21		3										21		3				21		3	
Dodds JT		Northern Star	1906	1908	Oldham Athletic	5		0										5		0				5		0	
Dodgin N		Whitehall Jnrs	1940	1950	Reading	84		1	2		0							86		1	46		1	132		2	
Domi D		Paris St-Germain (F)	1999	2001	Paris St-Germain (F)	44	11	3	5	3	1	2	1	0	4		0	55	15	4				55	15	4	
Donaldson A		Vickers Armstrong	1943	1949	Middlesbrough	19		6										19		6	12		3	31		9	
Donaldson RM		Juniors	2006	date			2	0		2	0	2		0				2	4	0				2	4	0	
Donaldson RS		Local	1943	1947	Hartlepools United																87		2	87		2	
Donaldson		Local	1894	1895		2		0										2		0				2		0	
Donnachie J	S	Morton	1905	1906	Everton	2		0										2		0				2		0	
Donnelly JW		Local	1918	1920																	5		1	5		1	
Doran JF	Ird	Coventry City	1918	1919	Brentford																4		1	4		1	
Douglas A	S	Chelsea	1913	1918	*Demise*	49		2	7		0							56		2				56		2	
Dowsey J		Hunswick Villa	1924	1926	West Ham United	3		0										3		0				3		0	
Dryden JR		Ashington	1932	1934	Exeter City	5		1	1		0							6		1				6		1	
Duff DA	RoI	Chelsea	2006	2009	Fulham	61	8	5	5		1	2	1	0	8	1	0	76	10	6				76	10	6	
Duffy A		Juniors	1966	1970	Brighton & Hove Albion	2	2	0										2	2	0				2	2	0	
Duffy CF		Middlesbrough	1906	1908	Bury	16		1										16		1				16		1	
Duffy RMD		Glasgow Celtic	1944	1945	*War-time guest*																21		0	21		0	
Dumas F		AS Monaco (F/PoM)	1999	2000	Olympique de Marseille (F)	6		0							1		0	7		0				7		0	
Duncan ASM		Dumbarton	1908	1913	Glasgow Rangers	73		10	8		1							81		11				81		11	
Duncan JG		Ayr United	1950	1953	*Retired*	5		3										5		3	1		0	6		3	
Duns L		Sunderland	1939	1942	*War-time guest*																20		8	20		8	
Dyer KC	E	Ipswich Town	1999	2007	West Ham United	169	21	23	17	1	5	6	3	3	30	3	5	222	28	36				222	28	36	
Dyson K		Juniors	1967	1971	Blackpool	74	2	22	4		1	1	1	1	13	1	2	92	4	26		2	0	92	6	26	
Eastham GE	E	Ards	1956	1960	Arsenal	124		29	5		5							129		34				129		34	
Eastham H		Liverpool	1942	1942	*War-time guest*																1		0	1		0	
Edgar DE	Ca	Juniors	2002	2009	Burnley	11	8	2	2		0		2	0				13	10	2				13	10	2	
Edgar E		Juniors	1973	1976	Hartlepool United				1		0							1		0				1		0	
Elliott D		Sunderland	1966	1971	Southend United	78	2	4	2	1	0	3		0	3	1	0	86	4	4				86	4	4	
Elliott RJ		Wallsend BC	1989	1997	Bolton Wanderers	126	16	11	12	4	0	9	1	0	17	2	1	164	23	12	1		0	165	23	12	
		Bolton Wanderers	2001	2006	*Released*																						
Ellison R		Juniors	1968	1973	Sunderland	5		0				1		0				6		0	1		0	7		0	
Emre B	T	Internazionale Milano (I)	2005	2008	Fenerbahce SK (T)	46	12	5	2	2	0	4	1	0	11	2	1	63	17	6				63	17	6	
English A		Coxlodge Jnrs	1940	1943	Local																23		6	23		6	
"Enrique", Jose Enrique SD		Villareal CF (Sp)	2007	date		111	8	1	6		0	4		0				121	8	1				121	8	1	
Evans R		Juniors	1956	1959	Charlton Athletic	4		0										4		0				4		0	
Evans TJ	W	Clapton Orient	1927	1929	*Retired*	13		1										13		1				13		1	
Fagan W	Swt	Liverpool	1942	1942	*War-time guest*																2		0	2		0	
Fairbrother J		Preston North End	1947	1952	Peterborough United	132		0	12		0							144		0				144		0	
Fairhurst DL	E	Walsall	1929	1946	*Retired*	266		2	18		0							284		2	1		0	285		2	
Farrier C		Local	1918	1920	Ashington																7		0	7		0	

F-G Player by Player Register

PLAYER	INT	JOINED FROM	YEAR	YEAR	LEFT TO	LEAGUE APP	LEAGUE SUB	LEAGUE GL	FA CUP APP	FA CUP SUB	FA CUP GL	FL CUP APP	FL CUP SUB	FL CUP GL	EUROPE APP	EUROPE SUB	EUROPE GL	TOTAL APP	TOTAL SUB	TOTAL GL	OTHERS APP	OTHERS SUB	OTHERS GL	GRAND TOTAL APP	GRAND TOTAL SUB	GRAND TOTAL GL	
Fashanu JS		Southall	1991	1991	Torquay United								1	0					1	0					1	0	
Faye AD	Sg	Bolton Wanderers	2007	2008	Stoke City	20	2	1	1		0	1		0				22	2	1				22	2	1	
Faye AM	Sg	Portsmouth	2005	2006	Charlton Athletic	22	9	0	3		0	1	1	0	9		0	35	10	0				35	10	0	
Feeney WT		Whitby United	1930	1932	Notts County	4		1										4		1				4		1	
Fell JI		Everton	1962	1963	Walsall	49		16	2		0	2		1				53		17				53		17	
Ferdinand L	E	Queens Park Rangers	1995	1997	Tottenham Hotspur	67	1	41	4	1	2	6		3	4		4	81	2	50	1		0	82	2	50	
Fereday W		Queens Park Rangers	1989	1990	AFC Bournemouth	27	6	0	1		0	3	1	0				31	7	0	1	2	0	32	9	0	
Ferguson BJ		Mansfield Town	1979	1980	Hull City	4	1	1										4	1	1				4	1	1	
Ferguson DC	S	Everton	1998	2000	Everton	24	6	8	6	2	3				2	1	1	32	9	12				32	9	12	
Ferguson RB		Dudley	1955	1962	Derby County	11		0	1		0							12		0				12		0	
Ferguson SK	NI	Juniors	2007	date		3	4	0				2		0				5	4	0				5	4	0	
Ferris PJ		Lisburn Jnrs	1981	1986	Gateshead	1	10	0					2	1				1	12	1				1	12	1	
Fidler A		Spen Black & White	1929	1930	Newburn	5		0										5		0				5		0	
Findlay J		Knibshill United	1905	1906	Vale of Leven	2		0										2		0				2		0	
Finlay J		Airdrieonians	1909	1927	*Retired, NU trainer*	153		8	8		0							161		8	12		1	173		9	
Finney T	E	Preston North End	1942	1942	*War-time guest*																6		3	6		3	
Flannigan D		Third Lanark	1928	1929	East Stirlingshire	3		0										3		0				3		0	
Fleming JBM		Edinburgh St Bernards	1911	1913	Tottenham Hotspur	4		0										4		0				4		0	
Foggon A		Juniors	1965	1971	Cardiff City	54	7	14	4		0	1	1	0	10	3	2	69	11	16				69	11	16	
Ford D		Sheffield Wednesday	1969	1971	Sheffield United	24	2	3	1	1	0				3		0	28	3	3				28	3	3	
Ford JC		Rosewell Rosedale	1931	1934	Partick Thistle	1		0										1		0				1		0	
Forster LJ		Blackpool	1943	1943	*War-time guest*																3		0	3		0	
Forster WB		Howdon British Legion	1932	1938	Southend United	3		0										3		0				3		0	
Foulkes WI	W	Chester	1951	1954	Southampton	58		8	10		1							68		9				68		9	
Fox RA		Norwich City	1994	1995	Tottenham Hotspur	56	2	12	5		0	3		1	4		1	68	2	14				68	2	14	
Foyers R	S	Edinburgh St Bernards	1895	1897	Edinburgh St Bernards	34		0	5		0							39		0				39		0	
Franks AJ		Sunderland	1953	1960	Glasgow Rangers	72		4	3		0							75		4				75		4	
Fraser J	S	Notts County	1899	1901	St Mirren	49		9	3		0							52		9				52		9	
Fraser R		Hibernian	1946	1950	*Retired*	26		0	1		0							27		0				27		0	
Frost AD		New Brighton	1939	1939	New Brighton	5		1										5		1				5		1	
Fulthorpe G		Local	1918	1919	Local																6		1	6		1	
"Fumaca", Antunes JRA		Crystal Palace	1999	2000	*Released*	1	4	0		1	0							1	5	0				1	5	0	
Gallacher HK	S	Airdrieonians	1925	1930	Chelsea	160		133	14		10							174		143				174		143	
Gallacher JA		Falkirk	1989	1992	Hartlepool United	22	7	6	2		0	3		1				27	7	7	3		1	30	7	8	
Gallacher KW	S	Blackburn Rovers	1999	2001	Preston North End	27	12	4	5	1	1	2		1				34	13	6				34	13	6	
Gallacher P	S	Stoke City	1939	1939	*War-time guest*																1		0	1		0	
Gallantree WL		Harton CW	1931	1936	Aldershot Town	9		2										9		2				9		2	
Garbutt EJE		Billingham	1939	1951	*Retired*	52		0	1		0							53		0	1		0	54		0	
Gardner Alec (Alex)		Leith Athletic	1899	1910	*Retired*	279		22	34		4							313		26	1		0	314		26	
Gardner And(rew)		Grimsby Town	1902	1903	Bolton Wanderers	9		3	1		0							10		3				10		3	
Gardner C		Local	1890	1892																	3		0	3		0	
Gardner DR	S	Third Lanark	1899	1902	Grimsby Town	76		2	2		0							78		2				78		2	
Garland PJ		Tottenham Hotspur	1992	1992	Charlton Athletic		2	0											2	0		1	0		3	0	
Garnham A		Birtley	1934	1939	Queen of the South	45		1	5		0							50		1	1		0	51		1	
Garrow HA		Fochabers	1960	1963	Horden CW	4		0										4		0				4		0	
Gascoigne PJ	E	Redheugh BC	1980	1988	Tottenham Hotspur	83	9	21	4		3	8		1				95	9	25	2	1	0	97	10	25	
Gaskell A		Southport	1953	1954	Mansfield Town	1		0										1		0				1		0	
Gavilan DAZ	Pa	Cerro Porteno (Pa)	2000	2003	SC Internacional (Br)	2	5	1					1	0				2	6	1				2	6	1	
Gayle HA		Liverpool	1982	1983	Liverpool	8		2										8		2				8		2	
Gaynor T		Nottingham Forest	1990	1990	Nottingham Forest	4		1										4		1				4		1	
Georgiadis G	Gr	Panathinaikos (Gr)	1998	1999	PAOK (Salonika) (Gr)	7	3	0		2	1	1		0				8	5	1				8	5	1	
"Geremi", Njitap FS	Cm	Chelsea	2007	2010	MKE Ankaragucu (T)	38	11	1				4	1	1				42	12	2				42	12	2	
Ghee T		Kilmarnock	1897	1902	*Retired, NU trainer*	134		4	10		1							144		5				144		5	
Gibb T		Partick Thistle	1968	1975	Sunderland	190	9	12	8	3	0	12		1	24		3	234	12	16	17	6	3	251	18	19	
Gibbon P		Bishop Auckland	1889	1890					2		2							2		2	8		3	10		5	
Gibson CH		Cardiff City	1948	1949	Aston Villa	23		5	1		0							24		5				24		5	
Gibson J		Linfield	1959	1961	Cambridge United	2		1										2		1				2		1	
Gibson RJ		Middlesbrough	1911	1912	Lincoln City	2		0										2		0	1		0	3		0	
		Third Lanark	1919	1920																							
Gibson WM		Ayr United	1923	1929	*Retired*	124		2	18		2							142		4				142		4	
Gilfillan RI		Cowdenbeath	1959	1961	St Johnstone	7		2										7		2				7		2	
Gilholme AG		Backworth	1939	1942	Horden CW																21		3	21		3	
Gillespie KR	NI	Manchester United	1995	1998	Blackburn Rovers	94	19	11	9	1	2	7	1	1	11	4	0	121	25	14		1	0	121	26	14	
Gillespie WF		East Fife	1927	1929	Bristol Rovers	9		0										9		0				9		0	
Gillespy T		Arthur's Hill	1893	1894	Hebburn Argyle	4		0										4		0				4		0	
Ginola DDM	F	Paris St-Germain (F)	1995	1997	Tottenham Hotspur	54	4	6	4		0	6		0	6	1	1	70	5	7	1		0	71	5	7	
Given SJJ	RoI	Blackburn Rovers	1997	2009	Manchester City	354		0	34		0	12	1	0	62		0	462	1	0				462	1	0	
Glass S	S	Aberdeen	1998	2001	Watford	24	19	7	3	4	0	3		0	2	3	0	32	26	7				32	26	7	
Glassey JR		Mansfield Town	1944	1944	*War-time guest*																2		0	2		0	
Goddard P	E	West Ham United	1986	1988	Derby County	61		19	6		3	3		1				70		23				70		23	
Golding W		Burradon Welfare	1944	1945	Local																2		0	2		0	
Goma A	F	Paris St-Germain (F)	1999	2001	Fulham	32	1	1	2		0	4		0	2		0	40	1	1				40	1	1	
Gonzalez IM	Ug	Valencia CF (Sp)	2008	2009	Valencia CF (Sp)		2	0											2	0					2	0	
Goodwill T		Seaton Delaval	1913	1916	*Demise*	52		4	8		2							60		6				60		6	
Gordon J		Wishaw Jnrs	1935	1945	Middlesbrough	132		2	11		1							143		3	110		18	253		21	x
Gorry MC		Barnsley	1976	1978	Hartlepool United		1	0											1	0					1	0	
Gosling D		Everton	2010	date			1	0											1	0					1	0	
Gosnell AA	E	Chatham	1904	1910	Tottenham Hotspur	106		15	18		3							124		18	1		0	125		18	
Gourlay AM		Morton	1988	1992	Motherwell	2	1	0					2	0				2	3	0				2	3	0	
Gowling AE		Huddersfield Town	1975	1978	Bolton Wanderers	91	1	30	15		8	9		7	3		3	118	1	48	4		4	122	1	52	

PLAYER	INT	JOINED FROM	YEAR	YEAR	LEFT TO	LEAGUE			FA CUP			FL CUP			EUROPE			TOTAL			OTHERS			GRAND TOTAL			
						APP	SUB	GL	APP	SUB	GL	APP	SUB	GL	APP	SUB	GL	APP	SUB	GL	APP	SUB	GL	APP	SUB	GL	
Graham D		Barrington United	1940	1950	Preston North End	71		0	3		0							74		0	90		1	164		1	
Graham JR		Workington Diamonds	1901	1903	Bradford City	6		0										6		0				6		0	
Graham S		Galston	1902	1905	Norwich City	5		0	1		0							6		0				6		0	
Graham W		New Cumnock	1892	1899		88		10	11		1							99		11	10		2	109		13	
Graver AM		Annfield Plain	1947	1950	Lincoln City	1		0										1		0				1		0	
Gray AD		Jesmond Villa	1920	1921	Leadgate Park	2		0										2		0				2		0	
Gray R		Gateshead	1940	1945	*War-time guest*																2		0	2		0	
Gray TD		Dundee	1945	1945	*War-time guest*																1		0	1		0	
Green A	S	Blackpool	1971	1973	*Retired*	33		3	2		0							35		3	3	1	0	38	1	3	
Green S		Ashington	1936	1941																	2		0	2		0	
Greener R		Easington Colliery	1951	1955	Darlington	3		0										3		0				3		0	
Grey TJ		Bedlington United	1908	1910	Blyth Spartans	1		0										1		0				1		0	
		Blyth Spartans	1911	1915	Local																						
Griffin A		Stoke City	1998	2004	Portsmouth	63	13	2	6		0	8		0	14		1	91	13	3				91	13	3	
Grundy AJ		Dunston CWS	1936	1944		2		0										2		0				2		0	
Guivarc'h S	F	AJ Auxerre (F)	1998	1998	Glasgow Rangers	2	2	1										2	2	1				2	2	1	
Guppy SA	E	Wycombe Wanderers	1994	1994	Port Vale								1	0					1	0					1	0	
Guthrie CW		Juniors	1970	1972	Southend United	3		0										3		0	1		0	4		0	
Guthrie DS		Liverpool	2008	date		68	8	6	4	1	0	4		1				76	9	7				76	9	7	
Guthrie RG		Juniors	1963	1973	Sunderland	52	3	2		1	0	2		0	3	2	0	57	6	2	3		0	60	6	2	
Gutierrez JM	Ag	RCD Mallorca (Sp)	2008	date		91	13	7	3	2	0	2	2	0				96	17	7				96	17	7	
Guy A		Juniors	1975	1979	Peterborough United	3	1	0	2		0	1		0				6	1	0	1		0	7	1	0	
Guy LB		Juniors	2001	2005	Doncaster Rovers											1	0		1	0					1	0	
Haddock PM		Cramlington Jnrs	1976	1986	Leeds United	53	4	0	3		0	5		0				61	4	0				61	4	0	
Hagan A		Washington CW	1919	1923	Cardiff City	21		5										21		5	4		1	25		6	
Hair G		Spen Jnrs	1943	1949	Grimsby Town	23		7	3		1							26		8	51		14	77		22	
Hale KO		Everton	1956	1962	Coventry City	30		15	1		0	4		1				35		16				35		16	
Hall AN		Edinburgh St Bernards	1907	1908	Dundee	6		2										6		2				6		2	
Hall E		West Wylam	1933	1937	Brighton & Hove Albion	2		0										2		0				2		0	
Hall FB		Queens Park Rangers	2010	2010	Queens Park Rangers	7		0										7		0				7		0	
Hall T		Sunderland	1913	1920	Gillingham	54		15	4		1							58		16				58		16	
Halliday B		Juniors	1977	1982	Bury	32		1	4		0	2		0				38		1				38		1	
Halliday W		Queen of the South	1927	1928	Third Lanark	1		0										1		0				1		0	
Hamann D	G	Bayern Munich (G)	1998	1999	Liverpool	22	1	4	7		1	1		0				30	1	5				30	1	5	
Hamilton DS		Shawfield Jnrs	1939	1946	Southend United																8		1	8		1	x
Hamilton DV		Bradford City	1997	2001	Cardiff City	7	5	0	1		0	1	1	1	2	1	0	11	7	1				11	7	1	
Hampson W		Norwich City	1914	1927	South Shields	163		1	11		0							174		1				174		1	
Hannah GL		Linfield	1949	1957	Lincoln City	167		41	8		2							175		43	2		0	177		43	
Hardinge HTW	E	Maidstone United	1905	1907	Sheffield United	9		1										9		1				9		1	
Hardwick S		Chesterfield	1976	1983	Oxford United	92		0	4		0	3		0	2		0	101		0				101		0	
Hardy S		Rutherford College	1911	1918	*Retired*	3		1										3		1				3		1	
Harewood MA		Aston Villa	2009	2010	Aston Villa	9	6	5										9	6	5				9	6	5	
Harford MG	E	Lincoln City	1980	1981	Bristol City	18	1	4										18	1	4				18	1	4	
Harker CJ		West Allotment	1955	1961	Bury	1		0										1		0				1		0	
Harnby DR		Darlington ATC	1944	1947	York City																8		0	8		0	
Harper SA		Seaham Red Star	1993	date		144	7	0	9	1	0	12		0	15	2	0	180	10	0				180	10	0	
Harris A		Blackhall CW	1935	1936	Barnsley	12		4										12		4				12		4	
Harris J	S	Middlesbrough	1925	1931	York City	149		2	8		0							157		2				157		2	
Harris NL	S	Partick Thistle	1920	1925	Notts County	174		87	20		14							194		101				194		101	
Harrower J		Liverpool	1961	1962	Falkirk	5		0	1		0							6		0				6		0	
Hart WR		Willington Quay	1940	1944	North Shields																38		1	38		1	
Harvey BR		Wisbech Town	1958	1961	Cambridge City	86		0	4		0	1		0				91		0				91		0	
Harvey Jn (John)		Sunderland	1897	1899	*Retired, NU trainer*	30		8	5		2							35		10				35		10	
Harvey Jos (Joseph)		Bradford City	1945	1954	*Retired, NU trainer*	224		12	23		0							247		12	34		1	281		13	
Hay J	S	Glasgow Celtic	1911	1919	Ayr United	132		8	17		0							149		8				149		8	
Haynes		Local	1894	1895		1		0										1		0				1		0	
Heard TP		Sheffield Wednesday	1984	1985	Middlesbrough	34		2	2		0							36		2				36		2	
Hedley G		Local	1907	1908	Knaresborough	1		0										1		0				1		0	
		Knaresborough	1910	1911																							
Hedley R		Newcastle Albion	1894	1894	Jarrow	3		1										3		1				3		1	
		Jarrow	1895	1896	Hebburn Argyle																						
Hedworth C		Juniors	1982	1986	Barnsley	8	1	0				1		0				9	1	0				9	1	0	
"Helder", Cristovao MR	P	Deportivo La Coruna (Sp)	1999	2000	Deportivo La Coruna (Sp)	8		1	4		0							12		1				12		1	
Henderson D		Kilmarnock	1889	1890	Middlesbrough Ironopolis				4		0							4		0	5		0	9		0	
Henderson HB		Throckley CW	1943	1944																	5		0	5		0	
Henderson Jas (James)		Cardiff City	1919	1920	Scotswood	6		1										6		1				6		1	
Henderson Jn (John)		Clyde	1895	1897		30		0	5		0							35		0				35		0	
Hendrie JG		Bradford City	1988	1989	Leeds United	34		4	4		0	2		1				40		5	3		0	43		5	
Herd A	Swt	Manchester City	1940	1941	*War-time guest*																4		3	4		3	
Heslop GW		Dudley Jnrs	1959	1962	Everton	27		0	1		0	4		0				32		0				32		0	
Heward HA		Herrington Swifts	1932	1934	Bradford Park Avenue	5		0										5		0				5		0	
Hewison R		Whitley Athletic	1908	1920	Northampton Town	67		0	3		0							70		0				70		0	
Heywood F		Turton	1900	1902	Blackpool	13		3										13		3				13		3	
Hibbert W	E	Bury	1911	1920	Bradford City	139		46	16		3							155		49	4		1	159		50	
Hibbitt TA		Leeds United	1971	1975	Birmingham City	227	1	12	14		1	16		0				257	1	13	33		5	290	1	18	x
		Birmingham City	1978	1981	Gateshead																						
Higgins A	S	Kilmarnock	1905	1919	Kilmarnock	126		36	24		5							150		41				150		41	
Higgins W		Bristol City	1898	1900	Middlesbrough	35		3	4		0							39		3				39		3	
Highmoor GW		Clara Vale Jnrs	1942	1946	Local																3		0	3		0	
Hill JH	E	Burnley	1928	1931	Bradford City	74		2	4		0							78		2				78		2	

H-K Player by Player Register

PLAYER	INT	JOINED FROM	YEAR	YEAR	LEFT TO	LEAGUE APP	LEAGUE SUB	LEAGUE GL	FA CUP APP	FA CUP SUB	FA CUP GL	FL CUP APP	FL CUP SUB	FL CUP GL	EUROPE APP	EUROPE SUB	EUROPE GL	TOTAL APP	TOTAL SUB	TOTAL GL	OTHERS APP	OTHERS SUB	OTHERS GL	GRAND TOTAL APP	GRAND TOTAL SUB	GRAND TOTAL GL	
Hill JM	NI	Linfield	1957	1958	Norwich City	11		2										11		2				11		2	
Hilley D		Third Lanark	1962	1967	Nottingham Forest	194		31	8		1	7		1				209		33				209		33	
Hindmarsh E		Hylton Jnrs	1942	1943	Sunderland																6		0	6		0	
Hindson G		Juniors	1968	1971	Luton Town	7		1								1	0	7	1	1				7	1	1	
Hiscock E		Local	1883	1889					1		0							1		0				1		0	
Hislop NS	Tr	Reading	1995	1998	West Ham United	53		0	6		0	8		0	4		0	71		0				71		0	
Hoban T		Newcastle Rangers	1884	1891	Hibernian				4		1							4		1	1		0	5		1	
Hockey T	W	Nottingham Forest	1963	1965	Birmingham City	52		3	2		0	2		0				56		3				56		3	
Hodges GP	W	Wimbledon	1987	1987	Watford	7		0										7		0				7		0	
Hodgson GH		Juniors	1971	1974	Mansfield Town	8	1	0	1		0							9	1	0	1	2	0	10	3	0	
Hodgson K		Montague & N Fenham YC	1959	1961	Scunthorpe United	6		0	1		0							7		0				7		0	
Holland CJ		Preston North End	1994	1996	Birmingham City	2	1	0					1	0				2	2	0				2	2	0	
Hollins DM	W	Brighton & Hove Albion	1961	1967	Mansfield Town	112		0	3		0	6		0				121		0				121		0	
Hooper MD		Liverpool	1993	1996	*Retired*	23	2	0	3		0	2		0				28	2	0				28	2	0	
Hope G1		Juniors	1971	1975	Charlton Athletic	6		1										6		1				6		1	
Hope G2		Scotswood	1943	1946	Local																1		0	1		0	
Hope JWM		Darlington	1969	1971	Sheffield United	1		0										1		0				1		0	
Horsfield A		Middlesbrough	1969	1969	Swindon Town	7	2	3							1		0	8	2	3				8	2	3	
Hottiger M	Sw	FC Sion (Sw)	1994	1996	Everton	38	1	1	4		1	6	1	0	4		0	52	2	2				52	2	2	
Houghton FC		Ballymena United	1948	1953	Exeter City	55		10	2		0							57		10				57		10	
Howard P		Barnsley	1971	1976	Arsenal	182	2	7	22		1	19		0				223	2	8	37		1	260	2	9	x
Howdon S		Ryton Jnrs	1941	1943	Gateshead																10		1	10		1	
Howe D		Bolton Wanderers	1939	1939	*War-time guest*																1		5	1		5	
Howey SN	E	Juniors	1986	2000	Manchester City	167	24	6	21	2	0	14	2	1	5	2	0	207	30	7	5		0	212	30	7	
Howie J	S	Bristol Rovers	1903	1910	Huddersfield Town	198		68	37		14							235		82	2		0	237		82	
Hubble L		Horden CW	1940	1946																	2		0	2		0	
Huckerby DC		Lincoln City	1995	1996	Coventry City		1	0		1	0								2	0					2	0	
Hudson J		Clara Vale Jnrs	1940	1945	West Stanley																3		0	3		0	
Hudson RW		Juniors	1973	1978	Fort Lauderdale Strikers (USA)	16	4	1	3		1	1		0		1	0	20	5	2	4		0	24	5	2	
Hudspeth FC	E	North Shields Athletic	1910	1929	Stockport County	430		34	42		3							472		37	10		1	482		38	
Hughes AW	NI	Irish Boys Brigade	1995	2005	Aston Villa	193	12	4	15	4	1	9	1	0	39	5	1	256	22	6				256	22	6	
Hughes G		Tow Law Town	1956	1963	Derby County	133		18	9		2	1		0				143		20				143		20	
Hughes Jn (John)		Tanfield Lea Institute	1932	1935	Aldershot	5		0										5		0				5		0	
Hughes Jos (Joseph)		Local	1938	1943																	2		0	2		0	
Hughes T		Wallsend Park Villa	1912	1915	*Demise*	2		0										2		0				2		0	
Hughes WJ		Rhyl Athletic	1908	1910	Huddersfield Town	1		0										1		0				1		0	
Hunt A		Kettering Town	1991	1993	West Bromwich Albion	34	9	11	2		2	3		1				39	9	14	3		0	42	9	14	
Hunter I		Local	1918	1920	Ashington																1		0	1		0	
Hunter JA			1919	1919	Motherwell	10		0	2		0							12		0				12		0	
		Falkirk	1924	1925	New Bedford Whalers (USA)																						
Hunter JB		Preston North End	1941	1941	*War-time guest*																8		0	8		0	
Huntington PD		Yewdale Pegasus	2002	2007	Leeds United	10	1	1	2		0	1		0	1	1	0	14	2	1				14	2	1	
Hutchinson R		St Mirren	1918	1920	Ashington																1		0	1		0	
Hutchison D		Dundee United	1929	1932	Derby County	40		16	6		5							46		21				46		21	
Hutton TO		Sleekburn Welfare	1939	1942	Accrington Stanley																3		0	3		0	
Hynd J		Cowdenbeath	1894	1895		9		0										9		0				9		0	
Iley J		Nottingham Forest	1962	1969	Peterborough United	227	5	15	9		0	7		1		1	0	243	6	16				243	6	16	
Imrie WN	S	Blackburn Rovers	1934	1938	Swansea Town	125		24	3		0							128		24				128		24	
Inglis J		Dalmuir Thistle	1893	1894		3		0										3		0				3		0	
Innerd W		Wallsend Park Villa	1900	1905	Crystal Palace	3		0										3		0				3		0	
Ireland SJ	RoI	Aston Villa	2011	2011	Aston Villa		2	0											2	0					2	0	
Jackson D	S	Meadowbank Thistle	1986	1988	Dundee United	53	16	7	5		1	5		1				63	16	9	4		0	67	16	9	
Jackson J		Glasgow Rangers	1897	1899	Woolwich Arsenal	62		1	6		2							68		3				68		3	
Jackson PA		Bradford City	1986	1988	Bradford City	60		3	6		0	3		0				69		3	3		0	72		3	
Jeffrey H		Newcastle West End	1892	1895	*Retired*	45		3	3		0							48		3	7		0	55		3	
Jeffrey MR		Doncaster Rovers	1993	1995	Rotherham United	2		0				1		1		2	0	3	2	1				3	2	1	
Jenas JA	E	Nottingham Forest	2002	2005	Tottenham Hotspur	86	24	9	6	1	1	3		1	28	4	1	123	29	12				123	29	12	
Jobey G		Morpeth Harriers	1906	1913	Woolwich Arsenal	47		2	6		0							53		2				53		2	
Johnsen JR	Nw	Free agent	2004	2004	Valerenga IF (Nw)	3		0				2		0				5		0				5		0	
Johnson H		Walker Park	1933	1937	Port Vale	5		0										5		0				5		0	
Johnson PE		Middlesbrough	1980	1983	Darlington	16		0	4		0							20		0				20		0	
Jones R		Blackburn Rovers	1976	1977	Stoke City	5		0										5		0	2		0	7		0	
Juliussen AL		Huddersfield Town	1944	1944	*War-time guest*																1		0	1		0	
Kadar T	H	Zalaegerszegi TE (H)	2008	date		6	7	0	2		0	3		0				11	7	0				11	7	0	
Karelse J		NAC Breda (N)	1999	2003	AGOVV Apeldoorn (N)	3		0										3		0				3		0	
Keating AE		Prudhoe Castle	1923	1925	Bristol City	12		3										12		3				12		3	
Keeble VAW		Colchester United	1952	1957	West Ham United	104		56	16		11							120		67	1		2	121		69	
Keegan JK	E	Southampton	1982	1984	*Retired*	78		48	3		0	4		1				85		49				85		49	
Keeley GM		Ipswich Town	1974	1976	Blackburn Rovers	43	1	2	8		0	10		2				61	1	4	11		0	72	1	4	
Keen ERL	E	Nuns Moor	1927	1930	Derby County	1		0										1		0				1		0	
Keen JF		Bristol City	1922	1923	Queens Park Rangers	2		0										2		0				2		0	
Keery S		Shrewsbury Town	1952	1957	Mansfield Town	19		1	1		0							20		1				20		1	
Keir M		Dalmuir Thistle	1893	1894		1		0										1		0				1		0	
Keith RM	NI	Linfield	1956	1964	Bournemouth & BA	208		2	11		0	4		0				223		2				223		2	
Kelly D		Leeds United	1938	1946		1		0										1		0	8		0	9		0	
Kelly DT	RoI	Leicester City	1991	1993	Wolverhampton Wanderers	70		35	5		1	4		2				79		38	4		1	83		39	
Kelly GA		Juniors	1984	1989	Bury	53		0	3		0	4		0				60		0	2		0	62		0	
Kelly J		Burnley	1933	1935	Leeds United	5		1										5		1				5		1	
Kelly PA		Juniors	1973	1981	*Retired*	31	2	0				3		0	1		0	35	2	0	1		0	36	2	0	
Kelly WB		Watford	1911	1911	Manchester City	6		0										6		0				6		0	

PLAYER	INT	JOINED FROM	YEAR	YEAR	LEFT TO	LEAGUE APP	LEAGUE SUB	LEAGUE GL	FA CUP APP	FA CUP SUB	FA CUP GL	FL CUP APP	FL CUP SUB	FL CUP GL	EUROPE APP	EUROPE SUB	EUROPE GL	TOTAL APP	TOTAL SUB	TOTAL GL	OTHERS APP	OTHERS SUB	OTHERS GL	GRAND TOTAL APP	GRAND TOTAL SUB	GRAND TOTAL GL	
Kelsey WJ		Boldon Star	1906	1908	Boldon Colliery	2		0										2		0				2		0	
Kennedy AP	E	Juniors	1971	1978	Liverpool	155	3	9	21	1	0	16		0	2		0	194	4	9	16	1	1	210	5	10	x
Kennedy KV		Juniors	1968	1972	Bury	1		0										1		0				1		0	
Kerr B	S	Juniors	1997	2004	Motherwell	4	5	0		2	0				1	1	0	5	8	0				5	8	0	
Kerray JR		Huddersfield Town	1962	1963	Dunfermline Athletic	38		10	1		0	1		0				40		10				40		10	
Ketsbaia T	Ge	AEK (Athens) (Gr)	1997	2000	Wolverhampton Wanderers	41	37	8	8	8	4	1	1	0	7	6	2	57	52	14				57	52	14	
Kettleborough KF		Sheffield United	1966	1966	Doncaster Rovers	30		0	2		0	1		0				33		0				33		0	
Khizanishvili Z	Ge	Blackburn Rovers	2009	2009	Blackburn Rovers	6	1	0										6	1	0				6	1	0	
Kilcline B		Oldham Athletic	1992	1994	Swindon Town	20	12	0	1	2	0	3	2	0				24	16	0	5		0	29	16	0	
King G		RAF	1946	1948	Hull City	2		0										2		0				2		0	
King J		Partick Thistle	1913	1920	Dykehead	54		8	7		2							61		10				61		10	
King R		Amble BC	1942	1946	Leyton Orient				2		0							2		0	31		0	33		0	
Kinghorn WJD		Liverpool	1942	1942	*War-time guest*																2		0	2		0	
Kingsley M	E	Darwen	1898	1904	West Ham United	180		0	9		0							189		0				189		0	
Kinsella J		Darwen	1897	1897		2		0										2		0				2		0	
Kirkaldy JW		Northern Temperance	1904	1907	Local	11		1										11		1				11		1	
Kirkman AJ		Rotherham United	1963	1963	Scunthorpe United	5		1										5		1				5		1	
Kitson P		Derby County	1994	1997	West Ham United	26	10	10	6	1	3	3	2	1		1	0	35	14	14				35	14	14	
Kluivert PS	N	FC Barcelona (Sp)	2004	2005	Valencia CF (Sp)	15	10	6	3	1	2	2		0	5	1	5	25	12	13				25	12	13	
Knox T		Chelsea	1965	1967	Mansfield Town	24	1	1				1		0				25	1	1				25	1	1	
Koenen FLA		NEC (Nijmegan) (N)	1980	1981	De Treffers (N)	11	1	1				2		0				13	1	1				13	1	1	
Kristensen B	D	Aarhus GF (D)	1989	1993	Portsmouth	71	11	4	6		0	3		0				80	11	4	6	1	1	86	12	5	
Krul TM	N	ADO Den Haag (N)	2005	date		21	3	0	4		0	5		0	1		0	31	3	0				31	3	0	
Kuqi S	Fn	Free agent	2011	2011	*Released*		6	0											6	0					6	0	
Lackenby G		Local	1950	1956	Exeter City	19		0										19		0	1		0	20		0	
Laidlaw JA		Burnley	1900	1901	Woolwich Arsenal	10		3	1		0							11		3				11		3	
Lang T		Larkhall Thistle	1926	1934	Huddersfield Town	215		53	14		5							229		58	1		0	230		58	
Larnach M		Clydebank	1977	1978	Motherwell	12	2	0										12	2	0				12	2	0	
Laughton D		Morton	1973	1975	*Retired*	7		0					1	0				7	1	0	1	1	0	8	2	0	
Laverick J		Local	1893	1894	Hebburn Argyle	4		0										4		0				4		0	
Law JA		Washington CW	1937	1944	Local																1		0	1		0	
Law JH		Everton	1893	1894		8		2	2		0							10		2				10		2	
Lawrence J	S	Glasgow Perthshire	1904	1922	*Retired*	432		0	64		0							496		0	11		0	507		0	
Leach TJ	E	Sheffield Wednesday	1934	1936	Stockport County	51		2	2		0							53		2				53		2	
Leaver PH		Juniors	1977	1982	Whitley Bay							1		0				1		0				1		0	
Lee R		Local	1943	1944																	2		0	2		0	
Lee RM	E	Charlton Athletic	1992	2002	Derby County	292	11	44	27		5	22	1	3	27		4	368	12	56	1		0	369	12	56	
Leek K	W	Leicester City	1961	1961	Birmingham City	13		6				1		0				14		6				14		6	
Leighton WA		Walker Park	1932	1938	Southend United	39		8	1		0							40		8				40		8	
Lennox M		Glasgow Perthshire	1895	1898	New Brompton	46		16	3		1							49		17				49		17	
Lewis DJ	W	Crystal Palace	1944	1944	*War-time guest*																1		0	1		0	
Liddell R		Westwood	1904	1911	Millwall Athletic	14		2										14		2				14		2	
Lightfoot L		Waterhouses	1943	1946	Consett																10		0	10		0	
Lindsay DM		Cowdenbeath	1930	1931	Bury	19		12										19		12				19		12	
Lindsay J		Jarrow	1899	1900	Burnley	2		0										2		0				2		0	
Lindsay WA		Grimsby Town	1898	1900	Luton Town	61		1	1		0							62		1				62		1	
Litchfield EB		Bedford Town	1937	1943																	2		0	2		0	
Little J		Crook Town	1927	1928	Southport	3		0										3		0				3		0	
Little R		Jarrow Croft	1912	1919	Hamilton Academicals	3		0										3		0	4		1	7		1	
Littlefair J		Burradon	1900	1902	Local	2		0										2		0				2		0	
Livingstone A		Dundee	1935	1938	Bury	33		5										33		5				33		5	
Lockey J		Willington Athletic	1895	1899	Grimsby Town	3		0										3		0				3		0	
Lockie AJ		Sunderland	1940	1940	*War-time guest*																1		0	1		0	
Logan J	S	Dundee	1895	1896	Loughborough	7		5	2		3							9		8				9		8	
Lormor A		Wallsend BC	1987	1990	Lincoln City	6	2	3										6	2	3				6	2	3	
Loughlin J		Darlington Railway Athletic	1924	1927	West Ham United	12		5										12		5				12		5	
Lovenkrands PR	D	Schalke 04 (G)	2009	2010	*Released*	45	21	22	2	1	3	4		1				51	22	26				51	22	26	
		Free agent	2010	date																							
Low J		Glasgow Rangers	1921	1928	*Retired*	108		8	13		1							121		9				121		9	
Low WL	S	Aberdeen	1909	1924	*Retired, NU trainer*	324		9	43		0							367		9	11		0	378		9	
Lowery J		Parsons Athletic	1947	1952	Lincoln City	6		0										6		0				6		0	
Lowery W		Blyth	1893	1895	Local	28		0	2		0							30		0				30		0	
Lowes T		Wallsend Park Villa	1910	1914	Coventry City	16		3										16		3				16		3	
Lowrie G	W	Coventry City	1948	1949	Bristol City	12		5										12		5				12		5	
LuaLua K		Juniors	2005	date			8	0		4	0	3		0				3	12	0				3	12	0	
LuaLua LT	Cg	Colchester United	2000	2004	Portsmouth	14	45	5		7	0	2	3	0	5	12	4	21	67	9				21	67	9	
Luke GT		Local	1950	1953	Hartlepools United	27		4	2		0							29		4				29		4	
		Hartlepools United	1959	1961	Darlington																						
Luque AM	Sp	Deportivo La Coruna (Sp)	2005	2007	Ajax Amsterdam (N)	6	15	1	1	2	0	1		0	6	3	2	14	20	3				14	20	3	
Macdonald MI	E	Luton Town	1971	1976	Arsenal	187		95	22		14	18		12				227		121	29	1	17	256	1	138	x
MacFarlane A	S	Airdrieonians	1898	1901	Dundee	84		17	2		0							86		17				86		17	
MacKenzie RR		Inverness Clacknacuddin	1922	1935	Gateshead	238		6	18		1							256		7				256		7	
Maguire GT	W	Portsmouth	1991	1991	Portsmouth	3		0										3		0				3		0	
Mahoney MJ		Torquay United	1975	1978	Chicago Stings (USA)	108		0	12		0	13		0	2		0	135		0	3		0	138		0	
Maitland AE		Middlesbrough	1924	1930	Jarrow	156		0	7		0							163		0				163		0	
Makel LR		Hilda Park Jnrs	1987	1992	Blackburn Rovers	6	6	1				1		0				7	6	1		1	0	7	7	1	
Malcolm WGL		Dalkeith Thistle	1957	1960	Raith Rovers	1		0										1		0				1		0	
Manners PJ		Juniors	1977	1979	Seiko Sports (HK)	2		0										2		0				2		0	
Marcelino ES	Sp	RCD Mallorca (Sp)	1999	2003	Polideportivo Ejido (Sp)	15	2	0	2	1	0				2		0	19	3	0				19	3	0	
Maric S	Cr	NK Croatia Zagreb (Cr)	1999	2000	FC Porto (P)	12	11	0	1	3	0	1		0	3		2	17	14	2				17	14	2	

M Player by Player Register

PLAYER	INT	JOINED FROM	YEAR	YEAR	LEFT TO	LEAGUE APP	LEAGUE SUB	LEAGUE GL	FA CUP APP	FA CUP SUB	FA CUP GL	FL CUP APP	FL CUP SUB	FL CUP GL	EUROPE APP	EUROPE SUB	EUROPE GL	TOTAL APP	TOTAL SUB	TOTAL GL	OTHERS APP	OTHERS SUB	OTHERS GL	GRAND TOTAL APP	GRAND TOTAL SUB	GRAND TOTAL GL	
Markie J		Bathgate St Mary's	1962	1964	Falkirk	2		0										2		0				2		0	
Marshall G		Heart of Midlothian	1963	1968	Nottingham Forest	177		0	6		0	4		0				187		0				187		0	
Marshall T		Pembroke	1887	1888					1		0							1		0				1		0	
Marshall TWJ		Wisbech Town	1958	1961	Wisbech Town	5		1										5		1				5		1	
Martin DW		Carlisle United	1977	1978	Mansfield Town	9	2	2										9	2	2				9	2	2	
Martin MP	RoI	West Bromwich Albion	1978	1983	Wolverhampton Wanderers	139	8	5	10		1	6		0				155	8	6				155	8	6	
Martins OA	Ng	Internazionale Milano (I)	2006	2009	VfL Wolfsburg (G)	76	12	28	2		0	4	1	1	7	2	6	89	15	35				89	15	35	
Mathie AM		Morton	1993	1995	Ipswich Town	3	22	4				2	2	0				5	24	4				5	24	4	
Mathison G		Walker Celtic	1926	1933	Lincoln City	20		0	2		0							22		0				22		0	
McBain T		Whifflet Emerald	1932	1932	Carlisle United	1		0										1		0				1		0	
McCaffery A		Juniors	1975	1978	Derby County	57	2	4	5		1	3	1	0	3		0	68	3	5				68	3	5	
McCall W		Aberdeen	1948	1948	Motherwell	16		4										16		4				16		4	
McClarence JP		Wallsend Park Villa	1904	1908	Bolton Wanderers	30		13	2		0							32		13				32		13	
McClen JD		Cramlington Jnrs	1994	2005	Carlisle United	7	7	0	3		1					5	0	10	12	1				10	12	1	
McColl RS	S	Queen's Park	1901	1904	Glasgow Rangers	64		18	3		2							67		20				67		20	
McCombie A	S	Sunderland	1904	1910	*Retired, NU trainer*	113		0	18		0							131		0				131		0	
McCormack CJ		Gateshead	1945	1945	*War-time guest*																1		0	1		0	
McCormack JA		Johnstone	1906	1909	Everton	2		1										2		1				2		1	
McCormack JH		Local	1942	1947																	2		1	2		1	
McCracken WR	NI	Belfast Distillery	1904	1923	*Retired*	377		6	55		2							432		8	12		0	444		8	
McCreery D	NI	Tulsa Roughnecks (USA)	1982	1989	GIF Sundsvall (Se)	237	6	2	10	1	0	15		0				262	7	2	3		0	265	7	2	
McCulloch A		Middlesbrough	1908	1908	Bradford Park Avenue	1		0										1		0				1		0	
McCurdie A		Clydebank	1889	1892	Newcastle West End				5		0							5		0	29		1	34		1	x
McCurley J		Third Lanark	1927	1930	East Fife	43		8	2		0							45		8				45		8	
McDermid R		Dundee Wanderers	1894	1897	Hebburn Argyle	56		2	8		0							64		2				64		2	
McDermott T	E	Bury	1973	1974	Liverpool	129	1	18	12		3	7		2				148	1	23	18		0	166	1	23	x
		Liverpool	1982	1984	*Retired*																						
McDonald J1		Glasgow Ashfield	1895	1899	Lincoln City	6		2										6		2				6		2	
McDonald J2		Liverpool	1912	1914	Raith Rovers	31		4	5		0							36		4				36		4	
McDonald NR		Carlisle United	1982	1988	Everton	163	17	24	10	1	1	12		3				185	18	28	3		0	188	18	28	
McDonald RR		PSV Eindhoven (N)	1988	1989	Besiktas JK (T)	6	4	1	1	3	0							7	7	1	1		1	8	7	2	
McDonald TH		Glasgow Rangers	1921	1931	York City	341		100	26		13							367		113				367		113	
McDonough DK		Luton Town	1992	1994	*Retired*	2	1	0										2	1	0				2	1	0	
McFaul WS	NI	Linfield	1966	1975	*Retired, NU coach/manager*	290		0	22		0	18		0	24		0	354		0	32		0	386		0	x
McGarry RJ		Bolton Wanderers	1962	1967	Barrow	118	3	41	6		3	5		2				129	3	46				129	3	46	
McGhee ME	S	Morton	1977	1979	Aberdeen	86	11	29	8	1	6	5	1	1				99	13	36	3		0	102	13	36	
		Glasgow Celtic	1989	1991	IK Brage (Se)																						
McGough R		Carlisle United	1914	1915	Portsmouth	2		0										2		0				2		0	
McGrath JT		Bury	1961	1968	Southampton	169	1	2	5		0	6		0				180	1	2				180	1	2	
McGuigan JJ		Southend United	1958	1962	Scunthorpe United	50		15	3		1	2		1				55		17				55		17	
McInnes JS		Liverpool	1941	1941	*War-time guest*				3		0										1		0	1		0	
McInnes T	S	Cowlairs	1890	1891	Newcastle West End				3		4							3		4	21		12	24		16	x
McInroy A	E	Sunderland	1929	1934	Sunderland	143		0	17		0							160		0				160		0	
McIntosh A		Wolverhampton Wanderers	1941	1941	*War-time guest*																3		2	3		2	
McIntosh RA		Dundee	1920	1924	Stockport County	101		2	2		0							103		2				103		2	
McIntyre EP		Allendale Park	1900	1906	Fulham	6		1										6		1				6		1	
McKane J		Clydebank	1889	1895	Blyth	41		0	11		0							52		0	44		0	96		0	x
McKay R	S	Glasgow Rangers	1926	1928	Sunderland	62		21	4		1							66		22				66		22	
McKay W		Glasgow Rangers	1895	1897		18		6	3		1							21		7				21		7	
McKellar DN		Hibernian	1986	1986	Hibernian	10		0										10		0				10		0	
McKerrell D		East Fife	1941	1941	*War-time guest*																2		0	2		0	
McKinney WE		Wallsend St Lukes	1956	1965	Bournemouth & BA	85		6	7		1	2		1				94		8				94		8	
McKinnon R	S	Rutherglen Glencairn	1984	1986	Hartlepool United	1		0										1		0				1		0	
McLaughlin H		Sunderland	1889	1890					3		0							3		0	11		4	14		4	
McLean DJ		Juniors	1975	1978	Carlisle United	7	2	0				1		0	1		0	9	2	0				9	2	0	
McMenemy H		Strathclyde Jnrs	1931	1937	Dundee	138		34	10		1							148		35	1		2	149		37	
McMichael A	NI	Linfield	1949	1963	South Shields	402		1	25		0	4		0				431		1	2		0	433		1	
McNamee J		Hibernian	1966	1971	Blackburn Rovers	115	2	8	6		0	1		0	7	1	0	129	3	8				129	3	8	
McNee J		Bolton Wanderers	1894	1895	Gateshead NER	21		4	2		0							23		4				23		4	
McNeil MA		Hibernian	1949	1951	Barnsley	9		0	2		0							11		0				11		0	
McPhillips WP		Musselburgh Bruntonians	1930	1938	Guildford City	33		0	1		0							34		0				34		0	
McQuade G		Annan	1942	1946																	1		0	1		0	
McTavish JK	S	Tottenham Hotspur	1912	1913	Partick Thistle	34		6	5		1							39		7				39		7	
McVay TL		Local	1939	1941																	1		0	1		0	
McWilliam P	S	Inverness Thistle	1902	1911	*Retired*	199		11	41		1							240		12	2		0	242		12	
Meek J		Swansea Town	1939	1942	*War-time guest*																2		2	2		2	
Megson GJ		Nottingham Forest	1984	1985	Sheffield Wednesday	21	3	1	2		1	1	1	0				24	4	2				24	4	2	
Mellor WG		Norwich City	1914	1920		23		0	2		0							25		0	1		0	26		0	
Metcalf A		North Shields Athletic	1909	1912	Liverpool	12		2										12		2				12		2	
Milburn JET	E	Ashington ATC	1943	1957	Linfield	353		177	44		23							397		200	97		38	494		238	x
Milburn JN		Stanley United	1940	1946	Local																1		0	1		0	
Miller Jas (James)		Kilmarnock	1888	1894	Hurlford Town	9		0	12		0							21		0	50		0	71		0	x
Miller Jn1 (John)		Kilmarnock	1889	1890					2		0							2		0	8		3	10		3	
Miller Jn2 (John)		(Glasgow)	1889	1889					1		1							1		1	5		4	6		5	
Miller W		Kilmarnock	1895	1897	Kilmarnock	42		2	6		0							48		2				48		2	
Mills DJ		West Bromwich Albion	1982	1982	West Bromwich Albion	33	6	9					2	0				33	8	9				33	8	9	
		Sheffield Wednesday	1983	1984	Middlesbrough																						
Milne WJ		Rutherford College	1894	1895	Sunderland	6		1										6		1				6		1	
Milner JP	E	Leeds United	2004	2008	Aston Villa	72	22	6	5	3	2	6		1	17	11	2	100	36	11				100	36	11	
"Mirandinha", da Silva FEL	Br	SE Palmeiras (Br)	1987	1989	SE Palmeiras (Br)	47	7	20	4	1	1	4		2				55	8	23	3	1	1	58	9	24	

PLAYER	INT	JOINED FROM	YEAR	YEAR	LEFT TO	LEAGUE APP	LEAGUE SUB	LEAGUE GL	FA CUP APP	FA CUP SUB	FA CUP GL	FL CUP APP	FL CUP SUB	FL CUP GL	EUROPE APP	EUROPE SUB	EUROPE GL	TOTAL APP	TOTAL SUB	TOTAL GL	OTHERS APP	OTHERS SUB	OTHERS GL	GRAND TOTAL APP	GRAND TOTAL SUB	GRAND TOTAL GL	
Mitchell DS	Aus	Chelsea	1991	1991	Chelsea	2		1										2		1				2		1	
Mitchell I		Dundee United	1970	1971	Dundee United	2	1	0	1		1					1	0	3	2	1				3	2	1	
Mitchell K		Juniors	1975	1981	Darlington	61	5	2	5		0		1	0				66	6	2	1		0	67	6	2	
Mitchell RC	S	Third Lanark	1949	1961	Berwick Rangers	367		95	41		18							408		113	2		0	410		113	
Mitchell SA		Benburb Jnrs	1953	1963	Third Lanark	45		0	3		0							48		0				48		0	
Mitchell TM		Spennymoor United	1920	1926	Leeds United	60		5	1		0							61		5				61		5	
Mitten JE		Mansfield Town	1958	1961	Leicester City	9		3				1		0				10		3				10		3	
Mole G		Stockton St Johns	1900	1900	Burnley	1		1										1		1				1		1	
Moncur R	S	Juniors	1960	1974	Sunderland	293	3	3	17		0	10		0	22		4	342	3	7	15		2	357	3	9	x
Monkhouse ATW		Millwall	1953	1956	York City	21		9	2		2							23		11				23		11	
Mooney E		Walker Celtic	1919	1927	Hull City	121		3	14		1							135		4				135		4	
Mooney T		Airdrieonians	1936	1944	Morton	75		17	5		2							80		19				80		19	x
Moore CA	Aus	Borussia Moenchengladbach (G)	2005	2007	Brisbane Roar (Aus)	25		0		1	0	1		0	3	1	0	29	2	0				29	2	0	
Moran P		Tottenham Hotspur	1991	1991	Tottenham Hotspur	1		0										1		0				1		0	
Mordue T		Horden Athletic	1925	1926	Sheffield United	5		2										5		2				5		2	
Mortensen SH	E	Blackpool	1943	1943	*War-time guest*																1		2	1		2	
Moses G		Local	1939	1946	Hartlepools United																9		6	9		6	
Mowatt A		Wallsend Park Villa	1891	1893	Hebburn Argyle	1		0										1		0				1		0	
		Hebburn Argyle	1898	1899	Lincoln City																						
		Lincoln City	1900	1900																							
Muir A		Cheviot	1887	1889					4		1							4		1				4		1	
Muir W		Newcastle Rangers	1885	1891	Rangers (SA)				1		2							1		2				1		2	
Mulgrew T		Northampton Town	1952	1954	Southampton	14		1	1		0							15		1				15		1	
Mulgrove KA		Juniors	1977	1980	Barrow		1	0											1	0					1	0	
Mullen J	E	Wolverhampton Wanderers	1942	1943	*War-time guest*																15		4	15		4	
Mulvey M		Motherwell	1887	1891	Gateshead NER				6		1							6		1	29		5	35		6	x
Murray JJ		Glasgow Rangers	1932	1936	Albion Rovers	92		10	4		0							96		10				96		10	
Mutch A		Huddersfield Town	1922	1924	*Retired, NU groundsman*	36		0	7		0							43		0				43		0	
Myers J		Ferryhill	1940	1941																	1		1	1		1	
Napier CRA		Workington	1965	1966	Brighton & Hove Albion	8		0										8		0				8		0	
Nattrass I		Juniors	1970	1979	Middlesbrough	226	12	16	23		1	22		3	4		0	275	12	20	25	1	2	300	13	22	
Naylor J		Huddersfield Town	1930	1932	Manchester City	30		0	2		0							32		0				32		0	
Neale DF		Ilford	1959	1963	Plymouth Argyle	88		8	6		3	4		1				98		12				98		12	
Neilson AB	W	Juniors	1989	1995	Southampton	35	7	1				4		0				39	7	1	4		0	43	7	1	
Nelson J	S	Cardiff City	1930	1935	Southend United	146		0	13		0							159		0	1		0	160		0	
Nesbit A		Juniors	1985	1987	Seaham Red Star	1	2	0										1	2	0		1	0	1	3	0	
Nesbitt J		South Shields	1955	1959		3		0										3		0				3		0	
Nevin GW		Dipton United	1925	c1925	White-le-Head Rangers	6		0										6		0				6		0	
		White-le-Head Rangers	1928	1930	Sheffield Wednesday																						
Nevins L		Local	1940	1947	Brighton & Hove Albion																33		5	33		5	
Niblo TB	S	Linthouse	1898	1902	Aston Villa	60		4										60		4				60		4	
		Watford	1907	1908	Hebburn Argyle																						
Nicholson B		Morpeth Harriers	1905	1907	Luton Town	1		0										1		0				1		0	
Nicholson GA		Juniors	1978	1981	Mansfield Town	7	5	0	1		0	3		0				11	5	0				11	5	0	
Nicholson WE	E	Tottenham Hotspur	1943	1944	*War-time guest*																19		0	19		0	
Noble P		Consett	1964	1968	Swindon Town	22	3	7										22	3	7				22	3	7	
Nolan KAJ		Bolton Wanderers	2009	2011	West Ham United	84	1	29	3		0	1	2	1				88	3	30				88	3	30	
Nulty GO		Burnley	1974	1978	Everton	101		11	10		1	10		2	2		0	123		14	4		0	127		14	
N'Zogbia CJ	F	Le Havre AC (F)	2004	2009	Wigan Athletic	86	32	9	8	2	0	7	1	1	13	5	1	114	40	11				114	40	11	
Oates G		Blackburn Rovers	1976	1978	Detroit Express (USA)	26	10	3				3		0				29	10	3	4		0	33	10	3	
O'Brien A	RoI	Juniors	2000	2007	Hibernian	1	4	0		3	0					1	0	1	8	0				1	8	0	
O'Brien AJ	RoI	Bradford City	2001	2005	Portsmouth	114	6	6	7	3	1	4	1	0	32	5	0	157	15	7				157	15	7	
O'Brien PG		Sheffield United	1894	1896	Hebburn Argyle	10		2	2		0							12		2				12		2	
O'Brien WF	RoI	Manchester United	1988	1994	Tranmere Rovers	131	22	19	12	2	1	9		1				152	24	21	9		1	161	24	22	
O'Neil LA		Blyth Spartans	1961	1965	Darlington	1		0										1		0				1		0	
O'Neil TH		Spennymoor United	1942	1948	Newport County																1		0	1		0	
O'Neill MAM	NI	Coleraine	1987	1989	Dundee United	36	12	15	3	2	1	2		0				41	14	16	2	1	1	43	15	17	
Onyewu OC	USA	Standard Liege (Bel)	2007	2007	Standard Liege (Bel)	7	4	0										7	4	0				7	4	0	
Orr R	S	St Mirren	1901	1908	Liverpool	160		61	20		9							180		70				180		70	
Osborne F		Aston Villa	1940	1940	*War-time guest*																1		0	1		0	
Ostler J		Motherwell	1896	1900	*Retired*	71		2	7		0							78		2				78		2	
Owen MJ	E	Real Madrid CF (Sp)	2005	2009	Manchester United	58	13	26	5		1	2	1	3				65	14	30				65	14	30	
Owens M		Juniors	1975	1977	Crook Town																1		0	1		0	
Pailor R		West Bromwich Albion	1914	1915	*Retired*	11		2	5		3							16		5				16		5	
Pancrate F		Paris St-Germain (F)	2009	2010	*Released*	5	11	1	3		0							8	11	1				8	11	1	
Papavasiliou N	Cy	OFI (Ct)	1993	1994	OFI (Ct)	7		0										7		0				7		0	
Park JB		Hamilton Academicals	1936	1941	*Retired*	60		11	1		1							61		12	12		2	73		14	
Park O		Darlington Railway Athletic	1924	1931	Northampton Town	42		0	1		0							43		0				43		0	
Parker SM	E	Chelsea	2005	2007	West Ham United	54	1	4	3		1	4		1	9	2	0	70	3	6				70	3	6	
Parkinson AJ	USA	Dynamos United (SA)	1978	1979	Peterborough United		3	0											3	0					3	0	
Parr J		Derby County	1944	1944	*War-time guest*																1		0	1		0	
Paterson TA		Leicester City	1950	1952	Watford	2		0										2		0				2		0	
Paterson WAK		Doncaster Rovers	1954	1958	Glasgow Rangers	22		1	5		1							27		2				27		2	
Paton HD		Clydebank	1921	1922	St Mirren	13		2										13		2				13		2	
Patten JT		Newcastle West End	1892	1897	Hebburn Argyle	1		0										1		0				1		0	
Pattinson D		Willington Athletic	1900	1902	Local	1		1										1		1				1		1	
Pattinson MJ	SA	Redheugh BC	1999	2008	Norwich City	4	6	0	2		0					3	0	6	9	0				6	9	0	
Payne LJ		Barnet	1988	1989	Reading	6	1	0										6	1	0				6	1	0	
Peacock D		Queens Park Rangers	1994	1998	Blackburn Rovers	131	2	2	11		0	13	1	2	16	1	0	171	4	4	1		0	172	4	4	
Peacock GK		AFC Bournemouth	1990	1993	Chelsea	102	3	35	6		2	6		5				114	3	42	3		4	117	3	46	

P-R Player by Player Register

PLAYER	INT	JOINED FROM	YEAR	YEAR	LEFT TO	LEAGUE			FA CUP			FL CUP			EUROPE			TOTAL			OTHERS			GRAND TOTAL			
						APP	SUB	GL	APP	SUB	GL	APP	SUB	GL	APP	SUB	GL	APP	SUB	GL	APP	SUB	GL	APP	SUB	GL	
Pearce S	E	Nottingham Forest	1997	1999	West Ham United	37		0	7		0	2		0	5	1	1	51	1	1				51	1	1	
Pears W		Crook Town	1936	1941		2		0										2		0				2		0	
Pearson JF		Everton	1978	1980	Barrow	11		3		1	0	2		1				13	1	4				13	1	4	
Pearson SC	E	Manchester United	1941	1942	*War-time guest*																5		0	5		0	
Pearson TU	S	Murrayfield Amateurs	1933	1948	Aberdeen	212		46	16		6							228		52	49		8	277		60	x
Peart JG		Stoke	1912	1913	Notts County	17		6										17		6				17		6	
Peddie JH		Third Lanark	1897	1902	Manchester United	126		71	10		5							136		76				136		76	
Penman WST		Glasgow Rangers	1963	1966	Swindon Town	62	1	18	2		0							64	1	18				64	1	18	
Peppitt S		Stoke City	1941	1941	*War-time guest*																2		0	2		0	
Perch JR		Nottingham Forest	2010	date		9	4	0	1		0	1		0				11	4	0				11	4	0	
Phillipson TW		Scotswood	1919	1921	Swindon Town	14		4	1		0							15		4				15		4	
Pingel FM	D	Aarhus GF (D)	1989	1989	Brondby IF (D)	13	1	1										13	1	1				13	1	1	
Pistone A		Internazionale Milano (I)	1997	2000	Everton	45	1	1	8		0	1	1	0	7		0	61	2	1				61	2	1	
Porter L		Redheugh Steelworks	1944	1949	York City																11		2	11		2	
Porter W		Shotton Colliery	1942	1946	Hartlepools United																6		0	6		0	
Price A		Spen Black & White	1939	1944	Consett																43		1	43		1	
Prior KG		Sunderland	1952	1954	Millwall	10		3										10		3				10		3	
		Millwall	1956	1957	Berwick Rangers																						
Pudan AE		Bristol Rovers	1906	1909	Leicester Fosse	24		0	6		0							30		0				30		0	
Pugh KJ		Juniors	1976	1982	Gateshead		1	0											1	0					1	0	
Punton WH		Portadown	1954	1958	Southend United	23		1	2		0							25		1	1		0	26		1	
Pyke GW		Rutherford College	1913	1922	Blyth Spartans	13		3										13		3				13		3	
Quinn C		Local	1893	1894	Manchester City	24		5	2		0							26		5				26		5	
		Manchester City	1895	1896																							
Quinn M		Portsmouth	1989	1992	Coventry City	112	5	59	7		4	7	2	0				126	7	63	6	1	8	132	8	71	
Quinn WR		Sheffield United	2001	2003	West Ham United	14	1	0		1	0	1		0	6	1	1	21	3	1				21	3	1	
Rafferty WH		Wolverhampton Wanderers	1979	1980	Portsmouth	34	5	6	1		0	2		2				37	5	8				37	5	8	
Raine JE		Sheffield United	1905	1906	Sunderland	4		1										4		1				4		1	
Rainnie A		South Shields	1919	1920	Darlington	1		0										1		0				1		0	
Ramage PI		Juniors	2000	2008	Queens Park Rangers	45	6	0	4	1	0	4	1	0	6	2	0	59	10	0				59	10	0	
Ramsay A		(Scotland)	1890	1892	Stockton	1		0										1		0				1		0	
		Stockton	1893	1893	Dundee																						
Ramsay AP		Swalwell	1919	1921	Queens Park Rangers	34		2	3		0							37		2	5		2	42		4	
Randall CE		Hobson Wanderers	1908	1911	Woolwich Arsenal	18		6	1		0							19		6				19		6	
Ranger N		Southampton	2008	date		5	44	2	1	3	0	5		1				11	47	3				11	47	3	
Ranson R		Birmingham City	1988	1993	Manchester City	79	5	1	10		0	4		0				93	5	1	3	1	0	96	6	1	
Raylstone J		Newcastle West End	1886	1889					3		1							3		1				3		1	
Reay H		Shankhouse Black Watch	1891	1893	Everton				6		5							6		5	24		9	30		14	
Redhead WS		George Angus	1954	1959	Gateshead	1		0										1		0				1		0	
Reed FTW		Gateshead	1918	1920																	2		0	2		0	
Reid AD		Dundee United	1971	1973	Morton	15	8	0		2	0							15	10	0	1		0	16	10	0	
Reid O		Rotherham	1895	1896		2		0										2		0				2		0	
Reid W		Kilmarnock	1899	1900	Kilmarnock	4		1										4		1				4		1	
Reilly GG		Watford	1985	1985	West Bromwich Albion	31		10				2		0				33		10				33		10	
Rendell T		Shankhouse Black Watch	1894	1895	Shankhouse Black Watch	23		0	2		2							25		2				25		2	
Richardson EG		South Shields	1922	1923	Huddersfield Town	2		0										2		0				2		0	
Richardson J	Ewt	Blyth Spartans	1929	1945	*Retired, NU trainer*	208		1	15		0							223		1	114		0	337		1	
Richardson JR	E	Blyth Spartans	1928	1934	Huddersfield Town	150		44	13		7							163		51	1		0	164		51	
		Huddersfield Town	1937	1938	Millwall																						
Richardson O		Wallsend Park Villa	1902	1903	Local	1		0										1		0				1		0	
Ridley J		Willington Athletic	1907	1911	Nottingham Forest	17		2										17		2				17		2	
Robert L	F	Paris St-Germain (F)	2001	2005	Portsmouth	110	19	22	10		3	6	1	2	29	6	5	155	26	32				155	26	32	
Roberts RJ		West Bromwich Albion	1901	1904	Middlesbrough	51		17	4		0							55		17				55		17	
Robertson JG	S	Heart of Midlothian	1988	1988	Heart of Midlothian	7	5	0					2	0				7	7	0	2		0	9	7	0	
Robinson DJ		Wallsend BC	1986	1992	Reading		8	0		1	1		1	0					10	1					10	1	
Robinson JA	E	Sheffield Wednesday	1942	1942	*War-time guest*																1		0	1		0	
Robinson JW		Scarborough	1931	1931		1		0										1		0				1		0	
Robinson MJ		Barnsley	1993	1994	Swindon Town	14	11	0	1		0							15	11	0				15	11	0	
Robinson PD		Darlington	1998	2000	Wimbledon	2	9	0					1	0		4	1	2	14	1				2	14	1	
Robinson R		Sunderland	1952	1954		5		0										5		0				5		0	
Robinson RW		Scotswood	1919	1920	Sunderland	27		4	2		0							29		4				29		4	
Robinson SA		Murton Colliery	1975	1980	Aldershot	11	1	2	2		1							13	1	3				13	1	3	
Robledo EO	Ch	Barnsley	1949	1953	CSD Colo-Colo (Ch)	37		0	8		0							45		0	2		0	47		0	
Robledo GO	Ch	Barnsley	1949	1953	CSD Colo-Colo (Ch)	146		82	18		9							164		91	2		0	166		91	
Robson BS		Clara Vale Jnrs	1962	1971	West Ham United	205	1	82	10		4	4		2	24		9	243	1	97				243	1	97	
Robson K		Juniors	1971	1974	West Ham United	14		3				1		2				15		5	3		1	18		6	
Robson R		Parsons Jnrs	1939	1942																	5		1	5		1	
Robson TH		Chelsea	1966	1968	Peterborough United	46	2	11	1		0	1		0				48	2	11				48	2	11	
Roche D		Wallsend BC	1986	1993	Doncaster Rovers	23	13	0	1		0	2		0				26	13	0	1	2	0	27	15	0	
Rodger T		St Johnstone	1893	1895	Local	22		0	2		0							24		0				24		0	
Roeder GV		Queens Park Rangers	1983	1989	Watford	193		8	11		1	11		1				215		10	2		0	217		10	
Rogers E	Wwt	Arsenal	1936	1939	Swansea Town	56		10	2		0							58		10				58		10	
Rogers JJ		Grimsby Town	1898	1901	Preston North End	54		10	3		1							57		11				57		11	
Ross EW	NI	Glentoran	1967	1969	Northampton Town	2		0				2		0				4		0				4		0	
Rossi G	I	Manchester United	2006	2007	Manchester United	3	8	0				2		1				5	8	1				5	8	1	
Routledge WNA		Queens Park Rangers	2010	date		25	9	3	1		0	1		0				27	9	3				27	9	3	
Rowlandson TS		Sunderland	1905	1906	Old Carthusians	1		0										1		0				1		0	
Roxburgh R		Morpeth Comrades	1920	1924	Blackburn Rovers	24		0										24		0				24		0	
Rozehnal DS	CzR	Paris St-Germain (F)	2007	2008	SS Lazio (I)	16	5	0	1	2	0	1		0				18	7	0				18	7	0	
Rush IJ	W	Leeds United	1997	1998	Wrexham	6	4	0		1	1	2		1	1		0	9	5	2				9	5	2	

PLAYER	INT	JOINED FROM	YEAR	YEAR	LEFT TO	LEAGUE APP	LEAGUE SUB	LEAGUE GL	FA CUP APP	FA CUP SUB	FA CUP GL	FL CUP APP	FL CUP SUB	FL CUP GL	EUROPE APP	EUROPE SUB	EUROPE GL	TOTAL APP	TOTAL SUB	TOTAL GL	OTHERS APP	OTHERS SUB	OTHERS GL	GRAND TOTAL APP	GRAND TOTAL SUB	GRAND TOTAL GL	
Rushton G		Shotton Jnrs	1944	1946	Horden CW																1		0	1		0	
Russell SR	NI	Old Park Corinthians	1920	1925	Shelbourne	28		0	3		0							31		0				31		0	
Russell T		Glasgow Rangers	1934	1937	Horden CW	7		0										7		0				7		0	
Rutherford J	E	Willington Athletic	1902	1913	Woolwich Arsenal	290		78	44		14							334		92	2		2	336		94	
Rutherford R		Wallsend St Lukes	1944	1946	Gateshead																19		2	19		2	
Rutherford RE		Local	1905	1906		1		0										1		0				1		0	
Rutherford TV		Scotswood	1938	1940	Ashington																25		0	25		0	
		Ashington	1940	1944																							
Ryan JB		Oldham Athletic	1983	1984	Sheffield Wednesday	28		1	1		0	2		0				31		1				31		1	
Ryder I		Local	1893	1895		1		0										1		0				1		0	
Ryder J		Newcastle West End	1892	1895	Hebburn Argyle	2		0										2		0				2		0	
Saha LL	F	FC Metz (F)	1999	1999	FC Metz (F)	5	6	1	1		1							6	6	2				6	6	2	
Sales RD		Reyrolles	1942	1947	Leyton Orient																42		0	42		0	
Salthouse W		Local	1940	1941																	1		0	1		0	
Sansom KG	E	Arsenal	1988	1989	Queens Park Rangers	20		0	4		0							24		0				24		0	
Saunders W		Juniors	1980	1985	Carlisle United	79		0	6		1	8		0				93		1				93		1	
Sawyers A		Clyde	1889	1889					2		0							2		0	7		0	9		0	
Scanlon AJ		Manchester United	1960	1962	Lincoln City	22		5	4		1	1		0				27		6				27		6	
Scarr R		Chester-le-Street Old Boys	1942	1944																	7		0	7		0	
Scott FH		York City	1945	1945	*War-time guest*																6		1	6		1	
Scott G		South Shields	1929	1930	Gillingham	7		2	3		0							10		2				10		2	
Scott J	S	Hibernian	1967	1970	Crystal Palace	70	4	6	4	1	1	4		0	14	1	5	92	6	12				92	6	12	
Scott JA		Juniors	1976	1980	Berwick Rangers	9	1	0										9	1	0				9	1	0	
Scott JG		Wallsend Slipway	1910	1913	Grimsby Town	8		1										8		1				8		1	
Scott KW		Eppleton CW	1984	1994	Tottenham Hotspur	229		8	15	1	1	18		0				262	1	9	10	2	2	272	3	11	
Scott M		Elswick Rangers	1889	1892	Sunderland				10		0							10		0	42		0	52		0	x
Scott ME		Cleadon Jnrs	1955	1961	Darlington	25		2	1		0							26		2				26		2	
Scott MM	S	Airdrieonians	1900	1901	Airdrieonians	5		0										5		0				5		0	
Scott W		Aberdeen	1938	1946	Consett	6		2	3		0							9		2	7		3	16		5	x
Scott WH		Airdrieonians	1923	1926	*Retired*	4		0										4		0				4		0	
Scoular J	S	Portsmouth	1953	1961	Bradford Park Avenue	247		6	24		0							271		6	1		0	272		6	
Sellars S		Leeds United	1993	1995	Bolton Wanderers	56	5	5	3		0	6	1	2	4		1	69	6	8				69	6	8	
Serrant C		Oldham Athletic	1998	2001	*Retired*	5	1	0								1	0	5	2	0				5	2	0	
Seymour CM		Gateshead	1939	1943	*Demise*																3		0	3		0	
Seymour GS		Morton	1920	1929	*Retired*	242		73	24		11							266		84				266		84	
Shackleton LF	E	Bradford Park Avenue	1946	1948	Sunderland	57		26	7		3							64		29				64		29	
Shankley R		Rutherglen Glencairn	1934	1935	Aldershot	6		0										6		0				6		0	
Shearer A	E	Blackburn Rovers	1996	2006	*Retired*	295	8	148	36		21	15	1	7	49		30	395	9	206	1		0	396	9	206	
Sheedy KM	RoI	Everton	1992	1993	Blackpool	36	1	4	2	1	1	4		0				42	2	5	4		1	46	2	6	
Shepherd A	E	Bolton Wanderers	1908	1914	Bradford City	104		76	19		16							123		92				123		92	
Shiel J		Seahouses	1936	1938	North Shields	1		0										1		0				1		0	
Shinton RT		Manchester City	1980	1982	Millwall	41	1	10	3	1	0	3		0				47	2	10				47	2	10	
Short J		Leeds United	1940	1943	*War-time guest*																43		35	43		35	
Shoulder A		Blyth Spartans	1978	1982	Carlisle United	99	8	35	3	1	1	4	2	2				106	11	38				106	11	38	
Sibierski AC		Manchester City	2006	2007	Wigan Athletic	14	12	3	2		0	1	1	1	8	1	4	25	14	8				25	14	8	
Sibley A		Southend United	1947	1950	Southend United	31		6	1		0							32		6				32		6	
Simm W		Trafalgar	1893	1894	Local	1		0										1		0				1		0	
Simpson DP		Manchester United	2009	date		69		1	2		0	1		0				72		1				72		1	
Simpson N	S	Aberdeen	1990	1991	Motherwell	1	3	0					1	0				1	4	0				1	4	0	
Simpson RC	S	Third Lanark	1951	1960	Hibernian	262		0	33		0							295		0	2		0	297		0	
Simpson TG		Local	1941	1943																	4		0	4		0	
Sinclair JEW	S	Leicester City	1967	1969	Sheffield Wednesday	42	1	6	1	1	0	1		1	4	2	1	48	4	8				48	4	8	
Sinclair TS		Glasgow Rangers	1907	1912	Dumbarton Harp	8		0										8		0				8		0	
Sloan J		Parsons Athletic	1945	1946	Hartlepools United																7		0	7		0	
Sloan SM		Berwick Rangers	1990	1991	Falkirk	11	5	1	1		0							12	5	1	1		0	13	5	1	
Smailes A		Blyth Spartans	1919	1922	Sheffield Wednesday	73		30	4		0							77		30				77		30	
Smallwood F		Reading	1943	1943	*War-time guest*																2		0	2		0	
Smellie RD		Nottingham Forest	1896	1897		26		15	1		0							27		15				27		15	
Smirk AH		Southend United	1940	1940	*War-time guest*																1		0	1		0	
Smith Alan	E	Manchester United	2007	date		68	14	0	5		0	4	1	0				77	15	0				77	15	0	
Smith Ant(hony)		Juniors	1975	1979	Peterborough United	1	1	0										1	1	0	1		0	2	1	0	
Smith D		Reyrolles	1935	1936	South Shields	1		0										1		0				1		0	
Smith Jas (James)	S	Aberdeen	1969	1976	*Retired*	124	5	13	13	1	0	9	1	0	5		0	151	7	13	18	2	3	169	9	16	x
Smith Jk (Jack)		Huddersfield Town	1934	1938	Manchester United	104		69	8		4							112		73				112		73	
Smith Jn (John)		Kilmarnock	1887	1889	Sunderland	25		10	5		0							30		10				30		10	
		Sheffield Wednesday	1894	1896	*Retired*																						
Smith S		Local	1918	1919																	1		0	1		0	
Smith T		Horden CW	1941	1952	Annfield Plain	8		0	2		0							10		0	145		0	155		0	
Smith W		Hibernian	1898	1899		19		6										19		6				19		6	
Solano NAT	Pe	CA Boca Juniors (Ag)	1998	2004	Aston Villa	210	20	37	25		2	15	3	2	37	5	7	287	28	48				287	28	48	
		Aston Villa	2005	2007	West Ham United																						
Soo F	Ewt	Stoke City	1941	1941	*War-time guest*																2		0	2		0	
Sorley J		Newmilns	1891	1893	Middlesbrough	1		1	6		5							7		6	28		21	35		27	x
Soulsby JN		Rodsley	1914	1919	Blyth Spartans	1		0										1		0				1		0	
Soye J		Southampton	1906	1909	Aberdeen	7		2										7		2				7		2	
Speed GA	W	Everton	1998	2004	Bolton Wanderers	206	7	29	22		5	9	2	1	39		5	276	9	40				276	9	40	
Speedie FB	S	Glasgow Rangers	1906	1908	Oldham Athletic	52		13	7		1							59		14	1		0	60		14	
Spence J		Sunderland	1891	1892					5		1							5		1	12		2	17		3	
Spencer CW	E	Washington Chemicals	1921	1928	Manchester United	161		1	14		0							175		1				175		1	
Spike S		Willington Athletic	1940	1942																	3		0	3		0	

S-V Player by Player Register

PLAYER	INT	JOINED FROM	YEAR	YEAR	LEFT TO	LEAGUE APP	LEAGUE SUB	LEAGUE GL	FA CUP APP	FA CUP SUB	FA CUP GL	FL CUP APP	FL CUP SUB	FL CUP GL	EUROPE APP	EUROPE SUB	EUROPE GL	TOTAL APP	TOTAL SUB	TOTAL GL	OTHERS APP	OTHERS SUB	OTHERS GL	GRAND TOTAL APP	GRAND TOTAL SUB	GRAND TOTAL GL	
Spink J		Craghead United	1913	1919	Hartlepools United	20		0	4		0							24		0				24		0	
Spuhler JO		Sunderland	1944	1944	*War-time guest*																2		1	2		1	
Srnicek P	CzR	Banik Ostrava (CzR)	1991	1998	Banik Ostrava (CzR)	149	2	0	11		0	10	1	0	10		0	180	3	0	7		0	187	3	0	
		SC Beira-Mar (P)	2006	2007	*Retired*																						
Starling RW	E	Hull City	1930	1932	Sheffield Wednesday	51		8	2		0							53		8				53		8	
Steel W		Local	1939	1942																	1		0	1		0	
Stenhouse H		Blyth Spartans	1902	1905	Ashington	6		0										6		0				6		0	
Stephenson P		St Marys BC	1984	1988	Millwall	58	3	1	2		0	3	1	0				63	4	1	2		0	65	4	1	
Stevenson J		Derby County	1898	1900	Bristol City	33		12	4		1							37		13				37		13	
Stewart AV		Huddersfield Town	1944	1944	*War-time guest*																2		0	2		0	
Stewart IE	Ni	Queens Park Rangers	1985	1987	Portsmouth	34	8	3	2	1	0	4	1	0				40	10	3				40	10	3	
Stewart J	E	Sheffield Wednesday	1908	1913	Glasgow Rangers	121		49	17		4							138		53				138		53	
Stewart T		Motherwell	1896	1898	Grimsby Town	27		0	3		0							30		0				30		0	
Stewart WG	S	Queen's Park	1901	1903		37		4	4		1							41		5				41		5	
Stimson MN		Tottenham Hotspur	1989	1992	Portsmouth	84	4	2	7		1	5		0				96	4	3	4		0	100	4	3	
Stobbart GC		Middlesbrough	1946	1949	Luton Town	66		21	6		1							72		22				72		22	
Stokoe R		Spen Jnrs	1947	1961	Bury	261		4	26		1							287		5	1		0	288		5	
Stones S		Guisborough	1887	1888					1		0							1		0				1		0	
Stott J		Grimsby Town	1895	1899	Middlesbrough	117		9	14		2							131		11				131		11	
Stubbins A	Ewt	Whitley & Monkseaton	1936	1946	Liverpool	27		5	3		1							30		6	187		231	217		237	x
Suddick A		Chester-le-Street Old Boys	1961	1966	Blackpool	144		41	4		1	4		1				152		43				152		43	
Suggett C		Norwich City	1978	1981	*Retired, NU coach*	20	3	0				1		0				21	3	0				21	3	0	
Surtees J		Nottingham Forest	1941	1942	*War-time guest*																2		2	2		2	
Swan CS		Local	1919	1923	Stockport County	4		0										4		0				4		0	
Sweeney PM		Raith Rovers	1989	1990	St Johnstone	28	8	0	3		0	2	1	0				33	9	0	2		0	35	9	0	
Swinburne TA	Ewt	Herrington Colliery	1934	1947	Consett	77		0	7		0							84		0	48		0	132		0	x
Tait A		Juniors	1952	1960	Bristol City	32		8	2		2							34		10				34		10	
Tapken NH		Wallsend Thermal Welfare	1933	1938	Manchester United	106		0	7		0							113		0	9		0	122		0	
		Manchester United	1942	1943	*War-time guest*																						
Tate IH		Marley Hill	1923	1927	West Ham United	4		0										4		0				4		0	
Tavernier JH		Leeds United/Juniors	2006	date								2		0				2		0				2		0	
Taylor A		North Shields	1925	1926	South Shields	1		0										1		0				1		0	
Taylor C		Walsall	1963	1964	Walsall	33		7				3		0				36		7				36		7	
Taylor E	E	Hylton Colliery Jnrs	1942	1951	Blackpool	107		19	10		2							117		21	26		7	143		28	
Taylor JD		Hylton Colliery	1939	1940																	1		2	1		2	
Taylor JH		Crawcrook	1952	1960	Chelmsford City	28		5	1		0							29		5				29		5	
Taylor PH	E	Liverpool	1941	1942	*War-time guest*																7		0	7		0	
Taylor RA		Wigan Athletic	2009	date		30	16	4	3		0	5		2				38	16	6				38	16	6	
Taylor SV		Juniors	2002	date		137	9	11	9		1	8		0	20	4	1	174	13	13				174	13	13	
Templeton RB	S	Aston Villa	1903	1904	Woolwich Arsenal	51		4	1		1							52		5				52		5	
Thain JW		Pelaw Jnrs	1921	1922	Brentford	1		0										1		0				1		0	
Theaker CA		Grimsby Town	1938	1947	Hartlepools United	13		0	3		0							16		0	65		0	81		0	
Thomas AM		Oxford United	1986	1988	Bradford City	24	7	6	3		1	1		0				28	7	7	1		2	29	7	9	
Thomas EB		Scunthorpe United	1962	1964	Scunthorpe United	73		48	2		1	3		1				78		50				78		50	
Thomas JW		Brighton & Hove Albion	1911	1912	Spennymoor United	1		0										1		0				1		0	
Thomas MR	W	Bristol Rovers	1983	1988	Birmingham City	118		0	5		0	7		0				130		0	1		0	131		0	
Thompson A	E	Juniors	1989	1993	Bolton Wanderers	13	3	0	1		0							14	3	0	3		0	17	3	0	
Thompson F		St Peter's Albion	1923	1925		2		1										2		1				2		1	
Thompson GA		Halesowen	1903	1905	Crystal Palace	1		0	1		0							2		0				2		0	
Thompson H		North Shields Athletic	1908	1910	Crystal Palace	2		0										2		0				2		0	
Thompson JH		Juniors	1950	1957	Lincoln City	8		0										8		0	1		0	9		0	
Thompson M		Local	1939	1941																	2		0	2		0	
Thompson T	E	Lumley YMCA	1946	1950	Aston Villa	20		6										20		6				20		6	
Thompson W		Juniors	1957	1967	Rotherham United	79	1	1	6		0	3		0				88	1	1				88	1	1	
Thompson WK		Shankhouse Black Watch	1889	1897	Jarrow	80		34	19		13							99		47	36		18	135		65	x
Thompson WN		Ashington	1940	1941																	1		0	1		0	
Thomson JA		Petershill Jnrs	1968	1971	Grimsby Town	4	1	0										4	1	0				4	1	0	
Thomson RW	S	Sunderland	1928	1934	Hull City	73		0	7		0							80		0				80		0	
Thorn AC		Wimbledon	1988	1989	Crystal Palace	36		2				4		1				40		3	3		0	43		3	
Tildesley J		Halesowen St John	1903	1906	Middlesbrough	21		0	1		0							22		0				22		0	
Tinlin C		Cheviot	1887	1895	*Retired, NU admin*																1		0	1		0	
Tinn		Local	1888	1889	Local																2		0	2		0	
Tinnion B		Juniors	1984	1989	Bradford City	30	2	2				5		0				35	2	2	1	1	0	36	3	2	
Tiote CI	IC	FC Twente (N)	2010	date		26		1		1	0		1	0				26	2	1				26	2	1	
Todd K		Ryhope CA	1981	1983	Darlington	5	2	3	2	1	0	1		0				8	3	3				8	3	3	
Tomasson JD	D	SC Heerenveen (N)	1997	1998	Feyenoord (N)	17	6	3	2		0	2	1	1	6	1	0	27	8	4				27	8	4	
Tozer BPA		Swindon Town	2008	2011	Northampton Town		1	0				1		0				1	1	0				1	1	0	
Trewick J		West Bromwich Albion	1980	1984	Oxford United	76	2	8	7		0	2		0				85	2	8				85	2	8	
Tudor JA		Sheffield United	1971	1976	Stoke City	161	3	53	14		3	8		1				183	3	57	32	1	15	215	4	72	x
Tuohy W	RoI	Shamrock Rovers	1960	1963	Shamrock Rovers	38		9	1		0	3		0				42		9				42		9	
Turner AD	E	Derby County	1903	1904	Tottenham Hotspur	13		1										13		1				13		1	
Turner DJ		Juniors	1960	1963	Brighton & Hove Albion	2		0				1		0				3		0				3		0	
Urwin T	E	Middlesbrough	1924	1930	Sunderland	188		22	12		1							200		23				200		23	
van Aanholt PJM		Chelsea	2010	2010	Chelsea	7		0										7		0				7		0	
Varadi I		Everton	1981	1983	Sheffield Wednesday	81		39	5		2	4		1				90		42				90		42	
Varty TH		Vickers Works	1940	1945	Darlington																1		0	1		0	
Veitch CCM	E	Rutherford College	1899	1915	*Retired, NU trainer*	276		43	45		6							321		49	1		0	322		49	
Venison B	E	Liverpool	1992	1995	Galatasaray SK (T)	108	1	1	11		0	9		0	1		0	129	1	1	3		0	132	1	1	
Viana HMF	P	Sporting Clube de Portugal (P)	2002	2006	Valencia CF (Sp)	16	23	2		1	0	2		0	10	9	2	28	33	4				28	33	4	
Viduka MA	Aus	Middlesbrough	2007	2009	*Retired*	25	13	7	2		0							27	13	7				27	13	7	

PLAYER	INT	JOINED FROM	YEAR	YEAR	LEFT TO	LEAGUE APP	LEAGUE SUB	LEAGUE GL	FA CUP APP	FA CUP SUB	FA CUP GL	FL CUP APP	FL CUP SUB	FL CUP GL	EUROPE APP	EUROPE SUB	EUROPE GL	TOTAL APP	TOTAL SUB	TOTAL GL	OTHERS APP	OTHERS SUB	OTHERS GL	GRAND TOTAL APP	GRAND TOTAL SUB	GRAND TOTAL GL	
Vuckic H		NK Domzale (Sl)	2009	date			2	0				4	1	0				4	3	0				4	3	0	
Waddle CR	E	Tow Law Town	1980	1985	Tottenham Hotspur	169	1	46	12		4	9		2				190	1	52				190	1	52	
Wake HW		Birtley	1919	1923	Cardiff City	3		0										3		0	1		0	4		0	
Walker AF	S	Glasgow Celtic	1991	1991	Glasgow Celtic	2		0				1		0				3		0				3		0	
Walker L		Spennymoor United	1963	1964	Aldershot	1		0				1		0				2		0				2		0	
Walker NS		Whickham	1977	1982	San Diego Sockers (USA)	65	5	3	3		0	1		0				69	5	3				69	5	3	
Walker TJ		Netherton Jnrs	1941	1954	Oldham Athletic	184		34	20		3							204		37	31		2	235		39	
Wall GH		Perkinsville	1919	1919	*Demise*																1		0	1		0	
Wallace J		Newmilns	1891	1895	Rendel	42		19	8		3							50		22	27		11	77		33	x
Wallace JL		Partick Thistle	1942	1942	*War-time guest*																1		0	1		0	
Walshaw K		Sunderland	1941	1941	*War-time guest*																4		0	4		0	
Warburton J		Local	1894	1895	Hebburn Argyle	3		0										3		0				3		0	
Ward E		Blyth Spartans	1920	1922	Crystal Palace	21		5	4		0							25		5				25		5	
Ward WA		Loughborough	1894	1896		18		0	3		0							21		0				21		0	
Wardrope W		Linthouse	1895	1900	Middlesbrough	131		48	14		7							145		55				145		55	
Ware H		Stoke City	1935	1937	Sheffield Wednesday	44		9	5		0							49		9				49		9	
Watkin G		Chopwell	1962	1963	King's Lynn	1		0										1		0				1		0	
Watson J		Clyde	1902	1903	New Brompton	3		0										3		0				3		0	
Watson JF		Bury	1941	1941	*War-time guest*																1		0	1		0	
Watson JI		Wallsend BC	1990	1993	Scunthorpe United		1	0											1	0		1	0		2	0	
Watson P		Newmilns	1891	1893	Rotherham Town				2		0							2		0	16		0	18		0	x
Watson R		Garton Villa	1889	1890					1		0							1		0	9		0	10		0	
Watson SC		Wallsend BC	1989	1998	Aston Villa	179	29	12	13	4	0	10	6	1	14	3	1	216	42	14	4	1	0	220	43	14	
Watters J		Glasgow Celtic	1941	1941	*War-time guest*																2		1	2		1	
Watts C		Burton Wanderers	1896	1906	*Retired, NU trainer*	93		0	8		0							101		0				101		0	
Waugh K		Film Renters	1952	1956	Hartlepools United	7		0										7		0				7		0	
Waugh R		Newcastle Bentonians	1908	1912	Derby County	11		1										11		1				11		1	
Wayman C		Spennymoor United	1941	1947	Southampton	47		32	6		4							53		36	71		35	124		71	
Weaver S	E	Hull City	1929	1936	Chelsea	204		41	25		2							229		43	1		0	230		43	
Westwood RW	E	Bolton Wanderers	1939	1939	*War-time guest*																1		3	1		3	
Wharton K		Grainger Park BC	1978	1989	*Retired*	268	22	26	22		0	13	2	1				303	24	27	6		0	309	24	27	
White AH		Newcastle Rangers	1882	1892	*Retired*				3		1							3		1	8		3	11		4	x
White J		Clyde	1896	1898	Dundee	48		1	5		0							53		1				53		1	
White LR		Rotherham United	1953	1962	Huddersfield Town	244		142	22		11	3		0				269		153	1		0	270		153	
Whitehead R		Fatfield	1954	1962	Darlington	20		0										20		0				20		0	
Whitehurst W		Hull City	1985	1986	Oxford United	28		7	1		0	1	1	0				30	1	7				30	1	7	
Whitson TT		Walker Parish	1905	1919	Carlisle United	124		0	21		0							145		0	1		0	146		0	
Whittle E		Quaking House Jnrs	1944	1946	Seaham CW																1		0	1		0	
Whitton D		Newcastle West End	1892	1893	Shankhouse Black Watch				1		0							1		0	10		0	11		0	
Wilkinson J		Sheffield Wednesday	1930	1932	Lincoln City	30		7	2		0							32		7				32		7	
Wilkinson JM		Crook Town	1927	1929	Everton	27		11										27		11				27		11	
Williams R	W	Swansea Town	1933	1935	Chester	35		14	1		0							36		14				36		14	
Williamson MJ		Portsmouth	2010	date		44	1	0	1		0	1	1	0				46	2	0				46	2	0	
Willis DL		Sunderland	1907	1913	Reading	95		3	12		1							107		4	1		0	108		4	
Willis R		Shankhouse Black Watch	1893	1895	Shankhouse Black Watch	34		18	2		0							36		18				36		18	
Willitts J		Shotton CW	1941	1943	Local																1		0	1		0	
Wills T		Ayr	1903	1906	Crystal Palace	18		0	1		0							19		0				19		0	
Wilson CA		Delves Lane Jnrs	1958	1959	Gateshead	1		0										1		0				1		0	
Wilson GW	S	Everton	1907	1919	Raith Rovers	176		25	41		8							217		33	1		0	218		33	
Wilson J		Shotts Bon Accord	1959	1962	Morton	12		2				1		0				13		2				13		2	
Wilson JA		Tanfield Lea Institute	1933	1936	Brighton & Hove Albion	28		5	2		0							30		5				30		5	
Wilson JH		Newcastle Bentonians	1912	1914	North Shields Athletic	3		0	1		0							4		0				4		0	
Wilson JT		Leadgate United	1919	1920	Leadgate Park	7		2										7		2	2		1	9		3	
Wilson JW		Stanley United	1927	1930	Southend United	1		0										1		0				1		0	
Wilson T		Nottingham Forest	1992	1992	Nottingham Forest	2		0										2		0				2		0	
Wilson WA1		Newcastle West End	1890	1892					6		0							6		0	29		0	35		0	x
Wilson WA2		Juniors	1919	1922	Merthyr Town																2		0	2		0	
Wilson WS		Walkerburn Jnrs	1960	1962	Gala Fairydene							1		0				1		0				1		0	
Wilson W1		Peebles Rovers	1925	1929	Millwall	127		0	7		0							134		0				134		0	
Wilson W2		South Shields Athletic	1900	1903	Bradford City	4		0										4		0				4		0	
Winstanley G		Juniors	1964	1969	Carlisle United	5	2	0	1		0				1		0	7	2	0				7	2	0	
Withe C		Juniors	1979	1983	Bradford City	2		0										2		0				2		0	
Withe P	E	Nottingham Forest	1978	1980	Aston Villa	76		25	4		2	3		0				83		27				83		27	
Wood EE		Rhyl Athletic	1928	1930		9		0										9		0				9		0	
Wood GA		Blucher United	1944	1946																	7		0	7		0	
Wood L		Science & Art	1889	1890	Science & Art																1		0	1		0	
Woodburn J		Coltness United	1938	1948	Gateshead	44		4	3		0							47		4	45		4	92		8	x
Woodgate JS	E	Leeds United	2003	2004	Real Madrid CF (Sp)	28		0	2		0				7		0	37		0				37		0	
Woods CMP		Cleator Moor Celtic	1959	1962	Bournemouth & BA	26		7	3		3	1		0				30		10				30		10	
Woods H		South Shields	1922	1923	Arsenal	14		2	2		0							16		2				16		2	
Woods PB		Bedewell	1943	1945	Hartlepools United																16		0	16		0	
Woollard AJ	Bm	Peterborough United	1952	1956	Bournemouth & BA	8		0	2		0							10		0				10		0	
Woollett C		Eppleton CW	1941	1946	Bradford City																75		13	75		13	
Wright BG		Juniors	1956	1963	Peterborough United	45		1	1		0	1		0				47		1				47		1	
Wright JD	E	Southend United	1938	1948	Lincoln City	72		1	10		0							82		1	23		0	105		1	x
Wright TJ	NI	Linfield	1988	1993	Nottingham Forest	75	1	0	4		0	6		0				85	1	0	1		0	86	1	0	
		Manchester City	1999	1999	Manchester City																						
Wright WJ		Leicester City	1958	1959	Plymouth Argyle	5		3										5		3				5		3	
Wrightson JG		Wallsend BC	1985	1987	Preston North End	3	1	0										3	1	0				3	1	0	
"Xisco", Jiminez Tejada F		Deportivo La Coruna (Sp)	2008	date		3	6	1	1		0		1	0				4	7	1				4	7	1	
Yeats J		Whitehall Jnrs	1940	1942																	4		0	4		0	
Young D		Juniors	1964	1973	Sunderland	41	2	2				4		0	5	1	0	50	3	2	2	1	0	52	4	2	
Young P			1890	1891																	1		0	1		0	
Young W		Kilmarnock	1888	1889					4		1							4		1				4		1	

Player appearances & goals relating to completed void and aborted fixtures

(In addition to the overall player schedule and indicated by 'x')

1890-91 v Newcastle West End (2 fixtures), Darlington St Augustine's (Northern League, declared as friendlies)

App: McCurdie A 3, McKane J 3, Miller Jas 3, Scott M 3, Thompson WK 3, Wallace J 3, Watson P 3, Wilson WA 3, Collins J 2, Creilly R 2, McInnes T 2, Mulvey M 1, Sorley J 1, White AH 1.
Goals: Collins J 2, Creilly R 2, McInnes T 2, Thompson WK 2, Mulvey M 1, Sorley J 1, Wallace J 1, White AH 1.

1939-40 v Millwall, Nottingham Forest, Swansea Town (FL Div 2, aborted season)

App: Ancell RFD 3, Bowden ER 3, Craig B 3, Denmark J 3, Scott W 3, Swinburne TA 3, Woodburn J 3, Cairns WH 2, Hamilton DS 2, Pearson TU 2, Wright JD 2, Birkett RJE 1, Gordon J 1, Mooney T 1, Stubbins A 1.
Goals: Bowden ER 3, Pearson TU 2, Cairns WH 1, Hamilton DS 1, Scott W 1.

1943-44 v Darlington (FL North, the Tyne-Wear-Tees Cup 'Golden Goal' not classed as first-class)

Goals: Milburn JET 1.

1973-74 v Nottingham Forest (FAC6, annulled by the FA)

App: 1 each; Barrowclough SJ, Clark FA, Craig DJ, Hibbitt TA, Howard P, Kennedy AP (sub app), Macdonald MI, McDermott T, McFaul WS, Moncur R, Smith Jas, Tudor JA.
Goals: 1 each; Craig DJ, McDermott T, Moncur R, Tudor JA.

Players selected as substitute in a first-class fixture, but not to have made their senior debut

Barrett PD (1996-97)
Caig T (2002-03, 03-04, 04-05, 05-06)
Caldwell GR (S) (1999-00)
Clarke DL (1968-69), Cormack P (1992-93)
Donaldson RM (2010-11)
Doninger M (2008-09)
Drysdale J (1994-95)
Elliott ST (1996-97, 97-98)
Forster FG (2006-07, 07-08, 08-09)
Gate K (2005-06)
Green S (1999-00, 2001-02)
Hallam D (1987-88)
Inman B (2008-09, 09-10)
Johnson T (1968-69)
Keen PA (1995-96, 98-99)
Keidel R (1997-98)
Melling T (1965-66)
Murray NA (1992-93)
Ngo Baheng WC (2009-10)
Orr BJ (2003-04)
Perez LPA (1998-99, 99-00)
Pinas B (1997-98)
Reid B (1993-94)
Richardson MS (2010-11)
Soderberg OP (2009-10, 2010-11)
Steele EG (1972-73, 73-74)
Terrier D (1997-98)
Troisi J (Aus) (2006-07)
Tunks RW (1974-75)
Wiafe Danquah F (2008-09)

Three nearly men in United colours
Top to bottom;
Goalkeeper Tony Caig, Gary Caldwell and Bradley Orr. Caldwell ended up appearing for Scotland alongside his brother Steven.

A first-class fixture or not?

United's FA Cup 6th Round tie against Nottingham Forest in 1974 was completed, a thrilling 4-3 victory. But the Football Association ordered a replay due to a crowd invasion when Forest were ahead. John Tudor dives to head a dramatic equaliser (right). Bob Moncur in joyous celebration with Macdonald (right) after grabbing the winner.

Two replays took place, both at Goodison Park. United eventually won again by 1-0.

United 4 Forest 3

Managers & Coaching Staff

Like many football clubs during the first 50 years or so of the game, affairs on the pitch at Newcastle United were largely managed by a Director's Committee and the Club Secretary, with senior players and the trainer also influential in team matters. United did not employ a manager until 1930 when Andy Cunningham was appointed. Even then, the post was far from the role football is accustomed to now. For another 30 years directors still held much control over the appointed boss, especially on transfer policy and even on team selection. When Joe Harvey was engaged in 1962 he could be termed the club's first autonomous manager with 'full control' of playing affairs – although of course every manager had a master, in Newcastle United's case, a sometimes difficult hierarchy.

The summary of the club's Managers & Coaching Staff include Caretaker Managers and it should be noted that in periods between managers departing and being appointed such temporary posts – usually taken by the first-team coach – are during a phase of change and unrest with the duties of the manager carried out by several individuals, including the directors. Even when a new manager arrived, sometimes the caretaker boss actually selected the team before the new man took charge completely.

Over the years many former players have moved from the dressing-room to a training or coaching role in various capacities. For much of football's past, coaches were referred to as trainers and were largely focussed on keeping the players fit, rather than tactical football matters. In modern football, managers have a whole team of backroom staff including assistant-managers, tactical coaches and fitness trainers as well as a physio and medical team. United's senior trainer/coach year by year is summarised together with assistant trainer/coaches who were on the staff during each season and who generally looked after the reserve and junior sides. Included are those individuals in charge of the recent Academy set-up, but not the wider coaching staff at the Little Benton complex.

Andy Cunningham

As a player north of the border, Andy Cunningham was one of the elite. A Rangers legend, at inside-forward he graced the field as a tall, commanding midfielder in almost 450 games. Winning no fewer than seven title and three Scottish Cup medals, he was a regular for his country. Well into his thirties, Newcastle saw his experience and know-how as the ideal candidate to become the club's first manager. He arrived on Tyneside during February 1929 still as a player – making his debut in English football at the age of 39 years old – and was in January of 1930 appointed boss as well. Cunningham had to not only try and forge a United side that had lost its way after League Championship success in 1927, but also cope with a Board of Directors who were loathe to relinquish control of team affairs, and which did not do so for another 30 years. Retiring from playing in the summer of 1930, the Scot started well, overcoming the difficulties of losing star asset Hughie Gallacher, to guide United from the bottom reaches of the First Division then to Wembley victory in 1932. It looked as though Andy had combined a good balance of wise heads and youthful promise in his Magpie side, but very quickly his plans fell apart. Within 12 months of FA Cup triumph the Magpies went through their worst season up to then, being relegated in 1934. Cunningham's stay at St James' Park was afterwards not to be long. He departed in May 1935 when he moved back to Scotland becoming a respected journalist for many a year.

Born Galston.
Manager, 1930 to 1935, 249 games.

Manager Register

	Manager	Appointed	Departed	Span	Games	First match				Result
	Committee/Director Committee	1881	Jan 1930							
1	**Cunningham AN**	Jan 1930	May 1935	5y 4m 22d	249g	11 Jan 1930	York City	H	FAC	D1-1
2	**Mather T**	June 1935	Oct 1939	4y 3m 26d	179g	31 Aug 1935	Bradford PA	H	Div 2	D3-3
	Seymour GS (Director, in a Honorary post)	Oct 1939	May 1947							
3	**Martin GS**	May 1947	Dec 1950	3y 6m 20d	154g	26 May 1947	West Ham Utd	H	Div 2	L2-3
	Seymour GS (Director, in a Honorary post)	Dec 1950	Dec 1954							
4	**Livingstone D**	Dec 1954	Jan 1956	1y 28d	58g	1 Jan 1955	Sheffield Utd	A	Div 1	L2-6
	Director Committee	Jan 1956	June 1958							
5	**Mitten C**	June 1958	Oct 1961	3y 4m 1d	150g	23 Aug 1958	Blackburn Rvs	H	Div 1	L1-5
	Director Committee	Oct 1961	Nov 1961							
6	**Smith N**	Nov 1961	June 1962	6m 9d	25g	25 Nov 1961	Stoke City	A	Div 2	L1-3
7	**Harvey J**	June 1962	June 1975	13y 0m 10d	628g*	18 Aug 1962	Cardiff City	A	Div 2	D4-4
8	**Lee GF**	June 1975	Jan 1977	1y 7m 13d	84g	16 Aug 1975	Ipswich Town	A	Div 1	W3-0
9	**Dinnis RR**	Feb 1977	Nov 1977	9m 6d	41g	5 Feb 1977	Bristol City	A	Div 1	D1-1
	McFaul WS (caretaker)	Nov 1977	Nov 1977		(1g)					
10	**McGarry WH**	Nov 1977	Aug 1980	2y 9m 11d	126g	19 Nov 1977	Arsenal	H	Div 1	L1-2
	Harvey J (caretaker)	Aug 1980	Sept 1980		(3g)					
11	**Cox A**	Sept 1980	June 1984	3y 8m 16d	181g*	13 Sept 1980	QPR	A	Div 2	W2-1
12	**Charlton J**	June 1984	Aug 1985	1y 1m 30d	48g	25 Aug 1984	Leicester City	A	Div 1	W3-2
	McFaul WS (caretaker)	Aug 1985	Sept 1985		(7g)					
13	**McFaul WS**	Sept 1985	Oct 1988	3y 1m 25d	148g*	17 Aug 1985	Southampton	A	Div 1	D1-1
	Suggett C (caretaker)	Oct 1988	Dec 1988		9g					
14	**Smith JM**	Dec 1988	Mrch 1991	2y 3m 21d	121g	10 Dec 1988	Wimbledon	H	Div 1	W2-1
	Saxton R (caretaker)	Mrch 1991	Mrch 1991		1g					
15	**Ardiles OC**	April 1991	Feb 1992	10m 3d	46g	1 April 1991	Bristol Rovers	H	Div 2	L0-2
16	**Keegan JK**	Feb 1992	Jan 1997	4y 11m 3d	272g*	8 Feb 1992	Bristol City	H	Div 2	W3-0
	McDermott T/Cox A (caretakers)	Jan 1997	Jan 1997		(2g)					
17	**Dalglish KM**	Jan 1997	Aug 1998	1y 7m 10d	77g	18 Jan 1997	Southampton	A	PL	D2-2
	Craig TB/Irvine AJ (caretakers)	Aug 1998	Aug 1998		1g					
18	**Gullit RD**	Aug 1998	Aug 1999	11m 28d	51g	9 Sept 1998	Aston Villa	A	PL	L0-1
	Clarke S (caretaker)	Aug 1999	Aug 1999		1g					
19	**Robson RW**	Sept 1999	Aug 2004	4y 11m 27d	255g	11 Sept 1999	Chelsea	A	PL	L0-1
	Carver JW (caretaker)	Sept 2004	Sept 2004		1g					
20	**Souness GJ**	Sept 2004	Feb 2006	1y 4m 20d	83g	16 Sept 2004	Hapoel BS	A	UEFAC	W2-0
	Roeder GV (caretaker, with Craig TB)	Feb 2006	May 2006		(17g)					
21	**Roeder GV**	May 2006	May 2007	1y 3m 4d	73g*	4 Feb 2006	Portsmouth	H	PL	W2-0
	Pearson NG (caretaker)	May 2007	May 2007		(1g)					
22	**Allardyce S**	May 2007	Jan 2008	7m 25d	24g	11 Aug 2007	Bolton Wand	A	PL	W3-1
	Pearson NG (caretaker)	Jan 2008	Jan 2008		3g*					
23	**Keegan JK**	Jan 2008	Sept 2008	7m 19d	(22g)	19 Jan 2008	Bolton Wand	H	PL	D0-0
	Hughton CWG (caretaker)	Sept 2008	Sept 2008		(3g)					
24	**Kinnear JP**	Sept 2008	Feb 2009	4m 12d	22g	27 Sept 2008	Blackburn Rvs	H	PL	L1-2
	Hughton CWG (caretaker)	Feb 2009	Mrch 2009		(5g)					
25	**Shearer A**	April 2009	May 2009	1m 23d	8g	4 April 2009	Chelsea	H	PL	L0-2
	Hughton CWG (caretaker)	May 2009	Oct 2009		(16g)					
26	**Hughton CWG**	Oct 2009	Dec 2010	1y 6m 11d	78g*	8 Aug 2009	WBA	A	Ch	D1-1
	Beardsley PA/Stone SB (caretakers)	Dec 2010	Dec 2010		0g					
27	**Pardew AS**	Dec 2010	to date		23g	11 Dec 2010	Liverpool	H	PL	W3-1

Notes:

Total games are for senior competitive matches only and allow for fixtures where the appointed manager may not have selected the team during periods with a caretaker boss.

Total games include second periods as manager (indicated*), and any additional spells as caretaker boss.

Periods as manager do not include isolated spans as caretaker manager, but do include periods when a caretaker role developed into a full-time position.

The appointments of Norman Smith (6), Joe Kinnear (24) and Alan Shearer (25) were short-term posts.
Kinnear's period in charge was curtailed due to illness.

Richard Dinnis (9) and Kevin Keegan (16) were initially appointed on a short-term basis and thereafter as permanent manager.

Alan Pardew's games are up to the end of the 2010-11 season.

Managerial & Coaching staff: season by season

Season	Manager	Coach/Trainer & Asst Manager	Asst Coach/Trainer & Other Coaching/Football staff	Physio
1881-82	Committee			
1882-83	Committee			
1883-84	Committee			
1884-85	Committee			
1885-86	Committee			
1886-87	Committee			
1887-88	Committee	TJ Dodds		
1888-89	Committee	TJ Dodds		
1889-90	Dir Committee	TJ Dodds		
1890-91	Dir Committee	TJ Dodds, W Bayles	H Nelson	
1891-92	Dir Committee	W Bayles		
1892-93	Dir Committee	W Bayles	J Pears	
1893-94	Dir Committee	W Bayles	J Pears, D Veitch	
1894-95	Dir Committee	W Bayles, H Kirk	J Pears	
1895-96	Dir Committee	J Pears	H Kirk	
1896-97	Dir Committee	W Leach	H Kirk, H Ryder	
1897-98	Dir Committee	TJ Dodds	H Ryder	
1898-99	Dir Committee	TJ Dodds	H Ryder	
1899-00	Dir Committee	TJ Dodds	J Harvey	
1900-01	Dir Committee	TJ Dodds		
1901-02	Dir Committee	TJ Dodds		
1902-03	Dir Committee	TJ Dodds	T Ghee	
1903-04	Dir Committee	JQ McPherson(s)	T Ghee	
1904-05	Dir Committee	JQ McPherson(s)	T Ghee	
1905-06	Dir Committee	JQ McPherson(s)	T Ghee	
1906-07	Dir Committee	JQ McPherson(s)	T Ghee, C Watts	
1907-08	Dir Committee	JQ McPherson(s)	T Ghee, C Watts	
1908-09	Dir Committee	JQ McPherson(s)	T Ghee, G Hardy	
1909-10	Dir Committee	JQ McPherson(s)	T Ghee, G Hardy	
1910-11	Dir Committee	JQ McPherson(s)	T Ghee, A McCombie	
1911-12	Dir Committee	JQ McPherson(s)	T Ghee, A McCombie	
1912-13	Dir Committee	JQ McPherson(s)	T Ghee, A McCombie, J Carr	
1913-14	Dir Committee	JQ McPherson(s)	T Ghee, A McCombie, J Carr	
1914-15	Dir Committee	JQ McPherson(s)	T Ghee, A McCombie, J Carr, CCM Veitch	
1915-16	Dir Committee	JQ McPherson(s)		
1916-17	Dir Committee	JQ McPherson(s)		
1917-18	Dir Committee	JQ McPherson(s)		
1918-19	Dir Committee	JQ McPherson(s)		
1919-20	Dir Committee	JQ McPherson(s)	A McCombie, J Carr, AA Gosnell, CCM Veitch	
1920-21	Dir Committee	JQ McPherson(s)	A McCombie, J Carr, AA Gosnell, CCM Veitch	
1921-22	Dir Committee	JQ McPherson(s)	A McCombie, J Carr, CCM Veitch	
1922-23	Dir Committee	JQ McPherson(s)	A McCombie, CCM Veitch	
1923-24	Dir Committee	JQ McPherson(s)	A McCombie, CCM Veitch	
1924-25	Dir Committee	JQ McPherson(s)	A McCombie, WL Low, CCM Veitch	
1925-26	Dir Committee	JQ McPherson(s)	A McCombie, WL Low, CCM Veitch	
1926-27	Dir Committee	JQ McPherson(s)	A McCombie, WL Low	
1927-28	Dir Committee	JQ McPherson(s), A McCombie	WL Low, J Finlay, JQ McPherson(s)	
1928-29	Dir Committee	A McCombie	WL Low, J Finlay, JQ McPherson(s)	
1929-30	Dir Committee/ AN Cunningham	A McCombie	WL Low, JQ McPherson(j), JQ McPherson(s), J Finlay	
1930-31	AN Cunningham	JQ McPherson(j)	A McCombie, JQ McPherson(s)	
1931-32	AN Cunningham	JQ McPherson(j)	A McCombie, JQ McPherson(s)	
1932-33	AN Cunningham	JQ McPherson(j)	A McCombie, A Mutch(j)	
1933-34	AN Cunningham	JQ McPherson(j)	A McCombie, A Mutch(j)	
1934-35	AN Cunningham	JQ McPherson(j)	A McCombie, A Mutch(j)	
1935-36	T Mather	JQ McPherson(j)	A McCombie, A Mutch(j)	
1936-37	T Mather	JQ McPherson(j)	A McCombie, A Mutch(j)	
1937-38	T Mather	H Bedford, A McCombie	A Mutch(j)	
1938-39	T Mather	N Smith	A McCombie, A Mutch(j)	
1939-40	Dir Committee	N Smith	A McCombie, A Mutch(j)	
1940-41	Dir Committee	N Smith	A McCombie, A Mutch(j)	
1941-42	Dir Committee	N Smith	A McCombie, A Mutch(j)	
1942-43	Dir Committee	N Smith	A McCombie, A Mutch(j)	
1943-44	Dir Committee	N Smith	A McCombie, A Mutch(j)	
1944-45	Dir Committee	N Smith	A McCombie, A Mutch(j)	
1945-46	Dir Committee	N Smith	A McCombie, A Mutch(j)	
1946-47	Dir Committee	N Smith	A McCombie, J Richardson, A Mutch(j)	
1947-48	GS Martin	N Smith	A McCombie, J Richardson, A Mutch(j)	
1948-49	GS Martin	N Smith	A McCombie, J Richardson, A Mutch(j)	
1949-50	GS Martin	N Smith	A McCombie, J Richardson, A Mutch(j)	
1950-51	Dir Committee	N Smith	A McCombie, J Richardson, B Craig, A Mutch(j)	
1951-52	Dir Committee	N Smith	J Richardson, B Craig, A Mutch(j)	
1952-53	Dir Committee	N Smith	J Richardson, B Craig, A Mutch(j)	
1953-54	Dir Committee	N Smith	J Richardson, B Craig, A Mutch(j), J Harvey	
1954-55	Dir Committee/ D Livingstone	N Smith	J Richardson, B Craig, A Mutch(j), J Harvey	
1955-56	D Livingstone/ Dir Committee	N Smith	J Richardson, B Craig, A Mutch(j)	
1956-57	Dir Committee	N Smith	J Richardson, B Craig, A Mutch(j)	
1957-58	Dir Committee	N Smith	J Richardson, B Craig	A Mutch(j)
1958-59	C Mitten	N Smith	J Richardson, B Craig	A Mutch(j)
1959-60	C Mitten	N Smith	J Richardson, B Craig	A Mutch(j)
1960-61	C Mitten	N Smith	J Richardson, B Craig	A Mutch(j)
1961-62	C Mitten, N Smith	N Smith	J Richardson, B Craig	A Mutch(j)
1962-63	J Harvey	N Smith, JR Greenhalgh	J Richardson, B Craig	A Mutch(j)
1963-64	J Harvey	JR Greenhalgh	J Richardson, B Craig	A Mutch(j)

James McPherson

Serving Newcastle United for almost 30 years, Jimmy McPherson was the old style of football trainer in days before managers and coaches as such. Originally from Fife, McPherson spent the early part of his sporting career as an athlete, then with Kilmarnock as their trainer. From a large footballing family, he is related to three noted Scottish players of that time, and later his own offspring also entered the coaching side of the game while he was to be related by marriage to another footballer, Edwin Dutton who appeared for Germany. James was appointed United trainer in the close season of 1903 and played an important role in the rise of the Magpies to become England's finest side during the Edwardian era. The Scot became the man to look after the players more than any other in United's hierarchy, possessing a character which created harmony in the dressing-room. His influence was huge and the Black'n'Whites went onto lift four titles and reach six FA Cup finals under McPherson's shrewd and sharp guidance. Full of wit and tact, he retired from first-team duties in January 1928, but remained associated with the club behind the scenes as masseur to his death in 1932. His son, James (Jnr) survived him as United's trainer and was part of another FA Cup success in 1932.

Born Coupar.
Trainer, 1903 to 1928.

Norman Smith

One of Huddersfield Town's fringe players as they won a treble of successive League Championship victories in the Twenties, Norman Smith was solid wing-half as a player. Also on the sidelines with Sheffield Wednesday as they won two titles, he moved to Queens Park Rangers then to Switzerland as a coach in 1932, one of several Englishmen to teach the game in Europe before the war. The appointment of Stan Seymour as director in the close season of 1938 saw the arrival of Smith as United's trainer, Seymour's right-hand man for two decades to follow. He was a key part of the club's backroom staff as United regained their glory, first securing promotion, then lifting a headlining treble of FA Cup victories in the first half of the Fifties decade. Norman became a stand-in manager after Charlie Mitten was sacked in October 1961 and as the club struggled in the aftermath of relegation. Smith retired during the summer of 1962 on the appointment of Joe Harvey as boss after 24 years with the Magpies. United's Duggie Graham was his son-in-law.

Born Newcastle upon Tyne.
Trainer & Manager 1938 to 1962.

eason	Manager	Coach/Trainer & Asst Manager	Asst Coach/Trainer & Other Coaching/Football staff	Physio
964-65	J Harvey	JR Greenhalgh	J Richardson, B Craig	A Mutch(j)
965-66	J Harvey	JR Greenhalgh	J Richardson, B Craig	A Mutch(j)
966-67	J Harvey	RD Lewin	J Richardson, B Craig	A Mutch(j)
967-68	J Harvey	RD Lewin	KH Burkinshaw, DB Smith, J Richardson, B Craig	A Mutch(j)
968-69	J Harvey	DB Smith	KH Burkinshaw, J Richardson, B Craig	A Mutch(j)
969-70	J Harvey	DB Smith	KH Burkinshaw, J Richardson, B Craig, GB Allen	A Mutch(j)
970-71	J Harvey	DB Smith	KH Burkinshaw, GB Allen, J Richardson, B Craig	A Mutch(j)
971-72	J Harvey	KH Burkinshaw	GB Allen, J Richardson, B Craig, K Oliver	A Mutch(j)
972-73	J Harvey	KH Burkinshaw	GB Allen, J Richardson, B Craig, K Oliver	A Mutch(j)
973-74	J Harvey	KH Burkinshaw	GB Allen, J Richardson, B Craig, K Oliver	A Mutch(j)
974-75	J Harvey	KH Burkinshaw	RD Lewin, GB Allen, J Richardson, B Craig	A Mutch(j)
975-76	GF Lee	RR Dinnis	RD Lewin, WS McFaul, GB Allen, B Craig	A Mutch(j)
976-77	GF Lee, RR Dinnis	RR Dinnis, WS McFaul	WS McFaul, G Herd, D Woodfield, GB Allen, B Craig	A Mutch(j)
977-78	RR Dinnis, WH McGarry	WS McFaul, PJ Morris	WS McFaul, GB Allen, F Spraggon, B Craig	A Mutch(j), B Collins
978-79	WH McGarry	PJ Morris	WS McFaul, GB Allen, B Craig	B Collins
979-80	WH McGarry	WS McFaul	GB Allen, B Craig	B Collins
980-81	WH McGarry, A Cox	WS McFaul	GB Allen, C Suggett, B Craig	B Collins
981-82	A Cox	TH Cavanagh	WS McFaul, C Suggett, B Craig	B Collins
982-83	A Cox	TH Cavanagh	WS McFaul, C Suggett	I Liversedge
983-84	A Cox	WS McFaul	C Suggett	I Liversedge
984-85	J Charlton	J Harvey, WS McFaul	C Suggett	D Wright
985-86	WS McFaul	J Harvey, C Suggett	IJ Hughes	D Wright
986-87	WS McFaul	J Harvey, C Suggett	J Pickering	D Wright
987-88	WS McFaul	J Harvey, J Pickering	C Suggett	D Wright
988-89	WS McFaul, JM Smith	R Saxton, J Pickering	C Suggett	D Wright
989-90	JM Smith	R Saxton	C Suggett, MP Martin	D Wright
990-91	JM Smith, OC Ardiles	R Saxton, A Galvin	DW Fazackerly, C Suggett, MP Martin	D Wright
991-92	OC Ardiles, JK Keegan	A Galvin, T McDermott, DW Fazackerly	C Suggett	D Wright
992-93	JK Keegan	T McDermott, DW Fazackerly	C Suggett, JCP Anderson, J Montgomery(G)	D Wright
993-94	JK Keegan	T McDermott, DW Fazackerly	A Cox, C McMenemy, C Suggett, JD Clarke, J Montgomery(G)/ J Burridge(G)	D Wright, PJ Ferris
994-95	JK Keegan	T McDermott, DW Fazackerly	A Cox, C McMenemy, JD Clarke, J Burridge(G)	D Wright, PJ Ferris
995-96	JK Keegan	T McDermott, DW Fazackerly, C McMenemy	A Cox, JD Clarke, J Burridge(G)/PP Bonetti(G)	D Wright, PJ Ferris
996-97	JK Keegan, KM Dalglish	T McDermott, C McMenemy	MT Lawrenson, JW Carver, AJ Irvine, PP Bonetti(G)	D Wright, PJ Ferris
997-98	KM Dalglish	T McDermott, T Burns	JW Carver, C McMenemy, AJ Irvine, TW Gennoe(G)	D Wright, PJ Ferris
998-99	KM Dalglish, RD Gullit	S Clarke, JW Carver	T McDermott, TB Craig, TW Gennoe(G), AJ Irvine(A)	D Wright, PJ Ferris
999-00	RD Gullit, RW Robson	G Milne, S Clarke, M Wadsworth, JW Carver	TB Craig, K Wharton, S Smith(G), AJ Irvine(A)	D Wright, PJ Ferris
2000-01	RW Robson	M Wadsworth	TB Craig, JW Carver, K Wharton, S Smith(G), AJ Irvine(A), G Milne(DoF)	D Wright, PJ Ferris
2001-02	RW Robson	JW Carver	D Geddis, TB Craig, K Wharton, S Smith(G), AJ Irvine(A), G Milne(DoF)	D Wright, PJ Ferris
2002-03	RW Robson	JW Carver	D Geddis, TB Craig, K Wharton, S Smith(G), G Milne(DoF), PA Beardsley(A)	D Wright, PJ Ferris
2003-04	RW Robson	JW Carver	D Geddis, TB Craig, K Wharton, S Smith(G), G Milne(DoF), B Eastick(A)	D Wright, PJ Ferris
2004-05	RW Robson, GJ Souness	JW Carver, A Murray, DN Saunders	P Boersma, TB Craig, K Wharton, S Smith(G)/RW Tunks(G), B Eastick(A), JW Carver(A)	D Wright, PJ Ferris
2005-06	GJ Souness, GV Roeder	A Murray, DN Saunders, A Shearer	T McDermott, TB Craig, RW Tunks(G)/A Sadler(G), GV Roeder(A)	D Wright, PJ Ferris
2006-07	GV Roeder	KJ Bond, NG Pearson	T McDermott, LR Clark, TW Gennoe(G), JP Joyce(A)	D Wright, K Bell
2007-08	S Allardyce, JK Keegan	NG Pearson, SJ Round	CWG Hughton, LR Clark, A Cox, T McDermott, TW Gennoe(G)/PG Barron(G), DF Wise(DoF), JP Joyce(A)	D Wright, J Murphy, D Henderson
2008-09	JK Keegan, JP Kinnear, A Shearer	CWG Hughton, I Dowie	A Cox, C Calderwood, PG Barron(G), DF Wise(DoF), JP Joyce(A), R Money(A)	D Wright, D Henderson
2009-10	CWG Hughton	C Calderwood	A Thompson, PG Barron(G), JP Joyce(A), R Money(A)	D Wright, D Henderson
2010-11	CWG Hughton, AS Pardew	C Calderwood, JW Carver	SB Stone, W Donachie, PG Barron(G)/AJ Woodman(G), JP Joyce(A)	D Wright, D Henderson

Notes:

n recent years where United have operated an Academy, the director or manager is included in the 'Assistant Coach' classification (indicated by A). Other coaches t the Academy are not included.

Prior to the Academy, the club's junior sides were looked after by Assistant Trainers/Coaches noted in the schedule. In addition, the incorporation f the N's within the club during 1948 saw a manager appointed to act alongside coaches. Ted Hughes fulfilled this role from 1948 to c1962.

Noted posts are for whole or part of the season.

Committee/Dir (Director) Committee, indicates the seasons when no manager was appointed and the Board of Directors (and Club Committee in earliest years) ppointed a *Selection Committee* to carry out the role of picking teams as well as the buying and selling players.

n earlier years the position of physio was usually taken by one of the Assistant Trainers with the assistance of the appointed Club Doctor.

Specific Abbreviations:

A) = Academy director or manager, Asst = Assistant, (DoF) = Director of Football role, (G) = goalkeeping coach,

j) = junior, (s) = senior, Span; 2y 3m 5d = 2 years 3 months 5 days.

Arthur Cox, led United to promotion and was later assistant to Kevin Keegan.

Sir Bobby Robson in tactical discussion with coach John Carver who was previously on United's books as a player.

Sir Bobby Robson

In an age of high profile managers, few were as respected as Bobby Robson. A fine wing-half as a player reaching England recognition during the Fifties, he served Fulham and West Bromwich Albion with distinction before moving into management at Craven Cottage during 1968. He became a noted boss with Ipswich, then with England before a successful career on the Continent with Porto, Sporting Clube, PSV and Barcelona. From County Durham and a household of Newcastle United supporters, although he left the region as a teenager, he never forgot his roots and was delighted when appointed United boss in September 1999. Knighted in 2002, he had to quickly repair a broken club. Robson did so in marvellous style, taking the Black'n'Whites back to the upper reaches of the Premier League and into the Champions League with an attractive line-up full of star quality. For five years he guided the Magpies, becoming revered and distinguished, yet, the axe fell on Sir Bobby too. In August 2004 he was controversially sacked after a poor start to the new season. Robson received much backing afterwards and became the game's iconic father figure. On several occasions he battled against cancer, sadly in 2009 he died of the disease. Tributes were overwhelming, the sign of his immense standing in football. His name lives on, *The Bobby Robson Foundation*, a well-known and active charity raising substantial sums. He earned the CBE as well as the Freedom of Newcastle, Ipswich and the City of Durham.

Born Sacriston.
Manager, 1999 to 2004, 255 games.

Corporate Newcastle United

For a century Newcastle United were controlled at the top by generation after generation of directors either linked by family or friendship way back to when the club first became a limited company as Newcastle East End in 1890. Over that period, ownership and control of the Magpies have been restricted to holders of the 2,000 ten-shilling shares, with the Board of Directors empowered to accept or reject the transfer or sale of such shares. It was in many respects a closed-shop until Sir John Hall's takeover as the 1990s opened, when, ironically the new ownership of Newcastle United was held by substantially one family.

While the club was run by a Board of Directors, much power was left in the hands of a dedicated Chairman. He was the authority behind Newcastle United and over generations, the Chairman's seat has been occupied by several colourful characters, often linked by family association. Past names with a major say in how the Black'n'Whites were run include the Bell, Oliver, Rutherford, Seymour and McKeag families, as well as Lord Westwood and his father.

By the end of the 1980s, Newcastle United's continued mediocrity in the football world – languishing in the second-tier – was the focus of a rebellion against the archaic regime of the club. With the emergence of big money into the game, something had to change in the hot-spot that was St James' Park. The Magpie Group was formed to create that change, to challenge the somewhat antiquated ownership and a bitter share-war for control of the Black'n'Whites raged for three years and more. Huge sums of money exchanged hands for the limited and now valuable share certificates. John Hall (later Sir John) led the crusade, and with his financial acumen eventually completed a full-blown takeover of the club. By the time the Premiership had been formed for the 1992-93 season, Newcastle United were ready to be dramatically transformed and join the modern elite. A new wave of football money swilled through the game as the Millennium opened and in 2007 this brought Mike Ashley north to initially buy-out the Cameron-Hall stake in the club and acquire all other shares soon after.

At the heart of Newcastle United for a century and more has been the Club's Secretary, the man who held the administrative controls. The name of Frank Watt figures prominently, both father and son, having served in the post with merit for almost 55 years. Russell Cushing was another long serving Secretary to control much of the Club's affairs for over three decades.

The summary of United's directors and officials include all those individuals to have held a position in the Boardroom as committee member, director, or as Secretary over the 130 years. Also included are modern posts of Chief Executive and the like. A separate table schedules the directors and officials of Newcastle United plc for the period the company was quoted on the Stock Exchange.

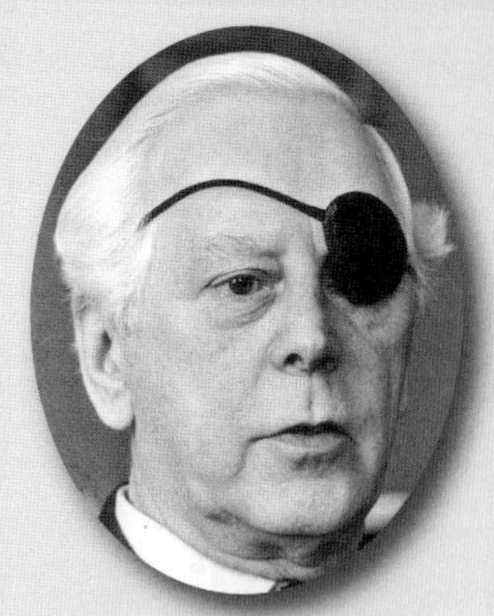

Lord Westwood, a powerful figure at St James' Park during the 60s and 70s era.

United's Board of Directors proudly display the Inter Cities Fairs Cup at their AGM at the County Hotel. Left to right: RR Mackenzie, WB Taylor, GS Seymour, JD Barker (Secretary), Lord Westwood (Chairman), RJ Rutherford, W McKeag, J Rush, F Braithwaite.

Club Names & Ownership

Newcastle United evolved from Stanley Football Club and have twice altered their title, to East End FC, then Newcastle United FC. The schedules below indicate the key dates of such changes together with the ultimate ownership status to the present day.

Names & Company Status

1881-1882	Stanley FC	Private organisation founded November 1881
1882-1890	East End FC	Name change October 1882. Private organisation
1890-1892	Newcastle East End Football Company Limited	Limited Company approved 11th March 1890
1892-date	Newcastle United Football Company Ltd	Name change December 1892, officially authorised 6th November 1895

Parent Company

1990	Newcastle United Limited	Formed August 1990
1990-1992	Newcastle United PLC	October 1990
1992-1997	Newcastle United Limited	July 1992
1997-2008	Newcastle United PLC	February 1997
2008-date	Newcastle United Limited	February 2008

Ownership status

		Owner	
1881-1890	Run by Committee	Not applicable	
1890-1992	Private company; Shareholders	Shareholders of 2,000, ten shilling (50p) original shares	7,987,936 new shares issued during 1990/91
1992-1997	Private company; Cameron-Hall (Sir John Hall & family) with majority stake	Sir John Hall & family	Majority control completed May 1992
1997-2007	Public quoted company on the London Stock Exchange, Newcastle United PLC	Shareholders of 133,107,121 shares	PLC status completed April 1997
2007-date	Private company; St James Holdings Limited	MJW Ashley	Reverted to private ownership July 2007

Mike Ashley, present-day owner of Newcastle United.

Jnited's original investors

 the Victorian years between the late 1880s and early 1890s there as a surge in the game's evolution and several clubs initially ecame fully professional and then rapidly developed into business entures complete with limited company status, including capital vestments, shareholders, boards of directors as well as yearly profit nd loss accounts and balance sheets. Newcastle East End were to e at the forefront of what was something of a corporate xperiment in the game.

he first of the present-day football clubs in England to try this orporate route was Small Heath (now Birmingham City). In 1888 hey became incorporated as a limited company, Small Heath ootball Club Ltd. It took a few years for the majority of clubs to ollow their lead but, in 1890, four clubs took the same gamble: otts County, Grimsby Town as well as East End and their rivals in lewcastle, West End. Several other clubs soon followed in the oming years including Everton, Liverpool, Preston North End, olton Wanderers and West Bromwich Albion. Middlesbrough were nother who did so although Sunderland did not become a limited ompany until 1906.

n Tyneside, East End were the first to take the plunge. Two neetings were held at Dr Rutherford's Infant School on Shields oad in Byker during January 1890 to make the transformation. lub secretary, Charles Tinlin, suggested forming a company by ssuing 2,000 shares at 10s 0d (50p) each, capital of £1,000. It was oted the cost would "suit the working classes who are the chief supporters of the institution". He proposed that extensive changes were needed within the club. Some £150 would have to be raised to put their ground in order and a further £100 to establish a really good team! It was further proposed that a Board of Management should be appointed consisting of between eight and twelve members holding at least five shares each.

Within a month, on 17th February, a public meeting was convened at the Leighton Schoolrooms on Heaton Road to launch the share issue and the Newcastle East End Football Company Limited formally came into being. Councillor James Birkett chaired the meeting and around 50 shares were sold in the first instance, over 70 by the end of the first month, and by the close of the season the total had risen substantially. By May, the company was able to hold its first Annual General Meeting when Adam Gilchrist was elected Chairman.

Among those first shareholders were, not surprisingly, prominent East Enders. All are logged in the surviving original East End share-ledger. East End's first director list, and in essence Newcastle United's first Board, was led by Gilchrist and consisted of: James Birkett, Alec White, James Peel, Matt Hiscock, John Dixon and Bill Woodman along with William Hudson, John Steel, Thomas Liddle, William Henry, William Richardson and John Armstrong. The qualification to become a director was that "he shall be a shareholder to the amount of £2 10s at least". Their occupations varied from that of a clerk to a pattern-maker and ironfounder. All resided in the Byker and Heaton area.

No. 24 Share Certificate. Five Shares.

The Newcastle United Football COMPANY, LIMITED.

Incorporated under "The Companies Acts, 1862 to 1890."

This is to Certify that Wm Robinson Hudson of 47 Bond St Newcastle is the Registered Proprietor of Five Shares of 10/- each, numbered 86 to 90 inclusive, in The Newcastle United Football Company, Limited, subject to the Memorandum and Articles of Association and Regulations of the said Company, and that there has been paid up in respect of each of such Shares the full sum of Ten Shillings.

Given under the Common Seal of the said Company, the 11th day of July 189

Secretary. Directors.

N.B.—This Certificate must accompany any transfer of these Shares lodged at the Company's Office for Registration.

One of the early Share Certificates as issued following the change to limited company status in 1890.

The first 18 shareholders

lewcastle United's first registered investors during the share launch in February 1890 totalled 18 different individuals who purchased 1 shares at an investment of £35 10s 0d (£35 50p). These residents, of again predominantly Byker and Heaton, are scheduled below. further 17 enthusiasts committed to acquiring 64 shares in March with 40 sales following during April and May. By the end of that nonth 75 people had collectively purchased 277 of the 2,000 shares on offer at an investment of £138 10s 0d (£138 50p). There was one ady shareholder, Mary Amelia Laing, the wife of engineer Christopher Laing, also a shareholder.

Birkett, James	Heaton Park Rd, Heaton	Ironfounder	1 share (10s 0d)
Cameron, John	Jesmond Vale Tce, Heaton	Commercial Traveller	10 shares (£5 0s 0d)
Cameron, Daniel	Holmside Place, Heaton	Clothier	5 shares (£2 10s 0d)
Cameron, James	Jesmond Vale Tce, Heaton	Clothier	5 shares (£2 10s 0d)
Cranston, James	Norfolk Rd, Byker	Porter	2 shares (£1 0s 0d)
Coburn, James	Shields Rd, Byker	Painter	2 shares (£1 0s 0d)
Dix, Walter	Tynemouth Rd, Heaton	Engineer	2 shares (£1 0s 0d)
Foggo, John	Langhorn St, Heaton	Gentleman	4 shares (£2 0s 0d)
Gent, Charles Frederick	Shields Rd, Byker	Tobacconist	2 shares (£1 0s 0d)
Liddle, Thomas	Ouseburn Glass Works	Glass manufacturer	6 shares (£3 0s 0d)
Liddle, John Walker	Heaton Grove, Heaton	Glass manufacturer	2 shares (£1 0s 0d)
Neylon, James Joseph	Wilfred St, Byker	Manager	10 shares (£5 0s 0d)
Peel, James Edward	Cardigan Tce, Heaton	Clerk	10 shares (£5 0s 0d)
Richardson, William John	Addison St, Heaton	Patternmaker	1 share (10s 0d)
Steel, John	Malcolm St, Heaton	School Attendance Officer	5 shares (£2 10s 0d)
Spence, Henry George	Chillingham Rd, Heaton	Plater	2 shares (£1 0s 0d)
White, Alexander Henry	Mowbray St, Heaton	Schoolmaster	1 share (10s 0d)
Waters, James	Albert St, Shieldfield	Compositor	1 share (10s 0d)

One of the original shareholders of the club, Walter Dix who also was a pioneer footballer on Tyneside.

The Newcastle United Sporting Club

For a short period in the club's recent history Newcastle United attempted to broaden their activities by forming the *Newcastle United Sporting Club.* Formed during the mid-1990s it was planned to encompass various sports other than football along the model successfully achieved in Europe and North America. Apart from the core football business, soon to be added were basketball, ice-hockey and rugby clubs. All were rebranded, and all sported colours of black-and-white. In addition United formed a venture in a health club operation, known as *Livingwell at Newcastle United.*

Ice Hockey In May 1995 Durham Wasps were purchased and somewhat controversially relocated and renamed as the Newcastle Cobras with a new base at Tyneside's Telewest Arena.

Basketball Formally the Sunderland Scorpions and Newcastle Comets, the club was secured in 1995 and branded the Newcastle Eagles.

Rugby Union A controlling interest in Newcastle Gosforth RFC was acquired in September 1995 and the club renamed Newcastle Falcons. Their stadium at Kingston Park was for a time used by the football club's reserve eleven.

Although on-the-field success was seen as the Falcons, led by Rob Andrew, became English Champions, lifting the Allied Dunbar Premiership in 1998, the overall financial equation for the Sporting Club never worked. The concept was short-lived and prior to Newcastle United's stock-market flotation in 1997, it was separated from the core football business and soon disbanded and sold off.

Rob Andrew was Director of Rugby at the Falcons in the 1990s.

Season	Chairman	Directors	Secretary
1881-82	*untraced*	Committee; WA Coulson & others *untraced*	W Findlay
1882-83	*untraced*	Committee; *untraced*	JP Cook
1883-84	*untraced*	Committee; J Broughton, R Cook, E Elliott, J Fenwick, J Speight, W Wilson	JP Cook
1884-85	JT Oliver(Pr)	Committee; *untraced*	MK Hiscock
1885-86	JT Oliver(Pr)	Committee; *untraced*	C Gray
1886-87	JT Oliver(Pr)	Committee; AP Arnold, D Crawford, R Crawford & others *untraced*	C Gray/WA Coulson
1887-88	JT Oliver(Pr)	Committee; J Birkett, D Crawford, R Crawford, C Fenwick, E Elliott, WJ Richardson	WA Coulson/C Tinlin
1888-89	*untraced*	Committee; *untraced*	T Watson/C Tinlin
1889-90	AB Gilchrist	J Armstrong, J Birkett, J Dixon, W Henry, MK Hiscock, WR Hudson, T Liddle, JE Peel, WJ Richardson, J Steel, AH White, W Woodman	J Steel/C Tinlin
1890-91	AB Gilchrist	J Armstrong, J Birkett, J Dixon, W Henry, MK Hiscock, WR Hudson, T Liddle, JE Peel, WJ Richardson, J Steel, A Turnbull, AH White, W Woodman	J Steel/WH Golding
1891-92	A Turnbull	J Bell, T Bell, J Cameron, T Carmichael, J Dixon, G Forster, WR Hudson, J Patterson, JE Peel	WH Golding/ JJ Neylon
1892-93	A Turnbull	J Bell, J Black, W Bramwell, J Cameron, J Dixon, J Graham, WR Hudson, R Johnson, GT Milne, G McConachie, D McPherson, JE Peel, J Telford, W Nesham	WH Golding/ JE Peel
1893-94	A Turnbull/ D McPherson	J Bell, T Bell, J Black, W Bramwell, John Cameron, James Cameron, M Carmichael, J Graham, WR Hudson, GT Milne, G McConachie, J Telford, W Nesham	J Dixon/ WJ Robinson/ JJ Neylon
1894-95	D McPherson/ J Cameron	J Bell, T Bell, J Black, W Bramwell, M Carmichael, J Graham, GT Milne, WR Hudson, G McConachie, A Turnbull, J Telford, W Nesham	JJ Neylon/ JS Ferguson
1895-96	W Nesham	J Bell, J Black, W Bramwell, J Cameron, M Carmichael, J Graham, GT Milne, G McConachie, D McPherson, J Telford, A Turnbull	JS Ferguson/WH Golding/ FG Watt(s)
1896-97	W Nesham	GG Archibald, J Bell, J Black, W Bramwell, J Cameron, M Carmichael, J Graham, J Lunn, GT Milne, G McConachie, WJ Sanderson, J Telford, A Turnbull	FG Watt(s)
1897-98	W Nesham	GG Archibald, JR Auld, J Bell, J Black, W Bramwell, J Cameron, M Carmichael, J Graham, J Lunn, GT Milne, G McConachie, J Telford, A Turnbull	FG Watt(s)
1898-99	W Nesham	GG Archibald, JR Auld, J Bell, J Black, W Bramwell, J Cameron, A Fox, J Graham, J Lunn, GT Milne, J Telford, A Turnbull	FG Watt(s)
1899-00	W Nesham	GG Archibald, JR Auld, J Bell, W Bramwell, J Cameron, A Fox, J Graham, J Lunn, GT Milne, J Telford, A Turnbull, L Zollner	FG Watt(s)
1900-01	W Nesham/ J Telford	GG Archibald, JR Auld, J Bell, J Cameron, A Fox, J Graham, J Lunn, A Turnbull, W Bramwell, GT Milne, L Zollner	FG Watt(s)
1901-02	W Nesham/ J Telford	GG Archibald, JR Auld, J Bell, W Bramwell, J Cameron, A Fox, J Graham, J Lunn, GT Milne, L Zollner	FG Watt(s)
1902-03	J Telford	GG Archibald, JR Auld, J Bell, W Bramwell, J Cameron, A Fox, J Graham, J Lunn, GT Milne, JP Oliver, L Zollner	FG Watt(s)
1903-04	J Telford	GG Archibald, JR Auld, J Bell, W Bramwell, J Cameron, A Fox, J Graham, J Lunn, GT Milne, JP Oliver, L Zollner	FG Watt(s)
1904-05	J Cameron	GG Archibald, JR Auld, J Bell, W Bramwell, D Crawford, J Graham, J Lunn, GT Milne, JP Oliver, R Oliver	FG Watt(s)
1905-06	J Cameron	GG Archibald, JR Auld, SF Bates, J Bell, JW Bell, W Bramwell, D Crawford, J Graham, GT Milne, J Lunn, RW Mackenzie, JP Oliver, R Oliver	FG Watt(s)
1906-07	J Cameron	GG Archibald, SF Bates, J Bell, JW Bell, D Crawford, J Graham, J Lunn, GT Milne, RW Mackenzie, JP Oliver, R Oliver	FG Watt(s)
1907-08	J Cameron	GG Archibald, SF Bates, J Bell, JW Bell, W Bramwell, D Crawford, J Graham, J Lunn, GT Milne, RW Mackenzie, JP Oliver, R Oliver	FG Watt(s)
1908-09	J Bell	GG Archibald, SF Bates, W Bramwell, J Cameron, D Crawford, J Graham, W Lilburn, J Lunn, RW Mackenzie, GT Milne, JP Oliver, R Oliver	FG Watt(s)
1909-10	J Lunn	GG Archibald, SF Bates, W Bramwell, J Cameron, D Crawford, J Graham, W Lilburn, GT Milne, RW Mackenzie, JP Oliver, R Oliver	FG Watt(s)
1910-11	J Lunn	GG Archibald, SF Bates, W Bramwell, J Cameron, D Crawford, J Graham, W Lilburn, GT Milne, RW Mackenzie, JP Oliver, R Oliver	FG Watt(s)
1911-12	GT Milne	GG Archibald, SF Bates, W Bramwell, J Cameron, D Crawford, J Graham, J Lunn, W Lilburn, RW Mackenzie, R Oliver, JP Oliver	FG Watt(s)
1912-13	GT Milne	GG Archibald, SF Bates, W Bramwell, J Cameron, D Crawford, J Graham, J Lunn, W Lilburn, RW Mackenzie, R Oliver, JP Oliver	FG Watt(s)
1913-14	GG Archibald	SF Bates, W Bramwell, J Cameron, D Crawford, J Graham, W Lilburn, J Lunn, GT Milne, RW Mackenzie, JP Oliver, R Oliver	FG Watt(s)
1914-15	GG Archibald	SF Bates, W Bramwell, J Cameron, D Crawford, J Graham, W Lilburn, J Lunn, GT Milne, RW Mackenzie, JP Oliver, R Oliver	FG Watt(s)
1915-16	J Graham	GG Archibald, SF Bates, W Bramwell, J Cameron, D Crawford, W Lilburn, J Lunn, RW Mackenzie, GT Milne, JP Oliver, R Oliver	FG Watt(s)
1916-17	J Graham	GG Archibald, SF Bates, W Bramwell, J Cameron, D Crawford, W Lilburn, J Lunn, RW Mackenzie, GT Milne, JP Oliver, R Oliver, RS Stewart	FG Watt(s)
1917-18	J Graham	GG Archibald, SF Bates, W Bramwell, D Crawford, W Lilburn, J Lunn, RW Mackenzie, GT Milne, JP Oliver, R Oliver, RS Stewart	FG Watt(s)
1918-19	J Graham/ JP Oliver	GG Archibald, SF Bates, W Bramwell, D Crawford, W Lilburn, J Lunn, RW Mackenzie, R Oliver, RW Simpson, RS Stewart	FG Watt(s)
1919-20	JP Oliver	GG Archibald, SF Bates, W Bramwell, D Crawford, J Graham, W Lilburn, J Lunn, RW Mackenzie, R Oliver, RW Simpson, RS Stewart	FG Watt(s)
1920-21	JP Oliver	SF Bates, W Bramwell, D Crawford, J Graham, W Lilburn, J Lunn, RW Mackenzie, R Oliver, RW Simpson, RS Stewart	FG Watt(s)
1921-22	JP Oliver	SF Bates, W Bramwell, D Crawford, J Graham, W Lilburn, J Lunn, RW Mackenzie, R Oliver, RW Simpson, RS Stewart,	FG Watt(s)
1922-23	JP Oliver	SF Bates, W Bramwell, D Crawford, J Graham, W Lilburn, J Lunn, RW Mackenzie, RW Nevin, R Oliver, RW Simpson, RS Stewart	FG Watt(s)
1923-24	JP Oliver	SF Bates, W Bramwell, D Crawford, J Graham, J Lunn, RW Mackenzie, RW Nevin, R Oliver, RW Simpson, RS Stewart	FG Watt(s)
1924-25	JP Oliver	SF Bates, D Crawford, J Graham, J Lewis, J Lunn, RW Nevin, RW Mackenzie, R Oliver, RW Simpson, RS Stewart	FG Watt(s)
1925-26	JP Oliver	SF Bates, D Crawford, J Graham, J Lunn, RW Mackenzie, RW Nevin, T Oliver, GF Rutherford, RW Simpson, RS Stewart	FG Watt(s)
1926-27	JP Oliver	SF Bates, D Crawford, J Graham, J Lunn, RW Mackenzie, RW Nevin, T Oliver, GF Rutherford, RW Simpson, RS Stewart	FG Watt(s)
1927-28	JP Oliver	SF Bates, D Crawford, J Graham, J Lunn, RW Mackenzie, RW Nevin, T Oliver, GF Rutherford, RW Simpson	FG Watt(s)
1928-29	D Crawford/ JP Oliver	SF Bates, J Graham, J Lunn, RW Mackenzie, RW Nevin, T Oliver, GF Rutherford, RW Simpson	FG Watt(s)
1929-30	J Lunn	SF Bates, D Crawford, J Graham, RW Mackenzie, W Molineux, RW Nevin, T Oliver, GF Rutherford, R Rutherford, RW Simpson	FG Watt(s)

George Milne was a noted Tynesider, a director of the club while his son William appeared for United on six occasions.

James Lunn

Associated with Newcastle United as a shareholder and Board member for over 45 years, James Lunn was perhaps typical of the club's directorate for a century. From a distinguished Newcastle family, related to Sir George Lunn who was a prominent Novocastrian too, a liberal politician and Lord Mayor of Newcastle. James ran a Building Contracting business, was a Councillor, and purchased shares in 1895, joining the Board of Directors a year later. Lunn was a prominent voice in all things Newcastle United during much of the club's pre-war success story. He became Chairman in two spells, firstly in 1909 for a short period before the Great War, then again in 1928 for a much longer spell of unbroken seasons up to the Second World War. On the Board as the club lifted four Football League titles and reached no fewer than seven FA Cup finals, he was then in the Chair when the Magpies were relegated for the first time in 1934. James was appointed Sheriff of Newcastle in 1922, remaining connected with the Black'n'Whites to his death.

Born Newcastle upon Tyne.
Director & Chairman, 1896 to 1941.

John Graham was a long-serving director and enthusiastic supporter of Tyneside football since earliest years.

eason	Chairman	Directors	Secretary
930-31	J Lunn	RB Bennie, J Graham, W Molineux, RW Nevin, T Oliver, GF Rutherford, R Rutherford, RW Simpson	FG Watt(s)
931-32	J Lunn	RB Bennie, J Graham, W Molineux, RW Nevin, T Oliver, GF Rutherford, R Rutherford, RW Simpson	FG Watt(s)/ FG Watt(j)
932-33	J Lunn	RB Bennie, J Graham, W Molineux, RW Nevin, T Oliver, GF Rutherford, R Rutherford, RW Simpson	FG Watt(j)
933-34	J Lunn	RB Bennie, J Graham, W Molineux, RW Nevin, T Oliver, GF Rutherford, R Rutherford, RW Simpson	FG Watt(j)
934-35	J Lunn	RB Bennie, JW Lee, W Molineux, RW Nevin, T Oliver, GF Rutherford, R Rutherford, RW Simpson	FG Watt(j)
935-36	J Lunn	RB Bennie, JW Lee, W Molineux, RW Nevin, T Oliver, GF Rutherford, R Rutherford, RW Simpson, AG Stableforth	FG Watt(j)
936-37	J Lunn	RB Bennie, JW Lee, W Molineux, RW Nevin, T Oliver, GF Rutherford, R Rutherford, AG Stableforth	FG Watt(j)
937-38	J Lunn	RB Bennie, JW Lee, W Molineux, RW Nevin, T Oliver, GF Rutherford, R Rutherford, AG Stableforth	FG Watt(j)
938-39	J Lunn	RB Bennie, JW Lee, W Molineux, RW Nevin, GF Rutherford, R Rutherford, GS Seymour, AG Stableforth	FG Watt(j)
939-40	J Lunn	RB Bennie, JW Lee, W Molineux, RW Nevin, GF Rutherford, R Rutherford, GS Seymour, AG Stableforth	FG Watt(j)
940-41	GF Rutherford/ J Lunn	RB Bennie, JW Lee, W Molineux, RW Nevin, R Rutherford, GS Seymour, AG Stableforth	FG Watt(j)
941-42	GF Rutherford	RB Bennie, JW Lee, W Molineux, RW Nevin, R Rutherford, GS Seymour, AG Stableforth, WB Taylor	FG Watt(j)
942-43	GF Rutherford	RB Bennie, JW Lee, W Molineux, RW Nevin, GS Seymour, AG Stableforth, WB Taylor, R Rutherford	FG Watt(j)
943-44	GF Rutherford	JW Lee, W Molineux, W McKeag, RW Nevin, R Rutherford, GS Seymour, AG Stableforth, WB Taylor, Lord Westwood(s)	FG Watt(j)
944-45	GF Rutherford	JW Lee, W McKeag, R Rutherford, GS Seymour, AG Stableforth, B Taylor, Lord Westwood(s)	FG Watt(j)
945-46	GF Rutherford	JW Lee, W McKeag, R Rutherford, GS Seymour, AG Stableforth, WB Taylor, Lord Westwood(s)	FG Watt(j)
946-47	GF Rutherford	JW Lee, W McKeag, R Rutherford, GS Seymour, AG Stableforth, WB Taylor, Lord Westwood(s)	FG Watt(j)
947-48	GF Rutherford	JW Lee, W McKeag, R Rutherford, GS Seymour, AG Stableforth, WB Taylor, Lord Westwood(s)	FG Watt(j)
948-49	GF Rutherford	JW Lee, W McKeag, R Rutherford, GS Seymour, AG Stableforth, WB Taylor, Lord Westwood(s)	FG Watt(j)
949-50	JW Lee/ GF Rutherford	WE Hurford, W McKeag, R Rutherford, GS Seymour, AG Stableforth, WB Taylor, Lord Westwood(s)	FG Watt(j)
950-51	JW Lee	WE Hurford, W McKeag, R Rutherford, RJ Rutherford, GS Seymour, AG Stableforth, WB Taylor, Lord Westwood(s)	FG Watt(j)/ E Hall
951-52	JW Lee/ R Rutherford	WE Hurford, W McKeag, GS Seymour, AG Stableforth, RJ Rutherford, WB Taylor, Lord Westwood(s)	E Hall
952-53	R Rutherford	WE Hurford, JW Lee, W McKeag, RJ Rutherford, GS Seymour, WB Taylor, Lord Westwood(s)	E Hall
953-54	R Rutherford/ GS Seymour	WE Hurford, JW Lee, RR Mackenzie, W McKeag, RJ Rutherford, WB Taylor, Lord Westwood(s)	E Hall
954-55	GS Seymour	H Davis, WE Hurford, JW Lee, RR Mackenzie, W McKeag, R Rutherford, RJ Rutherford, WB Taylor,	E Hall
955-56	WB Taylor	H Davis, WE Hurford, RR Mackenzie, W McKeag, R Rutherford, RJ Rutherford, GS Seymour	E Hall
956-57	WB Taylor	H Davis, WE Hurford, W McKeag, RR Mackenzie, R Rutherford, RJ Rutherford, GS Seymour	E Hall
957-58	WB Taylor/ W McKeag	H Davis, WE Hurford, RR Mackenzie, GS Seymour, R Rutherford, RJ Rutherford	E Hall
958-59	W McKeag	H Davis, WE Hurford, RR Mackenzie, R Rutherford, RJ Rutherford, GS Seymour, WB Taylor	E Hall/ JD Barker
959-60	W McKeag/ WE Hurford	H Davis, RR Mackenzie, R Rutherford, RJ Rutherford, GS Seymour, WB Taylor	JD Barker
960-61	WE Hurford	F Braithwaite, W McKeag, RR Mackenzie, RJ Rutherford, GS Seymour, WB Taylor, Lord Westwood(j)	JD Barker
961-62	WE Hurford	F Braithwaite, W McKeag, RR Mackenzie, RJ Rutherford, GS Seymour, WB Taylor, Lord Westwood(j)	JD Barker
962-63	WE Hurford	F Braithwaite, W McKeag, RR Mackenzie, RJ Rutherford, GS Seymour, WB Taylor, Lord Westwood(j)	JD Barker
963-64	WE Hurford	F Braithwaite, W McKeag, RR Mackenzie, RJ Rutherford, GS Seymour, WB Taylor, Lord Westwood(j)	JD Barker
964-65	WE Hurford/ Lord Westwood(j)	F Braithwaite, W McKeag, RR Mackenzie, RJ Rutherford, GS Seymour, WB Taylor	JD Barker
965-66	Lord Westwood(j)	F Braithwaite, WE Hurford, W McKeag, RR Mackenzie, RJ Rutherford, GS Seymour, WB Taylor	JD Barker
966-67	Lord Westwood(j)	F Braithwaite, WE Hurford, W McKeag, RR Mackenzie, J Rush, RJ Rutherford, GS Seymour, WB Taylor	JD Barker
967-68	Lord Westwood(j)	F Braithwaite, W McKeag, RR Mackenzie, J Rush, RJ Rutherford, GS Seymour, WB Taylor	JD Barker
968-69	Lord Westwood(j)	F Braithwaite, W McKeag, RR Mackenzie, J Rush, RJ Rutherford, GS Seymour, WB Taylor	JD Barker
969-70	Lord Westwood(j)	F Braithwaite, W McKeag, RR Mackenzie, J Rush, RJ Rutherford, GS Seymour, WB Taylor	JD Barker
970-71	Lord Westwood(j)	F Braithwaite, W McKeag, RR Mackenzie, J Rush, RJ Rutherford, GS Seymour, WB Taylor	JD Barker/ MG Hoole
971-72	Lord Westwood(j)	F Braithwaite, HH Dickson, W McKeag, RR Mackenzie, J Rush, RJ Rutherford, GS Seymour	MG Hoole
972-73	Lord Westwood(j)	F Braithwaite, HH Dickson, W McKeag, WG McKeag, RR Mackenzie, J Rush, RJ Rutherford, GS Seymour	MG Hoole
973-74	Lord Westwood(j)	F Braithwaite, HH Dickson, WG McKeag, RR Mackenzie, J Rush, RJ Rutherford, GS Seymour	R Cushing
974-75	Lord Westwood(j)	F Braithwaite, HH Dickson, WG McKeag, RR Mackenzie, J Rush, RJ Rutherford, GS Seymour	R Cushing
975-76	Lord Westwood(j)	F Braithwaite, HH Dickson, RR Mackenzie, WG McKeag, J Rush, RJ Rutherford, DV Salkeld, S Seymour, GS Seymour	R Cushing
976-77	Lord Westwood(j)	F Braithwaite, HH Dickson, WG McKeag, J Rush, RJ Rutherford, DV Salkeld, S Seymour	R Cushing
977-78	Lord Westwood(j)/ RJ Rutherford	F Braithwaite, HH Dickson, WG McKeag, R Mackenzie, J Rush, DV Salkeld, S Seymour	R Cushing

Frank Watt

One of the pioneers of the game in Scotland, Frank Watt was a player with early clubs Edinburgh Swifts, Third Edinburgh Rifle Volunteers as well as Hearts during the 1870s then Secretary of the Edinburgh FA. Often a referee and highly respected north of the border, he was due to take up a post with Dundee before being waylaid and redirected to Tyneside. He was appointed United Secretary in December 1895, a milestone date in the club's history. Watt was a first-class administrator and did much to create Newcastle's standing as one of the finest and most well-regarded clubs in the country. Within a decade the Magpies had narrowly missed securing the double and by the time he died when still in post, the club had lifted four Championship titles and reached six FA Cup finals. Sporting a magnificent moustache throughout his time in office at St James' Park, Frank became esteemed throughout football. He was acquainted with everyone worth knowing north and south of the border and his portly, well-dressed frame became one of football's senior figures, a genial character who was held in great reverence. His son, Frank Watt (Jnr) took over the Secretary role at Gallowgate on his death in 1932, and remained with the club until 1950; nearly 55 years unbroken family service with the club.

Born Edinburgh.
Secretary, 1895 to 1932.

Russell Cushing

From East Anglia, Russell Cushing first became involved in football as part of Norwich City's office staff, appointed Assistant Secretary in the close-season of 1965. When the same Newcastle United post became vacant he travelled north to land to job during June 1971. Appointed to the Secretary role two years later, Cushing soon became a valued official within football and saw it all happen at St James' Park. He worked through many highs and lows during more than 36 years at Gallowgate, a rollercoaster which took him from the depths of the second-tier, to the top of the Premiership, into the Champions League and dealing with multi-million pound transfers and super-star players from home and on the Continent. Cushing was appointed to the Board firstly in 1989 and held executive positions in addition to the traditional Company Secretary post; General Manager and Chief Operating Officer. Having to run day to day operations during the turbulent Magpie Group's takeover, and then be at the heart of the club's resurgence afterwards, Russell had to at times walk a fine line of diplomacy, testament to his integrity and ability as an administrator. Following accomplished service to the club, he left the scene in September 2007 soon afterwards operating a UEFA and FA licensed football agency. Residing in Northumberland, Cushing was awarded the Football League's Long Service award in 1993.

Born Norwich.
Secretary & Director, 1971 to 2007.

Season	Chairman	Directors	Secretary	Other
1978-79	RJ Rutherford	F Braithwaite, WG McKeag, R Mackenzie, J Rush, DV Salkeld, S Seymour, Lord Westwood(j)	R Cushing	
1979-80	RJ Rutherford	F Braithwaite, WG McKeag, R Mackenzie, J Rush, DV Salkeld, S Seymour, Lord Westwood(j)	R Cushing	
1980-81	RJ Rutherford/ S Seymour	Sir G Bowman, F Braithwaite, WP Catesby, WG McKeag, R Mackenzie, J Rush, DV Salkeld, Lord Westwood(j)	R Cushing	
1981-82	S Seymour	Sir G Bowman, F Braithwaite, WP Catesby, E Dunn, WG McKeag, R Mackenzie, J Rush	R Cushing	
1982-83	S Seymour	Sir G Bowman, F Braithwaite, WP Catesby, E Dunn, WG McKeag, R Mackenzie, J Rush	R Cushing	
1983-84	S Seymour	Sir G Bowman, F Braithwaite, WP Catesby, E Dunn, GR Forbes, WG McKeag, R Mackenzie, J Rush	R Cushing	
1984-85	S Seymour	Sir G Bowman, GR Dickson, E Dunn, GR Forbes, WG McKeag, R Mackenzie, J Rush	R Cushing	
1985-86	S Seymour	Sir G Bowman, GR Dickson, E Dunn, GR Forbes, WG McKeag, R Mackenzie, J Rush	R Cushing	
1986-87	S Seymour	Sir G Bowman, GR Dickson, E Dunn, GR Forbes, WG McKeag, R Mackenzie, J Rush	R Cushing	
1987-88	S Seymour/ WG McKeag	Sir G Bowman, GR Dickson, E Dunn, GR Forbes, R Mackenzie, J Rush	R Cushing	
1988-89	WG McKeag	Sir G Bowman, GR Dickson, E Dunn, GR Forbes, R Mackenzie, PC Mallinger, J Rush, S Seymour, R Young	R Cushing	
1989-90	WG McKeag	Sir G Bowman, R Cushing, GR Forbes, J Hall, PC Mallinger, J Rush, S Seymour, R Young	R Cushing	
1990-91	WG McKeag/ GR Forbes	Sir G Bowman, R Cushing, DS Hall, J Hall, PC Mallinger, S Seymour, R Young	R Cushing	
1991-92	GR Forbes/ Sir J Hall	R Cushing, DS Hall, S Seymour, WF Shepherd, PC Mallinger, WG McKeag, D McVickers, R Young	R Cushing	RND Stephenson (CE)/ AO Fletcher(CE)
1992-93	Sir J Hall	R Cushing, DS Hall, R Jones, WF Shepherd	R Cushing	AO Fletcher(CE)
1993-94	Sir J Hall	TL Bennett, R Cushing, DS Hall, R Jones, WF Shepherd	R Cushing	AO Fletcher(CE)
1994-95	Sir J Hall	TL Bennett, DS Hall, R Jones, WF Shepherd	R Cushing	AO Fletcher(CE)
1995-96	Sir J Hall	TL Bennett, DS Hall, R Jones, WF Shepherd	R Cushing	AO Fletcher(CE)
1996-97	Sir J Hall	TL Bennett, MA Corbidge, J Dixon, AO Fletcher, DS Hall, R Jones, WF Shepherd	R Cushing	AO Fletcher/M Corbidge(Joint CE)
1997-98	Sir J Hall/ WF Shepherd	J Dixon, AO Fletcher, DS Hall, R Jones, LA Wheatley, AM Wilson	R Cushing	AO Fletcher(CE)
1998-99	WF Shepherd	AO Fletcher, DS Hall, R Jones, LA Wheatley, AM Wilson	R Cushing	AO Fletcher(CE)
1999-00	WF Shepherd	AO Fletcher, DS Hall, R Jones, DC Stonehouse, LA Wheatley	R Cushing	AO Fletcher(CE)/ DC Stonehouse(CE)
2000-01	WF Shepherd	R Cushing, DS Hall, R Jones, K Slater, DC Stonehouse	R Cushing	DC Stonehouse(CE)
2001-02	WF Shepherd	R Cushing, DS Hall, LT Hatton, R Jones, K Slater	R Cushing	R Cushing(COO)
2002-03	WF Shepherd	R Cushing, DS Hall, LT Hatton, K Slater	R Cushing	R Cushing(COO)
2003-04	WF Shepherd	R Cushing, DS Hall, LT Hatton, K Slater	R Cushing	R Cushing(COO)
2004-05	WF Shepherd	R Cushing, DS Hall, LT Hatton, K Slater	R Cushing	R Cushing(COO)
2005-06	WF Shepherd	R Cushing, DS Hall, LT Hatton, K Slater	R Cushing	R Cushing(COO)
2006-07	WF Shepherd/ CA Mort	R Cushing, DS Hall, LT Hatton, K Slater, SJ Walton	R Cushing	SJ Walton(CE)
2007-08	CA Mort/ DD Llambias(MD)	R Cushing, JA Irving, K Slater, SJ Walton, DC Williamson, DF Wise	R Cushing/ JA Irving	L Charnley(FS)
2008-09	DD Llambias(MD)	L Charnley, JA Irving, DC Williamson, DF Wise	JA Irving	L Charnley(FS)
2009-10	DD Llambias(MD)	L Charnley, JA Irving	JA Irving	L Charnley(FS)
2010-11	DD Llambias(MD)	L Charnley, JA Irving	JA Irving	L Charnley(FS)

Notes:

Generally, directors listed are those in position at the start of each season, but also includes directors in post for part of any season.

For the period June 2008 to date, Newcastle United did not fill the position of Chairman.

Newcastle United as a PLC

Season	Chairman	Directors	Secretary	Other
1996-97	Sir T Harrison	DP Cassidy, MA Corbidge, J Dixon, AO Fletcher, DS Hall, R Jones, JC Mayo, WF Shepherd	AB Price	AO Fletcher/ MA Corbidge(Joint CE)
1997-98	Sir T Harrison/ DP Cassidy	J Dixon, JL Fender, T Fenton, AO Fletcher, DS Hall, JI Josephs, R Jones, JC Mayo, WF Shepherd, LA Wheatley	AB Price	AO Fletcher(CE)
1998-99	DP Cassidy/ AO Fletcher	DS Hall, JL Fender, T Fenton, R Jones, JI Josephs, WF Shepherd, LA Wheatley, IM Winskell	AB Price/ LA Wheatley/ IM Winskell	AO Fletcher(CE)
1999-00	AO Fletcher/ JL Fender	DS Hall, R Jones, WF Shepherd, DC Stonehouse, LA Wheatley IM Winskell	IM Winskell/ R Cushing	AO Fletcher(CE)/ DC Stonehouse(CE)
2000-01	JL Fender	DS Hall, R Jones, WF Shepherd, DC Stonehouse	R Cushing	DC Stonehouse(CE)/ R Cushing(COO)
2001-02	JL Fender/ WF Shepherd	DS Hall, R Jones, TJ Revill, BS Shepherd	R Cushing	R Cushing(COO)
2002-03	WF Shepherd	DS Hall, R Jones, TJ Revill, BS Shepherd	R Cushing	R Cushing(COO)
2003-04	WF Shepherd	A Antonopoulos, DS Hall, R Jones, TJ Revill, BS Shepherd	R Cushing	R Cushing(COO)
2004-05	WF Shepherd	A Antonopoulos, DS Hall, TJ Revill, BS Shepherd	R Cushing	R Cushing(COO)
2005-06	WF Shepherd	A Antonopoulos, DS Hall, TJ Revill, BS Shepherd	R Cushing	R Cushing(COO)
2006-07	WF Shepherd	A Antonopoulos, DS Hall, TJ Revill, BS Shepherd	R Cushing	R Cushing(COO)

Notes:

For the period 1997 to 2007 Newcastle United became a public company quoted on the London Stock Exchange and had a separate PLC Board of Directors to the Football Club board.

On 18th July 2007, following the acquisition of the club by MJW Ashley, the Company was delisted and reverted back to a private ownership.

Sir John Hall

Before Sir John Hall became connected with Newcastle United, the club was in a grim state. Turnover was a mere £4m, they had little capital, a stadium in need of vast improvement, and a team languishing in the second-tier of English football going nowhere fast – and if anywhere, towards the old Division Three for the first time. Becoming the figurehead for change as the Magpie Group started a takeover bid in 1988, the Northumberland-born entrepreneur, property developer and former Coal Board surveyor was determined to make Newcastle United one of the powers in football. As soon as his company Cameron-Hall took full control in 1992 the club was rapidly transformed. Funds were provided, almost without limit; the stadium rebuilt, the team changed beyond recognition with big-name stars galore. As a result United's status changed spectacularly with turnover approaching £100m. They challenged at the top of the Premier League and became one of Europe's giants. Knighted in 1991, Sir John takes the credit of making it all happen and few individuals in United's history has achieved as much. Yet one thing Hall did not accomplish, was to bring a principal trophy to St James' Park before he retired from the scene in 1998. He sold his majority stake in Newcastle United during 2007 while his son Douglas Hall was also part of the United directorate for over 15 years. To mark the contribution he made to the club, the Leazes End stand was renamed the Sir John Hall Stand in 1993 while he was awarded the Freedom of Gateshead during 2011.

Born North Seaton.
Director, Chairman 1990 to 1998
President, 1998 to date.

Reporting to The City.
2003 Annual Report from the PLC.

lub Presidents

76-1978	GS Seymour	As Vice-President
78-1983	Lord Westwood	As President
83-1985	F Braithwaite	As President
89-1992	S Seymour	As President
93-1997	TL Bennett	As President
98-2007	Sir John Hall	As President
93-date	R Young	As Honorary President
07-date	Sir John Hall	As Life President

tes:

rt from earliest pioneer years, Newcastle United first appointed a club figurehead in 1976, as a Vice-President. This was changed to the title of President during 1978.

The name of Seymour served United well in the Boardroom; Stan senior (above), and Stan junior (below).

lub Turnover

modern years an important gauge of how football clubs are viewed in the business world is by the turnover generated. The broadest asure of Newcastle United's trading since the Second World War has been charted and shows a gradual increase in revenue during the ar 50 years since 1946, then a surge during the 1990s when football changed rapidly on the advent of the FA Premier League, UEFA's ampions League and substantial television income which came with it.

1996 global accountancy firm Deloitte introduced an annual financial analysis of the world's top football clubs. Known as the *Deloitte otball Money League*, or more commonly as football's *Rich List*, it ranks clubs by corporate size. This has become an important indicator d grades the world's leading clubs by turnover, a key measure of their wealth and status in the game as a whole. Newcastle United's ranking oted from season 1996-97.

st-war Turnover per season

46-47	Div 2	*untraced*	1968-69	Div 1	£407,575*	1990-91	Div 2	£4.418m
47-48	Div 2	£128,161	1969-70	Div 1	£369,726	1991-92	Div 2	£5.875m
48-49	Div 1	£133,987	1970-71	Div 1	£349,023	1992-93	Div 1	£8.798m
49-50	Div 1	*untraced*	1971-72	Div 1	£381,831	1993-94	PL	£17.269m
50-51	Div 1	£128,542	1972-73	Div 1	£439,976	1994-95	PL	£24.723m*
51-52	Div 1	£145,967	1973-74	Div 1	£657,028	1995-96	PL	£28.970m
52-53	Div 1	£128,919	1974-75	Div 1	£670,983	1996-97	PL	£41.134m *RL 8th*
53-54	Div 1	£132,534	1975-76	Div 1	£940,280	1997-98	PL	£49.177m *RL 5th*
54-55	Div 1	£138,568	1976-77	Div 1	£809,981	1998-99	PL	£44.718m *RL 12th*
55-56	Div 1	£116,351	1977-78	Div 1	£899,491	1999-00	PL	£49.090m *RL 20th*
56-57	Div 1	£111,565	1978-79	Div 2	£809,510	2000-01	PL	£54.916m *RL 14th*
57-58	Div 1	£134,400	1979-80	Div 2	£1.140m	2001-02	PL	£70.858m *RL 13th*
58-59	Div 1	£145,335	1980-81	Div 2	£1.000m	2002-03	PL	£96.449m *RL 9th*
59-60	Div 1	£136,935	1981-82	Div 2	£1.646m	2003-04	PL	£90.161m *RL 11th*
60-61	Div 1	£155,100*	1982-83	Div 2	£2.222m	2004-05	PL	£86.982m *RL12th*
61-62	Div 2	£150,209	1983-84	Div 2	£2.481m	2005-06	PL	£83.086m* *RL 13th*
62-63	Div 2	£150,327	1984-85	Div 1	£2.658m*	2006-07	PL	£87.083m *RL 14th*
63-64	Div 2	£161,697	1985-86	Div 1	£2.462m	2007-08	PL	£99.358m *RL 17th*
64-65	Div 2	£173,627	1986-87	Div 1	£2.706m	2008-09	PL	£86.075m *RL 20th*
65-66	Div 1	£208,286	1987-88	Div 1	£2.645m	2009-10	Ch	£52.4m
66-67	Div 1	£223,648	1988-89	Div 1	£3.729m	2010-11	PL	*£80.0m estimate*
67-68	Div 1	*untraced*	1989-90	Div 2	£4.118m			

Newcastle United Football Coy.,

LIMITED.

DIRECTORS' REPORT

AND

BALANCE SHEET,

30th APRIL, 1899.

NOTICE IS HEREBY GIVEN that the ANNUAL GENERAL MEETING of this COMPANY will be held in the Hotel Metropole, Newcastle, on Thursday, the 25th day of May, 1899, at 7.30 p.m.

FRANK G. WATT,
Secretary.

3, St. James Street,
Newcastle,
May, 1899.

J. B. BOWES, PRINTER, PENKLE STREET, NEWCASTLE.

The club's Annual document dated 30th April 1899. A report has been produced every year since 1890. The year's meeting in 1899 was held at the Hotel Metropole.

tes:

ures are based on the club's published Annual Director's Report and audited Statement of Accounts since World War Two. Turnover is ascertained on overall Newcastle ted football related activities.

ounting legislation and procedures have changed over the years, to enable a general like for like comparison to be made, all figures are based upon published revenue, come before any shares to other clubs and football authorities. Added are all sundry receipts including the likes of broadcasting revenue, programme sales, Development ociation surplus, but exclude insurance, investment income as well as player trading. Figures are after any deductions for tax in the published Accounts documents.

Rich List ranking is taken from published Deloitte documents.

ere the financial year is either more or less than the normal 12 month period, this is indicated by *.

ecific Abbreviations used:

) = Chief Executive, (COO) = Chief Operating Officer, (FS) = Football Secretary, (j) = junior, (MD) = Managing Director, (Pr) = President, PLC = Public Limited Company, = Rich List, (s) = senior.

Section 4

A Fortress on Tyneside: St James' Park

- The St James' Park Story
- Other Grounds; Stanley & East End
- Other fixtures at St James' Park; internationals, representative & neutral club fixtures
- Other events at St James' Park

Notes on the statistics

Principal Fixtures

Apart from fixtures involving Newcastle United, St James' Park has hosted many other games, both first-class matches and contests of a secondary nature. Of course, both the Newcastle Rangers and Newcastle West End clubs were based at the ground prior to United taking up residence in 1892, and several FA Cup, Northern League and exhibition games against some of the country's top sides took place before East End's switch to Barrack Road. FA Cup fixtures are scheduled due to their importance at the time, however all other games involving the previous tenants of St James' Park are not.

Several major representative fixtures have been staged at Gallowgate including full international contests and matches from the European Championship of 1996 while the ground is scheduled to host part of the Olympic Games football tournament in 2012. Attendances have been significant for certain games. In the immediate post-war boom years the Football League versus Scottish League challenge attracted an attendance of nearly 65,000 with a reported 20,000 locked out. During the twenties Home Scots versus Anglo-Scots representative games took place on Tyneside to provide "funds to raise a memorial fitting to uphold the memory of the Immortal Bard"....Robbie Burns. Proceeds also went to Newcastle's Royal Victoria Infirmary and the matches saw a proverbial who's who of Scottish football talent on view.

During World War One, when Newcastle United closed down for much of the period, representative matches took place at the stadium. Celebrated full-back Bill McCracken gathered together a star-studded McCracken's XI to face an equally formidable Cuggy's XI for a handful of games.

All of these matches are regarded first-class fixtures along with other senior club games and prominent amateur contests such as FA Amateur Cup semi-finals and, on one occasion, the replayed final. All are detailed on the summaries.

Secondary Fixtures

Apart from senior games, numerous secondary matches have taken place over the years. In the pioneering days, an England versus Scotland confrontation of sorts took place with teams selected from North East based players to represent their countries. During May 1890, England won 3-0 in a game in aid of funds to purchase a local trophy, while two years later the Scots recorded a 2-0 victory in a testimonial match. However, these fixtures cannot be termed first-class contests.

There have been several youth and schools internationals, as well as boy's club, university and police internationals. County representative matches have been played at St James' Park since the formation of the local association, while various inter-city contests at a variety of levels took place too, including the prestigious English Schools Shield Final when, in 1930, a crowd of 25,000 saw Newcastle Boys take on Chesterfield Boys and win 1-0. Several fixtures were watched by substantial gates, the England versus Scotland Boys clash in 1949 saw a crowd of 44,605 inside the ground, while over 35,000 saw Newcastle Boys take on Leicester Boys in 1947.

Many reserve and local competitions have been played at the Gallowgate ground over the last century and more, especially semi-final and finals of competitions such as the Northumberland Challenge Cup, Aged Miners Cup and Tyne Charity Shield. Representative games featuring the likes of the North Eastern League or Central League elevens have taken place too. St James' Park often hosted wartime services games with over 50,000 watching the Army versus RAF contest in 1945. Even games of a secondary nature on occasion attracted extraordinary crowds. The Northern Command versus Western Command services fixture in 1944 saw 21,900 in the ground. Minor games aplenty have also used St James' Park and the stadium has seen matches featuring sides representing Newcastle Trams (1929) and the Law Students (1908). The Newcastle Gatemen defeated the Sunderland Gatemen 8-0 in 1908.

Ladies football has also made an appearance. In 1895 the British Ladies played a Reds versus Blues exhibition contest and 8,000 turned up while in 1908 England Ladies met Ireland Ladies in aid of the Lord Mayor's Relief Fund. A gate of 2,000 saw a 5-0 victory for the English. The wartime Munitionettes' combination also played games at Gallowgate while, in 1919, Newcastle Ladies drew 0-0 with Preston Ladies in front of a 25,000 crowd.

These secondary matches are not included in the summary of principal fixtures. The exception to this is where any fixtures involving senior clubs have resulted in largely a first-team XI being fielded, as was the case when Middlesbrough met Sunderland at Gallowgate in the final of the North East Counties Cup during 1920. In addition, details of national cup finals are shown when staged at St James' Park; these include the English Schools Shield and FA Sunday Cup finals.

Other Events

Apart from football, other sporting and non-sporting events have been staged at the Gallowgate arena while St James' Park is scheduled to host the Rugby World Cup in 2015. A brief account is included together with a digest of recent music gigs as attendances have at times been exceptional for these concerts.

St James' Park before development in 2000 when capacity was increased to over 52,000.

St James' Park

Fortress Facts

- **FIRST GAME:** 16th Oct 1880
  Newcastle Rangers Captain's XI v Others (6-1).
- **CLUBS:**
  Newcastle Rangers 1880 to 1882,
  Newcastle West End 1886 to 1892,
  Newcastle East End/Newcastle United 1892 to date.
  Minor club Newcastle Wednesday also played at the ground from 1888 for a period.
- **FIRST GAME AS EAST END/NEWCASTLE UNITED:**
  3rd Sept 1892, East End v Glasgow Celtic (0-1) Att: 7,000.
- **HIGHEST ATTENDANCE:**
  68,386 v Chelsea, 3rd Sept 1930 (Div 1).
- **HIGHEST AVERAGE ATTENDANCE:**
  56,298, League & Cup fixtures, 1947-48 (Div 2).

The enlarged St James' Park as viewed from the historic Leazes Park in winter.

The St James' Park story

United's famous and historic home of St James' Park is now one of the oldest football stadiums in the country. While football was more than likely played on the site in an unorganised fashion before the first club, Newcastle Rangers moved in, the earliest organised game took place during October 1880. Rangers held a trial game that lasted some two hours between a Rangers Captain's XI and an Others side which contained 15 players! Back on Victorian Tyneside there was no manicured pitch, no giant concrete, steel and glass structures, instead a rough patch of grazing land, part of the wider Castle Leazes and Town Moor. It was noted in the press that "the new ground is very nicely situated and is close to the centre of town. It is 120 yards x 60 yards broad and is completely level."

There was a touch of journalistic licence in the newspaper report, as the site actually had a pronounced fall of some 18 feet from the north to south goal. Although subsequent ground improvements at St James' Park have levelled the pitch off significantly, part of the original slope can still be seen in the impressive arena that is the modern home of Newcastle United.

An area of just over five acres, situated off Barrack Road and named after the nearby St James' Street, it was an advantageous setting and not far from the site of the old execution gallows – hence its other commonly used title of Gallowgate. St James' Park is positioned on historic land granted to the town by King John – the Town Moor. It is owned jointly by the City Freemen and City Council with Newcastle United long-term tenants and that arrangement has brought with it many a problem to the club over the years.

United's old Victorian Stand is captured in the background of this action shot at the turn of the century.

Rangers remained on the site until the end of the 1881-82 season when they moved to another pitch at Dalton Street in Byker. The Gallowgate field lay fallow for four years until the Newcastle West End club made St James' Park its home. They stayed there for six years before folding in 1892 inviting rivals Newcastle East End to take over the lease. Since then the location, with its marvellous backdrop of the Georgian Leazes Terrace as well as the adjoining Victorian Leazes Park, has been the headquarters of Newcastle United.

Limited development took place during those early years. West End roped off the pitch and erected substantial paling, eight feet high. The cost of these initial improvements was estimated at £200 and it gave the club an identity in the area. Thomas Bell, the Sheriff of Newcastle, formally opened the revamped St James' Park on 2nd October 1886 when the visitors were future tenants East End. A crowd of 2,000 were in attendance, the largest ever assembled for an 'ordinary' club match in Newcastle.

The press at the time published a contemporary view of West End's new home: "The ground is situated at the bottom end of Leazes Park and is called St James' Park. It is very large and, with improvements that are yet to take place, will make it one of the best, if not the best, grounds in the north." There were though very little facilities to speak of then, the players and officials using the Lord Hill public-house on Pitt Street, just across Barrack Road as their base. The pub, associated with director John Black, was to become an important venue for the club during the next few years as a meeting point – the players also using it to change there before and after games. The Black Bull Inn nearby was also used, under the stewardship of another supporter and director, George McConachie.

Just over a year later, during December 1887, St James' Park recorded a much bigger attendance when Shankhouse Black Watch borrowed the ground for a prestigious FA Cup-tie against team of the era, Aston Villa. Reports note that a crowd of anything between 5,000 and 7,000 gathered for what ended up a complete rout of the local side by 9-0. Prior to East End's move to St James' Park, that was the largest attendance to be recorded until West End met East End in another FA Cup contest in October 1891 when 8,000 fans were gathered around the pitch, although it should be noted that gate figures varied from report to report to make it difficult to establish definitive 'record' crowds.

Once East End moved across the city during the following year they started to improve facilities. A modest Victorian wooden stand was erected on the Barrack Road touchline with another planned at the Gallowgate End. The club's elevation into the top-tier of football during 1898 saw much needed expansion and improvement to the stands and terracing. The original central main stand was extended by adding extensions to either end, now running the full length of the west touchline. By the time the Magpies had become established as one of football's top sides, the stadium underwent a major redevelopment project. The arena was completely remodelled with vast terracing and a state-of-the-art barrel-vaulted main stand was erected along the Barrack Road touchline. Included was a much admired central bird's-eye press-box. The new St James' Park was opened during September 1905 with the capacity set at 60,000, although much more were to be admitted in the years to follow. It was a huge increase from the previous 30,000 limit. The ground was noted as "amongst the most perfectly appointed football enclosures in the country". Season-tickets for the new West Stand Centre-Pavilion prime seats were set at £2 2s 0d (£2 10p).

Although Newcastle United and St James' Park were at the forefront of stadium redevelopment at the start of the 20th century, for much of nearly 70 years to follow, the kindest thing said about the arena was that it has been inhabited by some of football's most exciting characters both on the pitch and on the terraces. Improvement and further development between the Twenties and Eighties decades floundered due to a long-running dispute between landlord and tenant which became a highly contentious issue. The only noticeable improvements being a cover over the Leazes End terrace, erected in 1929, the arrival of floodlighting – initially in 1953 – then with the installation of four giant pylons during 1958, as well as a new club entrance being constructed to the Edwardian West Stand in 1956.

Following much debate over development plans decade by decade, matters came to a head when Newcastle United – and the City – lost the chance of being a host venue for the 1966 World Cup because of this impasse. It was not until 1971 when a scheme was finally agreed and with it actual construction work planned. A modern concrete East Stand, with limited capacity due to planning restraints associated with the listed Leazes Terrace, was erected in 1973, but soon after plans were stalled due to further approval issues and a lack of finance. Newcastle had to act though, the club's 82-year-old West Stand had a timber seating deck and was demolished due to stringent safety requirements following the Bradford fire disaster. The long overdue replacement Milburn Stand was unveiled in 1988.

More progress did not materialise until the Cameron-Hall takeover of the club as the 1990s began. At last the largely deadlock position of the past was resolved and St James' Park was completely remodelled in rapid time into an all-seater arena to match the best. Capacity was restricted to only just over 36,500 but United's historic home became something of a cauldron with a very special atmosphere. It was a fortress to the club as they became a Premiership force.

Enlargement was a priority though as demand for tickets outstripped supply by thousands. Indeed in 1998 there was a reported waiting list of some 10,000 for season-tickets. A grandiose scheme was tabled in 1997 to relocate a short distance behind Leazes Park and create a brand new 70,000 seated stadium. This ambitious development plan would have involved utilising the site of St James' Park as a training and multi-purpose arena together with the regeneration of the historic public park. But opposition from largely conservation groups saw the plans called-in by the Secretary of State and a lengthy delay resulted. Newcastle United could not wait and decided instead to further expand the historic Gallowgate site.

United's Edwardian West Stand, opened in 1905 and demolished in 1987.

The ground was enlarged to a capacity of just over 52,500 (now set at 52,387) by substantially enlarging the existing Milburn and Leazes stands. Opened in August 2000 for the fixture against Derby County, St James' Park now houses several floors of corporate suites and apart from Old Trafford and Arsenal's Emirates Stadium, is the largest club ground in England.

Other Grounds

Newcastle United's pioneers Stanley and East End did play on other grounds prior to moving to St James' Park during the summer of 1892. All were based in the east of the city, in the neighbouring Byker and Heaton districts. Very little is known about the club's first three sites, and certainly it is unlikely there would have been any structures or stands to speak of, just a roughly marked out football pitch in the style of the day - that being only a rectangle - and maybe roped off. The playing surface would have been decidedly rutted and probably on a slope.

(see pages 31 and 33 for location plans of grounds).

Stanley Street 1881 to c1883

The club's first site was a pitch in the St Peter's area of South Byker, alongside the River Tyne near to Stanley Street which was part of Walker Road. The exact location is not featured on any town plans of the day, but they played more than likely on Stanley's cricket field or on a pitch nearby which was close to the local Methodist Chapel - these days near where St Peter's Social Club is located on Raby Street, all on the fringe of the modern award-winning Byker Wall development. Stanley's first match there was during November 1881. There were brick-works, potteries and tanneries as well as a manure works in the vicinity.

Byker Vicarage c1883 to 1884

The club soon moved to another site in the neighbourhood, at Byker Vicarage. There is no precise record as to when they did relocate, but before the start of season 1883-84 it was reported that their home ground was located on a field "behind the Byker Vicarage" not far away from Stanley Street. It is possible that they may have moved some time before this, perhaps in 1882 when they had changed their name. The vicarage was St Michael's Vicarage in Byker Village, an area that has since been developed, demolished and redeveloped again. Today, St Michael's Church still stands amidst the Byker Wall complex, high on a hill with a sweeping panorama down to the bridges over the Tyne, but now in a semi-derelict state and no longer used as a place of worship. The pitch behind Byker Vicarage was to be eventually taken over by another local club, Cheviot FC.

Dalton Street 1884 to 1886

In the summer of 1884, East End decided to move to an improved site near Dalton Street, not far away but regarded as a step forward. Tyneside pioneer club, Rangers FC, had also moved to Dalton Street two years earlier but they were now on the decline. The site was further up the incline of the valley, towards the main thoroughfare of Shields Road and alongside the newly built terrace houses of Byker which were being constructed all over the slopes to the riverside. A railway line and brick-works were nearby. Dalton Street still exists today, on the edge of the Byker Wall residential development.

Chillingham Road 1886 to 1882

Now acknowledged as a football force in the region, East End looked for a more favourable arena. An established site was found on the Byker and Heaton border less than a mile away and during the close-season of 1886 the club moved to a pitch off Chillingham Road, previously tenanted by the Heaton Athletic Club and adjoining the old base of North Eastern FC - one of the earliest clubs on Tyneside. This could be called a proper ground rather than merely a football pitch. It was to be the club's headquarters for the next six years until moving the two miles across the city to St James' Park.

The site was next to Heaton Junction, a giant railway intersection on the main Edinburgh to London railway line; hence its other commonly used title of the Heaton Junction Ground. Next door was a cricket arena while the football site was formally part of a recreation ground which saw athletics and cycling take place. Known also previously as the Heaton Bicycle Track or Heaton Athletics Field, a dedicated football ground was created also to be used for a time by the Heaton Association club. The ground was soon developed south of the established cricket area, at the end of Hartford Street and Spencer Street. East End erected a fence to enclose the playing area, had a new flag-pole installed and removed the cycle track. To follow in the months to come were turnstiles, an elevated press box for reporters - a first in the region. During the summer months of 1889 a timber pavilion building was constructed in characteristic Victorian style, able to seat the club's members, guests and ladies. It was described as a "large and comfortable stand". Yet, the Chillingham Road ground was not perfect. The pitch was often waterlogged due to drainage problems and was constantly criticised for its muddy approaches. Attendances rarely reached in excess of 4,000 or 5,000 during East's End's tenancy. The best gate recorded was the 6,000 crowd for the visit of Teesside's Ironopolis in 1892.

East End also had to contend with the threat of eviction as their landlords, the North Eastern Railway Company, notified the club that the Heaton ground would be required for development, although in the end that was delayed. However, as the future of the Chillingham Road ground was uncertain, when the invitation arrived in the summer of 1892 to takeover West End's site at St James' Park, as well as the prospect of moving to a permanent location near to the city-centre, all was very attractive.

Within 12 months of East End vacating the Heaton Junction Ground, a local club, Trafalgar FC, moved in. The site is now covered by terraced houses and industrial units. It is still adjacent the railway - near the England-Scotland main line and is a goal-kick from the present Chillingham Arms public-house.

Highest Attendances at Chillingham Road:

6,000 v Middlesbrough Ironopolis, 19th April 1892 (Northern Lg).

5,803 v Blackburn Rovers, 13th Feb 1892 (Fr).

St James' Park at the end of the 1920s, prior to construction of cover to the Leazes End (left). The Gallowgate End is to the right while the main West Stand, off Barrack Road, is the only structure to speak of.

ST JAMES' PARK: The Venue

World War One Charity Matches

A few games were arranged during the First World War to raise funds for charities. United star Bill McCracken was particularly active in organising such matches while teammate Bobby Hewison also arranged the occasional fixture. Sometimes the teams selected included a significant number of Newcastle players, although not played under the Newcastle United banner. Two of the most prominent games were played at St James' Park, two others elsewhere on Tyneside; at Brough Park in 1915 (Hewison XI v Mayson XI), and at Wallsend the following year (McCracken XI v Cuggy XI).

11 Nov 1916
W McCracken's XI v League Team 0-2 (0-0) 8,000
(War Funds/Charity Match)

24 May 1919
W McCracken's XI v F Cuggy's XI 1-0 (1-0) 15,000
(War Funds/Charity Match)

Programmes from internationals: England v Wales (1901) and the Euro 96 competition.

Other Events at St James' Park

•Athletics •Baseball •Basketball •Pushball
•Boxing •Rugby •Music •Royal Visits

Many events other than football have taken place at St James' Park over the years. Local sports days were staged at the stadium, featuring track, field and cycling activities before and after World War Two, branded for a period in the Forties as the 'Newcastle United Sports Event', and at a point formally recognised by the Amateur Athletic Association. St James' Park will be a host venue for the 2012 Olympic Games, staging both men and women's football matches.

Both baseball and basketball have been played on the St James' Park pitch. A US Navy side took on the US Army team in a wartime baseball exhibition in 1944 while the world famous Harlem Globetrotters entertained Tyneside during the 1950s. In September 1902 an unusual international took place under the rules of 'pushball' when England defeated the USA 15-9.

During August 1916 a top boxing event was staged at St James' Park in aid of local Red Cross Funds. The open-air promotion saw a healthy attendance of 11,847 (plus a number of wounded soldiers who were admitted free) with five bouts, top-of-the-bill being Bombardier Billy Wells (British Heavyweight Champion) against Sergeant Dick Smith (Light Heavyweight Champion). Not surprisingly perhaps, Wells was superior and won in the ninth round. He held the British title from 1911 to 1919, the first heavyweight to be awarded a Lonsdale Belt outright. His appearance was a headline act.

Rugby internationals have also been staged at the ground; during October 1906 Northumberland played South Africa (0-44) in front of 12,000, while in October 1908 a Northumberland and Cumberland side faced Australia (6-18). Then during January 1909 an England team met the Aussies in a Northern Union Test match (15-5) in front of 22,000. Two years later in 1911 Great Britain faced the Aussie touring side (10-19). During inter-war years the Aussies were back, in 1929 facing an England side under rugby league rules in front of 10,000. The tourists won 32-22. St James' Park is also a confirmed venue for the 2015 Rugby World Cup.

Principal Fixtures played at St James' Park

Matches not involving Newcastle United

Full Internationals

18 March 1901	England v Wales	HIC	6-0	(1-0)	11,439
6 April 1907	England v Scotland	HIC	1-1	(1-1)	35,829
15 Nov 1933	England v Wales	HIC	1-2	(0-1)	12,558
9 Nov 1938	England v Norway	Fr	4-0	(4-0)	39,887
10 June 1996	France v Romania	EC	1-0	(1-0)	26,323
13 June 1996	Bulgaria v Romania	EC	1-0	(1-0)	19,107
18 June 1996	France v Bulgaria	EC	3-1	(1-0)	26,976
5 Sept 2001	England v Albania	WC	2-0	(1-0)	51,046
18 Aug 2004	England v Ukraine	Fr	3-0	(1-0)	35,387
30 March 2005	England v Azerbaijan	WC	2-0	(0-0)	49,046

Wartime Internationals

2 Dec 1939	England v Scotland	WrF	2-1	(1-1)	15,000
8 Feb 1941	England v Scotland	WrF	2-3	(2-2)	25,000
17 May 1941	England* v Army	WrF	4-2	(3-2)	8,425
5 Dec 1942	RAF v Scotland*	WrF	4-0	(2-0)	28,750

*While the actual match programmes noted 'England' and 'Scotland', the teams on show were undoubtedly a Select XI on each occasion rather than the full international side.

B Level, Under-21 & Under-23 Internationals

22 Feb 1950	England B v Holland	Ch	1-0	(0-0)	43,068
2 Nov 1960	England u23 v Italy u23	Ch	1-1	(1-1)	15,064
5 Feb 1964	England u23 v Scotland u23	Ch	3-2	(2-2)	35,032
1 March 1967	England u23 v Scotland u23	Ch	1-3	(0-1)	22,097
13 March 1974	England u23 v Scotland u23	Ch	2-0	(1-0)	4,511
26 April 1983	England u21 v Hungary u21	Ch	1-0	(0-0)	7,810
15 Nov 1994	England u21 v Eire u21	Ch	1-0	(1-0)	25,863
1 April 2003	England u21 v Turkey u21	Chp	1-1	(1-1)	21,085

Full International Trials

25 Feb 1920	England v The North	Ch	5-3	(3-2)	27,024
10 Feb 1926	England v The Rest	Ch	3-4	(1-1)	13,145

Inter-League Internationals

8 March 1902	Football League v Scottish League	Ch	6-3	(5-0)	10,894
17 Feb 1923	Football League v Scottish League	Ch	2-1	(0-1)	27,049
21 Sept 1927	Football League v Irish League	Ch	9-1	(9-0)	1,123
17 March 1948	Football League v Scottish League	Ch	1-1	(0-0)	64,938
31 Oct 1956	Football League v Irish League	Ch	3-2	(1-1)	34,000
26 March 1958	Football League v Scottish League	Ch	4-1	(2-1)	46,800
16 March 1966	Football League v Scottish League	Ch	1-3	(1-0)	32,910

FA & Services Matches

10 March 1945	Army v RAF	Ch	0-0	(0-0)	51,375
3 March 1952	Scottish FA v Army	Ch	3-1	(2-1)	13,000
4 Nov 1953	FA XI v Army	Ch	3-1	(0-0)	15,360
9 Nov 1955	FA XI v Army	Ch	2-2	(0-0)	5,360
29 Oct 1958	FA XI v Army	Ch	4-1	(1-0)	20,738
21 Oct 1959	FA XI v Army	Ch	3-1	(0-0)	18,508

Other Representative Matches

22 April 1925	Home Scots v Anglo Scots		RB	1-0	(0-0)	22,000
28 April 1926	Home Scots v Anglo Scots	aet	RB	4-2	(2-2)	20,000
27 April 1927	Home Scots v Anglo Scots		RB	3-1	(3-1)	17,000
25 April 1928	Home Scots v Anglo Scots	aet	RB	2-4	(1-0)	15,000
22 April 1931	Home Scots v Anglo Scots		AMF	2-3	(2-1)	7,000
26 April 1933	Home Scots v Anglo Scots		Ch	3-2	(1-0)	10,000
29 Sept 1933	North v South (in aid of Wilf Low's dependants)		Ben	6-0	(2-0)	10,000
10 Oct 2004	Celebrities v Legends (The Match, Sky)		Ch	1-2	(0-1)	49,000
9 Oct 2005	Celebrities v Legends (The Match, Sky)		Ch	0-2	(0-1)	52,000
8 Oct 2006	Celebrities v Legends (The Match, Sky)		Ch	0-2	(0-1)	52,000
14 Oct 2007	Duke of Northumberland XI v Earl of Durham XI		PTT	5-3	(3-1)	18,000
26 July 2009	England XI v Germany XI		RFd	3-2	(2-2)	33,000

Club Matches

Date	Match		Comp	Score	HT	Att
13 Nov 1886	Newcastle West End v Sunderland		FACQ	1-0	(0-0)	4,000
20 Nov 1886	Newcastle West End v Gainsborough Trinity		FACQ	2-6	(2-4)	
15 Oct 1887	Newcastle West End v Redcar		FACQ	5-1	(2-0)	
17 Dec 1887	Shankhouse Black Watch v Aston Villa		FAC4	0-9	(0-4)	7,000
6 Oct 1888	Newcastle West End v Bishop Auckland Church Institute		FACQ	7-2	(1-1)	1,000
27 Oct 1888	Newcastle West End v Sunderland Albion (replay ordered)		FACQ	3-5	(2-1)	3,000
10 Nov 1888	Newcastle West End v Sunderland Albion	aet	FACQ	1-2	(1-1)	4,000
5 Oct 1889	Newcastle West End v Port Clarence		FACQ	9-1	(5-1)	1,500
16 Nov 1889	Newcastle West End v South Bank		FACQ	5-2	(1-2)	
18 Jan 1890	Newcastle West End v Grimsby Town		FAC1	1-2	(0-2)	3,000
25 Oct 1890	Newcastle West End v Southwick		FACQ	8-1	(5-1)	1,500
15 Nov 1890	Newcastle West End v Sunderland Albion		FACQ	0-3	(0-1)	3,000
24 Oct 1891	Newcastle West End v Newcastle East End		FACQ	0-3	(0-1)	8,000
18 April 1903	Sunderland v Middlesbrough		FL	2-1	(1-0)	26,554
1 Jan 1917	Liverpool v Leeds City		Ben	4-0	(1-0)	
28 April 1920	Middlesbrough v Sunderland		NECf	0-2	(0-1)	27,000
7 Dec 1925	Blyth Spartans v Hartlepools United	aet	FAC1r	1-1	(1-1)	3,098
19 Nov 1928	Jarrow v York City		FACQr	2-3	(0-3)	6,843
23 Dec 1935	Hartlepools United v Halifax Town	aet	FAC2	4-1	(1-0)	7,698
20 April 1940	Sunderland v Darlington		WrC	1-1	(0-1)	6,023
4 May 1940	Sunderland v Leeds United		WrC	0-0	(0-0)	11,226
26 May 1945	Sunderland v Gateshead		TTC	3-6	(0-3)	13,779
25 Nov 1946	Ashington v North Shields		FACQr	1-3	(1-0)	4,889
24 Sept 1947	Newcastle upon Tyne XI v Groningen (N)		Ch	2-1	(2-0)	7,949
6 Feb 1952	Gateshead v West Bromwich Albion		FAC4	0-2	(0-1)	39,287
13 March 1954	Bishop Auckland v Briggs Sports		FAAsf	5-1	(3-1)	54,210
28 Nov 1955	Carlisle United v Darlington		FAC1r	1-3	(0-1)	34,257
17 March 1956	Bishop Auckland v Kingstonian		FAAsf	5-1	(5-0)	26,890
16 March 1957	Bishop Auckland v Hayes		FAAsf	2-0	(0-0)	32,887
12 March 1960	Crook Town v Kingstonian		FAAsf	1-2	(1-1)	18,167
28 March 1964	Crook Town v Barnet		FAAsf	2-1	(1-0)	10,065
16 Jan 1967	Middlesbrough v York City		FAC2r	4-1	(2-0)	21,347
18 March 1972	Blyth Spartans v Enfield		FAAsf	0-2	(0-2)	18,650
27 Feb 1978	Blyth Spartans v Wrexham		FAC5r	1-2	(0-2)	42,157
8 Aug 1992	Real Sociedad (Sp) v Sporting Clube de Portugal (prior to Newcastle Utd fixture)		NES	2-3	(1-1)	8,548
9 Aug 1992	Middlesbrough v Real Sociedad (Sp) (prior to Newcastle Utd fixture) Real Sociedad won 5-4 on pens.		NES	3-3	(0-1)	7,764
3 Sept 1994	Gateshead v Yeovil Town		VC	0-3	(0-2)	2,734
31 July 2004	Sporting Clube de Portugal v Feyenoord (N) (prior to Newcastle Utd fixture) Sporting won 4-3 on pens.		NGC	1-1	(1-0)	31,554
1 Aug 2004	Glasgow Rangers v Feyenoord (N) (prior to Newcastle Utd fixture) Rangers won 8-7 on pens.		NGC	0-0	(0-0)	23,446

National Finals

Date	Match	Comp	Score	HT	Att
10 May 1913	Sunderland Boys v Watford Boys	ESS	1-1	(1-1)	1,000
17 May 1930	Newcastle Boys v Chesterfield Boys	ESS	1-0	(1-0)	25,000
19 April 1954	Bishop Auckland v Crook Town	FAAr	2-2	(0-2)	56,008
1 May 1988	Humbledon Plains Farm (Sunderland) v Nexday (Northampton)	FAS	0-2	(0-2)	3,000

ABBREVIATIONS

AMF = Aged Miners Fund
Ben = Benefit match
Ch = Challenge match
Chp = European Under-21 Championship
ESS = English Schools Shield
FAA = FA Amateur Cup
FAC = FA Cup
FACQ = FA Cup Qualifying tie
FAS = FA Sunday Cup
FL = Football League
Fr = Friendly match
EC = European Championship
HIC = Home International Championship
NECf = North East Counties Cup final
NES = Newcastle Exhibition Superchallenge Cup
NGC = Newcastle Gateshead Cup
PTT = Princes Trust Challenge Trophy
RB = Robert Burns Memorial Trophy Fund
RFd = Sir Bobby Robson Foundation charity
TTC = Tyne-Wear-Tees Cup
VC = Vauxhall Conference League
WC = World Cup qualifier
WrF = War Funds/Charity match
WrC = War Cup

In recent years St James' Park has been used as a venue for music concerts and has seen some of the biggest acts in the country at the stadium.

Date / Attendance	Act
23 June 1982 35,000	**Rolling Stones** The J Geils Band
5 July 1984 30,000	**Bob Dylan** Santana and Lindisfarne
4 June 1985 35,000	**Bruce Springsteen & The E Street Band**
5 June 1985 38,000	**Bruce Springsteen & The E Street Band**
9 July 1986 38,000	**Queen** Status Quo, Zeno
18 July 1990 30,000	**Rolling Stones** Dan Reed Network and The Quireboys
6 June 2006 20,000	**Bryan Adams** Beverley Knight
25 June 2007 20,000	**Rod Stewart** The Pretenders

The first visit by Royalty to St James' Park took place in 1917 when HM King George V and Queen Mary arrived for the investiture and decoration presentation following World War One. Other non-sporting gatherings have also taken place. The Prince of Wales, later HM King Edward VIII visited Tyneside in 1923 to unveil a World War One statue, The Response, at Barras Bridge. He was also present for a review of school children at St James' Park and around 42,000 were inside the stadium. The only occasion that Royalty has visited the ground for an actual football match was during April 1932 immediately after United's FA Cup final victory at Wembley against Arsenal. With Blackpool the opposition, the two teams were presented to HRH Prince of Wales and the FA Cup was paraded around at pitch-side. In addition, much later HM Queen Elizabeth II visited St James' Park (in 1997) while both HRH Princess Anne (1998) and HRH Prince Charles (2006) did likewise, all for appointments at the arena on non-match days.

Many other non-sporting events have taken place at Newcastle United's home, including scouting pageants, recently swish fashion shows, while even sheep-dog trials have been seen on the famous turf too. St James' Park has also been used as a location for films and television programmes.

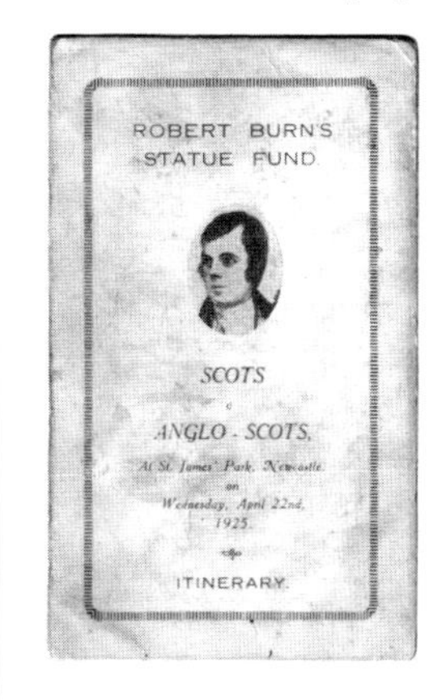

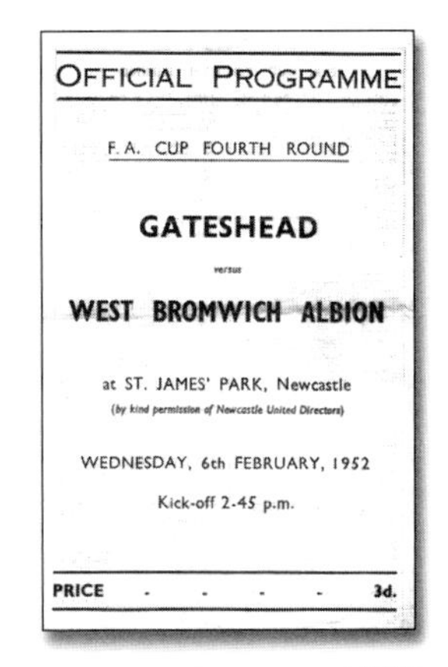

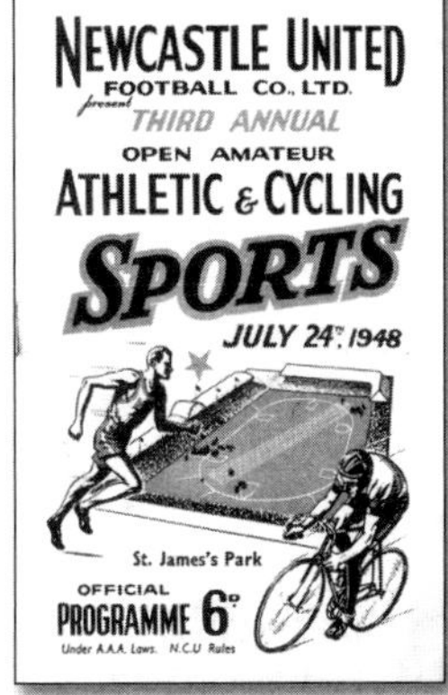

Memorabilia featuring St James' Park events: Player's card for the Scots v Anglo-Scots contest (1925), Gateshead v WBA FA Cup replay (1952), St James' Park Athletics Meeting (1948) and the Rolling Stones 'Urban Jungle' tour poster (1990).

Coca-Cola

- Pioneer Firsts • Football League & Premier League fixtures
- Season's Start, Unbeaten Runs, Consecutive Victories, Defeats & Draws, Without Victory
- FA Cup • Football League Cup • European Competition
- Penalty Shoot-outs • Fixtures • Opposition • Referees • Attendances
- Goals & Goalscorers • Goalkeepers • Players • Managers

Notes on the Statistics

The schedule of Newcastle United's *Facts, Figures & Records* charts the club's principal register of statistics at the close-season 2011 and since formation in 1881. These are perpetually moving and require review each season. Generally, unless detailed, statistics are for senior League, Cup and European fixtures, excluding competitions such as the Texaco Cup, Anglo-Italian Cup and the like although where appropriate other matches have been included or noted.

PIONEER FIRSTS

First fixture
26 Nov 1881 (as Stanley FC) v Elswick Leather Works 2nd XI (h) 5-0 (fr).

First competitive fixture
13 Jan 1883 v Elswick Leather Works (h) 1-2 (N&DCC1).

First league fixture
7 Sept 1889 v Darlington (h) 2-1 (NL).

FOOTBALL LEAGUE/ PREMIER LEAGUE

First fixture
2 Sept 1893 v Woolwich Arsenal (a) 2-2 (Div 2).
This was also Arsenal's first FL fixture.

First victory (& first home fixture)
30 Sept 1893 v Woolwich Arsenal (h) 6-0 (Div 2).

First defeat
23 Sept 1893 v Burton Swifts (a) 1-3 (Div 2).

First away victory
21 Oct 1893 v Ardwick (Manchester City) 3-2 (Div 2).

First top-tier fixture
3 Sept 1898 v Wolverhampton Wanderers (h) 2-4.

First top-tier victory
5 Nov 1898 v Liverpool (h) 3-0.

Overall Records: Home & Away in a season

Most wins
30 in 2009-10 (Ch).

Fewest wins
6 in 1977-78 (Div 1).

Undefeated
United have never gone through a season unbeaten. The best record is 4 defeats in 2009-10 (Ch).

Most defeats
26 in 1977-78 (Div 1).

Most draws
17 in 1990-91 (Div 2) & 2003-04 (PL).

Most points
Two-point system: 57 in 1964-65 (Div 2).
Three-point system: 102 in 2009-10 (Ch).

Fewest Points
Two-point system: 22 in 1977-78 (Div 1).
Three-point system: 31 in 1988-89 (Div 1).

Steven Taylor holds the Championship trophy aloft in 2010.

Overall Records: Home in a season

Most wins
19 in 1926-27 (Div 1).

Fewest wins
3 in 1988-89 (Div 1).

Undefeated
1906-07 (Div 1): P19 W18 D1 L0 & 2009-10 (Ch): P23 W18 D5 L0.
The draw in 1906-07 came in the last home game of the season.

Most defeats
11 in 1957-58 (Div 1) & 1977-78 (Div 1).

Most draws:
11 in 1933-34 (Div 1).

Overall Records: Away in a season

Most wins
13 in 1992-93 (Div 1).

Fewest wins
1 in 1894-95 (Div 2) & 1967-68 (Div 1).

Undefeated
United have never gone through a season unbeaten. The best record is 4 defeats in 2009-10 (Ch).

Most defeats
16 in 1929-30 (Div 1).

Most draws
12 in 2003-04 (PL).

Longest period in the top-tier
32 seasons, 1898-99 to 1933-34.
Top-tier: 80 seasons, 75%.
Second-tier: 27 seasons, 25%.

Lowest final position
Div 2: 20th 1991-92.

Never out of the top two tiers
United are one of only 8 clubs not to have played lower than tier 2 of English football since entering the Football League; *Newcastle United, Arsenal, Everton, Liverpool, Manchester United, Chelsea, West Ham United, Tottenham Hotspur.*

Leading medal holders
FL Championship (tier 1) winners; 3 by Colin Veitch, Jack Rutherford, Jimmy Lawrence.

Biggest victory
13-0 v Newport County (h) Oct 1946 (Div 2).
Largest score in the top 2 tiers of English football and the joint highest in all 4 tiers.

Heaviest defeat
0-9 v Burton Wanderers (a) April 1895 (Div 2).

Large victories; Home
8-0 v Notts County, Oct 1901 (Div 1).
8-0 v Wolves, Nov 1905 (Div 1).
8-0 v Birmingham, Nov 1907 (Div 1).
8-0 v Sheffield Wednesday, Sept 1999 (PL).
9-2 v Liverpool, Jan 1934 (Div 1).
United defeated Swansea Town 8-1 (Div 2) Sept 1939, but the match was later annulled on the outbreak of war.

Large victories; Away
6-0 v Everton, Oct 1912 (Div 1).
6-0 v Walsall, Sept 1962 (Div 2).
7-1 v Manchester United, Sept 1927 (Div 1).
7-2 v Bury, Oct 1961 (Div 2).

Heavy defeats; Home
1-9 v Sunderland, Dec 1908 (Div 1).
1-7 v Blackburn Rovers, Sept 1925 (Div 1).
1-6 v Manchester United, Oct 1907 (Div 1).
1-6 v Chelsea, March 1961 (Div 1).
2-7 v Burnley, Aug 1928 (Div 1).

Heavy defeats; Away
0-7 v Aston Villa, Nov 1902 (Div 1).
0-7 v Tottenham Hotspur, Nov 1950 (Div 1).
1-8 v Everton, Oct 1931 (Div 1).
1-8 v West Ham United, April 1986 (Div 1).

Large half-time leads; Home
7-0 v Newport County, Oct 1946 (Div 2) 13-0.
6-0 v Arsenal, Oct 1925 (Div 1) 7-0.
6-0 v Leicester City, May 1993 (Div 1) 7-1.

Large half-time leads; Away
4-0 v Sunderland, Dec 1955 (Div 1) 6-1.
4-0 v QPR, Sept 1984 (Div 1) 5-5.

Heaviest half-time deficit; Home
1-6 v Burnley Aug 1928 (Div 1) 2-7
In season 2010-11 United were 0-4 down at half-time to Arsenal, but drew 4-4.

Heaviest half-time deficit; Away
0-6 v Everton, Oct 1931 (Div 1) 1-8.

Second-half displays; Home
7 goals v Liverpool, Jan 1934 (Div 1) 9-2.
United scored 8 goals v York City, Oct 1939 (WL) 9-2.
Sunderland netted 8 goals against United, Dec 1908 (Div 1) 1-9.

Second-half displays; Away
5 goals v Everton, Jan 1911 (Div 1) 5-1.
5 goals v Manchester United, Sept 1927 (Div 1) 7-1.
5 goals v Bury, Oct 1961 (Div 2) 7-2.
Manchester United netted 6 goals, Jan 2008 (PL) 0-6, as did Chelsea, March 1961 (Div 1) 1-6.

High scoring games
13 goals: 13-0 v Newport County (h) Oct 1946 (Div 2).
12 goals: 7-5 v Aston Villa (h) March 1928 (Div 1).

High scoring draws
10 goals: 5-5 v West Ham United (h) Dec 1960 (Div 1).
10 goals: 5-5 v QPR (a) Sept 1984 (Div 1).

Most frequent score
Overall: 1-1, 450 times.
Home: 1-0, 208 times.
Away: 1-1, 254 times.

SEASON START

Best start to a season
6-0 v Stoke City (h) 1951-52 (Div 1).

Jackie Milburn, a hat-trick v Stoke in 1951.

Worst start to a season
0-5 v Darwen (a) 1894-95 (Div 2).
In consecutive seasons, 1958-59 and 1959-60 United lost their opening Div 1 fixture, 1-5 to Blackburn Rovers and Tottenham Hotspur respectively, both at home.

Unbeaten from the start of the season
11 games, 1950-51 (W5 D6, Div 1) & 1992-93 (W11, Div 1) & 1994-95 (W9 D2, PL).

Consecutive wins from the start of the season
11 games, 1992-93 (Div 1).

Without victory from the start of the season
10 games, 1898-99 (D4 L6, Div 1).

Consecutive defeats from the start of the season
4 games, 1934-35 (Div 2).

SEQUENCES

Unbeaten Runs

League, (overall)
Overall: 17 games, Feb to May 2010 (W13 D4, Ch).
Home: 31 games, Dec 1905 to Sept 1907 (W 27 D4, Div 1).
Away: 10 games, Nov 1907 to Mar 1908 (W3 D7, Div 1).

League, (within a season)
Overall: 17 games, Feb to May 2010 (W13 D4, Ch).
Home: 23 games (whole season) Aug 2009 to April 2010 (W18 D5, Ch).
Away: 10 games, Nov 1907 to March 1908 (W3 D7, Div 1).

League & Cup
Overall: 18 games, May to Oct 1994 (W16 D2).
Including AIC games, United went 19 competitive games without defeat, April to Oct 1992.
Home: 26 games, Aug 2009 to Aug 2010 (W21 D5).
Away: 11 games, Nov 1907 to March 1908 (W4 D7).

Consecutive Victories

League
Overall: 13 games, April to Oct 1992 (Div 2/1).
Home: 20 games, April 1906 to April 1907 (Div 1).
Away: 6 games, May to Oct 1992 (Div 2/Div 1).

League & Cup
Overall: 9 games, May to Sept 1994.
Home: 14 games, April 1895 to Jan 1896 & Dec 1926 to Sept 1927.
Away: 7 games, Aug to Oct 1994.

Consecutive Defeats

League
Overall: 10 games, Aug to Oct 1977 (Div 1).
Home: 6 games, Sept to Oct 1953 (Div 1).
Away: 10 games, Dec 1931 to April 1932 (Div 1).

League & Cup
Overall: 6 games, Jan to Feb 1937 & Oct to Nov 1963 & Oct 1971.
Home: 6 games, Sept to Oct 1953.
Away: 10 games, Sept to Dec 1960.

Consecutive Draws

League
Overall: 4 games on 15 occasions.
During April 1900 (Div 1) one such sequence included 3 consecutive 0-0 draws.
Home: 5 games, Dec 1960 to Feb 1961 (Div 1).
Away: 8 games, Dec 1969 to Mar 1970 (Div 1) *(last 8 away games of the season).*

League & Cup
Overall: 5 games, Oct to Nov 1984.
Home: 4 games, Feb 1936.
Away: 6 games, Dec 1907 to Mar 1908.

Without Victory

League
Overall: 21 games, Jan to Aug 1978 (D8 L13, Div 1/Div 2).
Within this run United failed to win any of the last 19 games of the 1977-78 season (D8 L11). United went 14 PL games without a win, April to Sept 1999, before ending the sequence by beating Sheffield Wednesday 8-0.
Home: 12 games, Dec 1977 to Aug 1978 (D5 L7, Div 1/Div 2).
Away: 18 games, Sept 1984 to April 1985 (D8 L10, Div 1).

League & Cup
Overall: 23 games, Jan to Aug 1978 (D9 L14).
Home: 11 games, Jan to Aug 1978 (D6 L5).
Away: 18 games April 1967 to Jan 1968 (D7 L11).
This run was part of a sequence of 1 victory in 23 games.

FA Cup glory in 1932.

FA CUP

First game
15 Oct 1887 v South Bank (a) 2-3 (R1Q).

First victory
6 Oct 1888 v Port Clarence (h) 3-1 (R1Q).

Biggest victory
9-0 v Southport (at Hillsborough) Feb 1932 (R4rr).

Heaviest defeat
1-7 v Aston Villa (a) Feb 1895 (R2).

Heaviest home defeat
0-5 v Sheffield United Jan 1914 (R1).

Biggest home win
8-0 v West Hartlepool NER Oct 1895 (R1Q).
8-1 v Notts County Jan 1927 (R3).
7-0 v Bishop Auckland Town Dec 1891 (R4Q).

Biggest away win
9-0 v Southport (at Hillsborough) Feb 1932 (R4rr).
6-0 v Fulham (at Anfield) March 1908 (SF).
The 6-0 victory remains the biggest in a semi-final.
7-2 v Oldham Athletic Jan 1950 (R3).
6-1 v Plymouth Argyle Jan 1958 (R3).
6-1 Bradford City March 1963 (R3).

Biggest half-time lead
6-0 v Notts County (h) Jan 1927 (R3) 8-1.
4-0 v Tow Law Town (a) Oct 1891 (R1Q) 5-1.
4-0 v West Hartlepool NER (h) Oct 1895 (R1Q) 8-0.
4-0 v Rendel (h) Nov 1895 (R3Q) 5-0.
4-0 v Southport (at Hillsborough) Feb 1932 (R4rr) 9-0.
4-0 v Crystal Palace (h) Jan 1947 (R3) 6-2.

Heaviest half-time deficit
1-6 v Aston Villa (a) Feb 1895 (R2) 1-7.

Longest ties
4 games (450m) v Watford, 1988-89 (R3).
4 games (420m) v Derby County, 1923-24 (R2).

Unbeaten run
16 games: 1950-51 (8 games), 1951-52 (7 games) & 1952-53 (1 game).
United went three seasons in which the only ties they lost were played at Wembley: 1997-98 (6 games to final), 1998-99 (6 games to final), 1999-2000 (5 games to semi-final) and they drew their first game in 2000-01 before losing the replay, making a run of 18 matches.

Scored in every round
Jack Milburn: 1950-51 (8 goals).

Semi-final venues
Most: 4 games at Hillsborough, Sheffield (P4 W1 D3 L0).

Non-League opponents
Excluding Qualifying rounds. Newcastle have drawn non-League opponents on 22 occasions, including when the likes of Tottenham Hotspur and West Ham United were members of the Southern League prior to 1919.
Bedford Town (1964), Chesterfield (1896), Corinthians (1927), Crystal Palace (1907, 1920), Hendon (1974), Hereford United (1972), Northampton Town (1911), Plymouth Argyle (1905), Reading (1900), Southampton (1898, 1900), Stevenage Borough (1998), Stoke (1910), Swansea Town (1915), Swindon Town (1910), Tottenham Hotspur (1905), West Ham United (1908, 1909, 1915), Wigan Athletic (1954), Yeading (2005).

Non-League clash with Corinthians.

Defeats by non-League sides
1898 v Southampton (a) R2 L0-1, 1900 v Southampton (a) R2 L1-4, 1907 v Crystal Palace (h) R1 L0-1, 1964 v Bedford Town (h) R3 L1-2, 1972 v Hereford United (a) R3r L1-2.

Extra-time matches
P25 W6 D14 L5.

Leading medal holders
Winners: 3 by Jack Milburn, Bobby Mitchell & Bobby Cowell.
Finalists: 5 by Colin Veitch, Jack Rutherford & Jimmy Lawrence.

Played in & managed a winning side
With United: Stan Seymour (player 1924, manager/director 1951 & 1952).
Joe Harvey played in winning sides (1951,1952), was on the coaching staff at the time of the 1955 victory, and managed United to a losing final (1974).
Played for United, managed elsewhere: Peter McWilliam (United 1910, Tottenham Hotspur 1921), Bob Stokoe (United 1955, Sunderland 1973).

First Football League Cup fixture.

FOOTBALL LEAGUE CUP

First game
10 Oct 1960 v Colchester United (a) 1-4 (R1).

First victory
13 Sept 1961 v Scunthorpe United (h) 2-0 (R1).

Biggest home victory
6-0 v Doncaster Rovers Oct 1973 (R2).
6-0 v Southport Sept 1975 (R2).

Biggest away victory
7-1 v Notts County Oct 1993 (R2).
5-0 v Bristol City Sept 1995 (R2).
4-0 v QPR Oct 1974 (R3).
4-0 v Stoke City Oct 1995 (R3).

Heaviest defeat
2-7 v Manchester United (a) Oct 1976 (R4).

Heaviest home defeat
0-4 v Arsenal Oct 2010 (R4).
1-4 v Leeds United Oct 1982 (R2).
0-3 v Blackpool Oct 1972 (R3).

Biggest half-time lead
4-0 v Ipswich Town (h)
Nov 2001 (R4) 4-1.

Heaviest half-time deficit
0-3 v Colchester United (a)
Oct 1960 (R1) 1-4.

Unbeaten run
5 games, Sept to Dec 1974 & Sept to Dec 1975.

Extra-time matches
P13 W2 D5 L6.

Jack Rutherford, five FA Cup medals.

Champions League action; Andy Griffin has just scored against Juventus.

EUROPEAN COMPETITION

Qualifying seasons

UEFA Champions League: 1997-98, 2002-03, 2003-04 (Qual).

Inter Cities/European Fairs Cup: 1968-69, 1969-70, 1970-71.

UEFA Cup: 1977-78, 1994-95, 1996-97, 1999-00, 2003-04, 2004-05, 2006-07.

UEFA Cup Winners Cup: 1998-99.

Intertoto Cup: 2001-02, 2005-06, 2006-07.

United are one of only 10 English clubs to have qualified for the UEFA Champions League and one of 16 sides to have appeared in the overall European Cup/Champions League since inception.

First game & First victory
11 Sept 1968 v Feyenoord (h) 4-0 (ICFC1).

Biggest home victory
5-0 v NAC Breda (h) Sept 2003 (UEFAC1).

Biggest away victory
5-0 v Royal Antwerp (a) Sept 1994 (UEFAC1).

Heaviest defeat
0-3 v AS Monaco (a) March 1997 (UEFAC4) & 1-4 v Internazionale Milano (h) Nov 2002 (CL) & 1-4 v Sporting Clube de Portugal (a) April 2005 (UEFAC5).

Heaviest home defeat
1-4 v Internazionale Milano (h) Nov 2002 (CL).

Biggest half-time lead
4-0 v Royal Antwerp (h) Sept 1994 (UEFAC1) 5-2.

Biggest half-time deficit
0-3 v Internazionale Milano (h) Nov 2002 (CL) 1-4.

Best aggregate victory
10-2 v Royal Antwerp 1994-95 (UEFAC1) 5-0 (a), 5-2 (h).

Worst aggregate defeat
0-4 v AS Monaco 1996-97 (UEFAC4) 0-1 (h), 0-3 (a).

Unbeaten run

Overall: 13 games 2006-07, Intertoto and UEFA Cups (W10, D3).

Home: 13 games 1968-69 to 1977-78, Inter Cities Fairs and UEFA Cups (W12 D1) & 2003-04 to 2005-06, UEFA and Intertoto Cups (W11 D2).

Away: 8 games 2002-03 to 2003-04, Champions League and UEFA Cup (W5 D3).

Consecutive victories

Overall: 5 games, 1968-69 to 1969-70 Inter Cities Fairs Cup & 2004-05 UEFA Cup (twice) & 2006-07 UEFA Cup.

Home: 8 games, 1968-69 to 1969-70 Inter Cities Fairs Cup.

Away: 5 games 2004-05 UEFA Cup.

Extra-time matches
P3 W0 D1 L2.

PENALTY SHOOT-OUTS

Overall: P8 W1 L7.

United have lost all 5 shoot-outs contested at home, having won only once v Watford (a) Nov 2006 (FLC R4).

FA Cup: Lost to AFC Bournemouth (h) 1991-92 (R3) & Chelsea (h) 1995-96 (R3).

League Cup: Lost to Sunderland (h) 1979-80 (R2) & Blackburn Rovers (h) 1998-99 (R4) & Everton (h) 2002-03 (R3).

Europe: Lost to Pecsi Dozsa (a) 1970-71 (ICFC2) & FK Partizan (h) 2003-04 (CLQ).

FIXTURES

Longest season
1968-69, 10 Aug to 11 June, 10m 2d.

Most games in a season
Overall: 59 in 1968-69 (42 FL, 3 FAC, 2 FLC, 12 ICFC).
FA Cup: 10 games in 1954-55.
FL Cup: 8 games in 1975-76.
Europe: 14 games in 2002-03 (CL) & 2003-04 (CL/UEFAC) & 2006-07 (ITC/UEFAC).

Longest game
Around 143m v Darlington May 1944 (h) 1-1 (FLN & TTWC).

Overall Competitive Record

Competition	Home								
First XI competitive fixtures.	P	W	%	D	%	L	%	F	A
FA Premier League (17 seasons)	327	175	54	83	25	69	21	580	341
FL Division 1/Tier 1 (63 seasons)	1272	689	54	284	22	299	24	2463	1512
FL Division 2/Tier 2 (27 seasons)	546	355	65	105	19	86	16	1210	540
FL Test Matches/Play-Offs	3	2	67	0	0	1	33	6	3
Northern League (4 seasons)	29	20	69	3	10	6	21	77	26
FA Cup	182	109	60	40	22	33	18	406	186
FL Cup	58	34	59	8	14	16	28	110	63
European	60	44	73	8	13	8	13	123	47
FA Charity Shield/SoL Shield	1	0	0	0	0	1	100	3	5
Wartime League & Cup	137	85	62	19	14	33	24	414	219
Texaco Cup	14	10	71	3	21	1	7	36	14
Anglo-Italian Cup	6	4	67	1	17	1	17	17	5
Anglo-Scottish Cup	3	1	33	1	33	1	33	5	4
Full Members Cup	3	3	100	0	0	0	0	7	3
Mercantile Cantenary Trophy	1	1	100	0	0	0	0	1	0
N&D/Northb Challenge Cup	12	7	58	2	17	3	25	67	15
FL/FA Cup annulled matches	2	2	100	0	0	0	0	12	4
Total	2656	1541	58	557	21	558	21	5537	2987

Competition	Away								
First XI competitive fixtures.	P	W	%	D	%	L	%	F	A
FA Premier League (17 seasons)	327	83	25	95	29	149	46	360	493
FL Division 1/Tier 1 (63 seasons)	1272	302	24	322	25	648	51	1492	2262
FL Division 2/Tier 2 (27 seasons)	546	156	29	125	23	265	48	678	933
FL Test Matches/Play-Offs	3	0	0	1	33	2	67	3	5
Northern League (4 seasons)	29	8	28	5	17	16	55	47	80
FA Cup	195	77	39	45	23	73	37	285	272
FL Cup	68	21	31	11	16	36	53	88	111
European	60	25	42	14	23	21	35	85	72
FA Charity Shield/SoL Shield	6	2	33	0	0	4	67	10	15
Wartime League & Cup	130	42	32	18	14	70	54	240	291
Texaco Cup	14	2	14	5	36	7	50	13	17
Anglo-Italian Cup	7	3	43	3	43	1	14	9	7
Anglo-Scottish Cup	4	1	25	1	25	2	50	1	5
Full Members Cup	6	0	0	1	17	5	83	11	18
Mercantile Cantenary Trophy	1	0	0	0	0	1	100	0	2
N&D/Northb Challenge Cup	9	4	44	1	11	4	44	19	15
FL/FA Cup annulled matches	2	0	0	0	0	2	100	0	5
Total	2679	726	27	647	24	1306	49	3341	4603

Competition	Total								
First XI competitive fixtures.	P	W	%	D	%	L	%	F	A
FA Premier League (17 seasons)	654	258	39	178	27	218	33	940	834
FL Division 1/Tier 1 (63 seasons)	2544	991	39	606	24	947	37	3955	3774
FL Division 2/Tier 2 (27 seasons)	1092	511	47	230	21	351	32	1888	1473
FL Test Matches/Play-Offs	6	2	33	1	17	3	50	9	8
Northern League (4 seasons)	58	28	48	8	14	22	38	124	106
FA Cup	377	186	49	85	22	106	28	691	458
FL Cup	126	55	44	19	15	52	41	198	174
European	120	69	58	22	18	29	24	208	119
FA Charity Shield/SoL Shield	7	2	29	0	0	5	71	13	20
Wartime League & Cup	267	127	48	37	14	103	39	654	510
Texaco Cup	28	12	43	8	29	8	29	49	31
Anglo-Italian Cup	13	7	54	4	31	2	15	26	12
Anglo-Scottish Cup	7	2	29	2	29	3	43	6	9
Full Members Cup	9	3	33	1	11	5	56	18	21
Mercantile Cantenary Trophy	2	1	50	0	0	1	50	1	2
N&D/Northb Challenge Cup	21	11	52	3	14	7	33	86	30
FL/FA Cup annulled matches	4	2	50	0	0	2	50	12	9
Total	5335	2267	42	1204	23	1864	35	8878	7590

Abandoned matches not included.

FA Cup record includes walkover when drawn away to Leadgate Exiles in 1895-96 as an away win

Away record includes all neutral ground fixtures.

OPPOSITION

Most games against one club

League & Cup: Arsenal P168 W66 D37 L65.
League: Arsenal P154 W62 D35 L57.
Cup football: Nottingham Forest P18 W6 D7 L5.
All matches: 236 v Sunderland (144 League & Cup, 25 Wartime, 67 Others).

Most frequent opponents in a season

7 games v Birmingham City 1973-74 (2 FL, 2 FLC, 3 TC).

Most League wins

Overall: 64 v Manchester City.
Home: 48 v Manchester City.
Away: 22 v Arsenal.

Most League draws

Overall: 41 v Sunderland.
Home: 23 v Liverpool.
Away: 24 v Sunderland.
The away Play-off match against Sunderland in May 1990 was also drawn.

Most League defeats

Overall: 72 Liverpool.
Home: 26 v Manchester United.
Away: 50 v Liverpool.

Most League goals scored

Overall: 231 v Aston Villa.
Home: 156 v Aston Villa.
Away: 90 v Everton.

Most League goals conceded

Overall: 272 v Manchester United.
Home: 110 v Manchester United.
Away: 172 v Liverpool.

PL/FL clubs United have not played in League or Cup football

Aldershot Town, Barnet, Burton Albion, Crawley Town, Dagenham & Redbridge, Milton Keynes Dons#, Macclesfield Town, Morecambe, Rochdale*, AFC Wimbledon#, Wycombe Wanderers, Yeovil Town.

Ex-League clubs United have not faced in League or Cup football

Aldershot, Ashington, Barrow, Bootle, Boston United, Darlington*, Durham City*, Kidderminster Harriers, Leeds City, Maidstone United, Merthyr Town, Nelson, New Brighton, Scarborough, South Shields/Gateshead*, Stalybridge Celtic, Thames, Wigan Borough, Workington.

** Identifies sides United have played in competitive Northern League or wartime football.*
 # United have played the Dons when they were based in London as Wimbledon, but have not faced either AFC Wimbledon or MK Dons.

Overseas Opponents

United have played football in 42 different countries out with the UK.

Matches against foreign opponents in European competition

14 Netherlands, 13 Spain, 11 France.

Tyne v Wear

First game: 3 Nov 1883
(as East End v Sunderland 'A') (h) 0-3 (fr).
First senior game: 17 Nov 1888
(as East End) (a) 0-2 (FACQ).
First League meeting: 24 Dec 1898 (a) 3-2 (Div 1).
Biggest victory: 6-1 (h) Oct 1920 (Div 1) & (a) Dec 1955 (Div 1).
Heaviest defeat: 1-9 (h) Dec 1908 (Div 1).
Overall record, League & Cup: P144 W52 D46 L46
(1979-80 FLC lost on pens taken as a defeat).
Derby Hat-tricks: Alex Tait (h) Dec 1956 (Div 1) & Peter Beardsley (h) Jan 1985 (Div 1) & Kevin Nolan (h) Oct 2010 (PL).

REFEREES

(Post-World War Two, League & Cup fixtures)

Most games: 39 MA Riley (1997-2007).
Most Wins: 17 DJ Gallacher (1991-2007) & SW Dunn (1995-2005).
Most defeats: 16 JB Worrall (1977-95).
No defeats (more than 6 games): 9 A Murdoch (1952-59).
No wins (more than 6 games): 10 KH Burns (1968-76).
Most dismissals: 6 B Knight, in 10 games (1999-2005).
Brian Coddington only refereed a single United fixture (v Derby Co, April 1992) when he sent-off 3 Newcastle players plus coach Terry McDermott.

ATTENDANCES

Record home attendance, progression

1890s: 30,000 v Burnley Dec 1897 (Div 2) & v Sheffield United Oct 1899 (Div 1).
1900s: 56,875 v Sunderland Sept 1906 (Div 1).
1910s: 61,761 v Sunderland Nov 1919 (Div 1).
1920s: 67,067 v Sunderland March 1927 (Div 1).
1930s: 68,386 v Chelsea Sept 1930 (Div 1).
A crowd reported as between 45,000 and as high as 70,000 were in and around St James' Park for the Div 1 fixture with Sunderland on Good Friday 1901. The match was abandoned before a ball was kicked.

Average Attendances (League & Cup)

Record at St James' Park: 56,298 (1947-48 Div 2).
Lowest at St James' Park: 3,769 (1893-94 Div 2).
Lowest at St James' Park (post-war): 17,307 (1990-91, Div 2).
United's average attendance in Premier League action since ground enlargement for 2000-01 is 50,891 (10 seasons).

Top aggregate attendance at St James' Park

1.327m spectators in season 2002-03
1.277m spectators in season 2001-02
1.206m spectators in season 2004-05
In total 79,398,862 fans have watched United's senior games on Tyneside to the end of the 2010-11 season. During the club's 130th Anniversary of 2011-12 a total of 80m spectators will have seen the Magpies on home turf.

Highest attendances, all games

League: 75,965 v Manchester United (a) Jan 2008 (PL).
FA Cup: 101,117 v Aston Villa (Crystal Palace) April 1905 (FACF).
FL Cup: 100,000 v Manchester City (Wembley) Feb 1976 (FLCF).
Europe: 98,000 v Dynamo Kyiv (a) Oct 1997 (CL).
Friendly: 61,300 v Celtic (a) Sept 1951.

Highest attendances, at St James' Park

League: 68,386 v Chelsea Sept 1930 (Div 1).
FA Cup: 67,596 v Bolton Wanderers Jan 1951 (R4).
FL Cup: 49,902 v Tottenham Hotspur Jan 1976 (SF).
Europe: 59,309 v RSC Anderlecht March 1970 (ICFC4).
Wartime: 54,954 v Manchester City Dec 1945 (WL).
Friendly: 51,257 v FC Barcelona Aug 2002.
Testimonial: 52,275 v Celtic (Alan Shearer) May 2006.
Other fixtures: 64,938 Football League v Scottish League March 1948.

Lowest attendances, all games (post-1900)
League: 2,000 v Wolves (a) March 1902 (Div 1).
FA Cup: 6,000 v Grimsby Town (a) Feb 1903 (R1).
FL Cup: 4,098 v Accrington Stanley (a) Aug 2010 (R2).
Europe: 2,425 v Sporting Lokeren (a) July 2001 (ITC3).
Other competitive: 744 v AS Lucchese (a) Nov 1992 (AIC).

Lowest attendances, at St James' Park (post-1900)
League: 3,867 v Nottingham Forest March 1937 (Div 2).
FA Cup: 11,953 v Bradford City Jan 1913 (R1).
FL Cup: 9,073 v Bury Aug 1980 (R2).
Europe: 19,046 v Bohemians Sept 1977 (UEFAC1).
Other competitive: 4,609 v AC Cesena Dec 1992 (AIC).

GOALS & GOALSCORERS

First Goals
League: Tom Crate v Woolwich Arsenal (a) Sept 1893 (Div 2).
FA Cup: William Muir v South Bank (a) Oct 1887 (RQ).
FL Cup: Duncan Neale v Colchester United (a) Oct 1960 (R1).
Europe: Jim Scott v Feyenoord (h) Sept 1968 (ICFC1).

Record Victories
Progression since entering the Football League
6-0 v Woolwich Arsenal (h) Sept 1893 (Div 2).
(equalled v Crewe Alex 1894-95)
8-0 v West Hartlepool NER (h) Oct 1895 (FACQ).
(equalled 3 times; v Notts Co 1901-02, v Wolves 1905-06, v Birmingham 1907-08).
9-0 v Southport (at Hillsborough) Feb 1932 (FAC4).
13-0 v Newport County (h) Oct 1946 (Div 2).

Heaviest Defeats
Progression since entering the Football League
0-5 v Darwen (a) Sept 1894 (Div 2).
1-7 v Aston Villa (a) Feb 1895 (FAC2).
0-9 v Burton Wanderers (a) April 1895 (Div 2).

Highest scoring victories, all fixtures
19-0 v Point Pleasant (as East End) (h) Jan 1888 (NCC).
16-2 v Alberta All Stars (a) June 1949 (fr).
14-1 v Beaumaris (a) Feb 1908 (fr).
13-0 v Newport County (h) Oct 1946 (Div 2).
13-2 v Saskatchewan (a) May 1949 (fr).
12-1 v Bela Vista (h) Oct 1958 (fr).
12-2 v Brampton Welfare (a) March 1899 (fr).
11-0 v Austria XI (a) May 1905 (fr).
11-0 v Bradford City (h) Nov 1944 (WL).
11-0 v Middlesbrough (h) May 1945 (WL).
11-1 v Washington State (a) June 1949 (fr).
11-2 v Paris Athletique (h) Sept 1904 (fr).
10-0 v Border Province (a) July 1952 (fr).
10-1 v Berlin British (a) May 1905 (fr).

High scoring draws, all fixtures
6-6 v Gateshead (h) Dec 1942 (WL).
6-6 v Tranmere Rovers (a) Oct 1991 (FMC).

Quickest Goals
4 seconds: Malcolm Macdonald v St Johnstone (a) July 1972 (fr).
8-10 seconds: Jack Milburn v Cardiff City (h) Nov 1947 (Div 2).
10 seconds: Alan Shearer v Manchester City (h) Jan 2003 (PL).
Jack Milburn scored after 45 seconds against Manchester City in the 1955 FA Cup final, at the time the fastest goal in a Wembley final.

Most Goals in a season
League & Cup: 113 goals 1951-52 (Div 1).
League only: 98 goals 1951-52 (Div 1).

Fewest Goals in a season
League & Cup: 36 goals 1988-89 (Div 1).
League only: 30 goals 1980-81 (Div 2).

Most Goals conceded in a season
League & Cup: 117 goals 1960-61 (Div 1).
League only: 109 goals 1960-61 (Div 1).

Fewest Goals conceded in a season
League & Cup: 37 goals 1901-02 (Div 1).
League only: 32 goals 1897-98 (Div 2).
United conceded a further 6 goals in the 1897-98 Test Matches.

Top-5 United Goalscorers, League & Cup
206 goals: Alan Shearer (1996-2006).
200 goals: Jack Milburn (1943-57).
153 goals: Len White (1953-62).
143 goals: Hughie Gallacher (1925-30).
121 goals: Malcolm Macdonald (1971-76).
152 own goals have also been scored.

Alan Shearer, most goals.

Most Goals, by competition
League & Cup: 206 by Alan Shearer (1996-2006).
League: 177 by Jack Milburn (1943-57).
FA Cup: 23 by Jack Milburn (1943-57).
FL Cup: 12 by Malcolm Macdonald (1971-76).
Europe: 30 by Alan Shearer (1996-2006).
Wartime: 231 by Albert Stubbins (1939-46).
League, Cup, Wartime games: 238 by Jack Milburn (1943-57).
Note: Jack Milburn also scored a 'Golden Goal' against Darlington in wartime football taking his tally to 239.

Best strike-rate in a career
82% by Hughie Gallacher, 143 goals in 174 games (1925-30).
Arthur Bottom (1958) had a strike rate of 91% but only played 11 games, scoring 10 goals.

Most Goals in a season, League & Cup
41 by Andy Cole 1993-94 (PL).
39 by George Robledo 1951-52 (Div 1).
39 by Hughie Gallacher 1926-27 (Div 1).
Albert Stubbins scored 43 goals in both wartime seasons 1943-44 & 1944-4, as well as 42 goals in 1942-43.

Lowest top-scorer in a season, League & Cup
7 by Bobby Shinton 1980-81 (Div 2) & John Barnes, Alan Shearer 1997-98 (PL) & Carl Cort, Alan Shearer, Nobby Solano, 2000-01 (PL).

Most goals home & away
Home; 131 Alan Shearer. Away; 80 Jack Milburn.

Most goals in a game
9 by Bill Appleyard v Beaumaris (a) Feb 1908 (fr).
7 by Alec White v Point Pleasant (h) Jan 1888 (NCC).
Some reports note White as scoring 8, 9 or even 10 goals.
7 by George Robledo v Border Province (a) July 1952 (fr).
6 by Len Shackleton v Newport County (h) Oct 1946 (Div 2).
6 by Eddie Carr v Bradford City (h) Nov 1944 (WL).
6 by Jack Milburn v Alberta All Stars (a) June 1949 (fr).
Albert Stubbins scored 5 goals in a match on 5 occasions in wartime football.
Ted Harper (Blackburn Rovers) netted 5 against United in Sept 1925, the highest individual tally by an opponent in League or Cup football.

Hat-tricks, League & Cup
First hat-trick: Tom McInnes v West End (h) Sept 1890 (NL).
McInnes also scored the club's first FA Cup hat-trick against Shankhouse Black Watch (h) Nov 1890.
Most hat-tricks in a season:
5 by Hughie Gallacher 1926-27 (Div 1).
Most hat-tricks in a career:
14 by Hughie Gallacher (1925-30).
Hat-trick as substitute: Craig Bellamy v Brentford (h) Sept 2001 (FLC2) (in extra-time).
Most club hat-tricks in a season: 9 in 1926-27.
Albert Stubbins scored 29 hat-tricks in wartime football including 7 in 1942-43. 11 hat-tricks were scored for United in the wartime 1942-43 season.
Most hat-tricks scored against opponents:
9 v Liverpool.
12 hat-tricks were scored against Middlesbrough in wartime football.

Premier League best (all clubs)
Most goals in a season: 34 by Andy Cole (for United) 1993-94 & Alan Shearer (for Blackburn Rovers) 1994-95.

Most goals in a game: 5 by Alan Shearer (for United) v Sheffield Wednesday Sept 1999 & Andy Cole (for Manchester United) v Ipswich Town, March 1995.

Most goals in a career: 260 by Alan Shearer.
Andy Cole (187), Les Ferdinand (149) and Michael Owen (149) are all featured in the top-ten goalscorers.*

Fastest 100 goals
Hughie Gallacher in 31 months (Dec 1925 to March 1929).

Penalties
First penalty: by Harry Jeffrey v Walsall Town Swifts (h) March 1894 (Div 2).

Most penalties scored in a match: 2 penalties have been scored in a match by United on 17 occasions.

Most penalties in a season:
9 by Alan Shoulder 1979-80 (Div 2).

Most penalties in a career: 46 by Alan Shearer 1996-2006, 34 by Frank Hudspeth 1910-29.

Most club penalties in a season, League & Cup:
11 in 1993-94.

Most penalties scored against opponents:
18 v Everton, Sunderland.

In January 1912, Manchester City missed 3 penalties against United.

Consecutive scoring, League
Overall: 25 games, April 1939 to Dec 1946 (W12 D7 L6, Div 2).
Home: 48 games, Sept 1894 to Nov 1897 (W42 D 2 L 4, Div 2).
Away: 19 games, Jan 1992 to Dec 1992 (W11 D2 L6, Div 2).

Consecutive scoring, League & Cup
Overall: 28 games, Nov 1954 to April 1955 (W15 D7 L6).
Home: 55 games, Sept 1894 to Nov 1897 (W48 D2 L5).
Away: 15 games, Nov 1954 to April 1955 (W5 D5 L5).

Consecutive non-scoring, League
Overall: 6 games, Dec 1938 to Feb 1939 (D2 L4, Div 2) & Oct 1988 to Dec 1988 (D2 L4, Div 1).
Home: 6 games, March 2007 to Aug 2007 (D4 L2, PL).
Away: 8 games, Oct 1913 to Jan 1914 (D2 L6, Div 1) & Feb 1981 to Sept 1981 (D2 L6, Div 2).

Consecutive non-scoring, League & Cup
Overall: 6 games, Oct to Dec 1988 (D2 L4).
Home: 5 games, April 1951 (D1 L4, Div 1) & March 2007 to Aug 2007 (D3 L2).
Away: 9 games, Feb 1981 to Sept 1981 (D2 L7).

Individual consecutive scoring
League & Cup: 9 games (13 goals) by Willie Wardrope, Oct to Dec 1895 Div 2.

League: 7 games (9 goals) by Len White, Dec 1960 to Feb 1961, Div 1 & Paul Goddard (7 goals) March to April 1987 Div 1.

FA Cup: 5 games (8 goals) by Bill Appleyard, Jan to March 1908.

FL Cup: 4 games (6 goals) by Malcolm Macdonald, Sept to Nov 1974.

Europe: 5 games (6 goals) by Alan Shearer, Feb to April 2005, UEFA Cup.

Wartime: 6 games (13 goals) by Albert Stubbins, Nov 1942 to Dec 1942 & (10 goals) Oct 1943 to Dec 1943.

Most own-goals conceded by opposition
League & Cup: 9 by Sheffield United.
League: 9 by Sheffield United.

Most own-goals in a season
6 in 1948-49.

Most Cup Final goals
3 by Jack Milburn (2 in 1951 FAC, 1 in 1955 FAC) & Bobby Moncur (2 in 1st leg, 1 in 2nd leg 1969 ICFC).

Bob Moncur, three goals v Ujpesti.

GOALKEEPERS

Top-5 'keepers; clean-sheets, League and Cup
173 by Jimmy Lawrence (1904-22).
131 by Shay Given (1997-2009).
103 by Willie McFaul (1966-75).
64 by Matt Kingsley (1898-04).
61 by Pavel Srnicek (1991-98, 2006-2007).

Most clean-sheets by competition
League and Cup: 173 by Jimmy Lawrence (1904-22).
League: 142 by Jimmy Lawrence (1904-22).
FA Cup: 31 by Jimmy Lawrence (1904-22).
FL Cup: 6 by Shaka Hislop (1995-98) & Willie McFaul (1966-75).
Europe: 21 by Shay Given (1997-2009).

Best League goals per game ratio in a career
0.95 by Bill Bradley (127 goals in 133 games, 1914-27).

Clean-sheets in a League season
22 in 2009-10 (Ch), 21 by Steve Harper & 1 by Tim Krul.
20 in 1947-48 (Div 2) 10 by Jack Fairbrother & 10 by Eric Garbutt.
Jimmy Lawrence kept 18 clean sheets in 1920-21 (Div 1) and 17 in 1908-09 (Div 1).

Most League clean-sheets against opposition
Overall: 48 v Everton.
Home: 34 v Everton. Away: 19 v Arsenal.

Consecutive clean-sheets, League
Overall: 6 games, March to April 1982 (W4 D2, Div 2).
Home: 6 games, Jan to April 1948 (W6, Div 2) & Sept to Dec 1979 (W5 D1, Div 2) & Feb to April 1982 (W4 D2, Div 2).
Away: 5 games, Jan to Feb 1909 (W5, Div 1).

Consecutive clean-sheets, League & Cup
Overall: 6 games, March to April 1982 (W4 D2).
Home: 6 games, Jan to Feb 1921 (W6) & Jan to April 1948 (W6) & Sept to Dec 1979 (W5 D1) & Feb to Apr 1982 (W4 D2).
Away: 7 games, Jan to March 1909 (W6 D1).

PLAYERS
Totals noted include substitute appearances.

Top-5 appearances, League & Cup
496 games: Jimmy Lawrence, goalkeeper (1904-22).
472 games: Frank Hudspeth, full-back (1910-29).
463 games: Shay Given, goalkeeper (1997-2009).
456 games: Frank Clark, full-back (1962-75).
432 games: Bill McCracken, full-back (1904-23).

Most Appearances, by competition
League & Cup: 496 by Jimmy Lawrence, goalkeeper (1904-22).

League: 432 by Jimmy Lawrence, goalkeeper (1904-22).

FA Cup: 64 by Jimmy Lawrence, goalkeeper (1904-22).

FL Cup: 23 by Robert Lee, midfield (1992-2002).

Europe: 62 by Shay Given, goalkeeper (1997-2009).

Wartime: 187 by Albert Stubbins, centre-forward (1939-46).

League, Cup, Wartime & Sundry competitive app: 507 Jimmy Lawrence, goalkeeper (1904-22).
Lawrence also appeared in an FA Cup match abandoned at half-time.
Consecutive League & Cup appearances: 171 by Tommy Gibb, midfield (Aug 1968 to Oct 1971).

400 games & 200 goals, League & Cup
Alan Shearer: 404 app, 206 goals.

League ever-presents in a season
4 times by Shay Given; 2001-02, 2002-03, 2003-04 & 2005-06.
3 times by Jimmy Lawrence; 1907-08, 1908-09 & 1920-21.

League ever-present in consecutive seasons
Excluding substitute appearances
Matt Kingsley 1898-99, 1899-1900.
Jimmy Lawrence 1907-08, 1908-09.
Bryan Robson 1968-69, 1969-70.
Tommy Gibb 1969-70, 1970-71.
Alan Kennedy 1975-76, 1976-77.
Shay Given 2001-02, 2002-03, 2003-04.

Shay Given, ever present in consecutive seasons.

Substitutes
First named substitute: Albert Bennett v Nottingham Forest (h) Aug 1965 (Div 1).
First substitute appearance: Ollie Burton (for Trevor Hockey) v Northampton Town (h) Sept 1965 (Div 1).
First substitute to score: Ollie Burton v Lincoln City (a) Sept 1967 (FLC2).
Most substitute appearances: 119 by Shola Ameobi (1995-date).
Most goals by a substitute: 8 by Shola Ameobi (1995-date).
Most substituted player: 130 by Nobby Solano (1998-2004, 2005-07)
Most unused substitute: 390 by Steve Harper (1993-date).
United's first substitute in any game was probably William Beattie in Jan 1895 v Sunderland (h) in a friendly contest when he replaced Harry Jeffrey.

Age
Youngest debutant: Steve Watson (16y 7m 9d) v Wolverhampton Wanderers (a) Nov 1990 as sub (Div 2).
Oldest debutant: Andy Cunningham (39y 2d) v Leicester City (a) Feb 1929 (Div 1).
Oldest player: Billy Hampson (42y 7m 14d) v Birmingham (a) April 1927 (Div 1).
Robert Gray was 16y 5m 25d old when he appeared for United during June 1940 v Bradford City in wartime.
Youngest team: 21y 51d (average) v Peterborough United (a) Sept 2009 (FLC3).
Krul, Tavernier, Taylor(S), Tozer, Taylor(R), Guthrie, Donaldson, LuaLua, Vuckic, Lovenkrands, Ranger.
Youngest scorer: Jack Rutherford (17y 4m 21d) v Bolton Wanderers (h) March 1902 (Div 1).
Oldest scorer: Billy Hampson (39y 2m 1d) v Middlesbrough (h) Oct 1923 (Div 1).

Youngest hat-trick scorer: Andy Aitken (18y 4m 24d) v Notts County (h) Sept 1895 (Div 2).

Ernie Taylor was 17y 1m 1d old when he scored a hat-trick v Leeds United in Oct 1942 in wartime football.

Oldest Defence: United's defensive trio against Cardiff City in Feb 1923 had an average age of almost 39 years old.

Sandy Mutch (38y 2m 1d), Billy Hampson (38y 5m 15d) & Bill McCracken (40y 12d).

Goalscoring debuts

6 goals by Len Shackleton v Newport County (h) Oct 1946 (Div 2).

4 goals by Mick Quinn (right) v Leeds United (h) Aug 1989 (Div 2).

3 goals by Harry Brown (v Birmingham (a) Sept 1906), Bob McKay (v WBA (h) Nov 1926) & Wilf Bott (v Bury (h) Jan 1935).

Donald Howe scored 5 goals as a wartime guest player v York City (h) Oct 1939, his only appearance for United.

Unlucky debuts

Joe Ford (broken leg) v Grimsby Town (h) Jan 1932 (Div 1).

Bob Blanthorne (broken leg) v Bradford City (h) Sept 1908 (Div 1).

Neither player appeared again for United.

Dismissals

Most times sent off: 4 by David Batty, Lee Bowyer, & Nicos Dabizas.

Most United dismissals in a match: 3 v Derby County (a) April 1992 (Div 2) Brock, O'Brien, Scott (Coach Terry McDermott was also sent-off) & 3 v Aston Villa (h) April 2005 (PL) Bowyer, Dyer, Taylor.

Most players in a match: 4 v Torino (h) May 1973 (AIC), Craig, Smith (for United), Cereser, Masiello (for Torino).

Most dismissals in a season: 7 in 2004-05, 2005-06, 2008-09.

Quickest dismissal: 53 secs, Jimmy Smith v Birmingham City (h) Dec 1973 (TC).

Long service

46y 3m 27d by Andy McCombie as player & trainer, 1904-50.

46y 1m 13d by Joe Richardson as player & trainer, 1929-77.

43y 2m 1d by Benny Craig as player & trainer, 1938-82.

Alex Mutch, son of United's goalkeeper of the same name, joined United in the close-season of 1929 as a young player, then became assistant trainer and physio. He did not retire until over 54 years later. His father spent almost 36 years at St James' Park as player and groundsman.

Long service as a player

18y 10m 10d by Frank Hudspeth, 1910-29.

18y 9m 25d by Bill McCracken, 1904-23.

Both Hudspeth and McCracken's periods included 3 seasons of wartime close-down.

18 years* by Steve Harper, 1993-date.

Harper's first appearance for United was in December 1991 before signing full-time and his overall period connected with the club increases.

Longest serving captain

7y 3m 27d by Joe Harvey, 1945-53.

Shortest stay

Mick Harford was a player for a matter of minutes, or as quick as it takes to sign a transfer form. Transferred to United for a second time in March 1982 from Bristol City, he was immediately released to join Birmingham City to allow outstanding monies to be paid to Newcastle.

Overseas nationalities

Excluding UK & Irish born.

United have fielded players from 38 different countries the most frequent being; 14 France, 5 Denmark, 5 Netherlands.

Transfers: Record fees paid, progression

1900s: £1,600 George Wilson (Everton) Nov 1907.

1910s: £1,950 Billy Hibbert (Bury) Oct 1911.

1920s: £8,100 Jack Hill (Burnley) Oct 1928.

1930s: £8,500 Harry Clifton (Chesterfield) June 1938.

1940s: £18,500 George Lowrie (Coventry City) March 1948.

1950s: £28,000 Ivor Allchurch (Swansea Town) Oct 1958.

1960s: £100,000 (£80,000) Jim Smith (Aberdeen) July 1969.

1970s: £200,000 Peter Withe (Nottingham Forest) Aug 1978.

1980s: £850,000 Dave Beasant (Wimbledon) June 1988.

1990s: £15m Alan Shearer (Blackburn Rovers) July 1996.

2000s: £16m Michael Owen (Real Madrid CF) Aug 2005.

Amounts generally exclude add-ons; tax, levy and sundry fees.

Top-5 expensive players

£16m Michael Owen (Real Madrid CF) Aug 2005.

£15m Alan Shearer (Blackburn Rovers) July 1996.

£11.4m Albert Luque (Deportivo La Coruna) Aug 2005.

£10.1m Obafemi Martins (Internazionale Milano) Aug 2006.

£10m Fabricio Coloccini (Deportivo La Coruna) Aug 2008.

Most expensive by position

Goalkeeper: £1.575m Shaka Hislop (Reading) Aug 1995.

Full-back: £6.3m Jose Enrique (Villareal CF) Aug 2007.

Centre-back: £10m Fabricio Coloccini (Deportivo La Coruna) Aug 2008.

Midfielder: £8.2m Hugo Viana (Sporting Clube de Portugal) July 2002.

Winger: £9.2m Laurent Robert (Paris St-Germain) Aug 2001.

Centre-forward: £15m Alan Shearer (Blackburn Rovers) July 1996.

Striker: £16m Michael Owen (Real Madrid CF) Aug 2005.

Record transfer fee received

£35m Andy Carroll (Liverpool) Jan 2011.

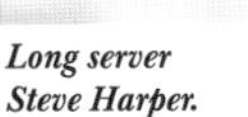

Long server Steve Harper.

Greatest transfer profit

£35m for Andy Carroll (bought for zero, sold for £35m).

Greatest transfer loss

£16m for Michael Owen (bought for £16m, sold for zero, out of contract).

Internationals

First full cap: Matt Kingsley (England) March 1901 v Wales.

Most caps with United: 81 by Shay Given (Republic of Ireland) 1997-2009.

Most capped player in a career: 118 by Geremi (Cameroon), 113* by Shay Given (Rep of Ireland), 112 by Jon Dahl Tomasson (Denmark).

First all-international line-up: v Everton (a) Feb 1998 (PL).

Given/Barton, Howey, Albert, Pearce/Lee, Batty, Speed, Gillespie (Ketsbaia)/Shearer, Andersson.

MANAGERS

Joe Harvey, longest serving boss.

First Manager: Andy Cunningham (Jan 1930).

Longest serving manager: Joe Harvey 13y 10d (1962-75, excluding caretaker period).

Shortest period as permanent manager: Kevin Keegan 7m 19d (2008) & Sam Allardyce 7m 25d (2007-08).

Shortest period as an interim manager: Alan Shearer 1m 23d (2009).

Two spells as manager: Stan Seymour (as director-manager) & Kevin Keegan.

Player, coach/manager & director: Stan Seymour.

Player, coach & manager: Joe Harvey, Willie McFaul, Glenn Roeder.

Alan Shearer also had a brief spell as an assistant to Glenn Roeder.

Player & manager: Andy Cunningham, Kevin Keegan, Alan Shearer.

Most games (excl caretaker): 625 Joe Harvey (1962-75), 255 Sir Bobby Robson (1999-2004), 272 Kevin Keegan (1992-97, 2008).

Most victories (excl caretaker): 240 Joe Harvey (1962-75), 145 Kevin Keegan (1992-97, 2008), 119 Sir Bobby Robson (1999-2004).

Best win ratio (excl caretaker): 56% by C Hughton, 53% K Keegan, 50% D Livingstone.

Presentation & Subscriber Roll

130th Anniversary Presentation Copies

1 **Newcastle United Football Club**
2 **Newcastle United Football Club**
3 **Paul Joannou**
4 **Alan Candlish**
5 **Bill Swann**
6 **Bob Moncur**
7 **Newcastle upon Tyne Central Library**
8 **Peter Beardsley MBE**
9 **Alan Shearer OBE**
10 **Newcastle Chronicle & Journal**
11 **National Football Museum**

130th Anniversary Subscriber Copies

12 **Kevin Steptoe** (England). For my Granddad, Francis Steptoe 1922-2006.
13 **Frank Moyle**, Newcastle upon Tyne. Happy Xmas from your wife Maureen.
14 **Tom, William and James Howes**, suffering fans for generations!
15 **Johnny Bewick**, Gateshead. For a true Geordie, dedicated to following the Toon no matter what.
16 **Steven O'Mara**. Everything is Black and White.
17 **James Savage**, Selsey. The highway's jammed with broken heroes on a last chance power drive.
18 **Aaron Hughes**. Fond memories of a great football club.
19 **Dean Paul Richardson**. Deano is, and always will be, innocent.
20 **Kevin Richardson**. Once a Mag always a Mag, regardless. The love never leaves you.
21 **David Haley and Sons**, Ponteland. East Stand Paddock, Black-and-White and Proud since 1966.
22 **Anthony Britton**, Braintree, Essex. To NUFC, for some of the greatest days of my life!
23 **Gavin Duncan**. The Shola Ameobi edition.
24 **Ryan Brown**, Newcastle United through and through.
25 **Keith McLellan**.
26 **Dr Nabeel Alsindi**, Doncaster. Thrilling, infuriating, exhilarating, disappointing, unpredictable. Wouldn't have it any other way.
27 **Andrew Morris**, Rhyl. Newcastle fan since 1990 on the Gallowgate and views from Leazes Terrace.
28 **Mark Pearce**, Willand, Devon. Forever Black and White.
29 **Barry Moyle**, Newcastle upon Tyne. Happy Xmas from Dad and Mam.
30 **Michael Hedley**, faithful supporter since Dad first took me to St James's in 1966.
31 **Oli Mussett**, Barton on Humber, North Lincs.
32 **Stewart Pearson**, Harrogate. Riding the rollercoaster since 1982 - Howay The Lads!
33 **Jim and Joy Farms**, Durham City. Hoping the Toon goes on to real glories!
34 **Stephen Faulkner**, Sheffield. Stephen, Travis, Maureen and Dave. Woodseats Mags forever.
35 **John Bolam**, Morpeth.
36 **David Bolam**, Morpeth.
37 **Michael Bolam**, Morpeth.
38 **Terence & Jemma Ross**. In memory of a dad & granddad, Alan Ross.
39 **Gary Langley**, South Shields. Gallowgate season ticket holder "eats, sleeps, breathes" Newcastle United Football Club.
40 **Duncan Walker**.
41 **Anthony Garforth Ryle**, 14/04/41.
42 **BW**, London. Remembering Tommy Hall, my father's cousin, who appeared for the Magpies years ago.
43 **Ross Alexander Bowman**, Newcastle upon Tyne.
44 **Gordon Barr**, South Shields. There's only one United and they play in black and white.
45 **Ken Pullar**. In Memory of my brother James "Oz" Pullar, 1965-2010, Toon Army!
46 **Les Wheatley**, Sheffield. Merry Christmas, love Neil and Jess.
47 **Chris Langshaw**, Newcastle. Ganning away in wor Freddies transit, cans, sarnies, no tickets, worra belta!
48 **Jonathan Waller**, proud lifetime supporter. Great Uncle Jimmy Woodburn played with Wor Jackie 1938-1948.
49 **Jim Walker**, Hetton. Thank you Dad for taking me to St James'. Your son, Michael.
50 **Bill Burnett**, lifelong Toon Fan.
51 **Paul Tully**, Hexham. A valuable and essential addition to the black-and-white library.
52 **Gerald M Graham**, Hawick. Toon Through Thick and Thin.
53 **David Taylor**.
54 **Richard McGrill**, Bristol. For my Father, taking me to my first game. Forever in Toon.
55 **Richard Barron**, Barnsley. Gallowgate season ticket holder since 1993, lifelong member of Toon Army.
56 **Peter Shiel**. Washington. From Milburn to Shearer, I've seen them all! 56 Years and still there!
57 **Hugh Collingwood**.
58 **Stuart Fitz-Gerald**, Heaton. To my Grandfather John Edward Fitz-Gerald, Captain of Newcastle United 'A' Team.
59 **Harry Peasland**, South Shields. Howay The Lads.
60 **Shaun Robson**, Fenham, Newcastle. Happy Christmas Shaun, Love Dad.
61 **John Hall**.
62 **Mick Tait**. The Toon, forever in our hearts no matter what. The passion never leaves us!
63 **Graeme and Ron Thompson**. Newcastle United 3 Leeds United 2 always remembered.
64 **Matthew Watson-Broughton**. NUFC has benefited our community for 130 years... long may it continue!
65 **Steve Field**, Walker. Lifelong Toon fan and a canny lad as well!
66 **Peter Stephenson**, West Boldon. In memory of Mark Stephenson 1927-2006.
67 **Alex Wolens** MSG (ex Blyth). 11-11-67 the day my life changed. Sorry to all affected.
68 **Philip Hughes**, a lifetime supporter of NUFC.
69 **Glenn Robison**, Cramlington. Supermac supreme!
70 **Tony Lister**, lifelong fan on his 70th birthday. From grandsons William, Patrick and Frankie.
71 **Mattias Cal Karlsson**, Helsingborg, Sweden: Here's to another century of pain, pints and pleasure!
72 **Paul Laverick**, Radio Tyneside Sports Editor. Haway the Lads!
73 **Alan Alsop**, a Newcastle United fan since 1958.
74 **Stephen Brennan**, Newcastle upon Tyne. Leazes End 1974, San Siro 2003, Accrington Stanley 2010.
75 **Alastaire Keith Brennan**, Newcastle upon Tyne. Some lights never go out Dad.
76 **Charlie Parwani**, Chicago, Illinois, USA. NUFC first; then the Bears, then the Cubs.
77 **Paul White**. To Dad, a lifelong fan, here is a lifetime history, enjoy...
78 **Andy Anderson**. Raised by his Dad to support "The Lads" through thick and (mostly!) thin.
79 **Darren Reeve**, Newcastle. Proud to be a Geordie, supporting NUFC is a way of life.
80 **Jim Mitchell**, Blaydon. Always kept the faith.
81 **Simon Harwood**. Born a Geordie, always a Geordie and a Toon supporter HWTL.
82 **Stephen Rowan**. NUFC forever, wishing the lads all the best for this season and many to come.
83 **Liam Murphy**. Sir John Hall Stand, Lower Tier, Row MM, Seat 33.
84 **Tony Fiddes**, Newcastle. One love, one life, one club - Newcastle United.
85 **Joe Fiddes**, Newcastle. Some people change - I'm always black and white!
86 **Anna Fiddes**, Newcastle. Newcastle United - it's a way of life!
87 **Dave Hill and Alastair Hill**. A lifelong devotion to Newcastle United. Braintree, Essex.
88 **Lee Guo Chun Hksar**, 04.Dec.1973.
89 **Glenn Hall**, Stakeford.
90 **Neil Rutherford**, hooked since 31 January 1970 v Crystal Palace.
91 **Robert Rutherford**, Basingstoke.
92 **Dave, Yuko and Ko Woodrow**. In loving memory of Ernie "Geordie" Woodrow.
93 **Jonathan Thompson**, Newcastle. Happy 18th Birthday son, love from Dad and all the family.
94 **Julie Stanford**, Glasson. East Stand season ticket holder since 1992, Toon Forever.
95 **Jerome Borkwood**, France. Leazes Ender.
96 **Adrian Borkwood**, London. 3rd generation supporter.
97 **John Bradley**, York. Toon Forever.
98 **Craig Nicholson**.
99 **Dave Goldsmith**. Cramlington Mag now living in Leicestershire.
100 For **Roy**, a loyal follower over many years and Rosamunde my wife, for her tolerance.
101 **Geoff Smithson**. Howay the Lads!
102 **Thomas Gordon**, Shenfield, Essex.
103 **Robert Gordon**, Shenfield, Essex.
104 **Colin McClenaghan**, Omagh, Northern Ireland. Proud to be a Toon supporter.
105 **Phil Mudie**, Bell's Close. Newcastle United will never be defeated.
106 **Michael Mudie**, Ponteland.
107 **Jonathan**, Nottingham. Once you're a fan it's in your blood forever, here's to some trophies!
108 **Malcolm Scott**, Berwick upon Tweed. East Stand Upper, supporter since 1964/65.
109 **Eamonn Byrd**, Dublin. From the Carlisle Grounds to Stade Vélodrome. To David, Mark, Daniel & Shane.
110 **Dan & Tara Devlin**. Two Yanks say THANKS NUFC for the "HoneyToon" experience of a lifetime!
111 **Philip Anthony George Dobbs**. Love and best wishes from Mam, NUFC forever.
112 **Christopher Brown**. Following the Toon with the Chapel Park Mags and the Scottish Mags.
113 **Jarrod Bailey**, Northumberland. Grandad Joe, thanks for being a Geordie and getting me hooked!
114 **David & Nat Mankelow**. Howay The Lads.
115 RIP **Matt Mankelow** (1969-2009). Toon forever.
116 **Graeme Parkin**, Sacriston. Loyal supporter since 1977 aged 7 when we beat Wolves 4-0!
117 **John Jobling**, Cramlington. Supporter since 1968, this club always in my Heart, Soul, and Blood.

118 WO **George Frizzell** (RAF). TOONY since 10 July 1959
119 **Daniel George Frizzell**. TOONY since 1 June 1985.
120 **Les Hancock**, Langley Park. Milburn Paddock, saw first match in 1961. What a journey!
121 **Martin Black**, Edinburgh. Mitra, Love of my life, here it is in Black'n'White!
122 **Martin Roberts**, Hexham. Popular Side 1964 to East Stand 2004 - now there in spirit only.
123 **John W Bradley**. No matter where I roam, St James' is my home.
124 **Melvyn Hughes**, Godden Green.
125 **David Hughes**, Godden Green.
126 **Richard Hughes**, Godden Green.
127 **Nigel Maddison**, Balham.
128 **Graeme Lomax**, Leeds. Happy Birthday to a Leazes stalwart and fantastic brother, love Adam.
129 **Rob Millican**, Carlisle. Proud to be supporting the most exciting club in football history.
130 **Trevor & Dawn Smith**, Newfield. United Forever.
131 **Andrew Veitch**.
132 **DG Brownlow**, Newcastle upon Tyne.
133 **Dave Greaves**: 61 Seasons and still making new friends following The Lads home and away.
134 **NUFC Midland Supporters Club**. A focal point for exiled Mags since 1976.
135 **David Emmerson** & family, Walker. NE6.
136 **David Pallister**, Bishop Auckland Mags.
137 **Keith Gunning**.
138 **Lovaine Donaldson**, Wellingborough. Born and raised in Black and White.
139 **Rob Wallace**.
140 **Shaun Carroll**, Chester-le-Street. East Stand season ticket holder, Black and White for life.
141 **Tyronne Browne**. Mag for life.
142 **Adrian & Melanie Freemantle**, Peterborough. Black'n'White for life!!
143 **Ethan Wiley**, born to be a Mag. Francine Wiley - Geordie chick.
144 **Nicola Atkinson**, Western Australia.
145 **Alex and Mark Sneddon**, Whitley Bay. There through thick and thin. Keep the faith.
146 **Warren**, too young for '69 and still waiting after all these years!
147 **Andrew Kirkham**, Queensland Australia. From Newcastle England to Noosa Australia.
148 **Andy Robson**, South Shields. To my niece and nephew, Kate and Jude Ramsey.
149 **Evelyn Talbott**.
150 **James Antonio Turner**, Piggy's Lonnen, Newcastle upon Tyne. Merry Christmas 2011, love Mam & Dad.
151 **Maurice Lockey**. To my dad and best mate.
152 **Christopher Coulthard**, New Jersey, USA.
153 **David MacLaren**, ex Kenton.
154 **Barry Barkes**, Winchester.
155 **Graham Armstrong**, the ultimate Newcastle United fan. Howay the Lads.
156 **Ian Shanks**, Amble, Northumberland.
157 **Stephen and Michael Minto**, Low Fell, Gallowgate End. Life is Black and White.
158 **Mark Adamson**, lifelong supporter and Toon Army member.
159 **Bruce Renwick**, Felling and East Stand - since April Fool's Day 1967.
160 **Geoff and Michael Davidson**, Black and White through thick and thin and proud of it.
161 **James Edes**. A long suffering, lifelong fan.
162 **Larry Lim Gim Lee** from Singapore. Love Newcastle United Football Club.
163 **Mark Oselton**, Gateshead. Fan since 1988. Hopefully a trophy won before the next edition!
164 **Peter Whitney**, Newcastle. Toon Toon.
165 **Jake Davey**, Newcastle.
166 **Trevor Stephenson**, Shildon. East Stand Paddock season ticket holder since 1974, first game Portsmouth (h) 1957.
167 **Rob Mason**, Sunderland AFC Club historian. With best wishes.
168 **Mick Hardman**. Howay the Lads from a Whitley Bay scorer. A lifelong passion never dimmed.
169 **Stephen King**.
170 **Kirk Leech**. Not believing in Newcastle United is the same as not believing in gravity.
171 **Lavender Lee-Flynn**, Vancouver, Canada. Newcastle United's newest fan, born in January 2011.
172 **Leazes Jack**. What a journey, but I wouldn't swap it.
173 **John Richards**. Proud to have been born looking out onto the Town Moor. Howay Toon!
174 **Sam Brent**.
175 **Peter Nelson**. Black and white since 1943.
176 **Stephen Hunter**. A journey made by many full of hope - one day the destination will be reached.
177 **Paul Ross**. Remembering Great Times with My Dad, Stan Ross.
178 **Bill Turnbull**, Wallsend. Lifelong Toon Fan.
179 **Gary Hughes**, Manchester.
180 **Gregory Hollin**. Doomed to support Newcastle United forever.
181 **Ian Gowens**. Merry Christmas Mam, enjoy reading the history of life's longest rollercoaster.
182 **Kevin Miles**, Howdon. 40 years, home and away. One day, I'll see us win something...
183 **Sam Maill**, Newcastle.
184 **Jamie Maill**, Newcastle.
185 **Dave & Jacqui Candlish**.
186 **Karen Candlish & John Price**.
187 **Ron Wilson**, Catterick Garrison, Allez les Magpies.
188 **Thomas Patrick Nolan**.
189 **George Vickers**. Jonesy - always remembered, never forgotten.
190 **John Alder**.
191 **Bill Bruce**.
192 **Anthony Hutchinson**.
193 **Craig Chalmers**, Southport. Happy Birthday, long time exile, find me in the Coronation, Southport.
194 **Scott Lohnes**, Canada.
195 **Anthony Taylor**.
196 **Keith Beveridge**, Club Doctor 1981-1998.
197 **Keith Mason**, South Shields. "There's always next season."
198 **Kev Lambert**, Season ticket holder Milburn Paddock. TOON 4 LIFE.
199 **Richard Lynch**, Whickham. Following the lads since 1960 from Newcastle to Milan & everywhere in-between.
200 **Tom Wales**.
201 **Anthony/Anth/Tony Nicholson**, Gallowgate. More than football, but our heritage, life and social upbringing.
202 **Jim Jobson**, Xmas 2011, from Emma, Marc, George and Lola.
203 **Colin Wafer**, Wallsend.
204 **Eric Hogg**, Stockton.
205 **John Gordon**. In memory of Peter (big Pete) Knox. Toon Army.
206 **Dale Lang**.
207 **Darren Barnes**, Prudhoe Mags. Season ticket holder, Sir John Hall Stand.
208 **Gary Dodd**, Hartlepool. To Carl, Luke and Anais, love Dad.
209 **Michael Wannop** , Andrea Wannop and Katie Wannop.
210 **James Addison**, Penicuik.
211 **Jon Steven White**, Leadgate. Lifelong Newcastle United supporter.
212 **John Paul Hardy**, Haydon Bridge. Gannin' alang the Scotswood Road for 40 years.
213 **Martin Waggott**. Merry Xmas, Kev.
214 **Michael Hicks**, Seaton Burn. Proud Geordie and loyal Toon Army member. Howay The Lads.
215 **Paul Rowe**, Durham.
216 **Tim Bell**, NZ born, Toon descent, black and white since 1971.
217 **Ian "mad dog" Harrison**, Portvasgo. NUFC born and bred.
218 **John, Sue and Daisy Feeona Yates**. Proud supporters of Bobby Robson's and Alan Shearer's team.
219 **Mr William A Powell**, Hemel Hempstead, Hertfordshire.
220 **David Garforth Ryle** 26/01/1969.
221 **Albert Robson**, Ashington, Northumberland. Merry Christmas Dad, Love Shaun.
222 **Alan Price**, Wardley, Gateshead. Geordies are black and white, on both sides of the Tyne.
223 **Clive Swinsco**. Here's to Bobby Moncur with the Fairs Cup in his hand.
224 **Si Martin**, Wallsend. For my Son Louie John George Martin, Born 6th March 2005.
225 **Paul Gordon**, Chester-le-Street. For Charlie.
226 **Pete Atkinson**. A Mag since 1966.
227 **Simon Pearce**. For all the Newcastle United fans within the family to treasure.
228 **Tony Ampleford**, Killingworth. John Hall Stand season ticket holder since 2000 and lifelong Toon Army member.
229 **Sushane Nair**. Never a dull moment!
230 **George Weatherstone**, North Shields. A loyal fan for over 50 years.
231 **Michael Harris**. A lifelong fan through good times and bad.
232 **John Howey**. Love from Mam and Dad.
233 **Elwyn Jones**. Lifelong Newcastle United supporter through thick and thin, but mostly....
234 **Jeff Wilson**. Geordie Boy Done Good. Love Fiona, Amy and Nathan
235 **Andrew Nugent**.
236 **David Dent**.
237 **Steven Cavagan**, Milburn Stand with daughter Sadie and wife Jill. Toon for Life.
238 **David Webster**. To David with love from Granddad.
239 **Fraser Browne**, Auckland. NUFC fan since 1992.
240 **Krzysztof Mrózek**, Columbus, Ohio, USA. I bleed Black and White - NUFC always number ONE!
241 **Eddie Kinney**, North Shields, Alexander and Imogen - Keep the faith!
242 **Kevin Silver**, Chelmsford. Proud to support the Toon!!
243 **Gary Dodd**, Consett. 27 March 2007, Rubie.
244 **Ian Gregg**, Bishop Auckland. Newcastle United - it's always emotional.
245 **Christopher, Victoria & Rachel Jensen**. Global Geordies.
246 **Abhisit Vejjajiva**.
247 **Graeme Milne**, North Shields - a long suffering NUFC fan.
248 **Bryan Milne**, Cramlington - a truly devoted dad and NUFC fan.
249 **Chris Urwin**, London.
250 **David & Jack Frame**. I love this city. I love this club. Black & White.
251 **David Armstrong**. To a very special son, with love from Mum and Dad.
252 **Michael Armstrong**. To a very special son, with love from Mum and Dad.

253 **Bill Stephenson**. An exiled Geordie living in Virginia - forever an avid fan of Newcastle United.
254 **Graeme N. Gilhespy**, Kingston Park. Once a Mag always a Mag.
255 **John Anderson**. The ultimate football book man. From all at Wearset.
256 **Lee Cowan**, Newcastle. From this point on to forever.
257 Toon Army **James Bunting, Peter O'Shaughnessy** (ONE POSH MAG)
258 **Louis Azzopardi**, Malta. Got all Paul's books on Newcastle, so not missing this updated one.
259 **Michael (Vimto) Vinton**, Cadishead. "Easy come easy go".
260 **David Thompson**.
261 **Michael P. Durham**. My Life.
262 **Michael Whitfield**.
263 **Peter Gibson**. It's Denty to blame!
264 **Samuel Villius**, Linkoping, Sweden. I will always be there. win or lose I do not care.
265 **Simon Youngson**, the best husband in the world. From Julie Youngson.
266 **Steve Sowden**. To Andrew, 1969 was my highlight - hope you see many. Happy 18th birthday son.
267 **Terje Kvicksson**, Bergen.
268 **Tony Conaboy**, Calgary, Canada. Till Death Do Us Part, and Thereafter.
269 **Ian Edgar**, Blackhill, Consett.
270 **David, Peter & Joseph Leech**.
271 **David Low**.
272 **Brian White**, Walker-Wallsend-Shieldfield. Howay, let's win the Premiership in my lifetime!
273 **Andy Gilbert**, Newcastle. Remember, through good times and bad times, always keep the faith.
274 **Colin Varty**, Edinburgh.
275 **David Claydon**. Ultimately, and for the record, there's never a dull moment.
276 **Kirsten Marsh**, Fenham. To K love Shar & Liam.
277 **Nick Pearson**, Jarrow. True Mag Forever.
278 **Ged Clarke**, Author, "Newcastle United: Fifty Years of Hurt." Still counting... but keeping the faith.
279 **Christo Patsan**.
280 **Ian Jobson**, Birtley. 47 years loyal. Very little success but priceless memories.
281 **Jordon Tinniswood**, High Spen. The research into the club's history is a labour of love.
282 **Luke**, I can't wait to read this book with you, Lots of Love, Dad.
283 **Peter Wilkinson**, Gosforth, fifty years a Black and White for better and for worse.
284 **Stephen Kettle**. Washington. Forever loyal.
285 **Nicholas Johnson**.
286 **Alan Shell**.
287 **Lasse Leipola**. Following the ups and downs of NUFC gets me through the Finnish winter.
288 **Roland Archibold**, whose Granddad was a director of NUFC 1906/07. RIP Granddad John Ring.
289 **Michael Le Hanie**.
290 **Spuddey**. Toon Army Forever.
291 **Cameron Shiels**.
292 **Derek Nesbitt**. Merry Christmas, you old Devil! Jamie.
293 **Malcolm Jackson**, 09.02.1949, Black & White forever!
294 **Peter Dunleavy**. Happy 60th birthday Dad.
295 **Stephen Hurst**, Whitley Bay. In memory of Archie Allen.
296 **Dr Anton Lang**. By the next edition can we please have won something important!
297 **Jared Robinson**. Forever NUFC.
298 **Bill Marsh**. Magpie Exile.
299 **Ian Lewis**, Leyland, Toon Toon!
300 **David Stonebanks**, London. Toon forever.
301 **Tony Noble**. To Granddad, With all of our love Thomas and William.
302 **John Kelters**.
303 **Harvey Lavelle**.
304 **Ian Ferguson**, Dunfermline.
305 **Kev Hill**. For all the Lads I've travelled with home & away, you know who you are.
306 **Colin Powell**.
307 **James Dawson**, carrying on a tradition. Let's hope for success with your generation!
308 **Tommy Thompson**.
309 **Tommy toon Arkley**. Born in Wallsend and will support the Toon 4 eva.
310 **Paul Durham**, Norfolk. I bless and curse the day I fell in love with you.
311 **Hollie Potts**, Newcastle. 31 Oct 10 - First day I stood up on my own.
312 **Keith Arthur**, York.
313 **Keith Bartley**: A gift of love. Mam.
314 **Trevor Clifford Bartley**: A gift of love. Mam.
315 **Roger Talbot**. Supporting from Rawai Beach, Phuket, Thailand.
316 To **Fen** with much love from Joan. Christmas 2011.
317 **David G Smith**, Shepshed.
318 **Fred Howitt**: To a great Dad, love Kevin, Stephen, Christine & Marie.
319 **Brad McLeod**. In memory of my Grandfather, William Bennett - a true Geordie.
320 **Philip Haggan**, Washington. East Stand.
321 **Gavin, Joe, John, Mark, Michael, Brian, Grant, Bill** and never forgetting **Mick**.
322 **Toon fans** forever.
323 **Keith Woollard**. Supported Newcastle since 1952 (Re: Arnold James Woollard) and have never left.
324 **The Fegans** of Canada - because we bleed black and white.
325 **Glenn Carver**, Woodford Green, Essex.
326 **Frank Carver**, Woodford Green, Essex.
327 **Alfonso Carver**, Woodford Green, Essex.
328 **Daniel Grayson**, Hartlepool. A 'Pooley Magpie.
329 **John P. Aliamus**. Brilliant 2011 Newcazzle.
330 **Harry Sanderson**. Newcastle upon Tyne. Proud to be a Geordie, love from Mam & Dad.
331 **Alastair FM Lambie**, Chester le Street. Black & White. Simples!
332 **Simon J Hill**, Bower Hinton. Somerset will be forever black and white!
333 To my Dad from Scott McBarron.
334 **Kurt Taylor**. One town, one team, one life.
335 **Duncan Mackay**, Harlow. Supporting the Toon since birth with black & white blood - TOON ARMY!
336 **Peter Foster**, Edinburgh. In memory of my dad Fred Foster (Forest Hall), Howay the Lads.
337 **Talal Altuwaijri**.
338 **Luke Henry**, aged 13, Bedworth. Granddad & me are passionate about NUFC, now & forever.
339 **Leonie Underdown**. My dad played for NUFC between the wars so this is a cherished possession.
340 **Stephen Baird**, Morpeth. Keep the faith you mighty Mags. Howay the Lads.
341 **Al & Al**, Aycliffe. For the Village Mags, Ben & Cal.
342 **Michael Purdy**.
343 **James Purdy**.
344 **Aidan Robertson**.
345 **Bob Carson**, Flitwick Mags. Number One Granddad to Ava, Benny, Charlotte and Harry.
346 **Daniel J Marshall**, Darlington. Lifelong NUFC supporter.
347 **David Lough**.
348 **James Barrie Gadsden**, Wideopen, Newcastle upon Tyne, lifelong NUFC fan.
349 **Jonathan Hope**.
350 **Mark Field**, Preston.
351 **Martin Wardhaugh**, North Shields.
352 **Michael Maloney**. Hastings. For my Dad with thanks for first taking me to the match.
353 **Neil and Jake Robinson**, High Heaton.
354 **Patrick Martin**.
355 **Paul Simpson**. Love always to Debra, Erin and Caitlin. Howay the Lads.
356 **Richard Rafeek**.
357 **Owen S Quigley**, Thornaby, Our own little number 9, Love Mam & Dad.
358 **Roger M Douglass**, Richmond, Surrey. Remembering the Best of Times and the Worst of Times.
359 **Stephen Glynn**, Loughborough. Matthew, Keep The Faith.
360 **Stephen Glynn**, Loughborough. Nathaniel, It Will Be Worth It.
361 **Stephen Parkin**, Newcastle. Hope we can win a trophy in my lifetime!
362 **Will Burns**.
363 **Benjamin Allen**, Perth, Australia. Black and White until I die. Long may NUFC continue.
364 **Chris Sheridan**.
365 **Arthur Preston**, Toon fan for 50 years.
366 In memory of my grandfather **Thomas Rodger**, b1871 Perth, d1946 Newcastle. Played for NUFC 1894.
367 **Jamie Stevenson**. Happy birthday from your wee man Peter and baby Peanut.
368 **John Edminson**, Corbridge. Lifelong supporter, attending games since 1951, following in my father's footsteps.
369 **Gordon (twitch) Mitchell**, Newcastle. Many happy times following the Toon.
370 **Jennifer Wright - Keith Maughan**. Support Newcastle United forever through thick and thin.
371 **Len and Ian Brooks**. Good luck with the new book Paul.
372 **Michael Murray**, Whitley Bay. To Will, never forget the black and white dream.
373 **Alan Cochrane**.
374 **David Potter**, Kirkcaldy. Et gloria olim fuit picis (the Magpies once had their glory).
375 **Iain Stewart**, Hexham, Northumberland, 2011.
376 **Paul, Lesley & Lauren Gowans**, Ashington. Proud to be Geordies, black & white hearts forever.
377 **Bob Borthwick**.
378 **David Bowman**.
379 **John Fergusson**, Newcastle. Black & White 4 EVER.
380 **Vince Edes**, supports Newcastle United as a birthright and because it's his duty.
381 **Jonathan Edes**, supports Newcastle United as a birthright and because it's his duty.
382 **Nathan Castle**, supports Newcastle United as a birthright and because it's his duty.
383 **Gary McIver**, Newcastle. In memory of Norrie, my father, who took me to my first match.
384 **Brian** (Australia). Hope you enjoy reading the book, Granda. Love Hayden, Tyler and Liam.
385 **Malcolm Dix**, Newcastle. "Walter Dix", original shareholder and player. He made my "exploits" possible!
386 **Stephen Nichols**.

387 **Danny Baines**. NUFC always and forever.
388 **Laura Pringle**.
389 **Martin Giles**, Norton.
390 **Horold Hodgson**, watching the Toon is like being on a white knuckle ride!
391 **Pam Colyer**. Proud to be the Great Granddaughter of former NUFC player Thomas Wills.
392 **Paul Winship**, Byker.
393 **John Brian Morrow**, Birtley.
394 **Leon Milner**.
395 **David Jones**, Whickham. Merry Christmas, love from Steve and Joyce.
396 **Spencer Stapleton**, Heaton.
397 **Frank Gilmour**, Newcastle.
398 **Paul John Carlton**. Not everything in life is black and white - but the most important things are.
399 **Rob Storey**. Win or lose, forever a Toon fan.
400 **Shaune**, Merry Christmas and a Happy New Year from Darren and Carol.
401 **Ross Muers**, Newcastle born and bred. Proud to be a Geordie. Love from Mam.
402 **Brian Flinn**.
403 **Deborah Brown**. Happy 40th, love Mam & Dad.
404 **Jules Lee**, Plymouth, Exiled Geordie (RN), United Forever.
405 **Arnold Langwell**.
406 **Edward Hogan**, Bedlington. Barrie Thomas was my favourite number nine.
407 **Barrie Wilson**, Wallsend. In loving memory of my Dad Stan and Granddad Stan, Toon Fans.
408 **David Briggs**, Crawcrook.
409 **Kevin, Brendon, Mark & Rhiannon Stubbs**, Yardley, Hastings. Toon Army.
410 **Roy Mitford**, Toon fan.
411 **John Headley**, Shotley Bridge. Here's to another 130 years at the top!
412 **Oskar Parish**, St Albans. NUFC since my arrival in 1994 (Thanks Dad).
413 **Kevin S Morris**. Supporter No: 17223, Gallowgate Stand Middle Tier. Row S, Seat 74. God Bless The Toon.
414 **Paul Hicks**. When the Toon go up, to lift the FA Cup, we'll be dead!
415 **Rachel Quinn**.
416 Happy birthday **Barry**. All my love Kathleen.
417 **Alan Small**, Low Fell. Toon Army foot soldier keeps the faith.
418 **Christopher Campbell**. Happy 21st birthday from Mam and Dad.
419 **Daniel Campbell**. Happy birthday from Granddad and Grandma.
420 **David Campbell**. Happy birthday from Mam and Dad.
421 **David Atkinson**, Greenside. An invaluable work of devotion!
422 **George Graham**, Morpeth.
423 **John Morrow**.
424 **Joseph Gaul**, Cullercoats.
425 **Mark Bridgett**. Proud to be a Geordie, Howay the Lads. God's grass! St James' Park.
426 **Paul, Cheryl, Stacey & Samantha Bell** of Benton, Newcastle.
427 **Peter Moyle**.
428 **Edward McKenzie**. I watched the Magpies with Bobby Robson and Basil Hume, about 70 years ago.
429 **Jeff Harper**, Cramlington. NUFC forever, from Phil and Frances.
430 **Richard K Johnston**, Gosforth.
431 **Scott**. Remember to Keep the Faith, love Nanna and Liam.
432 **William Gouldburn**. Memories both happy and sad.
433 **John, Laura and John**. Gateshead born and bred.
434 **Kenneth Elliott**.
435 **Chris Kelly**, Washington.
436 **John Annett**, Newcastle.
437 **John William Wallace**, Walker.
438 **David Jakeman**. Happy Birthday to a special brother and ardent Newcastle United fan.
439 **Alan McNeil**, Madrid. For Hannah, Daniel and Ruth. Keep the flame burning. Love from Dad.
440 **Chris Dixon**, born 16 April 1988. First match versus Bristol City 4 October 1995.
441 **Stephen Dixon**, born 19 February 1990. First match versus Halmstads BK 10 September 1996.
442 **Daniel Cook** (Legend), Weymouth. Football is my religion, St James' Park is my church.
443 **Derek Younger**.
444 **Simon McGeary**, loved by Cheryl, Milly and Poppy!
445 **Kevin Burn**.
446 **William O'Driscoll**. Sir Bobby Robson and Terry Hibbitt RIP.
447 **William McCartney**, Washington. Hope you enjoy this book. Love Marg.
448 **Rod Stockley**, Newcastle. Through thick and thin season ticket holder, Leazes End since 1992.
449 **David McCormack**, Gateshead.
450 **Thomas Bell**, Newcastle.
451 Very proud of **J.Q.McPherson Snr & J.Q.McPherson Jnr** - our Great Grandfather and Grandfather respectively.
452 **Geoff Dixon**, Birmingham. Lifelong fan of Newcastle United.
453 **James Austin**.
454 **Dave, Clare, Lydia and Georgia Crawford**.
455 **Michael Murray**, Newcastle upon Tyne.
456 **Gavin Haigh**, 4/11/68. Once a Mag, always a Mag - Keep the Faith.
457 **Joyce McKenzie**, South Shields.
458 **Tox te Boekhorst**, Maastricht, Nederland. Newcastle United FC for life.
459 **Simon Cruickshank**, our Geordie Kiwi son. Love from Mam and Dad on your 39th birthday.
460 The real **Dave McKie**, Witton Gilbert Geordie, it's a social thing, love Andrew and Hilary.
461 **Harry Oswell**.
462 **Josh Witherow**, Australia's Number One fan. Toon supporter for life!
463 **Mark Jensen**.
464 **Nick Embiricos**, now London prev Stamfordham. NUFC are up there with my wife, kids and dog! A Cup please!
465 **David Dickie**, Henley on Thames. It all started with Wor Jackie, who remained loyal to the end.
466 **Cliffy Ahmed**, South Shields. Leazes Ender since 1968.
467 **Zen Li**, who are running black & white blood and always with NUFC!
468 **Alana Miller**, Northampton.
469 **Lawrence Cook**, NUFC FOR LIFE.
470 **Peter Corrigan**, South Shields.
471 **Sneck**, the hardest ("I'm too emotional to speak, I'll call ya back") Boot Boy.
472 **George and Ann Stokes**, Bar 1892. Black and white love never dies.
473 **Ian & Aaron Smith**, Bridgend, Wales. Forever Black 'n' White - Toon 'til we die.
474 **John Campion**, Warwick.
475 **Paul Darling**, London. Jack Allen: the ball was not over the line.
476 **Richard Potrzeba**, Jersey, Bangkok, San Francisco. Forever black and white.
477 **The Carney Family**, Monkseaton.
478 **William Joseph Marlon McReavy**.
479 **Gavin Quinlan**, Portmarnock. Howay the Toon from Ireland.
480 **Paul Wardle**, Ryton. To Granddad Mac and all at Stanhope Street, for making NUFC my life.
481 **Raymond Walton**, Cockermouth, Cumbria. Hibbitt since 1963.
482 **Paul Bernard Gluza** and **Jozef Lawrence Gluza**. Lifetime Newcastle supporters.
483 **Bill Stainton**, Carlisle. Happy memories Dad.
484 **Dave Maughan**. In memory of my brother John and all who have lost loved ones.
485 **Euan McFarlane**, love Dad.
486 **Jason Jones**, age 10. Lifelong lover of the Toon Army.
487 **Ben Chapman**, South Cheam, Surrey. NUFC mascot Chelsea v NUFC FA Cup 6th round 22.03.2006.
488 **Ian Glen**, Hook Heath, Surrey Magpie.
489 **Steve Tansey**, Morpeth. How many Highs and Lows since 1963?
490 **Malcolm Gibson**. Was there in 1969 and held the Fairs Cup trophy. A Magpie forever.
491 **Tom Gibson**. First match Newcastle United v Leicester. Won 5-4. Became a Magpie forever.
492 **Bob Hogg**, Cannock, Staffordshire. Bedlington boy, lifelong Toon fan.
493 **Joshua Clark**, Hassocks. A great son and fine wingback. Toon for life!
494 **Eric Wilson**, Fenham. Bill Appleyard, one of the first No.9 legends - always remembered by family & friends.
495 **Adrian Clark**, Ashington. Adrian and Vicki - UNITED, always.
496 **David Dando**, Newcastle.
497 **Iain Colquhoun**, London.
498 **Kenneth Martin**, Newcastle.
499 **Phyllis Martin**, Newcastle.
500 **Greg Billington**, Preston. With Love to Corey and Matilda.
501 **Thomas Wilkinson**, South Shields.
502 **Bill & Norma Walker**, United forever.
503 **Councillor Michael Hood**, Lamesley Ward. Mayor of Gateshead 2010-2011.
504 **Anthony Ainsley**. Enjoy the history, the future is yet to be written!
505 **James Ainsley**. Enjoy the history, the future is yet to be written!
506 **Morgan David Cook**, Adelaide, Australia.
507 **The Park Family**. Following Newcastle through thick and thin. Howay the Lads.
508 **Jon Leon White**, Leadgate. Lifelong Newcastle United supporter.
509 **Nicholas Howorth**, Alan Walton, Aidan Walton. Three generations united in their love of The Toon.
510 **Callum Wilkie**, number one Toon fan and top centre-forward. From Granddad Wilkie.
511 **Chris Scott**, Hull. Happy 60th birthday.
512 For my wife **Anke Chapman**, adopted NUFC fan. All my love, Graham.
513 **Ray Mossom**. A fan since 1955 - and will be until the day I die.
514 **Phill Rochead**, Stakeford, Northumberland.
515 **Michael Walker**, North East England, Black and White forever.
516 **Simon Malia**, exiled in Liverpool. Essential for every true supporter.
517 **Steve Pharoah**, Dorchester. Colourful memories of a love that's black and white - Howay the Lads.
518 **Stuart Hutton**, Dunfermline. Emma and Cara - Loved too much to be forgotten.
519 **Ed Young**, Cullercoats. In honour of your dedication and suffering in following the Mags!
520 **James Brown**. The Club I have loved for 63 years. Now you take over son.
521 **Eddie McCoy**.
522 **Joe Davey**, Newcastle.
523 **Andrew Conway**. Some good, some bad times - need silverware before too old to enjoy it.

524 **Andrew Hayes**, Newcastle. Still keeping the faith, despite his Dad's advice and grey hair.
525 **Andrew Hedges**, Coleford.
526 **Bob Cook**, Farnborough.
527 **Colin Shield**, a Magpie till I die.
528 **George Shield**, Newcastle United's Number 1 fan.
529 **David Skipsey** RIP. Thought they were going to do it in your memory, so close.
530 **Gareth Furlong**, Dublin. Number 1 Newcastle fan!
531 **Gary Bellerby**, Chapel House, Newcastle. Geordies are the Pride of England.
532 **Ian Weller**, Darlington.
533 **Paul and Helen Tilley**. Still waiting for silverware.
534 **Peter Bennett**, Chapeltown.
535 **Vaughann Turnbull**. Toon 4 Ever.
536 **Arthur Farey**.
537 **Barry Foster**, Burnley.
538 **Brian James Hands**. An early Xmas present.
539 **Dennis Flynn**, Eccles, Manchester.
540 **Jean Barber**. 15 September 2001 - It doesn't get much better than this!
541 **Keith Mason**, Kenton. Season ticket holder since 1991 and lifelong Magpies fan. Love Dylan.
542 **Norman Dawe**, Australia.
543 **Paul Reed**, Consett/Western Australia.
544 **Arron Laverty**, Swanley.
545 **Michael Jones**, Brisbane, Australia.
546 **Rob Norton**, Auckland, New Zealand.
547 **Tom Cadwallender**, Northumberland. For my dad who took me to my first match - Bolton Wanderers 1965.
548 **Dave & David John Rowe**, East Stand.
549 **David Robertson**, Boston.
550 **Joel Blakey**, Toon Supporter. With much love, Granddad.
551 In memory of **Ron Renton**, a great man, wonderful dad and fantastic granddad.
552 **John Clouston**.
553 **Steve and George Curry**, Selby. Milburn Stand season ticket holders, Black and White Army.
554 **Ken Stark**, Darlington.
555 **Duffy**, a True and Faithful Supporter.
556 **Mick and Shirley**, Lichfield.
557 **Ron Rickeard**, Howay the Lads!
558 **Alistair Brett**. Northumbrian-born, a silverware optimist like Granddad Jack Smith.
559 **Jack Brett**. London born - Newcastle supporter nevertheless, like Dad Alistair and Great Granddad Jack Smith.
560 **Lawrence Kindley**. To my forebears, father, brothers and sons who all love the Toon.
561 **Robert Lee Woods**, Cheshunt, Hertfordshire. Age 28 - Newcastle United fan.
562 **Johnny Bruce**, London via Seaton Sluice.
563 **Richard Howarth**.
564 **Robin Taylor-Wilson**, Durham.
565 **Bill Veitch**, Darwen.
566 **Kevin Skinner**, following in Dad's footsteps.
567 **Shae Conway**, Ashington. Future Magpie? Keep the faith, Granddad Paul & Nanna Carol.
568 **Christopher Brennan**, Washington.
569 **Lawrence Brennan**, Washington.
570 **Neil Cockburn**. To Neil with love from Dad.
571 **John Moore**, USA. Thank You Alan Shearer.
572 **Des Duffy**, Low Fell. Black and White for 60 years.
573 **Chris Hurst**. As a lifetime 4th generation supporter, cherish the heritage of our club.
574 **Peter and Bethany Moreland**. Toon fanatics!
575 **Nick Duckworth**. You do not choose your football club, your football club chooses you.
576 **Peter Page**, Newcastle.
577 **Ben Lowans**, Menston, formerly Corbridge.
578 **David Gunn**. Toon fan for life.
579 **Robin Golding**, Woodbridge. In memory of my father Heath - a third generation Toon supporter.
580 **Colin McAllister**, Bromsgrove. Many happy memories, especially 1955 - I was there! Howay the Lads!
581 **M Henderson**, Hadrian Park.
582 **Chris Foster**, Wallsend. A lifelong fan and Toon Army member for 36 years.
583 **Peter Rae**, Wallsend. A lifelong fan and Toon Army member for 25 years.
584 **Les Rae**, Wallsend. A lifelong fan and Toon Army member for 47 years.
585 **Frank Cassidy**, Wallsend. A lifelong fan and Toon Army member for 30 years.
586 **Terry Cassidy**, Wallsend. A lifelong fan and Toon Army member.
587 **Seamus Michael Cassidy**. A lifelong fan and Toon Army member for 20 years.
588 **Steven R Milne**, Whitley Bay. Born 28-5-1986. Proud to be a Geordie.
589 **Robert W Milne**, Whitley Bay. Born 21-2-1950. Proud to be a Geordie.
590 **Les Pearson**. Like his Granddad John Henry Orange, a lifelong Newcastle United supporter.
591 **Wayne Allen**, Bangor NI. Forever a proud follower of the Toon.
592 **Mark and Matty Batey**. English by birth, Geordies by the grace of God.
593 **Peter Glass**, Southampton. Black and White forever.
594 **Alan Turner**, North Shields. Platinum Club, lifelong Toon Army supporter - forever hopeful.
595 **The Glennie Family**, Stannington. Who put the ball in the mackem net?
596 **Geoff, Gemma & Stuart Dick** - lifelong Newcastle United fans.
597 **John Wood**, Brighton. Huge fan of Alan Shearer and the Newcastle philosophy of exciting football.
598 **Stewart Kirkpatrick**, Manchester.
599 **Bryan Williams** RIP.
600 **Matthew Valentine**. Born 6th May 2011.
601 **John Hurst**. As a lifetime 3rd generation supporter, cherish the heritage of our club.
602 **Michael John Little**, father (23.12.66) and son (13.02.03).
603 **Ian Jack**. Greatest moments: Tino's third, Rob Lee at Wembley, Bob Moncur v Forest. Just Brill!!
604 **Matthew Maxwell**, Gateshead.
605 **Pat and Davie Kelly** RIP, **Lee Yellop** RIP, **Terry McGlade** RIP. Always Remembered.
606 **David Edward Kelly, Ian Gerard Kelly, Darren George Purvis, Sean David Purvis, Simon Lee Snowball**.
607 **Steven White**, USA. To Steven from Leon & Amy.
608 **Tom Mitchell**. Lifelong fan, who dreams of silverware at least once more in his lifetime.
609 **John Anderson**. Happy Birthday Dad, lots of love, Paul & Pauline.
610 **Robin Blagburn**, Newcastle.
611 **Colin Lisle**, [a loyal supporter] to mark your 60th. With best wishes, Gordon and Rob.
612 **Eddie & Kieran Richardson**, Somerset. Following the Toon together.
613 **Geoff Green**. Highs and lows over 50 years. Looking forward to more highs!
614 **George Mitchell (Mitch)**. Once a Mag always a Mag!
615 **Grainger Fenton**, Newcastle upon Tyne. Lifelong Newcastle supporter.
616 **Jack Ord**, Kirk Merrington. Dad, we support the greatest club in the World! Michael.
617 **Keith Topping**. First match April 1969 Popular Side (Sheffield Wednesday 3-2).
618 **Philip Brown**, Darlington.
619 **Steve, Claire, Zak and Ewan Corrigan**.
620 **Bernie Lamb**, Newcastle.
621 **Bill Corcoran**. Greetings to the invincible and legendary City and People of Newcastle upon Tyne.
622 **Josh Guy**, Cairns, Australia. The Ultimate Record for The Ultimate Supporter.
623 **Redcar Toontone**. For my late Dad, and son Richard, NUFC Forever
624 **Tony Hill**, Evesham, Worcestershire. To my Dad, quite simply the reason we are Newcastle fans.
625 **David White**, Wideopen. Happy Christmas 2011.We'll follow the Toon together forever. Love Dad.
626 **Robert Williams**. North Shields born, keeping the faith in Ramsbottom, Lancashire.
627 **Stuart Wigg**, Monkseaton.
628 **Paul Rudd** & family, South Shields. Always been watching, never stopped supporting.
629 **Oliver Smithson**, Newbury. Supporting Newcastle since 1999.
630 **Dennis Bryden**, North Shields.
631 **Gordon Smith**, Bedlington. A lifetime of love, joy and pain but always Newcastle United forever!
632 **James Wright**, High Heaton.
633 **John Lackenby**, Wallsend.
634 **David Malone**. Happy Christmas Dad, from Becky, Jack, Scarlett & Joseph.
635 **Michael Malone**. Happy Christmas Granddad, from Rebecca, Jack, Scarlett & Joseph.
636 **Kevin Nixon**. Happy Christmas Granddad, from Scarlett & Joseph.
637 **Peter Calleeuw**, Norway. From King Kevin Keegan, Prince Philippe Albert to Legend Alan Shearer: Passion!!
638 **Roger Burton**, Woolley Grange. Howay the Lads.
639 **Simon Gardner**, Durham. NUFC - nothing else matters.
640 **Dylan Hughes**. "Our Team". From Ed Wraith, Manchester.
641 **Tony Hogg**, in exile.
642 **Trevor Corbitt**, London. Dedicated to Newcastle United Supporters, everywhere, for their loyalty.
643 **David Watson**, Newcastle.
644 **Paul Wright**, Newcastle.
645 **Sam James Nesbitt**.
646 **Brian Longworth**.
647 **Tony Farrar**, Blackpool.
648 **James Odemuyiwa**, Banstead. Happy Birthday!!
649 **John Clark**, Canvey Island.
650 **Thomas McConnell** and his son **Darren McConnell**, Newcastle United supporters always and forever.
651 **Jimmy Beresford**, thoroughbred Geordie, lifelong NUFC supporter and true friend. Happy 50th.
652 The **Brown and O'Keefe** families, Wallsend.
653 **Tom Lynch**, Heaton, Newcastle. NUFC season ticket holder since 1992.
654 **Vincent and Lena McCormack**, Wardley. Lifelong fans and Toon Army members.
655 **Ray Smith**, Blaydon. Sir John Hall Stand season ticket holder - Toon Army for ever.
656 **Robert F Roddham**. A supporter of Newcastle United. 1946-2011.
657 **Dave Taylor**. Part of my life since 1964 - never lose the faith.
658 **Paul Elsender**, Lincoln. Geordie for Life.
659 **Scott Jon Stewart**.

660 **Andrew and Julie Huddart**. Newcastle United Will Never Be Defeated!
661 **Graham Gaffney**. Happy fiftieth - a lifelong loyal fan.
662 **Steve Wraith**.
663 **John Wraith**.
664 **Rob Wraith**.
665 **Stephen McMullen**.
666 **John Guy**. I loved The Entertainers.
667 **Gurdip Singh Kambo**, Newcastle upon Tyne. Newcastle United is my second home, supporter for life.
668 **George Green**, Newcastle.
669 **Allan, David and James**. Magpies in Newcastle, Australia. United forever.
670 **Anne, Susan and Jack**. Wife, daughter and grandson of Johnny Thompson - Newcastle United 50/57.
671 **Loudfoot, Ian & Jack Ross**. Big & Little Louders. NUFC from here to eternity.
672 **Nicky Jones**, Newcastle. Happy 70th Birthday Granddad. Love from Katie, Sam, Aidan & Robbie.
673 **Anthony 'The Rocker' Stobart**. Happy Birthday Sid. Best wishes mate, from the Hombletons.
674 **Scott Muncaster**.
675 **Ian Scott**, London. In memory of dwarfy, Black and White throughout - a Toon fan forever.
676 **David Littlewood**, Swindon. Toon follower since Sept 1966; 1-1 v Fulham, Sir Bobby No 4 for the opposition!
677 **Iain Hindhaugh**, originally from Blyth. Newcastle United will never be defeated.
678 **Ian Gibson**, originally from Blyth. Also known as Quicksilver. Still available for selection.
679 **Anthony Simm**, Gateshead.
680 **John Herbert**, Peterborough.
681 **Chris Shilton**. Flash of the Gallowgate.
682 **Wilfred Martin Renton**.
683 **David Ian Renton**.
684 **John Hackett**, Jarrow. With love to Kate and in memory of Johnathan and Johanna.
685 **Les Slater**, Heaton. RIP.
686 **Peter Child**. Ultimate club. Ultimate memories. Ultimate Record.
687 **Jack Mackenzie**, Newcastle.
688 **Duncan Mackenzie**, Newcastle.
689 **Iain Mackenzie**, Newcastle.
690 **Niall Mackenzie**, Newcastle.
691 **Joseph Moran**, born Blackhill, Consett, County Durham, 8th December. Happy 50th Birthday, Moran/Jack clans.
692 **David Clarke**, Harrold, Bedfordshire. A loyal supporter encouraged by an exiled Geordie Mum!
693 **Frank Hamill**, Grimsby.
694 **Les Storey**, Fenham. Thanks for all your help and advice in life - Tony and Laura.
695 **Mark Cripps**, New York City.
696 **David Andrew Robinson**, Coxhoe, Durham.
697 **Gerry Allan**, lifetime supporter.
698 **Trevor Hails**, lifetime supporter.
699 **Aidan James Bell**, Newcastle upon Tyne. Lifetime supporter.
700 **Chris Biskupek**, Mississauga, Ontario, Canada. To Nana Spalding, our true Geordie hero and legend 1918-2010.
701 **Daniel Bloyce**, Chester.
702 **Dominic Moore**, Wallsend. Newcastle United - more than just a football club.
703 **Paul (Wax) Walker**, Melbourne, Australia. Paul, a reminder of the games we attended. Love Dad.
704 **Kenny Owens**, Gateshead. One life, one dream, one team.
705 **Paul Mooney**, Wallsend 10/09/74. Proud To Be A Geordie.
706 **Peter Collyns**, Tasmania.
707 **Stuart McLeod**, Seaton Sluice & Weymouth. Supporter since 1965. Favourites: Wyn Davies & Supermac's debut.
708 **Ian Scott**, North Shields.
709 **Paul Marshall Scott**, Southampton. It all went wrong after 1955!!
710 **Martin Shillito**, Lincoln. Here's to success and happiness - Toon and beyond.
711 **John Robert Bell, Ken Bell, Paul and John Bell, Jordan Bell**. Four generations of support.
712 **Tommy Mackinnon**. Happy Birthday Brother.
713 **Marcus, Tony and Sean Martin**. Newcastle United always
714 **Piotr and Jakub Jozefowicz**, Gdansk, Poland. Lifelong Toon Army members.
715 **John Thomas, John William, Anthony John, Arnutchai John, Michael Nopadol Miller** - Newcastle United.
716 **Graham Fryer**. The pride. The passion. The Toon.
717 **Meg Hobson**, Tynemouth. Great days remembered at St James'. Love from Alex.
718 **Alski Broon**, Walker, Newcastle. Never stop believing!!
719 **William Kenneth Swaddle**, lifelong NUFC fan.
720 **Michael Stephenson**. A reminder of the years watching the Toon with my dad, Peter Stephenson.
721 **David Nicoll**, Ireland. Newcastle United supporter from birth!
722 **Stephen Wood Hutchinson** born 21/09/1933: a man for all seasons and lifelong supporter.
723 **John Johnson**, Germany. What a history!
724 **Ethan Gallagher**, Australia. Happy Birthday, love Auntie Ruth and Laraine.
725 **Shaun Turner**, Birtley.
726 **David Dobson**, Seat G46 Sir John Hall Stand, St James' Park, Newcastle.
727 **Alan Dormer**, Consett. Sixty years a fan - and counting!
728 **Kevin Brown**, Newcastle upon Tyne. Happy 38th lad!
729 **Graeme Brown**, Manchester.
730 **Gary Patterson**, North Shields. Happy Christmas, love Gavin.
731 **Scott Healey**, Wallsend. HWTL.
732 **Thomas Logan**, Bedlington, 21/09/1944. Happy Birthday Big T.
733 **Jamie**, Haway the Lads!
734 **Jon Lienard**, looking forward to watching Alex in the number nine shirt in 2030.
735 **Kevin Hinds**, North Shields. For Kieron Campbell, ball boy vs WBA, 22nd May 2011.
736 **Matthew Slater**, Whickham. Merry Christmas from Mam and Dad. Toon Toon!
737 **Michael Hogan**, Waterford, Ireland. Thanks for the memories, from an adopted Geordie.
738 **Micah**, NSW, Australia.
739 **Trev Parker**, Newcastle. No better place than SJP full of passionate Geordies in full voice.
740 **Ann Bell**, Stockton on Tees.
741 **Ewan Campbell**, Bearsden Mag.
742 **Elle Howe**, Morpeth.
743 **Andrew Hodgson**, Ingleby Barwick. Andrew & Natalie - 12.12.10 - a perfect match.
744 **Andy Griffin**. The Griffs: born black and white.
745 **Mike Evans**. In memory of my Mum and Dad. Love to Sonya, Simon and Sam.
746 **Rafferty family**, "4 more, you only need 4 more" Newcastle 5 Sunderland 1 31/10/10.
747 **Mike & Jean Bell**. Keeping the faith with sons overseas.
748 **Bob Holcroft**, South Shields.
749 **Callum Woodrow**, Hebburn. Proud supporter and Dad. Joy and despair since 1983. Always love.
750 **Lee Robertson**, Cramlington. Mam - thanks for the strips when I was a bairn. Miss you.
751 **Ian Robertson**, North Shields. Dad, Love you mate despite putting me through this for the last 40 years.
752 **John Clark**, Milburn Stand season ticket holder.
753 **Charly Curtis**, Durham City. Always a Toon fan.
754 **Brian Gowens**, Hebburn Lad and Great Dad. Black and White Forever.
755 **Brian Codling**. Loving Dad, Husband, Granddad.
756 **Colin Dixon**, St Neots. Howay the Lads!
757 **Paul 'Nutmeg' Robson**, Newcastle. You have the book now bring on the quiz...
758 **Iain Tipping**, Morpeth. Still keepin' the faith.
759 In memory of **Algy Sidney**, wonderful Geordie lad, dad and granddad: Wembley 1951, 1952, 1955.
760 **John Sinclair**. Loyal Mag.
761 **Brian Wilkin**, Throckley.
762 **Glynn McGee**.'People believe NUFC is a matter of life and death. It's more important than that'.
763 **George, Rhiannon and now Colin**. It is great when your blood is black and white.
764 **George Edward Bainbridge**. Many years of support and fellowship with brother Arthur, uncles and friends.
765 **Ray Duffell**, Morpeth. With love from Ian, Helen, Ben and Alice.
766 **John Aitman**. For Jimmy Aitman, a great Dad.
767 **Brian Jackson**. God bless Bobby Robson and NUFC.
768 **Paul Crozier**, Benton.
769 **Jeff Todd**, York. For Stan, Jeff, Simon, Samantha and Andrew.
770 **Jim Lamb**. Enjoy the ride.
771 **Jimmy Jones, John Farrage, Alan Walker, Bob Walker, Brian Richardson, Phil Walker**, Toon Army Soldiers.
772 **Jowls**, Belgium. 52 years of joy supporting United, and counting.
773 **Thomas James Burke**, born 7th February 2010. "Granda's Little Magpie."
774 **Ken Pollard**, Whickham. In memory of Stan Dobson - best friend, best man, Newcastle fans United.
775 **Kevin Ferguson**, Whickham. Newcastle UNITED till I die.
776 **Steven Carr**. Scottish Mags. In fond and loving memory of Gran and Granda Henderson.
777 **Kathleen Irene Carr**, lifelong Newcastle United supporter.
778 **Liam Errington**, Newcastle. NUFC till I die.
779 **Russell Gardiner**. Uncle Russ/Wor Kid, all our love, Laura & Shannon, Lisa & Rich.
780 **Howard Beckett**, Cramlington.
781 **Chris Baldry**, Cottenham. Celebrating 2011, the year of Chris' 21st Birthday. Love Mum & Dad.
782 **James Palmer**. 47 years of hurt but still the club I love.
783 **Mark and Paul Roadley**. East Stand Brothers. NUFC till we die.
784 **Jim Donaghan and Les & Joyce Roadley**. True Supporters. Together forever.
785 **Gordon Young**, Wallsend Magpie.
786 **Stew Waters**. Lipsy set text, salty biscuits, smarties, missed by many PABRO.
787 **Paddy Fagan**, Melrose. It's the hope that kills you.
788 **Steve Melia**, Hebburn (1959-2007). Much loved and sorely missed by family and friends.
789 **Jack Michael Bradbury and Phil Bradbury**, Keig Alford, Scotland. Newcastle United: great years will follow.

790 **Paul Mac**, Stockton. Living the lifelong obsession that is supporting NUFC home and away.
791 **Raymond Nicholson**.
792 **Richard Gibson**, Northampton. "We know what's around the corner, we just don't know where the corner is." KK
793 **Rob Armstrong**, Beverley.
794 **Roger Jennings**, Stockton on Tees.
795 **Steve Kirby**, Gallowgate End. Players, Managers, Directors come and go. We will always be there.
796 **Sean Stewart**. Forever loyal to Newcastle United.
797 **David Waggott**. Once black and white always black and white.
798 **Philip Johnson**, Wallsend. Thanks for all the memories Dad! Love Steven.
799 **Steve "WheelchairSteve" Wilkinson**, Newcastle. First game v Scunthorpe, March 1962. NUDSA co-founder, 1998.
800 **Laurence Thompson**.
801 **Sam Hall**, Whitley Bay. Destined by birthright to follow the Toon!
802 **Steve Evans**, lifelong fan. Happy Birthday lots of love Sue and Jess.
803 **Ernie Wilson**, Whitby Magpie. First match 1949 and counting, Gallowgate End season ticket holder.
804 **Graeme Robson**, Crawcrook. "The noise, passion, feeling of belonging and the pride in your city."
805 **Thomas McCruden**, Exeter.
806 **Andrew Bush**, supporter from 16 March 1983.
807 **Tony James**, Kenton Bar. Best wishes to the future of this club and all involved!
808 **Trevor Lee**. To John Lee, who could na make it!
809 **Will Gibson**, Benton.
810 **Alan Birbeck**, Langley Park. I love the Toon.
811 **Alan Bye**. Proud following this magnificent club's first team, reserves & juniors since 1982.
812 **Andrew McTernan**, Australia.
813 **The Nicholsons**. Black and White through and through, thanks Dad.
814 **Brent McIver**. Forever Black & White.
815 **Dean McIver**. Forever Black & White.
816 **Mark Slater**, Whickham - East Standers.
817 **Keith Hudson**, Newcastle.
818 **Ken 'Jinky Jim' Dartnall**. With all its sham, drudgery and broken dreams, it's still a beautiful world.
819 **John Charles Shutt**. A fanatical Geordie supporter and European traveller.
820 **James Chestney**. Number 1 Toon fan.
821 **South Shields Mags**: Toffa, Spug, Andy, Paul, Mark, Cus, Les & Dunny, & Tone, & AndyM. 40yrs Hurting...
822 **Dr Christopher Pentland**.
823 **Craig Hayton**, Basingstoke. Howay The Lads!
824 **Jill Morris**, York. My ultimate wife, recorded for life, within the ultimate records.
825 **Matthew Alexander**, Cramlington. Wherever you may wander in the world, you'll always be a Geordie.
826 **Ruth Irving**. Toon For Life.
827 **Dave Ridley**, Shire Oak Mags.
828 **David Jackson**, Barmston, Washington.
829 **Dennis Telford**. A regular at St James' Park since January 27th 1951: Newcastle 3 Bolton 2.
830 **Derek Cooper**, Dudley. Owners come and go, but we are always here. Keep the Faith!!
831 **Jack Luke**, Hebburn. Lukey Mags.
832 **Jimmy, Joe, Sally & David Morgan**. Devon's Black'n'White army.
833 **Paul Robinson**, Fenham. Your favourite memory is in here somewhere ... amongst ones to forget! David.
834 **Adam Bates**.
835 **Michael Farrow**. An amazing dad.
836 **David Lee**, Whitley Bay.
837 **Gary Davis**, Shildon. Black and White always. Howay the Toon.
838 **Gary Mark Coates**, Wallsend Mag.
839 **Ian Coates**, Cramlington Mag.
840 **Geoff Bell**, Newcastle. For Mam, Dad, Grandma and Margaret.
841 **Glenn Wallace**, Ashington.
842 **Tom McCallum**. With love from Helen.
843 **Ian Johnson**, Cumbria - Howay The Lads.
844 **David Jackson (jacko)**, Whitley Bay. Black and White, Geordie and proud!
845 **Cameron Howes**, all the future Howes Mags and in memory of Granddad.
846 **Harry Kidd**, Wallsend. Happy 60th from James & Andrea.
847 **Jim Thompson**, Cowling. St James' regular since 1957 - the passion never dies. Still dreaming!
848 **Jim Murray**, Perth, Australia. There's only one Toon, my beloved Newcastle.
849 **Robert William Sample**, Byker. A great Dad and a true football man.
850 **Geoff Buffey**, true Mag, RIP. Love from son Jon and new grandson Henry.
851 **Kev Taylor**, Gateshead. Trophy please before my toes turn up!
852 Down through the generations. All black & white daft. And still to continue. KNR.
853 **Kenneth Weall**, will be manager by 2020.
854 **Lawrence Connelly**, Ponteland. Looking forward to a really good read over Christmas.
855 **Lee Jones**, Australia.
856 **Lee Hodgkinson**, Canada.
857 **Colin Liddle**, Winlaton.
858 **Malcolm Bell**, Stakeford.
859 **Aaron James Henderson**, New Zealand. I'm proud of you son. Dad.
860 **Martyn Gray**.
861 **Matthew Cook**, Canterbury. This club has provided me with some unforgettable memories.
862 **Diddler, Wrighta and Buster**. Newcastle United Supporters Club - Jerusalem Branch 1984.
863 **Pete Murray**. Happy Retirement - from Megan, Bryony, Siobhan and Niamh Dale - Howay the Lad!
864 **Michael Dunn**, Monkseaton, 29/10/80.
865 **Mick & Tiffany Pilch, Dan Pope**, Watton, Norfolk. Keep the Faith.
866 **Mark Mulhern**, Killingworth. NUFC lost a true fan in my dad on 21.08.2009, RIP **Peter Mulhern**.
867 **Neil Thornton**, Ashington. John, Glenda, Mark, Elaine, James, Richard, Clare, Hannah, Neve, Emma.
868 **Paul Connelly**, Newcastle.
869 **Peter Bainbridge**.
870 **Derek Ginsberg**. My hero - finally writing his name in Newcastle United history!!
871 **Bryn Waller**, age 11. I hope that we win something in my lifetime.
872 **Liam Ramshaw**, Happy 18th Birthday 2011, love Mam and Dad.
873 **Daniel Ramshaw**, Happy 21st Birthday 2011, love Mam and Dad.
874 **Mark Allison** aka Run Geordie Run. Newcastle United for life, Howay the Lads.
875 **Oliver & Henry Smith**, Morpeth. Magpies for life!
876 **Brian Blenkinsop**, Newcastle. Lifetime supporter through thick and thin: still hoping for that elusive trophy.
877 **Robert Towers**, Barnoldswick.
878 **Barry Speker** OBE DL, Newcastle upon Tyne. Best Dad... Best Man! Love Robert (favourite son).
879 **Ronnie and Chris**, Whitehaven.
880 **Alexander Jackson**, Sheffield.
881 **Rob Sampson**, South Shields. Sammaz - Black and White until I die, 2011.
882 **Sean Douglass**.
883 **Simon Moran**. Oh that there were more time.
884 **Mick Thomson**. Watching Newcastle United since I was a young lad in the early sixties.
885 **George Rowan**. Lifelong Newcastle United fan from Westerhope.
886 **Ian Firth**. Gallowgate End season ticket holder, lifelong Toon supporter.
887 **Alastair Thomson**.
888 **Steve Hilditch and Simon Hilditch**.
889 **Steve Reynolds**.
890 **David Irving**. For Lee, Aidan, Harry, Matt and cousin John, where are you now?
891 **Lee Irving**, USA.
892 **Stuart Mather**, Hilversum. To the next 130 years - Haway the Lads of the future!
893 **Richie Gray**, Newcastle.
894 **Colin Taylor**, Ovingham. 32 years of pain and counting!
895 **Oscar James Aram**. Born, 17th June 2011 at Royal Berkshire Hospital, Reading. 8lb 5oz.
896 **Terry Warr**. Season Ticket in 'The Corner'. First game October 1968, Gallowgate End v Leeds.
897 **Thomas Joyce**. Season ticket holder at 81! Happy Christmas 2011.
898 **Toon Broon**, Reading. 40+ years of pain, but once a Geordie always a Geordie!
899 **Mal Broon**, Newcastle. "You spend your life waiting for a moment that just doesn't come."
900 **Sjur Grinde**, Norway.
901 **Stephen Bambrough**. It's all in Black & White.
902 **Andrew Sproat**.
903 **Andrew Smith**, Australia. Howay the Lads!
904 **Nikita (2009) and Monty (2010) Johnson**, Newcastle supporters born in Australia, coming home soon.
905 **David Kennedy**. Happy 50th birthday to a lifelong friend and Newcastle United fan.
906 **Brian Robinson**, Histon. Many years, many cheers, many tears, always a Mag. Womb to Tomb.
907 **Brian Hobson**. Black & White for 65 years - not given up yet! Howay the Lads!
908 **Bill Reay**. Old enough to remember winning trophies, daft enough to believe it'll happen again.
909 **Garry Cosgrove**, Morpeth.
910 **Kevin Taylor**, Newcastle.
911 **Billy Taylor**, lifelong Newcastle Fan.
912 **John Preston** (Garage). Welcome to a first grandchild arriving in time for the 2011/12 season.
913 **Paul, Sean & Mark Donnelly**, Leeds. One Family. One Club. One lifelong Love!
914 **Paul, Mark & Sean Donnelly**, Newcastle & Leeds. Forever Mags. Grandpops, dad, uncle & grandson!
915 **Allen Convery**. Happy 40th Birthday - Chris.
916 **Chris Octon**, Monterrey, Mexico.
917 **Carl Greener**, Northampton. Keep the faith. Our day will come!
918 **Bob Greener**, Welwyn, Hertfordshire. For you Dad. Keep the faith. Our day will come!
919 **Gary Holmes**, Gateshead.

920 **Trevor Holmes**, Gateshead.
921 **Bob Rayner**, Newcastle. Lifelong supporter.
922 **Brian Harrihill**.
923 **Douglas "Four Goal Margin" Bairstow**.
924 **Paul "Four nil, and you mucked it up!!" Maddison**.
925 **Philip McCahy**. Moving further and further from the action.
926 **Jim McCahy**. At least they have won something in your lifetime, Dad!
927 **David Todd**, Forest Hall. This season will be the one.
928 **Joseph Close**, Berwick upon Tweed, Happy 4th Birthday.
929 **Alex Chun**, from Manx boy to Toon man.
930 **Colin Hostler**, Hepscott. Maybe in my lifetime.....
931 **Charles Robertson Taylor**, Heaton. First attended St James' Park 1937, celebrating 75 years in 2012.
932 **Dave Newby**.
933 **Graeme E Cross**. A True Geordie.
934 **Malcolm A Hull**. A True Geordie.
935 **Derek Meehan**, Wakefield.
936 **Trevor Dunn**. Always with Newcastle United, through thick and thin. Good things to come.
937 **Drapes - Isaac, Norman, Jan, David & Jonny**.
938 **Aidan Gifford**. Forever a Magpie.
939 **Graham Crosby**, Leeds. Steve, David - We three are one! NUFC.
940 **Richard Laidlaw**, Teesdale. One big Mag.
941 **Gordon Small**, Preston. Hollins; McKinney, Ferguson; Neale, Thompson, Dalton; Hilley, Hale, Thomas, Kerray, Fell.
942 **Gregor Gregorc**, Slovenia.
943 **Peter Holgate**.
944 **Don Bankier**. A Magpie in the Garden of England.
945 **Hugh Macdonald**, happy 40th birthday, love from your brother Iain mac.
946 **Max Summers**, enjoy the rollercoaster that is Newcastle United.
947 **Ian Archbold**, Gerrards Cross.
948 **John Ryles**, Chippenham, lifelong NUFC fan.
949 **Jim McBurnie**, the book looks like a great job.
950 **Andrew Allister**.
951 **Malcolm Webb**.
952 **James Brown**, Dunston.
953 **Walter Scott**, Lobley Hill.
954 **Lewis Brown**, Heaton.
955 **Jason John Facer**, South Africa. Newcastle United's No 1 fan and South African Geordie!
956 **Jeremy Robson**, Spennymoor.
957 **John Kidd**, Cumbria. My Magpie-mad, big brother. From Elizabeth.
958 **Adrian Scott**, Newcastle. My Magpie-mad Antipodean-born Geordie. From Elizabeth.
959 **Michael Rochford**, Chester-le-Street. Toon Army Forever.
960 **John Rochford**, Esh Winning. Black & White Army.
961 **John Williamson**, Bedlington.
962 **Gordon Lundgren**. Born Amble, Northumberland in 1957. Newcastle United supporter for life.
963 **Irene & Eddie Lundgren**. Alnwick, Northumberland.
964 **Les Ruffell**, South Shields. Everything has to be black and white to you.
965 **Thomas Tomlin**, Barnard Castle. 60 - and still as daft as ever.
966 **Alan Gibson**, Doxford Park. Thanks for all the lifts - Tommy.
967 **Bob Wallis and Tommy Dickinson**, who are now with Wor Jackie.
968 **Steven Hughes**, Gateshead. Geordie boot boy, mental and mad.
969 **Mark Turnbull**, Norwich. Geordie through and through, will support you forever more NUFC.
970 **Malc Hetherington**. ne-doubleyou-see-a-ess-tea-ell-ee you-en-eye-tea-ee-dee.
971 **Mark Bowie**, Cullercoats. It's all here in black and white, Enjoy, Mam & Dad.
972 **Paul Bowie**, Cullercoats. The whole crazy rollercoaster ride documented. Enjoy, Mam & Dad.
973 **Mark Shaw**.
974 **Kay Langford**.
975 **Mick Percival**, Newcastle. First match 1/02/69 Bolton reserves. 0-0, raining, addicted ever since.
976 **Mick Rennison**, anywhere. 95-97. Immortal. The world's favourite team. Thanks again Kevin Keegan: LEGEND.
977 **Sam Brent**.
978 **Mike Rennie**, Aberdeen. Mike and Scott Rennie, loyal North East of Scotland Mags.
979 **Chris Smith**, Durham. Proud to be an adopted Geordie. Howay the Lads!
980 **Harry Galsworthy** 27/01/11. This is your life, enjoy every moment. Love Mam and Dad.
981 **Jeff Tate**. Have a long and Happy Retirement. Love from all the family. June 2011.
982 **Paul Moulding**, Hexham. 30 years season ticket holder, on the biggest rollercoaster ever.
983 **Eddie Howe**, Newcastle. I look forward to supporting Newcastle United like my Dad and hope for success!
984 **Peter Sylvestersson**, Helsinki, Finland.
985 **Steve Pringle**, NYC, USA. 35 years of ups and downs but still smiling.
986 **Bill Pringle**, Washington. Black and White since 1955 and counting.
987 **Paul Hundrup**. Burtonwood, Warrington. Born Wallsend, raised Southampton, lives in Warrington. Heart in Newcastle.
988 **Duncan James**, Wallsend. I saw Fumaca trap the ball!
989 **Paul Emmerson**, Cardiff. From father to son; we look before and after.
990 **Keith Faulkner**, Northwich. Dear Dad, the ultimate record for the ultimate dad!
991 **John Faulkner**, Liverpool. Our kid! Always keeping it Toon. Haway the Lads.
992 **Jimmy & James Burns**. 1992-2009. East Stand Row T seats 10 & 11. West End Geordies!
993 **Jimmy, James & Joseph Burns**. Three Generations of Geordies & Toon Fans!
994 **R Fletcher**, Newcastle upon Tyne. Thanks dad, granddad and Alan.
995 **Rich Meehan**, Doncaster. Welcome to the Toon, Will!
996 **Richard Greenwood**, Norwich. Geordie in exile but still keeping the faith. Howay The Lads!
997 **Anthony Joyce**, 09/10/10. One year on and counting!! FRO.
998 **John Taskas**, Lincoln. Dad, Merry Christmas 2011. Lots of Love, Gaynor and Tony.
999 **Joseph and Samuel Buck**, Cramlington. Newcastle United supporters forever!
1000 **Linda Nelson**. It's My Toon and it's my book. I'm loving this!!
1001 **Dave Green**. The Big Fella in the Gallowgate.
1002 **Lee, Matthew and Danielle Scott**, Chopwell. Enjoy reading the Toon Bible, love Dad.
1003 **The Jack family**. We took the Fulwell!
1004 **Andrew McQueen**, Leyton, London.
1005 **Eddie McQueen**, Winlaton, Tyne & Wear.
1006 **Dave Smith**. Happy Birthday Dad.
1007 **Peter McCartney**, Cochrane Park. Lifelong Newcastle United fan.
1008 **Vince** from Couldson. Happy memories of the only team.
1009 **Andrew Waddington**, New York. The best football club in the world, supported the world over.
1010 **Steve Murphy**. Will all of the effort, pain, toil & cost ever be worth it?
1011 **Jimmy Florance**, Wallsend.
1012 **Ian Nesbit**. A Mag amongst the Blades and Owls.
1013 **William Nesbit**. From Bedlington to Sheffield to Billingham, but still black 'n' white at heart.
1014 **Richard Spowart**.
1015 **Andrew Spowart**.
1016 **Malcolm Spowart**.
1017 **Billy (William) Wilson**. From Kay, Kenny and Chris, your loving children - always proud.
1018 **Harry & Paul Hewetson**, NUFC forever in our hearts.
1019 **Aarron Kimber**. Happy 16th birthday to a top Toon fan.
1020 **John Mayne**, loyal supporter.
1021 **Gary Staward**, Jarrow.
1022 **Keith Brewis**, Bristol.
1023 **Michael Murphy**, Ashington: Married Michelle on the 27 October 2006.
1024 **Craig Falcus**, Springwell Village. To the biggest Toon fan in the world, love Oliver Falcus.
1025 **Mick Hutchfield**, Happy 50th, lots of love Sarah, Andrew and Sebastian.
1026 **Darren Miller**, Merry Christmas with love from Aysha.
1027 **David Ware**, Maidenhead. NUFC is a part of you, and we are proud that you are a part of us. Sid & Moo.
1028 **Graeme Harwood**, To my dad Bryan for putting me on the rollercoaster that is supporting the Toon.
1029 **James Smith (senior)**. To the 'Old Man'. We came, we saw, we nearly conquered.
1030 **Calum Heslop**. Future success and trophies. Enjoy reading the NUFC history.
1031 **Stuart Seaborn**, with love from Carley
1032 **Mr George Robert Coulson**, Happy Birthday Dad. Love Robert, Karen, Amy, Adam. Newcastle United forever.
1033 **Stuart Black**, Catchgate, Stanley, Co Durham.
1034 **John Beavis**. Toon Lifer since 1982 and Scoreboard season ticket holder.
1035 **Trevor Ross**. Season ticket holder, Gallowgate End. Devoted fan since 1965.
1036 **Terry Turner**, Happy 60th Birthday, love Carol.
1037 **Ken Slater**, Belsay.
1038 **Newcastle John**. I am a Geordie, a Toon fan till the end. My love for the Toon will never end.
1039 **Richard Swann**.
1040 **Mark Swann**.
1041 **Karen Swann**.
1042 **Mark Hannen**, Newcastle. Centre Paddock to Leazes End to Gallowgate with Jen, Joseph & Jack.
1043 **Dave Hewson**, Tudhoe Village. Here's to the team on the Valley 1994-2008: TH, PT, IH, PJ, DH, SA, GW, DL, JG, MG, BS, and of course, FTF ... Great memories! With love to Helen, Claire, Rachael and Jacqueline.
1044 **Simon Arbon**, Whickham. Sorry for the late nights! ... Gill, Emily, Alice.
1045 **Kath Cassidy**, SJP T-Lady extraordinaire.
1046 **Steve Huddart**. Years of hurt but we wouldn't have it any other way...
1047 **Dag Martin Hagen**, Norway. I have supported Newcastle United since 1973.
1048 **Philip Hagen**, Blackhill. Consett Mags! Home or Away we always go. NUFC forever.
1049 **James Copner**. Look to the future. Remember the past.
1050 **Colin Hall**, Rowlands Gill. Merry Christmas Dad!
1051 **Iain Moir**, Alnwick. Lifelong Magpie.
1052 **Mitchell A Joannou**. Born a Scot but proud to have Black'n'White blood.
1053 **E 'Johnny' Joannou**. Introduced me to United's Greats. The result; Black-and-White Pride & Passion. PJ.

Abbreviations

General Abbreviations:

Note: *Specific abbreviations are also noted on individual data charts.*

A, a, (a)-away fixture
A-goals against (in season summary)
AGM-Annual General Meeting
AIC-Anglo-Italian Cup
Amat-Amateur club
ano-another, detail untraced
App-appearances
Asst-assistant
ATC-Air Training Corps
BBC-British Broadcasting Corporation
BB-Boy's Brigade team
BC-Boy's Club team
Champ-Champions or Championship
Ch-Championship (League Tier 2)
CL-(UEFA) Champions League
Clackn-(Inverness) Clacknacudden
Co-County
CS-(FA) Charity Shield
CW-Colliery Welfare club
CWS-Co-operative Wholesale Society team
Cy-Canada youth player
D-Drawn
d-player dismissal (in team line-up)
Div-Division
Dir-Director
Ea-England amateur player
Es-England schools player
Ey-England youth player
EFC-European Fairs Cup
F-Final, cup final
F-goals for (in season summary)
FA-Football Association
FAC-FA Cup
FC-Football Club
FL-Football League
FLC-Football League Cup
FLN-Football League North
FMC-Full Members Cup
Fr-Friendly
Free-free transfer, no fee
g-goals, or games
G, Gp-Group stage
H, h, (h)-Home fixture
HRH-His or Her Royal Highness
HM-His or Her Majesty
Hy-Hungary youth player
Inst-Institute club
ICFC-Inter Cities Fairs Cup
ITC-Intertoto Cup
Jas-James
Jn-John
Jnrs-Juniors club
Jnr/j-junior
L-Lost
Lg-League
m-matches
m-million, in a £3m fee
MBE-Member of the Order of the British Empire
MD-Managing Director
m, mins-minutes
n-neutral venue
N-North
NER-North Eastern Railway (Company)
NL-Northern League
Ny-Netherland youth player
NIy-Northern Ireland youth player
Northb-Northumberland
NCC-Northumberland FA Challenge Cup (Senior Cup)
N&D-Northumberland & Durham (Football Association)
NUFC, NU-Newcastle United Football Club
O-Olympique
OBE- Officer of the Order of the British Empire
og-own goal
P-Played (in season summary)
P-Preliminary, as in match or round
PA-(Bradford) Park Avenue
pen-penalty kick
PFA-Professional Footballer's Association
PL-Premier League
PM-Prime Minister
Posn-league position after fixture
Pts-points
Q-Qualifying stage or round
QPR-Queens Park Rangers
R-Round
r-replay (as R3r, Round Three replay)
rr-second replay
rrr-third replay
RAF-Royal Air Force
RFC-Rugby Football Club
RoIs-Republic of Ireland schools player
RoIy-Republic of Ireland youth player
RVI-Royal Victoria Infirmary
s-substitute appearance, appended by the player replaced, eg s4 (in team line-up)
sub-as a substitute
s-senior
sch-schools football
SF-semi-final
SoL-Sheriff of London (Charity Shield)
Ss-Scotland schools player
Sy-Scotland youth player
Synth-(Billingham) Synthonia
TC-Texaco Cup
TTWC-Tyne-Tees-Wear Cup
TUC-Trades Union Congress
TV-television
u-unused substitute (in team line-up)
unattached-transfer from no club
UEFA-Union of European Football Associations
UEFAC-UEFA Cup
Under-23/Under-21-age group for international team
u-fee-undisclosed transfer fee
Univ-university
v-versus
W-won
WBA-West Bromwich Albion
WW-World War
YC-youth club team
YMCA-Young Men's Christian Association team

Numeric & Other Abbreviations

2(1)-Second Round, First Leg match
2(2)-Second Round, Second Leg match
Y m d-years, months, days

Appearances: totals for each player noted as **23(5)** indicates 23 starts and 5 appearances as substitute.

*****-after the name of a player (in the Facts and Player Focus) indicates his career continues.

In the Player Focus, substitute appearances are included in the overall total.

Universal abbreviations have also been used in summaries for dates and club titles, while specific abbreviations for fixture competitions are included before each section.

Club Titles

Historic titles of clubs used in the data not generally recognisable:

AC Ambrosiana (Milan)-Internazionale Milano, **Ardwick**-Manchester City, **Newton Heath**-Manchester United, **Shaddongate United**-Carlisle United, **Small Heath**-Birmingham City.

Country Abbreviations

A-Austria, **Ag**-Argentina, **Aus**-Australia, **B**-Bohemia (Czech pre-1918), **Bel**-Belgium, **Br**-Brazil, **BH**-Bosnia Herzegovina (post-1992), **Bm**-Bermuda, **Bul**-Bulgaria, **Ca**-Canada, **Cg**-Congo, **Ch**-Chile, **Cm**-Cameroon, **Col**-Colombia, **Cr**-Croatia (post-1991), **Ct**-Crete, **Cz**-Czechoslovakia (1919-93), **CzR**-Czech Republic (post-93), **Cy**-Cyprus, **D**-Denmark, **EG**-East Germany (1945-90), **Es**-Estonia, **F**-France, **Fn**-Finland, **G**-Germany (pre-1919 & post-1990), **Ge**-Georgia, **Gr**-Greece, **H**-Hungary, **HK**-Hong Kong, **I**-Italy, **IC**-Ivory Coast, **Ir**-Iran, **Is**-Israel, **J**-Japan, **Jm**-Jamaica, **K**-Kosovo (post-2008), **L**-Latvia, **M**-Malta, **Mal**-Malaysia, **Mex**-Mexico, **N**-Netherlands, **Ng**-Nigeria, **Nw**-Norway, **NZ**-New Zealand, **P**-Portugal, **Pa**-Paraguay, **PEA**-Portuguese East Africa (Mozambique), **Pe**-Peru, **Pol**-Poland, **PoM**-Principality of Monaco, **R**-Romania, **Rh**-Rhodesia, **SA**-South Africa, **Sb**-Serbia (post-1992), **Se**-Sweden, **Sg**-Senegal, **Sl**-Slovenia (post-1991), **Sp**-Spain, **Sv**-Slovakia, **Sw**-Switzerland, **T**-Turkey, **Tr**-Trinidad, **Th**-Thailand, **U**-Ukraine (post-1993), **Ug**-Uraguay, **USA**-United States, **USSR**-Soviet Union (1922-91), **WG**-West Germany (1949-90), **Y**-Yugoslavia (1918-92).

Generally abbreviations are not used for the UK *Home* countries and Republic of Ireland, however player international classification included in the Player Register utilises the following:

E-England, **Ird**-Ireland prior to division, **NI**-Northern Ireland, **RoI**-Republic of Ireland , **S**-Scotland, **W**-Wales.

(Suffixes; **wt**-wartime international appearance).

NEWCASTLE UNITED HISTORY ... FURTHER READING

EARLY HISTORY

Pioneers of the North. The Birth of Football in the North East. (By Paul Joannou & Alan Candlish, p2009 Breedon Books/Derby Books Publishing, ISBN 978-1-85983-727-6).

GENERAL HISTORY

United: The First 100 Years & More - Millennium Edition. (By Paul Joannou, p2000 Polar Publishing, ISBN 1-899538-20-8).
Note: Now out of print and available on the second-hand market and in local libraries.

EUROPEAN

The Grand Tour. Newcastle United's Adventures in Europe. (By Paul Joannou, p2006 Mainstream Publishing, ISBN 1-84596-022 X).

PLAYERS

The Black'n'White Alphabet, A Complete Who's Who of Newcastle United Football Club. (By Paul Joannou, p1996 Polar Publishing, ISBN 1-899538-03-8).
Note: Now out of print and available on the second-hand market and in local libraries. A planned update volume is to be published.

Shirt of Legends. The Story of Newcastle United's No. 9 Legends. (By Paul Joannou, p2004 & 2005 Mainstream Publishing, ISBN 1-84018-962-2).

ST JAMES' PARK

Fortress St James. (By Paul Joannou, p2000 Ballast, ISBN 0-9539164-0-5).
Note: Now out of print and available on the second-hand market and in local libraries.

NEWCASTLE V SUNDERLAND

Ha'way/Howay The Lads. The History of the rivalry between Newcastle United and Sunderland. (By Alan Candlish, p2006 Sports Books, ISBN 1-899807-39 X).